Each and all time - 50-51
Sphitran
three
381 - Woodnater

Del

MAJOR AMERICAN POETS

SELECTED AND EDITED, WITH CHRONOLOGIES, BIBLIOGRAPHIES, AND NOTES

BY

HARRY HAYDEN CLARK

Professor of English, University of Wisconsin

NEW YORK CINCINNATI CHICAGO

AMERICAN BOOK COMPANY

BOSTON ATLANTA DALLAS SAN FRANCISCO

CLARK'S MAJOR AMERICAN POETS
E. P. 3

MADE IN U.S.A.

PREFACE

Ideally, of course, one cannot completely understand American poetry unless one reads all the poems of all our poets. In practice, however, few if any readers can do this, and it is utterly impossible in the limited time available in the average college course devoted to the subject. Selection becomes necessary, then, although the choice of poets and poems is perhaps justifiable only in the light of its guiding principles, and therefore the reader is entitled to a candid statement of the principles which have governed the making of the present book.

1. *The Poets Included.* Most teachers today agree that it is preferable to acquaint oneself thoroughly with a considerable body of the work of a relatively few major figures who are representative than to try to read snippets from a multitude who soon become mere names. Thus the present book includes the ten generally recognized major American poets, along with Freneau to illustrate the neglected but important early development of our poetry as inspired by scientific deism, and along with Robinson and Lindsay to represent two contrasting aspects of the modern temper in the East and the West, respectively.

2. *Range of Ideas.* One must follow the trail of a poet's thought wherever it may lead. Our poets were closely interested in the full cycle of the ideas of their time. An attempt has therefore been made to include not only poems which are intrinsically good as works of art but also those poems which express each poet's political, religious, social, economic, and æsthetic views. Not only do poems dealing with such a variety of ideas enable a reader to learn the logical articulation of a poet's thought but they illustrate the manner in which the poet inspired or was inspired by the life of his time and place. The poetry included thus constitutes an index to the intellectual history of America which parallels and helps to illuminate other aspects of American history.

3. *Genetic Development.* Some of our poets reveal themselves, when studied closely, as having gone through many changes of view from youth to old age, changes so striking in some cases as to make the same man seem composed of different individuals. By disregarding chronology, by artificially arranging the order of a poet's poems, or by omitting all his early or all his mature poems, one is in danger of securing a portrait of the poet which fails to present him faithfully proportioned and integrated as a "man against the sky." Materials have therefore been provided which should enable a reader to trace the growth of the poet's mind and art from his earliest to his latest expression in order that he may emerge as a complete, organic personality in his intellectual habit as he lived.

4. *Æsthetic Theory*. Modernist critics who emphasize appreciation and the enjoyment of poetry have long told us that in approaching a given poem for the first time one should try to divest himself of subjective biases and prejudices and try to ascertain to what extent the poet succeeded in fulfilling his own peculiar aim. In this anthology, then, an attempt has been made to include not only illustrations of the poets' practice but representative prose statements of the theories and aims which underlie and direct and in part explain their practice, their poetic art. This principle has been further elaborated by a considerable note summarizing the poetic theory of each poet. This material should insure not only a more sympathetic and intelligent understanding of the poems but, in providing a means of checking theory against practice, it should furnish at least one definite and clean-cut method for the study of a subject which is too apt to degenerate into subjectivity or chaos. While the present selection aims to give due emphasis to the poets' *ideas* in their full range, it also attempts to emphasize the importance of poetic *art*. While many ideas are apt to be common to all contemporaries of a given era, probably of a hundred poems embodying the same ideas only one poem endures. If one inquires the reason for this familiar phenomenon, it is likely to be found in the fact that distinction of *form* of expression, of prosodic art, constitutes in considerable measure a competitive power of appeal. I am grateful to Professor G. W. Allen for enabling me to quote liberally, in the notes, from his *American Prosody*, a book based on a doctoral dissertation done under my direction. Finally, it need hardly be said that this method of providing for an interpretation of a poet's practice in the light of his own theory is in no way incompatible with the necessary critical appraisal of the ultimate value of the poet's thought and art in the light of traditional and universal criteria; indeed it is the necessary means to such a desirable end.

5. *Relation to the History of Relevant Scholarship*. In the last third of a century a vast fraternity of scholars in Europe as well as in America, working largely under the stimulus of our competitive university system, have made immense contributions to our understanding of the full and rich significance of American poetry. These scholarly contributions, however, are often published in inaccessible journals, and their conclusions are unknown to many students. Furthermore, when individual studies are known, the student is often at a loss to know how their value compares with that of other similar studies and to what extent the conclusions have been modified by other research. As a help in remedying this situation, then, extensive bibliographies with interpretative or critical annotations have been provided for each poet, in order that the student may profit by what specialists have done in interpreting the significance of the poetic spokesmen of our American tradition.

6. *Interpretative Notes*. The rather full notes aim not only to suggest the

main outlines of the growth of each poet's mind and art as a whole but to illuminate individual poems and to cite passages in the poet's prose which testify to the genesis of such poems and which help to define and round out the poet's ideas. While there may be those who will think that the notes are needlessly full and that they include things the teacher may himself wish to say, long and realistic experience in the classroom has suggested that a slight repetition, from different angles, is not an unmitigated evil, especially where abstruse philosophical questions are involved. Furthermore an attempt has been made, by citing or quoting widely divergent interpretations and opinions, to make the notes suggestive rather than dogmatic and thus to leave the teacher free to develop his own point of view and to encourage the student to sharpen his critical evaluation.

I am grateful to Mrs. Hazen Carpenter for help in checking portions of the bibliographies in this book.

H. H. C.

ACKNOWLEDGMENTS

The editor very gratefully acknowledges the kindness of publishers and individuals in giving specific permission to include material indicated:

D. Appleton-Century Company: for quotations from T. W. Whipple's *Spokesmen.*

Coward-McCann, Inc.: for a passage from Alfred Kreymborg's *Our Singing Strength.*

Doubleday, Doran and Company: for selections from Walt Whitman's *Leaves of Grass.*

Ginn and Company: for an extract from Percy H. Boynton's *History of American Literature.*

Harcourt, Brace and Company: for quotations from Henry Seidel Canby's *Classic Americans* and Foerster's *Reinterpretation of American Literature.*

Harper and Brothers: for passages from the *Letters of James Russell Lowell*, edited by Charles Eliot Norton.

Houghton Mifflin Company (by permission of and by arrangement with): for poems and prose selections by Emerson, Holmes, Longfellow, Lowell, and Whittier, and for quotations from Foerster's *American Criticism*, Ferris Greenslet's *Lowell*, Albert Mordell's *Quaker Militant*, H. E. Scudder's *James Russell Lowell*, and E. C. Stedman's *Poets of America.*

The Judson Press: for quotations from A. H. Strong's *American Poets and Their Theology.*

Little, Brown and Company and Martha Dickinson Bianchi: for the poems by Emily Dickinson.

The Macmillan Company: for poems by Vachel Lindsay and Edwin Arlington Robinson, and for passages from W. A. Bradley's *Bryant*, Charles Cestre's *An Introduction to Edwin Arlington Robinson*, and *The Cambridge History of American Literature.*

Mr. Alfred Noyes and Frederick A. Stokes Company: for passages from Mr. Noyes's *Some Aspects of Modern Poetry.*

The Saturday Review of Literature (January 18, 1936) and the author: for an extract from F. O. Matthiessen's article on Emily Dickinson.

Charles Scribner's Sons: for poems and prose extracts from the work of Sidney Lanier, poems by Edwin Arlington Robinson, and a passage from Edgar Lee Masters's *Vachel Lindsay.*

The University of North Carolina Press: for passages from A. H. Starke's *Sidney Lanier*,

CONTENTS

Philip Freneau

William Cullen Bryant

John Greenleaf Whittier

Ralph Waldo Emerson

Edgar Allan Poe

James Russell Lowell

Oliver Wendell Holmes

Emily Dickinson

Sidney Lanier

Walt Whitman

Vachel Lindsay

Edwin Arlington Robinson

MAJOR AMERICAN POETS

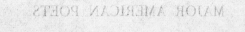

PHILIP FRENEAU

THE POWER OF FANCY [1]

WAKEFUL, vagrant, restless thing,
Ever wandering on the wing,
Who thy wondrous source can find,
Fancy, regent of the mind;
A spark from Jove's resplendent throne,
But thy nature all unknown.
This spark of bright, celestial flame,
From Jove's seraphic altar came,
And hence alone in man we trace,
Resemblance to the immortal race.
Ah! what is all this mighty whole,
These suns and stars that round us roll!
What are they all, where'er they shine,
But Fancies of the Power Divine!
What is this globe, these lands, and seas,
And heat, and cold, and flowers, and trees,
And life, and death, and beast, and man,
And time,—that with the sun began—
But thoughts on reason's scale combin'd,
Ideas of the Almighty mind?
On the surface of the brain
Night after night she walks unseen,
Noble fabrics doth she raise
In the woods or on the seas,
On some high, steep, pointed rock,
Where the billows loudly knock
And the dreary tempests sweep
Clouds along the uncivil deep.
Lo! she walks upon the moon,
Listens to the chimy tune
Of the bright, harmonious spheres,
And the song of angels hears;
Sees this earth a distant star,[2]
Pendant, floating in the air;
Leads me to some lonely dome,
Where Religion loves to come,
Where the bride of Jesus dwells,
And the deep ton'd organ swells
In notes with lofty anthems join'd,
Notes that half distract the mind.
Now like lightning she descends
To the prison of the fiends,
Hears the rattling of their chains,
Feels their never ceasing pains—
But, O never may she tell
Half the frightfulness of hell.
Now she views Arcadian rocks,
Where the shepherds guard their flocks,
And, while yet her wings she spreads,
Sees crystal streams and coral beds,
Wanders to some desert deep,
Or some dark, enchanted steep,
By the full moon light doth shew
Forests of a dusky blue,
Where, upon some mossy bed,
Innocence reclines her head.
Swift, she stretches o'er the seas
To the far off Hebrides,
Canvas on the lofty mast
Could not travel half so fast—
Swifter than the eagle's flight
Or instantaneous rays of light!
Lo! contemplative she stands
On Norwegia's rocky lands—
Fickle Goddess, set me down
Where the rugged winters frown
Upon Orca's howling steep,
Nodding o'er the northern deep,
Where the winds tumultuous roar,
Vext that Ossian sings no more.
Fancy, to that land repair,
Sweetest Ossian slumbers there;
Waft me far to southern isles
Where the soften'd winter smiles,
To Bermuda's orange shades,
Or Demarara's lovely glades;
Bear me o'er the sounding cape,
Painting death in every shape,
Where daring Anson spread the sail
Shatter'd by the stormy gale—
Lo! she leads me wide and far,
Sense can never follow her—
Shape thy course o'er land and sea,
Help me to keep pace with thee,
Lead me to yon' chalky cliff,

[1] Text from edition of 1786.

[2] Milton's *Paradise Lost*, B. II, v. 1052. [*Freneau's note.*]

Over rock and over reef,
Into Britain's fertile land,
Stretching far her proud command.
Look back and view, thro' many a year,
Caesar, Julius Caesar, there.
Now to Tempe's verdant wood,
Over the mid ocean flood
Lo! the islands of the sea
—Sappho, Lesbos mourns for thee:
Greece, arouse thy humbled head,
Where are all thy mighty dead,
Who states to endless ruin hurl'd
And carried vengeance through the world?—
Troy, thy vanish'd pomp resume,
Or, weeping at thy Hector's tomb,
Yet those faded scenes renew,
Whose memory is to Homer due.
Fancy, lead me wandering still
Up to Ida's cloud-topt hill;
Not a laurel there doth grow
But in vision thou shalt show,—
Every sprig on Virgil's tomb
Shall in livelier colors bloom,
And every triumph Rome has seen
Flourish on the years between.
Now she bears me far away
In the east to meet the day,
Leads me over Ganges' streams,
Mother of the morning beams—
O'er the ocean hath she ran,
Places me on Tinian;
Farther, farther in the east,
Till it almost meets the west,
Let us wandering both be lost
On Taitis sea-beat coast,
Bear me from that distant strand,
Over ocean, over land,
To California's golden shore—
Fancy, stop, and rove no more.
Now, tho' late, returning home,
Lead me to Belinda's tomb;
Let me glide as well as you
Through the shroud and coffin too,
And behold, a moment, there,
All that once was good and fair—
Who doth here so soundly sleep?
Shall we break this prison deep?—
Thunders cannot wake the maid,
Lightnings cannot pierce the shade,
And tho' wintry tempests roar,
Tempests shall disturb no more.
Yet must those eyes in darkness stay,
That once were rivals to the day—?
Like heaven's bright lamp beneath the main
They are but set to rise again.
Fancy, thou the muses' pride,
In thy painted realms reside
Endless images of things,
Fluttering each on golden wings,
Ideal objects, such a store,
The universe could hold no more:
Fancy, to thy power I owe
Half my happiness below;
By thee Elysian groves were made,
Thine were the notes that Orpheus play'd;
By thee was Pluto charm'd so well
While rapture seiz'd the sons of hell—
Come, O come—perceiv'd by none,
You and I will walk alone.

1770 1786

THE RISING GLORY OF AMERICA

Being part of a Dialogue pronounced on a public occasion

ARGUMENT

The subject proposed—The discovery of America by Columbus—A philosophical enquiry into the origin of the savages of America—The first planters from Europe—Causes of their migration to America—The difficulties they encountered from the jealousy of the natives—Agriculture descanted on—Commerce and navigation—Science—Future prospects of British usurpation, tyranny, and devastation on this side the Atlantic—The more comfortable one of Independence, Liberty and Peace—Conclusion.

Acasto

Now shall the adventurous muse attempt a theme
More new, more noble, and more flush of fame
Than all that went before—
Now through the veil of ancient days renew
The period famed when first Columbus touched
These shores so long unknown—through various toils,
Famine, and death, the hero forced his way,
Through oceans pregnant with perpetual storms,
And climates hostile to adventurous man.

But why, to prompt your tears, should we resume,
The tale of Cortez, furious chief, ordained
With Indian blood to dye the sands, and choke,
Famed Mexico, thy streams with dead? or why
Once more revive the tale so oft rehearsed
Of Atabilipa, by thirst of gold,
(Too conquering motive in the human breast,)
Deprived of life, which not Peru's rich ore
Nor Mexico's vast mines could then redeem?
Better these northern realms demand our song
Designed by nature for the rural reign,
For agriculture's toil.—No blood we shed
For metals buried in a rocky waste.—
Cursed be that ore, which brutal makes our race
And prompts mankind to shed their kindred blood.

Eugenio

——But whence arose
That vagrant race who love the shady vale,
And choose the forest for their dark abode?—
For long has this perplext the sages' skill
To investigate.—Tradition lends no aid
To unveil this secret to the human eye,
When first these various nations, north and south,
Possest these shores, or from what countries came,—
Whether they sprang from some primaeval head
In their own lands, like Adam in the east,—
Yet this the sacred oracles deny,
And reason, too, reclaims against the thought:
For when the general deluge drowned the world
Where could their tribes have found security,
Where find their fate, but in the ghastly deep?—
Unless, as others dream, some chosen few
High on the Andes 'scaped the general death,
High on the Andes, wrapt in endless snow,
Where winter in his wildest fury reigns,
And subtile æther scarce our life maintains.
But here philosophers oppose the scheme:
This earth, say they, nor hills nor mountains knew
Ere yet the universal flood prevailed;
But when the mighty waters rose aloft,
Roused by the winds, they shook their solid base,
And, in convulsions, tore the deluged world,
'Till by the winds assuaged, again they fell,
And all their ragged bed exposed to view.
Perhaps far wandering toward the northern pole
The straits of Zembla, and the frozen zone,
And where the eastern Greenland almost joins
America's north point, the hardy tribes
Of banished Jews, Siberians, Tartars wild
Came over icy mountains, or on floats,
First reached these coasts, hid from the world beside—
And yet another argument more strange,
Reserved for men of deeper thought, and late,
Presents itself to view.—In Peleg's days,[1]
(So says the Hebrew seer's unerring pen)
This mighty mass of earth, this solid globe,
Was cleft in twain,—"divided" east and west,
While then perhaps the deep Atlantic roll'd,—
Through the vast chasm, and laved the solid world;
And traces indisputable remain
Of this primeval land now sunk and lost.—
The islands rising in our eastern main
Are but small fragments of this continent,
Whose two extremities were Newfoundland
And St. Helena.—One far in the north,
Where shivering seamen view with strange surprise
The guiding pole-star glittering o'er their heads;
The other near the southern tropic rears
Its head above the waves—Bermuda's isles,
Cape Verde, Canary, Britain, and the Azores,
With fam'd Hibernia, are but broken parts
Of some prodigious waste, which once sustain'd
Nations and tribes, of vanished memory,
Forests and towns, and beasts of every class,
Where navies now explore their briny way.

Leander

Your sophistry, Eugenio, makes me smile;
The roving mind of man delights to dwell
On hidden things, merely because they're hid:
He thinks his knowledge far beyond all limit,

[1] *Gen.* X, 25. [*Freneau's note.*]

And boldly fathoms Nature's darkest haunts;—
But for uncertainties, your broken isles,
Your northern Tartars, and your wandering Jews,
(The flimsy cobwebs of a sophist's brain)
Hear what the voice of history proclaims—
The Carthagenians, ere the Roman yoke
Broke their proud spirits, and enslaved them too,
For navigation were renowned as much
As haughty Tyre with all her hundred fleets,
Full many a league their venturous seamen sailed
Through strait Gibraltar, down the western shore
Of Africa, to the Canary isles:
By them called Fortunate; so Flaccus[1] sings.
Because eternal spring there clothes the fields
And fruits delicious bloom throughout the year.—
From voyaging here, this inference I draw,
Perhaps some barque with all her numerous crew
Falling to leeward of her destined port,
Caught by the eastern Trade, was hurried on
Before the unceasing blast to Indian isles,
Brazil, La Plata, or the coasts more south—
There stranded, and unable to return,
Forever from their native skies estranged.
Doubtless they made these virgin climes their own,
And in the course of long revolving years
A numerous progeny from these arose,
And spread throughout the coasts—those whom we call
Brazilians, Mexicans, Peruvians rich,
The tribes of Chili, Patagon, and those
Who till the shores of Amazon's long stream.—
When first the power of Europe here attained,
Vast empires, kingdoms, cities, palaces
And polished nations stock'd the fertile land.
Who has not heard of Cusco, Lima, and
The town of Mexico—huge cities form'd
From Indian architecture; ere the arms
Of haughty Spain disturb'd the peaceful soil.—
But here, amid this northern dark domain
No towns were seen to rise.—No arts were here;
The tribes unskill'd to raise the lofty mast,
Or force the daring prow thro' adverse waves,
Gazed on the pregnant soil, and craved alone
Life from the unaided genius of the ground,—
This indicates they were a different race;
From whom descended, 'tis not ours to say—
That power, no doubt, who furnish'd trees, and plants,
And animals to this vast continent,
Spoke into being man among the rest,—
But what a change is here!—what arts arise!
What towns and capitals! how commerce waves
Her gaudy flags, where silence reign'd before!

Acasto

Speak, learned Eugenio, for I've heard you tell
The dismal story, and the cause that brought
The first adventurers to these western shores!
The glorious cause that urged our fathers first
To visit climes unknown, and wilder woods
Than e'er Tartarian or Norwegian saw,
And with fair culture to adorn a soil
That never felt the industrious swain before.

Eugenio

All this long story to rehearse, would tire;
Besides, the sun towards the west retreats,
Nor can the noblest theme retard his speed,
Nor loftiest verse—not that which sang the fall
Of Troy divine, and fierce Achilles' ire.—
Yet hear a part:—By persecution wronged,
And sacerdotal rage, our fathers came
From Europe's hostile shores to these abodes,
Here to enjoy a liberty in faith,
Secure from tyranny and base control.
For this they left their country and their friends,
And plough'd the Atlantic wave in quest of peace;
And found new shores, and sylvan settlements,
And men, alike unknowing and unknown.
Hence, by the care of each adventurous chief
New governments (their wealth unenvied yet)
Were form'd on liberty and virtue's plan.
These searching out uncultivated tracts
Conceived new plans of towns, and capitals,
And spacious provinces.—Why should I name
Thee, Penn, the Solon of our western lands;
Sagacious legislator, whom the world
Admires, long dead: an infant colony,
Nursed by thy care, now rises o'er the rest

[1] *Hor. Epod.* 16. [*Freneau's note.*]

Like that tall pyramid in Egypt's waste
O'er all the neighboring piles, they also great.
Why should I name those heroes so well known,
Who peopled all the rest from Canada
To Georgia's farthest coasts, West Florida,
Or Appalachian mountains?—Yet what streams
Of blood were shed! what Indian hosts were slain,
Before the days of peace were quite restored!

Leander

Yes, while they overturn'd the rugged soil
And swept the forests from the shaded plain
'Midst dangers, foes, and death, fierce Indian tribes
With vengeful malice arm'd, and black design,
Oft murdered, or dispersed, these colonies—
Encouraged, too, by Gallia's hostile sons,
A warlike race, who late their arms display'd,
At Quebec, Montreal, and farthest coasts
Of Labrador, or Cape Breton, where now
The British standard awes the subject host.
Here, those brave chiefs, who, lavish of their blood,
Fought in Britannia's cause, in battle fell!—
What heart but mourns the untimely fate of Wolfe,
Who, dying, conquered!—or what breast but beats
To share a fate like his, and die like him!

Acasto

But why alone commemorate the dead,
And pass those glorious heroes by, who yet
Breathe the same air, and see the light with us?—
The dead, Leander, are but empty names,
And they who fall today the same to us
As they who fell ten centuries ago!—
Lost are they all that shined on earth before;
Rome's boldest champions in the dust are laid,
Ajax and great Achilles are no more,
And Philip's warlike son, an empty shade!—
A Washington among our sons of fame
Will rise conspicuous as the morning star
Among the inferior lights:—
To distant wilds Virginia sent him forth—
With her brave sons he gallantly opposed
The bold invaders of his country's rights,
Where wild Ohio pours the mazy flood,
And mighty meadows skirt his subject streams.—
But now, delighting in his elm tree's shade,
Where deep Potowmac laves the enchanting shore,
He prunes the tender vine, or bids the soil
Luxuriant harvest to the sun display.—
Behold a different scene—not thus employed
Were Cortez, and Pizarro, pride of Spain,
Whom blood and murder only satisfied,
And all to glut their avarice and ambition!—

Eugenio

Such is the curse, Acasto, where the soul
Humane is wanting—but we boast no feats
Of cruelty like Europe's murdering breed—
Our milder epithet is merciful,
And each American, true hearted, learns
To conquer, and to spare; for coward souls
Alone seek vengeance on a vanquished foe.
Gold, fatal gold, was the alluring bait
To Spain's rapacious tribes—hence rose the wars
From Chili to the Caribbean sea,
And Montezuma's Mexican domains:
More blest are we, with whose unenvied soil
Nature decreed no mingling gold to shine,
No flashing diamond, precious emerald,
No blushing sapphire, ruby, chrysolite,
Or jasper red—more noble riches flow
From agriculture, and the industrious swain,
Who tills the fertile vale, or mountain's brow,
Content to lead a safe, a humble life,
Among his native hills, romantic shades
Such as the muse of Greece of old did feign,
Allured the Olympian gods from crystal skies,
Envying such lovely scenes to mortal man.

Leander

Long has the rural life been justly fam'd,
And bards of old their pleasing pictures drew
Of flowery meads, and groves, and gliding streams:
Hence, old Arcadia—wood-nymphs, satyrs, fauns;
And hence Elysium, fancied heaven below!—
Fair agriculture, not unworthy kings,
Once exercised the royal hand, or those
Whose virtues raised them to the rank of gods.

See, old Laertes [1] in his shepherd weeds
Far from his pompous throne and court august,
Digging the grateful soil, where round him rise,
Sons of the earth, the tall aspiring oaks,
Or orchards, boasting of more fertile boughs,
Laden with apples red, sweet scented peach,
Pear, cherry, apricot, or spungy plum;
While through the glebe the industrious oxen draw
The earth-inverting plough.—Those Romans too,
Fabricius and Camillus, loved a life
Of neat simplicity and rustic bliss,
And from the noisy Forum hastening far,
From busy camps, and sycophants, and crowns,
'Midst woods and fields spent the remains of life,
Where full enjoyment still awaits the wise.
  How grateful, to behold the harvests rise,
And mighty crops adorn the extended plains!—
Fair plenty smiles throughout, while lowing herds
Stalk o'er the shrubby hill or grassy mead,
Or at some shallow river slake their thirst.—
The inclosure, now, succeeds the shepherd's care,
Yet milk-white flocks adorn the well stock'd farm,
And court the attention of the industrious swain—
Their fleece rewards him well, and when the winds
Blow with a keener blast, and from the north
Pour mingled tempests through a sunless sky
(Ice, sleet, and rattling hail) secure he sits
Warm in his cottage, fearless of the storm,
Enjoying now the toils of milder moons,
Yet hoping for the spring.—Such are the joys,
And such the toils of those whom heaven hath bless'd
With souls enamored of a country life.

Acasto

Such are the visions of the rustic reign—
But this alone, the fountain of support,
Would scarce employ the varying mind of man;
Each seeks employ, and each a different way:
Strip Commerce of her sail, and men once more
Would be converted into savages;—
No nation e'er grew social and refined
'Till Commerce first had wing'd the adventurous prow,
Or sent the slow-paced caravan, afar,
To waft their produce to some other clime,
And bring the wished exchange—thus came, of old,
Golconda's golden ore, and thus the wealth
Of Ophir, to the wisest of mankind.

Eugenio

Great is the praise of Commerce, and the men
Deserve our praise, who spread the undaunted sail,
And traverse every sea—their dangers great,
Death still to combat in the unfeeling gale,
And every billow but a gaping grave:—
There, skies and waters, wearying on the eye,
For weeks and months no other prospect yield
But barren wastes, unfathomed depths, where not
The blissful haunt of human form is seen
To cheer the unsocial horrors of the way.—
Yet all these bold designs to Science owe
Their rise and glory—Hail, fair Science! thou,
Transplanted from the eastern skies, dost bloom
In these blest regions—Greece and Rome no more
Detain the Muses on Citheron's brow,
Or old Olympus, crowned with waving woods,
Or Haemus' top, where once was heard the harp,
Sweet Orpheus' harp, that gained his cause below,
And pierced the souls of Orcus and his bride;
That hushed to silence by its voice divine
Thy melancholy waters, and the gales
O Hebrus! that o'er thy sad surface blow.—
No more the maids round Alpheus' waters stray,
Where he with Arethusa's stream doth mix,
Or where swift Tiber disembogues his waves
Into the Italian sea, so long unsung;
Hither they wing their way, the last, the best
Of countries, where the arts shall rise and grow,
And arms shall have their day—even now we boast
A Franklin, prince of all philosophy,
A genius piercing as the electric fire,

[1] *Hom. Odyss.* B. 24. [*Freneau's note.*]

Bright as the lightning's flash, explained so well,
By him, the rival of Britannia's sage.[1]
This is the land of every joyous sound,
Of liberty and life, sweet liberty!
Without whose aid the noblest genius fails,
And Science irretrievably must die.

Leander

But come, Eugenio, since we know the past—
What hinders to pervade with searching eye
The mystic scenes of dark futurity!
Say, shall we ask what empires yet must rise,
What kingdoms, powers and states, where now are seen
Mere dreary wastes and awful solitude,
Where Melancholy sits, with eye forlorn,
And time anticipates, when we shall spread
Dominion from the north, and south, and west,
Far from the Atlantic to Pacific shores,
And people half the convex of the main!—
A glorious theme!—but how shall mortals dare
To pierce the dark events of future years
And scenes unravel, only known to fate?

Acasto

This might we do, if warmed by that bright coal
Snatch'd from the altar of cherubic fire
Which touched Isaiah's lips—or if the spirit
Of Jeremy and Amos, prophets old,
Might swell the heaving breast—I see, I see
Freedom's established reign; cities, and men,
Numerous as sands upon the ocean shore,
And empires rising where the sun descends!—
The Ohio soon shall glide by many a town
Of note; and where the Mississippi stream,
By forests shaded, now runs weeping on,
Nations shall grow, and states not less in fame
Than Greece and Rome of old!—we too shall boast
Our Scipios, Solons, Catos, sages, chiefs
That in the lap of time yet dormant lie,
Waiting the joyous hour of life and light—
O snatch me hence, ye muses, to those days
When, through the veil of dark antiquity,
A race shall hear of us as things remote,
That blossomed in the morn of days—Indeed,
How could I weep that we exist so soon,

[1] Newton. [*Freneau's note.*]

Just in the dawning of these mighty times,
Whose scenes are painting for eternity!
Dissensions that shall swell the trump of fame,
And ruin hovering o'er all monarchy!

Eugenio

Nor shall these angry tumults here subside
Nor murder [1] cease, through all these provinces,
Till foreign crowns have vanished from our view
And dazzle here no more—no more presume
To awe the spirit of fair Liberty—
Vengeance must cut the thread—and Britain, sure
Will curse her fatal obstinacy for it!
Bent on the ruin of this injured country,
She will not listen to our humble prayers,
Though offered with submission:
Like vagabonds and objects of destruction,
Like those whom all mankind are sworn to hate,
She casts us off from her protection,
And will invite the nations round about,
Russians and Germans, slaves and savages,
To come and have a share in our perdition—
O cruel race, O unrelenting Britain,
Who bloody beasts will hire to cut our throats,
Who war will wage with prattling innocence,
And basely murder unoffending women!—
Will stab their prisoners when they cry for quarter,
Will burn our towns, and from his lodging turn
The poor inhabitant to sleep in tempests!—
These will be wrongs, indeed, and all sufficient
To kindle up our souls to deeds of horror,
And give to every arm the nerves of Sampson—
These are the men that fill the world with ruin,
And every region mourns their greedy sway,—
Not only for ambition——
But what are this world's goods, that they for them
Should exercise perpetual butchery?
What are these mighty riches we possess,
That they should send so far to plunder them—?—

[1] The English massacre at Boston, March 5th, 1770, is here more particularly glanced at. [*Freneau's note.*]

Already have we felt their potent arm—
And ever since that inauspicious day,
When first Sir Francis Bernard
His ruffians planted at the council door,
And made the assembly room a home for vagrants,
And soldiers, rank and file—e'er since that day
This wretched land, that drinks its children's gore,
Has been a scene of tumult and confusion!—
Are there not evils in the world enough?
Are we so happy that they envy us?
Have we not toiled to satisfy their harpies,
Kings' deputies, that are insatiable;
Whose practice is to incense the royal mind
And make us despicable in his view?—
  Have we not all the evils to contend with
That, in this life, mankind are subject to,
Pain, sickness, poverty, and natural death—
But into every wound that nature gave
They will a dagger plunge, and make them mortal!

Leander

Enough, enough!—such dismal scenes you paint,
I almost shudder at the recollection—
What! are they dogs that they would mangle us?—
Are these the men that come with base design
To rob the hive, and kill the industrious bee!—
To brighter skies I turn my ravished view,
And fairer prospects from the future draw—
Here independent power shall hold her sway,
And public virtue warm the patriot breast:
No traces shall remain of tyranny,
And laws, a pattern to the world beside,
Be here enacted first.——

Acasto

And when a train of rolling years are past,
(So sung the exiled seer in Patmos isle)
A new Jerusalem, sent down from heaven,
Shall grace our happy earth,—perhaps this land,
Whose ample bosom shall receive, though late,
Myriads of saints, with their immortal king,
To live and reign on earth a thousand years,
Thence called Millennium. Paradise anew
Shall flourish, by no second Adam lost,
No dangerous tree with deadly fruit shall grow,
No tempting serpent to allure the soul
From native innocence.—A Canaan here,
Another Canaan shall excel the old,
And from a fairer Pisgah's top be seen.
No thistle here, nor thorn, nor briar shall spring,
Earth's curse before: the lion and the lamb
In mutual friendship linked, shall browse the shrub,
And timorous deer with softened tigers stray
O'er mead, or lofty hill, or grassy plain;
Another Jordan's stream shall glide along,
And Siloah's brook in circling eddies flow:
Groves shall adorn their verdant banks, on which
The happy people, free from toils and death,
Shall find secure repose. No fierce disease,
No fevers, slow consumption, ghastly plague,
(Fate's ancient ministers) again proclaim
Perpetual war with man: fair fruits shall bloom,
Fair to the eye, and sweeter to the taste;
Nature's loud storms be hushed, and seas no more
Rage hostile to mankind—and, worse than all,
The fiercer passions of the human breast
Shall kindle up to deeds of death no more,
But all subside in universal peace.——
                    —Such days the world,
And such America at last shall have
When ages, yet to come, have run their round,
And future years of bliss alone remain.

1771 1772, 1786

A POLITICAL LITANY

Libera Nos, Domine.—Deliver us, O Lord, not only from British Dependence, but also,

From a junto that labor with absolute power,
Whose schemes disappointed have made them look sour,
From the lords of the council, who fight against freedom,
Who still follow on where delusion shall lead them.

From the group at St. James's who slight our petitions,
And fools that are waiting for further submissions—

From a nation whose manners are rough and severe,
From scoundrels and rascals,—do keep us all clear.

From pirates sent out by command of the king
To murder and plunder, but never to swing;
From Wallace and Greaves, and *Vipers* and *Roses*,[1]
Whom, if heaven pleases, we'll give bloody noses.

From the valiant Dunmore, with his crew of banditti,
Who plunder Virginians at Williamsburg city,
From hot-headed Montague, mighty to swear,
The little fat man, with his pretty white hair.

From bishops in Britain, who butchers are grown,
From slaves, that would die for a smile from the throne,
From assemblies, that vote against Congress proceedings,
(Who now see the fruit of their stupid misleadings.)

From Tryon the mighty, who flies from our city,
And swelled with importance disdains the committee:
(But since he is pleased to proclaim us his foes,
What the devil care we where the devil he goes.)

From the caitiff, lord North, who would bind us in chains,
From a royal king Log, with his tooth-full of brains,
Who dreams, and is certain (when taking a nap)
He has conquered our lands, as they lay on his map.

From a kingdom that bullies, and hectors, and swears,
We send up to heaven our wishes and prayers
That we, disunited, may freemen be still,
And Britain go on—to be damned if she will.

New-York, June 1775 1775(?)

[1] Captains and ships in the British navy, then employed on the American coast. [*Freneau's note.*]

THE DYING ELM

SWEET, lovely Elm, who here dost grow
Companion of unsocial care,
Lo! thy dejected branches die
Amidst this torrid air—
Smit by the sun or blasting moon,
Like fainting flowers, their verdure gone.

Thy withering leaves, that drooping hang,
Presage thine end approaching nigh;
And lo! thy amber tears distill,
Attended with that last departing sigh—
O charming tree! no more decline,
But be thy shades and love-sick whispers mine.

Forbear to die—this weeping eve
Shall shed her little drops on you,
Shall o'er thy sad disaster grieve,
And wash your wounds with pearly dew,
Shall pity you, and pity me,
And heal the languor of my tree!

Short is thy life, if thou so soon must fade,
Like angry Jonah's gourd at Nineveh,
That, in a night, its bloomy branches spread,
And perished with the day.—
Come, then, revive, sweet lovely Elm, lest I,
Thro' vehemence of heat, like Jonah, wish to die.

1779, 1786

ON RETIREMENT

A HERMIT's house beside a stream
With forests planted round,
Whatever it to you may seem
More real happiness I deem
Than if I were a monarch crown'd.

A cottage I could call my own
Remote from domes of care;
A little garden, wall'd with stone,
The wall with ivy overgrown,
A limpid fountain near,

Would more substantial joys afford,
More real bliss impart
Than all the wealth that misers hoard,
Than vanquished worlds, or worlds restored—
Mere cankers of the heart!

Vain foolish man! how vast thy pride,
How little can thy wants supply!—
'Tis surely wrong to grasp so wide—
You act as if you only had
To vanquish—not to die!

1786

THE PICTURES OF COLUMBUS, THE GENOESE [1]

Picture I

COLUMBUS MAKING MAPS [2]

As o'er his charts Columbus ran,
Such disproportion he survey'd,
He thought he saw in art's mean plan
Blunders that Nature never made;
The land in one poor corner plac'd,
And all beside, a swelling waste!—
"It can't be so," Columbus said;

"This world on paper idly drawn,
O'er one small tract so often gone
The pencil tires; in this void space
Allow'd to find no resting place.

"But copying Nature's bold design,
If true to her, no fault is mine;
Perhaps in these moist regions dwell
Forms wrought like man, and lov'd as well.

"Yet to the west what lengthen'd seas!
Are no gay islands found in these,
No sylvan worlds that Nature meant
To balance Asia's vast extent?

"As late a mimic globe I made
(Imploring Fancy to my aid)
O'er these wild seas a shade I threw,
And a new world my pencil drew.

"But westward plac'd, and far away
In the deep seas this country lay
Beyond all climes already known,
In Neptune's bosom plac'd alone.

"Who knows but he that hung this ball
In the clear void, and governs all,
On those dread scenes, remote from view,
Has trac'd his great idea too.

"What can these idle charts avail—
O'er real seas I mean to sail;
If fortune aids the grand design,
Worlds yet unthought of shall be mine.

"But how shall I this country find!
Gay, painted picture of the mind!
Religion [1] holds my project vain,
And owns no worlds beyond the main.

"'Midst yonder hills long time has stay'd
In sylvan cells a wondrous maid,
Who things to come can truly tell,
Dread mistress of the magic spell.

"Whate'er the depths of time can shew
All pass before her in review,
And all events her eyes survey,
'Till time and nature both decay.

"I'll to her cave, enquiring there
What mighty things the fates prepare;
Whether my hopes and plans are vain,
Or I must give new worlds to Spain."

Picture II

THE CELL OF AN INCHANTRESS

Inchantress

Who dares attempt this gloomy grove
Where never shepherd dream'd of love,
And birds of night are only found,
And poisonous weeds bestrew the ground:
Hence, stranger, take some other road,
Nor dare profane my dark abode;
The winds are high, the moon is low—
Would you enter?—no, no, no:—

Columbus

Sorceress of mighty power! [2]
Hither at the midnight hour

[1] Text from the edition of 1788.

[2] History informs us this was his original profession: and from the disproportionate vacancy observable in the drafts of that time between Europe and Asia to the west, it is most probable he first took the idea of another continent, lying in a parallel direction to, and existing between both. [*Freneau's note.*]

[1] The Inquisition made it criminal to assert the existence of the Antipodes. [*Freneau's note.*]

[2] The fifteenth century was, like many of the preceding, an age of superstition, cruelty, and ignorance. When this circumstance, therefore, is brought into view, the mixture of truth and fiction will not appear altogether absurd or

Over hill and dale I've come,
Leaving ease and sleep at home:
With daring aims my bosom glows;
Long a stranger to repose,
I have come to learn from you
Whether phantoms I pursue,
Or if, as reason would persuade,
New worlds are on the ocean laid—
Tell me, wonder-working maid,
Tell me, dire inchantress, tell,
Mistress of the magic spell!

Inchantress

The staring owl her note has sung;
With gaping snakes my cave is hung;
Of maiden hair my bed is made,
Two winding sheets above it laid;
With bones of men my shelves are pil'd,
And toads are for my supper boil'd;
Three ghosts attend to fill my cup,
And four to serve my pottage up;
The crow is waiting to say grace:—
Wouldst thou in such a dismal place
The secrets of thy fortune trace?

Columbus

Though death and all his dreary crew
Were to be open'd on my view,
I would not from this threshold fly
'Till you had made a full reply.
Open wide this iron gate,
I must read the book of fate:
Tell me, if beyond the main
Islands are reserv'd for Spain;
Tell me, if beyond the sea
Worlds are to be found by me:
Bid your spirits disappear,
Phantoms of delusive fear,
These are visions I despise,
Shadows and uncertainties.

Inchantress

Must I, then, yield to your request!
Columbus, why disturb my rest!—
For this the ungrateful shall combine,
And hard misfortune shall be thine;—
For this the base reward remains
Of cold neglect and galling chains! [1]

In a poor solitude forgot,
Reproach and want shall be the lot
Of him that gives new worlds to Spain,
And westward spreads her golden reign.
Before you came to vex my bower
I slept away the evening hour,
Or watch'd the rising of the moon,
With hissing vipers keeping tune,
Or galloping along the glade
Took pleasure in the lunar shade,
And gather'd herbs, or made a prize
Of horses' tails and adders' eyes:
Now open flies the iron gate,
Advance, and read the book of fate!
On thy design what woes attend!
The nations at the ocean's end,
No longer destin'd to be free,
Shall owe distress and death to thee!
The seats of innocence and love
Shall soon the scenes of horror prove:
But why disturb these Indian climes,
The pictures of more happy times!
Has avarice, with unfeeling breast,
Has cruelty thy soul possess'd?
May ruin on thy boldness wait!—
Advance, and read the book of fate.
When vulture, fed but once a week,
And ravens three together shriek,
And skeleton for vengeance cries,
Then shall the fatal curtain rise!
Two lamps in yonder vaulted room,
Suspended o'er a brazen tomb,
Shall lend their glimmerings, as you pass,
To find your fortune in that glass
Whose wondrous virtue is, to show
Whate'er the inquirer wants to know.

PICTURE III

THE MIRROR

Columbus

Strange things I see, bright mirror, in thy
breast:—
There Perseverance stands, and nobly scorns
The gabbling tongue of busy calumny:

---

unnatural. At any rate, it has ever been tolerated in this species of poetry. [*Freneau's note.*]

[1] In 1498 he was superseded in his command at Hispaniola and sent home in irons. Soon after finishing his fourth voyage, finding himself neglected by the Court of Spain after all his services, he retired to Valladolid, in Old Castile, where he died on the 20th of May, A.D. 1506. [*Freneau's note.*]

Proud Erudition in a scholar's garb
Derides my plans and grins a jeering smile.
Hypocrisy, clad in a doctor's gown,
A western continent deems heresy:
The princes, kings, and nobles of the land
Smile at my projects, and report me mad:
One royal woman only stands my friend,
Bright Isabell, the lady of our hearts,
Whom avarice prompts to aid my purposes,
And love of toys—weak female vanity!—
She gains her point!—three slender barques I see
(Or else the witch's glass deceives mine eye)
Rigg'd trim, and furnish'd out with stores and men,
Fitted for tedious journeys o'er the main:
Columbus—ha!—their motions he directs;
Their captains come, and ask advice from him,
Holding him for the soul of resolution.
Now, now we launch from Palos! prosperous gales
Impel the canvas: now the far fam'd strait
Is pass'd, the pillars of the son of Jove,
Long held the limits of the paths of men:
Ah! what a waste of ocean here begins,
And lonely waves, so black and comfortless!
Light flies each bounding galley o'er the main;
Now Lancerota gathers on our view,
And Teneriffe her clouded summit rears:
Awhile we linger at these islands fair
That seem the utmost boundaries of the world,
Then westward aiming on the unfathom'd deep
Sorrowing, with heavy hearts we urge our way.
Now all is discontent—such oceans pass'd,
No land appearing yet, dejects the most;
Yet, fertile in expedients, I alone
The mask of mild content am forc'd to wear:
A thousand signs I see, or feign to see,
Of shores at hand, and bottoms underneath;
And not a bird that wanders o'er the main,
And not a cloud that traverses the sky
But brings me something to support their hopes:
All fails at last!—so frequently deceiv'd
They growl with anger—mad to look at death
They gnash their teeth, and will be led no more;
On me their vengeance turns: they look at me
As their conductor to the realms of ruin:
Plot after plot discover'd, not reveng'd,
They join against their chief in mutiny:
They urge to plunge him in the boiling deep
As one, the only one that would pursue
Imaginary worlds through boundless seas:—
The scene is chang'd—Fine islands greet mine eye,
Cover'd with trees, and beasts, and yellow men;
Eternal summer through the valleys smiles
And fragrant gales o'er golden meadows play!—
Inchantress, 'tis enough!—now veil your glass—
The curtain falls—and I must homeward pass.

Picture IV

COLUMBUS ADDRESSES KING FERDINAND

Prince and pride of Spain! while meaner crowns,
Pleas'd with the shadow of monarchial sway,
Exact obedience from some paltry tract
Scarce worth the pain and toil of governing,
Be thine the generous care to send thy fame
Beyond the knowledge, or the guess of man.
This gulphy deep (that bounds our western reign
So long by civil feuds and wars disgrac'd)
Must be the passage to some other shore
Where nations dwell, children of early time,
Basking in the warm sunshine of the south,
Who some false deity, no doubt, adore,
Owning no virtue in the potent cross:
What honor, sire, to plant your standards there,[1]
And souls recover to our holy faith
That now in paths of dark perdition stray
Warp'd to his worship by the evil one!
Think not that Europe and the Asian waste,
Or Africa, where barren sands abound,
Are the sole gems in Neptune's bosom laid:
Think not the world a vast extended plain:
See yon bright orbs, that through the ether move,
All globular; this earth a globe like them
Walks her own rounds, attended by the moon,
Bright comrade, but with a borrowed lustre bright.

[1] It is allowed by most historians that Ferdinand was an implicit believer and one of the most superstitious bigots of his age. [*Freneau's note.*]

If all the surface of this mighty round
Be one wide ocean of unfathom'd depth
Bounding the little space already known,
Nature must have forgot her wonted wit
And made a monstrous havoc of proportion.
If her proud depths were not restrain'd by
lands,
And broke by continents of vast extent
Existing somewhere under western skies,
Far other waves would roll before the storms
Than ever yet have burst on Europe's shores,
Driving before them deluge and confusion.
But Nature will preserve what she has plann'd:
And the whole suffrage of antiquity,
Platonic dreams, and reason's plainer page
All point at something that we ought to see
Buried behind the waters of the west,
Clouded with the shadows of uncertainty.
The time is come for some sublime event
Of mighty fame:—mankind are children yet,
And hardly dream what treasures they possess
In the dark bosom of the fertile main,
Unfathom'd, unattempted, unexplor'd.
These, mighty prince, I offer to reveal,
And by the magnet's aid, if you supply
Ships and some gallant hearts, will hope to
bring
From distant climes, news worthy of a king.

Picture V

FERDINAND AND HIS FIRST MINISTER

Ferdinand

What would this madman have, this odd projector!
A wild address I have today attended,
Mingling its folly with our great affairs,
Dreaming of islands and new hemispheres
Plac'd on the ocean's verge, we know not
where—
What shall I do with this petitioner?

Minister

Even send him, sire, to perish in his search:
He has so pester'd me these many years
With idle projects of discovery—
His name—I almost dread to hear it mention'd:
He is a Genoese of vulgar birth
And has been round all Europe with his plans
Presenting them to every potentate;
He lives, 'tis said, by vending maps and charts,
And being us'd to sketch imagin'd islands
On that blank space that represents the seas,
His head at last grows giddy with this folly,
And fancied isles are turned to real lands
With which he puzzles me perpetually:
What pains me too, is, that our royal lady
Lends him her ear, and reads his mad addresses,
Oppos'd to reason and philosophy.

Ferdinand

He acts the devil's part in Eden's garden;
Knowing the man was proof to his temptations
He whisper'd something in the ear of Eve,
And promis'd much, but meant not to perform.

Minister

I've treated all his schemes with such contempt
That any but a rank, mad-brain'd enthusiast,
Pushing his purpose to extremities,
Would have forsook your empire, royal sir,
Discourag'd, and forgotten long ago.

Ferdinand

Has he so long been busy at his projects?—
I scarcely heard of him till yesterday:
A plan pursued with so much obstinacy
Looks not like madness:—wretches of that
stamp
Survey a thousand objects in an hour,
In love with each, and yet attach'd to none
Beyond the moment that it meets the eye—
But him I honor, tho' in beggar's garbs,
Who has a soul of so much constancy
As to bear up against the hard rebuffs,
Sneers of great men, and insolence of power,
And through the opposition of them all
Pursues his object:—Minister, this man
Must have our notice:—Let him be commissioned
Viceroy of all the lands he shall discover,
Admiral and general in the fleets of Spain;
Let three stout ships be instantly selected,
The best and strongest ribb'd of all we own,
With men to man them, patient of fatigue:
But stay, attend! how stands our treasury?—

Minister

Empty—even to the bottom, royal sir!
We have not coin for bare necessities,
Much less, so pardon me, to spend on madmen.

Picture VI

COLUMBUS ADDRESSES QUEEN ISABELLA

While Turkish queens, dejected, pine,
Compell'd sweet freedom to resign;
And taught one virtue, to obey,
Lament some eastern tyrant's sway,

Queen of our hearts, bright Isabell!
A happier lot to you has fell,
Who makes a nation's bliss your own,
And share the rich Castilian throne.

Exalted thus, beyond all fame,
Assist, fair lady, that proud aim
Which would your native reign extend
To the wide world's remotest end.

From science, fed by busy thought,
New wonders to my view are brought:
The vast abyss beyond our shore
I deem impassable no more.

Let those that love to dream or sleep
Pretend no limits to the deep:
I see beyond the rolling main
Abounding wealth reserv'd for Spain.

From Nature's earliest days conceal'd,
Men of their own these climates yield,
And scepter'd dames, no doubt, are there,
Queens like yourself, but not so fair.

But what should most provoke desire
Are the fine pearls that they admire,
And diamonds bright and coral green
More fit to grace a Spanish queen.

Their yellow shells, and virgin gold,
And silver, for our trinkets sold,
Shall well reward this toil and pain,
And bid our commerce shine again.

As men were forc'd from Eden's shade
By errors that a woman made,
Permit me at a woman's cost
To find the climates that we lost.

He that with you partakes command,
The nation's hope, great Ferdinand,
Attends, indeed, to my request,
But wants no empires in the west.

Then, queen, supply the swelling sail,
For eastward breathes the steady gale
That shall the meanest barque convey
To regions richer than Cathay.[1]

Arriv'd upon that flowery coast
Whole towns of golden temples boast,
While these bright objects strike our view
Their wealth shall be reserv'd for you.

Each swarthy king shall yield his crown,
And smiling lay their sceptres down,
When they, not tam'd by force of arms,
Shall hear the story of your charms.

Did I an empty dream pursue
Great honor still must wait on you,
Who sent the lads of Spain to keep
Such vigils on the untravell'd deep,

Who fix'd the bounds of land and sea,
Trac'd Nature's works through each degree,
Imagin'd some unheard of shore
But prov'd that there was nothing more.

Yet happier prospects, I maintain,
Shall open on your female reign,
While ages hence with rapture tell
How much they owe to Isabell!

Picture VII

QUEEN ISABELLA'S PAGE OF HONOR WRITING A REPLY TO COLUMBUS

Your yellow shells, and coral green,
And gold, and silver—not yet seen,
Have made such mischief in a woman's mind
The queen could almost pillage from the crown,
And add some costly jewels of her own,
Thus sending you that charming coast to find
Where all these heavenly things abound,
Queens in the west, and chiefs renown'd.
But then no great men take you by the hand,
Nor are the nobles busied in your aid;
The clergy have no relish for your scheme,
And deem it madness—one archbishop said
You were bewilder'd in a paltry dream
That led directly to undoubted ruin,
Your own and other men's undoing:—

[1] The ancient name for China. [*Freneau's note.*]

And our confessor says it is not true,
And calls it heresy in you
Thus to assert the world is round,
And that Antipodes are found
Held to the earth, we can't tell how.—
  But you shall sail; I heard the queen declare
That mere geography is not her care;—
And thus she bids me say,
"Columbus, haste away,
Hasten to Palos, and if you can find
Three barques, of structure suited to your mind,
Straight make a purchase in the royal name;
Equip them for the seas without delay,
Since long the journey is (we heard you say)
To that rich country which we wish to claim—
Let them be small!—for know the crown is poor
Though basking in the sunshine of renown.
Long wars have wasted us: the pride of Spain
Was ne'er before so high, nor purse so mean;
Giving us ten years' war, the humbled Moor
Has left us little else but victory:
Time must restore past splendor to our reign."

Picture VIII

COLUMBUS AT THE HARBOR OF PALOS, IN ANDALUSIA

Columbus

  In three small barques to cross so vast a sea,
Held to be boundless, even in learning's eye,
And trusting only to a magic glass,
Which may have represented things untrue,
Shadows and visions for realities!—
It is a bold attempt!—Yet I must go,
Travelling the surge to its great boundary;
Far, far away beyond the reach of men,
Where never galley spread her milk-white sail
Or weary pilgrim bore the Christian name!
  But though I were confirm'd in my design
And saw the whole event with certainty,
How shall I so exert my eloquence,
And hold such arguments with vulgar minds
As to convince them I am not an idiot
Chasing the visions of a shatter'd brain,
Ending in their perdition and my own?
The world, and all its wisdom is against me;
The dreams of priests; philosophy in chains;
False learning swoln with self-sufficiency;
Men seated at the helm of royalty
Reasoning like school-boys;—what discouragements!
Experience holds herself mine enemy,
And one weak woman only hears my story!—
I'll make a speech—"Here jovial sailors, here!
Ye that would rise beyond the rags of fortune,
Struggling too long with hopeless poverty
Coasting your native shores on shallow seas,
Vex'd by the galleys of the Ottoman;
Now meditate with me a bolder plan,
Catching at fortune in her plenitude!
He that shall undertake this voyage with me
Shall be no longer held a vulgar man:
Princes shall wish they had been our companions,
And Science blush she did not go along
To learn a lesson that might humble pride
Now grinning idly from a pedant's cap,
Lurking behind the veil of cowardice.
  "Far in the west a golden region lies
Unknown, unvisited for many an age,
Teeming with treasures to enrich the brave.
Embark, embark—Columbus leads the way—
Why, friends, existence is alike to me
Dear and desirable with other men;
What good could I devise in seeking ruin?
Embark, I say; and he that sails with me
Shall reap a harvest of immortal honor:
Wealthier he shall return than they that now
Lounge in the lap of principalities,
Hoarding the gorgeous treasures of the east."—
  Alas, alas! they turn their backs upon me,
And rather choose to wallow in the mire
Of want, and torpid inactivity,
Than by one bold and masterly exertion
Themselves ennoble, and enrich their country!

Picture IX

A SAILOR'S HUT, NEAR THE SHORE

Thomas and Susan

Thomas

I wish I was over the water again!
'Tis a pity we cannot agree;
When I try to be merry 'tis labor in vain,
You always are scolding at me;

Then what shall I do
With this termagant Sue;
Tho' I hug her and squeeze her
I never can please her—
Was there ever a devil like you!

Susan

If I was a maid as I now am a wife
With a sot and a brat to maintain,
I think it should be the first care of my life,
To shun such a drunkard again:
Not one of the crew
Is so hated by Sue;
Though they always are bawling,
And pulling, and hauling—
Not one is a puppy like you.

Thomas

Dear Susan, I'm sorry that you should complain:
There is nothing indeed to be done;
If a war should break out, not a sailor in Spain
Would sooner be found at his gun:
Arriving from sea
I would kneel on one knee,
And the plunder presenting
To Susan relenting—
Who then would be honor'd like me!

Susan

Today as I came by the sign of the ship,
A mighty fine captain was there,
He was asking for sailors to take a small trip,
But I cannot remember well where:
He was hearty and free,
And if you can agree
To leave me, dear honey,
To bring me some money!—
How happy—indeed—I shall be!

Thomas

The man that you saw not a sailor can get,
'Tis a captain Columbus, they say;
To fit out a ship he is running in debt,
And our wages he never will pay:
Yes, yes, it is he,
And, Sue, do ye see,
On a wild undertaking
His heart he is breaking—
The devil may take him for me!

Picture X

BERNARDO, A SPANISH FRIAR, IN HIS CANONICALS

Did not our holy book most clearly say
This earth is built upon a pillar'd base;
And did not reason add convincing proofs
That this huge world is one continued plain
Extending onward to immensity,
Bounding with oceans these abodes of men,
I should suppose this dreamer had some hopes,
Some prospects built on probability.
What says our lord the pope—he cannot err—
He says, our world is not orbicular,
And has rewarded some with chains and death
Who dar'd defend such wicked heresies.
But we are turning heretics indeed!—
A foreigner, an idiot, an impostor,
An infidel (since he dares contradict
What our most holy order holds for truth)
Is pouring poison in the royal ear;
Telling him tales of islands in the moon,
Leading the nations into dangerous errors,
Slighting instruction from our brotherhood!—
O Jesu! Jesu! what an age is this!

Picture XI

OROSIO, A MATHEMATICIAN, WITH HIS SCALES AND COMPASSES

This persevering man succeeds at last!
The last gazette has publish'd to the world
That Ferdinand and Isabella grant
Three well-rigg'd ships to Christopher Columbus;
And have bestow'd the noble titles too
Of Admiral and Vice-Roy—great indeed!—
Who will not now project, and scrawl on paper—
Pretenders now shall be advanc'd to honor;
And every pedant that can frame a problem,
And every lad that can draw parallels
Or measure the subtension of an angle,
Shall now have ships to make discoveries.
This simple man would sail he knows not where;
Building on fables, schemes of certainty;—
Visions of Plato, mix'd with idle tales
Of later date, intoxicate his brain:
Let him advance beyond a certain point
In his fantastic voyage, and I foretell

He never can return: ay, let him go!—
There is a line towards the setting sun
Drawn on an ocean of tremendous depth,
(Where nature plac'd the limits of the day)
Haunted by dragons, fond of solitude,
Red serpents, fiery forms, and yelling hags,
Fit company for mad adventurers.—
There, when the sun descends, 'tis horror all;
His angry globe through vast abysses gliding
Burns in the briny bosom of the deep
Making a havoc so detestable,
And causing such a wasteful ebullition
That never island green, or continent
Could find foundation, there to grow upon.

Picture XII

COLUMBUS AND A PILOT

Columbus

To take on board the sweepings of a jail
Is inexpedient in a voyage like mine,
That will require most patient fortitude,
Strict vigilance and staid sobriety,
Contempt of death on cool reflection founded,
A sense of honor, motives of ambition,
And every sentiment that sways the brave.—
Princes should join me now!—not those I mean
Who lurk in courts, or revel in the shade
Of painted ceilings:—those I mean, more worthy,
Whose daring aims and persevering souls,
Soaring beyond the sordid views of fortune,
Bespeak the lineage of true royalty.

Pilot

A fleet arrived last month at Carthagene
From Smyrna, Cyprus, and the neighboring isles:
Their crews, releas'd from long fatigues at sea,
Have spent their earnings in festivity,
And hunger tells them they must out again.
Yet nothing instantly presents itself
Except your new and noble expedition:
The fleet must undergo immense repairs,
And numbers will be unemploy'd a while:
I'll take them in the hour of dissipation
(Before reflection has made cowards of them,
Suggesting questions of impertinence)
When desperate plans are most acceptable,
Impossibilities are possible,
And all the spring and vigor of the mind
Is strain'd to madness and audacity:
If you approve my scheme, our ninety men
(The number you pronounce to be sufficient)
Shall all be enter'd in a week, at most.

Columbus

Go, pilot, go—and every motive urge
That may put life into this expedition.
Early in August we must weigh our anchors.
Time wears apace—bring none but willing men,
So shall our orders be the better borne,
The people less inclin'd to mutiny.

Picture XIII

DISCONTENTS AT SEA

Antonio

Dreadful is death in his most gentle forms!—
More horrid still on this mad element,
So far remote from land—from friends remote!
So many thousand leagues already sail'd
In quest of visions!—what remains to us
But perishing in these moist solitudes;
Where many a day our corpses on the sea
Shall float unwept, unpitied, unentomb'd!
O fate most terrible!—undone Antonio!
Why didst thou listen to a madman's dreams,
Pregnant with mischief—why not, comrades, rise!—
See, Nature's self prepares to leave us here;
The needle, once so faithful to the pole,
Now quits his object and bewilders us;
Steering at random, just as chance directs—
O fate most terrible!—undone Antonio!—

Hernando

Borne to creation's utmost verge, I saw
New stars ascending, never view'd before!
Low sinks the bear!—O land, my native land,
Clear springs and shady groves! why did I change
Your aspect fair for these infernal wastes,
Peopled by monsters of another kind;
Ah me! design'd not for the view of man!

Columbus

Cease, dastards, cease; and be inform'd that man
Is nature's lord, and wields her to his will;

If her most noble works obey our aims,
How much more so ought worthless scum, like you,
Whose whole existence is a morning dream,
Whose life is sunshine on a wintry day,
Who shake at shadows, struck with palsied fear;
Measuring the limit of your lives by distance.

Antonio

Columbus, hear! when with the land we parted
You thirty days agreed to plough the main,
Directing westward.—Thirty have elaps'd,
And thirty more have now begun their round,
No land appearing yet, nor trace of land,
But distant fogs that mimic lofty isles,
Painting gay landscapes on the vaporish air,
Inhabited by fiends that mean our ruin—
You persevere, and have no mercy on us—
Then perish by yourself—we must return—
And know, our firm resolve is fix'd for Spain;
In this resolve we are unanimous.

Juan de Villa-Real to Columbus

(*A Billet*)

"I heard them over night a plot contriving
Of fatal purpose—have a care Columbus!—
They have resolv'd, as on the deck you stand,
Aiding the vigils of the midnight hour,
To plunge you headlong in the roaring deep,
And slaughter such as favor your design
Still to pursue this western continent."

Columbus, solus

Why, nature, hast thou treated those so ill,
Whose souls, capacious of immense designs,
Leave ease and quiet for a nation's glory,
Thus to subject them to these little things,
Insects, by heaven's decree in shapes of men!
But so it is, and so we must submit,
Bending to thee, the heaven's great chancellor!
But must I fail!—and by timidity!
Must thou to thy green waves receive me, Neptune,
Or must I basely with my ships return,
Nothing accomplish'd!—not one pearl discover'd,
One bit of gold to make our queen a bracelet,
One diamond for the crown of Ferdinand!
How will their triumph be confirm'd, who said
That I was mad!—Must I then change my course,
And quit the country that would straight appear,
If one week longer we pursued the sun!—
The witch's glass was not delusion, sure!—
All this, and more, she told me to expect!—

(*To the crew*)

"Assemble, friends; attend to what I say:
Signs unequivocal, at length, declare
That some great continent approaches us:
The sea no longer glooms unmeasur'd depths,
The setting sun discovers clouds that owe
Their origin to fens and woodland wastes,
Not such as breed on ocean's salt domain:—
Vast flocks of birds attend us on our way,
These all have haunts amidst the wat'ry void,
Sweet scenes of ease, and sylvan solitude,
And springs, and streams that we shall share with them.
Now, hear my most importunate request:
I call you all my friends; you are my equals,
Men of true worth and native dignity,
Whose spirits are too mighty to return
Most meanly home, when nothing is accomplish'd—
Consent to sail our wonted course with me
But one week longer, and if that be spent,
And nought appear to recompence our toil,
Then change our course and homeward haste away—
Nay, homeward not!—for that would be too base—
But to some negro coast, where we may hide,
And never think of Ferdinand again."

Hernando

One week!—too much—it shall not be, Columbus!
Already are we on the verge of ruin,
Warm'd by the sunshine of another sphere,
Fann'd by the breezes of the burning zone,
Launch'd out upon the world's extremities!—
Who knows where one week more may carry us?

Antonio

Nay, talk not to the traitor!—base Columbus,
To thee our ruin and our deaths we owe!
Away, away!—friends!—men at liberty,
Now free to act as best befits our case,

Appoint another pilot to the helm,
And Andalusia be our port again!

Columbus

Friends, is it thus you treat your admiral,
Who bears the honors of great Ferdinand,
The royal standard, and the arms of Spain!
Three days allow me—and I'll show new worlds.

Hernando

Three days!—one day will pass too tediously—
But in the name of all our crew, Columbus,
Whose speaker and controller I am own'd;
Since thou indeed art a most gallant man,
Three days we grant—but ask us not again!

Picture XIV

COLUMBUS AT CAT ISLAND

Columbus, solus

Hail, beauteous land! the first that greets mine eye
Since, bold, we left the cloud capp'd Teneriffe,
The world's last limit long suppos'd by men.—
Tir'd with dull prospects of the wat'ry waste
And midnight dangers that around us grew,
Faint hearts and feeble hands and traitors vile,
Thee, Holy Saviour, on this foreign land
We still adore, and name this coast from thee! [1]
In these green groves who would not wish to stay
Where guardian nature holds her quiet reign,
Where beardless men speak other languages,
Unknown to us, ourselves unknown to them.

Antonio

In tracing o'er the isle no gold I find—
Nought else but barren trees and craggy rocks
Where screaming sea-fowl mix their odious loves,
And fields of burning marle, where devils play
And men with copper skins talk barbarously—
What merit has our chief in sailing hither
Discovering countries of no real worth!

[1] He called the island San Salvador (Holy Saviour). It lies about 90 miles S. E. from Providence. [*Freneau's note.*]

Spain has enough of barren sands, no doubt,
And savages in crowds are found at home;—
Why then surmount the world's circumference
Merely to stock us with this Indian breed?

Hernando

Soft!—or Columbus will detect your murmuring—
This new found isle has re-instated him
In all our favors—see you yonder sands?—
Why, if you see them, swear that they are gold,
And gold like this shall be our homeward freight,
Gladding the heart of Ferdinand the great,
Who, when he sees it, shall say smilingly,
"Well done, advent'rous fellows, you have brought
The treasure we expected and deserv'd!"—
Hold!—I am wrong—there goes a savage man
With gold suspended from his ragged ears:
I'll brain the monster for the sake of gold;
There, savage, try the power of Spanish steel—
'Tis of Toledo [1]—true and trusty stuff!
He falls! he falls! the gold, the gold is mine!
First acquisition in this golden isle!—

Columbus, solus

Sweet sylvan scenes of innocence and ease,
How calm and joyous pass the seasons here!
No splendid towns or spiry turrets rise,
No lordly palaces—no tyrant kings
Enact hard laws to crush fair freedom here;
No gloomy jails to shut up wretched men;
All, all are free!—here God and nature reign;
Their works unsullied by the hands of men—
Ha! what is this—a murder'd wretch I see,
His blood yet warm—O hapless islander,
Who could have thus so basely mangled thee,
Who never offer'd insult to our shore—
Was it for those poor trinkets in your ears
Which by the custom of your tribe you wore,—
Now seiz'd away—and which would not have weigh'd
One poor piastre!
Is this the fruit of my discovery!
If the first scene is murder, what shall follow

[1] The best steel-blades in Spain are manufactured at Toledo and Bilboa. [*Freneau's note.*]

But havoc, slaughter, chains and devastation
In every dress and form of cruelty!
O injur'd Nature, whelm me in the deep,
And let not Europe hope for my return,
Or guess at worlds upon whose threshold now
So black a deed has just been perpetrated!—
We must away—enjoy your woods in peace,
Poor, wretched, injur'd, harmless islanders;—
On Hayti's [1] isle you say vast stores are found
Of this destructive gold—which without murder
Perhaps, we may possess!—away, away!
And southward, pilots, seek another isle,
Fertile they say, and of immense extent:
There we may fortune find without a crime.

Picture XV

Columbus in a Tempest, on His Return to Spain

The storm hangs low; the angry lightning glares
And menaces destruction to our masts;
The Corposant [2] is busy on the decks,
The soul, perhaps, of some lost admiral
Taking his walks about most leisurely,
Foreboding we shall be with him to-night:
See, now he mounts the shrouds—as he ascends
The gale grows bolder!—all is violence!
Seas, mounting from the bottom of their depths,
Hang o'er our heads with all their horrid curls
Threatening perdition to our feeble barques,
Which three hours longer cannot bear their fury,
Such heavy strokes already shatter them;
Who can endure such dreadful company!—
Then, must we die with our discovery!
Must all my labors, all my pains, be lost,
And my new world in old oblivion sleep?—
My name forgot, or if it be remember'd,
Only to have it said, "He was a madman
Who perish'd as he ought—deservedly—
In seeking what was never to be found!"—
Let's obviate what we can this horrid sentence,
And, lost ourselves, perhaps, preserve our name.
'Tis easy to contrive this painted casket,
(Caulk'd, pitch'd, secur'd with canvas round and round)
That it may float for months upon the main,
Bearing the freight within secure and dry:
In this will I an abstract of our voyage,
And islands found, in little space enclose:
The western winds in time may bear it home
To Europe's coasts: or some wide wandering ship
By accident may meet it toss'd about,
Charg'd with the story of another world.

Picture XVI

Columbus Visits the Court at Barcelona

Ferdinand

Let him be honor'd like a God, who brings
Tidings of islands at the ocean's end!
In royal robes let him be straight attir'd,
And seated next ourselves, the noblest peer.

Isabella

The merit of this gallant deed is mine:
Had not my jewels furnish'd out the fleet
Still had this world been latent in the main—
Since on this project every man look'd cold,
A woman, as his patroness, shall shine;
And through the world the story shall be told,
A woman gave new continents to Spain.

Columbus

A world, great prince, bright queen and royal lady,
Discover'd now, has well repaid our toils;
We to your bounty owe all that we are;
Men of renown and to be fam'd in story.
Islands of vast extent we have discover'd
With gold abounding: see a sample here
Of those most precious metals we admire;
And Indian men, natives of other climes,
Whom we have brought to do you princely homage,
Owning they hold their diadems from you.

[1] This island is now called Hispaniola. [*Freneau's note.*]

[2] A vapor common at sea in bad weather, something larger and rather paler than the light of a candle; which, seeming to rise out of the sea, first moves about the decks, and then ascends or descends the rigging in proportion to the increase or decrease of the storm. Superstition formerly imagined them to be the souls of drowned men. [*Freneau's note.*]

Ferdinand
To fifteen sail your charge shall be augmented:
Hasten to Palos, and prepare again
To sail in quest of this fine golden country,
The Ophir, never known to Solomon;
Which shall be held the brightest gem we have,
The richest diamond in the crown of Spain.

Picture XVII

COLUMBUS IN CHAINS [1]

Are these the honors they reserve for me,
Chains for the man that gave new worlds to Spain!
Rest here, my swelling heart!—O kings, O queens,
Patrons of monsters, and their progeny,
Authors of wrong, and slaves to fortune merely!
Why was I seated by my prince's side,
Honor'd, caress'd like some first peer of Spain?
Was it that I might fall most suddenly
From honor's summit to the sink of scandal!
'Tis done, 'tis done!—what madness is ambition!
What is there in that little breath of men,
Which they call Fame, that should induce the brave
To forfeit ease and that domestic bliss
Which is the lot of happy ignorance,
Less glorious aims, and dull humility.—
Whoe'er thou art that shalt aspire to honor,
And on the strength and vigor of the mind
Vainly depending, court a monarch's favor,
Pointing the way to vast extended empire;
First count your pay to be ingratitude,
Then chains and prisons, and disgrace like mine!
Each wretched pilot now shall spread his sails,
And treading in my footsteps, hail new worlds,
Which, but for me, had still been empty visions.

[1] During his third voyage, while in San Domingo, such unjust representations were made of his conduct to the Court of Spain, that a new admiral, Bovadilla, was appointed to supersede him, who sent Columbus home in irons. [*Freneau's note.*]

Picture XVIII

COLUMBUS AT VALLADOLID [1]

1

How sweet is sleep, when gain'd by length of toil!
No dreams disturb the slumbers of the dead—
To snatch existence from this scanty soil,
Were these the hopes deceitful fancy bred;
And were her painted pageants nothing more
Than this life's phantoms by delusion led?

2

The winds blow high: one other world remains;
Once more without a guide I find the way;
In the dark tomb to slumber with my chains—
Prais'd by no poet on my funeral day,
Nor even allow'd one dearly purchas'd claim—
My new found world not honor'd with my name.

3

Yet, in this joyless gloom while I repose,
Some comfort will attend my pensive shade,
When memory paints, and golden fancy shows
My toils rewarded, and my woes repaid;
When empires rise where lonely forests grew,
Where Freedom shall her generous plans pursue.

4

To shadowy forms, and ghosts and sleepy things,
Columbus, now with dauntless heart repair;
You liv'd to find new worlds for thankless kings,
Write this upon my tomb—yes—tell it there—
Tell of those chains that sullied all my glory—
Not mine, but their's—ah, tell the shameful story.

1774 1788

[1] After he found himself in disgrace with the Court of Spain, he retired to Valladolid, a town of Old Castile, where he died, it is said, more of a broken heart than of any other disease, on the 20th of May, 1506. [*Freneau's note.*]

THE HOUSE OF NIGHT[1]

A VISION

ADVERTISEMENT—This Poem is founded upon the authority of Scripture, inasmuch as these sacred books assert, that *the last enemy that shall be conquered is Death.* For the purposes of poetry he is here personified, and represented as on his dying bed. The scene is laid at a solitary palace, (the time midnight) which, tho' before beautiful and joyous, is now become sad and gloomy, as being the abode and receptacle of Death. Its owner, an amiable, majestic youth, who had lately lost a beloved consort, nevertheless with a noble philosophical fortitude and humanity, entertains him in a friendly manner, and by employing Physicians, endeavours to restore him to health, altho' an enemy; convinced of the excellence and propriety of that divine precept, *If thine enemy hunger, feed him; if he thirst, give him drink.* He nevertheless, as if by a spirit of prophecy, informs this (fictitiously) wicked being of the certainty of his doom, and represents to him in a pathetic manner the vanity of his expectations, either of a reception into the abodes of the just, or continuing longer to make havoc of mankind upon earth. The patient finding his end approaching, composes his epitaph, and orders it to be engraved on his tombstone, hinting to us thereby, that even Death and Distress have vanity; and would be remembered with honor after he is no more, altho' his whole life has been spent in deeds of devastation and murder. He dies at last in the utmost agonies of despair, after agreeing with the avaricious Undertaker to intomb his bones. This reflects upon the inhumanity of those men, who, not to mention an enemy, would scarcely cover a departed friend with a little dust, without the certainty of a reward for so doing. The circumstances of his funeral are then recited, and the visionary and fabulous part of the poem disappears. It concludes with a few reflections on the impropriety of a too great attachment to the present life, and incentives to such moral virtue as may assist in conducting us to a better.

1

TREMBLING I write my dream, and recollect
A fearful vision at the midnight hour;
So late, Death o'er me spread his sable wings,
Painted with fancies of malignant power!

2

Such was the dream the sage Chaldean saw
Disclos'd to him that felt heav'n's vengeful rod,
Such was the ghost, who through deep silence cry'd,
Shall mortal man—be juster than his God.

[1] Text from edition of 1786.

3

Let others draw from smiling skies their theme,
And tell of climes that boast unfading light,
I draw a darker scene, replete with gloom,
I sing the horrors of the House of Night.

4

Stranger, believe the truth experience tells,
Poetic dreams are of a finer cast
Than those which o'er the sober brain diffus'd,
Are but a repetition of some action past.

5

Fancy, I own thy power—when sunk in sleep
Thou play'st thy wild delusive part so well
You lift me into immortality,
Depict new heavens, or draw scenes of hell.

6

By some sad means, when Reason holds no sway,
Lonely I rov'd at midnight o'er a plain
Where murmuring streams and mingling rivers flow,
Far to their springs, or seek the sea again.

7

Sweet vernal May! tho' then thy woods in bloom
Flourish'd, yet nought of this could Fancy see,
No wild pinks bless'd the meads, no green the fields,
And naked seem'd to stand each lifeless tree:

8

Dark was the sky, and not one friendly star
Shone from the zenith or horizon, clear,
Mist sate upon the woods, and darkness rode
In her black chariot, with a wild career.

9

And from the woods the late resounding note
Issued of the loquacious Whip-poor-will,[1]
Hoarse, howling dogs, and nightly roving wolves
Clamor'd from far off cliffs invisible.

[1] A Bird peculiar to America, of a solitary nature, who sings but in the night. Her note resembles the name given to her by the country people. [*Freneau's note.*]

10

Rude, from the wide extended *Chesapeke*
I heard the winds the dashing waves assail,
And saw from far, by pictures fancy form'd,
The black ship travelling through the noisy gale.

11

At last, by chance and guardian fancy led,
I reach'd a noble dome, rais'd fair and high,
And saw the light from upper windows flame,
Presage of mirth and hospitality.

12

And by that light around the dome appear'd
A mournful garden of autumnal hue,
Its lately pleasing flowers all drooping stood
Amidst high weeds that in rank plenty grew.

13

The Primrose there, the violet darkly blue,
Daisies and fair Narcissus ceas'd to rise,
Gay spotted pinks their charming bloom withdrew,
And Polyanthus quench'd its thousand dyes.

14

No pleasant fruit or blossom gaily smil'd.
Nought but unhappy plants and trees were seen,
The yew, the myrtle, and the church-yard elm,
The cypress, with its melancholy green.

15

There cedars dark, the osier, and the pine,
Shorn tamarisks, and weeping willows grew,
The poplar tall, the lotos, and the lime,
And pyracantha did her leaves renew.

16

The poppy there, companion to repose,
Display'd her blossoms that began to fall,
And here the purple amaranthus rose
With mint strong-scented, for the funeral.

17

And here and there with laurel shrubs between
A tombstone lay, inscrib'd with strains of woe,
And stanzas sad, throughout the dismal green,
Lamented for the dead that slept below.

18

Peace to this awful dome!—when straight I heard
The voice of men in a secluded room,
Much did they talk of death, and much of life,
Of coffins, shrouds, and horrors of a tomb.

19

Pathetic were their words, and well they aim'd
To explain the mystic paths of providence,
Learn'd were they all, but there remain'd not I
To hear the upshot of their conference.

20

Meantime from an adjoining chamber came
Confused murmurings, half distinguish'd sounds,
And as I nearer drew, disputes arose
Of surgery, and remedies for wounds.

21

Dull were their feuds, for they went on to talk
Of *Anchylosis*,[1] and the shoulder blade,
Os Femoris,[1] *Trochanters*[1]—and whate'er
Has been discuss'd by Cheselden or Meade:

22

And often each, to prove his notion true
Brought proofs from Galen or Hippocrates—
But fancy led me hence—and left them so,
Firm at their points of hardy No and Yes.

23

Then up three winding stairs my feet were brought
To a high chamber, hung with mourning sad,
The unsnuff'd candles glar'd with visage dim,
'Midst grief, in ecstasy of woe run mad.

24

A wide leaf'd table stood on either side,
Well fraught with phials, half their liquids spent,
And from a couch, behind the curtain's veil,
I heard a hollow voice of loud lament.

[1] *Anchylosis*—a morbid contraction of the joints. *Os Femoris*—the thigh bone. *Trochanters*—two processes in the upper part of the thigh bone, otherwise called *rotator major et minor*, in which the tendons of many muscles terminate. [*Freneau's notes*.]

25

Turning to view the object whence it came,
My frighted eyes a horrid form survey'd;
Fancy, I own thy power—Death on the couch,
With fleshless limbs, at rueful length, was laid.

26

And o'er his head flew jealousies and cares,
Ghosts, imps, and half the black Tartarian crew,
Arch-angels damn'd, nor was their Prince remote,
Borne on the vaporous wings of Stygian dew.

27

Around his bed, by the dull flambeaux' glare,
I saw pale phantoms—Rage to madness vext,
Wan, wasting grief, and ever musing care,
Distressful pain, and poverty perplext.

28

Sad was his countenance, if we can call
That countenance, where only bones were seen
And eyes sunk in their sockets, dark and low,
And teeth, that only show'd themselves to grin.

29

Reft was his skull of hair, and no fresh bloom
Of cheerful mirth sate on his visage hoar:
Sometimes he rais'd his head, while deep-drawn groans
Were mixt with words that did his fate deplore.

30

Oft did he wish to see the daylight spring,
And often toward the window lean'd to hear,
Fore-runner of the scarlet-mantled morn,
The early note of wakeful Chanticleer.

31

Thus he—But at my hand a portly youth
Of comely countenance, began to tell,
"That this was Death upon his dying bed,
Sullen, morose, and peevish to be well;

32

"Fixt is his doom—the miscreant reigns no more
The tyrant of the dying or the dead;
This night concludes his all-consuming reign,
Pour out, ye heav'ns, your vengeance on his head.

33

"But since, my friend (said he), chance leads you here,
With me this night upon the sick attend,
You on this bed of death must watch, and I
Will not be distant from the fretful fiend.

34

"Before he made this lofty pile his home,
In undisturb'd repose I sweetly slept,
But when he came to this sequester'd dome
'Twas then my troubles came, and then I wept:

35

"Twice three long nights, in this sad chamber, I,
As though a brother languish'd in despair,
Have 'tended faithful round his gloomy bed,
Have been content to breathe this loathsome air.

36

"A while relieve the languors that I feel,
Sleep's magic forces close my weary eyes;
Soft o'er my soul unwonted slumbers steal,
Aid the weak patient till you see me rise.

37

"But let no slumbers on your eye-lids fall,
That if he ask for powder or for pill
You may be ready at the word to start,
And still seem anxious to perform his will.

38

"The bleeding Saviour of a world undone
Bade thy compassion rise toward thy foe;
Then, stranger, for the sake of Mary's son,
Thy tears of pity on this wretch bestow.

39

"'Twas he that stole from my adoring arms
Aspasia, she the loveliest of her kind,
Lucretia's virtue, with a Helen's charms,
Charms of the face, and beauties of the mind.

40

"The blushy cheek, the lively, beaming eye,
The ruby lip, the flowing jetty hair,
The stature tall, the aspect so divine,
All beauty, you would think, had center'd there.

41

"Each future age her virtues shall extol,
Nor the just tribute to her worth refuse;
Fam'd, to the stars Urania bids her rise,
Theme of the moral, and the tragic Muse.

42

"Sweet as the fragrance of the vernal morn,
Nipt in its bloom this faded flower I see;
The inspiring angel from that breast is gone,
And life's warm tide forever chill'd in thee!

43

"Such charms shall greet my longing soul no more,
Her lively eyes are clos'd in endless shade,
Torpid, she rests on yonder marble floor;
Approach, and see what havoc Death has made.

44

"Yet, stranger, hold—her charms are so divine,
Such tints of life still on her visage glow,
That even in death this slumbering bride of mine
May seize thy heart, and make thee wretched too.

45

"O shun the sight—forbid thy trembling hand
From her pale face to raise the enshrouding lawn,—
Death claims thy care, obey his stern command,
Trim the dull tapers, for I see no dawn!"

46

So said, at Death's left side I sate me down,
The mourning youth toward his right reclin'd;
Death in the middle lay, with all his groans,
And much he toss'd and tumbled, sigh'd and pin'd.

47

But now this man of hell toward me turn'd,
And straight, in hideous tone, began to speak,
Long held he sage discourse, but I forebore
To answer him, much less his news to seek.

48

He talk'd of tomb-stones and of monuments,
Of Equinoxial climes and India shores,
He talk'd of stars that shed their influence,
Fevers and plagues, and all their noxious stores.

49

He mention'd, too, the guileful *calenture*,[1]
Tempting the sailor on the deep sea main,
That paints gay groves upon the ocean floor,
Beckoning her victim to the faithless scene.

50

Much spoke he of the myrtle and the yew,
Of ghosts that nightly walk the church-yard o'er,
Of storms that through the wint'ry ocean blow
And dash the well-mann'd galley on the shore,

51

Of broad-mouth'd cannons, and the thunder-bolt,
Of sieges and convulsions, dearth and fire,
Of poisonous weeds—but seem'd to sneer at these
Who by the laurel o'er him did aspire.

52

Then with a hollow voice thus went he on,
"Get up, and search, and bring, when found, to me,
Some cordial, potion, or some pleasant draught,
Sweet, slumb'rous poppy, or the mild Bohea.

53

"But hark, my pitying friend!—and, if you can,
Deceive the grim physician at the door—
Bring half the mountain springs—ah! hither bring
The cold rock water from the shady bower.

54

"For till this night such thirst did ne'er invade,
A thirst provok'd by heav'n's avenging hand;

[1] *Calenture*—an inflammatory fever, attended with a delirium, common in long voyages at sea, in which the diseased persons fancy the sea to be green fields and meadows, and, if they are not hindered, will leap overboard. [*Freneau's note.*]

Hence bear me, friends, to quaff, and quaff again
The cool wave bubbling from the yellow sand.

55

"To these dark walls with stately step I came,
Prepar'd your drugs and doses to defy;
Smit with the love of never dying fame,
I came, alas! to conquer—not to die!"

56

Glad, from his side I sprang, and fetch'd the draught,
Which down his greedy throat he quickly swills,
Then on a second errand sent me straight,
To search in some dark corner for his pills.

57

Quoth he, "These pills have long compounded been,
Of dead men's bones and bitter roots, I trow;
But that I may to wonted health return,
Throughout my lank veins shall their substance go."

58

So down they went—He rais'd his fainting head
And oft in feeble tone essay'd to talk;
Quoth he, "Since remedies have small avail,
Assist unhappy Death once more to walk."

59

Then slowly rising from his loathsome bed,
On wasted legs the meagre monster stood,
Gap'd wide, and foam'd, and hungry seem'd to ask,
Tho' sick, an endless quantity of food.

60

Said he, "The sweet melodious flute prepare,
The anthem, and the organ's solemn sound,
Such as may strike my soul with ecstasy,
Such as may from yon' lofty wall rebound.

61

"Sweet music can the fiercest pains assuage,
She bids the soul to heav'n's blest mansions rise,
She calms despair, controls infernal rage
And deepest anguish, when it hears her, dies.

62

"And see, the mizzling, misty midnight reigns,
And no soft dews are on my eye-lids sent—!
Here, stranger, lend thy hand; assist me, pray,
To walk a circuit of no large extent."—

63

On my prest shoulders leaning, round he went,
And could have made the boldest spectre flee,
I led him up stairs, and I led him down,
But not one moment's rest from pain got he.

64

Then with his dart, its cusp unpointed now,
Thrice with main strength he smote the trembling floor;
The roof resounded to the fearful blow,
And Cleon started, doom'd to sleep no more.

65

When thus spoke Death, impatient of control,
"Quick, move, and bring from yonder black bureau
The sacred book that may preserve my soul
From long damnation, and eternal woe.

66

"And with it bring—for you may find them there,
The works of holy authors, dead and gone,
The sacred *tome* of moving Drelincourt,
Or what more solemn Sherlock mus'd upon:

67

"And read, my Cleon, what these sages say,
And what the sacred Penman hath declar'd,
That when the wicked leaves his odious way,
His sins shall vanish, and his soul be spar'd."

68

But he, unmindful of the vain command,
Reason'd with Death, nor were his reasonings few:
Quoth he—"My Lord, what frenzy moves your brain,
Pray, what, my Lord, can Sherlock be to you,

69

"Or all the sage divines that ever wrote,
Grave Drelincourt, or heaven's unerring page;

These point their arrows at your hostile breast,
And raise new pains that time must ne'er assuage.

70

"And why should thus thy woe disturb my rest?
Much of Theology I once did read,
And there 'tis fixt, sure as my God is so,
That Death shall perish, tho' a God should bleed.

71

"The martyr, doom'd the pangs of fire to feel,
Lives but a moment in the sultry blast;
The victim groans, and dies beneath the steel,
But thy severer pains shall always last.

72

"O miscreant vile, thy age has made thee dote—
If peace, if sacred peace were found for you,
Hell would cry out, and all the damn'd arise
And, more deserving, seek for pity too.

73

"Seek not for Paradise—'tis not for thee,
Where high in heaven its sweetest blossoms blow,
Nor even where, gliding to the Persian main
Thy waves, Euphrates, through the garden flow!

74

"Bloody has been thy reign, O man of hell,
Who sympathiz'd with no departing groan;
Cruel wast thou, and hardly dost deserve
To have *Hic Jacet* stampt upon thy stone.

75

"He that could build his mansion o'er the tombs,
Depending still on sickness and decay,
May dwell unmov'd amidst these drowsier glooms,
May laugh the dullest of these shades away.

76

"Remember how with unrelenting ire
You tore the infant from the unwilling breast—
Aspasia fell, and Cleon must expire,
Doom'd by the impartial God to endless rest:

77

"In vain with stars he deck'd yon' spangled skies,
And bade the mind to heaven's bright regions soar,
And brought so far to my admiring eyes
A glimpse of glories that shall blaze no more!

78

"Even now to glut thy devilish wrath, I see
From eastern realms a wasteful army rise:
Why else those lights that tremble in the north?
Why else yon' comet blazing through the skies?

79

"Rejoice, O fiend; Britannia's tyrant sends
From German plains his myriads to our shore.
The fierce Hibernian with the Briton join'd—
Bring them, ye winds!—but waft them back no more.

80

"To you, alas! the fates in wrath deny
The comforts to our parting moments due,
And leave you here to languish and to die,
Your crimes too many, and your tears too few.

81

"No cheering voice to thee shall cry, Repent!
As once it echoed through the wilderness—
No patron died for thee—damn'd, damn'd art thou
Like all the devils, nor one jot the less.

82

"A gloomy land, with sullen skies is thine,
Where never rose or amaranthus grow,
No daffodils, nor comely columbine,
No hyacinths nor asphodels for you.

83

"The barren trees that flourish on the shore
With leaves or fruit were never seen to bend,
O'er languid waves unblossom'd branches hang,
And every branch sustains some vagrant fiend.

84

"And now no more remains, but to prepare
To take possession of thy punishment,

That's thy inheritance, that thy domain,
A land of bitter woe, and loud lament.

85

"And oh that He, who spread the universe,
Would cast one pitying glance on thee below;
Millions of years in torments thou might'st fry,
But thy eternity!—who can conceive its woe!"

86

He heard, and round with his black eye-balls gaz'd, 341
Full of despair, and curs'd, and rav'd, and swore:
"And since this is my doom," said he, "call up
Your wood-mechanics to my chamber door:

87

"Blame not on me the ravage to be made;
Proclaim,—even Death abhors such woe to see;
I'll quit the world, while decently I can,
And leave the work to George my deputy."

88

Up rush'd a band, with compasses and scales
To measure his slim carcase, long and lean—
"Be sure," said he, "to frame my coffin strong,
You, master workman, and your men, I mean:

89

"For if the Devil, so late my trusty friend,
Should get one hint where I am laid, from you,
Not with my soul content, he'd seek to find
That moldering mass of bones, my body, too! 356

90

"Of hardest ebon let the plank be found,
With clamps and ponderous bars secur'd around,
That if the box by Satan should be storm'd,
It may be able for resistance found."

91

"Yes," said the master workman, "noble Death,
Your coffin shall be strong—that leave to me—
But who shall these your funeral dues discharge? 363
Nor friends nor pence you have, that I can see."

92

To this said Death—"You might have ask'd me, too,
Base caitiff, who are my executors,
Where my estate, and who the men that shall
Partake my substance, and be call'd my heirs.

93

"Know, then, that hell is my inheritance, 369
The devil himself my funeral dues must pay—
Go—since you must be paid—go, ask of him,
For he has gold, as fabling poets say."

94

Straight they retir'd—when thus he gave me charge,
Pointing from the light window to the west,
"Go three miles o'er the plain, and you shall see
A burying-yard of sinners dead, unblest.

95

"Amid the graves a spiry building stands
Whose solemn knell resounding through the gloom
Shall call thee o'er the circumjacent lands 379
To the dull mansion destin'd for my tomb.

96

"There, since 'tis dark, I'll plant a glimmering light
Just snatch'd from hell, by whose reflected beams
Thou shalt behold a tomb-stone, full eight feet,
Fast by a grave, replete with ghosts and dreams.

97

"And on that stone engrave this epitaph,
Since Death, it seems, must die like mortal men;
Yes—on that stone engrave this epitaph,
Though all hell's furies aim to snatch the pen.

98

"*Death in this tomb his weary bones hath laid,*
Sick of dominion o'er the human kind— 390
Behold what devastations he hath made,
Survey the millions by his arm confin'd.

99

"Six thousand years has sovereign sway been mine,
None, but myself, can real glory claim;
Great Regent of the world I reign'd alone,
And princes trembled when my mandate came.

100

"Vast and unmatch'd throughout the world, my fame
Takes place of gods, and asks no mortal date—
No; by myself, and by the heavens, I swear,
Not Alexander's name is half so great.

101

"Nor swords nor darts my prowess could withstand,
All quit their arms, and bow'd to my decree,
Even mighty Julius died beneath my hand,
For slaves and Cæsars were the same to me!

102

"Traveller, wouldst thou his noblest trophies seek,
Search in no narrow spot obscure for those;
The sea profound, the surface of all land
Is molded with the myriads of his foes."

103

Scarce had he spoke, when on the lofty dome
Rush'd from the clouds a hoarse resounding blast—
Round the four eaves so loud and sad it play'd
As though all music were to breathe its last.

104

Warm was the gale, and such as travellers say
Sport with the winds on Zaara's waste;
Black was the sky, a mourning carpet spread,
Its azure blotted, and its stars o'ercast!

105

Lights in the air like burning stars were hurl'd,
Dogs howl'd, heaven mutter'd, and the tempest blew,
The red half-moon peeped from behind a cloud
As if in dread the amazing scene to view.

106

The mournful trees that in the garden stood
Bent to the tempest as it rush'd along,
The elm, the myrtle, and the cypress sad
More melancholy tun'd its bellowing song.

107

No more that elm its noble branches spread,
The yew, the cypress, or the myrtle tree,
Rent from the roots the tempest tore them down,
And all the grove in wild confusion lay.

108

Yet, mindful of his dread command, I part
Glad from the magic dome—nor found relief;
Damps from the dead hung heavier round my heart,
While sad remembrance rous'd her stores of grief.

109

O'er a dark field I held my dubious way
Where Jack-a-lanthorn walk'd his lonely round,
Beneath my feet substantial darkness lay,
And screams were heard from the distemper'd ground.

110

Nor look'd I back, till to a far off wood
Trembling with fear, my weary feet had sped—
Dark was the night, but at the inchanted dome
I saw the infernal windows flaming red.

111

And from within the howls of Death I heard,
Cursing the dismal night that gave him birth,
Damning his ancient sire, and mother sin,
Who at the gates of hell, accursed, brought him forth.

112

[For fancy gave to my enraptur'd soul
An eagle's eye, with keenest glance to see,
And bade those distant sounds distinctly roll,
Which, waking, never had affected me.]

113

Oft his pale breast with cruel hand he smote,
And tearing from his limbs a winding sheet,
Roar'd to the black skies, while the woods around,
As wicked as himself, his words repeat.

114

Thrice tow'rd the skies his meagre arms he rear'd,
Invok'd all hell, and thunders on his head,
Bid light'nings fly, earth yawn, and tempests roar,
And the sea wrap him in its oozy bed.

115

"My life for one cool draught!—O, fetch your springs,
Can one unfeeling to my woes be found!
No friendly visage comes to my relief,
But ghosts impend, and spectres hover round.

116

"Though humbled now, dishearten'd and distrest,
Yet, when admitted to the peaceful ground,
With heroes, kings, and conquerors I shall rest,
Shall sleep as safely, and perhaps as sound."

117

Dim burnt the lamp, and now the phantom Death
Gave his last groans in horror and despair—
"All hell demands me hence,"—he said, and threw
The red lamp hissing through the midnight air.

118

Trembling, across the plain my course I held,
And found the grave-yard, loitering through the gloom,
And, in the midst, a hell-red, wandering light,
Walking in fiery circles round the tomb.

119

Among the graves a spiry building stood,
Whose tolling bell, resounding through the wood,
Sung doleful ditties to the adjacent wood,
And many a dismal drowsy thing it said.

120

This fabric tall, with towers and chancels grac'd,
Was rais'd by sinners' hands, in ages fled;
The roof they painted, and the beams they brac'd,
And texts from scripture o'er the walls they spread:

121

But wicked were their hearts, for they refus'd
To aid the helpless orphan, when distrest,
The shivering, naked stranger they mis-us'd,
And banish'd from their doors the starving guest.

122

By laws protected, cruel and profane,
The poor man's ox these monsters drove away;—
And left Distress to attend her infant train,
No friend to comfort, and no bread to stay.

123

But heaven look'd on with keen, resentful eye,
And doom'd them to perdition and the grave,
That as they felt not for the wretch distrest,
So heaven no pity on their souls would have.

124

In pride they rais'd this building tall and fair,
Their hearts were on perpetual mischief bent,
With pride they preach'd, and pride was in their prayer,
With pride they were deceiv'd, and so to hell they went.

125

At distance far approaching to the tomb,
By lamps and lanthorns guided through the shade,
A coal-black chariot hurried through the gloom,
Spectres attending, in black weeds array'd,

126

Whose woeful forms yet chill my soul with dread,
Each wore a vest in Stygian chambers wove,
Death's kindred all—Death's horses they bestrode,
And gallop'd fiercely, as the chariot drove.

127

Each horrid face a grisly mask conceal'd,
Their busy eyes shot terror to my soul
As now and then, by the pale lanthorn's glare,
I saw them for their parted friend condole.

128

Before the hearse Death's chaplain seem'd to go,
Who strove to comfort, what he could, the dead;
Talk'd much of Satan, and the land of woe,
And many a chapter from the scriptures read.

129

At last he rais'd the swelling anthem high,
In dismal numbers seem'd he to complain;
The captive tribes that by Euphrates wept,
Their song was jovial to his dreary strain.

130

That done, they plac'd the carcass in the tomb,
To dust and dull oblivion now resign'd,
Then turn'd the chariot tow'rd the House of Night,
Which soon flew off, and left no trace behind.

131

But as I stoop'd to write the appointed verse,
Swifter than thought the airy scene decay'd;
Blushing the morn arose, and from the east
With her gay streams of light dispell'd the shade.

132

What is this Death, ye deep read sophists, say?—
Death is no more than one unceasing change;
New forms arise, while other forms decay,
Yet all is Life throughout creation's range.

133

The towering *Alps*, the haughty *Appenine*,
The *Andes*, wrapt in everlasting snow,
The *Apalachian* and the *Ararat*
Sooner or later must to ruin go.

134

Hills sink to plains, and man returns to dust,
That dust supports a reptile or a flower;
Each changeful atom by some other nurs'd
Takes some new form, to perish in an hour.

135

Too nearly join'd to sickness, toils, and pains,
(Perhaps for former crimes imprison'd here)
True to itself the immortal soul remains,
And seeks new mansions in the starry sphere.

136

When Nature bids thee from the world retire,
With joy thy lodging leave, a fated guest;
In Paradise, the land of thy desire,
Existing always, always to be blest.

1779, 1786

THE BEAUTIES OF SANTA CRUZ [1]

1776

Sweet orange grove, the fairest of the isle,
In thy soft shade luxuriously reclined,
Where, round my fragrant bed, the flowrets smile,
In sweet delusions I deceive my mind.

But Melancholy's glooms assail my breast,
For potent nature reigns despotic there;—
A nation ruined, and a world oppressed,
Might rob the boldest Stoic of a tear.

Sick of thy northern glooms, come, shepherd, seek
More equal climes, and a serener sky:
Why shouldst thou toil amid thy frozen ground,
Where half years' snows, a barren prospect, lie,

When thou mayst go where never frost was seen,
Or north-west winds with cutting fury blow,
Where never ice congealed the limpid stream,
Where never mountain tipt its head with snow?

Twice ten days prosperous gales thy barque shall bear
To isles that flourish in perpetual green,
Where richest herbage glads each fertile vale,
And ever verdant plants on every hill are seen.

Nor dread the dangers of the billowy deep,
Autumnal winds shall safely waft thee o'er;
Put off the timid heart, or, man unblest,
Ne'er shalt thou reach this gay enchanting shore.

[1] Or St. Croix, a Danish island (in the American Archipelago), commonly, tho' erroneously, included in the cluster of the Virgin Islands; belonging to the crown of Denmark. [*Freneau's note.*]

Thus Judah's tribes beheld the promised land,
While Jordan's angry waters swelled between;
Thus trembling on the brink I see them stand,
Heav'n's type in view, the Canaanitish green.

Thus, some mean souls, in spite of age and care,
Are held so firmly to this earth below,
They never wish to cross fate's dusky main,
That parting them and happiness, doth flow.

Though Reason's voice might whisper to the soul
That nobler climes for man the heavens design—
Come, shepherd, haste—the northern breezes blow,
No more the slumbering winds thy barque confine.

Sweet orange grove, the fairest of the isle,
In thy soft shade luxuriously reclined,
Where, round my fragrant bed, the flowrets smile,
In sweet delusions I deceive my mind.

But Melancholy's glooms assail my breast,
For potent nature reigns despotic there;—
A nation ruined, and a world oppressed,
Might rob the boldest Stoic of a tear.

From the vast caverns of old Ocean's bed,
Fair Santa Cruz arising, laves her waist,
The threatening waters roar on every side,
For every side by ocean is embraced.

Sharp, craggy rocks repel the surging brine,
Whose caverned sides by restless billows wore,
Resemblance claim to that remoter isle
Where once the winds' proud lord the sceptre bore.

Betwixt old Cancer and the mid-way line,
In happiest climate, lies this envied isle:
Trees bloom throughout the year, soft breezes blow,
And fragrant Flora wears a lasting smile.

Cool, woodland streams from shaded cliffs descend,
The dripping rock no want of moisture knows,
Supplied by springs that on the skies depend,
That fountain feeding as the current flows.

Such were the isles which happy Flaccus sung,
Where one tree blossoms while another bears,
Where spring forever gay, and ever young,
Walks her gay round through her unceasing years.

Such were the climes which youthful Eden saw
Ere crossing fates destroyed her golden reign—
Reflect upon thy loss, unhappy man,
And seek the vales of Paradise again.

No lowering skies are here—the neighboring sun
Clear and unveiled, his brilliant journey goes,
Each morn emerging from the ambient main,
And sinking there, each evening, to repose.

In June's fair month the spangled traveller gains
The utmost limits of his northern way,
And blesses with his beams cold lands remote,
Sad Greenland's coast, and Hudson's frozen bay.

The shivering swains of those unhappy climes
Behold the side-way monarch through the trees,
Here glows his fiercer heat, his vertic beams,
Tempered with cooling gales and trade-wind breeze.

The native here, in golden plenty blest,
Bids from the soil the verdant harvests spring;
Feasts in the abundant dome, the joyous guest;
Time short,—life easy,—pleasure on the wing.

Here, fixt today in plenty's smiling vales,
Just as the year revolves, they laugh or groan;
September comes, seas swell with horrid gales,
And old Port-Royal's fate is found their own!

And, though so near heaven's blazing lamp doth run
They court the beam that sheds the golden day,
And hence are called the children of the sun,
Who, without fainting, bear his downward ray.

No threatening tides upon their island rise,
Gay Cynthia scarce disturbs the ocean here,
No waves approach her orb, and she, as kind,
Attracts no ocean to her silver sphere.

The happy waters boast, of various kinds,
Unnumbered myriads of the scaly race,
Sportive they glide above the deluged sand,
Gay as their clime, in ocean's ample vase.

Some streaked with burnished gold, resplendent, glare,
Some cleave the limpid deep, all silvered o'er,
Some, clad in living green, delight the eye,
Some red, some blue; of mingled colors more.

Here glides the spangled dolphin through the deep,
The giant carcased whales at distance stray,
The huge green turtles wallow through the wave,
Well pleas'd alike with land or water, they.

The Rainbow cuts the deep, of varied green,
The well-fed Grouper lurks remote, below,
The swift Bonetta coasts the watery scene,
The diamond-coated Angels kindle as they go,

Delicious to the taste, salubrious food,
Which might some temperate, studious sage allure
To curse the fare of his abstemious cell
And turn, for once, a cheerful epicure.

Unhurt mayest thou this luscious food enjoy,
To fulness feast upon the scaly kind;
These, well selected from a thousand more,
Delight the taste, and leave no bane behind.

Nor think Hygeia [1] is a stranger here—
To sensual souls the climate may fatal prove,
Anguish and death attend, and pain severe,
The midnight revel, and licentious love.

Full many a swain, in youth's serenest bloom,
Is borne untimely to this alien clay,
Constrained to slumber in a foreign tomb,
Far from his friends, his country far away.

[1] The goddess of health, in the Grecian mythology. [*Freneau's note.*]

Yet, if devoted to a sensual soul,
If fondly their own ruin they create,
These victims to the banquet and the bowl
Must blame their folly, only, not their fate.

But thou who first drew breath in northern air,
At early dawn ascend the sloping hills:
And oft, at noon, to lime-tree shades repair,
Where some soft stream from neighboring groves distills.

And with it mix the liquid of the lime,
The old-aged essence of the generous cane,
And sweetest syrups of this liquorish clime,
And drink, to cool thy thirst, and drink again.

This happy beverage, joy-inspiring bowl,
Dispelling far the shades of mental night,
Beams bright ideas on the awakened soul,
And sorrow turns to pleasure and delight.

Sweet verdant isle! through thy dark woods I rove,
And learn the nature of each native tree,
The fustic hard, the poisonous manchineel,
Which for its fragrant apple pleaseth thee;

Alluring to the smell, fair to the eye,
But deadliest poison in the taste is found—
O shun the dangerous tree, nor touch, like Eve,
This interdicted fruit, in Eden's ground.

The lowly mangrove fond of watery soil,
The white-barked gregory, rising high in air,
The mastic in the woods you may descry,
Tamarind, and lofty bay-trees flourish there.

Sweet orange groves in lonely valleys rise
And drop their fruits, unnoticed and unknown,
And cooling acid limes in hedges grow,
The juicy lemons swell in shades their own.

Sweet, spungy plums on trees wide spreading hang,
Bell-apples here, suspended, shade the ground,
Plump grenadilloes and güavas grey,
With melons in each plain and vale abound.

The conic-formed cashew, of juicy kind,
That bears at once an apple and a nut;

Whose poisonous coat, indignant to the lip,
Doth in its cell a wholesome kernel shut.

The prince of fruits, whom some jayama call,
Anana some, the happy flavored pine;
In which unite the tastes and juices all
Of apple, quince, peach, grape, and nectarine,

Grows to perfection here, and spreads his crest,
His diadem toward the parent sun;
His diadem, in fiery blossoms drest,
Stands armed with swords, from potent Nature won.

Yon' cotton shrubs with bursting knobs behold,
Their snow white locks these humbler groves array;
On slender trees the blushing coffee hangs,
Like thy fair cherry, and would tempt thy stay.

Safe from the winds, in deep retreats, they rise;
Their utmost summit may thy arm attain;
Taste the moist fruit, and from thy closing eyes
Sleep shall retire, with all his drowsy train.

The spicy berry, they güava call,
Swells in the mountains on a stripling tree;
These some admire, and value more than all,
My humble verse, besides, unfolds to thee.

The smooth white cedar, here, delights the eye,
The bay-tree, with its aromatic green,
The sea-side grapes, sweet natives of the sand,
And pulse, of various kinds, on trees are seen.

Here mingled vines, their downward shadows cast,
Here, clustered grapes from loaded boughs depend,
Their leaves no frosts, their fruits no cold winds blast,
But, reared by suns, to time alone they bend.

The plantane and banana flourish here,
Of hasty growth, and love to fix their root
Where some soft stream of ambling water flows,
To yield full moisture to their clustered fruit.

No other trees so vast a leaf can boast,
So broad, so long—through these, refreshed, we stray,
And though the noon-sun all his radiance shed,
These friendly leaves shall shade me all the way,

And tempt the cooling breeze to hasten there,
With its sweet odorous breath to charm the grove;
High shades and verdant seats, while underneath
A little stream by mossy banks doth rove,

Where once the Indian dames slept with their swains,
Or fondly kissed the moon-light eves away;—
The lovers fled, the tearful stream remains,
And only I console it with my lay!

Among the shades of yonder whispering grove
The green palmettoes mingle, tall and fair,
That ever murmur, and forever move,
Fanning with wavy bough the ambient air.

Pomegranates grace the wild, and sweet-sops there
Ready to fall, require the helping hand,
Nor yet neglect the papaw or mamee,
Whose slighted trees with fruits unheeded stand.

Those shaddocks juicy shall thy taste delight,
And yon' high fruits, the noblest of the wood,
That cling in clusters to the mother tree,
The cocoa-nut; rich, milky, healthful food.

O grant me, gods, if yet condemned to stray,
At least to spend life's sober evening here,
To plant a grove where winds yon' sheltered bay,
And pluck these fruits, that frost nor winter fear.

Cassada shrubs abound—transplanted here
From every clime, exotic blossoms blow;
Here Asia plants her flowers, here Europe trees,
And hyperborean herbs, unwintered, grow.

Here, a new herbage glads the generous steed,
Mules, goats, and sheep, enjoy these pastures fair,

And for thy hedges, Nature has decreed,
Guards of thy toils, the date and prickly pear.

But chief the glory of these Indian isles
Springs from the sweet, uncloying sugar-cane:
Hence comes the planter's wealth, hence commerce sends
Such floating piles, to traverse half the main.

Whoe'er thou art that leavest thy native shore
And shalt to fair West-India climates come,
Taste not the enchanting plant—to taste forbear,
If ever thou wouldst reach thy much-loved home.

Ne'er through the isle permit thy feet to rove,
Or, if thou dost, let prudence lead the way,
Forbear to taste the virtues of the cane,
Forbear to taste what will complete your stay.

Whoever sips of this enchanting juice,
Delicious nectar, fit for Jove's own hall,
Returns no more from his loved Santa Cruz,
But quits his friends, his country, and his all.

And thinks no more of home—Ulysses so
Dragged off by force his sailors from that shore
Where lotos grew, and, had not strength prevailed,
They never would have sought their country more.

No annual toil inters this thrifty plant,
The stalk lopt off, the freshening showers prolong
To future years, unfading and secure,
The root so vigorous, and the juice so strong.

Unnumbered plants, besides, these climates yield,
And grass peculiar to the soil that bears:
Ten thousand varied herbs array the field,
This glads thy palate, that thy health repairs.

Along the shore a wondrous flower is seen,
Where rocky ponds receive the surging wave,
Some drest in yellow, some attired in green,
Beneath the water their gay branches lave.

This mystic plant, with its bewitching charms,
Too surely springs from some enchanted bower,
Fearful it is, and dreads impending harms,
And animal, the natives call the flower.

From the smooth rock its little branches rise,
The object of thy view, and that alone,
Feast on its beauties with thy ravished eyes,
But aim to touch it, and—the flower is gone.

Nay, if thy shade but intercept the beam
That gilds their boughs beneath the briny lake,
Swift they retire, like a deluding dream,
And even a shadow for destruction take.

Warned by experience, hope not thou to gain
The magic plant thy curious hand invades;
Returning to the light, it mocks thy pain,
Deceives all grasp, and seeks its native shades!

On yonder blue-browed hill, fresh harvests rise,
Where the dark tribe from Afric's sunburnt plain,
Oft o'er the ocean turn their wishful eyes
To isles remote high looming o'er the main.

And view soft seats of ease and fancied rest,
Their native groves new painted on the eye,
Where no proud misers their gay hours molest,
No lordly despots pass, unsocial, by.

See, yonder slave that slowly bends this way,
With years, and pain, and ceaseless toil opprest,
Though no complaining words his woes betray,
The eye dejected proves the heart distrest.

Perhaps in chains he left his native shore,
Perhaps he left a helpless offspring there,
Perhaps a wife, that he must see no more,
Perhaps a father, who his love did share.

Cursed be the ship, that brought him o'er the main,
And cursed the men, who from his country tore;
May she be stranded, ne'er to float again,
May they be shipwrecked on some hostile shore—

O gold accurst, of every ill the spring,
For thee compassion flies the darkened mind,
Reason's plain dictates no conviction bring,
And madness only sways all human kind.

O gold accurst! for thee we madly run,
With murderous hearts across the briny flood,
Seek foreign climes beneath a foreign sun,
And, there, exult to shed a brother's blood.

But thou, who ownest this sugar-bearing soil,
To whom no good the great First Cause denies,
Let free-born hands attend thy sultry toil,
And fairer harvests to thy view shall rise,

The teeming earth will mightier stores disclose
Than ever struck the longing eye before,
And late content shall shed a soft repose—
Repose, so long a stranger at thy door.

Give me some clime, the favorite of the sky,
Where cruel slavery never sought to reign—
But shun the theme, sad muse, and tell me why
These abject trees lie scattered o'er the plain?

These isles, lest Nature should have proved too kind,
Or man have sought his happiest heaven below,
Are torn with mighty winds, fierce hurricanes,
Nature convulsed in every shape of woe.

Nor scorn yon' lonely vale of trees so reft:
There plantane groves late grew of liveliest green,
The orange flourished, and the lemon bore,
The genius of the isle dwelt there, unseen.

Wild were the skies, affrighted Nature groaned
As though approached her last decisive day.
Skies blazed around and bellowing winds had nigh
Dislodged these cliffs, and tore yon' hills away.

O'er the wild main, dejected and afraid,
The trembling pilot lashed his helm a-lee
Or swiftly scudding, asked thy potent aid,
Dear Pilot of the Galilean sea.

Low hung the glooms, distended with the gale
The clouds, dark brooding, winged their circling flight,
Tremendous thunders joined the hurricane,
Daughter of chaos, and eternal night!

And how, alas! could these fair trees withstand
The wasteful madness of so fierce a blast,
That stormed along the plain, seized every grove,
And deluged with a sea this mournful waste.

That plantane grove, where oft I fondly strayed,
Thy darts, dread Phoebus, in those glooms to shun,
Is now no more a refuge or a shade,
Is now with rocks and deep sands over-run.

Those late proud domes of splendor, pomp, and ease
No longer strike the view, in grand attire;
But, torn by winds, flew piece-meal to the seas,
Nor left one nook to lodge the astonished 'squire.

But other groves the hand of Time shall raise,
Again shall Nature smile, serenely gay:
So soon each scene revives, why haste I leave
These green retreats, o'er the dark seas to stray.

For I must go where the mad pirate roves,
A stranger on the inhospitable main,
Lost to the scenes of Hudson's sweetest groves,
Cesarea's forests, and my native plain.

There endless waves deject the wearied eye,
And hostile winds incessant toil prepare;
But should loud bellowing storms all art defy,
The manly heart alone must conquer there.—

There wakes my fears, the guileful Calenture
Tempting the wanderer on the deep-sea main,
That paints gay groves upon the ocean floor,
Beckoning her victim to the faithless scene!

On these blue hills, to cull bright Fancy's flowers,

Might yet awhile the unwelcome work delay,
Might yet beguile the few remaining hours—
Ere to those waves I take my destined way.

Thy vales, Bermuda, and thy sea-girt groves
Can never like these southern forests please;
And, lashed by stormy waves, you court in vain
The northern shepherd to your cedar trees.

Not o'er those isles such equal planets rule.
All, but the cedar, dread the wintry blast;
Too well thy charms the banished Waller sung;
Too near the pilot's star thy doom is cast.

Far o'er the waste of yonder surgy field
My native climes in fancied prospect lie,
Now hid in shades, and now by clouds concealed,
And now by tempests ravished from the eye.

There, triumphs to enjoy, are, Britain, thine,
There, thy proud navy awes the pillaged shore;
Nor sees the day when nations shall combine
That pride to humble, and our rights restore.

Yet o'er the globe shouldst thou extend thy reign,
Here may thy conquering arms one grotto spare;
Here—though thy conquests vex—in spite of pain,
We sip the enlivening glass, in spite of care.

What though we bend to a tyrannic crown;
Still Nature's charms in varied beauty shine—
What though we own the rude imperious Dane,
Gold is his sordid care, the Muses mine.

Winter, and winter's glooms are far removed,
Eternal spring with smiling summer joined:—
Absence, and death, and heart-corroding care,
Why should they cloud the sun-shine of the mind?

But, shepherd, haste, and leave behind thee far
Thy bloody plains, and iron glooms above;
Quit the cold northern star, and here enjoy,
Beneath the smiling skies, this land of love.

The drowsy pelican wings home his way,
The misty eve sits heavy on the sea,
And though yon' storm hangs brooding o'er the main,
Say, shall a moment's gloom discourage thee?

To-morrow's sun new paints the faded scene:
Though deep in ocean sink his western beams,
His spangled chariot shall ascend more clear,
More radiant from the drowsy land of dreams.

Of all the isles the neighboring ocean bears,
None can with this their equal landscapes boast,
What could we do on Saba's cloudy height;
Or what could please on 'Statia's barren coast?

Couldst thou content on rough Tortola stray,
Confest the fairest of the Virgin train; 422
Or couldst thou on those rocky summits play
Where high St. John stands frowning o'er the main?

Haste, shepherd, haste—Hesperian fruits for thee
And clustered grapes from mingled boughs depend—
What pleasure in thy forests can there be
That, leafless now, to every tempest bend?

To milder stars, and skies of clearer blue,
Sworn foe to tyrants, for a time repair:
And, till to mightier force proud Britain bends—
Despise her triumphs, and forget your care.

Soon shall the genius of the fertile soil
A new creation to thy view unfold—
Admire the works of Nature's magic hand,
But scorn that vulgar bait—the thirst for gold.—

Yet, if persuaded by no verse of mine,
You still admire your lands of frost and snow,
And pleased, prefer above these southern groves, 439
The darksome forests that around you grow:

Still there remain—your native air enjoy,
Repel the Tyrant, who thy peace invades:
While charmed, we trace the vales of Santa
Cruz,
And paint with rapture, her inspiring shades.

1776 1779

ON THE MEMORABLE VICTORY,

Obtained by the gallant Captain John Paul Jones, of *Le Bon Homme Richard*, (or father Richard) over the British ship of war *Seraphis*, of 44 guns, under the command of Captain Pearson

First published in Mr. Francis Bailey's Freeman's Journal, Philadelphia, 1781.

O'ER the rough main with flowing sheet
The guardian of a numerous fleet,
Seraphis from the Baltic came;
A ship of less tremendous force
Sailed by her side the self-same course,
Countess of Scarborough was her name.

And now their native coasts appear,
Britannia's hills their summits rear
Above the German main:
Fond to suppose their dangers o'er,
They southward coast along the shore,
Thy waters, gentle Thames, to gain.

Full forty guns *Seraphis* bore,
And *Scarborough's Countess* twenty-four,
Manned with Old England's boldest tars—
What flag that rides the Gallic seas
Shall dare attack such piles as these,
Designed for tumults and for wars!

Now from the top-mast's giddy height
A seaman cried—"Four sail in sight
Approach with favouring gales";
Pearson, resolved to save the fleet,
Stood off to sea, these ships to meet,
And closely braced his shivering sails.

With him advanced the *Countess* bold,
Like a black tar in wars grown old:
And now these floating piles drew nigh;
But, muse, unfold, what chief of fame
In the other warlike squadron came,
Whose standards at his mast-head fly.

'Twas Jones, brave Jones, to battle led
As bold a crew as ever bled
Upon the sky-surrounded main;
The standards of the western world
Were to the willing winds unfurled,
Denying Britain's tyrant reign.

The *Good Man Richard* led the line;
The *Alliance* next: with these combine
The Gallic ship they *Pallas* call:
The *Vengeance*, armed with sword and flame,
These to attack the Britons came—
But *two* accomplished all.

Now Phoebus sought his pearly bed:
But who can tell the scenes of dread,
The horrors of that fatal night!
Close up these floating castles came:
The *Good Man Richard* bursts in flame;
Seraphis trembled at the sight.

She felt the fury of *her* ball:
Down, prostrate down, the Britons fall;
The decks were strewed with slain:
Jones to the foe his vessel lashed;
And, while the black artillery flashed,
Loud thunders shook the main.

Alas! that mortals should employ
Such murdering engines, to destroy
That frame by heaven so nicely joined;
Alas! that e'er the god decreed
That brother should by brother bleed,
And poured such madness in the mind.

But thou, brave Jones, no blame shalt bear;
The rights of men demand thy care:
For *these* you dare the greedy waves—
No tyrant, on destruction bent,
Has planned thy conquests—thou art sent
To humble tyrants and their slaves.

See!—dread Seraphis flames again—
And art thou, Jones, among the slain,
And sunk to Neptune's caves below—
He lives—though crowds around him fall,
Still he, unhurt, survives them all;
Almost alone he fights the foe.

And can your ship these strokes sustain?
Behold thy brave companions slain,
All clasped in ocean's dark embrace.

"STRIKE, OR BE SUNK"—the Briton cries—
"SINK, IF YOU CAN"—the chief replies,
Fierce lightnings blazing in his face.

Then to the side three guns he drew,
(Almost deserted by his crew)
And charged them deep with woe;
By *Pearson's* flash he aimed hot balls;
His main-mast totters—down it falls—
O'erwhelming half below.

Pearson as yet disdained to yield,
But scarce his secret fears concealed,
And thus was heard to cry—
"With hell, not mortals, I contend;
What art thou—human or a fiend,
That dost my force defy?

"Return, my lads, the fight renew!"—
So called bold Pearson to his crew;
But called, alas! in vain;
Some on the decks lay maimed and dead;
Some to their deep recesses fled,
And hosts were shrouded in the main.

Distressed, forsaken, and alone,
He hauled his tattered standard down,
And yielded to his gallant foe;
Bold *Pallas* soon the *Countess* took,—
Thus both their haughty colours struck,
Confessing what the brave can do.

But, Jones, too dearly didst thou buy
These ships possest so gloriously,
Too many deaths disgraced the fray:
Your barque that bore the conquering flame,
That the proud Briton overcame,
Even she forsook thee on thy way;

For when the morn began to shine,
Fatal to her, the ocean brine
Poured through each spacious wound;
Quick in the deep she disappeared;
But Jones to friendly Belgia steered,
With conquest and with glory crowned.

Go on, great man, to scourge the foe,
And bid the haughty Britons know
They to our *Thirteen Stars* shall bend;
The *Stars* that clad in dark attire,
Long glimmered with a feeble fire,
But radiant now ascend.

Bend to the Stars that flaming rise
On western worlds, more brilliant skies,
Fair Freedom's reign restored—
So when the Magi, come from far,
Beheld the God-attending star,
They trembled and adored.

1781 1781

TO THE MEMORY OF THE BRAVE AMERICANS

Under General Greene, in South Carolina, who fell in the action of September 8, 1781

AT Eutaw Springs the valiant died;
Their limbs with dust are covered o'er—
Weep on, ye springs, your tearful tide;
How many heroes are no more!

If in this wreck of ruin, they
Can yet be thought to claim a tear,
O smite your gentle breast, and say
The friends of freedom slumber here!

Thou, who shalt trace this bloody plain,
If goodness rules thy generous breast,
Sigh for the wasted rural reign;
Sigh for the shepherds, sunk to rest!

Stranger, their humble graves adorn;
You too may fall, and ask a tear;
'Tis not the beauty of the morn
That proves the evening shall be clear.—

They saw their injured country's woe;
The flaming town, the wasted field;
Then rushed to meet the insulting foe;
They took the spear—but left the shield.

Led by thy conquering genius, Greene,
The Britons they compelled to fly;
None distant viewed the fatal plain,
None grieved, in such a cause to die—

But, like the Parthian, famed of old,
Who, flying, still their arrows threw,
These routed Britons, full as bold,
Retreated, and retreating slew.

Now rest in peace, our patriot band;
Though far from nature's limits thrown,
We trust they find a happier land,
A brighter sunshine of their own.

1781 1781

THE POLITICAL BALANCE

OR, THE FATES OF BRITAIN AND AMERICA COMPARED

A Tale

Deciding Fates, in Homer's style, we shew,
And bring contending gods once more to view.

As Jove the Olympian (who both I and you know,
Was brother to Neptune, and husband to Juno)
Was lately reviewing his papers of state,
He happened to light on the records of Fate:

In Alphabet order this volume was written—
So he opened at B, for the article Britain—
She struggles so well, said the god, I will see
What the sisters in Pluto's dominions decree.

And, first, on the top of a column he read
"Of a king, with a mighty soft place in his head,
Who should join in his temper the ass and the mule,
The third of his name, and by far the worst fool:

"His reign shall be famous for multiplication,
The sire and the king of a whelp generation:
But such is the will and the purpose of fate,
For each child he begets he shall forfeit a State:

"In the course of events, he shall find to his cost
That he cannot regain what he foolishly lost;
Of the nations around he shall be the derision,
And know, by experience, the rule of Division."

So Jupiter read—a god of first rank—
And still had read on—but he came to a blank:
For the Fates had neglected the rest to reveal—
They either forgot it, or chose to conceal:

When a leaf is torn out, or a blot on a page
That pleases our fancy, we fly in a rage—
So, curious to know what the Fates would say next,
No wonder if Jove, disappointed, was vext.

But still, as true genius not frequently fails,
He glanced at the Virgin, and thought of the Scales;
And said, "To determine the will of the Fates,
One scale shall weigh Britain, the other the States."

Then turning to Vulcan, his maker of thunder,
Said he, "My dear Vulcan, I pray you look yonder,
Those creatures are tearing each other to pieces,
And, instead of abating, the carnage increases.

"Now, as you are a blacksmith, and lusty stout ham-eater,
You must make me a globe of a shorter diameter;
The world in abridgement, and just as it stands
With all its proportions of waters and lands;

"But its various divisions must so be designed,
That I can unhinge it whene'er I've a mind—
How else should I know what the portions will weigh,
Or which of the combatants carry the day?"

Old Vulcan complied, (we've no reason to doubt it)
So he put on his apron and straight went about it—
Made center, and circles as round as a pancake,
And here the Pacific, and there the Atlantic.

An axis he hammered, whose ends were the poles,
(On which the whole body perpetually rolls)
A brazen meridian he added to these,
Where four times repeated were ninety degrees.

I am sure you had laughed to have seen his droll attitude,
When he bent round the surface the circles of latitude,
The zones, and the tropics, meridians, equator,
And other fine things that are drawn on salt water.

Away to the southward (instructed by Pallas)
He placed in the ocean the Terra Australis,
New Holland, New Guinea, and so of the rest—
America lay by herself in the west:

From the regions where winter eternally reigns,
To the climes of Peru he extended her plains;
Dark groves, and the zones did her bosom adorn,
And the Crosiers,[1] new burnished, he hung at Cape Horn.

The weight of two oceans she bore on her sides,
With all their convulsions of tempests and tides;
Vast lakes on her surface did fearfully roll,
And the ice from her rivers surrounded the pole.

Then Europe and Asia he northward extended,
Where under the Arctic with Zembla they ended;
(The length of these regions he took with his garters,
Including Siberia, the land of the Tartars).

In the African clime (where the cocoa-nut tree grows)
He laid down the deserts, and even the negroes,
The shores by the waves of four oceans embraced,
And elephants strolling about in the waste.

In forming East India, he had a wide scope,
Beginning his work at the cape of Good Hope;
Then eastward of that he continued his plan,
'Till he came to the empire and isles of Japan.

Adjacent to Europe he struck up an island,
(One part of it low, but the other was high land)
With many a comical creature upon it,
And one wore a hat, and another a bonnet.

Like emmits or ants in a fine summer's day,
They ever were marching in battle array,
Or skipping about on the face of the brine,
Like witches in egg-shells (their ships of the line).

These poor little creatures were all in a flame,
To the lands of America, urging their claim,

[1] Stars, in the form of a cross, which mark the South Pole in southern latitudes. [*Freneau's note.*]

Still biting, or stinging, or spreading their sails;
(For Vulcan had formed them with stings in their tails).

So poor and so lean, you might count all their ribs,[1]
Yet were so enraptured with crackers and squibs,
That Vulcan with laughter almost split asunder,
"Because they imagined their crackers were thunder."

Due westward from these, with a channel between,
A servant to slaves, Hibernia was seen,
Once crowded with monarchs, and high in renown,
But all she retained was the Harp and the Crown!

Insulted forever by nobles and priests,
And managed by bullies, and governed by beasts,
She looked!—to describe her I hardly know how—
Such an image of death in the scowl on her brow:

For scaffolds and halters were full in her view,
And the fiends of perdition their cutlasses drew:
And axes and gibbets around her were placed,
And the demons of murder her honors defaced—
With the blood of the worthy her mantle was stained,
And hardly a trace of her beauty remained.

Her genius, a female, reclined in the shade,
And, sick of oppression, so mournfully played,
That Jove was uneasy to hear her complain,
And ordered his blacksmith to loosen her chain:

Then tipt her a wink, saying, "Now is your time,
(To rebel is the sin, to revolt is no crime)
When your fetters are off, if you dare not be free
Be a slave and be damned, but complain not to me."

[1] Their national debt being now above £200,000,000 sterling. [*Freneau's note.*]

But finding her timid, he cried in a rage—
"Though the doors are flung open, she stays in the cage!
Subservient to Britain then let her remain,
And her freedom shall be, but the choice of her chain."

At length, to discourage all stupid pretensions,
Jove looked at the globe, and approved its dimensions,
And cried in a transport—"Why what have we here!
Friend Vulcan, it is a most beautiful sphere!

"Now while I am busy in taking apart
This globe that is formed with such exquisite art,
Go, Hermes, to Libra, (you're one of her gallants)
And ask, in my name, for the loan of her balance."

Away posted Hermes, as swift as the gales,
And as swiftly returned with the ponderous scales,
And hung them aloft to a beam in the air,
So equally poised, they had turned with a hair.

Now Jove to Columbia his shoulders applied,
But aiming to lift her, his strength she defied—
Then, turning about to their godships, he says—
"A body so vast is not easy to raise;

"But if you assist me, I still have a notion
Our forces, united, can put her in motion,
And swing her aloft, (though alone I might fail)
And place her, in spite of her bulk, in our scale;

"If six years together the Congress have strove,
And more than divided the empire with Jove;
With a Jove like myself, who am nine times as great,
You can join, like their soldiers, to heave up this weight."

So to it they went, with handspikes and levers,
And upward she sprung, with her mountains and rivers!
Rocks, cities, and islands, deep waters and shallows,
Ships, armies, and forests, high heads, and fine fellows:

"Stick to it!" cries Jove "now heave one and all!
At least we are lifting one-eighth of the ball!
If backward she tumbles—then trouble begins,
And then have a care, my dear boys, of your shins!"

When gods are determined what project can fail?
So they gave a hard shove, and she mounted the scale;
Suspended aloft, Jove viewed her with awe—
And the gods,[1] for their pay, had a hearty—huzza!

But Neptune bawled out— "Why Jove you're a noddy,
Is Britain sufficient to poise that vast body?
'Tis nonsense such castles to build in the air—
As well might an oyster with Britain compare."

"Away to your waters, you blustering bully,"
Said Jove, "or I'll make you repent of your folly,
Is Jupiter, Sir, to be tutored by you?—
Get out of my sight, for I know what to do!"

Then searching about with his fingers for Britain,
Thought he, "this same island I cannot well hit on!
The devil take him who first called her the Great:
If she was—she is vastly diminished of late!"

Like a man that is searching his thigh for a flea,
He peeped and he fumbled, but nothing could see;
At last he exclaimed—"I am surely upon it—
I think I have hold of a Highlander's bonnet."

But finding his error, he said with a sigh,
"This bonnet is only the island of Skie!" [2]
So away to his namesake the planet he goes,
And borrowed two moons to hang on his nose.

[1] American soldiers. [*Freneau's note.*]

[2] An Island on the north-west of Scotland. [*Freneau's note.*]

Through these, as through glasses, he saw her quite clear,
And in rapture cried out—"I have found her—she's here!
If this be not Britain, then call me an ass,
She looks like a gem in an ocean of glass.

"But faith, she's so small I must mind how I shake her:
In a box I'll enclose her, for fear I should break her:
Though a god, I might suffer for being aggressor,
Since scorpions, and vipers, and hornets possess her;

"The white cliffs of Albion I think I descry,
And the hills of Plinlimmon appear rather nigh—
But, Vulcan, inform me what creatures are these,
That smell so of onions, and garlic, and cheese?"

Old Vulcan replied—"Odds splutter a nails!
Why, these are the Welch, and the country is Wales!
When Taffy is vext, no devil is ruder—
Take care how you trouble the offspring of Tudor!

"On the crags of the mountains *hur* living *hur* seeks,
Hur country is planted with garlic and leeks;
So great is *hur* choler, beware how you tease *hur*,
For these are the Britons—unconquered by Caesar."

"But now, my dear Juno, pray give me my mittens,
(These insects I am going to handle are Britons)
I'll draw up their isle with a finger and thumb,
As the doctor extracts an old tooth from the gum."

Then he raised her aloft—but to shorten our tale,
She looked like a clod in the opposite scale—
Britannia so small, and Columbia so large—
A ship of first rate, and a ferryman's barge!

Cried Pallas to Vulcan, "Why, Jove's in a dream—
Observe how he watches the turn of the beam!
Was ever a mountain outweighed by a grain?
Or what is a drop when compared to the main?"

But Momus alleged—"In my humble opinion,
You should add to Great-Britain her foreign dominion,
When this is appended, perhaps she will rise,
And equal her rival in weight and in size."

"Alas! (said the monarch), your project is vain,
But little is left of her foreign domain;
And, scattered about in the liquid expanse,
That little is left to the mercy of France;

"However, we'll lift them, and give her fair play"—
And soon in the scale with their mistress they lay;
But the gods were confounded and struck with surprise,
And Vulcan could hardly believe his own eyes!

For (such was the purpose and guidance of fate)
Her foreign dominions diminished her weight—
By which it appeared, to Britain's disaster,
Her foreign possessions were changing their master.

Then, as he replaced them, said Jove with a smile—
"Columbia shall never be ruled by an isle—
But vapors and darkness around her may rise,
And tempests conceal her awhile from our eyes;

"So locusts in Egypt their squadrons display,
And rising, disfigure the face of the day;
So the moon, at her full, has a frequent eclipse,
And the sun in the ocean diurnally dips.

"Then cease your endeavours, ye vermin of
    Britain—
(And here, in derision, their island he spit on)
'Tis madness to seek what you never can find,
Or to think of uniting what nature disjoined;

"But still you may flutter awhile with your
    wings,
And spit out your venom and brandish your
    stings:
Your hearts are as black, and as bitter as gall,
A curse to mankind—and a blot on the Ball."[1]

1782

[1] It is hoped that such a sentiment may not be deemed wholly illiberal—Every candid person will certainly *draw a line between a brave and magnanimous people, and a most vicious and vitiating government.* Perhaps the following extract from a pamphlet lately published in London and republished at Baltimore (June, 1809) by Mr. *Bernard Dornin,* will place the preceding sentiment in a fair point of view:

"A better spirit than exists in the English people, never existed in any people in the world; it has been misdirected, and squandered upon party purposes in the most degrading and scandalous manner; they have been led to believe that they were benefiting the commerce of England by destroying the commerce of America, that they were defending their sovereign by perpetuating the bigoted oppression of their fellow subjects; their rulers and their guides have told them that they would equal the vigor of France by equalling her atrocity, and they have gone on, wasting that opulence, patience and courage, which if husbanded by prudent, and moderate counsels, might have proved the salvation of mankind. The same policy of turning the good qualities of Englishmen to their own destruction, which made Mr. Pitt omnipotent, continues his power to those who resemble him only in his vices: advantage is taken of the loyalty of Englishmen, to make them meanly submissive; their piety is turned into persecution; their courage into useless and obstinate contention; they are plundered because they are ready to pay, and soothed into asinine stupidity because they are full of virtuous patience. If England must perish at last, so let it be: that event is in the hands of God; we must dry up our tears, and submit. But that England should perish swindling and stealing; that it should perish waging war against lazar-houses and hospitals, that it should perish persecuting with monastic bigotry; that it should calmly give itself up to be ruined by the flashy arrogance of one man, and the narrow fanaticism of another; these events are within the power of human beings, but I did not think that the magnanimity of Englishmen would ever stoop to such degradations." [*Freneau's note.*]

BARNEY'S INVITATION

Come, all ye lads who know no fear,
To wealth and honor with me steer
In the *Hyder Ali* privateer,
    Commanded by brave Barney.

She's new and true, and tight and sound,
Well rigged aloft, and all well found—
Come away and be with laurel crowned,
    Away—and leave your lasses.

Accept our terms without delay,
And make your fortunes while you may,
Such offers are not every day
    In the power of a jolly sailor.

Success and fame attend the brave,
But death the coward and the slave,
Who fears to plow the Atlantic wave,
    To seek the bold invaders.

Come, then, and take a cruising bout,
Our ship sails well, there is no doubt,
She *has* been tried both in and out,
    And answers expectation.

Let no proud foes whom Europe bore,
Distress our trade, insult our shore—
Teach them to know their reign is o'er,
    Bold Philadelphia sailors!

We'll teach them how to sail so near,
Or to venture on the Delaware,
When we in warlike trim appear
    And cruise without Henlopen.

Who cannot wounds and battle dare
Shall never clasp the blooming fair;
The brave alone their charms should share,
    The brave are their protectors.

With hand and heart united all,
Prepared to conquer or to fall,
Attend, my lads, to honor's call,
    Embark in our *Hyder Ali.*

From an Eastern prince she takes her name,
Who, smit with Freedom's sacred flame,
Usurping Britons brought to shame,
    His country's wrongs avenging;

See, on her stern the waving stars—
Inured to blood, inured to wars,

Come, enter quick, my jolly tars,
To scourge these warlike Britons.

Here's grog enough—then drink about,
I know your hearts are firm and stout;
American blood will never give out,
And often we have proved it.

Though stormy oceans round us roll,
We'll keep a firm undaunted soul,
Befriended by the cheering bowl,
Sworn foes to melancholy:

While timorous landsmen lurk on shore,
'Tis ours to go where cannons roar—
On a coasting cruise we'll go once more,
Despisers of all danger;

And Fortune still, who crowns the brave,
Shall guard us over the gloomy wave;
A fearful heart betrays a knave;
Success to the *Hyder Ali.*

1786

SONG

ON CAPTAIN BARNEY'S VICTORY OVER THE SHIP *GENERAL MONK. APRIL 26, 1782*

O'ER the waste of waters cruising,
Long the *General Monk* had reigned;
All subduing, all reducing,
None her lawless rage restrained:
Many a brave and hearty fellow
Yielding to this warlike foe,
When her guns began to bellow
Struck his humbled colors low.

But grown bold with long successes,
Leaving the wide watery way,
She, a stranger to distresses,
Came to cruise within Cape May;
"Now we soon (said captain Rogers)
Shall their men of commerce meet;
In our hold we'll have them lodgers,
We shall capture half their fleet.

"Lo! I see their van appearing—
Back our topsails to the mast—
They toward us full are steering
With a gentle western blast;
I've a list of all their cargoes,
All their guns, and all their men:
I am sure these modern Argos
Can't escape us one in ten:

"Yonder comes the *Charming Sally*
Sailing with the *General Greene*—
First we'll fight the *Hyder Ali,*
Taking her is taking them:
She invites to give us battle,
Bearing down with all her sail—
Now, boys, let our cannon rattle!
To take her we cannot fail.

"Our eighteen guns, each a nine pounder,
Soon shall terrify this foe;
We shall maul her, we shall wound her,
Bringing rebel colors low."
While he thus anticipated
Conquests that he could not gain,
He in the Cape May channel waited
For the ship that caused his pain.

Captain Barney then preparing,
Thus addressed his gallant crew—
"Now, brave lads, be bold and daring,
Let your hearts be firm and true;
This is a proud English cruiser,
Roving up and down the main,
We must fight her—must reduce her,
Though our decks be strewed with slain.

"Let who will be the survivor,
We must conquer or must die,
We must take her up the river,
Whate'er comes of you or I:
Though she shews most formidable
With her eighteen pointed nines,
And her quarters clad in sable,
Let us balk her proud designs.

"With four nine pounders, and twelve sixes
We will face that daring band;
Let no dangers damp your courage,
Nothing can the brave withstand.
Fighting for your country's honor,
Now to gallant deeds aspire;
Helmsman, bear us down upon her,
Gunner, give the word to fire!"

Then yard arm and yard arm meeting,
Straight began the dismal fray,
Cannon mouths, each other greeting,
Belched their smoky flames away:

Soon the langrage, grape and chain shot,
  That from Barney's cannons flew,
Swept the *Monk*, and cleared each round top,
  Killed and wounded half her crew.

Captain Rogers strove to rally:
  But they from their quarters fled,
While the roaring *Hyder Ali*
  Covered o'er his decks with dead.
When from their tops their dead men tumbled,
  And the streams of blood did flow,
Then their proudest hopes were humbled
  By their brave inferior foe.

All aghast, and all confounded,
  They beheld their champions fall,
And their captain, sorely wounded,
  Bade them quick for quarters call.
Then the *Monk's* proud flag descended,
  And her cannon ceased to roar;
By her crew no more defended,
  She confessed the contest o'er.

Come, brave boys, and fill your glasses,
  You have humbled one proud foe,
No brave action this surpasses,
  Fame shall tell the nations so—
Thus be Britain's woes completed,
  Thus abridged her cruel reign,
'Till she ever, thus defeated,
  Yields the sceptre of the main.

1782

THE SEASONS MORALIZED

THEY, who to warmer regions run,
May bless the favor of the sun,
But seek in vain what charms us here,
Life's picture, varying with the year.

Spring, and her wanton train advance
Like Youth to lead the festive dance,
All, all her scenes are mirth and play,
And blushing blossoms own her sway.

The Summer next (those blossoms blown)
Brings on the fruits that spring had sown,
Thus men advance, impelled by time,
And Nature triumphs in her prime.

Then Autumn crowns the beauteous year,
The groves a sicklier aspect wear;
And mournful she (the lot of all)
Matures her fruits, to make them fall.

Clad in the vestments of a tomb,
Old age is only Winter's gloom—
Winter, alas! shall spring restore,
But youth returns to man no more.

1785

ON THE VICISSITUDES OF THINGS

"THE constant lapse of rolling years
Awakes our hopes, provokes our fears
Of something yet unknown;
We saw the last year pass away,
But who, that lives can safely say,
The next shall be his own?"

So hundreds talk—and thousands more
Descant their moral doctrines o'er;
And when the preaching's done,
Each goes his various, wonted way,
To labor some, and some to play—
So goes the folly on.

How swift the vagrant seasons fly;
They're hardly born before they die,
Yet in their wild career,
Like atoms round the rapid wheel,
We seem the same, though changing still,
Mere reptiles of a year.

Some haste to seek a wealthy bride,
Some, rhymes to make on one that died;
And millions curse the day,
When first in Hymen's silken bands
The parson joined mistaken hands,
And bade the bride obey.

While sad Amelia vents her sighs,
In epitaphs and elegies,
For her departed dear,
Who would suppose the muffled bell,
And mourning gowns, were meant to tell,
Her grief will last—a year?

In folly's path how many meet—
What hosts will live to lie and cheat—
How many empty pates
May, in this wise, eventful year,
In native dignity appear
To manage Rising States!

How vain to sigh!—the wheel must on
And straws are to the whirlpool drawn,
With ships of gallant mien—

What has been once, may time restore;
What now exists, has been before—
Years only change the scene.

In endless circles all things move;
Below, about, far off, above,
This motion all attain—
If Folly's self should flit away,
She would return some New Year's day,
With millions in her train.

Sun, moon, and stars, are each a sphere,
The earth the same, (or very near,)
Sir Isaac has defined—
In circles every coin is cast,
And hence our cash departs so fast,
Cash—that no charm can bind.

From you to us—from us it rolls
To comfort other cloudy souls:—
If again we make it square,[1]
Perhaps the uneasy guest will stay
To cheer us in some wintry day,
And smooth the brow of care.

1785

TO SYLVIUS

ON THE FOLLY OF WRITING POETRY

Of all the fools that haunt our coast
The scribbling tribe I pity most:
Their's is a standing scene of woes,
And their's no prospect of repose.

Then, Sylvius, why this eager claim
To light your torch at Clio's flame?
To few she shews sincere regard,
And none, from her, should hope reward.

A garret high, dark dismal room,
Is still the pensive poets' doom:
Hopes raised to heaven must be their lot,
Yet bear the curse, to be forgot.

Hourly they deal with Grecian Jove,
And draw their bills on banks above:
Yet stand abashed, with all their fire,
When brought to face some country 'squire.

To mend the world, is still their aim:
The world, alas! remains the same,
And so must stand to every age,
Proof to the morals of the page!

[1] The old Continental. [*Freneau's note.*]

The knave that keeps a tippling inn,
The red-nosed boy that deals out gin,
If aided by some paltry skill
May both be statesmen when they will.

The man that mends a beggar's shoes,
The quack that heals your negro's bruise,
The wretch that turns a cutler's stone,
Have wages they can call their own:

The head, that plods in trade's domains,
Gets something to reward its pains;
But Wit—that does the world beguile,
Takes for its pay—an empty smile!

Yet each presumes his works will rise,
And gain a name that never dies;
From earth, and cold oblivion freed,
Immortal, in the poets' creed!

Can Reason in that bosom reign
Which fondly feeds a hope so vain,
When every age that passes by
Beholds a crowd of poets die!

Poor Sappho's fate shall Milton know—
His scenes of grief and tales of woe
No honors, that all Europe gave,
No merit—shall from ruin save.—

To all that write and all that read
Fate shall, with hasty step, succeed!
Even Shakespeare's page, his mirth, his tears
May sink beneath this weight of years.

Old Spenser's doom shall, Pope, be thine
The music of each moving line
Scarce bribes an age or two to stay,
Admire your strain—then flit away.

The people of old Chaucer's times
Were once in raptures with his rhymes,
But Time—that over verse prevails,
To other ears tells other tales.

Why then so sad, dear rhyming friends—
One common fate on both attends,
The bards that soothe the statesman's ear,
And him—who finds no audience there.

Mere structures formed of common earth,
Not they from heaven derive their birth,
Or why through life, like vagrants, pass
To mingle with the moldering mass?—

Of all the souls, from Jove that came
To animate this mortal frame,
Of all the myriads, on the wing,
How few can taste the Muse's spring!

Sejanus, of mercantile skill,
Without whose aid the world stands still,
And by whose wonder-working play
The sun goes round—(his flatterers say)

Sejanus has in house declared
"These States, as yet, can boast no bard,
And all the sing-song of our clime
Is merely nonsense, fringed with rhyme."

With such a bold, conceited air
When such assume the critic's chair,
Low in the dust is genius laid,
The muses with the man in trade.

Then, Sylvius, come—let you and I
On Neptune's aid, once more rely:
Perhaps the muse may still impart
Her balm to ease the aching heart.

Though cold might chill and storms dismay,
Yet Zoilus will be far away:
With us at least, depart and share
No garret—but resentment there.

1788

THE WILD HONEY SUCKLE

Fair flower, that dost so comely grow,
Hid in this silent, dull retreat,
Untouched thy honied blossoms blow,
Unseen thy little branches greet:
No roving foot shall crush thee here,
No busy hand provoke a tear.

By Nature's self in white arrayed,
She bade thee shun the vulgar eye,
And planted here the guardian shade,
And sent soft waters murmuring by;
Thus quietly thy summer goes,
Thy days declining to repose.

Smit with those charms, that must decay,
I grieve to see your future doom;
They died—nor were those flowers more gay,
The flowers that did in Eden bloom;
Unpitying frosts, and Autumn's power
Shall leave no vestige of this flower.

From morning suns and evening dews
At first thy little being came:
If nothing once, you nothing lose,
For when you die you are the same;
The space between, is but an hour,
The frail duration of a flower.

1786

ON A BOOK CALLED *UNITARIAN THEOLOGY*[1]

In this choice work, with wisdom penned, we find
The noblest system to reform mankind,
Bold truths confirmed, that bigots have denied,
By most perverted, and which some deride.
Here, truths divine in easy language flow,
Truths long concealed, that now all climes shall know:
Here, like the blaze of our material sun,
Enlightened Reason proves, that GOD IS ONE—
As that, concentered in itself, a sphere,
Illumes all Nature with its radiance here,
Bids towards itself all trees and plants aspire,
Awakes the winds, impels the seeds of fire,
And still subservient to the Almighty plan,
Warms into life the changeful race of man;
So—like that sun—in heaven's bright realms we trace
One Power of Love, that fills unbounded space,
Existing always by no borrowed aid,
Before all worlds—eternal, and not made—
To That indebted, stars and comets burn,
Owe their swift movements, and to That return!
Prime source of wisdom, all-contriving mind,
First spring of Reason, that this globe designed;
Parent of order, whose unwearied hand
Upholds the fabric that his wisdom planned,
And, its due course assigned to every sphere,
Revolves the seasons, and sustains the year!—
Pure light of Truth! where'er thy splendors shine,
Thou art the image of the power divine;
Nought else, in life, that full resemblance bears,
No sun, that lights us through our circling years,

[1] First entitled "On the Honorable Emanuel Swedenborg's Universal Theology."

No stars, that through yon' charming azure stray,
No moon, that glads us with her evening ray,
No seas, that o'er their gloomy caverns flow,
No forms beyond us, and no shapes below!
Then slight—ah slight not, this instructive page,
For the mean follies of a dreaming age:
Here to the truth, by Reason's aid aspire,
Nor some dull preacher of romance admire;
See One, Sole God, in these convincing lines,
Beneath whose view perpetual day-light shines;
At whose command all worlds their circuits run,
And night, retiring, dies before the sun!
Here, Man no more disgraced by Time appears,
Lost in dull slumbers through ten thousand years:
Plunged in that gulf, whose dark unfathomed waves
Men of all ages to perdition gave;
An empty dream, or still more empty shade,
The substance vanished, and the form decayed!—
Here Reason proves, that when this life decays,
Instant, new life in the warm bosom plays,
As that expiring, still its course repairs
Through endless ages, and unceasing years.
Where parted souls with kindred spirits meet,
Wrapt to the bloom of beauty all complete;
In that celestial, vast, unclouded sphere,
Nought there exists but has its image here!
All there is Mind!—That Intellectual Flame,
From whose vast stores all human genius came,
In which all Nature forms on Reason's plan—
Flows to this abject world, and beams on Man!

1786

THE DYING INDIAN: TOMO-CHEQUI

"On yonder lake I spread the sail no more!
Vigor, and youth, and active days are past—
Relentless demons urge me to that shore
On whose black forests all the dead are cast:—
Ye solemn train, prepare the funeral song,
For I must go to shades below,
Where all is strange and all is new;
Companion to the airy throng!—
What solitary streams,
In dull and dreary dreams,
All melancholy, must I rove along!

To what strange lands must Chequi take his way!
Groves of the dead departed mortals trace:
No deer along those gloomy forests stray,
No huntsmen there take pleasure in the chase,
But all are empty unsubstantial shades,
That ramble through those visionary glades;
No spongy fruits from verdant trees depend,
But sickly orchards there
Do fruits as sickly bear,
And apples a consumptive visage shew,
And withered hangs the hurtle-berry blue.

Ah me! what mischiefs on the dead attend!
Wandering a stranger to the shores below,
Where shall I brook or real fountain find?
Lazy and sad deluding waters flow—
Such is the picture in my boding mind!
Fine tales, indeed, they tell
Of shades and purling rills,
Where our dead fathers dwell
Beyond the western hills,
But when did ghost return his state to shew;
Or who can promise half the tale is true?

I too must be a fleeting ghost!—no more—
None, none but shadows to those mansions go;
I leave my woods, I leave the Huron shore,
For emptier groves below!
Ye charming solitudes,
Ye tall ascending woods,
Ye glassy lakes and prattling streams,
Whose aspect still was sweet,
Whether the sun did greet,
Or the pale moon embraced you with her beams—
Adieu to all!
To all, that charmed me where I strayed,
The winding stream, the dark sequestered shade;
Adieu all triumphs here!
Adieu the mountain's lofty swell,

Adieu, thou little verdant hill,
And seas, and stars, and skies—farewell,
For some remoter sphere!

Perplexed with doubts, and tortured with despair,
Why so dejected at this hopeless sleep?
Nature at last these ruins may repair,
When fate's long dream is o'er, and she forgets to weep;
Some real world once more may be assigned,
Some new born mansion for the immortal mind!
Farewell, sweet lake; farewell surrounding woods,
To other groves, through midnight glooms, I stray,
Beyond the mountains, and beyond the floods,
Beyond the Huron bay!
Prepare the hollow tomb, and place me low,
My trusty bow and arrows by my side,
The cheerful bottle and the venison store;
For long the journey is that I must go,
Without a partner, and without a guide."
He spoke, and bid the attending mourners weep,
Then closed his eyes, and sunk to endless sleep!

1784

THE HURRICANE[1]

Happy the man who, safe on shore,
Now trims, at home, his evening fire;
Unmoved, he hears the tempests roar,
That on the tufted groves expire:
Alas! on us they doubly fall,
Our feeble barque must bear them all.

Now to their haunts the birds retreat,
The squirrel seeks his hollow tree,
Wolves in their shaded caverns meet,
All, all are blest but wretched we—
Foredoomed a stranger to repose,
No rest the unsettled ocean knows.

While o'er the dark abyss we roam,
Perhaps, with last departing gleam,
We saw the sun descend in gloom,
No more to see his morning beam;
But buried low, by far too deep,
On coral beds, unpitied, sleep!

But what a strange, uncoasted strand
Is that, where fate permits no day—
No charts have we to mark that land,
No compass to direct that way—
What Pilot shall explore that realm,
What new Columbus take the helm!

While death and darkness both surround,
And tempests rage with lawless power,
Of friendship's voice I hear no sound,
No comfort in this dreadful hour—
What friendship can in tempests be,
What comforts on this raging sea?

The barque, accustomed to obey,
No more the trembling pilots guide:
Alone she gropes her trackless way,
While mountains burst on either side—
Thus, skill and science both must fall;
And ruin is the lot of all.

1785

[1] Near the east end of Jamaica, July 30, 1784. [*Freneau's note.*]

THE INDIAN BURYING GROUND

In spite of all the learned have said,
I still my old opinion keep;
The posture, that we give the dead,
Points out the soul's eternal sleep.

Not so the ancients of these lands—
The Indian, when from life released,
Again is seated with his friends,
And shares again the joyous feast.[1]

His imaged birds, and painted bowl,
And venison, for a journey dressed,
Bespeak the nature of the soul,
Activity, that knows no rest.

His bow, for action ready bent,
And arrows, with a head of stone,
Can only mean that life is spent,
And not the old ideas gone.

[1] The North American Indians bury their dead in a sitting posture; decorating the corpse with wampum, the images of birds, quadrupeds, etc.: And (if that of a warrior) with bows, arrows, tomhawks, and other military weapons. [*Freneau's note.*]

Thou, stranger, that shalt come this way,
No fraud upon the dead commit—
Observe the swelling turf, and say
They do not lie, but here they sit.

Here still a lofty rock remains,
On which the curious eye may trace
(Now wasted, half, by wearing rains)
The fancies of a ruder race.

Here still an aged elm aspires,
Beneath whose far-projecting shade
(And which the shepherd still admires)
The children of the forest played!

There oft a restless Indian queen
(Pale Shebah, with her braided hair)
And many a barbarous form is seen
To chide the man that lingers there.

By midnight moons, o'er moistening dews,
In habit for the chase arrayed,
The hunter still the deer pursues,
The hunter and the deer, a shade!

And long shall timorous fancy see
The painted chief, and pointed spear,
And Reason's self shall bow the knee
To shadows and delusions here.

1788

MAY TO APRIL

Without your showers, I breed no flowers,
Each field a barren waste appears;
If you don't weep, my blossoms sleep,
They take such pleasures in your tears.

As your decay made room for May,
So I must part with all that's mine:
My balmy breeze, my blooming trees
To torrid suns their sweets resign!

O'er April dead, my shades I spread:
To her I owe my dress so gay—
Of daughters three, it falls on me
To close our triumphs on one day:

Thus, to repose, all Nature goes;
Month after month must find its doom:
Time on the wing, May ends the Spring,
And Summer dances on her tomb!

1787

TO AN AUTHOR

Your leaves bound up compact and fair,
In neat array at length prepare,
To pass their hour on learning's stage,
To meet the surly critic's rage;
The statesman's slight, the smatterer's sneer—
Were these, indeed, your only fear,
You might be tranquil and resigned:
What most should touch your fluttering mind;
Is that, few critics will be found
To sift your works, and deal the wound.

Thus, when one fleeting year is past
On some bye-shelf your book is cast—
Another comes, with something new,
And drives you fairly out of view:

With some to praise, but more to blame,
The mind returns to—whence it came;
And some alive, who scarce could read
Will publish satires on the dead.

Thrice happy Dryden,[1] who could meet
Some rival bard in every street!
When all were bent on writing well
It was some credit to excel:—

Thrice happy Dryden, who could find
A Milbourne for his sport designed—
And Pope, who saw the harmless rage
Of Dennis bursting o'er his page
Might justly spurn the critic's aim,
Who only helped to swell his fame.

On these bleak climes by Fortune thrown,
Where rigid Reason reigns alone,
Where lovely Fancy has no sway,
Nor magic forms about us play—
Nor nature takes her summer hue
Tell me, what has the muse to do?—

An age employed in edging steel
Can no poetic raptures feel;
No solitude's attracting power,
No leisure of the noon day hour,
No shaded stream, no quiet grove
Can this fantastic century move,

The muse of love in no request—
Go—try your fortune with the rest,

[1] See Johnson's lives of the English Poets. [*Freneau's note.*]

One of the nine you should engage,
To meet the follies of the age:—

On one, we fear, your choice must fall—
The least engaging of them all—
Her visage stern—an angry style—
A clouded brow—malicious smile—
A mind on murdered victims placed—
She, only she, can please the taste!

1788

ON THE SLEEP OF PLANTS

When suns are set, and stars in view,
Not only man to slumber yields;
But Nature grants this blessing too,
To yonder plants, in yonder fields.

The Summer heats and lengthening days
(To them the same as toil and care)
Thrice welcome make the evening breeze,
That kindly does their strength repair.

At early dawn each plant survey,
And see, revived by Nature's hand,
With youthful vigor, fresh and gay,
Their blossoms blow, their leaves expand.

Yon' garden plant, with weeds o'er-run,
Not void of thought, perceives its hour,
And, watchful of the parting sun,
Throughout the night conceals her flower.

Like us, the slave of cold and heat,
She too enjoys her little span—
With Reason, only less complete
Than that which makes the boast of man.

Thus, moulded from one common clay,
A varied life adorns the plain;
By Nature subject to decay,
By Nature meant to bloom again!

1790

TO THE PUBLIC [1]

This age is so fertile of mighty events,
That people complain, with some reason, no doubt,
Besides the time lost, and besides the expense,
With reading the papers they're fairly worn out:
The past is no longer an object of care,
The present consumes all the time they can spare.

Thus grumbles the reader, but still he reads on
With his pence and his paper unwilling to part:
He sees the world passing, men going and gone,
Some riding in coaches, and some in a cart:
For a peep at the farce a subscription he'll give,—
Revolutions must happen, and printers must live:

For a share of your favor we aim with the rest:
To enliven the scene we'll exert all our skill,
What we have to impart shall be some of the best,
And *Multum in Parvo* our text, if you will;
Since we never admitted a clause in our creed,
That the greatest employment of life is—to read.

The king of the French and the queen of the North
At the head of the play, for the season, we find:
From the spark that we kindled, a flame has gone forth
To astonish the world and enlighten mankind:
With a code of new doctrines the universe rings,
And Paine is addressing strange sermons to kings.

Thus launch'd, as we are, on the ocean of news,
In hopes that your pleasure our pains will repay,
All honest endeavors the author will use
To furnish a feast for the grave and the gay:
At least he'll essay such a track to pursue
That the world shall approve—and his news shall be true.

1791

[1] Text of edition of 1795.

TO MY BOOK [1]

Seven years are now elaps'd, dear rambling volume,
Since, to all knavish wights a foe,
I sent you forth to vex and gall 'em,
Or drive them to the shades below:

[1] Text of edition of 1795.

With spirit, still, of Democratic proof,
And still despising Shylock's canker'd hoof:
What doom the fates intend, is hard to say,
Whether to live to some far-distant day,
Or sickening in your prime,
In this bard-baiting clime,
Take pet, make wings, say prayers, and flit away.

"Virtue, order, and religion,
Haste, and seek some other region;
Your plan is laid, to hunt them down,
Destroy the mitre, rend the gown,
And that vile hag, Philosophy, restore"—
Did ever volume plan so much before?

For seven years past, a host of busy foes
Have buzz'd about your nose,
White, black, and grey, by night and day;
Garbling, lying, singing, sighing:
These eastern gales a cloud of insects bring
That fluttering, snivelling, whimpering—on the wing—
And, wafted still as discord's demon guides,
Flock round the flame, that yet shall singe their hides.

Well!—let the fates decree whate'er they please:
Whether you're doom'd to drink oblivion's cup,
Or Praise-God Barebones eats you up,
This I can say, you've spread your wings afar,
Hostile to garter, ribbon, crown, and star;
Still on the people's, still on Freedom's side,
With full determin'd aim, to baffle every claim
Of well-born wights, that aim to mount and ride.

1792

ON MR. PAINE'S *RIGHTS OF MAN*

Thus briefly sketched the sacred Rights of Man,
How inconsistent with the Royal Plan!
Which for itself exclusive honor craves,
Where some are masters born, and millions slaves.
With what contempt must every eye look down
On that base, childish bauble called a crown,
The gilded bait, that lures the crowd, to come,
Bow down their necks, and meet a slavish doom;
The source of half the miseries men endure,
The quack that kills them, while it seems to cure.
Roused by the reason of his manly page,
Once more shall Paine a listening world engage:
From Reason's source, a bold reform he brings,
In raising up mankind, he pulls down kings,
Who, source of discord, patrons of all wrong,
On blood and murder have been fed too long:
Hid from the world, and tutored to be base,
The curse, the scourge, the ruin of our race,
Their's was the task, a dull designing few,
To shackle beings that they scarcely knew,
Who made this globe the residence of slaves,
And built their thrones on systems formed by knaves
—Advance, bright years, to work their final fall,
And haste the period that shall crush them all.
Who, that has read and scanned the historic page
But glows, at every line, with kindling rage,
To see by them the rights of men aspersed,
Freedom restrained, and Nature's law reversed,
Men, ranked with beasts, by monarchs willed away,
And bound young fools, or madmen to obey:
Now driven to wars, and now oppressed at home,
Compelled in crowds o'er distant seas to roam,
From India's climes the plundered prize to bring
To glad the strumpet, or to glut the king.
Columbia, hail! immortal be thy reign:
Without a king, we till the smiling plain;
Without a king, we trace the unbounded sea,
And traffic round the globe, through each degree;
Each foreign clime our honor'd flag reveres,
Which asks no monarch, to support the stars:
Without a king, the laws maintain their sway,
While honor bids each generous heart obey.
Be our's the task the ambitious to restrain,
And this great lesson teach—that kings are vain;

That warring realms to certain ruin haste,
That kings subsist by war, and wars are waste:
So shall our nation, form'd on Virtue's plan,
Remain the guardian of the Rights of Man,
A vast Republic, famed through every clime,
Without a king, to see the end of time.

[1792] 1795

ODE [1]

God save the Rights of Man!
Give us a heart to scan
Blessings so dear:
Let them be spread around
Wherever man is found,
And with the welcome sound
Ravish his ear.

Let us with France agree,
And bid the world be free,
While tyrants fall!
Let the rude savage host
Of their vast numbers boast—
Freedom's almighty trust
Laughs at them all!

Though hosts of slaves conspire
To quench fair Gallia's fire,
Still shall they fail:
Though traitors round her rise,
Leagu'd with her enemies,
To war each patriot flies,
And will prevail.

No more is valor's flame
Devoted to a name,
Taught to adore—
Soldiers of Liberty
Disdain to bow the knee,
But teach Equality
To every shore.

The world at last will join
To aid thy grand design,
Dear Liberty!
To Russia's frozen lands
The generous flame expands:
On Afric's burning sands
Shall man be free!

In this our western world
Be Freedom's flag unfurl'd
Through all its shores!
May no destructive blast
Our heaven of joy o'ercast,
May Freedom's fabric last
While time endures.

If e'er her cause require!—
Should tyrants e'er aspire
To aim their stroke,
May no proud despot daunt—
Should he his standard plant,
Freedom will never want
Her hearts of oak!

1793 1795

[1] Text of edition of 1795.

ON THE DEATH OF A REPUBLICAN PRINTER [1]

[By his Partner and Successor]

Like Sybils' leaves, abroad he spread
His sheets, to awe the aspiring crew:
Stock-jobbers fainted while they read;
Each hidden scheme display'd to view—
Who could such doctrines spread abroad
So long, and not be clapper-claw'd!

Content with slow uncertain gains,
With heart and hand prepar'd he stood
To send his works to distant plains,
And hills beyond the Ohio-flood—
And, since he had no time to lose,
Preach'd whiggish lectures with his news.

Now death, with cold unsparing hand,
(At whose decree even Capets fall)
From life's poor glass has shook his sand,
And sent him, fainting, to the wall—
Because he gave you some sad wipes,
O Mammon! seize not thou his types.

What shall be done, in such a case?
Shall I, because my partner fails,
Call in his bull-dogs from the chase
To loll their tongues and drop their tails—
No, faith—the title-hunting crew
No longer fly than we pursue.

1793

[1] Text of edition of 1795.

ON THE ANNIVERSARY [1]

Of the storming of the Bastille, at Paris, July 14th, 1789

The chiefs that bow to Capet's reign,
In mourning, now, their weeds display;
But we, that scorn a monarch's chain,
Combine to celebrate the Day
Of Freedom's birth that put the seal,
And laid in dust the proud Bastille.

To Gallia's rich and splendid crown,
This mighty Day gave such a blow
As Time's recording hand shall own
No former age had power to do:
No single gem some Brutus stole,
But instant ruin seiz'd the whole.

Now tyrants rise, once more to bind
In royal chains a nation freed—
Vain hope! for they, to death consign'd,
Shall soon, like perjur'd Louis, bleed:
O'er every king, o'er every queen
Fate hangs the sword, and guillotine.

"Plung'd in a gulf of deep distress
France turns her back—(so traitors say)
Kings, priests, and nobles, round her press,
Resolv'd to seize their destin'd prey:
Thus Europe swears (in arms combin'd)
To Poland's doom is France consign'd."

Yet those, who now are thought so low
From conquests that were basely gain'd,
Shall rise tremendous from the blow
And free Two Worlds, that still are chain'd,
Restrict the Briton to his isle,
And Freedom plant in every soil.

Ye sons of this degenerate clime,
Haste, arm the barque, expand the sail;
Assist to speed that golden time
When Freedom rules, and monarchs fail;
All left to France—new powers may join,
And help to crush the cause divine.

Ah! while I write, dear France Allied,
My ardent wish I scarce restrain,
To throw these Sybil leaves aside,
And fly to join you on the main:
Unfurl the topsail for the chase
And help to crush the tyrant race!

1793

[1] Text of edition of 1795.

REFLECTIONS [1]

ON THE GRADUAL PROGRESS OF NATIONS FROM DEMOCRATICAL STATES TO DESPOTIC EMPIRES

Mantua vae miserae nimium vicina Cremonae!
—Virgil

Oh fatal day! when to the Atlantic shore,
European despots sent the doctrine o'er,
That man's vast race was born to lick the dust;
Feed on the Winds, or toil through life accurst;
Poor and despised, that rulers might be great
And swell to monarchs, to devour the state.

Whence came these ills, or from what causes grew,
This vortex vast, that only spares the few,
Despotic sway, where every plague combined,
Distracts, degrades, and swallows up mankind;
Takes from the intellectual sun its light,
And shrouds the world in universal night?

Accuse not nature for the dreary scene,
That glooms her stage or hides her heaven serene,
She, equal still in all her varied ways,
An equal blessing to the world displays.
The suns that now on northern climates glow,
Will soon retire to melt Antarctic snow,
The seas she robb'd to form her clouds and rain,
Return in rivers to that source again;
But man, wrong'd man, borne down, deceived and vex'd,
Groans on through life, bewilder'd and perplex'd;
No suns on him but suns of misery shine,
Now march'd to war, now grovelling in the mine.
Chain'd, fetter'd, prostrate, sent from earth a slave,
To seek rewards in worlds beyond the grave.

If in her general system, just to all,
We nature an impartial parent call,
Why did she not on man's whole race bestow,
Those fine sensations angels only know;
Who, sway'd by reason, with superior mind

[1] Text of edition of 1815.

In nature's state all nature's blessings find,
Which shed through all, does all their race pervade,
In streams not niggard by a despot made?

Leave this a secret in great nature's breast,
Confess that all her works tend to the best,
Or own that man's neglected culture here
Breeds all the mischiefs that we feel or fear.
In all, except the skill to rule her race,
Man, wise and skillful, gives each part its place:
Each nice machine he plans, to reason true,
Adapting all things to the end in view,
But taught in this, the art himself to rule
His sense is folly, and himself a fool.

Where social strength resides, there rests, 'tis plain,
The power, mankind to govern and restrain:
This strength is not but in the social plan
Controling all, the common good of man,
That power concentred by the general voice,
In honest men, an honest people's choice,
With frequent change, to keep the patriot pure,
And from vain views of power the heart secure:
Here lies the secret, hid from Rome or Greece,
That holds a state in awe, yet holds in peace.

See through the world, in ages now retired,
Man foe to man, as policy required:
At some proud tyrant's nod what millions rose,
To extend their sway, and make a world their foes.
View Asia ravaged, Europe drench'd with blood,
In feuds whose cause no nation understood.
The cause we fear, of so much misery sown,
Known at the helm of state, and there alone.

Left to himself, wherever man is found,
In peace he aims to walk life's little round;
In peace to sail, in peace to till the soil,
Nor force false grandeur from a brother's toil.
All but the base, designing, scheming, few,
Who seize on nations with a robber's view,
With crowns and sceptres awe his dazzled eye,
And priests that hold the artillery of the sky;
These, these, with armies, navies, potent grown,
Impoverish man and bid the nations groan.
These with pretended balances of states
Keep worlds at variance, breed eternal hates,
Make man the poor base slave of low design,
Degrade his nature to its last decline,
Shed hell's worse blots on his exalted race,
And make them poor and mean, to make them base.

Shall views like these assail our happy land,
Where embryo monarchs thirst for wide command,
Shall a whole nation's strength and fair renown
Be sacrificed, to prop a tottering throne,
That, ages past, the world's great curse has stood,
Has throve on plunder, and been fed on blood.—
Americans! will you control such views?
Speak—for you must—you have no hour to lose.

1815

ON THE UNIVERSALITY AND OTHER ATTRIBUTES OF THE GOD OF NATURE[1]

ALL that we see, about, abroad,
What is it all, but nature's God?
In meaner works discover'd here
No less than in the starry sphere.

In seas, on earth, this God is seen;
All that exist, upon him lean;
He lives in all, and never stray'd
A moment from the works he made:

His system fix'd on general laws
Bespeaks a wise creating cause;
Impartially he rules mankind
And all that on this globe we find.

Unchanged in all that seems to change,
Unbounded space is his great range;
To one vast purpose always true,
No time, with him, is old or new.

In all the attributes divine
Unlimited perfectings shine;
In these enwrapt, in these complete,
All virtues in that centre meet.

[1] Text of edition of 1815.

This power who doth all powers transcend,
To all intelligence a friend,
Exists, the greatest and the best [1]
Throughout all worlds, to make them blest.

All that he did he first approved,
He all things into *being* loved;
O'er all he made he still presides,
For them in life, or death provides.

1815

ON THE UNIFORMITY AND PERFECTION OF NATURE

On one fix'd point all nature moves,
Nor deviates from the track she loves;
Her system, drawn from reason's source,
She scorns to change her wonted course.

Could she descend from that great plan
To work unusual things for man,
To suit the insect of an hour—
This would betray a want of power,

Unsettled in its first design
And erring, when it did combine
The parts that form the vast machine,
The figures sketch'd on nature's scene.

Perfections of the great first cause
Submit to no contracted laws,
But all-sufficient, all-supreme,
Include no trivial views in them.

Who looks through nature with an eye
That would the scheme of heaven descry,
Observes her constant, still the same,
In all her laws, through all her frame.

No imperfection can be found
In all that is, above, around,—
All, nature made, in reason's sight
Is order all and all is right.

1815

ON THE RELIGION OF NATURE [2]

The power, that gives with liberal hand
The blessings man enjoys, while here,
And scatters through a smiling land
The abundant products of the year;
That power of nature, ever bless'd,
Bestow'd religion with the rest.

Born with ourselves, her early sway
Inclines the tender mind to take
The path of right, fair virtue's way
Its own felicity to make.
This universally extends
And leads to no mysterious ends.

Religion, such as nature taught,
With all divine perfection suits;
Had all mankind this system sought
Sophists would cease their vain disputes,
And from this source would nations know
All that can make their heaven below.

This deals not curses on mankind,
Or dooms them to perpetual grief,
If from its aid no joys they find,
It damns them not for unbelief;
Upon a more exalted plan
Creatress nature dealt with man—

Joy to the day, when all agree
On such grand systems to proceed,
From fraud, design, and error free,
And which to truth and goodness lead:
Then persecution will retreat
And man's religion be complete.

1815

ADVICE TO AUTHORS [1]

BY THE LATE MR. ROBERT SLENDER

There are few writers of books in this new world, and amongst these very few that deal in works of imagination, and, I am sorry to say, fewer still that have any success attending their lucubrations. Perhaps, however, the world thinks justly on this subject. The productions of the most brilliant imagination are at best but mere beautiful flowers, that may amuse us in a walk through a garden in a fine afternoon, but can by no means be expected to engage much of that time which God and nature designed to be spent in very different employments. In a country, which two hundred years ago was peopled only by savages, and where the government has ever, in effect, since the first establishment of the white men in these parts, been no other than republican, it is

[1] Jupiter, optimus.—Cicero. [*Freneau's note.*]
[2] Text of edition of 1815.

[1] Text of edition of 1788. Freneau occasionally used such pseudonyms as Robert Slender and Hezekiah Salem.

really wonderful there should be any polite original authors at all in any line, especially when it is considered, that according to the common course of things, any particular nation or people must have arrived to, or rather passed, their meridian of opulence and refinement, before they consider the professors of the fine arts in any other light than a nuisance to the community. This is evidently the case at present in our age and country; all you have to do then, my good friends, is to graft your authorship upon some other calling, or support drooping genius by the assistance of some mechanical employment, in the same manner as the helpless ivy takes hold of the vigorous oak, and cleaves to it for support—I mean to say, in plain language, that you may make something by weaving garters, or mending old sails, when an Epic poem would be your utter destruction.

But I see no reason that, because we are all striving to live by the same idle trade, we should suffer ourselves to be embittered against each other, like a fraternity of rival mechanics in the same street. Authors (such I mean as are not possessed of fortunes) are at present considered as the dregs of the community: their situation and prospects are truly humiliating, and any other set of men in a similar state of calamitous adversity would unite together for their mutual defence, instead of worrying and lampooning each other for the amusement of the illiberal vulgar. —And I cannot do otherwise than freely declare, that where the whole profits of a company amount to little or nothing at all, there ought not, in the nature of things, to be any quarrelling about shares and dividends.

As to those authors who have lately exported themselves from Britain and Ireland, and boast that they have introduced the Muses among us since the conclusion of the late war, I really believe them to be a very good natured set of gentlemen, notwithstanding they, in the course of the last winter, called me *poetaster* and *scribbler*, and some other names still more unsavory. They are, however, excusable in treating the American authors as inferiors; a political and a literary independence of their nation being two very different things—the first was accomplished in about seven years, the latter will not be completely effected, perhaps, in as many centuries. It is my opinion, nevertheless, that a duty ought to be laid upon all imported authors, the net proceeds of which should be appropriated to the benefit of real American writers, when become old and helpless, and no longer able to wield the pen to advantage.

If a coach or a chariot constructed in Britain pays an impost of twenty pounds at the custom-house, why should not at least twice that sum be laid upon all imported authors who are able to do twice as much mischief with their rumbling pindaric odes, and gorgeous apparatus of strophes, antistrophes and recitativos? —I, for my own part, am clearly of opinion that these gentlemen should be taxed; not that I would wish to nip their buds of beauty with the untimely frost of excise, but merely to teach them that our own natural manufactures ought to be primarily attended to and encouraged.

I will now, gentlemen, with your leave, lay down a few simple rules, to which, in my opinion, every genuine author will make no difficulty to conform.

1. When you write a book for the public, have nothing to do with *Epistles dedicatory*. They were first invented by slaves, and have been continued by fools and sycophants. I would not give a farthing more for a book on account of its being patronized by all the noblemen or crowned heads in Christendom. If it does not possess intrinsic merit enough to protect itself, and force its way through the world, their supposed protection will be of no avail: besides, by this ridiculous practice you degrade the *dignity authorial*, the honor of authorship, which ought evermore to be uppermost in your thoughts. The silly unthinking author addresses a great man in the style of a servile dependent, whereas a real author, and a man of true genius, has upon all occasions a bold, disinterested and daring confidence in himself, and considers the common cant of adulation to the sons of fortune as the basest and most abominable of all prostitution.

2. Be particularly careful to avoid all connexion with doctors of law and divinity, masters of arts, professors of colleges, and in general all those that wear square black caps.

A mere scholar and an original author are two animals as different from each other as a fresh and salt water sailor. There has been an old rooted enmity between them from the earliest ages, and which it is likely will forever continue. The scholar is not unlike that piddling orator, who, cold and inanimate, not roused into action by the impelling flame of inspiration, can only pronounce the oration he has learned by rote; the real author, on the contrary, is the nervous Demosthenes, who stored with an immensity of ideas, awakened within him he knows not how, has them at command upon every occasion; and must therefore be disregarded as a madman or an enthusiast by the narrow and limited capacity, as well as the natural self-sufficiency of the other.

3. It is risking a great deal to propose a subscription for an original work. The world will be ready enough to anticipate your best endeavors; and that which has been long and anxiously expected, rarely or never comes up to their expectations at last.

4. If you are so poor that you are compelled to live in some miserable garret or cottage; do not repine, but give thanks to heaven that you are not forced to pass your life in a tub, as was the fate of Diogenes of old. Few authors in any country are rich, because a man must first be reduced to a state of penury before he will commence author. Being poor therefore in externals, take care, gentlemen, that you say or do nothing that may argue a poverty of spirit. Riches, we have often heard, are by no means the standard of the value of a man. This maxim the world allows to be true, and yet contradicts it every hour and minute in the year. Fortune most commonly bestows wealth and abundance upon fools and idiots; and men of the dullest natural parts are, notwithstanding, generally best calculated to acquire large estates, and hoard up immense sums from small beginnings.

5. Never borrow money of any man, for if you should once be mean enough to fall into such a habit you will find yourselves unwelcome guests every where. If upon actual trial you are at length convinced you possess no abilities that will command the esteem, veneration or gratitude of mankind, apply yourselves without loss of time to some of the lower arts, since it is far more honorable to be a good bricklayer or a skilful weaver than an indifferent poet. —If you cannot at all exist without now and then gratifying your itch for scribbling, follow my example who can both weave stockings and write poems. —But, if you really possess that sprightliness of fancy and elevation of soul which alone constitute an author, do not on that account be troublesome to your friends. A little reflection will point out other means to extract money from the hands and pockets of your fellow citizens than by poorly borrowing what, perhaps, you will never be able to repay.

6. Never engage in any business as an inferior or understrapper. I cannot endure to see an author debase his profession so far as to submit to be second or third in any office or employment whatever. If fortune, or the ill taste of the public compels you even to turn shallopman on the Delaware, let it be your first care to have the command of the boat. Beggary itself, with all its hideous apparatus of rags and misery, becomes at once respectable whenever it exhibits the least token of independence of spirit and a single spark of laudable ambition.

7. If you are in low circumstances, do not forget that there is such a thing in the world as a decent pride. They are only cowards and miscreants that poverty can render servile in their behaviour. Your haughtiness should always rise in proportion to the wretchedness and desperation of your circumstances. If you have only a single guinea in the world be complaisant and obliging to every one: if you are absolutely destitute of a shilling, immediately assume the air of a despot, pull off your hat to no one, let your discourse, in every company, turn upon the vanity of riches, the insignificancy of the great men of the earth, the revolution of empires, and the final consummation of all things. —By such means you will at least conceal a secret of some importance to yourself—that you have not a shilling in the world to pay for your last night's lodging.

8. Should you ever be prevailed upon to dedicate your book to any great man or woman, consider first, whether the tenor and subject of it be such as may in some measure coincide with the age, temper, education,

business and general conversation of the person whose patronage is requested. A friend of mine once committed a great error on this score. He wrote a bawdy poem, and dedicated it to the principal in the department of finance.

9. Never make a present of your works to great men. If they do not think them worth purchasing, trust me, they will never think them worth reading.

10. If fortune seems absolutely determined to starve you, and you can by no means whatever make your works sell; to keep up as much as in you lies, the expiring dignity of authorship, do not take to drinking, gambling or bridge-building as some have done, thereby bringing the trade of authorship into disrepute; but retire to some uninhabited island or desert, and there, at your leisure, end your life with decency.

1788

WILLIAM CULLEN BRYANT

THANATOPSIS

To him who in the love of Nature holds
Communion with her visible forms, she speaks
A various language; for his gayer hours
She has a voice of gladness, and a smile
And eloquence of beauty, and she glides
Into his darker musings, with a mild
And healing sympathy, that steals away
Their sharpness, ere he is aware. When thoughts
Of the last bitter hour come like a blight
Over thy spirit, and sad images
Of the stern agony, and shroud, and pall,
And breathless darkness, and the narrow house,
Make thee to shudder, and grow sick at heart;—
Go forth, under the open sky, and list
To Nature's teachings, while from all around—
Earth and her waters, and the depths of air—
Comes a still voice—Yet a few days, and thee
The all-beholding sun shall see no more
In all his course; nor yet in the cold ground,
Where thy pale form was laid, with many tears,
Nor in the embrace of ocean, shall exist
Thy image. Earth, that nourished thee, shall claim
Thy growth, to be resolved to earth again,
And, lost each human trace, surrendering up
Thine individual being, shalt thou go
To mix forever with the elements,
To be a brother to the insensible rock
And to the sluggish clod, which the rude swain
Turns with his share, and treads upon. The oak
Shall send his roots abroad, and pierce thy mould.

Yet not to thine eternal resting-place
Shalt thou retire alone, nor couldst thou wish
Couch more magnificent. Thou shalt lie down
With patriarchs of the infant world—with kings,
The powerful of the earth—the wise, the good,
Fair forms, and hoary seers of ages past,
All in one mighty sepulchre. The hills
Rock-ribbed and ancient as the sun,—the vales
Stretching in pensive quietness between;
The venerable woods—rivers that move
In majesty, and the complaining brooks
That make the meadows green; and, poured round all,
Old Ocean's gray and melancholy waste,—
Are but the solemn decorations all
Of the great tomb of man. The golden sun,
The planets, all the infinite host of heaven,
Are shining on the sad abodes of death,
Through the still lapse of ages. All that tread
The globe are but a handful to the tribes
That slumber in its bosom.—Take the wings
Of morning, pierce the Barcan wilderness,
Or lose thyself in the continuous woods
Where rolls the Oregon, and hears no sound,
Save his own dashings—yet the dead are there:
And millions in those solitudes, since first
The flight of years began, have laid them down
In their last sleep—the dead reign there alone.
So shalt thou rest, and what if thou withdraw
In silence from the living, and no friend
Take note of thy departure? All that breathe
Will share thy destiny. The gay will laugh
When thou art gone, the solemn brood of care
Plod on, and each one as before will chase
His favorite phantom; yet all these shall leave
Their mirth and their employments, and shall come
And make their bed with thee. As the long train
Of ages glide away, the sons of men,
The youth in life's green spring, and he who goes
In the full strength of years, matron and maid,
The speechless babe, and the gray-headed man—
Shall one by one be gathered to thy side,
By those, who in their turn shall follow them.

So live, that when thy summons comes to join
The innumerable caravan, which moves

To that mysterious realm, where each shall take
His chamber in the silent halls of death,
Thou go not, like the quarry-slave at night,
Scourged to his dungeon, but, sustained and soothed
By an unfaltering trust, approach thy grave,
Like one who wraps the drapery of his couch
About him, and lies down to pleasant dreams.

1811? 1817, 1821

INSCRIPTION FOR THE ENTRANCE TO A WOOD

STRANGER, if thou hast learned a truth which needs
No school of long experience, that the world
Is full of guilt and misery, and hast seen
Enough of all its sorrows, crimes, and cares,
To tire thee of it, enter this wild wood
And view the haunts of Nature. The calm shade
Shall bring a kindred calm, and the sweet breeze
That makes the green leaves dance, shall waft a balm
To thy sick heart. Thou wilt find nothing here
Of all that pained thee in the haunts of men,
And made thee loathe thy life. The primal curse
Fell, it is true, upon the unsinning earth,
But not in vengeance. God hath yoked to guilt
Her pale tormentor, misery. Hence, these shades
Are still the abodes of gladness; the thick roof
Of green and stirring branches is alive
And musical with birds, that sing and sport
In wantonness of spirit; while below
The squirrel, with raised paws and form erect,
Chirps merrily. Throngs of insects in the shade
Try their thin wings and dance in the warm beam
That waked them into life. Even the green trees
Partake the deep contentment; as they bend
To the soft winds, the sun from the blue sky
Looks in and sheds a blessing on the scene.
Scarce less the cleft-born wild-flower seems to enjoy
Existence, than the wingèd plunderer
That sucks its sweets. The mossy rocks themselves,
And the old and ponderous trunks of prostrate trees
That lead from knoll to knoll a causey rude
Or bridge the sunken brook, and their dark roots,
With all their earth upon them, twisting high,
Breathe fixed tranquillity. The rivulet
Sends forth glad sounds, and tripping o'er its bed
Of pebbly sands, or leaping down the rocks,
Seems, with continuous laughter, to rejoice
In its own being. Softly tread the marge,
Lest from her midway perch thou scare the wren
That dips her bill in water. The cool wind,
That stirs the stream in play, shall come to thee,
Like one that loves thee nor will let thee pass
Ungreeted, and shall give its light embrace.

1815 1817

TO A WATERFOWL

WHITHER, midst falling dew,
While glow the heavens with the last steps of day,
Far, through their rosy depths, dost thou pursue
Thy solitary way?

Vainly the fowler's eye
Might mark thy distant flight to do thee wrong,
As, darkly seen against the crimson sky,
Thy figure floats along.

Seek'st thou the plashy brink
Of weedy lake, or marge of river wide,
Or where the rocking billows rise and sink
On the chafed ocean-side?

There is a Power whose care
Teaches thy way along that pathless coast—
The desert and illimitable air—
Lone wandering, but not lost.

All day thy wings have fanned,
At that far height, the cold, thin atmosphere,
Yet stoop not, weary, to the welcome land,
Though the dark night is near.

And soon that toil shall end;
Soon shalt thou find a summer home, and rest,
And scream among thy fellows; reeds shall bend,
Soon, o'er thy sheltered nest.

Thou'rt gone, the abyss of heaven
Hath swallowed up thy form; yet, on my heart
Deeply has sunk the lesson thou hast given,
And shall not soon depart.

He who, from zone to zone,
Guides through the boundless sky thy certain flight,
In the long way that I must tread alone,
Will lead my steps aright.

1815 1818

GREEN RIVER

When breezes are soft and skies are fair,
I steal an hour from study and care,
And hie me away to the woodland scene,
Where wanders the stream with waters of green,
As if the bright fringe of herbs on its brink
Had given their stain to the waves they drink;
And they, whose meadows it murmurs through,
Have named the stream from its own fair hue.

Yet pure its waters—its shallows are bright
With colored pebbles and sparkles of light,
And clear the depths where its eddies play,
And dimples deepen and whirl away,
And the plane-tree's speckled arms o'ershoot
The swifter current that mines its root,
Through whose shifting leaves, as you walk the hill,
The quivering glimmer of sun and rill
With a sudden flash on the eye is thrown,
Like the ray that streams from the diamond-stone.
Oh, loveliest there the spring days come,
With blossoms, and birds, and wild-bees' hum;
The flowers of summer are fairest there,
And freshest the breath of the summer air;
And sweetest the golden autumn day
In silence and sunshine glides away.

Yet, fair as thou art, thou shunnest to glide,
Beautiful stream! by the village side;
But windest away from haunts of men,
To quiet valley and shaded glen;
And forest, and meadow, and slope of hill,
Around thee, are lonely, lovely, and still,
Lonely—save when, by thy rippling tides,
From thicket to thicket the angler glides;
Or the simpler comes, with basket and book,
For herbs of power on thy banks to look;
Or haply, some idle dreamer, like me,
To wander, and muse, and gaze on thee,
Still—save the chirp of birds that feed
On the river cherry and seedy reed,
And thy own wild music gushing out
With mellow murmur of fairy shout,
From dawn to the blush of another day,
Like traveller singing along his way.

That fairy music I never hear,
Nor gaze on those waters so green and clear,
And mark them winding away from sight,
Darkened with shade or flashing with light,
While o'er them the vine to its thicket clings,
And the zephyr stoops to freshen his wings,
But I wish that fate had left me free
To wander these quiet haunts with thee,
Till the eating cares of earth should depart,
And the peace of the scene pass into my heart;
And I envy thy stream, as it glides along
Through its beautiful banks in a trance of song.

Though forced to drudge for the dregs of men,
And scrawl strange words with the barbarous pen,
And mingle among the jostling crowd,
Where the sons of strife are subtle and loud—
I often come to this quiet place,
To breathe the airs that ruffle thy face,
And gaze upon thee in silent dream,
For in thy lonely and lovely stream
An image of that calm life appears
That won my heart in my greener years.

1818 1821

A WINTER PIECE

The time has been that these wild solitudes,
Yet beautiful as wild, were trod by me
Oftener than now; and when the ills of life
Had chafed my spirit—when the unsteady pulse

Beat with strange flutterings—I would wander forth
And seek the woods. The sunshine on my path
Was to me as a friend. The swelling hills,
The quiet dells retiring far between,
With gentle invitation to explore
Their windings, were a calm society
That talked with me and soothed me. Then the chant
Of birds, and chime of brooks, and soft caress
Of the fresh sylvan air, made me forget
The thoughts that broke my peace, and I began
To gather simples by the fountain's brink,
And lose myself in day-dreams. While I stood
In Nature's loneliness, I was with one
With whom I early grew familiar, one
Who never had a frown for me, whose voice
Never rebuked me for the hours I stole
From cares I loved not, but of which the world
Deems highest, to converse with her. When shrieked
The bleak November winds, and smote the woods,
And the brown fields were herbless, and the shades,
That met above the merry rivulet,
Were spoiled, I sought, I loved them still; they seemed
Like old companions in adversity.
Still there was beauty in my walks; the brook,
Bordered with sparkling frost-work, was as gay
As with its fringe of summer flowers. Afar,
The village with its spires, the path of streams
And dim receding valleys, hid before
By interposing trees, lay visible
Through the bare grove, and my familiar haunts
Seemed new to me. Nor was I slow to come
Among them, when the clouds, from their still skirts,
Had shaken down on earth the feathery snow,
And all was white. The pure keen air abroad,
Albeit it breathed no scent of herb, nor heard
Love-call of bird nor merry hum of bee,
Was not the air of death. Bright mosses crept
Over the spotted trunks, and the close buds,
That lay along the boughs, instinct with life,
Patient, and waiting the soft breath of Spring,
Feared not the piercing spirit of the North.
The snow-bird twittered on the beechen bough,
And 'neath the hemlock, whose thick branches bent
Beneath its bright cold burden, and kept dry
A circle, on the earth, of withered leaves,
The partridge found a shelter. Through the snow
The rabbit sprang away. The lighter track
Of fox, and the raccoon's broad path, were there,
Crossing each other. From his hollow tree
The squirrel was abroad, gathering the nuts
Just fallen, that asked the winter cold and sway
Of winter blast, to shake them from their hold.

But Winter has yet brighter scenes—he boasts
Splendors beyond what gorgeous Summer knows;
Or Autumn with his many fruits, and woods
All flushed with many hues. Come when the rains
Have glazed the snow and clothed the trees with ice,
While the slant sun of February pours
Into the bowers a flood of light. Approach!
The incrusted surface shall upbear thy steps,
And the broad arching portals of the grove
Welcome thy entering. Look! the massy trunks
Are cased in the pure crystal; each light spray,
Nodding and tinkling in the breath of heaven,
Is studded with its trembling water-drops,
That glimmer with an amethystine light.
But round the parent-stem the long low boughs
Bend, in a glittering ring, and arbors hide
The glassy floor. Oh! you might deem the spot
The spacious cavern of some virgin mine,
Deep in the womb of earth—where the gems grow,
And diamonds put forth radiant rods and bud
With amethyst and topaz—and the place
Lit up, most royally, with the pure beam
That dwells in them. Or haply the vast hall
Of fairy palace, that outlasts the night,
And fades not in the glory of the sun;—
Where crystal columns send forth slender shafts
And crossing arches; and fantastic aisles
Wind from the sight in brightness, and are lost
Among the crowded pillars. Raise thine eye;

Thou seest no cavern roof, no palace vault;
There the blue sky and the white drifting cloud
Look in. Again the wildered fancy dreams
Of spouting fountains, frozen as they rose,
And fixed, with all their branching jets, in air,
And all their sluices sealed. All, all is light;
Light without shade. But all shall pass away
With the next sun. From numberless vast trunks
Loosened, the crashing ice shall make a sound
Like the far roar of rivers, and the eve
Shall close o'er the brown woods as it was wont.

And it is pleasant, when the noisy streams
Are just set free, and milder suns melt off
The plashy snow, save only the firm drift
In the deep glen or the close shade of pines—
'Tis pleasant to behold the wreaths of smoke
Roll up among the maples of the hill,
Where the shrill sound of youthful voices wakes
The shriller echo, as the clear pure lymph,
That from the wounded trees, in twinkling drops,
Falls, mid the golden brightness of the morn,
Is gathered in with brimming pails, and oft,
Wielded by sturdy hands, the stroke of axe
Makes the woods ring. Along the quiet air,
Come and float calmly off the soft light clouds,
Such as you see in summer, and the winds
Scarce stir the branches. Lodged in sunny cleft,
Where the cold breezes come not, blooms alone
The little wind-flower, whose just opened eye
Is blue as the spring heaven it gazes at—
Startling the loiterer in the naked groves
With unexpected beauty, for the time
Of blossoms and green leaves is yet afar.
And ere it comes, the encountering winds shall oft
Muster their wrath again, and rapid clouds
Shade heaven, and bounding on the frozen earth
Shall fall their volleyed stores, rounded like hail
And white like snow, and the loud North again
Shall buffet the vexed forest in his rage.

1820 1821

"OH FAIREST OF THE RURAL MAIDS"

Oh fairest of the rural maids!
Thy birth was in the forest shades;
Green boughs, and glimpses of the sky,
Were all that met thine infant eye.

Thy sports, thy wanderings, when a child,
Were ever in the sylvan wild;
And all the beauty of the place
Is in thy heart and on thy face.

The twilight of the trees and rocks
Is in the light shade of thy locks;
Thy step is as the wind, that weaves
Its playful way among the leaves.

Thine eyes are springs, in whose serene
And silent waters heaven is seen;
Their lashes are the herbs that look
On their young figures in the brook.

The forest depths, by foot unpressed,
Are not more sinless than thy breast;
The holy peace, that fills the air
Of those calm solitudes, is there.

1820 1832

HYMN TO DEATH

Oh! could I hope the wise and pure in heart
Might hear my song without a frown, nor deem
My voice unworthy of the theme it tries,—
I would take up the hymn to Death, and say
To the grim power, The world hath slandered thee
And mocked thee. On thy dim and shadowy brow
They place an iron crown, and call thee king
Of terrors, and the spoiler of the world,
Deadly assassin, that strik'st down the fair,
The loved, the good—that breathest on the lights
Of virtue set along the vale of life,
And they go out in darkness. I am come,
Not with reproaches, not with cries and prayers,
Such as have stormed thy stern, insensible ear
From the beginning; I am come to speak
Thy praises. True it is, that I have wept

Thy conquests, and may weep them yet again,
And thou from some I love will take a life
Dear to me as my own. Yet while the spell
Is on my spirit, and I talk with thee
In sight of all thy trophies, face to face,
Meet is it that my voice should utter forth
Thy nobler triumphs; I will teach the world
To thank thee. Who are thine accusers?—Who?
The living!—they who never felt thy power,
And know thee not. The curses of the wretch
Whose crimes are ripe, his sufferings when thy hand
Is on him, and the hour he dreads is come,
Are writ among thy praises. But the good—
Does he whom thy kind hand dismissed to peace,
Upbraid the gentle violence that took off
His fetters, and unbarred his prison-cell?

Raise then the hymn to Death. Deliverer!
God hath anointed thee to free the oppressed
And crush the oppressor. When the armed chief,
The conqueror of nations, walks the world,
And it is changed beneath his feet, and all
Its kingdoms melt into one mighty realm—
Thou, while his head is loftiest and his heart
Blasphemes, imagining his own right hand
Almighty, thou dost set thy sudden grasp
Upon him, and the links of that strong chain
Which bound mankind are crumbled; thou dost break
Sceptre and crown, and beat his throne to dust.
Then the earth shouts with gladness, and her tribes
Gather within their ancient bounds again.
Else had the mighty of the olden time,
Nimrod, Sesostris, or the youth who feigned
His birth from Libyan Ammon, smitten yet
The nations with a rod of iron, and driven
Their chariot o'er our necks. Thou dost avenge,
In thy good time, the wrongs of those who know
No other friend. Nor dost thou interpose
Only to lay the sufferer asleep,
Where he who made him wretched troubles not
His rest—thou dost strike down his tyrant too.
Oh, there is joy when hands that held the scourge
Drop lifeless, and the pitiless heart is cold.
Thou too dost purge from earth its horrible
And old idolatries;—from the proud fanes
Each to his grave their priests go out, till none
Is left to teach their worship; then the fires
Of sacrifice are chilled, and the green moss
O'ercreeps their altars; the fallen images
Cumber the weedy courts, and for loud hymns,
Chanted by kneeling multitudes, the wind
Shrieks in the solitary aisles. When he
Who gives his life to guilt, and laughs at all
The laws that God or man has made, and round
Hedges his seat with power, and shines in wealth,—
Lifts up his atheist front to scoff at Heaven,
And celebrates his shame in open day,
Thou, in the pride of all his crimes, cutt'st off
The horrible example. Touched by thine,
The extortioner's hard hand foregoes the gold
Wrung from the o'er-worn poor. The perjurer,
Whose tongue was lithe, e'en now, and voluble
Against his neighbor's life, and he who laughed
And leaped for joy to see a spotless fame
Blasted before his own foul calumnies,
Are smit with deadly silence. He, who sold
His conscience to preserve a worthless life,
Even while he hugs himself on his escape,
Trembles, as, doubly terrible, at length,
Thy steps o'ertake him, and there is no time
For parley, nor will bribes unclench thy grasp.
Oft, too, dost thou reform thy victim, long
Ere his last hour. And when the reveller,
Mad in the chase of pleasure, stretches on,
And strains each nerve, and clears the path of life
Like wind, thou point'st him to the dreadful goal,
And shak'st thy hour-glass in his reeling eye,
And check'st him in mid course. Thy skeleton hand
Shows to the faint of spirit the right path,
And he is warned, and fears to step aside.
Thou sett'st between the ruffian and his crime
Thy ghastly countenance, and his slack hand

Drops the drawn knife. But, oh, most fearfully
Dost thou show forth Heaven's justice, when thy shafts
Drink up the ebbing spirit—then the hard
Of heart and violent of hand restores
The treasure to the friendless wretch he wronged.
Then from the writhing bosom thou dost pluck
The guilty secret; lips, for ages sealed,
Are faithless to their dreadful trust at length,
And give it up; the felon's latest breath
Absolves the innocent man who bears his crime;
The slanderer, horror-smitten, and in tears,
Recalls the deadly obloquy he forged
To work his brother's ruin. Thou dost make
Thy penitent victim utter to the air
The dark conspiracy that strikes at life,
And aims to whelm the laws; ere yet the hour
Is come, and the dread sign of murder given.

Thus, from the first of time, hast thou been found
On virtue's side; the wicked, but for thee,
Had been too strong for the good; the great of earth
Had crushed the weak for ever. Schooled in guile
For ages, while each passing year had brought
Its baneful lesson, they had filled the world
With their abominations; while its tribes,
Trodden to earth, imbruted, and despoiled,
Had knelt to them in worship; sacrifice
Had smoked on many an altar, temple-roofs
Had echoed with the blasphemous prayer and hymn:
But thou, the great reformer of the world,
Tak'st off the sons of violence and fraud
In their green pupilage, their lore half learned—
Ere guilt had quite o'errun the simple heart
God gave them at their birth, and blotted out
His image. Thou dost mark them flushed with hope,
As on the threshold of their vast designs
Doubtful and loose they stand, and strik'st them down.

. . . .

Alas! I little thought that the stern power,
Whose fearful praise I sang, would try me thus
Before the strain was ended. It must cease—
For he is in his grave who taught my youth
The art of verse, and in the bud of life
Offered me to the Muses. Oh, cut off
Untimely! when thy reason in its strength,
Ripened by years of toil and studious search
And watch of Nature's silent lessons, taught
Thy hand to practise best the lenient art
To which thou gavest thy laborious days,
And, last, thy life. And, therefore, when the earth
Received thee, tears were in unyielding eyes
And on hard cheeks, and they who deemed thy skill
Delayed their death-hour, shuddered and turned pale
When thou wert gone. This faltering verse, which thou
Shalt not, as wont, o'erlook, is all I have
To offer at thy grave—this—and the hope
To copy thy example, and to leave
A name of which the wretched shall not think
As of an enemy's, whom they forgive
As all forgive the dead. Rest, therefore, thou
Whose early guidance trained my infant steps—
Rest, in the bosom of God, till the brief sleep
Of death is over, and a happier life
Shall dawn to waken thine insensible dust.

Now thou art not—and yet the men whose guilt
Has wearied Heaven for vengeance—he who bears
False witness—he who takes the orphan's bread,
And robs the widow—he who spreads abroad
Polluted hands in mockery of prayer,
Are left to cumber earth. Shuddering I look
On what is written, yet I blot not out
The desultory numbers; let them stand,
The record of an idle revery.

1820 1825

THE AGES

I

WHEN to the common rest that crowns our days,
Called in the noon of life, the good man goes,

Or full of years, and ripe in wisdom, lays
His silver temples in their last repose;
When, o'er the buds of youth, the death-wind blows
And blights the fairest; when our bitter tears
Stream, as the eyes of those that love us close,
We think on what they were, with many fears
Lest goodness die with them, and leave the coming years.

II

And therefore, to our hearts, the days gone by,
When lived the honored sage whose death we wept,
And the soft virtues beamed from many an eye,
And beat in many a heart that long has slept—
Like spots of earth where angel-feet have stepped,
Are holy; and high-dreaming bards have told
Of times when worth was crowned, and faith was kept,
Ere friendship grew a snare, or love waxed cold—
Those pure and happy times—the golden days of old.

III

Peace to the just man's memory; let it grow
Greener with years, and blossom through the flight
Of ages; let the mimic canvas show
His calm benevolent features; let the light
Stream on his deeds of love, that shunned the sight
Of all but heaven, and in the book of fame
The glorious record of his virtues write
And hold it up to men, and bid them claim
A palm like his, and catch from him the hallowed flame.

IV

But oh, despair not of their fate who rise
To dwell upon the earth when we withdraw!
Lo! the same shaft by which the righteous dies,
Strikes through the wretch that scoffed at mercy's law
And trode his brethren down, and felt no awe
Of Him who will avenge them. Stainless worth,
Such as the sternest age of virtue saw,
Ripens, meanwhile, till time shall call it forth
From the low modest shade, to light and bless the earth.

V

Has Nature, in her calm, majestic march,
Faltered with age at last? does the bright sun
Grow dim in heaven? or, in their far blue arch,
Sparkle the crowd of stars, when day is done,
Less brightly? when the dew-lipped Spring comes on,
Breathes she with airs less soft, or scents the sky
With flowers less fair than when her reign begun?
Does prodigal Autumn, to our age, deny
The plenty that once swelled beneath his sober eye?

VI

Look on this beautiful world, and read the truth
In her fair page; see, every season brings
New change, to her, of everlasting youth;
Still the green soil, with joyous living things,
Swarms, the wide air is full of joyous wings,
And myriads, still, are happy in the sleep
Of ocean's azure gulfs, and where he flings
The restless surge. Eternal Love doth keep,
In his complacent arms, the earth, the air, the deep.

VII

Will then the merciful One, who stamped our race
With his own image, and who gave them sway
O'er earth, and the glad dwellers on her face,
Now that our swarming nations far away

Are spread, where'er the moist earth drinks the day,
Forget the ancient care that taught and nursed
His latest offspring? will he quench the ray
Infused by his own forming smile at first,
And leave a work so fair all blighted and accursed?

VIII

Oh, no! a thousand cheerful omens give
Hope of yet happier days, whose dawn is nigh.
He who has tamed the elements, shall not live
The slave of his own passions; he whose eye
Unwinds the eternal dances of the sky,
And in the abyss of brightness dares to span
The sun's broad circle, rising yet more high,
In God's magnificent works his will shall scan—
And love and peace shall make their paradise with man.

IX

Sit at the feet of History—through the night
Of years the steps of virtue she shall trace,
And show the earlier ages, where her sight
Can pierce the eternal shadows o'er their face;—
When, from the genial cradle of our race,
Went forth the tribes of men, their pleasant lot
To choose, where palm-groves cooled their dwelling-place,
Or freshening rivers ran; and there forgot
The truth of heaven, and kneeled to gods that heard them not.

X

Then waited not the murderer for the night,
But smote his brother down in the bright day,
And he who felt the wrong, and had the might,
His own avenger, girt himself to slay;
Beside the path the unburied carcass lay;
The shepherd, by the fountains of the glen,
Fled, while the robber swept his flock away,
And slew his babes. The sick, untended then,
Languished in the damp shade, and died afar from men.

XI

But misery brought in love; in passion's strife
Man gave his heart to mercy, pleading long,
And sought out gentle deeds to gladden life;
The weak, against the sons of spoil and wrong,
Banded, and watched their hamlets, and grew strong;
States rose, and, in the shadow of their might,
The timid rested. To the reverent throng,
Grave and time-wrinkled men, with locks all white,
Gave laws, and judged their strifes, and taught the way of right;

XII

Till bolder spirits seized the rule, and nailed
On men the yoke that man should never bear,
And drave them forth to battle. Lo! unveiled
The scene of those stern ages! What is there!
A boundless sea of blood, and the wild air
Moans with the crimson surges that entomb
Cities and bannered armies; forms that wear
The kingly circlet rise, amid the gloom,
O'er the dark wave, and straight are swallowed in its womb.

XIII

Those ages have no memory, but they left
A record in the desert—columns strown
On the waste sands, and statues fallen and cleft,
Heaped like a host in battle overthrown;
Vast ruins, where the mountain's ribs of stone
Were hewn into a city; streets that spread
In the dark earth, where never breath has blown
Of heaven's sweet air, nor foot of man dares tread
The long and perilous ways—the Cities of the Dead!

XIV

And tombs of monarchs to the clouds uppiled—
They perished, but the eternal tombs remain—

And the black precipice, abrupt and wild,
Pierced by long toil and hollowed to a fane;—
Huge piers and frowning forms of gods sustain
The everlasting arches, dark and wide,
Like the night-heaven, when clouds are black with rain.
But idly skill was tasked, and strength was plied,
All was the work of slaves to swell a despot's pride.

XV

And Virtue cannot dwell with slaves, nor reign
O'er those who cower to take a tyrant's yoke;
She left the down-trod nations in disdain,
And flew to Greece, when Liberty awoke,
New-born, amid those glorious vales, and broke
Sceptre and chain with her fair youthful hands:
As rocks are shivered in the thunder-stroke.
And lo! in full-grown strength, an empire stands
Of leagued and rival states, the wonder of the lands.

XVI

Oh, Greece! thy flourishing cities were a spoil
Unto each other; thy hard hand oppressed
And crushed the helpless; thou didst make thy soil
Drunk with the blood of those that loved thee best;
And thou didst drive, from thy unnatural breast,
Thy just and brave to die in distant climes;
Earth shuddered at thy deeds, and sighed for rest
From thine abominations; after-times,
That yet shall read thy tale, will tremble at thy crimes!

XVII

Yet there was that within thee which has saved
Thy glory, and redeemed thy blotted name;
The story of thy better deeds, engraved
On fame's unmouldering pillar, puts to shame
Our chiller virtue; the high art to tame
The whirlwind of the passions was thine own;
And the pure ray, that from thy bosom came,
Far over many a land and age has shone,
And mingles with the light that beams from God's own throne.

XVIII

And Rome—thy sterner, younger sister, she
Who awed the world with her imperial frown—
Rome drew the spirit of her race from thee,
The rival of thy shame and thy renown.
Yet her degenerate children sold the crown
Of earth's wide kingdoms to a line of slaves;
Guilt reigned, and woe with guilt, and plagues came down,
Till the North broke its floodgates, and the waves
Whelmed the degraded race, and weltered o'er their graves.

XIX

Vainly that ray of brightness from above,
That shone around the Galilean lake,
The light of hope, the leading star of love,
Struggled, the darkness of that day to break;
Even its own faithless guardians strove to slake,
In fogs of earth, the pure ethereal flame;
And priestly hands, for Jesus' blessed sake,
Were red with blood, and charity became,
In that stern war of forms, a mockery and a name.

XX

They triumphed, and less bloody rites were kept
Within the quiet of the convent-cell;
The well-fed inmates pattered prayer, and slept,
And sinned, and liked their easy penance well.
Where pleasant was the spot for men to dwell,

Amid its fair broad lands the abbey lay,
Sheltering dark orgies that were shame to tell,
And cowled and barefoot beggars swarmed the way,
All in their convent weeds, of black, and white, and gray.

XXI

Oh, sweetly the returning muses' strain
Swelled over that famed stream, whose gentle tide
In their bright lap the Etrurian vales detain,
Sweet, as when winter storms have ceased to chide,
And all the new-leaved woods, resounding wide,
Send out wild hymns upon the scented air.
Lo! to the smiling Arno's classic side
The emulous nations of the West repair,
And kindle their quenched urns, and drink fresh spirit there.

XXII

Still, Heaven deferred the hour ordained to rend
From saintly rottenness the sacred stole;
And cowl and worshipped shrine could still defend
The wretch with felon stains upon his soul;
And crimes were set to sale, and hard his dole
Who could not bribe a passage to the skies;
And vice, beneath the mitre's kind control,
Sinned gayly on, and grew to giant size,
Shielded by priestly power, and watched by priestly eyes.

XXIII

At last the earthquake came—the shock, that hurled
To dust, in many fragments dashed and strown,
The throne, whose roots were in another world,
And whose far-stretching shadow awed our own.
From many a proud monastic pile, o'erthrown,
Fear-struck, the hooded inmates rushed and fled;
The web, that for a thousand years had grown
O'er prostrate Europe, in that day of dread
Crumbled and fell, as fire dissolves the flaxen thread.

XXIV

The spirit of that day is still awake,
And spreads himself, and shall not sleep again;
But through the idle mesh of power shall break
Like billows o'er the Asian monarch's chain;
Till men are filled with him, and feel how vain,
Instead of the pure heart and innocent hands,
Are all the proud and pompous modes to gain
The smile of Heaven;—till a new age expands
Its white and holy wings above the peaceful lands.

XXV

For look again on the past years;—behold,
How like the nightmare's dreams have flown away
Horrible forms of worship, that, of old,
Held, o'er the shuddering realms, unquestioned sway:
See crimes, that feared not once the eye of day,
Rooted from men, without a name or place:
See nations blotted out from earth, to pay
The forfeit of deep guilt;—with glad embrace
The fair disburdened lands welcome a nobler race.

XXVI

Thus error's monstrous shapes from earth are driven;
They fade, they fly—but Truth survives their flight;
Earth has no shades to quench that beam of heaven;
Each ray that shone, in early time, to light
The faltering footstep in the path of right,
Each gleam of clearer brightness shed to aid
In man's maturer day his bolder sight,

All blended, like the rainbow's radiant braid,
Pour yet, and still shall pour, the blaze that cannot fade.

XXVII

Late, from this Western shore, that morning chased
The deep and ancient night, which threw its shroud
O'er the green land of groves, the beautiful waste,
Nurse of full streams, and lifter-up of proud
Sky-mingling mountains that o'erlook the cloud.
Erewhile, where yon gay spires their brightness rear,
Trees waved, and the brown hunter's shouts were loud
Amid the forest; and the bounding deer
Fled at the glancing plume, and the gaunt wolf yelled near.

XXVIII

And where his willing waves yon bright blue bay
Sends up, to kiss his decorated brim,
And cradles, in his soft embrace, the gay
Young group of grassy islands born of him,
And crowding nigh, or in the distance dim,
Lift the white throng of sails, that bear or bring
The commerce of the world;—with tawny limb,
And belt and beads in sunlight glistening,
The savage urged his skiff like wild bird on the wing.

XXIX

Then all this youthful paradise around,
And all the broad and boundless mainland, lay
Cooled by the interminable wood, that frowned
O'er mount and vale, where never summer ray
Glanced, till the strong tornado broke his way
Through the gray giants of the sylvan wild;
Yet many a sheltered glade, with blossoms gay
Beneath the showery sky and sunshine mild,
Within the shaggy arms of that dark forest smiled.

XXX

There stood the Indian hamlet, there the lake
Spread its blue sheet that flashed with many an oar,
Where the brown otter plunged him from the brake,
And the deer drank: as the light gale flew o'er,
The twinkling maize-field rustled on the shore;
And while that spot, so wild, and lone, and fair,
A look of glad and guiltless beauty wore,
And peace was on the earth and in the air,
The warrior lit the pile, and bound his captive there.

XXXI

Not unavenged—the foeman, from the wood,
Beheld the deed, and, when the midnight shade
Was stillest, gorged his battle-axe with blood;
All died—the wailing babe—the shrinking maid—
And in the flood of fire that scathed the glade,
The roofs went down; but deep the silence grew,
When on the dewy woods the day-beam played;
No more the cabin-smokes rose wreathed and blue,
And ever, by their lake, lay moored the bark canoe.

XXXII

Look now abroad—another race has filled
These populous borders—wide the wood recedes,
And towns shoot up, and fertile realms are tilled;
The land is full of harvests and green meads;
Streams numberless, that many a fountain feeds,

Shine, disembowered, and give to sun and
breeze
Their virgin waters; the full region leads
New colonies forth, that toward the western
seas
Spread, like a rapid flame among the autumnal
trees.

XXXIII

Here the free spirit of mankind, at length,
Throws its last fetters off; and who shall
place
A limit to the giant's unchained strength,
Or curb his swiftness in the forward race?
On, like the comet's way through infinite
space,
Stretches the long untravelled path of light,
Into the depths of ages; we may trace,
Afar, the brightening glory of its flight,
Till the receding rays are lost to human sight.

XXXIV

Europe is given a prey to sterner fates,
And writhes in shackles; strong the arms
that chain
To earth her struggling multitude of states;
She too is strong, and might not chafe in vain
Against them, but might cast to earth the
train
That trample her, and break their iron net.
Yes, she shall look on brighter days and gain
The meed of worthier deeds; the moment set
To rescue and raise up, draws near—but is
not yet.

XXXV

But thou, my country, thou shalt never fall,
Save with thy children—thy maternal care,
Thy lavish love, thy blessings showered on
all—
These are thy fetters—seas and stormy air
Are the wide barrier of thy borders, where,
Among thy gallant sons that guard thee
well,
Thou laugh'st at enemies: who shall then
declare
The date of thy deep-founded strength, or
tell
How happy, in thy lap, the sons of men shall
dwell?

1821 1821

THE INDIAN GIRL'S LAMENT

An Indian girl was sitting where
Her lover, slain in battle, slept;
Her maiden veil, her own black hair,
Came down o'er eyes that wept;
And wildly, in her woodland tongue,
This sad and simple lay she sung:

"I've pulled away the shrubs that grew
Too close above thy sleeping head,
And broke the forest-boughs that threw
Their shadows o'er thy bed,
That, shining from the sweet southwest,
The sunbeams might rejoice thy rest.

"It was a weary, weary road
That led thee to the pleasant coast,
Where thou, in his serene abode,
Hast met thy father's ghost;
Where everlasting autumn lies
On yellow woods and sunny skies.

"'Twas I the broidered mocsen made,
That shod thee for that distant land;
'Twas I thy bow and arrows laid
Beside thy still cold hand;
Thy bow in many a battle bent,
Thy arrows never vainly sent.

"With wampum-belts I crossed thy breast,
And wrapped thee in the bison's hide,
And laid the food that pleased thee best,
In plenty, by thy side,
And decked thee bravely, as became
A warrior of illustrious name.

"Thou'rt happy now, for thou hast passed
The long dark journey of the grave,
And in the land of light, at last,
Hast joined the good and brave;
Amid the flushed and balmy air,
The bravest and the loveliest there.

"Yet, oft to thine own Indian maid
Even there thy thoughts will earthward
stray—
To her who sits where thou wert laid,
And weeps the hours away,
Yet almost can her grief forget,
To think that thou dost love her yet.

"And thou, by one of those still lakes
That in a shining cluster lie,
On which the south wind scarcely breaks
The image of the sky,
A bower for thee and me hast made
Beneath the many-colored shade.

"And thou dost wait and watch to meet
My spirit sent to join the blessed,
And, wondering what detains my feet
From that bright land of rest,
Dost seem, in every sound, to hear
The rustling of my footsteps near."

1823 1826

MUTATION

THEY talk of short-lived pleasure—be it so—
Pain dies as quickly: stern, hard-featured Pain
Expires, and lets her weary prisoner go.
The fiercest agonies have shortest reign;
And after dreams of horror, comes again
The welcome morning with its rays of peace.
Oblivion, softly wiping out the stain,
Makes the strong secret pangs of shame to cease:
Remorse is virtue's root; its fair increase
Are fruits of innocence and blessedness:
Thus joy, o'erborne and bound, doth still release
His young limbs from the chains that round him press.
Weep not that the world changes—did it keep
A stable, changeless state, 'twere cause indeed to weep.

1824 1824

AUTUMN WOODS

ERE, in the northern gale,
The summer tresses of the trees are gone,
The woods of Autumn, all around our vale,
Have put their glory on.

The mountains that infold,
In their wide sweep, the colored landscape round,
Seem groups of giant kings, in purple and gold,
That guard the enchanted ground.

I roam the woods that crown
The uplands, where the mingled splendors glow,
Where the gay company of trees look down
On the green fields below.

My steps are not alone
In these bright walks; the sweet southwest, at play,
Flies, rustling, where the painted leaves are strown
Along the winding way.

And far in heaven, the while,
The sun, that sends that gale to wander here,
Pours out on the fair earth his quiet smile—
The sweetest of the year.

Where now the solemn shade,
Verdure and gloom where many branches meet;
So grateful, when the noon of summer made
The valleys sick with heat?

Let in through all the trees
Come the strange rays; the forest depths are bright;
Their sunny colored foliage, in the breeze,
Twinkles, like beams of light.

The rivulet, late unseen,
Where bickering through the shrubs its waters run,
Shines with the image of its golden screen,
And glimmerings of the sun.

But 'neath yon crimson tree,
Lover to listening maid might breathe his flame,
Nor mark, within its roseate canopy,
Her blush of maiden shame.

Oh, Autumn! why so soon
Depart the hues that make thy forests glad,
Thy gentle wind and thy fair sunny noon,
And leave thee wild and sad!

Ah! 'twere a lot too blest
Forever in thy colored shades to stray;
Amid the kisses of the soft southwest
To roam and dream for aye;

And leave the vain low strife
That makes men mad—the tug for wealth and power—
The passions and the cares that wither life,
And waste its little hour.

1824 1824

"I BROKE THE SPELL THAT HELD ME LONG"

I BROKE the spell that held me long,
The dear, dear witchery of song.
I said, the poet's idle lore
Shall waste my prime of years no more,
For Poetry, though heavenly born,
Consorts with poverty and scorn.

I broke the spell—nor deemed its power
Could fetter me another hour.
Ah, thoughtless! how could I forget
Its causes were around me yet?
For wheresoe'er I looked, the while,
Was Nature's everlasting smile.

Still came and lingered on my sight
Of flowers and streams the bloom and light,
And glory of the stars and sun;—
And these and poetry are one.
They, ere the world had held me long,
Recalled me to the love of song.

1824 1824

A FOREST HYMN

THE groves were God's first temples. Ere man learned
To hew the shaft, and lay the architrave,
And spread the roof above them—ere he framed
The lofty vault, to gather and roll back
The sound of anthems; in the darkling wood,
Amid the cool and silence, he knelt down,
And offered to the Mightiest solemn thanks
And supplication. For his simple heart
Might not resist the sacred influences
Which, from the stilly twilight of the place,
And from the gray old trunks that high in heaven
Mingled their mossy boughs, and from the sound
Of the invisible breath that swayed at once
All their green tops, stole over him, and bowed
His spirit with the thought of boundless power
And inaccessible majesty. Ah, why
Should we, in the world's riper years, neglect
God's ancient sanctuaries, and adore
Only among the crowd, and under roofs
That our frail hands have raised? Let me, at least,
Here, in the shadow of this aged wood,
Offer one hymn—thrice happy, if it find
Acceptance in His ear.

Father, thy hand
Hath reared these venerable columns, thou
Didst weave this verdant roof. Thou didst look down
Upon the naked earth, and, forthwith, rose
All these fair ranks of trees. They, in thy sun,
Budded, and shook their green leaves in thy breeze,
And shot toward heaven. The century-living crow,
Whose birth was in their tops, grew old and died
Among their branches, till, at last, they stood,
As now they stand, massy, and tall, and dark,
Fit shrine for humble worshipper to hold
Communion with his Maker. These dim vaults,
These winding aisles, of human pomp or pride
Report not. No fantastic carvings show
The boast of our vain race to change the form
Of thy fair works. But thou art here—thou fill'st
The solitude. Thou art in the soft winds
That run along the summit of these trees
In music; thou art in the cooler breath
That from the inmost darkness of the place
Comes, scarcely felt; the barky trunks, the ground,
The fresh moist ground, are all instinct with thee.
Here is continual worship;—Nature, here,
In the tranquillity that thou dost love,
Enjoys thy presence. Noiselessly, around,
From perch to perch, the solitary bird
Passes; and yon clear spring, that, midst its herbs,
Wells softly forth and wandering steeps the roots
Of half the mighty forest, tells no tale

Of all the good it does. Thou hast not left
Thyself without a witness, in the shades,
Of thy perfections. Grandeur, strength, and grace
Are here to speak of thee. This mighty oak—
By whose immovable stem I stand and seem
Almost annihilated—not a prince,
In all that proud old world beyond the deep,
E'er wore his crown as loftily as he
Wears the green coronal of leaves with which
Thy hand has graced him. Nestled at his root
Is beauty, such as blooms not in the glare
Of the broad sun. That delicate forest flower,
With scented breath and look so like a smile,
Seems, as it issues from the shapeless mould,
An emanation of the indwelling Life,
A visible token of the upholding Love,
That are the soul of this great universe.

My heart is awed within me when I think
Of the great miracle that still goes on,
In silence, round me—the perpetual work
Of thy creation, finished, yet renewed
Forever. Written on thy works I read
The lesson of thy own eternity.
Lo! all grow old and die—but see again,
How on the faltering footsteps of decay
Youth presses—ever gay and beautiful youth
In all its beautiful forms. These lofty trees
Wave not less proudly that their ancestors
Moulder beneath them. Oh, there is not lost
One of earth's charms: upon her bosom yet,
After the flight of untold centuries,
The freshness of her far beginning lies
And yet shall lie. Life mocks the idle hate
Of his arch-enemy Death—yea, seats himself
Upon the tyrant's throne—the sepulchre,
And of the triumphs of his ghastly foe
Makes his own nourishment. For he came forth
From thine own bosom, and shall have no end.

There have been holy men who hid themselves
Deep in the woody wilderness, and gave
Their lives to thought and prayer, till they outlived
The generation born with them, nor seemed
Less aged than the hoary trees and rocks
Around them;—and there have been holy men
Who deemed it were not well to pass life thus.
But let me often to these solitudes
Retire, and in thy presence reassure
My feeble virtue. Here its enemies,
The passions, at thy plainer footsteps shrink
And tremble and are still. O God! when thou
Dost scare the world with tempests, set on fire
The heavens with falling thunderbolts, or fill,
With all the waters of the firmament,
The swift dark whirlwind that uproots the woods
And drowns the villages; when, at thy call,
Uprises the great deep and throws himself
Upon the continent, and overwhelms
Its cities—who forgets not, at the sight
Of these tremendous tokens of thy power,
His pride, and lays his strifes and follies by?
Oh, from these sterner aspects of thy face
Spare me and mine, nor let us need the wrath
Of the mad unchained elements to teach
Who rules them. Be it ours to meditate,
In these calm shades, thy milder majesty,
And to the beautiful order of thy works
Learn to conform the order of our lives.

1825 1825

THE DEATH OF THE FLOWERS

THE melancholy days are come, the saddest of the year,
Of wailing winds, and naked woods, and meadows brown and sere.
Heaped in the hollows of the grove, the autumn leaves lie dead;
They rustle to the eddying gust, and to the rabbit's tread;
The robin and the wren are flown, and from the shrubs the jay,
And from the wood-top calls the crow through all the gloomy day.

Where are the flowers, the fair young flowers, that lately sprang and stood
In brighter light and softer airs, a beauteous sisterhood?
Alas! they all are in their graves, the gentle race of flowers
Are lying in their lowly beds, with the fair and good of ours.
The rain is falling where they lie, but the cold November rain
Calls not from out the gloomy earth the lovely ones again.

The wind-flower and the violet, they perished long ago,
And the brier-rose and the orchis died amid the summer glow;
But on the hills the golden-rod, and the aster in the wood,
And the yellow sun-flower by the brook in autumn beauty stood,
Till fell the frost from the clear cold heaven, as falls the plague on men,
And the brightness of their smile was gone, from upland, glade, and glen.

And now, when comes the calm mild day, as still such days will come,
To call the squirrel and the bee from out their winter home;
When the sound of dropping nuts is heard, though all the trees are still,
And twinkle in the smoky light the waters of the rill,
The south wind searches for the flowers whose fragrance late he bore,
And sighs to find them in the wood and by the stream no more.

And then I think of one who in her youthful beauty died,
The fair meek blossom that grew up and faded by my side.
In the cold moist earth we laid her, when the forests cast the leaf,
And we wept that one so lovely should have a life so brief:
Yet not unmeet it was that one, like that young friend of ours,
So gentle and so beautiful, should perish with the flowers.

1825 1825

JUNE

I GAZED upon the glorious sky
  And the green mountains round,
And thought that when I came to lie
  At rest within the ground,
'Twere pleasant, that in flowery June,
When brooks send up a cheerful tune,
  And groves a joyous sound,
The sexton's hand, my grave to make,
The rich, green mountain-turf should break.

A cell within the frozen mould,
  A coffin borne through sleet,
And icy clods above it rolled,
  While fierce the tempests beat—
Away!—I will not think of these—
Blue be the sky and soft the breeze,
  Earth green beneath the feet,
And be the damp mould gently pressed
Into my narrow place of rest.

There through the long, long summer hours,
  The golden light should lie,
And thick young herbs and groups of flowers
  Stand in their beauty by.
The oriole should build and tell
His love-tale close beside my cell;
  The idle butterfly
Should rest him there, and there be heard
The housewife bee and humming-bird.

And what if cheerful shouts at noon
  Come, from the village sent,
Or songs of maids, beneath the moon
  With fairy laughter blent?
And what if, in the evening light,
Betrothèd lovers walk in sight
  Of my low monument?
I would the lovely scene around
Might know no sadder sight nor sound.

I know that I no more should see
  The season's glorious show,
Nor would its brightness shine for me,
  Nor its wild music flow;
But if, around my place of sleep,
The friends I love should come to weep,
  They might not haste to go.
Soft airs, and song, and light, and bloom
Should keep them lingering by my tomb.

These to their softened hearts should bear
  The thought of what has been,
And speak of one who cannot share
  The gladness of the scene;
Whose part, in all the pomp that fills
The circuit of the summer hills,
  Is that his grave is green;
And deeply would their hearts rejoice
To hear again his living voice.

1825 1826

THE AFRICAN CHIEF

Chained in the market-place he stood,
  A man of giant frame,
Amid the gathering multitude
  That shrunk to hear his name—
All stern of look and strong of limb,
  His dark eye on the ground:—
And silently they gazed on him,
  As on a lion bound.

Vainly, but well, that chief had fought,
  He was a captive now,
Yet pride, that fortune humbles not,
  Was written on his brow.
The scars his dark broad bosom wore
  Showed warrior true and brave;
A prince among his tribe before,
  He could not be a slave.

Then to his conqueror he spake:
  "My brother is a king;
Undo this necklace from my neck,
  And take this bracelet ring,
And send me where my brother reigns,
  And I will fill thy hands
With store of ivory from the plains,
  And gold-dust from the sands."

"Not for thy ivory nor thy gold
  Will I unbind thy chain;
That bloody hand shall never hold
  The battle-spear again.
A price thy nation never gave
  Shall yet be paid for thee;
For thou shalt be the Christian's slave,
  In lands beyond the sea."

Then wept the warrior chief, and bade
  To shred his locks away;
And one by one, each heavy braid
  Before the victor lay.
Thick were the platted locks, and long,
  And closely hidden there
Shone many a wedge of gold among
  The dark and crispèd hair.

"Look, feast thy greedy eye with gold
  Long kept for sorest need:
Take it—thou askest sums untold—
  And say that I am freed.
Take it—my wife, the long, long day,
  Weeps by the cocoa-tree,
And my young children leave their play,
  And ask in vain for me."

"I take thy gold, but I have made
  Thy fetters fast and strong,
And ween that by the cocoa-shade
  Thy wife will wait thee long."
Strong was the agony that shook
  The captive's frame to hear,
And the proud meaning of his look
  Was changed to mortal fear.

His heart was broken—crazed his brain:
  At once his eye grew wild;
He struggled fiercely with his chain,
  Whispered, and wept, and smiled;
Yet wore not long those fatal bands,
  And once, at shut of day,
They drew him forth upon the sands,
  The foul hyena's prey.

1825 1826

OCTOBER

Ay, thou art welcome, heaven's delicious
  breath!
When woods begin to wear the crimson leaf,
And suns grow meek, and the meek suns grow
  brief,
And the year smiles as it draws near its death.
Wind of the sunny south! oh, still delay
In the gay woods and in the golden air,
Like to a good old age released from care,
Journeying, in long serenity, away.
In such a bright, late quiet, would that I
Might wear out life like thee, 'mid bowers and
  brooks,
And, dearer yet, the sunshine of kind looks,
And music of kind voices ever nigh;
And when my last sand twinkled in the glass,
Pass silently from men, as thou dost pass.

1826 1826

THE PAST

Thou unrelenting Past!
Strong are the barriers round thy dark do-
  main,
And fetters, sure and fast,
Hold all that enter thy unbreathing reign.

Far in thy realm withdrawn,
Old empires sit in sullenness and gloom,
And glorious ages gone
Lie deep within the shadow of thy womb.

Childhood, with all its mirth,
Youth, Manhood, Age that draws us to the ground,
And last, Man's Life on earth,
Glide to thy dim dominions, and are bound.

Thou hast my better years;
Thou hast my earlier friends, the good, the kind,
Yielded to thee with tears—
The venerable form, the exalted mind.

My spirit yearns to bring
The lost ones back—yearns with desire intense,
And struggles hard to wring
Thy bolts apart, and pluck thy captives thence.

In vain; thy gates deny
All passage save to those who hence depart;
Nor to the streaming eye
Thou giv'st them back—nor to the broken heart.

In thy abysses hide
Beauty and excellence unknown; to thee
Earth's wonder and her pride
Are gathered, as the waters to the sea;

Labors of good to man,
Unpublished charity, unbroken faith,
Love, that midst grief began,
And grew with years, and faltered not in death.

Full many a mighty name
Lurks in thy depths, unuttered, unrevered;
With thee are silent fame,
Forgotten arts, and wisdom disappeared.

Thine for a space are they—
Yet shalt thou yield thy treasures up at last:
Thy gates shall yet give way,
Thy bolts shall fall, inexorable Past!

All that of good and fair
Has gone into thy womb from earliest time,
Shall then come forth to wear
The glory and the beauty of its prime.

They have not perished—no!
Kind words, remembered voices once so sweet,
Smiles, radiant long ago,
And features, the great soul's apparent seat.

All shall come back; each tie
Of pure affection shall be knit again;
Alone shall Evil die,
And Sorrow dwell a prisoner in thy reign.

And then shall I behold
Him, by whose kind paternal side I sprung,
And her, who, still and cold,
Fills the next grave—the beautiful and young.

1828 1828

THE EVENING WIND

SPIRIT that breathest through my lattice, thou
That cool'st the twilight of the sultry day,
Gratefully flows thy freshness round my brow;
Thou hast been out upon the deep at play,
Riding all day the wild blue waves till now,
Roughening their crests, and scattering high their spray,
And swelling the white sail. I welcome thee
To the scorched land, thou wanderer of the sea!

Nor I alone; a thousand bosoms round
Inhale thee in the fulness of delight;
And languid forms rise up, and pulses bound
Livelier, at coming of the wind of night;
And, languishing to hear thy grateful sound,
Lies the vast inland stretched beyond the sight.
Go forth into the gathering shade; go forth,
God's blessing breathed upon the fainting earth!

Go, rock the little wood-bird in his nest,
Curl the still waters, bright with stars, and rouse
The wide old wood from his majestic rest,
Summoning from the innumerable boughs
The strange, deep harmonies that haunt his breast:
Pleasant shall be thy way where meekly bows
The shutting flower, and darkling waters pass,
And where the o'ershadowing branches sweep the grass.

The faint old man shall lean his silver head
  To feel thee; thou shalt kiss the child asleep,
And dry the moistened curls that overspread
  His temples, while his breathing grows more deep;
And they who stand about the sick man's bed,
  Shall joy to listen to thy distant sweep,
And softly part his curtains to allow
Thy visit, grateful to his burning brow.

Go—but the circle of eternal change,
  Which is the life of Nature, shall restore,
With sounds and scents from all thy mighty range,
  Thee to thy birthplace of the deep once more;
Sweet odors in the sea-air, sweet and strange,
  Shall tell the home-sick mariner of the shore;
And, listening to thy murmur, he shall deem
He hears the rustling leaf and running stream.

1829 1829

TO THE FRINGED GENTIAN

Thou blossom bright with autumn dew,
And colored with the heaven's own blue,
That openest when the quiet light
Succeeds the keen and frosty night—

Thou comest not when violets lean
O'er wandering brooks and springs unseen,
Or columbines, in purple dressed,
Nod o'er the ground-bird's hidden nest.

Thou waitest late and com'st alone,
When woods are bare and birds are flown,
And frosts and shortening days portend
The aged year is near his end.

Then doth thy sweet and quiet eye
Look through its fringes to the sky,
Blue—blue—as if that sky let fall
A flower from its cerulean wall.

I would that thus, when I shall see
The hour of death draw near to me,
Hope, blossoming within my heart,
May look to heaven as I depart.

1829 1832

HYMN OF THE CITY

Not in the solitude
Alone may man commune with Heaven, or see,
  Only in savage wood
And sunny vale, the present Deity;
  Or only hear his voice
Where the winds whisper and the waves rejoice.

  Even here do I behold
Thy steps, Almighty!—here, amidst the crowd
  Through the great city rolled,
With everlasting murmur deep and loud—
  Choking the ways that wind
'Mongst the proud piles, the work of human kind.

  Thy golden sunshine comes
From the round heaven, and on their dwellings lies
  And lights their inner homes;
For them Thou fill'st with air the unbounded skies,
  And givest them the stores
Of ocean, and the harvests of its shores.

  Thy Spirit is around,
Quickening the restless mass that sweeps along;
  And this eternal sound—
Voices and footfalls of the numberless throng—
  Like the resounding sea,
Or like the rainy tempest, speaks of Thee.

  And when the hour of rest
Comes, like a calm upon the mid-sea brine,
  Hushing its billowy breast—
The quiet of that moment too is thine;
  It breathes of Him who keeps
The vast and helpless city while it sleeps.

1830 1830

SONG OF MARION'S MEN

Our band is few but true and tried,
  Our leader frank and bold;
The British soldier trembles
  When Marion's name is told.

Our fortress is the good greenwood,
Our tent the cypress-tree;
We know the forest round us,
As seamen know the sea.
We know its walls of thorny vines,
Its glades of reedy grass,
Its safe and silent islands
Within the dark morass.

Woe to the English soldiery
That little dread us near!
On them shall light at midnight
A strange and sudden fear:
When, waking to their tents on fire,
They grasp their arms in vain,
And they who stand to face us
Are beat to earth again;
And they who fly in terror deem
A mighty host behind,
And hear the tramp of thousands
Upon the hollow wind.

Then sweet the hour that brings release
From danger and from toil:
We talk the battle over,
And share the battle's spoil.
The woodland rings with laugh and shout,
As if a hunt were up,
And woodland flowers are gathered
To crown the soldier's cup.
With merry songs we mock the wind
That in the pine-top grieves,
And slumber long and sweetly
On beds of oaken leaves.

Well knows the fair and friendly moon
The band that Marion leads—
The glitter of their rifles,
The scampering of their steeds.
'Tis life to guide the fiery barb
Across the moonlight plain;
'Tis life to feel the night-wind
That lifts the tossing mane.
A moment in the British camp—
A moment—and away
Back to the pathless forest,
Before the peep of day.

Grave men there are by broad Santee,
Grave men with hoary hairs;
Their hearts are all with Marion,
For Marion are their prayers.
And lovely ladies greet our band
With kindliest welcoming,
With smiles like those of summer,
And tears like those of spring.
For them we wear these trusty arms,
And lay them down no more
Till we have driven the Briton,
Forever, from our shore.

1831 1831

THE PRAIRIES

THESE are the gardens of the Desert, these
The unshorn fields, boundless and beautiful,
For which the speech of England has no name—
The Prairies. I behold them for the first,
And my heart swells, while the dilated sight
Takes in the encircling vastness. Lo! they stretch,
In airy undulations, far away,
As if the ocean, in his gentlest swell,
Stood still, with all his rounded billows fixed,
And motionless forever.—Motionless?—
No—they are all unchained again. The clouds
Sweep over with their shadows, and, beneath,
The surface rolls and fluctuates to the eye;
Dark hollows seem to glide along and chase
The sunny ridges. Breezes of the South!
Who toss the golden and the flame-like flowers,
And pass the prairie-hawk that, poised on high,
Flaps his broad wings, yet moves not—ye have played
Among the palms of Mexico and vines 19
Of Texas, and have crisped the limpid brooks
That from the fountains of Sonora glide
Into the calm Pacific—have ye fanned
A nobler or a lovelier scene than this?
Man hath no power in all this glorious work:
The hand that built the firmament hath heaved
And smoothed these verdant swells, and sown their slopes
With herbage, planted them with island groves,
And hedged them round with forests. Fitting floor
For this magnificent temple of the sky—
With flowers whose glory and whose multitude
Rival the constellations! The great heavens

Seem to stoop down upon the scene in love,—
A nearer vault, and of a tenderer blue,
Than that which bends above our eastern hills.

As o'er the verdant waste I guide my steed,
Among the high rank grass that sweeps his sides
The hollow beating of his footstep seems
A sacrilegious sound. I think of those
Upon whose rest he tramples. Are they here—
The dead of other days?—and did the dust
Of these fair solitudes once stir with life
And burn with passion? Let the mighty mounds
That overlook the rivers, or that rise
In the dim forest crowded with old oaks,
Answer. A race, that long has passed away,
Built them;—a disciplined and populous race
Heaped, with long toil, the earth, while yet the Greek
Was hewing the Pentelicus to forms
Of symmetry, and rearing on its rock
The glittering Parthenon. These ample fields
Nourished their harvests, here their herds were fed,
When haply by their stalls the bison lowed,
And bowed his manèd shoulder to the yoke.
All day this desert murmured with their toils,
Till twilight blushed, and lovers walked, and wooed
In a forgotten language, and old tunes,
From instruments of unremembered form,
Gave the soft winds a voice. The red man came—
The roaming hunter tribes, warlike and fierce,
And the mound-builders vanished from the earth.
The solitude of centuries untold
Has settled where they dwelt. The prairie-wolf
Hunts in their meadows, and his fresh-dug den
Yawns by my path. The gopher mines the ground
Where stood their swarming cities. All is gone;
All—save the piles of earth that hold their bones,
The platforms where they worshipped unknown gods,
The barriers which they builded from the soil
To keep the foe at bay—till o'er the walls
The wild beleaguerers broke, and, one by one,
The strongholds of the plain were forced, and heaped
With corpses. The brown vultures of the wood
Flocked to those vast uncovered sepulchres,
And sat unscared and silent at their feast.
Haply some solitary fugitive,
Lurking in marsh and forest, till the sense
Of desolation and of fear became
Bitterer than death, yielded himself to die.
Man's better nature triumphed then. Kind words
Welcomed and soothed him; the rude conquerors
Seated the captive with their chiefs; he chose
A bride among their maidens, and at length
Seemed to forget—yet ne'er forgot—the wife
Of his first love, and her sweet little ones,
Butchered, amid their shrieks, with all his race.

Thus change the forms of being. Thus arise
Races of living things, glorious in strength,
And perish, as the quickening breath of God
Fills them, or is withdrawn. The red man, too,
Has left the blooming wilds he ranged so long,
And, nearer to the Rocky Mountains, sought
A wilder hunting-ground. The beaver builds
No longer by these streams, but far away,
On waters whose blue surface ne'er gave back
The white man's face—among Missouri's springs,
And pools whose issues swell the Oregon—
He rears his little Venice. In these plains
The bison feeds no more. Twice twenty leagues
Beyond remotest smoke of hunter's camp,
Roams the majestic brute, in herds that shake
The earth with thundering steps—yet here I meet
His ancient footprints stamped beside the pool.

Still this great solitude is quick with life.
Myriads of insects, gaudy as the flowers
They flutter over, gentle quadrupeds,
And birds, that scarce have learned the fear of man,
Are here, and sliding reptiles of the ground,
Startlingly beautiful. The graceful deer
Bounds to the wood at my approach. The bee,
A more adventurous colonist than man,

With whom he came across the eastern deep,
Fills the savannas with his murmurings,
And hides his sweets, as in the golden age,
Within the hollow oak. I listen long
To his domestic hum, and think I hear
The sound of that advancing multitude
Which soon shall fill these deserts. From the ground
Comes up the laugh of children, the soft voice
Of maidens, and the sweet and solemn hymn
Of Sabbath worshippers. The low of herds
Blends with the rustling of the heavy grain
Over the dark brown furrows. All at once
A fresher wind sweeps by, and breaks my dream,
And I am in the wilderness alone.

1832 1833

EARTH

A MIDNIGHT black with clouds is in the sky;
I seem to feel, upon my limbs, the weight
Of its vast brooding shadow. All in vain
Turns the tired eye in search of form; no star
Pierces the pitchy veil; no ruddy blaze,
From dwellings lighted by the cheerful hearth,
Tinges the flowering summits of the grass.
No sound of life is heard, no village hum,
Nor measured tramp of footstep in the path,
Nor rush of wind, while, on the breast of Earth,
I lie and listen to her mighty voice:
A voice of many tones—sent up from streams
That wander through the gloom, from woods unseen
Swayed by the sweeping of the tides of air,
From rocky chasms where darkness dwells all day,
And hollows of the great invisible hills,
And sands that edge the ocean, stretching far
Into the night—a melancholy sound!

O Earth! dost thou too sorrow for the past
Like man thy offspring? Do I hear thee mourn
Thy childhood's unreturning hours, thy springs
Gone with their genial airs and melodies,
The gentle generations of thy flowers,
And thy majestic groves of olden time,
Perished with all their dwellers? Dost thou wail
For that fair age of which the poets tell,
Ere yet the winds grew keen with frost, or fire
Fell with the rains or spouted from the hills,
To blast thy greenness, while the virgin night
Was guiltless and salubrious as the day?
Or haply dost thou grieve for those that die—
For living things that trod thy paths awhile,
The love of thee and heaven—and now they sleep
Mixed with the shapeless dust on which thy herds
Trample and graze? I too must grieve with thee,
O'er loved ones lost. Their graves are far away
Upon thy mountains; yet, while I recline
Alone, in darkness, on thy naked soil,
The mighty nourisher and burial-place
Of man, I feel that I embrace their dust.

Ha! how the murmur deepens! I perceive
And tremble at its dreadful import. Earth
Uplifts a general cry for guilt and wrong,
And heaven is listening. The forgotten graves
Of the heart-broken utter forth their plaint.
The dust of her who loved and was betrayed,
And him who died neglected in his age;
The sepulchres of those who for mankind
Labored, and earned the recompense of scorn;
Ashes of martyrs for the truth, and bones
Of those who, in the strife for liberty,
Were beaten down, their corses given to dogs,
Their names to infamy, all find a voice.
The nook in which the captive, overtoiled,
Lay down to rest at last, and that which holds
Childhood's sweet blossoms, crushed by cruel hands,
Send up a plaintive sound. From battle-fields,
Where heroes madly drave and dashed their hosts
Against each other, rises up a noise,
As if the armèd multitudes of dead
Stirred in their heavy slumber. Mournful tones
Come from the green abysses of the sea—
A story of the crimes the guilty sought
To hide beneath its waves. The glens, the groves,
Paths in the thicket, pools of running brook,
And banks and depths of lake, and streets and lanes
Of cities, now that living sounds are hushed,
Murmur of guilty force and treachery.

Here, where I rest, the vales of Italy
Are round me, populous from early time,
And field of the tremendous warfare waged
'Twixt good and evil. Who, alas! shall dare
Interpret to man's ear the mingled voice
That comes from her old dungeons yawning now
To the black air, her amphitheatres,
Where the dew gathers on the mouldering stones,
And fanes of banished gods, and open tombs,
And roofless palaces, and streets and hearths
Of cities dug from their volcanic graves?
I hear a sound of many languages,
The utterance of nations now no more,
Driven out by mightier, as the days of heaven
Chase one another from the sky. The blood
Of freemen shed by freemen, till strange lords
Came in their hour of weakness, and made fast
The yoke that is worn, cries out to Heaven.

What then shall cleanse thy bosom, gentle Earth,
From all its painful memories of guilt?
The whelming flood, or the renewing fire,
Or the slow change of time?—that so, at last,
The horrid tale of perjury and strife,
Murder and spoil, which men call history,
May seem a fable, like the inventions told
By poets of the gods of Greece. O thou,
Who sittest far beyond the Atlantic deep,
Among the sources of thy glorious streams,
My native Land of Groves! a newer page
In the great record of the world is thine;
Shall it be fairer? Fear, and friendly Hope,
And Envy, watch the issue, while the lines,
By which thou shalt be judged, are written down.

1834 1835

THE BATTLE-FIELD

ONCE this soft turf, this rivulet's sands,
Were trampled by a hurrying crowd,
And fiery hearts and armèd hands
Encountered in the battle-cloud.

Ah! never shall the land forget
How gushed the life-blood of her brave—
Gushed, warm with hope and courage yet,
Upon the soil they fought to save.

Now all is calm, and fresh, and still;
Alone the chirp of flitting bird,
And talk of children on the hill,
And bell of wandering kine, are heard.

No solemn host goes trailing by
The black-mouthed gun and staggering wain;
Men start not at the battle-cry,
Oh, be it never heard again!

Soon rested those who fought; but thou
Who minglest in the harder strife
For truths which men receive not now,
Thy warfare only ends with life.

A friendless warfare! lingering long
Through weary day and weary year,
A wild and many-weaponed throng
Hang on thy front, and flank, and rear.

Yet nerve thy spirit to the proof,
And blench not at thy chosen lot.
The timid good may stand aloof,
The sage may frown—yet faint thou not.

Nor heed the shaft too surely cast,
The foul and hissing bolt of scorn;
For with thy side shall dwell, at last,
The victory of endurance born.

Truth, crushed to earth, shall rise again;
Th' eternal years of God are hers;
But Error, wounded, writhes in pain,
And dies among his worshippers.

Yea, though thou lie upon the dust,
When they who helped thee flee in fear,
Die full of hope and manly trust,
Like those who fell in battle here.

Another hand thy sword shall wield,
Another hand the standard wave,
Till from the trumpet's mouth is pealed
The blast of triumph o'er thy grave.

1837 1837

AN EVENING REVERY

THE summer day is closed—the sun is set:
Well they have done their office, those bright hours,
The latest of whose train goes softly out
In the red west. The green blade of the ground

Has risen, and herds have cropped it; the young twig
Has spread its plaited tissues to the sun;
Flowers of the garden and the waste have blown
And withered; seeds have fallen upon the soil,
From bursting cells, and in their graves await
Their resurrection. Insects from the pools
Have filled the air awhile with humming wings,
That now are still for ever; painted moths
Have wandered the blue sky, and died again;
The mother-bird hath broken for her brood
Their prison shell, or shoved them from the nest,
Plumed for their earliest flight. In bright alcoves,
In woodland cottages with barky walls,
In noisome cells of the tumultuous town,
Mothers have clasped with joy the new-born babe.
Graves by the lonely forest, by the shore
Of rivers and of ocean, by the ways
Of the thronged city, have been hollowed out
And filled, and closed. This day hath parted friends
That ne'er before were parted; it hath knit
New friendships; it hath seen the maiden plight
Her faith, and trust her peace to him who long
Had wooed; and it hath heard, from lips which late
Were eloquent of love, the first harsh word,
That told the wedded one her peace was flown.
Farewell to the sweet sunshine! One glad day
Is added now to Childhood's merry days,
And one calm day to those of quiet Age.
Still the fleet hours run on; and as I lean,
Amid the thickening darkness, lamps are lit,
By those who watch the dead, and those who twine
Flowers for the bride. The mother from the eyes
Of her sick infant shades the painful light,
And sadly listens to his quick-drawn breath.

O thou great Movement of the Universe,
Or Change, or Flight of Time—for ye are one!
That bearest, silently, this visible scene
Into night's shadow and the streaming rays
Of starlight, whither art thou bearing me?
I feel the mighty current sweep me on,
Yet know not whither. Man foretells afar
The courses of the stars; the very hour
He knows when they shall darken or grow bright;
Yet doth the eclipse of Sorrow and of Death
Come unforewarned. Who next, of those I love,
Shall pass from life, or, sadder yet, shall fall
From virtue? Strife with foes, or bitterer strife
With friends, or shame and general scorn of men—
Which who can bear?—or the fierce rack of pain—
Lie they within my path? Or shall the years
Push me, with soft and inoffensive pace,
Into the stilly twilight of my age?
Or do the portals of another life
Even now, while I am glorying in my strength,
Impend around me? Oh! beyond that bourne,
In the vast cycle of being which begins
At that dread threshold, with what fairer forms
Shall the great law of change and progress clothe
Its workings? Gently—so have good men taught—
Gently, and without grief, the old shall glide
Into the new; the eternal flow of things,
Like a bright river of the fields of heaven,
Shall journey onward in perpetual peace.

1840 1841

THE ANTIQUITY OF FREEDOM

Here are old trees, tall oaks, and gnarlèd pines,
That stream with gray-green mosses; here the ground
Was never trenched by spade, and flowers spring up
Unsown, and die ungathered. It is sweet
To linger here, among the flitting birds
And leaping squirrels, wandering brooks, and winds
That shake the leaves, and scatter, as they pass,
A fragrance from the cedars, thickly set
With pale-blue berries. In these peaceful shades—
Peaceful, unpruned, immeasurably old—
My thoughts go up the long dim path of years,
Back to the earliest days of liberty.

O Freedom! thou art not, as poets dream,
A fair young girl, with light and delicate limbs,
And wavy tresses gushing from the cap
With which the Roman master crowned his slave
When he took off the gyves. A bearded man,
Armed to the teeth, art thou; one mailèd hand
Grasps the broad shield, and one the sword; thy brow,
Glorious in beauty though it be, is scarred
With tokens of old wars; thy massive limbs
Are strong with struggling. Power at thee has launched
His bolts, and with his lightnings smitten thee;
They could not quench the life thou hast from heaven;
Merciless Power has dug thy dungeon deep,
And his swart armorers, by a thousand fires,
Have forged thy chain; yet, while he deems thee bound,
The links are shivered, and the prison-walls
Fall outward; terribly thou springest forth,
As springs the flame above a burning pile,
And shoutest to the nations, who return
Thy shoutings, while the pale oppressor flies.

Thy birthright was not given by human hands:
Thou wert twin-born with man. In pleasant fields,
While yet our race was few, thou sat'st with him,
To tend the quiet flock and watch the stars,
And teach the reed to utter simple airs.
Thou by his side, amid the tangled wood,
Didst war upon the panther and the wolf,
His only foes; and thou with him didst draw
The earliest furrow on the mountain-side,
Soft with the deluge. Tyranny himself,
Thy enemy, although of reverend look,
Hoary with many years, and far obeyed,
Is later born than thou; and as he meets
The grave defiance of thine elder eye,
The usurper trembles in his fastnesses.

Thou shalt wax stronger with the lapse of years,
But he shall fade into a feebler age—
Feebler, yet subtler. He shall weave his snares,
And spring them on thy careless steps, and clap
His withered hands, and from their ambush call
His hordes to fall upon thee. He shall send
Quaint maskers, wearing fair and gallant forms
To catch thy gaze, and uttering graceful words
To charm thy ear; while his sly imps, by stealth,
Twine round thee threads of steel, light thread on thread,
That grow to fetters; or bind down thy arms
With chains concealed in chaplets. Oh! not yet
Mayst thou unbrace thy corslet, nor lay by
Thy sword; nor yet, O Freedom! close thy lids
In slumber; for thine enemy never sleeps,
And thou must watch and combat till the day
Of the new earth and heaven. But wouldst thou rest
Awhile from tumult and the frauds of men,
These old and friendly solitudes invite
Thy visit. They, while yet the forest-trees
Were young upon the unviolated earth,
And yet the moss-stains on the rock were new,
Beheld thy glorious childhood, and rejoiced.

1842 1842

"OH MOTHER OF A MIGHTY RACE"

Oh mother of a mighty race,
Yet lovely in thy youthful grace!
The elder dames, thy haughty peers,
Admire and hate thy blooming years.
With words of shame
And taunts of scorn they join thy name.

For on thy cheeks the glow is spread
That tints thy morning hills with red;
Thy step—the wild-deer's rustling feet
Within thy woods are not more fleet;
Thy hopeful eye
Is bright as thine own sunny sky.

Ay, let them rail—those haughty ones,
While safe thou dwellest with thy sons.
They do not know how loved thou art,
How many a fond and fearless heart
Would rise to throw
Its life between thee and the foe.

They know not, in their hate and pride,
What virtues with thy children bide;

How true, how good, thy graceful maids
Make bright, like flowers, the valley-shades;
What generous men
Spring, like thine oaks, by hill and glen;—
What cordial welcomes greet the guest
By thy lone rivers of the West;
How faith is kept, and truth revered,
And man is loved, and God is feared,
In woodland homes,
And where the ocean border foams.

There's freedom at thy gates and rest
For Earth's down-trodden and opprest,
A shelter for the hunted head,
For the starved laborer toil and bread.
Power, at thy bounds,
Stops and calls back his baffled hounds.

Oh fair young mother! on thy brow
Shall sit a nobler grace than now.
Deep in the brightness of the skies
The thronging years in glory rise,
And, as they fleet,
Drop strength and riches at thy feet.

Thine eye, with every coming hour,
Shall brighten, and thy form shall tower;
And when thy sisters, elder born,
Would brand thy name with words of scorn,
Before thine eye,
Upon their lips the taunt shall die.

1846 1847

ITALY

VOICES from the mountains speak,
Apennines to Alps reply;
Vale to vale and peak to peak
Toss an old-remembered cry:
"Italy
Shall be free!"
Such the mighty shout that fills
All the passes of her hills.

All the old Italian lakes
Quiver at that quickening word;
Como with a thrill awakes;
Garda to her depths is stirred;
Mid the steeps
Where he sleeps,
Dreaming of the elder years,
Startled Thrasymenus hears.

Sweeping Arno, swelling Po,
Murmur freedom to their meads.
Tiber swift and Liris slow
Send strange whispers from their reeds.
"Italy
Shall be free!"
Sing the glittering brooks that slide,
Toward the sea, from Etna's side.

Long ago was Gracchus slain;
Brutus perished long ago;
Yet the living roots remain
Whence the shoots of greatness grow;
Yet again,
Godlike men,
Sprung from that heroic stem,
Call the land to rise with them.

They who haunt the swarming street,
They who chase the mountain-boar,
Or, where cliff and billow meet,
Prune the vine or pull the oar,
With a stroke
Break their yoke;
Slaves but yestereve were they—
Freemen with the dawning day.

Looking in his children's eyes,
While his own with gladness flash,
"These," the Umbrian father cries,
"Ne'er shall crouch beneath the lash!
These shall ne'er
Brook to wear
Chains whose cruel links are twined
Round the crushed and withering mind."

Monarchs! ye whose armies stand
Harnessed for the battle-field!
Pause, and from the lifted hand
Drop the bolt of war ye wield.
Stand aloof
While the proof
Of the people's might is given;
Leave their kings to them and Heaven!

Stand aloof, and see the oppressed
Chase the oppressor, pale with fear,
As the fresh winds of the west
Blow the misty valleys clear.
Stand and see
Italy
Cast the gyves she wears no more
To the gulfs that steep her shore.

1860 1860

THE POET

Thou, who wouldst wear the name
Of poet mid thy brethren of mankind,
And clothe in words of flame
Thoughts that shall live within the general mind!
Deem not the framing of a deathless lay
The pastime of a drowsy summer day.

But gather all thy powers,
And wreak them on the verse that thou dost weave,
And in thy lonely hours,
At silent morning or at wakeful eve,
While the warm current tingles through thy veins,
Set forth the burning words in fluent strains.

No smooth array of phrase,
Artfully sought and ordered though it be,
Which the cold rhymer lays
Upon his page with languid industry,
Can wake the listless pulse to livelier speed,
Or fill with sudden tears the eyes that read.

The secret wouldst thou know
To touch the heart or fire the blood at will?
Let thine own eyes o'erflow;
Let thy lips quiver with the passionate thrill;
Seize the great thought, ere yet its power be past,
And bind, in words, the fleet emotion fast.

Then, should thy verse appear
Halting and harsh, and all unaptly wrought,
Touch the crude line with fear,
Save in the moment of impassioned thought;
Then summon back the original glow, and mend
The strain with rapture that with fire was penned.

Yet let no empty gust
Of passion find an utterance in thy lay,
A blast that whirls the dust
Along the howling street and dies away;
But feelings of calm power and mighty sweep,
Like currents journeying through the windless deep.

Seek'st thou, in living lays,
To limn the beauty of the earth and sky?
Before thine inner gaze
Let all that beauty in clear vision lie;
Look on it with exceeding love, and write
The words inspired by wonder and delight.

Of tempests wouldst thou sing,
Or tell of battles—make thyself a part
Of the great tumult; cling
To the tossed wreck with terror in thy heart;
Scale, with the assaulting host, the rampart's height,
And strike and struggle in the thickest fight.

So shalt thou frame a lay
That haply may endure from age to age,
And they who read shall say:
"What witchery hangs upon this poet's page!
What art is his the written spells to find
That sway from mood to mood the willing mind!"

1863 1864

THE FLOOD OF YEARS

A mighty Hand, from an exhaustless Urn,
Pours forth the never-ending Flood of Years,
Among the nations. How the rushing waves
Bear all before them! On their foremost edge,
And there alone, is Life. The Present there
Tosses and foams, and fills the air with roar
Of mingled noises. There are they who toil,
And they who strive, and they who feast, and they
Who hurry to and fro. The sturdy swain—
Woodman and delver with the spade—is there,
And busy artisan beside his bench,
And pallid student with his written roll.
A moment on the mounting billow seen,
The flood sweeps over them and they are gone.
There groups of revellers whose brows are twined
With roses, ride the topmost swell awhile,
And as they raise their flowing cups and touch
The clinking brim to brim, are whirled beneath
The waves and disappear. I hear the jar
Of beaten drums, and thunders that break forth

From cannon, where the advancing billow sends
Up to the sight long files of armèd men,
That hurry to the charge through flame and smoke.
The torrent bears them under, whelmed and hid
Slayer and slain, in heaps of bloody foam.
Down go the steed and rider, the plumed chief
Sinks with his followers; the head that wears
The imperial diadem goes down beside
The felon's with cropped ear and branded cheek.
A funeral-train—the torrent sweeps away
Bearers and bier and mourners. By the bed
Of one who dies men gather sorrowing,
And women weep aloud; the flood rolls on;
The wail is stifled and the sobbing group
Borne under. Hark to that shrill, sudden shout,
The cry of an applauding multitude,
Swayed by some loud-voiced orator who wields
The living mass as if he were its soul!
The waters choke the shout and all is still.
Lo! next a kneeling crowd, and one who spreads
The hands in prayer—the engulfing wave o'ertakes
And swallows them and him. A sculptor wields
The chisel, and the stricken marble grows
To beauty; at his easel, eager-eyed,
A painter stands, and sunshine at his touch
Gathers upon his canvas, and life glows;
A poet, as he paces to and fro,
Murmurs his sounding lines. Awhile they ride
The advancing billow, till its tossing crest
Strikes them and flings them under, while their tasks
Are yet unfinished. See a mother smile
On her young babe that smiles to her again;
The torrent wrests it from her arms; she shrieks
And weeps, and midst her tears is carried down.
A beam like that of moonlight turns the spray
To glistening pearls; two lovers, hand in hand,
Rise on the billowy swell and fondly look
Into each other's eyes. The rushing flood
Flings them apart: the youth goes down; the maid
With hands outstretched in vain, and streaming eyes,
Waits for the next high wave to follow him.
An aged man succeeds; his bending form
Sinks slowly. Mingling with the sullen stream
Gleam the white locks, and then are seen no more.

Lo! wider grows the stream—a sea-like flood
Saps earth's walled cities; massive palaces
Crumble before it; fortresses and towers
Dissolve in the swift waters; populous realms
Swept by the torrent see their ancient tribes
Engulfed and lost; their very languages
Stifled, and never to be uttered more.

I pause and turn my eyes, and looking back
Where that tumultuous flood has been, I see
The silent ocean of the Past, a waste
Of waters weltering over graves, its shores
Strewn with the wreck of fleets where mast and hull
Drop away piecemeal; battlemented walls
Frown idly, green with moss, and temples stand
Unroofed, forsaken by the worshipper.
There lie memorial stones, whence time has gnawed
The graven legends, thrones of kings o'erturned,
The broken altars of forgotten gods,
Foundations of old cities and long streets
Where never fall of human foot is heard,
On all the desolate pavement. I behold
Dim glimmerings of lost jewels, far within
The sleeping waters, diamond, sardonyx,
Ruby and topaz, pearl and chrysolite,
Once glittering at the banquet on fair brows
That long ago were dust, and all around
Strewn on the surface of that silent sea
Are withering bridal wreaths, and glossy locks
Shorn from dear brows, by loving hands, and scrolls
O'erwritten, haply with fond words of love
And vows of friendship, and fair pages flung
Fresh from the printer's engine. There they lie
A moment, and then sink away from sight.

I look, and the quick tears are in my eyes,
For I behold in every one of these
A blighted hope, a separate history
Of human sorrows, telling of dear ties
Suddenly broken, dreams of happiness

Dissolved in air, and happy days too brief
That sorrowfully ended, and I think
How painfully must the poor heart have beat
In bosoms without number, as the blow
Was struck that slew their hope and broke
their peace.
Sadly I turn and look before, where yet
The Flood must pass, and I behold a mist
Where swarm dissolving forms, the brood of
Hope, 110
Divinely fair, that rest on banks of flowers,
Or wander among rainbows, fading soon
And reappearing, haply giving place
To forms of grisly aspect such as Fear
Shapes from the idle air—where serpents lift
The head to strike, and skeletons stretch forth
The bony arm in menace. Further on
A belt of darkness seems to bar the way, 118
Long, low, and distant, where the Life to come
Touches the Life that is. The Flood of Years
Rolls toward it near and nearer. It must pass
That dismal barrier. What is there beyond?
Hear what the wise and good have said. Be-
yond
That belt of darkness, still the Years roll on
More gently, but with not less mighty sweep.
They gather up again and softly bear
All the sweet lives that late were overwhelmed
And lost to sight, all that in them was good,
Noble, and truly great, and worthy of love—
The lives of infants and ingenuous youths,
Sages and saintly women who have made
Their households happy; all are raised and
borne 132
By that great current in its onward sweep,
Wandering and rippling with caressing waves
Around green islands with the breath
Of flowers that never wither. So they pass
From stage to stage along the shining course
Of that bright river, broadening like a sea.
As its smooth eddies curl along their way
They bring old friends together; hands are
clasped 140
In joy unspeakable; the mother's arms
Again are folded round the child she loved
And lost. Old sorrows are forgotten now,
Or but remembered to make sweet the hour
That overpays them; wounded hearts that
bled
Or broke are healed forever. In the room
Of this grief-shadowed present, there shall be
A Present in whose reign no grief shall gnaw
The heart, and never shall a tender tie 149
Be broken; in whose reign the eternal Change
That waits on growth and action shall pro-
ceed
With everlasting Concord hand in hand.

1876 1876

EARLY AMERICAN VERSE

Of the poetry of the United States different opinions have been entertained, and prejudice on the one side, and partiality on the other, have equally prevented a just and rational estimate of its merits. Abroad, our literature has fallen under unmerited contumely, from those who were but slenderly acquainted with the subject on which they professed to decide; and at home, it must be confessed, that the swaggering and pompous pretensions of many have done not a little to provoke and excuse the ridicule of foreigners. Either of these extremes exerts an injurious influence on the cause of letters in our country. To encourage exertion and embolden merit to come forward, it is necessary that they should be acknowledged and rewarded—few will have the confidence to solicit what has been withheld from claims as strong as theirs, or the courage to tread a path which presents no prospect but the melancholy wrecks of those who have gone before them. National gratitude—national pride—every high and generous feeling that attaches us to the land of our birth, or that exalts our characters as individuals, ask of us that we should foster the infant literature of our country, and that genius and industry, employing their efforts to hasten its perfection, should receive, from our hands, that celebrity which reflects as much honor on the nation which confers it as on those to whom it is extended. On the other hand, it is not necessary for these purposes—it is even detrimental to bestow on mediocrity the praise due to excellence, and still more so is the attempt to persuade ourselves and others into an admiration of the faults of favorite writers. We make but a contemptible figure in the eyes of the world, and set ourselves up as objects of pity to our posterity, when we affect to rank the poets of our own country with those mighty masters of song who have flourished in Greece, Italy and Britain. Such extravagant admiration may spring from a praiseworthy and patriotic motive, but it seems to us that it defeats its own object of encouraging our literature, by seducing those, who would aspire to the favor of the public, into an imitation of imperfect models, and leading them to rely too much on the partiality of their countrymen to overlook their deficiencies. Were our rewards to be bestowed only on what is intrinsically meritorious, merit alone would have any apology for appearing before the public. The poetical adventurer should be taught that it is only the productions of genius, taste and diligence that can find favor at the bar of criticism—that his writings are not to be applauded merely because they are written by an American, and are not decidedly bad; and that he must produce some more satisfactory evidence of his claim to celebrity than an extract from the parish register. To show him what we expect of him, it is necessary to point out the faults of his predecessors, and to commend their excellencies. He must be taught, as well what to avoid, as what to imitate. This is the only way of diffusing and preserving a pure taste, both among those who read and those who write, and, in our opinion, the only way of affording merit a proper and effectual encouragement.

It must however be allowed, that the poetry of the United States, though it has not reached that perfection to which some other countries have carried theirs, is yet even better than we could have been expected to produce, considering that our nation has scarcely seen two centuries since the first of its founders erected their cabins on its soil, that our literary institutions are yet in their infancy, and that our citizens are just beginning to find leisure to attend to intellectual refinement and indulge in intellectual luxury, and the means of rewarded intellectual excellence. For the first century after the settlement of this country, the few quaint and unskilful specimens of poetry which yet remain to us, are looked upon merely as objects of curiosity, are preserved only in the cabinet of the antiquary, and give little pleasure, if read without reference to the age and people which produced them. A purer taste began after this period to prevail—the poems of the Rev. John Adams, written in the early part of the eighteenth century, which have been considered as no bad specimen of the poetry of his time, are tolerably free from the faults of the generation that preceded him, and show the dawnings of an ambition of correctness and elegance. The poetical writings of Joseph Green, Esq., who wrote about the middle of the same century, have been admired for their humor and the playful ease of their composition.

But, previous to the contest which terminated in the independence of the United States, we can hardly be said to have had any national poetry. Literary ambition was not then frequent amongst us—there was little motive for it, and few rewards. We were contented with considering ourselves as participating in the literary fame of that nation, of which we were a part, and of which many of us were natives, and aspired to no separate distinction. And indeed we might well lay an equal claim, with those who remained on the British soil, to whatever glory the genius and learning as well as the virtue and bravery of other times reflected on the British name. These were qualities which ennobled our common ancestors; and though their graves were not with us, and we were at a distance from the scenes and haunts which were hallowed by their deeds, their studies, and their contemplations, yet we brought with us, and preserved all the more valuable gifts which they left to their posterity and to mankind—their illumination—their piety—their spirit of liberty—reverence for their memory and example and all the proud tokens of a generous descent.

Yet here was no theatre for the display of literary talent—the worshippers of fame could find no altars erected to that divinity in America, and he who would live by his pen must seek patronage in the parent country. Some men of taste and learning amongst us, might occasionally amuse their leisure with poetical trifles, but a country struggling with the difficulties of colonization, and possessing no superfluous wealth, wanted any other class of men rather than poets. Accordingly we find the specimens of American poetry, before this period, mostly desultory and occasional—rare and delicate exotics, cultivated only by the curious.

On our becoming an independent empire, a different spirit began to manifest itself, and the general ambition to distinguish ourselves as a nation was not without its effect on our literature. It seems to us, that it is from this time only that we can be said to have poets of our own, and from this period it is that we must date the origin of American poetry. About this time, flourished Francis Hopkinson, whose humorous ballad, entitled the Battle of the Kegs, is in most of our memories, and some of whose attempts, though deficient in vigor, are not inelegant. The keen and forcible invectives of Dr. Church, which are still recollected by his contemporaries, received an additional edge and sharpness from the exasperated feelings of the times. A writer in verse of inferior note was Philip Freneau, whose pen seems to have been chiefly employed on political subjects, and whose occasional productions, distinguished by a coarse strength of sarcasm, and abounding with allusions to passing events, which is perhaps their greatest merit, attracted in their time considerable notice, and in the year 1786 were collected into a volume. But the influence of that principle which awoke and animated the exertions of all who participated in the political enthusiasm of that time, was still more strongly exemplified in the Connecticut poets—Trumbull, Dwight, Barlow, Humphreys, and Hopkins—who began to write about this period. In all the productions of these authors, there is a pervading spirit of *nationality* and patriotism—a desire to reflect credit on the country to which they belonged, which seems, as much as individual ambition, to have prompted their efforts, and which at times gives a certain glow and interest to their manner.

McFingal, the most popular of the writings of the former of these poets, first appeared in the year 1782. This pleasant satire on the adherents of Britain in those times, may be pronounced a tolerably successful imitation of the great work of Butler—though, like every other imitation of that author, it wants that varied and inexhaustible fertility of allusion, which made all subjects of thought—the lightest and most abstruse parts of learning—every thing in the physical and moral world—in art or nature, the playthings of his wit. The work of Trumbull cannot be much praised for the purity of its diction. Yet perhaps great scrupulousness in this particular was not consistent with the plan of the author, and, to give the scenes of his poem their full effect, it might have been thought necessary to adopt the familiar dialect of the country and the times. We think his Progress of Dulness a more pleasing poem, as more finished, and more perfect in its kind, and though written in the same manner, more free from the constraint and servility of imitation. The graver poems of Trumbull contain some vigorous and animated declamation.

Of Dr. Dwight we would speak with all the respect due to talents, to learning, to piety, and a long life of virtuous usefulness—but we must be excused from feeling any high admiration of his poetry. It seems to us modelled upon a manner altogether too artificial and mechanical. There is something strained, violent, and out of nature, in all his attempts. His Conquest of Canaan will not secure immortality to its author. In this work the author has been considered by some as by no means happy in the choice of his fable—however this may be, he has certainly failed to avail himself of the advantages it offered him—his epic wants the creations and colorings of an inventive and poetical fancy—the charm, which, in the hands of genius, communicates interest to the simplest incidents, and something of the illusion of reality to the most improbable fictions. The versification is remarkable for its unbroken monotony. Yet it contains splendid passages, which, separated from the body of the work, might be admired, but a few pages pall both on the ear and the imagination. It has been urged in its favor that the writer was young—the poetry of his maturer years does not however seem to possess greater beauties or fewer faults. The late Mr. Dennie at one time exerted his ingenuity to render this poem popular with his countrymen; in the year 1800 he published, in the *Farmer's Museum*, a paper printed at Walpole, of which he was the editor, a series of observations and criticisms on the Conquest of Canaan, after the manner of Addison in those numbers of the *Spectator* which made Milton a favorite with the English people. But this attempt did not meet with success—the work would not sell, and loads of copies yet cumber the shelves of our booksellers. In the other poems of Dr. Dwight, which are generally obnoxious to the same criticisms, he sometimes endeavors to descend to a more familiar style, and entertains his reader with laborious attempts at wit, and here he is still unsuccessful. Parts of his Greenfield Hill, and that most unfortunate of his productions, the Triumph of Infidelity, will confirm the truth of this remark.

Barlow, when he began to write, was a poet of no inconsiderable promise. His Hasty Pudding, one of his earliest productions, is a good specimen of mock-heroic poetry, and his Vision of Columbus, at the time of its first appearance, attracted much attention and was hailed as an earnest of better things. It is no small praise to say, that when appointed by the General Assembly of Churches in Connecticut, to revise Watts' Version of the Psalms, and to versify such as were omitted in that work, he performed the task in a manner which made a near approach to the simplicity and ease of that poet, who, according to Dr. Johnson, "has done better than any body else what nobody has done well." In his maturer years, Barlow became ambitious of distinguishing himself and doing honor to his country, by some more splendid and important exertion of his talents, and, for this purpose, projected a national epic, in which was sung the Discovery of America, the successful struggle of the states in the defence of their liberties, and the exalted prospects which were opening before them. It is to be regretted that a design, so honorable and so generously conceived, should have failed. In 1807 appeared the Columbiad, which was his poem of the Vision of Columbus, much enlarged, and with such variations as the feelings and reflections of his riper age and judgment led him to make. The Columbiad is not, in our opinion, so pleasing a poem, in its present form, as in that in which it was originally written. The plan of the work is utterly destitute of interest, and that, which was at first sufficiently wearisome, has become doubly so by being drawn out to its present length. Nor are the additions of much value, on account of the taste in which they are composed. Barlow, in his later poetry, attempted to invigorate his style, but instead of drawing strength and salubrity, from the pure wells of ancient English, he corrupted and debased it with foreign infusions. The imposing but unchaste glitter, which distinguished the manner of Darwin and his imitators, appears likewise to have taken strong hold on his fancy, and he has not scrupled to bestow on his poem much of this meretricious decoration. But notwithstanding the bad taste in which his principal work is composed—notwithstanding he cannot be said to write with much pathos, or many of the native felicities of fancy, there is yet enough, in the poetry of Mr. Barlow to prove, that, had he fixed his eye on purer models, he might have excelled, not indeed in epic or narrative poetry, nor in the delineation of passion and feeling, but in that calm, lofty, sustained style, which suits best with topics of morality and philosophy, and for which the vigor and spirit of his natural manner, whenever he permits it to appear, shew him to have been well qualified. . . .

With respect to the prevailing style of poetry, at the present day, in our country, we apprehend that it will be found, in too many instances, tinged with a sickly and affected imitation of the peculiar manner of some of the late popular poets of England. We speak not of a disposition to enumerate whatever is beautiful and excellent in their writings,—still less would we be understood as intending to censure that sort of imitation which, exploring all the treasures of English poetry, culls from all a diction, that shall form a natural and becoming dress for the conceptions of the writer,—this is a course of preparation which every one ought to go through before he appears before the public—but we desire to set a mark on that servile habit of copying, which adopts the vocabulary of some favorite author, and apes the fashions of his sentences, and cramps and forces the ideas into a shape, which they would not naturally have taken, and of which the only recommendation is, not that it is most elegant or most striking, but that it bears some resemblance to the manner of him who is proposed as a model. This way of writing has an air of poverty and meanness—it seems to indicate a paucity of reading as well as perversion of taste—it might almost lead us to suspect that the writer had but one or two examples of poetical composition in his hands, and was afraid of expressing himself, except according to some formula which they might contain—and it ever has been, and ever will be, the resort of those who are sensible that their works need some factitious recommendation, to give them even a temporary popularity.

We have now given a brief summary of what we conceived to be the characteristic merits and defects of our most celebrated American poets. Some names, of which we are not at present aware, equally deserving of notice with those whom we have mentioned, may have been omitted—some we have passed over, because we would not willingly disturb their passage to that oblivion, towards which, to the honor of our country, they are hastening—and some elegant productions of later date we have not commented on, because we were unwilling to tire our readers with a discussion which they may think already exhausted.

On the whole there seems to be more good taste among those who read, than those who write poetry in our country. With respect to the poets whom we have enumerated, and whose merits we have discussed, we think the judgment pronounced on their works by the public will be found, generally speaking, just. They hold that station in our literature to which they are entitled, and could hardly be admired more than they are, without danger to the taste of the nation. We know of no instance in which great poetical merit has come forward, and finding its claims unallowed, been obliged to retire to the shade from which it emerged. Whenever splendid talents of this description shall appear, we believe that there will be found a disposition to encourage and reward them. The fondness for literature is fast increasing in our country—and if this were not the case, the patrons of literature have multiplied, of course, and will continue to multiply with the mere growth of our population. The popular English works of the day are reprinted in our country—they are dispersed all over the union—they are to be found in every body's hands—they are made the subject of every body's conversation. What should hinder our native works, if equal in merit, from meeting an equally favorable reception? . . .

1818 1818

From LECTURES ON POETRY

LECTURE FIRST

On the Nature of Poetry

. . . Of the nature of poetry different ideas have been entertained. The ancient critics seemed to suppose that they did something toward giving a tolerable notion of it by calling it a mimetic or imitative art, and classing it with sculpture and painting. Of its affinity with these arts there can be no doubt; but that affinity seems to me to consist almost wholly in the principles by which they all produce their effect, and not in the manner in which those principles are reduced to practice. There is no propriety in applying to poetry the term *imitative* in a literal and philosophical sense, as there is in applying it to painting and sculpture. The latter speak to the senses; poetry speaks directly to the mind. They reproduce sensible objects, and, by means of these, suggest the feeling or sentiment connected with them; poetry, by the symbols of words, suggests both the sensible object and the association. I should be glad to learn how a poem descriptive of a scene or an event is any more an imitation of that scene or that event than a prose description would be. A prose composition giving an account of the proportions and dimensions of a building, and the materials of which it is constructed, is certainly, so far as mere exactness is concerned, a better imitation of it than the finest poem that could be written about it. Yet who, after all, ever thought of giving such a composition the name of an imitation? The truth is, painting and sculpture are, literally, imitative arts, while poetry is only metaphorically so. The epithet as applied to poetry may be well enough, perhaps, as a figure of speech, but to make a metaphor the foundation of a philosophical classification is putting it to a service in which it is sure to confuse what it professes to make clear.

I would rather call poetry a suggestive art. Its power of affecting the mind by pure suggestion, and employing, instead of a visible or tangible imitation, arbitrary symbols, as unlike as possible to the things with which it deals, is what distinguishes this from its two sister arts. It is owing to its operation by means of suggestion that it affects different minds with such different degrees of force. In a picture or a statue the colors and forms employed by the artist impress the senses with the greatest distinctness. In painting, there is little—in sculpture, there is less—for the imagination to supply. It is true that different minds, according to their several degrees of cultivation, will receive different degrees of pleasure from the productions of these arts, and that the moral associations they suggest will be variously felt, and in some instances variously interpreted. Still, the impression made on the senses is in all cases the same; the same figures, the same lights and shades, are seen by all beholders alike. But the creations of Poetry have in themselves nothing of this precision and fixedness of form, and depend greatly for their vividness and clearness of impression upon the mind to which they are presented. Language, the great machine with which her miracles are wrought, is contrived to have an application to all possible things; and wonderful as this contrivance is, and numerous and varied as are its combinations, it is still limited and imperfect, and, in point of comprehensiveness, distinctness, and variety, falls infinitely short of the mighty and diversified world of matter and mind of which it professes to be the representative. It is, however, to the very limitation of this power of language, as it seems to me, that Poetry owes her magic. The most detailed of her descriptions, which, by the way, are not always the most striking, are composed of a few touches; they are glimpses of things thrown into the mind; here and there a trace of the outline; here a gleam of light, and there a dash of shade. But these very touches act like a spell upon the imagination and awaken it to greater activity, and fill it, perhaps, with greater delight than the best defined objects could do. The imagination is the most active and the least susceptible of fatigue of all the faculties of the human mind; its more intense exercise is tremendous, and sometimes unsettles the reason; its repose is only a gentle sort of activity; nor am I certain that it is ever quite unemployed, for even in our sleep it is still awake and busy, and amuses itself with fabricating our dreams. To this restless faculty—which is unsatisfied when the whole of its work is done to its hands, and which is ever wandering from the combination of ideas directly presented to it to other combinations of its own—it is the office of poetry to furnish the exercise in which it delights. Poetry is that art which selects and arranges the symbols of thought in such a manner as to excite it the most powerfully and delightfully. The imagination of the reader is guided, it is true, by the poet, and it is his business to guide it skilfully and agreeably; but the imagination in the mean time is by no means passive. It pursues the path which the poet only points out, and shapes its visions from the scenes and allusions which he gives. It fills up his sketches of beauty with what suits its own highest conceptions of the beautiful, and completes his outline of grandeur with the noblest images its own stores can furnish. It is obvious that the degree of perfection with which this is done must depend greatly upon the strength and cultivation of that faculty. For example, in the following passage, in which Milton describes the general mother passing to her daily task among the flowers:

> "With goddess-like demeanor forth she went
> Not unattended, for on her as queen
> A pomp of winning graces waited still."

The coldest imagination, on reading it, will figure to itself, in the person of Eve, the finest forms, attitudes, and movements of female loveliness and dignity, which, after all, are not described, but only hinted at by the poet. A warmer fancy, kindling at the delicate allusions in these lines, will not only bestow these attractions on the principal figure, but will fill the air around her with beauty, and people it with the airy forms of the graces; it will see the delicate proportions of their limbs, the lustre of their flowing hair, and the soft light of their eyes. Take, also, the following passage from the same poet, in which, speaking of Satan, he says:

"His face
Deep scars of thunder had entrenched, and care
Sat on his faded cheek—but under brows
Of dauntless courage and considerate pride
Waiting revenge; cruel his eye but cast
Signs of remorse and passion to behold
The fellows of his crime, the followers rather,
(Far other once beheld in bliss), condemned
For evermore to have their lot in pain."

The imagination of the reader is stimulated by the hints in this powerful passage to form to itself an idea of the features in which reside this strong expression of malignity and dejection—the brow, the cheek, the eye of the fallen angel, bespeaking courage, pride, the settled purpose of revenge, anxiety, sorrow for the fate of his followers, and fearfully marked with the wrath of the Almighty. There can be no doubt that the picture which this passage calls up in the minds of different individuals will vary accordingly as the imagination is more or less vivid, or more or less excited in the perusal. It will vary, also, accordingly as the individual is more or less experienced in the visible expression of strong passion, and as he is in the habit of associating the idea of certain emotions with certain configurations of the countenance.

There is no question that one principal office of poetry is to excite the imagination, but this is not its sole, nor perhaps its chief, province; another of its ends is to touch the heart, and, as I expect to show in this lecture, it has something to do with the understanding. I know that some critics have made poetry to consist solely in the exercise of the imagination. They distinguish poetry from pathos. They talk of pure poetry, and by this phrase they mean passages of mere imagery, with the least possible infusion of human emotion. I do not know by what authority these gentlemen take the term poetry from the people, and thus limit its meaning.

In its ordinary acceptation, it has, in all ages and all countries, included something more. When we speak of a poem, we do not mean merely a tissue of striking images. The most beautiful poetry is that which takes the strongest hold of the feelings, and, if it is really the most beautiful, then it is poetry in the highest sense. Poetry is constantly resorting to the language of the passions to heighten the effect of her pictures; and, if this be not enough to entitle that language to the appellation of poetical, I am not aware of the meaning of the term. Is there no poetry in the wrath of Achilles? Is there no poetry in the passage where Lear, in the tent of Cordelia, just recovered from his frenzy, his senses yet infirm and unassured, addresses his daughter as she kneels to ask his blessing?

"Pray do not mock me;
I am a very foolish, fond old man,
Fourscore and upward:
Not an hour more or less, and to deal plainly
I fear I am not in my perfect mind."

Is there no poetry in the remorse of Othello, in the terrible consciousness of guilt which haunts Macbeth, or the lamentations of Antony over the body of his friend, the devoted love of Juliet, and the self-sacrificing affection of Cleopatra? In the immortal work of Milton, is there no poetry in the penitence of Adam, or in the sorrows of Eve at being excluded from Paradise? The truth is, that poetry which does not find its way to the heart is scarcely deserving of the name; it may be brilliant and ingenious, but it soon wearies the attention. The feelings and the imagination, when skilfully touched, act reciprocally on each other. For example, when the poet introduces Ophelia, young, beautiful, and unfortunate, the wildness of frenzy in her eye, dressed with fantastic garlands of wild flowers, and singing snatches of old tunes, there is a picture for the imagination, but it is one which affects the heart. But when, in the midst of her incoherent talk, she utters some simple allusion to her own sorrows, as when she says,

"We know what we are, but know not what we
may be,"

this touching sentence, addressed merely to our sympathy, strongly excites the imagination. It sets before us the days when she knew sorrow only by name, before her father was slain by the hand of her lover, and before her lover was estranged, and makes us feel the heaviness of that affliction which crushed a being so gentle and innocent and happy.

Those poems, however, as I have already hinted, which are apparently the most affluent of imagery, are not always those which most kindle the reader's imagination. It is because the ornaments with which they abound are not naturally suggested by the subject, not poured forth from a mind warmed and occupied by it; but a forced fruit of the fancy, produced by labor, without spontaneity or excitement.

The language of passion is naturally figurative, but its figures are only employed to heighten the intensity of the expression; they are never introduced for their own sake. Important, therefore, as may be the office of the imagination in poetry, the great spring of poetry is emotion. It is this power that holds the key of the storehouse where the mind has laid up its images, and that alone can open it without violence. All the forms of fancy stand ever in its sight, ready to execute its bidding. Indeed, I doubt not that most of the offences against good taste in this kind of composition are to be traced to the absence of emotion. A desire to treat agreeably or impressively a subject by which the writer is himself little moved, leads him into great mistakes about the means of effecting his purpose. This is the origin of cold conceits, of prosing reflections, of the minute painting of uninteresting circumstances, and of the opposite extremes of tameness and extravagance. On the other hand, strong feeling is always a sure guide. It rarely offends against good taste, because it instinctively chooses the most effectual means of communicating itself to others. It gives a variety to the composition it inspires, with which the severest taste is delighted. It may sometimes transgress arbitrary rules, or offend against local associations, but it speaks a language which reaches the heart in all countries and all times. Everywhere are the sentiments of fortitude and magnanimity uttered in strains that brace our own nerves, and the dead mourned in accents that draw our tears.

But poetry not only addresses the passions and the imagination; it appeals to the understanding also. So far as this position relates to the principles of taste which lie at the foundation of all poetry, and by which its merits are tried, I believe its truth will not be doubted. These principles have their origin in the reason of things, and are investigated and applied by the judgment. True it is that they may be observed by one who has never speculated about them, but it is no less true that their observance always gratifies the understanding with the fitness, the symmetry, and the congruity it produces. To write fine poetry requires intellectual faculties of the highest order, and among these, not the least important, is the faculty of reason. Poetry is the worst mask in the world behind which folly and stupidity could attempt to hide their features. Fitter, safer, and more congenial to them is the solemn discussion of unprofitable questions. Any obtuseness of apprehension or incapacity for drawing conclusions, which shows a deficiency or want of cultivation of the reasoning power, is sure to expose the unfortunate poet to contempt and ridicule.

But there is another point of view in which poetry may be said to address the understanding—I mean in the direct lessons of wisdom that it delivers. Remember that it does not concern itself with abstract reasonings, nor with any course of investigation that fatigues the mind. Nor is it merely didactic; but this does not prevent it from teaching truths which the mind instinctively acknowledges. The elements of moral truth are few and simple, but their combinations with human actions are as innumerable and diversified as the combinations of language. Thousands of inductions resulting from the application of great principles to human life and conduct lie, as it were, latent in our minds, which we have never drawn for ourselves, but which we admit the moment they are hinted at, and which, though not abstruse, are yet new. Nor are these of less value because they require no laborious research to discover them. The best riches of the earth are produced on its surface, and we need no reasoning to teach us the folly of a people who should leave its harvest ungathered to dig for its ores. The truths of which I have spoken, when possessing any peculiar force or beauty, are properly within the province of the art of which I am treating, and, when recommended by harmony of numbers, become poetry of the highest kind. Accordingly, they abound in the works of the most celebrated poets. When Shakespeare says of mercy,

"it is twice blessed—
It blesses him that gives and him that takes,"

does he not utter beautiful poetry as well as unquestionable truth? There are passages also in Milton of the same kind, which sink into the heart like the words of an oracle. For instance:

"Evil into the mind of God or man
May come and go so unapproved, and leave
No spot or blame behind."

Take, also, the following example from Cowper, in which he bears witness against the guilt and folly of princes:

"War is a game which, were their subjects wise,
Kings should not play at. Nations would do well
To extort their truncheons from the puny hands
Of heroes whose infirm and baby minds
Are gratified with mischief, and who spoil,
Because men suffer it, their toy—the world."

I call these passages poetry, because the mind instantly acknowledges their truth and feels their force, and is moved and filled and elevated by them. Nor does poetry refuse to carry on a sort of process of reasoning by deducing one truth from another. Her demonstrations differ, however, from ordinary ones by requiring that each step should be in itself beautiful or striking, and that they all should carry the mind to the final conclusion without the consciousness of labor.

All the ways by which poetry affects the mind are open also to the prose-writer. All that kindles the imagination, all that excites emotion, all those moral truths that find an echo in our bosoms, are his property as well as that of the poet. It is true that in the ornaments of style the poet is allowed a greater license, but there are many excellent poems which are not distinguished by any liberal use of the figures of speech from prose writings composed with the same degree of excitement. What, then, is the ground of the distinction between prose and poetry? This is a question about which there has been much debate, but one which seems to me of easy solution to those who are not too ambitious of distinguishing themselves by profound researches into things already sufficiently clear. I suppose that poetry differs from prose, in the first place, by the employment of metrical harmony. It differs from it, in the next place, by excluding all that disgusts, all that tasks and fatigues the understanding, and all matters which are too trivial and common to excite any emotion whatever. Some of these, verse cannot raise into dignity; to others, verse is an encumbrance: they are, therefore, all unfit for poetry; put them into verse, and they are prose still.

A distinction has been attempted to be made between poetry and eloquence, and I acknowledge that there is one; but it seems to me that it consists solely in metrical arrangement. Eloquence is the poetry of prose; poetry is the eloquence of verse. The maxim that the poet is born and the orator made is a pretty antithesis, but a moment's reflection will convince us that one can become neither without natural gifts improved by cultivation. By eloquence I do not mean mere persuasiveness: there are many processes of argument that are not susceptible of eloquence, because they require close and painful attention. But by eloquence I understand those appeals to our moral perceptions that produce emotion as soon as they are uttered. It is in these that the orator is himself affected with the feelings he would communicate, that his eyes glisten, and his frame seems to dilate, and his voice acquires an unwonted melody, and his sentences arrange themselves into a sort of measure and harmony, and the listener is chained in involuntary and breathless attention. This is the very enthusiasm that is the parent of poetry. Let the same man go to his closet and clothe in numbers conceptions full of the same fire and spirit, and they will be poetry.

In conclusion, I will observe that the elements of poetry make a part of our natures, and that every individual is more or less a poet. In this "bank-note world," as it has been happily denominated, we sometimes meet with individuals who declare that they have no taste for poetry. But by their leave I will assert they are mistaken; they have it, although they may have never cultivated it. Is there any one among them who will confess himself insensible to the beauty of order or to the pleasure of variety—two principles, the happy mingling of which makes the perfection of poetic numbers? Is there any one whose eye is undelighted with beautiful forms and colors, whose ear is not charmed by sweet sounds, and who sees no loveliness in the returns of light and darkness, and the changes of the seasons? Is there any one for whom the works of Nature have no associations but such as relate to his animal wants? Is there any one to whom her great courses and operations show no majesty, to whom they impart no knowledge, and from whom they hide no secrets? Is there any one who is attached by no ties to his fellow-beings, who has no hopes for the future, and no memory of the past? Have they all forgotten the days and the friends of their childhood, and do they all shut their eyes to the advances of age? Have they nothing to desire and nothing to lament, and are their minds never darkened with the shadows of fear? Is it, in short, for these men that life has no pleasures and no pains, the grave no solemnity, and the world to come no mysteries? All these things are the sources of poetry, and they are not only part of ourselves, but of the universe, and will expire only with the last of the creatures of God.

1825 1884

LECTURE FOURTH

ON ORIGINALITY AND IMITATION

I propose in this lecture to say a few words on the true use and value of imitation in poetry. I mean not what is technically called the imitation of nature, but the studying and copying of models of poetic composition. There is hardly any praise of which writers in the present age, particularly writers in verse, are more ambitious than that of originality. This ambition is a laudable one, for a captivating originality is everything in the art. Whether it consists in presenting familiar things in a new and striking yet natural light, or in revealing secrets of emotion and thought which have lain undetected from the birth of literature, it is one of the most abundant and sure sources of poetic delight. It strikes us with the same sort of feeling as the finding of some beautiful spot in our familiar walks which we had never observed before, or the exhibition of some virtue in the character of a friend which we were ignorant that he possessed. It is of itself a material addition to the literary riches of the country in which it is produced; and it impresses something of its character upon that literature, which lasts as long as the productions in which it is contained are read and remembered.

Nor does it lose its peculiar charm with the lapse of time, for there is an enduring freshness and vividness in its pictures of nature, of action and emotion, that fade not with years. The poetry of Shakespeare, for instance, maintains its original power over the mind, and no more loses its living beauty by the lapse of ages than the universe grows dim and deformed in the sight of men.

It is not at all strange that a quality of so much importance to the poet should be sought after with great ardor, and that, in the zeal of pursuit, mistakes should sometimes be made as to that characteristic of it which alone is really valuable. Poets have often been willing to purchase the praise of it at the sacrifice of what is better. They have been led, by their overeagerness to attain it, into puerile conceits, into extravagant vagaries of imagination, into overstrained exaggerations of passion, into mawkish and childish simplicity. It has given birth to outrages upon moral principle, upon decency, upon common sense; it has produced, in short, irregularities and affectations of every kind. The grandiloquous nonsense of euphuism, which threatened to overlay and smother English literature in its very cradle, the laborious wit of the metaphysical poets who were contemporaries of Milton, the puling effeminacy of the cockney school, which has found no small favor at the present day—are all children of this fruitful parent.

It seems to me that all these errors arise from not paying sufficient attention to the consideration that poetry is an art; that, like all other arts, it is founded upon a series of experiments—experiments, in this instance, made upon the imagination and the feelings of mankind; that a great deal of its effect depends upon the degree of success with which a sagacious and strong mind seizes and applies the skill of others, and that to slight the experiences of our predecessors on this subject is a pretty certain way to go wrong. For, if we consider the matter a little more narrowly, we shall find that the most original of poets is not without very great obligations to his predecessors and his contemporaries. The art of poetry is not perfected in a day. It is brought to excellence, by slow degrees, from the first rude and imperfect attempts at versification to the finished productions of its greatest masters. The gorgeousness of poetic imagery, the curious felicities of poetic language, the music of poetic numbers, the spells of words that act like magic on the heart, are not created by one poet in any language, in any country. An innumerable multitude of sentiments, of illustrations, of impassioned forms of expression, of harmonious combinations of words, both fixed in books and floating in conversation, must previously exist either in the vernacular language of the poet or in some other which he has studied, and whose beauties and riches he seeks to transplant into his own, before he can produce any work which is destined to live.

Genius, therefore, with all its pride in its own strength, is but a dependent quality, and cannot put forth its whole powers nor claim all its honors without an amount of aid from the talents and labors of others which it is difficult to calculate. In those fortunate circumstances which permit its most perfect exercises, it takes, it is true, a pre-eminent station; but, after all, it is elevated upon the shoulders of its fellows. It may create something in literature, but it does not create all, great as its merit may be. What it does is infinitely less than what is done for it; the new treasures it finds are far less in value than the old of which it makes use. There is no warrant for the notion maintained by some, that the first poets in any language were great poets, or that, whatever their rank, they did not learn their art from the great poets in other languages. It might as well be expected that a self-taught architect would arise in a country whose inhabitants live in caves, and, without models or instruction, raise the majestic Parthenon and pile up St. Peter's into the clouds.

That there were poets in the English language before Chaucer, some of whom were not unworthy to be his predecessors, is attested by extant monuments of their verse; and, if there had not been, he might have learned his art from the polished poets of Italy, whom he studied and loved. Italy had versifiers before Dante, and, if they were not his masters, he at least found masters in the harmonious poets of a kindred dialect, the Provençal. In the Provençal language, the earliest of the cultivated tongues of modern Europe, there arose no great poet. The reason was that their literature had scarcely been brought to that degree of perfection which produces the finest specimens of poetry when the hour of its decline had come. It possessed, it is true, authors innumerable, revivers of the same art, enrichers of the same idiom, and polishers of the same system of versification, yet they never looked for models out of their own literature; they did not study the remains of ancient poetry to avail themselves of its riches; they confined themselves to such improvements and enlargements of the art as were made among themselves; and therefore their progress, though wonderful for the circumstances in which they were placed, was yet limited in comparison with that of those nations who have had access to the treasures they neglected.

In Roman literature there were poets before Lucretius, who is thought to have carried the poetry of the Latins to its highest measure of perfection; before even Ennius, who boasted of having introduced the melody of the hexameter into Latin verse. But Ennius and Lucretius and Horace and Virgil, and all the Roman poets, were, moreover, disciples of the Greeks, and sought to transfuse the spirit of the Grecian literature into their domestic tongue. Of the Greek poets we discover no instructors. The oldest of their poems which we possess, the writings of Homer, are also among the most perfect. Yet we should forget all reverence for probability were we to suppose that the art of poetry was born with him. The inferior and more mechanical parts of it must have been the fruit of long and zealous cultivation; centuries must have elapsed, and thousands of trials must have been made, before the musical and various hexameter could have been brought to the perfection in which we find it in his works. His poems themselves are full of allusions to a long antiquity of poetry. All the early traditions of Greece are sprinkled with the names of its minstrels, and the heroic fables of that country are probably, in a great measure, the work of these primitive bards. Orpheus, whose verse recalled the dead, Sinus and Musæus, whom Virgil, the disciple of Homer, seats in that elysium where he forgets to place his master, are examples of a sort of immortality conferred on mere names in literature, the dim but venerable shadows of the fathers of poetry, whose works have been lost for thousands of years. These were undoubtedly the ancient bards from whose compositions Homer kindled his imagination, and, catching a double portion of their spirit, emulated and surpassed them.

At the present day, however, a writer of poems writes in a language which preceding poets have polished, refined, and filled with forcible, graceful, and musical expressions. He is not only taught by them to overcome the difficulties of rhythmical construction, but he is shown, as it were, the secrets of the mechanism by which he moves the mind of his reader; he is shown ways of kindling the imagination and of interesting the passions which his own sagacity might never have discovered; his mind is filled with the beauty of their sentiments, and their enthusiasm is breathed into his soul. He owes much, also, to his contemporaries as well as to those who have gone before him. He reads their works, and whatever excellence he beholds in them, inspires him with a strong desire to rival it—stronger, perhaps, than that excited by the writings of his predecessors; for such is our reverence for the dead that we are willing to concede to them that superiority which we are anxious to snatch from the living. Even if he should refuse to read the writings of his brethren, he cannot escape the action of their minds on his own. He necessarily comes to partake somewhat of the character of their genius, which is impressed not only on all contemporary literature, but even on the daily thoughts of those with whom he associates. In short, his mind is in a great degree formed by the labors of others; he walks in a path which they have made smooth and plain, and is supported by their strength. Whoever would entirely disclaim imitation, and aspire to the praises of complete originality, should be altogether ignorant of any poetry written by others, and of all those aids which the cultivation of poetry has lent to prose. Deprive an author of these advantages, and what sort of poetry does any one imagine that he would produce? I dare say it would be sufficiently original, but who will affirm that it could be read?

The poet must do precisely what is done by the mathematician, who takes up his science where his predecessors have left it, and pushes its limits as much farther, and makes as many new applications of principles, as he can. He must found himself on the excellence already attained in his art, and if, in addition to this, he delights us with new modes of sublimity, of beauty, and of human emotion, he deserves the praise of originality and of genius. If he has nothing of all this, he is entitled to no other honor than belongs to him who keeps alive the practice of a delightful and beautiful art.

This very necessity, however, of a certain degree of dependence upon models in poetry has at some periods led into an opposite fault to the inordinate desire of originality. The student, instead of copying nature with the aid of knowledge derived from these models, has been induced to make them the original, from which the copy was to be drawn. He has been led to take an imperfect work—and all human works are imperfect—as the standard of perfection, and to dwell upon it with such reverence that he comes to see beauties where no beauties are, and excellence in place of positive defects. Thus the study of poetry, which should encourage the free and unlimited aspirations of the mind after all that is noble and beautiful, has been perverted into a contrivance to chill and repress them. It has seduced its admirers from an admiration of the works of God to an idolatry for the works of men; it has carried them from living and inexhaustible sources of poetic inspiration to drink at comparatively scanty and impure channels; it has made them to linger by the side of these instead of using them as guides to ascend to their original fountain.

It is of high importance, then, to inquire what are the proper limits of poetic imitation, or, in other words, by what means the examples and labors of others may be made use of in strengthening, and prevented from enfeebling, the native vigor of genius. No better rule has been given for this purpose than to take no particular poem nor poet, nor class of poets, as the pattern of poetic composition, but to study the beauties of all. All good poems have their peculiar merits and faults, all great poets their points of strength and weakness, all schools of poetry their agreements with good taste and their offences against it. To confine the attention and limit the admiration to one particular sort of excellence, not only tends to narrow the range of the intellectual powers, but most surely brings along with it the peculiar defects to which that sort of excellence is allied, and into which it is most apt to deviate. Thus, a poet of the Lake school, by endeavoring too earnestly after simplicity, may run into childishness; a follower of Byron, in his pursuit of energy of thought, and the intense expression of passion, may degenerate into abruptness, extravagance, or obscurity; a disciple of Scott, in his zeal for easy writing, may find himself inditing something little better than doggerel, or, at least, very dull and feeble verse; an imitator of Leigh Hunt, too intent on keeping up the vivacity and joyousness of the poetic temperament, may forget his common sense; and a poet of the school of Pope may write very polished, well-balanced verses with a great deal of antithesis and very little true feeling.

Still, these several schools have all their excellences; they have all some qualities to be admired and loved and dwelt upon. Let the student of poetry dwell upon them as long as he pleases, let him study them until they are incorporated into his mind, but let him give his admiration to no one of them exclusively. It is remarkable to what degree the great founders of the several styles of English poetry, even of the least lofty, varied, and original, have pursued this universal search after excellence. When Pope—brilliant, witty, harmonious, and, within a certain compass, a great master of language—had fixed the poetical taste of his age, we all know what a crowd of imitators arose in his train, and how rapidly poetry declined. But the imitators of Pope failed to do what Pope did. Great as was his partiality for the French school, and closely as he formed himself on the model of Boileau, he yet disdained not to learn much from other instructors. He went back for gems of thought and graces of style to the earlier writers of English verse—to the poets of the Elizabethan age, and, farther still, to the venerable Chaucer. He was a passionate admirer and a restorer of Shakespeare, and, by recommending him to the English people, prepared the way for the downfall of his own school, but not, I hope, for the oblivion of his own writings.

This relish of poetic excellence in all its forms, and in whatever school or style of poetry it is found, does not, I apprehend, lead to a less lively apprehension of the several merits of these styles, while at the same time it opens the eyes of the student to their several defects and errors. In this way the mind forms to itself a higher standard of excellence than exists in any of them—a standard compounded of the characteristic merits of all, and free from any of their imperfections. To this standard it will refer all their compositions; to this it will naturally aspire; and, by the contemplation of this, it will divest itself of that blind and idolatrous reverence for certain models of composition and certain dogmas of ancient criticism which are the death of the hopes and inspirations of the poet.

It is long since the authority of great names was disregarded in matters of science. Ages ago the schools shook themselves loose from the fetters of Aristotle. He no more now delivers the oracles of philosophy than the priests of Apollo deliver the oracles of religion. Why should the chains of authority be worn any longer by the heart and the imagination than by the reason? This is a question which the age has already answered. The genius of modern times has gone out in every direction in search of originality. Its ardor has not always been compensated by the discovery of its object, but under its auspices a fresh, vigorous, and highly original poetry has grown up. The fertile soil of modern literature has thrown up, it is true, weeds among the flowers, but the flowers are of immortal bloom and fragrance, and the weeds are soon outworn. It is no longer necessary that a narrative poem should be written on the model of the ancient epic; a lyric composition is not relished the more, perhaps not so much, for being Pindaric or Horatian; and it is not required that a satire should remind the reader of Juvenal. It is enough for the age if beautiful diction, glowing imagery, strong emotion, and fine thought are so combined as to give them their fullest effect upon the mind. The end of poetry is then attained, no matter by what system of rules.

If it were to be asked which is the more likely to produce specimens of poetry worthy of going down to posterity, which is the more favorable to the enlargement of the human mind and the vigorous action of all its faculties on the variety of objects and their relations by which it is surrounded—an age distinguished for too great carefulness of imitation, or an age remarkable for an excessive ambition of originality—I think that a wise decision must be in favor of the latter. Whatever errors in taste may spring from the zeal for new developments of genius and the disdain of imitation, their influence is of short duration. The fantastic brood of extravagances and absurdities to which they give birth soon die and are forgotten, for nothing is immortal in literature but what is truly excellent. On the other hand, such an age may and does produce poems worthy to live. The works of the early Italian poets were composed in such an age; the proudest monuments of English verse are the growth of such a spirit; the old poetry of Spain, the modern poetry of Germany, grew into beauty and strength under such auspices. Men walked, as they should ever do, with a confident step by the side of these ancient masters, of whom they learned this art; they studied their works, not that they might resemble, but that they might surpass them.

But one of the best fruits of such an age is the remarkable activity into which it calls the human intellect. Those things which are ours rather by memory than by the natural growth of the mind lie on its surface, already wrought into distinct shape, and are brought into use with little effort. But for the native conceptions of the mind, the offspring of strong mental excitement, it is necessary to go deeper and to toil more intensely. It is not without a vigorous exercise that the intellect searches for these among its stores, extricates them from the obscurity in which they are first beheld, ascertains their parts and detains them until they are moulded into distinctness and symmetry, and embodied in language.

But when once a tame and frigid taste has possessed the tribe of poets, when all their powers are employed in servilely copying the works of their predecessors, it is not only impossible that any great work should be produced among them, but the period of a literary reformation, of the awakening of genius, is postponed to a distant futurity. It is the quality of such a state of literature, by the imposing precision of its rules and the ridicule it throws on everything out of its own beaten track, to perpetuate itself indefinitely. The happy appearance of some extraordinary genius, educated under different influences than those operating on the age, and compelling admiration by the force of his talents; or, perhaps, some great moral or political revolution, by unsettling old opinions and familiarizing men to daring speculations—can alone have any effect to remove it. The mind grows indolent, or, at least, enfeebled, by the want of those higher exercises to which it was destined. At the same time, the spirit of poetry, as seen in its power of elevating the mind, of humanizing the affections, and expelling sordid appetites, is no longer felt, or only felt by a few, who conceal in their own bosoms the secret of its power over them.

1825 1884

From INTRODUCTION TO A LIBRARY OF POETRY AND SONG

There are two tendencies by which the seekers after poetic fame in our day are apt to be misled, through both the example of others and the applause of critics. One of these is the desire to extort admiration by striking novelties of expression; and the other, the ambition to distinguish themselves by subtilties of thought, remote from the common apprehension.

With regard to the first of these I have only to say what has been often said before, that, however favorable may be the idea which this luxuriance of poetic imagery and of epithet at first gives us of the author's talent, our admiration soon exhausts itself. We feel that the thought moves heavily under its load of garments, some of which perhaps strike us as tawdry and others as ill-fitting, and we lay down the book to take it up no more.

The other mistake, if I may so call it, deserves more attention, since we find able critics speaking with high praise of passages in the poetry of the day to which the general reader is puzzled to attach a meaning. This is often the case when the words themselves seem simple enough, and keep within the range of the Saxon or household element of our language. The obscurity lies sometimes in the phrase itself, and sometimes in the recondite or remote allusion. I will not say that certain minds are not affected by this, as others are by verses in plainer English. To the few it may be genuine poetry, although it may be a riddle to the mass of readers. I remember reading somewhere of a mathematician who was affected with a sense of sublimity by the happy solution of an algebraical or geometrical problem, and I have been assured by one who devoted himself to the science of mathematics that the phenomenon is no uncommon one. Let us beware, therefore, of assigning too narrow limits to the causes which produce the poetic exaltation of mind. The genius of those who write in this manner may be freely acknowledged, but they do not write for mankind at large.

To me it seems that one of the most important requisites for a great poet is a luminous style. The elements of poetry lie in natural objects, in the vicissitudes of human life, in the emotions of the human heart, and the relations of man to man. He who can present them in combinations and lights which at once affect the mind with a deep sense of their truth and beauty is the poet for his own age and the ages that succeed it. It is no disparagement either to his skill or his power that he finds them near at hand; the nearer they lie to the common track of the human intelligence, the more certain is he of the sympathy of his own generation, and of those which shall come after him. The metaphysician, the subtile thinker, the dealer in abstruse speculations, whatever his skill in versification, misapplies it when he abandons the more convenient form of prose and perplexes himself with the attempt to express his ideas in poetic numbers.

Let me say for the poets of the present day, that in one important respect they have profited by the example of their immediate predecessors; they have learned to go directly to nature for their imagery, instead of taking it from what had once been regarded as the common stock of the guild of poets. I have often had occasion to verify this remark with no less delight than surprise on meeting in recent verse new images in their untarnished lustre, like coins fresh from the mint, unworn and unsoiled by passing from pocket to pocket. It is curious, also, to observe how a certain set of hackneyed phrases, which Leigh Hunt, I believe, was the first to ridicule, and which were once used for the convenience of rounding out a line or supplying a rhyme, have disappeared from our poetry, and how our blank verse in the hands of the most popular writers has dropped its stiff Latinisms and all the awkward distortions resorted to by those who thought that by putting a sentence out of its proper shape they were writing like Milton.

1870 1871

JOHN GREENLEAF WHITTIER

THE DEMON'S CAVE

THE moon is bright on the rocky hill,
But the dwarfish pines are gloomy and still,
Fixed, motionless forms in the upper air,—
The moonlight rests o'er them but darkness is there—
Like the fitful play of the stormfire's light
On the black, wild clouds of an evil night,
Or the smile which sometimes quivers upon
The faded cheek of the sorrowing one—
A wasted light, a radiance lost
On the gloom which its kindly glow had crossed!

A dim cave yawns in the rude hill-side
Like the jaws of a monster opened wide,
Where a few wild bushes of thorn and fern
Their leaves from the breath of the night air turn,
And half with twining foliage cover
The mouth of that shadowy cavern over.
Above it—the rock hangs gloomy and high
Like a rent in the blue of the beautiful sky,
Which seems as it opens on either hand
Like some bright sea laving a desolate land.

Below it—a stream on its bed of stone
From a rift in the rock comes brawling down,
Telling forever the same wild tale
Of its loftier home to the lowly vale;—
And over its waters an oak is bending—
Its boughs like a skeleton's arms extending—
A shattered tree—by the lightning shorn
With trunk all sere and branches torn;
And the rocks beneath it blackened and rent
Tell where the path of the thunder went!

'Tis said that the cave is an evil place—
The chosen haunt of a fallen race—
That the midnight traveller oft hath seen
A red flame tremble its jaws between,
And lighten and quiver the boughs among
Like the fiery play of a serpent's tongue—
The sounds of fear from its chambers swell—
The ghostly gibber—the demon's yell,—
That bodiless hands at its portals wave;—
And hence they have named it the *Demon's Cave!*

It is strange how man to this spot hath lent
A terror which Nature never meant—
For none who wander with curious eye
This dim and shadowy cavern by—
Have seen in the sun or starlight aught
Which might not beseem so lonely a spot,—
The stealthy fox and shy racoon—
The night bird's wing in the shining moon—
The frog's low croak—, and, upon the hill
The steady chant of the whippoorwill.

And yet there is something to romance dear,
In this shadowy cave and its lingering fear,
Something which tells of another age—
Of the wizard's wand and the sybil's page—
Of the fairy ring, and the haunted glen—
Of the restless phantoms of murdered men—
Of the fears and visions of dreamy youth
Ere they pass away at the glance of truth;—
And I love even now to list the tale
Of the Demon's Cave and its haunted vale!

1831

TO WILLIAM LLOYD GARRISON

CHAMPION of those who groan beneath
Oppression's iron hand:
In view of penury, hate, and death,
I see thee fearless stand.
Still bearing up thy lofty brow,
In the steadfast strength of truth,
In manhood sealing well the vow
And promise of thy youth.

Go on, for thou hast chosen well;
On in the strength of God!
Long as one human heart shall swell
Beneath the tyrant's rod.
Speak in a slumbering nation's ear,
As thou hast ever spoken,
Until the dead in sin shall hear,
The fetter's link be broken!

I love thee with a brother's love,
  I feel my pulses thrill,
To mark thy spirit soar above
  The cloud of human ill.
My heart hath leaped to answer thine,
  And echo back thy words,
As leaps the warrior's at the shine
  And flash of kindred swords!

They tell me thou art rash and vain,
  A searcher after fame;
That thou art striving but to gain
  A long-enduring name;
That thou hast nerved the Afric's hand
  And steeled the Afric's heart,
To shake aloft his vengeful brand,
  And rend his chain apart.

Have I not known thee well, and read
  Thy mighty purpose long?
And watched the trials which have made
  Thy human spirit strong?
And shall the slanderer's demon breath
  Avail with one like me,
To dim the sunshine of my faith
  And earnest trust in thee?

Go on, the dagger's point may glare
  Amid thy pathway's gloom;
The fate which sternly threatens there
  Is glorious martyrdom!
Then onward with a martyr's zeal;
  And wait thy sure reward
When man to man no more shall kneel,
  And God alone be Lord!

1832 1838

TO ——

WITH A COPY OF WOOLMAN'S JOURNAL

"Get the writings of John Woolman by heart."
—*Essays of Elia.*

MAIDEN! with the fair brown tresses
  Shading o'er thy dreamy eye,
Floating on thy thoughtful forehead
  Cloud wreaths of its sky.

Youthful years and maiden beauty,
  Joy with them should still abide,—
Instinct take the place of Duty,
  Love, not Reason, guide,

Ever in the New rejoicing,
  Kindly beckoning back the Old,
Turning, with the gift of Midas,
  All things into gold,

And the passing shades of sadness
  Wearing even a welcome guise,
As, when some bright lake lies open
  To the sunny skies,

Every wing of bird above it,
  Every light cloud floating on,
Glitters like that flashing mirror
  In the self-same sun.

But upon thy youthful forehead
  Something like a shadow lies;
And a serious soul is looking
  From thy earnest eyes.

With an early introversion,
  Through the forms of outward things,
Seeking for the subtle essence,
  And the hidden springs,

Deeper than the gilded surface
  Hath thy wakeful vision seen,
Farther than the narrow present
  Have thy journeyings been.

Thou hast midst Life's empty noises
  Heard the solemn steps of Time,
And the low mysterious voices
  Of another clime.

All the mystery of Being
  Hath upon thy spirit pressed,—
Thoughts which, like the Deluge wanderer,
  Find no place of rest:

That which mystic Plato pondered,
  That which Zeno heard with awe,
And the star-rapt Zoroaster
  In his night-watch saw.

From the doubt and darkness springing
  Of the dim, uncertain Past,
Moving to the dark still shadows
  O'er the Future cast,

Early hath Life's mighty question
  Thrilled within thy heart of youth,
With a deep and strong beseeching:
  What and where is Truth?

Hollow creed and ceremonial,
  Whence the ancient life hath fled,
Idle faith unknown to action,
  Dull and cold and dead,

Oracles, whose wire-worked meanings
  Only wake a quiet scorn,—
Not from these thy seeking spirit
  Hath its answer drawn.

But, like some tired child at even,
  On thy mother Nature's breast,
Thou, methinks, art vainly seeking
  Truth, and peace, and rest.

O'er that mother's rugged features
  Thou art throwing Fancy's veil,
Light and soft as woven moonbeams,
  Beautiful and frail!

O'er the rough chart of Existence,
  Rocks of sin and wastes of woe,
Soft airs breathe, and green leaves tremble,
  And cool fountains flow.

And to thee an answer cometh
  From the earth and from the sky,
And to thee the hills and waters
  And the stars reply.

But a soul-sufficing answer
  Hath no outward origin;
More than Nature's many voices
  May be heard within.

Even as the great Augustine
  Questioned earth and sea and sky,
And the dusty tomes of learning
  And old poesy.

But his earnest spirit needed
  More than outward Nature taught;
More than blest the poet's vision
  Or the sage's thought.

Only in the gathered silence
  Of a calm and waiting frame,
Light and wisdom as from Heaven
  To the seeker came.

Not to ease and aimless quiet
  Doth that inward answer tend,
But to works of love and duty
  As our being's end;

Not to idle dreams and trances,
  Length of face, and solemn tone,
But to Faith, in daily striving
  And performance shown.

Earnest toil and strong endeavor
  Of a spirit which within
Wrestles with familiar evil
  And besetting sin;

And without, with tireless vigor,
  Steady heart, and weapon strong,
In the power of truth assailing
  Every form of wrong.

Guided thus, how passing lovely
  Is the track of Woolman's feet!
And his brief and simple record
  How serenely sweet!

O'er life's humblest duties throwing
  Light the earthling never knew,
Freshening all its dark waste places
  As with Hermon's dew.

All which glows in Pascal's pages,
  All which sainted Guion sought,
Or the blue-eyed German Rahel
  Half-unconscious taught:

Beauty, such as Goethe pictured,
  Such as Shelley dreamed of, shed
Living warmth and starry brightness
  Round that poor man's head.

Not a vain and cold ideal,
  Not a poet's dream alone,
But a presence warm and real,
  Seen and felt and known.

When the red right-hand of slaughter
  Moulders with the steel it swung,
When the name of seer and poet
  Dies on Memory's tongue,

All bright thoughts and pure shall gather
  Round that meek and suffering one,—
Glorious, like the seer-seen angel
  Standing in the sun!

Take the good man's book and ponder
  What its pages say to thee;
Blessed as the hand of healing
  May its lesson be.

If it only serves to strengthen
  Yearnings for a higher good,
For the fount of living waters
  And diviner food;

If the pride of human reason
  Feels its meek and still rebuke,
Quailing like the eye of Peter
  From the Just One's look!

If with readier ear thou heedest
  What the Inward Teacher saith,
Listening with a willing spirit
  And a childlike faith,—

Thou mayst live to bless the giver,
  Who, himself but frail and weak,
Would at least the highest welfare
  Of another seek;

And his gift, though poor and lowly
  It may seem to other eyes,
Yet may prove an angel holy
  In a pilgrim's guise.

1840

HAMPTON BEACH

The sunlight glitters keen and bright,
  Where, miles away,
Lies stretching to my dazzled sight
A luminous belt, a misty light,
Beyond the dark pine bluffs and wastes of sandy gray.

The tremulous shadow of the Sea!
  Against its ground
Of silvery light, rock, hill, and tree,
Still as a picture, clear and free,
With varying outline mark the coast for miles around.

On—on—we tread with loose-flung rein
  Our seaward way,
Through dark-green fields and blossoming grain,
Where the wild brier-rose skirts the lane,
And bends above our heads the flowering locust spray.

Ha! like a kind hand on my brow
  Comes this fresh breeze,
Cooling its dull and feverish glow,
While through my being seems to flow
The breath of a new life, the healing of the seas!

Now rest we, where this grassy mound
  His feet hath set
In the great waters, which have bound
His granite ankles greenly round
With long and tangled moss, and weeds with cool spray wet.

Good-by to Pain and Care! I take
  Mine ease today:
Here where these sunny waters break,
And ripples this keen breeze, I shake
All burdens from the heart, all weary thoughts away.

I draw a freer breath, I seem
  Like all I see—
Waves in the sun, the white-winged gleam
Of sea-birds in the slanting beam,
And far-off sails which flit before the south-wind free.

So when Time's veil shall fall asunder,
  The soul may know
No fearful change, nor sudden wonder,
Nor sink the weight of mystery under,
But with the upward rise, and with the vastness grow.

And all we shrink from now may seem
  No new revealing;
Familiar as our childhood's stream,
Or pleasant memory of a dream
The loved and cherished Past upon the new life stealing.

Serene and mild the untried light
  May have its dawning;
And, as in summer's northern night
The evening and the dawn unite,
The sunset hues of Time blend with the soul's new morning.

I sit alone; in foam and spray
  Wave after wave
Breaks on the rocks which, stern and gray,
Shoulder the broken tide away,
Or murmurs hoarse and strong through mossy cleft and cave.

What heed I of the dusty land
And noisy town?
I see the mighty deep expand
From its white line of glimmering sand
To where the blue of heaven on bluer waves
shuts down!

In listless quietude of mind,
I yield to all
The change of cloud and wave and wind;
And passive on the flood reclined,
I wander with the waves, and with them rise
and fall.

But look, thou dreamer! wave and shore
In shadow lie;
The night-wind warns me back once more
To where, my native hill-tops o'er,
Bends like an arch of fire the glowing sunset
sky.

So then, beach, bluff, and wave, farewell!
I bear with me
No token stone nor glittering shell,
But long and oft shall Memory tell
Of this brief thoughtful hour of musing by the
Sea.

1843

CASSANDRA SOUTHWICK

In 1658 two young persons, son and daughter of Lawrence Southwick of Salem, who had himself been imprisoned and deprived of nearly all his property for having entertained Quakers at his house, were fined for non-attendance at church. They being unable to pay the fine, the General Court issued an order empowering "the Treasurer of the County to sell the said persons to any of the English nation of *Virginia* or *Barbadoes*, to answer said fines." An attempt was made to carry this order into execution, but no shipmaster was found willing to convey them to the West Indies.

To the God of all sure mercies let my blessing
rise today,
From the scoffer and the cruel He hath plucked
the spoil away;
Yea, He who cooled the furnace around the
faithful three,
And tamed the Chaldean lions, hath set His
handmaid free!

Last night I saw the sunset melt through my
prison bars,
Last night across my damp earth-floor fell the
pale gleam of stars;
In the coldness and the darkness all through
the long night-time,
My grated casement whitened with autumn's
early rime.

Alone, in that dark sorrow, hour after hour
crept by;
Star after star looked palely in and sank adown
the sky;
No sound amid night's stillness, save that
which seemed to be
The dull and heavy beating of the pulses of the
sea;

All night I sat unsleeping, for I knew that on
the morrow
The ruler and the cruel priest would mock me
in my sorrow,
Dragged to their place of market, and bargained for and sold,
Like a lamb before the shambles, like a heifer
from the fold!

Oh, the weakness of the flesh was there,—the
shrinking and the shame;
And the low voice of the Tempter like whispers to me came:
"Why sit'st thou thus forlornly," the wicked
murmur said,
"Damp walls thy bower of beauty, cold earth
thy maiden bed?

"Where be the smiling faces, and voices soft
and sweet,
Seen in thy father's dwelling, heard in the
pleasant street?
Where be the youths whose glances, the summer Sabbath through,
Turned tenderly and timidly unto thy father's
pew?

"Why sit'st thou here, Cassandra?—Bethink
thee with what mirth
Thy happy schoolmates gather around the
warm, bright hearth;
How the crimson shadows tremble on foreheads white and fair,
On eyes of merry girlhood, half hid in golden
hair.

"Not for thee the hearth-fire brightens, not for thee kind words are spoken,
Not for thee the nuts of Wenham woods by laughing boys are broken;
No first-fruits of the orchard within thy lap are laid,
For thee no flowers of autumn the youthful hunters braid.

"O weak, deluded maiden!—by crazy fancies led,
With wild and raving railers an evil path to tread;
To leave a wholesome worship, and teaching pure and sound,
And mate with maniac women, loose-haired and sackcloth bound,—

"Mad scoffers of the priesthood, who mock at things divine,
Who rail against the pulpit, and holy bread and wine;
Sore from their cart-tail scourgings, and from the pillory lame,
Rejoicing in their wretchedness, and glorying in their shame.

"And what a fate awaits thee!—a sadly toiling slave,
Dragging the slowly lengthening chain of bondage to the grave!
Think of thy woman's nature, subdued in hopeless thrall,
The easy prey of any, the scoff and scorn of all!"

Oh, ever as the Tempter spoke, and feeble Nature's fears
Wrung drop by drop the scalding flow of unavailing tears,
I wrestled down the evil thoughts, and strove in silent prayer,
To feel, O Helper of the weak! that Thou indeed wert there!

I thought of Paul and Silas, within Philippi's cell,
And how from Peter's sleeping limbs the prison shackles fell,
Till I seemed to hear the trailing of an angel's robe of white,
And to feel a blessed presence invisible to sight.

Bless the Lord for all His mercies!—for the peace and love I felt,
Like dew of Hermon's holy hill, upon my spirit melt;
When "Get behind me, Satan!" was the language of my heart,
And I felt the Evil Tempter with all his doubts depart.

Slow broke the gray cold morning; again the sunshine fell,
Flecked with the shade of bar and grate within my lonely cell;
The hoar-frost melted on the wall, and upward from the street
Came careless laugh and idle word, and tread of passing feet.

At length the heavy bolts fell back, my door was open cast,
And slowly at the sheriff's side, up the long street I passed;
I heard the murmur round me, and felt, but dared not see,
How, from every door and window, the people gazed on me.

And doubt and fear fell on me, shame burned upon my cheek,
Swam earth and sky around me, my trembling limbs grew weak:
"O Lord! support Thy handmaid; and from her soul cast out
The fear of man, which brings a snare, the weakness and the doubt."

Then the dreary shadows scattered, like a cloud in morning's breeze,
And a low deep voice within me seemed whispering words like these:
"Though thy earth be as the iron, and thy heaven a brazen wall,
Trust still His loving-kindness whose power is over all."

We paused at length, where at my feet the sunlit waters broke
On glaring reach of shining beach, and shingly wall of rock;
The merchant-ships lay idly there, in hard clear lines on high,
Tracing with rope and slender spar their network on the sky.

And there were ancient citizens, cloak-wrapped and grave and cold,
And grim and stout sea-captains with faces bronzed and old,
And on his horse, with Rawson, his cruel clerk at hand,
Sat dark and haughty Endicott, the ruler of the land.

And poisoning with his evil words the ruler's ready ear,
The priest leaned o'er his saddle, with laugh and scoff and jeer;
It stirred my soul, and from my lips the seal of silence broke,
As if through woman's weakness a warning spirit spoke.

I cried, "The Lord rebuke thee, thou smiter of the meek,
Thou robber of the righteous, thou trampler of the weak!
Go light the dark, cold hearth-stones,—go turn the prison lock
Of the poor hearts thou hast hunted, thou wolf amid the flock!"

Dark lowered the brows of Endicott, and with a deeper red
O'er Rawson's wine-empurpled cheek the flush of anger spread;
"Good people," quoth the white-lipped priest, "heed not her words so wild,
Her Master speaks within her,—the Devil owns his child!"

But gray heads shook, and young brows knit, the while the sheriff read
That law the wicked rulers against the poor have made,
Who to their house of Rimmon and idol priesthood bring
No bended knee of worship, nor gainful offering.

Then to the stout sea-captains the sheriff, turning, said,—
"Which of ye, worthy seamen, will take this Quaker maid?
In the Isle of fair Barbadoes, or on Virginia's shore,
You may hold her at a higher price than Indian girl or Moor."

Grim and silent stood the captains; and when again he cried,
"Speak out, my worthy seamen!"—no voice, no sign replied;
But I felt a hard hand press my own, and kind words met my ear,—
"God bless thee, and preserve thee, my gentle girl and dear!"

A weight seemed lifted from my heart, a pitying friend was nigh,—
I felt it in his hard, rough hand, and saw it in his eye;
And when again the sheriff spoke, that voice, so kind to me,
Growled back its stormy answer like the roaring of the sea,—

"Pile my ship with bars of silver, pack with coins of Spanish gold,
From keel-piece up to deck-plank, the roomage of her hold,
By the living God who made me!—I would sooner in your bay
Sink ship and crew and cargo, than bear this child away!"

"Well answered, worthy captain, shame on their cruel laws!"
Ran through the crowd in murmurs loud the people's just applause.
"Like the herdsman of Tekoa, in Israel of old,
Shall we see the poor and righteous again for silver sold?"

I looked on haughty Endicott; with weapon half-way drawn,
Swept round the throng his lion glare of bitter hate and scorn;
Fiercely he drew his bridle-rein, and turned in silence back,
And sneering priest and baffled clerk rode murmuring in his track.

Hard after them the sheriff looked, in bitterness of soul;
Thrice smote his staff upon the ground, and crushed his parchment roll.
"Good friends," he said, "since both have fled, the ruler and the priest,
Judge ye, if from their further work I be not well released."

Loud was the cheer which, full and clear, swept round the silent bay,
As, with kind words and kinder looks, he bade me go my way;
For He who turns the courses of the streamlet of the glen,
And the river of great waters, had turned the hearts of men.

Oh, at that hour the very earth seemed changed beneath my eye,
A holier wonder round me rose the blue walls of the sky,
A lovelier light on rock and hill and stream and woodland lay,
And softer lapsed on sunnier sands the waters of the bay.

Thanksgiving to the Lord of life! to Him all praises be,
Who from the hands of evil men hath set His handmaid free;
All praise to Him before whose power the mighty are afraid,
Who takes the crafty in the snare which for the poor is laid!

Sing, O my soul, rejoicingly, on evening's twilight calm
Uplift the loud thanksgiving, pour forth the grateful psalm;
Let all dear hearts with me rejoice, as did the saints of old,
When of the Lord's good angel the rescued Peter told.

And weep and howl, ye evil priests and mighty men of wrong,
The Lord shall smite the proud, and lay His hand upon the strong.
Woe to the wicked rulers in His avenging hour!
Woe to the wolves who seek the flocks to raven and devour!

But let the humble ones arise, the poor in heart be glad,
And let the mourning ones again with robes of praise be clad.
For He who cooled the furnace, and smoothed the stormy wave,
And tamed the Chaldean lions, is mighty still to save!

1843

MEMORIES

A BEAUTIFUL and happy girl,
With step as light as summer air,
Eyes glad with smiles, and brow of pearl,
Shadowed by many a careless curl
Of unconfined and flowing hair;
A seeming child in everything,
Save thoughtful brow and ripening charms,
As Nature wears the smile of Spring
When sinking into Summer's arms.

A mind rejoicing in the light
Which melted through its graceful bower,
Leaf after leaf, dew-moist and bright,
And stainless in its holy white,
Unfolding like a morning flower:
A heart, which, like a fine-toned lute,
With every breath of feeling woke,
And, even when the tongue was mute,
From eye and lip in music spoke.

How thrills once more the lengthening chain
Of memory, at the thought of thee!
Old hopes which long in dust have lain,
Old dreams, come thronging back again,
And boyhood lives again in me;
I feel its glow upon my cheek,
Its fulness of the heart is mine,
As when I leaned to hear thee speak,
Or raised my doubtful eye to thine.

I hear again thy low replies,
I feel thy arm within my own,
And timidly again uprise
The fringèd lids of hazel eyes,
With soft brown tresses overblown.
Ah! memories of sweet summer eves,
Of moonlit wave and willowy way,
Of stars and flowers, and dewy leaves,
And smiles and tones more dear than they!

Ere this, thy quiet eye hath smiled
My picture of thy youth to see,
When, half a woman, half a child,
Thy very artlessness beguiled,
And folly's self seemed wise in thee;
I too can smile, when o'er that hour
The lights of memory backward stream,
Yet feel the while that manhood's power
Is vainer than my boyhood's dream.

Years have passed on, and left their trace,
  Of graver care and deeper thought;
And unto me the calm, cold face
Of manhood, and to thee the grace
  Of woman's pensive beauty brought.
More wide, perchance, for blame than praise,
  The school-boy's humble name has flown;
Thine, in the green and quiet ways
  Of unobtrusive goodness known.

And wider yet in thought and deed
  Diverge our pathways, one in youth;
Thine the Genevan's sternest creed,
While answers to my spirit's need
  The Derby dalesman's simple truth.
For thee, the priestly rite and prayer,
  And holy day, and solemn psalm;
For me, the silent reverence where
  My brethren gather, slow and calm.

Yet hath thy spirit left on me
  An impress Time has worn not out,
And something of myself in thee,
A shadow from the past, I see,
  Lingering, even yet, thy way about;
Not wholly can the heart unlearn
  That lesson of its better hours,
Not yet has Time's dull footstep worn
  To common dust that path of flowers.

Thus, while at times before our eyes
  The shadows melt, and fall apart,
And, smiling through them, round us lies
The warm light of our morning skies,—
  The Indian Summer of the heart!
In secret sympathies of mind,
  In founts of feeling which retain
Their pure, fresh flow, we yet may find
  Our early dreams not wholly vain!

1841 1843

EGO

WRITTEN IN THE ALBUM OF A FRIEND

On page of thine I cannot trace
The cold and heartless commonplace,
A statue's fixed and marble grace.

For ever as these lines I penned,
Still with the thought of thee will blend
That of some loved and common friend,

Who in life's desert track has made
His pilgrim tent with mine, or strayed
Beneath the same remembered shade.

And hence my pen unfettered moves
In freedom which the heart approves,
The negligence which friendship loves.

And wilt thou prize my poor gift less
For simple air and rustic dress,
And sign of haste and carelessness?

Oh, more than specious counterfeit
Of sentiment or studied wit,
A heart like thine should value it.

Yet half I fear my gift will be
Unto thy book, if not to thee,
Of more than doubtful courtesy.

A banished name from Fashion's sphere,
A lay unheard of Beauty's ear,
Forbid, disowned,—what do they here?

Upon my ear not all in vain
Came the sad captive's clanking chain,
The groaning from his bed of pain.

And sadder still, I saw the woe
Which only wounded spirits know
When Pride's strong footsteps o'er them go.

Spurned not alone in walks abroad,
But from the temples of the Lord
Thrust out apart, like things abhorred.

Deep as I felt, and stern and strong,
In words which Prudence smothered long,
My soul spoke out against the wrong;

Not mine alone the task to speak
Of comfort to the poor and weak,
And dry the tear on Sorrow's cheek;

But, mingled in the conflict warm,
To pour the fiery breath of storm
Through the harsh trumpet of Reform;

To brave Opinion's settled frown,
From ermined robe and saintly gown,
While wrestling reverenced Error down.

Founts gushed beside my pilgrim way,
Cool shadows on the greensward lay,
Flowers swung upon the bending spray.

And, broad and bright, on either hand,
Stretched the green slopes of Fairy-land,
With Hope's eternal sunbow spanned;

Whence voices called me like the flow,
Which on the listener's ear will grow,
Of forest streamlets soft and low.

And gentle eyes, which still retain
Their picture on the heart and brain,
Smiled, beckoning from that path of pain.

In vain! nor dream, nor rest, nor pause
Remain for him who round him draws
The battered mail of Freedom's cause.

From youthful hopes, from each green spot
Of young Romance, and gentle Thought,
Where storm and tumult enter not;

From each fair altar, where belong
The offerings Love requires of Song
In homage to her bright-eyed throng;

With soul and strength, with heart and hand,
I turned to Freedom's struggling band,
To the sad Helots of our land.

What marvel then that Fame should turn
Her notes of praise to those of scorn;
Her gifts reclaimed, her smiles withdrawn?

What matters it? a few years more,
Life's surge so restless heretofore
Shall break upon the unknown shore!

In that far land shall disappear
The shadows which we follow here,
The mist-wreaths of our atmosphere!

Before no work of mortal hand,
Of human will or strength expand
The pearl gates of the Better Land;

Alone in that great love which gave
Life to the sleeper of the grave,
Resteth the power to seek and save.

Yet, if the spirit gazing through
The vista of the past can view
One deed to Heaven and virtue true;

If through the wreck of wasted powers,
Of garlands wreathed from Folly's bowers,
Of idle aims and misspent hours,

The eye can note one sacred spot
By Pride and Self profanèd not,
A green place in the waste of thought,

Where deed or word hath rendered less
The sum of human wretchedness,
And Gratitude looks forth to bless;

The simple burst of tenderest feeling
From sad hearts worn by evil-dealing,
For blessing on the hand of healing;

Better than Glory's pomp will be
That green and blessed spot to me,
A palm-shade in Eternity!

Something of Time which may invite
The purified and spiritual sight
To rest on with a calm delight.

And when the summer winds shall sweep
With their light wings my place of sleep,
And mosses round my headstone creep;

If still, as Freedom's rallying sign,
Upon the young heart's altars shine
The very fires they caught from mine;

If words my lips once uttered still,
In the calm faith and steadfast will
Of other hearts, their work fulfil;

Perchance with joy the soul may learn
These tokens, and its eye discern
The fires which on those altars burn;

A marvellous joy that even then,
The spirit hath its life again,
In the strong hearts of mortal men.

Take, lady, then, the gift I bring,
No gay and graceful offering,
No flower-smile of the laughing spring.

Midst the green buds of Youth's fresh May,
With Fancy's leaf-enwoven bay,
My sad and sombre gift I lay.

And if it deepens in thy mind
A sense of suffering human-kind,—
The outcast and the spirit-blind;

Oppressed and spoiled on every side,
By Prejudice, and Scorn, and Pride,
Life's common courtesies denied;

Sad mothers mourning o'er their trust,
Children by want and misery nursed,
Tasting life's bitter cup at first;

If to their strong appeals which come
From fireless hearth, and crowded room,
And the close alley's noisome gloom,—

Though dark the hands upraised to thee
In mute beseeching agony,
Thou lend'st thy woman's sympathy;

Not vainly on thy gentle shrine,
Where Love, and Mirth, and Friendship twine
Their varied gifts, I offer mine.

1843

FORGIVENESS

My heart was heavy, for its trust had been
  Abused, its kindness answered with foul wrong;
So, turning gloomily from my fellow-men,
  One summer Sabbath day I strolled among
The green mounds of the village burial-place;
  Where, pondering how all human love and hate
  Find one sad level; and how, soon or late,
Wronged and wrongdoer, each with meekened face,
  And cold hands folded over a still heart,
Pass the green threshold of our common grave,
  Whither all footsteps tend, whence none depart,
Awed for myself, and pitying my race,
Our common sorrow, like a mighty wave,
Swept all my pride away, and trembling I forgave!

1846

MASSACHUSETTS TO VIRGINIA

The blast from Freedom's Northern hills, upon its Southern way,
Bears greeting to Virginia from Massachusetts Bay:
No word of haughty challenging, nor battle bugle's peal,
Nor steady tread of marching files, nor clang of horsemen's steel,

No trains of deep-mouthed cannon along our highways go;
Around our silent arsenals untrodden lies the snow;
And to the land-breeze of our ports, upon their errands far,
A thousand sails of commerce swell, but none are spread for war.

We hear thy threats, Virginia! thy stormy words and high
Swell harshly on the Southern winds which melt along our sky;
Yet not one brown, hard hand foregoes its honest labor here,
No hewer of our mountain oaks suspends his axe in fear.

Wild are the waves which lash the reefs along St. George's bank;
Cold on the shores of Labrador the fog lies white and dank;
Through storm, and wave, and blinding mist, stout are the hearts which man
The fishing-smacks of Marblehead, the sea-boats of Cape Ann.

The cold north light and wintry sun glare on their icy forms,
Bent grimly o'er their straining lines or wrestling with the storms;
Free as the winds they drive before, rough as the waves they roam,
They laugh to scorn the slaver's threat against their rocky home.

What means the Old Dominion? Hath she forgot the day
When o'er her conquered valleys swept the Briton's steel array?
How, side by side with sons of hers, the Massachusetts men
Encountered Tarleton's charge of fire, and stout Cornwallis, then?

Forgets she how the Bay State, in answer to the call
Of her old House of Burgesses, spoke out from Faneuil Hall?
When, echoing back her Henry's cry, came pulsing on each breath
Of Northern winds the thrilling sounds of "Liberty or Death!"

What asks the Old Dominion? If now her sons have proved
False to their fathers' memory, false to the faith they loved;

If she can scoff at Freedom, and its great charter spurn,
Must we of Massachusetts from truth and duty turn?

We hunt your bondmen, flying from Slavery's hateful hell;
Our voices, at your bidding, take up the bloodhound's yell;
We gather, at your summons, above our fathers' graves,
From Freedom's holy altar-horns to tear your wretched slaves!

Thank God! not yet so vilely can Massachusetts bow;
The spirit of her early time is with her even now;
Dream not because her Pilgrim blood moves slow and calm and cool,
She thus can stoop her chainless neck, a sister's slave and tool!

All that a sister State should do, all that a free State may,
Heart, hand, and purse we proffer, as in our early day;
But that one dark loathsome burden ye must stagger with alone,
And reap the bitter harvest which ye yourselves have sown!

Hold, while ye may, your struggling slaves, and burden God's free air
With woman's shriek beneath the lash, and manhood's wild despair;
Cling closer to the "cleaving curse" that writes upon your plains
The blasting of Almighty wrath against a land of chains.

Still shame your gallant ancestry, the cavaliers of old,
By watching round the shambles where human flesh is sold;
Gloat o'er the new-born child, and count his market value, when
The maddened mother's cry of woe shall pierce the slaver's den!

Lower than plummet soundeth, sink the Virginia name;
Plant, if ye will, your fathers' graves with rankest weeds of shame;
Be, if ye will, the scandal of God's fair universe;
We wash our hands forever of your sin and shame and curse.

A voice from lips whereon the coal from Freedom's shrine hath been,
Thrilled, as but yesterday, the hearts of Berkshire's mountain men:
The echoes of that solemn voice are sadly lingering still
In all our sunny valleys, on every wind-swept hill.

And when the prowling man-thief came hunting for his prey
Beneath the very shadow of Bunker's shaft of gray,
How, through the free lips of the son, the father's warning spoke;
How, from its bonds of trade and sect, the Pilgrim city broke!

A hundred thousand right arms were lifted up on high,
A hundred thousand voices sent back their loud reply;
Through the thronged towns of Essex the startling summons rang,
And up from bench and loom and wheel her young mechanics sprang!

The voice of free, broad Middlesex, of thousands as of one,
The shaft of Bunker calling to that of Lexington;
From Norfolk's ancient villages, from Plymouth's rocky bound
To where Nantucket feels the arms of ocean close her round;

From rich and rural Worcester, where through the calm repose
Of cultured vales and fringing woods the gentle Nashua flows,
To where Wachuset's wintry blasts the mountain larches stir,
Swelled up to Heaven the thrilling cry of "God save Latimer!"

And sandy Barnstable rose up, wet with the salt sea spray;
And Bristol sent her answering shout down Narragansett Bay!

Along the broad Connecticut old Hampden felt the thrill,
And the cheer of Hampshire's woodmen swept down from Holyoke Hill.

The voice of Massachusetts! Of her free sons and daughters,
Deep calling unto deep aloud, the sound of many waters!
Against the burden of that voice what tyrant power shall stand?
No fetters in the Bay State! No slave upon her land!

Look to it well, Virginians! In calmness we have borne,
In answer to our faith and trust, your insult and your scorn;
You've spurned our kindest counsels; you've hunted for our lives;
And shaken round our hearths and homes your manacles and gyves!

We wage no war, we lift no arm, we fling no torch within
The fire-damps of the quaking mine beneath your soil of sin;
We leave ye with your bondmen, to wrestle, while ye can,
With the strong upward tendencies and godlike soul of man!

But for us and for our children, the vow which we have given
For freedom and humanity is registered in heaven;
No slave-hunt in our borders,—no pirate on our strand!
No fetters in the Bay State,—no slave upon our land!

1842 1843

SONGS OF LABOR

DEDICATION

I WOULD the gift I offer here
Might graces from thy favor take,
And, seen through Friendship's atmosphere,
On softened lines and coloring, wear
The unaccustomed light of beauty, for thy sake.

Few leaves of Fancy's spring remain:
But what I have I give to thee,
The o'er-sunned bloom of summer's plain,
And paler flowers, the latter rain
Calls from the westering slope of life's autumnal lea.

Above the fallen groves of green,
Where youth's enchanted forest stood,
Dry root and mossèd trunk between,
A sober after-growth is seen,
As springs the pine where falls the gay-leafed maple wood!

Yet birds will sing, and breezes play
Their leaf-harps in the sombre tree;
And through the bleak and wintry day
It keeps its steady green alway,—
So, even my after-thoughts may have a charm for thee.

Art's perfect forms no moral need,
And beauty is its own excuse;
But for the dull and flowerless weed
Some healing virtue still must plead,
And the rough ore must find its honors in its use.

So haply these, my simple lays
Of homely toil, may serve to show
The orchard bloom and tasselled maize
That skirt and gladden duty's ways,
The unsung beauty hid life's common things below.

Haply from them the toiler, bent
Above his forge or plough, may gain
A manlier spirit of content,
And feel that life is wisest spent
Where the strong working hand makes strong the working brain.

The doom which to the guilty pair
Without the walls of Eden came,
Transforming sinless ease to care
And rugged toil, no more shall bear
The burden of old crime, or mark of primal shame.

A blessing now, a curse no more;
Since He, whose name we breathe with awe,
The coarse mechanic vesture wore,
A poor man toiling with the poor,
In labor, as in prayer, fulfilling the same law.

1850

THE SHOEMAKERS

Ho! workers of the old time styled
  The Gentle Craft of Leather!
Young brothers of the ancient guild,
  Stand forth once more together!
Call out again your long array,
  In the olden merry manner!
Once more, on gay St. Crispin's day,
  Fling out your blazoned banner!

Rap, rap! upon the well-worn stone
  How falls the polished hammer!
Rap, rap! the measured sound has grown
  A quick and merry clamor.
Now shape the sole! now deftly curl
  The glossy vamp around it,
And bless the while the bright-eyed girl
  Whose gentle fingers bound it!

For you, along the Spanish main
  A hundred keels are ploughing;
For you, the Indian on the plain
  His lasso-coil is throwing;
For you, deep glens with hemlock dark
  The woodman's fire is lighting;
For you, upon the oak's gray bark,
  The woodman's axe is smiting.

For you, from Carolina's pine
  The rosin-gum is stealing;
For you, the dark-eyed Florentine
  Her silken skein is reeling;
For you, the dizzy goatherd roams
  His rugged Alpine ledges;
For you, round all her shepherd homes,
  Bloom England's thorny hedges.

The foremost still, by day or night,
  On moated mound or heather,
Where'er the need of trampled right
  Brought toiling men together;
Where the free burghers from the wall
  Defied the mail-clad master,
Than yours, at Freedom's trumpet-call,
  No craftsmen rallied faster.

Let foplings sneer, let fools deride,
  Ye heed no idle scorner;
Free hands and hearts are still your pride,
  And duty done your honor.
Ye dare to trust, for honest fame,
  The jury Time empanels,
And leave to truth each noble name
  Which glorifies your annals.

Thy songs, Hans Sachs, are living yet,
  In strong and hearty German;
And Bloomfield's lay, and Gifford's wit,
  And patriot fame of Sherman;
Still from his book, a mystic seer,
  The soul of Behmen teaches,
And England's priestcraft shakes to hear
  Of Fox's leathern breeches.

The foot is yours; where'er it falls,
  It treads your well-wrought leather,
On earthern floor, in marble halls
  On carpet, or on heather.
Still there the sweetest charm is found
  Of matron grace or vestal's,
As Hebe's foot bore nectar round
  Among the old celestials!

Rap, rap!—your stout and bluff brogan,
  With footsteps slow and weary,
May wander where the sky's blue span
  Shuts down upon the prairie.
On Beauty's foot your slippers glance,
  By Saratoga's fountains,
Or twinkle down the summer dance
  Beneath the Crystal Mountains!

The red brick to the mason's hand,
  The brown earth to the tiller's,
The shoe in yours shall wealth command,
  Like fairy Cinderella's!
As they who shunned the household maid
  Beheld the crown upon her,
So all shall see your toil repaid
  With hearth and home and honor.

Then let the toast be freely quaffed,
  In water cool and brimming,—
"All honor to the good old Craft,
  Its merry men and women!"
Call out again your long array,
  In the old time's pleasant manner:
Once more, on gay St. Crispin's day,
  Fling out his blazoned banner!

1845 1845

THE HUSKERS

It was late in mild October, and the long autumnal rain
Had left the summer harvest-fields all green with grass again;
The first sharp frosts had fallen, leaving all the woodlands gay
With the hues of summer's rainbow, or the meadow-flowers of May.

Through a thin, dry mist, that morning, the sun rose broad and red,
At first a rayless disk of fire, he brightened as he sped;
Yet even his noontide glory fell chastened and subdued,
On the cornfields and the orchards and softly pictured wood.

And all that quiet afternoon, slow sloping to the night,
He wove with golden shuttle the haze with yellow light;
Slanting through the painted beeches, he glorified the hill;
And, beneath it, pond and meadow lay brighter, greener still.

And shouting boys in woodland haunts caught glimpses of that sky,
Flecked by the many-tinted leaves, and laughed, they knew not why;
And school-girls, gay with aster-flowers, beside the meadow brooks,
Mingled the glow of autumn with the sunshine of sweet looks.

From spire and barn looked westerly the patient weathercocks;
But even the birches on the hill stood motionless as rocks.
No sound was in the woodlands, save the squirrel's dropping shell,
And the yellow leaves among the boughs, low rustling as they fell.

The summer grains were harvested; the stubble-fields lay dry,
Where June winds rolled, in light and shade, the pale green waves of rye;
But still, on gentle hill-slopes, in valleys fringed with wood,
Ungathered, bleaching in the sun, the heavy corn crop stood.

Bent low, by autumn's wind and rain, through husks that, dry and sere,
Unfolded from their ripened charge, shone out the yellow ear;
Beneath, the turnip lay concealed, in many a verdant fold,
And glistened in the slanting light the pumpkin's sphere of gold.

There wrought the busy harvesters; and many a creaking wain
Bore slowly to the long barn-floor its load of husk and grain;
Till broad and red, as when he rose, the sun sank down, at last,
And like a merry guest's farewell, the day in brightness passed.

And lo! as through the western pines, on meadow, stream, and pond,
Flamed the red radiance of a sky, set all afire beyond,
Slowly o'er the eastern sea-bluffs a milder glory shone,
And the sunset and the moonrise were mingled into one!

As thus into the quiet night the twilight lapsed away,
And deeper in the brightening moon the tranquil shadows lay;
From many a brown old farm-house, and hamlet without name,
Their milking and their home-tasks done, the merry huskers came.

Swung o'er the heaped-up harvest, from pitchforks in the mow,
Shone dimly down the lanterns on the pleasant scene below;
The growing pile of husks behind, the golden ears before,
And laughing eyes and busy hands and brown cheeks glimmering o'er.

Half hidden, in a quiet nook, serene of look and heart,
Talking their old times over, the old men sat apart;
While up and down the unhusked pile, or nestling in its shade,
At hide-and-seek, with laugh and shout, the happy children played.

Urged by the good host's daughter, a maiden young and fair,
Lifting to light her sweet blue eyes and pride of soft brown hair,
The master of the village school, sleek of hair and smooth of tongue,
To the quaint tune of some old psalm, a husking-ballad sung.

THE CORN-SONG

Heap high the farmer's wintry hoard!
Heap high the golden corn!
No richer gift has Autumn poured
From out her lavish horn!

Let other lands, exulting, glean
The apple from the pine,
The orange from its glossy green,
The cluster from the vine;

We better love the hardy gift
Our rugged vales bestow,
To cheer us when the storm shall drift
Our harvest-fields with snow.

Through vales of grass and meads of flowers
Our ploughs their furrows made,
While on the hills the sun and showers
Of changeful April played.

We dropped the seed o'er hill and plain
Beneath the sun of May,
And frightened from our sprouting grain
The robber crows away.

All through the long, bright days of June
Its leaves grew green and fair,
And waved in hot midsummer's noon
Its soft and yellow hair.

And now, with autumn's moonlit eves,
Its harvest-time has come,
We pluck away the frosted leaves,
And bear the treasure home.

There, when the snows about us drift,
And winter winds are cold,
Fair hands the broken grain shall sift,
And knead its meal of gold.

Let vapid idlers loll in silk
Around their costly board;
Give us the bowl of samp and milk,
By homespun beauty poured!

Where'er the wide old kitchen hearth
Sends up its smoky curls,
Who will not thank the kindly earth,
And bless our farmer girls!

Then shame on all the proud and vain,
Whose folly laughs to scorn
The blessing of our hardy grain,
Our wealth of golden corn!

Let earth withhold her goodly root,
Let mildew blight the rye,
Give to the worm the orchard's fruit,
The wheat-field to the fly:

But let the good old crop adorn
The hills our fathers trod;
Still let us, for His golden corn,
Send up our thanks to God!

1847

THE REFORMER

All grim and soiled and brown with tan,
I saw a Strong One, in his wrath,
Smiting the godless shrines of man
Along his path.

The Church, beneath her trembling dome,
Essayed in vain her ghostly charm:
Wealth shook within his gilded home
With strange alarm.

Fraud from his secret chambers fled
Before the sunlight bursting in:
Sloth drew her pillow o'er her head
To drown the din.

"Spare," Art implored, "yon holy pile;
That grand, old, time-worn turret spare;"
Meek Reverence, kneeling in the aisle,
Cried out, "Forbear!"

Gray-bearded Use, who, deaf and blind,
  Groped for his old accustomed stone,
Leaned on his staff, and wept to find
    His seat o'erthrown.

Young Romance raised his dreamy eyes,
  O'erhung with paly locks of gold,—
"Why smite," he asked in sad surprise,
    "The fair, the old?"

Yet louder rang the Strong One's stroke,
  Yet nearer flashed his axe's gleam;
Shuddering and sick of heart I woke,
    As from a dream.

I looked: aside the dust-cloud rolled,
  The Waster seemed the Builder too;
Upspringing from the ruined Old
    I saw the New.

'Twas but the ruin of the bad,—
  The wasting of the wrong and ill;
Whate'er of good the old time had
    Was living still.

Calm grew the brows of him I feared;
  The frown which awed me passed away,
And left behind a smile which cheered
    Like breaking day.

The grain grew green on battle-plains,
  O'er swarded war-mounds grazed the cow;
The slave stood forging from his chains
    The spade and plough.

Where frowned the fort, pavilions gay
  And cottage windows, flower-entwined,
Looked out upon the peaceful bay
    And hills behind.

Through vine-wreathed cups with wine once red,
  The lights on brimming crystal fell,
Drawn, sparkling, from the rivulet head
    And mossy well.

Through prison walls, like Heaven-sent hope,
  Fresh breezes blew, and sunbeams strayed,
And with the idle gallows-rope
    The young child played.

Where the doomed victim in his cell
  Had counted o'er the weary hours,
Glad school-girls, answering to the bell,
    Came crowned with flowers.

Grown wiser for the lesson given,
  I fear no longer, for I know
That, where the share is deepest driven,
    The best fruits grow.

The outworn rite, the old abuse,
  The pious fraud transparent grown,
The good held captive in the use
    Of wrong alone,—

These wait their doom, from that great law
  Which makes the past time serve today;
And fresher life the world shall draw
    From their decay.

Oh, backward-looking son of time!
  The new is old, the old is new,
The cycle of a change sublime
    Still sweeping through.

So wisely taught the Indian seer;
  Destroying Seva, forming Brahm,
Who wake by turns Earth's love and fear,
    Are one, the same.

Idly as thou, in that old day
  Thou mournest, did thy sire repine;
So, in his time, thy child grown gray
    Shall sigh for thine.

But life shall on and upward go;
  Th' eternal step of Progress beats
To that great anthem, calm and slow,
    Which God repeats.

Take heart! the Waster builds again,—
  A charmèd life old Goodness hath;
The tares may perish, but the grain
    Is not for death.

God works in all things; all obey
  His first propulsion from the night:
Wake thou and watch! the world is gray
    With morning light!

1846

SONG OF SLAVES IN THE DESERT

WHERE are we going? where are we going,
  Where are we going, Rubee?
Lord of peoples, lord of lands,
Look across these shining sands,
Through the furnace of the noon,
Through the white light of the moon.

Strong the Ghiblee wind is blowing,
Strange and large the world is growing!
Speak and tell us where we are going,
Where are we going, Rubee?

Bornou land was rich and good,
Wells of water, fields of food,
Dourra fields, and bloom of bean,
And the palm-tree cool and green:
Bornou land we see no longer,
Here we thirst and here we hunger,
Here the Moor-man smites in anger:
Where are we going, Rubee?

When we went from Bornou land,
We were like the leaves and sand,
We were many, we are few;
Life has one, and death has two:
Whitened bones our path are showing,
Thou All-seeing, thou All-knowing!
Hear us, tell us, where are we going,
Where are we going, Rubee?

Moons of marches from our eyes
Bornou land behind us lies;
Stranger round us day by day
Bends the desert circle gray;
Wild the waves of sand are flowing,
Hot the winds above them blowing,—
Lord of all things! where are we going?
Where are we going, Rubee?

We are weak, but Thou art strong;
Short our lives, but Thine is long;
We are blind, but Thou hast eyes;
We are fools, but Thou art wise!
Thou, our morrow's pathway knowing
Through the strange world round us growing,
Hear us, tell us where are we going,
Where are we going, Rubee?

1847 1847

PROEM

I LOVE the old melodious lays
Which softly melt the ages through,
The songs of Spenser's golden days,
Arcadian Sidney's silvery phrase,
Sprinkling our noon of time with freshest morning dew.

Yet, vainly in my quiet hours
To breathe their marvellous notes I try;
I feel them, as the leaves and flowers
In silence feel the dewy showers,
And drink with glad still lips the blessing of the sky.

The rigor of a frozen clime,
The harshness of an untaught ear,
The jarring words of one whose rhyme
Beat often Labor's hurried time,
Or Duty's rugged march through storm and strife, are here.

Of mystic beauty, dreamy grace,
No rounded art the lack supplies;
Unskilled the subtle lines to trace,
Or softer shades of Nature's face,
I view her common forms with unanointed eyes.

Nor mine the seer-like power to show
The secrets of the heart and mind;
To drop the plummet-line below
Our common world of joy and woe,
A more intense despair or brighter hope to find.

Yet here at least an earnest sense
Of human right and weal is shown;
A hate of tyranny intense,
And hearty in its vehemence,
As if my brother's pain and sorrow were my own.

O Freedom! if to me belong
Nor mighty Milton's gift divine,
Nor Marvell's wit and graceful song,
Still with a love as deep and strong
As theirs, I lay, like them, my best gifts on thy shrine!

1847 1849

BARCLAY OF URY

Among the earliest converts to the doctrines of Friends in Scotland was Barclay of Ury, an old and distinguished soldier, who had fought under Gustavus Adolphus, in Germany. As a Quaker, he became the object of persecution and abuse at the hands of the magistrates and the populace. None bore the indignities of the mob with greater patience and nobleness of soul than this once proud gentleman and soldier. One of his friends, on an occasion of uncommon rudeness, lamented that he should be treated so harshly in his old age who had been so honored before. "I find more satisfaction," said Barclay, "as well as honor, in being thus insulted for my religious principles, than when, a few years ago, it was usual for the magistrates, as I passed the city of Aberdeen, to meet me on the road and conduct me to public entertainment in their hall, and then escort me out again, to gain my favor."

Up the streets of Aberdeen,
By the kirk and college green,
  Rode the Laird of Ury;
Close behind him, close beside,
Foul of mouth and evil-eyed,
  Pressed the mob in fury.

Flouted him the drunken churl,
Jeered at him the serving-girl,
  Prompt to please her master;
And the begging carlin, late
Fed and clothed at Ury's gate,
  Cursed him as he passed her.

Yet, with calm and stately mien,
Up the streets of Aberdeen
  Came he slowly riding;
And, to all he saw and heard,
Answering not with bitter word,
  Turning not for chiding.

Came a troop with broadswords swinging,
Bits and bridles sharply ringing,
  Loose and free and froward;
Quoth the foremost, "Ride him down!
Push him! prick him! through the town
  Drive the Quaker coward!"

But from out the thickening crowd
Cried a sudden voice and loud:
  "Barclay! Ho! a Barclay!"
And the old man at his side
Saw a comrade, battle-tried,
  Scarred and sunburned darkly;

Who with ready weapon bare,
Fronting to the troopers there,
  Cried aloud: "God save us,
Call ye coward him who stood
Ankle-deep in Lützen's blood,
  With the brave Gustavus?"

"Nay, I do not need thy sword,
Comrade mine," said Ury's lord;
  "Put it up, I pray thee:
Passive to His holy will,
Trust I in my Master still,
  Even though He slay me.

"Pledges of thy love and faith,
Proved on many a field of death,
  Not by me are needed."
Marvelled much that henchman bold,
That his laird, so stout of old,
  Now so meekly pleaded.

"Woe's the day!" he sadly said,
With a slowly shaking head,
  And a look of pity;
"Ury's honest lord reviled,
Mock of knave and sport of child,
  In his own good city!

"Speak the word, and, master mine,
As we charged on Tilly's line,
  And his Walloon lancers,
Smiting through their midst we'll teach
Civil look and decent speech
  To these boyish prancers!"

"Marvel not, mine ancient friend,
Like beginning, like the end,"
  Quoth the Laird of Ury;
"Is the sinful servant more
Than his gracious Lord who bore
  Bonds and stripes in Jewry?

"Give me joy that in His name
I can bear, with patient frame,
  All these vain ones offer;
While for them He suffereth long,
Shall I answer wrong with wrong,
  Scoffing with the scoffer?

"Happier I, with loss of all,
Hunted, outlawed, held in thrall,
  With few friends to greet me,
Than when reeve and squire were seen,
Riding out from Aberdeen,
  With bared heads to meet me.

"When each goodwife, o'er and o'er,
Blessed me as I passed her door;
  And the snooded daughter,

Through her casement glancing down,
Smiled on him who bore renown
From red fields of slaughter.

"Hard to feel the stranger's scoff,
Hard the old friend's falling off,
Hard to learn forgiving;
But the Lord His own rewards,
And His love with theirs accords,
Warm and fresh and living.

"Through this dark and stormy night
Faith beholds a feeble light
Up the blackness streaking;
Knowing God's own time is best,
In a patient hope I rest
For the full day-breaking!"

So the Laird of Ury said,
Turning slow his horse's head
Towards the Tolbooth prison,
Where, through iron gates, he heard
Poor disciples of the Word
Preach of Christ arisen!

Not in vain, Confessor old,
Unto us the tale is told
Of thy day of trial;
Every age on him who strays
From its broad and beaten ways
Pours its seven-fold vial.

Happy he whose inward ear
Angel comfortings can hear,
O'er the rabble's laughter;
And while Hatred's fagots burn,
Glimpses through the smoke discern
Of the good hereafter.

Knowing this, that never yet
Share of Truth was vainly set
In the world's wide fallow;
After hands shall sow the seed,
After hands from hill and mead
Reap the harvests yellow.

Thus, with somewhat of the Seer,
Must the moral pioneer
From the Future borrow;
Clothe the waste with dreams of grain,
And, on midnight's sky of rain,
Paint the golden morrow!

1847 1847

WHAT THE VOICE SAID

MADDENED by Earth's wrong and evil,
"Lord!" I cried in sudden ire,
"From Thy right hand, clothed with thunder,
Shake the bolted fire!

"Love is lost, and Faith is dying;
With the brute the man is sold;
And the dropping blood of labor
Hardens into gold.

"Here the dying wail of Famine,
There the battle's groan of pain;
And, in silence, smooth-faced Mammon
Reaping men like grain.

" 'Where is God, that we should fear Him?'
Thus the earth-born Titans say;
'God! if Thou art living, hear us!'
Thus the weak ones pray."

"Thou, the patient Heaven upbraiding,"
Spake a solemn Voice within;
"Weary of our Lord's forbearance,
Art thou free from sin?

"Fearless brow to Him uplifting,
Canst thou for His thunders call,
Knowing that to guilt's attraction
Evermore they fall?

"Know'st thou not all germs of evil
In thy heart await their time?
Not thyself, but God's restraining,
Stays their growth of crime.

"Couldst thou boast, O child of weakness!
O'er the sons of wrong and strife,
Were their strong temptations planted
In thy path of life?

"Thou hast seen two streamlets gushing
From one fountain, clear and free,
But by widely varying channels
Searching for the sea.

"Glideth one through greenest valleys,
Kissing them with lips still sweet;
One, mad roaring down the mountains,
Stagnates at their feet.

"Is it choice whereby the Parsee
Kneels before his mother's fire?
In his black tent did the Tartar
Choose his wandering sire?

"He alone, whose hand is bounding
Human power and human will,
Looking through each soul's surrounding,
Knows its good or ill.

"For thyself, while wrong and sorrow
Make to thee their strong appeal,
Coward wert thou not to utter
What the heart must feel.

"Earnest words must needs be spoken
When the warm heart bleeds or burns
With its scorn of wrong, or pity
For the wronged, by turns.

"But, by all thy nature's weakness,
Hidden faults and follies known,
Be thou, in rebuking evil,
Conscious of thine own.

"Not the less shall stern-eyed Duty
To thy lips her trumpet set,
But with harsher blasts shall mingle
Wailings of regret."

Cease not, Voice of holy speaking,
Teacher sent of God, be near,
Whispering through the day's cool silence,
Let my spirit hear!

So, when thoughts of evil-doers
Waken scorn, or hatred move,
Shall a mournful fellow-feeling
Temper all with love.

1847 1847

MY SOUL AND I

STAND still, my soul, in the silent dark
I would question thee,
Alone in the shadow drear and stark
With God and me!

What, my soul, was thy errand here?
Was it mirth or ease,
Or heaping up dust from year to year?
"Nay, none of these!"

Speak, soul, aright in His holy sight
Whose eye looks still
And steadily on thee through the night:
"To do His will!"

What hast thou done, O soul of mine,
That thou tremblest so?
Hast thou wrought His task, and kept the line
He bade thee go?

What, silent all! art sad of cheer?
Art fearful now?
When God seemed far and men were near,
How brave wert thou!

Aha! thou tremblest!—well I see
Thou'rt craven grown.
Is it so hard with God and me
To stand alone?

Summon thy sunshine bravery back,
O wretched sprite!
Let me hear thy voice through this deep and black
Abysmal night.

What hast thou wrought for Right and Truth,
For God and Man,
From the golden hours of bright-eyed youth
To life's mid span?

Ah, soul of mine, thy tones I hear,
But weak and low,
Like far sad murmurs on my ear
They come and go.

"I have wrestled stoutly with the Wrong,
And borne the Right
From beneath the footfall of the throng
To life and light.

"Wherever Freedom shivered a chain,
God speed, quoth I;
To Error amidst her shouting train
I gave the lie."

Ah, soul of mine! ah, soul of mine!
Thy deeds are well:
Were they wrought for Truth's sake or for thine?
My soul, pray tell.

"Of all the work my hand hath wrought
Beneath the sky,
Save a place in kindly human thought,
No gain have I."

Go to, go to! for thy very self
Thy deeds were done:
Thou for fame, the miser for pelf,
Your end is one!

And where art thou going, soul of mine?
Canst see the end?
And whither this troubled life of thine
Evermore doth tend?

What daunts thee now? what shakes thee so?
My sad soul, say.
"I see a cloud like a curtain low
Hang o'er my way.

"Whither I go I cannot tell:
That cloud hangs black,
High as the heaven and deep as hell
Across my track.

"I see its shadow coldly enwrap
The souls before.
Sadly they enter it, step by step,
To return no more.

"They shrink, they shudder, dear God! they kneel
To Thee in prayer.
They shut their eyes on the cloud, but feel
That it still is there.

"In vain they turn from the dread Before
To the Known and Gone;
For while gazing behind them evermore
Their feet glide on.

"Yet, at times, I see upon sweet pale faces
A light begin
To tremble, as if from holy places
And shrines within.

"And at times methinks their cold lips move
With hymn and prayer,
As if somewhat of awe, but more of love
And hope were there.

"I call on the souls who have left the light
To reveal their lot;
I bend mine ear to that wall of night,
And they answer not.

"But I hear around me sighs of pain
And the cry of fear,
And a sound like the slow sad dropping of rain,
Each drop a tear!

"Ah, the cloud is dark, and day by day
I am moving thither:
I must pass beneath it on my way—
God pity me!—whither?"

Ah, soul of mine! so brave and wise
In the life-storm loud,
Fronting so calmly all human eyes
In the sunlit crowd!

Now standing apart with God and me
Thou art weakness all,
Gazing vainly after the things to be
Through Death's dread wall.

But never for this, never for this
Was thy being lent;
For the craven's fear is but selfishness,
Like his merriment.

Folly and Fear are sisters twain:
One closing her eyes,
The other peopling the dark inane
With spectral lies.

Know well, my soul, God's hand controls
Whate'er thou fearest;
Round Him in calmest music rolls
Whate'er thou hearest.

What to thee is shadow, to Him is day,
And the end He knoweth,
And not on a blind and aimless way
The spirit goeth.

Man sees no future,—a phantom show
Is alone before him;
Past Time is dead, and the grasses grow,
And flowers bloom o'er him.

Nothing before, nothing behind;
The steps of Faith
Fall on the seeming void, and find
The rock beneath.

The Present, the Present is all thou hast
For thy sure possessing;
Like the patriarch's angel hold it fast
Till it gives its blessing.

Why fear the night? why shrink from Death,
That phantom wan?
There is nothing in heaven or earth beneath
Save God and man.

Peopling the shadows we turn from Him
And from one another;
All is spectral and vague and dim
Save God and our brother!

Like warp and woof all destinies
Are woven fast,
Linked in sympathy like the keys
Of an organ vast.

Pluck one thread, and the web ye mar;
Break but one
Of a thousand keys, and the paining jar
Through all will run.

O restless spirit! wherefore strain
Beyond thy sphere?
Heaven and hell, with their joy and pain,
Are now and here.

Back to thyself is measured well
All thou hast given;
Thy neighbor's wrong is thy present hell,
His bliss, thy heaven.

And in life, in death, in dark and light,
All are in God's care:
Sound the black abyss, pierce the deep of night,
And He is there!

All which is real now remaineth,
And fadeth never:
The hand which upholds it now sustaineth
The soul forever.

Leaning on Him, make with reverent meekness
His own thy will,
And with strength from Him shall thy utter weakness
Life's task fulfil;

And that cloud itself, which now before thee
Lies dark in view,
Shall with beams of light from the inner glory
Be stricken through.

And like meadow mist through autumn's dawn
Uprolling thin,
Its thickest folds when about thee drawn
Let sunlight in.

Then of what is to be, and of what is done,
Why queriest thou?
The past and the time to be are one,
And both are now!

1847

WORSHIP

Pure religion and undefiled before God and the Father is this, To visit the fatherless and widows in their affliction, and to keep himself unspotted from the world.—James i. 27.

The Pagan's myths through marble lips are spoken,
And ghosts of old Beliefs still flit and moan
Round fane and altar overthrown and broken,
O'er tree-grown barrow and gray ring of stone.

Blind Faith had martyrs in those old high places,
The Syrian hill grove and the Druid's wood,
With mothers offering, to the Fiend's embraces,
Bone of their bone, and blood of their own blood.

Red altars, kindling through that night of error,
Smoked with warm blood beneath the cruel eye
Of lawless Power and sanguinary Terror,
Throned on the circle of a pitiless sky;

Beneath whose baleful shadow, overcasting
All heaven above, and blighting earth below,
The scourge grew red, the lip grew pale with fasting,
And man's oblation was his fear and woe!

Then through great temples swelled the dismal moaning
Of dirge-like music and sepulchral prayer;
Pale wizard priests, o'er occult symbols droning,
Swung their white censers in the burdened air:

As if the pomp of rituals, and the savor
Of gums and spices could the Unseen One please;
As if His ear could bend, with childish favor,
To the poor flattery of the organ keys!

Feet red from war-fields trod the church aisles holy,
With trembling reverence: and the oppressor there,

Kneeling before his priest, abased and lowly,
  Crushed human hearts beneath his knee of
    prayer.

Not such the service the benignant Father
  Requireth at His earthly children's hands:
Not the poor offering of vain rites, but rather
  The simple duty man from man demands.

For Earth He asks it: the full joy of heaven
  Knoweth no change of waning or increase;
The great heart of the Infinite beats even,
  Untroubled flows the river of His peace.

He asks no taper lights, on high surrounding
  The priestly altar and the saintly grave,
No dolorous chant nor organ music sounding,
  Nor incense clouding up the twilight nave.

For he whom Jesus loved hath truly spoken:
  The holier worship which he deigns to bless
Restores the lost, and binds the spirit broken,
  And feeds the widow and the fatherless!

Types of our human weakness and our sorrow!
  Who lives unhaunted by his loved ones
    dead?
Who, with vain longing, seeketh not to bor-
    row
  From stranger eyes the home lights which
    have fled?

O brother man! fold to thy heart thy brother;
  Where pity dwells, the peace of God is
    there;
To worship rightly is to love each other,
  Each smile a hymn, each kindly deed a
    prayer.

Follow with reverent steps the great example
  Of Him whose holy work was "doing
    good;"
So shall the wide earth seem our Father's
    temple,
  Each loving life a psalm of gratitude.

Then shall all shackles fall; the stormy clan-
    gor
  Of wild war music o'er the earth shall cease;
Love shall tread out the baleful fire of anger,
  And in its ashes plant the tree of peace!

1848 1848

THE POOR VOTER ON ELECTION DAY

The proudest now is but my peer,
  The highest not more high;
Today, of all the weary year,
  A king of men am I.
Today alike are great and small,
  The nameless and the known;
My palace is the people's hall,
  The ballot-box my throne!

Who serves today upon the list
  Beside the served shall stand;
Alike the brown and wrinkled fist,
  The gloved and dainty hand!
The rich is level with the poor,
  The weak is strong today;
And sleekest broadcloth counts no more
  Than homespun frock of gray.

Today let pomp and vain pretence
  My stubborn right abide;
I set a plain man's common sense
  Against the pedant's pride.
Today shall simple manhood try
  The strength of gold and land;
The wide world has not wealth to buy
  The power in my right hand!

While there's a grief to seek redress,
  Or balance to adjust,
Where weighs our living manhood less
  Than Mammon's vilest dust,—
While there's a right to need my vote,
  A wrong to sweep away,
Up! clouted knee and ragged coat!
  A man's a man today!

1848 1852

ICHABOD

So fallen! so lost! the light withdrawn
  Which once he wore!
The glory from his gray hairs gone
  Forevermore!

Revile him not, the Tempter hath
  A snare for all;
And pitying tears, not scorn and wrath,
  Befit his fall!

Oh, dumb be passion's stormy rage,
When he who might
Have lighted up and led his age,
Falls back in night.

Scorn! would the angels laugh, to mark
A bright soul driven,
Fiend-goaded, down the endless dark,
From hope and heaven!

Let not the land once proud of him
Insult him now,
Nor brand with deeper shame his dim,
Dishonored brow.

But let its humbled sons, instead,
From sea to lake,
A long lament, as for the dead,
In sadness make.

Of all we loved and honored, naught
Save power remains;
A fallen angel's pride of thought,
Still strong in chains.

All else is gone; from those great eyes
The soul has fled:
When faith is lost, when honor dies,
The man is dead!

Then pay the reverence of old days
To his dead fame;
Walk backward, with averted gaze,
And hide the shame!

1850 1850

WORDSWORTH

WRITTEN ON A BLANK LEAF OF HIS MEMOIRS

DEAR friends, who read the world aright,
And in its common forms discern
A beauty and a harmony
The many never learn!

Kindred in soul of him who found
In simple flower and leaf and stone
The impulse of the sweetest lays
Our Saxon tongue has known,—

Accept this record of a life
As sweet and pure, as calm and good,
As a long day of blandest June
In green field and in wood.

How welcome to our ears, long pained
By strife of sect and party noise,
The brook-like murmur of his song
Of nature's simple joys!

The violet by its mossy stone,
The primrose by the river's brim,
And chance-sown daffodil, have found
Immortal life through him.

The sunrise on his breezy lake,
The rosy tints his sunset brought,
World-seen, are gladdening all the vales
And mountain-peaks of thought.

Art builds on sand; the works of pride
And human passion change and fall;
But that which shares the life of God
With Him surviveth all.

1851

A SABBATH SCENE

This poem finds its justification in the readiness with which, even in the North, clergymen urged the prompt execution of the Fugitive Slave Law as a Christian duty, and defended the system of slavery as a Bible institution.

SCARCE had the solemn Sabbath-bell
Ceased quivering in the steeple,
Scarce had the parson to his desk
Walked stately through his people,

When down the summer-shaded street
A wasted female figure,
With dusky brow and naked feet,
Came rushing wild and eager.

She saw the white spire through the trees,
She heard the sweet hymn swelling:
O pitying Christ! a refuge give
That poor one in Thy dwelling!

Like a scared fawn before the hounds,
Right up the aisle she glided,
While close behind her, whip in hand,
A lank-haired hunter strided.

She raised a keen and bitter cry,
  To Heaven and Earth appealing;
Were manhood's generous pulses dead?
  Had woman's heart no feeling?

A score of stout hands rose between
  The hunter and the flying:
Age clenched his staff, and maiden eyes
  Flashed tearful, yet defying.

"Who dares profane this house and day?"
  Cried out the angry pastor.
"Why, bless your soul, the wench's a slave,
  And I'm her lord and master!

"I've law and gospel on my side,
  And who shall dare refuse me?"
Down came the parson, bowing low,
  "My good sir, pray excuse me!

"Of course I know your right divine
  To own and work and whip her;
Quick, deacon, throw that Polyglott
  Before the wench, and trip her!"

Plump dropped the holy tome, and o'er
  Its sacred pages stumbling,
Bound hand and foot, a slave once more,
  The hapless wretch lay trembling.

I saw the parson tie the knots,
  The while his flock addressing,
The Scriptural claims of slavery
  With text on text impressing.

"Although," said he, "on Sabbath day
  All secular occupations
Are deadly sins, we must fulfil
  Our moral obligations:

"And this commends itself as one
  To every conscience tender;
As Paul sent back Onesimus,
  My Christian friends, we send her!"

Shriek rose on shriek,—the Sabbath air
  Her wild cries tore asunder;
I listened, with hushed breath, to hear
  God answering with his thunder!

All still! the very altar's cloth
  Has smothered down her shrieking,
And, dumb, she turned from face to face,
  For human pity seeking!

I saw her dragged along the aisle,
  Her shackles harshly clanking;
I heard the parson, over all,
  The Lord devoutly thanking!

My brain took fire: "Is this," I cried,
  "The end of prayer and preaching?
Then down with pulpit, down with priest,
  And give us Nature's teaching!

"Foul shame and scorn be on ye all
  Who turn the good to evil,
And steal the Bible from the Lord,
  To give it to the Devil!

"Than garbled text or parchment law
  I own a statute higher;
And God is true, though every book
  And every man's a liar!"

Just then I felt the deacon's hand
  In wrath my coat-tail seize on;
I heard the priest cry, "Infidel!"
  The lawyer mutter, "Treason!"

I started up,—where now were church,
  Slave, master, priest, and people?
I only heard the supper-bell,
  Instead of clanging steeple.

But, on the open window's sill,
  O'er which the white blooms drifted,
The pages of a good old Book
  The wind of summer lifted,

And flower and vine, like angel wings
  Around the Holy Mother,
Waved softly there, as if God's truth
  And Mercy kissed each other.

And freely from the cherry-bough
  Above the casement swinging,
With golden bosom to the sun,
  The oriole was singing.

As bird and flower made plain of old
  The lesson of the Teacher,
So now I heard the written Word
  Interpreted by Nature!

For to my ear methought the breeze
  Bore Freedom's blessed word on;
Thus saith the Lord: Break every yoke,
  Undo the heavy burden!

1850

THE PEACE OF EUROPE

"Great peace in Europe! Order reigns
From Tiber's hills to Danube's plains!"
So say her kings and priests; so say
The lying prophets of our day.

Go lay to earth a listening ear;
The tramp of measured marches hear;
The rolling of the cannon's wheel,
The shotted musket's murderous peal,
The night alarm, the sentry's call,
The quick-eared spy in hut and hall!
From Polar sea and tropic fen
The dying-groans of exiled men!
The bolted cell, the galley's chains,
The scaffold smoking with its stains!
Order, the hush of brooding slaves!
Peace, in the dungeon-vaults and graves!

O Fisher! of the world-wide net,
With meshes in all waters set,
Whose fabled keys of heaven and hell
Bolt hard the patriot's prison-cell,
And open wide the banquet-hall,
Where kings and priests hold carnival!
Weak vassal tricked in royal guise,
Boy Kaiser with thy lip of lies;
Base gambler for Napoleon's crown,
Barnacle on his dead renown!
Thou, Bourbon Neapolitan,
Crowned scandal, loathed of God and man;
And thou, fell Spider of the North!
Stretching thy giant feelers forth,
Within whose web the freedom dies
Of nations eaten up like flies!
Speak, Prince and Kaiser, Priest and Czar!
If this be Peace, pray what is War?

White Angel of the Lord! unmeet
That soil accursed for thy pure feet.
Never in Slavery's desert flows
The fountain of thy charmed repose;
No tyrant's hand thy chaplet weaves
Of lilies and of olive-leaves;
Not with the wicked shalt thou dwell,
Thus saith the Eternal Oracle;
Thy home is with the pure and free!
Stern herald of thy better day,
Before thee, to prepare thy way,
The Baptist Shade of Liberty,
Gray, scarred and hairy-robed, must press
With bleeding feet the wilderness!
Oh that its voice might pierce the ear
Of princes, trembling while they hear
A cry as of the Hebrew seer:
Repent! God's kingdom draweth near!

1852 1852

ASTRÆA

"Jove means to settle
Astræa in her seat again,
And let down from his golden chain
An age of better metal."
— Ben Jonson, 1615.

O poet rare and old!
Thy words are prophecies;
Forward the age of gold,
The new Saturnian lies.

The universal prayer
And hope are not in vain;
Rise, brothers! and prepare
The way for Saturn's reign.

Perish shall all which takes
From labor's board and can;
Perish shall all which makes
A spaniel of the man!

Free from its bonds the mind,
The body from the rod;
Broken all chains that bind
The image of our God.

Just men no longer pine
Behind their prison-bars;
Through the rent dungeon shine
The free sun and the stars.

Earth own, at last, untrod
By sect, or caste, or clan,
The fatherhood of God,
The brotherhood of man!

Fraud fail, craft perish, forth
The money-changers driven,
And God's will done on earth,
As now in heaven!

1852 1852

SUMMER BY THE LAKESIDE

Lake Winnipesaukee

I. NOON

White clouds, whose shadows haunt the deep,
Light mists, whose soft embraces keep
The sunshine on the hills asleep!

O isles of calm! O dark, still wood!
And stiller skies that overbrood
Your rest with deeper quietude!

O shapes and hues, dim beckoning, through
Yon mountain gaps, my longing view
Beyond the purple and the blue,

To stiller sea and greener land,
And softer lights and airs more bland,
And skies,—the hollow of God's hand!

Transfused through you, O mountain friends!
With mine your solemn spirit blends,
And life no more hath separate ends.

I read each misty mountain sign,
I know the voice of wave and pine,
And I am yours, and ye are mine.

Life's burdens fall, its discords cease,
I lapse into the glad release
Of Nature's own exceeding peace.

O welcome calm of heart and mind!
As falls yon fir-tree's loosened rind
To leave a tenderer growth behind,

So fall the weary years away;
A child again, my head I lay
Upon the lap of this sweet day.

This western wind hath Lethean powers,
Yon noonday cloud nepenthe showers,
The lake is white with lotus-flowers!

Even Duty's voice is faint and low,
And slumberous Conscience, waking slow,
Forgets her blotted scroll to show.

The Shadow which pursues us all,
Whose ever-nearing steps appall,
Whose voice we hear behind us call,—

That Shadow blends with mountain gray,
It speaks but what the light waves say,—
Death walks apart from Fear today!

Rocked on her breast, these pines and I
Alike on Nature's love rely;
And equal seems to live or die.

Assured that He whose presence fills
With light the spaces of these hills
No evil to His creatures wills,

The simple faith remains, that He
Will do, whatever that may be,
The best alike for man and tree.

What mosses over one shall grow,
What light and life the other know,
Unanxious, leaving Him to show.

II. EVENING

Yon mountain's side is black with night,
  While, broad-orbed, o'er its gleaming crown
The moon, slow-rounding into sight,
  On the hushed inland sea looks down.

How start to light the clustering isles,
  Each silver-hemmed! How sharply show
The shadows of their rocky piles,
  And tree-tops in the wave below!

How far and strange the mountains seem,
  Dim-looming through the pale, still light!
The vague, vast grouping of a dream,
  They stretch into the solemn night.

Beneath, lake, wood, and peopled vale,
  Hushed by that presence grand and grave,
Are silent, save the cricket's wail,
  And low response of leaf and wave.

Fair scenes! whereto the Day and Night
  Make rival love, I leave ye soon,
What time before the eastern light
  The pale ghost of the setting moon

Shall hide behind yon rocky spines,
  And the young archer, Morn, shall break
His arrows on the mountain pines,
  And, golden-sandalled, walk the lake!

Farewell! around this smiling bay
  Gay-hearted Health, and Life in bloom,
With lighter steps than mine, may stray
  In radiant summers yet to come.

But none shall more regretful leave
  These waters and these hills than I:

Or, distant, fonder dream how eve
  Or dawn is painting wave and sky;

How rising moons shine sad and mild
  On wooded isle and silvering bay;
Or setting suns beyond the piled
  And purple mountains lead the day;

Nor laughing girl, nor bearding boy,
  Nor full-pulsed manhood, lingering here,
Shall add, to life's abounding joy,
  The charmed repose to suffering dear.

Still waits kind Nature to impart
  Her choicest gifts to such as gain
An entrance to her loving heart
  Through the sharp discipline of pain.

Forever from the Hand that takes
  One blessing from us others fall;
And, soon or late, our Father makes
  His perfect recompense to all!

Oh, watched by Silence and the Night,
  And folded in the strong embrace
Of the great mountains, with the light
  Of the sweet heavens upon thy face,

Lake of the Northland! keep thy dower
  Of beauty still, and while above
Thy solemn mountains speak of power,
  Be thou the mirror of God's love.

1853 1853

FIRST-DAY THOUGHTS

In calm and cool and silence, once again
  I find my old accustomed place among
  My brethren, where, perchance, no human tongue
  Shall utter words; where never hymn is sung,
  Nor deep-toned organ blown, nor censer swung,
Nor dim light falling through the pictured pane!
There, syllabled by silence, let me hear
The still small voice which reached the prophet's ear;
Read in my heart a still diviner law
Than Israel's leader on his tables saw!
There let me strive with each besetting sin,
  Recall my wandering fancies, and restrain
  The sore disquiet of a restless brain;
  And, as the path of duty is made plain,
May grace be given that I may walk therein,
  Not like the hireling, for his selfish gain,
With backward glances and reluctant tread,
Making a merit of his coward dread,
  But, cheerful, in the light around me thrown,
  Walking as one to pleasant service led;
  Doing God's will as if it were my own,
Yet trusting not in mine, but in His strength alone!

1852 1852

MAUD MULLER

Maud Muller on a summer's day
Raked the meadow sweet with hay.

Beneath her torn hat glowed the wealth
Of simple beauty and rustic health.

Singing, she wrought, and her merry glee
The mock-bird echoed from his tree.

But when she glanced to the far-off town,
White from its hill-slope looking down,

The sweet song died, and a vague unrest
And a nameless longing filled her breast,—

A wish that she hardly dared to own,
For something better than she had known.

The Judge rode slowly down the lane,
Smoothing his horse's chestnut mane.

He drew his bridle in the shade
Of the apple-trees, to greet the maid,

And asked a draught from the spring that flowed
Through the meadow across the road.

She stooped where the cool spring bubbled up,
And filled for him her small tin cup,

And blushed as she gave it, looking down
On her feet so bare, and her tattered gown.

"Thanks!" said the Judge; "a sweeter draught
From a fairer hand was never quaffed."

He spoke of the grass and flowers and trees,
Of the singing birds and the humming bees;

Then talked of the haying, and wondered whether
The cloud in the west would bring foul weather.

And Maud forgot her brier-torn gown,
And her graceful ankles bare and brown;

And listened, while a pleased surprise
Looked from her long-lashed hazel eyes.

At last, like one who for delay
Seeks a vain excuse, he rode away.

Maud Muller looked and sighed: "Ah me!
That I the Judge's bride might be!

"He would dress me up in silks so fine,
And praise and toast me at his wine.

"My father should wear a broadcloth coat;
My brother should sail a painted boat.

"I'd dress my mother so grand and gay,
And the baby should have a new toy each day.

"And I'd feed the hungry and clothe the poor,
And all should bless me who left our door."

The Judge looked back as he climbed the hill,
And saw Maud Muller standing still.

"A form more fair, a face more sweet,
Ne'er hath it been my lot to meet.

"And her modest answer and graceful air
Show her wise and good as she is fair.

"Would she were mine, and I today,
Like her, a harvester of hay;

"No doubtful balance of rights and wrongs,
Nor weary lawyers with endless tongues,

"But low of cattle and song of birds,
And health and quiet and loving words."

But he thought of his sisters, proud and cold,
And his mother, vain of her rank and gold.

So, closing his heart, the Judge rode on,
And Maud was left in the field alone.

But the lawyers smiled that afternoon,
When he hummed in court an old love-tune;

And the young girl mused beside the well
Till the rain on the unraked clover fell.

He wedded a wife of richest dower,
Who lived for fashion, as he for power.

Yet oft, in his marble hearth's bright glow,
He watched a picture come and go;

And sweet Maud Muller's hazel eyes
Looked out in their innocent surprise.

Oft, when the wine in his glass was red,
He longed for the wayside well instead;

And closed his eyes on his garnished rooms
To dream of meadows and clover-blooms.

And the proud man sighed, with a secret pain,
"Ah, that I were free again!

"Free as when I rode that day,
Where the barefoot maiden raked her hay."

She wedded a man unlearned and poor,
And many children played round her door.

But care and sorrow, and childbirth pain,
Left their traces on heart and brain.

And oft, when the summer sun shone hot
On the new-mown hay in the meadow lot,

And she heard the little spring brook fall
Over the roadside, through the wall,

In the shade of the apple-tree again
She saw a rider draw his rein;

And, gazing down with timid grace,
She felt his pleased eyes read her face.

Sometimes her narrow kitchen walls
Stretched away into stately halls;

The weary wheel to a spinnet turned,
The tallow candle an astral burned,

And for him who sat by the chimney lug,
Dozing and grumbling o'er pipe and mug,

A manly form at her side she saw,
And joy was duty and love was law.

Then she took up her burden of life again,
Saying only, "It might have been."

Alas for maiden, alas for Judge,
For rich repiner and household drudge!

God pity them both! and pity us all,
Who vainly the dreams of youth recall.

For of all sad words of tongue or pen,
The saddest are these: "It might have been!"

Ah, well! for us all some sweet hope lies
Deeply buried from human eyes;

And, in the hereafter, angels may
Roll the stone from its grave away!

1854 1854

BURNS

ON RECEIVING A SPRIG OF HEATHER IN BLOSSOM

No more these simple flowers belong
  To Scottish maid and lover;
Sown in the common soil of song,
  They bloom the wide world over.

In smiles and tears, in sun and showers,
  The minstrel and the heather,
The deathless singer and the flowers
  He sang of live together.

Wild heather-bells and Robert Burns!
  The moorland flower and peasant!
How, at their mention, memory turns
  Her pages old and pleasant!

The gray sky wears again its gold
  And purple of adorning,
And manhood's noonday shadows hold
  The dews of boyhood's morning.

The dews that washed the dust and soil
  From off the wings of pleasure,
The sky, that flecked the ground of toil
  With golden threads of leisure.

I call to mind the summer day,
  The early harvest mowing,
The sky with sun and clouds at play,
  And flowers with breezes blowing.

I hear the blackbird in the corn,
  The locust in the haying;
And, like the fabled hunter's horn,
  Old tunes my heart is playing.

How oft that day, with fond delay,
  I sought the maple's shadow,
And sang with Burns the hours away,
  Forgetful of the meadow!

Bees hummed, birds twittered, overhead
  I heard the squirrels leaping,
The good dog listened while I read,
  And wagged his tail in keeping.

I watched him while in sportive mood
  I read "*The Twa Dogs*' " story,
And half believed he understood
  The poet's allegory.

Sweet day, sweet songs! The golden hours
  Grew brighter for that singing,
From brook and bird and meadow flowers
  A dearer welcome bringing.

New light on home-seen Nature beamed,
  New glory over Woman;
And daily life and duty seemed
  No longer poor and common.

I woke to find the simple truth
  Of fact and feeling better
Than all the dreams that held my youth
  A still repining debtor:

That Nature gives her handmaid, Art,
  The themes of sweet discoursing;
The tender idyls of the heart
  In every tongue rehearsing.

Why dream of lands of gold and pearl,
  Of loving knight and lady,
When farmer boy and barefoot girl
  Were wandering there already?

I saw through all familiar things
  The romance underlying;
The joys and griefs that plume the wings
  Of Fancy skyward flying.

I saw the same blithe day return,
  The same sweet fall of even,
That rose on wooded Craigie-burn,
  And sank on crystal Devon.

I matched with Scotland's heathery hills
  The sweetbrier and the clover;
With Ayr and Doon, my native rills,
  Their wood hymns chanting over.

O'er rank and pomp, as he had seen,
  I saw the Man uprising;
No longer common or unclean,
  The child of God's baptizing!

With clearer eyes I saw the worth
  Of life among the lowly;
The Bible at his Cotter's hearth
  Had made my own more holy.

And if at times an evil strain,
  To lawless love appealing,
Broke in upon the sweet refrain
  Of pure and healthful feeling,

It died upon the eye and ear,
  No inward answer gaining;
No heart had I to see or hear
  The discord and the staining.

Let those who never erred forget
  His worth, in vain bewailings;
Sweet Soul of Song! I own my debt
  Uncancelled by his failings!

Lament who will the ribald line
  Which tells his lapse from duty,
How kissed the maddening lips of wine
  Or wanton ones of beauty;

But think, while falls that shade between
  The erring one and Heaven,
That he who loved like Magdalen,
  Like her may be forgiven.

Not his the song whose thunderous chime
  Eternal echoes render;
The mournful Tuscan's haunted rhyme,
  And Milton's starry splendor!

But who his human heart has laid
  To Nature's bosom nearer?
Who sweetened toil like him, or paid
  To love a tribute dearer?

Through all his tuneful art, how strong
  The human feeling gushes!
The very moonlight of his song
  Is warm with smiles and blushes!

Give lettered pomp to teeth of Time,
  So "Bonnie Doon" but tarry;
Blot out the Epic's stately rhyme,
  But spare his Highland Mary!

1854 1854

THE RENDITION

On the 2d of June, 1854, Anthony Burns, a fugitive slave from Virginia, after being under arrest for ten days in the Boston Court House, was remanded to slavery under the Fugitive Slave Act, and taken down State Street to a steamer chartered by the United States Government, under guard of United States troops and artillery, Massachusetts militia and Boston police. Public excitement ran high, a futile attempt to rescue Burns having been made during his confinement, and the streets were crowded with tens of thousands of people, of whom many came from other towns and cities of the State to witness the humiliating spectacle.

I HEARD the train's shrill whistle call,
  I saw an earnest look beseech,
  And rather by that look than speech
My neighbor told me all.

And, as I thought of Liberty
  Marched handcuffed down that sworded street,
  The solid earth beneath my feet
Reeled fluid as the sea.

I felt a sense of bitter loss,—
  Shame, tearless grief, and stifling wrath,
  And loathing fear, as if my path
A serpent stretched across.

All love of home, all pride of place,
  All generous confidence and trust,
  Sank smothering in that deep disgust
And anguish of disgrace.

Down on my native hills of June,
  And home's green quiet, hiding all,
  Fell sudden darkness like the fall
Of midnight upon noon!

And Law, an unloosed maniac, strong,
  Blood-drunken, through the blackness trod,
  Hoarse-shouting in the ear of God
The blasphemy of wrong.

"O Mother, from thy memories proud,
  Thy old renown, dear Commonwealth,
  Lend this dead air a breeze of health,
And smite with stars this cloud.

"Mother of Freedom, wise and brave,
  Rise awful in thy strength," I said;
  Ah me! I spake but to the dead;
I stood upon her grave!

1854 1854

ARISEN AT LAST

I SAID I stood upon thy grave,
My Mother State, when last the moon
Of blossoms clomb the skies of June.

And, scattering ashes on my head,
I wore, undreaming of relief,
The sackcloth of thy shame and grief.

Again that moon of blossoms shines
On leaf and flower and folded wing,
And thou hast risen with the spring!

Once more thy strong maternal arms
Are round about thy children flung,—
A lioness that guards her young!

No threat is on thy closèd lips,
But in thine eye a power to smite
The mad wolf backward from its light.

Southward the baffled robber's track
Henceforth runs only; hereaway,
The fell lycanthrope finds no prey.

Henceforth, within thy sacred gates,
His first low howl shall downward draw
The thunder of thy righteous law.

Not mindless of thy trade and gain,
But, acting on the wiser plan,
Thou'rt grown conservative of man.

So shalt thou clothe with life the hope,
Dream-painted on the sightless eyes
Of him who sang of Paradise,—

The vision of a Christian man,
In virtue, as in stature great
Embodied in a Christian State.

And thou, amidst thy sisterhood
Forbearing long, yet standing fast,
Shalt win their grateful thanks at last;

When North and South shall strive no more,
And all their feuds and fears be lost
In Freedom's holy Pentecost.

1855 1855

FOR RIGHTEOUSNESS' SAKE

Inscribed to friends under arrest for treason against the slave power.

THE age is dull and mean. Men creep,
Not walk; with blood too pale and tame
To pay the debt they owe to shame;
Buy cheap, sell dear; eat, drink, and sleep
Down-pillowed, deaf to moaning want;
Pay tithes for soul-insurance; keep
Six days to Mammon, one to Cant.

In such a time, give thanks to God,
That somewhat of the holy rage
With which the prophets in their age
On all its decent seemings trod,
Has set your feet upon the lie,
That man and ox and soul and clod
Are market stock to sell and buy!

The hot words from your lips, my own,
To caution trained, might not repeat;
But if some tares among the wheat
Of generous thought and deed were sown,
No common wrong provoked your zeal;
The silken gauntlet that is thrown
In such a quarrel rings like steel.

The brave old strife the fathers saw
For Freedom calls for men again
Like those who battled not in vain
For England's Charter, Alfred's law;
And right of speech and trial just
Wage in your name their ancient war
With venal courts and perjured trust.

God's ways seem dark, but, soon or late,
They touch the shining hills of day;
The evil cannot brook delay,
The good can well afford to wait.
Give ermined knaves their hour of crime;
Ye have the future grand and great,
The safe appeal of Truth to Time!

1855 1855

THE LAST WALK IN AUTUMN

I

O'ER the bare woods, whose outstretched hands
Plead with the leaden heavens in vain,
I see, beyond the valley lands,
The sea's long level dim with rain.

Around me all things, stark and dumb,
Seem praying for the snows to come,
And, for the summer bloom and greenness gone,
With winter's sunset lights and dazzling morn atone.

II

Along the river's summer walk,
The withered tufts of asters nod;
And trembles on its arid stalk
The hoar plume of the golden-rod.
And on a ground of sombre fir,
And azure-studded juniper,
The silver birch its buds of purple shows,
And scarlet berries tell where bloomed the sweet wild-rose!

III

With mingled sound of horns and bells,
A far-heard clang, the wild geese fly,
Storm-sent, from Arctic moors and fells,
Like a great arrow through the sky,
Two dusky lines converged in one,
Chasing the southward-flying sun;
While the brave snow-bird and the hardy jay
Call to them from the pines, as if to bid them stay.

IV

I passed this way a year ago:
The wind blew south; the noon of day
Was warm as June's; and save that snow
Flecked the low mountains far away,
And that the vernal-seeming breeze
Mocked faded grass and leafless trees,
I might have dreamed of summer as I lay,
Watching the fallen leaves with the soft wind at play.

V

Since then, the winter blasts have piled
The white pagodas of the snow
On these rough slopes, and, strong and wild,
Yon river, in its overflow
Of spring-time rain and sun, set free,
Crashed with its ices to the sea;
And over these gray fields, then green and gold,
The summer corn has waved, the thunder's organ rolled.

VI

Rich gift of God! A year of time!
What pomp of rise and shut of day,
What hues wherewith our Northern clime
Makes autumn's dropping woodlands gay,
What airs outblown from ferny dells,
And clover-bloom and sweetbrier smells,
What songs of brooks and birds, what fruits and flowers,
Green woods and moonlit snows, have in its round been ours!

VII

I know not how, in other lands,
The changing seasons come and go;
What splendors fall on Syrian sands,
What purple lights on Alpine snow!
Nor how the pomp of sunrise waits
On Venice at her watery gates;
A dream alone to me is Arno's vale,
And the Alhambra's halls are but a traveller's tale.

VIII

Yet, on life's current, he who drifts
Is one with him who rows or sails;
And he who wanders widest lifts
No more of beauty's jealous veils
Than he who from his doorway sees
The miracle of flowers and trees,
Feels the warm Orient in the noonday air,
And from cloud minarets hears the sunset call to prayer!

IX

The eye may well be glad that looks
Where Pharpar's fountains rise and fall;
But he who sees his native brooks
Laugh in the sun, has seen them all.
The marble palaces of Ind
Rise round him in the snow and wind;
From his lone sweetbrier Persian Hafiz smiles,
And Rome's cathedral awe is in his woodland aisles.

X

And thus it is my fancy blends
The near at hand and far and rare;
And while the same horizon bends
Above the silver-sprinkled hair
Which flashed the light of morning skies
On childhood's wonder-lifted eyes,

Within its round of sea and sky and field,
Earth wheels with all her zones, the Kosmos stands revealed.

XI

And thus the sick man on his bed,
The toiler to his task-work bound,
Behold their prison-walls outspread,
Their clipped horizon widen round!
While freedom-giving fancy waits,
Like Peter's angel at the gates,
The power is theirs to baffle care and pain,
To bring the lost world back, and make it theirs again!

XII

What lack of goodly company,
When masters of the ancient lyre
Obey my call, and trace for me
Their words of mingled tears and fire!
I talk with Bacon, grave and wise,
I read the world with Pascal's eyes;
And priest and sage, with solemn brows austere,
And poets, garland-bound, the Lords of Thought, draw near.

XIII

Methinks, O friend, I hear thee say,
"In vain the human heart we mock;
Bring living guests who love the day,
Not ghosts who fly at crow of cock!
The herbs we share with flesh and blood
Are better than ambrosial food
With laurelled shades." I grant it, nothing loath,
But doubly blest is he who can partake of both.

XIV

He who might Plato's banquet grace,
Have I not seen before me sit,
And watched his puritanic face,
With more than Eastern wisdom lit?
Shrewd mystic! who, upon the back
Of his Poor Richard's Almanac
Writing the Sufi's song, the Gentoo's dream,
Links Manu's age of thought to Fulton's age of steam!

XV

Here too, of answering love secure,
Have I not welcomed to my hearth
The gentle pilgrim troubadour,
Whose songs have girdled half the earth;
Whose pages, like the magic mat
Whereon the Eastern lover sat,
Have borne me over Rhine-land's purple vines,
And Nubia's tawny sands, and Phrygia's mountain pines!

XVI

And he, who to the lettered wealth
Of ages adds the lore unpriced,
The wisdom and the moral health,
The ethics of the school of Christ;
The statesman to his holy trust,
As the Athenian archon, just,
Struck down, exiled like him for truth alone,
Has he not graced my home with beauty all his own?

XVII

What greetings smile, what farewells wave,
What loved ones enter and depart!
The good, the beautiful, the brave,
The Heaven-lent treasures of the heart!
How conscious seems the frozen sod
And beechen slope whereon they trod!
The oak-leaves rustle, and the dry grass bends
Beneath the shadowy feet of lost or absent friends.

XVIII

Then ask not why to these bleak hills
I cling, as clings the tufted moss,
To bear the winter's lingering chills,
The mocking spring's perpetual loss.
I dream of lands where summer smiles,
And soft winds blow from spicy isles,
But scarce would Ceylon's breath of flowers be sweet,
Could I not feel thy soil, New England, at my feet!

XIX

At times I long for gentler skies,
And bathe in dreams of softer air,
But homesick tears would fill the eyes
That saw the Cross without the Bear.
The pine must whisper to the palm,
The north-wind break the tropic calm;
And with the dreamy languor of the Line,
The North's keen virtue blend, and strength to beauty join.

XX

Better to stem with heart and hand
The roaring tide of life, than lie,
Unmindful, on its flowery strand,
Of God's occasions drifting by!
Better with naked nerve to bear
The needles of this goading air,
Than, in the lap of sensual ease, forego
The godlike power to do, the godlike aim to know.

XXI

Home of my heart! to me more fair
Than gay Versailles or Windsor's halls,
The painted, shingly town-house where
The freeman's vote for Freedom falls!
The simple roof where prayer is made,
Than Gothic groin and colonnade;
The living temple of the heart of man,
Than Rome's sky-mocking vault, or many-spired Milan!

XXII

More dear thy equal village schools,
Where rich and poor the Bible read,
Than classic halls where Priestcraft rules,
And Learning wears the chains of Creed;
Thy glad Thanksgiving, gathering in
The scattered sheaves of home and kin,
Than the mad license ushering Lenten pains,
Or holidays of slaves who laugh and dance in chains.

XXIII

And sweet homes nestle in these dales,
And perch along these wooded swells;
And, blest beyond Arcadian vales,
They hear the sound of Sabbath bells!
Here dwells no perfect man sublime,
Nor woman winged before her time,
But with the faults and follies of the race,
Old home-bred virtues hold their not unhonored place.

XXIV

Here manhood struggles for the sake
Of mother, sister, daughter, wife,
The graces and the loves which make
The music of the march of life;
And woman, in her daily round
Of duty, walks on holy ground.
No unpaid menial tills the soil, nor here
Is the bad lesson learned at human rights to sneer.

XXV

Then let the icy north-wind blow
The trumpets of the coming storm,
To arrowy sleet and blinding snow
Yon slanting lines of rain transform.
Young hearts shall hail the drifted cold,
As gaily as I did of old;
And I, who watch them through the frosty pane,
Unenvious, live in them my boyhood o'er again.

XXVI

And I will trust that He who heeds
The life that hides in mead and wold,
Who hangs yon alder's crimson beads,
And stains these mosses green and gold,
Will still, as He hath done, incline
His gracious care to me and mine;
Grant what we ask aright, from wrong debar,
And, as the earth grows dark, make brighter every star!

XXVII

I have not seen, I may not see,
My hopes for man take form in fact,
But God will give the victory
In due time; in that faith I act.
And he who sees the future sure,
The baffling present may endure,
And bless, meanwhile, the unseen Hand that leads
The heart's desires beyond the halting step of deeds.

XXVIII

And thou, my song, I send thee forth,
Where harsher songs of mine have flown;
Go, find a place at home and hearth
Where'er thy singer's name is known;
Revive for him the kindly thought
Of friends; and they who love him not,
Touched by some strain of thine, perchance may take
The hand he proffers all, and thank him for thy sake.

1856 1857

SKIPPER IRESON'S RIDE

Of all the rides since the birth of time,
Told in story or sung in rhyme,—
On Apuleius's Golden Ass,
Or one-eyed Calendar's horse of brass,
Witch astride of a human back,
Islam's prophet on Al-Borák,—
The strangest ride that ever was sped
Was Ireson's, out from Marblehead!
Old Floyd Ireson, for his hard heart,
Tarred and feathered and carried in a cart
By the women of Marblehead!

Body of turkey, head of owl,
Wings a-droop like a rained-on fowl,
Feathered and ruffled in every part,
Skipper Ireson stood in the cart.
Scores of women, old and young,
Strong of muscle, and glib of tongue,
Pushed and pulled up the rocky lane,
Shouting and singing the shrill refrain:
"Here's Flud Oirson, fur his horrd horrt,
Torr'd an' futherr'd an' corr'd in a corrt
By the women o' Morble'ead!"

Wrinkled scolds with hands on hips,
Girls in bloom of cheek and lips,
Wild-eyed, free-limbed, such as chase
Bacchus round some antique vase,
Brief of skirt, with ankles bare,
Loose of kerchief and loose of hair,
With conch-shells blowing and fish-horns' twang,
Over and over the Mænads sang:
"Here's Flud Oirson, fur his horrd horrt,
Torr'd an' futherr'd an' corr'd in a corrt
By the women o' Morble'ead!"

Small pity for him!—He sailed away
From a leaking ship, in Chaleur Bay,—
Sailed away from a sinking wreck,
With his own town's-people on her deck!
"Lay by! lay by!" they called to him.
Back he answered, "Sink or swim!
Brag of your catch of fish again!"
And off he sailed through the fog and rain!
Old Floyd Ireson, for his hard heart,
Tarred and feathered and carried in a cart
By the women of Marblehead!

Fathoms deep in dark Chaleur
That wreck shall lie forevermore.
Mother and sister, wife and maid,
Looked from the rocks of Marblehead
Over the moaning and rainy sea,—
Looked for the coming that might not be!
What did the winds and the sea-birds say
Of the cruel captain who sailed away?—
Old Floyd Ireson, for his hard heart,
Tarred and feathered and carried in a cart
By the women of Marblehead!

Through the street, on either side,
Up flew windows, doors swung wide;
Sharp-tongued spinsters, old wives gray,
Treble lent the fish-horn's bray.
Sea-worn grandsires, cripple-bound,
Hulks of old sailors run aground,
Shook head, and fist, and hat, and cane,
And cracked with curses the hoarse refrain:
"Here's Flud Oirson, fur his horrd horrt,
Torr'd an' futherr'd an' corr'd in a corrt
By the women o' Morble'ead!"

Sweetly along the Salem road
Bloom of orchard and lilac showed.
Little the wicked skipper knew
Of the fields so green and the sky so blue.
Riding there in his sorry trim,
Like an Indian idol glum and grim,
Scarcely he seemed the sound to hear
Of voices shouting, far and near:
"Here's Flud Oirson, fur his horrd horrt,
Torr'd an' futherr'd an' corr'd in a corrt
By the women o' Morble'ead!"

"Hear me, neighbors!" at last he cried,—
"What to me is this noisy ride?
What is the shame that clothes the skin
To the nameless horror that lives within?
Waking or sleeping, I see a wreck,
And hear a cry from a reeling deck!
Hate me and curse me,—I only dread
The hand of God and the face of the dead!"
Said old Floyd Ireson, for his hard heart,
Tarred and feathered and carried in a cart
By the women of Marblehead!

Then the wife of the skipper lost at sea
Said, "God has touched him! why should we!"
Said an old wife mourning her only son,

"Cut the rogue's tether and let him run!"
So with soft relentings and rude excuse,
Half scorn, half pity, they cut him loose,
And gave him a cloak to hide him in,
And left him alone with his shame and sin.
Poor Floyd Ireson, for his hard heart,
Tarred and feathered and carried in a cart
By the women of Marblehead!

1828, 1857 1857

TELLING THE BEES

Here is the place; right over the hill
Runs the path I took;
You can see the gap in the old wall still,
And the stepping-stones in the shallow brook.

There is the house, with the gate red-barred,
And the poplars tall;
And the barn's brown length, and the cattle-yard,
And the white horns tossing above the wall.

There are the beehives ranged in the sun;
And down by the brink
Of the brook are her poor flowers, weed-o'er-run,
Pansy and daffodil, rose and pink.

A year has gone, as the tortoise goes,
Heavy and slow;
And the same rose blows, and the same sun glows,
And the same brook sings of a year ago.

There's the same sweet clover-smell in the breeze;
And the June sun warm
Tangles his wings of fire in the trees,
Setting, as then, over Fernside farm.

I mind me how with a lover's care
From my Sunday coat
I brushed off the burrs, and smoothed my hair,
And cooled at the brookside my brow and throat.

Since we parted, a month had passed,—
To love, a year;
Down through the beeches I looked at last
On the little red gate and the well-sweep near.

I can see it all now,—the slantwise rain
Of light through the leaves,
The sundown's blaze on her window-pane,
The bloom of her roses under the eaves.

Just the same as a month before,—
The house and the trees,
The barn's brown gable, the vine by the door,—
Nothing changed but the hives of bees.

Before them, under the garden wall,
Forward and back,
Went drearily singing the chore-girl small,
Draping each hive with a shred of black.

Trembling, I listened: the summer sun
Had the chill of snow;
For I knew she was telling the bees of one
Gone on the journey we all must go!

Then I said to myself, "My Mary weeps
For the dead today:
Haply her blind old grandsire sleeps
The fret and the pain of his age away."

But her dog whined low; on the doorway sill,
With his cane to his chin,
The old man sat; and the chore-girl still
Sung to the bees stealing out and in.

And the song she was singing ever since
In my ear sounds on:—
"Stay at home, pretty bees, fly not hence!
Mistress Mary is dead and gone!"

1858 1858

THE OVER-HEART

For of Him, and through Him, and to Him, are all things: to whom be glory for ever!—Romans xi. 36.

Above, below, in sky and sod,
In leaf and spar, in star and man,
Well might the wise Athenian scan
The geometric signs of God,
The measured order of His plan.

And India's mystics sang aright
Of the One Life pervading all,—
One Being's tidal rise and fall
In soul and form, in sound and sight,—
Eternal outflow and recall.

God is: and man in guilt and fear
The central fact of Nature owns;
Kneels, trembling, by his altar stones,
And darkly dreams the ghastly smear
Of blood appeases and atones.

Guilt shapes the Terror: deep within
The human heart the secret lies
Of all the hideous deities;
And, painted on a ground of sin,
The fabled gods of torment rise!

And what is He? The ripe grain nods,
The sweet dews fall, the sweet flowers blow;
But darker signs His presence show:
The earthquake and the storm are God's,
And good and evil interflow.

O hearts of love! O souls that turn
Like sunflowers to the pure and best!
To you the truth is manifest:
For they the mind of Christ discern
Who lean like John upon His breast!

In him of whom the sibyl told,
For whom the prophet's harp was toned,
Whose need the sage and magian owned,
The loving heart of God behold,
The hope for which the ages groaned!

Fade, pomp of dreadful imagery
Wherewith mankind have deified
Their hate, and selfishness, and pride!
Let the scared dreamer wake to see
The Christ of Nazareth at his side!

What doth that holy Guide require?
No rite of pain, nor gift of blood,
But man a kindly brotherhood,
Looking, where duty is desire,
To Him, the beautiful and good.

Gone be the faithlessness of fear,
And let the pitying heaven's sweet rain
Wash out the altar's bloody stain;
The law of Hatred disappear,
The law of Love alone remain.

How fall the idols false and grim!
And lo! their hideous wreck above
The emblems of the Lamb and Dove!
Man turns from God, not God from him;
And guilt, in suffering, whispers Love!

The world sits at the feet of Christ,
Unknowing, blind, and unconsoled;
It yet shall touch His garment's fold,
And feel the heavenly Alchemist
Transform its very dust to gold.

The theme befitting angel tongues
Beyond a mortal's scope has grown.
O heart of mine! with reverence own
The fulness which to it belongs,
And trust the unknown for the known.

1859? 1859

MY PLAYMATE

The pines were dark on Ramoth hill,
Their song was soft and low;
The blossoms in the sweet May wind
Were falling like the snow.

The blossoms drifted at our feet,
The orchard birds sang clear;
The sweetest and the saddest day
It seemed of all the year.

For, more to me than birds or flowers,
My playmate left her home,
And took with her the laughing spring,
The music and the bloom.

She kissed the lips of kith and kin,
She laid her hand in mine:
What more could ask the bashful boy
Who fed her father's kine?

She left us in the bloom of May:
The constant years told o'er
Their seasons with as sweet May morns,
But she came back no more.

I walk, with noiseless feet, the round
Of uneventful years;
Still o'er and o'er I sow the spring
And reap the autumn ears.

She lives where all the golden year
Her summer roses blow;
The dusky children of the sun
Before her come and go.

There haply with her jewelled hands
She smooths her silken gown,—
No more the homespun lap wherein
I shook the walnuts down.

The wild grapes wait us by the brook,
The brown nuts on the hill,
And still the May-day flowers make sweet
The woods of Follymill.

The lilies blossom in the pond,
The bird builds in the tree,
The dark pines sing on Ramoth hill
The slow song of the sea.

I wonder if she thinks of them,
And how the old time seems,—
If ever the pines of Ramoth wood
Are sounding in her dreams.

I see her face, I hear her voice;
Does she remember mine?
And what to her is now the boy
Who fed her father's kine?

What cares she that the orioles build
For other eyes than ours,—
That other hands with nuts are filled,
And other laps with flowers?

O playmate in the golden time!
Our mossy seat is green,
Its fringing violets blossom yet,
The old trees o'er it lean.

The winds so sweet with birch and fern
A sweeter memory blow;
And there in spring the veeries sing
The song of long ago.

And still the pines of Ramoth wood
Are moaning like the sea,—
The moaning of the sea of change
Between myself and thee!

1860 1860

THE SHADOW AND THE LIGHT

"And I sought, whence is Evil: I set before the eye of my spirit the whole creation; whatsoever we see therein,—sea, earth, air, stars, trees, moral creatures,—yea, whatsoever there is we do not see,—angels and spiritual powers. Where is evil, and whence comes it, since God the Good hath created all things? Why made He anything at all of evil, and not rather by His Almightiness cause it not to be? These thoughts I turned in my miserable heart, overcharged with most gnawing cares." "And, admonished to return to myself, I entered even into my inmost soul, Thou being my guide, and beheld even beyond my soul and mind the Light unchangeable. He who knows the Truth knows what that Light is, and he that knows it knows Eternity! O Truth, who art Eternity! Love, who art Truth! Eternity, who art Love! And I beheld that Thou madest all things good, and to Thee is nothing whatsoever evil. From the angel to the worm, from the first motion to the last, Thou settest each in its place, and everything is good in its kind. Woe is me!—how high art Thou in the highest, how deep in the deepest! and Thou never departest from us, and we scarcely return to Thee."—AUGUSTINE'S *Soliloquies*, Book VII.

THE fourteen centuries fall away
Between us and the Afric saint,
And at his side we urge, today,
The immemorial quest and old complaint.

No outward sign to us is given,—
From sea or earth comes no reply;
Hushed as the warm Numidian heaven
He vainly questioned bends our frozen sky.

No victory comes of all our strife,—
From all we grasp the meaning slips;
The Sphinx sits at the gate of life,
With the old question on her awful lips.

In paths unknown we hear the feet
Of fear before, and guilt behind;
We pluck the wayside fruit, and eat
Ashes and dust beneath its golden rind.

From age to age descends unchecked
The sad bequest of sire to son,
The body's taint, the mind's defect;
Through every web of life the dark threads run.

Oh, why and whither? God knows all;
I only know that He is good,
And that whatever may befall
Or here or there, must be the best that could.

Between the dreadful cherubim
A Father's face I still discern,
As Moses looked of old on Him,
And saw His glory into goodness turn!

For He is merciful as just;
And so, by faith correcting sight,
I bow before His will, and trust
Howe'er they seem He doeth all things right;

And dare to hope that He will make
The rugged smooth, the doubtful plain;
His mercy never quite forsake;
His healing visit every realm of pain;

That suffering is not His revenge
Upon His creatures weak and frail,
Sent on a pathway new and strange
With feet that wander and with eyes that fail;

That, o'er the crucible of pain,
Watches the tender eye of Love
The slow transmuting of the chain
Whose links are iron below to gold above!

Ah me! we doubt the shining skies,
Seen through our shadows of offence,
And drown with our poor childish cries
The cradle-hymn of kindly Providence.

And still we love the evil cause,
And of the just effect complain:
We tread upon life's broken laws,
And murmur at our self-inflicted pain;

We turn us from the light, and find
Our spectral shapes before us thrown,
As they who leave the sun behind
Walk in the shadows of themselves alone.

And scarce by will or strength of ours
We set our faces to the day;
Weak, wavering, blind, the Eternal Powers
Alone can turn us from ourselves away.

Our weakness is the strength of sin,
But love must needs be stronger far,
Outreaching all and gathering in
The erring spirit and the wandering star.

A Voice grows with the growing years;
Earth, hushing down her bitter cry,
Looks upward from her graves, and hears,
"The Resurrection and the Life am I."

O Love Divine!—whose constant beam
Shines on the eyes that will not see,
And waits to bless us, while we dream
Thou leavest us because we turn from Thee!

All souls that struggle and aspire,
All hearts of prayer by Thee are lit;
And, dim or clear, Thy tongues of fire
On dusky tribes and twilight centuries sit.

Nor bounds, nor clime, nor creed Thou know'st,
Wide as our need Thy favors fall;
The white wings of the Holy Ghost
Stoop, seen or unseen, o'er the heads of all.

O Beauty, old yet ever new!
Eternal Voice, and Inward Word,
The Logos of the Greek and Jew,
The old sphere-music which the Samian heard!

Truth which the sage and prophet saw,
Long sought without, but found within,
The Law of Love beyond all law,
The Life o'erflooding mortal death and sin!

Shine on us with the light which glowed
Upon the trance-bound shepherd's way,
Who saw the Darkness overflowed
And drowned by tides of everlasting Day.

Shine, light of God!—make broad thy scope
To all who sin and suffer; more
And better than we dare to hope
With Heaven's compassion make our longings poor!

1860 1860

THE WAITING

I WAIT and watch: before my eyes
Methinks the night grows thin and gray;
I wait and watch the eastern skies
To see the golden spears uprise
Beneath the oriflamme of day!

Like one whose limbs are bound in trance
I hear the day-sounds swell and grow,
And see across the twilight glance,
Troop after troop, in swift advance,
The shining ones with plumes of snow!

I know the errand of their feet,
I know what mighty work is theirs;
I can but lift up hands unmeet,
The threshing-floors of God to beat,
And speed them with unworthy prayers.

I will not dream in vain despair
The steps of progress wait for me:
The puny leverage of a hair
The planet's impulse well may spare,
A drop of dew the tided sea.

The loss, if loss there be, is mine,
And yet not mine if understood;
For one shall grasp and one resign,
One drink life's rue, and one its wine,
And God shall make the balance good.

Oh power to do! Oh baffled will!
Oh prayer and action! ye are one.
Who may not strive, may yet fulfil
The harder task of standing still,
And good but wished with God is done!

1862? 1865

AMY WENTWORTH

TO WILLIAM BRADFORD

As they who watch by sick-beds find relief
Unwittingly from the great stress of grief
And anxious care, in fantasies outwrought
From the hearth's embers flickering low, or caught
From whispering wind, or tread of passing feet,
Or vagrant memory calling up some sweet
Snatch of old song or romance, whence or why
They scarcely know or ask,—so, thou and I,
Nursed in the faith that Truth alone is strong
In the endurance which outwearies Wrong,
With meek persistence baffling brutal force,
And trusting God against the universe,—
We, doomed to watch a strife we may not share
With other weapons than the patriot's prayer,
Yet owning, with full hearts and moistened eyes,
The awful beauty of self-sacrifice,
And wrung by keenest sympathy for all
Who give their loved ones for the living wall
'Twixt law and treason,—in this evil day
May haply find, through automatic play
Of pen and pencil, solace to our pain,
And hearten others with the strength we gain.
I know it has been said our times require
No play of art, nor dalliance with the lyre,
No weak essay with Fancy's chloroform
To calm the hot, mad pulses of the storm,
But the stern war-blast rather, such as sets
The battle's teeth of serried bayonets,
And pictures grim as Vernet's. Yet with these
Some softer tints may blend, and milder keys
Relieve the storm-stunned ear. Let us keep sweet,
If so we may, our hearts, even while we eat
The bitter harvest of our own device
And half a century's moral cowardice.
As Nürnberg sang while Wittenberg defied,
And Kranach painted by his Luther's side,
And through the war-march of the Puritan
The silver stream of Marvell's music ran,
So let the household melodies be sung,
The pleasant pictures on the wall be hung,—
So let us hold against the hosts of night
And slavery all our vantage-ground of light.
Let Treason boast its savagery, and shake
From its flag-folds its symbol rattlesnake,
Nurse its fine arts, lay human skins in tan,
And carve its pipe-bowls from the bones of man,
And make the tale of Fijian banquets dull
By drinking whiskey from a loyal skull,—
But let us guard, till this sad war shall cease,
(God grant it soon!) the graceful arts of peace:
No foes are conquered who the victors teach
Their vandal manners and barbaric speech.

And while, with hearts of thankfulness, we bear
Of the great common burden our full share,
Let none upbraid us that the waves entice
The sea-dipped pencil, or some quaint device,
Rhythmic and sweet, beguiles my pen away
From the sharp strifes and sorrows of today.
Thus, while the east-wind keen from Labrador
Sings in the leafless elms, and from the shore
Of the great sea comes the monotonous roar
Of the long-breaking surf, and all the sky
Is gray with cloud, home-bound and dull, I try
To time a simple legend to the sounds
Of wind in the woods, and waves on pebbled bounds,—
A song for oars to chime with, such as might
Be sung by tired sea-painters, who at night
Look from their hemlock camps, by quiet cove
Or beach, moon-lighted, on the waves they love.
(So hast thou looked, when level sunset lay
On the calm bosom of some Eastern bay,
And all the spray-moist rocks and waves that rolled
Up the white sand-slopes flashed with ruddy gold.)
Something it has—a flavor of the sea,
And the sea's freedom—which reminds of thee.
Its faded picture, dimly smiling down
From the blurred fresco of the ancient town,

I have not touched with warmer tints in vain,
If, in this dark, sad year, it steals one thought
from pain.

Her fingers shame the ivory keys
They dance so light along;
The bloom upon her parted lips
Is sweeter than the song.

O perfumed suitor, spare thy smiles!
Her thoughts are not of thee;
She better loves the salted wind,
The voices of the sea.

Her heart is like an outbound ship
That at its anchor swings;
The murmur of the stranded shell
Is in the song she sings.

She sings, and, smiling, hears her praise,
But dreams the while of one
Who watches from his sea-blown deck
The icebergs in the sun.

She questions all the winds that blow,
And every fog-wreath dim,
And bids the sea-birds flying north
Bear messages to him.

She speeds them with the thanks of men
He perilled life to save,
And grateful prayers like holy oil
To smooth for him the wave.

Brown Viking of the fishing-smack!
Fair toast of all the town!—
The skipper's jerkin ill beseems
The lady's silken gown!

But ne'er shall Amy Wentworth wear
For him the blush of shame
Who dares to set his manly gifts
Against her ancient name.

The stream is brightest at its spring,
And blood is not like wine;
Nor honored less than he who heirs
Is he who founds a line.

Full lightly shall the prize be won,
If love be Fortune's spur;
And never maiden stoops to him
Who lifts himself to her.

Her home is brave in Jaffrey Street,
With stately stairways worn
By feet of old Colonial knights
And ladies gentle-born.

Still green about its ample porch
The English ivy twines,
Trained back to show in English oak
The herald's carven signs.

And on her, from the wainscot old,
Ancestral faces frown,—
And this has worn the soldier's sword,
And that the judge's gown.

But, strong of will and proud as they,
She walks the gallery floor
As if she trod her sailor's deck
By stormy Labrador!

The sweetbrier blooms on Kittery-side,
And green are Elliot's bowers;
Her garden is the pebbled beach,
The mosses are her flowers.

She looks across the harbor-bar
To see the white gulls fly;
His greeting from the Northern sea
Is in their clanging cry.

She hums a song, and dreams that he,
As in its romance old,
Shall homeward ride with silken sails
And masts of beaten gold!

Oh, rank is good, and gold is fair,
And high and low mate ill;
But love has never known a law
Beyond its own sweet will!

1862 1862

ANDREW RYKMAN'S PRAYER

ANDREW RYKMAN's dead and gone;
You can see his leaning slate
In the graveyard, and thereon
Read his name and date.

"*Trust is truer than our fears,*"
Runs the legend through the moss,
"*Gain is not in added years,*
Nor in death is loss."

Still the feet that thither trod,
All the friendly eyes are dim;
Only Nature, now, and God
Have a care for him.

There the dews of quiet fall,
  Singing birds and soft winds stray:
Shall the tender Heart of all
  Be less kind than they?

What he was and what he is
  They who ask may haply find,
If they read this prayer of his
  Which he left behind.

Pardon, Lord, the lips that dare
Shape in words a mortal's prayer!
Prayer, that, when my day is done,
And I see its setting sun,
Shorn and beamless, cold and dim,
Sink beneath the horizon's rim,—
When this ball of rock and clay
Crumbles from my feet away,
And the solid shores of sense
Melt into the vague immense,
Father! I may come to Thee
Even with the beggar's plea,
As the poorest of Thy poor,
With my needs, and nothing more.

Not as one who seeks his home
With a step assured I come;
Still behind the tread I hear
Of my life-companion, Fear;
Still a shadow deep and vast
From my westering feet is cast,
Wavering, doubtful, undefined,
Never shapen nor outlined:
From myself the fear has grown,
And the shadow is my own.
Yet, O Lord, through all a sense
Of Thy tender providence
Stays my failing heart on Thee,
And confirms the feeble knee;
And, at times, my worn feet press
Spaces of cool quietness,
Lilied whiteness shone upon
Not by light of moon or sun.
Hours there be of inmost calm,
Broken but by grateful psalm,
When I love Thee more than fear Thee,
And Thy blessed Christ seems near me,
With forgiving look, as when
He beheld the Magdalen.
Well I know that all things move
To the spheral rhythm of love,—
That to Thee, O Lord of all!
Nothing can of chance befall:
Child and seraph, mote and star,
Well Thou knowest what we are!
Through Thy vast creative plan
Looking, from the worm to man,
There is pity in Thine eyes,
But no hatred nor surprise.
Not in blind caprice of will,
Not in cunning sleight of skill,
Not for show of power, was wrought
Nature's marvel in Thy thought.
Never careless hand and vain
Smites these chords of joy and pain;
No immortal selfishness
Plays the game of curse and bless:
Heaven and earth are witnesses
That Thy glory goodness is.
Not for sport of mind and force
Hast Thou made Thy universe,
But as atmosphere and zone
Of Thy loving heart alone.
Man, who walketh in a show,
Sees before him, to and fro,
Shadow and illusion go;
All things flow and fluctuate,
Now contract and now dilate.
In the welter of this sea,
Nothing stable is but Thee;
In this whirl of swooning trance,
Thou alone art permanence;
All without Thee only seems,
All beside is choice of dreams.
Never yet in darkest mood
Doubted I that Thou wast good,
Nor mistook my will for fate,
Pain of sin for heavenly hate,—
Never dreamed the gates of pearl
Rise from out the burning marl,
Or that good can only live
Of the bad conservative,
And through counterpoise of hell
Heaven alone be possible.

For myself alone I doubt;
All is well, I know, without;
I alone the beauty mar,
I alone the music jar.
Yet, with hands by evil stained,
And an ear by discord pained,
I am groping for the keys
Of the heavenly harmonies;

Still within my heart I bear
Love for all things good and fair.
Hands of want or souls in pain
Have not sought my door in vain;
I have kept my fealty good
To the human brotherhood;
Scarcely have I asked in prayer
That which others might not share.
I, who hear with secret shame
Praise that paineth more than blame,
Rich alone in favors lent,
Virtuous by accident,
Doubtful where I fain would rest,
Frailest where I seem the best,
Only strong for lack of test,—
What am I, that I should press
Special pleas of selfishness,
Coolly mounting into heaven
On my neighbor unforgiven?
Ne'er to me, howe'er disguised,
Comes a saint unrecognized;
Never fails my heart to greet
Noble deed with warmer beat;
Halt and maimed, I own not less
All the grace of holiness;
Nor, through shame or self-distrust,
Less I love the pure and just.
Lord, forgive these words of mine:
What have I that is not Thine?
Whatsoe'er I fain would boast
Needs Thy pitying pardon most.
Thou, O Elder Brother! who
In Thy flesh our trial knew,
Thou, who hast been touched by these
Our most sad infirmities,
Thou alone the gulf canst span
In the dual heart of man,
And between the soul and sense
Reconcile all difference,
Change the dream of me and mine
For the truth of Thee and Thine,
And, through chaos, doubt, and strife,
Interfuse Thy calm of life.
Haply, thus by Thee renewed,
In Thy borrowed goodness good,
Some sweet morning yet in God's
Dim, æonian periods,
Joyful I shall wake to see
Those I love who rest in Thee,
And to them in Thee allied,
Shall my soul be satisfied.
Scarcely Hope hath shaped for me
What the future life may be.
Other lips may well be bold;
Like the publican of old,
I can only urge the plea,
"Lord, be merciful to me!"
Nothing of desert I claim,
Unto me belongeth shame.
Not for me the crowns of gold,
Palms, and harpings manifold;
Not for erring eye and feet
Jasper wall and golden street.
What Thou wilt, O Father, give!
All is gain that I receive.
If my voice I may not raise
In the elders' song of praise,
If I may not, sin-defiled,
Claim my birthright as a child,
Suffer it that I to Thee
As an hired servant be;
Let the lowliest task be mine,
Grateful, so the work be Thine;
Let me find the humblest place
In the shadow of Thy grace:
Blest to me were any spot
Where temptation whispers not.
If there be some weaker one,
Give me strength to help him on;
If a blinder soul there be,
Let me guide him nearer Thee.
Make my mortal dreams come true
With the work I fain would do;
Clothe with life the weak intent,
Let me be the thing I meant;
Let me find in Thy employ
Peace that dearer is than joy;
Out of self to love be led
And to heaven acclimated,
Until all things sweet and good
Seem my natural habitude.

So we read the prayer of him
  Who, with John of Labadie,
Trod, of old, the oozy rim
  Of the Zuyder Zee.

Thus did Andrew Rykman pray.
  Are we wiser, better grown,
That we may not, in our day,
  Make his prayer our own?

1862 1863

BRYANT ON HIS BIRTHDAY

We praise not now the poet's art,
The rounded beauty of his song;
Who weighs him from his life apart
Must do his nobler nature wrong.

Not for the eye, familiar grown
With charms to common sight denied,—
The marvellous gift he shares alone
With him who walked on Rydal-side;

Not for rapt hymn nor woodland lay,
Too grave for smiles, too sweet for tears;
We speak his praise who wears today
The glory of his seventy years.

When Peace brings Freedom in her train,
Let happy lips his songs rehearse:
His life is now his noblest strain,
His manhood better than his verse!

Thank God! his hand on Nature's keys
Its cunning keeps at life's full span;
But, dimmed and dwarfed, in times like these,
The poet seems beside the man!

So be it! let the garlands die,
The singer's wreath, the painter's meed,
Let our names perish, if thereby
Our country may be saved and freed!

1864 1865

THE VANISHERS

Sweetest of all childlike dreams
In the simple Indian lore
Still to me the legend seems
Of the shapes who flit before.

Flitting, passing, seen and gone,
Never reached nor found at rest,
Baffling search, but beckoning on
To the Sunset of the Blest.

From the clefts of mountain rocks,
Through the dark of lowland firs,
Flash the eyes and flow the locks
Of the mystic Vanishers!

And the fisher in his skiff,
And the hunter on the moss,
Hear their call from cape and cliff,
See their hands the birch-leaves toss.

Wistful, longing, through the green
Twilight of the clustered pines,
In their faces rarely seen
Beauty more than mortal shines.

Fringed with gold their mantles flow
On the slopes of westering knolls;
In the wind they whisper low
Of the Sunset Land of Souls.

Doubt who may, O friend of mine!
Thou and I have seen them too;
On before with beck and sign
Still they glide, and we pursue.

More than clouds of purple trail
In the gold of setting day;
More than gleams of wing or sail
Beckon from the sea-mist gray.

Glimpses of immortal youth,
Gleams and glories seen and flown,
Far-heard voices sweet with truth,
Airs from viewless Eden blown;

Beauty that eludes our grasp,
Sweetness that transcends our taste,
Loving hands we may not clasp,
Shining feet that mock our haste;

Gentle eyes we closed below,
Tender voices heard once more,
Smile and call us, as they go
On and onward, still before.

Guided thus, O friend of mine!
Let us walk our little way,
Knowing by each beckoning sign
That we are not quite astray.

Chase we still, with baffled feet,
Smiling eye and waving hand,
Sought and seeker soon shall meet,
Lost and found, in Sunset Land!

1864 1864

LAUS DEO!

It is done!
Clang of bell and roar of gun
Send the tidings up and down.
How the belfries rock and reel!
How the great guns, peal on peal,
Fling the joy from town to town!

Ring, O bells!
Every stroke exulting tells
Of the burial hour of crime.
Loud and long, that all may hear,
Ring for every listening ear
Of Eternity and Time!

Let us kneel:
God's own voice is in that peal,
And this spot is holy ground.
Lord, forgive us! What are we,
That our eyes this glory see,
That our ears have heard the sound!

For the Lord
On the whirlwind is abroad;
In the earthquake He has spoken;
He has smitten with His thunder
The iron walls asunder,
And the gates of brass are broken!

Loud and long
Lift the old exulting song;
Sing with Miriam by the sea,
He has cast the mighty down;
Horse and rider sink and drown;
"He hath triumphed gloriously!"

Did we dare,
In our agony of prayer,
Ask for more than He has done?
When was ever His right hand
Over any time or land
Stretched as now beneath the sun?

How they pale,
Ancient myth and song and tale,
In this wonder of our days,
When the cruel rod of war
Blossoms white with righteous law,
And the wrath of man is praise!

Blotted out!
All within and all about
Shall a fresher life begin;
Freer breathe the universe
As it rolls its heavy curse
On the dead and buried sin!

It is done!
In the circuit of the sun
Shall the sound thereof go forth.
It shall bid the sad rejoice,
It shall give the dumb a voice,
It shall belt with joy the earth!

Ring and swing,
Bells of joy! On morning's wing
Send the song of praise abroad!
With a sound of broken chains
Tell the nations that He reigns,
Who alone is Lord and God!

1865 1865

THE ETERNAL GOODNESS

O FRIENDS! with whom my feet have trod
The quiet aisles of prayer,
Glad witness to your zeal for God
And love of man I bear.

I trace your lines of argument;
Your logic linked and strong
I weigh as one who dreads dissent,
And fears a doubt as wrong.

But still my human hands are weak
To hold your iron creeds:
Against the words ye bid me speak
My heart within me pleads.

Who fathoms the Eternal Thought?
Who talks of scheme and plan?
The Lord is God! He needeth not
The poor device of man.

I walk with bare, hushed feet the ground
Ye tread with boldness shod;
I dare not fix with mete and bound
The love and power of God.

Ye praise His justice; even such
His pitying love I deem:
Ye seek a king; I fain would touch
The robe that hath no seam.

Ye see the curse which overbroods
A world of pain and loss;
I hear our Lord's beatitudes
And prayer upon the cross.

More than your schoolmen teach, within
Myself, alas! I know:
Too dark ye cannot paint the sin,
Too small the merit show.

I bow my forehead to the dust,
I veil mine eyes for shame,
And urge, in trembling self-distrust,
A prayer without a claim.

I see the wrong that round me lies,
  I feel the guilt within;
I hear, with groan and travail-cries,
  The world confess its sin.

Yet, in the maddening maze of things,
  And tossed by storm and flood,
To one fixed trust my spirit clings;
  I know that God is good!

Not mine to look where cherubim
  And seraphs may not see,
But nothing can be good in Him
  Which evil is in me.

The wrong that pains my soul below
  I dare not throne above,
I know not of His hate,—I know
  His goodness and His love.

I dimly guess from blessings known
  Of greater out of sight,
And, with the chastened Psalmist, own
  His judgments too are right.

I long for household voices gone,
  For vanished smiles I long,
But God hath led my dear ones on,
  And He can do no wrong.

I know not what the future hath
  Of marvel or surprise,
Assured alone that life and death
  His mercy underlies.

And if my heart and flesh are weak
  To bear an untried pain,
The bruisèd reed He will not break,
  But strengthen and sustain.

No offering of my own I have,
  Nor works my faith to prove;
I can but give the gifts He gave,
  And plead His love for love.

And so beside the Silent Sea
  I wait the muffled oar;
No harm from Him can come to me
  On ocean or on shore.

I know not where His islands lift
  Their fronded palms in air;
I only know I cannot drift
  Beyond His love and care.

O brothers! if my faith is vain,
  If hopes like these betray,
Pray for me that my feet may gain
  The sure and safer way.

And Thou, O Lord! by whom are seen
  Thy creatures as they be,
Forgive me if too close I lean
  My human heart on Thee!

1865 1867

OUR MASTER

IMMORTAL Love, forever full,
  Forever flowing free,
Forever shared, forever whole,
  A never-ebbing sea!

Our outward lips confess the name
  All other names above;
Love only knoweth whence it came,
  And comprehendeth love.

Blow, winds of God, awake and blow
  The mists of earth away!
Shine out, O Light Divine, and show
  How wide and far we stray!

Hush every lip, close every book,
  The strife of tongues forbear;
Why forward reach, or backward look,
  For love that clasps like air?

We may not climb the heavenly steeps
  To bring the Lord Christ down:
In vain we search the lowest deeps,
  For Him no depths can drown.

Nor holy bread, nor blood of grape,
  The lineaments restore
Of Him we know in outward shape
  And in the flesh no more.

He cometh not a king to reign;
  The world's long hope is dim;
The weary centuries watch in vain
  The clouds of heaven for Him.

Death comes, life goes; the asking eye
  And ear are answerless;
The grave is dumb, the hollow sky
  Is sad with silentness.

The letter fails, and systems fall,
  And every symbol wanes;
The Spirit over-brooding all
  Eternal Love remains.

And not for signs in heaven above
  Or earth below they look,
Who know with John His smile of love,
  With Peter His rebuke.

In joy of inward peace, or sense
  Of sorrow over sin,
He is His own best evidence,
  His witness is within.

No fable old, nor mythic lore,
  Nor dream of bards and seers,
No dead fact stranded on the shore
  Of the oblivious years;—

But warm, sweet, tender, even yet
  A present help is He;
And faith has still its Olivet,
  And love its Galilee.

The healing of His seamless dress
  Is by our beds of pain;
We touch Him in life's throng and press,
  And we are whole again.

Through Him the first fond prayers are said
  Our lips of childhood frame,
The last low whispers of our dead
  Are burdened with His name.

Our Lord and Master of us all!
  Whate'er our name or sign,
We own Thy sway, we hear Thy call,
  We test our lives by Thine.

Thou judgest us; Thy purity
  Doth all our lusts condemn;
The love that draws us nearer Thee
  Is hot with wrath to them.

Our thoughts lie open to Thy sight;
  And, naked to Thy glance,
Our secret sins are in the light
  Of Thy pure countenance.

Thy healing pains, a keen distress
  Thy tender light shines in;
Thy sweetness is the bitterness,
  Thy grace the pang of sin.

Yet, weak and blinded though we be,
  Thou dost our service own;
We bring our varying gifts to Thee,
  And Thou rejectest none.

To Thee our full humanity,
  Its joys and pains, belong;
The wrong of man to man on Thee
  Inflicts a deeper wrong.

Who hates, hates Thee, who loves becomes
  Therein to Thee allied;
All sweet accords of hearts and homes
  In Thee are multiplied.

Deep strike Thy roots, O heavenly Vine,
  Within our earthly sod,
Most human and yet most divine,
  The flower of man and God!

O Love! O Life! Our faith and sight
  Thy presence maketh one,
As through transfigured clouds of white
  We trace the noon-day sun.

So, to our mortal eyes subdued,
  Flesh-veiled, but not concealed,
We know in Thee the fatherhood
  And heart of God revealed.

We faintly hear, we dimly see,
  In differing phrase we pray;
But, dim or clear, we own in Thee
  The Light, the Truth, the Way!

The homage that we render Thee
  Is still our Father's own;
No jealous claim or rivalry
  Divides the Cross and Throne.

To do Thy will is more than praise,
  As words are less than deeds,
And simple trust can find Thy ways
  We miss with chart of creeds.

No pride of self Thy service hath,
  No place for me and mine;
Our human strength is weakness, death
  Our life, apart from Thine.

Apart from Thee all gain is loss,
  All labor vainly done;
The solemn shadow of Thy Cross
  Is better than the sun.

Alone, O Love ineffable!
  Thy saving name is given;
To turn aside from Thee is hell,
  To walk with Thee is heaven!

How vain, secure in all Thou art,
  Our noisy championship!
The sighing of the contrite heart
  Is more than flattering lip.

Not Thine the bigot's partial plea,
  Nor Thine the zealot's ban;
Thou well canst spare a love of Thee
  Which ends in hate of man.

Our Friend, our Brother, and our Lord,
  What may Thy service be?—
Nor name, nor form, nor ritual word,
  But simply following Thee.

We bring no ghastly holocaust,
  We pile no graven stone;
He serves Thee best who loveth most
  His brothers and Thy own.

Thy litanies, sweet offices
  Of love and gratitude;
Thy sacramental liturgies,
  The joy of doing good.

In vain shall waves of incense drift
  The vaulted nave around,
In vain the minster turret lift
  Its brazen weights of sound.

The heart must ring Thy Christmas bells,
  Thy inward altars raise;
Its faith and hope Thy canticles,
  And its obedience praise!

1866? 1866

SNOW-BOUND

A WINTER IDYL

"As the Spirits of Darkness be stronger in the dark, so Good Spirits, which be Angels of Light, are augmented not only by the Divine light of the Sun, but also by our common VVood Fire: and as the Celestial Fire drives away dark spirits, so also this our Fire of VVood doth the same."—Cor. Agrippa, *Occult Philosophy*, Book I. ch. v.

"Announced by all the trumpets of the sky,
Arrives the snow, and, driving o'er the fields,
Seems nowhere to alight: the whited air
Hides hills and woods, the river and the heaven,
And veils the farm-house at the garden's end.
The sled and traveller stopped, the courier's feet
Delayed, all friends shut out, the housemates sit
Around the radiant fireplace, enclosed
In a tumultuous privacy of storm."
—Emerson, *The Snow-Storm.*

The sun that brief December day
Rose cheerless over hills of gray,
And, darkly circled, gave at noon
A sadder light than waning moon.
Slow tracing down the thickening sky
Its mute and ominous prophecy,
A portent seeming less than threat,
It sank from sight before it set.
A chill no coat, however stout,
Of homespun stuff could quite shut out,
A hard, dull bitterness of cold,
That checked, mid-vein, the circling race
Of life-blood in the sharpened face,
The coming of the snow-storm told.
The wind blew east; we heard the roar
Of Ocean on his wintry shore,
And felt the strong pulse throbbing there
Beat with low rhythm our inland air.

Meanwhile we did our nightly chores,—
Brought in the wood from out of doors,
Littered the stalls, and from the mows
Raked down the herd's-grass for the cows:
Heard the horse whinnying for his corn;
And, sharply clashing horn on horn,
Impatient down the stanchion rows
The cattle shake their walnut bows;
While, peering from his early perch
Upon the scaffold's pole of birch,
The cock his crested helmet bent
And down his querulous challenge sent.

Unwarmed by any sunset light
The gray day darkened into night,
A night made hoary with the swarm
And whirl-dance of the blinding storm,
As zigzag, wavering to and fro,
Crossed and recrossed the wingèd snow:
And ere the early bedtime came
The white drift piled the window-frame,
And through the glass the clothes-line posts
Looked in like tall and sheeted ghosts.

So all night long the storm roared on:
The morning broke without a sun;
In tiny spherule traced with lines

Of Nature's geometric signs,
In starry flake, and pellicle,
All day the hoary meteor fell;
And, when the second morning shone,
We looked upon a world unknown,
On nothing we could call our own.
Around the glistening wonder bent
The blue walls of the firmament,
No cloud above, no earth below,—
A universe of sky and snow!
The old familiar sights of ours
Took marvellous shapes; strange domes and towers
Rose up where sty or corn-crib stood,
Or garden-wall, or belt of wood;
A smooth white mound the brush-pile showed,
A fenceless drift what once was road;
The bridle-post an old man sat
With loose-flung coat and high cocked hat;
The well-curb had a Chinese roof;
And even the long sweep, high aloof,
In its slant splendor, seemed to tell
Of Pisa's leaning miracle.

A prompt, decisive man, no breath
Our father wasted: "Boys, a path!"
Well pleased, (for when did farmer boy
Count such a summons less than joy?)
Our buskins on our feet we drew;
With mittened hands, and caps drawn low,
To guard our necks and ears from snow,
We cut the solid whiteness through.
And, where the drift was deepest, made
A tunnel walled and overlaid
With dazzling crystal: we had read
Of rare Aladdin's wondrous cave,
And to our own his name we gave,
With many a wish the luck were ours
To test his lamp's supernal powers.
We reached the barn with merry din,
And roused the prisoned brutes within.
The old horse thrust his long head out,
And grave with wonder gazed about;
The cock his lusty greeting said,
And forth his speckled harem led;
The oxen lashed their tails, and hooked,
And mild reproach of hunger looked;
The hornèd patriarch of the sheep,
Like Egypt's Amun roused from sleep,
Shook his sage head with gesture mute,
And emphasized with stamp of foot.

All day the gusty north-wind bore
The loosening drift its breath before;
Low circling round its southern zone,
The sun through dazzling snow-mist shone.
No church-bell lent its Christian tone
To the savage air, no social smoke
Curled over woods of snow-hung oak.
A solitude made more intense
By dreary-voicèd elements,
The shrieking of the mindless wind,
The moaning tree-boughs swaying blind,
And on the glass the unmeaning beat
Of ghostly finger-tips of sleet.
Beyond the circle of our hearth
No welcome sound of toil or mirth
Unbound the spell, and testified
Of human life and thought outside.
We minded that the sharpest ear
The buried brooklet could not hear,
The music of whose liquid lip
Had been to us companionship,
And, in our lonely life, had grown
To have an almost human tone.

As night drew on, and, from the crest
Of wooded knolls that ridged the west,
The sun, a snow-blown traveller, sank
From sight beneath the smothering bank,
We piled, with care, our nightly stack
Of wood against the chimney-back,—
The oaken log, green, huge, and thick,
And on its top the stout back-stick;
The knotty forestick laid apart,
And filled between with curious art
The ragged brush; then, hovering near,
We watched the first red blaze appear,
Heard the sharp crackle, caught the gleam
On whitewashed wall and sagging beam,
Until the old, rude-furnished room
Burst, flower-like, into rosy bloom;
While radiant with a mimic flame
Outside the sparkling drift became,
And through the bare-boughed lilac-tree
Our own warm hearth seemed blazing free.
The crane and pendent trammels showed,
The Turks' heads on the andirons glowed;
While childish fancy, prompt to tell
The meaning of the miracle,
Whispered the old rhyme: "*Under the tree,*
When fire outdoors burns merrily,
There the witches are making tea."

The moon above the eastern wood
Shone at its full; the hill-range stood
Transfigured in the silver flood,
Its blown snows flashing cold and keen,
Dead white, save where some sharp ravine
Took shadow, or the sombre green
Of hemlocks turned to pitchy black
Against the whiteness at their back.
For such a world and such a night
Most fitting that unwarming light,
Which only seemed where'er it fell
To make the coldness visible.

Shut in from all the world without,
We sat the clean-winged hearth about,
Content to let the north-wind roar
In baffled rage at pane and door,
While the red logs before us beat
The frost-line back with tropic heat;
And ever, when a louder blast
Shook beam and rafter as it passed,
The merrier up its roaring draught
The great throat of the chimney laughed;
The house-dog on his paws outspread
Laid to the fire his drowsy head,
The cat's dark silhouette on the wall
A couchant tiger's seemed to fall;
And, for the winter fireside meet,
Between the andirons' straddling feet,
The mug of cider simmered slow,
The apples sputtered in a row,
And, close at hand, the basket stood
With nuts from brown October's wood.

What matter how the night behaved?
What matter how the north-wind raved?
Blow high, blow low, not all its snow
Could quench our hearth-fire's ruddy glow.
O Time and Change!—with hair as gray
As was my sire's that winter day,
How strange it seems, with so much gone
Of life and love, to still live on!
Ah, brother! only I and thou
Are left of all that circle now,—
The dear home faces whereupon
That fitful firelight paled and shone.
Henceforth, listen as we will,
The voices of that hearth are still;
Look where we may, the wide earth o'er
Those lighted faces smile no more.
We tread the paths their feet have worn,
We sit beneath their orchard trees,
We hear, like them, the hum of bees
And rustle of the bladed corn;
We turn the pages that they read,
Their written words we linger o'er,
But in the sun they cast no shade,
No voice is heard, no sign is made,
No step is on the conscious floor!
Yet Love will dream, and Faith will trust,
(Since He who knows our need is just,)
That somehow, somewhere, meet we must.
Alas for him who never sees
The stars shine through his cypress-trees!
Who, hopeless, lays his dead away,
Nor looks to see the breaking day
Across the mournful marbles play!
Who hath not learned, in hours of faith,
The truth to flesh and sense unknown,
That Life is ever lord of Death,
And Love can never lose its own!

We sped the time with stories old,
Wrought puzzles out, and riddles told,
Or stammered from our school-book lore
"The Chief of Gambia's golden shore."
How often since, when all the land
Was clay in Slavery's shaping hand,
As if a far-blown trumpet stirred
The languorous sin-sick air, I heard:
"*Does not the voice of reason cry,*
Claim the first right which Nature gave,
From the red scourge of bondage fly,
Nor deign to live a burdened slave!"
Our father rode again his ride
On Memphremagog's wooded side;
Sat down again to moose and samp
In trapper's hut and Indian camp;
Lived o'er the old idyllic ease
Beneath St. François' hemlock-trees;
Again for him the moonlight shone
On Norman cap and bodiced zone;
Again he heard the violin play
Which led the village dance away.
And mingled in its merry whirl
The grandam and the laughing girl.
Or, nearer home, our steps he led
Where Salisbury's level marshes spread
Mile-wide as flies the laden bee;
Where merry mowers, hale and strong,
Swept, scythe on scythe, their swaths along
The low green prairies of the sea.

We shared the fishing off Boar's Head,
  And round the rocky Isles of Shoals
  The hake-broil on the drift-wood coals;
The chowder on the sand-beach made,
Dipped by the hungry, steaming hot
With spoons of clam-shell from the pot.
We heard the tales of witchcraft old,
And dream and sign and marvel told
To sleepy listeners as they lay
Stretched idly on the salted hay,
Adrift along the winding shores,
When favoring breezes deigned to blow
The square sail of the gundelow
And idle lay the useless oars.

Our mother, while she turned her wheel
Or run the new-knit stocking-heel,
Told how the Indian hordes came down
At midnight on Cocheco town,
And how her own great-uncle bore
His cruel scalp-mark to fourscore.
Recalling, in her fitting phrase,
  So rich and picturesque and free,
  (The common unrhymed poetry
Of simple life and country ways,)
The story of her early days,—
She made us welcome to her home;
Old hearths grew wide to give us room;
We stole with her a frightened look
At the gray wizard's conjuring-book,
The fame whereof went far and wide
Through all the simple country-side;
We heard the hawks at twilight play,
The boat-horn on Piscataqua,
The loon's weird laughter far away;
We fished her little trout-brook, knew
What flowers in wood and meadow grew,
What sunny hillsides autumn-brown
She climbed to shake the ripe nuts down,
Saw where in sheltered cove and bay
The ducks' black squadron anchored lay,
And heard the wild-geese calling loud
Beneath the gray November cloud.

Then, haply, with a look more grave,
And soberer tone, some tale she gave
From painful Sewel's ancient tome,
Beloved in every Quaker home,
Of faith fire-winged by martyrdom,
Or Chalkley's Journal, old and quaint,—
Gentlest of skippers, rare sea-saint!—
Who, when the dreary calms prevailed,
And water-butt and bread-cask failed,
And cruel, hungry eyes pursued
His portly presence mad for food,
With dark hints muttered under breath
Of casting lots for life or death,
Offered, if Heaven withheld supplies,
To be himself the sacrifice.
Then, suddenly, as if to save
The good man from his living grave,
A ripple on the water grew,
A school of porpoise flashed in view.
"Take, eat," he said, "and be content;
These fishes in my stead are sent
By Him who gave the tangled ram
To spare the child of Abraham."

Our uncle, innocent of books,
Was rich in lore of fields and brooks,
The ancient teachers never dumb
Of Nature's unhoused lyceum.
In moons and tides and weather wise,
He read the clouds as prophecies,
And foul or fair could well divine,
By many an occult hint and sign,
Holding the cunning-warded keys
To all the woodcraft mysteries;
Himself to Nature's heart so near
That all her voices in his ear
Of beast or bird had meanings clear,
Like Apollonius of old,
Who knew the tales the sparrows told,
Or Hermes, who interpreted
What the sage cranes of Nilus said;
A simple, guileless, childlike man,
Content to live where life began;
Strong only on his native grounds,
The little world of sights and sounds
Whose girdle was the parish bounds,
Whereof his fondly partial pride
The common features magnified,
As Surrey hills to mountains grew
In White of Selborne's loving view,—
He told how teal and loon he shot,
And how the eagle's eggs he got,
The feats on pond and river done,
The prodigies of rod and gun;
Till, warming with the tales he told,
Forgotten was the outside cold,
The bitter wind unheeded blew,
From ripening corn the pigeons flew,
The partridge drummed i' the wood, the mink

Went fishing down the river-brink;
In fields with bean or clover gay,
The woodchuck, like a hermit gray,
  Peered from the doorway of his cell;
The muskrat plied the mason's trade,
And tier by tier his mud-walls laid;
And from the shagbark overhead
  The grizzled squirrel dropped his shell.

Next, the dear aunt, whose smile of cheer
And voice in dreams I see and hear,—
The sweetest woman ever Fate
Perverse denied a household mate,
Who, lonely, homeless, not the less
Found peace in love's unselfishness,
And welcome wheresoe'er she went,
A calm and gracious element,
Whose presence seemed the sweet income
And womanly atmosphere of home,—
Called up her girlhood memories,
The huskings and the apple-bees,
The sleigh-rides and the summer sails,
Weaving through all the poor details
And homespun warp of circumstance
A golden woof-thread of romance.
For well she kept her genial mood
And simple faith of maidenhood;
Before her still a cloud-land lay,
The mirage loomed across her way;
The morning dew, that dries so soon
With others, glistened at her noon;
Through years of toil and soil and care,
From glossy tress to thin gray hair,
All unprofaned she held apart
The virgin fancies of the heart.
Be shame to him of woman born
Who hath for such but thought of scorn.

There, too, our elder sister plied
Her evening task the stand beside;
A full, rich nature, free to trust,
Truthful and almost sternly just,
Impulsive, earnest, prompt to act,
And make her generous thought a fact,
Keeping with many a light disguise
The secret of self-sacrifice.
O heart sore-tried! thou hast the best,
That Heaven itself could give thee,—rest,
Rest from all bitter thoughts and things!
  How many a poor one's blessing went
  With thee beneath the low green tent
Whose curtain never outward swings!

As one who held herself a part
Of all she saw, and let her heart
  Against the household bosom lean,
Upon the motley-braided mat
Our youngest and our dearest sat,
Lifting her large, sweet, asking eyes,
  Now bathed in the unfading green
And holy peace of Paradise.
Oh, looking from some heavenly hill,
  Or from the shade of saintly palms,
  Or silver reach of river calms,
Do those large eyes behold me still?
With me one little year ago:—
The chill weight of the winter snow
  For months upon her grave has lain;
And now, when summer south-winds blow
  And brier and harebell bloom again,
I tread the pleasant paths we trod,
I see the violet-sprinkled sod
Whereon she leaned, too frail and weak
The hillside flowers she loved to seek,
Yet following me where'er I went
With dark eyes full of love's content.
The birds are glad; the brier-rose fills
The air with sweetness; all the hills
Stretch green to June's unclouded sky;
But still I wait with ear and eye
For something gone which should be nigh,
A loss in all familiar things,
In flower that blooms, and bird that sings.
And yet, dear heart! remembering thee,
  Am I not richer than of old?
Safe in thy immortality,
  What change can reach the wealth I hold?
  What chance can mar the pearl and gold
Thy love hath left in trust with me?
And while in life's late afternoon,
  Where cool and long the shadows grow,
I walk to meet the night that soon
  Shall shape and shadow overflow,
I cannot feel that thou art far,
Since near at need the angels are;
And when the sunset gates unbar,
  Shall I not see thee waiting stand,
And, white against the evening star,
  The welcome of thy beckoning hand?

Brisk wielder of the birch and rule,
The master of the district school
Held at the fire his favored place,
Its warm glow lit a laughing face

Fresh-hued and fair, where scarce appeared
The uncertain prophecy of beard.
He teased the mitten-blinded cat,
Played cross-pins on my uncle's hat,
Sang songs, and told us what befalls
In classic Dartmouth's college halls.
Born the wild Northern hills among,
From whence his yeoman father wrung
By patient toil subsistence scant,
Not competence and yet not want,
He early gained the power to pay
His cheerful, self-reliant way;
Could doff at ease his scholar's gown
To peddle wares from town to town;
Or through the long vacation's reach
In lonely lowland districts teach,
Where all the droll experience found
At stranger hearths in boarding round,
The moonlit skater's keen delight,
The sleigh-drive through the frosty night,
The rustic-party, with its rough
Accompaniment of blind-man's-buff,
And whirling-plate, and forfeits paid,
His winter task a pastime made.
Happy the snow-locked homes wherein
He tuned his merry violin,
Or played the athlete in the barn,
Or held the good dame's winding-yarn,
Or mirth-provoking versions told
Of classic legends rare and old,
Wherein the scenes of Greece and Rome
Had all the commonplace of home,
And little seemed at best the odds
'Twixt Yankee pedlers and old gods;
Where Pindus-born Arachthus took
The guise of any grist-mill brook,
And dread Olympus at his will
Became a huckleberry hill.

A careless boy that night he seemed;
But at his desk he had the look
And air of one who wisely schemed,
And hostage from the future took
In trainèd thought and lore of book.
Large-brained, clear-eyed, of such as he
Shall Freedom's young apostles be,
Who, following in War's bloody trail,
Shall every lingering wrong assail;
All chains from limb and spirit strike,
Uplift the black and white alike;
Scatter before their swift advance
The darkness and the ignorance,
The pride, the lust, the squalid sloth,
Which nurtured Treason's monstrous growth,
Made murder pastime, and the hell
Of prison-torture possible;
The cruel lie of caste refute,
Old forms remould, and substitute
For Slavery's lash the freeman's will,
For blind routine, wise-handed skill;
A school-house plant on every hill,
Stretching in radiate nerve-lines thence
The quick wires of intelligence;
Till North and South together brought
Shall own the same electric thought,
In peace a common flag salute,
And, side by side in labor's free
And unresentful rivalry,
Harvest the fields wherein they fought.

Another guest that winter night
Flashed back from lustrous eyes the light.
Unmarked by time, and yet not young,
The honeyed music of her tongue
And words of meekness scarcely told
A nature passionate and bold,
Strong, self-concentred, spurning guide,
Its milder features dwarfed beside
Her unbent will's majestic pride.
She sat among us, at the best,
A not unfeared, half-welcome guest,
Rebuking with her cultured phrase
Our homeliness of words and ways.
A certain pard-like, treacherous grace
Swayed the lithe limbs and dropped the lash,
Lent the white teeth their dazzling flash;
And under low brows, black with night,
Rayed out at times a dangerous light;
The sharp heat-lightnings of her face
Presaging ill to him whom Fate
Condemned to share her love or hate.
A woman tropical, intense
In thought and act, in soul and sense,
She blended in a like degree
The vixen and the devotee,
Revealing with each freak or feint
The temper of Petruchio's Kate,
The raptures of Siena's saint.
Her tapering hand and rounded wrist
Had facile power to form a fist;
The warm, dark languish of her eyes
Was never safe from wrath's surprise.

Brows saintly calm and lips devout
Knew every change of scowl and pout;
And the sweet voice had notes more high
And shrill for social battle-cry.

Since then what old cathedral town
Has missed her pilgrim staff and gown,
What convent-gate has held its lock
Against the challenge of her knock!
Through Smyrna's plague-hushed thorough-
fares,
Up sea-set Malta's rocky stairs,
Gray olive slopes of hills that hem
Thy tombs and shrines, Jerusalem,
Or startling on her desert throne
The crazy Queen of Lebanon
With claims fantastic as her own,
Her tireless feet have held their way;
And still, unrestful, bowed, and gray,
She watches under Eastern skies,
With hope each day renewed and fresh,
The Lord's quick coming in the flesh,
Whereof she dreams and prophesies!

Where'er her troubled path may be,
The Lord's sweet pity with her go!
The outward wayward life we see,
The hidden springs we may not know.
Nor is it given us to discern
What threads the fatal sisters spun,
Through what ancestral years has run
The sorrow with the woman born,
What forged her cruel chain of moods,
What set her feet in solitudes,
And held the love within her mute,
What mingled madness in the blood,
A life-long discord and annoy,
Water of tears with oil of joy,
And hid within the folded bud
Perversities of flower and fruit.
It is not ours to separate
The tangled skein of will and fate,
To show what metes and bounds should stand
Upon the soul's debatable land,
And between choice and Providence
Divide the circle of events;
But He who knows our frame is just,
Merciful and compassionate,
And full of sweet assurances
And hope for all the language is,
That He remembereth we are dust!

At last the great logs, crumbling low,
Sent out a dull and duller glow,
The bull's-eye watch that hung in view,
Ticking its weary circuit through,
Pointed with mutely warning sign
Its black hand to the hour of nine.
That sign the pleasant circle broke:
My uncle ceased his pipe to smoke,
Knocked from its bowl the refuse gray,
And laid it tenderly away;
Then roused himself to safely cover
The dull red brands with ashes over.
And while, with care, our mother laid
The work aside, her steps she stayed
One moment, seeking to express
Her grateful sense of happiness
For food and shelter, warmth and health,
And love's contentment more than wealth,
With simple wishes (not the weak,
Vain prayers which no fulfilment seek,
But such as warm the generous heart,
O'er-prompt to do with Heaven its part)
That none might lack, that bitter night,
For bread and clothing, warmth and light.

Within our beds awhile we heard
The wind that round the gables roared,
With now and then a ruder shock,
Which made our very bedsteads rock.
We heard the loosened clapboards tost,
The board-nails snapping in the frost;
And on us, through the unplastered wall,
Felt the light sifted snow-flakes fall.
But sleep stole on, as sleep will do
When hearts are light and life is new;
Faint and more faint the murmurs grew,
Till in the summer-land of dreams
They softened to the sound of streams,
Low stir of leaves, and dip of oars,
And lapsing waves on quiet shores.

Next morn we wakened with the shout
Of merry voices high and clear;
And saw the teamsters drawing near
To break the drifted highways out.
Down the long hillside treading slow
We saw the half-buried oxen go,
Shaking the snow from heads uptost,
Their straining nostrils white with frost.
Before our door the straggling train
Drew up, an added team to gain.

The elders threshed their hands a-cold,
Passed, with the cider-mug, their jokes
From lip to lip; the younger folks
Down the loose snow-banks, wrestling, rolled,
Then toiled again the cavalcade
O'er windy hill, through clogged ravine,
And woodland paths that wound between
Low drooping pine-boughs winter-weighed.
From every barn a team afoot,
At every house a new recruit,
Where, drawn by Nature's subtlest law,
Haply the watchful young men saw
Sweet doorway pictures of the curls
And curious eyes of merry girls,
Lifting their hands in mock defence
Against the snow-ball's compliments,
And reading in each missive tost
The charm with Eden never lost.

We heard once more the sleigh-bells' sound;
And, following where the teamsters led,
The wise old Doctor went his round,
Just pausing at our door to say,
In the brief autocratic way
Of one who, prompt at Duty's call,
Was free to urge her claim on all,
That some poor neighbor sick abed
At night our mother's aid would need.
For, one in generous thought and deed,
What mattered in the sufferer's sight
The Quaker matron's inward light,
The Doctor's mail of Calvin's creed?
All hearts confess the saints elect
Who, twain in faith, in love agree,
And melt not in an acid sect
The Christian pearl of charity!

So days went on: a week had passed
Since the great world was heard from last.
The Almanac we studied o'er,
Read and reread our little store
Of books and pamphlets, scarce a score;
One harmless novel, mostly hid
From younger eyes, a book forbid,
And poetry, (or good or bad,
A single book was all we had,)
Where Ellwood's meek, drab-skirted Muse,
A stranger to the heathen Nine,
Sang, with a somewhat nasal whine,
The wars of David and the Jews.
At last the floundering carrier bore
The village paper to our door.
Lo! broadening outward as we read,
To warmer zones the horizon spread;
In panoramic length unrolled
We saw the marvels that it told.
Before us passed the painted Creeks,
And daft McGregor on his raids
In Costa Rica's everglades.
And up Taygetos winding slow
Rode Ypsilanti's Mainote Greeks,
A Turk's head at each saddle-bow!
Welcome to us its week-old news,
Its corner for the rustic Muse,
Its monthly gauge of snow and rain,
Its record, mingling in a breath
The wedding bell and dirge of death:
Jest, anecdote, and love-lorn tale,
The latest culprit sent to jail;
Its hue and cry of stolen and lost,
Its vendue sales and goods at cost,
And traffic calling loud for gain.
We felt the stir of hall and street,
The pulse of life that round us beat;
The chill embargo of the snow
Was melted in the genial glow;
Wide swung again our ice-locked door,
And all the world was ours once more!

Clasp, Angel of the backward look
And folded wings of ashen gray
And voice of echoes far away,
The brazen covers of thy book;
The weird palimpsest old and vast,
Wherein thou hid'st the spectral past;
Where, closely mingling, pale and glow
The characters of joy and woe;
The monographs of outlived years,
Or smile-illumed or dim with tears,
Green hills of life that slope to death,
And haunts of home, whose vistaed trees
Shade off to mournful cypresses
With the white amaranths underneath.
Even while I look, I can but heed
The restless sands' incessant fall,
Importunate hours that hours succeed,
Each clamorous with its own sharp need,
And duty keeping pace with all.
Shut down and clasp the heavy lids;
I hear again the voice that bids
The dreamer leave his dream midway
For larger hopes and graver fears:

Life greatens in these later years,
The century's aloe flowers today!

Yet, haply, in some lull of life,
Some Truce of God which breaks its strife,
The worldling's eyes shall gather dew,
  Dreaming in throngful city ways
Of winter joys his boyhood knew;
And dear and early friends—the few
Who yet remain—shall pause to view
  These Flemish pictures of old days;
Sit with me by the homestead hearth,
And stretch the hands of memory forth
  To warm them at the wood-fire's blaze!
And thanks untraced to lips unknown
Shall greet me like the odors blown
From unseen meadows newly mown,
Or lilies floating in some pond,
Wood-fringed, the wayside gaze beyond;
The traveller owns the grateful sense
Of sweetness near, he knows not whence,
And, pausing, takes with forehead bare
The benediction of the air.

1865 *1866*

ABRAHAM DAVENPORT

In the old days (a custom laid aside
With breeches and cocked hats) the people sent
Their wisest men to make the public laws.
And so, from a brown homestead, where the Sound
Drinks the small tribute of the Mianas,
Waved over by the woods of Rippowams,
And hallowed by pure lives and tranquil deaths,
Stamford sent up to the councils of the State
Wisdom and grace in Abraham Davenport.

'Twas on a May-day of the far old year
Seventeen hundred eighty, that there fell
Over the bloom and sweet life of the Spring,
Over the fresh earth and the heaven of noon,
A horror of great darkness, like the night
In day of which the Norland sagas tell,—
The Twilight of the Gods. The low-hung sky
Was black with ominous clouds, save where its rim
Was fringed with a dull glow, like that which climbs
The crater's sides from the red hell below.
Birds ceased to sing, and all the barn-yard fowls
Roosted; the cattle at the pasture bars
Lowed, and looked homeward; bats on leathern wings
Flitted abroad; the sounds of labor died;
Men prayed, and women wept; all ears grew sharp
To hear the doom-blast of the trumpet shatter
The black sky, that the dreadful face of Christ
Might look from the rent clouds, not as He looked
A loving guest at Bethany, but stern
As Justice and inexorable Law.

Meanwhile in the old State House, dim as ghosts,
Sat the lawgivers of Connecticut,
Trembling beneath their legislative robes.
"It is the Lord's Great Day! Let us adjourn,"
Some said; and then, as if with one accord,
All eyes were turned to Abraham Davenport.
He rose, slow cleaving with his steady voice
The intolerable hush. "This well may be
The Day of Judgment which the world awaits;
But be it so or not, I only know
My present duty, and my Lord's command
To occupy till He come. So at the post
Where He hath set me in His providence,
I choose, for one, to meet Him face to face,—
No faithless servant frightened from my task,
But ready when the Lord of the harvest calls;
And therefore, with all reverence, I would say,
Let God do His work, we will see to ours.
Bring in the candles." And they brought them in.

Then by the flaring lights the Speaker read,
Albeit with husky voice and shaking hands,
An act to amend an act to regulate
The shad and alewive fisheries. Whereupon
Wisely and well spake Abraham Davenport,
Straight to the question, with no figures of speech
Save the ten Arab signs, yet not without
The shrewd dry humor natural to the man:
His awe-struck colleagues listening all the while,
Between the pauses of his argument,
To hear the thunder of the wrath of God
Break from the hollow trumpet of the cloud.

And there he stands in memory to this day,
Erect, self-poised, a rugged face, half seen
Against the background of unnatural dark,
A witness to the ages as they pass,
That simple duty hath no place for fear.

1866 1866

THE MEETING

The elder folks shook hands at last,
Down seat by seat the signal passed.
To simple ways like ours unused,
Half solemnized and half amused,
With long-drawn breath and shrug, my guest
His sense of glad relief expressed.
Outside, the hills lay warm in sun;
The cattle in the meadow-run
Stood half-leg deep; a single bird
The green repose above us stirred.
"What part or lot have you," he said,
"In these dull rites of drowsy-head?
Is silence worship? Seek it where
It soothes with dreams the summer air,
Not in this close and rude-benched hall,
But where soft lights and shadows fall,
And all the slow, sleep-walking hours
Glide soundless over grass and flowers!
From time and place and form apart,
Its holy ground the human heart,
Nor ritual-bound nor templeward
Walks the free spirit of the Lord!
Our common Master did not pen
His followers up from other men;
His service liberty indeed,
He built no church, He framed no creed;
But while the saintly Pharisee
Made broader his phylactery,
As from the synagogue was seen
The dusty-sandalled Nazarene
Through ripening cornfields lead the way
Upon the awful Sabbath day,
His sermons were the healthful talk
That shorter made the mountain-walk,
His wayside texts were flowers and birds,
Where mingled with His gracious words
The rustle of the tamarisk-tree
And ripple-wash of Galilee."

"Thy words are well, O friend," I said;
"Unmeasured and unlimited,
With noiseless slide of stone to stone,
The mystic Church of God has grown.
Invisible and silent stands
The temple never made with hands,
Unheard the voices still and small
Of its unseen confessional.
He needs no special place of prayer
Whose hearing ear is everywhere;
He brings not back the childish days
That ringed the earth with stones of praise,
Roofed Karnak's hall of gods, and laid
The plinths of Philæ's colonnade.
Still less He owns the selfish good
And sickly growth of solitude,—
The worthless grace that, out of sight,
Flowers in the desert anchorite;
Dissevered from the suffering whole,
Love hath no power to save a soul.
Not out of Self, the origin
And native air and soil of sin,
The living waters spring and flow,
The trees with leaves of healing grow.

"Dream not, O friend, because I seek
This quiet shelter twice a week,
I better deem its pine-laid floor
Than breezy hill or sea-sung shore;
But nature is not solitude:
She crowds us with her thronging wood;
Her many hands reach out to us,
Her many tongues are garrulous;
Perpetual riddles of surprise
She offers to our ears and eyes;
She will not leave our senses still,
But drags them captive at her will:
And, making earth too great for heaven,
She hides the Giver in the given.

"And so I find it well to come
For deeper rest to this still room,
For here the habit of the soul
Feels less the outer world's control;
The strength of mutual purpose pleads
More earnestly our common needs;
And from the silence multiplied
By these still forms on either side,
The world that time and sense have known
Falls off and leaves us God alone.

"Yet rarely through the charmed repose
Unmixed the stream of motive flows,
A flavor of its many springs,
The tints of earth and sky it brings;

In the still waters needs must be
Some shade of human sympathy;
And here, in its accustomed place,
I look on memory's dearest face;
The blind by-sitter guesseth not
What shadow haunts that vacant spot;
No eyes save mine alone can see
The love wherewith it welcomes me!
And still, with those alone my kin,
In doubt and weakness, want and sin,
I bow my head, my heart I bare,
As when that face was living there,
And strive (too oft, alas! in vain)
The peace of simple trust to gain,
Fold fancy's restless wings, and lay
The idols of my heart away.

"Welcome the silence all unbroken,
Nor less the words of fitness spoken,—
Such golden words as hers for whom
Our autumn flowers have just made room;
Whose hopeful utterance through and through
The freshness of the morning blew;
Who loved not less the earth that light
Fell on it from the heavens in sight,
But saw in all fair forms more fair
The Eternal beauty mirrored there.
Whose eighty years but added grace
And saintlier meaning to her face,—
The look of one who bore away
Glad tidings from the hills of day,
While all our hearts went forth to meet
The coming of her beautiful feet!
Or haply hers, whose pilgrim tread
Is in the paths where Jesus led;
Who dreams her childhood's sabbath dream
By Jordan's willow-shaded stream,
And, of the hymns of hope and faith,
Sung by the monks of Nazareth,
Hears pious echoes, in the call
To prayer, from Moslem minarets fall,
Repeating where His works were wrought
The lesson that her Master taught,
Of whom an elder Sibyl gave,
The prophecies of Cumæ's cave!

"I ask no organ's soulless breath
To drone the themes of life and death,
No altar candle-lit by day,
No ornate wordsman's rhetoric-play,
No cool philosophy to teach
Its bland audacities of speech
To double-tasked idolaters
Themselves their gods and worshippers,
No pulpit hammered by the fist
Of loud-asserting dogmatist,
Who borrows for the Hand of love
The smoking thunderbolts of Jove.
I know how well the fathers taught,
What work the later schoolmen wrought;
I reverence old-time faith and men,
But God is near us now as then;
His force of love is still unspent,
His hate of sin as imminent;
And still the measure of our needs
Outgrows the cramping bounds of creeds;
The manna gathered yesterday
Already savors of decay;
Doubts to the world's child-heart unknown
Question us now from star and stone;
Too little or too much we know,
And sight is swift and faith is slow;
The power is lost to self-deceive
With shallow forms of make-believe.
We walk at high noon, and the bells
Call to a thousand oracles,
But the sound deafens, and the light
Is stronger than our dazzled sight;
The letters of the sacred Book
Glimmer and swim beneath our look;
Still struggles in the Age's breast
With deepening agony of quest
The old entreaty: 'Art thou He,
Or look we for the Christ to be?'

"God should be most where man is least:
So, where is neither church nor priest,
And never rag of form or creed
To clothe the nakedness of need,—
Where farmer-folk in silence meet,—
I turn my bell-unsummoned feet;
I lay the critic's glass aside,
I tread upon my lettered pride,
And, lowest-seated, testify
To the oneness of humanity;
Confess the universal want,
And share whatever Heaven may grant.
He findeth not who seeks his own,
The soul is lost that's saved alone.
Not on one favored forehead fell
Of old the fire-tongued miracle,
But flamed o'er all the thronging host

The baptism of the Holy Ghost;
Heart answers heart: in one desire
The blending lines of prayer aspire;
'Where, in my name, meet two or three,'
Our Lord hath said, 'I there will be!'

"So sometimes comes to soul and sense
The feeling which is evidence
That very near about us lies
The realm of spiritual mysteries.
The sphere of the supernal powers
Impinges on this world of ours.
The low and dark horizon lifts,
To light the scenic terror shifts;
The breath of a diviner air
Blows down the answer of a prayer:
That all our sorrow, pain, and doubt
A great compassion clasps about,
And law and goodness, love and force,
Are wedded fast beyond divorce.
Then duty leaves to love its task,
The beggar Self forgets to ask;
With smile of trust and folded hands,
The passive soul in waiting stands
To feel, as flowers the sun and dew,
The One true Life its own renew.

"So to the calmly gathered thought
The innermost of truth is taught,
The mystery dimly understood,
That love of God is love of good,
And, chiefly, its divinest trace
In Him of Nazareth's holy face;
That to be saved is only this,—
Salvation from our selfishness,
From more than elemental fire,
The soul's unsanctified desire,
From sin itself, and not the pain
That warns us of its chafing chain;
That worship's deeper meaning lies
In mercy, and not sacrifice,
Not proud humilities of sense
And posturing of penitence,
But love's unforced obedience;
That Book and Church and Day are given
For man, not God,—for earth, not heaven,—
The blessed means to holiest ends,
Not masters, but benignant friends;
That the dear Christ dwells not afar,
The king of some remoter star,
Listening, at times, with flattered ear
To homage wrung from selfish fear,
But here, amidst the poor and blind,
The bound and suffering of our kind,
In works we do, in prayers we pray,
Life of our life, He lives today."

1868 1868

AMONG THE HILLS

PRELUDE

Along the roadside, like the flowers of gold
That tawny Incas for their gardens wrought,
Heavy with sunshine droops the golden-rod,
And the red pennons of the cardinal-flowers
Hang motionless upon their upright staves.
The sky is hot and hazy, and the wind,
Wing-weary with its long flight from the south,
Unfelt; yet, closely scanned, yon maple leaf
With faintest motion, as one stirs in dreams,
Confesses it. The locust by the wall
Stabs the noon-silence with his sharp alarm.
A single hay-cart down the dusty road
Creaks slowly, with its driver fast asleep
On the load's top. Against the neighboring hill,
Huddled along the stone wall's shady side,
The sheep show white, as if a snowdrift still
Defied the dog-star. Through the open door
A drowsy smell of flowers—gray heliotrope,
And white sweet clover, and shy mignonette—
Comes faintly in, and silent chorus lends
To the pervading symphony of peace.

No time is this for hands long over-worn
To task their strength: and (unto Him be praise
Who giveth quietness!) the stress and strain
Of years that did the work of centuries
Have ceased, and we can draw our breath once more
Freely and full. So, as yon harvesters
Make glad their nooning underneath the elms
With tale and riddle and old snatch of song,
I lay aside grave themes, and idly turn
The leaves of memory's sketch-book, dreaming o'er
Old summer pictures of the quiet hills,
And human life, as quiet, at their feet.

And yet not idly all. A farmer's son,
Proud of field-lore and harvest craft, and feeling

All their fine possibilities, how rich
And restful even poverty and toil
Become when beauty, harmony, and love
Sit at their humble hearth as angels sat
At evening in the patriarch's tent, when man
Makes labor noble, and his farmer's frock
The symbol of a Christian chivalry,
Tender and just and generous to her
Who clothes with grace all duty; still, I know
Too well the picture has another side,—
How wearily the grind of toil goes on
Where love is wanting, how the eye and ear
And heart are starved amidst the plenitude
Of nature, and how hard and colorless
Is life without an atmosphere. I look
Across the lapse of half a century,
And call to mind old homesteads, where no flower
Told that the spring had come, but evil weeds,
Nightshade and rough-leaved burdock in the place
Of the sweet doorway greeting of the rose
And honeysuckle, where the house walls seemed
Blistering in sun, without a tree or vine
To cast the tremulous shadow of its leaves
Across the curtainless windows, from whose panes
Fluttered the signal rags of shiftlessness.
Within, the cluttered kitchen floor, unwashed
(Broom-clean I think they called it); the best room
Stifling with cellar-damp, shut from the air
In hot midsummer, bookless, pictureless
Save the inevitable sampler hung
Over the fireplace, or a mourning piece,
A green-haired woman, peony-cheeked, beneath
Impossible willows; the wide-throated hearth
Bristling with faded pine-boughs half concealing
The piled-up rubbish at the chimney's back;
And, in sad keeping with all things about them,
Shrill, querulous women, sour and sullen men,
Untidy, loveless, old before their time,
With scarce a human interest save their own
Monotonous round of small economies,
Or the poor scandal of the neighborhood;
Blind to the beauty everywhere revealed,
Treading the May-flowers with regardless feet;
For them the song-sparrow and the bobolink
Sang not, nor winds made music in the leaves;
For them in vain October's holocaust
Burned, gold and crimson, over all the hills,
The sacramental mystery of the woods.
Church-goers, fearful of the unseen Powers,
But grumbling over pulpit-tax and pew-rent,
Saving, as shrewd economists, their souls
And winter pork with the least possible outlay
Of salt and sanctity; in daily life
Showing as little actual comprehension
Of Christian charity and love and duty,
As if the Sermon on the Mount had been
Outdated like a last year's almanac:
Rich in broad woodlands and in half-tilled fields,
And yet so pinched and bare and comfortless,
The veriest straggler limping on his rounds,
The sun and air his sole inheritance,
Laughed at poverty that paid its taxes,
And hugged his rags in self-complacency!

Not such should be the homesteads of a land
Where whoso wisely wills and acts may dwell
As king and lawgiver, in broad-acred state,
With beauty, art, taste, culture, books, to make
His hour of leisure richer than a life
Of fourscore to the barons of old time,
Our yeoman should be equal to his home
Set in the fair, green valleys, purple walled,
A man to match his mountains, not to creep
Dwarfed and abased below them. I would fain
In this light way (of which I needs must own
With the knife-grinder of whom Canning sings,
"Story, God bless you! I have none to tell you!")
Invite the eye to see and heart to feel
The beauty and the joy within their reach,—
Home, and home loves, and the beatitudes
Of nature free to all. Haply in years
That wait to take the places of our own,
Heard where some breezy balcony looks down
On happy homes, or where the lake in the moon
Sleeps dreaming of the mountains, fair as Ruth,
In the old Hebrew pastoral, at the feet
Of Boaz, even this simple lay of mine
May seem the burden of a prophecy,
Finding its late fulfilment in a change
Slow as the oak's growth, lifting manhood up

Through broader culture, finer manners, love,
And reverence, to the level of the hills.

O Golden Age, whose light is of the dawn,
And not of sunset, forward, not behind,
Flood the new heavens and earth, and with thee bring
All the old virtues, whatsoever things
Are pure and honest and of good repute,
But add thereto whatever bard has sung
Or seer has told of when in trance and dream
They saw the Happy Isles of prophecy!
Let Justice hold her scale, and Truth divide
Between the right and wrong; but give the heart
The freedom of its fair inheritance;
Let the poor prisoner, cramped and starved so long,
At Nature's table feast his ear and eye
With joy and wonder; let all harmonies
Of sound, form, color, motion, wait upon
The princely guest, whether in soft attire
Of leisure clad, or the coarse frock of toil,
And, lending life to the dead form of faith,
Give human nature reverence for the sake
Of One who bore it, making it divine
With the ineffable tenderness of God;
Let common need, the brotherhood of prayer,
The heirship of an unknown destiny,
The unsolved mystery round about us, make
A man more precious than the gold of Ophir.
Sacred, inviolate, unto whom all things
Should minister, as outward types and signs
Of the eternal beauty which fulfils
The one great purpose of creation, Love,
The sole necessity of Earth and Heaven!

For weeks the clouds had raked the hills
And vexed the vales with raining,
And all the woods were sad with mist,
And all the brooks complaining.

At last, a sudden night-storm tore
The mountain veils asunder,
And swept the valleys clean before
The besom of the thunder.

Through Sandwich notch the west-wind sang
Good morrow to the cotter;
And once again Chocorua's horn
Of shadow pierced the water.

Above his broad lake Ossipee,
Once more the sunshine wearing,
Stooped, tracing on that silver shield
His grim armorial bearing.

Clear drawn against the hard blue sky,
The peaks had winter's keenness;
And, close on autumn's frost, the vales
Had more than June's fresh greenness.

Again the sodden forest floors
With golden lights were checkered,
Once more rejoicing leaves in wind
And sunshine danced and flickered.

It was as if the summer's late
Atoning for its sadness
Had borrowed every season's charm
To end its days in gladness.

I call to mind those banded vales
Of shadow and of shining,
Through which, my hostess at my side,
I drove in day's declining.

We held our sideling way above
The river's whitening shallows,
By homesteads old, with wide-flung barns
Swept through and through by swallows;

By maple orchards, belts of pine
And larches climbing darkly
The mountain slopes, and, over all,
The great peaks rising starkly.

You should have seen that long hill-range
With gaps of brightness riven,—
How through each pass and hollow streamed
The purpling lights of heaven,—

Rivers of gold-mist flowing down
From far celestial fountains,—
The great sun flaming through the rifts
Beyond the wall of mountains!

We paused at last where home-bound cows
Brought down the pasture's treasure,
And in the barn the rhythmic flails
Beat out a harvest measure.

We heard the night-hawk's sullen plunge,
The crow his tree-mates calling:
The shadows lengthening down the slopes
About our feet were falling,

And through them smote the level sun
  In broken lines of splendor,
Touched the gray rocks and made the green
  Of the shorn grass more tender.

The maples bending o'er the gate,
  Their arch of leaves just tinted
With yellow warmth, the golden glow
  Of coming autumn hinted.

Keen white between the farm-house showed,
  And smiled on porch and trellis
The fair democracy of flowers
  That equals cot and palace.

And weaving garlands for her dog,
  'Twixt chidings and caresses,
A human flower of childhood shook
  The sunshine from her tresses.

On either hand we saw the signs
  Of fancy and of shrewdness,
Where taste had wound its arms of vines
  Round thrift's uncomely rudeness.

The sun-brown farmer in his frock
  Shook hands, and called to Mary:
Bare-armed, as Juno might, she came,
  White-aproned from her dairy.

Her air, her smile, her motions, told
  Of womanly completeness;
A music as of household songs
  Was in her voice of sweetness.

Not fair alone in curve and line,
  But something more and better,
The secret charm eluding art,
  Its spirit, not its letter;—

An inborn grace that nothing lacked
  Of culture or appliance,—
The warmth of genial courtesy,
  The calm of self-reliance.

Before her queenly womanhood
  How dared our hostess utter
The paltry errand of her need
  To buy her fresh-churned butter?

She led the way with housewife pride,
  Her goodly store disclosing,
Full tenderly the golden balls
  With practised hands disposing.

Then, while along the western hills
  We watched the changeful glory
Of sunset, on our homeward way,
  I heard her simple story.

The early crickets sang; the stream
  Plashed through my friend's narration:
Her rustic patois of the hills
  Lost in my free translation.

"More wise," she said, "than those who swarm
  Our hills in middle summer,
She came, when June's first roses blow,
  To greet the early comer.

"From school and ball and rout she came,
  The city's fair, pale daughter,
To drink the wine of mountain air
  Beside the Bearcamp Water.

"Her step grew firmer on the hills
  That watch our homesteads over;
On cheek and lip, from summer fields,
  She caught the bloom of clover.

"For health comes sparkling in the streams
  From cool Chocorua stealing:
There's iron in our Northern winds;
  Our pines are trees of healing.

"She sat beneath the broad-armed elms
  That skirt the mowing meadow,
And watched the gentle west-wind weave
  The grass with shine and shadow.

"Beside her, from the summer heat
  To share her grateful screening,
With forehead bared, the farmer stood,
  Upon his pitchfork leaning.

"Framed in its damp, dark locks, his face
  Had nothing mean or common,—
Strong, manly, true, the tenderness
  And pride beloved of woman.

"She looked up, glowing with the health
  The country air had brought her,
And, laughing, said: 'You lack a wife,
  Your mother lacks a daughter.

" 'To mend your frock and bake your bread
  You do not need a lady:
Be sure among these brown old homes
  Is some one waiting ready,—

" 'Some fair, sweet girl with skilful hand
And cheerful heart for treasure,
Who never played with ivory keys,
Or danced the polka's measure.'

"He bent his black brows to a frown,
He set his white teeth tightly.
''Tis well,' he said, 'for one like you
To choose for me so lightly.

" 'You think because my life is rude
I take no note of sweetness:
I tell you love has naught to do
With meetness or unmeetness.

" 'Itself its best excuse, it asks
No leave of pride or fashion
When silken zone or homespun frock
It stirs with throbs of passion.

" 'You think me deaf and blind: you bring
Your winning graces hither
As free as if from cradle-time
We two had played together.

" 'You tempt me with your laughing eyes,
Your cheek of sundown's blushes,
A motion as of waving grain,
A music as of thrushes.

" 'The plaything of your summer sport,
The spells you weave around me
You cannot at your will undo,
Nor leave me as you found me.

" 'You go as lightly as you came,
Your life is well without me;
What care you that these hills will close
Like prison-walls about me?

" 'No mood is mine to seek a wife,
Or daughter for my mother:
Who loves you loses in that love
All power to love another!

" 'I dare your pity or your scorn,
With pride your own exceeding;
I fling my heart into your lap
Without a word of pleading.'

"She looked up in his face of pain
So archly, yet so tender:
'And if I lend you mine,' she said,
'Will you forgive the lender?

" 'Nor frock nor tan can hide the man;
And see you not, my farmer,
How weak and fond a woman waits
Behind this silken armor?

" 'I love you: on that love alone,
And not my worth, presuming,
Will you not trust for summer fruit
The tree in May-day blooming?'

"Alone the hangbird overhead,
His hair-swung cradle straining,
Looked down to see love's miracle,—
The giving that is gaining.

"And so the farmer found a wife,
His mother found a daughter:
There looks no happier home than hers
On pleasant Bearcamp Water.

"Flowers spring to blossom where she walks
The careful ways of duty;
Our hard, stiff lines of life with her
Are flowing curves of beauty.

"Our homes are cheerier for her sake,
Our door-yards brighter blooming,
And all about the social air
Is sweeter for her coming.

"Unspoken homilies of peace
Her daily life is preaching;
The still refreshment of the dew
Is her unconscious teaching.

"And never tenderer hand than hers
Unknits the brow of ailing;
Her garments to the sick man's ear
Have music in their trailing.

"And when, in pleasant harvest moons,
The youthful huskers gather,
Or sleigh-drives on the mountain ways
Defy the winter weather,—

"In sugar-camps, when south and warm
The winds of March are blowing,
And sweetly from its thawing veins
The maple's blood is flowing,—

"In summer, where some lilied pond
Its virgin zone is baring,
Or where the ruddy autumn fire
Lights up the apple-paring,—

"The coarseness of a ruder time
Her finer mirth displaces,
A subtler sense of pleasure fills
Each rustic sport she graces.

"Her presence lends its warmth and health
To all who come before it.
If woman lost us Eden, such
As she alone restore it.

"For larger life and wiser aims
The farmer is her debtor;
Who holds to his another's heart
Must needs be worse or better.

"Through her his civic service shows
A purer-toned ambition;
No double consciousness divides
The man and politician.

"In party's doubtful ways he trusts
Her instincts to determine;
At the loud polls, the thought of her
Recalls Christ's Mountain Sermon.

"He owns her logic of the heart,
And wisdom of unreason,
Supplying, while he doubts and weighs,
The needed word in season.

"He sees with pride her richer thought,
Her fancy's freer ranges;
And love thus deepened to respect
Is proof against all changes.

"And if she walks at ease in ways
His feet are slow to travel,
And if she reads with cultured eyes
What his may scarce unravel,

"Still clearer, for her keener sight
Of beauty and of wonder,
He learns the meaning of the hills
He dwelt from childhood under.

"And higher, warmed with summer lights,
Or winter-crowned and hoary,
The ridged horizon lifts for him
Its inner veils of glory.

"He has his own free, bookless lore,
The lessons nature taught him,
The wisdom which the woods and hills
And toiling men have brought him:

"The steady force of will whereby
Her flexile grace seems sweeter;
The sturdy counterpoise which makes
Her woman's life completer;

"A latent fire of soul which lacks
No breath of love to fan it;
And wit, that, like his native brooks,
Plays over solid granite.

"How dwarfed against his manliness
She sees the poor pretension,
The wants, the aims, the follies, born
Of fashion and convention!

"How life behind its accidents
Stands strong and self-sustaining,
The human fact transcending all
The losing and the gaining.

"And so, in grateful interchange
Of teacher and of hearer,
Their lives their true distinctness keep
While daily drawing nearer.

"And if the husband or the wife
In home's strong light discovers
Such slight defaults as failed to meet
The blinded eyes of lovers,

"Why need we care to ask?—who dreams
Without their thorns of roses,
Or wonders that the truest steel
The readiest spark discloses?

"For still in mutual sufferance lies
The secret of true living:
Love scarce is love that never knows
The sweetness of forgiving.

"We send the Squire to General Court,
He takes his young wife thither;
No prouder man election day
Rides through the sweet June weather.

"He sees with eyes of manly trust
All hearts to her inclining;
Not less for him his household light
That others share its shining."

Thus, while my hostess spake, there grew
Before me, warmer tinted
And outlined with a tenderer grace,
The picture that she hinted.

The sunset smoldered as we drove
Beneath the deep hill-shadows.
Below us wreaths of white fog walked
Like ghosts the haunted meadows.

Sounding the summer night, the stars
Dropped down their golden plummets;
The pale arc of the Northern lights
Rose o'er the mountain summits,

Until, at last, beneath its bridge,
We heard the Bearcamp flowing,
And saw across the mapled lawn
The welcome home-lights glowing.

And, musing on the tale I heard,
'Twere well, thought I, if often
To rugged farm-life came the gift
To harmonize and soften;

If more and more we found the troth
Of fact and fancy plighted,
And culture's charm and labor's strength
In rural homes united,—

The simple life, the homely hearth,
With beauty's sphere surrounding,
And blessing toil where toil abounds
With graces more abounding.

1867, 1868 1868

THE PENNSYLVANIA PILGRIM

INTRODUCTORY NOTE

The beginning of German emigration to America may be traced to the personal influence of William Penn, who in 1677 visited the Continent, and made the acquaintance of an intelligent and highly cultivated circle of Pietists, or Mystics, who, reviving in the seventeenth century the spiritual faith and worship of Tauler and the "Friends of God" in the fourteenth, gathered about the pastor Spener, and the young and beautiful Eleonora Johanna Von Merlau. In this circle originated the Frankfort Land Company, which bought of William Penn, the Governor of Pennsylvania, a tract of land near the new city of Philadelphia.

The company's agent in the New World was a rising young lawyer, Francis Daniel Pastorius, son of Judge Pastorius, of Windsheim, who, at the age of seventeen, entered the University of Altorf. He studied law at Strasburg, Basle, and Jena, and at Ratisbon, the seat of the Imperial Government, obtained a practical knowledge of international polity. Successful in all his examinations and disputations, he received the degree of Doctor of Law at Nuremberg in 1676. In 1679 he was a law-lecturer at Frankfort, where he became deeply interested in the teachings of Dr. Spener. In 1680–81 he travelled in France, England, Ireland, and Italy with his friend Herr Von Rodeck. "I was," he says, "glad to enjoy again the company of my Christian friends, rather than be with Von Rodeck feasting and dancing." In 1683, in company with a small number of German Friends, he emigrated to America, settling upon the Frankfort Company's tract between the Schuylkill and the Delaware rivers. The township was divided into four hamlets, namely, Germantown, Krisheim, Crefield, and Sommerhausen. Soon after his arrival he united himself with the Society of Friends and became one of its most able and devoted members, as well as the recognized head and lawgiver of the settlement. He married, two years after his arrival, Anneke (Anna), daughter of Dr. Klosterman, of Muhlheim.

In the year 1688 he drew up a memorial against slaveholding, which was adopted by the Germantown Friends and sent up to the Monthly Meeting, and thence to the Yearly Meeting at Philadelphia. It is noteworthy as the first protest made by a religious body against Negro Slavery. The original document was discovered in 1844 by the Philadelphian antiquarian, Nathan Kite, and published in *The Friend* (Vol. XVIII, No. 16). It is a bold and direct appeal to the best instincts of the heart. "Have not," he asks, "these negroes as much right to fight for their freedom as you have to keep them slaves?"

Under the wise direction of Pastorius, the Germantown settlement grew and prospered. The inhabitants planted orchards and vineyards, and surrounded themselves with souvenirs of their old home. A large number of them were linen-weavers, as well as small farmers. The Quakers were the principal sect, but men of all religions were tolerated, and lived together in harmony. In 1692 Richard Frame published, in what he called verse, a *Description of Pennsylvania*, in which he alludes to the settlement:

"The German town of which I spoke before,
Which is at least in length one mile or more,
Where lives High German people and Low Dutch,
Whose trade in weaving linen cloth is much,—
There grows the flax, as also you may know
That from the same they do divide the tow.
Their trade suits well their habitation,—
We find convenience for their occupation."

Pastorius seems to have been on intimate terms with William Penn, Thomas Lloyd, Chief Justice Logan, Thomas Story, and other leading men in the Province belonging to his own religious society, as also with Kelpius, the learned Mystic of the Wissahickon, with the pastor of the Swedes' church, and the leaders of the Mennonites. He wrote a description of Pennsylvania, which was published at Frankfort and Leipsic in 1700 and 1701. His *Lives of the Saints*, etc., written in German and dedicated to Professor Schurmberg, his old teacher, was published in 1690. He left behind him many unpublished manuscripts covering a very wide range of subjects, most of which are now lost. One huge manuscript folio, entitled *Hive Beestock, Melliotropheum Alucar, or Rusca Apium*, still remains, containing one thousand pages with about one hundred lines to a page. It is a medley of knowledge and fancy, history, philosophy, and poetry, written in seven languages. A large portion of his poetry is devoted to the pleasures of gardening, the description of flowers, and the care of bees. The following specimen of his punning Latin is addressed to an orchard-pilferer:

"Quisquis in haec furtim reptas viridaria nostra
Tangere fallaci poma caveto manu,
Si non obsequeris faxit Deus omne quod opto,
Cum malis nostris ut mala cuncta feras."

Professor Oswald Seidensticker, to whose papers in *Der Deutsche Pioneer* and that able periodical *The Penn Monthly*, of Philadelphia, I am indebted for many of the foregoing facts in regard to the German pilgrims of the New World, thus closes his notice of Pastorius:

"No tombstone, not even a record of burial, indicates where his remains have found their last resting-place, and the pardonable desire to associate the homage due to this distinguished man with some visible memento cannot be gratified. There is no reason to suppose that he was interred in any other place than the Friends' old burying-ground in Germantown, though the fact is not attested by any definite source of information. After all, this obliteration of the last trace of his earthly existence is but typical of what has overtaken the times which he represents; *that* Germantown which he founded, which saw him live and move, is at present but a quaint idyl of the past, almost a myth, barely remembered and little cared for by the keener race that has succeeded."

The Pilgrims of Plymouth have not lacked historian and poet. Justice has been done to their faith, courage, and self-sacrifice and to the mighty influence of their endeavors to establish righteousness on the earth. The Quaker pilgrims of Pennsylvania, seeking the same object by different means, have not been equally fortunate. The power of their testimony for truth and holiness, peace and freedom, enforced only by what Milton calls "the unresistible might of meekness," has been felt through two centuries in the amelioration of penal severities, the abolition of slavery, the reform of the erring, the relief of the poor and suffering,—felt, in brief, in every step of human progress. But of the men themselves, with the single exception of William Penn, scarcely anything is known. Contrasted, from the outset, with the stern, aggressive Puritans of New England, they have come to be regarded as "a feeble folk," with a personality as doubtful as their unrecorded graves. They were not soldiers, like Miles Standish; they had no figure so picturesque as Vane, no leader so rashly brave and haughty as Endicott. No Cotton Mather wrote their *Magnalia;* they had no awful drama of supernaturalism in which Satan and his angels were actors; and the only witch mentioned in their simple annals was a poor old Swedish woman, who, on complaint of her countrywomen, was tried and acquitted of everything but imbecility and folly. Nothing but commonplace offices of civility came to pass between them and the Indians; indeed, their enemies taunted them with the fact that the savages did not regard them as Christians, but just such men as themselves. Yet it must be apparent to every careful observer of the progress of American civilization that its two principal currents had their sources in the entirely opposite directions of the Puritan and Quaker colonies. To use the words of a late writer: "The historical forces, with which no others may be compared in their influence on the people, have been those of the Puritan and the Quaker. The strength of the one was in the confession of an invisible Presence, a righteous, eternal Will, which would establish righteousness on earth; and thence arose the conviction of a direct personal responsibility, which could be tempted by no external splendor and could be shaken by no internal agitation, and could not be evaded or transferred. The strength of the other was the witness in the human spirit to an eternal Word, an Inner Voice which spoke to each alone, while yet it spoke to every man; a Light which each was to follow, and which yet was the light of the world; and all other voices were silent before this, and the solitary path whither it led was more sacred than the worn ways of cathedral-aisles." (Mulford's *The Nation*, pp. 267, 268.)

It will be sufficiently apparent to the reader that, in the poem which follows, I have attempted nothing beyond a study of the life and times of the Pennsylvania colonist,—a simple picture of a noteworthy man and his locality. The colors of my sketch are all very sober, toned down to the quiet and dreamy atmosphere through which its subject is visible. Whether, in the glare and tumult of the present time, such a picture will find favor may well be questioned. I only know that it has beguiled for me some hours of weariness, and that, whatever may be its measure of public appreciation, it has been to me its own reward.

AMESBURY, *5th mo.*, 1872 J. G. W.

HAIL to posterity!
Hail, future men of Germanopolis!
Let the young generations yet to be
Look kindly upon this.

Think how your fathers left their native land,—
  Dear German-land! O sacred hearths and homes!—
  And, where the wild beast roams,
      In patience planned
New forest-homes beyond the mighty sea,
    There undisturbed and free
To live as brothers of one family.
    What pains and cares befell,
      What trials and what fears,
Remember, and wherein we have done well
  Follow our footsteps, men of coming years!
    Where we have failed to do
      Aright, or wisely live,
Be warned by us, the better way pursue,
And, knowing we were human, even as you,
      Pity us and forgive!
    Farewell, Posterity!
  Farewell, dear Germany!
    Forevermore farewell!

From the Latin of FRANCIS DANIEL PASTORIUS *in the Germantown Records.* 1688.

PRELUDE

I SING the Pilgrim of a softer clime
  And milder speech than those brave men's who brought
To the ice and iron of our winter time
  A will as firm, a creed as stern, and wrought
  With one mailed hand, and with the other fought.
Simply, as fits my theme, in homely rhyme
  I sing the blue-eyed German Spener taught,
Through whose veiled, mystic faith the Inward Light,
  Steady and still, an easy brightness, shone,
Transfiguring all things in its radiance white.
The garland which his meekness never sought
  I bring him; over fields of harvest sown
  With seeds of blessing, now to ripeness grown,
I bid the sower pass before the reapers' sight.

Never in tenderer quiet lapsed the day
From Pennsylvania's vales of spring away,
Where, forest-walled, the scattered hamlets lay

Along the wedded rivers. One long bar
Of purple cloud, on which the evening star
Shone like a jewel on a scimitar,

Held the sky's golden gateway. Through the deep
Hush of the woods a murmur seemed to creep,
The Schuylkill whispering in a voice of sleep.

All else was still. The oxen from their ploughs
Rested at last, and from their long day's browse
Came the dun files of Krisheim's home-bound cows.

And the young city, round whose virgin zone
The rivers like two mighty arms were thrown,
Marked by the smoke of evening fires alone,

Lay in the distance, lovely even then
With its fair women and its stately men
Gracing the forest court of William Penn,

Urban yet sylvan; in its rough-hewn frames
Of oak and pine the dryads held their claims,
And lent its streets their pleasant woodland names.

Anna Pastorius down the leafy lane
Looked city-ward, then stooped to prune again
Her vines and simples, with a sigh of pain.

For fast the streaks of ruddy sunset paled
In the oak clearing, and, as daylight failed,
Slow, overhead, the dusky night-birds sailed.

Again she looked: between green walls of shade,
With low-bent head as if with sorrow weighed,
Daniel Pastorius slowly came and said,

"God's peace be with thee, Anna!" Then he stood
Silent before her, wrestling with the mood
Of one who sees the evil and not good.

"What is it, my Pastorius?" As she spoke,
A slow, faint smile across his features broke,
Sadder than tears. "Dear heart," he said, "our folk

"Are even as others. Yea, our goodliest Friends
Are frail; our elders have their selfish ends,
And few dare trust the Lord to make amends

"For duty's loss. So even our feeble word
For the dumb slaves the startled meeting heard
As if a stone its quiet waters stirred;

"And, as the clerk ceased reading, there began
A ripple of dissent which downward ran
In widening circles, as from man to man.

"Somewhat was said of running before sent,
Of tender fear that some their guide outwent,
Troublers of Israel. I was scarce intent

"On hearing, for behind the reverend row
Of gallery Friends, in dumb and piteous show,
I saw, methought, dark faces full of woe.

"And, in the spirit, I was taken where
They toiled and suffered; I was made aware
Of shame and wrath and anguish and despair!

"And while the meeting smothered our poor plea
With cautious phrase, a Voice there seemed to be,
'As ye have done to these ye do to Me!'

"So it all passed; and the old tithe went on
Of anise, mint, and cumin, till the sun
Set, leaving still the weightier work undone.

"Help, for the good man faileth! Who is strong,
If these be weak? Who shall rebuke the wrong,
If these consent? How long, O Lord! how long!"

He ceased; and, bound in spirit with the bound,
With folded arms, and eyes that sought the ground,
Walked musingly his little garden round.

About him, beaded with the falling dew,
Rare plants of power and herbs of healing grew,
Such as Van Helmont and Agrippa knew.

For, by the lore of Gorlitz' gentle sage,
With the mild mystics of his dreamy age
He read the herbal signs of nature's page,

As once he heard in sweet Von Merlau's bowers
Fair as herself, in boyhood's happy hours,
The pious Spener read his creed in flowers.

"The dear Lord give us patience!" said his wife,
Touching with finger-tip an aloe, rife
With leaves sharp-pointed like an Aztec knife

Or Carib spear, a gift to William Penn
From the rare gardens of John Evelyn,
Brought from the Spanish Main by merchant-men.

"See this strange plant its steady purpose hold,
And, year by year, its patient leaves unfold,
Till the young eyes that watched it first are old.

"But some time, thou hast told me, there shall come
A sudden beauty, brightness, and perfume;
The century-moulded bud shall burst in bloom.

"So may the seed which hath been sown to-day
Grow with the years, and, after long delay,
Break into bloom, and God's eternal Yea

"Answer at last the patient prayers of them
Who now, by faith alone, behold its stem
Crowned with the flowers of Freedom's diadem.

"Meanwhile, to feel and suffer, work and wait,
Remains for us. The wrong indeed is great,
But love and patience conquer soon or late."

"Well hast thou said, my Anna!" Tenderer
Than youth's caress upon the head of her
Pastorius laid his hand. "Shall we demur

"Because the vision tarrieth? In an hour
We dream not of, the slow-grown bud may flower,
And what was sown in weakness rise in power!"

Then through the vine-draped door whose legend read,
"*Procul este profani!*" Anna led
To where their child upon his little bed

Looked up and smiled. "Dear heart," she said, "if we
Must bearers of a heavy burden be,
Our boy, God willing, yet the day shall see

"When from the gallery to the farthest seat,
Slave and slave-owner shall no longer meet,
But all sit equal at the Master's feet."

On the stone hearth the blazing walnut block
Set the low walls a-glimmer, showed the cock
Rebuking Peter on the Van Wyck clock,

Shone on old tomes of law and physic, side
By side with Fox and Behmen, played at hide
And seek with Anna, midst her household pride
Of flaxen webs, and on the table, bare
Of costly cloth or silver cup, but where,
Tasting the fat shads of the Delaware,
The courtly Penn had praised the goodwife's cheer,
And quoted Horace o'er her home-brewed beer,
Till even grave Pastorius smiled to hear.

In such a home, beside the Schuylkill's wave,
He dwelt in peace with God and man, and gave
Food to the poor and shelter to the slave.
For all too soon the New World's scandal shamed
The righteous code by Penn and Sidney framed,
And men withheld the human rights they claimed.

And slowly wealth and station sanction lent,
And hardened avarice, on its gains intent,
Stifled the inward whisper of dissent.

Yet all the while the burden rested sore
On tender hearts. At last Pastorius bore
Their warning message to the Church's door

In God's name; and the leaven of the word
Wrought ever after in the souls who heard,
And a dead conscience in its grave-clothes stirred

To troubled life, and urged the vain excuse
Of Hebrew custom, patriarchal use,
Good in itself if evil in abuse.

Gravely Pastorius listened, not the less
Discerning through the decent fig-leaf dress
Of the poor plea its shame of selfishness.

One Scripture rule, at least, was unforgot;
He hid the outcast, and bewrayed him not;
And, when his prey the human hunter sought,

He scrupled not, while Anna's wise delay
And proffered cheer prolonged the master's stay,
To speed the black guest safely on his way.

Yet, who shall guess his bitter grief who lends
His life to some great cause, and finds his friends
Shame or betray it for their private ends?

How felt the Master when His chosen strove
In childish folly for their seats above;
And that fond mother, blinded by her love,

Besought Him that her sons, beside His throne,
Might sit on either hand? Amidst his own
A stranger oft, companionless and lone,

God's priest and prophet stands. The martyr's pain
Is not alone from scourge and cell and chain;
Sharper the pang when, shouting in his train,
His weak disciples by their lives deny
The loud hosannas of their daily cry,
And make their echo of his truth a lie.

His forest home no hermit's cell he found,
Guests, motley-minded, drew his hearth around,
And held armed truce upon its neutral ground.

There Indian chiefs with battle-bows unstrung,
Strong, hero-limbed, like those whom Homer sung,
Pastorius fancied, when the world was young,

Came with their tawny women, lithe and tall,
Like bronzes in his friend Von Rodeck's hall,
Comely, if black, and not unpleasing all.

There hungry folk in homespun drab and gray
Drew round his board on Monthly Meeting day,
Genial, half merry in their friendly way,

Or, haply, pilgrims from the Fatherland,
Weak, timid, homesick, slow to understand
The New World's promise, sought his helping hand.

Or painful Kelpius from his hermit den
By Wissahickon, maddest of good men,
Dreamed o'er the Chiliast dreams of Petersen.

Deep in the woods, where the small river slid
Snake-like in shade, the Helmstadt Mystic hid,
Weird as a wizard, over arts forbid,

Reading the books of Daniel and of John,
And Behmen's Morning-Redness, through the Stone
Of Wisdom, vouchsafed to his eyes alone,

Whereby he read what man ne'er read before,
And saw the visions man shall see no more,
Till the great angel, striding sea and shore,

Shall bid all flesh await, on land or ships,
The warning trump of the Apocalypse,
Shattering the heavens before the dread eclipse.

Or meek-eyed Mennonist his bearded chin
Leaned o'er the gate; or Ranter, pure within,
Aired his perfection in a world of sin.

Or, talking of old home scenes, Op der Graaf
Teased the low back-log with his shodden staff,
Till the red embers broke into a laugh

And dance of flame, as if they fain would cheer
The rugged face, half tender, half austere,
Touched with the pathos of a homesick tear!

Or Sluyter, saintly familist, whose word
As law the Brethren of the Manor heard,
Announced the speedy terrors of the Lord,

And turned, like Lot at Sodom, from his race,
Above a wrecked world with complacent face
Riding secure upon his plank of grace!

Haply, from Finland's birchen groves exiled,
Manly in thought, in simple ways a child,
His white hair floating round his visage mild,

The Swedish pastor sought the Quaker's door,
Pleased from his neighbor's lips to hear once more
His long-disused and half-forgotten lore.

For both could baffle Babel's lingual curse,
And speak in Bion's Doric, and rehearse
Cleanthes' hymn or Virgil's sounding verse.

And oft Pastorius and the meek old man
Argued as Quaker and as Lutheran,
Ending in Christian love, as they began.

With lettered Lloyd on pleasant morns he strayed
Where Sommerhausen over vales of shade
Looked miles away, by every flower delayed,

Or song of bird, happy and free with one
Who loved, like him, to let his memory run
Over old fields of learning, and to sun

Himself in Plato's wise philosophies,
And dream with Philo over mysteries
Whereof the dreamer never finds the keys;

To touch all themes of thought, nor weakly stop
For doubt of truth, but let the buckets drop
Deep down and bring the hidden waters up.

For there was freedom in that wakening time
Of tender souls; to differ was not crime;
The varying bells made up the perfect chime.

On lips unlike was laid the altar's coal,
The white, clear light, tradition-colored, stole
Through the stained oriel of each human soul.

Gathered from many sects, the Quaker brought
His old beliefs, adjusting to the thought
That moved his soul the creed his fathers taught.

One faith alone, so broad that all mankind
Within themselves its secret witness find,
The soul's communion with the Eternal Mind,

The Spirit's law, the Inward Rule and Guide,
Scholar and peasant, lord and serf, allied,
The polished Penn and Cromwell's Ironside.

As still in Hemskerck's Quaker Meeting, face
By face in Flemish detail, we may trace
How loose-mouthed boor and fine ancestral grace

Sat in close contrast,—the clipt-headed churl,
Broad market-dame, and simple serving-girl
By skirt of silk and periwig in curl!

For soul touched soul; the spiritual treasure-trove
Made all men equal, none could rise above
Nor sink below that level of God's love.

So, with his rustic neighbors sitting down,
The homespun frock beside the scholar's gown,
Pastorius to the manners of the town

Added the freedom of the woods, and sought
The bookless wisdom by experience taught,
And learned to love his new-found home, while not

Forgetful of the old; the seasons went
Their rounds, and somewhat to his spirit lent
Of their own calm and measureless content.

Glad even to tears, he heard the robin sing
His song of welcome to the Western spring,
And bluebird borrowing from the sky his wing.

And when the miracle of autumn came,
And all the woods with many-colored flame
Of splendor, making summer's greenness tame,

Burned, unconsumed, a voice without a sound
Spake to him from each kindled bush around,
And made the strange, new landscape holy ground!

And when the bitter north-wind, keen and swift,
Swept the white street and piled the dooryard drift,
He exercised, as Friends might say, his gift

Of verse, Dutch, English, Latin, like the hash
Of corn and beans in Indian succotash;
Dull, doubtless, but with here and there a flash

Of wit and fine conceit,—the good man's play
Of quiet fancies, meet to while away
The slow hours measuring off an idle day.

At evening, while his wife put on her look
Of love's endurance, from its niche he took
The written pages of his ponderous book.

And read, in half the languages of man,
His "Rusca Apium," which with bees began,
And through the gamut of creation ran.

Or, now and then, the missive of some friend
In gray Altorf or storied Nürnberg penned
Dropped in upon him like a guest to spend

The night beneath his roof-tree. Mystical
The fair Von Merlau spake as waters fall
And voices sound in dreams, and yet withal

Human and sweet, as if each far, low tone,
Over the roses of her gardens blown,
Brought the warm sense of beauty all her own.

Wise Spener questioned what his friend could trace
Of spiritual influx or of saving grace
In the wild natures of the Indian race.

And learned Schurmberg, fain, at times, to look
From Talmud, Koran, Veds, and Pentateuch,
Sought out his pupil in his far-off nook,

To query with him of climatic change,
Of bird, beast, reptile, in his forest range,
Of flowers and fruits and simples new and strange.

And thus the Old and New World reached their hands
Across the water, and the friendly lands
Talked with each other from their severed strands.

Pastorius answered all: while seed and root
Sent from his new home grew to flower and fruit
Along the Rhine and at the Spessart's foot;

And, in return, the flowers his boyhood knew
Smiled at his door, the same in form and hue,
And on his vines the Rhenish clusters grew.

No idler he; whoever else might shirk,
He set his hand to every honest work,—
Farmer and teacher, court and meeting clerk.

Still on the town seal his device is found,
Grapes, flax, and thread-spool on a trefoil ground,
With "*Vinum, Linum et Textrinum*" wound.

One house sufficed for gospel and for law,
Where Paul and Grotius, Scripture text and saw,
Assured the good, and held the rest in awe.

Whatever legal maze he wandered through,
He kept the Sermon on the Mount in view,
And justice always into mercy grew.

No whipping-post he needed, stocks, nor jail,
Nor ducking-stool; the orchard-thief grew pale
At his rebuke, the vixen ceased to rail,

The usurer's grasp released the forfeit land;
The slanderer faltered at the witness-stand,
And all men took his counsel for command.

Was it caressing air, the brooding love
Of tenderer skies than German land knew of,
Green calm below, blue quietness above,

Still flow of water, deep repose of wood
That, with a sense of loving Fatherhood
And childlike trust in the Eternal Good,

Softened all hearts, and dulled the edge of hate,
Hushed strife, and taught impatient zeal to wait
The slow assurance of the better state?

Who knows what goadings in their sterner way
O'er jagged ice, relieved by granite gray,
Blew round the men of Massachusetts Bay?

What hate of heresy the east-wind woke?
What hints of pitiless power and terror spoke
In waves that on their iron coast-line broke?

Be it as it may: within the Land of Penn
The sectary yielded to the citizen,
And peaceful dwelt the many-creeded men.

Peace brooded over all. No trumpet stung
The air to madness, and no steeple flung
Alarums down from bells at midnight rung.

The land slept well. The Indian from his face
Washed all his war-paint off, and in the place
Of battle-marches sped the peaceful chase,

Or wrought for wages at the white man's side,—
Giving to kindness what his native pride
And lazy freedom to all else denied.

And well the curious scholar loved the old
Traditions that his swarthy neighbors told
By wigwam-fires when nights were growing cold,

Discerned the fact round which their fancy drew
Its dreams, and held their childish faith more true
To God and man than half the creeds he knew.

The desert blossomed round him; wheat-fields rolled
Beneath the warm wind waves of green and gold;
The planted ear returned its hundred-fold.

Great clusters ripened in a warmer sun
Than that which by the Rhine stream shines upon
The purpling hillsides with low vines o'errun.

About each rustic porch the humming-bird
Tried with light bill, that scarce a petal stirred,
The Old World flowers to virgin soil transferred;

And the first-fruits of pear and apple, bending
The young boughs down, their gold and russet blending,
Made glad his heart, familiar odors lending

To the fresh fragrance of the birch and pine,
Life-everlasting, bay, and eglantine,
And all the subtle scents the woods combine.

Fair First-Day mornings, steeped in summer calm,
Warm, tender, restful, sweet with woodland balm,
Came to him, like some mother-hallowed psalm

To the tired grinder at the noisy wheel
Of labor, winding off from memory's reel
A golden thread of music. With no peal

Of bells to call them to the house of praise,
The scattered settlers through green forest-ways
Walked meeting-ward. In reverent amaze

The Indian trapper saw them, from the dim
Shade of the alders on the rivulet's rim,
Seek the Great Spirit's house to talk with Him.

There, through the gathered stillness multiplied
And made intense by sympathy, outside
The sparrows sang, and the gold-robin cried,

A-swing upon his elm. A faint perfume
Breathed through the open windows of the room
From locust-trees, heavy with clustered bloom.

Thither, perchance, sore-tried confessors came,
Whose fervor jail nor pillory could tame,
Proud of the cropped ears meant to be their shame,

Men who had eaten slavery's bitter bread
In Indian isles; pale women who had bled
Under the hangman's lash, and bravely said

God's message through their prison's iron bars;
And gray old soldier-converts, seamed with scars
From every stricken field of England's wars.

Lowly before the Unseen Presence knelt
Each waiting heart, till haply some one felt
On his moved lips the seal of silence melt.

Or, without spoken words, low breathings stole
Of a diviner life from soul to soul,
Baptizing in one tender thought the whole.

When shaken hands announced the meeting o'er,
The friendly group still lingered at the door,
Greeting, inquiring, sharing all the store

Of weekly tidings. Meanwhile youth and maid
Down the green vistas of the woodland strayed,
Whispered and smiled and oft their feet delayed.

Did the boy's whistle answer back the thrushes?
Did light girl laughter ripple through the bushes,
As brooks make merry over roots and rushes?

Unvexed the sweet air seemed. Without a wound
The ear of silence heard, and every sound
Its place in Nature's fine accordance found.

And solemn meeting, summer sky and wood,
Old kindly faces, youth and maidenhood
Seemed, like God's new creation, very good!

And, greeting all with quiet smile and word,
Pastorius went his way. The unscared bird
Sang at his side; scarcely the squirrel stirred

At his hushed footstep on the mossy sod;
And, wheresoe'er the good man looked or trod,
He felt the peace of nature and of God.

His social life wore no ascetic form,
He loved all beauty, without fear of harm,
And in his veins his Teuton blood ran warm.

Strict to himself, of other men no spy,
He made his own no circuit-judge to try
The freer conscience of his neighbors by.

With love rebuking, by his life alone,
Gracious and sweet, the better way was shown,
The joy of one, who, seeking not his own,

And faithful to all scruples, finds at last
The thorns and shards of duty overpast,
And daily life, beyond his hope's forecast,

Pleasant and beautiful with sight and sound,
And flowers upspringing in its narrow round,
And all his days with quiet gladness crowned.

He sang not; but, if sometimes tempted strong,
He hummed what seemed like Altorf's Burschen-song,
His good wife smiled and did not count it wrong.

For well he loved his boyhood's brother band;
His Memory, while he trod the New World's strand,
A double-ganger walked the Fatherland!

If, when on frosty Christmas eves the light
Shone on his quiet hearth, he missed the sight
Of Yule-log, Tree, and Christ-child all in white;

And closed his eyes, and listened to the sweet
Old wait-songs sounding down his native street,
And watched again the dancers' mingling feet;

Yet not the less, when once the vision passed,
He held the plain and sober maxims fast
Of the dear Friends with whom his lot was cast.

Still all attuned to nature's melodies,
He loved the bird's song in his dooryard trees,
And the low hum of home-returning bees;

The blossomed flax, the tulip-trees in bloom
Down the long street, the beauty and perfume
Of apple-boughs, the mingling light and gloom

Of Sommerhausen's woodlands, woven through
With sun-threads; and the music the wind drew,
Mournful and sweet, from leaves it overblew.

And evermore, beneath this outward sense,
And through the common sequence of events,
He felt the guiding hand of Providence

Reach out of space. A Voice spake in his ear,
And lo! all other voices far and near
Died at that whisper, full of meanings clear.

The Light of Life shone round him; one by one
The wandering lights, that all-misleading run,
Went out like candles paling in the sun.

That Light he followed, step by step, where'er
It led, as in the vision of the seer
The wheels moved as the spirit in the clear

And terrible crystal moved, with all their eyes
Watching the living splendor sink or rise,
Its will their will, knowing no otherwise.

Within himself he found the law of right,
He walked by faith and not the letter's sight,
And read his Bible by the Inward Light.

And if sometimes the slaves of form and rule,
Frozen in their creeds like fish in winter's pool,
Tried the large tolerance of his liberal school,

His door was free to men of every name,
He welcomed all the seeking souls who came,
And no man's faith he made a cause of blame.

But best he loved in leisure hours to see
His own dear Friends sit by him knee to knee,
In social converse, genial, frank, and free.

There sometimes silence (it were hard to tell
Who owned it first) upon the circle fell,
Hushed Anna's busy wheel, and laid its spell

On the black boy who grimaced by the hearth,
To solemnize his shining face of mirth;
Only the old clock ticked amidst the dearth

Of sound; nor eye was raised nor hand was stirred
In that soul-sabbath, till at last some word
Of tender counsel or low prayer was heard.

Then guests, who lingered but farewell to say
And take love's message, went their homeward way;
So passed in peace the guileless Quaker's day.

His was the Christian's unsung Age of Gold,
A truer idyl than the bards have told
Of Arno's banks or Arcady of old.

Where still the Friends their place of burial keep,
And century-rooted mosses o'er it creep,
The Nürnberg scholar and his helpmeet sleep.

And Anna's aloe? If it flowered at last
In Bartram's garden, did John Woolman cast
A glance upon it as he meekly passed?

And did a secret sympathy possess
That tender soul, and for the slave's redress
Lend hope, strength, patience? It were vain to guess.

Nay, were the plant itself but mythical,
Set in the fresco of tradition's wall
Like Jotham's bramble, mattereth not at all.

Enough to know that, through the winter's frost
And summer's heat, no seed of truth is lost,
And every duty pays at last its cost.

For, ere Pastorius left the sun and air,
God sent the answer to his life-long prayer;
The child was born beside the Delaware,

Who, in the power a holy purpose lends,
Guided his people unto nobler ends,
And left them worthier of the name of Friends.

And lo! the fullness of the time has come,
And over all the exile's Western home,
From sea to sea the flowers of freedom bloom!

And joy-bells ring, and silver trumpets blow;
But not for thee, Pastorius! Even so
The world forgets, but the wise angels know.

1872 1872

A SEA DREAM

We saw the slow tides go and come,
The curving surf-lines lightly drawn,
The gray rocks touched with tender bloom
Beneath the fresh-blown rose of dawn.

We saw in richer sunsets lost
The sombre pomp of showery noons;
And signalled spectral sails that crossed
The weird, low light of rising moons.

On stormy eves from cliff and head
We saw the white spray tossed and spurned;

While over all, in gold and red,
  Its face of fire the lighthouse turned.

The rail-car brought its daily crowds,
  Half curious, half indifferent,
Like passing sails or floating clouds,
  We saw them as they came and went.

But, one calm morning, as we lay
  And watched the mirage-lifted wall
Of coast, across the dreamy bay,
  And heard afar the curlew call,

And nearer voices, wild or tame,
  Of airy flock and childish throng,
Up from the water's edge there came
  Faint snatches of familiar song.

Careless we heard the singer's choice
  Of old and common airs; at last
The tender pathos of his voice
  In one low chanson held us fast.

A song that mingled joy and pain,
  And memories old and sadly sweet;
While, timing to its minor strain,
  The waves in lapsing cadence beat.

The waves are glad in breeze and sun;
  The rocks are fringed with foam;
I walk once more a haunted shore,
  A stranger, yet at home,
  A land of dreams I roam.

Is this the wind, the soft sea-wind
  That stirred thy locks of brown?
Are these the rocks whose mosses knew
  The trail of thy light gown,
  Where boy and girl sat down?

I see the gray fort's broken wall,
  The boats that rock below;
And, out at sea, the passing sails
  We saw so long ago
  Rose-red in morning's glow.

The freshness of the early time
  On every breeze is blown;
As glad the sea, as blue the sky,—
  The change is ours alone;
  The saddest is my own.

A stranger now, a world-worn man,
  Is he who bears my name;
But thou, methinks, whose mortal life
  Immortal youth became,
  Art evermore the same.

Thou art not here, thou art not there,
  Thy place I cannot see;
I only know that where thou art
  The blessed angels be,
  And heaven is glad for thee.

Forgive me if the evil years
  Have left on me their sign;
Wash out, O soul so beautiful,
  The many stains of mine
  In tears of love divine!

I could not look on thee and live,
  If thou wert by my side;
The vision of a shining one,
  The white and heavenly bride,
  Is well to me denied.

But turn to me thy dear girl-face
  Without the angel's crown,
The wedded roses of thy lips,
  Thy loose hair rippling down
  In waves of golden brown.

Look forth once more through space and time,
  And let thy sweet shade fall
In tenderest grace of soul and form
  On memory's frescoed wall,
  A shadow, and yet all!

Draw near, more near, forever dear!
  Where'er I rest or roam,
Or in the city's crowded streets,
  Or by the blown sea foam,
  The thought of thee is home!

At breakfast hour the singer read
  The city news, with comment wise,
Like one who felt the pulse of trade
  Beneath his finger fall and rise.

His look, his air, his curt speech, told
  The man of action, not of books,
To whom the corners made in gold
  And stocks were more than seaside nooks.

Of life beneath the life confessed
  His song had hinted unawares;
Of flowers in traffic's ledgers pressed,
  Of human hearts in bulls and bears.

But eyes in vain were turned to watch
That face so hard and shrewd and strong;
And ears in vain grew sharp to catch
The meaning of that morning song.

In vain some sweet-voiced querist sought
To sound him, leaving as she came;
Her baited album only caught
A common, unromantic name.

No word betrayed the mystery fine,
That trembled on the singer's tongue;
He came and went, and left no sign
Behind him save the song he sung.

1874

THE FRIEND'S BURIAL

My thoughts are all in yonder town,
Where, wept by many tears,
Today my mother's friend lays down
The burden of her years.

True as in life, no poor disguise
Of death with her is seen,
And on her simple casket lies
No wreath of bloom and green.

Oh, not for her the florist's art,
The mocking weeds of woe;
Dear memories in each mourner's heart
Like heaven's white lilies blow.

And all about the softening air
Of new-born sweetness tells,
And the ungathered May-flowers wear
The tints of ocean shells.

The old, assuring miracle
Is fresh as heretofore;
And earth takes up its parable
Of life from death once more.

Here organ-swell and church-bell toll
Methinks but discord were;
The prayerful silence of the soul
Is best befitting her.

No sound should break the quietude
Alike of earth and sky;
O wandering wind in Seabrook wood,
Breathe but a half-heard sigh!

Sing softly, spring-bird, for her sake;
And thou not distant sea,
Lapse lightly as if Jesus spake,
And thou wert Galilee!

For all her quiet life flowed on
As meadow streamlets flow,
Where fresher green reveals alone
The noiseless ways they go.

From her loved place of prayer I see
The plain-robed mourners pass,
With slow feet treading reverently
The graveyard's springing grass.

Make room, O mourning ones, for me,
Where, like the friends of Paul,
That you no more her face shall see
You sorrow most of all.

Her path shall brighten more and more
Unto the perfect day;
She cannot fail of peace who bore
Such peace with her away.

O sweet, calm face that seemed to wear
The look of sins forgiven!
O voice of prayer that seemed to bear
Our own needs up to heaven!

How reverent in our midst she stood,
Or knelt in grateful praise!
What grace of Christian womanhood
Was in her household ways!

For still her holy living meant
No duty left undone;
The heavenly and the human blent
Their kindred loves in one.

And if her life small leisure found
For feasting ear and eye,
And Pleasure, on her daily round,
She passed unpausing by,

Yet with her went a secret sense
Of all things sweet and fair,
And Beauty's gracious providence
Refreshed her unaware.

She kept her line of rectitude
With love's unconscious ease;
Her kindly instincts understood
All gentle courtesies.

An inborn charm of graciousness
  Made sweet her smile and tone,
And glorified her farm-wife dress
  With beauty not its own.

The dear Lord's best interpreters
  Are humble human souls;
The Gospel of a life like hers
  Is more than books or scrolls.

From scheme and creed the light goes out,
  The saintly fact survives;
The blessed Master none can doubt
  Revealed in holy lives.

1873 1874

A MYSTERY

THE river hemmed with leaning trees
  Wound through its meadows green;
A low, blue line of mountains showed
  The open pines between.

One sharp, tall peak above them all
  Clear into sunlight sprang:
I saw the river of my dreams,
  The mountains that I sang!

No clue of memory led me on,
  But well the ways I knew;
A feeling of familiar things
  With every footstep grew.

Not otherwise above its crag
  Could lean the blasted pine;
Not otherwise the maple hold
  Aloft its red ensign.

So up the long and shorn foot-hills
  The mountain road should creep;
So, green and low, the meadow fold
  Its red-haired kine asleep.

The river wound as it should wind;
  Their place the mountains took;
The white torn fringes of their clouds
  Wore no unwonted look.

Yet ne'er before that river's rim
  Was pressed by feet of mine,
Never before mine eyes had crossed
  That broken mountain line.

A presence, strange at once and known,
  Walked with me as my guide;
The skirts of some forgotten life
  Trailed noiseless at my side.

Was it a dim-remembered dream?
  Or glimpse through æons old?
The secret which the mountains kept
  The river never told.

But from the vision ere it passed
  A tender hope I drew,
And, pleasant as a dawn of spring,
  The thought within me grew,

That love would temper every change,
  And soften all surprise,
And, misty with the dreams of earth,
  The hills of Heaven arise.

1873? 1873

VESTA

O CHRIST of God! whose life and death
  Our own have reconciled,
Most quietly, most tenderly
  Take home Thy star-named child!

Thy grace is in her patient eyes,
  Thy words are on her tongue;
The very silence round her seems
  As if the angels sung.

Her smile is as a listening child's
  Who hears its mother call;
The lilies of Thy perfect peace
  About her pillow fall.

She leans from out our clinging arms
  To rest herself in Thine;
Alone to Thee, dear Lord, can we
  Our well-beloved resign!

Oh, less for her than for ourselves
  We bow our heads and pray;
Her setting star, like Bethlehem's,
  To Thee shall point the way!

1874

THE PROBLEM

I

NOT without envy Wealth at times must look
On their brown strength who wield the reap-
  ing-hook
And scythe, or at the forge-fire shape the
  plough

Or the steel harness of the steeds of steam;
All who, by skill and patience, anyhow
Make service noble, and the earth redeem
From savageness. By kingly accolade
Than theirs was never worthier knighthood made.
Well for them, if, while demagogues their vain
And evil counsels proffer, they maintain
Their honest manhood unseduced, and wage
No war with Labor's right to Labor's gain
Of sweet home-comfort, rest of hand and brain,
And softer pillow for the head of Age.

II

And well for Gain if it ungrudging yields
Labor its just demand; and well for Ease
If in the uses of its own, it sees
No wrong to him who tills its pleasant fields
And spreads the table of its luxuries.
The interests of the rich man and the poor
Are one and same, inseparable evermore;
And, when scant wage or labor fail to give
Food, shelter, raiment, wherewithal to live,
Need has its rights, necessity its claim.
Yea, even self-wrought misery and shame
Test well the charity suffering long and kind.
The home-pressed question of the age can find
No answer in the catch-words of the blind
Leaders of blind. Solution there is none
Save in the Golden Rule of Christ alone.

1876? 1877

THE TRAILING ARBUTUS

I WANDERED lonely where the pine-trees made
Against the bitter East their barricade,
And, guided by its sweet
Perfume, I found, within a narrow dell,
The trailing spring flower tinted like a shell
Amid dry leaves and mosses at my feet.

From under dead boughs, for whose loss the pines
Moaned ceaseless overhead, the blossoming vines
Lifted their glad surprise,
While yet the bluebird smoothed in leafless trees
His feathers ruffled by the chill sea-breeze,
And snow-drifts lingered under April skies.

As, pausing, o'er the lonely flower I bent,
I thought of lives thus lowly, clogged and pent,
Which yet find room,
Through care and cumber, coldness and decay,
To lend a sweetness to the ungenial day,
And make the sad earth happier for their bloom.

1879? 1879

SUNSET ON THE BEARCAMP

A GOLD fringe on the purpling hem
Of hills the river runs,
As down its long, green valley falls
The last of summer's suns.
Along its tawny gravel-bed
Broad-flowing, swift, and still,
As if its meadow levels felt
The hurry of the hill,
Noiseless between its banks of green
From curve to curve it slips;
The drowsy maple-shadows rest
Like fingers on its lips.

A waif from Carroll's wildest hills,
Unstoried and unknown;
The ursine legend of its name
Prowls on its banks alone.
Yet flowers as fair its slopes adorn
As ever Yarrow knew,
Or, under rainy Irish skies,
By Spenser's Mulla grew;
And through the gaps of leaning trees
Its mountain cradle shows:
The gold against the amethyst,
The green against the rose.

Touched by a light that hath no name,
A glory never sung,
Aloft on sky and mountain wall
Are God's great pictures hung.
How changed the summits vast and old!
No longer granite-browed,
They melt in rosy mist; the rock
Is softer than the cloud;
The valley holds its breath; no leaf
Of all its elms is twirled:
The silence of eternity
Seems falling on the world.

The pause before the breaking seals
Of mystery is this;
Yon miracle-play of night and day
Makes dumb its witnesses.
What unseen altar crowns the hills
That reach up stair on stair?
What eyes look through, what white wings fan
These purple veils of air?
What Presence from the heavenly heights
To those of earth stoops down?
Not vainly Hellas dreamed of gods
On Ida's snowy crown!

Slow fades the vision of the sky,
The golden water pales,
And over all the valley-land
A gray-winged vapor sails.
I go the common way of all;
The sunset fires will burn,
The flowers will blow, the river flow,
When I no more return.
No whisper from the mountain pine
Nor lapsing stream shall tell
The stranger, treading where I tread,
Of him who loved them well.

But beauty seen is never lost,
God's colors all are fast;
The glory of this sunset heaven
Into my soul has passed,
A sense of gladness unconfined
To mortal date or clime;
As the soul liveth, it shall live
Beyond the years of time.
Beside the mystic asphodels
Shall bloom the home-born flowers,
And new horizons flush and glow
With sunset hues of ours.

Farewell! these smiling hills must wear
Too soon their wintry frown,
And snow-cold winds from off them shake
The maple's red leaves down.
But I shall see a summer sun
Still setting broad and low;
The mountain slopes shall blush and bloom,
The golden water flow.
A lover's claim is mine on all
I see to have and hold,—
The rose-light of perpetual hills,
And sunsets never cold!

1876 1878

From PREFACE TO LEGENDS OF NEW ENGLAND (1831)

In the following pages I have to present in an interesting form some of the popular traditions and legends of New England. The field is a new one—and I have but partially explored it. New England is rich in traditionary lore—a thousand associations of superstition and manly daring and romantic adventure are connected with her green hills and her pleasant rivers. I leave the task of rescuing these associations from oblivion to some more fortunate individual, and if this little volume shall have the effect to induce such an effort, I shall at least be satisfied, whatever may be the judgment of the public upon my own humble production . . . written during the anxieties and perplexing cares attendant upon the management of a political and literary periodical.

From ROBERT DINSMORE

The great charm of Scottish poetry consists in its simplicity, and genuine, unaffected sympathy with the common joys and sorrows of daily life. It is a home-taught, household melody. It calls to mind the pastoral bleat on the hillsides, the kirk-bells of a summer Sabbath, the song of the lark in the sunrise, the cry of the quail in the corn-land, the low of cattle, and the blithe carol of milkmaids "when the kye come hame" at gloaming. Meetings at fair and market, blushing betrothments, merry weddings, the joy of young maternity, the lights and shades of domestic life, its bereavements and partings, its chances and changes, its holy death-beds, and funerals solemnly beautiful in quiet kirkyards,—these furnish the hints of the immortal melodies of Burns, the sweet ballads of the Ettrick Shepherd and Allan Cunningham, and the rustic drama of Ramsay. It is the poetry of home, of nature, and the affections.

All this is sadly wanting in our young literature. We have no songs; American domestic life has never been hallowed and beautified by the sweet and graceful and tender associations of poetry. We have no Yankee pastorals. Our rivers and streams turn mills and float rafts, and are otherwise as commendably useful as those of Scotland; but no quaint ballad or simple song reminds us that men and women have loved, met, and parted on their banks, or that beneath each roof within their valleys the tragedy and comedy of life have been enacted. Our poetry is cold and imitative; it seems more the product of over-strained intellects than the spontaneous outgushing of hearts warm with love, and strongly sympathizing with human nature as it actually exists about us, with the joys and griefs of the men and women whom we meet daily. Unhappily, the opinion prevails that a poet must be also a philosopher, and hence it is that much of our poetry is as indefinable in its mysticism as an Indian Brahmin's commentary on his sacred books, or German metaphysics subjected to homœopathic dilution. It assumes to be prophetical, and its utterances oracular. It tells of strange, vague emotions and yearnings, painfully suggestive of spiritual "groanings which cannot be uttered." If it "babbles o' green fields" and the common sights and sounds of nature, it is only for the purpose of finding some vague analogy between them and its internal experiences and longings. It leaves the warm and comfortable fireside of actual knowledge and human comprehension, and goes wailing and gibbering like a ghost about the impassable doors of mystery:—

"It fain would be resolved
How things are done,
And who the tailor is
That works for the man i' the sun."

How shall we account for this marked tendency in the literature of a shrewd, practical people? Is it that real life in New England lacks those conditions of poetry and romance which age, reverence, and superstition have gathered about it in the Old World? Is it that

"Ours are not Tempe's nor Arcadia's vales,"

but are more famous for growing Indian corn and potatoes, and the manufacture of wooden ware and pedler notions, than for romantic associations and legendary interest? That our huge, unshapely shingle structures, blistering in the sun and glaring with windows, were evidently never reared by the spell of pastoral harmonies, as the walls of Thebes rose at the sound of the lyre of Amphion? That the habits of our people are too cool, cautious, undemonstrative, to furnish the warp and woof of song and pastoral, and that their dialect and figures of speech, however richly significant and expressive in the autobiography of Sam Slick, or the satire of Hosea Biglow and Ethan Spike, form a very awkward medium of sentiment and pathos? All this may be true. But the Yankee, after all, is a man, and as such his history, could it be got at, must have more or less of poetic material in it; moreover, whether conscious of it or not, he also stands relieved against the background of Nature's beauty or sublimity. There is a poetical side to the commonplace of his incomings and outgoings; study him well, and you may frame an idyl of some sort from his apparently prosaic existence. Our poets, we must needs think, are deficient in that shiftiness, ready adaptation to circumstances, and ability of making the most of things, for which, as a people, we are proverbial. Can they make nothing of our Thanksgiving, that annual gathering of long-severed friends? Do they find nothing to their purpose in our apple-bees, huskings, berry-pickings, summer picnics, and winter sleigh-rides? Is there nothing available in our peculiarities of climate, scenery, customs, and political institutions? Does the Yankee leap into life, shrewd, hard, and speculating, armed, like Pallas, for a struggle with fortune? Are there not boys and girls, school loves and friendship, courtings and match-makings, hope and fear, and all the varied play of human passions,—the keen struggles of gain, the mad grasping of ambition,—sin and remorse, tearful repentance and holy aspirations? Who shall say that we have not all the essentials of the poetry of human life and simple nature, of the hearth and the farm-field? Here, then, is a mine unworked, a harvest ungathered. Who shall sink the shaft and thrust in the sickle?

And here let us say that the mere dilettante and the amateur ruralist may as well keep their hands off. The prize is not for them. He who would successfully strive for it must be himself what he sings,—part and parcel of the rural life of New England,—one who has grown strong amidst its healthful influences, familiar with all its details, and capable of detecting whatever of beauty, humor, or pathos pertain to it,—one who has added to his book-lore the large experience of an active participation in the rugged toil, the hearty amusements, the trials, and the pleasures he describes.

1828–1850

THE BEAUTIFUL

"A beautiful form is better than a beautiful face; a beautiful behavior is better than a beautiful form; it gives a higher pleasure than statues or pictures; it is the finest of the fine arts."

— Emerson's *Essays,* Second Series, iv., p. 162.

A few days since I was walking with a friend, who, unfortunately for himself, seldom meets with anything in the world of realities worthy of comparison with the ideal of his fancy, which, like the bird in the Arabian tale, glides perpetually before him, always near yet never overtaken. He was half humorously, half seriously, complaining of the lack of beauty in the faces and forms that passed us on the crowded sidewalk. Some defect was noticeable in all: one was too heavy, another too angular; here a nose was at fault, there a mouth put a set of otherwise fine features out of countenance; the fair complexions had red hair, and glossy black locks were wasted upon dingy ones. In one way or another all fell below his impossible standard.

The beauty which my friend seemed in search of was that of proportion and coloring; mechanical exactness; a due combination of soft curves and obtuse angles, of warm carnation and marble purity. Such a man, for aught I can see, might love a graven image, like the girl of Florence who pined into a shadow for the Apollo Belvidere, looking coldly on her with stony eyes from his niche in the Vatican. One thing is certain,—he will never find his faultless piece of artistical perfection by searching for it amidst flesh-and-blood realities. Nature does not, as far as I can perceive, work with square and compass, or lay on her colors by the rules of royal artists or the dunces of the academies. She eschews regular outlines. She does not shape her forms by a common model. Not one of Eve's numerous progeny in all respects resembles her who first culled the flowers of Eden. To the infinite variety and picturesque inequality of Nature we owe the great charm of her uncloying beauty. Look at her primitive woods; scattered trees, with moist sward and bright mosses at their roots; great clumps of green shadow, where limb intwists with limb and the rustle of one leaf stirs a hundred others,—stretching up steep hill-sides, flooding with green beauty the valleys, or arching over with leaves the sharp ravines, every tree and shrub unlike its neighbor in size and proportion,—the old and storm-broken leaning on the young and vigorous,—intricate and confused, without order or method. Who would exchange this for artificial French gardens, where every tree stands stiff and regular, clipped and trimmed into unvarying conformity, like so many grenadiers under review? Who wants eternal sunshine or shadow? Who would fix forever the loveliest cloudwork of an autumn sunset, or hang over him an everlasting moonlight? If the stream had no quiet eddying place, could we so admire its cascade over the rocks? Were there no clouds, could we so hail the sky shining through them in its still, calm purity? Who shall venture to ask our kind Mother Nature to remove from our sight any one of her forms or colors? Who shall decide which is beautiful, or otherwise, in itself considered?

There are too many, like my fastidious friend, who go through the world "from Dan to Beersheba, finding all barren,"—who have always some fault or other to find with Nature and Providence, seeming to consider themselves especially ill used because the one does not always coincide with their taste, nor the other with their narrow notions of personal convenience. In one of his early poems, Coleridge has well expressed a truth, which is not the less important because it is not generally admitted. The idea is briefly this: that the mind gives to all things their coloring, their gloom, or gladness; that the pleasure we derive from external nature is primarily from ourselves:—

> "from the mind itself must issue forth
> A light, a glory, a fair luminous mist,
> Enveloping the earth."

The real difficulty of these lifelong hunters after the beautiful exists in their own spirits. They set up certain models of perfection in their imaginations, and then go about the world in the vain expectation of finding them actually wrought out according to pattern; very unreasonably calculating that Nature will suspend her everlasting laws for the purpose of creating faultless prodigies for their especial gratification.

The authors of *Gayeties and Gravities* give it as their opinion that no object of sight is regarded by us as a simple disconnected form, but that an instantaneous reflection as to its history, purpose, or associations converts it into a concrete one,—a process, they shrewdly remark, which no thinking being can prevent, and which can only be avoided by the unmeaning and stolid stare of "a goose on the common or a cow on the green." The senses and the faculties of the understanding are so blended with and dependent upon each other that not one of them can exercise its office alone and without the modification of some extrinsic interference or suggestion. Grateful or unpleasant associations cluster around all which sense takes cognizance of; the beauty which we discern in an external object is often but the reflection of our own minds.

What is beauty, after all? Ask the lover who kneels in homage to one who has no attractions for others. The cold onlooker wonders that he can call that unclassic combination of features and that awkward form beautiful. Yet so it is. He sees, like Desdemona, her "visage in her mind," or her affections. A light from within shines through the external uncomeliness,—softens, irradiates, and glorifies it. That which to others seems commonplace and unworthy of note is to him, in the words of Spenser,—

> "A sweet, attractive kind of grace;
> A full assurance given by looks;
> Continual comfort in a face;
> The lineaments of Gospel books."

"Handsome is that handsome does,—hold up your heads, girls!" was the language of Primrose in the play when addressing her daughters. The worthy matron was right. Would that all my female readers who are sorrowing foolishly because they are not in all respects like Dubufe's Eve, or that statue of the Venus "which enchants the world," could be persuaded to listen to her. What is good looking, as Horace Smith remarks, but looking good? Be good, be womanly, be gentle,—generous in your sympathies, heedful of the well-being of all around you; and, my word for it, you will not lack kind words of admiration. Loving and pleasant associations will gather about you. Never mind the ugly reflection which your glass may give you. That mirror has no heart. But quite another picture is yours on the retina of human sympathy. There the beauty of holiness, of purity, of that inward grace which passeth show, rests over it, softening and mellowing its features just as the full calm moonlight melts those of a rough landscape into harmonious loveliness. "Hold up your heads, girls!" I repeat after Primrose. Why should you not? Every mother's daughter of you *can* be beautiful. You can envelop yourselves in an atmosphere of moral and intellectual beauty, through which your otherwise plain faces will look forth like those of angels. Beautiful to Ledyard, stiffening in the cold of a northern winter, seemed the diminutive, smoke-stained women of Lapland, who wrapped him in their furs and ministered to his necessities with kindness and gentle words of compassion. Lovely to the homesick heart of Park seemed the dark maids of Sego, as they sung their low and simple song of welcome beside his bed, and sought to comfort the white stranger, who had "no mother to bring him milk and no wife to grind him corn." Oh, talk as we may of beauty as a thing to be chiselled from marble or wrought out on canvas, speculate as we may upon its colors and outlines, what is it but an intellectual abstraction, after all? The heart feels a beauty of another kind; looking through the outward environment, it discovers a deeper and more real loveliness.

This was well understood by the old painters. In their pictures of Mary, the virgin mother, the beauty which melts and subdues the gazer is that of the soul and the affections, uniting the awe and mystery of that mother's miraculous allotment with the irrepressible love, the unutterable tenderness, of young maternity,—Heaven's crowning miracle with Nature's holiest and sweetest instinct. And their pale Magdalens, holy with the look of sins forgiven,—how the divine beauty of their penitence sinks into the heart! Do we not feel that the only real deformity is sin, and that goodness evermore hallows and sanctifies its dwelling-place? When the soul is at rest, when the passions and desires are all attuned to the divine harmony,—

> "Spirits moving musically
> To a lute's well-ordered law," [1]

do we not read the placid significance thereof in the human countenance? "I have seen," said Charles Lamb, "faces upon which the dove of peace sat brooding." In that simple and beautiful record of a holy life, the *Journal of John Woolman*, there is a passage of which I have been more than once reminded in my intercourse with my fellow-beings: "Some glances of real beauty may be seen in their faces who dwell in true meekness. There is a harmony in the sound of that voice to which divine love gives utterance."

Quite the ugliest face I ever saw was that of a woman whom the world calls beautiful. Through its "silver veil" the evil and ungentle passions looked out hideous and hateful. On the other hand, there are faces which the multitude at the first glance pronounce homely, unattractive, and such as "Nature fashions by the gross," which I always recognize with a warm heart-thrill; not for the world would I have one feature changed; they please me as they are; they are hallowed by kind memories; they are beautiful through their associations; nor are they any the less welcome that with my admiration of them "the stranger intermeddleth not."

1844

[1] *The Haunted Palace*, by Edgar A. Poe. [*Whittier's note.*]

RALPH WALDO EMERSON

GOOD-BYE

Good-bye, proud world! I'm going home:
Thou art not my friend, and I'm not thine.
Long through thy weary crowds I roam;
A river-ark on the ocean brine,
Long I've been tossed like the driven foam;
But now, proud world! I'm going home.

Good-bye to Flattery's fawning face;
To Grandeur with his wise grimace;
To upstart Wealth's averted eye;
To supple Office, low and high;
To crowded halls, to court and street;
To frozen hearts and hasting feet;
To those who go, and those who come;
Good-bye, proud world! I'm going home.

I am going to my own hearth-stone,
Bosomed in yon green hills alone,—
A secret nook in a pleasant land,
Whose groves the frolic fairies planned;
Where arches green, the livelong day,
Echo the blackbird's roundelay,
And vulgar feet have never trod
A spot that is sacred to thought and God.

O, when I am safe in my sylvan home,
I tread on the pride of Greece and Rome;
And when I am stretched beneath the pines,
Where the evening star so holy shines,
I laugh at the lore and the pride of man,
At the sophist schools and the learned clan;
For what are they all, in their high conceit,
When man in the bush with God may meet?

1823 1839

THOUGHT

I am not poor, but I am proud,
Of one inalienable right,
Above the envy of the crowd,—
Thought's holy light.

Better it is than gems or gold,
And oh! it cannot die,
But thought will glow when the sun grows cold,
And mix with Deity.

1823

WEBSTER

Ill fits the abstemious Muse a crown to weave
For living brows; ill fits them to receive:
And yet, if virtue abrogate the law,
One portrait—fact or fancy—we may draw;
A form which Nature cast in the heroic mould
Of them who rescued liberty of old;
He, when the rising storm of party roared,
Brought his great forehead to the council board,
There, while hot heads perplexed with fears the state,
Calm as the morn the manly patriot sate;
Seemed, when at last his clarion accents broke,
As if the conscience of the country spoke.
Not on its base Monadnoc surer stood,
Than he to common sense and common good:
No mimic; from his breast his counsel drew,
Believed the eloquent was aye the true;
He bridged the gulf from th' alway good and wise
To that within the vision of small eyes.
Self-centred; when he launched the genuine word
It shook or captivated all who heard,
Ran from his mouth to mountains and the sea,
And burned in noble hearts proverb and prophecy.

1834 1883

THE RHODORA:

ON BEING ASKED, WHENCE IS THE FLOWER?

In May, when sea-winds pierced our solitudes,
I found the fresh Rhodora in the woods,
Spreading its leafless blooms in a damp nook,
To please the desert and the sluggish brook.
The purple petals, fallen in the pool,
Made the black water with their beauty gay;
Here might the redbird come his plumes to cool,
And court the flower that cheapens his array.
Rhodora! if the sages ask thee why
This charm is wasted on the earth and sky,
Tell them, dear, that if eyes were made for seeing,

Then Beauty is its own excuse for being:
Why thou wert there, O rival of the rose!
I never thought to ask, I never knew:
But, in my simple ignorance, suppose
The self-same Power that brought me there
brought you.

1834 *1839*

EACH AND ALL

Little thinks, in the field, yon red-cloaked
clown
Of thee from the hill-top looking down;
The heifer that lows in the upland farm,
Far-heard, lows not thine ear to charm;
The sexton, tolling his bell at noon,
Deems not that great Napoleon
Stops his horse, and lists with delight,
Whilst his files sweep round yon Alpine
height;
Nor knowest thou what argument
Thy life to thy neighbor's creed has lent.
All are needed by each one;
Nothing is fair or good alone.
I thought the sparrow's note from heaven,
Singing at dawn on the alder bough;
I brought him home, in his nest, at even;
He sings the song, but it cheers not now,
For I did not bring home the river and sky;—
He sang to my ear,—they sang to my eye.
The delicate shells lay on the shore;
The bubbles of the latest wave
Fresh pearls to their enamel gave,
And the bellowing of the savage sea
Greeted their safe escape to me.
I wiped away the weeds and foam,
I fetched my sea-born treasures home;
But the poor, unsightly, noisome things
Had left their beauty on the shore
With the sun and the sand and the wild up-
roar.
The lover watched his graceful maid,
As 'mid the virgin train she strayed,
Nor knew her beauty's best attire
Was woven still by the snow-white choir.
At last she came to his hermitage,
Like the bird from the woodlands to the
cage;—
The gay enchantment was undone,
A gentle wife, but fairy none.
Then I said, "I covet truth;
Beauty is unripe childhood's cheat;
I leave it behind with the games of youth:"—
As I spoke, beneath my feet
The ground-pine curled its pretty wreath,
Running over the club-moss burrs;
I inhaled the violet's breath;
Around me stood the oaks and firs;
Pine-cones and acorns lay on the ground;
Over me soared the eternal sky,
Full of light and of deity;
Again I saw, again I heard,
The rolling river, the morning bird;—
Beauty through my senses stole;
I yielded myself to the perfect whole.

1834? *1839*

THE APOLOGY

Think me not unkind and rude
That I walk alone in grove and glen;
I go to the god of the wood
To fetch his word to men.

Tax not my sloth that I
Fold my arms beside the brook;
Each cloud that floated in the sky
Writes a letter in my book.

Chide me not, laborious band,
For the idle flowers I brought;
Every aster in my hand
Goes home loaded with a thought.

There was never mystery
But 'tis figured in the flowers;
Was never secret history
But birds tell it in the bowers.

One harvest from thy field
Homeward brought the oxen strong;
A second crop thine acres yield,
Which I gather in a song.

1834? *1847*

NATURE

A subtle chain of countless rings
The next unto the farthest brings;
The eye reads omens where it goes,
And speaks all languages the rose;
And, striving to be man, the worm
Mounts through all the spires of form.

1836 *1836*

THE HUMBLE-BEE

Burly, dozing humble-bee,
Where thou art is clime for me.
Let them sail for Porto Rique,
Far-off heats through seas to seek;
I will follow thee alone,
Thou animated torrid-zone!
Zigzag steerer, desert cheerer,
Let me chase thy waving lines;
Keep me nearer, me thy hearer,
Singing over shrubs and vines.

Insect lover of the sun,
Joy of thy dominion!
Sailor of the atmosphere;
Swimmer through the waves of air;
Voyager of light and noon;
Epicurean of June;
Wait, I prithee, till I come
Within earshot of thy hum,—
All without is martyrdom.

When the south wind, in May days,
With a net of shining haze
Silvers the horizon wall,
And with softness touching all,
Tints the human countenance
With a color of romance,
And infusing subtle heats,
Turns the sod to violets,
Thou, in sunny solitudes,
Rover of the underwoods,
The green silence dost displace
With thy mellow, breezy bass.

Hot midsummer's petted crone,
Sweet to me thy drowsy tone
Tells of countless sunny hours,
Long days, and solid banks of flowers;
Of gulfs of sweetness without bound
In Indian wildernesses found;
Of Syrian peace, immortal leisure,
Firmest cheer, and bird-like pleasure.

Aught unsavory or unclean
Hath my insect never seen;
But violets and bilberry bells,
Maple-sap and daffodels,
Grass with green flag half-mast high,
Succory to match the sky,
Columbine with horn of honey,
Scented fern, and agrimony,
Clover, catchfly, adder's-tongue
And brier-roses, dwelt among;
All beside was unknown waste,
All was picture as he passed.

Wiser far than human seer,
Yellow-breeched philosopher!
Seeing only what is fair,
Sipping only what is sweet,
Thou dost mock at fate and care,
Leave the chaff, and take the wheat.
When the fierce northwestern blast
Cools sea and land so far and fast,
Thou already slumberest deep;
Woe and want thou canst outsleep;
Want and woe, which torture us,
Thy sleep makes ridiculous.

1837? 1839

THE POET

I

Right upward on the road of fame
With sounding steps the poet came;
Born and nourished in miracles,
His feet were shod with golden bells,
Or where he stepped the soil did peal
As if the dust were glass and steel.
The gallant child where'er he came
Threw to each fact a tuneful name.
The things whereon he cast his eyes
Could not the nations rebaptize,
Nor Time's snows hide the names he set,
Nor last posterity forget.
Yet every scroll whereon he wrote
In latent fire his secret thought,
Fell unregarded to the ground,
Unseen by such as stood around.
The pious wind took it away,
The reverent darkness hid the lay.
Methought like water-haunting birds
Divers or dippers were his words,
And idle clowns beside the mere
At the new vision gape and jeer.
But when the noisy scorn was past,
Emerge the wingèd words in haste.
New-bathed, new-trimmed, on healthy wing,
Right to the heaven they steer and sing.

A Brother of the world, his song
Sounded like a tempest strong

Which tore from oaks their branches broad,
And stars from the ecliptic road.
Times wore he as his clothing-weeds,
He sowed the sun and moon for seeds.
As melts the iceberg in the seas,
As clouds give rain to the eastern breeze,
As snow-banks thaw in April's beam,
The solid kingdoms like a dream
Resist in vain his motive strain,
They totter now and float amain.
For the Muse gave special charge
His learning should be deep and large,
And his training should not scant
The deepest lore of wealth or want:
His flesh should feel, his eyes should read
Every maxim of dreadful Need;
In its fulness he should taste
Life's honeycomb, but not too fast;
Full fed, but not intoxicated;
He should be loved; he should be hated;
A blooming child to children dear,
His heart should palpitate with fear.

And well he loved to quit his home
And, Calmuck, in his wagon roam
To read new landscapes and old skies;—
But oh, to see his solar eyes
Like meteors which chose their way
And rived the dark like a new day!
Not lazy grazing on all they saw,
Each chimney-pot and cottage door,
Farm-gear and village picket-fence,
But, feeding on magnificence,
They bounded to the horizon's edge
And searched with the sun's privilege.
Landward they reached the mountains old
Where pastoral tribes their flocks infold,
Saw rivers run seaward by cities high
And the seas wash the low-hung sky;
Saw the endless rack of the firmament
And the sailing moon where the cloud was rent,
And through man and woman and sea and star
Saw the dance of Nature forward and far,
Through worlds and races and terms and times
Saw musical order and pairing rhymes.

II

The gods talk in the breath of the woods,
They talk in the shaken pine,
And fill the long reach of the old seashore
With dialogue divine;
And the poet who overhears
Some random word they say
Is the fated man of men
Whom the ages must obey:
One who having nectar drank
Into blissful orgies sank;
He takes no mark of night or day,
He cannot go, he cannot stay,
He would, yet would not, counsel keep,
But, like a walker in his sleep
With staring eye that seeth none,
Ridiculously up and down
Seeks how he may fitly tell
The heart-o'erlading miracle.

Not yet, not yet,
Impatient friend,—
A little while attend;
Not yet I sing: but I must wait,
My hand upon the silent string,
Fully until the end.
I see the coming light,
I see the scattered gleams,
Aloft, beneath, on left and right
The stars' own ether beams;
These are but seeds of days,
Not yet a steadfast morn,
An intermittent blaze,
An embryo god unborn.
How all things sparkle,
The dust is alive,
To the birth they arrive:
I snuff the breath of my morning afar,
I see the pale lustres condense to a star:
The fading colors fix,
The vanishing are seen,
And the world that shall be
Twins the world that has been.
I know the appointed hour,
I greet my office well,
Never faster, never slower
Revolves the fatal wheel!
The Fairest enchants me,
The Mighty commands me,
Saying, "Stand in thy place;
Up and eastward turn thy face;
As mountains for the morning wait,
Coming early, coming late,
So thou attend the enriching Fate
Which none can stay, and none accelerate."
I am neither faint nor weary,

Fill thy will, O faultless heart!
Here from youth to age I tarry,—
Count it flight of bird or dart.
My heart at the heart of things
Heeds no longer lapse of time,
Rushing ages moult their wings,
Bathing in thy day sublime.

The sun set, but set not his hope:—
Stars rose, his faith was earlier up:
Fixed on the enormous galaxy,
Deeper and older seemed his eye,
And matched his sufferance sublime
The taciturnity of Time.

Beside his hut and shading oak,
Thus to himself the poet spoke,
"I have supped tonight with gods,
I will not go under a wooden roof:
As I walked among the hills
In the love which Nature fills,
The great stars did not shine aloof,
They hurried down from their deep abodes
And hemmed me in their glittering troop.

"Divine Inviters! I accept
The courtesy ye have shown and kept
From ancient ages for the bard,
To modulate
With finer fate
A fortune harsh and hard.
With aim like yours
I watch your course,
Who never break your lawful dance
By error or intemperance.
O birds of ether without wings!
O heavenly ships without a sail!
O fire of fire! O best of things!
O mariners who never fail!
Sail swiftly through your amber vault,
An animated law, a presence to exalt."

Ah, happy if a sun or star
Could chain the wheel of Fortune's car,
And give to hold an even state,
Neither dejected nor elate,
That haply man upraised might keep
The height of Fancy's far-eyed steep.
In vain: the stars are glowing wheels,
Giddy with motion Nature reels,
Sun, moon, man, undulate and stream,
The mountains flow, the solids seem,
Change acts, reacts; back, forward hurled,
And pause were palsy to the world.—
The morn is come: the starry crowds
Are hid behind the thrice-piled clouds;
The new day lowers, and equal odds
Have changed not less the guest of gods;
Discrowned and timid, thoughtless, worn,
The child of genius sits forlorn:
Between two sleeps a short day's stealth,
'Mid many ails a brittle health,
A cripple of God, half true, half formed,
And by great sparks Promethean warmed,
Constrained by impotence to adjourn
To infinite time his eager turn,
His lot of action at the urn.
He by false usage pinned about
No breath therein, no passage out,
Cast wishful glances at the stars
And wishful saw the Ocean stream:—
"Merge me in the brute universe,
Or lift to a diviner dream!"

Beside him sat enduring love,
Upon him noble eyes did rest,
Which, for the Genius that there strove,
The follies bore that it invest.
They spoke not, for their earnest sense
Outran the craft of eloquence.

He whom God had thus preferred,—
To whom sweet angels ministered,
Saluted him each morn as brother,
And bragged his virtues to each other,—
Alas! how were they so beguiled,
And they so pure? He, foolish child,
A facile, reckless, wandering will,
Eager for good, not hating ill,
Thanked Nature for each stroke she dealt;
On his tense chords all strokes were felt, 211
The good, the bad with equal zeal,
He asked, he only asked, to feel.
Timid, self-pleasing, sensitive,
With Gods, with fools, content to live;
Bended to fops who bent to him;
Surface with surfaces did swim.

"Sorrow, sorrow!" the angels cried,
"Is this dear Nature's manly pride?
Call hither thy mortal enemy,
Make him glad thy fall to see!
Yon waterflag, yon sighing osier,
A drop can shake, a breath can fan;

Maidens laugh and weep; Composure
Is the pudency of man."

Again by night the poet went
From the lighted halls
Beneath the darkling firmament
To the seashore, to the old seawalls,
Out shone a star beneath the cloud,
The constellation glittered soon,—
"You have no lapse; so have ye glowed
But once in your dominion.
And yet, dear stars, I know ye shine
Only by needs and loves of mine;
Light-loving, light-asking life in me
Feeds those eternal lamps I see.
And I to whom your light has spoken,
I, pining to be one of you,
I fall, my faith is broken,
Ye scorn me from your deeps of blue.
Or if perchance, ye orbs of Fate,
Your ne'er averted glance
Beams with a will compassionate
On sons of time and chance,
Then clothe these hands with power
In just proportion,
Nor plant immense designs
Where equal means are none."

CHORUS OF SPIRITS

Means, dear brother, ask them not;
  Soul's desire is means enow,
Pure content is angel's lot,
  Thine own theatre art thou.

Gentler far than falls the snow
In the woodwalks still and low
Fell the lesson on his heart
And woke the fear lest angels part.

POET

I see your forms with deep content,
I know that ye are excellent,
  But will ye stay?
I hear the rustle of wings,
Ye meditate what to say
Ere ye go to quit me for ever and aye.

SPIRITS

Brother, we are no phantom band;
Brother, accept this fatal hand.
Aches thine unbelieving heart
With the fear that we must part?
See, all we are rooted here
By one thought to one same sphere;
From thyself thou canst not flee,—
From thyself no more can we.

POET

Suns and stars their courses keep,
But not angels of the deep:
Day and night their turn observe,
But the day of day may swerve.
Is there warrant that the waves
Of thought in their mysterious caves
Will heap in me their highest tide,
In me therewith beatified?
Unsure the ebb and flood of thought,
The moon comes back,—the Spirit not.

SPIRITS

Brother, sweeter is the Law
Than all the grace Love ever saw;
We are its suppliants. By it, we
Draw the breath of Eternity;
Serve thou it not for daily bread,—
Serve it for pain and fear and need.
Love it, though it hide its light;
By love behold the sun at night.
If the Law should thee forget,
More enamored serve it yet;
Though it hate thee, suffer long;
Put the Spirit in the wrong;
Brother, no decrepitude
  Chills the limbs of Time;
As fleet his feet, his hands as good,
  His vision as sublime:
On Nature's wheels there is no rust;
Nor less on man's enchanted dust
  Beauty and Force alight.

1838–44?

URIEL

It fell in the ancient periods
  Which the brooding soul surveys,
Or ever the wild Time coined itself
  Into calendar months and days.

This was the lapse of Uriel,
Which in Paradise befell.
Once, among the Pleiads walking,
Seyd overheard the young gods talking;

And the treason, too long pent,
To his ears was evident.
The young deities discussed
Laws of form, and metre just,
Orb, quintessence, and sunbeams,
What subsisteth, and what seems.
One, with low tones that decide,
And doubt and reverend use defied,
With a look that solved the sphere,
And stirred the devils everywhere,
Gave his sentiment divine
Against the being of a line.
"Line in nature is not found;
Unit and universe are round;
In vain produced, all rays return;
Evil will bless, and ice will burn."

As Uriel spoke with piercing eye,
A shudder ran around the sky;
The stern old war-gods shook their heads,
The seraphs frowned from myrtle-beds;
Seemed to the holy festival
The rash word boded ill to all;
The balance-beam of Fate was bent;
The bounds of good and ill were rent;
Strong Hades could not keep his own,
But all slid to confusion.

A sad self-knowledge, withering, fell
On the beauty of Uriel;
In heaven once eminent, the god
Withdrew, that hour, into his cloud;
Whether doomed to long gyration
In the sea of generation,
Or by knowledge grown too bright
To hit the nerve of feebler sight.
Straightway, a forgetting wind
Stole over the celestial kind,
And their lips the secret kept,
If in ashes the fire-seed slept.
But now and then, truth-speaking things
Shamed the angels' veiling wings;
And, shrilling from the solar course,
Or from fruit of chemic force,
Procession of a soul in matter,
Or the speeding change of water,
Or out of the good of evil born,
Came Uriel's voice of cherub scorn,
And a blush tinged the upper sky,
And the gods shook, they knew not why.

1838 1846

THE PROBLEM

I LIKE a church; I like a cowl;
I love a prophet of the soul;
And on my heart monastic aisles
Fall like sweet strains, or pensive smiles;
Yet not for all his faith can see
Would I that cowlèd churchman be.

Why should the vest on him allure,
Which I could not on me endure?

Not from a vain or shallow thought
His awful Jove young Phidias brought;
Never from lips of cunning fell
The thrilling Delphic oracle;
Out from the heart of nature rolled
The burdens of the Bible old;
The litanies of nations came,
Like the volcano's tongue of flame,
Up from the burning core below,—
The canticles of love and woe:
The hand that rounded Peter's dome
And groined the aisles of Christian Rome
Wrought in a sad sincerity;
Himself from God he could not free;
He builded better than he knew;—
The conscious stone to beauty grew.

Know'st thou what wove yon woodbird's nest
Of leaves, and feathers from her breast?
Or how the fish outbuilt her shell,
Painting with morn each annual cell?
Or how the sacred pine-tree adds
To her old leaves new myriads?
Such and so grew these holy piles,
Whilst love and terror laid the tiles.
Earth proudly wears the Parthenon,
As the best gem upon her zone,
And Morning opes with haste her lids
To gaze upon the Pyramids;
O'er England's abbeys bends the sky,
As on its friends, with kindred eye;
For out of Thought's interior sphere
These wonders rose to upper air;
And Nature gladly gave them place,
Adopted them into her race,
And granted them an equal date
With Andes and with Ararat.

These temples grew as grows the grass;
Art might obey, but not surpass.

The passive Master lent his hand
To the vast soul that o'er him planned;
And the same power that reared the shrine
Bestrode the tribes that knelt within.
Ever the fiery Pentecost
Girds with one flame the countless host,
Trances the heart through chanting choirs,
And through the priest the mind inspires.
The word unto the prophet spoken
Was writ on tables yet unbroken;
The word by seers or sibyls told,
In groves of oak, or fanes of gold,
Still floats upon the morning wind,
Still whispers to the willing mind.
One accent of the Holy Ghost
The heedless world hath never lost.
I know what say the fathers wise,—
The Book itself before me lies,
Old *Chrysostom*, best Augustine,
And he who blent both in his line,
The younger *Golden Lips* or mines,
Taylor, the Shakspeare of divines.
His words are music in my ear,
I see his cowlèd portrait dear;
And yet, for all his faith could see,
I would not the good bishop be.

1839 1840

COMPENSATION

The wings of Time are black and white,
Pied with morning and with night.
Mountain tall and ocean deep
Trembling balance duly keep.
In changing moon and tidal wave
Glows the feud of Want and Have.
Gauge of more and less through space,
Electric star or pencil plays,
The lonely Earth amid the balls
That hurry through the eternal halls,
A makeweight flying to the void,
Supplemental asteroid,
Or compensatory spark,
Shoots across the neutral Dark.

Man's the elm, and Wealth the vine;
Stanch and strong the tendrils twine:
Though the frail ringlets thee deceive,
None from its stock that vine can reave.
Fear not, then, thou child infirm,
There's no god dare wrong a worm;
Laurel crowns cleave to deserts,
And power to him who power exerts.
Hast not thy share? On wingèd feet,
Lo! it rushes thee to meet;
And all that Nature made thy own,
Floating in air or pent in stone,
Will rive the hills and swim the sea,
And, like thy shadow, follow thee.

1841

ART

Give to barrows, trays, and pans
Grace and glimmer of romance;
Bring the moonlight into noon
Hid in gleaming piles of stone;
On the city's paved street
Plant gardens lined with lilacs sweet;
Let spouting fountains cool the air,
Singing in the sun-baked square;
Let statue, picture, park, and hall,
Ballad, flag, and festival,
The past restore, the day adorn,
And make tomorrow a new morn.
So shall the drudge in dusty frock
Spy behind the city clock
Retinues of airy kings,
Skirts of angels, starry wings,
His fathers shining in bright fables,
His children fed at heavenly tables.
'Tis the privilege of Art
Thus to play its cheerful part,
Man on earth to acclimate
And bend the exile to his fate,
And, moulded of one element
With the days and firmament,
Teach him on these as stairs to climb,
And live on even terms with Time;
Whilst upper life the slender rill
Of human sense doth overfill.

1841

UNITY

Space is ample, east and west,
But two cannot go abreast,
Cannot travel in it two:
Yonder masterful cuckoo
Crowds every egg out of the nest,
Quick or dead, except its own;
A spell is laid on sod and stone,

Night and Day were tampered with,
Every quality and pith
Surcharged and sultry with a power
That works its will on age and hour.

1841

PRUDENCE

THEME no poet gladly sung,
Fair to old and foul to young;
Scorn not thou the love of parts,
And the articles of arts.
Grandeur of the perfect sphere
Thanks the atoms that cohere.

1841

HEROISM

RUBY wine is drunk by knaves,
Sugar spends to fatten slaves,
Rose and vine-leaf deck buffoons;
Thunder-clouds are Jove's festoons,
Drooping oft in wreaths of dread,
Lightning-knotted round his head;
The hero is not fed on sweets,
Daily his own heart he eats;
Chambers of the great are jails,
And head-winds right for royal sails.

1841

SPIRITUAL LAWS

THE living Heaven thy prayers respect,
House at once and architect,
Quarrying man's rejected hours,
Builds therewith eternal towers;
Sole and self-commanded works,
Fears not undermining days,
Grows by decays,
And, by the famous might that lurks
In reaction and recoil,
Makes flame to freeze and ice to boil;
Forging, through swart arms of Offence,
The silver seat of Innocence.

1841

WOODNOTES

I

1

WHEN the pine tosses its cones
To the song of its waterfall tones,
Who speeds to the woodland walks?
To birds and trees who talks?
Cæsar of his leafy Rome,
There the poet is at home.
He goes to the river-side,—
Not hook nor line hath he;
He stands in the meadows wide,—
Nor gun nor scythe to see.
Sure some god his eye enchants:
What he knows nobody wants.
In the wood he travels glad,
Without better fortune had,
Melancholy without bad.
Knowledge this man prizes best
Seems fantastic to the rest:
Pondering shadows, colors, clouds,
Grass-buds and caterpillar-shrouds,
Boughs on which the wild bees settle,
Tints that spot the violet's petal,
Why Nature loves the number five,
And why the star-form she repeats:
Lover of all things alive,
Wonderer at all he meets,
Wonderer chiefly at himself,
Who can tell him what he is?
Or how meet in human elf
Coming and past eternities?

2

And such I knew, a forest seer,
A minstrel of the natural year,
Foreteller of the vernal ides,
Wise harbinger of spheres and tides,
A lover true, who knew by heart
Each joy the mountain dales impart;
It seemed that Nature could not raise
A plant in any secret place,
In quaking bog, on snowy hill,
Beneath the grass that shades the rill,
Under the snow, between the rocks,
In damp fields known to bird and fox,
But he would come in the very hour
It opened in its virgin bower,
As if a sunbeam showed the place,
And tell its long-descended race.
It seemed as if the breezes brought him,
It seemed as if the sparrows taught him;
As if by secret sight he knew
Where, in far fields, the orchis grew.
Many haps fall in the field
Seldom seen by wishful eyes,
But all her shows did Nature yield,
To please and win this pilgrim wise.

He saw the partridge drum in the woods;
He heard the woodcock's evening hymn;
He found the tawny thrushes' broods;
And the shy hawk did wait for him;
What others did at distance hear,
And guessed within the thicket's gloom,
Was shown to this philosopher,
And at his bidding seemed to come.

3

In unploughed Maine he sought the lumberers' gang
Where from a hundred lakes young rivers sprang;
He trod the unplanted forest floor, whereon
The all-seeing sun for ages hath not shone;
Where feeds the moose, and walks the surly bear,
And up the tall mast runs the woodpecker.
He saw beneath dim aisles, in odorous beds,
The slight Linnæa hang its twin-born heads,
And blessed the monument of the man of flowers,
Which breathes his sweet fame through the northern bowers.
He heard, when in the grove, at intervals,
With sudden roar the aged pine-tree falls,—
One crash, the death-hymn of the perfect tree,
Declares the close of its green century.
Low lies the plant to whose creation went
Sweet influence from every element;
Whose living towers the years conspired to build,
Whose giddy top the morning loved to gild.
Through these green tents, by eldest Nature dressed,
He roamed, content alike with man and beast.
Where darkness found him he lay glad at night;
There the red morning touched him with its light.
Three moons his great heart him a hermit made,
So long he roved at will the boundless shade.
The timid it concerns to ask their way,
And fear what foe in caves and swamps can stray,
To make no step until the event is known,
And ills to come as evils past bemoan.
Not so the wise; no coward watch he keeps
To spy what danger on his pathway creeps;
Go where he will, the wise man is at home,
His hearth the earth,—his hall the azure dome;
Where his clear spirit leads him, there's his road
By God's own light illumined and foreshowed.

4

'Twas one of the charmèd days
When the genius of God doth flow;
The wind may alter twenty ways,
A tempest cannot blow;
It may blow north, it still is warm;
Or south, it still is clear;
Or east, it smells like a clover-farm;
Or west, no thunder fear.
The musing peasant, lowly great,
Beside the forest water sate;
The rope-like pine-roots crosswise grown
Composed the network of his throne;
The wide lake, edged with sand and grass,
Was burnished to a floor of glass,
Painted with shadows green and proud
Of the tree and of the cloud.
He was the heart of all the scene;
On him the sun looked more serene;
To hill and cloud his face was known,—
It seemed the likeness of their own;
They knew by secret sympathy
The public child of earth and sky.
"You ask," he said, "what guide
Me through trackless thickets led,
Through thick-stemmed woodlands rough and wide.
I found the water's bed.
The watercourses were my guide;
I travelled grateful by their side,
Or through their channel dry;
They led me through the thicket damp,
Through brake and fern, the beavers' camp,
Through beds of granite cut my road,
And their resistless friendship showed:
The falling waters led me,
The foodful waters fed me,
And brought me to the lowest land,
Unerring to the ocean sand.
The moss upon the forest bark
Was pole-star when the night was dark;
The purple berries in the wood
Supplied me necessary food;
For Nature ever faithful is
To such as trust her faithfulness.
When the forest shall mislead me,

When the night and morning lie,
When sea and land refuse to feed me,
'Twill be time enough to die;
Then will yet my mother yield
A pillow in her greenest field,
Nor the June flowers scorn to cover
The clay of their departed lover."

1840

II

As sunbeams stream through liberal space
And nothing jostle or displace,
So waved the pine-tree through my thought
And fanned the dreams it never brought.

"Whether is better, the gift or the donor?
Come to me,"
Quoth the pine-tree,
"I am the giver of honor.
My garden is the cloven rock,
And my manure the snow;
And drifting sand-heaps feed my stock,
In summer's scorching glow.
He is great who can live by me:
The rough and bearded forester
Is better than the lord;
God fills the scrip and canister,
Sin piles the loaded board.
The lord is the peasant that was,
The peasant the lord that shall be;
The lord is hay, the peasant grass,
One dry, and one the living tree.
Who liveth by the ragged pine
Foundeth a heroic line;
Who liveth in the palace hall
Waneth fast and spendeth all.
He goes to my savage haunts,
With his chariot and his care;
My twilight realm he disenchants,
And finds his prison there.

"What prizes the town and the tower?
Only what the pine-tree yields;
Sinew that subdued the fields;
The wild-eyed boy, who in the woods
Chants his hymn to hills and floods,
Whom the city's poisoning spleen
Made not pale, or fat, or lean;
Whom the rain and the wind purgeth,
Whom the dawn and the day-star urgeth,
In whose cheek the rose-leaf blusheth,
In whose feet the lion rusheth,
Iron arms, and iron mould,
That know not fear, fatigue, or cold.
I give my rafters to his boat,
My billets to his boiler's throat,
And I will swim the ancient sea
To float my child to victory,
And grant to dwellers with the pine
Dominion o'er the palm and vine.
Who leaves the pine-tree, leaves his friend,
Unnerves his strength, invites his end.
Cut a bough from my parent stem,
And dip it in thy porcelain vase;
A little while each russet gem
Will swell and rise with wonted grace;
But when it seeks enlarged supplies,
The orphan of the forest dies.
Whoso walks in solitude
And inhabiteth the wood,
Choosing light, wave, rock, and bird,
Before the money-loving herd,
Into that forester shall pass,
From these companions, power and grace.
Clean shall he be, without, within,
From the old adhering sin,
All ill dissolving in the light
Of his triumphant piercing sight:
Not vain, sour, nor frivolous;
Not mad, athirst, nor garrulous;
Grave, chaste, contented, though retired,
And of all other men desired.
On him the light of star and moon
Shall fall with purer radiance down;
All constellations of the sky
Shed their virtue through his eye.
Him Nature giveth for defence
His formidable innocence;
The mounting sap, the shells, the sea,
All spheres, all stones, his helpers be;
He shall meet the speeding year,
Without wailing, without fear;
He shall be happy in his love,
Like to like shall joyful prove;
He shall be happy whilst he woos,
Muse-born, a daughter of the Muse.
But if with gold she bind her hair,
And deck her breast with diamond,
Take off thine eyes, thy heart forbear,
Though thou lie alone on the ground.

"Heed the old oracles,
Ponder my spells;

Song wakes in my pinnacles
When the wind swells.
Soundeth the prophetic wind,
The shadows shake on the rock behind,
And the countless leaves of the pine are strings
Tuned to the lay the wood-god sings.
Hearken! Hearken!
If thou wouldst know the mystic song
Chanted when the sphere was young.
Aloft, abroad, the pæan swells;
O wise man! hear'st thou half it tells?
O wise man! hear'st thou the least part?
'Tis the chronicle of art.
To the open ear it sings
Sweet the genesis of things,
Of tendency through endless ages,
Of star-dust, and star-pilgrimages,
Of rounded worlds, of space and time,
Of the old flood's subsiding slime,
Of chemic matter, force and form,
Of poles and powers, cold, wet, and warm:
The rushing metamorphosis
Dissolving all that fixture is,
Melts things that be to things that seem,
And solid nature to a dream.
O, listen to the undersong,
The ever old, the ever young;
And, far within those cadent pauses,
The chorus of the ancient Causes!
Delights the dreadful Destiny
To fling his voice into the tree,
And shock thy weak ear with a note
Breathed from the everlasting throat.
In music he repeats the pang
Whence the fair flock of Nature sprang.
O mortal! thy ears are stones;
These echoes are laden with tones
Which only the pure can hear;
Thou canst not catch what they recite
Of Fate and Will, of Want and Right,
Of man to come, of human life,
Of Death and Fortune, Growth and Strife."

Once again the pine-tree sung:—
"Speak not thy speech my boughs among:
Put off thy years, wash in the breeze;
My hours are peaceful centuries.
Talk no more with feeble tongue;
No more the fool of space and time,
Come weave with mine a nobler rhyme.
Only thy Americans
Can read thy line, can meet thy glance,
But the runes that I rehearse
Understands the universe;
The least breath my boughs which tossed
Brings again the Pentecost;
To every soul resounding clear
In a voice of solemn cheer,—
'Am I not thine? Are not these thine?'
And they reply, 'Forever mine!'
My branches speak Italian,
English, German, Basque, Castilian,
Mountain speech to Highlanders,
Ocean tongues to islanders,
To Fin and Lap and swart Malay,
To each his bosom-secret say.

"Come learn with me the fatal song
Which knits the world in music strong,
Come lift thine eyes to lofty rhymes,
Of things with things, of times with times,
Primal chimes of sun and shade,
Of sound and echo, man and maid,
The land reflected in the flood,
Body with shadow still pursued.
For Nature beats in perfect tune,
And rounds with rhyme her every rune,
Whether she work in land or sea,
Or hide underground her alchemy.
Thou canst not wave thy staff in air,
Or dip thy paddle in the lake,
But it carves the bow of beauty there,
And the ripples in rhymes the oar forsake.
The wood is wiser far than thou;
The wood and wave each other know
Not unrelated, unaffied,
But to each thought and thing allied,
Is perfect Nature's every part,
Rooted in the mighty Heart.
But thou, poor child! unbound, unrhymed,
Whence camest thou, misplaced, mistimed,
Whence, O thou orphan and defrauded?
Is thy land peeled, thy realm marauded?
Who thee divorced, deceived and left?
Thee of thy faith who hath bereft,
And torn the ensigns from thy brow,
And sunk the immortal eye so low?
Thy cheek too white, thy form too slender,
Thy gait too slow, thy habits tender
For royal man;—they thee confess
An exile from the wilderness,—

The hills where health with health agrees,
And the wise soul expels disease.
Hark! in thy ear I will tell the sign
By which thy hurt thou may'st divine.
When thou shalt climb the mountain cliff,
Or see the wide shore from thy skiff,
To thee the horizon shall express
But emptiness on emptiness;
There lives no man of Nature's worth
In the circle of the earth;
And to thine eye the vast skies fall,
Dire and satirical,
On clucking hens and prating fools,
On thieves, on drudges, and on dolls.
And thou shalt say to the Most High,
'Godhead! all this astronomy,
And fate and practice and invention,
Strong art and beautiful pretension,
This radiant pomp of sun and star,
Throes that were, and worlds that are,
Behold! were in vain and in vain;—
It cannot be,—I will look again.
Surely now will the curtain rise,
And earth's fit tenant me surprise;—
But the curtain doth *not* rise,
And Nature has miscarried wholly
Into failure, into folly.'

"Alas! thine is the bankruptcy,
Blessed Nature so to see.
Come, lay thee in my soothing shade,
And heal the hurts which sin has made.
I see thee in the crowd alone;
I will be thy companion.
Quit thy friends as the dead in doom,
And build to them a final tomb;
Let the starred shade that nightly falls
Still celebrate their funerals,
And the bell of beetle and of bee
Knell their melodious memory.
Behind thee leave thy merchandise,
Thy churches and thy charities;
And leave thy peacock wit behind;
Enough for thee the primal mind
That flows in streams, that breathes in wind:
Leave all thy pedant lore apart;
God hid the whole world in thy heart.
Love shuns the sage, the child it crowns,
Gives all to them who all renounce.
The rain comes when the wind calls;
The river knows the way to the sea;
Without a pilot it runs and falls,
Blessing all lands with its charity;
The sea tosses and foams to find
Its way up to the cloud and wind;
The shadow sits close to the flying ball;
The date fails not on the palm-tree tall;
And thou,—go burn thy wormy pages,—
Shalt outsee seers, and outwit sages.
Oft didst thou thread the woods in vain
To find what bird had piped the strain:—
Seek not, and the little eremite
Flies gayly forth and sings in sight.

"Hearken once more!
I will tell thee the mundane lore.
Older am I than thy numbers wot,
Change I may, but I pass not.
Hitherto all things fast abide,
And anchored in the tempest ride.
Trenchant time behoves to hurry
All to yean and all to bury:
All the forms are fugitive,
But the substances survive.
Ever fresh the broad creation,
A divine improvisation,
From the heart of God proceeds,
A single will, a million deeds.
Once slept the world an egg of stone,
And pulse, and sound, and light was none;
And God said, 'Throb!' and there was motion
And the vast mass became vast ocean.
Onward and on, the eternal Pan,
Who layeth the world's incessant plan,
Halteth never in one shape,
But forever doth escape,
Like wave or flame, into new forms
Of gem, and air, of plants, and worms.
I, that today am a pine,
Yesterday was a bundle of grass.
He is free and libertine,
Pouring of his power the wine
To every age, to every race;
Unto every race and age
He emptieth the beverage;
Unto each, and unto all,
Maker and original.
The world is the ring of his spells,
And the play of his miracles.
As he giveth to all to drink,
Thus or thus they are and think.
With one drop sheds form and feature;

With the next a special nature;
The third adds heat's indulgent spark;
The fourth gives light which eats the dark;
Into the fifth himself he flings,
And conscious Law is King of kings.
As the bee through the garden ranges,
From world to world the godhead changes;
As the sheep go feeding in the waste,
From form to form He maketh haste;
This vault which glows immense with light
Is the inn where he lodges for a night.
What recks such Traveller if the bowers
Which bloom and fade like meadow flowers
A bunch of fragrant lilies be,
Or the stars of eternity?
Alike to him the better, the worse,—
The glowing angel, the outcast corse.
Thou metest him by centuries,
And lo! he passes like the breeze;
Thou seek'st in globe and galaxy,
He hides in pure transparency;
Thou askest in fountains and in fires,
He is the essence that inquires.
He is the axis of the star;
He is the sparkle of the spar;
He is the heart of every creature;
He is the meaning of each feature;
And his mind is the sky,
Than all it holds more deep, more high."

1841

THE SNOW-STORM

Announced by all the trumpets of the sky,
Arrives the snow, and, driving o'er the fields,
Seems nowhere to alight: the whited air
Hides hills and woods, the river, and the heaven,
And veils the farm-house at the garden's end.
The sled and traveller stopped, the courier's feet
Delayed, all friends shut out, the housemates sit
Around the radiant fireplace, enclosed
In a tumultuous privacy of storm.

Come see the north wind's masonry.
Out of an unseen quarry evermore
Furnished with tile, the fierce artificer
Curves his white bastions with projected roof
Round every windward stake, or tree, or door.
Speeding, the myriad-handed, his wild work
So fanciful, so savage, nought cares he
For number or proportion. Mockingly,
On coop or kennel he hangs Parian wreaths;
A swan-like form invests the hidden thorn;
Fills up the farmer's lane from wall to wall,
Maugre the farmer's sighs; and at the gate
A tapering turret overtops the work.
And when his hours are numbered, and the world
Is all his own, retiring, as he were not,
Leaves, when the sun appears, astonished Art
To mimic in slow structures, stone by stone,
Built in an age, the mad wind's night-work,
The frolic architecture of the snow.

1841

FRIENDSHIP

A ruddy drop of manly blood
The surging sea outweighs,
The world uncertain comes and goes;
The lover rooted stays.
I fancied he was fled,—
And, after many a year,
Glowed unexhausted kindliness,
Like daily sunrise there.
My careful heart was free again,
O friend, my bosom said,
Through thee alone the sky is arched,
Through thee the rose is red;
All things through thee take nobler form,
And look beyond the earth,
The mill-round of our fate appears
A sun-path in thy worth.
Me too thy nobleness has taught
To master my despair;
The fountains of my hidden life
Are through thy friendship fair.

1841

THE SPHINX

The Sphinx is drowsy,
Her wings are furled:
Her ear is heavy,
She broods on the world.
"Who'll tell me my secret,
The ages have kept?—
I awaited the seer
While they slumbered and slept:—

"The fate of the man-child,
The meaning of man;
Known fruit of the unknown;
Dædalian plan;
Out of sleeping a waking,
Out of waking a sleep;
Life death overtaking;
Deep underneath deep?

"Erect as a sunbeam,
Upspringeth the palm;
The elephant browses,
Undaunted and calm;
In beautiful motion
The thrush plies his wings;
Kind leaves of his covert,
Your silence he sings.

"The waves, unashamèd,
In difference sweet,
Play glad with the breezes,
Old playfellows meet;
The journeying atoms,
Primordial wholes,
Firmly draw, firmly drive,
By their animate poles.

"Sea, earth, air, sound, silence,
Plant, quadruped, bird,
By one music enchanted,
One deity stirred,—
Each the other adorning,
Accompany still;
Night veileth the morning,
The vapor the hill.

"The babe by its mother
Lies bathèd in joy;
Glide its hours uncounted,—
The sun is its toy;
Shines the peace of all being,
Without cloud, in its eyes;
And the sum of the world
In soft miniature lies.

"But man crouches and blushes,
Absconds and conceals;
He creepeth and peepeth,
He palters and steals;
Infirm, melancholy,
Jealous glancing around,
An oaf, an accomplice,
He poisons the ground.

"Out spoke the great mother,
Beholding his fear;—
At the sound of her accents
Cold shuddered the sphere:—
'Who has drugged my boy's cup?
Who has mixed my boy's bread?
Who, with sadness and madness,
Has turned my child's head?'"

I heard a poet answer
Aloud and cheerfully,
"Say on, sweet Sphinx! thy dirges
Are pleasant songs to me.
Deep love lieth under
These pictures of time;
They fade in the light of
Their meaning sublime.

"The fiend that man harries
Is love of the Best;
Yawns the pit of the Dragon,
Lit by rays from the Blest.
The Lethe of Nature
Can't trance him again,
Whose soul sees the perfect,
Which his eyes seek in vain.

"To vision profounder,
Man's spirit must dive;
His aye-rolling orb
At no goal will arrive;
The heavens that now draw him
With sweetness untold,
Once found,—for new heavens
He spurneth the old.

"Pride ruined the angels,
Their shame them restores;
Lurks the joy that is sweetest
In stings of remorse.
Have I a lover
Who is noble and free?—
I would he were nobler
Than to love me.

"Eterne alternation
Now follows, now flies;
And under pain, pleasure,—
Under pleasure, pain lies.
Love works at the centre,
Heart-heaving alway;
Forth speed the strong pulses
To the borders of day.

"Dull Sphinx, Jove keep thy five wits;
Thy sight is growing blear;
Rue, myrrh and cummin for the Sphinx,
Her muddy eyes to clear!"
The old Sphinx bit her thick lip,—
Said, "Who taught thee me to name?
I am thy spirit, yoke-fellow;
Of thine eye I am eyebeam.

"Thou art the unanswered question;
Couldst see thy proper eye,
Alway it asketh, asketh;
And each answer is a lie.
So take thy quest through nature,
It through thousand natures ply:
Ask on, thou clothed eternity;
Time is the false reply."

Uprose the merry Sphinx,
And crouched no more in stone;
She melted into purple cloud,
She silvered in the moon;
She spired into a yellow flame;
She flowered in blossoms red;
She flowed into a foaming wave;
She stood Monadnoc's head.

Thorough a thousand voices
Spoke the universal dame;
"Who telleth one of my meanings,
Is master of all I am."

1841

GRACE

How much, preventing God! how much I owe
To the defences thou hast round me set:
Example, custom, fear, occasion slow,—
These scornèd bondmen were my parapet.
I dare not peep over this parapet
To gauge with glance the roaring gulf below,
The depths of sin to which I had descended,
Had not these me against myself defended.

1842

THRENODY

The South-wind brings
Life, sunshine and desire,
And on every mount and meadow
Breathes aromatic fire;
But over the dead he has no power,
The lost, the lost, he cannot restore;
And, looking over the hills, I mourn
The darling who shall not return.

I see my empty house,
I see my trees repair their boughs;
And he, the wondrous child,
Whose silver warble wild
Outvalued every pulsing sound
Within the air's cerulean round,—
The hyacinthine boy, for whom
Morn well might break and April bloom,
The gracious boy, who did adorn
The world whereinto he was born,
And by his countenance repay
The favor of the loving Day,—
Has disappeared from the Day's eye;
Far and wide she cannot find him;
My hopes pursue, they cannot bind him.
Returned this day, the South-wind searches,
And finds young pines and budding birches;
But finds not the budding man;
Nature, who lost, cannot remake him;
Fate let him fall, Fate can't retake him;
Nature, Fate, men, him seek in vain.

And whither now, my truant wise and sweet,
O, whither tend thy feet?
I had the right, few days ago,
Thy steps to watch, thy place to know:
How have I forfeited the right?
Hast thou forgot me in a new delight?
I hearken for thy household cheer,
O eloquent child!
Whose voice, an equal messenger,
Conveyed thy meaning mild.
What though the pains and joys
Whereof it spoke were toys
Fitting his age and ken,
Yet fairest dames and bearded men,
Who heard the sweet request,
So gentle, wise, and grave,
Bended with joy to his behest
And let the world's affairs go by,
A while to share his cordial game,
Or mend his wicker wagon-frame,
Still plotting how their hungry ear
That winsome voice again might hear;
For his lips could well pronounce
Words that were persuasions.

Gentlest guardians marked serene
His early hope, his liberal mien;

Took counsel from his guiding eyes
To make this wisdom earthly wise.
Ah, vainly do these eyes recall
The school-march, each day's festival,
When every morn my bosom glowed
To watch the convoy on the road;
The babe in willow wagon closed,
With rolling eyes and face composed;
With children forward and behind,
Like Cupids studiously inclined;
And he the chieftain paced beside,
The centre of the troop allied,
With sunny face of sweet repose,
To guard the babe from fancied foes.
The little captain innocent
Took the eye with him as he went;
Each village senior paused to scan
And speak the lovely caravan.
From the window I look out
To mark thy beautiful parade,
Stately marching in cap and coat
To some tune by fairies played;—
A music heard by thee alone
To works as noble led thee on.

Now Love and Pride, alas! in vain,
Up and down their glances strain.
The painted sled stands where it stood;
The kennel by the corded wood;
His gathered sticks to stanch the wall
Of the snow-tower, when snow should fall;
The ominous hole he dug in the sand,
And childhood's castles built or planned;
His daily haunts I well discern,—
The poultry-yard, the shed, the barn,—
And every inch of garden ground
Paced by the blessed feet around,
From the roadside to the brook
Whereinto he loved to look.
Step the meek fowls where erst they ranged;
The wintry garden lies unchanged;
The brook into the stream runs on;
But the deep-eyed boy is gone.

On that shaded day,
Dark with more clouds than tempests are,
When thou didst yield thy innocent breath
In birdlike heavings unto death,
Night came, and Nature had not thee;
I said, "We are mates in misery."
The morrow dawned with needless glow;
Each snowbird chirped, each fowl must crow;
Each tramper started; but the feet
Of the most beautiful and sweet
Of human youth had left the hill
And garden,—they were bound and still.
There's not a sparrow or a wren,
There's not a blade of autumn grain,
Which the four seasons do not tend
And tides of life and increase lend;
And every chick of every bird,
And weed and rock-moss is preferred.
O ostrich-like forgetfulness!
O loss of larger in the less!
Was there no star that could be sent,
No watcher in the firmament,
No angel from the countless host
That loiters round the crystal coast,
Could stoop to heal that only child,
Nature's sweet marvel undefiled,
And keep the blossom of the earth,
Which all her harvests were not worth?
Not mine,—I never called thee mine,
But Nature's heir,—if I repine,
And seeing rashly torn and moved
Not what I made, but what I loved,
Grow early old with grief that thou
Must to the wastes of Nature go,—
'Tis because a general hope
Was quenched, and all must doubt and grope.
For flattering planets seemed to say
This child should ills of ages stay,
By wondrous tongue, and guided pen,
Bring the flown Muses back to men.
Perchance not he but Nature ailed,
The world and not the infant failed.
It was not ripe yet to sustain
A genius of so fine a strain,
Who gazed upon the sun and moon
As if he came unto his own,
And, pregnant with his grander thought,
Brought the old order into doubt.
His beauty once their beauty tried;
They could not feed him, and he died,
And wandered backward as in scorn,
To wait an æon to be born.
Ill day which made this beauty waste,
Plight broken, this high face defaced!
Some went and came about the dead;
And some in books of solace read;
Some to their friends the tidings say;
Some went to write, some went to pray;

One tarried here, there hurried one;
But their heart abode with none.
Covetous death bereaved us all,
To aggrandize one funeral.
The eager fate which carried thee
Took the largest part of me:
For this losing is true dying;
This is lordly man's down-lying,
This his slow but sure reclining,
Star by star his world resigning.

O child of paradise,
Boy who made dear his father's home,
In whose deep eyes
Men read the welfare of the times to come,
I am too much bereft.
The world dishonored thou hast left.
O truth's and nature's costly lie!
O trusted broken prophecy!
O richest fortune sourly crossed!
Born for the future, to the future lost!

The deep Heart answered, "Weepest thou?
Worthier cause for passion wild
If I had not taken the child.
And deemest thou as those who pore,
With aged eyes, short way before,—
Think'st Beauty vanished from the coast
Of matter, and thy darling lost?
Taught he not thee—the man of eld,
Whose eyes within his eyes beheld
Heaven's numerous hierarchy span
The mystic gulf from God to man?
To be alone wilt thou begin
When worlds of lovers hem thee in?
To-morrow, when the masks shall fall
That dizen Nature's carnival,
The pure shall see by their own will,
Which overflowing Love shall fill,
'Tis not within the force of fate
The fate-conjoined to separate.
But thou, my votary, weepest thou?
I gave thee sight—where is it now?
I taught thy heart beyond the reach
Of ritual, bible, or of speech;
Wrote in thy mind's transparent table,
As far as the incommunicable;
Taught thee each private sign to raise
Lit by the supersolar blaze.
Past utterance, and past belief,
And past the blasphemy of grief,
The mysteries of Nature's heart;
And though no Muse can these impart,
Throb thine with Nature's throbbing breast,
And all is clear from east to west.

"I came to thee as to a friend;
Dearest, to thee I did not send
Tutors, but a joyful eye,
Innocence that matched the sky,
Lovely locks, a form of wonder,
Laughter rich as woodland thunder,
That thou might'st entertain apart
The richest flowering of all art:
And, as the great all-loving Day
Through smallest chambers takes its way,
That thou might'st break thy daily bread
With prophet, savior and head;
That thou might'st cherish for thine own
The riches of sweet Mary's Son,
Boy-Rabbi, Israel's paragon.
And thoughtest thou such guest
Would in thy hall take up his rest?
Would rushing life forget her laws,
Fate's glowing revolution pause?
High omens ask diviner guess;
Not to be conned to tediousness
And know my higher gifts unbind
The zone that girds the incarnate mind.
When the scanty shores are full
With Thought's perilous, whirling pool;
When frail Nature can no more,
Then the Spirit strikes the hour:
My servant Death, with solving rite,
Pours finite into infinite.
Wilt thou freeze love's tidal flow,
Whose streams through Nature circling go?
Nail the wild star to its track
On the half-climbed zodiac?
Light is light which radiates,
Blood is blood which circulates,
Life is life which generates,
And many-seeming life is one,—
Wilt thou transfix and make it none?
Its onward force too starkly pent
In figure, bone and lineament?
Wilt thou, uncalled, interrogate,
Talker! the unreplying Fate?
Nor see the genius of the whole
Ascendant in the private soul,
Beckon it when to go and come,
Self-announced its hour of doom?

Fair the soul's recess and shrine,
Magic-built to last a season;
Masterpiece of love benign,
Fairer that expansive reason
Whose omen 'tis, and sign.
Wilt thou not ope thy heart to know
What rainbows teach, and sunsets show?
Verdict which accumulates
From lengthening scroll of human fates,
Voice of earth to earth returned,
Prayers of saints that inly burned,—
Saying, *What is excellent,*
As God lives, is permanent;
Hearts are dust, hearts' loves remain;
Heart's love will meet thee again.
Revere the Maker; fetch thine eye
Up to his style, and manners of the sky.
Not of adamant and gold
Built he heaven stark and cold;
No, but a nest of bending reeds,
Flowering grass and scented weeds;
Or like a traveller's fleeing tent,
Or bow above the tempest bent;
Built of tears and sacred flames,
And virtue reaching to its aims;
Built of furtherance and pursuing,
Not of spent deeds, but of doing.
Silent rushes the swift Lord
Through ruined systems still restored,
Broadsowing, bleak and void to bless,
Plants with worlds the wilderness;
Waters with tears of ancient sorrow
Apples of Eden ripe to-morrow.
House and tenant go to ground,
Lost in God, in Godhead found."

1842–46 1847

CHARACTER

THE sun set, but set not his hope:
Stars rose; his faith was earlier up:
Fixed on the enormous galaxy,
Deeper and older seemed his eye;
And matched his sufferance sublime
The taciturnity of time.
He spoke, and words more soft than rain
Brought the Age of Gold again:
His action won such reverence sweet
As hid all measure of the feat.

1844

POLITICS

GOLD and iron are good
To buy iron and gold;
All earth's fleece and food
For their like are sold.
Boded Merlin wise,
Proved Napoleon great,
Nor kind nor coinage buys
Aught above its rate.
Fear, Craft and Avarice
Cannot rear a State.
Out of dust to build
What is more than dust,—
Walls Amphion piled
Phœbus stablish must.
When the Muses nine
With the Virtues meet,
Find to their design
An Atlantic seat,
By green orchard boughs
Fended from the heat,
Where the statesman ploughs
Furrow for the wheat,—
When the Church is social worth,
When the state-house is the hearth,
Then the perfect State is come,
The republican at home.

1844

EXPERIENCE

THE lords of life, the lords of life,—
I saw them pass
In their own guise,
Like and unlike,
Portly and grim,—
Use and Surprise,
Surface and Dream,
Succession swift and spectral Wrong,
Temperament without a tongue,
And the inventor of the game
Omnipresent without name;—
Some to see, some to be guessed,
They marched from east to west:
Little man, least of all,
Among the legs of his guardians tall,
Walked about with puzzled look.
Him by the hand dear Nature took,
Dearest Nature, strong and kind,
Whispered, "Darling, never mind!

To-morrow they will wear another face,
The founder thou; these are thy race!"

1844

FABLE

The mountain and the squirrel
Had a quarrel,
And the former called the latter "Little Prig";
Bun replied,
"You are doubtless very big;
But all sorts of things and weather
Must be taken in together,
To make up a year
And a sphere.
And I think it no disgrace
To occupy my place.
If I'm not so large as you,
You are not so small as I,
And not half so spry.
I'll not deny you make
A very pretty squirrel track;
Talents differ; all is well and wisely put;
If I cannot carry forests on my back,
Neither can you crack a nut."

1845 1847

THE DAY'S RATION

When I was born,
From all the seas of strength Fate filled a chalice,
Saying, "This be thy portion, child; this chalice,
Less than a lily's, thou shalt daily draw
From my great arteries,—nor less, nor more."
All substances the cunning chemist Time
Melts down into that liquor of my life,—
Friends, foes, joys, fortunes, beauty and disgust.
And whether I am angry or content,
Indebted or insulted, loved or hurt,
All he distils into sidereal wine
And brims my little cup; heedless, alas!
Of all he sheds how little it will hold,
How much runs over on the desert sands.
If a new Muse draw me with splendid ray,
And I uplift myself into its heaven,
The needs of the first sight absorb my blood,
And all the following hours of the day
Drag a ridiculous age.
Today, when friends approach, and every hour
Brings book, or starbright scroll of genius,
The little cup will hold not a bead more,
And all the costly liquor runs to waste;
Nor gives the jealous lord one diamond drop
So to be husbanded for poorer days.
Why need I volumes, if one word suffice?
Why need I galleries, when a pupil's draught
After the master's sketch fills and o'erfills
My apprehension? Why seek Italy,
Who cannot circumnavigate the sea
Of thoughts and things at home, but still adjourn
The nearest matters for a thousand days?

1846

BACCHUS

Bring me wine, but wine which never grew
In the belly of the grape,
Or grew on vine whose tap-roots, reaching through
Under the Andes to the Cape,
Suffer no savor of the earth to scape.

Let its grapes the morn salute
From a nocturnal root,
Which feels the acrid juice
Of Styx and Erebus;
And turns the woe of Night,
By its own craft, to a more rich delight.

We buy ashes for bread;
We buy diluted wine;
Give me of the true,—
Whose ample leaves and tendrils curled
Among the silver hills of heaven
Draw everlasting dew;
Wine of wine,
Blood of the world,
Form of forms, and mould of statures,
That I intoxicated,
And by the draught assimilated,
May float at pleasure through all natures;
The bird-language rightly spell,
And that which roses say so well.

Wine that is shed
Like the torrents of the sun
Up the horizon walls,
Or like the Atlantic streams, which run
When the South Sea calls.

Water and bread,
Food which needs no transmuting,
Rainbow-flowering, wisdom-fruiting,
Wine which is already man,
Food which teach and reason can.

Wine which Music is,—
Music and wine are one,—
That I, drinking this,
Shall hear far Chaos talk with me;
Kings unborn shall walk with me;
And the poor grass shall plot and plan
What it will do when it is man.
Quickened so, will I unlock
Every crypt of every rock.

I thank the joyful juice
For all I know;—
Winds of remembering
Of the ancient being blow,
And seeming-solid walls of use
Open and flow.

Pour, Bacchus! the remembering wine;
Retrieve the loss of me and mine!
Vine for vine be antidote,
And the grape requite the lote!
Haste to cure the old despair,—
Reason in Nature's lotus drenched,
The memory of ages quenched;
Give them again to shine;
Let wine repair what this undid;
And where the infection slid,
A dazzling memory revive;
Refresh the faded tints,
Recut the aged prints,
And write my old adventures with the pen
Which on the first day drew,
Upon the tablets blue,
The dancing Pleiads and eternal men.

1846 1847

ODE

INSCRIBED TO W. H. CHANNING

THOUGH loath to grieve
The evil time's sole patriot,
I cannot leave
My honied thought
For the priest's cant,
Or statesman's rant.

If I refuse
My study for their politique,
Which at the best is trick,
The angry Muse
Puts confusion in my brain.

But who is he that prates
Of the culture of mankind,
Of better arts and life?
Go, blindworm, go,
Behold the famous States
Harrying Mexico
With rifle and with knife!

Or who, with accent bolder,
Dare praise the freedom-loving mountaineer?
I found by thee, O rushing Contoocook!
And in thy valleys, Agiochook!
The jackals of the negro-holder.

The God who made New Hampshire
Taunted the lofty land
With little men;—
Small bat and wren
House in the oak:—
If earth-fire cleave
The upheaved land, and bury the folk,
The southern crocodile would grieve.
Virtue palters; Right is hence;
Freedom praised, but hid;
Funeral eloquence
Rattles the coffin-lid.

What boots thy zeal,
O glowing friend,
That would indignant rend
The northland from the south?
Wherefore? to what good end?
Boston Bay and Bunker Hill
Would serve things still;—
Things are of the snake.

The horseman serves the horse,
The neatherd serves the neat,
The merchant serves the purse,
The eater serves his meat;
'Tis the day of the chattel,
Web to weave, and corn to grind;
Things are in the saddle,
And ride mankind.

There are two laws discrete,
Not reconciled,—

Law for man, and law for thing;
The last builds town and fleet,
But it runs wild,
And doth the man unking.

'Tis fit the forest fall,
The steep be graded,
The mountain tunnelled,
The sand shaded,
The orchard planted,
The glebe tilled,
The prairie granted,
The steamer built.

Let man serve law for man;
Live for friendship, live for love,
For truth's and harmony's behoof;
The state may follow how it can,
As Olympus follows Jove.

Yet do not I implore
The wrinkled shopman to my sounding woods,
Nor bid the unwilling senator
Ask votes of thrushes in the solitudes.
Every one to his chosen work;—
Foolish hands may mix and mar;
Wise and sure the issues are.
Round they roll till dark is light,
Sex to sex, and even to odd;—
The over-god
Who marries Right to Might,
Who peoples, unpeoples,—
He who exterminates
Races by stronger races,
Black by white faces,—
Knows to bring honey
Out of the lion;
Grafts gentlest scion
On pirate and Turk.

The Cossack eats Poland,
Like stolen fruit;
Her last noble is ruined,
Her last poet mute:
Straight, into double band
The victors divide;
Half for freedom strike and stand;—
The astonished Muse finds thousands at her side.

1847

MERLIN

I

Thy trivial harp will never please
Or fill my craving ear;
Its chords should ring as blows the breeze,
Free, peremptory, clear.
No jingling serenader's art,
Nor tinkle of piano strings,
Can make the wild blood start
In its mystic springs.
The kingly bard
Must smite the chords rudely and hard,
As with hammer or with mace;
That they may render back
Artful thunder, which conveys
Secrets of the solar track,
Sparks of the supersolar blaze.
Merlin's blows are strokes of fate,
Chiming with the forest tone,
When boughs buffet boughs in the wood;
Chiming with the gasp and moan
Of the ice-imprisoned flood;
With the pulse of manly hearts;
With the voice of orators;
With the din of city arts;
With the cannonade of wars;
With the marches of the brave;
And prayers of might from martyrs' cave.

Great is the art,
Great be the manners, of the bard.
He shall not his brain encumber
With the coil of rhythm and number;
But, leaving rule and pale forethought,
He shall aye climb
For his rhyme.
"Pass in, pass in," the angels say,
"In to the upper doors,
Nor count compartments of the floors,
But mount to paradise
By the stairway of surprise."

Blameless master of the games,
King of sport that never shames,
He shall daily joy dispense
Hid in song's sweet influence.
Forms more cheerly live and go,
What time the subtle mind
Sings aloud the tune whereto
Their pulses beat,

And march their feet,
And their members are combined.

By Sybarites beguiled,
He shall no task decline;
Merlin's mighty line
Extremes of nature reconciled,—
Bereaved a tyrant of his will,
And made the lion mild.
Songs can the tempest still,
Scattered on the stormy air,
Mould the year to fair increase,
And bring in poetic peace.

He shall not seek to weave,
In weak, unhappy times,
Efficacious rhymes;
Wait his returning strength.
Bird that from the nadir's floor
To the zenith's top can soar,—
The soaring orbit of the muse exceeds that journey's length.
Nor profane affect to hit
Or compass that, by meddling wit,
Which only the propitious mind
Publishes when 'tis inclined.
There are open hours
When the God's will sallies free,
And the dull idiot might see
The flowing fortunes of a thousand years;—
Sudden, at unawares,
Self-moved, fly-to the doors,
Nor sword of angels could reveal
What they conceal.

1846

II

THE rhyme of the poet
Modulates the king's affairs;
Balance-loving Nature
Made all things in pairs.
To every foot its antipode;
Each color with its counter glowed;
To every tone beat answering tones,
Higher or graver;
Flavor gladly blends with flavor;
Leaf answers leaf upon the bough;
And match the paired cotyledons.
Hands to hands, and feet to feet,
In one body grooms and brides;
Eldest rite, two married sides
In every mortal meet.
Light's far furnace shines,
Smelting balls and bars,
Forging double stars,
Glittering twins and trines.
The animals are sick with love,
Lovesick with rhyme;
Each with all propitious Time
Into chorus wove.

Like the dancers' ordered band,
Thoughts come also hand in hand;
In equal couples mated,
Or else alternated;
Adding by their mutual gage,
One to other, health and age.
Solitary fancies go
Short-lived wandering to and fro,
Most like to bachelors,
Or an ungiven maid,
Not ancestors,
With no posterity to make the lie afraid,
Or keep truth undecayed.
Perfect-paired as eagle's wings,
Justice is the rhyme of things;
Trade and counting use
The self-same tuneful muse;
And Nemesis,
Who with even matches odd,
Who athwart space redresses
The partial wrong,
Fills the just period,
And finishes the song.

Subtle rhymes, with ruin rife,
Murmur in the house of life,
Sung by the Sisters as they spin;
In perfect time and measure they
Build and unbuild our echoing clay,
As the two twilights of the day
Fold us music-drunken in.

1847

THE WORLD-SOUL

THANKS to the morning light,
Thanks to the foaming sea,
To the uplands of New Hampshire,
To the green-haired forest free;
Thanks to each man of courage,
To the maids of holy mind,
To the boy with his games undaunted
Who never looks behind.

Cities of proud hotels,
  Houses of rich and great,
Vice nestles in your chambers,
  Beneath your roofs of slate.
It cannot conquer folly,—
  Time-and-space-conquering steam,—
And the light-outspeeding telegraph
  Bears nothing on its beam.

The politics are base;
  The letters do not cheer;
And 'tis far in the deeps of history,
  The voice that speaketh clear.
Trade and the streets ensnare us,
  Our bodies are weak and worn;
We plot and corrupt each other,
  And we despoil the unborn.

Yet there in the parlor sits
  Some figure of noble guise,—
Our angel, in a stranger's form,
  Or woman's pleading eyes;
Or only a flashing sunbeam
  In at the window-pane;
Or Music pours on mortals
  Its beautiful disdain.

The inevitable morning
  Finds them who in cellars be;
And be sure the all-loving Nature
  Will smile in a factory.
Yon ridge of purple landscape,
  Yon sky between the walls,
Hold all the hidden wonders
  In scanty intervals.

Alas! the Sprite that haunts us
  Deceives our rash desire;
It whispers of the glorious gods,
  And leaves us in the mire.
We cannot learn the cipher
  That's writ upon our cell;
Stars taunt us by a mystery
  Which we could never spell.

If but one hero knew it,
  The world would blush in flame;
The sage, till he hit the secret,
  Would hang his head for shame.
Our brothers have not read it,
  Not one has found the key;
And henceforth we are comforted,—
  We are but such as they.

Still, still the secret presses;
  The nearing clouds draw down;
The crimson morning flames into
  The fopperies of the town.
Within, without the idle earth,
  Stars weave eternal rings;
The sun himself shines heartily,
  And shares the joy he brings.

And what if Trade sow cities
  Like shells along the shore,
And thatch with towns the prairie broad
  With railways ironed o'er?—
They are but sailing foam-bells
  Along Thought's causing stream,
And take their shape and sun-color
  From him that sends the dream.

For Destiny never swerves
  Nor yields to men the helm;
He shoots his thought, by hidden nerves,
  Throughout the solid realm.
The patient Dæmon sits,
  With roses and a shroud;
He has his way, and deals his gifts,—
  But ours is not allowed.

He is no churl nor trifler,
  And his viceroy is none,—
Love-without-weakness,—
  Of Genius sire and son.
And his will is not thwarted;
  The seeds of land and sea
Are the atoms of his body bright,
  And his behest obey.

He serveth the servant,
  The brave he loves amain;
He kills the cripple and the sick,
  And straight begins again;
For gods delight in gods,
  And thrust the weak aside;
To him who scorns their charities
  Their arms fly open wide.

When the old world is sterile
  And the ages are effete,
He will from wrecks and sediment
  The fairer world complete.
He forbids to despair;
  His cheeks mantle with mirth;
And the unimagined good of men
  Is yeaning at the birth.

Spring still makes spring in the mind
When sixty years are told;
Love wakes anew this throbbing heart,
And we are never old;
Over the winter glaciers
I see the summer glow,
And through the wild-piled snowdrift
The warm rosebuds below.

1847

INITIAL, DÆMONIC, AND CELESTIAL LOVE

I

THE INITIAL LOVE

VENUS, when her son was lost,
Cried him up and down the coast,
In hamlets, palaces, and parks,
And told the truant by his marks,—
Golden curls, and quiver and bow.
This befell how long ago!
Time and tide are strangely changed,
Men and manners much deranged:
None will now find Cupid latent
By this foolish antique patent.
He came late along the waste,
Shod like a traveller for haste;
With malice dared me to proclaim him,
That the maids and boys might name him.

Boy no more, he wears all coats,
Frocks and blouses, capes, capotes;
He bears no bow, or quiver, or wand,
Nor chaplet on his head or hand.
Leave his weeds and heed his eyes,—
All the rest he can disguise.
In the pit of his eye's a spark
Would bring back day if it were dark;
And, if I tell you all my thought,
Though I comprehend it not,
In those unfathomable orbs
Every function he absorbs;
Doth eat, and drink, and fish, and shoot,
And write, and reason, and compute,
And ride, and run, and have, and hold,
And whine, and flatter, and regret,
And kiss, and couple, and beget,
By those roving eyeballs bold.
Undaunted are their courages,
Right Cossacks in their forages;
Fleeter they than any creature,—
They are his steeds, and not his feature;
Inquisitive, and fierce, and fasting,
Restless, predatory, hasting;
And they pounce on other eyes
As lions on their prey;
And round their circles is writ,
Plainer than the day,
Underneath, within, above,—
Love—love—love—love.
He lives in his eyes;
There doth digest, and work, and spin,
And buy, and sell, and lose, and win;
He rolls them with delighted motion,
Joy-tides swell their mimic ocean.
Yet holds he them with tautest rein,
That they may seize and entertain
The glance that to their glance opposes,
Like fiery honey sucked from roses.
He palmistry can understand,
Imbibing virtue by his hand
As if it were a living root;
The pulse of hands will make him mute;
With all his force he gathers balms
Into those wise, thrilling palms.

Cupid is a casuist,
A mystic and a cabalist,—
Can your lurking thought surprise,
And interpret your device.
He is versed in occult science,
In magic and in clairvoyance,
Oft he keeps his fine ear strained,
And Reason on her tiptoe pained
For aëry intelligence,
And for strange coincidence.
But it touches his quick heart
When Fate by omens takes his part,
And chance-dropped hints from Nature's sphere
Deeply soothe his anxious ear.

Heralds high before him run;
He has ushers many a one;
He spreads his welcome where he goes,
And touches all things with his rose.
All things wait for and divine him,—
How shall I dare to malign him,
Or accuse the god of sport?

I must end my true report,
Painting him from head to foot,
In as far as I took note,
Trusting well the matchless power
Of this young-eyed emperor
Will clear his fame from every cloud
With the bards and with the crowd.

He is wilful, mutable,
Shy, untamed, inscrutable,
Swifter-fashioned than the fairies,
Substance mixed of pure contraries;
His vice some elder virtue's token,
And his good is evil-spoken.
Failing sometimes of his own,
He is headstrong and alone;
He affects the wood and wild,
Like a flower-hunting child;
Buries himself in summer waves,
In trees, with beasts, in mines and caves,
Loves nature like a hornèd cow,
Bird, or deer, or caribou.

Shun him, nymphs, on the fleet horses!
He has a total world of wit;
O how wise are his discourses!
But he is the arch-hypocrite,
And, through all science and all art,
Seeks alone his counterpart.
He is a Pundit of the East,
He is an augur and a priest,
And his soul will melt in prayer,
But word and wisdom is a snare;
Corrupted by the present toy
He follows joy, and only joy.
There is no mask but he will wear;
He invented oaths to swear;
He paints, he carves, he chants, he prays,
And holds all stars in his embrace.
He takes a sovran privilege
Not allowed to any liege;
For Cupid goes behind all law,
And right into himself does draw;
For he is sovereignly allied,—
Heaven's oldest blood flows in his side,—
And interchangeably at one
With every king on every throne,
That no god dare say him nay,
Or see the fault, or seen betray:
He has the Muses by the heart,
And the stern Parcæ on his part.
His many signs cannot be told;
He has not one mode, but manifold,
Many fashions and addresses,
Piques, reproaches, hurts, caresses.
He will preach like a friar,
And jump like Harlequin;
He will read like a crier,
And fight like a Paladin.
Boundless is his memory;
Plans immense his term prolong;
He is not of counted age,
Meaning always to be young.
And his wish is intimacy,
Intimater intimacy,
And a stricter privacy;
The impossible shall yet be done,
And, being two, shall still be one.
As the wave breaks to foam on shelves,
Then runs into a wave again,
So lovers melt their sundered selves,
Yet melted would be twain.

II

THE DÆMONIC LOVE

Man was made of social earth,
Child and brother from his birth,
Tethered by a liquid cord
Of blood through veins of kindred poured.
Next his heart the fireside band
Of mother, father, sister, stand;
Names from awful childhood heard
Throbs of a wild religion stirred;—
Virtue, to love, to hate them, vice;
Till dangerous Beauty came, at last,
Till Beauty came to snap all ties;
The maid, abolishing the past,
With lotus wine obliterates
Dear memory's stone-incarved traits,
And, by herself, supplants alone
Friends year by year more inly known.
When her calm eyes opened bright,
All else grew foreign in their light.
It was ever the self-same tale,
The first experience will not fail;
Only two in the garden walked,
And with snake and seraph talked.

Close, close to men,
Like undulating layer of air,
Right above their heads,

The potent plain of Dæmons spreads.
Stands to each human soul its own,
For watch and ward and furtherance,
In the snares of Nature's dance;
And the lustre and the grace
To fascinate each youthful heart,
Beaming from its counterpart,
Translucent through the mortal covers,
Is the Dæmon's form and face.
To and fro the Genius hies,—
A gleam which plays and hovers
Over the maiden's head,
And dips sometimes as low as to her eyes.
Unknown, albeit lying near,
To men, the path to the Dæmon sphere;
And they that swiftly come and go
Leave no track on the heavenly snow.
Sometimes the airy synod bends,
And the mighty choir descends,
And the brains of men thenceforth,
In crowded and in still resorts,
Teem with unwonted thoughts:
As, when a shower of meteors
Cross the orbit of the earth,
And, lit by fringent air,
Blaze near and far,
Mortals deem the planets bright
Have slipped their sacred bars,
And the lone seaman all the night
Sails, astonished, amid stars.

Beauty of a richer vein,
Graces of a subtler strain,
Unto men these moonmen lend,
And our shrinking sky extend.
So is man's narrow path
By strength and terror skirted;
Also (from the song the wrath
Of the Genii be averted!
The Muse the truth uncolored speaking)
The Dæmons are self-seeking:
Their fierce and limitary will
Draws men to their likeness still.
The erring painter made Love blind,—
Highest Love who shines on all;
Him, radiant, sharpest-sighted god,
None can bewilder;
Whose eyes pierce
The universe,
Path-finder, road-builder,
Mediator, royal giver;
Rightly seeing, rightly seen,
Of joyful and transparent mien.
'Tis a sparkle passing
From each to each, from thee to me,
To and fro perpetually;
Sharing all, daring all,
Levelling, displacing
Each obstruction, it unites
Equals remote, and seeming opposites.
And ever and forever Love
Delights to build a road:
Unheeded Danger near him strides,
Love laughs, and on a lion rides.
But Cupid wears another face,
Born into Dæmons less divine:
His roses bleach apace,
His nectar smacks of wine.
The Dæmon ever builds a wall,
Himself encloses and includes,
Solitude in solitudes:
In like sort his love doth fall.
He doth elect
The beautiful and fortunate,
And the sons of intellect,
And the souls of ample fate,
Who the Future's gates unbar,—
Minions of the Morning Star.
In his prowess he exults,
And the multitude insults.
His impatient looks devour
Oft the humble and the poor;
And, seeing his eye glare,
They drop their few pale flowers
Gathered with hope to please,
Along the mountain towers,—
Lose courage, and despair.
He will never be gainsaid,—
Pitiless, will not be stayed;
His hot tyranny
Burns up every other tie.
Therefore comes an hour from Jove
Which his ruthless will defies,
And the dogs of Fate unties.
Shiver the palaces of glass;
Shrivel the rainbow-colored walls,
Where in bright Art each god and sibyl dwelt
Secure as in the zodiac's belt;
And the galleries and halls,
Wherein every siren sung,
Like a meteor pass.
For this fortune wanted root

In the core of God's abysm,—
Was a weed of self and schism;
And ever the Dæmonic Love
Is the ancestor of wars
And the parent of remorse.

III

THE CELESTIAL LOVE

But God said,
"I will have a purer gift;
There is smoke in the flame;
New flowerets bring, new prayers uplift,
And love without a name.
Fond children, ye desire
To please each other well;
Another round, a higher,
Ye shall climb on the heavenly stair,
And selfish preference forbear;
And in right deserving,
And without a swerving
Each from your proper state,
Weave roses for your mate.

"Deep, deep are loving eyes,
Flowed with naphtha fiery sweet;
And the point is paradise,
Where their glances meet:
Their reach shall yet be more profound,
And a vision without bound:
The axis of those eyes sun-clear
Be the axis of the sphere:
So shall the lights ye pour amain
Go, without check or intervals,
Through from the empyrean walls
Unto the same again."

Higher far into the pure realm,
Over sun and star,
Over the flickering Dæmon film,
Thou must mount for love;
Into vision where all form
In one only form dissolves;
In a region where the wheel
On which all beings ride
Visibly revolves;
Where the starred, eternal worm
Girds the world with bound and term;
Where unlike things are like;
Where good and ill,
And joy and moan,
Melt into one.

There Past, Present, Future, shoot
Triple blossoms from one root;
Substances at base divided,
In their summits are united;
There the holy essence rolls,
One through separated souls;
And the sunny Æon sleeps
Folding Nature in its deeps,
And every fair and every good,
Known in part, or known impure,
To men below,
In their archetypes endure.
The race of gods,
Or those we erring own,
Are shadows flitting up and down
In the still abodes.
The circles of that sea are laws
Which publish and which hide the cause.

Pray for a beam
Out of that sphere,
Thee to guide and to redeem.
O, what a load
Of care and toil,
By lying use bestowed,
From his shoulders falls who sees
The true astronomy,
The period of peace.
Counsel which the ages kept
Shall the well-born soul accept.
As the overhanging trees
Fill the lake with images,—
As garment draws the garment's hem,
Men their fortunes bring with them.
By right or wrong,
Lands and goods go to the strong.
Property will brutely draw
Still to the proprietor;
Silver to silver creep and wind,
And kind to kind.

Nor less the eternal poles
Of tendency distribute souls.
There need no vows to bind
Whom not each other seek, but find.
They give and take no pledge or oath,—
Nature is the bond of both:
No prayer persuades, no flattery fawns,—
Their noble meanings are their pawns.
Plain and cold is their address,
Power have they for tenderness;
And, so thoroughly is known

Each other's counsel by his own,
They can parley without meeting;
Need is none of forms of greeting;
They can well communicate
In their innermost estate;
When each the other shall avoid,
Shall each by each be most enjoyed.

Not with scarfs or perfumed gloves
Do these celebrate their loves:
Not by jewels, feasts and savors,
Not by ribbons or by favors,
But by the sun-spark on the sea,
And the cloud-shadow on the lea,
The soothing lapse of morn to mirk,
And the cheerful round of work.
Their cords of love so public are,
They intertwine the farthest star:
The throbbing sea, the quaking earth,
Yield sympathy and signs of mirth;
Is none so high, so mean is none,
But feels and seals this union;
Even the fell Furies are appeased,
The good applaud, the lost are eased.

Love's hearts are faithful, but not fond,
Bound for the just, but not beyond;
Not glad, as the low-loving herd,
Of self in other still preferred,
But they have heartily designed
The benefit of broad mankind.
And they serve men austerely,
After their own genius, clearly,
Without a false humility;
For this is Love's nobility,—
Not to scatter bread and gold,
Goods and raiment bought and sold;
But to hold fast his simple sense,
And speak the speech of innocence,
And with hand and body and blood,
To make his bosom-counsel good.
He that feeds men serveth few;
He serves all who dares be true.

1847

ALPHONSO OF CASTILE

I, ALPHONSO, live and learn,
Seeing Nature go astern.
Things deteriorate in kind;
Lemons run to leaves and rind;
Meagre crop of figs and limes;
Shorter days and harder times.
Flowering April cools and dies
In the insufficient skies.
Imps, at high midsummer, blot
Half the sun's disk with a spot:
'Twill not now avail to tan
Orange cheek or skin of man.
Roses bleach, the goats are dry,
Lisbon quakes, the people cry.
Yon pale, scrawny fisher fools,
Gaunt as bitterns in the pools,
Are no brothers of my blood;—
They discredit Adamhood.
Eyes of gods! ye must have seen,
O'er your ramparts as ye lean,
The general debility;
Of genius the sterility;
Mighty projects countermanded;
Rash ambition, brokenhanded;
Puny man and scentless rose
Tormenting Pan to double the dose.
Rebuild or ruin: either fill
Of vital force the wasted rill,
Or tumble all again in heap
To weltering chaos and to sleep.

Say, Seigniors, are the old Niles dry,
Which fed the veins of earth and sky,
That mortals miss the loyal heats,
Which drove them erst to social feats;
Now, to a savage selfness grown,
Think nature barely serves for one;
With science poorly mask their hurt,
And vex the gods with question pert,
Immensely curious whether you
Still are rulers, or Mildew?

Masters, I'm in pain with you;
Masters, I'll be plain with you;
In my palace of Castile,
I, a king, for kings can feel.
There my thoughts the matter roll,
And solve and oft resolve the whole.
And, for I'm styled Alphonse the Wise,
Ye shall not fail for sound advice.
Before ye want a drop of rain,
Hear the sentiment of Spain.

You have tried famine: no more try it;
Ply us now with a full diet;
Teach your pupils now with plenty,
For one sun supply us twenty.

I have thought it thoroughly over,—
State of hermit, state of lover;
We must have society,
We cannot spare variety.
Hear you, then, celestial fellows!
Fits not to be overzealous;
Steads not to work on the clean jump,
Nor wine nor brains perpetual pump.
Men and gods are too extense;
Could you slacken and condense?
Your rank overgrowths reduce
Till your kinds abound with juice?
Earth, crowded, cries, "Too many men!"
My counsel is, kill nine in ten,
And bestow the shares of all
On the remnant decimal.
Add their nine lives to this cat;
Stuff their nine brains in one hat;
Make his frame and forces square
With the labors he must dare;
Thatch his flesh, and even his years
With the marble which he rears.
There, growing slowly old at ease
No faster than his planted trees,
He may, by warrant of his age,
In schemes of broader scope engage.
So shall ye have a man of the sphere
Fit to grace the solar year.

1847

DAYS

Daughters of Time, the hypocritic Days,
Muffled and dumb like barefoot dervishes,
And marching single in an endless file,
Bring diadems and fagots in their hands.
To each they offer gifts after his will,
Bread, kingdoms, stars, and sky that holds them all.
I, in my pleached garden, watched the pomp,
Forgot my morning wishes, hastily
Took a few herbs and apples, and the Day
Turned and departed silent. I, too late,
Under her solemn fillet saw the scorn.

1852 1857

WALDEINSAMKEIT

I do not count the hours I spend
In wandering by the sea;
The forest is my loyal friend,
Like God it useth me.

In plains that room for shadows make
Of skirting hills to lie,
Bound in by streams which give and take
Their colors from the sky;

Or on the mountain-crest sublime,
Or down the oaken glade,
O what have I to do with time?
For this the day was made.

Cities of mortals woe-begone
Fantastic care derides,
But in the serious landscape lone
Stern benefit abides.

Sheen will tarnish, honey cloy,
And merry is only a mask of sad,
But, sober on a fund of joy,
The woods at heart are glad.

There the great Planter plants
Of fruitful worlds the grain,
And with a million spells enchants
The souls that walk in pain.

Still on the seeds of all he made
The rose of beauty burns;
Through times that wear and forms that fade,
Immortal youth returns.

The black ducks mounting from the lake,
The pigeon in the pines,
The bittern's boom, a desert make
Which no false art refines.

Down in yon watery nook,
Where bearded mists divide,
The gray old gods whom Chaos knew,
The sires of Nature, hide.

Aloft, in secret veins of air,
Blows the sweet breath of song,
O, few to scale those uplands dare,
Though they to all belong!

See thou bring not to field or stone
The fancies found in books;
Leave authors' eyes, and fetch your own,
To brave the landscape's looks.

Oblivion here thy wisdom is,
Thy thrift, the sleep of cares;
For a proud idleness like this
Crowns all thy mean affairs.

1858

CULTURE

CAN rules or tutors educate
The semigod whom we await?
He must be musical,
Tremulous, impressional,
Alive to gentle influence
Of landscape and of sky,
And tender to the spirit-touch
Of man's or maiden's eye:
But, to his native centre fast,
Shall into Future fuse the Past,
And the world's flowing fates in his own mould
recast.

1860

WEALTH

WHO shall tell what did befall,
Far away in time, when once,
Over the lifeless ball,
Hung idle stars and suns?
What god the element obeyed?
Wings of what wind the lichen bore,
Wafting the puny seeds of power,
Which, lodged in rock, the rock abrade?
And well the primal pioneer
Knew the strong task to it assigned,
Patient through Heaven's enormous year
To build in matter home for mind.
From air the creeping centuries drew
The matted thicket low and wide,
This must the leaves of ages strew
The granite slab to clothe and hide,
Ere wheat can wave its golden pride.
What smiths, and in what furnace, rolled
(In dizzy æons dim and mute
The reeling brain can ill compute)
Copper and iron, lead and gold?
What oldest star the fame can save
Of races perishing to pave
The planet with a floor of lime?
Dust is their pyramid and mole:
Who saw what ferns and palms were pressed
Under the tumbling mountain's breast,
In the safe herbal of the coal?
But when the quarried means were piled,
All is waste and worthless, till
Arrives the wise selecting will,
And, out of slime and chaos, Wit
Draws the threads of fair and fit.
Then temples rose, and towns, and marts,
The shop of toil, the hall of arts;
Then flew the sail across the seas
To feed the North from tropic trees;
The storm-wind wove, the torrent span,
Where they were bid, the rivers ran;
New slaves fulfilled the poet's dream,
Galvanic wire, strong-shouldered steam.
Then docks were built, and crops were stored,
And ingots added to the hoard.
But though light-headed man forget,
Remembering Matter pays her debt:
Still, through her motes and masses, draw
Electric thrills and ties of law,
Which bind the strengths of Nature wild
To the conscience of a child.

1860

BEAUTY

WAS never form and never face
So sweet to Seyd as only grace
Which did not slumber like a stone,
But hovered gleaming and was gone.
Beauty chased he everywhere,
In flame, in storm, in clouds of air.
He smote the lake to feed his eye
With the beryl beam of the broken wave;
He flung in pebbles well to hear
The moment's music which they gave.
Oft pealed for him a lofty tone
From nodding pole and belting zone.
He heard a voice none else could hear
From centred and from errant sphere.
The quaking earth did quake in rhyme,
Seas ebbed and flowed in epic chime.
In dens of passion, and pits of woe,
He saw strong Eros struggling through,
To sun the dark and solve the curse,
And beam to the bounds of the universe.
While thus to love he gave his days
In loyal worship, scorning praise,
How spread their lures for him in vain
Thieving Ambition and paltering Gain!
He thought it happier to be dead,
To die for Beauty, than live for bread.

1860

ILLUSIONS

FLOW, flow the waves hated,
Accursed, adored,
The waves of mutation;

No anchorage is.
Sleep is not, death is not;
Who seem to die live.
House you were born in,
Friends of your spring-time,
Old man and young maid,
Day's toil and its guerdon,
They are all vanishing,
Fleeing to fables,
Cannot be moored.
See the stars through them,
Through treacherous marbles.
Know the stars yonder,
The stars everlasting,
Are fugitive also,
And emulate, vaulted,
The lambent heat lightning
And fire-fly's flight.

When thou dost return
On the wave's circulation,
Behold the shimmer,
The wild dissipation,
And, out of endeavor
To change and to flow,
The gas become solid,
And phantoms and nothings
Return to be things,
And endless imbroglio
Is law and the world,—
Then first shalt thou know,
That in the wild turmoil,
Horsed on the Proteus,
Thou ridest to power,
And to endurance.

1860

WORSHIP

This is he, who, felled by foes,
Sprung harmless up, refreshed by blows:
He to captivity was sold,
But him no prison-bars would hold:
Though they sealed him in a rock,
Mountain chains he can unlock:
Thrown to lions for their meat,
The crouching lion kissed his feet;
Bound to the stake, no flames appalled,
But arched o'er him an honoring vault.
This is he men miscall Fate,
Threading dark ways, arriving late,
But ever coming in time to crown
The truth, and hurl wrong-doers down.
He is the oldest, and best known,
More near than aught thou call'st thy own,
Yet, greeted in another's eyes,
Disconcerts with glad surprise.
This is Jove, who, deaf to prayers,
Floods with blessings unawares.
Draw, if thou canst, the mystic line
Severing rightly his from thine,
Which is human, which divine.

1860

THE TEST

(Musa loquitur.)

I hung my verses in the wind,
Time and tide their faults may find.
All were winnowed through and through,
Five lines lasted sound and true;
Five were smelted in a pot
Than the South more fierce and hot;
These the siroc could not melt,
Fire their fiercer flaming felt,
And the meaning was more white
Than July's meridian light.
Sunshine cannot bleach the snow,
Nor time unmake what poets know.
Have you eyes to find the five
Which five hundred did survive?

1861

VOLUNTARIES

I

Low and mournful be the strain,
Haughty thought be far from me;
Tones of penitence and pain,
Moanings of the tropic sea;
Low and tender in the cell
Where a captive sits in chains,
Crooning ditties treasured well
From his Afric's torrid plains.
Sole estate his sire bequeathed,—
Hapless sire to hapless son,—
Was the wailing song he breathed,
And his chain when life was done.

What his fault, or what his crime?
Or what ill planet crossed his prime?
Heart too soft and will too weak
To front the fate that crouches near,—
Dove beneath the vulture's beak;—

Will song dissuade the thirsty spear?
Dragged from his mother's arms and breast,
Displaced, disfurnished here,
His wistful toil to do his best
Chilled by a ribald jeer.
Great men in the Senate sate,
Sage and hero, side by side,
Building for their sons the State,
Which they shall rule with pride.
They forbore to break the chain
Which bound the dusky tribe,
Checked by the owners' fierce disdain,
Lured by "Union" as the bribe.
Destiny sat by, and said,
"Pang for pang your seed shall pay,
Hide in false peace your coward head,
I bring round the harvest day."

II

Freedom all winged expands,
Nor perches in a narrow place;
Her broad van seeks unplanted lands;
She loves a poor and virtuous race.
Clinging to a colder zone
Whose dark sky sheds the snowflake down,
The snowflake is her banner's star,
Her stripes the boreal streamers are.
Long she loved the Northman well;
Now the iron age is done,
She will not refuse to dwell
With the offspring of the Sun;
Foundling of the desert far,
Where palms plume, siroccos blaze,
He roves unhurt the burning ways
In climates of the summer star.
He has avenues to God
Hid from men of Northern brain,
Far beholding, without cloud,
What these with slowest steps attain.
If once the generous chief arrive
To lead him willing to be led,
For freedom he will strike and strive,
And drain his heart till he be dead.

III

In an age of fops and toys,
Wanting wisdom, void of right,
Who shall nerve heroic boys
To hazard all in Freedom's fight,—
Break sharply off their jolly games,
Forsake their comrades gay
And quit proud homes and youthful dames
For famine, toil and fray?
Yet on the nimble air benign
Speed nimbler messages,
That waft the breath of grace divine
To hearts in sloth and ease.
So nigh is grandeur to our dust,
So near is God to man,
When Duty whispers low, *Thou must*,
The youth replies, *I can*.

IV

O, well for the fortunate soul
Which Music's wings infold,
Stealing away the memory
Of sorrows new and old!
Yet happier he whose inward sight,
Stayed on his subtile thought,
Shuts his sense on toys of time,
To vacant bosoms brought.
But best befriended of the God
He who, in evil times,
Warned by an inward voice,
Heeds not the darkness and the dread,
Biding by his rule and choice,
Feeling only the fiery thread
Leading over heroic ground,
Walled with mortal terror round,
To the aim which him allures,
And the sweet heaven his deed secures.
Peril around, all else appalling,
Cannon in front and leaden rain
Him duty through the clarion calling
To the van called not in vain.

Stainless soldier on the walls,
Knowing this,—and knows no more,—
Whoever fights, whoever falls,
Justice conquers evermore,
Justice after as before,—
And he who battles on her side,
God, though he were ten times slain,
Crowns him victor glorified,
Victor over death and pain.

V

Blooms the laurel which belongs
To the valiant chief who fights;
I see the wreath, I hear the songs
Lauding the Eternal Rights,
Victors over daily wrongs:

Awful victors, they misguide
Whom they will destroy,
And their coming triumph hide
In our downfall, or our joy:
They reach no term, they never sleep,
In equal strength through space abide;
Though, feigning dwarfs, they crouch and
creep,
The strong they slay, the swift outstride:
Fate's grass grows rank in valley clods,
And rankly on the castled steep,—
Speak it firmly, these are gods,
All are ghosts beside.

1863

MANNERS

GRACE, Beauty, and Caprice
Build this golden portal;
Graceful women, chosen men,
Dazzle every mortal.
Their sweet and lofty countenance
His enchanted food;
He need not go to them, their forms
Beset his solitude.
He looketh seldom in their face,
His eyes explore the ground,—
The green grass is a looking-glass
Whereon their traits are found.
Little and less he says to them,
So dances his heart in his breast;
Their tranquil mien bereaveth him
Of wit, of words, of rest.
Too weak to win, too fond to shun
The tyrants of his doom,
The much deceived Endymion
Slips behind a tomb.

1867

MAY–DAY

DAUGHTER of Heaven and Earth, coy Spring,
With sudden passion languishing,
Teaching barren moors to smile,
Painting pictures mile on mile,
Holds a cup with cowslip-wreaths,
Whence a smokeless incense breathes.
The air is full of whistlings bland;
What was that I heard
Out of the hazy land?
Harp of the wind, or song of bird,
Or vagrant booming of the air,
Voice of a meteor lost in day?
Such tidings of the starry sphere
Can this elastic air convey.
Or haply 'twas the cannonade
Of the pent and darkened lake,
Cooled by the pendent mountain's shade,
Whose deeps, till beams of noonday break,
Afflicted moan, and latest hold
Even into May the iceberg cold.
Was it a squirrel's pettish bark,
Or clarionet of jay? or hark
Where yon wedged line the Nestor leads,
Steering north with raucous cry
Through tracts and provinces of sky,
Every night alighting down
In new landscapes of romance,
Where darkling feed the clamorous clans
By lonely lakes to men unknown.
Come the tumult whence it will,
Voice of sport, or rush of wings,
It is a sound, it is a token
That the marble sleep is broken,
And a change has passed on things.

When late I walked, in earlier days,
All was stiff and stark;
Knee-deep snows choked all the ways,
In the sky no spark;
Firm-braced I sought my ancient woods,
Struggling through the drifted roads;
The whited desert knew me not,
Snow-ridges masked each darling spot;
The summer dells, by genius haunted,
One arctic moon had disenchanted.
All the sweet secrets therein hid
By Fancy, ghastly spells undid.
Eldest mason, Frost, had piled
Swift cathedrals in the wild;
The piny hosts were sheeted ghosts
In the star-lit minster aisled.
I found no joy: the icy wind
Might rule the forest to his mind.
Who would freeze on frozen lakes?
Back to books and sheltered home,
And wood-fire flickering on the walls,
To hear, when, 'mid our talk and games,
Without the baffled North-wind calls.
But soft! a sultry morning breaks;
The ground-pines wash their rusty green,
The maple-tops their crimson tint,
On the soft path each track is seen,

The girl's foot leaves its neater print.
The pebble loosened from the frost
Asks of the urchin to be tost.
In flint and marble beats a heart,
The kind Earth takes her children's part,
The green lane is the school-boy's friend,
Low leaves his quarrel apprehend,
The fresh ground loves his top and ball,
The air rings jocund to his call,
The brimming brook invites a leap,
He dives the hollow, climbs the steep.
The youth sees omens where he goes,
And speaks all languages the rose,
The wood-fly mocks with tiny voice
The far halloo of human voice;
The perfumed berry on the spray
Smacks of faint memories far away.
A subtle chain of countless rings
The next into the farthest brings,
And, striving to be man, the worm
Mounts through all the spires of form.

The cagèd linnet in the Spring
Hearkens for the choral glee,
When his fellows on the wing
Migrate from the Southern Sea;
When trellised grapes their flowers unmask,
And the new-born tendrils twine,
The old wine darkling in the cask
Feels the bloom on the living vine,
And bursts the hoops at hint of Spring:
And so, perchance, in Adam's race,
Of Eden's bower some dream-like trace
Survived the Flight and swam the Flood,
And wakes the wish in youngest blood
To tread the forfeit Paradise,
And feed once more the exile's eyes;
And ever when the happy child
In May beholds the blooming wild,
And hears in heaven the bluebird sing,
"Onward," he cries, "your baskets bring,—
In the next field is air more mild,
And o'er yon hazy crest is Eden's balmier spring."

Not for a regiment's parade,
Nor evil laws or rulers made,
Blue Walden rolls its cannonade,
But for a lofty sign
Which the Zodiac threw,
That the bondage-days are told,
And waters free as winds shall flow.
Lo! how all the tribes combine
To rout the flying foe.
See, every patriot oak-leaf throws
His elfin length upon the snows,
Not idle, since the leaf all day
Draws to the spot the solar ray,
Ere sunset quarrying inches down,
And halfway to the mosses brown;
While the grass beneath the rime
Has hints of the propitious time,
And upward pries and perforates
Through the cold slab a thousand gates,
Till green lances peering through
Bend happy in the welkin blue.

As we thaw frozen flesh with snow,
So Spring will not her time forerun,
Mix polar night with tropic glow,
Nor cloy us with unshaded sun,
Nor wanton skip with bacchic dance,
But she has the temperance
Of the gods, whereof she is one,—
Masks her treasury of heat
Under east winds crossed with sleet.
Plants and birds and humble creatures
Well accept her rule austere;
Titan-born, to hardy natures
Cold is genial and dear.
As Southern wrath to Northern right
Is but straw to anthracite;
As in the day of sacrifice,
When heroes piled the pyre,
The dismal Massachusetts ice
Burned more than others' fire,
So Spring guards with surface cold
The garnered heat of ages old.
Hers to sow the seed of bread,
That man and all the kinds be fed;
And, when the sunlight fills the hours,
Dissolves the crust, displays the flowers.

Beneath the calm, within the light,
A hid unruly appetite
Of swifter life, a surer hope,
Strains every sense to larger scope,
Impatient to anticipate
The halting steps of aged Fate.
Slow grows the palm, too slow the pearl:
When Nature falters, fain would zeal
Grasp the felloes of her wheel,

And grasping give the orbs another whirl.
Turn swiftlier round, O tardy ball!
And sun this frozen side.
Bring hither back the robin's call,
Bring back the tulip's pride.

Why chidest thou the tardy Spring?
The hardy bunting does not chide;
The blackbirds make the maples ring
With social cheer and jubilee;
The redwing flutes his *o-ka-lee*,
The robins know the melting snow;
The sparrow meek, prophetic-eyed,
Her nest beside the snow-drift weaves,
Secure the osier yet will hide
Her callow brood in mantling leaves,—
And thou, by science all undone,
Why only must thy reason fail
To see the southing of the sun?

The world rolls round,—mistrust it not,—
Befalls again what once befell;
All things return, both sphere and mote,
And I shall hear my bluebird's note,
And dream the dream of Auburn dell.

April cold with dropping rain
Willows and lilacs brings again,
The whistle of returning birds,
And trumpet-lowing of the herds.
The scarlet maple-keys betray
What potent blood hath modest May,
What fiery force the earth renews,
The wealth of forms, the flush of hues;
What joy in rosy waves outpoured
Flows from the heart of Love, the Lord.

Hither rolls the storm of heat;
I feel its finer billows beat
Like a sea which me infolds;
Heat with viewless fingers moulds,
Swells, and mellows, and matures,
Paints, and flavors, and allures,
Bird and brier inly warms,
Still enriches and transforms,
Gives the reed and lily length,
Adds to oak and oxen strength,
Transforming what it doth infold,
Life out of death, new out of old,
Painting fawns' and leopards' fells,
Seethes the gulf-encrimsoning shells,
Fires gardens with a joyful blaze
Of tulips, in the morning's rays.
The dead log touched bursts into leaf,
The wheat-blade whispers of the sheaf.
What god is this imperial Heat,
Earth's prime secret, sculpture's seat?
Doth it bear hidden in its heart
Water-line patterns of all art?
Is it Dædalus? is it Love?
Or walks in mask almighty Jove,
And drops from Power's redundant horn
All seeds of beauty to be born?

Where shall we keep the holiday,
And duly greet the entering May?
Too strait and low our cottage doors,
And all unmeet our carpet floors;
Nor spacious court, nor monarch's hall,
Suffice to hold the festival.
Up and away! where haughty woods
Front the liberated floods:
We will climb the broad-backed hills,
Hear the uproar of their joy;
We will mark the leaps and gleams
Of the new-delivered streams,
And the murmuring rivers of sap
Mount in the pipes of the trees,
Giddy with day, to the topmost spire,
Which for a spike of tender green
Bartered its powdery cap;
And the colors of joy in the bird,
And the love in its carol heard,
Frog and lizard in holiday coats,
And turtle brave in his golden spots;
While cheerful cries of crag and plain
Reply to the thunder of river and main.

As poured the flood of the ancient sea
Spilling over mountain chains,
Bending forests as bends the sedge,
Faster flowing o'er the plains,—
A world-wide wave with a foaming edge
That rims the running silver sheet,—
So pours the deluge of the heat
Broad northward o'er the land,
Painting artless paradises,
Drugging herbs with Syrian spices,
Fanning secret fires which glow
In columbine and clover-blow,
Climbing the northern zones,
Where a thousand pallid towns
Lie like cockles by the main,

Or tented armies on a plain.
The million-handed sculptor moulds
Quaintest bud and blossom folds,
The million-handed painter pours
Opal hues and purple dye;
Azaleas flush the island floors,
And the tints of heaven reply.

Wreaths for the May! for happy Spring
Today shall all her dowry bring,
The love of kind, the joy, the grace,
Hymen of element and race,
Knowing well to celebrate
With song and hue and star and state,
With tender light and youthful cheer,
The spousals of the new-born year.

Spring is strong and virtuous,
Broad-sowing, cheerful, plenteous,
Quickening underneath the mould
Grains beyond the price of gold.
So deep and large her bounties are,
That one broad, long midsummer day
Shall to the planet overpay
The ravage of a year of war.

Drug the cup, thou butler sweet,
And send the nectar round;
The feet that slid so long on sleet
Are glad to feel the ground.
Fill and saturate each kind
With good according to its mind,
Fill each kind and saturate
With good agreeing with its fate,
And soft perfection of its plan—
Willow and violet, maiden and man.

The bitter-sweet, the haunting air
Creepeth, bloweth everywhere;
It preys on all, all prey on it,
Blooms in beauty, thinks in wit,
Stings the strong with enterprise,
Makes travellers long for Indian skies,
And where it comes this courier fleet
Fans in all hearts expectance sweet,
As if tomorrow should redeem
The vanished rose of evening's dream.
By houses lies a fresher green,
On men and maids a ruddier mien,
As if Time brought a new relay
Of shining virgins every May,
And Summer came to ripen maids
To a beauty that not fades.

I saw the bud-crowned Spring go forth,
Stepping daily onward north
To greet staid ancient cavaliers
Filing single in stately train.
And who, and who are the travellers?
They were Night and Day, and Day and
Night,
Pilgrims wight with step forthright.
I saw the Days deformed and low,
Short and bent by cold and snow;
The merry Spring threw wreaths on them,
Flower-wreaths gay with bud and bell;
Many a flower and many a gem,
They were refreshed by the smell,
They shook the snow from hats and shoon,
They put their April raiment on;
And those eternal forms,
Unhurt by a thousand storms,
Shot up to the height of the sky again,
And danced as merrily as young men.
I saw them mask their awful glance
Sidewise meek in gossamer lids;
And to speak my thought if none forbids
It was as if the eternal gods,
Tired of their starry periods,
Hid their majesty in cloth
Woven of tulips and painted moth.
On carpets green the maskers march
Below May's well-appointed arch,
Each star, each god, each grace amain,
Every joy and virtue speed,
Marching duly in her train,
And fainting Nature at her need
Is made whole again.

'Twas the vintage-day of field and wood,
When magic wine for bards is brewed;
Every tree and stem and chink
Gushed with syrup to the brink.
The air stole into the streets of towns,
Refreshed the wise, reformed the clowns,
And betrayed the fund of joy
To the high-school and medalled boy:
On from hall to chamber ran,
From youth to maid, from boy to man,
To babes, and to old eyes as well.
"Once more," the old man cried, "ye clouds,
Airy turrets purple-piled,

Which once my infancy beguiled,
Beguile me with the wonted spell.
I know ye skilful to convoy
The total freight of hope and joy
Into rude and homely nooks,
Shed mocking lustres on shelf of books,
On farmer's byre, on pasture rude,
And stony pathway to the wood.
I care not if the pomps you show
Be what they soothfast appear,
Or if yon realms in sunset glow
Be bubbles of the atmosphere.
And if it be to you allowed
To fool me with a shining cloud,
So only new griefs are consoled
By new delights, as old by old,
Frankly I will be your guest,
Count your change and cheer the best.
The world hath overmuch of pain,—
If Nature give me joy again,
Of such deceit I'll not complain."

Ah! well I mind the calendar,
Faithful through a thousand years,
Of the painted race of flowers,
Exact to days, exact to hours,
Counted on the spacious dial
Yon broidered zodiac girds.
I know the trusty almanac
Of the punctual coming-back,
On their due days, of the birds.
I marked them yestermorn,
A flock of finches darting
Beneath the crystal arch,
Piping, as they flew, a march,—
Belike the one they used in parting
Last year from yon oak or larch;
Dusky sparrows in a crowd,
Diving, darting northward free,
Suddenly betook them all,
Every one to his hole in the wall,
Or to his niche in the apple-tree.
I greet with joy the choral trains
Fresh from palms and Cuba's canes.
Best gems of Nature's cabinet,
With dews of tropic morning wet,
Beloved of children, bards and Spring,
O birds, your perfect virtues bring,
Your song, your forms, your rhythmic flight,
Your manners for the heart's delight,
Nestle in hedge, or barn, or roof,
Here weave your chamber weather-proof,
Forgive our harms, and condescend
To man, as to a lubber friend,
And, generous, teach his awkward race
Courage and probity and grace!

Poets praise that hidden wine
Hid in milk we drew
At the barrier of Time,
When our life was new.
We had eaten fairy fruit,
We were quick from head to foot,
All the forms we looked on shone
As with diamond dews thereon.
What cared we for costly joys,
The Museum's far-fetched toys?
Gleam of sunshine on the wall
Poured a deeper cheer than all
The revels of the Carnival.
We a pine-grove did prefer
To a marble theatre,
Could with gods on mallows dine,
Nor cared for spices or for wine.
Wreaths of mist and rainbow spanned,
Arch on arch, the grimmest land;
Whistle of a woodland bird
Made the pulses dance,
Note of horn in valleys heard
Filled the region with romance.

None can tell how sweet,
How virtuous, the morning air;
Every accent vibrates well;
Not alone the wood-bird's call,
Or shouting boys that chase their ball,
Pass the height of minstrel skill,
But the ploughman's thoughtless cry,
Lowing oxen, sheep that bleat,
And the joiner's hammer-beat,
Softened are above their will,
Take tones from groves they wandered through
Or flutes which passing angels blew.
All grating discords melt,
No dissonant note is dealt,
And though thy voice be shrill
Like rasping file on steel,
Such is the temper of the air,
Echo waits with art and care,
And will the faults of song repair.

So by remote Superior Lake,
And by resounding Mackinac,
When northern storms the forest shake,
And billows on the long beach break,
The artful Air will separate
Note by note all sounds that grate,
Smothering in her ample breast
All but godlike words,
Reporting to the happy ear
Only purified accords.
Strangely wrought from barking waves,
Soft music daunts the Indian braves,—
Convent-chanting which the child
Hears pealing from the panther's cave
And the impenetrable wild.

Soft on the South-wind sleeps the haze:
So on thy broad mystic van
Lie the opal-colored days,
And waft the miracle to man.
Soothsayer of the eldest gods,
Repairer of what harms betide,
Revealer of the inmost powers
Prometheus proffered, Jove denied;
Disclosing treasures more than true,
Or in what far tomorrow due;
Speaking by the tongues of flowers,
By the ten-tongued laurel speaking,
Singing by the oriole songs,
Heart of bird the man's heart seeking;
Whispering hints of treasure hid
Under Morn's unlifted lid,
Islands looming just beyond
The dim horizon's utmost bound;—
Who can, like thee, our rags upbraid,
Or taunt us with our hope decayed?
Or who like thee persuade,
Making the splendor of the air,
The morn and sparkling dew, a snare?
Or who resent
Thy genius, wiles, and blandishment?

There is no orator prevails
To beckon or persuade
Like thee the youth or maid:
Thy birds, thy songs, thy brooks, thy gales,
Thy blooms, thy kinds,
Thy echoes in the wilderness,
Soothe pain, and age, and love's distress,
Fire fainting will, and build heroic minds.

For thou, O Spring! canst renovate
All that high God did first create.
Be still his arm and architect,
Rebuild the ruin, mend defect;
Chemist to vamp old worlds with new,
Coat sea and sky with heavenlier blue,
New tint the plumage of the birds,
And slough decay from grazing herds,
Sweep ruins from the scarped mountain,
Cleanse the torrent at the fountain,
Purge alpine air by towns defiled,
Bring to fair mother fairer child,
Not less renew the heart and brain,
Scatter the sloth, wash out the stain,
Make the aged eye sun-clear,
To parting soul bring grandeur near.
Under gentle types, my Spring
Masks the might of Nature's king,
An energy that searches thorough
From Chaos to the dawning morrow;
Into all our human plight,
The soul's pilgrimage and flight;
In city or in solitude,
Step by step, lifts bad to good,
Without halting, without rest,
Lifting Better up to Best;
Planting seeds of knowledge pure,
Through earth to ripen, through heaven endure.

1845–67 1867

TERMINUS

It is time to be old,
To take in sail:—
The god of bounds,
Who sets to seas a shore,
Came to me in his fatal rounds,
And said: "No more!
No farther shoot
Thy broad ambitious branches, and thy root.
Fancy departs: no more invent;
Contract thy firmament
To compass of a tent.
There's not enough for this and that,
Make thy option which of two;
Economize the failing river,
Not the less revere the Giver,
Leave the many and hold the few.
Timely wise accept the terms,
Soften the fall with wary foot;

A little while
Still plan and smile,
And,—fault of novel germs,—
Mature the unfallen fruit.
Curse, if thou wilt, thy sires,
Bad husbands of their fires,
Who, when they gave thee breath,
Failed to bequeath
The needful sinew stark as once,
The Baresark marrow to thy bones,
But left a legacy of ebbing veins,
Inconstant heat and nerveless reins,—
Amid the Muses, left thee deaf and dumb,
Amid the gladiators, halt and numb."

As the bird trims her to the gale,
I trim myself to the storm of time,
I man the rudder, reef the sail,
Obey the voice at eve obeyed at prime:
"Lowly faithful, banish fear,
Right onward drive unharmed;
The port, well worth the cruise, is near,
And every wave is charmed."

1867

THE POET

A moody child and wildly wise
Pursued the game with joyful eyes,
Which chose, like meteors, their way,
And rived the dark with private ray:
They overleapt the horizon's edge,
Searched with Apollo's privilege;
Through man, and woman, and sea, and star
Saw the dance of nature forward far;
Through worlds, and races, and terms, and times
Saw musical order, and pairing rhymes.

Olympian bards who sung
Divine ideas below,
Which always find us young,
And always keep us so.

Those who are esteemed umpires of taste are often persons who have acquired some knowledge of admired pictures or sculptures, and have an inclination for whatever is elegant; but if you inquire whether they are beautiful souls, and whether their own acts are like fair pictures, you learn that they are selfish and sensual. Their cultivation is local, as if you should rub a log of dry wood in one spot to produce fire, all the rest remaining cold. Their knowledge of the fine arts is some study of rules and particulars, or some limited judgment of color or form, which is exercised for amusement or for show. It is a proof of the shallowness of the doctrine of beauty as it lies in the minds of our amateurs, that men seem to have lost the perception of the instant dependence of form upon soul. There is no doctrine of forms in our philosophy. We were put into our bodies, as fire is put into a pan to be carried about; but there is no accurate adjustment between the spirit and the organ, much less is the latter the germination of the former. So in regard to other forms, the intellectual men do not believe in any essential dependence of the material world on thought and volition. Theologians think it a pretty air-castle to talk of the spiritual meaning of a ship or a cloud, of a city or a contract, but they prefer to come again to the solid ground of historical evidence; and even the poets are contented with a civil and conformed manner of living, and to write poems from the fancy, at a safe distance from their own experience. But the highest minds of the world have never ceased to explore the double meaning, or shall I say the quadruple or the centuple or much more manifold meaning, of every sensuous fact; Orpheus, Empedocles, Heraclitus, Plato, Plutarch, Dante, Swedenborg, and the masters of sculpture, picture, and poetry. For we are not pans and barrows, nor even porters of the fire and torch-bearers, but children of the fire, made of it, and only the same divinity transmuted and at two or three removes, when we know least about it. And this hidden truth, that the fountains whence all this river of Time and its creatures floweth are intrinsically ideal and beautiful, draws us to the consideration of the nature and functions of the Poet, or the man of Beauty; to the means and materials he uses, and to the general aspect of the art in the present time.

The breadth of the problem is great, for the poet is representative. He stands among partial men for the complete man, and apprises us not of his wealth, but of the common wealth. The young man reveres men of genius, because, to speak truly, they are more himself than he is. They receive of the soul as he also receives, but they more. Nature enhances her beauty, to the eye of loving men, from their belief that the poet is beholding her shows at the same time. He is isolated among his contemporaries by truth and by his art, but with this consolation in his pursuits, that they will draw all men sooner or later. For all men live by truth and stand in need of expression. In love, in art, in avarice, in politics, in labor, in games, we study to utter our painful secret. The man is only half himself, the other half is his expression.

Notwithstanding this necessity to be published, adequate expression is rare. I know not how it is that we need an interpreter, but the great majority of men seem to be minors, who have not yet come into possession of their own, or mutes, who cannot report the conversation they have had with nature. There is no man who does not anticipate a supersensual utility in the sun and stars, earth and water. These stand and wait to render him a peculiar service. But there is some obstruction or some excess of phlegm in our constitution, which does not suffer them to yield the due effect. Too feeble fall the impressions of nature on us to make us artists. Every touch should thrill. Every man should be so much an artist that he could report in conversation what had befallen him. Yet, in our experience, the rays or appulses have sufficient force to arrive at the senses, but not enough to reach the quick and compel the reproduction of themselves in speech. The poet is the person in whom these powers are in balance, the man without impediment, who sees and handles that which others dream of, traverses the whole scale of experience, and is representative of man, in virtue of being the largest power to receive and to impart.

For the Universe has three children, born at one time, which reappear under different names, in every system of thought, whether they be called cause, operation, and effect; or, more poetically, Jove, Pluto, Neptune; or, theologically, the Father, the Spirit, and the Son; but which we will call here the Knower, the Doer, and the Sayer. These stand respectively for the love of truth, for the love of good, and for the love of beauty. These three are equal. Each is that which he is, essentially, so that he cannot be surmounted or analyzed, and each of these three has the power of the others latent in him and his own, patent.

The poet is the sayer, the namer, and represents beauty. He is a sovereign, and stands on the centre. For the world is not painted or adorned, but is from the beginning beautiful; and God has not made some beautiful things, but Beauty is the creator of the universe. Therefore the poet is not any permissive potentate, but is emperor in his own right. Criticism is infested with a cant of materialism, which assumes that manual skill and activity is the first merit of all men, and disparages such as say and do not, overlooking the fact that some men, namely poets, are natural sayers, sent into the world to the end of expression, and confounds them with those whose province is action but who quit it to imitate the sayers. But Homer's words are as costly and admirable to Homer as Agamemnon's victories are to Agamemnon. The poet does not wait for the hero or the sage, but, as they act and think primarily, so he writes primarily what will and must be spoken, reckoning the others, though primaries also, yet, in respect to him, secondaries and servants; as sitters or models in the studio of a painter, or as assistants who bring building-materials to an architect.

For poetry was all written before time was, and whenever we are so finely organized that we can penetrate into that region where the air is music, we hear those primal warblings and attempt to write them down, but we lose ever and anon a word or a verse and substitute something of our own, and thus miswrite the poem. The men of more delicate ear write down these cadences more faithfully, and these transcripts, though imperfect, become the songs of the nations. For nature is as truly beautiful as it is good, or as it is reasonable, and must as much appear as it must be done, or be known. Words and deeds are quite indifferent modes of the divine energy. Words are also actions, and actions are a kind of words.

The sign and credentials of the poet are that he announces that which no man foretold. He is the true and only doctor; he knows and tells; he is the only teller of news, for he was present and privy to the appearance which he describes. He is a beholder of ideas and an utterer of the necessary and causal. For we do not speak now of men of poetical talents, or of industry and skill in metre, but of the true poet. I took part in a conversation the other day concerning a recent writer of lyrics, a man of subtle mind, whose head appeared to be a music-box of delicate tunes and rhythms, and whose skill and command of language we could not sufficiently praise. But when the question arose whether he was not only a lyrist but a poet, we were obliged to confess that he is plainly a contemporary, not an eternal man. He does not stand out of our low limitations, like a Chimborazo under the line, running up from a torrid base through all the climates of the globe, with belts of the herbage of every latitude on its high and mottled sides; but this genius is the landscape-garden of a modern house, adorned with fountains and statues, with well-bred men and women standing and sitting in the walks and terraces. We hear, through all the varied music, the ground-tone of conventional life. Our poets are men of talents who sing, and not the children of music. The argument is secondary, the finish of the verse is primary.

For it is not metres, but a metre-making argument that makes a poem—a thought so passionate and alive that like the spirit of a plant or an animal it has an architecture of its own, and adorns nature with a new thing. The thought and the form are equal in the order of time, but in the order of genesis the thought is prior to the form. The poet has a new thought; he has a whole new experience to unfold; he will tell us how it was with him, and all men will be the richer in his fortune. For the experience of each new age requires a new confession, and the world seems always waiting for its poet. I remember when I was young how much I was moved one morning by tidings that genius had appeared in a youth who sat near me at table. He had left his work and gone rambling none knew whither, and had written hundreds of lines, but could not tell whether that which was in him was therein told; he could tell nothing but that all was changed,—man, beast, heaven, earth, and sea. How gladly we listened! how credulous! Society seemed to be compromised. We sat in the aurora of a sunrise which was to put out all the stars. Boston seemed to be at twice the distance it had the night before, or was much farther than that. Rome—what was Rome? Plutarch and Shakespeare were in the yellow leaf, and Homer no more should be heard of. It is much to know that poetry has been written this very day, under this very roof, by your side. What! that wonderful spirit has not expired! These stony moments are still sparkling and animated! I had fancied that the oracles were all silent, and nature had spent her fires; and behold! all night, from every pore, these fine auroras have been streaming. Every one has some interest in the advent of the poet, and no one knows how much it may concern him. We know that the secret of the world is profound, but who or what shall be our interpreter, we know not. A mountain ramble, a new style of face, a new person, may put the key into our hands. Of course the value of genius to us is in the veracity of its report. Talent may frolic and juggle; genius realizes and adds. Mankind, in good earnest, have availed so far in understanding themselves and their work, that the foremost watchman on the peak announces his news. It is the truest word ever spoken, and the phrase will be the fittest, most musical, and the unerring voice of the world for that time.

All that we call sacred history attests that the birth of a poet is the principal event in chronology. Man, never so often deceived, still watches for the arrival of a brother who can hold him steady to a truth, until he has made it his own. With what joy I begin to read a poem, which I confide in as an inspiration! And now my chains are to be broken; I shall mount above these clouds and opaque airs in which I live,—opaque, though they seem transparent,—and from the heaven of truth I shall see and comprehend my relations. That will reconcile me to life and renovate nature, to see trifles animated by a tendency, and to know what I am doing. Life will no more be a noise; now I shall see men and women, and know the signs by which they may be discerned from fools and satans. This day shall be better than my birthday: then I became an animal; now I am invited into the science of the real. Such is the hope, but the fruition is postponed. Oftener it falls that this winged man, who will carry me into the heaven, whirls me into mists, then leaps and frisks about with me as it were from cloud to cloud, still affirming that he is bound heavenward; and I, being myself a novice, am slow in perceiving that he does not know the way into the heavens, and is merely bent that I should admire his skill to rise like a fowl or a flying fish, a little way from the ground or the water; but the all-piercing, all-feeding, and ocular air of heaven that man shall never inhabit. I tumble down again soon into my old nooks, and lead the life of exaggerations as before, and have lost my faith in the possibility of any guide who can lead me thither where I would be.

But, leaving these victims of vanity, let us, with new hope, observe how nature, by worthier impulses, has insured the poet's fidelity to his office of announcement and affirming, namely by the beauty of things, which becomes a new and higher beauty when expressed. Nature offers all her creatures to him as a picture-language. Being used as a type, a second wonderful value appears in the object, far better than its old value; as the carpenter's stretched cord, if you hold your ear close enough, is musical in the breeze. "Things more excellent than every image," says Jamblichus, "are expressed through images." Things admit of being used as symbols, because nature is a symbol, in the whole, and in every part. Every line we can draw in the sand has expression; and there is no body without its spirit or genius. All form is an effect of character; all condition, of the quality of the life; all harmony, of health; and for this reason a perception of beauty should be sympathetic, or proper only to the good. The beautiful rests on the foundations of the necessary. The soul makes the body, as the wise Spenser teaches:—

"So every spirit, as it is more pure,
And hath in it the more of heavenly light,
So it the fairer body doth procure
To habit in, and it more fairly dight,
With cheerful grace and amiable sight.
For, of the soul, the body form doth take,
For soul is form, and doth the body make."

Here we find ourselves suddenly not in a critical speculation but in a holy place, and should go very warily and reverently. We stand before the secret of the world, there where Being passes into Appearance and Unity into Variety.

The Universe is the externization of the soul. Wherever the life is, that bursts into appearance around it. Our science is sensual, and therefore superficial. The earth and the heavenly bodies, physics and chemistry, we sensually treat, as if they were self-existent; but these are the retinue of that Being we have. "The mighty heaven," said Proclus, "exhibits, in its transfigurations, clear images of the splendor of intellectual perceptions; being moved in conjunction with the unapparent periods of intellectual natures." Therefore science always goes abreast with the just elevation of the man, keeping step with religion and metaphysics; or the state of science is an index of our self-knowledge. Since every thing in nature answers to a moral power, if any phenomenon remains brute and dark it is because the corresponding faculty in the observer is not yet active.

No wonder then, if these waters be so deep, that we hover over them with a religious regard. The beauty of the fable proves the importance of the sense; to the poet, and to all others; or, if you please, every man is so far a poet as to be susceptible of these enchantments of nature; for all men have the thoughts whereof the universe is the celebration. I find that the fascination resides in the symbol. Who loves nature? Who does not? Is it only poets, and men of leisure and cultivation, who live with her? No; but also hunters, farmers, grooms, and butchers, though they express their affection in their choice of life, and not in their choice of words. The writer wonders what the coachman or the hunter values in riding, in horses and dogs. It is not superficial qualities. When you talk with him, he holds these at as slight a rate as you. His worship is sympathetic; he has no definitions, but he is commanded in nature by the living power which he feels to be there present. No imitation or playing of these things would content him; he loves the earnest of the north wind, of rain, of stone and wood and iron. A beauty not explicable is dearer than a beauty which we can see to the end of. It is nature the symbol, nature certifying the supernatural, body overflowed by life which he worships with coarse but sincere rites.

The inwardness and mystery of this attachment drive men of every class to the use of emblems. The schools of poets and philosophers are not more intoxicated with their symbols than the populace with theirs. In our political parties, compute the power of badges and emblems. See the great ball which they roll from Baltimore to Bunker Hill! In the political processions, Lowell goes in a loom, and Lynn in a shoe, and Salem in a ship. Witness the cider-barrel, the log-cabin, the hickory-stick, the palmetto, and all the cognizances of party. See the power of national emblems. Some stars, lilies, leopards, a crescent, a lion, an eagle, or other figure which came into credit God knows how, on an old rag of bunting, blowing in the wind on a fort at the ends of the earth, shall make the blood tingle under the rudest or the most conventional exterior. The people fancy they hate poetry, and they are all poets and mystics!

Beyond this universality of the symbolic language, we are apprised of the divineness of this superior use of things, whereby the world is a temple whose walls are covered with emblems, pictures, and commandments of the Deity,—in this, that there is no fact in nature which does not carry the whole sense of nature; and the distinctions which we make in events, and in affairs, of low and high, honest and base, disappear when nature is used as a symbol. Thought makes everything fit for use. The vocabulary of an omniscient man would embrace words and images excluded from polite conversation. What would be base, or even obscene, to the obscene, becomes illustrious, spoken in a new connection of thought. The piety of the Hebrew prophets purges their grossness. The circumcision is an example of the power of poetry to raise the low and offensive. Small and mean things serve as well as great symbols. The meaner the type by which a law is expressed, the more pungent it is, and the more lasting in the memories of men; just as we choose the smallest box or case in which any needful utensil can be carried. Bare lists of words are found suggestive to an imaginative and excited mind; as it is related of Lord Chatham that he was accustomed to read in Bailey's Dictionary when he was preparing to speak in Parliament. The poorest experience is rich enough for all the purposes of expressing thought. Why covet a knowledge of new facts? Day and night, house and garden, a few books, a few actions, serve us as well as would all trades and all spectacles. We are far from having exhausted the significance of the few symbols we use. We can come to use them yet with a terrible simplicity. It does not need that a poem should be long. Every word was once a poem. Every new relation is a new word. Also we use defects and deformities to a sacred purpose, so expressing our sense that the evils of the world are such only to the evil eye. In the old mythology, mythologists observe, defects are ascribed to divine natures, as lameness to Vulcan, blindness to Cupid, and the like,—to signify exuberances.

For as it is dislocation and detachment from the life of God that makes things ugly, the poet, who re-attaches things to nature and the Whole,—re-attaching even artificial things, and violations of nature, to nature, by a deeper insight,—disposes very easily of the most disagreeable facts. Readers of poetry see the factory-village and the railway, and fancy that the poetry of the landscape is broken up by these; for these works of art are not yet consecrated in their reading; but the poet sees them fall within the great Order not less than the beehive or the spider's geometrical web. Nature adopts them very fast into her vital circles, and the gliding train of cars she loves like her own. Besides, in a centred mind, it signifies nothing how many mechanical inventions you exhibit. Though you add millions, and never so surprising, the fact of mechanics has not gained a grain's weight. The spiritual fact remains unalterable by many or by few particulars; as no mountain is of any appreciable height to break the curve of the sphere. A shrewd country-boy goes to the city for the first time, and the complacent citizen is not satisfied with his little wonder. It is not that he does not see all the fine houses and know that he never saw such before, but he disposes of them as easily as the poet finds place for the railway. The chief value of the new fact is to enhance the great and constant fact of Life, which can dwarf any and every circumstance, and to which the belt of wampum and the commerce of America are alike.

The world being thus put under the mind for verb and noun, the poet is he who can articulate it. For, though life is great, and fascinates and absorbs; and though all men are intelligent of the symbols through which it is named; yet they cannot originally use them. We are symbols and inhabit symbols; workmen, work, and tools, words and things, birth and death, all are emblems; but we sympathize with the symbols, and being infatuated with the economical uses of things, we do not know that they are thoughts. The poet, by an ulterior intellectual perception, gives them a power which makes their old use forgotten, and puts eyes and a tongue into every dumb and inanimate object. He perceives the independence of the thought on the symbol, the stability of the thought, the accidency and fugacity of the symbol. As the eyes of Lyncæus were said to see through the earth, so the poet turns the world to glass, and shows us all things in their right series and procession. For through that better perception he stands one step nearer to things, and sees the flowing or metamorphosis; perceives that thought is multiform; that within the form of every creature is a force impelling it to ascend into a higher form; and following with his eyes the life, uses the forms which express that life, and so his speech flows with the flowing of nature. All the facts of the animal economy, sex, nutriment, gestation, birth, growth, are symbols of the passage of the world into the soul of man, to suffer there a change and reappear a new and higher fact. He uses forms according to the life, and not according to the form. This is true science. The poet alone knows astronomy, chemistry, vegetation, and animation, for he does not stop at these facts, but employs them as signs. He knows why the plain or meadow of space was strown with these flowers we call suns and moons and stars; why the great deep is adorned with animals, with men, and gods; for in every word he speaks he rides on them as the horses of thought.

By virtue of this science the poet is the Namer, or Language-maker, naming things sometimes after their appearance, sometimes after their essence, and giving to every one its own name and not another's, thereby rejoicing the intellect, which delights in detachment or boundary. The poets made all the words, and therefore language is the archives of history, and, if we must say it, a sort of tomb of the muses. For though the origin of most of our words is forgotten, each word was at first a stroke of genius, and obtained currency because for the moment it symbolized the world to the first speaker and to the hearer. The etymologist finds the deadest word to have been once a brilliant picture. Language is fossil poetry. As the limestone of the continent consists of infinite masses of the shells of animalcules, so language is made up of images or tropes, which now, in their secondary use, have long ceased to remind us of their poetic origin. But the poet names the thing because he sees it, or comes one step nearer to it than any other. This expression or naming is not art, but a second nature, grown out of the first, as a leaf out of a tree. What we call nature is a certain self-regulated motion or change; and nature does all things by her own hands, and does not leave another to baptize her but baptizes herself; and this through the metamorphosis again. I remember that a certain poet described it to me thus:—

Genius is the activity which repairs the decays of things, whether wholly or partly of a material and finite kind. Nature, through all her kingdoms, insures herself. Nobody cares for planting the poor fungus; so she shakes down from the gills of one agaric countless spores, any one of which, being preserved, transmits new billions of spores to-morrow or next day. The new agaric of this hour has a chance which the old one had not. This atom of seed is thrown into a new place, not subject to the accidents which destroyed its parent two rods off. She makes a man; and having brought him to ripe age, she will no longer run the risk of losing this wonder at a blow, but she detaches from him a new self, that the kind may be safe from accidents to which the individual is exposed. So when the soul of the poet has come to ripeness of thought, she detaches and sends away from it its poems or songs,—a fearless, sleepless, deathless progeny, which is not exposed to the accidents of the weary kingdom of time; a fearless, vivacious offspring, clad with wings (such was the virtue of the soul out of which they came), which carry them fast and far, and infix them irrecoverably into the hearts of men. These wings are the beauty of the poet's soul. The songs, thus flying immortal from their mortal parent, are pursued by clamorous flights of censures, which swarm in far greater numbers and threaten to devour them; but these last are not winged. At the end of a very short leap they fall plump down and rot, having received from the souls out of which they came no beautiful wings. But the melodies of the poet ascend and leap and pierce into the deeps of infinite time.

So far the bard taught me, using his freer speech. But nature has a higher end, in the production of new individuals, than security, namely *ascension*, or the passage of the soul into higher forms. I knew in my younger days the sculptor who made the statue of the youth which stands in the public garden. He was, as I remember, unable to tell directly what made him happy or unhappy, but by wonderful indirections he could tell. He rose one day, according to his habit, before the dawn, and saw the morning break, grand as the eternity out of which it came, and for many days after, he strove to express this tranquillity, and lo! his chisel had fashioned out of marble the form of a beautiful youth, Phosphorus, whose aspect is such that it is said all persons who look on it become silent. The poet also resigns himself to his mood, and that thought which agitated him is expressed, but *alter idem*, in a manner totally new. The expression is organic, or the new type which things themselves take when liberated. As, in the sun, objects paint their images on the retina of the eye, so they, sharing the aspiration of the whole universe, tend to paint a far more delicate copy of their essence in his mind. Like the metamorphosis of things into higher organic forms is their change into melodies. Over everything stands its dæmon or soul, and, as the form of the thing is reflected by the eye, so the soul of the thing is reflected by a melody. The sea, the mountain-ridge, Niagara, and every flower-bed, pre-exist, or super-exist, in pre-cantations, which sail like odors in the air, and when any man goes by with an ear sufficiently fine, he overhears them and endeavors to write down the notes without diluting or depraving them. And herein is the legitimation of criticism, in the mind's faith that the poems are a corrupt version of some text in nature with which they ought to be made to tally. A rhyme in one of our sonnets should not be less pleasing than the iterated nodes of a seashell, or the resembling difference of a group of flowers. The pairing of the birds is an idyl, not tedious as our idyls are; a tempest is a rough ode, without falsehood or rant; a summer, with its harvest sown, reaped, and stored, is an epic song, subordinating how many admirably executed parts. Why should not the symmetry and truth that modulate these, glide into our spirits, and we participate the invention of nature?

This insight, which expresses itself by what is called Imagination, is a very high sort of seeing, which does not come by study, but by the intellect being where and what it sees; by sharing the path or circuit of things through forms, and so making them translucid to others. The path of things is silent. Will they suffer a speaker to go with them? A spy they will not suffer; a lover, a poet, is the transcendency of their own nature,—him they will suffer. The condition of true naming, on the poet's part, is his resigning himself to the divine *aura* which breathes through forms, and accompanying that.

It is a secret which every intellectual man quickly learns, that beyond the energy of his possessed and conscious intellect, he is capable of a new energy (as of an intellect doubled on itself), by abandonment to the nature of things; that beside his privacy of power as an individual man, there is a great public power on which he can draw, by unlocking, at all risks, his human doors, and suffering the ethereal tides to roll and circulate through him; then he is caught up into the life of the Universe, his speech is thunder, his thought is law, and his words are universally intelligible as the plants and animals. The poet knows that he speaks adequately then only when he speaks somewhat wildly, or "with the flower of the mind;" not with the intellect used as an organ, but with the intellect released from all service and suffered to take its direction from its celestial life; or as the ancients were wont to express themselves, not with intellect alone but with the intellect inebriated by nectar. As the traveller who has lost his way throws his reins on his horse's neck and trusts to the instinct of the animal to find his road, so must we do with the divine animal who carries us through this world. For if in any manner we can stimulate this instinct, new passages are opened for us into nature; the mind flows into and through things hardest and highest, and the metamorphosis is possible.

This is the reason why bards love wine, mead, narcotics, coffee, tea, opium, the fumes of sandalwood and tobacco, or whatever other procurers of animal exhilaration. All men avail themselves of such means as they can, to add this extraordinary power to their normal powers; and to this end they prize conversation, music, pictures, sculpture, dancing, theatres, travelling, war, mobs, fires, gaming, politics, or love, or science, or animal intoxication,—which are several coarser or finer *quasi*-mechanical substitutes for the true nectar, which is the ravishment of the intellect by coming nearer to the fact. These are auxiliaries to the centrifugal tendency of a man, to his passage out into free space, and they help him to escape the custody of that body in which he is pent up, and of that jail-yard of individual relations in which he is enclosed. Hence a great number of such as were professionally expressers of Beauty, as painters, poets, musicians, and actors, have been more than others wont to lead a life of pleasure and indulgence; all but the few who received the true nectar; and, as it was a spurious mode of attaining freedom, as it was an emancipation not into the heavens but into the freedom of baser places, they were punished for that advantage they won, by a dissipation and deterioration. But never can any advantage be taken of nature by a trick. The spirit of the world, the great calm presence of the Creator, comes not forth to the sorceries of opium or of wine. The sublime vision comes to the pure and simple soul in a clean and chaste body. That is not an inspiration, which we owe to narcotics, but some counterfeit excitement and fury. Milton says that the lyric poet may drink wine and live generously, but the epic poet, he who shall sing of the gods and their descent unto men, must drink water out of a wooden bowl. For poetry is not "Devil's wine," but God's wine. It is with this as it is with toys. We fill the hands and nurseries of our children with all manner of dolls, drums, and horses; withdrawing their eyes from the plain face and sufficing objects of nature, the sun and moon, the animals, the water and stones, which should be their toys. So the poet's habit of living should be set on a key so low that the common influences should delight him. His cheerfulness should be the gift of the sunlight; the air should suffice for his inspiration, and he should be tipsy with water. That spirit which suffices quiet hearts, which seems to come forth to such from every dry knoll of sere grass, from every pine stump and half-imbedded stone on which the dull March sun shines, comes forth to the poor and hungry, and such as are of simple taste. If thou fill thy brain with Boston and New York, with fashion and covetousness, and wilt stimulate thy jaded senses with wine and French coffee, thou shalt find no radiance of wisdom in the lonely waste of the pine woods.

If the imagination intoxicates the poet, it is not inactive in other men. The metamorphosis excites in the beholder an emotion of joy. The use of symbols has a certain power of emancipation and exhilaration for all men. We seem to be touched by a wand which makes us dance and run about happily, like children. We are like persons who come out of a cave or cellar into the open air. This is the effect on us of tropes, fables, oracles, and all poetic forms. Poets are thus liberating gods. Men have really got a new sense, and found within their world another world, or nest of worlds; for, the metamorphosis once seen, we divine that it does not stop. I will not now consider how much this makes the charm of algebra and the mathematics, which also have their tropes, but it is felt in every definition; as when Aristotle defines *space* to be an immovable vessel in which things are contained;—

or when Plato defines a *line* to be a flowing point; or *figure* to be a bound of solid; and many the like. What a joyful sense of freedom we have when Vitruvius announces the old opinion of artists that no architect can build any house well who does not know something of anatomy. When Socrates, in Charmides, tells us that the soul is cured of its maladies by certain incantations, and that these incantations are beautiful reasons, from which temperance is generated in souls; when Plato calls the world an animal, and Timæus affirms that the plants also are animals; or affirms a man to be a heavenly tree, growing with his root, which is his head, upward; and, as George Chapman, following him, writes—

> "So in our tree of man, whose nervie root
> Springs in his top;"—

when Orpheus speaks of hoariness as "that white flower which marks extreme old age;" when Proclus calls the universe the statue of the intellect; when Chaucer, in his praise of "Gentilesse," compares good blood in mean condition to fire, which, though carried to the darkest house betwixt this and the mount of Caucasus, will yet hold its natural office and burn as bright as if twenty thousand men did it behold; when John saw, in the Apocalypse, the ruin of the world through evil, and the stars fall from heaven, as the figtree casteth her untimely fruit; when Æsop reports the whole catalogue of common daily relations through the masquerade of birds and beasts;—we take the cheerful hint of the immortality of our essence and its versatile habit and escapes, as when the gypsies say of themselves, "it is in vain to hang them, they cannot die."

The poets are thus liberating gods. The ancient British bards had for the title of their order, "Those who are free throughout the world." They are free, and they make free. An imaginative book renders us much more service at first, by stimulating us through its tropes, than afterward when we arrive at the precise sense of the author. I think nothing is of any value in books excepting the transcendental and extraordinary. If a man is inflamed and carried away by his thought, to that degree that he forgets the authors and the public and heeds only this one dream which holds him like an insanity, let me read his paper, and you may have all the arguments and histories and criticism. All the value which attaches to Pythagoras, Paracelsus, Cornelius Agrippa, Cardan, Kepler, Swedenborg, Schelling, Oken, or any other who introduces questionable facts into his cosmogony, as angels, devils, magic, astrology, palmistry, mesmerism, and so on, is the certificate we have of departure from routine, and that here is a new witness. That also is the best success in conversation, the magic of liberty, which puts the world like a ball in our hands. How cheap even the liberty then seems; how mean to study, when an emotion communicates to the intellect the power to sap and upheave nature: how great the perspective! nations, times, systems, enter and disappear like threads in tapestry of large figure and many colors; dream delivers us to dream, and while the drunkenness lasts we will sell our bed, our philosophy, our religion, in our opulence.

There is good reason why we should prize this liberation. The fate of the poor shepherd, who, blinded and lost in the snowstorm, perishes in a drift within a few feet of his cottage door, is an emblem of the state of man. On the brink of the waters of life and truth, we are miserably dying. The inaccessibleness of every thought but that we are in, is wonderful. What if you come near to it; you are as remote when you are nearest as when you are farthest. Every thought is also a prison; every heaven is also a prison. Therefore we love the poet, the inventor, who in any form, whether in an ode or in an action or in looks and behavior, has yielded us a new thought. He unlocks our chains and admits us to a new scene.

This emancipation is dear to all men, and the power to impart it, as it must come from greater depth and scope of thought, is a measure of intellect. Therefore all books of the imagination endure, all which ascend to that truth that the writer sees nature beneath him, and uses it as his exponent. Every verse or sentence possessing this virtue will take care of its own immortality. The religions of the world are the ejaculations of a few imaginative men.

But the quality of the imagination is to flow,

and not to freeze. The poet did not stop at the color, or the form, but read their meaning; neither may he rest in this meaning, but he makes the same objects exponents of his new thought. Here is the difference betwixt the poet and the mystic, that the last nails a symbol to one sense, which was a true sense for a moment, but soon becomes old and false. For all symbols are fluxional; all language is vehicular and transitive, and is good, as ferries and horses are, for conveyance, not as farms and houses are, for homestead. Mysticism consists in the mistake of an accidental and individual symbol for an universal one. The morning-redness happens to be the favorite meteor to the eyes of Jacob Behmen, and comes to stand to him for truth and faith; and, he believes, should stand for the same realities to every reader. But the first reader prefers as naturally the symbol of a mother and child, or a gardener and his bulb, or a jeweller polishing a gem. Either of these, or of a myriad more, are equally good to the person to whom they are significant. Only they must be held lightly, and be very willingly translated into the equivalent terms which others use. And the mystic must be steadily told,—All that you say is just as true without the tedious use of that symbol as with it. Let us have a little algebra, instead of this trite rhetoric,—universal signs, instead of these village symbols,—and we shall both be gainers. The history of hierarchies seems to show that all religious error consisted in making the symbol too stark and solid, and was at last, nothing but an excess of the organ of language.

Swedenborg, of all men in the recent ages, stands eminently for the translator of nature into thought. I do not know the man in history to whom things stood so uniformly for words. Before him the metamorphosis continually plays. Everything on which his eye rests, obeys the impulses of moral nature. The figs become grapes whilst he eats them. When some of his angels affirmed a truth, the laurel twig which they held blossomed in their hands. The noise which at a distance appeared like gnashing and thumping, on coming nearer was found to be the voice of disputants. The men in one of his visions, seen in heavenly light, appeared like dragons, and seemed in darkness; but to each other they appeared as men, and when the light from heaven shone into their cabin, they complained of the darkness, and were compelled to shut the window that they might see.

There was this perception in him which makes the poet or seer an object of awe and terror, namely that the same man or society of men may wear one aspect to themselves and their companions, and a different aspect to higher intelligences. Certain priests, whom he describes as conversing very learnedly together, appeared to the children, who were at some distance, like dead horses; and many the like misappearances. And instantly the mind inquires whether these fishes under the bridge, yonder oxen in the pasture, those dogs in the yard, are immutably fishes, oxen, and dogs, or only so appear to me, and perchance to themselves appear upright men; and whether I appear as a man to all eyes. The Brahmins and Pythagoras propounded the same question, and if any poet has witnessed the transformation he doubtless found it in harmony with various experiences. We have all seen changes as considerable in wheat and caterpillars. He is the poet and shall draw us with love and terror, who sees through the flowing vest the firm nature, and can declare it.

I look in vain for the poet whom I describe. We do not with sufficient plainness or sufficient profoundness address ourselves to life, nor dare we chaunt our own times and social circumstance. If we filled the day with bravery, we should not shrink from celebrating it. Time and nature yield us many gifts, but not yet the timely man, the new religion, the reconciler, whom all things await. Dante's praise is that he dared to write his autobiography in colossal cipher, or into universality. We have yet had no genius in America, with tyrannous eye, which knew the value of our incomparable materials, and saw, in the barbarism and materialism of the times, another carnival of the same gods whose picture he so much admires in Homer; then in the Middle Age; then in Calvinism. Banks and tariffs, the newspaper and caucus, Methodism and Unitarianism, are flat and dull to dull people, but rest on the same foundations of wonder as the town of Troy, and the temple of Delphi, and are as swiftly passing away. Our log-rolling, our stumps and their politics, our fisheries, our Negroes, and Indians, our boats and our repudiations, the wrath of rogues and the pusillanimity of honest men, the northern trade, the southern planting, the western clearing, Oregon, and Texas, are yet unsung. Yet America is a poem in our eyes; its ample geography dazzles the imagination, and it will not wait long for metres. If I have not found that excellent combination of gifts in my countrymen which I seek, neither could I aid myself to fix the idea of the poet by reading now and then in Chalmers's collection of five centuries of English poets. These are wits more than poets, though there have been poets among them. But when we adhere to the ideal of the poet, we have our difficulties even with Milton and Homer. Milton is too literary, and Homer too literal and historical.

But I am not wise enough for a national criticism, and must use the old largeness a little longer, to discharge my errand from the muse to the poet concerning his art.

Art is the path of the creator to his work. The paths or methods are ideal and eternal, though few men ever see them; not the artist himself for years, or for a lifetime, unless he come into the conditions. The painter, the sculptor, the composer, the epic rhapsodist, the orator, all partake one desire, namely to express themselves symmetrically and abundantly, not dwarfishly and fragmentarily. They found or put themselves in certain conditions, as, the painter and sculptor before some impressive human figures; the orator into the assembly of the people; and the others in such scenes as each has found exciting to his intellect; and each presently feels the new desire. He hears a voice, he sees a beckoning. Then he is apprised, with wonder, what herds of dæmons hem him in. He can no more rest; he says, with the old painter, "By God it is in me and must go forth of me." He pursues a beauty, half seen, which flies before him. The poet pours out verses in every solitude. Most of the things he says are conventional, no doubt; but by and by he says something which is original and beautiful. That charms him. He would say nothing else but such things. In our way of talking we say, "That is yours, this is mine;" but the poet knows well that it is not his; that it is as strange and beautiful to him as to you; he would fain hear the like eloquence at length. Once having tasted this immortal ichor, he cannot have enough of it, and as an admirable creative power exists in these intellections, it is of the last importance that these things get spoken. What a little of all we know is said! What drops of all the sea of our science are baled up! and by what accident it is that these are exposed, when so many secrets sleep in nature! Hence the necessity of speech and song; hence these throbs and heart-beatings in the orator, at the door of the assembly, to the end namely that thought may be ejaculated as Logos, or Word.

Doubt not, O poet, but persist. Say, "It is in me, and shall out." Stand there, balked and dumb, stuttering and stammering, hissed and hooted, stand and strive, until at last rage draw out of thee that *dream*-power which every night shows thee is thine own; a power transcending all limit and privacy, and by virtue of which a man is the conductor of the whole river of electricity. Nothing walks, or creeps, or grows, or exists, which must not in turn arise and walk before him as exponent of his meaning. Comes he to that power, his genius is no longer exhaustible. All the creatures by pairs and by tribes pour into his mind as into a Noah's ark, to come forth again to people a new world. This is like the stock of air for our respiration or for the combustion of our fireplace; not a measure of gallons, but the entire atmosphere if wanted. And therefore the rich poets, as Homer, Chaucer, Shakespeare, and Raphael, have obviously no limits to their works except the limits of their lifetime, and resemble a mirror carried through the street, ready to render an image of every created thing.

O poet! a new nobility is conferred in groves and pastures, and not in castles by the sword-blade any longer. The conditions are hard, but equal. Thou shalt leave the world, and know the muse only. Thou shalt not know any longer the times, customs, graces, politics, or opinions of men, but shalt take all from the muse. For the time of towns is tolled from the world by funereal chimes, but in nature the universal hours are counted by succeeding tribes of animals and plants, and by growth of joy on joy. God wills also that thou abdicate a manifold and duplex life, and that thou be content that others speak for thee. Others shall be thy gentlemen, and shall represent all courtesy and worldly life for thee; others shall do the great and resounding actions also. Thou shalt lie close hid with nature, and canst not be afforded to the Capitol or the Exchange. The world is full of renunciations and apprenticeships, and this is thine; thou must pass for a fool and a churl for a long season. This is the screen and sheath in which Pan has protected his well-beloved flower, and thou shalt be known only to thine own, and they shall console thee with tenderest love. And thou shalt not be able to rehearse the names of thy friends in thy verse, for an old shame before the holy ideal. And this is the reward; that the ideal shall be real to thee, and the impressions of the actual world shall fall like summer rain, copious, but not troublesome to thy invulnerable essence. Thou shalt have the whole land for thy park and manor, the sea for thy bath and navigation, without tax and without envy; the woods and the rivers thou shalt own, and thou shalt possess that wherein others are only tenants and boarders. Thou true landlord! sea-lord! air-lord! Wherever snow falls or water flows, or birds fly, wherever day and night meet in twilight, wherever the blue heaven is hung by clouds or sown with stars, wherever are forms with transparent boundaries, wherever are outlets into celestial space, wherever is danger, and awe, and love,—there is Beauty, plenteous as rain, shed for thee, and though thou shouldst walk the world over, thou shalt not be able to find a condition inopportune or ignoble.

1844

EDGAR ALLAN POE

TAMERLANE

KIND solace in a dying hour!
Such, father, is not (now) my theme—
I will not madly deem that power
Of Earth may shrive me of the sin
Unearthly pride hath revell'd in—
I have no time to dote or dream:
You call it hope—that fire of fire!
It is but agony of desire:
If I *can* hope—oh, God! I can—
Its fount is holier—more divine—
I would not call thee fool, old man,
But such is not a gift of thine.

Know thou the secret of a spirit
Bow'd from its wild pride into shame.
O yearning heart! I did inherit
Thy withering portion with the fame,
The searing glory which hath shone
Amid the jewels of my throne,
Halo of Hell! and with a pain
Not Hell shall make me fear again—
O craving heart, for the lost flowers
And sunshine of my summer hours!
The undying voice of that dead time,
With its interminable chime,
Rings, in the spirit of a spell,
Upon thy emptiness—a knell.

I have not always been as now:
The fever'd diadem on my brow
I claim'd and won usurpingly—
Hath not the same fierce heirdom given
Rome to the Cæsar—this to me?
The heritage of a kingly mind,
And a proud spirit which hath striven
Triumphantly with human kind.

On mountain soil I first drew life:
The mists of the Taglay have shed
Nightly their dews upon my head,
And, I believe, the winged strife
And tumult of the headlong air
Have nestled in my very hair.

So late from Heaven—that dew—it fell
('Mid dreams of an unholy night)
Upon me with the touch of Hell,
While the red flashing of the light
From clouds that hung, like banners, o'er,
Appeared to my half-closing eye
The pageantry of monarchy,
And the deep trumpet-thunder's roar
Came hurriedly upon me, telling
Of human battle, where my voice,
My own voice, silly child! was swelling
(O! how my spirit would rejoice,
And leap within me at the cry)
The battle-cry of Victory!

The rain came down upon my head
Unshelter'd—and the heavy wind
Rendered me mad and deaf and blind.
It was but man, I thought, who shed
Laurels upon me: and the rush,
The torrent of the chilly air
Gurgled within my ear the crush
Of empires—with the captive's prayer—
The hum of suitors—and the tone
Of flattery round a sovereign's throne.

My passions, from that hapless hour,
Usurp'd a tyranny which men
Have deem'd, since I have reach'd to power,
My innate nature—be it so:
But, father, there liv'd one who, then,
Then—in my boyhood—when their fire
Burn'd with a still intenser glow
(For passion must, with youth, expire)
E'en *then* who knew this iron heart
In woman's weakness had a part.

I have no words—alas!—to tell
The loveliness of loving well!
Nor would I now attempt to trace
The more than beauty of a face
Whose lineaments, upon my mind,
Are—shadows on th' unstable wind:
Thus I remember having dwelt
Some page of early lore upon,
With loitering eye, till I have felt

The letters—with their meaning—melt
To fantasies—with none.

O, she was worthy of all love!
Love—as in infancy was mine—
'Twas such as angel minds above
Might envy; her young heart the shrine
On which my every hope and thought
Were incense—then a goodly gift,
For they were childish and upright—
Pure—as her young example taught:
Why did I leave it, and, adrift,
Trust to the fire within, for light?

We grew in age—and love—together—
Roaming the forest and the wild;
My breast her shield in wintry weather—
And, when the friendly sunshine smil'd,
And she would mark the opening skies,
I saw no Heaven—but in her eyes.

Young Love's first lesson is—the heart:
For 'mid that sunshine and those smiles,
When, from our little cares apart,
And laughing at her girlish wiles,
I'd throw me on her throbbing breast,
And pour my spirit out in tears—
There was no need to speak the rest—
No need to quiet any fears
Of her—who ask'd no reason why,
But turned on me her quiet eye!

Yet *more* than worthy of the love
My spirit struggled with, and strove,
When, on the mountain peak, alone,
Ambition lent it a new tone—
I had no being—but in thee:
The world, and all it did contain
In the earth—the air—the sea—
Its joy—its little lot of pain
That was new pleasure—the ideal,
Dim, vanities of dreams by night—
And dimmer nothings which were real—
(Shadows—and a more shadowy light!)
Parted upon their misty wings,
And, so, confusedly, became
Thine image and—a name—a name!
Two separate—yet most intimate things.

I was ambitious—have you known
The passion, father? You have not:
A cottager, I mark'd a throne
Of half the world as all my own,
And murmur'd at such lowly lot—
But, just like any other dream,
Upon the vapor of the dew
My own had past, did not the beam
Of beauty which did while it thro'
The minute—the hour—the day—oppress
My mind with double loveliness.

We walk'd together on the crown
Of a high mountain which look'd down
Afar from its proud natural towers
Of rock and forest, on the hills—
The dwindled hills! begirt with bowers
And shouting with a thousand rills.

I spoke to her of power and pride,
But mystically—in such guise
That she might deem it nought beside
The moment's converse; in her eyes
I read, perhaps too carelessly,
A mingled feeling with my own—
The flush on her bright cheek, to me
Seem'd to become a queenly throne
Too well that I should let it be
Light in the wilderness alone.

I wrapp'd myself in grandeur then
And donn'd a visionary crown—
Yet it was not that Fantasy
Had thrown her mantle over me—
But that, among the rabble—men,
Lion ambition is chain'd down—
And crouches to a keeper's hand—
Not so in deserts where the grand—
The wild—the terrible conspire
With their own breath to fan his fire.

Look round thee now on Samarcand!—
Is she not queen of Earth? her pride
Above all cities? in her hand
Their destinies? in all beside
Of glory which the world hath known
Stands she not nobly and alone?
Falling—her veriest stepping-stone
Shall form the pedestal of a throne—
And who her sovereign? Timour—he
Whom the astonished people saw
Striding o'er empires haughtily
A diadem'd outlaw!

O, human love! thou spirit given,
On Earth, of all we hope in Heaven!

Which fall'st into the soul like rain
Upon the Siroc-wither'd plain,
And, failing in thy power to bless,
But leav'st the heart a wilderness!
Idea! which bindest life around
With music of so strange a sound
And beauty of so wild a birth—
Farewell! for I have won the Earth.

When Hope, the eagle that tower'd, could see
No cliff beyond him in the sky,
His pinions were bent droopingly—
And homeward turn'd his soften'd eye.
'Twas sunset: when the sun will part
There comes a sullenness of heart
To him who still would look upon
The glory of the summer sun.
That soul will hate the ev'ning mist
So often lovely, and will list
To the sound of the coming darkness (known
To those whose spirits harken) as one
Who, in a dream of night, *would* fly
But *cannot* from a danger nigh.

What tho' the moon—the white moon—
Shed all the splendor of her noon,
Her smile is chilly—and *her* beam,
In that time of dreariness, will seem
(So like you gather in your breath)
A portrait taken after death.
And boyhood is a summer sun
Whose waning is the dreariest one.
For all we live to know is known,
And all we seek to keep hath flown.
Let life, then, as the day-flower, fall
With the noon-day beauty—which is all.

I reach'd my home—my home no more—
For all had flown who made it so.
I pass'd from out its mossy door,
And, tho' my tread was soft and low,
A voice came from the threshold stone
Of one whom I had earlier known—
O, I defy thee, Hell, to show
On beds of fire that burn below,
An humbler heart—a deeper wo.

Father, I firmly do believe—
I *know*—for Death who comes for me
From regions of the blest afar,
Where there is nothing to deceive,
Hath left his iron gate ajar,
And rays of truth you cannot see
Are flashing thro' Eternity—
I do believe that Eblis hath
A snare in every human path—
Else how, when in the holy grove
I wandered of the idol, Love,
Who daily scents his snowy wings
With incense of burnt offerings
From the most unpolluted things,
Whose pleasant bowers are yet so riven
Above with trellis'd rays from Heaven
No mote may shun—no tiniest fly—
The light'ning of his eagle eye—
How was it that Ambition crept,
Unseen, amid the revels there,
Till growing bold, he laughed and leapt
In the tangles of Love's very hair?

1826 1827

SONG

I SAW thee on thy bridal day,
When a burning blush came o'er thee,
Though happiness around thee lay,
The world all love before thee:

And in thine eye a kindling light
(Whatever it might be)
Was all on Earth my aching sight
Of Loveliness could see.

That blush, perhaps, was maiden shame—
As such it well may pass—
Though its glow hath raised a fiercer flame
In the breast of him, alas!

Who saw thee on that bridal day,
When that deep blush *would* come o'er thee,
Though happiness around thee lay,
The world all love before thee.

1827

SONNET—TO SCIENCE

SCIENCE! true daughter of Old Time thou art!
Who alterest all things with thy peering eyes.
Why preyest thou thus upon the poet's heart,
Vulture, whose wings are dull realities?
How should he love thee? or how deem thee wise,
Who wouldst not leave him in his wandering

To seek for treasure in the jewelled skies,
  Albeit he soared with an undaunted wing?
Hast thou not dragged Diana from her car,
  And driven the Hamadryad from the wood
To seek a shelter in some happier star?
  Hast thou not torn the Naiad from her flood,
The Elfin from the green grass, and from me
The summer dream beneath the tamarind tree?

1829

AL AARAAF

Part I

O! NOTHING earthly save the ray
(Thrown back from flowers) of Beauty's eye,
As in those gardens where the day
Springs from the gems of Circassy—
O! nothing earthly save the thrill
Of melody in woodland rill—
Or (music of the passion-hearted)
Joy's voice so peacefully departed
That, like the murmur in the shell,
Its echo dwelleth and will dwell—
Oh, nothing of the dross of ours—
Yet all the beauty—all the flowers
That list our Love, and deck our bowers—
Adorn yon world afar, afar—
The wandering star.

'Twas a sweet time for Nesace—for there
Her world lay lolling on the golden air,
Near four bright suns—a temporary rest—
An oasis in desert of the blest.
Away—away—'mid seas of rays that roll
Empyrean splendor o'er th' unchained soul—
The soul that scarce (the billows are so dense)
Can struggle to its destin'd eminence—
To distant spheres, from time to time, she rode,
And late to ours, the favor'd one of God—
But, now, the ruler of an anchor'd realm,
She throws aside the sceptre—leaves the helm,
And, amid incense and high spiritual hymns,
Laves in quadruple light her angel limbs.

Now happiest, loveliest in yon lovely Earth,
Whence sprang the "Idea of Beauty" into birth
(Falling in wreaths thro' many a startled star,
Like woman's hair 'mid pearls, until, afar,
It lit on hills Achaian, and there dwelt),
She look'd into Infinity—and knelt.
Rich clouds, for canopies, about her curled—
Fit emblems of the model of her world—
Seen but in beauty—not impeding sight
Of other beauty glittering thro' the light—
A wreath that twined each starry form around,
And all the opal'd air in color bound.

All hurriedly she knelt upon a bed
Of flowers: of lilies such as rear'd the head
On the fair Capo Deucato, and sprang
So eagerly around about to hang
Upon the flying footsteps of—deep pride—
Of her who lov'd a mortal—and so died.
The Sephalica, budding with young bees,
Uprear'd its purple stem around her knees:
And gemmy flower, of Trebizond misnam'd—
Inmate of highest stars, where erst it sham'd
All other loveliness: its honied dew
(The fabled nectar that the heathen knew)
Deliriously sweet, was dropp'd from Heaven,
And fell on gardens of the unforgiven
In Trebizond—and on a sunny flower
So like its own above, that, to this hour,
It still remaineth, torturing the bee
With madness, and unwonted reverie:
In Heaven, and all its environs, the leaf
And blossom of the fairy plant, in grief
Disconsolate linger—grief that hangs her head,
Repenting follies that full long have fled,
Heaving her white breast to the balmy air,
Like guilty beauty, chasten'd, and more fair:
Nyctanthes, too, as sacred as the light
She fears to perfume, perfuming the night:
And Clytia pondering between many a sun,
While pettish tears adown her petals run:
And that aspiring flower that sprang on Earth—
And died, ere scarce exalted into birth,
Bursting its odorous heart in spirit to wing
Its way to Heaven, from garden of a king:
And Valisnerian lotus thither flown
From struggling with the waters of the Rhone:
And thy most lovely purple perfume, Zante!
Isola d'oro!—Fior di Levante!
And the Nelumbo bud that floats for ever
With Indian Cupid down the holy river—
Fair flowers, and fairy! to whose care is given
To bear the Goddess' song, in odors, up to Heaven:

"Spirit! that dwellest where,
In the deep sky,
The terrible and fair,
In beauty vie!
Beyond the line of blue—
The boundary of the star
Which turneth at the view
Of thy barrier and thy bar—
Of the barrier overgone
By the comets who were cast
From their pride and from their throne,
To be drudges till the last—
To be carriers of fire
(The red fire of their heart)
With speed that may not tire
And with pain that shall not part—
Who livest—*that* we know—
In Eternity—we feel—
But the shadow of whose brow
What spirit shall reveal?
Tho' the beings whom thy Nesace,
Thy messenger, hath known,
Have dream'd for thy Infinity
A model of their own—
Thy will is done, oh, God!
The star hath ridden high
Thro' many a tempest, but she rode
Beneath thy burning eye;
And here, in thought, to thee—
In thought that can alone
Ascend thy empire and so be
A partner of thy throne—
By winged Fantasy,
My embassy is given,
Till secrecy shall knowledge be
In the environs of Heaven."

She ceas'd—and buried then her burning cheek
Abash'd, amid the lilies there, to seek
A shelter from the fervour of His eye;
For the stars trembled at the Deity.
She stirr'd not—breath'd not—for a voice was there
How solemnly pervading the calm air!
A sound of silence on the startled ear
Which dreamy poets name "the music of the sphere."
Ours is a world of words: Quiet we call
"Silence"—which is the merest word of all.
All Nature speaks, and ev'n ideal things
Flap shadowy sounds from visionary wings—
But ah! not so when, thus, in realms on high
The eternal voice of God is passing by;
And the red winds are withering in the sky!

"What tho' in worlds which sightless cycles run,
Link'd to a little system and one sun—
Where all my love is folly, and the crowd
Still think my terrors but the thunder cloud,
The storm, the earthquake, and the ocean wrath
(Ah! will they cross me in my angrier path?)—
What tho' in worlds which own a single sun
The sands of Time grow dimmer as they run,
Yet thine is my resplendency, so given
To bear my secrets thro' the upper Heaven.
Leave tenantless thy crystal home, and fly,
With all thy train, athwart the moony sky—
Apart—like fire-flies in Sicilian night,
And wing to other worlds another light!
Divulge the secrets of thy embassy
To the proud orbs that twinkle—and so be
To ev'ry heart a barrier and a ban
Lest the stars totter in the guilt of man!"

Up rose the maiden in the yellow night,
The single-mooned eve!—on Earth we plight
Our faith to one love—and one moon adore—
The birth-place of young Beauty had no more.
As sprang that yellow star from downy hours
Up rose the maiden from her shrine of flowers,
And bent o'er sheeny mountain and dim plain
Her way—but left not yet her Therasæan reign.

Part II

High on a mountain of enamell'd head—
Such as the drowsy shepherd on his bed
Of giant pasturage lying at his ease,
Raising his heavy eyelid, starts and sees
With many a mutter'd "hope to be forgiven,"
What time the moon is quadrated in Heaven—
Of rosy head, that towering far away
Into the sunlit ether, caught the ray
Of sunken suns at eve—at noon of night,
While the moon danc'd with the fair stranger light—
Uprear'd upon such height arose a pile
Of gorgeous columns on th' unburthen'd air,
Flashing from Parian marble that twin smile

Far down upon the wave that sparkled there,
And nursled the young mountain in its lair.
Of molten stars their pavement, such as fall
Thro' the ebon air, besilvering the pall
Of their own dissolution, while they die—
Adorning then the dwellings of the sky.
A dome, by linked light from Heaven let down,
Sat gently on these columns as a crown—
A window of one circular diamond, there,
Look'd out above into the purple air,
And rays from God shot down that meteor chain
And hallow'd all the beauty twice again,
Save when, between th' Empyrean and that ring,
Some eager spirit flapp'd his dusky wing.
But on the pillars Seraph eyes have seen
The dimness of this world: that greyish green
That Nature loves the best for Beauty's grave
Lurk'd in each cornice, round each architrave—
And every sculptur'd cherub thereabout
That from his marble dwelling peeréd out,
Seem'd earthly in the shadow of his niche—
Achaian statues in a world so rich!
Friezes from Tadmor and Persepolis,
From Balbec, and the stilly, clear abyss
Of beautiful Gomorrah! O, the wave
Is now upon thee—but too late to save!

Sound loves to revel in a summer night:
Witness the murmur of the grey twilight
That stole upon the ear, in Eyraco,
Of many a wild star gazer long ago—
That stealeth ever on the ear of him
Who, musing, gazeth on the distance dim,
And sees the darkness coming as a cloud—
Is not its form—its voice—most palpable and loud?

But what is this?—it cometh—and it brings
A music with it—'tis the rush of wings—
A pause—and then a sweeping, falling strain,
And Nesace is in her halls again.
From the wild energy of wanton haste
Her cheeks were flushing, and her lips apart;
And zone that clung around her gentle waist
Had burst beneath the heaving of her heart.
Within the centre of that hall to breathe
She paus'd and panted, Zanthe! all beneath,
The fairy light that kiss'd her golden hair
And long'd to rest, yet could but sparkle there!

Young flowers were whispering in melody
To happy flowers that night—and tree to tree;
Fountains were gushing music as they fell
In many a star-lit grove, or moon-lit dell;
Yet silence came upon material things—
Fair flowers, bright waterfalls, and angel wings—
And sound alone, that from the spirit sprang,
Bore burthen to the charm the maiden sang:

"'Neath blue-bell or streamer—
Or tufted wild spray
That keeps from the dreamer
The moonbeam away—
Bright beings! that ponder,
With half closing eyes,
On the stars which your wonder
Hath drawn from the skies,
Till they glance thro' the shade, and
Come down to your brow
Like—eyes of the maiden
Who calls on you now—
Arise! from your dreaming
In violet bowers,
To duty beseeming
These star-litten hours—
And shake from your tresses,
Encumber'd with dew,
The breath of those kisses
That cumber them too
(O, how, without you, Love!
Could angels be blest?)—
Those kisses of true love
That lull'd ye to rest!
Up!—shake from your wing
Each hindering thing:
The dew of the night—
It would weigh down your flight;
And true love caresses—
O! leave them apart:
They are light on the tresses,
But lead on the heart.

"Ligeia! Ligeia!
My beautiful one!
Whose harshest idea
Will to melody run,

O! is it thy will
On the breezes to toss?
Or, capriciously still,
Like the lone Albatross,
Incumbent on night
(As she on the air)
To keep watch with delight
On the harmony there?

"Ligeia! wherever
Thy image may be,
No magic shall sever
Thy music from thee.
Thou hast bound many eyes
In a dreamy sleep—
But the strains still arise
Which *thy* vigilance keep:
The sound of the rain
Which leaps down to the flower,
And dances again
In the rhythm of the shower—
The murmur that springs
From the growing of grass
Are the music of things—
But are modell'd, alas!—
Away, then, my dearest,
O! hie thee away
To springs that lie clearest
Beneath the moon-ray—
To lone lake that smiles,
In its dream of deep rest,
At the many star-isles
That enjewel its breast—
Where wild flowers, creeping,
Have mingled their shade,
On its margin is sleeping
Full many a maid—
Some have left the cool glade, and
Have slept with the bee—
Arouse them, my maiden,
On moorland and lea—
Go! breathe on their slumber,
All softly in ear,
The musical number
They slumber'd to hear—
For what can awaken
An angel so soon,
Whose sleep hath been taken
Beneath the cold moon,
As the spell which no slumber
Of witchery may test,
The rhythmical number
Which lull'd him to rest?"

Spirits in wing, and angels to the view,
A thousand seraphs burst th' Empyrean thro',
Young dreams still hovering on their drowsy flight,
Seraphs in all but "Knowledge," the keen light
That fell, refracted, thro' thy bounds, afar,
O Death! from eye of God upon that star:
Sweet was that error—sweeter still that death—
Sweet was that error—ev'n with *us* the breath
Of Science dims the mirror of our joy—
To them 'twere the Simoom, and would destroy—
For what (to them) availeth it to know
That Truth is Falsehood—or that Bliss is Woe?
Sweet was their death—with them to die was rife
With the last ecstasy of satiate life—
Beyond that death no immortality—
But sleep that pondereth and is not "to be"—
And there—oh! may my weary spirit dwell—
Apart from Heaven's Eternity—and yet how far from Hell!

What guilty spirit, in what shrubbery dim,
Heard not the stirring summons of that hymn?
But two: they fell: for Heaven no grace imparts
To those who hear not for their beating hearts.
A maiden-angel and her seraph-lover—
O! where (and ye may seek the wide skies over)
Was Love, the blind, near sober Duty known?
Unguided Love hath fallen—'mid "tears of perfect moan."

He was a goodly spirit—he who fell:
A wanderer by moss-y-mantled well—
A gazer on the lights that shine above—
A dreamer in the moonbeam by his love:
What wonder? for each star is eye-like there,
And looks so sweetly down on Beauty's hair;
And they, and ev'ry mossy spring were holy
To his love-haunted heart and melancholy.
The night had found (to him a night of wo)
Upon a mountain crag, young Angelo—
Beetling it bends athwart the solemn sky,
And scowls on starry worlds that down beneath it lie.
Here sate he with his love—his dark eye bent

With eagle gaze along the firmament:
Now turn'd it upon her—but ever then
It trembled to the orb of EARTH again.

"Ianthe, dearest, see! how dim that ray!
How lovely 'tis to look so far away!
She seemed not thus upon that autumn eve
I left her gorgeous halls—nor mourn'd to leave.
That eve—that eve—I should remember well—
The sun-ray dropp'd, in Lemnos, with a spell
On th' Arabesque carving of a gilded hall
Wherein I sate, and on the draperied wall—
And on my eyelids—O the heavy light!
How drowsily it weigh'd them into night!
On flowers, before, and mist, and love they ran
With Persian Saadi in his Gulistan:
But O that light!—I slumber'd—Death, the while,
Stole o'er my senses in that lovely isle
So softly that no single silken hair
Awoke that slept—or knew that he was there.

"The last spot of Earth's orb I trod upon
Was a proud temple call'd the Parthenon.
More beauty clung around her column'd wall
Than ev'n thy glowing bosom beats withal,
And when old Time my wing did disenthral—
Thence sprang I—as the eagle from his tower,
And years I left behind me in an hour.
What time upon her airy bounds I hung,
One half the garden of her globe was flung,
Unrolling as a chart unto my view—
Tenantless cities of the desert too!
Ianthe, beauty crowded on me then,
And half I wish'd to be again of men."

"My Angelo! and why of them to be?
A brighter dwelling-place is here for thee,
And greener fields than in yon world above,
And woman's loveliness—and passionate love."

"But, list, Ianthe! when the air so soft
Fail'd, as my pennon'd spirit leapt aloft,
Perhaps my brain grew dizzy—but the world
I left so late was into chaos hurl'd—
Sprang from her station, on the winds apart,
And roll'd, a flame, the fiery Heaven athwart.
Methought, my sweet one, then I ceased to soar,
And fell—not swiftly as I rose before,
But with a downward, tremulous motion thro'
Light, brazen rays, this golden star unto!
Nor long the measure of my falling hours,
For nearest of all stars was thine to ours—
Dread star! that came, amid a night of mirth,
A red Dædalion on the timid Earth."

"We came—and to thy Earth—but not to us
Be given our lady's bidding to discuss:
We came, my love; around, above, below,
Gay fire-fly of the night we come and go,
Nor ask a reason save the angel-nod
She grants to us, as granted by her God—
But, Angelo, than thine grey Time unfurl'd
Never his fairy wing o'er fairier world!
Dim was its little disk, and angel eyes
Alone could see the phantom in the skies,
When first Al Aaraaf knew her course to be
Headlong thitherward o'er the starry sea—
But when its glory swell'd upon the sky,
As glowing Beauty's bust beneath man's eye,
We paus'd before the heritage of men,
And thy star trembled—as doth Beauty then!"

Thus, in discourse, the lovers whiled away
The night that waned and waned and brought no day.
They fell: for Heaven to them no hope imparts
Who hear not for the beating of their hearts.

1827–1829 1829

ROMANCE

ROMANCE, who loves to nod and sing,
With drowsy head and folded wing,
Among the green leaves as they shake
Far down within some shadowy lake,
To me a painted paroquet
Hath been—a most familiar bird—
Taught me my alphabet to say,
To lisp my very earliest word,
While in the wild wood I did lie,
A child—with a most knowing eye.

Of late, eternal Condor years
So shake the very Heaven on high
With tumult as they thunder by,
I have no time for idle cares

Through gazing on the unquiet sky.
And when an hour with calmer wings
Its down upon my spirit flings—
That little time with lyre and rhyme
To while away—forbidden things!
My heart would feel to be a crime
Unless it trembled with the strings.

1829

TO ——

THE bowers whereat, in dreams, I see
The wantonest singing birds,
Are lips—and all thy melody
Of lip-begotten words.

Thine eyes, in Heaven of heart enshrined,
Then desolately fall,
O, God! on my funereal mind
Like starlight on a pall.

Thy heart—*thy* heart!—I wake and sigh,
And sleep to dream till day
Of the truth that gold can never buy—
Of the baubles that it may.

1829

TO ——

I HEED not that my earthly lot
Hath—little of Earth in it—
That years of love have been forgot
In the hatred of a minute:—
I mourn not that the desolate
Are happier, sweet, than I,
But that *you* sorrow for *my* fate
Who am a passer by.

1829

TO HELEN

HELEN, thy beauty is to me
Like those Nicéan barks of yore,
That gently, o'er a perfumed sea,
The weary, way-worn wanderer bore
To his own native shore.

On desperate seas long wont to roam,
Thy hyacinth hair, thy classic face,
Thy Naiad airs have brought me home
To the glory that was Greece
And the grandeur that was Rome.

Lo! in yon brilliant window-niche
How statue-like I see thee stand,
The agate lamp within thy hand!
Ah, Psyche, from the regions which
Are Holy Land!

1831

LENORE

AH, broken is the golden bowl!—the spirit flown forever!
Let the bell toll!—a saintly soul floats on the Stygian river:—
And, Guy De Vere, hast *thou* no tear?—weep now or never more!
See! on yon drear and rigid bier low lies thy love, Lenore!
Come, let the burial rite be read—the funeral song be sung!—
An anthem for the queenliest dead that ever died so young—
A dirge for her the doubly dead in that she died so young.

"Wretches! ye loved her for her wealth, and ye hated her for her pride;
And, when she fell in feeble health, ye blessed her—that she died:—
How *shall* the ritual, then, be read—the requiem how be sung
By you—by yours, the evil eye,—by yours, the slanderous tongue
That did to death the innocence that died, and died so young?"

Peccavimus; yet rave not thus! but let a Sabbath song
Go up to God so solemnly the dead may feel no wrong!
The sweet Lenore hath gone before, with Hope that flew beside,
Leaving thee wild for the dear child that should have been thy bride—
For her, the fair and debonair, that now so lowly lies,
The life upon her yellow hair, but not within her eyes—
The life still there upon her hair, the death upon her eyes.

"Avaunt!—avaunt! to friends from fiends the indignant ghost is riven—
From Hell unto a high estate within the utmost Heaven—

From moan and groan to a golden throne beside the King of Heaven:—
Let *no* bell toll, then, lest her soul, amid its hallowed mirth,
Should catch the note as it doth float up from the damnéd Earth!
And I—to-night my heart is light:—no dirge will I upraise,
But waft the angel on her flight with a Pæan of old days!"

1831

ISRAFEL

And the angel Israfel, whose heart-strings are a lute, and who has the sweetest voice of all God's creatures.—KORAN.

In Heaven a spirit doth dwell
"Whose heart-strings are a lute";
None sing so wildly well
As the angel Israfel,
And the giddy stars (so legends tell),
Ceasing their hymns, attend the spell
Of his voice, all mute.

Tottering above
In her highest noon,
The enamoured moon
Blushes with love,
While, to listen, the red levin
(With the rapid Pleiads, even,
Which were seven,)
Pauses in Heaven.

And they say (the starry choir
And the other listening things)
That Israfeli's fire
Is owing to that lyre
By which he sits and sings—
The trembling living wire
Of those unusual strings.

But the skies that angel trod,
Where deep thoughts are a duty,
Where Love's a grown-up God,
Where the Houri glances are
Imbued with all the beauty
Which we worship in a star.

Therefore, thou art not wrong,
Israfeli, who despisest
An unimpassioned song;
To thee the laurels belong,
Best bard, because the wisest!
Merrily live, and long!

The ecstasies above
With thy burning measures suit—
Thy grief, thy joy, thy hate, thy love,
With the fervour of thy lute—
Well may the stars be mute!

Yes, Heaven is thine; but this
Is a world of sweets and sours;
Our flowers are merely—flowers,
And the shadow of thy perfect bliss
Is the sunshine of ours.

If I could dwell
Where Israfel
Hath dwelt, and he where I,
He might not sing so wildly well
A mortal melody,
While a bolder note than this might swell
From my lyre within the sky.

1831

THE CITY IN THE SEA

Lo! Death has reared himself a throne
In a strange city lying alone
Far down within the dim West,
Where the good and the bad and the worst and the best
Have gone to their eternal rest.
There shrines and palaces and towers
(Time-eaten towers that tremble not!)
Resemble nothing that is ours.
Around, by lifting winds forgot,
Resignedly beneath the sky
The melancholy waters lie.

No rays from the holy heaven come down
On the long night-time of that town;
But light from out the lurid sea
Streams up the turrets silently—
Gleams up the pinnacles far and free—
Up domes—up spires—up kingly halls—
Up fanes—up Babylon-like walls—
Up shadowy long-forgotten bowers
Of sculptured ivy and stone flowers—
Up many and many a marvellous shrine
Whose wreathéd friezes intertwine
The viol, the violet, and the vine.

Resignedly beneath the sky
The melancholy waters lie.
So blend the turrets and shadows there
That all seem pendulous in air,
While from a proud tower in the town
Death looks gigantically down.

There open fanes and gaping graves
Yawn level with the luminous waves;
But not the riches there that lie
In each idol's diamond eye—
Not the gaily-jewelled dead
Tempt the waters from their bed;
For no ripples curl, alas!
Along that wilderness of glass—
No swellings tell that winds may be
Upon some far-off happier sea—
No heavings hint that winds have been
On seas less hideously serene.

But lo, a stir is in the air!
The wave—there is a movement there!
As if the towers had thrust aside,
In slightly sinking, the dull tide—
As if their tops had feebly given
A void within the filmy Heaven.
The waves have now a redder glow—
The hours are breathing faint and low—
And when, amid no earthly moans,
Down, down that town shall settle hence,
Hell, rising from a thousand thrones,
Shall do it reverence.

1831

THE SLEEPER

At midnight, in the month of June,
I stand beneath the mystic moon.
An opiate vapor, dewy, dim,
Exhales from out her golden rim,
And softly dripping, drop by drop,
Upon the quiet mountain top,
Steals drowsily and musically
Into the universal valley.
The rosemary nods upon the grave;
The lily lolls upon the wave;
Wrapping the fog about its breast,
The ruin moulders into rest;
Looking like Lethe, see! the lake
A conscious slumber seems to take,
And would not, for the world, awake.
All Beauty sleeps!—and lo! where lies
Irene, with her Destinies!

Oh, lady bright! can it be right—
This window open to the night?
The wanton airs, from the tree-top,
Laughingly through the lattice drop—
The bodiless airs, a wizard rout,
Flit through thy chamber in and out,
And wave the curtain canopy
So fitfully—so fearfully—
Above the closed and fringéd lid
'Neath which thy slumb'ring soul lies hid,
That, o'er the floor and down the wall,
Like ghosts the shadows rise and fall!
Oh, lady dear, hast thou no fear?
Why and what art thou dreaming here?
Sure thou art come o'er far-off seas,
A wonder to these garden trees!
Strange is thy pallor! strange thy dress!
Strange, above all, thy length of tress,
And this all solemn silentness!

The lady sleeps! Oh, may her sleep,
Which is enduring, so be deep!
Heaven have her in its sacred keep!
This chamber changed for one more holy,
This bed for one more melancholy,
I pray to God that she may lie
Forever with unopened eye,
While the pale sheeted ghosts go by!

My love, she sleeps! Oh, may her sleep,
As it is lasting, so be deep!
Soft may the worms about her creep!
Far in the forest, dim and old,
For her may some tall vault unfold—
Some vault that oft hath flung its black
And wingéd pannels fluttering back,
Triumphant, o'er the crested palls
Of her grand family funerals—

Some sepulchre, remote, alone,
Against whose portal she hath thrown,
In childhood, many an idle stone—
Some tomb from out whose sounding door
She ne'er shall force an echo more,
Thrilling to think, poor child of sin!
It was the dead who groaned within.

1831

THE VALLEY OF UNREST

Once it smiled a silent dell
Where the people did not dwell;
They had gone unto the wars,
Trusting to the mild-eyed stars,
Nightly, from their azure towers,
To keep watch above the flowers,
In the midst of which all day
The red sun-light lazily lay.
Now each visitor shall confess
The sad valley's restlessness.
Nothing there is motionless—
Nothing save the airs that brood
Over the magic solitude.
Ah, by no wind are stirred those trees
That palpitate like the chill seas
Around the misty Hebrides!
Ah, by no wind those clouds are driven
That rustle through the unquiet Heaven
Uneasily, from morn till even,
Over the violets there that lie
In myriad types of the human eye—
Over the lilies there that wave
And weep above a nameless grave!
They wave:—from out their fragrant tops
Eternal dews come down in drops.
They weep:—from off their delicate stems
Perennial tears descend in gems.

1831

THE COLISEUM

Type of the antique Rome! Rich reliquary
Of lofty contemplation left to Time
By buried centuries of pomp and power!
At length—at length—after so many days
Of weary pilgrimage and burning thirst
(Thirst for the springs of lore that in thee lie),
I kneel, an altered and an humble man,
Amid thy shadows, and so drink within
My very soul thy grandeur, gloom, and glory!

Vastness! and Age! and Memories of Eld!
Silence! and Desolation! and dim Night!
I feel ye now—I feel ye in your strength—
O spells more sure than e'er Judæan king
Taught in the gardens of Gethsemane!
O charms more potent than the rapt Chaldee
Ever drew down from out the quiet stars!
Here, where a hero fell, a column falls!
Here, where the mimic eagle glared in gold,
A midnight vigil holds the swarthy bat!
Here, where the dames of Rome their gilded hair
Waved to the wind, now wave the reed and thistle!
Here, where on golden throne the monarch lolled,
Glides, spectre-like, unto his marble home,
Lit by the wan light of the hornéd moon,
The swift and silent lizard of the stones!

But stay! these walls—these ivy-clad arcades—
These mouldering plinths—these sad and blackened shafts—
These vague entablatures—this crumbling frieze—
These shattered cornices—this wreck—this ruin—
These stones—alas! these gray stones—are they all—
All of the famed and the colossal left
By the corrosive Hours to Fate and me?

"Not all"—the Echoes answer me—"not all!
Prophetic sounds and loud, arise forever
From us, and from all Ruin, unto the wise,
As melody from Memnon to the Sun.
We rule the hearts of mightiest men—we rule
With a despotic sway all giant minds.
We are not impotent—we pallid stones.
Not all our power is gone—not all our fame—
Not all the magic of our high renown—
Not all the wonder that encircles us—
Not all the mysteries that in us lie—
Not all the memories that hang upon
And cling around about us as a garment,
Clothing us in a robe of more than glory."

1833

TO ONE IN PARADISE

Thou wast that all to me, love,
For which my soul did pine—
A green isle in the sea, love,
A fountain and a shrine,
All wreathed with fairy fruits and flowers,
And all the flowers were mine.

Ah, dream too bright to last!
Ah, starry Hope! that didst arise

But to be overcast!
  A voice from out the Future cries,
"On! on!"—but o'er the Past
  (Dim gulf!) my spirit hovering lies
Mute, motionless, aghast!

For, alas! alas! with me
  The light of Life is o'er!
No more—no more—no more—
  (Such language holds the solemn sea
To the sands upon the shore)
  Shall bloom the thunder-blasted tree,
Or the stricken eagle soar!

And all my days are trances,
  And all my nightly dreams
Are where thy grey eye glances,
  And where thy footstep gleams—
In what ethereal dances,
  By what eternal streams.

1834

HYMN

At morn—at noon—at twilight dim—
Maria! thou hast heard my hymn!
In joy and wo—in good and ill—
Mother of God, be with me still!
When the Hours flew brightly by,
And not a cloud obscured the sky,
My soul, lest it should truant be,
Thy grace did guide to thine and thee;
Now, when storms of Fate o'ercast
Darkly my Present and my Past,
Let my Future radiant shine
With sweet hopes of thee and thine!

1835

TO F——

Beloved! amid the earnest woes
  That crowd around my earthly path—
(Drear path, alas! where grows
Not even one lonely rose)—
  My soul at least a solace hath
In dreams of thee, and therein knows
An Eden of bland repose.

And thus thy memory is to me
  Like some enchanted far-off isle
In some tumultuous sea—
  Some ocean throbbing far and free
  With storms—but where meanwhile
Serenest skies continually
  Just o'er that one bright island smile.

1835

TO F——S S. O——D

Thou wouldst be loved?—then let thy heart
  From its present pathway part not!
Being everything which now thou art,
  Be nothing which thou art not.
So with the world thy gentle ways,
  Thy grace, thy more than beauty,
Shall be an endless theme of praise,
  And love—a simple duty.

1835

SONNET—TO ZANTE

Fair isle, that from the fairest of all flowers
  Thy gentlest of all gentle names dost take,
How many memories of what radiant hours
  At sight of thee and thine at once awake!
How many scenes of what departed bliss!
  How many thoughts of what entombéd hopes!
How many visions of a maiden that is
  No more—no more upon thy verdant slopes!
No more! alas, that magical sad sound
  Transforming all! Thy charms shall please *no more,*—
Thy memory *no more!* Accurséd ground
  Henceforth I hold thy flower-enamelled shore,
O hyacinthine isle! O purple Zante!
"Isola d'oro! Fior di Levante!"

1837

THE HAUNTED PALACE

In the greenest of our valleys
  By good angels tenanted,
Once a fair and stately palace—
  Radiant palace—reared its head.
In the monarch Thought's dominion,
  It stood there!
Never seraph spread a pinion
  Over fabric half so fair!

Banners yellow, glorious, golden,
  On its roof did float and flow
(This—all this—was in the olden
  Time long ago),
And every gentle air that dallied,
  In that sweet day,
Along the ramparts plumed and pallid,
  A wingéd odor went away.

Wanderers in that happy valley,
  Through two luminous windows, saw
Spirits moving musically,
  To a lute's well-tunéd law,
Round about a throne where, sitting,
  Porphyrogene!
In state his glory well befitting,
  The ruler of the realm was seen.

And all with pearl and ruby glowing
  Was the fair palace door,
Through which came flowing, flowing, flowing,
  And sparkling evermore,
A troop of Echoes, whose sweet duty
  Was but to sing,
In voices of surpassing beauty,
  The wit and wisdom of their king.

But evil things, in robes of sorrow,
  Assailed the monarch's high estate.
(Ah, let us mourn!—for never morrow
  Shall dawn upon him, desolate!)
And round about his home the glory
  That blushed and bloomed,
Is but a dim-remembered story
  Of the old time entombed.

And travellers, now, within that valley,
  Through the red-litten windows see
Vast forms that move fantastically
  To a discordant melody,
While, like a ghastly rapid river,
  Through the pale door
A hideous throng rush out forever,
  And laugh—but smile no more.

1839

SONNET—SILENCE

There are some qualities—some incorporate things,
  That have a double life, which thus is made
A type of that twin entity which springs
  From matter and light, evinced in solid and shade.
There is a two-fold *Silence*—sea and shore—
  Body and soul. One dwells in lonely places,
  Newly with grass o'ergrown; some solemn graces,
Some human memories and tearful lore,
Render him terrorless: his name's "No More."
He is the corporate Silence: dread him not!
  No power hath he of evil in himself;
But should some urgent fate (untimely lot!)
  Bring thee to meet his shadow (nameless elf,
That haunteth the lone regions where hath trod
No foot of man), commend thyself to God!

1840

THE CONQUEROR WORM

Lo! 'tis a gala night
  Within the lonesome latter years!
An angel throng, bewinged, bedight
  In veils, and drowned in tears,
Sit in a theatre, to see
  A play of hopes and fears,
While the orchestra breathes fitfully
  The music of the spheres.

Mimes, in the form of God on high,
  Mutter and mumble low,
And hither and thither fly—
  Mere puppets they, who come and go
At bidding of vast formless things
  That shift the scenery to and fro,
Flapping from out their Condor wings
  Invisible Wo!

That motley drama—oh, be sure
  It shall not be forgot!
With its Phantom chased for evermore
  By a crowd that seize it not,
Through a circle that ever returneth in
  To the self-same spot,
And much of Madness, and more of Sin,
  And Horror the soul of the plot.

But see, amid the mimic rout,
  A crawling shape intrude!
A blood-red thing that writhes from out
  The scenic solitude!
It writhes!—it writhes!—with mortal pangs
  The mimes become its food,

And seraphs sob at vermin fangs
In human gore imbued.

Out—out are the lights—out all!
And, over each quivering form,
The curtain, a funeral pall,
Comes down with the rush of a storm,
While the angels, all pallid and wan,
Uprising, unveiling, affirm
That the play is the tragedy, "Man,"
And its hero, the Conqueror Worm.

1843

DREAM-LAND

By a route obscure and lonely,
Haunted by ill angels only,
Where an Eidolon, named Night,
On a black throne reigns upright,
I have reached these lands but newly
From an ultimate dim Thule—
From a wild weird clime that lieth, sublime,
Out of Space—out of Time.

Bottomless vales and boundless floods,
And chasms, and caves, and Titan woods,
With forms that no man can discover
For the tears that drip all over;
Mountains toppling evermore
Into seas without a shore;
Seas that restlessly aspire,
Surging, unto skies of fire;
Lakes that endlessly outspread
Their lone waters, lone and dead,—
Their still waters, still and chilly
With the snows of the lolling lily.

By the lakes that thus outspread
Their lone waters, lone and dead,—
Their sad waters, sad and chilly
With the snows of the lolling lily,—
By the mountains—near the river
Murmuring lowly, murmuring ever,—
By the grey woods,—by the swamp
Where the toad and the newt encamp,—
By the dismal tarns and pools
Where dwell the Ghouls,—
By each spot the most unholy—
In each nook most melancholy,—
There the traveller meets, aghast,
Sheeted Memories of the Past—
Shrouded forms that start and sigh
As they pass the wanderer by—
White-robed forms of friends long given,
In agony, to the Earth—and Heaven.

For the heart whose woes are legion
'Tis a peaceful, soothing region—
For the spirit that walks in shadow
'Tis—oh, 'tis an Eldorado!
But the traveller, travelling through it,
May not—dare not openly view it;
Never its mysteries are exposed
To the weak human eye unclosed;
So wills its King, who hath forbid
The uplifting of the fringéd lid;
And thus the sad Soul that here passes
Beholds it but through darkened glasses.

By a route obscure and lonely,
Haunted by ill angels only,
Where an Eidolon, named Night,
On a black throne reigns upright,
I have wandered home but newly
From this ultimate dim Thule.

1844

THE RAVEN

Once upon a midnight dreary, while I pondered, weak and weary,
Over many a quaint and curious volume of forgotten lore—
While I nodded, nearly napping, suddenly there came a tapping,
As of some one gently rapping, rapping at my chamber door.
"'Tis some visitor," I muttered, "tapping at my chamber door—
Only this and nothing more."

Ah, distinctly I remember it was in the bleak December;
And each separate dying ember wrought its ghost upon the floor.
Eagerly I wished the morrow;—vainly I had sought to borrow
From my books surcease of sorrow—sorrow for the lost Lenore—
For the rare and radiant maiden whom the angels name Lenore—
Nameless *here* for evermore.

And the silken, sad, uncertain rustling of each purple curtain
Thrilled me—filled me with fantastic terrors never felt before;
So that now, to still the beating of my heart, I stood repeating,
"'Tis some visitor entreating entrance at my chamber door—
Some late visitor entreating entrance at my chamber door;—
This it is and nothing more."

Presently my soul grew stronger; hesitating then no longer,
"Sir," said I, "or Madam, truly your forgiveness I implore;
But the fact is I was napping, and so gently you came rapping,
And so faintly you came tapping, tapping at my chamber door,
That I scarce was sure I heard you"—here I opened wide the door;—
Darkness there and nothing more.

Deep into that darkness peering, long I stood there wondering, fearing,
Doubting, dreaming dreams no mortal ever dared to dream before;
But the silence was unbroken, and the stillness gave no token,
And the only word there spoken was the whispered word, "Lenore?"
This I whispered, and an echo murmured back the word, "Lenore!"
Merely this and nothing more.

Back into the chamber turning, all my soul within me burning,
Soon again I heard a tapping somewhat louder than before.
"Surely," said I, "surely that is something at my window lattice;
Let me see, then, what thereat is, and this mystery explore—
Let my heart be still a moment and this mystery explore;—
'Tis the wind and nothing more!"

Open here I flung the shutter, when, with many a flirt and flutter,
In there stepped a stately Raven of the saintly days of yore;
Not the least obeisance made he; not a minute stopped or stayed he;
But, with mien of lord or lady, perched above my chamber door—
Perched upon a bust of Pallas just above my chamber door—
Perched, and sat, and nothing more.

Then this ebony bird beguiling my sad fancy into smiling,
By the grave and stern decorum of the countenance it wore,
"Though thy crest be shorn and shaven, thou," I said, "art sure no craven,
Ghastly grim and ancient Raven wandering from the Nightly shore—
Tell me what thy lordly name is on the Night's Plutonian shore!"
Quoth the Raven, "Nevermore."

Much I marvelled this ungainly fowl to hear discourse so plainly,
Though its answer little meaning—little relevancy bore;
For we cannot help agreeing that no living human being
Ever yet was blessed with seeing bird above his chamber door—
Bird or beast upon the sculptured bust above his chamber door,
With such name as "Nevermore."

But the Raven, sitting lonely on the placid bust, spoke only
That one word, as if his soul in that one word he did outpour.
Nothing farther then he uttered—not a feather then he fluttered—
Till I scarcely more than muttered, "Other friends have flown before—
On the morrow *he* will leave me, as my Hopes have flown before."
Then the bird said, "Nevermore."

Startled at the stillness broken by reply so aptly spoken,
"Doubtless," said I, "what it utters is its only stock and store
Caught from some unhappy master whom unmerciful Disaster
Followed fast and followed faster till his songs one burden bore—

Till the dirges of his Hope that melancholy burden bore
Of 'Never—nevermore.' "

But the Raven still beguiling my sad fancy into smiling,
Straight I wheeled a cushioned seat in front of bird and bust and door;
Then, upon the velvet sinking, I betook myself to linking
Fancy unto fancy, thinking what this ominous bird of yore—
What this grim, ungainly, ghastly, gaunt, and ominous bird of yore
Meant in croaking "Nevermore."

This I sat engaged in guessing, but no syllable expressing
To the fowl whose fiery eyes now burned into my bosom's core;
This and more I sat divining, with my head at ease reclining
On the cushion's velvet lining that the lamp-light gloated o'er,
But whose velvet-violet lining with the lamp-light gloating o'er,
Lenore She shall press, ah, nevermore!

Then, methought, the air grew denser, perfumed from an unseen censer
Swung by seraphim whose foot-falls tinkled on the tufted floor.
"Wretch," I cried, "thy God hath lent thee—by these angels he hath sent thee
Respite—respite and nepenthe from thy memories of Lenore;
Quaff, oh, quaff this kind nepenthe and forget this lost Lenore!"
Quoth the Raven, "Nevermore."

"Prophet!" said I, "thing of evil!—prophet still, if bird or devil!—
Whether Tempter sent, or whether tempest tossed thee here ashore,
Desolate yet all undaunted, on this desert land enchanted—
On this home by Horror haunted—tell me truly, I implore—
Is there—*is* there balm in Gilead?—tell me—tell me, I implore!"
Quoth the Raven, "Nevermore."

"Prophet!" said I, "thing of evil!—prophet still, if bird or devil!
By that Heaven that bends above us—by that God we both adore—
Tell this soul with sorrow laden if, within the distant Aidenn,
It shall clasp a sainted maiden whom the angels name Lenore—
Clasp a rare and radiant maiden whom the angels name Lenore."
Quoth the Raven, "Nevermore."

"Be that word our sign of parting, bird or fiend!" I shrieked, upstarting—
"Get thee back into the tempest and the Night's Plutonian shore!
Leave no black plume as a token of that lie thy soul hath spoken!
Leave my loneliness unbroken!—quit the bust above my door!
Take thy beak from out my heart, and take thy form from off my door!"
Quoth the Raven, "Nevermore."

And the Raven, never flitting, still is sitting, *still* is sitting
On the pallid bust of Pallas just above my chamber door;
And his eyes have all the seeming of a demon's that is dreaming,
And the lamp-light o'er him streaming throws his shadow on the floor;
And my soul from out that shadow that lies floating on the floor
Shall be lifted—nevermore!

It shall never be free from
the thought of Lenore—

1845

EULALIE—A SONG

I DWELT alone
In a world of moan,
And my soul was a stagnant tide,
Till the fair and gentle Eulalie became my blushing bride—
Till the yellow-haired young Eulalie became my smiling bride.

Ah, less—less bright
The stars of the night
Than the eyes of the radiant girl!
And never a flake

That the vapor can make
With the moon-tints of purple and pearl,
Can vie with the modest Eulalie's most unregarded curl—
Can compare with the bright-eyed Eulalie's most humble and careless curl.

Now Doubt—now Pain
Come never again,
For her soul gives me sigh for sigh,
And all day long
Shines, bright and strong,
Astarte within the sky,
While ever to her dear Eulalie upturns her matron eye—
While ever to her young Eulalie upturns her violet eye.

1845

ULALUME—A BALLAD

The skies they were ashen and sober;
The leaves they were crispéd and sere—
The leaves they were withering and sere:
It was night, in the lonesome October
Of my most immemorial year:
It was hard by the dim lake of Auber,
In the misty mid region of Weir—
It was down by the dank tarn of Auber,
In the ghoul-haunted woodland of Weir.

Here once, through an alley Titanic,
Of cypress, I roamed with my Soul—
Of cypress, with Psyche, my Soul.
These were days when my heart was volcanic
As the scoriac rivers that roll—
As the lavas that restlessly roll
Their sulphurous currents down Yaanek
In the ultimate climes of the Pole—
That groan as they roll down Mount Yaanek
In the realms of the Boreal Pole.

Our talk had been serious and sober,
But our thoughts they were palsied and sere—
Our memories were treacherous and sere;
For we knew not the month was October,
And we marked not the night of the year
(Ah, night of all nights in the year!)—
We noted not the dim lake of Auber
(Though once we had journeyed down here)—
We remembered not the dank tarn of Auber,
Nor the ghoul-haunted woodland of Weir.

And now, as the night was senescent
And star-dials pointed to morn—
As the star-dials hinted of morn—
At the end of our path a liquescent
And nebulous lustre was born,
Out of which a miraculous crescent
Arose with a duplicate horn—
Astarte's bediamonded crescent
Distinct with its duplicate horn.

And I said: "She is warmer than Dian;
She rolls through an ether of sighs—
She revels in a region of sighs.
She has seen that the tears are not dry on
These cheeks, where the worm never dies,
And has come past the stars of the Lion,
To point us the path to the skies—
To the Lethean peace of the skies—
Come up, in despite of the Lion,
To shine on us with her bright eyes—
Come up through the lair of the Lion,
With love in her luminous eyes."

But Psyche, uplifting her finger,
Said: "Sadly this star I mistrust—
Her pallor I strangely mistrust:
Ah, hasten!—ah, let us not linger!
Ah, fly!—let us fly!—for we must."
In terror she spoke, letting sink her
Wings till they trailed in the dust—
In agony sobbed, letting sink her
Plumes till they trailed in the dust—
Till they sorrowfully trailed in the dust.

I replied: "This is nothing but dreaming:
Let us on by this tremulous light!
Let us bathe in this crystalline light!
Its Sibyllic splendor is beaming
With Hope and in Beauty to-night:—
See!—it flickers up the sky through the night!
Ah, we safely may trust to its gleaming,
And be sure it will lead us aright—
We surely may trust to a gleaming,
That cannot but guide us aright,
Since it flickers up to Heaven through the night."

Thus I pacified Psyche and kissed her,
And tempted her out of her gloom—
And conquered her scruples and gloom;
And we passed to the end of the vista,
But were stopped by the door of a tomb—
By the door of a legended tomb;
And I said: "What is written, sweet sister,
On the door of this legended tomb?"
She replied: "Ulalume—Ulalume!—
'Tis the vault of thy lost Ulalume!"

Then my heart it grew ashen and sober
As the leaves that were crispéd and sere—
As the leaves that were withering and sere;
And I cried: "It was surely October
On *this* very night of last year
That I journeyed—I journeyed down here!—
That I brought a dread burden down here—
On this night of all nights in the year,
Ah, what demon hath tempted me here?
Well I know, now, this dim lake of Auber—
This misty mid region of Weir—
Well I know, now, this dank tarn of Auber,
This ghoul-haunted woodland of Weir."

Said we, then—the two, then: "Ah, can it
Have been that the woodlandish ghouls—
The pitiful, the merciful ghouls—
To bar up our way and to ban it
From the secret that lies in these wolds—
From the thing that lies hidden in these wolds—
Have drawn up the spectre of a planet
From the limbo of lunary souls—
This sinfully scintillant planet
From the Hell of the planetary souls?"

1847

TO HELEN

I SAW thee once—once only—years ago:
I must not say *how* many—but *not* many.
It was a July midnight; and from out
A full-orbed moon, that, like thine own soul, soaring,
Sought a precipitate pathway up through heaven,
There fell a silvery-silken veil of light,
With quietude, and sultriness, and slumber,
Upon the upturn'd faces of a thousand
Roses that grew in an enchanted garden,
Where no wind dared to stir, unless on tip-toe—
Fell on the upturn'd faces of these roses
That gave out, in return for the love-light,
Their odorous souls in an ecstatic death—
Fell on the upturn'd faces of these roses
That smiled and died in this parterre, enchanted
By thee, and by the poetry of thy presence.

Clad all in white, upon a violet bank
I saw thee half reclining; while the moon
Fell on the upturn'd faces of the roses,
And on thine own, upturn'd—alas, in sorrow!

Was it not Fate that, on this July midnight—
Was it not Fate (whose name is also Sorrow)
That bade me pause before that garden-gate,
To breathe the incense of those slumbering roses?
No footstep stirred: the hated world all slept,
Save only thee and me. (Oh, Heaven!—oh, God!
How my heart beats in coupling those two words!
Save only thee and me). I paused—I looked—
And in an instant all things disappeared.
(Ah, bear in mind this garden was enchanted!)
The pearly lustre of the moon went out:
The mossy banks and the meandering paths,
The happy flowers and the repining trees,
Were seen no more: the very roses' odors
Died in the arms of the adoring airs.
All—all expired save thee—save less than thou:
Save only the divine light in thine eyes—
Save but the soul in thine uplifted eyes.
I saw but them—they were the world to me.
I saw but them—saw only them for hours—
Saw only them until the moon went down.
What wild heart-histories seemed to lie enwritten
Upon those crystalline, celestial spheres!
How dark a wo! yet how sublime a hope!
How silently serene a sea of pride!
How daring an ambition! yet how deep—
How fathomless a capacity for love!

But now, at length, dear Dian sank from sight,
Into a western couch of thunder-cloud;
And thou, a ghost, amid the entombing trees

Didst glide away. *Only thine eyes remained.*
They *would not* go—they never yet have gone.
Lighting my lonely pathway home that night,
They have not left me (as my hopes have) since.
They follow me—they lead me through the years.
They are my ministers—yet I their slave.
Their office is to illumine and enkindle—
My duty, *to be saved* by their bright light,
And purified in their electric fire,
And sanctified in their elysian fire.
They fill my soul with Beauty (which is Hope),
And are far up in Heaven—the stars I kneel to
In the sad, silent watches of my night;
While even in the meridian glare of day
I see them still—two sweetly scintillant
Venuses, unextinguished by the sun!

1848

THE BELLS

I

HEAR the sledges with the bells—
Silver bells!
What a world of merriment their melody foretells!
How they tinkle, tinkle, tinkle,
In the icy air of night!
While the stars that oversprinkle
All the heavens, seem to twinkle
With a crystalline delight;
Keeping time, time, time,
In a sort of Runic rhyme,
To the tintinnabulation that so musically wells
From the bells, bells, bells, bells,
Bells, bells, bells—
From the jingling and the tinkling of the bells.

II

Hear the mellow wedding bells—
Golden bells!
What a world of happiness their harmony foretells!
Through the balmy air of night
How they ring out their delight!—
From the molten-golden notes,
And all in tune,
What a liquid ditty floats
To the turtle-dove that listens, while she gloats
On the moon!
Oh, from out the sounding cells,
What a gush of euphony voluminously wells!
How it swells!
How it dwells
On the Future!—how it tells
Of the rapture that impels
To the swinging and the ringing
Of the bells, bells, bells—
Of the bells, bells, bells, bells,
Bells, bells, bells—
To the rhyming and the chiming of the bells!

III

Hear the loud alarum bells—
Brazen bells!
What a tale of terror, now, their turbulency tells!
In the startled ear of night
How they scream out their affright!
Too much horrified to speak,
They can only shriek, shriek,
Out of tune,
In a clamorous appealing to the mercy of the fire,
In a mad expostulation with the deaf and frantic fire,
Leaping higher, higher, higher,
With a desperate desire,
And a resolute endeavor
Now—now to sit, or never,
By the side of the pale-faced moon.
Oh, the bells, bells, bells!
What a tale their terror tells
Of Despair!
How they clang, and clash, and roar!
What a horror they outpour
On the bosom of the palpitating air!
Yet the ear, it fully knows,
By the twanging
And the clanging,
How the danger ebbs and flows;
Yet the ear distinctly tells,
In the jangling
And the wrangling,
How the danger sinks and swells,
By the sinking or the swelling in the anger of the bells—
Of the bells,—

Of the bells, bells, bells, bells,
Bells, bells, bells—
In the clamor and the clangor of the bells!

IV

Hear the tolling of the bells—
Iron bells!
What a world of solemn thought their monody compels!
In the silence of the night,
How we shiver with affright
At the melancholy menace of their tone!
For every sound that floats
From the rust within their throats
Is a groan.
And the people—ah, the people—
They that dwell up in the steeple,
All alone,
And who tolling, tolling, tolling,
In that muffled monotone,
Feel a glory in so rolling
On the human heart a stone—
They are neither man nor woman—
They are neither brute nor human—
They are Ghouls:—
And their king it is who tolls:—
And he rolls, rolls, rolls,
Rolls
A pæan from the bells!
And his merry bosom swells
With the pæan of the bells!
And he dances, and he yells;
Keeping time, time, time,
In a sort of Runic rhyme,
To the pæan of the bells—
Of the bells:—
Keeping time, time, time,
In a sort of Runic rhyme,
To the throbbing of the bells—
Of the bells, bells, bells—
To the sobbing of the bells;
Keeping time, time, time,
As he knells, knells, knells,
In a happy Runic rhyme,
To the rolling of the bells—
Of the bells, bells, bells:—
To the tolling of the bells—
Of the bells, bells, bells, bells,
Bells, bells, bells—
To the moaning and the groaning of the bells.

1849

ELDORADO

Gaily bedight,
A gallant knight,
In sunshine and in shadow,
Had journeyed long,
Singing a song,
In search of Eldorado.

But he grew old—
This knight so bold—
And o'er his heart a shadow
Fell as he found
No spot of ground
That looked like Eldorado.

And, as his strength
Failed him at length,
He met a pilgrim shadow—
"Shadow," said he,
"Where can it be—
This land of Eldorado?"

"Over the Mountains
Of the Moon,
Down the Valley of the Shadow,
Ride, boldly ride,"
The shade replied,—
"If you seek for Eldorado!"

1849

FOR ANNIE

Thank Heaven! the crisis,
The danger, is past,
And the lingering illness
Is over at last—
And the fever called "Living"
Is conquered at last.

Sadly, I know
I am shorn of my strength,
And no muscle I move
As I lie at full length—
But no matter!—I feel
I am better at length.

And I rest so composedly,
Now, in my bed,
That any beholder
Might fancy me dead—
Might start at beholding me,
Thinking me dead.

The moaning and groaning,
The sighing and sobbing,
Are quieted now,
With that horrible throbbing
At heart:—ah, that horrible,
Horrible throbbing!

The sickness—the nausea—
The pitiless pain—
Have ceased, with the fever
That maddened my brain—
With the fever called "Living"
That burned in my brain.

And oh! of all tortures
That torture the worst
Has abated—the terrible
Torture of thirst
For the naphthaline river
Of Passion accurst:—
I have drank of a water
That quenches all thirst:—

Of a water that flows,
With a lullaby sound,
From a spring but a very few
Feet under ground—
From a cavern not very far
Down under ground.

And ah! let it never
Be foolishly said
That my room it is gloomy
And narrow my bed;
For man never slept
In a different bed—
And, to *sleep*, you must slumber
In just such a bed.

My tantalized spirit
Here blandly reposes,
Forgetting, or never
Regretting, its roses—
Its old agitations
Of myrtles and roses:

For now, while so quietly
Lying, it fancies
A holier odor
About it, of pansies—
A rosemary odor,
Commingled with pansies—
With rue and the beautiful
Puritan pansies.

And so it lies happily,
Bathing in many
A dream of the truth
And the beauty of Annie—
Drowned in a bath
Of the tresses of Annie.

She tenderly kissed me,
She fondly caressed,
And then I fell gently
To sleep on her breast—
Deeply to sleep
From the heaven of her breast.

When the light was extinguished,
She covered me warm,
And she prayed to the angels
To keep me from harm—
To the queen of the angels
To shield me from harm.

And I lie so composedly,
Now, in my bed
(Knowing her love),
That you fancy me dead—
And I rest so contentedly,
Now, in my bed
(With her love at my breast),
That you fancy me dead—
That you shudder to look at me,
Thinking me dead:—

But my heart is brighter
Than all of the many
Stars in the sky,
For it sparkles with Annie—
It glows with the light
Of the love of my Annie—
With the thought of the light
Of the eyes of my Annie.

1849

TO MY MOTHER

BECAUSE I feel that, in the Heavens above,
The angels, whispering to one another,
Can find, among their burning terms of love,
None so devotional as that of "Mother,"
Therefore by that dear name I long have called you—

You who are more than mother unto me,
And fill my heart of hearts, where Death installed you
In setting my Virginia's spirit free.
My mother—my own mother, who died early,
Was but the mother of myself; but you
Are mother to the one I loved so dearly,
And thus are dearer than the mother I knew
By that infinity with which my wife
Was dearer to my soul than its soul-life.

1849

ANNABEL LEE

It was many and many a year ago,
In a kingdom by the sea,
That a maiden there lived whom you may know
By the name of Annabel Lee;—
And this maiden she lived with no other thought
Than to love and be loved by me.

She was a child and *I* was a child,
In this kingdom by the sea,
But we loved with a love that was more than love—
I and my Annabel Lee—
With a love that the wingéd seraphs of Heaven
Coveted her and me.

And this was the reason that, long ago,
In this kingdom by the sea,
A wind blew out of a cloud by night
Chilling my Annabel Lee;
So that her highborn kinsmen came
And bore her away from me,
To shut her up in a sepulchre
In this kingdom by the sea.

The angels, not half so happy in Heaven,
Went envying her and me:—
Yes! that was the reason (as all men know,
In this kingdom by the sea)
That the wind came out of the cloud, chilling
And killing my Annabel Lee.

But our love it was stronger by far than the love
Of those who were older than we—
Of many far wiser than we—
And neither the angels in Heaven above
Nor the demons down under the sea,
Can ever dissever my soul from the soul
Of the beautiful Annabel Lee:—

For the moon never beams without bringing me dreams
Of the beautiful Annabel Lee;
And the stars never rise but I see the bright eyes
Of the beautiful Annabel Lee;
And so, all the night-tide, I lie down by the side
Of my darling, my darling, my life and my bride,
In her sepulchre there by the sea—
In her tomb by the side of the sea.

1849

THE PHILOSOPHY OF COMPOSITION

Charles Dickens, in a note now lying before me, alluding to an examination I once made of the mechanism of "Barnaby Rudge," says—"By the way, are you aware that Godwin wrote his 'Caleb Williams' backwards? He first involved his hero in a web of difficulties, forming the second volume, and then, for the first, cast about him for some mode of accounting for what had been done."

I cannot think this the *precise* mode of procedure on the part of Godwin—and indeed what he himself acknowledges is not altogether in accordance with Mr. Dickens' idea; but the author of "Caleb Williams" was too good an artist not to perceive the advantage derivable from at least a somewhat similar process. Nothing is more clear than that every plot, worth the name, must be elaborated to its *dénouement* before anything be attempted with the pen. It is only with the *dénouement* constantly in view that we can give a plot its indispensable air of consequence, or causation, by making the incidents, and especially the tone at all points, tend to the development of the intention.

There is a radical error, I think, in the usual mode of constructing a story. Either history affords a thesis, or one is suggested by an incident of the day, or, at best, the author sets himself to work in the combination of striking events to form merely the basis of his narrative, designing, generally, to fill in with description, dialogue, or autorial comment, whatever crevices of fact, or action, may, from page to page, render themselves apparent.

I prefer commencing with the consideration of an *effect*. Keeping originality *always* in view—for he is false to himself who ventures to dispense with so obvious and so easily attainable a source of interest—I say to myself, in the first place,—"Of the innumerable effects, or impressions, of which the heart, the intellect, or (more generally) the soul is susceptible, what one shall I, on the present occasion, select?" Having chosen a novel, first, and secondly a vivid effect, I consider whether it can be best wrought by incident or tone—whether by ordinary incidents and peculiar tone, or the converse, or by peculiarity both of incident and tone—afterward looking about me (or rather within) for such combinations of event, or tone, as shall best aid me in the construction of the effect.

I have often thought how interesting a magazine paper might be written by any author who would—that is to say, who could—detail, step by step, the processes by which any one of his compositions attained its ultimate point of completion. Why such a paper has never been given to the world, I am much at a loss to say; but, perhaps, the autorial vanity has had more to do with the omission than any one other cause. Most writers—poets in especial—prefer having it understood that they compose by a species of fine frenzy—an ecstatic intuition; and would positively shudder at letting the public take a peep behind the scenes, at the elaborate and vacillating crudities of thought, at the true purposes seized only at the last moment, at the innumerable glimpses of idea that arrived not at the maturity of full view, at the fully matured fancies discarded in despair as unmanageable, at the cautious selections and rejections, at the painful erasures and interpolations—in a word, at the wheels and pinions, the tackle for scene-shifting, the step-ladders and demon-traps—the cock's feathers, the red paint and the black patches, which, in ninety-nine cases out of the hundred, constitute the properties of the literary *histrio*.

I am aware, on the other hand, that the case is by no means common, in which an author is at all in condition to retrace the steps by which his conclusions have been attained. In general, suggestions, having arisen pell-mell, are pursued and forgotten in a similar manner.

For my own part, I have neither sympathy with the repugnance alluded to, nor, at any time the least difficulty in recalling to mind the progressive steps of any of my compositions; and, since the interest of an analysis, or reconstruction, such as I have considered a *desideratum*, is quite independent of any real or fancied interest in the thing analyzed, it will not be regarded as a breach of decorum on my part to show the *modus operandi* by which some one of my own works was put together. I select "The Raven" as most generally known. It is my design to render it manifest that no one point in its composition is referable either to accident or intuition; that the work proceeded, step by step, to its completion with the precision and rigid consequence of a mathematical problem.

Let us dismiss, as irrelevant to the poem, *per se*, the circumstance—or say the necessity—which, in the first place, gave rise to the intention of composing *a* poem that should suit at once the popular and the critical taste.

We commence, then, with this intention.

The initial consideration was that of extent. If any literary work is too long to be read at one sitting, we must be content to dispense with the immensely important effect derivable from unity of impression; for, if two sittings be required, the affairs of the world interfere, and everything like totality is at once destroyed. But since, *ceteris paribus*, no poet can afford to dispense with *anything* that may advance his design, it but remains to be seen whether there is, in extent, any advantage to counterbalance the loss of unity which attends it. Here I say no, at once. What we term a long poem is, in fact, merely a succession of brief ones—that is to say, of brief poetical effects. It is needless to demonstrate that a poem is such, only inasmuch as it intensely excites, by elevating, the soul; and all intense excitements are, through a psychal necessity, brief. For this reason, at least one half of the "Paradise Lost" is essentially prose—a succession of poetical excitements interspersed, *inevitably*, with corresponding depressions—the whole being deprived, through the extremeness of its length, of the vastly important artistic element, totality, or unity, of effect.

It appears evident, then, that there is a distinct limit, as regards length, to all works of literary art—the limit of a single sitting; and that, although in certain classes of prose composition, such as "Robinson Crusoe" (demanding no unity), this limit may be advantageously overpassed, it can never properly be overpassed in a poem. Within this limit, the extent of a poem may be made to bear mathematical relation to its merit—in other words, to the excitement or elevation—again, in other words, to the degree of the true poetical effect which it is capable of inducing; for it is clear that the brevity must be in direct ratio of the intensity of the intended effect:—this, with one proviso—that a certain degree of duration is absolutely requisite for the production of any effect at all.

Holding in view these considerations, as well as that degree of excitement which I deemed not above the popular, while not below the critical, taste, I reached at once what I conceived the proper *length* for my intended poem—a length of about one hundred lines. It is, in fact, a hundred and eight.

My next thought concerned the choice of an impression, or effect, to be conveyed: and here I may as well observe that, throughout the construction, I kept steadily in view the design of rendering the work *universally* appreciable. I should be carried too far out of my immediate topic were I to demonstrate a point upon which I have repeatedly insisted, and which, with the poetical, stands not in the slightest need of demonstration—the point, I mean, that Beauty is the sole legitimate province of the poem. A few words, however, in elucidation of my real meaning, which some of my friends have evinced a disposition to misrepresent. That pleasure which is at once the most intense, the most elevating, and the most pure, is, I believe, found in the contemplation of the beautiful. When, indeed, men speak of Beauty, they mean, precisely, not a quality, as is supposed, but an effect—they refer, in short, just to that intense and pure elevation of *soul*—*not* of intellect, or of heart—upon which I have commented, and which is experienced in consequence of contemplating "the beautiful." Now I designate Beauty as the province of the poem, merely because it is an obvious rule of Art that effects should be made to spring from direct causes—that objects should be attained through means best adapted for their attainment—no one as yet having been weak enough to deny that the peculiar elevation alluded to is *most readily* attained in the poem. Now the object, Truth, or the satisfaction of the intellect, and the object Passion, or the excitement of the heart, are, although attainable, to a certain extent in poetry, far more readily attainable in prose. Truth, in fact, demands a precision, and Passion a *homeliness* (the truly passionate will comprehend me), which are absolutely antagonistic to that Beauty which, I maintain, is the excitement, or pleasurable elevation, of the soul. It by no means follows from anything here said, that passion, or even truth, may not be introduced, and even profitably introduced, into a poem—for they may serve in elucidation, or aid the general effect, as do discords in music, by contrast; but the true artist will always contrive, first, to tone them into proper subservience to the predominant aim, and, secondly, to enveil them, as far as possible, in that Beauty which is the atmosphere and the essence of the poem.

Regarding, then, Beauty as my province, my next question referred to the *tone* of its highest manifestation; and all experience has shown that this tone is one of *sadness*. Beauty of whatever kind, in its supreme development, invariably excites the sensitive soul to tears. Melancholy is thus the most legitimate of all the poetical tones.

The length, the province, and the tone, being thus determined, I betook myself to ordinary induction, with the view of obtaining some artistic piquancy which might serve me as a key-note in the construction of the poem—some pivot upon which the whole structure might turn. In carefully thinking over all the usual artistic effects—or more properly *points*, in the theatrical sense—I did not fail to perceive immediately that no one had been so universally employed as that of the *refrain.* The universality of its employment sufficed to assure me of its intrinsic value, and spared me the necessity of submitting it to analysis. I considered it, however, with regard to its susceptibility of improvement, and soon saw it to be in a primitive condition. As commonly used, the *refrain*, or burden, not only is limited to lyric verse, but depends for its impression upon the force of monotone—both in sound and thought. The pleasure is deduced solely from the sense of identity—of repetition. I resolved to diversify, and so heighten, the effect, by adhering, in general, to the monotone of sound, while I continually varied that of thought: that is to say, I determined to produce continuously novel effects, by the variation *of the application* of the *refrain*—the *refrain* itself remaining, for the most part, unvaried.

These points being settled, I next bethought me of the *nature* of my *refrain.* Since its application was to be repeatedly varied, it was clear that the *refrain* itself must be brief, for there would have been an insurmountable difficulty in frequent variations of application in any sentence of length. In proportion to the brevity of the sentence, would, of course, be the facility of the variation. This led me at once to a single word as the best *refrain.*

The question now arose as to the *character* of the word. Having made up my mind to a *refrain*, the division of the poem into stanzas was, of course, a corollary: the *refrain* forming the close to each stanza. That such a close, to have force, must be sonorous and susceptible of protracted emphasis, admitted no doubt; and these considerations inevitably led me to the long *o* as the most sonorous vowel, in connection with *r* as the most producible consonant.

The sound of the *refrain* being thus determined, it became necessary to select a word embodying this sound and at the same time in the fullest possible keeping with that melancholy which I had predetermined as the tone of the poem. In such a search it would have been absolutely impossible to overlook the word "Nevermore." In fact, it was the very first which presented itself.

The next *desideratum* was a pretext for the continuous use of the one word "Nevermore." In observing the difficulty which I at once found in inventing a sufficiently plausible reason for its continuous repetition, I did not fail to perceive that this difficulty arose solely from the pre-assumption that the word was to be so continuously or monotonously spoken by a *human* being; I did not fail to perceive, in short, that the difficulty lay in the reconciliation of this monotony with the exercise of reason on the part of the creature repeating the word. Here, then, immediately arose the idea of a *non*-reasoning creature capable of speech; and, very naturally, a parrot, in the first instance, suggested itself, but was superseded forthwith by a Raven, as equally capable of speech, and infinitely more in keeping with the intended *tone.*

I had now gone so far as the conception of a Raven—the bird of ill omen—monotonously repeating the one word, "Nevermore," at the conclusion of each stanza, in a poem of melancholy tone, and in length about one hundred lines. Now, never losing sight of the object *supremeness*, or perfection, at all points, I asked myself—"Of all melancholy topics, what, according to the *universal* understanding of mankind, is the *most* melancholy?" Death—was the obvious reply. "And when," I said, "is this most melancholy of topics most poetical?" From what I have already explained at some length, the answer, here also, is obvious—"When it most closely allies itself to *Beauty;* the death, then, of a beautiful woman is, unquestionably, the most poetical topic in the world—and equally is it beyond doubt that the lips best suited for such topic are those of a bereaved lover."

I had now to combine the two ideas, of a lover lamenting his deceased mistress and a Raven continuously repeating the word "Nevermore." I had to combine these, bearing in mind my design of varying at every turn the *application* of the word repeated; but the only intelligible mode of such combination is that of imagining the Raven employing the word in answer to the queries of the lover. And here it was that I saw at once the opportunity afforded for the effect on which I had been depending—that is to say, the effect of the *variation of appli-*

cation. I saw that I could make the first query propounded by the lover—the first query to which the Raven should reply "Nevermore"—that I could make this first query a commonplace one, the second less so, the third still less, and so on, until at length the lover, startled from his original *nonchalance* by the melancholy character of the word itself, by its frequent repetition, and by a consideration of the ominous reputation of the fowl that uttered it, is at length excited to superstition, and wildly propounds queries of a far different character—queries whose solution he has passionately at heart—propounds them half in superstition and half in that species of despair which delights in self-torture—propounds them not altogether because he believes in the prophetic or demoniac character of the bird (which, reason assures him, is merely repeating a lesson learned by rote) but because he experiences a frenzied pleasure in so modeling his questions as to receive from the *expected* "Nevermore" the most delicious because the most intolerable of sorrow. Perceiving the opportunity thus afforded me—or, more strictly, thus forced upon me in the progress of the construction—I first established in mind the climax, or concluding query—that query to which "Nevermore" should be in the last place an answer—that query in reply to which this word "Nevermore" should involve the uttermost conceivable amount of sorrow and despair.

Here then the poem may be said to have its beginning—at the end, where all works of art should begin; for it was here, at this point of my preconsiderations, that I first put pen to paper in the composition of the stanza:—

"Prophet," said I, "thing of evil! prophet still if bird or devil!
By that heaven that bends above us—by that God we both adore,
Tell this soul with sorrow laden if, within the distant Aidenn,
It shall clasp a sainted maiden whom the angels name Lenore—
Clasp a rare and radiant maiden whom the angels name Lenore."
Quoth the Raven "Nevermore."

I composed this stanza, at this point, first that, by establishing the climax, I might the better vary and graduate, as regards seriousness and importance, the preceding queries of the lover, and, secondly, that I might definitely settle the rhythm, the metre, and the length and general arrangement of the stanza, as well as graduate the stanzas which were to precede, so that none of them might surpass this in rhythmical effect. Had I been able, in the subsequent composition, to construct more vigorous stanzas, I should, without scruple, have purposely enfeebled them, so as not to interfere with the climacteric effect.

And here I may as well say a few words of the versification. My first object (as usual) was originality. The extent to which this has been neglected, in versification, is one of the most unaccountable things in the world. Admitting that there is little possibility of variety in mere *rhythm*, it is still clear that the possible varieties of metre and stanza are absolutely infinite—and yet, *for centuries, no man, in verse, has ever done, or ever seemed to think of doing, an original thing*. The fact is, that originality (unless in minds of very unusual force) is by no means a matter, as some suppose, of impulse or intuition. In general, to be found, it must be elaborately sought, and although a positive merit of the highest class, demands in its attainment less of invention than negation.

Of course, I pretend to no originality in either the rhythm or metre of the "Raven." The former is trochaic, the latter is octameter acatalectic, alternating with heptameter catalectic repeated in the *refrain* of the fifth verse, and terminating with tetrameter catalectic. Less pedantically—the feet employed throughout (trochees) consist of a long syllable followed by a short; the first line of the stanza consists of eight of these feet, the second of seven and a half (in effect two-thirds), the third of eight, the fourth of seven and a half, the fifth the same, the sixth three and a half. Now, each of these lines, taken individually, has been employed before, and what originality the "Raven" has, is in their *combination into stanza;* nothing even remotely approaching this combination has ever been attempted. The effect of this originality of combination is aided by other unusual, and some altogether novel effects, arising from an extension of the application of the principles of rhyme and alliteration.

The next point to be considered was the mode of bringing together the lover and the

Raven; and the first branch of this consideration was the *locale*. For this the most natural suggestion might seem to be a forest, or the fields; but it has always appeared to me that a close *circumscription of space* is absolutely necessary to the effect of insulated incident:—it has the force of a frame to a picture. It has an indisputable moral power in keeping concentrated the attention, and, of course, must not be confounded with mere unity of place.

I determined, then, to place the lover in his chamber—in a chamber rendered sacred to him by memories of her who had frequented it. The room is represented as richly furnished—this in mere pursuance of the ideas I have already explained on the subject of Beauty, as the sole true poetical thesis.

The *locale* being thus determined, I had now to introduce the bird—and the thought of introducing him through the window was inevitable. The idea of making the lover suppose, in the first instance, that the flapping of the wings of the bird against the shutter, is a "tapping" at the door, originated in a wish to increase, by prolonging, the reader's curiosity, and in a desire to admit the incidental effect arising from the lover's throwing open the door, finding all dark, and thence adopting the half-fancy that it was the spirit of his mistress that knocked.

I made the night tempestuous, first, to account for the Raven's seeking admission, and secondly, for the effect of contrast with the (physical) serenity within the chamber.

I made the bird alight on the bust of Pallas, also for the effect of contrast between the marble and the plumage—it being understood that the bust was absolutely *suggested* by the bird; the bust of *Pallas* being chosen, first, as most in keeping with the scholarship of the lover, and, secondly, for the sonorousness of the word, Pallas, itself.

About the middle of the poem, also, I have availed myself of the force of contrast, with a view of deepening the ultimate impression. For example, an air of the fantastic, approaching as nearly to the ludicrous as was admissible, is given to the Raven's entrance. He comes in "with many a flirt and flutter."

Not the *least obeisance made he;* not a moment stopped or stayed he;
But with mien of lord or lady, perched above my chamber door.

In the two stanzas which follow, the design is more obviously carried out:—

Then this ebony bird beguiling my sad fancy into smiling
By the *grave and stern decorum of the countenance it wore,*—
"Though thy *crest be shorn and shaven,* thou," I said, "art sure no craven,
Ghastly grim and ancient Raven wandering from the nightly shore:
Tell me what thy lordly name is on the Night's Plutonian shore?"
Quoth the Raven "Nevermore."

Much I marvelled *this ungainly fowl* to hear discourse so plainly,
Though its answer little meaning—little relevancy bore;
For we cannot help agreeing that no living human being
Ever yet was blessed with seeing bird above his chamber door—
Bird or beast upon the sculptured bust above his chamber door,
With such name as "Nevermore."

The effect of the *dénouement* being thus provided for, I immediately drop the fantastic for a tone of the most profound seriousness:—this tone commencing in the stanza directly following the one last quoted, with the line,

But the Raven, sitting lonely on that placid bust, spoke only, etc.

From this epoch the lover no longer jests—no longer sees anything even of the fantastic in the Raven's demeanor. He speaks of him as a "grim, ungainly, ghastly, gaunt, and ominous bird of yore," and feels the "fiery eyes" burning into his "bosom's core." This revolution of thought, or fancy, on the lover's part, is intended to induce a similar one on the part of the reader—to bring the mind into a proper frame for the *dénouement*, which is now brought about as rapidly and as *directly* as possible.

With the *dénouement* proper—with the Raven's reply, "Nevermore," to the lover's final demand if he shall meet his mistress in another world—the poem, in its obvious phase, that of a simple narrative, may be said to have its completion. So far, everything is within the limits of the accountable, of the real. A raven, having learned by rote the single word "Nevermore," and having escaped from the custody of its owner, is driven at midnight, through the violence of a storm, to seek admission at a window from which a light still gleams—the chamber-window of a student, occupied half in poring over a volume, half in dreaming of a beloved mistress deceased. The casement being thrown open at the fluttering of the bird's wings, the bird itself perches on the most convenient seat out of the immediate reach of the student, who, amused by the incident and the oddity of the visitor's demeanor, demands of it, in jest and without looking for a reply, its name. The raven addressed, answers with its customary word, "Nevermore"—a word which finds immediate echo in the melancholy heart of the student, who, giving utterance aloud to certain thoughts suggested by the occasion, is again startled by the fowl's repetition of "Nevermore." The student now guesses the state of the case, but is impelled, as I have before explained, by the human thirst for self-torture, and in part by superstition, to propound such queries to the bird as will bring him, the lover, the most of the luxury of sorrow, through the anticipated answer "Nevermore." With the indulgence, to the extreme, of this self-torture, the narration, in what I have termed its first or obvious phase, has a natural termination, and so far there has been no overstepping of the limits of the real.

But in subjects so handled, however skilfully, or with however vivid an array of incident, there is always a certain hardness or nakedness, which repels the artistical eye. Two things are invariably required: first, some amount of complexity, or more properly, adaptation; and, secondly, some amount of suggestiveness, some under-current, however indefinite, of meaning. It is this latter, in especial, which imparts to a work of art so much of that *richness* (to borrow from colloquy a forcible term) which we are too fond of confounding with *the ideal*. It is the *excess* of the suggested meaning—it is rendering this the upper instead of the under-current of the theme—which turns into prose (and that of the very flattest kind) the so-called poetry of the so-called transcendentalists.

Holding these opinions, I added the two concluding stanzas of the poem—their suggestiveness being thus made to pervade all the narrative which has preceded them. The under-current of meaning is rendered first apparent in the lines—

"Take thy beak from out *my heart*, and take thy form from off my door!"
Quoth the Raven, "Nevermore!"

It will be observed that the words, "from out my heart," involve the first metaphorical expression in the poem. They, with the answer, "Nevermore," dispose the mind to seek a moral in all that has been previously narrated. The reader begins now to regard the Raven as emblematical—but it is not until the very last line of the very last stanza, that the intention of making him emblematical of *Mournful and Never-ending Remembrance* is permitted distinctly to be seen:—

And the Raven, never flitting, still is sitting, still is sitting,
On the pallid bust of Pallas just above my chamber door;
And his eyes have all the seeming of a demon's that is dreaming,
And the lamplight o'er him streaming throws his shadow on the floor;
And my soul *from out that shadow* that lies floating on the floor
Shall be lifted—nevermore.

1846

From EUREKA

AN ESSAY ON THE MATERIAL AND SPIRITUAL UNIVERSE

It is with humility really unassumed—it is with a sentiment even of awe—that I pen the opening sentence of this work: for of all conceivable subjects I approach the reader with the most solemn—the most comprehensive—the most difficult—the most august.

What terms shall I find sufficiently simple in their sublimity—sufficiently sublime in their simplicity—for the mere enunciation of my theme?

I design to speak of the *Physical, Metaphysical and Mathematical—of the Material and Spiritual Universe:—of its Essence, its Origin, its Creation, its Present Condition and its Destiny.* I shall be so rash, moreover, as to challenge the conclusions, and thus, in effect, to question the sagacity, of many of the greatest and most justly reverenced of men.

In the beginning, let me as distinctly as possible announce—not the theorem which I hope to demonstrate—for, whatever the mathematicians may assert, there is, in this world at least, *no such thing* as demonstration—but the ruling idea which, throughout this volume, I shall be continually endeavoring to suggest.

My general proposition, then, is this:—*In the Original Unity of the First Thing lies the Secondary Cause of All Things, with the Germ of their Inevitable Annihilation.*

In illustration of this idea, I propose to take such a survey of the Universe that the mind may be able really to receive and to perceive an individual impression. . . .

Oneness, then, is all that I predicate of the originally created Matter; but I propose to show that this *Oneness is a principle abundantly sufficient to account for the constitution, the existing phænomena and the plainly inevitable annihilation of at least the material Universe.*

The willing into being the primordial particle, has completed the act, or more properly the *conception*, of Creation. We now proceed to the ultimate purpose for which we are to suppose the Particle created—that is to say, the ultimate purpose so far as our considerations *yet* enable us to see it—the constitution of the Universe from it, the Particle.

This constitution has been effected by *forcing* the originally and therefore normally *One* into the abnormal condition of *Many*. An action of this character implies reaction. A diffusion from Unity, under the conditions, involves a tendency to return into Unity—a tendency ineradicable until satisfied. . . .

Discarding now the two equivocal terms, "gravitation" and "electricity," let us adopt the more definite expressions, "*attraction*" and "*repulsion*." The former is the body; the latter the soul: the one is the material; the other the spiritual, principle of the Universe. *No other principles exist. All* phænomena are referable to one, or to the other, or to both combined. So rigorously is this the case—so thoroughly demonstrable is it that attraction and repulsion are the *sole* properties through which we perceive the Universe—in other words, by which Matter is manifested to Mind—that, for all merely argumentative purposes, we are fully justified in assuming that matter *exists* only as attraction and repulsion—that attraction and repulsion *are* matter:—there being no conceivable case in which we may not employ the term "matter" and the terms "attraction" and "repulsion," taken together, as equivalent, and therefore convertible, expressions in Logic.

I said, just now, that what I have described as the tendency of the diffused atoms to return into their original unity, would be understood as the principle of the Newtonian law of gravity: and, in fact, there can be but little difficulty in such an understanding, if we look at the Newtonian gravity in a merely general view, as a force impelling matter to seek matter; that is to say, when we pay no attention to the known *modus operandi* of the Newtonian force. The general coincidence satisfies us; but, upon looking closely, we see, in detail, much that appears *in*coincident, and much in regard to which no coincidence, at least, is established. For example; the Newtonian gravity, when we think of it in certain moods, does *not* seem to be a tendency to *oneness* at all, but rather a tendency of all bodies in all directions—a phrase apparently expressive of a tendency to diffusion. Here, then, is an *in*coincidence. Again; when we reflect on the mathematical *law* governing the Newtonian tendency, we see clearly that no coincidence has been made good, in respect of the *modus operandi*, at least, between gravitation as known to exist and that seemingly simple and direct tendency which I have assumed.

In fact, I have attained a point at which it will be advisable to strengthen my position by reversing my processes. So far, we have gone on *à priori*, from an abstract consideration of *Simplicity*, as that quality most likely to have characterized the original action of God. Let us now see whether the established facts of the Newtonian Gravitation may not afford us, *à posteriori*, some legitimate inductions.

What does the Newtonian law declare?—That all bodies attract each other with forces proportional to their quantities of matter and inversely proportional to the squares of their distances. Purposely, I have here given, in the first place, the vulgar version of the law; and I confess that in this, as in most other vulgar versions of great truths, we find little of a suggestive character. Let us now adopt a more philosophical phraseology:—*Every atom, of every body, attracts every other atom, both of its own and of every other body, with a force which varies inversely as the squares of the distances between the attracting and attracted atom.*—Here, indeed, a flood of suggestion bursts upon the mind. . . .

Does not so evident a brotherhood among the atoms point to a common parentage? Does not a sympathy so omniprevalent, so ineradicable, and so thoroughly irrespective, suggest a common paternity as its source? Does not one extreme impel the reason to the other? Does not the infinitude of division refer to the utterness of individuality? Does not the entireness of the complex hint at the perfection of the simple? It is *not* that the atoms, as we see them, are divided or that they are complex in their relations—but that they are inconceivably divided and unutterably complex:—it is the extremeness of the conditions to which I now allude, rather than to the conditions themselves. In a word, not because the atoms were, at some remote epoch of time, even *more than together*—is it not because originally, and therefore normally, they were *One*—that now, in all circumstances—at all points—in all directions —by all modes of approach—in all relations and through all conditions—they struggle *back* to this absolutely, this irrelatively, this unconditionally *one?* . . .

Throughout all this we have no difficulty in understanding the absolute accuracy of the Divine *adaptation*. The density of the stars, respectively, proceeds, of course, as their condensation diminishes; condensation and heterogeneity keep pace with each other; through the latter, which is the index of the former, we estimate the vitalic and spiritual development. Thus, in the density of the globes, we have the measure in which their purposes are fulfilled. *As* density proceeds—*as* the divine intentions *are* accomplished—*as* less and still less remains *to be* accomplished—so—in the same ratio—should we expect to find an acceleration of *the End:*—and thus the philosophical mind will easily comprehend that the Divine designs in constituting the stars, advance *mathematically* to their fulfilment:—and more; it will readily give the advance a mathematical expression; it will decide that this advance is inversely proportional with the squares of the distances of all created things from the starting-point and goal of their creation.

Not only is this Divine adaptation, however, mathematically accurate, but there is that about it which stamps it *as divine*, in distinction from that which is merely the work of human constructiveness. I allude to the complete *mutuality* of adaptation. For example; in human constructions a particular cause has a particular effect; a particular intention brings to pass a particular object; but this is all; we see no reciprocity. The effect does not re-act upon the cause; the intention does not change relations with the object. In Divine constructions the object is either design or object as we choose to regard it—and we may take at any time a cause for an effect, or the converse—so that we can never absolutely decide which is which.

To give an instance:—In polar climates the human frame, to maintain its animal heat, requires, for combustion in the capillary system, an abundant supply of highly azotized food, such as train-oil. But again:—in polar climates nearly the sole food afforded man is the oil of abundant seals and whales. Now, whether is oil at hand because imperatively demanded, or the only thing demanded because the only thing to be obtained? It is impossible to decide. There is an absolute *reciprocity of adaptation.*

The pleasure which we derive from any display of human ingenuity is in the ratio of *the approach* to this species of reciprocity. In the construction of *plot*, for example, in fictitious literature, we should aim at so arranging the incidents that we shall not be able to determine, of any one of them, whether it depends from any one other or upholds it. In this sense, of course, *perfection* of *plot* is really, or practically, unattainable—but only because it is a finite intelligence that constructs. The plots of God are perfect. The Universe is a plot of God.

And now we have reached a point at which the intellect is forced, again, to struggle against its propensity for analogical inference—against its monomaniac grasping at the infinite. Moons have been seen *revolving* about planets; planets about stars; and the poetical instinct of humanity—its instinct of the symmetrical, if the symmetry be but a symmetry of surface:—this *instinct*, which the Soul, not only of Man but of all created beings, took up, in the beginning, from the *geometrical* basis of the Universal irradiation—impels us to the fancy of an endless extension of this system of *cycles*. Closing our eyes equally to *de*duction and *in*duction, we insist upon imagining a *revolution* of all the orbs of the Galaxy about some gigantic globe which we take to be the central pivot of the whole. Each cluster in the great cluster of clusters is imagined, of course, to be similarly supplied and constructed; while, that the "analogy" may be wanting at no point, we go on to conceive these clusters themselves, again, as *revolving* about some still more august sphere;—this latter, still again, *with* its encircling clusters, as but one of a yet more magnificent series of agglomerations, *gyrating* about yet another orb central *to them*—some orb still more unspeakably sublime—some orb, let us rather say, of infinite sublimity endlessly multiplied by the infinitely sublime. Such are the conditions, continued in perpetuity, which the voice of what some people term "analogy" calls upon the Fancy to depict and the Reason to contemplate, if possible, without becoming dissatisfied with the picture. Such, *in general*, are the interminable gyrations beyond gyration which we have been instructed by Philosophy to comprehend and to account for, at least in the best manner we can. . . .

I have already alluded to that absolute *reciprocity of adaptation* which is the idiosyncrasy of the divine Art—stamping it divine. Up to this point of our reflections, we have been regarding the electrical influence as a something by dint of whose repulsion alone Matter is enabled to exist in that state of diffusion demanded for the fulfilment of its purposes:—so far, in a word, we have been considering the influence in question as ordained for Matter's sake—to subserve the objects of matter. With a perfectly legitimate reciprocity, we are now permitted to look at Matter, as created *solely for the sake of this influence*—solely to serve the objects of this spiritual Ether. Through the aid—by the means—through the agency of Matter, and by dint of its heterogeneity—is this Ether manifested—is *Spirit individualized*. It is merely in the development of this Ether, through heterogeneity, that particular masses of Matter become animate—sensitive—and in the ratio of their heterogeneity;—some reaching a degree of sensitiveness involving what we call *Thought* and thus attaining Conscious Intelligence.

In this view, we are enabled to perceive Matter as a Means—not as an End. Its purposes are thus seen to have been comprehended in its diffusion; and with the return into Unity these purposes cease. The absolutely consolidated globe of globes would be *objectless*:—therefore not for a moment could it continue to exist. Matter, created for an end, would unquestionably, on fulfilment of that end, be Matter no longer. Let us endeavor to understand that it would disappear, and that God would remain all in all. . . .

But are we here to pause? Not so. On the Universal agglomeration and dissolution, we can readily conceive that a new and perhaps totally different series of conditions may ensue—another creation and irradiation, returning into itself—another action and reaction of the Divine Will. Guiding our imaginations by that omniprevalent law of laws, the law of periodicity, are we not, indeed, more than justified in entertaining a belief—let us say, rather, in indulging a hope—that the processes we have here ventured to contemplate will be renewed forever, and forever, and forever; a novel Universe swelling into existence, and then subsiding into nothingness, at every throb of the Heart Divine?

And now—this Heart Divine—what is it? *It is our own*. . . .

In this view [that each soul is in part its own God] and in this view alone, we comprehend the riddles of Divine Injustice—of Inexorable Fate. In this view alone the existence of Evil becomes intelligible; but in this view it becomes more—it becomes endurable. Our souls no longer rebel at a *Sorrow* which we ourselves have imposed upon ourselves, in furtherance of our own purposes—with a view—even with a futile view—to the extension of our own *Joy*.

I have spoken of *Memories* that haunt us during our youth. They sometimes pursue us even during our Manhood:—assume gradually less and less indefinite shapes:—and now and then speak to us in low voices, saying:

"There was an epoch in the Night of Time, when a still-existent Being existed—one of an absolutely infinite number of similar Beings that people the absolutely infinite domains of absolutely infinite space. It was not and is not in the power of this Being—any more than it is in your own—to extend, by actual increase, the joy of his Existence; but just as it *is* in your power to expand or to concentrate your pleasures (the absolute amount of happiness remaining always the same) so did and does a similar capability appertain to the Divine Being, who thus passes his Eternity in perpetual variation of Concentrated Self and almost infinite Self-Diffusion. What you call The Universe is but his present expansive existence. He now feels his life through an infinity of imperfect pleasures—the partial and pain-intertangled pleasures of those inconceivably numerous things which you designate as his creatures, but which are really but infinite individualizations of Himself. All these creatures—*all*—those which you term animate, as well as those to whom you deny life for no better reason than that you do not behold it in operation—*all* these creatures have, in a greater or less degree, a capacity for pleasure and for pain:—*but the general sum of their sensations is precisely that amount of Happiness which appertains by right to the Divine Being when concentrated within Himself.* These creatures are all too, more or less conscious Intelligences; conscious, first, of a proper identity; conscious, secondly and by faint indeterminate glimpses, of an identity with the Divine Being of whom we speak—of an identity with God. Of the two classes of consciousness, fancy that the former will grow weaker, the latter stronger, during the long succession of ages which must elapse before these myriads of individual Intelligences become blended—into One. Think that the sense of individual identity will be gradually merged in the general consciousness—that Man, for example, ceasing imperceptibly to feel himself Man, will at length attain that awfully triumphant epoch when he shall recognize his existence as that of Jehovah. In the mean time bear in mind that all is Life—Life—Life within Life—the less within the greater, and all within the *Spirit Divine.*"

1848

THE POETIC PRINCIPLE

In speaking of the Poetic Principle, I have no design to be either thorough or profound. While discussing, very much at random, the essentiality of what we call Poetry, my principal purpose will be to cite for consideration, some few of those minor English or American poems which best suit my own taste, or which, upon my own fancy, have left the most definite impression. By "minor poems" I mean, of course, poems of little length. And here, in the beginning, permit me to say a few words in regard to a somewhat peculiar principle, which, whether rightfully or wrongfully, has always had its influence in my own critical estimate of the poem. I hold that a long poem does not exist. I maintain that the phrase, "a long poem," is simply a flat contradiction in terms.

I need scarcely observe that a poem deserves its title only inasmuch as it excites, by elevating the soul. The value of the poem is in the ratio of this elevating excitement. But all excitements are, through a psychal necessity, transient. That degree of excitement which would entitle a poem to be so called at all, cannot be sustained throughout a composition of any great length. After the lapse of half an hour, at the very utmost, it flags—fails—a revulsion ensues—and then the poem is, in effect, and in fact, no longer such.

There are, no doubt, many who have found difficulty in reconciling the critical dictum that the *Paradise Lost* is to be devoutly admired throughout, with the absolute impossibility of maintaining for it, during perusal, the amount of enthusiasm which that critical dictum would demand. This great work, in fact, is to be regarded as poetical, only when, losing sight of that vital requisite in all works of Art, Unity, we view it merely as a series of minor poems. If, to preserve its Unity—its totality of effect or impression—we read it (as would be necessary) at a single sitting, the result is but a constant alternation of excitement and depression. After a passage of what we feel to be true poetry, there follows, inevitably, a passage of platitude which no critical pre-judgment can force us to admire; but if, upon completing the work, we read it again; omitting the first book—that is to say, commencing with the second

—we shall be surprised at now finding that admirable which we before condemned—that damnable which we had previously so much admired. It follows from all this that the ultimate, aggregate, or absolute effect of even the best epic under the sun, is a nullity:—and this is precisely the fact.

In regard to the *Iliad*, we have, if not positive proof, at least very good reason, for believing it intended as a series of lyrics; but, granting the epic intention, I can say only that the work is based on an imperfect sense of Art. The modern epic is, of the supposititious ancient model, but an inconsiderate and blindfold imitation. But the day of these artistic anomalies is over. If, at any time, any very long poem *were* popular in reality, which I doubt, it is at least clear that no very long poem will ever be popular again.

That the extent of a poetical work is, *ceteris paribus*, the measure of its merit, seems undoubtedly, when we thus state it, a proposition sufficiently absurd—yet we are indebted for it to the Quarterly Reviews. Surely there can be nothing in mere *size*, abstractly considered—there can be nothing in mere *bulk*, so far as a volume is concerned, which has so continuously elicited admiration from these saturnine pamphlets! A mountain, to be sure, by the mere sentiment of physical magnitude which it conveys, *does* impress us with a sense of the sublime—but no man is impressed after *this* fashion by the material grandeur of even *The Columbiad*. Even the Quarterlies have not instructed us to be so impressed by it. *As yet*, they have not *insisted* on our estimating Lamartine by the cubic foot, or Pollok by the pound—but what else are we to *infer* from their continual prating about "sustained effort"? If, by "sustained effort," any little gentleman has accomplished an epic, let us frankly commend him for the effort—if this indeed be a thing commendable—but let us forbear praising the epic on the effort's account. It is to be hoped that common sense, in the time to come, will prefer deciding upon a work of art, rather by the impression it makes, by the effect it produces, than by the time it took to impress the effect or by the amount of "sustained effort" which had been found necessary in effecting the impression. The fact is, that perseverance is one thing, and genius quite another—nor can all the Quarterlies in Christendom confound them. By-and-by, this proposition, with many which I have been just urging, will be received as self-evident. In the meantime, by being generally condemned as falsities, they will not be essentially damaged as truths.

On the other hand, it is clear that a poem may be improperly brief. Undue brevity degenerates into mere epigrammatism. A *very* short poem, while now and then producing a brilliant or vivid, never produces a profound or enduring effect. There must be the steady pressing down of the stamp upon the wax. De Béranger has wrought innumerable things, pungent and spirit-stirring; but, in general, they have been too imponderous to stamp themselves deeply into the public attention; and thus, as so many feathers of fancy, have been blown aloft only to be whistled down the wind.

A remarkable instance of the effect of undue brevity in depressing a poem—in keeping it out of the popular view—is afforded by the following exquisite little Serenade:

I arise from dreams of thee
  In the first sweet sleep of night,
When the winds are breathing low,
  And the stars are shining bright;
I arise from dreams of thee,
  And a spirit in my feet
Has led me—who knows how?—
  To thy chamber-window, sweet!

The wandering airs, they faint
  On the dark, the silent stream—
The champak odors fail
  Like sweet thoughts in a dream;
The nightingale's complaint,
  It dies upon her heart,
As I must die on thine,
  O, beloved as thou art!

O, lift me from the grass!
  I die, I faint, I fail!
Let thy love in kisses rain
  On my lips and eyelids pale.
My cheek is cold and white, alas!
  My heart beats loud and fast:
Oh! press it close to thine again,
  Where it will break at last!

Very few, perhaps, are familiar with these lines—yet no less a poet than Shelley is their author. Their warm, yet delicate and ethereal imagination will be appreciated by all—but by none so thoroughly as by him who has himself arisen from sweet dreams of one beloved to bathe in the aromatic air of a southern midsummer night.

One of the finest poems by Willis—the very best, in my opinion, which he has ever written—has, no doubt, through this same defect of undue brevity, been kept back from its proper position, not less in the critical than in the popular view.

The shadows lay along Broadway,
'Twas near the twilight-tide—
And slowly there a lady fair
Was walking in her pride.
Alone walk'd she; but, viewlessly,
Walk'd spirits at her side.

Peace charm'd the street beneath her feet,
And Honor charm'd the air;
And all astir looked kind on her,
And call'd her good as fair—
For all God ever gave to her
She kept with chary care.

She kept with care her beauties rare
From lovers warm and true—
For her heart was cold to all but gold,
And the rich came not to woo—
But honor'd well are charms to sell,
If priests the selling do.

Now walking there was one more fair—
A slight girl, lily-pale;
And she had unseen company
To make the spirit quail—
'Twixt Want and Scorn she walk'd forlorn,
And nothing could avail.

No mercy now can clear her brow
For this world's peace to pray;
For, as love's wild prayer dissolved in air,
Her woman's heart gave way!—
But the sin forgiven by Christ in Heaven
By man is cursed alway!

In this composition we find it difficult to recognize the Willis who has written so many mere "verses of society." The lines are not only richly ideal, but full of energy; while they breathe an earnestness—an evident sincerity of sentiment—for which we look in vain throughout all the other works of this author.

While the epic mania—while the idea that, to merit in poetry, prolixity is indispensable—has, for some years past, been gradually dying out of the public mind, by mere dint of its own absurdity—we find it succeeded by a heresy too palpably false to be long tolerated, but one which, in the brief period it has already endured, may be said to have accomplished more in the corruption of our Poetical Literature than all its other enemies combined. I allude to the heresy of *The Didactic*. It has been assumed, tacitly and avowedly, directly and indirectly, that the ultimate object of all Poetry is Truth. Every poem, it is said, should inculcate a moral; and by this moral is the poetical merit of the work to be adjudged. We Americans especially have patronized this happy idea; and we Bostonians, very especially, have developed it in full. We have taken it into our heads that to write a poem simply for the poem's sake, and to acknowledge such to have been our design, would be to confess ourselves radically wanting in the true Poetic dignity and force:—but the simple fact is, that, would we but permit ourselves to look into our own souls, we should immediately there discover that under the sun there neither exists nor *can* exist any work more thoroughly dignified—more supremely noble than this very poem—this poem *per se*—this poem which is a poem and nothing more—this poem written solely for the poem's sake.

With as deep a reverence for the True as ever inspired the bosom of man, I would, nevertheless, limit, in some measure, its modes of inculcation. I would limit to enforce them. I would not enfeeble them by dissipation. The demands of Truth are severe. She has no sympathy with the myrtles. All *that* which is so indispensable in Song, is precisely all *that* with which *she* has nothing whatever to do. It is but making her a flaunting paradox, to wreathe her in gems and flowers. In enforcing a truth, we need severity rather than efflorescence of language. We must be simple, precise, terse. We must be cool, calm, unimpassioned. In a word, we must be in that mood which, as nearly as possible, is the exact converse of the poetical. *He* must be blind, indeed, who does not perceive the radical and chasmal differences between the truthful and the poetical modes of inculcation. He must be theory-mad beyond redemption who, in spite of these differences, shall still persist in attempting to reconcile the obstinate oils and waters of Poetry and Truth.

Dividing the world of mind into its three

most obvious distinctions, we have the Pure Intellect, Taste, and the Moral Sense. I place Taste in the middle, because it is just this position which, in the mind, it occupies. It holds intimate relations with either extreme; but from the Moral Sense is separated by so faint a difference that Aristotle has not hesitated to place some of its operations among the virtues themselves. Nevertheless, we find the *offices* of the trio marked with a sufficient distinction. Just as the Intellect concerns itself with Truth, so Taste informs us of the Beautiful while the Moral Sense is regardful of Duty. Of this latter, while Conscience teaches the obligation, and Reason the expediency, Taste contents herself with displaying the charms:—waging war upon Vice solely on the ground of her deformity—her disproportion, her animosity to the fitting, to the appropriate, to the harmonious—in a word, to Beauty.

An immortal instinct, deep within the spirit of man, is thus, plainly, a sense of the Beautiful. This it is which administers to his delight in the manifold forms, and sounds, and odors, and sentiments amid which he exists. And just as the lily is repeated in the lake, or the eyes of Amaryllis in the mirror, so is the mere oral or written repetition of these forms, and sounds, and colors, and odors, and sentiments, a duplicate source of delight. But this mere repetition is not poetry. He who shall simply sing, with however glowing enthusiasm, or with however vivid a truth of description, of the sights, and sounds, and odors, and colors, and sentiments, which greet *him* in common with all mankind—he, I say, has yet failed to prove his divine title. There is still a something in the distance which he has been unable to attain. We have still a thirst unquenchable, to allay which he has not shown us the crystal springs. This thirst belongs to the immortality of Man. It is at once a consequence and an indication of his perennial existence. It is the desire of the moth for the star. It is no mere appreciation of the Beauty before us—but a wild effort to reach the Beauty above. Inspired by an ecstatic prescience of the glories beyond the grave, we struggle, by multiform combinations among the things and thoughts of Time, to attain a portion of that Loveliness whose very elements, perhaps, appertain to eternity alone. And thus when by Poetry—or when by Music, the most entrancing of the Poetic moods—we find ourselves melted into tears—we weep then—not as the Abbaté Gravina supposes—through excess of pleasure, but through a certain, petulant, impatient sorrow at our inability to grasp *now*, wholly, here on earth, at once and forever, those divine and rapturous joys, of which *through* the poem, or *through* the music, we attain to but brief and indeterminate glimpses.

The struggle to apprehend the supernal Loveliness—this struggle, on the part of souls fittingly constituted—has given to the world all *that* which it (the world) has ever been enabled at once to understand and *to feel* as poetic.

The Poetic Sentiment, of course, may develop itself in various modes—in Painting, in Sculpture, in Architecture, in the Dance—very especially in Music—and very peculiarly, and with a wide field, in the composition of the Landscape Garden. Our present theme, however, has regard only to its manifestation in words. And here let me speak briefly on the topic of rhythm. Contenting myself with the certainty that Music, in its various modes of metre, rhythm, and rhyme, is of so vast a moment in Poetry as never to be wisely rejected—is so vitally important an adjunct, that he is simply silly who declines its assistance, I will not now pause to maintain its absolute essentiality. It is in Music, perhaps, that the soul most nearly attains the great end for which, when inspired by the Poetic Sentiment, it struggles—the creation of supernal Beauty. It *may* be, indeed, that here this sublime end is, now and then, attained *in fact*. We are often made to feel, with a shivering delight, that from an earthly harp are stricken notes which *cannot* have been unfamiliar to the angels. And thus there can be little doubt that in the union of Poetry with Music in its popular sense, we shall find the widest field for the Poetic development. The old Bards and Minnesingers had advantages which we do not possess—and Thomas Moore, singing his own songs, was, in the most legitimate manner, perfecting them as poems.

To recapitulate, then:—I would define, in brief, the Poetry of words as *The Rhythmical*

Creation of Beauty. Its sole arbiter is Taste. With the Intellect or with the Conscience, it has only collateral relations. Unless incidentally, it has no concern whatever either with Duty or with Truth.

A few words, however, in explanation. *That* pleasure which is at once the most pure, the most elevating, and the most intense, is derived, I maintain, from the contemplation of the Beautiful. In the contemplation of Beauty we alone find it possible to attain that pleasurable elevation, or excitement, *of the soul*, which we recognize as the Poetic Sentiment, and which is so easily distinguished from Truth, which is the satisfaction of the Reason, or from Passion, which is the excitement of the heart. I make Beauty, therefore—using the word as inclusive of the sublime—I make Beauty the province of the poem, simply because it is an obvious rule of Art that effects should be made to spring as directly as possible from their causes:—no one as yet having been weak enough to deny that the peculiar elevation in question is at least *most readily* attainable in the poem. It by no means follows, however, that the incitements of Passion, or the precepts of Duty, or even the lessons of Truth, may not be introduced into a poem, and with advantage; for they may subserve, incidentally, in various ways, the general purposes of the work:—but the true artist will always contrive to tone them down in proper subjection to that *Beauty* which is the atmosphere and the real essence of the poem.

I cannot better introduce the few poems which I shall present for your consideration, than by the citation of the Proem to Mr. Longfellow's "Waif":

The day is done, and the darkness
  Falls from the wings of Night,
As a feather is wafted downward
  From an Eagle in his flight.

I see the lights of the village
  Gleam through the rain and the mist,
And a feeling of sadness comes o'er me,
  That my soul cannot resist;

A feeling of sadness and longing,
  That is not akin to pain,
And resembles sorrow only
  As the mist resembles the rain.

Come, read to me some poem,
  Some simple and heartfelt lay,
That shall soothe this restless feeling,
  And banish the thoughts of day.

Not from the grand old masters,
  Not from the bards sublime,
Whose distant footsteps echo
  Through the corridors of Time.

For, like strains of martial music,
  Their mighty thoughts suggest
Life's endless toil and endeavor;
  And to-night I long for rest.

Read from some humbler poet,
  Whose songs gushed from his heart,
As showers from the clouds of summer,
  Or tears from the eyelids start;

Who through long days of labor,
  And nights devoid of ease,
Still heard in his soul the music
  Of wonderful melodies.

Such songs have power to quiet
  The restless pulse of care,
And come like the benediction
  That follows after prayer.

Then read from the treasured volume
  The poem of thy choice,
And lend to the rhyme of the poet
  The beauty of thy voice.

And the night shall be filled with music,
  And the cares that infest the day,
Shall fold their tents, like the Arabs,
  And as silently steal away.

With no great range of imagination, these lines have been justly admired for their delicacy of expression. Some of the images are very effective. Nothing can be better than—

———The bards sublime,
Whose distant footsteps echo
Down the corridors of Time.

The idea of the last quatrain is also very effective. The poem, on the whole, however, is chiefly to be admired for the graceful *insouciance* of its metre, so well in accordance with the character of the sentiments, and especially for the *ease* of the general manner. This "ease," or naturalness, in a literary style, it has long been the fashion to regard as ease in appearance alone—as a point of really difficult attainment. But not so:—a natural manner is difficult only to him who should never meddle with it—to the unnatural. It is but the result of writing with the understanding, or with the instinct, that *the tone*, in composition, should always be that which the mass of mankind would adopt—and must perpetually vary, of course, with the occasion. The author who, after the fashion of the *North American Review*, should be, upon *all* occasions, merely "quiet," must necessarily upon *many* occasions, be simply silly, or stupid; and has no more right to be considered "easy," or "natural," than a Cockney exquisite, or than the sleeping Beauty in the wax-works.

Among the minor poems of Bryant, none has so much impressed me as the one which he entitles "June." I quote only a portion of it:

> There, through the long, long summer hours,
> The golden light should lie,
> And thick young herbs and groups of flowers
> Stand in their beauty by.
> The oriole should build and tell
> His love-tale, close beside my cell;
> The idle butterfly
> Should rest him there, and there be heard
> The housewife-bee and humming-bird.
>
> And what if cheerful shouts at noon
> Come, from the village sent,
> Or songs of maids, beneath the moon,
> With fairy laughter blent?
> And what if, in the evening light,
> Betrothed lovers walk in sight
> Of my low monument?
> I would the lovely scene around
> Might know no sadder sight nor sound.
>
> I know, I know I should not see
> The season's glorious show,
> Nor would its brightness shine for me,
> Nor its wild music flow;
> But if, around my place of sleep,
> The friends I love should come to weep,
> They might not haste to go.
> Soft airs, and song, and light, and bloom
> Should keep them lingering by my tomb.
>
> These to their softened hearts should bear
> The thought of what has been,
> And speak of one who cannot share
> The gladness of the scene;
> Whose part, in all the pomp that fills
> The circuit of the summer hills,
> Is—that his grave is green;
> And deeply would their hearts rejoice
> To hear again his living voice.

The rhythmical flow, here, is even voluptuous—nothing could be more melodious. The poem has always affected me in a remarkable manner. The intense melancholy which seems to well up, perforce, to the surface of all the poet's cheerful sayings about his grave, we find thrilling us to the soul—while there is the truest poetic elevation in the thrill. The impression left is one of a pleasurable sadness. And if, in the remaining compositions which I shall introduce to you, there be more or less of a similar tone always apparent, let me remind you that (how or why we know not) this certain taint of sadness is inseparably connected with all the higher manifestations of true Beauty. It is, nevertheless,

> A feeling of sadness and longing
> That is not akin to pain,
> And resembles sorrow only
> As the mist resembles the rain.

The taint of which I speak is clearly perceptible even in a poem so full of brilliancy and spirit as the "Health" of Edward Coate Pinckney:

> I fill this cup to one made up
> Of loveliness alone,
> A woman, of her gentle sex
> The seeming paragon;
> To whom the better elements
> And kindly stars have given
> A form so fair, that, like the air,
> 'Tis less of earth than heaven.
>
> Her every tone is music's own,
> Like those of morning birds,
> And something more than melody
> Dwells ever in her words;
> The coinage of her heart are they,
> And from her lips each flows
> As one may see the burden'd bee
> Forth issue from the rose.
>
> Affections are as thoughts to her,
> The measures of her hours;
> Her feelings have the fragrancy,
> The freshness of young flowers;
> And lovely passions, changing oft,
> So fill her, she appears
> The image of themselves by turns,—
> The idol of past years!
>
> Of her bright face one glance will trace
> A picture on the brain,
> And of her voice in echoing hearts
> A sound must long remain;
> But memory, such as mine of her,
> So very much endears,
> When death is nigh, my latest sigh
> Will not be life's but hers.

I fill this cup to one made up
Of loveliness alone,
A woman, of her gentle sex
The seeming paragon—
Her health! and would on earth there stood
Some more of such a frame,
That life might be all poetry,
And weariness a name.

It was the misfortune of Mr. Pinckney to have been born too far south. Had he been a New Englander, it is probable that he would have been ranked as the first of American lyrists, by that magnanimous cabal which has so long controlled the destinies of American Letters, in conducting the thing called the *North American Review*. The poem just cited is especially beautiful; but the poetic elevation which it induces, we must refer chiefly to our sympathy in the poet's enthusiasm. We pardon his hyperboles for the evident earnestness with which they are uttered.

It was by no means my design, however, to expatiate upon the *merits* of what I should read you. These will necessarily speak for themselves. Boccalini, in his *Advertisements from Parnassus*, tells us that Zoilus once presented Apollo a very caustic criticism upon a very admirable book:—whereupon the god asked him for the beauties of the work. He replied that he only busied himself about the errors. On hearing this, Apollo, handing him a sack of unwinnowed wheat, bade him pick out *all the chaff* for his reward.

Now this fable answers very well as a hit at the critics—but I am by no means sure that the god was in the right. I am by no means certain that the true limits of the critical duty are not grossly misunderstood. Excellence, in a poem especially, may be considered in the light of an axiom, which need only be properly *put*, to become self-evident. It is *not* excellence if it require to be demonstrated as such:—and thus, to point out too particularly the merits of a work of Art, is to admit that they are *not* merits altogether.

Among the "Melodies" of Thomas Moore, is one whose distinguished character as a poem proper, seems to have been singularly left out of view. I allude to his lines beginning—"Come rest in this bosom." The intense energy of their expression is not surpassed by anything in Byron. There are two of the lines in which a sentiment is conveyed that embodies the *all in all* of the divine passion of love—a sentiment which, perhaps, has found its echo in more, and in more passionate, human hearts than any other single sentiment ever embodied in words:

Come, rest in this bosom, my own stricken deer,
Though the herd have fled from thee, thy home is still here;
Here still is the smile, that no cloud can o'ercast,
And a heart and a hand all thy own to the last.

Oh! what was love made for, if 'tis not the same
Through joy and through torment, through glory and shame?
I know not, I ask not, if guilt's in that heart,
I but know that I love thee, whatever thou art.

Thou hast call'd me thy Angel in moments of bliss,
And thy Angel I'll be, 'mid the horrors of this,—
Through the furnace, unshrinking, thy steps to pursue,
And shield thee, and save thee,—or perish there too!

It has been the fashion, of late days, to deny Moore imagination, while granting him fancy—a distinction originating with Coleridge—than whom no man more fully comprehended the great powers of Moore. The fact is, that the fancy of this poet so far predominates over all his other faculties, and over the fancy of all other men, as to have induced, very naturally, the idea that he is fanciful *only*. But never was there a greater mistake. Never was a grosser wrong done the fame of a true poet. In the compass of the English language I can call to mind no poem more profoundly—more weirdly *imaginative*, in the best sense, than the lines commencing—"I would I were by that dim lake"—which are the composition of Thomas Moore. I regret that I am unable to remember them.

One of the noblest—and, speaking of fancy, one of the most singularly fanciful of modern poets, was Thomas Hood. His "Fair Ines" had always, for me, an inexpressible charm:

O saw ye not fair Ines?
She's gone into the West,
To dazzle when the sun is down,
And rob the world of rest:
She took our daylight with her,
The smiles that we love best,
With morning blushes on her cheek,
And pearls upon her breast.

O turn again, fair Ines,
  Before the fall of night,
For fear the Moon should shine alone,
  And stars unrivall'd bright;
And blessed will the lover be
  That walks beneath their light,
And breathes the love against thy cheek
  I dare not even write!

Would I had been, fair Ines,
  That gallant cavalier,
Who rode so gaily by thy side,
  And whisper'd thee so near!
Were there no bonny dames at home,
  Or no true lovers here,
That he should cross the seas to win
  The dearest of the dear?

I saw thee, lovely Ines,
  Descend along the shore,
With bands of noble gentlemen,
  And banners wav'd before;
And gentle youth and maidens gay,
  And snowy plumes they wore;
It would have been a beauteous dream,
  If it had been no more!

Alas, alas, fair Ines,
  She went away with song,
With Music waiting on her steps,
  And shoutings of the throng;
But some were sad, and felt no mirth,
  But only Music's wrong,
In sounds that sang Farewell, Farewell,
  To her you've loved so long.

Farewell, farewell, fair Ines,
  That vessel never bore
So fair a lady on its deck,
  Nor danced so light before,—
Alas for pleasure on the sea,
  And sorrow on the shore!
The smile that blest one lover's heart
  Has broken many more!

"The Haunted House," by the same author, is one of the truest poems ever written—one of the *truest*—one of the most unexceptionable—one of the most thoroughly artistic, both in its theme and in its execution. It is, moreover, powerfully ideal—imaginative. I regret that its length renders it unsuitable for the purposes of this Lecture. In place of it, permit me to offer the universally appreciated "Bridge of Sighs."

One more Unfortunate,
Weary of breath,
Rashly importunate,
Gone to her death!

Take her up tenderly,
Lift her with care;—
Fashion'd so slenderly,
Young, and so fair!

Look at her garments
Clinging like cerements;
Whilst the wave constantly
Drips from her clothing;
Take her up instantly,
Loving, not loathing.

Touch her not scornfully;
Think of her mournfully,
Gently and humanly;
Not of the stains of her,
All that remains of her
Now is pure womanly.

Make no deep scrutiny
Into her mutiny
Rash and undutiful;
Past all dishonor,
Death has left on her
Only the beautiful.

Still, for all slips of hers,
One of Eve's family—
Wipe those poor lips of hers
Oozing so clammily.
Loop up her tresses
Escaped from the comb,
Her fair auburn tresses;
Whilst wonderment guesses
Where was her home?

Who was her father?
Who was her mother?
Had she a sister?
Had she a brother?
Or was there a dearer one
Still, and a nearer one
Yet, than all other?

Alas! for the rarity
Of Christian charity
Under the sun!
Oh! it was pitiful!
Near a whole city full,
Home she had none.

Sisterly, brotherly,
Fatherly, motherly
Feelings had changed:
Love, by harsh evidence,
Thrown from its eminence;
Even God's providence
Seeming estranged.

Where the lamps quiver
So far in the river,
With many a light
From window and casement,

From garret to basement,
She stood, with amazement,
Houseless by night.

The bleak wind of March
Made her tremble and shiver;
But not the dark arch,
Or the black flowing river:
Mad from life's history,
Glad to death's mystery,
Swift to be hurl'd—
Anywhere, anywhere
Out of the world!

In she plunged boldly,
No matter how coldly
The rough river ran,—
Over the brink of it,
Picture it—think of it,
Dissolute Man!
Lave in it, drink of it
Then, if you can!

Take her up tenderly,
Lift her with care;
Fashion'd so slenderly,
Young, and so fair!

Ere her limbs frigidly
Stiffen too rigidly,
Decently,—kindly,—
Smooth, and compose them;
And her eyes, close them,
Staring so blindly!

Dreadfully staring
Through muddy impurity,
As when with the daring
Last look of despairing
Fixed on futurity.

Perishing gloomily,
Spurred by contumely,
Cold inhumanity,
Burning insanity,
Into her rest,—
Cross her hands humbly,
As if praying dumbly,
Over her breast!
Owning her weakness,
Her evil behavior,
And leaving, with meekness,
Her sins to her Savior!

The vigor of this poem is no less remarkable than its pathos. The versification, although carrying the fanciful to the very verge of the fantastic, is nevertheless admirably adapted to the wild insanity which is the thesis of the poem.

Among the minor poems of Lord Byron, is one which has never received from the critics the praise which it undoubtedly deserves:

Though the day of my destiny's over,
And the star of my fate hath declined,
Thy soft heart refused to discover
The faults which so many could find;
Though thy soul with my grief was acquainted,
It shrunk not to share it with me,
And the love which my spirit hath painted
It never hath found but in *thee*.

Then when nature around me is smiling,
The last smile which answers to mine,
I do not believe it beguiling,
Because it reminds me of thine;
And when winds are at war with the ocean,
As the breasts I believed in with me,
If their billows excite an emotion,
It is that they bear me from *thee*.

Though the rock of my last hope is shivered,
And its fragments are sunk in the wave,
Though I feel that my soul is delivered
To pain—it shall not be its slave.
There is many a pang to pursue me:
They may crush, but they shall not contemn—
They may torture, but shall not subdue me—
'Tis of *thee* that I think—not of them.

Though human, thou didst not deceive me,
Though woman, thou didst not forsake,
Though loved, thou forborest to grieve me,
Though slandered, thou never couldst shake,—
Though trusted, thou didst not disclaim me,
Though parted, it was not to fly,
Though watchful, 'twas not to defame me,
Nor mute, that the world might belie.

Yet I blame not the world, nor despise it,
Nor the war of the many with one
If my soul was not fitted to prize it,
'Twas folly not sooner to shun:
And if dearly that error hath cost me,
And more than I once could foresee,
I have found that whatever it lost me,
It could not deprive me of *thee*.

From the wreck of the past, which hath perished,
Thus much I at least may recall,
It hath taught me that what I most cherished
Deserved to be dearest of all:
In the desert a fountain is springing,
In the wide waste there still is a tree,
And a bird in the solitude singing,
Which speaks to my spirit of *thee*.

Although the rhythm here is one of the most difficult, the versification could scarcely be improved. No nobler *theme* ever engaged the pen of poet. It is the soul-elevating idea, that no man can consider himself entitled to complain of Fate while, in his adversity, he still retains the unwavering love of woman.

From Alfred Tennyson—although in perfect sincerity I regard him as the noblest poet that ever lived—I have left myself time to cite only a very brief specimen. I call him, and *think* him the noblest of poets—*not* because the impressions he produces are, at *all* times, the most profound—*not* because the poetical excitement which he induces is, at *all* times, the most intense—but because it *is*, at all times, the most ethereal—in other words, the most elevating and the most pure. No poet is so little of the earth, earthy. What I am about to read is from his last long poem, *The Princess:*

Tears, idle tears, I know not what they mean,
Tears from the depth of some divine despair
Rise in the heart, and gather to the eyes,
In looking on the happy Autumn-fields,
And thinking of the days that are no more.

Fresh as the first beam glittering on a sail
That brings our friends up from the underworld,
Sad as the last which reddens over one
That sinks with all we love below the verge;
So sad, so fresh, the days that are no more.

Ah, sad and strange as in dark summer dawns
The earliest pipe of half-awaken'd birds
To dying ears, when unto dying eyes
The casement slowly grows a glimmering square;
So sad, so strange, the days that are no more.

Dear as remember'd kisses after death,
And sweet as those by hopeless fancy feign'd
On lips that are for others; deep as love,
Deep as first love, and wild with all regret;
O Death in Life, the days that are no more!

Thus, although in a very cursory and imperfect manner, I have endeavoured to convey to you my conception of the Poetic Principle. It has been my purpose to suggest that, while this Principle itself is, strictly and simply, the Human Aspiration for Supernal Beauty, the manifestation of the Principle is always found in *an elevating excitement of the Soul*—quite independent of that passion which is the intoxication of the Heart—or of that Truth which is the satisfaction of the Reason. For, in regard to Passion, alas! its tendency is to degrade, rather than to elevate the Soul. Love, on the contrary—Love—the true, the divine Eros—the Uranian, as distinguished from the Dionæan Venus—is unquestionably the purest and truest of all poetical themes. And in regard to Truth—if, to be sure, through the attainment of a truth, we are led to perceive a harmony where none was apparent before, we experience, at once, the true poetical effect—but this effect is referable to the harmony alone, and not in the least degree to the truth which merely served to render the harmony manifest.

We shall reach, however, more immediately a distinct conception of what the true Poetry is, by mere reference to a few of the simple elements which induce in the Poet himself the true poetical effect. He recognizes the ambrosia which nourishes his soul, in the bright orbs that shine in Heaven—in the volutes of the flower—in the clustering of low shrubberies—in the waving of the grain-fields—in the slanting of tall, Eastern trees—in the blue distance of mountains—in the grouping of clouds—in the twinkling of half-hidden brooks—in the gleaming of silver rivers—in the repose of sequestered lakes—in the star-mirroring depths of lonely wells. He perceives it in the songs of birds—in the harp of Æolus—in the sighing of the night-wind—in the repining voice of the forest—in the surf that complains to the shore—in the fresh breath of the woods—in the scent of the violet—in the voluptuous perfume of the hyacinth—in the suggestive odor that comes to him, at eventide, from far-distant, undiscovered islands, over dim oceans, illimitable and unexplored. He owns it in all noble thoughts—in all unworldly motives—in all holy impulses—in all chivalrous, generous, and self-sacrificing deeds. He feels it in the beauty of woman—in the grace of her step—in the lustre of her eye—in the melody of her voice—in her soft laughter—in her sigh—in the harmony of the rustling of her robes. He deeply feels it in her winning endearments—in her burning enthusiasms—in her gentle charities—in her meek and devotional endurances—but above all—ah, far above all—he kneels to it—he worships it in the faith, in the purity, in the strength, in the altogether divine majesty—of her *love*.

Let me conclude—by the recitation of yet another brief poem—one very different in character from any that I have before quoted. It is by Motherwell, and is called "The Song of the Cavalier." With our modern and altogether rational ideas of the absurdity and impiety of warfare, we are not precisely in that frame of mind best adapted to sympathize with the sentiments, and thus to appreciate the real excellence of the poem. To do this fully, we must identify ourselves, in fancy, with the soul of the old cavalier.

Then mounte! then mounte, brave gallants, all,
   And don your helmes amaine:
Death's couriers, Fame and Honor, call
   Us to the field againe.
No shrewish teares shall fill our eye
   When the sword-hilt's in our hand,—
Heart-whole we'll part, and no whit sighe
   For the fayrest of the land;
Let piping swaine, and craven wight,
   Thus weepe and puling crye,
Our business is like men to fight,
   And hero-like to die!

1848-1849 1850

HENRY WADSWORTH LONGFELLOW

PRELUDE

PLEASANT it was, when woods were green
  And winds were soft and low,
To lie amid some sylvan scene,
Where, the long drooping boughs between,
Shadows dark and sunlight sheen
  Alternate come and go;

Or where the denser grove receives
  No sunlight from above,
But the dark foliage interweaves
In one unbroken roof of leaves,
Underneath whose sloping eaves
  The shadows hardly move.

Beneath some patriarchal tree
  I lay upon the ground;
His hoary arms uplifted he,
And all the broad leaves over me
Clapped their little hands in glee,
  With one continuous sound;—

A slumberous sound, a sound that brings
  The feelings of a dream,
As of innumerable wings,
As, when a bell no longer swings,
Faint the hollow murmur rings
  O'er meadow, lake, and stream.

And dreams of that which cannot die,
  Bright visions, came to me,
As lapped in thought I used to lie,
And gaze into the summer sky,
Where the sailing clouds went by,
  Like ships upon the sea;

Dreams that the soul of youth engage
  Ere Fancy has been quelled;
Old legends of the monkish page,
Traditions of the saint and sage,
Tales that have the rime of age,
  And chronicles of eld.

And, loving still these quaint old themes,
  Even in the city's throng
I feel the freshness of the streams,
That, crossed by shades and sunny gleams,
Water the green land of dreams,
  The holy land of song.

Therefore, at Pentecost, which brings
  The Spring, clothed like a bride,
When nestling buds unfold their wings,
And bishop's-caps have golden rings,
Musing upon many things,
  I sought the woodlands wide.

The green trees whispered low and mild;
  It was a sound of joy!
They were my playmates when a child,
And rocked me in their arms so wild!
Still they looked at me and smiled,
  As if I were a boy;

And ever whispered, mild and low,
  "Come, be a child once more!"
And waved their long arms to and fro,
And beckoned solemnly and slow;
Oh, I could not choose but go
  Into the woodlands hoar,—

Into the blithe and breathing air,
  Into the solemn wood,
Solemn and silent everywhere!
Nature with folded hands seemed there,
Kneeling at her evening prayer!
  Like one in prayer I stood.

Before me rose an avenue
  Of tall and sombrous pines;
Abroad their fan-like branches grew,
And, where the sunshine darted through,
Spread a vapor soft and blue,
  In long and sloping lines.

And, falling on my weary brain,
  Like a fast-falling shower,
The dreams of youth came back again,—
Low lispings of the summer rain,
Dropping on the ripened grain,
  As once upon the flower.

Visions of childhood! Stay, oh, stay!
Ye were so sweet and wild!
And distant voices seemed to say,
"It cannot be! They pass away!
Other themes demand thy lay;
Thou art no more a child!

"The land of Song within thee lies,
Watered by living springs;
The lids of Fancy's sleepless eyes
Are gates unto that Paradise;
Holy thoughts, like stars, arise;
Its clouds are angels' wings.

"Learn, that henceforth thy song shall be,
Not mountains capped with snow,
Nor forests sounding like the sea,
Nor rivers flowing ceaselessly,
Where the woodlands bend to see
The bending heavens below.

"There is a forest where the din
Of iron branches sounds!
A mighty river roars between,
And whosoever looks therein
Sees the heavens all black with sin,
Sees not its depths, nor bounds.

"Athwart the swinging branches cast,
Soft rays of sunshine pour;
Then comes the fearful wintry blast;
Our hopes, like withered leaves, fall fast;
Pallid lips say, 'It is past!
We can return no more!'

"Look, then, into thine heart, and write!
Yes, into Life's deep stream!
All forms of sorrow and delight,
All solemn Voices of the Night,
That can soothe thee, or affright,—
Be these henceforth thy theme."

1839 1839

A PSALM OF LIFE

WHAT THE HEART OF THE YOUNG MAN SAID TO THE PSALMIST

TELL me not, in mournful numbers,
Life is but an empty dream!—
For the soul is dead that slumbers,
And things are not what they seem.

Life is real! Life is earnest!
And the grave is not its goal;
Dust thou art, to dust returnest,
Was not spoken of the soul.

Not enjoyment, and not sorrow,
Is our destined end or way;
But to act, that each tomorrow
Find us farther than today.

Art is long, and Time is fleeting,
And our hearts, though stout and brave,
Still, like muffled drums, are beating
Funeral marches to the grave.

In the world's broad field of battle,
In the bivouac of Life,
Be not like dumb, driven cattle!
Be a hero in the strife!

Trust no Future, howe'er pleasant!
Let the dead Past bury its dead!
Act,—act in the living Present!
Heart within, and God o'erhead!

Lives of great men all remind us
We can make our lives sublime,
And, departing, leave behind us
Footprints on the sands of time;

Footprints, that perhaps another,
Sailing o'er life's solemn main,
A forlorn and shipwrecked brother,
Seeing, shall take heart again.

Let us, then, be up and doing,
With a heart for any fate;
Still achieving, still pursuing,
Learn to labor and to wait.

1838 1838

THE REAPER AND THE FLOWERS

THERE is a Reaper, whose name is Death,
And, with his sickle keen,
He reaps the bearded grain at a breath,
And the flowers that grow between.

"Shall I have naught that is fair?" saith he;
"Have naught but the bearded grain?
Though the breath of these flowers is sweet to me,
I will give them all back again."

He gazed at the flowers with tearful eyes,
He kissed their drooping leaves;

It was for the Lord of Paradise
  He bound them in his sheaves.

"My Lord has need of these flowerets gay,"
  The Reaper said, and smiled;
"Dear tokens of the earth are they,
  Where He was once a child.

"They shall all bloom in fields of light,
  Transplanted by my care,
And saints, upon their garments white,
  These sacred blossoms wear."

And the mother gave, in tears and pain,
  The flowers she most did love;
She knew she should find them all again
  In the fields of light above.

Oh, not in cruelty, not in wrath,
  The Reaper came that day;
'Twas an angel visited the green earth,
  And took the flowers away.

1838 1838

THE LIGHT OF STARS

The night is come, but not too soon;
  And sinking silently,
All silently, the little moon
  Drops down behind the sky.

There is no light in earth or heaven
  But the cold light of stars;
And the first watch of night is given
  To the red planet Mars.

Is it the tender star of love?
  The star of love and dreams?
Oh no! from that blue tent above
  A hero's armor gleams.

And earnest thoughts within me rise,
  When I behold afar,
Suspended in the evening skies,
  The shield of that red star.

O star of strength! I see thee stand
  And smile upon my pain;
Thou beckonest with thy mailèd hand,
  And I am strong again.

Within my breast there is no light
  But the cold light of stars;
I give the first watch of the night
  To the red planet Mars.

The star of the unconquered will,
  He rises in my breast,
Serene, and resolute, and still,
  And calm, and self-possessed.

And thou, too, whosoe'er thou art,
  That readest this brief psalm,
As one by one thy hopes depart,
  Be resolute and calm.

Oh, fear not in a world like this,
  And thou shalt know erelong,
Know how sublime a thing it is
  To suffer and be strong.

1838 1838

✓ old ballad form

THE WRECK OF THE HESPERUS

It not a very adult poem—

It was the schooner Hesperus,
  That sailed the wintry sea;
And the skipper had taken his little daughtèr,
  To bear him company.

Blue were her eyes as the fairy-flax,
  Her cheeks like the dawn of day,
And her bosom white as the hawthorn buds,
  That ope in the month of May.

The skipper he stood beside the helm,
  His pipe was in his mouth,
And he watched how the veering flaw did blow
  The smoke now West, now South.

Then up and spake an old Sailòr,
  Had sailed to the Spanish Main,
"I pray thee, put into yonder port,
  For I fear a hurricane.

similar to Sir Patrick Spence—

"Last night, the moon had a golden ring,
  And tonight no moon we see!"
The skipper, he blew a whiff from his pipe,
  And a scornful laugh laughed he.

Colder and louder blew the wind,
  A gale from the Northeast,
The snow fell hissing in the brine,
  And the billows frothed like yeast.

Down came the storm, and smote amain
  The vessel in its strength;
She shuddered and paused, like a frighted steed,
  Then leaped her cable's length.

"Come hither! come hither! my little daughtèr,
And do not tremble so;
For I can weather the roughest gale
That ever wind did blow."

He wrapped her warm in his seaman's coat
Against the stinging blast;
He cut a rope from a broken spar,
And bound her to the mast.

"O father! I hear the church-bells ring,
Oh say, what may it be?"
"'Tis a fog-bell on a rock-bound coast!"—
And he steered for the open sea.

"O father! I hear the sound of guns,
Oh say, what may it be?"
"Some ship in distress, that cannot live
In such an angry sea!"

"O father! I see a gleaming light,
Oh say, what may it be?"
But the father answered never a word,
A frozen corpse was he.

Lashed to the helm, all stiff and stark,
With his face turned to the skies,
The lantern gleamed through the gleaming snow
On his fixed and glassy eyes.

Then the maiden clasped her hands and prayed
That savèd she might be;
And she thought of Christ, who stilled the wave,
On the Lake of Galilee.

And fast through the midnight dark and drear,
Through the whistling sleet and snow,
Like a sheeted ghost, the vessel swept
Tow'rds the reef of Norman's Woe.

And ever the fitful gusts between
A sound came from the land;
It was the sound of the trampling surf
On the rocks and the hard sea-sand.

The breakers were right beneath her bows,
She drifted a dreary wreck,
And a whooping billow swept the crew
Like icicles from her deck.

She struck where the white and fleecy waves
Looked soft as carded wool,
But the cruel rocks, they gored her side
Like the horns of an angry bull.

Her rattling shrouds, all sheathed in ice,
With the masts went by the board;
Like a vessel of glass, she stove and sank,
Ho! ho! the breakers roared!

At daybreak, on the bleak sea-beach,
A fisherman stood aghast,
To see the form of a maiden fair,
Lashed close to a drifting mast.

The salt sea was frozen on her breast,
The salt tears in her eyes;
And he saw her hair, like the brown seaweed,
On the billows fall and rise.

Such was the wreck of the Hesperus,
In the midnight and the snow!
Christ save us all from a death like this,
On the reef of Norman's Woe!

1839 1840

✓

THE VILLAGE BLACKSMITH

does not tell us too much other than physical qualities

UNDER a spreading chestnut-tree
The village smithy stands;
The smith, a mighty man is he,
With large and sinewy hands;
And the muscles of his brawny arms
Are strong as iron bands.

His hair is crisp, and black, and long,
His face is like the tan;
His brow is wet with honest sweat,
He earns whate'er he can,
And looks the whole world in the face,
For he owes not any man.

Week in, week out, from morn till night,
You can hear his bellows blow;
You can hear him swing his heavy sledge,
With measured beat and slow,
Like a sexton ringing the village bell,
When the evening sun is low.

And children coming home from school
Look in at the open door;
They love to see the flaming forge,
And hear the bellows roar,
And catch the burning sparks that fly
Like chaff from a threshing-floor.

He goes on Sunday to the church,
And sits among his boys;

He hears the parson pray and preach,
He hears his daughter's voice,
Singing in the village choir,
And it makes his heart rejoice.

It sounds to him like her mother's voice,
Singing in Paradise!
He needs must think of her once more
How in the grave she lies;
And with his hard, rough hand he wipes
A tear out of his eyes.

Toiling,—rejoicing,—sorrowing,
Onward through life he goes;
Each morning sees some task begin,
Each evening sees it close;
Something attempted, something done,
Has earned a night's repose.

Thanks, thanks to thee, my worthy friend,
For the lesson thou hast taught!
Thus at the flaming forge of life
Our fortunes must be wrought;
Thus on its sounding anvil shaped
Each burning deed and thought.

1839 1840

HYMN TO THE NIGHT

'Ασπασίη, τρίλλιστος

I HEARD the trailing garments of the Night
Sweep through her marble halls!
I saw her sable skirts all fringed with light
From the celestial walls!

I felt her presence, by its spell of might,
Stoop o'er me from above;
The calm, majestic presence of the Night,
As of the one I love.

I heard the sounds of sorrow and delight,
The manifold, soft chimes,
That fill the haunted chambers of the Night,
Like some old poet's rhymes.

From the cool cisterns of the midnight air
My spirit drank repose;
The fountain of perpetual peace flows there,—
From those deep cisterns flows.

O holy Night! from thee I learn to bear
What man has borne before!
Thou layest thy finger on the lips of Care,
And they complain no more.

Peace! Peace! Orestes-like I breathe this prayer!
Descend with broad-winged flight,
The welcome, the thrice-prayed for, the most fair,
The best-belovèd Night!

1839 1839

FOOTSTEPS OF ANGELS

WHEN the hours of Day are numbered,
And the voices of the Night
Wake the better soul, that slumbered,
To a holy, calm delight;

Ere the evening lamps are lighted,
And, like phantoms grim and tall,
Shadows from the fitful firelight
Dance upon the parlor wall;

Then the forms of the departed
Enter at the open door;
The beloved, the true-hearted,
Come to visit me once more;

He, the young and strong, who cherished
Noble longings for the strife,
By the roadside fell and perished,
Weary with the march of life!

They, the holy ones and weakly,
Who the cross of suffering bore,
Folded their pale hands so meekly,
Spake with us on earth no more!

And with them the Being Beauteous,
Who unto my youth was given,
More than all things else to love me,
And is now a saint in heaven.

With a slow and noiseless footstep
Comes that messenger divine,
Takes the vacant chair beside me,
Lays her gentle hand in mine.

And she sits and gazes at me
With those deep and tender eyes,
Like the stars, so still and saint-like,
Looking downward from the skies.

Uttered not, yet comprehended,
Is the spirit's voiceless prayer,
Soft rebukes, in blessings ended,
Breathing from her lips of air.

Oh, though oft depressed and lonely,
  All my fears are laid aside,
If I but remember only
  Such as these have lived and died!

1839 1839

THE BELEAGUERED CITY

I HAVE read, in some old, marvellous tale,
  Some legend strange and vague,
That a midnight host of spectres pale
  Beleaguered the walls of Prague.

Beside the Moldau's rushing stream,
  With the wan moon overhead,
There stood, as in an awful dream,
  The army of the dead.

White as a sea-fog, landward bound,
  The spectral camp was seen,
And, with a sorrowful, deep sound,
  The river flowed between.

No other voice nor sound was there,
  No drum, nor sentry's pace;
The mist-like banners clasped the air
  As clouds with clouds embrace.

But when the old cathedral bell
  Proclaimed the morning prayer,
The white pavilions rose and fell
  On the alarmèd air.

Down the broad valley fast and far
  The troubled army fled;
Up rose the glorious morning star,
  The ghastly host was dead.

I have read, in the marvellous heart of man,
  That strange and mystic scroll,
That an army of phantoms vast and wan
  Beleaguer the human soul.

Encamped beside Life's rushing stream,
  In Fancy's misty light,
Gigantic shapes and shadows gleam
  Portentous through the night.

Upon its midnight battle-ground
  The spectral camp is seen,
And, with a sorrowful, deep sound,
  Flows the River of Life between.

No other voice nor sound is there,
  In the army of the grave;
No other challenge breaks the air,
  But the rushing of Life's wave.

And when the solemn and deep church-bell
  Entreats the soul to pray,
The midnight phantoms feel the spell,
  The shadows sweep away.

Down the broad Vale of Tears afar
  The spectral camp is fled;
Faith shineth as a morning star,
  Our ghastly fears are dead.

1839 1839

SERENADE

FROM "THE SPANISH STUDENT"

STARS of the summer night!
  Far in yon azure deeps,
Hide, hide your golden light!
  She sleeps!
My lady sleeps!
  Sleeps!

Moon of the summer night!
  Far down yon western steeps,
Sink, sink in silver light!
  She sleeps!
My lady sleeps!
  Sleeps!

Wind of the summer night!
  Where yonder woodbine creeps,
Fold, fold thy pinions light!
  She sleeps!
My lady sleeps!
  Sleeps!

Dreams of the summer night!
  Tell her, her lover keeps
Watch! while in slumbers light
  She sleeps!
My lady sleeps!
  Sleeps!

1840 1842

THE SKELETON IN ARMOR

"SPEAK! speak! thou fearful guest!
Who, with thy hollow breast
Still in rude armor drest,
  Comest to daunt me!

Wrapt not in Eastern balms,
But with thy fleshless palms
Stretched, as if asking alms,
  Why dost thou haunt me?"

Then, from those cavernous eyes
Pale flashes seemed to rise,
As when the Northern skies
  Gleam in December;
And, like the water's flow
Under December's snow,
Came a dull voice of woe
  From the heart's chamber.

"I was a Viking old!
My deeds, though manifold,
No Skald in song has told,
  No Saga taught thee!
Take heed, that in thy verse
Thou dost the tale rehearse,
Else dread a dead man's curse;
  For this I sought thee.

"Far in the Northern Land,
By the wild Baltic's strand,
I, with my childish hand,
  Tamed the gerfalcon;
And, with my skates fast-bound,
Skimmed the half-frozen Sound,
That the poor whimpering hound
  Trembled to walk on.

"Oft to his frozen lair
Tracked I the grisly bear,
While from my path the hare
  Fled like a shadow;
Oft through the forest dark
Followed the were-wolf's bark,
Until the soaring lark
  Sang from the meadow.

"But when I older grew,
Joining a corsair's crew,
O'er the dark sea I flew
  With the marauders.
Wild was the life we led;
Many the souls that sped,
Many the hearts that bled,
  By our stern orders.

"Many a wassail-bout
Wore the long Winter out;
Often our midnight shout
  Set the cocks crowing,
As we the Berserk's tale
Measured in cups of ale,
Draining the oaken pail,
  Filled to o'erflowing.

"Once as I told in glee
Tales of the stormy sea,
Soft eyes did gaze on me,
  Burning yet tender;
And as the white stars shine
On the dark Norway pine,
On that dark heart of mine
  Fell their soft splendor.

"I wooed the blue-eyed maid,
Yielding, yet half afraid,
And in the forest's shade
  Our vows were plighted.
Under its loosened vest
Fluttered her little breast,
Like birds within their nest
  By the hawk frighted.

"Bright in her father's hall
Shields gleamed upon the wall,
Loud sang the minstrels all,
  Chanting his glory;
When of old Hildebrand
I asked his daughter's hand,
Mute did the minstrels stand
  To hear my story.

"While the brown ale he quaffed,
Loud then the champion laughed,
And as the wind-gusts waft
  The sea-foam brightly,
So the loud laugh of scorn,
Out of those lips unshorn,
From the deep drinking-horn
  Blew the foam lightly.

"She was a Prince's child,
I but a Viking wild,
And though she blushed and smiled,
  I was discarded!
Should not the dove so white
Follow the sea-mew's flight,
Why did they leave that night
  Her nest unguarded?

"Scarce had I put to sea,
Bearing the maid with me,
Fairest of all was she
  Among the Norsemen!

When on the white sea-strand,
Waving his armèd hand,
Saw we old Hildebrand,
With twenty horsemen.

"Then launched they to the blast,
Bent like a reed each mast,
Yet we were gaining fast,
When the wind failed us;
And with a sudden flaw
Came round the gusty Skaw,
So that our foe we saw
Laugh as he hailed us.

"And as to catch the gale
Round veered the flapping sail,
'Death!' was the helmsman's hail,
'Death without quarter!'
Mid-ships with iron keel
Struck we her ribs of steel;
Down her black hulk did reel
Through the black water!

this poem is clear and direct; to the point, no wasted words.

crashes to the King's ship broadside they sank the ship

"As with his wings aslant,
Sails the fierce cormorant,
Seeking some rocky haunt,
With his prey laden,—
So toward the open main,
Beating to sea again,
Through the wild hurricane,
Bore I the maiden.

"Three weeks we westward bore,
And when the storm was o'er,
Cloud-like we saw the shore
Stretching to leeward;
There for my lady's bower
Built I the lofty tower,
Which, to this very hour,
Stands looking seaward.

"There lived we many years;
Time dried the maiden's tears;
She had forgot her fears,
She was a mother;
Death closed her mild blue eyes,
Under that tower she lies;
Ne'er shall the sun arise
On such another!

"Still grew my bosom then,
Still as a stagnant fen!
Hateful to me were men,
The sunlight hateful!
In the vast forest here,
Clad in my warlike gear,
Fell I upon my spear,
Oh, death was grateful!

"Thus, seamed with many scars,
Bursting these prison bars,
Up to its native stars
My soul ascended!
There from the flowing bowl
Deep drinks the warrior's soul,
Skoal! to the Northland! *skoal!*"
Thus the tale ended.

1840 1841

ENDYMION

THE rising moon has hid the stars;
Her level rays, like golden bars,
Lie on the landscape green,
With shadows brown between.

And silver white the river gleams,
As if Diana, in her dreams,
Had dropt her silver bow
Upon the meadows low.

On such a tranquil night as this,
She woke Endymion with a kiss,
When, sleeping in the grove,
He dreamed not of her love.

Like Dian's kiss, unasked, unsought,
Love gives itself, but is not bought;
Nor voice, nor sound betrays
Its deep, impassioned gaze.

It comes,—the beautiful, the free,
The crown of all humanity,—
In silence and alone
To seek the elected one.

It lifts the boughs, whose shadows deep
Are Life's oblivion, the soul's sleep,
And kisses the closed eyes
Of him who slumbering lies.

O weary hearts! O slumbering eyes!
O drooping souls, whose destinies
Are fraught with fear and pain,
Ye shall be loved again!

No one is so accursed by fate,
No one so utterly desolate,
But some heart, though unknown,
Responds unto his own.

Responds,—as if with unseen wings,
An angel touched its quivering strings;
And whispers, in its song,
"Where hast thou stayed so long?"

1841 1841

THE RAINY DAY

THE day is cold, and dark, and dreary;
It rains, and the wind is never weary;
The vine still clings to the mouldering wall,
But at every gust the dead leaves fall,
And the day is dark and dreary.

My life is cold, and dark, and dreary;
It rains, and the wind is never weary;
My thoughts still cling to the mouldering Past,
But the hopes of youth fall thick in the blast,
And the days are dark and dreary.

Be still, sad heart! and cease repining;
Behind the clouds is the sun still shining;
Thy fate is the common fate of all,
Into each life some rain must fall,
Some days must be dark and dreary.

1841 1841

EXCELSIOR

THE shades of night were falling fast,
As through an Alpine village passed
A youth, who bore, 'mid snow and ice,
A banner with the strange device,
Excelsior!

His brow was sad; his eye beneath,
Flashed like a falchion from its sheath,
And like a silver clarion rung
The accents of that unknown tongue,
Excelsior!

In happy homes he saw the light
Of household fires gleam warm and bright;
Above, the spectral glaciers shone,
And from his lips escaped a groan,
Excelsior!

"Try not the Pass!" the old man said;
"Dark lowers the tempest overhead,
The roaring torrent is deep and wide!"
And loud that clarion voice replied,
Excelsior!

"Oh stay," the maiden said, "and rest
Thy weary head upon this breast!"
A tear stood in his bright blue eye,
But still he answered, with a sigh,
Excelsior!

"Beware the pine-tree's withered branch!
Beware the awful avalanche!"
This was the peasant's last Good-night,
A voice replied, far up the height,
Excelsior!

At break of day, as heavenward
The pious monks of Saint Bernard
Uttered the oft-repeated prayer,
A voice cried through the startled air,
Excelsior!

A traveller, by the faithful hound,
Half-buried in the snow was found,
Still grasping in his hand of ice
That banner with the strange device,
Excelsior!

There in the twilight cold and gray,
Lifeless, but beautiful, he lay,
And from the sky, serene and far,
A voice fell, like a falling star,
Excelsior!

1841 1841

THE SLAVE'S DREAM

BESIDE the ungathered rice he lay,
His sickle in his hand;
His breast was bare, his matted hair
Was buried in the sand.
Again, in the mist and shadow of sleep,
He saw his Native Land.

Wide through the landscape of his dreams
The lordly Niger flowed;
Beneath the palm-trees on the plain
Once more a king he strode;
And heard the tinkling caravans
Descend the mountain road.

He saw once more his dark-eyed queen
  Among her children stand;
They clasped his neck, they kissed his cheeks,
  They held him by the hand!—
A tear burst from the sleeper's lids
  And fell into the sand.

And then at furious speed he rode
  Along the Niger's bank;
His bridle-reins were golden chains,
  And, with a martial clank,
At each leap he could feel his scabbard of steel
  Smiting his stallion's flank.

Before him, like a blood-red flag,
  The bright flamingoes flew;
From morn till night he followed their flight,
  O'er plains where the tamarind grew,
Till he saw the roofs of Caffre huts,
  And the ocean rose to view.

At night he heard the lion roar,
  And the hyena scream,
And the river-horse, as he crushed the reeds
  Beside some hidden stream;
And it passed, like a glorious roll of drums,
  Through the triumph of his dream.

The forests, with their myriad tongues,
  Shouted of liberty;
And the Blast of the Desert cried aloud,
  With a voice so wild and free,
That he started in his sleep and smiled
  At their tempestuous glee.

He did not feel the driver's whip,
  Nor the burning heat of day;
For Death had illumined the Land of Sleep,
  And his lifeless body lay
A worn-out fetter, that the soul
  Had broken and thrown away!

1842 1842

THE WARNING

Beware! The Israelite of old, who tore
  The lion in his path,—when, poor and blind,
He saw the blessed light of heaven no more,
  Shorn of his noble strength and forced to grind
In prison, and at last led forth to be
A pander to Philistine revelry,—
Upon the pillars of the temple laid
  His desperate hands, and in its overthrow
Destroyed himself, and with him those who made
  A cruel mockery of his sightless woe;
The poor, blind Slave, the scoff and jest of all,
Expired, and thousands perished in the fall!

There is a poor, blind Samson in this land,
  Shorn of his strength and bound in bonds of steel,
Who may, in some grim revel, raise his hand,
  And shake the pillars of this Commonweal,
Till the vast Temple of our liberties
A shapeless mass of wreck and rubbish lies.

1842

THE BELFRY OF BRUGES

CARILLON

In the ancient town of Bruges,
In the quaint old Flemish city,
As the evening shades descended,
Low and loud and sweetly blended,
Low at times and loud at times,
And changing like a poet's rhymes,
Rang the beautiful wild chimes
From the Belfry in the market
Of the ancient town of Bruges.

Then, with deep sonorous clangor
Calmly answering their sweet anger,
When the wrangling bells had ended,
Slowly struck the clock eleven,
And, from out the silent heaven,
Silence on the town descended.
Silence, silence everywhere,
On the earth and in the air,
Save that footsteps here and there
Of some burgher home returning,
By the street lamps faintly burning,
For a moment woke the echoes
Of the ancient town of Bruges.

But amid my broken slumbers
Still I heard those magic numbers,
As they loud proclaimed the flight
And stolen marches of the night;
Till their chimes in sweet collision
Mingled with each wandering vision,
Mingled with the fortune-telling
Gypsy-bands of dreams and fancies,

Which amid the waste expanses
Of the silent land of trances
Have their solitary dwelling;
All else seemed asleep in Bruges,
In the quaint old Flemish city.

And I thought how like these chimes
Are the poet's airy rhymes,
All his rhymes and roundelays,
His conceits, and songs, and ditties,
From the belfry of his brain,
Scattered downward, though in vain,
On the roofs and stones of cities!
For by night the drowsy ear
Under its curtains cannot hear,
And by day men go their ways,
Hearing the music as they pass,
But deeming it no more, alas!
Than the hollow sound of brass.

Yet perchance a sleepless wight,
Lodging at some humble inn
In the narrow lanes of life,
When the dusk and hush of night
Shut out the incessant din
Of daylight and its toil and strife,
May listen with a calm delight
To the poet's melodies,
Till he hears, or dreams he hears,
Intermingled with the song,
Thoughts that he has cherished long;
Hears amid the chime and singing
The bells of his own village ringing,
And wakes, and finds his slumberous eyes
Wet with most delicious tears.

Thus dreamed I, as by night I lay
In Bruges, at the Fleur-de-Blé,
Listening with a wild delight
To the chimes that, through the night,
Rang their changes from the Belfry
Of that quaint old Flemish city.

1842 1843

MEZZO CAMMIN

Half of my life is gone, and I have let
The years slip from me and have not fulfilled
The aspiration of my youth, to build
Some tower of song with lofty parapet.
Not indolence, nor pleasure, nor the fret
Of restless passions that would not be stilled,
But sorrow, and a care that almost killed,
Kept me from what I may accomplish yet;
Though, half-way up the hill, I see the Past
Lying beneath me with its sounds and sights,—
A city in the twilight dim and vast,
With smoking roofs, soft bells, and gleaming lights,—
And hear above me on the autumnal blast
The cataract of Death far thundering from the heights.

1842 1886

THE ARSENAL AT SPRINGFIELD

This is the Arsenal. From floor to ceiling,
Like a huge organ, rise the burnished arms;
But from their silent pipes no anthem pealing
Startles the villages with strange alarms.

Ah! what a sound will rise, how wild and dreary,
When the death-angel touches those swift keys!
What loud lament and dismal Miserere
Will mingle with their awful symphonies!

I hear even now the infinite fierce chorus,
The cries of agony, the endless groan,
Which, through the ages that have gone before us,
In long reverberations reach our own.

On helm and harness rings the Saxon hammer,
Through Cimbric forest roars the Norseman's song,
And loud, amid the universal clamor,
O'er distant deserts sounds the Tartar gong.

I hear the Florentine, who from his palace
Wheels out his battle-bell with dreadful din,
And Aztec priests upon their teocallis
Beat the wild war-drums made of serpent's skin;

The tumult of each sacked and burning village;
The shout that every prayer for mercy drowns;
The soldiers' revels in the midst of pillage;
The wail of famine in beleaguered towns;

The bursting shell, the gateway wrenched asunder,
The rattling musketry, the clashing blade;
And ever and anon, in tones of thunder
The diapason of the cannonade.

Is it, O man, with such discordant noises,
With such accursed instruments as these,
Thou drownest Nature's sweet and kindly voices,
And jarrest the celestial harmonies?

Were half the power that fills the world with terror,
Were half the wealth bestowed on camps and courts,
Given to redeem the human mind from error,
There were no need of arsenals or forts:

The warrior's name would be a name abhorrèd!
And every nation, that should lift again
Its hand against a brother, on its forehead
Would wear forevermore the curse of Cain!

Down the dark future, through long generations,
The echoing sounds grow fainter and then cease;
And like a bell, with solemn, sweet vibrations,
I hear once more the voice of Christ say, "Peace!"

Peace! and no longer from its brazen portals
The blast of War's great organ shakes the skies!
But beautiful as songs of the immortals,
The holy melodies of love arise.

1844 1844

NUREMBERG

In the valley of the Pegnitz, where across broad meadow-lands
Rise the blue Franconian mountains, Nuremberg, the ancient, stands.

Quaint old town of toil and traffic, quaint old town of art and song,
Memories haunt thy pointed gables, like the rooks that round them throng:

Memories of the Middle Ages, when the emperors, rough and bold,
Had their dwelling in thy castle, time-defying, centuries old;

And thy brave and thrifty burghers boasted, in their uncouth rhyme,
That their great imperial city stretched its hand through every clime.

In the court-yard of the castle, bound with many an iron band,
Stands the mighty linden planted by Queen Cunigunde's hand;

On the square the oriel window, where in old heroic days
Sat the poet Melchior singing Kaiser Maximilian's praise.

Everywhere I see around me rise the wondrous world of Art:
Fountains wrought with richest sculpture standing in the common mart;

And above cathedral doorways saints and bishops carved in stone,
By a former age commissioned as apostles to our own.

In the church of sainted Sebald sleeps enshrined his holy dust,
And in bronze the Twelve Apostles guard from age to age their trust;

In the church of sainted Lawrence stands a pix of sculpture rare,
Like the foamy sheaf of fountains, rising through the painted air.

Here, when Art was still religion, with a simple, reverent heart,
Lived and labored Albrecht Dürer, the Evangelist of Art;

Hence in silence and in sorrow, toiling still with busy hand,
Like an emigrant he wandered, seeking for the Better Land.

Emigravit is the inscription on the tombstone where he lies;
Dead he is not, but departed,—for the artist never dies.

Fairer seems the ancient city, and the sunshine seems more fair,
That he once has trod its pavement, that he once has breathed its air!

Through these streets so broad and stately, these obscure and dismal lanes,
Walked of yore the Mastersingers, chanting rude poetic strains.

From remote and sunless suburbs came they to the friendly guild,
Building nests in Fame's great temple, as in spouts the swallows build.

As the weaver plied the shuttle, wove he too the mystic rhyme,
And the smith his iron measures hammered to the anvil's chime;

Thanking God, whose boundless wisdom makes the flowers of poesy bloom
In the forge's dust and cinders, in the tissues of the loom.

Here Hans Sachs, the cobbler-poet, laureate of the gentle craft,
Wisest of the Twelve Wise Masters, in huge folios sang and laughed.

But his house is now an ale-house, with a nicely sanded floor,
And a garland in the window, and his face above the door;

Painted by some humble artist, as in Adam Puschman's song,
As the old man gray and dove-like, with his great beard white and long.

And at night the swart mechanic comes to drown his cark and care,
Quaffing ale from pewter tankards, in the master's antique chair.

Vanished is the ancient splendor, and before my dreamy eye
Wave these mingled shapes and figures, like a faded tapestry.

Not thy Councils, not thy Kaisers, win for thee the world's regard;
But thy painter, Albrecht Dürer, and Hans Sachs thy cobbler bard.

Thus, O Nuremberg, a wanderer from a region far away,
As he paced thy streets and court-yards, sang in thought his careless lay:

Gathering from the pavement's crevice, as a floweret of the soil,
The nobility of labor,—the long pedigree of toil.

1844 1844

SEAWEED

When descends on the Atlantic
The gigantic
Storm-wind of the equinox,
Landward in his wrath he scourges
The toiling surges,
Laden with seaweed from the rocks:

From Bermuda's reefs; from edges
Of sunken ledges,
In some far-off, bright Azore;
From Bahama, and the dashing,
Silver-flashing
Surges of San Salvador;

From the tumbling surf, that buries
The Orkneyan skerries,
Answering the hoarse Hebrides;
And from wrecks of ships, and drifting
Spars, uplifting
On the desolate, rainy seas;—

Ever drifting, drifting, drifting
On the shifting
Currents of the restless main;
Till in sheltered coves, and reaches
Of sandy beaches,
All have found repose again.

So when storms of wild emotion
Strike the ocean
Of the poet's soul, erelong
From each cave and rocky fastness,
In its vastness,
Floats some fragment of a song:

From the far-off isles enchanted,
Heaven has planted
With the golden fruit of Truth;
From the flashing surf, whose vision
Gleams Elysian
In the tropic clime of Youth;

From the strong Will, and the Endeavor
That forever
Wrestle with the tides of Fate;
From the wreck of Hopes far-scattered,
Tempest-shattered,
Floating waste and desolate;—

Ever drifting, drifting, drifting
On the shifting
Currents of the restless heart;
Till at length in books recorded,
They, like hoarded
Household words, no more depart.

1844 1845

THE DAY IS DONE

THE day is done, and the darkness
Falls from the wings of Night,
As a feather is wafted downward
From an eagle in his flight.

I see the lights of the village
Gleam through the rain and the mist,
And a feeling of sadness comes o'er me
That my soul cannot resist:

A feeling of sadness and longing,
That is not akin to pain,
And resembles sorrow only
As the mist resembles the rain.

Come, read to me some poem,
Some simple and heartfelt lay,
That shall soothe this restless feeling,
And banish the thoughts of day.

Not from the grand old masters,
Not from the bards sublime,
Whose distant footsteps echo
Through the corridors of Time.

For, like strains of martial music,
Their mighty thoughts suggest
Life's endless toil and endeavor;
And tonight I long for rest.

Read from some humbler poet,
Whose songs gushed from his heart,
As showers from the clouds of summer,
Or tears from the eyelids start;

Who, through long days of labor,
And nights devoid of ease,
Still heard in his soul the music
Of wonderful melodies.

Such songs have power to quiet
The restless pulse of care,
And come like the benediction
That follows after prayer.

Then read from the treasured volume
The poem of thy choice,
And lend to the rhyme of the poet
The beauty of thy voice.

And the night shall be filled with music,
And the cares, that infest the day,
Shall fold their tents, like the Arabs,
And as silently steal away.

1844 1844

THE BRIDGE

I STOOD on the bridge at midnight,
As the clocks were striking the hour,
And the moon rose o'er the city,
Behind the dark church-tower.

I saw her bright reflection
In the waters under me,
Like a golden goblet falling
And sinking into the sea.

And far in the hazy distance
Of that lovely night in June,
The blaze of the flaming furnace
Gleamed redder than the moon.

Among the long, black rafters
The wavering shadows lay,
And the current that came from the ocean
Seemed to lift and bear them away;

As, sweeping and eddying through them,
Rose the belated tide,
And, streaming into the moonlight,
The seaweed floated wide.

And like those waters rushing
Among the wooden piers,
A flood of thoughts came o'er me
That filled my eyes with tears.

How often, oh how often,
In the days that had gone by,
I had stood on that bridge at midnight
And gazed on that wave and sky!

How often, oh how often,
  I had wished that the ebbing tide
Would bear me away on its bosom
  O'er the ocean wild and wide!

For my heart was hot and restless,
  And my life was full of care,
And the burden laid upon me
  Seemed greater than I could bear.

But now it has fallen from me,
  It is buried in the sea;
And only the sorrow of others
  Throws its shadow over me.

Yet whenever I cross the river
  On its bridge with wooden piers,
Like the odor of brine from the ocean
  Comes the thought of other years.

And I think how many thousands
  Of care-encumbered men,
Each bearing his burden of sorrow,
  Have crossed the bridge since then.

I see the long procession
  Still passing to and fro,
The young heart hot and restless,
  And the old subdued and slow!

And forever and forever,
  As long as the river flows,
As long as the heart has passions,
  As long as life has woes;

The moon and its broken reflection
  And its shadows shall appear,
As the symbol of love in heaven,
  And its wavering image here.

1845 1845

AFTERNOON IN FEBRUARY

The day is ending,
The night is descending;
The marsh is frozen,
  The river dead.

Through clouds like ashes
The red sun flashes
On village windows
  That glimmer red.

The snow recommences;
The buried fences
Mark no longer
  The road o'er the plain;

While through the meadows,
Like fearful shadows,
Slowly passes
  A funeral train.

The bell is pealing,
And every feeling
Within me responds
  To the dismal knell;

Shadows are trailing,
My heart is bewailing
And tolling within
  Like a funeral bell.

1845 1845

THE OLD CLOCK ON THE STAIRS

Somewhat back from the village street
Stands the old-fashioned country-seat.
Across its antique portico
Tall poplar-trees their shadows throw;
And from its station in the hall
An ancient timepiece says to all,—
    "Forever—never!
    Never—forever!"

Half-way up the stairs it stands,
And points and beckons with its hands
From its case of massive oak,
Like a monk, who, under his cloak,
Crosses himself, and sighs, alas!
With sorrowful voice to all who pass,—
    "Forever—never!
    Never—forever!"

By day its voice is low and light;
But in the silent dead of night,
Distinct as a passing footstep's fall,
It echoes along the vacant hall,
Along the ceiling, along the floor,
And seems to say, at each chamber-door,—
    "Forever—never!
    Never—forever!"

Through days of sorrow and of mirth,
Through days of death and days of birth,
Through every swift vicissitude

Of changeful time, unchanged it has stood,
And as if, like God, it all things saw,
It calmly repeats those words of awe,—
"Forever—never!
Never—forever!"

In that mansion used to be
Free-hearted Hospitality;
His great fires up the chimney roared;
The stranger feasted at his board;
But, like the skeleton at the feast,
That warning timepiece never ceased,—
"Forever—never!
Never—forever!"

There groups of merry children played,
There youths and maidens dreaming strayed;
O precious hours! O golden prime,
And affluence of love and time!
Even as a miser counts his gold,
Those hours the ancient timepiece told,—
"Forever—never!
Never—forever!"

From that chamber, clothed in white,
The bride came forth on her wedding night;
There, in that silent room below,
The dead lay in his shroud of snow;
And in the hush that followed the prayer,
Was heard the old clock on the stair,—
"Forever—never!
Never—forever!"

All are scattered now and fled,
Some are married, some are dead;
And when I ask, with throbs of pain,
"Ah! when shall they all meet again?"
As in the days long since gone by,
The ancient timepiece makes reply,—
"Forever—never!
Never—forever!"

Never here, forever there,
Where all parting, pain, and care,
And death, and time shall disappear,—
Forever there, but never here!
The horologe of Eternity
Sayeth this incessantly,—
"Forever—never!
Never—forever!"

1845 1845

THE ARROW AND THE SONG

I SHOT an arrow into the air,
It fell to earth, I knew not where;
For, so swiftly it flew, the sight
Could not follow it in its flight.

I breathed a song into the air,
It fell to earth, I knew not where;
For who has sight so keen and strong,
That it can follow the flight of song?

Long, long afterward, in an oak
I found the arrow, still unbroke;
And the song, from beginning to end,
I found again in the heart of a friend.

1845 1845

CURFEW

I

SOLEMNLY, mournfully,
Dealing its dole,
The Curfew Bell
Is beginning to toll.

Cover the embers,
And put out the light;
Toil comes with the morning,
And rest with the night.

Dark grow the windows,
And quenched is the fire;
Sound fades into silence,—
All footsteps retire.

No voice in the chambers,
No sound in the hall!
Sleep and oblivion
Reign over all!

II

The book is completed,
And closed, like the day;
And the hand that has written it
Lays it away.

Dim grow its fancies;
Forgotten they lie;
Like coals in the ashes,
They darken and die.

Song sinks into silence,
The story is told,

The windows are darkened,
The hearth-stone is cold.

Darker and darker
The black shadows fall;
Sleep and oblivion
Reign over all.

1845 1845

TO THE DRIVING CLOUD

Gloomy and dark art thou, O chief of the mighty Omahas;
Gloomy and dark as the driving cloud, whose name thou hast taken!
Wrapped in thy scarlet blanket, I see thee stalk through the city's
Narrow and populous streets, as once by the margin of rivers
Stalked those birds unknown, that have left us only their footprints.
What, in a few short years, will remain of thy race but the footprints?

How canst thou walk these streets, who hast trod the green turf of the prairies?
How canst thou breathe this air, who hast breathed the sweet air of the mountains?
Ah! 'tis in vain that with lordly looks of disdain thou dost challenge
Looks of disdain in return, and question these walls and these pavements,
Claiming the soil for thy hunting-grounds, while down-trodden millions
Starve in the garrets of Europe, and cry from its caverns that they, too,
Have been created heirs of the earth, and claim its division!

Back, then, back to thy woods in the regions west of the Wabash!
There as a monarch thou reignest. In autumn the leaves of the maple
Pave the floors of thy palace-halls with gold, and in summer
Pine-trees waft through its chambers the odorous breath of their branches.
There thou art strong and great, a hero, a tamer of horses!
There thou chasest the stately stag on the banks of the Elkhorn,
Or by the roar of the Running-Water, or where the Omaha
Calls thee, and leaps through the wild ravine like a brave of the Blackfeet!

Hark! what murmurs arise from the heart of those mountainous deserts?
Is it the cry of the Foxes and Crows, or the mighty Behemoth,
Who, unharmed, on his tusks once caught the bolts of the thunder,
And now lurks in his lair to destroy the race of the red man?
Far more fatal to thee and thy race than the Crows and the Foxes,
Far more fatal to thee and thy race than the tread of Behemoth,
Lo! the big thunder-canoe, that steadily breasts the Missouri's
Merciless current! and yonder, afar on the prairies, the camp-fires
Gleam through the night; and the cloud of dust in the gray of the daybreak
Marks not the buffalo's track, nor the Mandan's dexterous horse-race;
It is a caravan, whitening the desert where dwell the Camanches!
Ha! how the breath of these Saxons and Celts, like the blast of the east-wind,
Drifts evermore to the west the scanty smokes of thy wigwams!

1845 1845

WANDERER'S NIGHT-SONGS

(WANDRERS NACHTLIED AND EIN GLEICHES)

FROM GOETHE

I

Thou that from the heavens art,
Every pain and sorrow stillest,
And the doubly wretched heart
Doubly with refreshment fillest,
I am weary with contending!
Why this rapture and unrest?
Peace descending
Come, ah, come into my breast!

II

O'er all the hill-tops
Is quiet now,

In all the tree-tops
Hearest thou
Hardly a breath;
The birds are asleep in the trees:
Wait; soon like these
Thou too shalt rest.

1845 1870

THE BUILDERS

All are architects of Fate,
Working in these walls of Time;
Some with massive deeds and great,
Some with ornaments of rhyme.

Nothing useless is, or low;
Each thing in its place is best;
And what seems but idle show
Strengthens and supports the rest.

For the structure that we raise,
Time is with materials filled;
Our todays and yesterdays
Are the blocks with which we build.

Truly shape and fashion these;
Leave no yawning gaps between;
Think not, because no man sees,
Such things will remain unseen.

In the elder days of Art,
Builders wrought with greatest care
Each minute and unseen part;
For the Gods see everywhere.

Let us do our work as well,
Both the unseen and the seen;
Make the house, where Gods may dwell,
Beautiful, entire, and clean.

Else our lives are incomplete,
Standing in these walls of Time,
Broken stairways, where the feet
Stumble as they seek to climb.

Build today, then, strong and sure,
With a firm and ample base;
And ascending and secure
Shall tomorrow find its place.

Thus alone can we attain
To those turrets, where the eye
Sees the world as one vast plain,
And one boundless reach of sky.

1846 1849

THE SECRET OF THE SEA

Ah! what pleasant visions haunt me
As I gaze upon the sea!
All the old romantic legends,
All my dreams, come back to me.

Sails of silk and ropes of sandal,
Such as gleam in ancient lore;
And the singing of the sailors,
And the answer from the shore!

Most of all, the Spanish ballad
Haunts me oft, and tarries long,
Of the noble Count Arnaldos
And the sailor's mystic song.

Like the long waves on a sea-beach,
Where the sand as silver shines,
With a soft, monotonous cadence,
Flow its unrhymed lyric lines;—

Telling how the Count Arnaldos,
With his hawk upon his hand,
Saw a fair and stately galley,
Steering onward to the land;—

How he heard the ancient helmsman
Chant a song so wild and clear,
That the sailing sea-bird slowly
Poised upon the mast to hear,

Till his soul was full of longing,
And he cried, with impulse strong,—
"Helmsman! for the love of heaven,
Teach me, too, that wondrous song!"

"Wouldst thou,"—so the helmsman answered,
"Learn the secret of the sea?
Only those who brave its dangers
Comprehend its mystery!"

In each sail that skims the horizon,
In each landward-blowing breeze,
I behold that stately galley,
Hear those mournful melodies;

Till my soul is full of longing
For the secret of the sea,
And the heart of the great ocean
Sends a thrilling pulse through me.

1848 1849

RESIGNATION

There is no flock, however watched and tended,
But one dead lamb is there!
There is no fireside, howsoe'er defended,
But has one vacant chair!

The air is full of farewells to the dying,
And mournings for the dead;
The heart of Rachel, for her children crying,
Will not be comforted!

Let us be patient! These severe afflictions
Not from the ground arise,
But oftentimes celestial benedictions
Assume this dark disguise.

We see but dimly through the mists and vapors;
Amid these earthly damps
What seem to us but sad, funereal tapers
May be heaven's distant lamps.

There is no Death! What seems so is transition;
This life of mortal breath
Is but a suburb of the life elysian,
Whose portal we call Death.

She is not dead,—the child of our affection,—
But gone unto that school
Where she no longer needs our poor protection,
And Christ himself doth rule.

In that great cloister's stillness and seclusion,
By guardian angels led,
Safe from temptation, safe from sin's pollution,
She lives, whom we call dead.

Day after day we think what she is doing
In those bright realms of air;
Year after year, her tender steps pursuing,
Behold her grown more fair.

Thus do we walk with her, and keep unbroken
The bond which nature gives,
Thinking that our remembrance, though unspoken,
May reach her where she lives.

Not as a child shall we again behold her;
For when with raptures wild
In our embraces we again enfold her,
She will not be a child;

But a fair maiden, in her Father's mansion,
Clothed with celestial grace;
And beautiful with all the soul's expansion
Shall we behold her face.

And though at times impetuous with emotion
And anguish long suppressed,
The swelling heart heaves moaning like the ocean,
That cannot be at rest,—

We will be patient, and assuage the feeling
We may not wholly stay;
By silence sanctifying, not concealing,
The grief that must have way.

1848 1849

THE BUILDING OF THE SHIP

"Build me straight, O worthy Master!
Stanch and strong, a goodly vessel,
That shall laugh at all disaster,
And with wave and whirlwind wrestle!"

The merchant's word
Delighted the Master heard;
For his heart was in his work, and the heart
Giveth grace unto every Art.
A quiet smile played round his lips,
As the eddies and dimples of the tide
Play round the bows of ships,
That steadily at anchor ride.
And with a voice that was full of glee,
He answered, "Erelong we will launch
A vessel as goodly, and strong, and stanch,
As ever weathered a wintry sea!"
And first with nicest skill and art,
Perfect and finished in every part,
A little model the Master wrought,
Which should be to the larger plan
What the child is to the man,
Its counterpart in miniature;
That with a hand more swift and sure
The greater labor might be brought
To answer to his inward thought.
And as he labored, his mind ran o'er
The various ships that were built of yore,
And above them all, and strangest of all
Towered the Great Harry, crank and tall,
Whose picture was hanging on the wall,

With bows and stern raised high in air,
And balconies hanging here and there,
And signal lanterns and flags afloat,
And eight round towers, like those that frown
From some old castle, looking down
Upon the drawbridge and the moat.
And he said with a smile, "Our ship, I wis,
Shall be of another form than this!"
It was of another form, indeed;
Built for freight, and yet for speed,
A beautiful and gallant craft;
Broad in the beam, that the stress of the blast,
Pressing down upon sail and mast,
Might not the sharp bows overwhelm;
Broad in the beam, but sloping aft
With graceful curve and slow degrees,
That she might be docile to the helm,
And that the currents of parted seas,
Closing behind, with mighty force,
Might aid and not impede her course.

In the ship-yard stood the Master,
With the model of the vessel,
That should laugh at all disaster,
And with wave and whirlwind wrestle!

Covering many a rood of ground,
Lay the timber piled around;
Timber of chestnut, and elm, and oak,
And scattered here and there, with these,
The knarred and crooked cedar knees;
Brought from regions far away,
From Pascagoula's sunny bay,
And the banks of the roaring Roanoke!
Ah! what a wondrous thing it is
To note how many wheels of toil
One thought, one word, can set in motion!
There's not a ship that sails the ocean,
But every climate, every soil,
Must bring its tribute, great or small,
And help to build the wooden wall!

The sun was rising o'er the sea,
And long the level shadows lay,
As if they, too, the beams would be
Of some great, airy argosy,
Framed and launched in a single day.
That silent architect, the sun,
Had hewn and laid them every one,
Ere the work of man was yet begun.
Beside the Master, when he spoke,
A youth, against an anchor leaning,
Listened, to catch his slightest meaning,
Only the long waves, as they broke
In ripples on the pebbly beach,
Interrupted the old man's speech.

Beautiful they were, in sooth,
The old man and the fiery youth!
The old man, in whose busy brain
Many a ship that sailed the main
Was modelled o'er and o'er again;—
The fiery youth, who was to be
The heir of his dexterity,
The heir of his house, and his daughter's hand,
When he had built and launched from land
What the elder head had planned.

"Thus," said he, "will we build this ship!
Lay square the blocks upon the slip,
And follow well this plan of mine.
Choose the timbers with greatest care;
Of all that is unsound beware;
For only what is sound and strong
To this vessel shall belong.
Cedar of Maine and Georgia pine
Here together shall combine.
A goodly frame, and a goodly fame,
And the UNION be her name!
For the day that gives her to the sea
Shall give my daughter unto thee!"

The Master's word
Enraptured the young man heard;
And as he turned his face aside,
With a look of joy and a thrill of pride
Standing before
Her father's door,
He saw the form of his promised bride.
The sun shone on her golden hair,
And her cheek was glowing fresh and fair,
With the breath of morn and the soft sea air.
Like a beauteous barge was she,
Still at rest on the sandy beach,
Just beyond the billow's reach;
But he
Was the restless, seething, stormy sea!
Ah, how skilful grows the hand
That obeyeth Love's command!
It is the heart, and not the brain,
That to the highest doth attain,
And he who followeth Love's behest
Far excelleth all the rest!

Thus with the rising of the sun
Was the noble task begun,
And soon throughout the ship-yard's bounds
Were heard the intermingled sounds
Of axes and of mallets, plied
With vigorous arms on every side;
Plied so deftly and so well,
That, ere the shadows of evening fell,
The keel of oak for a noble ship,
Scarfed and bolted, straight and strong,
Was lying ready, and stretched along
The blocks, well placed upon the slip.
Happy, thrice happy, every one
Who sees his labor well begun,
And not perplexed and multiplied,
By idly waiting for time and tide!

And when the hot, long day was o'er,
The young man at the Master's door
Sat with the maiden calm and still,
And within the porch, a little more
Removed beyond the evening chill,
The father sat, and told them tales
Of wrecks in the great September gales,
Of pirates coasting the Spanish Main,
And ships that never came back again,
The chance and change of a sailor's life,
Want and plenty, rest and strife,
His roving fancy, like the wind,
That nothing can stay and nothing can bind,
And the magic charm of foreign lands,
With shadows of palms, and shining sands,
Where the tumbling surf,
O'er the coral reefs of Madagascar,
Washes the feet of the swarthy Lascar,
As he lies alone and asleep on the turf.
And the trembling maiden held her breath
At the tales of that awful, pitiless sea,
With all its terror and mystery,
The dim, dark sea, so like unto Death,
That divides and yet unites mankind!
And whenever the old man paused, a gleam
From the bowl of his pipe would awhile illume
The silent group in the twilight gloom,
And thoughtful faces, as in a dream;
And for a moment one might mark
What had been hidden by the dark,
That the head of the maiden lay at rest,
Tenderly, on the young man's breast!

Day by day the vessel grew,
With timbers fashioned strong and true,
Stemson and keelson and sternson-knee,
Till, framed with perfect symmetry,
A skeleton ship rose up to view!
And around the bows and along the side
The heavy hammers and mallets plied,
Till after many a week, at length,
Wonderful for form and strength,
Sublime in its enormous bulk,
Loomed aloft the shadowy hulk!
And around it columns of smoke, upwreathing,
Rose from the boiling, bubbling, seething
Caldron, that glowed,
And overflowed
With the black tar, heated for the sheathing.
And amid the clamors
Of clattering hammers,
He who listened heard now and then
The song of the Master and his men:—

"Build me straight, O worthy Master,
Stanch and strong, a goodly vessel,
That shall laugh at all disaster,
And with wave and whirlwind wrestle!"

With oaken brace and copper band,
Lay the rudder on the sand,
That, like a thought, should have control
Over the movement of the whole;
And near it the anchor, whose giant hand
Would reach down and grapple with the land,
And immovable and fast
Hold the great ship against the bellowing blast!
And at the bows an image stood,
By a cunning artist carved in wood,
With robes of white, that far behind
Seemed to be fluttering in the wind.
It was not shaped in a classic mould,
Not like a Nymph or Goddess of old,
Or Naiad rising from the water,
But modelled from the Master's daughter!
On many a dreary and misty night,
'Twill be seen by the rays of the signal light,
Speeding along through the rain and the dark,
Like a ghost in its snow-white sark,
The pilot of some phantom bark,
Guiding the vessel, in its flight,
By a path none other knows aright!

Behold, at last,
Each tall and tapering mast
Is swung into its place;
Shrouds and stays
Holding it firm and fast!

Long ago,
In the deer-haunted forests of Maine,
When upon mountain and plain
Lay the snow,
They fell,—those lordly pines!
Those grand, majestic pines!
'Mid shouts and cheers
The jaded steers,
Panting beneath the goad,
Dragged down the weary, winding road
Those captive kings so straight and tall,
To be shorn of their streaming hair,
And naked and bare,
To feel the stress and the strain
Of the wind and the reeling main,
Whose roar
Would remind them forevermore
Of their native forests they should not see again.

And everywhere
The slender, graceful spars
Poise aloft in the air,
And at the mast-head,
White, blue, and red,
A flag unrolls the stripes and stars.
Ah! when the wanderer, lonely, friendless,
In foreign harbors shall behold
That flag unrolled,
'Twill be as a friendly hand
Stretched out from his native land,
Filling his heart with memories sweet and endless!

All is finished! and at length
Has come the bridal day
Of beauty and of strength.
Today the vessel shall be launched!
With fleecy clouds the sky is blanched,
And o'er the bay,
Slowly, in all his splendors dight,
The great sun rises to behold the sight.
The ocean old,
Centuries old,
Strong as youth, and as uncontrolled,
Paces restless to and fro,
Up and down the sands of gold.
His beating heart is not at rest;
And far and wide,
With ceaseless flow,
His beard of snow
Heaves with the heaving of his breast.
He waits impatient for his bride.
There she stands,
With her foot upon the sands,
Decked with flags and streamers gay,
In honor of her marriage day,
Her snow-white signals fluttering, blending,
Round her like a veil descending,
Ready to be
The bride of the gray old sea.

On the deck another bride
Is standing by her lover's side.
Shadows from the flags and shrouds,
Like the shadows cast by clouds,
Broken by many a sudden fleck,
Fall around them on the deck.

The prayer is said,
The service read,
The joyous bridegroom bows his head;
And in tears the good old Master
Shakes the brown hand of his son,
Kisses his daughter's glowing cheek
In silence, for he cannot speak,
And ever faster
Down his own the tears begin to run.
The worthy pastor—
The shepherd of that wandering flock,
That has the ocean for its wold,
That has the vessel for its fold,
Leaping ever from rock to rock—
Spake, with accents mild and clear,
Words of warning, words of cheer,
But tedious to the bridegroom's ear.
He knew the chart
Of the sailor's heart,
All its pleasures and its griefs,
All its shallows and rocky reefs,
All those secret currents, that flow
With such resistless undertow,
And lift and drift, with terrible force,
The will from its moorings and its course.
Therefore he spake, and thus said he:—
"Like unto ships far off at sea,
Outward or homeward bound, are we.

Before, behind, and all around,
Floats and swings the horizon's bound,
Seems at its distant rim to rise
And climb the crystal wall of the skies,
And then again to turn and sink,
As if we could slide from its outer brink.
Ah! it is not the sea,
It is not the sea that sinks and shelves,
But ourselves
That rock and rise
With endless and uneasy motion,
Now touching the very skies,
Now sinking into the depths of ocean.
Ah! if our souls but poise and swing
Like the compass in its brazen ring,
Ever level and ever true
To the toil and the task we have to do,
We shall sail securely, and safely reach
The Fortunate Isles, on whose shining beach
The sights we see, and the sounds we hear,
Will be those of joy and not of fear!"

Then the Master,
With a gesture of command,
Waved his hand;
And at the word,
Loud and sudden there was heard,
All around them and below,
The sound of hammers, blow on blow,
Knocking away the shores and spurs.
And see! she stirs!
She starts,—she moves,—she seems to feel
The thrill of life along her keel,
And, spurning with her foot the ground,
With one exulting, joyous bound,
She leaps into the ocean's arms!

And lo! from the assembled crowd
There rose a shout, prolonged and loud,
That to the ocean seemed to say,
"Take her, O bridegroom, old and gray,
Take her to thy protecting arms,
With all her youth and all her charms!"

How beautiful she is! How fair
She lies within those arms, that press
Her form with many a soft caress
Of tenderness and watchful care!
Sail forth into the sea, O ship!
Through wind and wave, right onward steer!
The moistened eye, the trembling lip,
Are not the signs of doubt or fear.

Sail forth into the sea of life,
O gentle, loving, trusting wife,
And safe from all adversity
Upon the bosom of that sea
Thy comings and thy goings be!
For gentleness and love and trust
Prevail o'er angry wave and gust;
And in the wreck of noble lives
Something immortal still survives!

Thou, too, sail on, O Ship of State!
Sail on, O UNION, strong and great!
Humanity with all its fears,
With all the hopes of future years,
Is hanging breathless on thy fate!
We know what Master laid thy keel,
What Workmen wrought thy ribs of steel,
Who made each mast, and sail, and rope,
What anvils rang, what hammers beat,
In what a forge and what a heat
Were shaped the anchors of thy hope!
Fear not each sudden sound and shock,
'Tis of the wave and not the rock;
'Tis but the flapping of the sail,
And not a rent made by the gale!
In spite of rock and tempest's roar,
In spite of false lights on the shore,
Sail on, nor fear to breast the sea!
Our hearts, our hopes, are all with thee,
Our hearts, our hopes, our prayers, our tears,
Our faith triumphant o'er our fears,
Are all with thee,—are all with thee!

1849 1849

GASPAR BECERRA

BY his evening fire the artist
Pondered o'er his secret shame;
Baffled, weary, and disheartened,
Still he mused, and dreamed of fame.

'Twas an image of the Virgin
That had tasked his utmost skill;
But, alas! his fair ideal
Vanished and escaped him still.

From a distant Eastern island
Had the precious wood been brought;
Day and night the anxious master
At his toil untiring wrought;

Till, discouraged and desponding,
Sat he now in shadows deep,

And the day's humiliation
  Found oblivion in sleep.

Then a voice cried, "Rise, O master!
  From the burning brand of oak
Shape the thought that stirs within thee!"—
  And the startled artist woke,—

Woke, and from the smoking embers
  Seized and quenched the glowing wood;
And therefrom he carved an image,
  And he saw that it was good.

O thou sculptor, painter, poet!
  Take this lesson to thy heart:
That is best which lieth nearest;
  Shape from that thy work of art.

1849 1849

THE LADDER OF SAINT AUGUSTINE

Saint Augustine! well hast thou said,
  That of our vices we can frame
A ladder, if we will but tread
  Beneath our feet each deed of shame!

All common things, each day's events,
  That with the hour begin and end,
Our pleasures and our discontents,
  Are rounds by which we may ascend.

The low desire, the base design,
  That makes another's virtues less;
The revel of the ruddy wine,
  And all occasions of excess;

The longing for ignoble things;
  The strife for triumph more than truth;
The hardening of the heart, that brings
  Irreverence for the dreams of youth;

All thoughts of ill; all evil deeds,
  That have their root in thoughts of ill;
Whatever hinders or impedes
  The action of the nobler will;—

All these must first be trampled down
  Beneath our feet, if we would gain
In the bright fields of fair renown
  The right of eminent domain.

We have not wings, we cannot soar;
  But we have feet to scale and climb
By slow degrees, by more and more,
  The cloudy summits of our time.

The mighty pyramids of stone
  That wedge-like cleave the desert airs,
When nearer seen, and better known,
  Are but gigantic flights of stairs.

The distant mountains, that uprear
  Their solid bastions to the skies,
Are crossed by pathways, that appear
  As we to higher levels rise.

The heights by great men reached and kept
  Were not attained by sudden flight,
But they, while their companions slept,
  Were toiling upward in the night.

Standing on what too long we bore
  With shoulders bent and downcast eyes,
We may discern—unseen before—
  A path to higher destinies,

Nor deem the irrevocable Past
  As wholly wasted, wholly vain,
If, rising on its wrecks, at last
  To something nobler we attain.

1850 1858

THE GOLDEN LEGEND

PROLOGUE—THE SPIRE OF STRASBURG CATHEDRAL

Night and storm. Lucifer, *with the Powers of the Air, trying to tear down the Cross*

LUCIFER

Hasten! hasten!
O ye spirits!
From its station drag the ponderous
Cross of iron, that to mock us
Is uplifted high in air!

VOICES

Oh, we cannot!
For around it
All the Saints and Guardian Angels
Throng in legions to protect it;
They defeat us everywhere!

THE BELLS

Laudo Deum verum!
Plebem voco!
Congrego clerum!

LUCIFER

Lower! lower!
Hover downward!
Seize the loud, vociferous bells, and
Clashing, clanging, to the pavement
Hurl them from their windy tower!

VOICES

All thy thunders
Here are harmless!
For these bells have been anointed,
And baptized with holy water!
They defy our utmost power.

THE BELLS

Defunctos ploro!
Pestem fugo!
Festa decoro!

LUCIFER

Shake the casements!
Break the painted
Panes, that flame with gold and crimson;
Scatter them like leaves of Autumn,
Swept away before the blast!

VOICES

Oh, we cannot!
The Archangel
Michael flames from every window,
With the sword of fire that drove us
Headlong, out of heaven, aghast!

THE BELLS

Funera plango!
Fulgura frango!
Sabbata pango!

LUCIFER

Aim your lightnings
At the oaken,
Massive, iron-studded portals!
Sack the house of God, and scatter
Wide the ashes of the dead!

VOICES

Oh, we cannot!
The Apostles
And the Martyrs, wrapped in mantles,
Stand as warders at the entrance,
Stand as sentinels o'erhead!

THE BELLS

Excito lentos!
Dissipo ventos!
Paco cruentos!

LUCIFER

Baffled! baffled!
Inefficient,
Craven spirits! leave this labor
Unto Time, the great Destroyer!
Come away, ere night is gone!

VOICES

Onward! onward!
With the night-wind,
Over field and farm and forest,
Lonely homestead, darksome hamlet,
Blighting all we breathe upon!

They sweep away. Organ and Gregorian Chant

CHOIR

Nocte surgentes
Vigilemus omnes!

I

THE CASTLE OF VAUTSBERG ON THE RHINE

A chamber in a tower. PRINCE HENRY, *sitting alone, ill and restless. Midnight*

PRINCE HENRY

I cannot sleep! my fervid brain
Calls up the vanished Past again,
And throws its misty splendors deep
Into the pallid realms of sleep!
A breath from that far-distant shore
Comes freshening ever more and more,
And wafts o'er intervening seas
Sweet odors from the Hesperides!
A wind, that through the corridor
Just stirs the curtain, and no more,
And, touching the æolian strings,
Faints with the burden that it brings!
Come back! ye friendships long departed!
That like o'erflowing streamlets started,
And now are dwindled, one by one,
To stony channels in the sun!
Come back! ye friends, whose lives are ended,
Come back, with all that light attended,
Which seemed to darken and decay
When ye arose and went away!

They come, the shapes of joy and woe,
The airy crowds of long ago,
The dreams and fancies known of yore,
That have been, and shall be no more.
They change the cloisters of the night
Into a garden of delight;
They make the dark and dreary hours
Open and blossom into flowers!
I would not sleep! I love to be
Again in their fair company;
But ere my lips can bid them stay,
They pass and vanish quite away!
Alas! our memories may retrace
Each circumstance of time and place,
Season and scene come back again,
And outward things unchanged remain;
The rest we cannot reinstate;
Ourselves we cannot re-create,
Nor set our souls to the same key
Of the remembered harmony!

Rest! rest! Oh, give me rest and peace!
The thought of life that ne'er shall cease
Has something in it like despair,
A weight I am too weak to bear!
Sweeter to this afflicted breast
The thought of never-ending rest!
Sweeter the undisturbed and deep
Tranquillity of endless sleep!

A flash of lightning, out of which LUCIFER *appears, in the garb of a travelling Physician*

LUCIFER

All hail, Prince Henry!

PRINCE HENRY, *starting*

Who is it speaks?
Who and what are you?

LUCIFER

One who seeks
A moment's audience with the Prince.

PRINCE HENRY

When came you in?

LUCIFER

A moment since.
I found your study door unlocked,
And thought you answered when I knocked.

PRINCE HENRY

I did not hear you.

LUCIFER

You heard the thunder;
It was loud enough to waken the dead.
And it is not a matter of special wonder
That, when God is walking overhead,
You should not hear my feeble tread.

PRINCE HENRY

What may your wish or purpose be?

LUCIFER

Nothing or everything, as it pleases
Your Highness. You behold in me
Only a travelling Physician;
One of the few who have a mission
To cure incurable diseases,
Or those that are called so.

PRINCE HENRY

Can you bring
The dead to life?

LUCIFER

Yes; very nearly.
And, what is a wiser and better thing,
Can keep the living from ever needing
Such an unnatural, strange proceeding,
By showing conclusively and clearly
That death is a stupid blunder merely,
And not a necessity of our lives.
My being here is accidental;
The storm, that against your casement drives,
In the little village below waylaid me.
And there I heard with a secret delight,
Of your maladies physical and mental,
Which neither astonished nor dismayed me.
And I hastened hither, though late in the night,
To proffer my aid!

PRINCE HENRY, *ironically*

For this you came!
Ah, how can I ever hope to requite
This honor from one so erudite?

LUCIFER

The honor is mine, or will be when
I have cured your disease.

PRINCE HENRY

But not till then.

LUCIFER

What is your illness?

PRINCE HENRY

It has no name.
A smouldering, dull, perpetual flame,
As in a kiln, burns in my veins,
Sending up vapors to the head;
My heart has become a dull lagoon,
Which a kind of leprosy drinks and drains;
I am accounted as one who is dead,
And, indeed, I think that I shall be soon.

LUCIFER

And has Gordonius the Divine,
In his famous Lily of Medicine,—
I see the book lies open before you,—
No remedy potent enough to restore you?

PRINCE HENRY

None whatever!

LUCIFER

The dead are dead,
And their oracles dumb, when questionèd
Of the new diseases that human life
Evolves in its progress, rank and rife.
Consult the dead upon things that were,
But the living only on things that are.
Have you done this, by the appliance
And aid of doctors?

PRINCE HENRY

Ay, whole schools
Of doctors, with their learned rules;
But the case is quite beyond their science.
Even the doctors of Salern
Send me back word they can discern
No cure for a malady like this,
Save one which in its nature is
Impossible and cannot be!

LUCIFER

That sounds oracular!

PRINCE HENRY

Unendurable!

LUCIFER

What is their remedy?

PRINCE HENRY

You shall see;
Writ in this scroll is the mystery.

LUCIFER, *reading*

"Not to be cured, yet not incurable!
The only remedy that remains
Is the blood that flows from a maiden's veins,
Who of her own free will shall die,
And give her life as the price of yours!"

That is the strangest of all cures,
And one, I think, you will never try;
The prescription you may well put by,
As something impossible to find
Before the world itself shall end!
And yet who knows? One cannot say
That into some maiden's brain that kind
Of madness will not find its way.
Meanwhile permit me to recommend,
As the matter admits of no delay,
My wonderful Catholicon,
Of very subtile and magical powers!

PRINCE HENRY

Purge with your nostrums and drugs infernal
The spouts and gargoyles of these towers,
Not me! My faith is utterly gone
In every power but the Power Supernal!
Pray tell me, of what school are you?

LUCIFER

Both of the Old and of the New!
The school of Hermes Trismegistus,
Who uttered his oracles sublime
Before the Olympiads, in the dew
Of the early dusk and dawn of time,
The reign of dateless old Hephæstus!
As northward, from its Nubian springs,
The Nile, forever new and old,
Among the living and the dead,
Its mighty, mystic stream has rolled;
So, starting from its fountain-head
Under the lotus-leaves of Isis,
From the dead demigods of eld,
Through long, unbroken lines of kings
Its course the sacred art has held,
Unchecked, unchanged by man's devices.
This art the Arabian Geber taught,
And in alembics, finely wrought,
Distilling herbs and flowers, discovered
The secret that so long had hovered
Upon the misty verge of Truth,
The Elixir of Perpetual Youth,
Called Alcohol, in the Arab speech!
Like him, this wondrous lore I teach!

PRINCE HENRY

What! an adept?

LUCIFER

Nor less, nor more!

PRINCE HENRY

I am a reader of your books,
A lover of that mystic lore!
With such a piercing glance it looks
Into great Nature's open eye,
And sees within it trembling lie
The portrait of the Deity!
And yet, alas! with all my pains,
The secret and the mystery
Have baffled and eluded me,
Unseen the grand result remains!

LUCIFER, *showing a flask*

Behold it here! this little flask
Contains the wonderful quintessence,
The perfect flower and efflorescence,
Of all the knowledge man can ask!
Hold it up thus against the light!

PRINCE HENRY

How limpid, pure, and crystalline,
How quick, and tremulous, and bright
The little wavelets dance and shine,
As were it the Water of Life in sooth!

LUCIFER

It is! It assuages every pain,
Cures all disease, and gives again
To age the swift delights of youth.
Inhale its fragrance.

PRINCE HENRY

It is sweet.
A thousand different odors meet
And mingle in its rare perfume,
Such as the winds of summer waft
At open windows through a room!

LUCIFER

Will you not taste it?

PRINCE HENRY

Will one draught
Suffice?

LUCIFER

If not, you can drink more.

PRINCE HENRY

Into this crystal goblet pour
So much as safely I may drink.

LUCIFER, *pouring*

Let not the quantity alarm you;
You may drink all; it will not harm you.

PRINCE HENRY

I am as one who on the brink
Of a dark river stands and sees
The waters flow, the landscape dim
Around him waver, wheel, and swim,
And, ere he plunges, stops to think
Into what whirlpools he may sink;
One moment pauses, and no more,
Then madly plunges from the shore!
Headlong into the mysteries
Of life and death I boldly leap,
Nor fear the fateful current's sweep,
Nor what in ambush lurks below!
For death is better than disease!

An ANGEL *with an æolian harp hovers in the air*

ANGEL

Woe! woe! eternal woe!
Not only the whispered prayer
Of love,
But the imprecations of hate,
Reverberate
For ever and ever through the air
Above!
This fearful curse
Shakes the great universe!

LUCIFER, *disappearing*

Drink! drink!
And thy soul shall sink
Down into the dark abyss,
Into the infinite abyss,
From which no plummet nor rope
Ever drew up the silver sand of hope!

PRINCE HENRY, *drinking*

It is like a draught of fire!
Through every vein
I feel again
The fever of youth, the soft desire;
A rapture that is almost pain
Throbs in my heart and fills my brain!
O joy! O joy! I feel

The band of steel
That so long and heavily has pressed
Upon my breast
Uplifted, and the malediction
Of my affliction
Is taken from me, and my weary breast
At length finds rest.

THE ANGEL

It is but the rest of the fire, from which the air has been taken!
It is but the rest of the sand, when the hour-glass is not shaken!
It is but the rest of the tide between the ebb and the flow!
It is but the rest of the wind between the flaws that blow!
With fiendish laughter,
Hereafter,
This false physician
Will mock thee in thy perdition.

PRINCE HENRY

Speak! speak!
Who says that I am ill?
I am not ill! I am not weak!
The trance, the swoon, the dream, is o'er!
I feel the chill of death no more!
At length,
I stand renewed in all my strength!
Beneath me I can feel
The great earth stagger and reel,
As if the feet of a descending God
Upon its surface trod,
And like a pebble it rolled beneath his heel!
This, O brave physician! this
Is thy great Palingenesis!

Drinks again

THE ANGEL

Touch the goblet no more!
It will make thy heart sore
To its very core!
Its perfume is the breath
Of the Angel of Death,
And the light that within it lies
Is the flash of his evil eyes.
Beware! Oh, beware!
For sickness, sorrow, and care
All are there!

PRINCE HENRY, *sinking back*

O thou voice within my breast!
Why entreat me, why upbraid me,
When the steadfast tongues of truth
And the flattering hopes of youth
Have all deceived me and betrayed me?
Give me, give me rest, oh rest!
Golden visions wave and hover,
Golden vapors, waters streaming,
Landscapes moving, changing, gleaming!
I am like a happy lover,
Who illumines life with dreaming!
Brave physician! Rare physician!
Well hast thou fulfilled thy mission!

His head falls on his book

THE ANGEL, *receding*

Alas! alas!
Like a vapor the golden vision
Shall fade and pass,
And thou wilt find in thy heart again
Only the blight of pain,
And bitter, bitter, bitter contrition!

COURT-YARD OF THE CASTLE

HUBERT *standing by the gateway*

HUBERT

How sad the grand old castle looks!
O'erhead, the unmolested rooks
Upon the turret's windy top
Sit, talking of the farmer's crop;
Here in the court-yard springs the grass,
So few are now the feet that pass;
The stately peacocks, bolder grown,
Come hopping down the steps of stone,
As if the castle were their own;
And I, the poor old seneschal,
Haunt, like a ghost, the banquet-hall.
Alas! the merry guests no more
Crowd through the hospitable door;
No eyes with youth and passion shine,
No cheeks glow redder than the wine;
No song, no laugh, no jovial din
Of drinking wassail to the pin;
But all is silent, sad, and drear,
And now the only sounds I hear
Are the hoarse rooks upon the walls,
And horses stamping in their stalls!

A horn sounds

What ho! that merry, sudden blast
Reminds me of the days long past!
And, as of old resounding, grate
The heavy hinges of the gate,
And, clattering loud, with iron clank,
Down goes the sounding bridge of plank,
As if it were in haste to greet
The pressure of a traveller's feet!

Enter WALTER *the Minnesinger*

WALTER

How now, my friend! This looks quite lonely!
No banner flying from the walls,
No pages and no seneschals,
No warders, and one porter only!
Is it you, Hubert?

HUBERT

Ah! Master Walter!

WALTER

Alas! how forms and faces alter!
I did not know you. You look older!
Your hair has grown much grayer and thinner,
And you stoop a little in the shoulder!

HUBERT

Alack! I am a poor old sinner,
And, like these towers, begin to moulder;
And you have been absent many a year!

WALTER

How is the Prince?

HUBERT

He is not here;
He has been ill: and now has fled.

WALTER

Speak it out frankly: say he's dead!
Is it not so?

HUBERT

No; if you please,
A strange, mysterious disease
Fell on him with a sudden blight.
Whole hours together he would stand
Upon the terrace, in a dream,
Resting his head upon his hand,
Best pleased when he was most alone,
Like Saint John Nepomuck in stone,
Looking down into a stream.
In the Round Tower, night after night,
He sat and bleared his eyes with books;
Until one morning we found him there
Stretched on the floor, as if in a swoon
He had fallen from his chair.
We hardly recognized his sweet looks!

WALTER

Poor Prince!

HUBERT

I think he might have mended;
And he did mend; but very soon
The priests came flocking in, like rooks,
With all their crosiers and their crooks,
And so at last the matter ended.

WALTER

How did it end?

HUBERT

Why, in Saint Rochus
They made him stand, and wait his doom;
And, as if he were condemned to the tomb,
Began to mutter their hocus-pocus.
First, the Mass for the Dead they chanted,
Then three times laid upon his head
A shovelful of churchyard clay,
Saying to him, as he stood undaunted,
"This is a sign that thou art dead,
So in thy heart be penitent!"
And forth from the chapel door he went
Into disgrace and banishment,
Clothed in a cloak of hodden gray,
And bearing a wallet, and a bell,
Whose sound should be a perpetual knell
To keep all travellers away.

WALTER

Oh, horrible fate! Outcast, rejected,
As one with pestilence infected!

HUBERT

Then was the family tomb unsealed,
And broken helmet, sword, and shield,
Buried together, in common wreck,
As is the custom, when the last
Of any princely house has passed,
And thrice, as with a trumpet-blast,
A herald shouted down the stair
The words of warning and despair,—
"O Hoheneck! O Hoheneck!"

WALTER

Still in my soul that cry goes on,—
Forever gone! forever gone!
Ah, what a cruel sense of loss,
Like a black shadow, would fall across
The hearts of all, if he should die!
His gracious presence upon earth
Was as a fire upon a hearth;
As pleasant songs, at morning sung,
The words that dropped from his sweet tongue
Strengthened our hearts; or heard at night,
Made all our slumbers soft and light.
Where is he?

HUBERT

In the Odenwald.
Some of his tenants, unappalled
By fear of death, or priestly word,—
A holy family, that make
Each meal a Supper of the Lord,—
Have him beneath their watch and ward,
For love of him, and Jesus' sake!
Pray you come in. For why should I
With out-door hospitality
My prince's friend thus entertain?

WALTER

I would a moment here remain.
But you, good Hubert, go before,
Fill me a goblet of May-drink,
As aromatic as the May
From which it steals the breath away,
And which he loved so well of yore;
It is of him that I would think.
You shall attend me, when I call,
In the ancestral banquet-hall.
Unseen companions, guests of air,
You cannot wait on, will be there;
They taste not food, they drink not wine,
But their soft eyes look into mine,
And their lips speak to me, and all
The vast and shadowy banquet-hall
Is full of looks and words divine!

Leaning over the parapet

The day is done; and slowly from the scene
The stooping sun up-gathers his spent shafts,
And puts them back into his golden quiver!
Below me in the valley, deep and green
As goblets are, from which in thirsty draughts
We drink its wine, the swift and mantling river
Flows on triumphant through these lovely regions,
Etched with the shadows of its sombre margent,
And soft, reflected clouds of gold and argent!
Yes, there it flows, forever, broad and still
As when the vanguard of the Roman legions
First saw it from the top of yonder hill!
How beautiful it is! Fresh fields of wheat,
Vineyard, and town, and tower with fluttering flag,
The consecrated chapel on the crag,
And the white hamlet gathered round its base,
Like Mary sitting at her Saviour's feet,
And looking up at his beloved face!
O friend! O best of friends! Thy absence more
Than the impending night darkens the landscape o'er!

II

A FARM IN THE ODENWALD

A garden; morning; PRINCE HENRY *seated, with a book.* ELSIE *at a distance gathering flowers*

PRINCE HENRY, *reading*

One morning, all alone,
Out of his convent of gray stone,
Into the forest older, darker, grayer,
His lips moving as if in prayer,
His head sunken upon his breast
As in a dream of rest,
Walked the Monk Felix. All about
The broad, sweet sunshine lay without,
Filling the summer air;
And within the woodlands as he trod,
The dusk was like the Truce of God
With worldly woe and care;
Under him lay the golden moss;
And above him the boughs of hoary trees
Waved, and made the sign of the cross,
And whispered their Benedicites;
And from the ground
Rose an odor sweet and fragrant
Of the wild-flowers and the vagrant
Vines that wandered,
Seeking the sunshine, round and round.

These he heeded not, but pondered
On the volume in his hand,
Wherein amazed he read:

"A thousand years in thy sight
Are but as yesterday when it is past,
And as a watch in the night!"
And with his eyes downcast
In humility he said:
"I believe, O Lord,
What is written in thy Word,
But alas! I do not understand!"

And lo! he heard
The sudden singing of a bird,
A snow-white bird, that from a cloud
Dropped down,
And among the branches brown
Sat singing,
So sweet, and clear, and loud,
It seemed a thousand harp-strings ringing.
And the Monk Felix closed his book,
And long, long,
With rapturous look,
He listened to the song,
And hardly breathed or stirred,
Until he saw, as in a vision,
The land Elysian,
And in the heavenly city heard
Angelic feet
Fall on the golden flagging of the street.
And he would fain
Have caught the wondrous bird,
But strove in vain;
For it flew away, away,
Far over hill and dell,
And instead of its sweet singing
He heard the convent bell
Suddenly in the silence ringing
For the service of noonday.
And he retraced
His pathway homeward sadly and in haste.

In the convent there was a change!
He looked for each well-known face,
But the faces were new and strange;
New figures sat in the oaken stalls,
New voices chanted in the choir;
Yet the place was the same place,
The same dusky walls
Of cold, gray stone,
The same cloisters and belfry and spire.

A stranger and alone
Among that brotherhood
The Monk Felix stood.
"Forty years," said a Friar,
"Have I been Prior
Of this convent in the wood,
But for that space
Never have I beheld thy face!"

The heart of the Monk Felix fell:
And he answered, with submissive tone,
"This morning, after the hour of Prime,
I left my cell,
And wandered forth alone,
Listening all the time
To the melodious singing
Of a beautiful white bird,
Until I heard
The bells of the convent ringing
Noon from their noisy towers.
It was as if I dreamed;
For what to me had seemed
Moments only, had been hours!"

"Years!" said a voice close by.
It was an aged monk who spoke,
From a bench of oak
Fastened against the wall;—
He was the oldest monk of all.
For a whole century
Had he been there,
Serving God in prayer,
The meekest and humblest of his creatures.
He remembered well the features
Of Felix, and he said,
Speaking distinct and slow:
"One hundred years ago,
When I was a novice in this place,
There was here a monk, full of God's grace,
Who bore the name
Of Felix, and this man must be the same."

And straightway
They brought forth to the light of day
A volume old and brown,
A huge tome, bound
In brass and wild-boar's hide,
Wherein were written down
The names of all who had died
In the convent, since it was edified.
And there they found,
Just as the old monk said,
That on a certain day and date,
One hundred years before,
Had gone forth from the convent gate

The Monk Felix, and never more
Had entered that sacred door.
He had been counted among the dead!
And they knew, at last,
That, such had been the power
Of that celestial and immortal song,
A hundred years had passed,
And had not seemed so long
As a single hour!

ELSIE *comes in with flowers*

ELSIE

Here are flowers for you,
But they are not all for you.
Some of them are for the Virgin
And for Saint Cecilia.

PRINCE HENRY

As thou standest there,
Thou seemest to me like the angel
That brought the immortal roses
To Saint Cecilia's bridal chamber.

ELSIE

But these will fade.

PRINCE HENRY

Themselves will fade,
But not their memory,
And memory has the power
To re-create them from the dust.
They remind me, too,
Of martyred Dorothea,
Who from celestial gardens sent
Flowers as her witnesses
To him who scoffed and doubted.

ELSIE

Do you know the story
Of Christ and the Sultan's daughter?
That is the prettiest legend of them all.

PRINCE HENRY

Then tell it to me.
But first come hither.
Lay the flowers down beside me,
And put both thy hands in mine.
Now tell me the story.

ELSIE

Early in the morning
The Sultan's daughter
Walked in her father's garden,
Gathering the bright flowers,
All full of dew.

PRINCE HENRY

Just as thou hast been doing
This morning, dearest Elsie.

ELSIE

And as she gathered them
She wondered more and more
Who was the Master of the Flowers,
And made them grow
Out of the cold, dark earth.
"In my heart," she said,
"I love him; and for him
Would leave my father's palace,
To labor in his garden."

PRINCE HENRY

Dear, innocent child!
How sweetly thou recallest
The long-forgotten legend,
That in my early childhood
My mother told me!
Upon my brain
It reappears once more,
As a birth-mark on the forehead
When a hand suddenly
Is laid upon it, and removed!

ELSIE

And at midnight,
As she lay upon her bed,
She heard a voice
Call to her from the garden,
And, looking forth from her window,
She saw a beautiful youth
Standing among the flowers.
It was the Lord Jesus;
And she went down to Him,
And opened the door for Him;
And He said to her, "O maiden!
Thou hast thought of me with love,
And for thy sake
Out of my Father's kingdom
Have I come hither:
I am the Master of the Flowers.
My garden is in Paradise,
And if thou wilt go with me,
Thy bridal garland
Shall be of bright red flowers."

And then He took from his finger
A golden ring,
And asked the Sultan's daughter
If she would be his bride.
And when she answered Him with love,
His wounds began to bleed,
And she said to him,
"O Love! how red thy heart is,
And thy hands are full of roses."
"For thy sake," answered He,
"For thy sake is my heart so red,
For thee I bring these roses;
I gathered them at the cross
Whereon I died for thee!
Come, for my Father calls.
Thou art my elected bride!"
And the Sultan's daughter
Followed Him to his Father's garden.

PRINCE HENRY

Wouldst thou have done so, Elsie?

ELSIE

Yes, very gladly.

PRINCE HENRY

Then the Celestial Bridegroom
Will come for thee also.
Upon thy forehead He will place,
Not his crown of thorns,
But a crown of roses.
In thy bridal chamber,
Like Saint Cecilia,
Thou shalt hear sweet music,
And breathe the fragrance
Of flowers immortal!
Go now and place these flowers
Before her picture.

A ROOM IN THE FARM-HOUSE

Twilight. URSULA *spinning.* GOTTLIEB *asleep in his chair*

URSULA

Darker and darker! Hardly a glimmer
Of light comes in at the window-pane;
Or is it my eyes are growing dimmer?
I cannot disentangle this skein,
Nor wind it rightly upon the reel.
Elsie!

GOTTLIEB, *starting*

The stopping of thy wheel
Has awakened me out of a pleasant dream.
I thought I was sitting beside a stream,
And heard the grinding of a mill,
When suddenly the wheels stood still,
And a voice cried "Elsie" in my ear!
It startled me, it seemed so near.

URSULA

I was calling her: I want a light.
I cannot see to spin my flax.
Bring the lamp, Elsie. Dost thou hear?

ELSIE, *within*

In a moment!

GOTTLIEB

Where are Bertha and Max?

URSULA

They are sitting with Elsie at the door.
She is telling them stories of the wood,
And the Wolf, and little Red Ridinghood.

GOTTLIEB

And where is the Prince?

URSULA

In his room overhead;
I heard him walking across the floor,
As he always does, with a heavy tread.

ELSIE *comes in with a lamp.* MAX *and* BERTHA *follow her; and they all sing the Evening Song on the lighting of the lamps*

EVENING SONG

O gladsome light
Of the Father Immortal,
And of the celestial
Sacred and blessed
Jesus, our Saviour!

Now to the sunset
Again hast thou brought us;
And, seeing the evening
Twilight, we bless thee,
Praise thee, adore thee!

Father omnipotent!
Son, the Life-giver!
Spirit, the Comforter!
Worthy at all times
Of worship and wonder!

PRINCE HENRY, *at the door*

Amen!

URSULA

Who was it said Amen?

ELSIE

It was the Prince: he stood at the door,
And listened a moment, as we chanted
The evening song. He is gone again.
I have often seen him there before.

URSULA

Poor Prince!

GOTTLIEB

I thought the house was haunted!
Poor Prince, alas! and yet as mild
And patient as the gentlest child!

MAX

I love him because he is so good,
And makes me such fine bows and arrows,
To shoot at the robins and the sparrows,
And the red squirrels in the wood!

BERTHA

I love him, too!

GOTTLIEB

Ah, yes! we all
Love him, from the bottom of our hearts;
He gave us the farm, the house, and the grange,
He gave us the horses and the carts,
And the great oxen in the stall,
The vineyard, and the forest range!
We have nothing to give him but our love!

BERTHA

Did he give us the beautiful stork above
On the chimney-top, with its large, round nest?

GOTTLIEB

No, not the stork; by God in heaven,
As a blessing, the dear white stork was given,
But the Prince has given us all the rest.
God bless him, and make him well again.

ELSIE

Would I could do something for his sake,
Something to cure his sorrow and pain!

GOTTLIEB

That no one can; neither thou nor I,
Nor any one else.

ELSIE

And must he die?

URSULA

Yes; if the dear God does not take
Pity upon him, in his distress,
And work a miracle!

GOTTLIEB

Or unless
Some maiden, of her own accord,
Offers her life for that of her lord,
And is willing to die in his stead.

ELSIE

I will!

URSULA

Prithee, thou foolish child, be still!
Thou shouldst not say what thou dost not mean!

ELSIE

I mean it truly!

MAX

O father! this morning,
Down by the mill, in the ravine,
Hans killed a wolf, the very same
That in the night to the sheepfold came,
And ate up my lamb, that was left outside.

GOTTLIEB

I am glad he is dead. It will be a warning
To the wolves in the forest, far and wide.

MAX

And I am going to have his hide!

BERTHA

I wonder if this is the wolf that ate
Little Red Ridinghood!

URSULA

Oh, no!
That wolf was killed a long while ago.
Come, children, it is growing late.

MAX

Ah, how I wish I were a man,
As stout as Hans is, and as strong!
I would do nothing else, the whole day long,
But just kill wolves.

GOTTLIEB

Then go to bed,
And grow as fast as a little boy can.
Bertha is half asleep already.
See how she nods her heavy head,
And her sleepy feet are so unsteady
She will hardly be able to creep upstairs.

URSULA

Good night, my children. Here's the light.
And do not forget to say your prayers
Before you sleep.

GOTTLIEB

Good night!

MAX *and* BERTHA

Good night!

They go out with ELSIE

URSULA, *spinning*

She is a strange and wayward child,
That Elsie of ours. She looks so old,
And thoughts and fancies weird and wild
Seem of late to have taken hold
Of her heart, that was once so docile and mild!

GOTTLIEB

She is like all girls.

URSULA

Ah no, forsooth!
Unlike all I have ever seen.
For she has visions and strange dreams,
And in all her words and ways, she seems
Much older than she is in truth.
Who would think her but fifteen?
And there has been of late such a change!
My heart is heavy with fear and doubt
That she may not live till the year is out.
She is so strange,—so strange,—so strange!

GOTTLIEB

I am not troubled with any such fear;
She will live and thrive for many a year.

ELSIE'S CHAMBER

Night. ELSIE *praying*

ELSIE

My Redeemer and my Lord,
I beseech thee, I entreat thee,
Guide me in each act and word,
That hereafter I may meet thee,
Watching, waiting, hoping, yearning,
With my lamp well trimmed and burning!

Interceding
With these bleeding
Wounds upon thy hands and side,
For all who have lived and errèd
Thou hast suffered, thou hast died,
Scourged, and mocked, and crucified,
And in the grave hast thou been buried!

If my feeble prayer can reach thee.
O my Saviour, I beseech thee,
Even as thou hast died for me,
More sincerely
Let me follow where thou leadest,
Let me, bleeding as thou bleedest,
Die, if dying I may give
Life to one who asks to live,
And more nearly,
Dying thus, resemble thee!

THE CHAMBER OF GOTTLIEB AND URSULA

Midnight. ELSIE *standing by their bedside, weeping*

GOTTLIEB

The wind is roaring; the rushing rain
Is loud upon roof and window-pane,
As if the Wild Huntsman of Rodenstein,
Boding evil to me and mine,
Were abroad tonight with his ghostly train!
In the brief lulls of the tempest wild,
The dogs howl in the yard; and hark!
Some one is sobbing in the dark,
Here in the chamber!

ELSIE

It is I.

URSULA

Elsie! what ails thee, my poor child?

ELSIE

I am disturbed and much distressed,
In thinking our dear Prince must die;
I cannot close mine eyes, nor rest.

GOTTLIEB

What wouldst thou? In the Power Divine
His healing lies, not in our own;
It is in the hand of God alone.

ELSIE

Nay, He has put it into mine,
And into my heart!

GOTTLIEB

Thy words are wild!

URSULA

What dost thou mean? my child! my child!

ELSIE

That for our dear Prince Henry's sake
I will myself the offering make,
And give my life to purchase his.

URSULA

Am I still dreaming, or awake?
Thou speakest carelessly of death,
And yet thou knowest not what it is.

ELSIE

'Tis the cessation of our breath.
Silent and motionless we lie;
And no one knoweth more than this.
I saw our little Gertrude die;
She left off breathing, and no more
I smoothed the pillow beneath her head.
She was more beautiful than before.
Like violets faded were her eyes;
By this we knew that she was dead.
Through the open window looked the skies
Into the chamber where she lay,
And the wind was like the sound of wings,
As if angels came to bear her away.
Ah! when I saw and felt these things,
I found it difficult to stay;
I longed to die, as she had died,
And go forth with her, side by side.
The Saints are dead, the Martyrs dead,
And Mary, and our Lord; and I
Would follow in humility
The way by them illumined!

URSULA

My child! my child! thou must not die!

ELSIE

Why should I live? Do I not know
The life of woman is full of woe?
Toiling on and on and on,
With breaking heart, and tearful eyes,
And silent lips, and in the soul
The secret longings that arise,
Which this world never satisfies!
Some more, some less, but of the whole
Not one quite happy, no, not one!

URSULA

It is the malediction of Eve!

ELSIE

In place of it, let me receive
The benediction of Mary, then.

GOTTLIEB

Ah, woe is me! Ah, woe is me!
Most wretched am I among men!

URSULA

Alas! that I should live to see
Thy death, beloved, and to stand
Above thy grave! Ah, woe the day!

ELSIE

Thou wilt not see it. I shall lie
Beneath the flowers of another land,
For at Salerno, far away
Over the mountains, over the sea,
It is appointed me to die!
And it will seem no more to thee
Than if at the village on market-day
I should a little longer stay
Than I am wont.

URSULA

Even as thou sayest!
And how my heart beats, when thou stayest!
I cannot rest until my sight
Is satisfied with seeing thee.
What then, if thou wert dead?

GOTTLIEB

Ah me!
Of our old eyes thou art the light!
The joy of our old hearts art thou!
And wilt thou die?

URSULA

Not now! not now!

ELSIE

Christ died for me, and shall not I
Be willing for my Prince to die?
You both are silent; you cannot speak.
This said I at our Saviour's feast
After confession, to the priest,

And even he made no reply.
Does he not warn us all to seek
The happier, better land on high,
Where flowers immortal never wither;
And could he forbid me to go thither?

GOTTLIEB

In God's own time, my heart's delight!
When He shall call thee, not before!

ELSIE

I heard Him call. When Christ ascended
Triumphantly, from star to star,
He left the gates of heaven ajar.
I had a vision in the night,
And saw Him standing at the door
Of his Father's mansion, vast and splendid,
And beckoning to me from afar.
I cannot stay!

GOTTLIEB

She speaks almost
As if it were the Holy Ghost
Spake through her lips, and in her stead!
What if this were of God?

URSULA

Ah, then
Gainsay it dare we not.

GOTTLIEB

Amen!
Elsie! the words that thou hast said
Are strange and new for us to hear,
And fill our hearts with doubt and fear.
Whether it be a dark temptation
Of the Evil One, or God's inspiration,
We in our blindness cannot say.
We must think upon it, and pray;
For evil and good it both resembles.
If it be of God, his will be done!
May He guard us from the Evil One!
How hot thy hand is! how it trembles!
Go to thy bed, and try to sleep.

URSULA

Kiss me. Good night; and do not weep!

ELSIE *goes out*

Ah, what an awful thing is this!
I almost shuddered at her kiss,
As if a ghost had touched my cheek,
I am so childish and so weak!
As soon as I see the earliest gray
Of morning glimmer in the east,
I will go over to the priest,
And hear what the good man has to say!

A VILLAGE CHURCH

A woman kneeling at the confessional

THE PARISH PRIEST, *from within*

Go, sin no more! Thy penance o'er,
A new and better life begin!
God maketh thee forever free
From the dominion of thy sin!
Go, sin no more! He will restore
The peace that filled thy heart before,
And pardon thine iniquity!

The woman goes out. The Priest comes forth, and walks slowly up and down the church

O blessed Lord! how much I need
Thy light to guide me on my way!
So many hands, that, without heed,
Still touch thy wounds, and make them bleed!
So many feet, that, day by day,
Still wander from thy fold astray!
Unless thou fill me with thy light,
I cannot lead thy flock aright;
Nor, without thy support, can bear
The burden of so great a care,
But am myself a castaway!

A pause

The day is drawing to its close;
And what good deeds, since first it rose,
Have I presented, Lord, to thee,
As offerings of my ministry?
What wrong repressed, what right maintained,
What struggle passed, what victory gained,
What good attempted and attained?
Feeble, at best, is my endeavor!
I see, but cannot reach, the height
That lies forever in the light,
And yet forever and forever,
When seeming just within my grasp,
I feel my feeble hands unclasp,
And sink discouraged into night!
For thine own purpose, thou hast sent
The strife and the discouragement!

A pause

Why stayest thou, Prince of Hoheneck?
Why keep me pacing to and fro
Amid these aisles of sacred gloom,
Counting my footsteps as I go,

And marking with each step a tomb?
Why should the world for thee make room,
And wait thy leisure and thy beck?
Thou comest in the hope to hear
Some word of comfort and of cheer.
What can I say? I cannot give
The counsel to do this and live;
But rather, firmly to deny
The tempter, though his power be strong,
And, inaccessible to wrong,
Still like a martyr live and die!

A pause

The evening air grows dusk and brown;
I must go forth into the town,
To visit beds of pain and death,
Of restless limbs, and quivering breath,
And sorrowing hearts, and patient eyes
That see, through tears, the sun go down,
But never more shall see it rise.
The poor in body and estate,
The sick and the disconsolate,
Must not on man's convenience wait.

Goes out

Enter LUCIFER, *as a Priest*

LUCIFER, *with a genuflexion, mocking*

This is the Black Pater-noster.
God was my foster,
He fostered me
Under the book of the Palm-tree!
St. Michael was my dame.
He was born at Bethlehem,
He was made of flesh and blood.
God send me my right food,
My right food, and shelter too,
That I may to yon kirk go,
To read upon yon sweet book
Which the mighty God of heaven shook.
Open, open, hell's gates!
Shut, shut, heaven's gates!
All the devils in the air
The stronger be, that hear the Black Prayer!

Looking round the church

What a darksome and dismal place!
I wonder that any man has the face
To call such a hole the House of the Lord,
And the Gate of Heaven,—yet such is the word.
Ceiling, and walls, and windows old,
Covered with cobwebs, blackened with mould;
Dust on the pulpit, dust on the stairs,
Dust on the benches, and stalls, and chairs!
The pulpit, from which such ponderous sermons
Have fallen down on the brains of the Germans,
With about as much real edification
As if a great Bible, bound in lead,
Had fallen, and struck them on the head;
And I ought to remember that sensation!
Here stands the holy-water stoup!
Holy-water it may be to many,
But to me, the veriest Liquor Gehennæ!
It smells like a filthy fast-day soup!
Near it stands the box for the poor,
With its iron padlock, safe and sure.
I and the priest of the parish know
Whither all these charities go;
Therefore, to keep up the institution,
I will add my little contribution!

He puts in money

Underneath this mouldering tomb,
With statue of stone, and scutcheon of brass,
Slumbers a great lord of the village.
All his life was riot and pillage,
But at length, to escape the threatened doom
Of the everlasting penal fire,
He died in the dress of a mendicant friar,
And bartered his wealth for a daily mass.
But all that afterwards came to pass,
And whether he finds it dull or pleasant,
Is kept a secret for the present,
At his own particular desire.

And here, in a corner of the wall,
Shadowy, silent, apart from all,
With its awful portal open wide,
And its latticed windows on either side,
And its step well worn by the bended knees
Of one or two pious centuries,
Stands the village confessional!
Within it, as an honored guest,
I will sit down awhile and rest!

Seats himself in the confessional

Here sits the priest; and faint and low,
Like the sighing of an evening breeze,
Comes through these painted lattices
The ceaseless sound of human woe;
Here, while her bosom aches and throbs
With deep and agonizing sobs,
That half are passion, half contrition,
The luckless daughter of perdition

Slowly confesses her secret shame!
The time, the place, the lover's name!
Here the grim murderer, with a groan,
From his bruised conscience rolls the stone,
Thinking that thus he can atone
For ravages of sword and flame!

Indeed, I marvel, and marvel greatly,
How a priest can sit here so sedately,
Reading, the whole year out and in,
Naught but the catalogue of sin,
And still keep any faith whatever
In human virtue! Never! never!

I cannot repeat a thousandth part
Of the horrors and crimes and sins and woes
That arise, when with palpitating throes
The graveyard in the human heart
Gives up its dead, at the voice of the priest,
As if he were an archangel, at least.
It makes a peculiar atmosphere,
This odor of earthly passions and crimes,
Such as I like to breathe, at times,
And such as often brings me here
In the hottest and most pestilential season.
Today, I come for another reason;
To foster and ripen an evil thought
In a heart that is almost to madness wrought,
And to make a murderer out of a prince,
A sleight of hand I learned long since!
He comes. In the twilight he will not see
The difference between his priest and me!
In the same net was the mother caught!

PRINCE HENRY, *entering and kneeling at the confessional*

Remorseful, penitent, and lowly,
I come to crave, O Father holy,
Thy benediction on my head.

LUCIFER

The benediction shall be said
After confession, not before!
'Tis a God-speed to the parting guest,
Who stands already at the door,
Sandalled with holiness, and dressed
In garments pure from earthly stain.
Meanwhile, hast thou searched well thy breast?
Does the same madness fill thy brain?
Or have thy passion and unrest
Vanished forever from thy mind?

PRINCE HENRY

By the same madness still made blind,
By the same passion still possessed,
I come again to the house of prayer,
A man afflicted and distressed!
As in a cloudy atmosphere,
Through unseen sluices of the air,
A sudden and impetuous wind
Strikes the great forest white with fear,
And every branch, and bough, and spray
Points all its quivering leaves one way,
And meadows of grass, and fields of grain,
And the clouds above, and the slanting rain,
And smoke from chimneys of the town,
Yield themselves to it, and bow down,
So does this dreadful purpose press
Onward, with irresistible stress,
And all my thoughts and faculties,
Struck level by the strength of this,
From their true inclination turn,
And all stream forward to Salern!

LUCIFER

Alas! we are but eddies of dust,
Uplifted by the blast, and whirled
Along the highway of the world
A moment only, then to fall
Back to a common level all,
At the subsiding of the gust!

PRINCE HENRY

O holy Father! pardon in me
The oscillation of a mind
Unsteadfast, and that cannot find
Its centre of rest and harmony!
For evermore before mine eyes
This ghastly phantom flits and flies,
And as a madman through a crowd,
With frantic gestures and wild cries,
It hurries onward, and aloud
Repeats its awful prophecies!
Weakness is wretchedness! To be strong
Is to be happy! I am weak,
And cannot find the good I seek,
Because I feel and fear the wrong!

LUCIFER

Be not alarmed! The Church is kind,
And in her mercy and her meekness
She meets half-way her children's weakness,
Writes their trangressions in the dust!

Though in the Decalogue we find
The mandate written, "Thou shalt not kill!"
Yet there are cases when we must.
In war, for instance, or from scathe
To guard and keep the one true Faith
We must look at the Decalogue in the light
Of an ancient statute, that was meant
For a mild and general application,
To be understood with the reservation
That in certain instances the Right
Must yield to the Expedient!
Thou art a Prince. If thou shouldst die,
What hearts and hopes would prostrate lie!
What noble deeds, what fair renown,
Into the grave with thee go down!
What acts of valor and courtesy
Remain undone, and die with thee!
Thou art the last of all thy race!
With thee a noble name expires,
And vanishes from the earth's face
The glorious memory of thy sires!
She is a peasant. In her veins
Flows common and plebeian blood;
It is such as daily and hourly stains
The dust and the turf of battle plains,
By vassals shed, in a crimson flood,
Without reserve, and without reward,
At the slightest summons of their lord!
But thine is precious; the fore-appointed
Blood of kings, of God's anointed!
Moreover, what has the world in store
For one like her, but tears and toil?
Daughter of sorrow, serf of the soil,
A peasant's child and a peasant's wife,
And her soul within her sick and sore
With the roughness and barrenness of life!
I marvel not at the heart's recoil
From a fate like this, in one so tender,
Nor at its eagerness to surrender
All the wretchedness, want, and woe
That await it in this world below,
Nor the unutterable splendor
Of the world of rest beyond the skies.
So the Church sanctions the sacrifice:
Therefore inhale this healing balm,
And breathe this fresh life into thine;
Accept the comfort and the calm
She offers, as a gift divine;
Let her fall down and anoint thy feet
With the ointment costly and most sweet
Of her young blood, and thou shalt live.

PRINCE HENRY

And will the righteous Heaven forgive?
No action, whether foul or fair,
Is ever done, but it leaves somewhere
A record, written by fingers ghostly,
As a blessing or a curse, and mostly
In the greater weakness or greater strength
Of the acts which follow it, till at length
The wrongs of ages are redressed,
And the justice of God made manifest!

LUCIFER

In ancient records it is stated
That, whenever an evil deed is done,
Another devil is created
To scourge and torment the offending one!
But evil is only good perverted,
And Lucifer, the bearer of Light,
But an angel fallen and deserted,
Thrust from his Father's house with a curse
Into the black and endless night.

PRINCE HENRY

If justice rules the universe,
From the good actions of good men
Angels of light should be begotten,
And thus the balance restored again.

LUCIFER

Yes; if the world were not so rotten,
And so given over to the Devil!

PRINCE HENRY

But this deed, is it good or evil?
Have I thine absolution free
To do it, and without restriction?

LUCIFER

Ay; and from whatsoever sin
Lieth around it and within,
From all crimes in which it may involve thee,
I now release thee and absolve thee!

PRINCE HENRY

Give me thy holy benediction.

LUCIFER, *stretching forth his hand and muttering*

Maledictione perpetua
Maledicat vos
Pater eternus!

THE ANGEL, *with the æolian harp*

Take heed! take heed!
Noble art thou in thy birth,
By the good and the great of earth
Hast thou been taught!
Be noble in every thought
And in every deed!
Let not the illusion of thy senses
Betray thee to deadly offences.
Be strong! be good! be pure!
The right only shall endure,
All things else are but false pretences.
I entreat thee, I implore,
Listen no more
To the suggestions of an evil spirit,
That even now is there,
Making the foul seem fair,
And selfishness itself a virtue and a merit!

A ROOM IN THE FARM-HOUSE

GOTTLIEB

It is decided! For many days,
And nights as many, we have had
A nameless terror in our breast,
Making us timid, and afraid
Of God, and his mysterious ways!
We have been sorrowful and sad;
Much have we suffered, much have prayed
That he would lead us as is best,
And show us what his will required.
It is decided; and we give
Our child, O Prince, that you may live!

URSULA

It is of God. He has inspired
This purpose in her; and through pain,
Out of a world of sin and woe,
He takes her to Himself again.
The mother's heart resists no longer;
With the Angel of the Lord in vain
It wrestled, for he was the stronger.

GOTTLIEB

As Abraham offered long ago
His son unto the Lord, and even
The Everlasting Father in heaven
Gave his, as a lamb unto the slaughter,
So do I offer up my daughter!

URSULA *hides her face*

ELSIE

My life is little,
Only a cup of water,
But pure and limpid.
Take it, O my Prince!
Let it refresh you,
Let it restore you.
It is given willingly,
It is given freely;
May God bless the gift!

PRINCE HENRY

And the giver!

GOTTLIEB

Amen!

PRINCE HENRY

I accept it!

GOTTLIEB

Where are the children?

URSULA

They are already asleep.

GOTTLIEB

What if they were dead?

IN THE GARDEN

ELSIE

I have one thing to ask of you.

PRINCE HENRY

What is it?
It is already granted.

ELSIE

Promise me,
When we are gone from here, and on our way
Are journeying to Salerno, you will not,
By word or deed, endeavor to dissuade me
And turn me from my purpose; but remember
That as a pilgrim to the Holy City
Walks unmolested, and with thoughts of pardon
Occupied wholly, so would I approach
The gates of Heaven, in this great jubilee,
With my petition, putting off from me
All thoughts of earth, as shoes from off my feet.
Promise me this.

PRINCE HENRY

Thy words fall from thy lips
Like roses from the lips of Angelo: and angels
Might stoop to pick them up!

ELSIE

Will you not promise?

PRINCE HENRY

If ever we depart upon this journey,
So long to one or both of us, I promise.

ELSIE

Shall we not go, then? Have you lifted me
Into the air, only to hurl me back
Wounded upon the ground? and offered me
The waters of eternal life, to bid me
Drink the polluted puddles of this world?

PRINCE HENRY

O Elsie! what a lesson thou dost teach me!
The life which is, and that which is to come,
Suspended hang in such nice equipoise
A breath disturbs the balance; and that scale
In which we throw our hearts preponderates,
And the other, like an empty one, flies up,
And is accounted vanity and air!
To me the thought of death is terrible,
Having such hold on life. To thee it is not
So much even as the lifting of a latch;
Only a step into the open air
Out of a tent already luminous
With light that shines through its transparent
walls!
O pure in heart! from thy sweet dust shall
grow
Lilies, upon whose petals will be written
"Ave Maria" in characters of gold!

III

A STREET IN STRASBURG

Night. PRINCE HENRY *wandering alone, wrapped in a cloak*

PRINCE HENRY

Still is the night. The sound of feet
Has died away from the empty street,
And like an artisan, bending down
His head on his anvil, the dark town
Sleeps, with a slumber deep and sweet.
Sleepless and restless, I alone,
In the dusk and damp of these walls of stone,
Wander and weep in my remorse!

CRIER OF THE DEAD, *ringing a bell*

Wake! wake!
All ye that sleep!
Pray for the Dead!
Pray for the Dead!

PRINCE HENRY

Hark! with what accents loud and hoarse
This warder on the walls of death
Sends forth the challenge of his breath!
I see the dead that sleep in the grave!
They rise up and their garments wave,
Dimly and spectral, as they rise,
With the light of another world in their eyes!

CRIER OF THE DEAD

Wake! wake!
All ye that sleep!
Pray for the Dead!
Pray for the Dead!

PRINCE HENRY

Why for the dead, who are at rest?
Pray for the living, in whose breast
The struggle between right and wrong
Is raging terrible and strong,
As when good angels war with devils!
This is the Master of the Revels,
Who, at Life's flowing feast, proposes
The health of absent friends, and pledges,
Not in bright goblets crowned with roses,
And tinkling as we touch their edges,
But with his dismal, tinkling bell,
That mocks and mimics their funeral knell!

CRIER OF THE DEAD

Wake! wake!
All ye that sleep!
Pray for the Dead!
Pray for the Dead!

PRINCE HENRY

Wake not, beloved! be thy sleep
Silent as night is, and as deep!
There walks a sentinel at thy gate
Whose heart is heavy and desolate,
And the heavings of whose bosom number
The respirations of thy slumber,

As if some strange, mysterious fate
Had linked two hearts in one, and mine
Went madly wheeling about thine,
Only with wider and wilder sweep!

CRIER OF THE DEAD, *at a distance*

Wake! wake!
All ye that sleep!
Pray for the Dead!
Pray for the Dead!

PRINCE HENRY

Lo! with what depth of blackness thrown
Against the clouds, far up the skies
The walls of the cathedral rise,
Like a mysterious grove of stone,
With fitful lights and shadows blending,
As from behind, the moon, ascending,
Lights its dim aisles and paths unknown!
The wind is rising; but the boughs
Rise not and fall not with the wind,
That through their foliage sobs and soughs;
Only the cloudy rack behind,
Drifting onward, wild and ragged,
Gives to each spire and buttress jagged
A seeming motion undefined.
Below on the square, an armèd knight,
Still as a statue and as white,
Sits on his steed, and the moonbeams quiver
Upon the points of his armor bright
As on the ripples of a river.
He lifts the visor from his cheek,
And beckons, and makes as he would speak.

WALTER *the Minnesinger*

Friend! can you tell me where alight
Thuringia's horsemen for the night?
For I have lingered in the rear,
And wander vainly up and down.

PRINCE HENRY

I am a stranger in the town,
As thou art; but the voice I hear
Is not a stranger to mine ear.
Thou art Walter of the Vogelweid!

WALTER

Thou hast guessed rightly; and thy name
Is Henry of Hoheneck!

PRINCE HENRY

Ay, the same.

WALTER, *embracing him*

Come closer, closer to my side!
What brings thee hither? What potent charm
Has drawn thee from thy German farm
Into the old Alsatian city?

PRINCE HENRY

A tale of wonder and of pity!
A wretched man, almost by stealth
Dragging my body to Salern,
In the vain hope and search for health,
And destined never to return.
Already thou hast heard the rest.
But what brings thee, thus armed and dight
In the equipments of a knight?

WALTER

Dost thou not see upon my breast
The cross of the Crusaders shine?
My pathway leads to Palestine.

PRINCE HENRY

Ah, would that way were also mine!
O noble poet! thou whose heart
Is like a nest of singing-birds
Rocked on the topmost bough of life,
Wilt thou, too, from our sky depart,
And in the clangor of the strife
Mingle the music of thy words?

WALTER

My hopes are high, my heart is proud,
And like a trumpet long and loud,
Thither my thoughts all clang and ring!
My life is in my hand, and lo!
I grasp and bend it as a bow,
And shoot forth from its trembling string
An arrow, that shall be, perchance,
Like the arrow of the Israelite king
Shot from the window toward the east,
That of the Lord's deliverance!

PRINCE HENRY

My life, alas! is what thou seest!
O enviable fate! to be
Strong, beautiful, and armed like thee
With lyre and sword, with song and steel;
A hand to smite, a heart to feel!
Thy heart, thy hand, thy lyre, thy sword,
Thou givest all unto thy Lord;
While I, so mean and abject grown,
Am thinking of myself alone.

WALTER

Be patient: Time will reinstate
Thy health and fortunes.

PRINCE HENRY

'Tis too late!
I cannot strive against my fate!

WALTER

Come with me; for my steed is weary;
Our journey has been long and dreary,
And, dreaming of his stall, he dints
With his impatient hoofs the flints.

PRINCE HENRY, *aside*

I am ashamed, in my disgrace,
To look into that noble face!
Tomorrow, Walter, let it be.

WALTER

Tomorrow, at the dawn of day,
I shall again be on my way.
Come with me to the hostelry,
For I have many things to say.
Our journey into Italy
Perchance together we may make;
Wilt thou not do it for my sake?

PRINCE HENRY

A sick man's pace would but impede
Thine eager and impatient speed.
Besides, my pathway leads me round
To Hirschau, in the forest's bound,
Where I assemble man and steed,
And all things for my journey's need.

They go out

LUCIFER, *flying over the city*

Sleep, sleep, O city! till the light
Wake you to sin and crime again,
Whilst on your dreams, like dismal rain,
I scatter downward through the night
My maledictions dark and deep.
I have more martyrs in your walls
Than God has; and they cannot sleep;
They are my bondsmen and my thralls;
Their wretched lives are full of pain,
Wild agonies of nerve and brain;
And every heart-beat, every breath,
Is a convulsion worse than death!
Sleep, sleep, O city! though within
The circuit of your walls there be
No habitation free from sin,
And all its nameless misery;
The aching heart, the aching head,
Grief for the living and the dead,
And foul corruption of the time,
Disease, distress, and want, and woe,
And crimes, and passions that may grow
Until they ripen into crime!

SQUARE IN FRONT OF THE CATHEDRAL

Easter Sunday. FRIAR CUTHBERT *preaching to the crowd from a pulpit in the open air*
PRINCE HENRY *and* ELSIE *crossing the square*

PRINCE HENRY

This is the day, when from the dead
Our Lord arose; and everywhere,
Out of their darkness and despair,
Triumphant over fears and foes,
The hearts of his disciples rose,
When to the women, standing near,
The Angel in shining vesture said,
"The Lord is risen; he is not here!"
And, mindful that the day is come,
On all the hearths in Christendom
The fires are quenched, to be again
Rekindled from the sun, that high
Is dancing in the cloudless sky.
The churches are all decked with flowers,
The salutations among men
Are but the Angel's words divine,
"Christ is arisen!" and the bells
Catch the glad murmur, as it swells,
And chant together in their towers.
All hearts are glad; and free from care
The faces of the people shine.
See what a crowd is in the square,
Gayly and gallantly arrayed!

ELSIE

Let us go back; I am afraid!

PRINCE HENRY

Nay, let us mount the church-steps here,
Under the doorway's sacred shadow;
We can see all things, and be freer
From the crowd that madly heaves and presses!

ELSIE

What a gay pageant! what bright dresses!
It looks like a flower-besprinkled meadow.
What is that yonder on the square?

PRINCE HENRY

A pulpit in the open air,
And a Friar, who is preaching to the crowd
In a voice so deep and clear and loud,
That, if we listen, and give heed,
His lowest words will reach the ear.

FRIAR CUTHBERT, *gesticulating and cracking a postilion's whip*

What ho! good people! do you not hear?
Dashing along at the top of his speed,
Booted and spurred, on his jaded steed,
A courier comes with words of cheer.
Courier! what is the news, I pray?
"Christ is arisen!" Whence come you? "From court."
Then I do not believe it; you say it in sport.

Cracks his whip again

Ah, here comes another, riding this way;
We soon shall know what he has to say.
Courier! what are the tidings today?
"Christ is arisen!" Whence come you? "From town."
Then I do not believe it; away with you, clown.

Cracks his whip more violently

And here comes a third, who is spurring amain;
What news do you bring, with your loose-hanging rein,
Your spurs wet with blood, and your bridle with foam?
"Christ is arisen!" Whence come you? "From Rome."
Ah, now I believe. He is risen, indeed.
Ride on with the news, at the top of your speed!

Great applause among the crowd

To come back to my text! When the news was first spread
That Christ was arisen indeed from the dead,
Very great was the joy of the angels in heaven;
And as great the dispute as to who should carry
The tidings thereof to the Virgin Mary,
Pierced to the heart with sorrows seven.
Old Father Adam was first to propose,
As being the author of all our woes;
But he was refused, for fear, said they,
He would stop to eat apples on the way!
Abel came next, but petitioned in vain,
Because he might meet with his brother Cain!
Noah, too, was refused, lest his weakness for wine
Should delay him at every tavern-sign;
And John the Baptist could not get a vote,
On account of his old-fashioned camel's-hair coat;
And the Penitent Thief, who died on the cross,
Was reminded that all his bones were broken!
Till at last, when each in turn had spoken,
The company being still at loss,
The Angel, who rolled away the stone,
Was sent to the sepulchre, all alone.
And filled with glory that gloomy prison,
And said to the Virgin, "The Lord is arisen!"

The Cathedral bells ring

But hark! the bells are beginning to chime;
And I feel that I am growing hoarse.
I will put an end to my discourse,
And leave the rest for some other time.
For the bells themselves are the best of preachers;
Their brazen lips are learned teachers,
From their pulpits of stone, in the upper air,
Sounding aloft, without crack or flaw,
Shriller than trumpets under the Law,
Now a sermon, and now a prayer.
The clangorous hammer is the tongue,
This way, that way, beaten and swung,
That from mouth of brass, as from Mouth of Gold,
May be taught the Testaments, New and Old.
And above it the great cross-beam of wood
Representeth the Holy Rood,
Upon which, like the bell, our hopes are hung.
And the wheel wherewith it is swayed and rung
Is the mind of man, that round and round
Sways, and maketh the tongue to sound!
And the rope, with its twisted cordage three,
Denoteth the Scriptural Trinity
Of Morals, and Symbols, and History;
And the upward and downward motion show
That we touch upon matters high and low;
And the constant change and transmutation
Of action and of contemplation,
Downward, the Scripture brought from on high,
Upward, exalted again to the sky;
Downward, the literal interpretation,
Upward, the Vision and Mystery!

And now, my hearers, to make an end,
I have only one word more to say;
In the church, in honor of Easter day
Will be presented a Miracle Play;
And I hope you will all have the grace to attend.
Christ bring us at last to his felicity!
Pax vobiscum! et Benedicite!

IN THE CATHEDRAL

CHANT

Kyrie Eleison!
Christe Eleison!

ELSIE

I am at home here in my Father's house!
These paintings of the Saints upon the walls
Have all familiar and benignant faces.

PRINCE HENRY

The portraits of the family of God!
Thine own hereafter shall be placed among them.

ELSIE

How very grand it is and wonderful!
Never have I beheld a church so splendid!
Such columns, and such arches, and such windows,
So many tombs and statues in the chapels,
And under them so many confessionals.
They must be for the rich. I should not like
To tell my sins in such a church as this.
Who built it?

PRINCE HENRY

A great master of his craft,
Erwin von Steinbach; but not he alone,
For many generations labored with him.
Children that came to see these Saints in stone,
As day by day out of the blocks they rose,
Grew old and died, and still the work went on,
And on, and on, and is not yet completed.
The generation that succeeds our own
Perhaps may finish it. The architect
Built his great heart into these sculptured stones,
And with him toiled his children, and their lives
Were builded, with his own, into the walls,
As offerings unto God. You see that statue
Fixing its joyous, but deep-wrinkled eyes
Upon the Pillars of the Angels yonder.
That is the image of the master, carved
By the fair hand of his own child, Sabina.

ELSIE

How beautiful is the column that he looks at!

PRINCE HENRY

That, too, she sculptured. At the base of it
Stand the Evangelists; above their heads
Four Angels blowing upon marble trumpets,
And over them the blessed Christ, surrounded
By his attendant ministers, upholding
The instruments of his passion.

ELSIE

O my Lord!
Would I could leave behind me upon earth
Some monument to thy glory, such as this!

PRINCE HENRY

A greater monument than this thou leavest
In thine own life, all purity and love!
See, too, the Rose, above the western portal
Resplendent with a thousand gorgeous colors,
The perfect flower of Gothic loveliness!

ELSIE

And, in the gallery, the long line of statues,
Christ with his twelve Apostles watching us!

A BISHOP *in armor, booted and spurred, passes with his train*

PRINCE HENRY

But come away; we have not time to look.
The crowd already fills the church, and yonder
Upon a stage, a herald with a trumpet,
Clad like the Angel Gabriel, proclaims
The Mystery that will now be represented.

THE NATIVITY

A MIRACLE-PLAY

INTROITUS

PRÆCO

Come, good people, all and each,
Come and listen to our speech!
In your presence here I stand,
With a trumpet in my hand,
To announce the Easter Play,

Which we represent today!
First of all we shall rehearse,
In our action and our verse,
The Nativity of our Lord,
As written in the old record
Of the Protevangelion,
So that he who reads may run!

Blows his trumpet

I. Heaven

MERCY, *at the feet of God*

Have pity, Lord! be not afraid
To save mankind, whom thou hast made,
Nor let the souls that were betrayed
Perish eternally!

JUSTICE

It cannot be, it must not be!
When in the garden placed by thee,
The fruit of the forbidden tree
He ate, and he must die!

MERCY

Have pity, Lord! let penitence
Atone for disobedience,
Nor let the fruit of man's offence
Be endless misery!

JUSTICE

What penitence proportionate
Can e'er be felt for sin so great?
Of the forbidden fruit he ate,
And damnèd must he be!

GOD

He shall be saved, if that within
The bounds of earth one free from sin
Be found, who for his kith and kin
Will suffer martyrdom.

THE FOUR VIRTUES

Lord! we have searched the world around,
From centre to the utmost bound,
But no such mortal can be found;
Despairing, back we come.

WISDOM

No mortal, but a God made man,
Can ever carry out this plan,
Achieving what none other can,
Salvation unto all!

GOD

Go, then, O my beloved Son!
It can by thee alone be done;
By thee the victory shall be won
O'er Satan and the Fall!

Here the ANGEL GABRIEL *shall leave Paradise and fly towards the earth; the jaws of Hell open below, and the Devils walk about, making a great noise*

II. Mary at the Well

MARY

Along the garden walk, and thence
Through the wicket in the garden fence,
I steal with quiet pace,
My pitcher at the well to fill,
That lies so deep and cool and still
In this sequestered place.

These sycamores keep guard around;
I see no face, I hear no sound,
Save bubblings of the spring,
And my companions, who, within,
The threads of gold and scarlet spin,
And at their labor sing.

THE ANGEL GABRIEL

Hail, Virgin Mary, full of grace!

Here MARY *looketh around her, trembling, and then saith:*

MARY

Who is it speaketh in this place,
With such a gentle voice?

GABRIEL

The Lord of heaven is with thee now!
Blessed among all women thou,
Who art his holy choice!

MARY, *setting down the pitcher*

What can this mean? No one is near,
And yet, such sacred words I hear,
I almost fear to stay.

Here the ANGEL, *appearing to her, shall say:*

GABRIEL

Fear not, O Mary! but believe!
For thou, a Virgin, shalt conceive
A child this very day.

Fear not, O Mary! from the sky
The majesty of the Most High
Shall overshadow thee!

MARY

Behold the handmaid of the Lord!
According to thy holy word,
So be it unto me!

Here the Devils shall again make a great noise, under the stage

III. The Angels of the Seven Planets, bearing the Star of Bethlehem

THE ANGELS

The Angels of the Planets Seven,
Across the shining fields of heaven
The natal star we bring!
Dropping our sevenfold virtues down
As priceless jewels in the crown
Of Christ, our new-born King.

RAPHAEL

I am the Angel of the Sun,
Whose flaming wheels began to run
When God's almighty breath
Said to the darkness and the Night,
Let there be light! and there was light!
I bring the gift of Faith.

ONAFIEL

I am the Angel of the Moon,
Darkened to be rekindled soon
Beneath the azure cope!
Nearest to earth, it is my ray
That best illumes the midnight way;
I bring the gift of Hope!

ANAEL

The Angel of the Star of Love,
The Evening Star, that shines above
The place where lovers be,
Above all happy hearths and homes,
On roofs of thatch, or golden domes,
I give him Charity!

ZOBIACHEL

The Planet Jupiter is mine!
The mightiest star of all that shine,
Except the sun alone!
He is the High Priest of the Dove,
And sends, from his great throne above,
Justice, that shall atone!

MICHAEL

The Planet Mercury, whose place
Is nearest to the sun in space,
Is my allotted sphere!
And with celestial ardor swift
I bear upon my hands the gift
Of heavenly Prudence here!

URIEL

I am the Minister of Mars,
The strongest star among the stars!
My songs of power prelude
The march and battle of man's life,
And for the suffering and the strife,
I give him Fortitude!

ORIFEL

The Angel of the uttermost
Of all the shining, heavenly host,
From the far-off expanse
Of the Saturnian, endless space
I bring the last, the crowning grace,
The gift of Temperance!

A sudden light shines from the windows of the stable in the village below

IV. The Wise Men of the East

The stable of the Inn. The VIRGIN *and* CHILD. *Three Gypsy Kings*, GASPAR, MELCHIOR, *and* BELSHAZZAR, *shall come in*

GASPAR

Hail to thee, Jesus of Nazareth!
Though in a manger thou draw breath,
Thou art greater than Life and Death,
Greater than Joy or Woe!
This cross upon the line of life
Portendeth struggle, toil, and strife,
And through a region with peril rife
In darkness shalt thou go!

MELCHIOR

Hail to thee, King of Jerusalem!
Though humbly born in Bethlehem,
A sceptre and a diadem
Await thy brow and hand!
The sceptre is a simple reed,
The crown will make thy temples bleed,

And in thine hour of greatest need,
  Abashed thy subjects stand!

BELSHAZZAR

Hail to thee, Christ of Christendom!
O'er all the earth thy kingdom come!
From distant Trebizond to Rome
  Thy name shall men adore!
Peace and good-will among all men,
The Virgin has returned again,
Returned the old Saturnian reign
  And Golden Age once more.

THE CHILD CHRIST

Jesus, the Son of God, am I,
Born here to suffer and to die
According to the prophecy,
  That other men may live!

THE VIRGIN

And now these clothes, that wrapped Him, take
And keep them precious, for his sake;
Our benediction thus we make,
  Naught else have we to give.

She gives them swaddling-clothes, and they depart

V. The Flight into Egypt

Here Joseph *shall come in, leading an ass, on which are seated* Mary *and the* Child

MARY

Here will we rest us, under these
O'erhanging branches of the trees,
Where robins chant their Litanies
  And canticles of joy.

JOSEPH

My saddle-girths have given way
With trudging through the heat today;
To you I think it is but play
  To ride and hold the boy.

MARY

Hark! how the robins shout and sing,
As if to hail their infant King!
I will alight at yonder spring
  To wash his little coat.

JOSEPH

And I will hobble well the ass,
Lest, being loose upon the grass,
He should escape; for, by the mass,
  He's nimble as a goat.

Here Mary *shall alight and go to the spring*

MARY

O Joseph! I am much afraid,
For men are sleeping in the shade;
I fear that we shall be waylaid,
  And robbed and beaten sore!

Here a band of robbers shall be seen sleeping, two of whom shall rise and come forward

DUMACHUS

Cock's soul! deliver up your gold!

JOSEPH

I pray you, Sirs, let go your hold!
You see that I am weak and old,
  Of wealth I have no store.

DUMACHUS

Give up your money!

TITUS

Prithee cease.
Let these people go in peace.

DUMACHUS

First let them pay for their release,
  And then go on their way.

TITUS

These forty groats I give in fee,
If thou wilt only silent be.

MARY

May God be merciful to thee
  Upon the Judgment Day!

JESUS

When thirty years shall have gone by,
I at Jerusalem shall die,
By Jewish hands exalted high
  On the accursed tree,
Then on my right and on my left side,
These thieves shall both be crucified,
And Titus thenceforth shall abide
  In paradise with me.

Here a great rumor of trumpets and horses, like the noise of a king with his army, and the robbers shall take flight

VI. The Slaughter of the Innocents

KING HEROD

Potz-tausend! Himmel-sacrament!
Filled am I with great wonderment
At this unwelcome news!
Am I not Herod? Who shall dare
My crown to take, my sceptre bear,
As king among the Jews?

Here he shall stride up and down and flourish his sword

What ho! I fain would drink a can
Of the strong wine of Canaan!
The wine of Helbon bring
I purchased at the Fair of Tyre,
As red as blood, as hot as fire,
And fit for any king!

He quaffs great goblets of wine

Now at the window will I stand,
While in the street the armèd band
The little children slay;
The babe just born in Bethlehem
Will surely slaughtered be with them,
Nor live another day!

Here a voice of lamentation shall be heard in the street

RACHEL

O wicked king! O cruel speed!
To do this most unrighteous deed!
My children all are slain!

HEROD

Ho seneschal! another cup!
With wine of Sorek fill it up!
I would a bumper drain!

RAHAB

May maledictions fall and blast
Thyself and lineage, to the last
Of all thy kith and kin!

HEROD

Another goblet! quick! and stir
Pomegranate juice and drops of myrrh
And calamus therein!

SOLDIERS, *in the street*

Give up thy child into our hands!
It is King Herod who commands
That he should thus be slain!

THE NURSE MEDUSA

O monstrous men! What have ye done!
It is King Herod's only son
That ye have cleft in twain!

HEROD

Ah, luckless day! What words of fear
Are these that smite upon my ear
With such a doleful sound!
What torments rack my heart and head!
Would I were dead! would I were dead,
And buried in the ground!

He falls down and writhes as though eaten by worms. Hell opens, and SATAN *and* ASTAROTH *come forth, and drag him down*

VII. Jesus at Play with His Schoolmates

JESUS

The shower is over. Let us play,
And make some sparrows out of clay,
Down by the river's side.

JUDAS

See, how the stream has overflowed
Its banks, and o'er the meadow road
Is spreading far and wide!

They draw water out of the river by channels, and form little pools. JESUS *makes twelve sparrows of clay, and the other boys do the same*

JESUS

Look! look how prettily I make
These little sparrows by the lake
Bend down their necks and drink!
Now will I make them sing and soar
So far, they shall return no more
Unto this river's brink.

JUDAS

That canst thou not! They are but clay.
They cannot sing, nor fly away
Above the meadow lands!

JESUS

Fly, fly! ye sparrows! you are free!
And while you live, remember me,
Who made you with my hands.

Here JESUS *shall clap his hands, and the sparrows shall fly away, chirruping*

JUDAS

Thou art a sorcerer, I know;
Oft has my mother told me so,
I will not play with thee!

He strikes JESUS *in the right side*

JESUS

Ah, Judas! thou hast smote my side,
And when I shall be crucified,
There shall I piercèd be!

Here JOSEPH *shall come in and say:*

JOSEPH

Ye wicked boys! why do ye play,
And break the holy Sabbath day?
What, think ye, will your mothers say
To see you in such plight!
In such a sweat and such a heat,
With all that mud upon your feet!
There's not a beggar in the street
Makes such a sorry sight!

VIII. The Village School

The RABBI BEN ISRAEL, *sitting on a high stool, with a long beard, and a rod in his hand*

RABBI

I am the Rabbi Ben Israel,
Throughout this village known full well,
And, as my scholars all will tell,
Learned in things divine;
The Cabala and Talmud hoar
Than all the prophets prize I more,
For water is all Bible lore,
But Mishna is strong wine.

My fame extends from West to East,
And always, at the Purim feast,
I am as drunk as any beast
That wallows in his sty;
The wine it so elateth me,
That I no difference can see
Between "Accursed Haman be!"
And "Blessed be Mordecai!"

Come hither, Judas Iscariot;
Say, if thy lesson thou hast got
From the Rabbinical Book or not.
Why howl the dogs at night?

JUDAS

In the Rabbinical Book, it saith
The dogs howl, when with icy breath
Great Sammael, the Angel of Death,
Takes through the town his flight!

RABBI

Well, boy! now say, if thou art wise,
When the Angel of Death, who is full of eyes,
Comes where a sick man dying lies,
What doth he to the wight?

JUDAS

He stands beside him, dark and tall,
Holding a sword, from which doth fall
Into his mouth a drop of gall,
And so he turneth white.

RABBI

And now, my Judas, say to me
What the great Voices Four may be,
That quite across the world do flee,
And are not heard by men?

JUDAS

The Voice of the Sun in heaven's dome,
The Voice of the Murmuring of Rome,
The Voice of a Soul that goeth home,
And the Angel of the Rain!

RABBI

Right are thine answers every one!
Now little Jesus, the carpenter's son,
Let us see how thy task is done;
Canst thou thy letters say?

JESUS

Aleph.

RABBI

What next? Do not stop yet!
Go on with all the alphabet.
Come, Aleph, Beth; dost thou forget?
Cock's soul! thou'dst rather play!

JESUS

What Aleph means I fain would know,
Before I any farther go!

RABBI

Oh, by Saint Peter! wouldst thou so?
Come hither, boy, to me.
As surely as the letter Jod
Once cried aloud, and spake to God,

So surely shalt thou feel this rod,
  And punished shalt thou be!

Here RABBI BEN ISRAEL *shall lift up his rod to strike* JESUS, *and his right arm shall be paralyzed*

IX. CROWNED WITH FLOWERS

JESUS *sitting among his playmates crowned with flowers as their King*

BOYS

We spread our garments on the ground!
With fragrant flowers thy head is crowned
While like a guard we stand around,
  And hail thee as our King!
Thou art the new King of the Jews!
Nor let the passers-by refuse
To bring that homage which men use
  To majesty to bring.

Here a traveller shall go by, and the boys shall lay hold of his garments and say:

BOYS

Come hither! and all reverence pay
Unto our monarch, crowned today!
Then go rejoicing on your way,
  In all prosperity!

TRAVELLER

Hail to the King of Bethlehem,
Who weareth in his diadem
The yellow crocus for the gem
  Of his authority!

He passes by; and others come in, bearing on a litter a sick child

BOYS

Set down the litter and draw near!
The King of Bethlehem is here!
What ails the child, who seems to fear
  That we shall do him harm?

THE BEARERS

He climbed up to the robin's nest,
And out there darted, from his rest,
A serpent with a crimson crest,
  And stung him in the arm.

JESUS

Bring him to me, and let me feel
The wounded place; my touch can heal
The sting of serpents, and can steal
  The poison from the bite!

He touches the wound, and the boy begins to cry

Cease to lament! I can foresee
That thou hereafter known shalt be,
Among the men who follow me,
  As Simon the Canaanite!

EPILOGUE

In the after part of the day
Will be represented another play,
Of the Passion of our Blessed Lord,
Beginning directly after Nones!
At the close of which we shall accord,
By way of benison and reward,
The sight of a holy Martyr's bones!

IV

THE ROAD TO HIRSCHAU

PRINCE HENRY *and* ELSIE, *with their attendants on horseback*

ELSIE

Onward and onward the highway runs to the distant city, impatiently bearing
Tidings of human joy and disaster, of love and of hate, of doing and daring!

PRINCE HENRY

This life of ours is a wild æolian harp of many a joyous strain,
But under them all there runs a loud perpetual wail, as of souls in pain.

ELSIE

Faith alone can interpret life, and the heart that aches and bleeds with the stigma
Of pain, alone bears the likeness of Christ, and can comprehend its dark enigma.

PRINCE HENRY

Man is selfish, and seeketh pleasure with little care of what may betide,
Else why am I travelling here beside thee, a demon that rides by an angel's side?

ELSIE

All the hedges are white with dust, and the great dog under the creaking wain

Hangs his head in the lazy heat, while onward
the horses toil and strain.

PRINCE HENRY

Now they stop at the wayside inn, and the
wagoner laughs with the landlord's
daughter,
While out of the dripping trough the horses
distend their leathern sides with water.

ELSIE

All through life there are wayside inns, where
man may refresh his soul with love;
Even the lowest may quench his thirst at
rivulets fed by springs from above.

PRINCE HENRY

Yonder, where rises the cross of stone, our
journey along the highway ends, 2109
And over the fields, by a bridle path, down
into the broad green valley descends.

ELSIE

I am not sorry to leave behind the beaten
road with its dust and heat;
The air will be sweeter far, and the turf will
be softer under our horses' feet.

They turn down a green lane

ELSIE

Sweet is the air with the budding haws, and
the valley stretching for miles below
Is white with blossoming cherry-trees, as if
just covered with lightest snow.

PRINCE HENRY

Over our heads a white cascade is gleaming
against the distant hill;
We cannot hear it, nor see it move, but it
hangs like a banner when winds are still.

ELSIE

Damp and cool is this deep ravine, and cool
the sound of the brook by our side!
What is this castle that rises above us, and
lords it over a land so wide?

PRINCE HENRY

It is the home of the Counts of Calva; well
have I known these scenes of old,
Well I remember each tower and turret, remember the brooklet, the wood, and the
wold. 2120

ELSIE

Hark! from the little village below us the bells
of the church are ringing for rain!
Priests and peasants in long procession come
forth and kneel on the arid plain.

PRINCE HENRY

They have not long to wait, for I see in the
south uprising a little cloud,
That before the sun shall be set will cover
the sky above us as with a shroud.

They pass on

THE CONVENT OF HIRSCHAU IN THE
BLACK FOREST

The Convent Cellar. FRIAR CLAUS *comes in
with a light and a basket of empty flagons*

FRIAR CLAUS

I always enter this sacred place
With a thoughtful, solemn, and reverent pace,
Pausing long enough on each stair
To breathe an ejaculatory prayer,
And a benediction on the vines 2129
That produce these various sorts of wines!
For my part, I am well content
That we have got through with the tedious
Lent!
Fasting is all very well for those
Who have to contend with invisible foes;
But I am quite sure it does not agree
With a quiet, peaceable man like me,
Who am not of that nervous and meagre kind,
That are always distressed in body and mind!
And at times it really does me good 2139
To come down among this brotherhood,
Dwelling forever underground,
Silent, contemplative, round and sound;
Each one old, and brown with mould,
But filled to the lips with the ardor of youth,
With the latent power and love of truth,
And with virtues fervent and manifold.

I have heard it said, that at Easter-tide
When buds are swelling on every side,
And the sap begins to move in the vine,
Then in all cellars, far and wide, 2150
The oldest as well as the newest wine
Begins to stir itself, and ferment,
With a kind of revolt and discontent
At being so long in darkness pent,

And fain would burst from its sombre tun
To bask on the hillside in the sun;
As in the bosom of us poor friars,
The tumult of half-subdued desires
For the world that we have left behind
Disturbs at times all peace of mind!
And now that we have lived through Lent,
My duty it is, as often before,
To open awhile the prison-door,
And give these restless spirits vent.

Now here is a cask that stands alone,
And has stood a hundred years or more,
Its beard of cobwebs, long and hoar,
Trailing and sweeping along the floor,
Like Barbarossa, who sits in his cave,
Taciturn, sombre, sedate, and grave,
Till his beard has grown through the table of stone!
It is of the quick and not of the dead!
In its veins the blood is hot and red,
And a heart still beats in those ribs of oak
That time may have tamed, but has not broke!
It comes from Bacharach on the Rhine,
Is one of the three best kinds of wine,
And costs some hundred florins the ohm;
But that I do not consider dear,
When I remember that every year
Four butts are sent to the Pope of Rome.
And whenever a goblet thereof I drain,
The old rhyme keeps running in my brain:

At Bacharach on the Rhine,
At Hochheim on the Main,
And at Würzburg on the Stein,
Grow the three best kinds of wine!

They are all good wines, and better far
Than those of the Neckar, or those of the Ahr.
In particular, Würzburg well may boast
Of its blessed wine of the Holy Ghost,
Which of all wines I like the most.
This I shall draw for the Abbot's drinking,
Who seems to be much of my way of thinking.

Fills a flagon

Ah! how the streamlet laughs and sings!
What a delicious fragrance springs
From the deep flagon, while it fills,
As of hyacinths and daffodils!
Between this cask and the Abbot's lips
Many have been the sips and slips;
Many have been the draughts of wine,
On their way to his, that have stopped at mine;
And many a time my soul has hankered
For a deep draught out of his silver tankard,
When it should have been busy with other affairs,
Less with its longings and more with its prayers.
But now there is no such awkward condition,
No danger of death and eternal perdition;
So here's to the Abbot and Brothers all,
Who dwell in this convent of Peter and Paul!

He drinks

O cordial delicious! O soother of pain!
It flashes like sunshine into my brain!
A benison rest on the Bishop who sends
Such a fudder of wine as this to his friends!
And now a flagon for such as may ask
A draught from the noble Bacharach cask,
And I will be gone, though I know full well
The cellar's a cheerfuller place than the cell.
Behold where he stands, all sound and good,
Brown and old in his oaken hood;
Silent he seems externally
As any Carthusian monk may be;
But within, what a spirit of deep unrest!
What a seething and simmering in his breast!
As if the heaving of his great heart
Would burst his belt of oak apart!
Let me unloose this button of wood,
And quiet a little his turbulent mood.

Sets it running

See! how its currents gleam and shine,
As if they had caught the purple hues
Of autumn sunsets on the Rhine,
Descending and mingling with the dews;
Or as if the grapes were stained with the blood
Of the innocent boy, who, some years back,
Was taken and crucified by the Jews,
In that ancient town of Bacharach;
Perdition upon those infidel Jews,
In that ancient town of Bacharach!
The beautiful town, that gives us wine
With the fragrant odor of Muscadine!
I should deem it wrong to let this pass
Without first touching my lips to the glass,
For here in the midst of the current I stand
Like the stone Pfalz in the midst of the river,

Taking toll upon either hand,
And much more grateful to the giver.

He drinks

Here, now, is a very inferior kind,
Such as in any town you may find,
Such as one might imagine would suit
The rascal who drank wine out of a boot.
And, after all, it was not a crime,
For he won thereby Dorf Hüffelsheim.
A jolly old toper! who at a pull
Could drink a postilion's jack-boot full,
And ask with a laugh, when that was done,
If the fellow had left the other one!
This wine is as good as we can afford
To the friars, who sit at the lower board,
And cannot distinguish bad from good,
And are far better off than if they could,
Being rather the rude disciples of beer
Than of anything more refined and dear!

Fills the flagon and departs

THE SCRIPTORIUM

FRIAR PACIFICUS *transcribing and illuminating*

FRIAR PACIFICUS

It is growing dark! Yet one line more,
And then my work for today is o'er.
I come again to the name of the Lord!
Ere I that awful name record,
That is spoken so lightly among men,
Let me pause awhile, and wash my pen;
Pure from blemish and blot must it be
When it writes that word of mystery!

Thus have I labored on and on,
Nearly through the Gospel of John.
Can it be that from the lips
Of this same gentle Evangelist,
That Christ himself perhaps has kissed,
Came the dread Apocalypse!
It has a very awful look,
As it stands there at the end of the book,
Like the sun in an eclipse.
Ah me! when I think of that vision divine,
Think of writing it, line by line,
I stand in awe of the terrible curse,
Like the trump of doom, in the closing verse!
God forgive me! if ever I
Take aught from the book of that Prophecy,
Lest my part too should be taken away
From the Book of Life on the Judgment Day.
This is well written, though I say it!
I should not be afraid to display it
In open day, on the selfsame shelf
With the writings of St. Thecla herself,
Or of Theodosius, who of old
Wrote the Gospels in letters of gold!
That goodly folio standing yonder,
Without a single blot or blunder,
Would not bear away the palm from mine,
If we should compare them line for line.

There, now, is an initial letter!
Saint Ulric himself never made a better!
Finished down to the leaf and the snail,
Down to the eyes on the peacock's tail!
And now, as I turn the volume over,
And see what lies between cover and cover,
What treasures of art these pages hold,
All ablaze with crimson and gold,
God forgive me! I seem to feel
A certain satisfaction steal
Into my heart, and into my brain,
As if my talent had not lain
Wrapped in a napkin, and all in vain.
Yes, I might almost say to the Lord,
Here is a copy of thy Word,
Written out with much toil and pain;
Take it, O Lord, and let it be
As something I have done for thee!

He looks from the window

How sweet the air is! How fair the scene!
I wish I had as lovely a green
To paint my landscapes and my leaves!
How the swallows twitter under the eaves!
There, now, there is one in her nest;
I can just catch a glimpse of her head and breast,
And will sketch her thus, in her quiet nook,
For the margin of my Gospel book.

He makes a sketch

I can see no more. Through the valley yonder
A shower is passing; I hear the thunder
Mutter its curses in the air,
The devil's own and only prayer!
The dusty road is brown with rain,
And, speeding on with might and main,
Hitherward rides a gallant train.
They do not parley, they cannot wait,
But hurry in at the convent gate.
What a fair lady! and beside her

What a handsome, graceful, noble rider!
Now she gives him her hand to alight;
They will beg a shelter for the night.
I will go down to the corridor,
And try to see that face once more;
It will do for the face of some beautiful Saint,
Or for one of the Maries I shall paint.

Goes out

THE CLOISTERS

The ABBOT ERNESTUS *pacing to and fro*

ABBOT

Slowly, slowly up the wall
Steals the sunshine, steals the shade;
Evening damps begin to fall,
Evening shadows are displayed.
Round me, o'er me, everywhere,
All the sky is grand with clouds,
And athwart the evening air
Wheel the swallows home in crowds.
Shafts of sunshine from the west
Paint the dusky windows red;
Darker shadows, deeper rest,
Underneath and overhead.
Darker, darker, and more wan,
In my breast the shadows fall;
Upward steals the life of man,
As the sunshine from the wall.
From the wall into the sky,
From the roof along the spire;
Ah, the souls of those that die
Are but sunbeams lifted higher.

Enter PRINCE HENRY

PRINCE HENRY

Christ is arisen!

ABBOT

Amen! He is arisen!
His peace be with you!

PRINCE HENRY

Here it reigns forever!
The peace of God, that passeth understanding,
Reigns in these cloisters and these corridors.
Are you Ernestus, Abbot of the convent?

ABBOT

I am.

PRINCE HENRY

And I Prince Henry of Hoheneck,
Who crave your hospitality tonight.

ABBOT

You are thrice welcome to our humble walls.
You do us honor; and we shall requite it,
I fear, but poorly, entertaining you
With Paschal eggs, and our poor convent wine,
The remnants of our Easter holidays.

PRINCE HENRY

How fares it with the holy monks of Hirschau?
Are all things well with them?

ABBOT

All things are well.

PRINCE HENRY

A noble convent! I have known it long
By the report of travellers. I now see
Their commendations lag behind the truth.
You lie here in the valley of the Nagold
As in a nest: and the still river, gliding
Along its bed, is like an admonition
How all things pass. Your lands are rich and ample,
And your revenues large. God's benediction
Rests on your convent.

ABBOT

By our charities
We strive to merit it. Our Lord and Master,
When He departed, left us in his will,
As our best legacy on earth, the poor!
These we have always with us; had we not,
Our hearts would grow as hard as are these stones.

PRINCE HENRY

If I remember right, the Counts of Calva
Founded your convent.

ABBOT

Even as you say.

PRINCE HENRY

And, if I err not, it is very old.

ABBOT

Within these cloisters lie already buried
Twelve holy Abbots. Underneath the flags
On which we stand, the Abbot William lies,
Of blessed memory.

PRINCE HENRY

And whose tomb is that,
Which bears the brass escutcheon?

ABBOT

A benefactor's.
Conrad, a Count of Calva, he who stood
Godfather to our bells.

PRINCE HENRY

Your monks are learned
And holy men, I trust.

ABBOT

There are among them
Learned and holy men. Yet in this age
We need another Hildebrand, to shake
And purify us like a mighty wind.
The world is wicked, and sometimes I wonder
God does not lose his patience with it wholly,
And shatter it like glass! Even here, at times,
Within these walls, where all should be at
peace,
I have my trials. Time has laid his hand
Upon my heart, gently, not smiting it,
But as a harper lays his open palm
Upon his harp, to deaden its vibrations.
Ashes are on my head, and on my lips
Sackcloth, and in my breast a heaviness
And weariness of life, that makes me ready
To say to the dead Abbots under us,
"Make room for me!" Only I see the dusk
Of evening twilight coming, and have not
Completed half my task; and so at times
The thought of my shortcomings in this life
Falls like a shadow on the life to come.

PRINCE HENRY

We must all die, and not the old alone;
The young have no exemption from that
doom.

ABBOT

Ah, yes! the young may die, but the old must!
That is the difference.

PRINCE HENRY

I have heard much laud
Of your transcribers. Your Scriptorium
Is famous among all; your manuscripts
Praised for their beauty and their excellence.

ABBOT

That is indeed our boast. If you desire it,
You shall behold these treasures. And mean-
while
Shall the Refectorarius bestow
Your horses and attendants for the night.

They go in. The Vesper-bell rings

THE CHAPEL

Vespers; after which the monks retire, a chorister leading an old monk who is blind

PRINCE HENRY

They are all gone, save one who lingers,
Absorbed in deep and silent prayer.
As if his heart could find no rest,
At times he beats his heaving breast
With clenchèd and convulsive fingers,
Then lifts them trembling in the air.
A chorister, with golden hair,
Guides hitherward his heavy pace.
Can it be so? Or does my sight
Deceive me in the uncertain light?
Ah no! I recognize that face,
Though Time has touched it in his flight,
And changed the auburn hair to white.
It is Count Hugo of the Rhine,
The deadliest foe of all our race,
And hateful unto me and mine!

THE BLIND MONK

Who is it that doth stand so near
His whispered words I almost hear?

PRINCE HENRY

I am Prince Henry of Hoheneck,
And you, Count Hugo of the Rhine!
I know you, and I see the scar,
The brand upon your forehead, shine
And redden like a baleful star!

THE BLIND MONK

Count Hugo once, but now the wreck
Of what I was. O Hoheneck!
The passionate will, the pride, the wrath
That bore me headlong on my path,
Stumbled and staggered into fear,
And failed me in my mad career,
As a tired steed some evil-doer,
Alone upon a desolate moor,
Bewildered, lost, deserted, blind,
And hearing loud and close behind
The o'ertaking steps of his pursuer.
Then suddenly from the dark there came
A voice that called me by my name,

And said to me, "Kneel down and pray!"
And so my terror passed away,
Passed utterly away forever.
Contrition, penitence, remorse,
Came on me, with o'erwhelming force;
A hope, a longing, an endeavor,
By days of penance and nights of prayer,
To frustrate and defeat despair!
Calm, deep, and still is now my heart,
With tranquil waters overflowed;
A lake whose unseen fountains start,
Where once the hot volcano glowed.
And you, O Prince of Hoheneck!
Have known me in that earlier time,
A man of violence and crime,
Whose passions brooked no curb nor check,
Behold me now, in gentler mood,
One of this holy brotherhood.
Give me your hand; here let me kneel;
Make your reproaches sharp as steel;
Spurn me, and smite me on each cheek;
No violence can harm the meek,
There is no wound Christ cannot heal!
Yes; lift your princely hand, and take
Revenge, if 'tis revenge you seek;
Then pardon me, for Jesus' sake!

PRINCE HENRY

Arise, Count Hugo! let there be
No further strife nor enmity
Between us twain; we both have erred!
Too rash in act, too wroth in word,
From the beginning have we stood
In fierce, defiant attitude,
Each thoughtless of the other's right,
And each reliant on his might.
But now our souls are more subdued;
The hand of God, and not in vain,
Has touched us with the fire of pain.
Let us kneel down and side by side
Pray, till our souls are purified,
And pardon will not be denied!

They kneel

THE REFECTORY

Gaudiolum of Monks at midnight. LUCIFER *disguised as a Friar*

FRIAR PAUL *sings*

Ave! color vini clari,
Dulcis potus, non amari,
Tua nos inebriari
Digneris potentia!

FRIAR CUTHBERT

Not so much noise, my worthy frères,
You'll disturb the Abbot at his prayers.

FRIAR PAUL *sings*

O! quam placens in colore!
O! quam fragrans in odore!
O! quam sapidum in ore!
Dulce linguæ vinculum!

FRIAR CUTHBERT

I should think your tongue had broken its chain!

FRIAR PAUL *sings*

Felix venter quem intrabis!
Felix guttur quod rigabis!
Felix os quod tu lavabis!
Et beata labia!

FRIAR CUTHBERT

Peace! I say, peace!
Will you never cease!
You will rouse up the Abbot, I tell you again!

FRIAR JOHN

No danger! tonight he will let us alone,
As I happen to know he has guests of his own.

FRIAR CUTHBERT

Who are they?

FRIAR JOHN

A German Prince and his train,
Who arrived here just before the rain.
There is with him a damsel fair to see,
As slender and graceful as a reed!
When she alighted from her steed,
It seemed like a blossom blown from a tree.

FRIAR CUTHBERT

None of your pale-faced girls for me!
None of your damsels of high degree!

FRIAR JOHN

Come, old fellow, drink down to your peg!
But do not drink any further, I beg!

FRIAR PAUL *sings*

In the days of gold,
The days of old,

Crosier of wood
And bishop of gold!

FRIAR CUTHBERT

What an infernal racket and riot!
Can you not drink your wine in quiet?
Why fill the convent with such scandals,
As if we were so many drunken Vandals?

FRIAR PAUL *continues*

Now we have changed
That law so good
To crosier of gold
And bishop of wood!

FRIAR CUTHBERT

Well, then, since you are in the mood
To give your noisy humors vent,
Sing and howl to your heart's content!

CHORUS OF MONKS

Funde vinum, funde!
Tanquam sint fluminis undæ,
Nec quæras unde,
Sed fundas semper abunde!

FRIAR JOHN

What is the name of yonder friar,
With an eye that glows like a coal of fire,
And such a black mass of tangled hair?

FRIAR PAUL

He who is sitting there,
With a rollicking,
Devil may care,
Free and easy look and air,
As if he were used to such feasting and
frolicking?

FRIAR JOHN

The same.

FRIAR PAUL

He's a stranger. You had better ask his name,
And where he is going and whence he came.

FRIAR JOHN

Hallo! Sir Friar!

FRIAR PAUL

You must raise your voice a little higher,
He does not seem to hear what you say.
Now, try again! He is looking this way.

FRIAR JOHN

Hallo! Sir Friar,
We wish to inquire
Whence you came, and where you are going,
And anything else that is worth the knowing.
So be so good as to open your head.

LUCIFER

I am a Frenchman born and bred,
Going on a pilgrimage to Rome.
My home
Is the convent of St. Gildas de Rhuys,
Of which, very like, you never have heard.

MONKS

Never a word!

LUCIFER

You must know, then, it is in the diocese
Called the Diocese of Vannes,
In the province of Brittany.
From the gray rocks of Morbihan
It overlooks the angry sea;
The very sea-shore where,
In his great despair,
Abbot Abelard walked to and fro,
Filling the night with woe,
And wailing aloud to the merciless seas
The name of his sweet Heloise,
Whilst overhead
The convent windows gleamed as red
As the fiery eyes of the monks within,
Who with jovial din
Gave themselves up to all kinds of sin!
Ha! that is a convent! that is an abbey!
Over the doors,
None of your death-heads carved in wood,
None of your Saints looking pious and good,
None of your Patriarchs old and shabby!
But the heads and tusks of boars,
And the cells
Hung all round with the fells
Of the fallow-deer.
And then what cheer!
What jolly, fat friars,
Sitting round the great, roaring fires,
Roaring louder than they,
With their strong wines,
And their concubines,
And never a bell,
With its swagger and swell,
Calling you up with a start of affright

In the dead of night,
To send you grumbling down dark stairs,
To mumble your prayers;
But the cheery crow
Of cocks in the yard below,
After daybreak, an hour or so,
And the barking of deep-mouthed hounds,
These are the sounds
That, instead of bells, salute the ear.
And then all day
Up and away
Through the forest, hunting the deer!
Ah, my friends! I'm afraid that here
You are a little too pious, a little too tame,
And the more is the shame.
'Tis the greatest folly
Not to be jolly;
That's what I think!
Come, drink, drink,
Drink, and die game!

MONKS

And your Abbot What's-his-name?

LUCIFER

Abelard!

MONKS

Did he drink hard?

LUCIFER

Oh, no! Not he!
He was a dry old fellow,
Without juice enough to get thoroughly mel-
low.
There he stood,
Lowering at us in sullen mood,
As if he had come into Brittany
Just to reform our brotherhood!

A roar of laughter

But you see
It never would do!
For some of us knew a thing or two,
In the Abbey of St. Gildas de Rhuys!
For instance, the great ado
With old Fulbert's niece,
The young and lovely Heloise.

FRIAR JOHN

Stop there, if you please,
Till we drink to the fair Heloise.

ALL, *drinking and shouting*

Heloise! Heloise!

The Chapel-bell tolls

LUCIFER, *starting*

What is that bell for? Are you such asses
As to keep up the fashion of midnight masses?

FRIAR CUTHBERT

It is only a poor, unfortunate brother,
Who is gifted with most miraculous powers
Of getting up at all sorts of hours,
And, by way of penance and Christian meek-
ness,
Of creeping silently out of his cell
To take a pull at that hideous bell;
So that all the monks who are lying awake
May murmur some kind of prayer for his
sake,
And adapted to his peculiar weakness!

FRIAR JOHN

From frailty and fall—

ALL

Good Lord, deliver us all!

FRIAR CUTHBERT

And before the bell for matins sounds,
He takes his lantern, and goes the rounds,
Flashing it into our sleepy eyes,
Merely to say it is time to arise.
But enough of that. Go on, if you please,
With your story about St. Gildas de Rhuys.

LUCIFER

Well, it finally came to pass
That, half in fun and half in malice,
One Sunday at Mass
We put some poison into the chalice.
But, either by accident or design,
Peter Abelard kept away
From the chapel that day,
And a poor young friar, who in his stead
Drank the sacramental wine,
Fell on the steps of the altar, dead!
But look! do you see at the window there
That face, with a look of grief and despair,
That ghastly face, as of one in pain?

MONKS

Who? where?

LUCIFER

As I spoke, it vanished away again.

FRIAR CUTHBERT

It is that nefarious
Siebald the Refectorarius.
That fellow is always playing the scout,
Creeping and peeping and prowling about;
And then he regales
The Abbot with scandalous tales.

LUCIFER

A spy in the convent? One of the brothers
Telling scandalous tales of the others?
Out upon him, the lazy loon!
I would put a stop to that pretty soon,
In a way he should rue it.

MONKS

How shall we do it?

LUCIFER

Do you, brother Paul,
Creep under the window, close to the wall,
And open it suddenly when I call.
Then seize the villain by the hair,
And hold him there,
And punish him soundly, once for all.

FRIAR CUTHBERT

As St. Dunstan of old,
We are told,
Once caught the Devil by the nose!

LUCIFER

Ha! ha! that story is very clever,
But has no foundation whatsoever.
Quick! for I see his face again
Glaring in at the window-pane;
Now! now! and do not spare your blows.

FRIAR PAUL *opens the window suddenly, and seizes* SIEBALD

They beat him

FRIAR SIEBALD

Help! help! are you going to slay me?

FRIAR PAUL

That will teach you again to betray me!

FRIAR SIEBALD

Mercy! mercy!

FRIAR PAUL, *shouting and beating*

Rumpas bellorum lorum
Vim confer amorum
Morum verorum rorum
Tu plena polorum!

LUCIFER

Who stands in the doorway yonder,
Stretching out his trembling hand,
Just as Abelard used to stand,
The flash of his keen, black eyes
Forerunning the thunder?

THE MONKS, *in confusion*

The Abbot! the Abbot!

FRIAR CUTHBERT

And what is the wonder!
He seems to have taken you by surprise.

FRIAR FRANCIS

Hide the great flagon
From the eyes of the dragon!

FRIAR CUTHBERT

Pull the brown hood over your face!
This will bring us into disgrace!

ABBOT

What means this revel and carouse?
Is this a tavern and drinking-house?
Are you Christian monks, or heathen devils,
To pollute this convent with your revels?
Were Peter Damian still upon earth,
To be shocked by such ungodly mirth,
He would write your names, with pen of gall,
In his Book of Gomorrah, one and all!
Away, you drunkards! to your cells,
And pray till you hear the matin-bells;
You, Brother Francis, and you, Brother Paul!
And as a penance mark each prayer
With the scourge upon your shoulders bare;
Nothing atones for such a sin
But the blood that follows the discipline.
And you, Brother Cuthbert, come with me
Alone into the sacristy;
You, who should be a guide to your brothers,
And are ten times worse than all the others,
For you I've a draught that has long been brewing,
You shall do a penance worth the doing!
Away to your prayers, then, one and all!
I wonder the very convent wall
Does not crumble and crush you in its fall!

THE NEIGHBORING NUNNERY

The ABBESS IRMINGARD *sitting with* ELSIE *in the moonlight*

IRMINGARD

The night is silent, the wind is still,
The moon is looking from yonder hill
Down upon convent, and grove, and garden;
The clouds have passed away from her face,
Leaving behind them no sorrowful trace,
Only the tender and quiet grace
Of one whose heart has been healed with pardon!

And such am I. My soul within
Was dark with passion and soiled with sin.
But now its wounds are healed again;
Gone are the anguish, the terror, and pain;
For across that desolate land of woe,
O'er whose burning sands I was forced to go,
A wind from heaven began to blow;
And all my being trembled and shook,
As the leaves of the tree, or the grass of the field,
And I was healed, as the sick are healed,
When fanned by the leaves of the Holy Book!

As thou sittest in the moonlight there,
Its glory flooding thy golden hair,
And the only darkness that which lies
In the haunted chambers of thine eyes,
I feel my soul drawn unto thee,
Strangely, and strongly, and more and more,
As to one I have known and loved before;
For every soul is akin to me
That dwells in the land of mystery!
I am the Lady Irmingard,
Born of a noble race and name!
Many a wandering Suabian bard,
Whose life was dreary, and bleak, and hard,
Has found through me the way to fame.

Brief and bright were those days, and the night
Which followed was full of a lurid light.
Love, that of every woman's heart
Will have the whole, and not a part,
That is to her, in Nature's plan,
More than ambition is to man,
Her light, her life, her very breath,
With no alternative but death,
Found me a maiden soft and young,
Just from the convent's cloistered school,
And seated on my lowly stool,
Attentive while the minstrels sung.

Gallant, graceful, gentle, tall,
Fairest, noblest, best of all,
Was Walter of the Vogelweid;
And, whatsoever may betide,
Still I think of him with pride!
His song was of the summer-time,
The very birds sang in his rhyme;
The sunshine, the delicious air,
The fragrance of the flowers, were there;
And I grew restless as I heard,
Restless and buoyant as a bird,
Down soft, aerial currents sailing,
O'er blossomed orchards, and fields in bloom,
And through the momentary gloom
Of shadows o'er the landscape trailing,
Yielding and borne I knew not where,
But feeling resistance unavailing.

And thus, unnoticed and apart,
And more by accident than choice,
I listened to that single voice
Until the chambers of my heart
Were filled with it by night and day.
One night,—it was a night in May,—
Within the garden, unawares,
Under the blossoms in the gloom,
I heard it utter my own name
With protestations and wild prayers;
And it rang through me, and became
Like the archangel's trump of doom,
Which the soul hears, and must obey;
And mine arose as from a tomb.
My former life now seemed to me
Such as hereafter death may be,
When in the great Eternity
We shall awake and find it day.

It was a dream, and would not stay;
A dream, that in a single night
Faded and vanished out of sight.
My father's anger followed fast
This passion, as a freshening blast
Seeks out and fans the fire, whose rage
It may increase, but not assuage.
And he exclaimed: "No wandering bard
Shall win thy hand, O Irmingard!
For which Prince Henry of Hoheneck
By messenger and letter sues."

Gently, but firmly, I replied:
"Henry of Hoheneck I discard!
Never the hand of Irmingard
Shall lie in his as the hand of a bride!"
This said I, Walter, for thy sake;
This said I, for I could not choose.
After a pause, my father spake
In that cold and deliberate tone
Which turns the hearer into stone,
And seems itself the act to be
That follows with such dread certainty:
"This or the cloister and the veil!"
No other words than these he said,
But they were like a funeral wail;
My life was ended, my heart was dead.

That night from the castle-gate went down,
With silent, slow, and stealthy pace,
Two shadows, mounted on shadowy steeds,
Taking the narrow path that leads
Into the forest dense and brown.
In the leafy darkness of the place,
One could not distinguish form nor face,
Only a bulk without a shape,
A darker shadow in the shade;
One scarce could say it moved or stayed.
Thus it was we made our escape!
A foaming brook, with many a bound,
Followed us like a playful hound;
Then leaped before us, and in the hollow
Paused, and waited for us to follow,
And seemed impatient, and afraid
That our tardy flight should be betrayed
By the sound our horses' hoof-beats made.
And when we reached the plain below,
We paused a moment and drew rein
To look back at the castle again;
And we saw the windows all aglow
With lights, that were passing to and fro;
Our hearts with terror ceased to beat;
The brook crept silent to our feet;
We knew what most we feared to know.
Then suddenly horns began to blow;
And we heard a shout, and a heavy tramp,
And our horses snorted in the damp
Night-air of the meadows green and wide,
And in a moment, side by side,
So close, they must have seemed but one,
The shadows across the moonlight run,
And another came, and swept behind,
Like the shadow of clouds before the wind!

How I remember that breathless flight
Across the moors, in the summer night!
How under our feet the long, white road
Backward like a river flowed,
Sweeping with it fences and hedges,
Whilst farther away and overhead,
Paler than I, with fear and dread,
The moon fled with us as we fled
Along the forest's jagged edges!

All this I can remember well;
But of what afterwards befell
I nothing further can recall
Than a blind, desperate, headlong fall;
The rest is a blank and darkness all.
When I awoke out of this swoon,
The sun was shining, not the moon,
Making a cross upon the wall
With the bars of my windows narrow and tall;
And I prayed to it, as I had been wont to pray,
From early childhood, day by day,
Each morning, as in bed I lay!
I was lying again in my own room!
And I thanked God, in my fever and pain,
That those shadows on the midnight plain
Were gone, and could not come again!
I struggled no longer with my doom!

This happened many years ago.
I left my father's home to come
Like Catherine to her martyrdom,
For blindly I esteemed it so.
And when I heard the convent door
Behind me close, to ope no more,
I felt it smite me like a blow.
Through all my limbs a shudder ran,
And on my bruisèd spirit fell
The dampness of my narrow cell
As night-air on a wounded man,
Giving intolerable pain.

But now a better life began.
I felt the agony decrease
By slow degrees, then wholly cease,
Ending in perfect rest and peace!
It was not apathy, nor dulness,
That weighed and pressed upon my brain,
But the same passion I had given
To earth before, now turned to heaven
With all its overflowing fulness.

Alas! the world is full of peril!
The path that runs through the fairest meads,
On the sunniest side of the valley, leads
Into a region bleak and sterile!
Alike in the high-born and the lowly,
The will is feeble, and passion strong.
We cannot sever right from wrong;
Some falsehood mingles with all truth;
Nor is it strange the heart of youth
Should waver and comprehend but slowly
The things that are holy and unholy!
But in this sacred, calm retreat,
We are all well and safely shielded
From winds that blow, and waves that beat,
From the cold, and rain, and blighting heat,
To which the strongest hearts have yielded.
Here we stand as the Virgins Seven,
For our celestial bridegroom yearning;
Our hearts are lamps forever burning,
With a steady and unwavering flame,
Pointing upward, forever the same,
Steadily upward toward the heaven!

The moon is hidden behind a cloud;
A sudden darkness fills the room,
And thy deep eyes, amid the gloom,
Shine like jewels in a shroud.
On the leaves is a sound of falling rain;
A bird, awakened in its nest,
Gives a faint twitter of unrest,
Then smoothes its plumes and sleeps again.
No other sounds than these I hear;
The hour of midnight must be near.
Thou art o'erspent with the day's fatigue
Of riding many a dusty league;
Sink, then, gently to thy slumber;
Me so many cares encumber,
So many ghosts, and forms of fright,
Have started from their graves tonight,
They have driven sleep from mine eyes away:
I will go down to the chapel and pray.

V

A COVERED BRIDGE AT LUCERNE

PRINCE HENRY

God's blessing on the architects who build
The bridges o'er swift rivers and abysses
Before impassable to human feet,
No less than on the builders of cathedrals,
Whose massive walls are bridges thrown across
The dark and terrible abyss of Death.
Well has the name of Pontifex been given
Unto the Church's head, as the chief builder
And architect of the invisible bridge
That leads from earth to heaven.

ELSIE

How dark it grows!
What are these paintings on the walls around us?

PRINCE HENRY

The Dance Macaber!

ELSIE

What?

PRINCE HENRY

The Dance of Death!
All that go to and fro must look upon it,
Mindful of what they shall be, while beneath,
Among the wooden piles, the turbulent river
Rushes, impetuous as the river of life,
With dimpling eddies, ever green and bright,
Save where the shadow of this bridge falls on it.

ELSIE

Oh yes! I see it now!

PRINCE HENRY

The grim musician
Leads all men through the mazes of that dance,
To different sounds in different measures moving;
Sometimes he plays a lute, sometimes a drum,
To tempt or terrify.

ELSIE

What is this picture?

PRINCE HENRY

It is a young man singing to a nun,
Who kneels at her devotions, but in kneeling
Turns round to look at him; and Death, meanwhile,
Is putting out the candles on the altar!

ELSIE

Ah, what a pity 'tis that she should listen
Unto such songs, when in her orisons
She might have heard in heaven the angels singing!

PRINCE HENRY

Here he has stolen a jester's cap and bells,
And dances with the Queen.

ELSIE

A foolish jest!

PRINCE HENRY

And here the heart of the new-wedded wife,
Coming from church with her beloved lord,
He startles with the rattle of his drum.

ELSIE

Ah, that is sad! And yet perhaps 'tis best
That she should die, with all the sunshine on
her,
And all the benedictions of the morning,
Before this affluence of golden light
Shall fade into a cold and clouded gray,
Then into darkness!

PRINCE HENRY

Under it is written,
"Nothing but death shall separate thee and
me!"

ELSIE

And what is this, that follows close upon it?

PRINCE HENRY

Death, playing on a dulcimer. Behind him,
A poor old woman, with a rosary,
Follows the sound, and seems to wish her
feet
Were swifter to o'ertake him. Underneath,
The inscription reads, "Better is Death than
Life."

ELSIE

Better is Death than Life! Ah yes! to thousands
Death plays upon a dulcimer, and sings
That song of consolation, till the air
Rings with it, and they cannot choose but
follow
Whither he leads. And not the old alone,
But the young also hear it, and are still.

PRINCE HENRY

Yes, in their sadder moments. 'Tis the sound
Of their own hearts they hear, half full of
tears,
Which are like crystal cups, half filled with
water,
Responding to the pressure of a finger
With music sweet and low and melancholy.
Let us go forward, and no longer stay
In this great picture-gallery of Death!
I hate it! ay, the very thought of it!

ELSIE

Why is it hateful to you?

PRINCE HENRY

For the reason
That life, and all that speaks of life, is lovely,
And death, and all that speaks of death, is
hateful.

ELSIE

The grave itself is but a covered bridge,
Leading from light to light, through a brief
darkness!

PRINCE HENRY, *emerging from the bridge*

I breathe again more freely! Ah, how pleasant
To come once more into the light of day,
Out of that shadow of death! To hear again
The hoof-beats of our horses on firm ground,
And not upon those hollow planks, resound-
ing
With a sepulchral echo, like the clods
On coffins in a churchyard! Yonder lies
The Lake of the Four Forest-Towns, ap-
parelled
In light, and lingering, like a village maiden,
Hid in the bosom of her native mountains,
Then pouring all her life into another's,
Changing her name and being! Overhead,
Shaking his cloudy tresses loose in air,
Rises Pilatus, with his windy pines.

They pass on

THE DEVIL'S BRIDGE

PRINCE HENRY *and* ELSIE *crossing with attendants*

GUIDE

This bridge is called the Devil's Bridge.
With a single arch, from ridge to ridge,
It leaps across the terrible chasm
Yawning beneath us, black and deep,
As if, in some convulsive spasm,
The summits of the hills had cracked,
And made a road for the cataract
That raves and rages down the steep!

LUCIFER, *under the bridge*

Ha! ha!

GUIDE

Never any bridge but this
Could stand across the wild abyss;
All the rest, of wood or stone,
By the Devil's hand were overthrown.
He toppled crags from the precipice,
And whatsoe'er was built by day
In the night was swept away;
None could stand but this alone.

LUCIFER, *under the bridge*

Ha! ha!

GUIDE

I showed you in the valley a boulder
Marked with the imprint of his shoulder;
As he was bearing it up this way,
A peasant, passing, cried, "Herr Jé!"
And the Devil dropped it in his fright,
And vanished suddenly out of sight!

LUCIFER, *under the bridge*

Ha! ha!

GUIDE

Abbot Giraldus of Einsiedel,
For pilgrims on their way to Rome,
Built this at last, with a single arch,
Under which, on its endless march,
Runs the river, white with foam,
Like a thread through the eye of a needle.
And the Devil promised to let it stand,
Under compact and condition
That the first living thing which crossed
Should be surrendered into his hand,
And be beyond redemption lost.

LUCIFER, *under the bridge*

Ha! ha! perdition!

GUIDE

At length, the bridge being all completed,
The Abbot, standing at its head,
Threw across it a loaf of bread,
Which a hungry dog sprang after,
And the rocks reëchoed with the peals of laughter
To see the Devil thus defeated!

They pass on

LUCIFER, *under the bridge*

Ha! ha! defeated!
For journeys and for crimes like this
I let the bridge stand o'er the abyss!

THE ST. GOTHARD PASS

PRINCE HENRY

This is the highest point. Two ways the rivers
Leap down to different seas, and as they roll
Grow deep and still, and their majestic presence
Becomes a benefaction to the towns
They visit, wandering silently among them,
Like patriarchs old among their shining tents.

ELSIE

How bleak and bare it is! Nothing but mosses
Grow on these rocks.

PRINCE HENRY

Yet are they not forgotten;
Beneficent Nature sends the mists to feed them.

ELSIE

See yonder little cloud, that, borne aloft
So tenderly by the wind, floats fast away
Over the snowy peaks! It seems to me
The body of St. Catherine, borne by angels!

PRINCE HENRY

Thou art St. Catherine, and invisible angels
Bear thee across these chasms and precipices,
Lest thou shouldst dash thy feet against a stone!

ELSIE

Would I were borne unto my grave, as she was,
Upon angelic shoulders! Even now
I seem uplifted by them, light as air!
What sound is that?

PRINCE HENRY

The tumbling avalanches!

ELSIE

How awful, yet how beautiful!

PRINCE HENRY

These are
The voices of the mountains! Thus they ope
Their snowy lips, and speak unto each other,
In the primeval language, lost to man.

ELSIE

What land is this that spreads itself beneath us?

PRINCE HENRY

Italy! Italy!

ELSIE

Land of the Madonna,
How beautiful it is! It seems a garden
Of Paradise!

PRINCE HENRY

Nay, of Gethsemane
To thee and me, of passion and of prayer!
Yet once of Paradise. Long years ago
I wandered as a youth among its bowers,
And never from my heart has faded quite
Its memory, that, like a summer sunset,
Encircles with a ring of purple light
All the horizon of my youth.

GUIDE

O friends!
The days are short, the way before us long;
We must not linger, if we think to reach
The inn at Belinzona before vespers!

They pass on

AT THE FOOT OF THE ALPS

A halt under the trees at noon

PRINCE HENRY

Here let us pause a moment in the trembling
Shadow and sunshine of the roadside trees,
And, our tired horses in a group assembling,
Inhale long draughts of this delicious breeze.
Our fleeter steeds have distanced our attendants;
They lag behind us with a slower pace;
We will await them under the green pendants
Of the great willows in this shady place.
Ho, Barbarossa! how thy mottled haunches
Sweat with this canter over hill and glade!
Stand still, and let these overhanging branches
Fan thy hot sides and comfort thee with shade!

ELSIE

What a delightful landscape spreads before us,
Marked with a whitewashed cottage here and there!
And, in luxuriant garlands drooping o'er us,
Blossoms of grape-vines scent the sunny air.

PRINCE HENRY

Hark! what sweet sounds are those, whose accents holy
Fill the warm noon with music sad and sweet!

ELSIE

It is a band of pilgrims, moving slowly
On their long journey, with uncovered feet.

PILGRIMS, *chanting the Hymn of St. Hildebert*

Me receptet Sion illa,
Sion David, urbs tranquilla,
Cujus faber auctor lucis,
Cujus portæ lignum crucis,
Cujus claves lingua Petri,
Cujus cives semper læti,
Cujus muri lapis vivus,
Cujus custos Rex festivus!

LUCIFER, *as a Friar in the procession*

Here am I, too, in the pious band,
In the garb of a barefooted Carmelite dressed!
The soles of my feet are as hard and tanned
As the conscience of old Pope Hildebrand,
The Holy Satan, who made the wives
Of the bishops lead such shameful lives.
All day long I beat my breast,
And chant with a most particular zest
The Latin hymns, which I understand
Quite as well, I think, as the rest.
And at night such lodging in barns and sheds,
Such a hurly-burly in country inns,
Such a clatter of tongues in empty heads,
Such a helter-skelter of prayers and sins!
Of all the contrivances of the time
For sowing broadcast the seeds of crime,
There is none so pleasing to me and mine
As a pilgrimage to some far-off shrine!

PRINCE HENRY

If from the outward man we judge the inner,
And cleanliness is godliness, I fear
A hopeless reprobate, a hardened sinner,
Must be that Carmelite now passing near.

LUCIFER

There is my German Prince again,
Thus far on his journey to Salern,
And the lovesick girl, whose heated brain
Is sowing the cloud to reap the rain;
But it's a long road that has no turn!
Let them quietly hold their way,

I have also a part in the play.
But first I must act to my heart's content
This mummery and this merriment,
And drive this motley flock of sheep
Into the fold, where drink and sleep
The jolly old friars of Benevent.
Of a truth, it often provokes me to laugh
To see these beggars hobble along,
Lamed and maimed, and fed upon chaff,
Chanting their wonderful piff and paff,
And, to make up for not understanding the song,
Singing it fiercely, and wild, and strong!
Were it not for my magic garters and staff,
And the goblets of goodly wine I quaff,
And the mischief I make in the idle throng,
I should not continue the business long.

PILGRIMS, *chanting*

In hâc urbe, lux solennis,
Ver æternum, pax perennis;
In hâc odor implens cælos,
In hâc semper festum melos!

PRINCE HENRY

Do you observe that monk among the train,
Who pours from his great throat the roaring bass,
As a cathedral spout pours out the rain,
And this way turns his rubicund, round face?

ELSIE

It is the same who, on the Strasburg square,
Preached to the people in the open air.

PRINCE HENRY

And he has crossed o'er mountain, field, and fell,
On that good steed, that seems to bear him well,
The hackney of the Friars of Orders Gray,
His own stout legs! He, too, was in the play,
Both as King Herod and Ben Israel.
Good morrow, Friar!

FRIAR CUTHBERT

Good morrow, noble Sir!

PRINCE HENRY

I speak in German, for, unless I err,
You are a German.

FRIAR CUTHBERT

I cannot gainsay you.
But by what instinct, or what secret sign,
Meeting me here, do you straightway divine
That northward of the Alps my country lies?

PRINCE HENRY

Your accent, like St. Peter's, would betray you,
Did not your yellow beard and your blue eyes.
Moreover, we have seen your face before,
And heard you preach at the Cathedral door
On Easter Sunday, in the Strasburg square.
We were among the crowd that gathered there,
And saw you play the Rabbi with great skill,
As if, by leaning o'er so many years
To walk with little children, your own will
Had caught a childish attitude from theirs,
A kind of stooping in its form and gait,
And could no longer stand erect and straight.
Whence come you now?

FRIAR CUTHBERT

From the old monastery
Of Hirschau, in the forest; being sent
Upon a pilgrimage to Benevent,
To see the image of the Virgin Mary,
That moves its holy eyes, and sometimes speaks,
And lets the piteous tears run down its cheeks,
To touch the hearts of the impenitent.

PRINCE HENRY

Oh, had I faith, as in the days gone by,
That knew no doubt, and feared no mystery!

LUCIFER, *at a distance*

Ho, Cuthbert! Friar Cuthbert!

FRIAR CUTHBERT

Farewell, Prince!
I cannot stay to argue and convince.

PRINCE HENRY

This is indeed the blessed Mary's land,
Virgin and Mother of our dear Redeemer!
All hearts are touched and softened at her name,
Alike the bandit, with the bloody hand,
The priest, the prince, the scholar, and the peasant,
The man of deeds, the visionary dreamer,

Pay homage to her as one ever present!
And even as children, who have much offended
A too indulgent father, in great shame,
Penitent, and yet not daring unattended
To go into his presence, at the gate
Speak with their sister, and confiding wait
Till she goes in before and intercedes;
So men, repenting of their evil deeds,
And yet not venturing rashly to draw near
With their requests an angry father's ear,
Offer to her their prayers and their confession,
And she for them in heaven makes intercession.
And if our Faith had given us nothing more
Than this example of all womanhood,
So mild, so merciful, so strong, so good,
So patient, peaceful, loyal, loving, pure,
This were enough to prove it higher and truer
Than all the creeds the world had known before.

PILGRIMS, *chanting afar off*

Urbs cœlestis, urbs beata,
Supra petram collocata,
Urbs in portu satis tuto
De longinquo te saluto,
Te saluto, te suspiro,
Te affecto, te requiro!

THE INN AT GENOA

A terrace overlooking the sea. Night

PRINCE HENRY

It is the sea, it is the sea,
In all its vague immensity,
Fading and darkening in the distance!
Silent, majestical, and slow,
The white ships haunt it to and fro,
With all their ghostly sails unfurled,
As phantoms from another world
Haunt the dim confines of existence!
But ah! how few can comprehend
Their signals, or to what good end
From land to land they come and go!
Upon a sea more vast and dark
The spirits of the dead embark,
All voyaging to unknown coasts.
We wave our farewells from the shore,
And they depart, and come no more,
Or come as phantoms and as ghosts.

Above the darksome sea of death
Looms the great life that is to be,
A land of cloud and mystery,
A dim mirage, with shapes of men
Long dead, and passed beyond our ken.
Awe-struck we gaze, and hold our breath
Till the fair pageant vanisheth,
Leaving us in perplexity,
And doubtful whether it has been
A vision of the world unseen,
Or a bright image of our own
Against the sky in vapors thrown.

LUCIFER, *singing from the sea*

Thou didst not make it, thou canst not mend it,
But thou hast the power to end it!
The sea is silent, the sea is discreet,
Deep it lies at thy very feet;
There is no confessor like unto Death!
Thou canst not see him, but he is near;
Thou needst not whisper above thy breath,
And he will hear;
He will answer the questions,
The vague surmises and suggestions,
That fill thy soul with doubt and fear!

PRINCE HENRY

The fisherman, who lies afloat,
With shadowy sail, in yonder boat,
Is singing softly to the Night!
But do I comprehend aright
The meaning of the words he sung
So sweetly in his native tongue?
Ah yes! the sea is still and deep;
All things within its bosom sleep!
A single step, and all is o'er;
A plunge, a bubble, and no more;
And thou, dear Elsie, wilt be free
From martyrdom and agony.

ELSIE, *coming from her chamber upon the terrace*

The night is calm and cloudless,
And still as still can be,
And the stars come forth to listen
To the music of the sea.
They gather, and gather, and gather,
Until they crowd the sky,
And listen, in breathless silence,
To the solemn litany.
It begins in rocky caverns,

As a voice that chants alone
To the pedals of the organ
In monotonous undertone;
And anon from shelving beaches,
And shallow sands beyond,
In snow-white robes uprising
The ghostly choirs respond.
And sadly and unceasing
The mournful voice sings on,
And the snow-white choirs still answer
Christe eleison!

PRINCE HENRY

Angel of God! thy finer sense perceives
Celestial and perpetual harmonies!
Thy purer soul, that trembles and believes,
Hears the archangel's trumpet in the breeze,
And where the forest rolls, or ocean heaves,
Cecilia's organ sounding in the seas,
And tongues of prophets speaking in the leaves.
But I hear discord only and despair,
And whispers as of demons in the air!

AT SEA

IL PADRONE

The wind upon our quarter lies,
And on before the freshening gale,
That fills the snow-white lateen sail,
Swiftly our light felucca flies.
Around, the billows burst and foam;
They lift her o'er the sunken rock,
They beat her sides with many a shock,
And then upon their flowing dome
They poise her, like a weathercock!
Between us and the western skies
The hills of Corsica arise;
Eastward, in yonder long blue line,
The summits of the Apennine,
And southward, and still far away,
Salerno, on its sunny bay.
You cannot see it, where it lies.

PRINCE HENRY

Ah, would that never more mine eyes
Might see its towers by night or day!

ELSIE

Behind us, dark and awfully,
There comes a cloud out of the sea,
That bears the form of a hunted deer,
With hide of brown, and hoofs of black,
And antlers laid upon its back,
And fleeing fast and wild with fear,
As if the hounds were on its track!

PRINCE HENRY

Lo! while we gaze, it breaks and falls
In shapeless masses, like the walls
Of a burnt city. Broad and red
The fires of the descending sun
Glare through the windows, and o'erhead,
Athwart the vapors, dense and dun,
Long shafts of silvery light arise,
Like rafters that support the skies!

ELSIE

See! from its summit the lurid levin
Flashes downward without warning,
As Lucifer, son of the morning,
Fell from the battlements of heaven!

IL PADRONE

I must entreat you, friends, below!
The angry storm begins to blow,
For the weather changes with the moon.
All this morning, until noon,
We had baffling winds, and sudden flaws
Struck the sea with their cat's-paws.
Only a little hour ago
I was whistling to Saint Antonio
For a capful of wind to fill our sail,
And instead of a breeze he has sent a gale.
Last night I saw Saint Elmo's stars,
With their glimmering lanterns, all at play
On the tops of the masts and the tips of the spars,
And I knew we should have foul weather to-day.
Cheerily, my hearties! yo heave ho!
Brail up the mainsail, and let her go
As the winds will and Saint Antonio!
Do you see that Livornese felucca,
That vessel to the windward yonder,
Running with her gunwale under?
I was looking when the wind o'ertook her.
She had all sail set, and the only wonder
Is that at once the strength of the blast
Did not carry away her mast.
She is a galley of the Gran Duca,
That, through the fear of the Algerines,
Convoys those lazy brigantines,

Laden with wine and oil from Lucca.
Now all is ready, high and low;
Blow, blow, good Saint Antonio!

Ha! that is the first dash of the rain,
With a sprinkle of spray above the rails,
Just enough to moisten our sails,
And make them ready for the strain.
See how she leaps, as the blasts o'ertake her,
And speeds away with a bone in her mouth!
Now keep her head toward the south,
And there is no danger of bank or breaker.
With the breeze behind us, on we go;
Not too much, good Saint Antonio!

VI

THE SCHOOL OF SALERNO

A travelling Scholastic affixing his Theses to the gate of the College

SCHOLASTIC

There, that is my gauntlet, my banner, my shield,
Hung up as a challenge to all the field!
One hundred and twenty-five propositions,
Which I will maintain with the sword of the tongue
Against all disputants, old and young.
Let us see if doctors or dialecticians
Will dare to dispute my definitions,
Or attack any one of my learned theses.
Here stand I; the end shall be as God pleases.
I think I have proved, by profound researches,
The error of all those doctrines so vicious
Of the old Areopagite Dionysius,
That are making such terrible work in the churches,
By Michael the Stammerer sent from the East,
And done into Latin by that Scottish beast,
Johannes Duns Scotus, who dares to maintain,
In the face of the truth, the error infernal,
That the universe is and must be eternal;
At first laying down, as a fact fundamental,
That nothing with God can be accidental;
Then asserting that God before the creation
Could not have existed, because it is plain
That, had He existed, He would have created;
Which is begging the question that should be debated,
And moveth me less to anger than laughter.
All nature, he holds, is a respiration
Of the Spirit of God, who, in breathing, hereafter
Will inhale it into his bosom again,
So that nothing but God alone will remain.
And therein he contradicteth himself;
For he opens the whole discussion by stating,
That God can only exist in creating.
That question I think I have laid on the shelf!

He goes out. Two Doctors come in disputing, and followed by pupils

DOCTOR SERAFINO

I, with the Doctor Seraphic, maintain,
That a word which is only conceived in the brain
Is a type of eternal Generation;
The spoken word is the Incarnation.

DOCTOR CHERUBINO

What do I care for the Doctor Seraphic,
With all his wordy chaffer and traffic?

DOCTOR SERAFINO

You make but a paltry show of resistance;
Universals have no real existence!

DOCTOR CHERUBINO

Your words are but idle and empty chatter;
Ideas are eternally joined to matter!

DOCTOR SERAFINO

May the Lord have mercy on your position,
You wretched, wrangling culler of herbs!

DOCTOR CHERUBINO

May he send your soul to eternal perdition,
For your Treatise on the Irregular Verbs!

They rush out fighting. Two Scholars come in

FIRST SCHOLAR

Monte Cassino, then, is your College.
What think you of ours here at Salern?

SECOND SCHOLAR

To tell the truth, I arrived so lately,
I hardly yet have had time to discern.
So much, at least, I am bound to acknowledge:
The air seems healthy, the buildings stately,
And on the whole I like it greatly.

FIRST SCHOLAR

Yes, the air is sweet; the Calabrian hills
Send us down puffs of mountain air;
And in summer-time the sea-breeze fills
With its coolness cloister, and court, and square.
Then at every season of the year
There are crowds of guests and travellers here;
Pilgrims, and mendicant friars, and traders
From the Levant, with figs and wine,
And bands of wounded and sick Crusaders,
Coming back from Palestine.

SECOND SCHOLAR

And what are the studies you pursue?
What is the course you here go through?

FIRST SCHOLAR

The first three years of the college course
Are given to Logic alone, as the source
Of all that is noble, and wise, and true.

SECOND SCHOLAR

That seems rather strange, I must confess,
In a Medical School; yet, nevertheless,
You doubtless have reasons for that.

FIRST SCHOLAR

Oh yes!
For none but a clever dialectician
Can hope to become a great physician;
That has been settled long ago.
Logic makes an important part
Of the mystery of the healing art;
For without it how could you hope to show
That nobody knows so much as you know?
After this there are five years more
Devoted wholly to medicine,
With lectures on chirurgical lore,
And dissections of the bodies of swine,
As likest the human form divine.

SECOND SCHOLAR

What are the books now most in vogue?

FIRST SCHOLAR

Quite an extensive catalogue;
Mostly, however, books of our own;
As Gariopontus' Passionarius,
And the writings of Matthew Platearius;
And a volume universally known
As the Regimen of the School of Salern,
For Robert of Normandy written in terse
And very elegant Latin verse.
Each of these writings has its turn.
And when at length we have finished these,
Then comes the struggle for degrees,
With all the oldest and ablest critics;
The public thesis and disputation,
Question, and answer, and explanation
Of a passage out of Hippocrates,
Or Aristotle's Analytics.
There the triumphant Magister stands!
A book is solemnly placed in his hands,
On which he swears to follow the rule
And ancient forms of the good old School;
To report if any confectionarius
Mingles his drugs with matters various,
And to visit his patients twice a day,
And once in the night, if they live in town,
And if they are poor, to take no pay.
Having faithfully promised these,
His head is crowned with a laurel crown;
A kiss on his cheek, a ring on his hand,
The Magister Artium et Physices
Goes forth from the school like a lord of the land.
And now, as we have the whole morning before us,
Let us go in, if you make no objection,
And listen awhile to a learned prelection
On Marcus Aurelius Cassiodorus.

They go in. Enter LUCIFER *as a Doctor*

LUCIFER

This is the great School of Salern!
A land of wrangling and of quarrels,
Of brains that seethe, and hearts that burn,
Where every emulous scholar hears,
In every breath that comes to his ears,
The rustling of another's laurels!
The air of the place is called salubrious;
The neighborhood of Vesuvius lends it
An odor volcanic, that rather mends it,
And the buildings have an aspect lugubrious,
That inspires a feeling of awe and terror
Into the heart of the beholder,
And befits such an ancient homestead of error,
Where the old falsehoods moulder and smoulder,
And yearly by many hundred hands
Are carried away, in the zeal of youth,
And sown like tares in the field of truth,
To blossom and ripen in other lands.

What have we here, affixed to the gate?
The challenge of some scholastic wight,
Who wishes to hold a public debate
On sundry questions wrong or right!
Ah, now this is my great delight!
For I have often observed of late
That such discussions end in a fight.
Let us see what the learned wag maintains
With such a prodigal waste of brains.

Reads

"Whether angels in moving from place to place
Pass through the intermediate space.
Whether God himself is the author of evil,
Or whether that is the work of the Devil.
When, where, and wherefore Lucifer fell,
And whether he now is chained in hell."
I think I can answer that question well!
So long as the boastful human mind
Consents in such mills as this to grind,
I sit very firmly upon my throne!
Of a truth it almost makes me laugh,
To see men leaving the golden grain
To gather in piles the pitiful chaff
That old Peter Lombard thrashed with his brain,
To have it caught up and tossed again
On the horns of the Dumb Ox of Cologne!

But my guests approach! there is in the air
A fragrance, like that of the Beautiful Garden
Of Paradise, in the days that were!
An odor of innocence and of prayer,
And of love, and faith that never fails,
Such as the fresh young heart exhales
Before it begins to wither and harden!
I cannot breathe such an atmosphere!
My soul is filled with a nameless fear,
That, after all my trouble and pain,
After all my restless endeavor,
The youngest, fairest soul of the twain,
The most ethereal, most divine,
Will escape from my hands for ever and ever.
But the other is already mine!
Let him live to corrupt his race,
Breathing among them, with every breath,
Weakness, selfishness, and the base
And pusillanimous fear of death.
I know his nature, and I know
That of all who in my ministry
Wander the great earth to and fro,
And on my errands come and go,
The safest and subtlest are such as he.

Enter PRINCE HENRY *and* ELSIE, *with attendants*

PRINCE HENRY

Can you direct us to Friar Angelo?

LUCIFER

He stands before you.

PRINCE HENRY

Then you know our purpose.
I am Prince Henry of Hoheneck, and this
The maiden that I spake of in my letters.

LUCIFER

It is a very grave and solemn business!
We must not be precipitate. Does she
Without compulsion, of her own free will,
Consent to this?

PRINCE HENRY

Against all opposition,
Against all prayers, entreaties, protestations.
She will not be persuaded.

LUCIFER

That is strange!
Have you thought well of it?

ELSIE

I come not here
To argue, but to die. Your business is not
To question, but to kill me. I am ready.
I am impatient to be gone from here
Ere any thoughts of earth disturb again
The spirit of tranquillity within me.

PRINCE HENRY

Would I had not come here! Would I were dead,
And thou wert in thy cottage in the forest,
And hadst not known me! Why have I done this?
Let me go back and die.

ELSIE

It cannot be;
Not if these cold, flat stones on which we tread
Were coulters heated white, and yonder gateway

Flamed like a furnace with a sevenfold heat.
I must fulfil my purpose.

PRINCE HENRY

I forbid it!
Not one step further. For I only meant
To put thus far thy courage to the proof.
It is enough. I, too, have strength to die,
For thou hast taught me!

ELSIE

O my Prince! remember
Your promises. Let me fulfil my errand.
You do not look on life and death as I do.
There are two angels, that attend unseen
Each one of us, and in great books record
Our good and evil deeds. He who writes down
The good ones, after every action closes
His volume, and ascends with it to God.
The other keeps his dreadful day-book open
Till sunset, that we may repent; which doing,
The record of the action fades away,
And leaves a line of white across the page.
Now if my act be good, as I believe,
It cannot be recalled. It is already
Sealed up in heaven, as a good deed accomplished.
The rest is yours. Why wait you? I am ready.

To her attendants

Weep not, my friends! rather rejoice with me.
I shall not feel the pain, but shall be gone,
And you will have another friend in heaven.
Then start not at the creaking of the door
Through which I pass. I see what lies beyond it.

To PRINCE HENRY

And you, O Prince! bear back my benison
Unto my father's house, and all within it.
This morning in the church I prayed for them,
After confession, after absolution,
When my whole soul was white, I prayed for them.
God will take care of them, they need me not.
And in your life let my remembrance linger,
As something not to trouble and disturb it,
But to complete it, adding life to life.
And if at times beside the evening fire
You see my face among the other faces,
Let it not be regarded as a ghost
That haunts your house, but as a guest that loves you.
Nay, even as one of your own family,
Without whose presence there were something wanting.
I have no more to say. Let us go in.

PRINCE HENRY

Friar Angelo! I charge you on your life,
Believe not what she says, for she is mad,
And comes here not to die, but to be healed.

ELSIE

Alas! Prince Henry!

LUCIFER

Come with me; this way.

ELSIE *goes in with* LUCIFER, *who thrusts* PRINCE HENRY *back and closes the door*

PRINCE HENRY

Gone! and the light of all my life gone with her!
A sudden darkness falls upon the world!
Oh, what a vile and abject thing am I
That purchase length of days at such a cost!
Not by her death alone, but by the death
Of all that's good and true and noble in me!
All manhood, excellence, and self-respect,
All love, and faith, and hope, and heart are dead!
All my divine nobility of nature
By this one act is forfeited forever.
I am a Prince in nothing but in name!

To the attendants

Why did you let this horrible deed be done?
Why did you not lay hold on her, and keep her
From self-destruction? Angelo! murderer!

Struggles at the door, but cannot open it

ELSIE, *within*

Farewell, dear Prince! farewell!

PRINCE HENRY

Unbar the door!

LUCIFER

It is too late!

PRINCE HENRY

It shall not be too late!

They burst the door open and rush in

THE FARM-HOUSE IN THE ODENWALD

URSULA *spinning. A summer afternoon. A table spread*

URSULA

I have marked it well,—it must be true,—
Death never takes one alone, but two!
Whenever he enters in at a door,
Under roof of gold or roof of thatch,
He always leaves it upon the latch,
And comes again ere the year is o'er.
Never one of a household only!
Perhaps it is a mercy of God,
Lest the dead there under the sod,
In the land of strangers, should be lonely!
Ah me! I think I am lonelier here!
It is hard to go,—but harder to stay!
Were it not for the children, I should pray
That Death would take me within the year!
And Gottlieb!—he is at work all day,
In the sunny field, or the forest murk,
But I know that his thoughts are far away,
I know that his heart is not in his work!
And when he comes home to me at night
He is not cheery, but sits and sighs,
And I see the great tears in his eyes,
And try to be cheerful for his sake.
Only the children's hearts are light.
Mine is weary, and ready to break.
God help us! I hope we have done right;
We thought we were acting for the best!

Looking through the open door

Who is it coming under the trees?
A man, in the Prince's livery dressed!
He looks about him with doubtful face,
As if uncertain of the place.
He stops at the beehives;—now he sees
The garden gate;—he is going past!
Can he be afraid of the bees?
No; he is coming in at last!
He fills my heart with strange alarm!

Enter a Forester

FORESTER

Is this the tenant Gottlieb's farm?

URSULA

This is his farm, and I his wife.
Pray sit. What may your business be!

FORESTER

News from the Prince!

URSULA

Of death or life?

FORESTER

You put your questions eagerly!

URSULA

Answer me, then! How is the Prince?

FORESTER

I left him only two hours since
Homeward returning down the river,
As strong and well as if God, the Giver,
Had given him back his youth again.

URSULA, *despairing*

Then Elsie, my poor child, is dead!

FORESTER

That, my good woman, I have not said.
Don't cross the bridge till you come to it,
Is a proverb old, and of excellent wit.

URSULA

Keep me no longer in this pain!

FORESTER

It is true your daughter is no more;—
That is, the peasant she was before.

URSULA

Alas! I am simple and lowly bred,
I am poor, distracted, and forlorn.
And it is not well that you of the court
Should mock me thus, and make a sport
Of a joyless mother whose child is dead,
For you, too, were of mother born!

FORESTER

Your daughter lives, and the Prince is well!
You will learn erelong how it all befell.
Her heart for a moment never failed;
But when they reached Salerno's gate,
The Prince's nobler self prevailed,
And saved her for a noble fate.
And he was healed, in his despair,
By the touch of St. Matthew's sacred bones;
Though I think the long ride in the open air,
That pilgrimage over stocks and stones,
In the miracle must come in for a share!

URSULA

Virgin! who lovest the poor and lowly,
If the loud cry of a mother's heart
Can ever ascend to where thou art,
Into thy blessed hands and holy
Receive my prayer of praise and thanksgiving!
Let the hands that bore our Saviour bear it
Into the awful presence of God;
For thy feet with holiness are shod,
And if thou bearest it He will hear it.
Our child who was dead again is living!

FORESTER

I did not tell you she was dead;
If you thought so 'twas no fault of mine;
At this very moment, while I speak,
They are sailing homeward down the Rhine,
In a splendid barge, with golden prow,
And decked with banners white and red
As the colors on your daughter's cheek.
They call her the Lady Alicia now;
For the Prince in Salerno made a vow
That Elsie only would he wed.

URSULA

Jesu Maria! what a change!
All seems to me so weird and strange!

FORESTER

I saw her standing on the deck,
Beneath an awning cool and shady;
Her cap of velvet could not hold
The tresses of her hair of gold,
That flowed and floated like the stream,
And fell in masses down her neck.
As fair and lovely did she seem
As in a story or a dream
Some beautiful and foreign lady.
And the Prince looked so grand and proud,
And waved his hand thus to the crowd
That gazed and shouted from the shore,
All down the river, long and loud.

URSULA

We shall behold our child once more;
She is not dead! She is not dead!
God, listening, must have overheard
The prayers, that, without sound or word,
Our hearts in secrecy have said!
Oh, bring me to her; for mine eyes
Are hungry to behold her face;
My very soul within me cries;
My very hands seem to caress her,
To see her, gaze at her, and bless her;
Dear Elsie, child of God and grace!

Goes out toward the garden

FORESTER

There goes the good woman out of her head;
And Gottlieb's supper is waiting here;
A very capacious flagon of beer,
And a very portentous loaf of bread.
One would say his grief did not much oppress
him.
Here's to the health of the Prince, God bless
him!

He drinks

Ha! it buzzes and stings like a hornet!
And what a scene there, through the door!
The forest behind and the garden before,
And midway an old man of threescore,
With a wife and children that caress him.
Let me try still further to cheer and adorn it
With a merry, echoing blast of my cornet!

Goes out blowing his horn

THE CASTLE OF VAUTSBERG ON THE RHINE

PRINCE HENRY *and* ELSIE *standing on the terrace at evening*

The sound of bells heard from a distance

PRINCE HENRY

We are alone. The wedding guests
Ride down the hill, with plumes and cloaks,
And the descending dark invests
The Niederwald, and all the nests
Among its hoar and haunted oaks.

ELSIE

What bells are those, that ring so slow,
So mellow, musical, and low?

PRINCE HENRY

They are the bells of Geisenheim,
That with their melancholy chime
Ring out the curfew of the sun.

ELSIE

Listen, beloved.

PRINCE HENRY

They are done!
Dear Elsie! many years ago

Those same soft bells at eventide
Rang in the ears of Charlemagne,
As, seated by Fastrada's side
At Ingelheim, in all his pride
He heard their sound with secret pain.

ELSIE

Their voices only speak to me
Of peace and deep tranquillity,
And endless confidence in thee!

PRINCE HENRY

Thou knowest the story of her ring,
How, when the court went back to Aix,
Fastrada died; and how the king
Sat watching by her night and day,
Till into one of the blue lakes,
Which water that delicious land,
They cast the ring, drawn from her hand:
And the great monarch sat serene
And sad beside the fated shore,
Nor left the land forevermore.

ELSIE

That was true love.

PRINCE HENRY

For him the queen
Ne'er did what thou hast done for me.

ELSIE

Wilt thou as fond and faithful be?
Wilt thou so love me after death?

PRINCE HENRY

In life's delight, in death's dismay,
In storm and sunshine, night and day,
In health, in sickness, in decay,
Here and hereafter, I am thine!
Thou hast Fastrada's ring. Beneath
The calm, blue waters of thine eyes,
Deep in thy steadfast soul it lies,
And, undisturbed by this world's breath,
With magic light its jewels shine!
This golden ring, which thou hast worn
Upon thy finger since the morn,
Is but a symbol and a semblance,
An outward fashion, a remembrance,
Of what thou wearest within unseen,
O my Fastrada, O my queen!
Behold! the hill-tops all aglow
With purple and with amethyst;
While the whole valley deep below
Is filled, and seems to overflow,
With a fast-rising tide of mist.
The evening air grows damp and chill;
Let us go in.

ELSIE

Ah, not so soon.
See yonder fire! It is the moon
Slow rising o'er the eastern hill.
It glimmers on the forest tips,
And through the dewy foliage drips
In little rivulets of light,
And makes the heart in love with night.

PRINCE HENRY

Oft on this terrace, when the day
Was closing, have I stood and gazed,
And seen the landscape fade away,
And the white vapors rise and drown
Hamlet and vineyard, tower and town,
While far above the hill-tops blazed.
But then another hand than thine
Was gently held and clasped in mine;
Another head upon my breast
Was laid, as thine is now, at rest.
Why dost thou lift those tender eyes
With so much sorrow and surprise?
A minstrel's, not a maiden's hand,
Was that which in my own was pressed.
A manly form usurped thy place,
A beautiful, but bearded face,
That now is in the Holy Land,
Yet in my memory from afar
Is shining on us like a star.
But linger not. For while I speak,
A sheeted spectre white and tall,
The cold mist climbs the castle wall,
And lays his hand upon thy cheek!

They go in

EPILOGUE—THE TWO RECORDING ANGELS ASCENDING

THE ANGEL OF GOOD DEEDS, *with closed book*

God sent his messenger the rain,
And said unto the mountain brook,
"Rise up, and from thy caverns look
And leap, with naked, snow-white feet,
From the cool hills into the heat
Of the broad, arid plain."

God sent his messenger of faith,
And whispered in the maiden's heart,
"Rise up, and look from where thou art,
And scatter with unselfish hands
Thy freshness on the barren sands
And solitudes of Death."

O beauty of holiness,
Of self-forgetfulness, of lowliness!
O power of meekness,
Whose very gentleness and weakness
Are like the yielding, but irresistible air!
Upon the pages
Of the sealed volume that I bear,
The deed divine
Is written in characters of gold,
That never shall grow old,
But through all ages
Burn and shine,
With soft effulgence!
O God! it is thy indulgence
That fills the world with the bliss
Of a good deed like this!

THE ANGEL OF EVIL DEEDS, *with open book*

Not yet, not yet
Is the red sun wholly set,
But evermore recedes,
While open still I bear
The Book of Evil Deeds,
To let the breathings of the upper air
Visit its pages and erase
The records from its face!
Fainter and fainter as I gaze
In the broad blaze
The glimmering landscape shines,
And below me the black river
Is hidden by wreaths of vapor!
Fainter and fainter the black lines
Begin to quiver
Along the whitening surface of the paper;
Shade after shade
The terrible words grow faint and fade,
And in their place
Runs a white space!

Down goes the sun!
But the soul of one,
Who by repentance
Hath escaped the dreadful sentence,
Shines bright below me as I look.
It is the end!
With closèd Book
To God do I ascend.

Lo! over the mountain steeps
A dark, gigantic shadow sweeps
Beneath my feet;
A blackness inwardly brightening
With sullen heat,
As a storm-cloud lurid with lightning.
And a cry of lamentation,
Repeated and again repeated,
Deep and loud
As the reverberation
Of cloud answering unto cloud,
Swells and rolls away in the distance,
As if the sheeted
Lightning retreated,
Baffled and thwarted by the wind's resistance.

It is Lucifer,
The son of mystery;
And since God suffers him to be,
He, too, is God's minister,
And labors for some good
By us not understood!

SECOND INTERLUDE

MARTIN LUTHER

A CHAMBER IN THE WARTBURG. MORNING.
MARTIN LUTHER WRITING

MARTIN LUTHER

Our God, a Tower of Strength is He,
A goodly wall and weapon;
From all our need He helps us free,
That now to us doth happen.
The old evil foe
Doth in earnest grow,
In grim armor dight,
Much guile and great might;
On earth there is none like him.

OH yes; a tower of strength indeed,
A present help in all our need,
A sword and buckler is our God.
Innocent men have walked unshod
O'er burning ploughshares, and have trod
Unharmed on serpents in their path,
And laughed to scorn the Devil's wrath!

Safe in this Wartburg tower I stand
Where God hath led me by the hand,
And look down, with a heart at ease,

Over the pleasant neighborhoods,
Over the vast Thuringian Woods,
With flash of river, and gloom of trees,
With castles crowning the dizzy heights,
And farms and pastoral delights,
And the morning pouring everywhere
Its golden glory on the air.
Safe, yes, safe am I here at last,
Safe from the overwhelming blast
Of the mouths of Hell, that followed me fast,
And the howling demons of despair
That hunted me like a beast to his lair.

> Of our own might we nothing can;
> We soon are unprotected;
> There fighteth for us the right Man,
> Whom God himself elected.
>   Who is He; ye exclaim?
>   Christus is his name,
>   Lord of Sabaoth,
>   Very God in troth;
> The field He holds forever.

Nothing can vex the Devil more
Than the name of Him whom we adore.
Therefore doth it delight me best
To stand in the choir among the rest,
With the great organ trumpeting
Through its metallic tubes, and sing:
Et verbum caro factum est!
These words the Devil cannot endure,
For he knoweth their meaning well!
Him they trouble and repel,
Us they comfort and allure,
And happy it were, if our delight
Were as great as his affright!

Yea, music is the Prophets' art;
Among the gifts that God hath sent,
One of the most magnificent!
It calms the agitated heart;
Temptations, evil thoughts, and all
The passions that disturb the soul,
Are quelled by its divine control,
As the Evil Spirit fled from Saul,
And his distemper was allayed,
When David took his harp and played.

> This world may full of Devils be,
> All ready to devour us;
> Yet not so sore afraid are we,
> They shall not overpower us.
>   This World's Prince, howe'er
>   Fierce he may appear,
>   He can harm us not,
>   He is doomed, God wot!
> One little word can slay him!

Incredible it seems to some
And to myself a mystery,
That such weak flesh and blood as we,
Armed with no other shield or sword,
Or other weapon than the Word,
Should combat and should overcome
A spirit powerful as he!
He summons forth the Pope of Rome
With all his diabolic crew,
His shorn and shaven retinue
Of priests and children of the dark;
Kill! kill! they cry, the Heresiarch,
Who rouseth up all Christendom
Against us; and at one fell blow
Seeks the whole Church to overthrow!
Not yet; my hour is not yet come.

Yesterday in an idle mood,
Hunting with others in the wood,
I did not pass the hours in vain,
For in the very heart of all
The joyous tumult raised around,
Shouting of men, and baying of hound,
And the bugle's blithe and cheery call,
And echoes answering back again,
From crags of the distant mountain chain,—
In the very heart of this, I found
A mystery of grief and pain.
It was an image of the power
Of Satan, hunting the world about,
With his nets and traps and well-trained dogs,
His bishops and priests and theologues,
And all the rest of the rabble rout,
Seeking whom he may devour!
Enough I have had of hunting hares,
Enough of these hours of idle mirth,
Enough of nets and traps and gins!
The only hunting of any worth
Is where I can pierce with javelins
The cunning foxes and wolves and bears,
The whole iniquitous troop of beasts,
The Roman Pope and the Roman priests
That sorely infest and afflict the earth!

Ye nuns, ye singing birds of the air!
The fowler hath caught you in his snare,
And keeps you safe in his gilded cage,
Singing the song that never tires,
To lure down others from their nests;
How ye flutter and beat your breasts,
Warm and soft with young desires
Against the cruel, pitiless wires,

Reclaiming your lost heritage!
Behold! a hand unbars the door,
Ye shall be captives held no more.

The Word they shall perforce let stand,
And little thanks they merit!
For He is with us in the land,
With gifts of his own Spirit!
Though they take our life,
Goods, honors, child and wife,
Let these pass away,
Little gain have they;
The Kingdom still remaineth!

Yea, it remaineth forevermore,
However Satan may rage and roar,
Though often he whispers in my ears:
What if thy doctrines false should be?
And wrings from me a bitter sweat.
Then I put him to flight with jeers,
Saying: Saint Satan! pray for me;
If thou thinkest I am not saved yet!

And my mortal foes that lie in wait
In every avenue and gate!
As to that odious monk John Tetzel,
Hawking about his hollow wares
Like a huckster at village fairs,
And those mischievous fellows, Wetzel,
Campanus, Carlstadt, Martin Cellarius,
And all the busy, multifarious
Heretics, and disciples of Arius,
Half-learned, dunce-bold, dry and hard,
They are not worthy of my regard,
Poor and humble as I am.

But ah! Erasmus of Rotterdam,
He is the vilest miscreant
That ever walked this world below!
A Momus, making his mock and mow,
At Papist and at Protestant,
Sneering at St. John and St. Paul,
At God and Man, at one and all;
And yet as hollow and false and drear,
As a cracked pitcher to the ear,
And ever growing worse and worse!
Whenever I pray, I pray for a curse
On Erasmus, the Insincere!

Philip Melancthon! thou alone
Faithful among the faithless known,
Thee I hail, and only thee!
Behold the record of us three!
Res et verba Philippus,
Res sine verbis Lutherus;
Erasmus verba sine re!

My Philip, prayest thou for me?
Lifted above all earthly care,
From these high regions of the air,
Among the birds that day and night
Upon the branches of tall trees
Sing their lauds and litanies,
Praising God with all their might,
My Philip, unto thee I write.

My Philip! thou who knowest best
All that is passing in this breast;
The spiritual agonies,
The inward deaths, the inward hell,
And the divine new births as well,
That surely follow after these,
As after winter follows spring;
My Philip, in the night-time sing
This song of the Lord I send to thee;
And I will sing it for thy sake,
Until our answering voices make
A glorious antiphony,
And choral chant of victory!

1850–51 1851

THE WARDEN OF THE CINQUE PORTS

A MIST was driving down the British Channel,
The day was just begun,
And through the window-panes, on floor and panel,
Streamed the red autumn sun.

It glanced on flowing flag and rippling pennon,
And the white sails of ships;
And, from the frowning rampart, the black cannon
Hailed it with feverish lips.

Sandwich and Romney, Hastings, Hithe, and Dover
Were all alert that day,
To see the French war-steamers speeding over,
When the fog cleared away.

Sullen and silent, and like couchant lions,
Their cannon, through the night,
Holding their breath, had watched, in grim defiance,
The sea-coast opposite.

And now they roared at drum-beat from their stations
On every citadel;
Each answering each, with morning salutations,
That all was well.

And down the coast, all taking up the burden,
Replied the distant forts,
As if to summon from his sleep the Warden
And Lord of the Cinque Ports.

Him shall no sunshine from the fields of azure,
No drum-beat from the wall,
No morning gun from the black fort's embrasure,
Awaken with its call!

No more, surveying with an eye impartial
The long line of the coast,
Shall the gaunt figure of the old Field Marshal
Be seen upon his post!

For in the night, unseen, a single warrior,
In sombre harness mailed,
Dreaded of man, and surnamed the Destroyer,
The rampart wall had scaled.

He passed into the chamber of the sleeper,
The dark and silent room,
And as he entered, darker grew, and deeper,
The silence and the gloom.

He did not pause to parley or dissemble,
But smote the Warden hoar;
Ah! what a blow! that made all England tremble
And groan from shore to shore.

Meanwhile, without, the surly cannon waited,
The sun rose bright o'erhead;
Nothing in Nature's aspect intimated
That a great man was dead.

1852 1852

DAYLIGHT AND MOONLIGHT

In broad daylight, and at noon,
Yesterday I saw the moon
Sailing high, but faint and white,
As a schoolboy's paper kite.

In broad daylight, yesterday,
I read a Poet's mystic lay;
And it seemed to me at most
As a phantom, or a ghost.

But at length the feverish day
Like a passion died away,
And the night, serene and still,
Fell on village, vale, and hill.

Then the moon, in all her pride,
Like a spirit glorified,
Filled and overflowed the night
With revelations of her light.

And the Poet's song again
Passed like music through my brain;
Night interpreted to me
All its grace and mystery.

1852 1858

THE ROPEWALK

In that building, long and low,
With its windows all a-row,
Like the port-holes of a hulk,
Human spiders spin and spin,
Backward down their threads so thin
Dropping, each a hempen bulk.

At the end, an open door;
Squares of sunshine on the floor
Light the long and dusky lane;
And the whirring of a wheel,
Dull and drowsy, makes me feel
All its spokes are in my brain.

As the spinners to the end
Downward go and reascend,
Gleam the long threads in the sun;
While within this brain of mine
Cobwebs brighter and more fine
By the busy wheel are spun.

Two fair maidens in a swing,
Like white doves upon the wing,
First before my vision pass;
Laughing, as their gentle hands
Closely clasp the twisted strands,
At their shadow on the grass.

Then a booth of mountebanks,
With its smell of tar and planks,
And a girl poised high in air
On a cord, in spangled dress,
With a faded loveliness,
And a weary look of care.

Then a homestead among farms,
And a woman with bare arms
Drawing water from a well;
As the bucket mounts apace,
With it mounts her own fair face,
As at some magician's spell.

Then an old man in a tower,
Ringing loud the noontide hour,
While the rope coils round and round
Like a serpent at his feet,
And again, in swift retreat,
Nearly lifts him from the ground.

Then within a prison-yard,
Faces fixed, and stern, and hard,
Laughter and indecent mirth;
Ah! it is the gallows-tree!
Breath of Christian charity,
Blow, and sweep it from the earth!

Then a school-boy, with his kite
Gleaming in a sky of light,
And an eager, upward look;
Steeds pursued through lane and field;
Fowlers with their snares concealed;
And an angler by a brook.

Ships rejoicing in the breeze,
Wrecks that float o'er unknown seas,
Anchors dragged through faithless sand;
Sea-fog drifting overhead,
And, with lessening line and lead,
Sailors feeling for the land.

All these scenes do I behold,
These, and many left untold,
In that building long and low;
While the wheel goes round and round,
With a drowsy, dreamy sound,
And the spinners backward go.

1854

THE SONG OF HIAWATHA

INTRODUCTION

SHOULD you ask me, whence these stories?
Whence these legends and traditions,
With the odors of the forest,
With the dew and damp of meadows,
With the curling smoke of wigwams,
With the rushing of great rivers,
With their frequent repetitions,
And their wild reverberations,
As of thunder in the mountains?
I should answer, I should tell you,
"From the forests and the prairies,
From the great lakes of the Northland,
From the land of the Ojibways,
From the land of the Dacotahs,
From the mountains, moors, and fen-lands,
Where the heron, the Shuh-shuh-gah,
Feeds among the reeds and rushes.
I repeat them as I heard them
From the lips of Nawadaha,
The musician, the sweet singer."
Should you ask where Nawadaha
Found these songs, so wild and wayward,
Found these legends and traditions,
I should answer, I should tell you,
"In the bird's-nests of the forest,
In the lodges of the beaver,
In the hoof-prints of the bison,
In the eyry of the eagle!
"All the wild-fowl sang them to him,
In the moorlands and the fen-lands,
In the melancholy marshes;
Chetowaik, the plover, sang them,
Mahng, the loon, the wild-goose, Wawa,
The blue heron, the Shuh-shuh-gah,
And the grouse, the Mushkodasa!"
If still further you should ask me,
Saying, "Who was Nawadaha?
Tell us of this Nawadaha,"
I should answer your inquiries
Straightway in such words as follow.
"In the Vale of Tawasentha,
In the green and silent valley,
By the pleasant water-courses,
Dwelt the singer Nawadaha.
Round about the Indian village
Spread the meadows and the corn-fields,
And beyond them stood the forest,
Stood the groves of singing pine-trees,
Green in Summer, white in Winter,
Ever sighing, ever singing.
"And the pleasant water-courses,
You could trace them through the valley,
By the rushing in the Spring-time,
By the alders in the Summer,
By the white fog in the Autumn,
By the black line in the Winter;
And beside them dwelt the singer,

In the vale of Tawasentha,
In the green and silent valley.
"There he sang of Hiawatha,
Sang the Song of Hiawatha,
Sang his wondrous birth and being,
How he prayed and how he fasted,
How he lived, and toiled, and suffered,
That the tribes of men might prosper,
That he might advance his people!"
Ye who love the haunts of Nature,
Love the sunshine of the meadow,
Love the shadow of the forest,
Love the wind among the branches,
And the rain-shower and the snow-storm,
And the rushing of great rivers
Through their palisades of pine-trees,
And the thunder in the mountains,
Whose innumerable echoes
Flap like eagles in their eyries;—
Listen to these wild traditions,
To this Song of Hiawatha!
Ye who love a nation's legends,
Love the ballads of a people,
That like voices from afar off
Call to us to pause and listen,
Speak in tones so plain and childlike,
Scarcely can the ear distinguish
Whether they are sung or spoken;—
Listen to this Indian Legend,
To this Song of Hiawatha!
Ye whose hearts are fresh and simple,
Who have faith in God and Nature,
Who believe, that in all ages
Every human heart is human,
That in even savage bosoms
There are longings, yearnings, strivings
For the good they comprehend not,
That the feeble hands and helpless,
Groping blindly in the darkness,
Touch God's right hand in that darkness
And are lifted up and strengthened;—
Listen to this simple story,
To this Song of Hiawatha!
Ye, who sometimes, in your rambles
Through the green lanes of the country,
Where the tangled barberry-bushes
Hang their tufts of crimson berries
Over stone walls gray with mosses,
Pause by some neglected graveyard,
For a while to muse, and ponder
On a half-effaced inscription,
Written with little skill of song-craft,
Homely phrases, but each letter
Full of hope and yet of heart-break,
Full of all the tender pathos
Of the Here and the Hereafter;—
Stay and read this rude inscription,
Read this Song of Hiawatha!

III

HIAWATHA'S CHILDHOOD

DOWNWARD through the evening twilight,
In the days that are forgotten,
In the unremembered ages,
From the full moon fell Nokomis,
Fell the beautiful Nokomis,
She a wife, but not a mother.
She was sporting with her women,
Swinging in a swing of grape-vines,
When her rival the rejected,
Full of jealousy and hatred,
Cut the leafy swing asunder,
Cut in twain the twisted grape-vines,
And Nokomis fell affrighted
Downward through the evening twilight,
On the Muskoday, the meadow,
On the prairie full of blossoms.
"See! a star falls!" said the people;
"From the sky a star is falling!"
There among the ferns and mosses,
There among the prairie lilies,
On the Muskoday, the meadow,
In the moonlight and the starlight,
Fair Nokomis bore a daughter.
And she called her name Wenonah,
As the first-born of her daughters.
And the daughter of Nokomis
Grew up like the prairie lilies,
Grew a tall and slender maiden,
With the beauty of the moonlight,
With the beauty of the starlight.
And Nokomis warned her often,
Saying oft, and oft repeating,
"Oh, beware of Mudjekeewis,
Of the West-Wind, Mudjekeewis;
Listen not to what he tells you;
Lie not down upon the meadow,
Stoop not down among the lilies,
Lest the West-Wind come and harm you!"
But she heeded not the warning,
Heeded not those words of wisdom,
And the West-Wind came at evening,

Walking lightly o'er the prairie,
Whispering to the leaves and blossoms,
Bending low the flowers and grasses,
Found the beautiful Wenonah,
Lying there among the lilies,
Wooed her with his words of sweetness,
Wooed her with his soft caresses,
Till she bore a son in sorrow,
Bore a son of love and sorrow.

Thus was born my Hiawatha,
Thus was born the child of wonder;
But the daughter of Nokomis,
Hiawatha's gentle mother,
In her anguish died deserted
By the West-Wind, false and faithless,
By the heartless Mudjekeewis.

For her daughter long and loudly
Wailed and wept the sad Nokomis;
"Oh that I were dead!" she murmured,
"Oh that I were dead, as thou art!
No more work, and no more weeping,
Wahonowin! Wahonowin!"

By the shores of Gitche Gumee,
By the shining Big-Sea-Water,
Stood the wigwam of Nokomis,
Daughter of the Moon, Nokomis.
Dark behind it rose the forest,
Rose the black and gloomy pine-trees,
Rose the firs with cones upon them;
Bright before it beat the water,
Beat the clear and sunny water,
Beat the shining Big-Sea-Water.

There the wrinkled old Nokomis
Nursed the little Hiawatha,
Rocked him in his linden cradle,
Bedded soft in moss and rushes,
Safely bound with reindeer sinews;
Stilled his fretful wail by saying,
"Hush! the Naked Bear will hear thee!"
Lulled him into slumber, singing,
"Ewa-yea! my little owlet!
Who is this, that lights the wigwam?
With his great eyes lights the wigwam?
Ewa-yea! my little owlet!"

Many things Nokomis taught him
Of the stars that shine in heaven;
Showed him Ishkoodah, the comet,
Ishkoodah, with fiery tresses;
Showed the Death-Dance of the spirits,
Warriors with their plumes and war-clubs,
Flaring far away to northward
In the frosty nights of Winter;
Showed the broad white road in heaven,
Pathway of the ghosts, the shadows,
Running straight across the heavens,
Crowded with the ghosts, the shadows.

At the door on summer evenings
Sat the little Hiawatha;
Heard the whispering of the pine-trees,
Heard the lapping of the waters,
Sounds of music, words of wonder;
"Minne-wawa!" said the pine-trees,
"Mudway-aushka!" said the water.

Saw the fire-fly, Wah-wah-taysee,
Flitting through the dusk of evening,
With the twinkle of its candle
Lighting up the brakes and bushes,
And he sang the song of children,
Sang the song Nokomis taught him:
"Wah-wah-taysee, little fire-fly,
Little, flitting, white-fire insect,
Little, dancing, white-fire creature,
Light me with your little candle,
Ere upon my bed I lay me,
Ere in sleep I close my eyelids!"

Saw the moon rise from the water
Rippling, rounding from the water,
Saw the flecks and shadows on it,
Whispered, "What is that, Nokomis?"
And the good Nokomis answered:
"Once a warrior, very angry,
Seized his grandmother, and threw her
Up into the sky at midnight;
Right against the moon he threw her;
'Tis her body that you see there."

Saw the rainbow in the heaven,
In the eastern sky, the rainbow,
Whispered, "What is that, Nokomis?"
And the good Nokomis answered:
"'Tis the heaven of flowers you see there;
All the wild-flowers of the forest,
All the lilies of the prairie,
When on earth they fade and perish,
Blossom in that heaven above us."

When he heard the owls at midnight,
Hooting, laughing in the forest,
"What is that?" he cried in terror,
"What is that," he said, "Nokomis?"
And the good Nokomis answered:
"That is but the owl and owlet,
Talking in their native language,
Talking, scolding at each other."

Then the little Hiawatha
Learned of every bird its language,
Learned their names and all their secrets,
How they built their nests in Summer,
Where they hid themselves in Winter,
Talked with them whene'er he met them,
Called them "Hiawatha's Chickens."
Of all beasts he learned the language,
Learned their names and all their secrets,
How the beavers built their lodges,
Where the squirrels hid their acorns,
How the reindeer ran so swiftly,
Why the rabbit was so timid,
Talked with them whene'er he met them,
Called them "Hiawatha's Brothers."
Then Iagoo, the great boaster,
He the marvellous story-teller,
He the traveller and the talker,
He the friend of old Nokomis,
Made a bow for Hiawatha;
From a branch of ash he made it,
From an oak-bough made the arrows,
Tipped with flint, and winged with feathers,
And the cord he made of deer-skin.
Then he said to Hiawatha:
"Go, my son, into the forest,
Where the red deer herd together,
Kill for us a famous roebuck,
Kill for us a deer with antlers!"
Forth into the forest straightway
All alone walked Hiawatha
Proudly, with his bow and arrows;
And the birds sang round him, o'er him,
"Do not shoot us, Hiawatha!"
Sang the robin, the Opechee,
Sang the bluebird, the Owaissa,
"Do not shoot us, Hiawatha!"
Up the oak-tree, close beside him,
Sprang the squirrel, Adjidaumo,
In and out among the branches,
Coughed and chattered from the oak-tree,
Laughed, and said between his laughing,
"Do not shoot me, Hiawatha!"
And the rabbit from his pathway
Leaped aside, and at a distance
Sat erect upon his haunches,
Half in fear and half in frolic,
Saying to the little hunter,
"Do not shoot me, Hiawatha!"
But he heeded not, nor heard them,
For his thoughts were with the red deer;
On their tracks his eyes were fastened,
Leading downward to the river,
To the ford across the river,
And as one in slumber walked he.
Hidden in the alder-bushes,
There he waited till the deer came,
Till he saw two antlers lifted,
Saw two eyes look from the thicket,
Saw two nostrils point to windward,
And a deer came down the pathway,
Flecked with leafy light and shadow.
And his heart within him fluttered,
Trembled like the leaves above him,
Like the birch-leaf palpitated,
As the deer came down the pathway.
Then, upon one knee uprising,
Hiawatha aimed an arrow;
Scarce a twig moved with his motion,
Scarce a leaf was stirred or rustled,
But the wary roebuck started,
Stamped with all his hoofs together,
Listened with one foot uplifted,
Leaped as if to meet the arrow;
Ah! the singing, fatal arrow,
Like a wasp it buzzed and stung him!
Dead he lay there in the forest,
By the ford across the river;
Beat his timid heart no longer,
But the heart of Hiawatha
Throbbed and shouted and exulted,
As he bore the red deer homeward,
And Iagoo and Nokomis
Hailed his coming with applauses.
From the red deer's hide Nokomis
Made a cloak for Hiawatha,
From the red deer's flesh Nokomis
Made a banquet to his honor.
All the village came and feasted,
All the guests praised Hiawatha,
Called him Strong-Heart, Soan-ge-taha!
Called him Loon-Heart, Mahn-go-taysee!

X

HIAWATHA'S WOOING

"As unto the bow the cord is,
So unto the man is woman;
Though she bends him, she obeys him,
Though she draws him, yet she follows;
Useless each without the other!"
Thus the youthful Hiawatha
Said within himself and pondered,

Much perplexed by various feelings,
Listless, longing, hoping, fearing.
Dreaming still of Minnehaha,
Of the lovely Laughing Water,
In the land of the Dacotahs.
"Wed a maiden of your people,"
Warning said the old Nokomis;
"Go not eastward, go not westward,
For a stranger, whom we know not!
Like a fire upon the hearth-stone
Is a neighbor's homely daughter,
Like the starlight or the moonlight
Is the handsomest of strangers!"
Thus dissuading spake Nokomis,
And my Hiawatha answered
Only this: "Dear old Nokomis,
Very pleasant is the firelight,
But I like the starlight better,
Better do I like the moonlight!"
Gravely then said old Nokomis:
"Bring not here an idle maiden,
Bring not here a useless woman,
Hands unskilful, feet unwilling;
Bring a wife with nimble fingers,
Heart and hand that move together,
Feet that run on willing errands!"
Smiling answered Hiawatha:
"In the land of the Dacotahs
Lives the Arrow-maker's daughter,
Minnehaha, Laughing Water,
Handsomest of all the women.
I will bring her to your wigwam,
She shall run upon your errands,
Be your starlight, moonlight, firelight,
Be the sunlight of my people!"
Still dissuading said Nokomis:
"Bring not to my lodge a stranger
From the land of the Dacotahs!
Very fierce are the Dacotahs,
Often is there war between us,
There are feuds yet unforgotten,
Wounds that ache and still may open!"
Laughing answered Hiawatha:
"For that reason, if no other,
Would I wed the fair Dacotah,
That our tribes might be united,
That old feuds might be forgotten,
And old wounds be healed forever!"
Thus departed Hiawatha
To the land of the Dacotahs,
To the land of handsome women;
Striding over moor and meadow,
Through interminable forests,
Through uninterrupted silence.
With his moccasins of magic,
At each stride a mile he measured;
Yet the way seemed long before him,
And his heart outran his footsteps;
And he journeyed without resting,
Till he heard the cataract's laughter,
Heard the Falls of Minnehaha
Calling to him through the silence.
"Pleasant is the sound!" he murmured,
"Pleasant is the voice that calls me!"
On the outskirts of the forests,
'Twixt the shadow and the sunshine,
Herds of fallow deer were feeding,
But they saw not Hiawatha;
To his bow he whispered, "Fail not!"
To his arrow whispered, "Swerve not!"
Sent it singing on its errand,
To the red heart of the roebuck;
Threw the deer across his shoulder,
And sped forward without pausing.
At the doorway of his wigwam
Sat the ancient Arrow-maker,
In the land of the Dacotahs,
Making arrow-heads of jasper,
Arrow-heads of chalcedony.
At his side, in all her beauty,
Sat the lovely Minnehaha,
Sat his daughter, Laughing Water,
Plaiting mats of flags and rushes;
Of the past the old man's thoughts were,
And the maiden's of the future.
He was thinking, as he sat there,
Of the days when with such arrows
He had struck the deer and bison,
On the Muskoday, the meadow;
Shot the wild goose, flying southward,
On the wing, the clamorous Wawa;
Thinking of the great war-parties,
How they came to buy his arrows,
Could not fight without his arrows.
Ah, no more such noble warriors
Could be found on earth as they were!
Now the men were all like women,
Only used their tongues for weapons!
She was thinking of a hunter,
From another tribe and country,
Young and tall and very handsome,
Who one morning, in the Spring-time,

Came to buy her father's arrows,
Sat and rested in the wigwam,
Lingered long about the doorway,
Looking back as he departed.
She had heard her father praise him,
Praise his courage and his wisdom;
Would he come again for arrows
To the Falls of Minnehaha?
On the mat her hands lay idle,
And her eyes were very dreamy.
  Through their thoughts they heard a footstep,
Heard a rustling in the branches,
And with glowing cheek and forehead,
With the deer upon his shoulders,
Suddenly from out the woodlands
Hiawatha stood before them.
  Straight the ancient Arrow-maker
Looked up gravely from his labor,
Laid aside the unfinished arrow,
Bade him enter at the doorway,
Saying, as he rose to meet him,
"Hiawatha, you are welcome!"
  At the feet of Laughing Water
Hiawatha laid his burden,
Threw the red deer from his shoulders;
And the maiden looked up at him,
Looked up from her mat of rushes,
Said with gentle look and accent,
"You are welcome, Hiawatha!"
  Very spacious was the wigwam,
Made of deer-skins dressed and whitened,
With the Gods of the Dacotahs
Drawn and painted on its curtains,
And so tall the doorway, hardly
Hiawatha stooped to enter,
Hardly touched his eagle-feathers
As he entered at the doorway.
  Then uprose the Laughing Water,
From the ground fair Minnehaha,
Laid aside her mat unfinished,
Brought forth food and set before them,
Water brought them from the brooklet,
Gave them food in earthen vessels,
Gave them drink in bowls of basswood,
Listened while the guest was speaking,
Listened while her father answered,
But not once her lips she opened,
Not a single word she uttered.
  Yes, as in a dream she listened
To the words of Hiawatha,
As he talked of old Nokomis,
Who had nursed him in his childhood,
As he told of his companions,
Chibiabos, the musician,
And the very strong man, Kwasind,
And of happiness and plenty
In the land of the Ojibways,
In the pleasant land and peaceful.
  "After many years of warfare,
Many years of strife and bloodshed,
There is peace between the Ojibways
And the tribe of the Dacotahs."
Thus continued Hiawatha,
And then added, speaking slowly,
"That this peace may last forever,
And our hands be clasped more closely,
And our hearts be more united,
Give me as my wife this maiden,
Minnehaha, Laughing Water,
Loveliest of Dacotah women!"
  And the ancient Arrow-maker
Paused a moment ere he answered,
Smoked a little while in silence,
Looked at Hiawatha proudly,
Fondly looked at Laughing Water,
And made answer very gravely:
"Yes, if Minnehaha wishes;
Let your heart speak, Minnehaha!"
  And the lovely Laughing Water
Seemed more lovely as she stood there,
Neither willing nor reluctant,
As she went to Hiawatha,
Softly took the seat beside him,
While she said, and blushed to say it,
"I will follow you, my husband!"
  This was Hiawatha's wooing!
Thus it was he won the daughter
Of the ancient Arrow-maker,
In the land of the Dacotahs!
  From the wigwam he departed,
Leading with him Laughing Water;
Hand in hand they went together,
Through the woodland and the meadow,
Left the old man standing lonely
At the doorway of his wigwam,
Heard the Falls of Minnehaha
Calling to them from the distance,
Crying to them from afar off,
"Fare thee well, O Minnehaha!"
  And the ancient Arrow-maker
Turned again unto his labor,

Sat down by his sunny doorway,
Murmuring to himself, and saying:
"Thus it is our daughters leave us,
Those we love, and those who love us!
Just when they have learned to help us,
When we are old and lean upon them,
Comes a youth with flaunting feathers,
With his flute of reeds, a stranger
Wanders piping through the village,
Beckons to the fairest maiden,
And she follows where he leads her,
Leaving all things for the stranger!"
Pleasant was the journey homeward,
Through interminable forests,
Over meadow, over mountain,
Over river, hill, and hollow.
Short it seemed to Hiawatha,
Though they journeyed very slowly,
Though his pace he checked and slackened
To the steps of Laughing Water.
Over wide and rushing rivers
In his arms he bore the maiden;
Light he thought her as a feather,
As the plume upon his head-gear;
Cleared the tangled pathway for her,
Bent aside the swaying branches,
Made at night a lodge of branches,
And a bed with boughs of hemlock,
And a fire before the doorway
With the dry cones of the pine-tree.
All the travelling winds went with them,
O'er the meadows, through the forest;
All the stars of night looked at them,
Watched with sleepless eyes their slumber;
From his ambush in the oak-tree
Peeped the squirrel, Adjidaumo,
Watched with eager eyes the lovers;
And the rabbit, the Wabasso,
Scampered from the path before them,
Peering, peeping from his burrow,
Sat erect upon his haunches,
Watched with curious eyes the lovers.
Pleasant was the journey homeward!
All the birds sang loud and sweetly
Songs of happiness and heart's-ease;
Sang the bluebird, the Owaissa,
"Happy are you, Hiawatha,
Having such a wife to love you!"
Sang the robin, the Opechee,
"Happy are you, Laughing Water,
Having such a noble husband!"
From the sky the sun benignant
Looked upon them through the branches,
Saying to them, "O my children,
Love is sunshine, hate is shadow,
Life is checkered shade and sunshine,
Rule by love, O Hiawatha!"
From the sky the moon looked at them,
Filled the lodge with mystic splendors,
Whispered to them, "O my children,
Day is restless, night is quiet,
Man imperious, woman feeble;
Half is mine, although I follow;
Rule by patience, Laughing Water!"
Thus it was they journeyed homeward;
Thus it was that Hiawatha
To the lodge of old Nokomis
Brought the moonlight, starlight, firelight,
Brought the sunshine of his people,
Minnehaha, Laughing Water,
Handsomest of all the women
In the land of the Dacotahs,
In the land of handsome women.

XI

HIAWATHA'S WEDDING-FEAST

You shall hear how Pau-Puk-Keewis,
How the handsome Yenadizze
Danced at Hiawatha's wedding;
How the gentle Chibiabos,
He the sweetest of musicians,
Sang his songs of love and longing;
How Iagoo, the great boaster,
He the marvellous story-teller,
Told his tales of strange adventure,
That the feast might be more joyous,
That the time might pass more gayly,
And the guests be more contented.
Sumptuous was the feast Nokomis
Made at Hiawatha's wedding;
All the bowls were made of basswood,
White and polished very smoothly,
All the spoons of horn of bison,
Black and polished very smoothly.
She had sent through all the village
Messengers with wands of willow,
As a sign of invitation,
As a token of the feasting;
And the wedding guests assembled,
Clad in all their richest raiment,
Robes of fur and belts of wampum,

Splendid with their paint and plumage,
Beautiful with beads and tassels.
First they ate the sturgeon, Nahma,
And the pike, the Maskenozha,
Caught and cooked by old Nokomis;
Then on pemican they feasted,
Pemican and buffalo marrow,
Haunch of deer and hump of bison,
Yellow cakes of the Mondamin,
And the wild rice of the river.
But the gracious Hiawatha,
And the lovely Laughing Water,
And the careful old Nokomis,
Tasted not the food before them,
Only waited on the others,
Only served their guests in silence.
And when all the guests had finished,
Old Nokomis, brisk and busy,
From an ample pouch of otter,
Filled the red-stone pipes for smoking
With tobacco from the South-land,
Mixed with bark of the red willow,
And with herbs and leaves of fragrance.
Then she said, "O Pau-Puk-Keewis,
Dance for us your merry dances,
Dance the Beggar's Dance to please us,
That the feast may be more joyous,
That the time may pass more gayly,
And our guests be more contented!"
Then the handsome Pau-Puk-Keewis,
He the idle Yenadizze,
He the merry mischief-maker,
Whom the people called the Storm-Fool,
Rose among the guests assembled.
Skilled was he in sports and pastimes,
In the merry dance of snow-shoes,
In the play of quoits and ball-play;
Skilled was he in games of hazard,
In all games of skill and hazard,
Pugasaing, the Bowl and Counters,
Kuntassoo, the Game of Plum-stones.
Though the warriors called him Faint-Heart,
Called him coward, Shaugodaya,
Idler, gambler, Yenadizze,
Little heeded he their jesting,
Little cared he for their insults,
For the women and the maidens
Loved the handsome Pau-Puk-Keewis.
He was dressed in shirt of doeskin,
White and soft, and fringed with ermine,
All inwrought with beads of wampum;
He was dressed in deer-skin leggings,
Fringed with hedgehog quills and ermine,
And in moccasins of buck-skin,
Thick with quills and beads embroidered.
On his head were plumes of swan's down,
On his heels were tails of foxes,
In one hand a fan of feathers,
And a pipe was in the other.
Barred with streaks of red and yellow,
Streaks of blue and bright vermilion,
Shone the face of Pau-Puk-Keewis.
From his forehead fell his tresses,
Smooth, and parted like a woman's,
Shining bright with oil, and plaited,
Hung with braids of scented grasses,
As among the guests assembled,
To the sound of flutes and singing,
To the sound of drums and voices,
Rose the handsome Pau-Puk-Keewis,
And began his mystic dances.
First he danced a solemn measure,
Very slow in step and gesture,
In and out among the pine-trees,
Through the shadows and the sunshine,
Treading softly like a panther.
Then more swiftly and still swifter,
Whirling, spinning round in circles,
Leaping o'er the guests assembled,
Eddying round and round the wigwam,
Till the leaves went whirling with him,
Till the dust and wind together
Swept in eddies round about him.
Then along the sandy margin
Of the lake, the Big-Sea-Water,
On he sped with frenzied gestures,
Stamped upon the sand, and tossed it
Wildly in the air around him;
Till the wind became a whirlwind,
Till the sand was blown and sifted
Like great snowdrifts o'er the landscape,
Heaping all the shores with Sand Dunes,
Sand Hills of the Nagow Wudjoo!
Thus the merry Pau-Puk-Keewis
Danced his Beggar's Dance to please them,
And, returning, sat down laughing
There among the guests assembled,
Sat and fanned himself serenely
With his fan of turkey-feathers.
Then they said to Chibiabos,
To the friend of Hiawatha,
To the sweetest of all singers,

To the best of all musicians,
"Sing to us, O Chibiabos!
Songs of love and songs of longing,
That the feast may be more joyous,
That the time may pass more gayly,
And our guests be more contented!"
  And the gentle Chibiabos
Sang in accents sweet and tender,
Sang in tones of deep emotion,
Songs of love and songs of longing;
Looking still at Hiawatha,
Looking at fair Laughing Water,
Sang he softly, sang in this wise:
  "Onaway! Awake, beloved!
Thou the wild-flower of the forest!
Thou the wild-bird of the prairie!
Thou with eyes so soft and fawn-like!
  "If thou only lookest at me,
I am happy, I am happy,
As the lilies of the prairie,
When they feel the dew upon them!
  "Sweet thy breath is as the fragrance
Of the wild-flowers in the morning,
As their fragrance is at evening,
In the Moon when leaves are falling.
  "Does not all the blood within me
Leap to meet thee, leap to meet thee,
As the springs to meet the sunshine,
In the Moon when nights are brightest?
  "Onaway! my heart sings to thee,
Sings with joy when thou art near me,
As the sighing, singing branches
In the pleasant Moon of Strawberries!
  "When thou art not pleased, beloved,
Then my heart is sad and darkened,
As the shining river darkens
When the clouds drop shadows on it!
  "When thou smilest, my beloved,
Then my troubled heart is brightened,
As in sunshine gleam the ripples
That the cold wind makes in rivers.
  "Smiles the earth, and smile the waters,
Smile the cloudless skies above us,
But I lose the way of smiling
When thou art no longer near me!
  "I myself, myself! behold me!
Blood of my beating heart, behold me!
Oh awake, awake, beloved!
Onaway! awake, beloved!"
  Thus the gentle Chibiabos
Sang his song of love and longing;
And Iagoo, the great boaster,
He the marvellous story-teller,
He the friend of old Nokomis,
Jealous of the sweet musician,
Jealous of the applause they gave him,
Saw in all the eyes around him,
Saw in all their looks and gestures,
That the wedding guests assembled
Longed to hear his pleasant stories,
His immeasurable falsehoods.
  Very boastful was Iagoo;
Never heard he an adventure
But himself had met a greater;
Never any deed of daring
But himself had done a bolder;
Never any marvellous story
But himself could tell a stranger.
  Would you listen to his boasting,
Would you only give him credence,
No one ever shot an arrow
Half so far and high as he had;
Ever caught so many fishes,
Ever killed so many reindeer,
Ever trapped so many beaver!
  None could run so fast as he could,
None could dive so deep as he could,
None could swim so far as he could,
None had made so many journeys,
None had seen so many wonders,
As this wonderful Iagoo,
As this marvellous story-teller!
  Thus his name became a by-word
And a jest among the people;
And whene'er a boastful hunter
Praised his own address too highly,
Or a warrior, home returning,
Talked too much of his achievements,
All his hearers cried, "Iagoo!
Here's Iagoo come among us!"
  He it was who carved the cradle
Of the little Hiawatha,
Carved its framework out of linden,
Bound it strong with reindeer sinews;
He it was who taught him later
How to make his bows and arrows,
How to make the bows of ash-tree,
And the arrows of the oak-tree.
So among the guests assembled
At my Hiawatha's wedding
Sat Iagoo, old and ugly,
Sat the marvellous story-teller.

And they said, "O good Iagoo,
Tell us now a tale of wonder,
Tell us of some strange adventure,
That the feast may be more joyous,
That the time may pass more gayly,
And our guests be more contented!"
And Iagoo answered straightway,
"You shall hear a tale of wonder,
You shall hear the strange adventures
Of Osseo, the Magician,
From the Evening Star descended."

XX
THE FAMINE

Oh, the long and dreary Winter!
Oh, the cold and cruel Winter!
Ever thicker, thicker, thicker
Froze the ice on lake and river,
Ever deeper, deeper, deeper
Fell the snow o'er all the landscape,
Fell the covering snow, and drifted
Through the forest, round the village.
Hardly from his buried wigwam
Could the hunter force a passage;
With his mittens and his snow-shoes
Vainly walked he through the forest,
Sought for bird or beast and found none,
Saw no track of deer or rabbit,
In the snow beheld no footprints,
In the ghastly, gleaming forest
Fell, and could not rise from weakness,
Perished there from cold and hunger.
Oh the famine and the fever!
Oh the wasting of the famine!
Oh the blasting of the fever!
Oh the wailing of the children!
Oh the anguish of the women!
All the earth was sick and famished;
Hungry was the air around them,
Hungry was the sky above them,
And the hungry stars in heaven
Like the eyes of wolves glared at them!
Into Hiawatha's wigwam
Came two other guests, as silent
As the ghosts were, and as gloomy,
Waited not to be invited,
Did not parley at the doorway,
Sat there without word of welcome
In the seat of Laughing Water;
Looked with haggard eyes and hollow
At the face of Laughing Water.
And the foremost said: "Behold me!
I am Famine, Bukadawin!"
And the other said: "Behold me!
I am Fever, Ahkosewin!"
And the lovely Minnehaha
Shuddered as they looked upon her,
Shuddered at the words they uttered,
Lay down on her bed in silence,
Hid her face, but made no answer;
Lay there trembling, freezing, burning
At the looks they cast upon her,
At the fearful words they uttered.
Forth into the empty forest
Rushed the maddened Hiawatha;
In his heart was deadly sorrow,
In his face a stony firmness;
On his brow the sweat of anguish
Started, but it froze and fell not.
Wrapped in furs and armed for hunting,
With his mighty bow of ash-tree,
With his quiver full of arrows,
With his mittens, Minjekahwun,
Into the vast and vacant forest
On his snow-shoes strode he forward.
"Gitche Manito, the Mighty!"
Cried he with his face uplifted
In that bitter hour of anguish,
"Give your children food, O father!
Give us food, or we must perish!
Give me food for Minnehaha,
For my dying Minnehaha!"
Through the far-resounding forest,
Through the forest vast and vacant
Rang that cry of desolation,
But there came no other answer
Than the echo of his crying,
Than the echo of the woodlands,
"Minnehaha! Minnehaha!"
All day long roved Hiawatha
In that melancholy forest,
Through the shadow of whose thickets,
In the pleasant days of Summer,
Of that ne'er forgotten Summer,
He had brought his young wife homeward
From the land of the Dacotahs;
When the birds sang in the thickets,
And the streamlets laughed and glistened,
And the air was full of fragrance,
And the lovely Laughing Water
Said with voice that did not tremble,
"I will follow you, my husband!"

In the wigwam with Nokomis,
With those gloomy guests that watched her,
With the Famine and the Fever,
She was lying, the Beloved,
She, the dying Minnehaha.
"Hark!" she said; "I hear a rushing,
Hear a roaring and a rushing,
Hear the Falls of Minnehaha
Calling to me from a distance!"
"No, my child!" said old Nokomis,
"'Tis the night-wind in the pine-trees!"
"Look!" she said; "I see my father
Standing lonely at his doorway,
Beckoning to me from his wigwam
In the land of the Dacotahs!"
"No, my child!" said old Nokomis,
"'Tis the smoke, that waves and beckons!"
"Ah!" said she, "the eyes of Pauguk
Glare upon me in the darkness,
I can feel his icy fingers
Clasping mine amid the darkness!
Hiawatha! Hiawatha!"
And the desolate Hiawatha,
Far away amid the forest,
Miles away among the mountains,
Heard that sudden cry of anguish,
Heard the voice of Minnehaha
Calling to him in the darkness,
"Hiawatha! Hiawatha!"
Over snow-fields waste and pathless,
Under snow-encumbered branches,
Homeward hurried Hiawatha,
Empty-handed, heavy-hearted,
Heard Nokomis moaning, wailing:
"Wahonowin! Wahonowin!
Would that I had perished for you,
Would that I were dead as you are!
Wahonowin! Wahonowin!"
And he rushed into the wigwam,
Saw the old Nokomis slowly
Rocking to and fro and moaning,
Saw his lovely Minnehaha
Lying dead and cold before him,
And his bursting heart within him
Uttered such a cry of anguish,
That the forest moaned and shuddered,
That the very stars in heaven
Shook and trembled with his anguish.
Then he sat down, still and speechless,
On the bed of Minnehaha,
At the feet of Laughing Water,
At those willing feet, that never
More would lightly run to meet him,
Never more would lightly follow.
With both hands his face he covered,
Seven long days and nights he sat there,
As if in a swoon he sat there,
Speechless, motionless, unconscious
Of the daylight or the darkness.
Then they buried Minnehaha;
In the snow a grave they made her,
In the forest deep and darksome,
Underneath the moaning hemlocks;
Clothed her in her richest garments,
Wrapped her in her robes of ermine,
Covered her with snow, like ermine;
Thus they buried Minnehaha.
And at night a fire was lighted,
On her grave four times was kindled,
For her soul upon its journey
To the Islands of the Blessed.
From his doorway Hiawatha
Saw it burning in the forest,
Lighting up the gloomy hemlocks;
From his sleepless bed uprising,
From the bed of Minnehaha,
Stood and watched it at the doorway,
That it might not be extinguished,
Might not leave her in the darkness.
"Farewell!" said he, "Minnehaha!
Farewell, O my Laughing Water!
All my heart is buried with you,
All my thoughts go onward with you!
Come not back again to labor,
Come not back again to suffer,
Where the Famine and the Fever
Wear the heart and waste the body.
Soon my task will be completed,
Soon your footsteps I shall follow
To the Islands of the Blessed,
To the Kingdom of Ponemah,
To the Land of the Hereafter!"

XXI
THE WHITE MAN'S FOOT

In his lodge beside a river,
Close beside a frozen river,
Sat an old man, sad and lonely.
White his hair was as a snow-drift;
Dull and low his fire was burning,
And the old man shook and trembled,
Folded in his Waubewyon,

In his tattered white-skin-wrapper,
Hearing nothing but the tempest
As it roared along the forest,
Seeing nothing but the snow-storm,
As it whirled and hissed and drifted.
All the coals were white with ashes,
And the fire was slowly dying,
As a young man, walking lightly,
At the open doorway entered.
Red with blood of youth his cheeks were,
Soft his eyes, as stars in Spring-time,
Bound his forehead was with grasses;
Bound and plumed with scented grasses,
On his lips a smile of beauty,
Filling all the lodge with sunshine,
In his hand a bunch of blossoms
Filling all the lodge with sweetness.
"Ah, my son!" exclaimed the old man,
"Happy are my eyes to see you.
Sit here on the mat beside me,
Sit here by the dying embers,
Let us pass the night together,
Tell me of your strange adventures,
Of the lands where you have travelled;
I will tell you of my prowess,
Of my many deeds of wonder."
From his pouch he drew his peace-pipe,
Very old and strangely fashioned;
Made of red stone was the pipe-head,
And the stem a reed with feathers;
Filled the pipe with bark of willow,
Placed a burning coal upon it,
Gave it to his guest, the stranger,
And began to speak in this wise:
"When I blow my breath about me,
When I breathe upon the landscape,
Motionless are all the rivers,
Hard as stone becomes the water!"
And the young man answered, smiling:
"When I blow my breath about me,
When I breathe upon the landscape,
Flowers spring up o'er all the meadows,
Singing, onward rush the rivers!"
"When I shake my hoary tresses,"
Said the old man darkly frowning,
"All the land with snow is covered;
All the leaves from all the branches
Fall and fade and die and wither,
For I breathe, and lo! they are not.
From the waters and the marshes
Rise the wild goose and the heron,
Fly away to distant regions,
For I speak, and lo! they are not.
And where'er my footsteps wander,
All the wild beasts of the forest
Hide themselves in holes and caverns,
And the earth becomes as flintstone!"
"When I shake my flowing ringlets,"
Said the young man, softly laughing,
"Showers of rain fall warm and welcome,
Plants lift up their heads rejoicing,
Back into their lakes and marshes
Come the wild goose and the heron,
Homeward shoots the arrowy swallow,
Sing the bluebird and the robin,
And where'er my footsteps wander,
All the meadows wave with blossoms,
All the woodlands ring with music,
All the trees are dark with foliage!"
While they spake, the night departed:
From the distant realms of Wabun,
From his shining lodge of silver,
Like a warrior robed and painted,
Came the sun, and said, "Behold me
Gheezis, the great sun, behold me!"
Then the old man's tongue was speechless
And the air grew warm and pleasant,
And upon the wigwam sweetly
Sang the bluebird and the robin,
And the stream began to murmur,
And a scent of growing grasses
Through the lodge was gently wafted.
And Segwun, the youthful stranger,
More distinctly in the daylight
Saw the icy face before him;
It was Peboan, the Winter!
From his eyes the tears were flowing,
As from melting lakes the streamlets,
And his body shrunk and dwindled
As the shouting sun ascended,
Till into the air it faded,
Till into the ground it vanished,
And the young man saw before him,
On the hearth-stone of the wigwam,
Where the fire had smoked and smouldered,
Saw the earliest flower of Spring-time,
Saw the Beauty of the Spring-time,
Saw the Miskodeed in blossom.
Thus it was that in the North-land
After that unheard-of coldness,
That intolerable Winter,
Came the Spring with all its splendor,

All its birds and all its blossoms,
All its flowers and leaves and grasses.
  Sailing on the wind to northward,
Flying in great flocks, like arrows,
Like huge arrows shot through heaven,
Passed the swan, the Mahnahbezee,
Speaking almost as a man speaks;
And in long lines waving, bending
Like a bow-string snapped asunder,
Came the white goose, Waw-be-wawa;
And in pairs, or singly flying,
Mahng the loon, with clangorous pinions,
The blue heron, the Shuh-shuh-gah,
And the grouse, the Mushkodasa.
  In the thickets and the meadows
Piped the bluebird, the Owaissa,
On the summit of the lodges
Sang the robin, the Opechee,
In the covert of the pine-trees
Cooed the pigeon, the Omemee;
And the sorrowing Hiawatha,
Speechless in his infinite sorrow,
Heard their voices calling to him,
Went forth from his gloomy doorway,
Stood and gazed into the heaven,
Gazed upon the earth and waters.
  From his wanderings far to eastward,
From the regions of the morning,
From the shining land of Wabun,
Homeward now returned Iagoo,
The great traveller, the great boaster,
Full of new and strange adventures,
Marvels many and many wonders.
  And the people of the village
Listened to him as he told them
Of his marvellous adventures,
Laughing answered him in this wise:
"Ugh! it is indeed Iagoo!
No one else beholds such wonders!"
  He had seen, he said, a water
Bigger than the Big-Sea-Water,
Broader than the Gitche Gumee,
Bitter so that none could drink it!
At each other looked the warriors,
Looked the women at each other,
Smiled, and said, "It cannot be so!
Kaw!" they said, "it cannot be so!"
  O'er it, said he, o'er this water
Came a great canoe with pinions,
A canoe with wings came flying,
Bigger than a grove of pine-trees,
Taller than the tallest tree-tops!
And the old men and the women
Looked and tittered at each other;
"Kaw!" they said, "we don't believe it!"
  From its mouth, he said, to greet him,
Came Waywassimo, the lightning,
Came the thunder, Annemeekee!
And the warriors and the women
Laughed aloud at poor Iagoo;
"Kaw!" they said, "what tales you tell us!"
  In it, said he, came a people,
In the great canoe with pinions
Came, he said, a hundred warriors;
Painted white were all their faces
And with hair their chins were covered!
And the warriors and the women
Laughed and shouted in derision,
Like the ravens on the tree-tops,
Like the crows upon the hemlocks.
"Kaw!" they said, "what lies you tell us!
Do not think that we believe them!"
  Only Hiawatha laughed not,
But he gravely spake and answered
To their jeering and their jesting:
"True is all Iagoo tells us;
I have seen it in a vision,
Seen the great canoe with pinions,
Seen the people with white faces,
Seen the coming of this bearded
People of the wooden vessel
From the regions of the morning,
From the shining lands of Wabun.
  "Gitche Manito, the Mighty,
The Great Spirit, the Creator,
Sends them hither on his errand,
Sends them to us with his message.
Wheresoe'er they move, before them
Swarms the stinging fly, the Ahmo,
Swarms the bee, the honey-maker;
Wheresoe'er they tread, beneath them
Springs a flower unknown among us,
Springs the White-man's Foot in blossom.
  "Let us welcome, then, the strangers,
Hail them as our friends and brothers,
And the heart's right hand of friendship
Give them when they come to see us.
Gitche Manito, the Mighty,
Said this to me in my vision.
  "I beheld, too, in that vision
All the secrets of the future,
Of the distant days that shall be.

I beheld the westward marches
Of the unknown, crowded nations.
All the land was full of people,
Restless, struggling, toiling, striving,
Speaking many tongues, yet feeling
But one heart-beat in their bosoms.
In the woodlands rang their axes,
Smoked their towns in all the valleys,
Over all the lakes and rivers
Rushed their great canoes of thunder.
"Then a darker, drearier vision
Passed before me, vague and cloud-like;
I beheld our nation scattered,
All forgetful of my counsels,
Weakened, warring with each other:
Saw the remnants of our people
Sweeping westward, wild and woful,
Like the cloud-rack of a tempest,
Like the withered leaves of Autumn!"

XXII
HIAWATHA'S DEPARTURE

By the shore of Gitche Gumee,
By the shining Big-Sea-Water,
At the doorway of his wigwam,
In the pleasant Summer morning,
Hiawatha stood and waited.
All the air was full of freshness,
All the earth was bright and joyous,
And before him, through the sunshine,
Westward toward the neighboring forest
Passed in golden swarms the Ahmo,
Passed the bees, the honey-makers,
Burning, singing in the sunshine.
Bright above him shone the heavens,
Level spread the lake before him;
From its bosom leaped the sturgeon,
Sparkling, flashing in the sunshine;
On its margin the great forest
Stood reflected in the water,
Every tree-top had its shadow,
Motionless beneath the water.
From the brow of Hiawatha
Gone was every trace of sorrow,
As the fog from off the water,
As the mist from off the meadow.
With a smile of joy and triumph,
With a look of exultation,
As of one who in a vision
Sees what is to be, but is not,
Stood and waited Hiawatha.
Toward the sun his hands were lifted,
Both the palms spread out against it,
And between the parted fingers
Fell the sunshine on his features,
Flecked with light his naked shoulders,
As it falls and flecks an oak-tree
Through the rifted leaves and branches.
O'er the water floating, flying,
Something in the hazy distance,
Something in the mists of morning,
Loomed and lifted from the water,
Now seemed floating, now seemed flying,
Coming nearer, nearer, nearer.
Was it Shingebis the diver?
Or the pelican, the Shada?
Or the heron, the Shuh-shuh-gah?
Or the white goose, Waw-be-wawa,
With the water dripping, flashing,
From its glossy neck and feathers?
It was neither goose nor diver,
Neither pelican nor heron,
O'er the water floating, flying,
Through the shining mist of morning,
But a birch canoe with paddles,
Rising, sinking on the water,
Dripping, flashing in the sunshine;
And within it came a people
From the distant land of Wabun,
From the farthest realms of morning
Came the Black-Robe chief, the Prophet,
He the Priest of Prayer, the Pale-face,
With his guides and his companions.
And the noble Hiawatha,
With his hands aloft extended,
Held aloft in sign of welcome,
Waited, full of exultation,
Till the birch canoe with paddles
Grated on the shining pebbles,
Stranded on the sandy margin,
Till the Black-Robe chief, the Pale-face,
With the cross upon his bosom,
Landed on the sandy margin.
Then the joyous Hiawatha
Cried aloud and spake in this wise:
"Beautiful is the sun, O strangers,
When you come so far to see us!
All our town in peace awaits you,
All our doors stand open for you;
You shall enter all our wigwams,
For the heart's right hand we give you.
"Never bloomed the earth so gayly,

Never shone the sun so brightly,
As today they shine and blossom
When you come so far to see us!
Never was our lake so tranquil,
Nor so free from rocks and sand-bars;
For your birch canoe in passing
Has removed both rock and sand-bar.
"Never before had our tobacco
Such a sweet and pleasant flavor,
Never the broad leaves of our cornfields
Were so beautiful to look on,
As they seem to us this morning,
When you come so far to see us!"
And the Black-Robe chief made answer,
Stammered in his speech a little,
Speaking words yet unfamiliar:
"Peace be with you, Hiawatha,
Peace be with you and your people,
Peace of prayer, and peace of pardon,
Peace of Christ, and joy of Mary!"
Then the generous Hiawatha
Led the strangers to his wigwam,
Seated them on skins of bison,
Seated them on skins of ermine,
And the careful old Nokomis
Brought them food in bowls of basswood,
Water brought in birchen dippers,
And the calumet, the peace-pipe,
Filled and lighted for their smoking.
All the old men of the village,
All the warriors of the nation,
All the Jossakeeds, the Prophets,
The magicians, the Wabenos,
And the Medicine-men, the Medas,
Came to bid the strangers welcome;
"It is well," they said, "O brothers,
That you come so far to see us!"
In a circle round the doorway,
With their pipes they sat in silence,
Waiting to behold the strangers,
Waiting to receive their message;
Till the Black-Robe chief, the Pale-face,
From the wigwam came to greet them,
Stammering in his speech a little,
Speaking words yet unfamiliar;
"It is well," they said, "O brother,
That you come so far to see us!"
Then the Black-Robe chief, the Prophet,
Told his message to the people,
Told the purport of his mission,
Told them of the Virgin Mary,
And her blessed Son, the Saviour,
How in distant lands and ages
He had lived on earth as we do;
How he fasted, prayed, and labored;
How the Jews, the tribe accursed,
Mocked him, scourged him, crucified him;
How he rose from where they laid him,
Walked again with his disciples,
And ascended into heaven.
And the chiefs made answer, saying:
"We have listened to your message,
We have heard your words of wisdom,
We will think on what you tell us.
It is well for us, O brothers,
That you come so far to see us!"
Then they rose up and departed
Each one homeward to his wigwam,
To the young men and the women
Told the story of the strangers
Whom the Master of Life had sent them
From the shining land of Wabun.
Heavy with the heat and silence
Grew the afternoon of Summer;
With a drowsy sound the forest
Whispered round the sultry wigwam,
With a sound of sleep the water
Rippled on the beach below it;
From the cornfields shrill and ceaseless
Sang the grasshopper, Pah-puk-keena;
And the guests of Hiawatha,
Weary with the heat of Summer,
Slumbered in the sultry wigwam.
Slowly o'er the simmering landscape
Fell the evening's dusk and coolness,
And the long and level sunbeams
Shot their spears into the forest,
Breaking through its shields of shadow,
Rushed into each secret ambush,
Searched each thicket, dingle, hollow;
Still the guests of Hiawatha
Slumbered in the silent wigwam.
From his place rose Hiawatha,
Bade farewell to old Nokomis,
Spake in whispers, spake in this wise,
Did not wake the guests, that slumbered:
"I am going, O Nokomis,
On a long and distant journey,
To the portals of the Sunset,
To the regions of the home-wind,
Of the Northwest-Wind, Keewaydin.
But these guests I leave behind me,

In your watch and ward I leave them;
See that never harm comes near them,
See that never fear molests them,
Never danger nor suspicion,
Never want of food or shelter,
In the lodge of Hiawatha!"
  Forth into the village went he,
Bade farewell to all the warriors,
Bade farewell to all the young men,
Spake persuading, spake in this wise:
  "I am going, O my people,
On a long and distant journey;
Many moons and many winters
Will have come, and will have vanished,
Ere I come again to see you.
But my guests I leave behind me;
Listen to their words of wisdom,
Listen to the truth they tell you,
For the Master of Life has sent them
From the land of light and morning!"
  On the shore stood Hiawatha,
Turned and waved his hand at parting;
On the clear and luminous water
Launched his birch canoe for sailing,
From the pebbles of the margin
Shoved it forth into the water;
Whispered to it, "Westward! westward!"
And with speed it darted forward.
  And the evening sun descending
Set the clouds on fire with redness,
Burned the broad sky, like a prairie,
Left upon the level water
One long track and trail of splendor,
Down whose stream, as down a river,
Westward, westward, Hiawatha
Sailed into the fiery sunset,
Sailed into the purple vapors,
Sailed into the dusk of evening.
  And the people from the margin
Watched him floating, rising, sinking,
Till the birch canoe seemed lifted
High into that sea of splendor,
Till it sank into the vapors
Like the new moon slowly, slowly
Sinking in the purple distance.
  And they said, "Farewell forever!"
Said, "Farewell, O Hiawatha!"
And the forests, dark and lonely,
Moved through all their depths of darkness,
Sighed, "Farewell, O Hiawatha!"
And the waves upon the margin
Rising, rippling on the pebbles,
Sobbed, "Farewell, O Hiawatha!"
And the heron, the Shuh-shuh-gah,
From her haunts among the fen-lands,
Screamed, "Farewell, O Hiawatha!"
  Thus departed Hiawatha,
Hiawatha the Beloved,
In the glory of the sunset,
In the purple mists of evening,
To the regions of the home-wind,
Of the Northwest-Wind, Keewaydin,
To the Islands of the Blessed,
To the Kingdom of Ponemah,
To the Land of the Hereafter!

1854–1855 1855

MY LOST YOUTH

Often I think of the beautiful town
  That is seated by the sea;
Often in thought go up and down
The pleasant streets of that dear old town,
  And my youth comes back to me.
    And a verse of a Lapland song
    Is haunting my memory still:
  "A boy's will is the wind's will,
And the thoughts of youth are long, long thoughts."

I can see the shadowy lines of its trees,
  And catch, in sudden gleams,
The sheen of the far-surrounding seas,
And islands that were the Hesperides
  Of all my boyish dreams.
    And the burden of that old song,
    It murmurs and whispers still:
  "A boy's will is the wind's will,
And the thoughts of youth are long, long thoughts."

I remember the black wharves and the slips,
  And the sea-tides tossing free;
And Spanish sailors with bearded lips,
And the beauty and mystery of the ships,
  And the magic of the sea.
    And the voice of that wayward song
    Is singing and saying still:
  "A boy's will is the wind's will,
And the thoughts of youth are long, long thoughts."

I remember the bulwarks by the shore,
And the fort upon the hill;
The sunrise gun, with its hollow roar,
The drum-beat repeated o'er and o'er,
And the bugle wild and shrill.
And the music of that old song
Throbs in my memory still:
"A boy's will is the wind's will,
And the thoughts of youth are long, long thoughts."

I remember the sea-fight far away,
How it thundered o'er the tide!
And the dead captains, as they lay
In their graves, o'erlooking the tranquil bay,
Where they in battle died. 41
And the sound of that mournful song
Goes through me with a thrill:
"A boy's will is the wind's will,
And the thoughts of youth are long, long thoughts."

I can see the breezy dome of groves,
The shadows of Deering's Woods;
And the friendships old and the early loves
Come back with a sabbath sound, as of doves
In quiet neighborhoods.
And the verse of that sweet old song,
It flutters and murmurs still:
"A boy's will is the wind's will,
And the thoughts of youth are long, long thoughts."

I remember the gleams and glooms that dart
Across the school-boy's brain;
The song and the silence in the heart,
That in part are prophecies, and in part
Are longings wild and vain.
And the voice of that fitful song
Sings on, and is never still:
"A boy's will is the wind's will,
And the thoughts of youth are long, long thoughts."

There are things of which I may not speak;
There are dreams that cannot die;
There are thoughts that make the strong heart weak,
And bring a pallor into the cheek,
And a mist before the eye.
And the words of that fatal song
Come over me like a chill:
"A boy's will is the wind's will,
And the thoughts of youth are long, long thoughts."

Strange to me now are the forms I meet
When I visit the dear old town;
But the native air is pure and sweet,
And the trees that o'ershadow each well-known street,
As they balance up and down,
Are singing the beautiful song,
Are sighing and whispering still:
"A boy's will is the wind's will,
And the thoughts of youth are long, long thoughts."

And Deering's Woods are fresh and fair,
And with joy that is almost pain
My heart goes back to wander there,
And among the dreams of the days that were,
I find my lost youth again.
And the strange and beautiful song,
The groves are repeating it still:
"A boy's will is the wind's will,
And the thoughts of youth are long, long thoughts."

1855 1855

DAYBREAK

A WIND came up out of the sea,
And said, "O mists, make room for me."

It hailed the ships, and cried, "Sail on,
Ye mariners, the night is gone."

And hurried landward far away,
Crying, "Awake! it is the day."

It said unto the forest, "Shout!
Hang all your leafy banners out!"

It touched the wood-bird's folded wing,
And said, "O bird, awake and sing."

And o'er the farms, "O chanticleer,
Your clarion blow; the day is near."

It whispered to the fields of corn,
"Bow down, and hail the coming morn."

It shouted through the belfry-tower,
"Awake, O bell! proclaim the hour."

It crossed the churchyard with a sigh,
And said, "Not yet! in quiet lie."

1857 1857

SANDALPHON

Have you read in the Talmud of old,
In the Legends the Rabbins have told
Of the limitless realms of the air,
Have you read it,—the marvellous story
Of Sandalphon, the Angel of Glory,
Sandalphon, the Angel of Prayer?

How, erect, at the outermost gates
Of the City Celestial he waits,
With his feet on the ladder of light,
That, crowded with angels unnumbered,
By Jacob was seen, as he slumbered
Alone in the desert at night?

The Angels of Wind and of Fire
Chant only one hymn, and expire
With the song's irresistible stress;
Expire in their rapture and wonder,
As harp-strings are broken asunder
By music they throb to express.

But serene in the rapturous throng,
Unmoved by the rush of the song,
With eyes unimpassioned and slow,
Among the dead angels, the deathless
Sandalphon stands listening breathless
To sounds that ascend from below;—

From the spirits on earth that adore,
From the souls that entreat and implore
In the fervor and passion of prayer;
From the hearts that are broken with losses,
And weary with dragging the crosses
Too heavy for mortals to bear.

And he gathers the prayers as he stands,
And they change into flowers in his hands,
Into garlands of purple and red;
And beneath the great arch of the portal,
Through the streets of the City Immortal
Is wafted the fragrance they shed.

It is but a legend, I know,—
A fable, a phantom, a show,
Of the ancient Rabbinical lore;
Yet the old mediæval tradition,
The beautiful, strange superstition,
But haunts me and holds me the more.

When I look from my window at night,
And the welkin above is all white,
All throbbing and panting with stars,
Among them majestic is standing
Sandalphon the angel, expanding
His pinions in nebulous bars.

And the legend, I feel, is a part
Of the hunger and thirst of the heart,
The frenzy and fire of the brain,
That grasps at the fruitage forbidden,
The golden pomegranates of Eden,
To quiet its fever and pain.

1857 1858

THE COURTSHIP OF MILES STANDISH

I

MILES STANDISH

In the Old Colony days, in Plymouth the land of the Pilgrims,
To and fro in a room of his simple and primitive dwelling,
Clad in doublet and hose, and boots of Cordovan leather,
Strode, with a martial air, Miles Standish the Puritan Captain.
Buried in thought he seemed, with his hands behind him, and pausing
Ever and anon to behold his glittering weapons of warfare,
Hanging in shining array along the walls of the chamber,—
Cutlass and corselet of steel, and his trusty sword of Damascus,
Curved at the point and inscribed with its mystical Arabic sentence,
While underneath, in a corner, were fowling-piece, musket, and matchlock.
Short of stature he was, but strongly built and athletic,
Broad in the shoulders, deep-chested, with muscles and sinews of iron;
Brown as a nut was his face, but his russet beard was already
Flaked with patches of snow, as hedges sometimes in November.
Near him was seated John Alden, his friend and household companion,
Writing with diligent speed at a table of pine by the window;

Fair-haired, azure-eyed, with delicate Saxon complexion,
Having the dew of his youth, and the beauty thereof, as the captives
Whom Saint Gregory saw, and exclaimed, "Not Angles, but Angels."
Youngest of all was he of the men who came in the Mayflower.

Suddenly breaking the silence, the diligent scribe interrupting,
Spake, in the pride of his heart, Miles Standish the Captain of Plymouth.
"Look at these arms," he said, "the warlike weapons that hang here
Burnished and bright and clean, as if for parade or inspection!
This is the sword of Damascus I fought with in Flanders; this breastplate,
Well I remember the day! once saved my life in a skirmish;
Here in front you can see the very dint of the bullet
Fired point-blank at my heart by a Spanish arcabucero.
Had it not been of sheer steel, the forgotten bones of Miles Standish
Would at this moment be mould, in their grave in the Flemish morasses."
Thereupon answered John Alden, but looked not up from his writing:
"Truly the breath of the Lord hath slackened the speed of the bullet;
He in his mercy preserved you, to be our shield and our weapon!"
Still the Captain continued, unheeding the words of the stripling:
"See, how bright they are burnished, as if in an arsenal hanging;
That is because I have done it myself, and not left it to others.
Serve yourself, would you be well served, is an excellent adage;
So I take care of my arms, as you of your pens and your inkhorn.
Then, too, there are my soldiers, my great, invincible army,
Twelve men, all equipped, having each his rest and his matchlock,
Eighteen shillings a month, together with diet and pillage,
And, like Cæsar, I know the name of each of my soldiers!"
This he said with a smile, that danced in his eyes, as the sunbeams
Dance on the waves of the sea, and vanish again in a moment.
Alden laughed as he wrote, and still the Captain continued:
"Look! you can see from this window my brazen howitzer planted
High on the roof of the church, a preacher who speaks to the purpose,
Steady, straightforward, and strong, with irresistible logic,
Orthodox, flashing conviction right into the hearts of the heathen.
Now we are ready, I think, for any assault of the Indians;
Let them come, if they like, and the sooner they try it the better,—
Let them come, if they like, be it sagamore, sachem, or pow-wow,
Aspinet, Samoset, Corbitant, Squanto, or Tokamahamon!"

Long at the window he stood, and wistfully gazed on the landscape,
Washed with a cold gray mist, the vapory breath of the east-wind,
Forest and meadow and hill, and the steel-blue rim of the ocean,
Lying silent and sad, in the afternoon shadows and sunshine.
Over his countenance flitted a shadow like those on the landscape,
Gloom intermingled with light; and his voice was subdued with emotion,
Tenderness, pity, regret, as after a pause he proceeded:
"Yonder there, on the hill by the sea, lies buried Rose Standish;
Beautiful rose of love, that bloomed for me by the wayside!
She was the first to die of all who came in the Mayflower!
Green above her is growing the field of wheat we have sown there,
Better to hide from the Indian scouts the graves of our people,
Lest they should count them and see how many already have perished!"

Sadly his face he averted, and strode up and down, and was thoughtful.

Fixed to the opposite wall was a shelf of books, and among them
Prominent three, distinguished alike for bulk and for binding;
Bariffe's Artillery Guide, and the Commentaries of Cæsar
Out of the Latin translated by Arthur Goldinge of London,
And, as if guarded by these, between them was standing the Bible.
Musing a moment before them, Miles Standish paused, as if doubtful
Which of the three he should choose for his consolation and comfort,
Whether the wars of the Hebrews, the famous campaigns of the Romans,
Or the Artillery practice, designed for belligerent Christians.
Finally down from its shelf he dragged the ponderous Roman,
Seated himself at the window, and opened the book, and in silence
Turned o'er the well-worn leaves, where thumb-marks thick on the margin,
Like the trample of feet, proclaimed the battle was hottest.
Nothing was heard in the room but the hurrying pen of the stripling,
Busily writing epistles important, to go by the Mayflower,
Ready to sail on the morrow, or next day at latest, God willing!
Homeward bound with the tidings of all that terrible winter,
Letters written by Alden, and full of the name of Priscilla!
Full of the name and the fame of the Puritan maiden Priscilla!

II

LOVE AND FRIENDSHIP

Nothing was heard in the room but the hurrying pen of the stripling,
Or an occasional sigh from the laboring heart of the Captain,
Reading the marvellous words and achievements of Julius Cæsar.
After a while he exclaimed, as he smote with his hand, palm downwards,
Heavily on the page: "A wonderful man was this Cæsar!
You are a writer, and I am a fighter, but here is a fellow
Who could both write and fight, and in both was equally skilful!"
Straightway answered and spake John Alden, the comely, the youthful:
"Yes, he was equally skilled, as you say, with his pen and his weapons.
Somewhere have I read, but where I forget, he could dictate
Seven letters at once, at the same time writing his memoirs."
"Truly," continued the Captain, not heeding or hearing the other,
"Truly a wonderful man was Caius Julius Cæsar!
Better be first, he said, in a little Iberian village,
Than be second in Rome, and I think he was right when he said it.
Twice was he married before he was twenty, and many times after;
Battles five hundred he fought, and a thousand cities he conquered;
He, too, fought in Flanders, as he himself has recorded;
Finally he was stabbed by his friend, the orator Brutus!
Now, do you know what he did on a certain occasion in Flanders,
When the rear-guard of his army retreated, the front giving way too,
And the immortal Twelfth Legion was crowded so closely together
There was no room for their swords? Why, he seized a shield from a soldier,
Put himself straight at the head of his troops, and commanded the captains,
Calling on each by his name, to order forward the ensigns;
Then to widen the ranks, and give more room for their weapons;
So he won the day, the battle of something-or-other.
That's what I always say; if you wish a thing to be well done,
You must do it yourself, you must not leave it to others!"

All was silent again; the Captain continued his reading.
Nothing was heard in the room but the hurrying pen of the stripling
Writing epistles important to go next day by the Mayflower,
Filled with the name and the fame of the Puritan maiden Priscilla;
Every sentence began or closed with the name of Priscilla,
Till the treacherous pen, to which he confided the secret,
Strove to betray it by singing and shouting the name of Priscilla!
Finally closing his book, with a bang of the ponderous cover,
Sudden and loud as the sound of a soldier grounding his musket,
Thus to the young man spake Miles Standish the Captain of Plymouth:
"When you have finished your work, I have something important to tell you.
Be not however in haste; I can wait; I shall not be impatient!"
Straightway Alden replied, as he folded the last of his letters,
Pushing his papers aside, and giving respectful attention:
"Speak; for whenever you speak, I am always ready to listen,
Always ready to hear whatever pertains to Miles Standish."
Thereupon answered the Captain, embarrassed, and culling his phrases:
"'Tis not good for a man to be alone, say the Scriptures.
This I have said before, and again and again I repeat it;
Every hour in the day, I think it, and feel it, and say it.
Since Rose Standish died, my life has been weary and dreary;
Sick at heart have I been, beyond the healing of friendship;
Oft in my lonely hours have I thought of the maiden Priscilla.
She is alone in the world; her father and mother and brother
Died in the winter together; I saw her going and coming,
Now to the grave of the dead, and now to the bed of the dying,
Patient, courageous, and strong, and said to myself, that if ever
There were angels on earth, as there are angels in heaven,
Two have I seen and known; and the angel whose name is Priscilla
Holds in my desolate life the place which the other abandoned.
Long have I cherished the thought, but never have dared to reveal it,
Being a coward in this, though valiant enough for the most part.
Go to the damsel Priscilla, the loveliest maiden of Plymouth,
Say that a blunt old Captain, a man not of words but of actions,
Offers his hand and his heart, the hand and heart of a soldier.
Not in these words, you know, but this in short is my meaning;
I am a maker of war, and not a maker of phrases.
You, who are bred as a scholar, can say it in elegant language,
Such as you read in your books of the pleadings and wooings of lovers,
Such as you think best adapted to win the heart of a maiden."

When he had spoken, John Alden, the fair-haired, taciturn stripling,
All aghast at his words, surprised, embarrassed, bewildered,
Trying to mask his dismay by treating the subject with lightness,
Trying to smile, and yet feeling his heart stand still in his bosom,
Just as a timepiece stops in a house that is stricken by lightning,
Thus made answer and spake, or rather stammered than answered:
"Such a message as that, I am sure I should mangle and mar it;
If you would have it well done,—I am only repeating your maxim,—
You must do it yourself, you must not leave it to others!"
But with the air of a man whom nothing can turn from his purpose,

Gravely shaking his head, made answer the Captain of Plymouth:
"Truly the maxim is good, and I do not mean to gainsay it;
But we must use it discreetly, and not waste powder for nothing.
Now, as I said before, I was never a maker of phrases.
I can march up to a fortress and summon the place to surrender,
But march up to a woman with such a proposal, I dare not.
I'm not afraid of bullets, nor shot from the mouth of a cannon,
But of a thundering 'No!' point-blank from the mouth of a woman,
That I confess I'm afraid of, nor am I ashamed to confess it!
So you must grant my request, for you are an elegant scholar,
Having the graces of speech, and skill in the turning of phrases."
Taking the hand of his friend, who still was reluctant and doubtful,
Holding it long in his own, and pressing it kindly, he added:
"Though I have spoken thus lightly, yet deep is the feeling that prompts me;
Surely you cannot refuse what I ask in the name of our friendship!"
Then made answer John Alden: "The name of friendship is sacred;
What you demand in that name, I have not the power to deny you!"
So the strong will prevailed, subduing and moulding the gentler,
Friendship prevailed over love, and Alden went on his errand.

III

THE LOVER'S ERRAND

So the strong will prevailed, and Alden went on his errand,
Out of the street of the village, and into the paths of the forest,
Into the tranquil woods, where bluebirds and robins were building
Towns in the populous trees, with hanging gardens of verdure,
Peaceful, aerial cities of joy and affection and freedom.
All around him was calm, but within him commotion and conflict,
Love contending with friendship, and self with each generous impulse.
To and fro in his breast his thoughts were heaving and dashing,
As in a foundering ship, with every roll of the vessel,
Washes the bitter sea, the merciless surge of the ocean!
"Must I relinquish it all," he cried with a wild lamentation,—
"Must I relinquish it all, the joy, the hope, the illusion?
Was it for this I have loved, and waited, and worshipped in silence?
Was it for this I have followed the flying feet and the shadow
Over the wintry sea, to the desolate shores of New England?
Truly the heart is deceitful, and out of its depths of corruption
Rise, like an exhalation, the misty phantoms of passion;
Angels of light they seem, but are only delusions of Satan.
All is clear to me now; I feel it, I see it distinctly!
This is the hand of the Lord; it is laid upon me in anger,
For I have followed too much the heart's desires and devices,
Worshipping Astaroth blindly, and impious idols of Baal.
This is the cross I must bear; the sin and the swift retribution."

So through the Plymouth woods John Alden went on his errand;
Crossing the brook at the ford, where it brawled over pebble and shallow,
Gathering still, as he went, the May-flowers blooming around him,
Fragrant, filling the air with a strange and wonderful sweetness,
Children lost in the woods, and covered with leaves in their slumber.
"Puritan flowers," he said, "and the type of Puritan maidens,

Modest and simple and sweet, the very type of Priscilla!
So I will take them to her; to Priscilla the Mayflower of Plymouth,
Modest and simple and sweet, as a parting gift will I take them;
Breathing their silent farewells, as they fade and wither and perish,
Soon to be thrown away as is the heart of the giver."
So through the Plymouth woods John Alden went on his errand;
Came to an open space, and saw the disk of the ocean,
Sailless, sombre and cold with the comfortless breath of the east-wind;
Saw the new-built house, and people at work in a meadow;
Heard, as he drew near the door, the musical voice of Priscilla
Singing the hundredth Psalm, the grand old Puritan anthem,
Music that Luther sang to the sacred words of the Psalmist,
Full of the breath of the Lord, consoling and comforting many.
Then, as he opened the door, he beheld the form of the maiden
Seated beside her wheel, and the carded wool like a snow-drift
Piled at her knee, her white hands feeding the ravenous spindle,
While with her foot on the treadle she guided the wheel in its motion.
Open wide on her lap lay the well-worn psalm-book of Ainsworth,
Printed in Amsterdam, the words and the music together,
Rough-hewn, angular notes, like stones in the wall of a churchyard,
Darkened and overhung by the running vine of the verses.
Such was the book from whose pages she sang the old Puritan anthem,
She, the Puritan girl, in the solitude of the forest,
Making the humble house and the modest apparel of homespun
Beautiful with her beauty, and rich with the wealth of her being!
Over him rushed, like a wind that is keen and cold and relentless,
Thoughts of what might have been, and the weight and woe of his errand;
All the dreams that had faded, and all the hopes that had vanished,
All his life henceforth a dreary and tenantless mansion,
Haunted by vain regrets, and pallid, sorrowful faces.
Still he said to himself, and almost fiercely he said it,
"Let not him that putteth his hand to the plough look backwards;
Though the ploughshare cut through the flowers of life to its fountains,
Though it pass o'er the graves of the dead and the hearths of the living,
It is the will of the Lord; and his mercy endureth forever!"

So he entered the house: and the hum of the wheel and the singing
Suddenly ceased; for Priscilla, aroused by his step on the threshold,
Rose as he entered, and gave him her hand, in signal of welcome,
Saying, "I knew it was you, when I heard your step in the passage;
For I was thinking of you, as I sat there singing and spinning."
Awkward and dumb with delight, that a thought of him had been mingled
Thus in the sacred psalm, that came from the heart of the maiden,
Silent before her he stood, and gave her the flowers for an answer,
Finding no words for his thought. He remembered that day in the winter,
After the first great snow, when he broke a path from the village,
Reeling and plunging along through the drifts that encumbered the doorway,
Stamping the snow from his feet as he entered the house, and Priscilla
Laughed at his snowy locks, and gave him a seat by the fireside,
Grateful and pleased to know he had thought of her in the snow-storm.
Had he but spoken then! perhaps not in vain had he spoken;

Now it was all too late; the golden moment had vanished!
So he stood there abashed, and gave her the flowers for an answer.

Then they sat down and talked of the birds and the beautiful Spring-time,
Talked of their friends at home, and the May-flower that sailed on the morrow.
"I have been thinking all day," said gently the Puritan maiden,
"Dreaming all night, and thinking all day, of the hedge-rows of England,—
They are in blossom now, and the country is all like a garden:
Thinking of lanes and fields, and the song of the lark and the linnet,
Seeing the village street, and familiar faces of neighbors
Going about as of old, and stopping to gossip together,
And, at the end of the street, the village church, with the ivy
Climbing the old gray tower, and the quiet graves in the churchyard.
Kind are the people I live with, and dear to me my religion;
Still my heart is so sad, that I wish myself back in Old England.
You will say it is wrong, but I cannot help it: I almost
Wish myself back in Old England, I feel so lonely and wretched."

Thereupon answered the youth: "Indeed I do not condemn you;
Stouter hearts than a woman's have quailed in this terrible winter.
Yours is tender and trusting, and needs a stronger to lean on;
So I have come to you now, with an offer and proffer of marriage
Made by a good man and true, Miles Standish the Captain of Plymouth!"

Thus he delivered his message, the dexterous writer of letters,—
Did not embellish the theme, nor array it in beautiful phrases,
But came straight to the point, and blurted it out like a school-boy;
Even the Captain himself could hardly have said it more bluntly.
Mute with amazement and sorrow, Priscilla the Puritan maiden
Looked into Alden's face, her eyes dilated with wonder,
Feeling his words like a blow, that stunned her and rendered her speechless;
Till at length she exclaimed, interrupting the ominous silence:
"If the great Captain of Plymouth is so very eager to wed me,
Why does he not come himself, and take the trouble to woo me?
If I am not worth the wooing, I surely am not worth the winning!"
Then John Alden began explaining and smoothing the matter,
Making it worse as he went, by saying the Captain was busy,—
Had no time for such things—such things! the words grating harshly
Fell on the ear of Priscilla; and swift as a flash she made answer:
"Has he no time for such things, as you call it, before he is married,
Would he be likely to find it, or make it, after the wedding?
That is the way with you men; you don't understand us, you cannot.
When you have made up your minds, after thinking of this one and that one,
Choosing, selecting, rejecting, comparing one with another,
Then you make known your desire, with abrupt and sudden avowal,
And are offended and hurt, and indignant perhaps, that a woman
Does not respond at once to a love that she never suspected,
Does not attain at a bound the height to which you have been climbing.
This is not right nor just: for surely a woman's affection
Is not a thing to be asked for, and had for only the asking.
When one is truly in love, one not only says it, but shows it.
Had he but waited awhile, had he only showed that he loved me,

Even this Captain of yours—who knows?—at last might have won me,
Old and rough as he is; but now it never can happen."

Still John Alden went on, unheeding the words of Priscilla,
Urging the suit of his friend, explaining, persuading, expanding;
Spoke of his courage and skill, and of all his battles in Flanders,
How with the people of God he had chosen to suffer affliction;
How, in return for his zeal, they had made him Captain of Plymouth;
He was a gentleman born, could trace his pedigree plainly
Back to Hugh Standish of Duxbury Hall, in Lancashire, England,
Who was the son of Ralph, and the grandson of Thurston de Standish;
Heir unto vast estates, of which he was basely defrauded,
Still bore the family arms, and had for his crest a cock argent,
Combed and wattled gules, and all the rest of the blazon.
He was a man of honor, of noble and generous nature;
Though he was rough, he was kindly; she knew how during the winter
He had attended the sick, with a hand as gentle as woman's;
Somewhat hasty and hot, he could not deny it, and headstrong,
Stern as a soldier might be, but hearty, and placable always,
Not to be laughed at and scorned, because he was little of stature;
For he was great of heart, magnanimous, courtly, courageous;
Any woman in Plymouth, nay, any woman in England,
Might be happy and proud to be called the wife of Miles Standish!

But as he warmed and glowed, in his simple and eloquent language,
Quite forgetful of self, and full of the praise of his rival,
Archly the maiden smiled, and, with eyes overrunning with laughter,
Said, in a tremulous voice, "Why don't you speak for yourself, John?"

IV

JOHN ALDEN

Into the open air John Alden, perplexed and bewildered,
Rushed like a man insane, and wandered alone by the sea-side;
Paced up and down the sands, and bared his head to the east-wind,
Cooling his heated brow, and the fire and fever within him.
Slowly as out of the heavens, with apocalyptical splendors,
Sank the City of God, in the vision of John the Apostle,
So, with its cloudy walls of chrysolite, jasper, and sapphire,
Sank the broad red sun, and over its turrets uplifted
Glimmered the golden reed of the angel who measured the city.

"Welcome, O wind of the East!" he exclaimed in his wild exultation,
"Welcome, O wind of the East, from the caves of the misty Atlantic!
Blowing o'er fields of dulse, and measureless meadows of sea-grass,
Blowing o'er rocky wastes, and the grottoes and gardens of ocean!
Lay thy cold, moist hand on my burning forehead, and wrap me
Close in thy garments of mist, to allay the fever within me!"

Like an awakened conscience, the sea was moaning and tossing,
Beating remorseful and loud the mutable sands of the sea-shore.
Fierce in his soul was the struggle and tumult of passions contending;
Love triumphant and crowned, and friendship wounded and bleeding,
Passionate cries of desire, and importunate pleadings of duty!

"Is it my fault," he said, "that the maiden has chosen between us?
Is it my fault that he failed,—my fault that I am the victor?"
Then within him there thundered a voice, like the voice of the Prophet:
"It hath displeased the Lord!"—and he thought of David's transgression,
Bathsheba's beautiful face, and his friend in the front of the battle!
Shame and confusion of guilt, and abasement and self-condemnation,
Overwhelmed him at once; and he cried in the deepest contrition:
"It hath displeased the Lord! It is the temptation of Satan!"

Then, uplifting his head, he looked at the sea, and beheld there
Dimly the shadowy form of the Mayflower riding at anchor,
Rocked on the rising tide, and ready to sail on the morrow;
Heard the voices of men through the mist, the rattle of cordage
Thrown on the deck, the shouts of the mate, and the sailors' "Ay, ay, Sir!"
Clear and distinct, but not loud, in the dripping air of the twilight.
Still for a moment he stood, and listened, and stared at the vessel,
Then went hurriedly on, as one who, seeing a phantom,
Stops, then quickens his pace, and follows the beckoning shadow.
"Yes, it is plain to me now," he murmured; "the hand of the Lord is
Leading me out of the land of darkness, the bondage of error,
Through the sea, that shall lift the walls of its waters around me,
Hiding me, cutting me off, from the cruel thoughts that pursue me.
Back will I go o'er the ocean, this dreary land will abandon,
Her whom I may not love, and him whom my heart has offended.
Better to be in my grave in the green old churchyard in England,
Close by my mother's side, and among the dust of my kindred;
Better be dead and forgotten, than living in shame and dishonor;
Sacred and safe and unseen, in the dark of the narrow chamber
With me my secret shall lie, like a buried jewel that glimmers
Bright on the hand that is dust, in the chambers of silence and darkness,—
Yes, as the marriage ring of the great espousal hereafter!"

Thus as he spake, he turned, in the strength of his strong resolution,
Leaving behind him the shore, and hurried along in the twilight,
Through the congenial gloom of the forest silent and sombre,
Till he beheld the lights in the seven houses of Plymouth,
Shining like seven stars in the dusk and mist of the evening.
Soon he entered his door, and found the redoubtable Captain
Sitting alone, and absorbed in the martial pages of Cæsar,
Fighting some great campaign in Hainault or Brabant or Flanders.
"Long have you been on your errand," he said with a cheery demeanor,
Even as one who is waiting an answer, and fears not the issue.
"Not far off is the house, although the woods are between us;
But you have lingered so long, that while you were going and coming
I have fought ten battles and sacked and demolished a city.
Come, sit down, and in order relate to me all that has happened."

Then John Alden spake, and related the wondrous adventure,
From beginning to end, minutely, just as it happened;
How he had seen Priscilla, and how he had sped in his courtship,
Only smoothing a little, and softening down her refusal.
But when he came at length to the words Priscilla had spoken,

Words so tender and cruel: "Why don't you speak for yourself, John?"
Up leaped the Captain of Plymouth, and stamped on the floor, till his armor
Clanged on the wall, where it hung, with a sound of sinister omen.
All his pent-up wrath burst forth in a sudden explosion,
E'en as a hand-grenade, that scatters destruction around it.
Wildly he shouted, and loud: "John Alden! you have betrayed me!
Me, Miles Standish, your friend! have supplanted, defrauded, betrayed me!
One of my ancestors ran his sword through the heart of Wat Tyler;
Who shall prevent me from running my own through the heart of a traitor?
Yours is the greater treason, for yours is a treason to friendship!
You, who lived under my roof, whom I cherished and loved as a brother;
You, who have fed at my board, and drunk at my cup, to whose keeping
I have intrusted my honor, my thoughts the most sacred and secret,—
You too, Brutus! ah woe to the name of friendship hereafter!
Brutus was Cæsar's friend, and you were mine, but henceforward
Let there be nothing between us save war, and implacable hatred!"

So spake the Captain of Plymouth, and strode about in the chamber,
Chafing and choking with rage; like cords were the veins on his temples.
But in the midst of his anger a man appeared at the doorway,
Bringing in uttermost haste a message of urgent importance,
Rumors of danger and war and hostile incursions of Indians!
Straightway the Captain paused, and, without further question or parley,
Took from the nail on the wall his sword with its scabbard of iron,
Buckled the belt round his waist, and, frowning fiercely, departed.
Alden was left alone. He heard the clank of the scabbard
Growing fainter and fainter, and dying away in the distance.
Then he arose from his seat, and looked forth into the darkness,
Felt the cool air blow on his cheek that was hot with the insult,
Lifted his eyes to the heavens, and, folding his hands as in childhood,
Prayed in the silence of night to the Father who seeth in secret.

Meanwhile the choleric Captain strode wrathful away to the council,
Found it already assembled, impatiently waiting his coming;
Men in the middle of life, austere and grave in deportment,
Only one of them old, the hill that was nearest to heaven,
Covered with snow, but erect, the excellent Elder of Plymouth.
God had sifted three kingdoms to find the wheat for his planting,
Then had sifted the wheat, as the living seed of a nation;
So say the chronicles old, and such is the faith of the people!
Near them was standing an Indian, in attitude stern and defiant,
Naked down to the waist, and grim and ferocious in aspect;
While on the table before them was lying unopened a Bible,
Ponderous, bound in leather, brass-studded, printed in Holland,
And beside it outstretched the skin of a rattlesnake glittered,
Filled, like a quiver, with arrows; a signal and challenge of warfare,
Brought by the Indian, and speaking with arrowy tongues of defiance.
This Miles Standish beheld, as he entered, and heard them debating
What were an answer befitting the hostile message and menace,
Talking of this and of that, contriving, suggesting, objecting;
One voice only for peace, and that the voice of the Elder,
Judging it wise and well that some at least were converted,

Rather than any were slain, for this was but Christian behavior!
Then out spake Miles Standish, the stalwart Captain of Plymouth,
Muttering deep in his throat, for his voice was husky with anger,
"What! do you mean to make war with milk and the water of roses?
Is it to shoot red squirrels you have your howitzer planted
There on the roof of the church, or is it to shoot red devils?
Truly the only tongue that is understood by a savage
Must be the tongue of fire that speaks from the mouth of the cannon!"
Thereupon answered and said the excellent Elder of Plymouth,
Somewhat amazed and alarmed at this irreverent language:
"Not so thought St. Paul, nor yet the other Apostles;
Not from the cannon's mouth were the tongues of fire they spake with!"
But unheeded fell this mild rebuke on the Captain,
Who had advanced to the table, and thus continued discoursing:
"Leave this matter to me, for to me by right it pertaineth.
War is a terrible trade; but in the cause that is righteous,
Sweet is the smell of powder; and thus I answer the challenge!"

Then from the rattlesnake's skin, with a sudden, contemptuous gesture,
Jerking the Indian arrows, he filled it with powder and bullets
Full to the very jaws, and handed it back to the savage,
Saying, in thundering tones: "Here, take it! this is your answer!"
Silently out of the room then glided the glistening savage,
Bearing the serpent's skin, and seeming himself like a serpent,
Winding his sinuous way in the dark to the depths of the forest.

V

THE SAILING OF THE MAYFLOWER

JUST in the gray of the dawn, as the mists uprose from the meadows,
There was a stir and a sound in the slumbering village of Plymouth;
Clanging and clicking of arms, and the order imperative, "Forward!"
Given in tone suppressed, a tramp of feet, and then silence.
Figures ten, in the mist, marched slowly out of the village.
Standish the stalwart it was, with eight of his valorous army,
Led by their Indian guide, by Hobomok, friend of the white men,
Northward marching to quell the sudden revolt of the savage.
Giants they seemed in the mist, or the mighty men of King David;
Giants in heart they were, who believed in God and the Bible,—
Ay, who believed in the smiting of Midianites and Philistines.
Over them gleamed far off the crimson banners of morning;
Under them loud on the sands, the serried billows, advancing,
Fired along the line, and in regular order retreated.

Many a mile had they marched, when at length the village of Plymouth
Woke from its sleep, and arose, intent on its manifold labors.
Sweet was the air and soft; and slowly the smoke from the chimneys
Rose over roofs of thatch, and pointed steadily eastward;
Men came forth from the doors, and paused and talked of the weather,
Said that the wind had changed, and was blowing fair for the Mayflower;
Talked of their Captain's departure, and all the dangers that menaced,
He being gone, the town, and what should be done in his absence.
Merrily sang the birds, and the tender voices of women

Consecrated with hymns the common cares of the household.
Out of the sea rose the sun, and the billows rejoiced at his coming;
Beautiful were his feet on the purple tops of the mountains;
Beautiful on the sails of the Mayflower riding at anchor,
Battered and blackened and worn by all the storms of the winter.
Loosely against her masts was hanging and flapping her canvas,
Rent by so many gales, and patched by the hands of the sailors.
Suddenly from her side, as the sun rose over the ocean,
Darted a puff of smoke, and floated seaward; anon rang
Loud over field and forest the cannon's roar, and the echoes
Heard and repeated the sound, the signal-gun of departure!
Ah! but with louder echoes replied the hearts of the people!
Meekly, in voices subdued, the chapter was read from the Bible,
Meekly the prayer was begun, but ended in fervent entreaty!
Then from their houses in haste came forth the Pilgrims of Plymouth,
Men and women and children, all hurrying down to the sea-shore,
Eager, with tearful eyes, to say farewell to the Mayflower,
Homeward bound o'er the sea, and leaving them here in the desert.

Foremost among them was Alden. All night he had lain without slumber,
Turning and tossing about in the heat and unrest of his fever.
He had beheld Miles Standish, who came back late from the council,
Stalking into the room, and heard him mutter and murmur;
Sometimes it seemed a prayer, and sometimes it sounded like swearing.
Once he had come to the bed, and stood there a moment in silence;
Then he had turned away, and said: "I will not awake him;
Let him sleep on, it is best; for what is the use of more talking!"
Then he extinguished the light, and threw himself down on his pallet,
Dressed as he was, and ready to start at the break of the morning,—
Covered himself with the cloak he had worn in his campaigns in Flanders,—
Slept as a soldier sleeps in his bivouac, ready for action.
But with the dawn he arose; in the twilight Alden beheld him
Put on his corselet of steel, and all the rest of his armor,
Buckle about his waist his trusty blade of Damascus,
Take from the corner his musket, and so stride out of the chamber.
Often the heart of the youth had burned and yearned to embrace him,
Often his lips had essayed to speak, imploring for pardon;
All the old friendship came back, with its tender and grateful emotions;
But his pride overmastered the nobler nature within him,—
Pride, and the sense of his wrong, and the burning fire of the insult.
So he beheld his friend departing in anger, but spake not,
Saw him go forth to danger, perhaps to death, and he spake not!
Then he arose from his bed, and heard what the people were saying,
Joined in the talk at the door, with Stephen and Richard and Gilbert,
Joined in the morning prayer, and in the reading of Scripture,
And, with the others, in haste went hurrying down to the sea-shore,
Down to the Plymouth Rock, that had been to their feet as a doorstep
Into a world unknown,—the corner-stone of a nation!

There with his boat was the Master, already a little impatient
Lest he should lose the tide, or the wind might shift to the eastward,
Square-built, hearty, and strong, with an odor of ocean about him,

Speaking with this one and that, and cramming letters and parcels
Into his pockets capacious, and messages mingled together
Into his narrow brain, till at last he was wholly bewildered.
Nearer the boat stood Alden, with one foot placed on the gunwale,
One still firm on the rock, and talking at times with the sailors,
Seated erect on the thwarts, all ready and eager for starting.
He too was eager to go, and thus put an end to his anguish,
Thinking to fly from despair, that swifter than keel is or canvas,
Thinking to drown in the sea the ghost that would rise and pursue him.
But as he gazed on the crowd, he beheld the form of Priscilla
Standing dejected among them, unconscious of all that was passing.
Fixed were her eyes upon his, as if she divined his intention,
Fixed with a look so sad, so reproachful, imploring, and patient,
That with a sudden revulsion his heart recoiled from its purpose,
As from the verge of a crag, where one step more is destruction.
Strange is the heart of man, with its quick, mysterious instincts!
Strange is the life of man, and fatal or fated are moments,
Whereupon turn, as on hinges, the gates of the wall adamantine!
"Here I remain!" he exclaimed, as he looked at the heavens above him,
Thanking the Lord whose breath had scattered the mist and the madness,
Wherein, blind and lost, to death he was staggering headlong.
"Yonder snow-white cloud, that floats in the ether above me,
Seems like a hand that is pointing and beckoning over the ocean.
There is another hand, that is not so spectral and ghost-like,
Holding me, drawing me back, and clasping mine for protection.
Float, O hand of cloud, and vanish away in the ether!
Roll thyself up like a fist, to threaten and daunt me; I heed not
Either your warning or menace, or any omen of evil!
There is no land so sacred, no air so pure and so wholesome,
As is the air she breathes, and the soil that is pressed by her footsteps.
Here for her sake will I stay, and like an invisible presence
Hover around her forever, protecting, supporting her weakness;
Yes! as my foot was the first that stepped on this rock at the landing,
So, with the blessing of God, shall it be the last at the leaving!"

Meanwhile the Master alert, but with dignified air and important,
Scanning with watchful eye the tide and the wind and the weather,
Walked about on the sands, and the people crowded around him
Saying a few last words, and enforcing his careful remembrance.
Then, taking each by the hand, as if he were grasping a tiller,
Into the boat he sprang, and in haste shoved off to his vessel,
Glad in his heart to get rid of all this worry and flurry,
Glad to be gone from a land of sand and sickness and sorrow,
Short allowance of victual, and plenty of nothing but Gospel!
Lost in the sound of the oars was the last farewell of the Pilgrims.
O strong hearts and true! not one went back in the Mayflower!
No, not one looked back, who had set his hand to this ploughing!

Soon were heard on board the shouts and songs of the sailors
Heaving the windlass round, and hoisting the ponderous anchor.
Then the yards were braced, and all sails set to the west-wind,

Blowing steady and strong; and the Mayflower sailed from the harbor,
Rounded the point of the Gurnet, and leaving far to the southward
Island and cape of sand, and the Field of the First Encounter,
Took the wind on her quarter, and stood for the open Atlantic,
Borne on the send of the sea, and the swelling hearts of the Pilgrims.

Long in silence they watched the receding sail of the vessel,
Much endeared to them all, as something living and human;
Then, as if filled with the spirit, and wrapt in a vision prophetic,
Baring his hoary head, the excellent Elder of Plymouth
Said, "Let us pray!" and they prayed, and thanked the Lord and took courage.
Mournfully sobbed the waves at the base of the rock, and above them
Bowed and whispered the wheat on the hill of death, and their kindred
Seemed to awake in their graves, and to join in the prayer that they uttered.
Sun-illumined and white, on the eastern verge of the ocean
Gleamed the departing sail, like a marble slab in a graveyard;
Buried beneath it lay forever all hope of escaping.
Lo! as they turned to depart, they saw the form of an Indian,
Watching them from the hill; but while they spake with each other,
Pointing with outstretched hands, and saying, "Look!" he had vanished.
So they returned to their homes; but Alden lingered a little,
Musing alone on the shore, and watching the wash of the billows
Round the base of the rock, and the sparkle and flash of the sunshine,
Like the spirit of God, moving visibly over the waters.

VI

PRISCILLA

Thus for a while he stood, and mused by the shore of the ocean,
Thinking of many things, and most of all of Priscilla;
And as if thought had the power to draw to itself, like the loadstone,
Whatsoever it touches, by subtile laws of its nature,
Lo! as he turned to depart, Priscilla was standing beside him.

"Are you so much offended, you will not speak to me?" said she.
"Am I so much to blame, that yesterday, when you were pleading
Warmly the cause of another, my heart, impulsive and wayward,
Pleaded your own, and spake out, forgetful perhaps of decorum?
Certainly you can forgive me for speaking so frankly, for saying
What I ought not to have said, yet now I can never unsay it;
For there are moments in life, when the heart is so full of emotion,
That if by chance it be shaken, or into its depths like a pebble
Drops some careless word, it overflows, and its secret,
Spilt on the ground like water, can never be gathered together.
Yesterday I was shocked, when I heard you speak of Miles Standish,
Praising his virtues, transforming his very defects into virtues,
Praising his courage and strength, and even his fighting in Flanders,
As if by fighting alone you could win the heart of a woman,
Quite overlooking yourself and the rest, in exalting your hero.
Therefore I spake as I did, by an irresistible impulse.
You will forgive me, I hope, for the sake of the friendship between us,
Which is too true and too sacred to be so easily broken!"

Thereupon answered John Alden, the scholar, the friend of Miles Standish:
"I was not angry with you, with myself alone I was angry,
Seeing how badly I managed the matter I had in my keeping."
"No!" interrupted the maiden, with answer prompt and decisive;
"No; you were angry with me, for speaking so frankly and freely.
It was wrong, I acknowledge; for it is the fate of a woman
Long to be patient and silent, to wait like a ghost that is speechless,
Till some questioning voice dissolves the spell of its silence.
Hence is the inner life of so many suffering women
Sunless and silent and deep, like subterranean rivers
Running through caverns of darkness, unheard, unseen, and unfruitful,
Chafing their channels of stone, with endless and profitless murmurs."
Thereupon answered John Alden, the young man, the lover of women:
"Heaven forbid it, Priscilla; and truly they seem to me always
More like the beautiful rivers that watered the garden of Eden,
More like the river Euphrates, through deserts of Havilah flowing,
Filling the land with delight, and memories sweet of the garden!"
"Ah, by these words, I can see," again interrupted the maiden,
"How very little you prize me, or care for what I am saying.
When from the depths of my heart, in pain and with secret misgiving,
Frankly I speak to you, asking for sympathy only and kindness,
Straightway you take up my words, that are plain and direct and in earnest,
Turn them away from their meaning, and answer with flattering phrases.
This is not right, is not just, is not true to the best that is in you;
For I know and esteem you, and feel that your nature is noble,
Lifting mine up to a higher, a more ethereal level.
Therefore I value your friendship, and feel it perhaps the more keenly
If you say aught that implies I am only as one among many,
If you make use of those common and complimentary phrases
Most men think so fine, in dealing and speaking with women,
But which women reject as insipid, if not as insulting."

Mute and amazed was Alden; and listened and looked at Priscilla,
Thinking he never had seen her more fair, more divine in her beauty.
He who but yesterday pleaded so glibly the cause of another,
Stood there embarrassed and silent, and seeking in vain for an answer.
So the maiden went on, and little divined or imagined
What was at work in his heart, that made him so awkward and speechless.
"Let us, then, be what we are, and speak what we think, and in all things
Keep ourselves loyal to truth, and the sacred professions of friendship.
It is no secret I tell you, nor am I ashamed to declare it:
I have liked to be with you, to see you, to speak with you always.
So I was hurt at your words, and a little affronted to hear you
Urge me to marry your friend, though he were the Captain Miles Standish.
For I must tell you the truth: much more to me is your friendship
Than all the love he could give, were he twice the hero you think him."
Then she extended her hand, and Alden, who eagerly grasped it,
Felt all the wounds in his heart, that were aching and bleeding so sorely,
Healed by the touch of that hand, and he said, with a voice full of feeling:
"Yes, we must ever be friends; and of all who offer you friendship
Let me be ever the first, the truest, the nearest and dearest!"

Casting a farewell look at the glimmering sail of the Mayflower,
Distant, but still in sight, and sinking below the horizon,
Homeward together they walked, with a strange, indefinite feeling,
That all the rest had departed and left them alone in the desert.
But, as they went through the fields in the blessing and smile of the sunshine,
Lighter grew their hearts, and Priscilla said very archly:
"Now that our terrible Captain has gone in pursuit of the Indians,
Where he is happier far than he would be commanding a household,
You may speak boldly, and tell me of all that happened between you,
When you returned last night, and said how ungrateful you found me."
Thereupon answered John Alden, and told her the whole of the story,—
Told her his own despair, and the direful wrath of Miles Standish.
Whereat the maiden smiled, and said between laughing and earnest,
"He is a little chimney, and heated hot in a moment!"
But as he gently rebuked her, and told her how he had suffered,—
How he had even determined to sail that day in the Mayflower,
And had remained for her sake, on hearing the dangers that threatened,—
All her manner was changed, and she said with a faltering accent,
"Truly I thank you for this: how good you have been to me always!"

Thus, as a pilgrim devout, who toward Jerusalem journeys,
Taking three steps in advance, and one reluctantly backward,
Urged by importunate zeal, and withheld by pangs of contrition;
Slowly but steadily onward, receding yet ever advancing,
Journeyed this Puritan youth to the Holy Land of his longings,
Urged by the fervor of love, and withheld by remorseful misgivings.

VII

THE MARCH OF MILES STANDISH

Meanwhile the stalwart Miles Standish was marching steadily northward,
Winding through forest and swamp, and along the trend of the sea-shore,
All day long, with hardly a halt, the fire of his anger
Burning and crackling within, and the sulphurous odor of powder
Seeming more sweet to his nostrils than all the scents of the forest.
Silent and moody he went, and much he revolved his discomfort;
He who was used to success, and to easy victories always,
Thus to be flouted, rejected, and laughed to scorn by a maiden,
Thus to be mocked and betrayed by the friend whom most he had trusted!
Ah! 'twas too much to be borne, and he fretted and chafed in his armor!

"I alone am to blame," he muttered, "for mine was the folly.
What has a rough old soldier, grown grim and gray in the harness,
Used to the camp and its ways, to do with the wooing of maidens?
'Twas but a dream,—let it pass,—let it vanish like so many others!
What I thought was a flower, is only a weed and is worthless;
Out of my heart will I pluck it, and throw it away, and henceforward
Be but a fighter of battles, a lover and wooer of dangers!"
Thus he revolved in his mind his sorry defeat and discomfort,
While he was marching by day or lying at night in the forest,
Looking up at the trees, and the constellations beyond them.

After a three days' march he came to an Indian encampment
Pitched on the edge of a meadow, between the sea and the forest;
Women at work by the tents, and warriors, horrid with war-paint,

Seated about a fire, and smoking and talking together;
Who, when they saw from afar the sudden approach of the white men,
Saw the flash of the sun on breastplate and sabre and musket,
Straightway leaped to their feet, and two, from among them advancing,
Came to parley with Standish, and offer him furs as a present;
Friendship was in their looks, but in their hearts there was hatred.
Braves of the tribe were these, and brothers, gigantic in stature,
Huge as Goliath of Gath, or the terrible Og, king of Bashan;
One was Pecksuot named, and the other was called Wattawamat.
Round their necks were suspended their knives in scabbards of wampum,
Two-edged, trenchant knives, with points as sharp as a needle.
Other arms had they none, for they were cunning and crafty.
"Welcome, English!" they said,—these words they had learned from the traders
Touching at times on the coast, to barter and chaffer for peltries.
Then in their native tongue they began to parley with Standish,
Through his guide and interpreter, Hobomok, friend of the white man,
Begging for blankets and knives, but mostly for muskets and powder,
Kept by the white man, they said, concealed, with the plague, in his cellars,
Ready to be let loose, and destroy his brother the red man!
But when Standish refused, and said he would give them the Bible,
Suddenly changing their tone, they began to boast and to bluster.
Then Wattawamat advanced with a stride in front of the other,
And, with a lofty demeanor, thus vauntingly spake to the Captain:
"Now Wattawamat can see, by the fiery eyes of the Captain,
Angry is he in his heart; but the heart of the brave Wattawamat
Is not afraid at the sight. He was not born of a woman,
But on a mountain at night, from an oak-tree riven by lightning,
Forth he sprang at a bound, with all his weapons about him,
Shouting, 'Who is there here to fight with the brave Wattawamat?' "
Then he unsheathed his knife, and, whetting the blade on his left hand,
Held it aloft and displayed a woman's face on the handle;
Saying, with bitter expression and look of sinister meaning:
"I have another at home, with the face of a man on the handle;
By and by they shall marry; and there will be plenty of children!"

Then stood Pecksuot forth, self-vaunting, insulting Miles Standish:
While with his fingers he patted the knife that hung at his bosom,
Drawing it half from its sheath, and plunging it back, as he muttered,
"By and by it shall see; it shall eat; ah, ha! but shall speak not!
This is the mighty Captain the white men have sent to destroy us!
He is a little man; let him go and work with the women!"

Meanwhile Standish had noted the faces and figures of Indians
Peeping and creeping about from bush to tree in the forest,
Feigning to look for game, with arrows set on their bow-strings,
Drawing about him still closer and closer the net of their ambush.
But undaunted he stood, and dissembled and treated them smoothly;
So the old chronicles say, that were writ in the days of the fathers.
But when he heard their defiance, the boast, the taunt, and the insult,
All the hot blood of his race, of Sir Hugh and of Thurston de Standish,
Boiled and beat in his heart, and swelled in the veins of his temples.

Headlong he leaped on the boaster, and, snatching his knife from its scabbard,
Plunged it into his heart, and, reeling backward, the savage
Fell with his face to the sky, and a fiendlike fierceness upon it.
Straight there arose from the forest the awful sound of the war-whoop.
And, like a flurry of snow on the whistling wind of December,
Swift and sudden and keen came a flight of feathery arrows.
Then came a cloud of smoke, and out of the cloud came the lightning,
Out of the lightning thunder; and death unseen ran before it.
Frightened the savages fled for shelter in swamp and in thicket,
Hotly pursued and beset; but their sachem, the brave Wattawamat,
Fled not; he was dead. Unswerving and swift had a bullet
Passed through his brain, and he fell with both hands clutching the greensward,
Seeming in death to hold back from his foe the land of his fathers.

There on the flowers of the meadow the warriors lay, and above them,
Silent, with folded arms, stood Hobomok, friend of the white man.
Smiling at length he exclaimed to the stalwart Captain of Plymouth:—
"Pecksuot bragged very loud, of his courage, his strength, and his stature,—
Mocked the great Captain, and called him a little man; but I see now
Big enough have you been to lay him speechless before you!"

Thus the first battle was fought and won by the stalwart Miles Standish.
When the tidings thereof were brought to the village of Plymouth,
And as a trophy of war the head of the brave Wattawamat
Scowled from the roof of the fort, which at once was a church and a fortress,
All who beheld it rejoiced, and praised the Lord, and took courage.
Only Priscilla averted her face from this spectre of terror,
Thanking God in her heart that she had not married Miles Standish;
Shrinking, fearing almost, lest, coming home from his battles,
He should lay claim to her hand, as the prize and reward of his valor.

VIII

THE SPINNING-WHEEL

MONTH after month passed away, and in autumn the ships of the merchants
Came with kindred and friends, with cattle and corn for the Pilgrims.
All in the village was peace; the men were intent on their labors,
Busy with hewing and building, with garden-plot and with merestead,
Busy with breaking the glebe, and mowing the grass in the meadows,
Searching the sea for its fish, and hunting the deer in the forest.
All in the village was peace; but at times the rumor of warfare
Filled the air with alarm, and the apprehension of danger.
Bravely the stalwart Standish was scouring the land with his forces,
Waxing valiant in fight and defeating the alien armies,
Till his name had become a sound of fear to the nations.
Anger was still in his heart, but at times the remorse and contrition
Which in all noble natures succeed the passionate outbreak,
Came like a rising tide, that encounters the rush of a river,
Staying its current awhile, but making it bitter and brackish.

Meanwhile Alden at home had built him a new habitation,
Solid, substantial, of timber rough-hewn from the firs of the forest.
Wooden-barred was the door, and the roof was covered with rushes;
Latticed the windows were, and the window-panes were of paper,

Oiled to admit the light, while wind and rain were excluded.
There too he dug a well, and around it planted an orchard:
Still may be seen to this day some trace of the well and the orchard.
Close to the house was the stall, where, safe and secure from annoyance,
Raghorn, the snow-white bull, that had fallen to Alden's allotment
In the division of cattle, might ruminate in the night-time
Over the pastures he cropped, made fragrant by sweet pennyroyal.

Oft when his labor was finished, with eager feet would the dreamer
Follow the pathway that ran through the woods to the house of Priscilla,
Led by illusions romantic and subtile deceptions of fancy,
Pleasure disguised as duty, and love in the semblance of friendship.
Ever of her he thought, when he fashioned the walls of his dwelling;
Ever of her he thought, when he delved in the soil of his garden;
Ever of her he thought, when he read in his Bible on Sunday
Praise of the virtuous woman, as she is described in the Proverbs,—
How the heart of her husband doth safely trust in her always,
How all the days of her life she will do him good, and not evil,
How she seeketh the wool and the flax and worketh with gladness,
How she layeth her hand to the spindle and holdeth the distaff,
How she is not afraid of the snow for herself or her household,
Knowing her household are clothed with the scarlet cloth of her weaving!

So as she sat at her wheel one afternoon in the Autumn,
Alden, who opposite sat, and was watching her dexterous fingers,
As if the thread she was spinning were that of his life and his fortune,
After a pause in their talk, thus spake to the sound of the spindle.
"Truly, Priscilla," he said, "when I see you spinning and spinning,
Never idle a moment, but thrifty and thoughtful of others,
Suddenly you are transformed, are visibly changed in a moment;
You are no longer Priscilla, but Bertha the Beautiful Spinner."
Here the light foot on the treadle grew swifter and swifter; the spindle
Uttered an angry snarl, and the thread snapped short in her fingers;
While the impetuous speaker, not heeding the mischief, continued:
"You are the beautiful Bertha, the spinner, the queen of Helvetia;
She whose story I read at a stall in the streets of Southampton,
Who, as she rode on her palfrey, o'er valley and meadow and mountain,
Ever was spinning her thread from a distaff fixed to her saddle.
She was so thrifty and good, that her name passed into a proverb.
So shall it be with your own, when the spinning-wheel shall no longer
Hum in the house of the farmer, and fill its chambers with music.
Then shall the mothers, reproving, relate how it was in their childhood,
Praising the good old times, and the days of Priscilla the spinner!"
Straight uprose from her wheel the beautiful Puritan maiden,
Pleased with the praise of her thrift from him whose praise was the sweetest,
Drew from the reel on the table a snowy skein of her spinning,
Thus making answer, meanwhile, to the flattering phrases of Alden:
"Come, you must not be idle; if I am a pattern for housewives,
Show yourself equally worthy of being the model of husbands.
Hold this skein on your hands, while I wind it, ready for knitting;
Then who knows but hereafter, when fashions have changed and the manners,

Fathers may talk to their sons of the good old times of John Alden!"
Thus, with a jest and a laugh, the skein on his hands she adjusted,
He sitting awkwardly there, with his arms extended before him,
She standing graceful, erect, and winding the thread from his fingers,
Sometimes chiding a little his clumsy manner of holding,
Sometimes touching his hands, as she disentangled expertly
Twist or knot in the yarn, unawares—for how could she help it?—
Sending electrical thrills through every nerve in his body.

Lo! in the midst of this scene, a breathless messenger entered,
Bringing in hurry and heat the terrible news from the village.
Yes; Miles Standish was dead!—an Indian had brought them the tidings,—
Slain by a poisoned arrow, shot down in the front of the battle,
Into an ambush beguiled, cut off with the whole of his forces;
All the town would be burned, and all the people be murdered!
Such were the tidings of evil that burst on the hearts of the hearers.
Silent and statue-like stood Priscilla, her face looking backward
Still at the face of the speaker, her arms uplifted in horror;
But John Alden, upstarting, as if the barb of the arrow
Piercing the heart of his friend had struck his own, and had sundered
Once and forever the bonds that held him bound as a captive,
Wild with excess of sensation, the awful delight of his freedom,
Mingled with pain and regret, unconscious of what he was doing,
Clasped, almost with a groan, the motionless form of Priscilla,
Pressing her close to his heart, as forever his own, and exclaiming:
"Those whom the Lord hath united, let no man put them asunder!"

Even as rivulets twain, from distant and separate sources,
Seeing each other afar, as they leap from the rocks, and pursuing
Each one its devious path, but drawing nearer and nearer,
Rush together at last, at their trysting-place in the forest;
So these lives that had run thus far in separate channels,
Coming in sight of each other, then swerving and flowing asunder,
Parted by barriers strong, but drawing nearer and nearer,
Rushed together at last, and one was lost in the other.

IX

THE WEDDING-DAY

Forth from the curtain of clouds, from the tent of purple and scarlet,
Issued the sun, the great High-Priest, in his garments resplendent,
Holiness unto the Lord, in letters of light, on his forehead,
Round the hem of his robe the golden bells and pomegranates.
Blessing the world he came, and the bars of vapor beneath him
Gleamed like a grate of brass, and the sea at his feet was a laver!

This was the wedding morn of Priscilla the Puritan maiden.
Friends were assembled together; the Elder and Magistrate also
Graced the scene with their presence, and stood like the Law and the Gospel,
One with the sanction of earth and one with the blessing of heaven.
Simple and brief was the wedding, as that of Ruth and of Boaz.
Softly the youth and the maiden repeated the words of betrothal,
Taking each other for husband and wife in the Magistrate's presence,
After the Puritan way, and the laudable custom of Holland.
Fervently then, and devoutly, the excellent Elder of Plymouth

Prayed for the hearth and the home, that were founded that day in affection,
Speaking of life and of death, and imploring Divine benedictions.

Lo! when the service was ended, a form appeared on the threshold,
Clad in armor of steel, a sombre and sorrowful figure!
Why does the bridegroom start and stare at the strange apparition?
Why does the bride turn pale, and hide her face on his shoulder?
Is it a phantom of air,—a bodiless, spectral illusion?
Is it a ghost from the grave, that has come to forbid the betrothal?
Long has it stood there unseen, a guest uninvited, unwelcomed;
Over its clouded eyes there had passed at times an expression
Softening the gloom and revealing the warm heart hidden beneath them,
As when across the sky the driving rack of the rain-cloud
Grows for a moment thin, and betrays the sun by its brightness.
Once it had lifted its hand, and moved its lips, but was silent,
As if an iron will had mastered the fleeting intention.
But when were ended the troth and the prayer and the last benediction,
Into the room it strode, and the people beheld with amazement
Bodily there in his armor Miles Standish, the Captain of Plymouth!
Grasping the bridegroom's hand, he said with emotion, "Forgive me!
I have been angry and hurt,—too long have I cherished the feeling;
I have been cruel and hard, but now, thank God! it is ended.
Mine is the same hot blood that leaped in the veins of Hugh Standish,
Sensitive, swift to resent, but as swift in atoning for error.
Never so much as now was Miles Standish the friend of John Alden."
Thereupon answered the bridegroom: "Let all be forgotten between us,—
All save the dear old friendship, and that shall grow older and dearer!"
Then the Captain advanced, and, bowing, saluted Priscilla,
Gravely, and after the manner of old-fashioned gentry in England,
Something of camp and of court, of town and of country, commingled,
Wishing her joy of her wedding, and loudly lauding her husband.
Then he said with a smile: "I should have remembered the adage,—
If you would be well served, you must serve yourself; and moreover,
No man can gather cherries in Kent at the season of Christmas!"

Great was the people's amazement, and greater yet their rejoicing,
Thus to behold once more the sunburnt face of their Captain,
Whom they had mourned as dead; and they gathered and crowded about him,
Eager to see him and hear him, forgetful of bride and of bridegroom,
Questioning, answering, laughing, and each interrupting the other,
Till the good Captain declared, being quite overpowered and bewildered,
He had rather by far break into an Indian encampment,
Than come again to a wedding to which he had not been invited.

Meanwhile the bridegroom went forth and stood with the bride at the doorway,
Breathing the perfumed air of that warm and beautiful morning.
Touched with autumnal tints, but lonely and sad in the sunshine,
Lay extended before them the land of toil and privation;
There were the graves of the dead, and the barren waste of the sea-shore,
There the familiar fields, the groves of pine, and the meadows;
But to their eyes transfigured, it seemed as the Garden of Eden,
Filled with the presence of God, whose voice was the sound of the ocean.

Soon was their vision disturbed by the noise and stir of departure,
Friends coming forth from the house, and impatient of longer delaying,
Each with his plan for the day, and the work that was left uncompleted.
Then from a stall near at hand, amid exclamations of wonder,
Alden the thoughtful, the careful, so happy, so proud of Priscilla,
Brought out his snow-white bull, obeying the hand of its master,
Led by a cord that was tied to an iron ring in its nostrils,
Covered with crimson cloth, and a cushion placed for a saddle.
She should not walk, he said, through the dust and heat of the noonday;
Nay, she should ride like a queen, not plod along like a peasant.
Somewhat alarmed at first, but reassured by the others,
Placing her hand on the cushion, her foot in the hand of her husband,
Gayly, with joyous laugh, Priscilla mounted her palfrey.
"Nothing is wanting now," he said with a smile, "but the distaff;
Then you would be in truth my queen, my beautiful Bertha!"

Onward the bridal procession now moved to their new habitation,
Happy husband and wife, and friends conversing together.
Pleasantly murmured the brook, as they crossed the ford in the forest,
Pleased with the image that passed, like a dream of love, through its bosom,
Tremulous, floating in air, o'er the depths of the azure abysses.
Down through the golden leaves the sun was pouring his splendors,
Gleaming on purple grapes, that, from branches above them suspended,
Mingled their odorous breath with the balm of the pine and the fir-tree,
Wild and sweet as the clusters that grew in the valley of Eshcol.
Like a picture it seemed of the primitive, pastoral ages,
Fresh with the youth of the world, and recalling Rebecca and Isaac,
Old and yet ever new, and simple and beautiful always,
Love immortal and young in the endless succession of lovers.
So through the Plymouth woods passed onward the bridal procession.

1857–58 1858

THE CHILDREN'S HOUR

BETWEEN the dark and the daylight,
When the night is beginning to lower,
Comes a pause in the day's occupations,
That is known as the Children's Hour.

I hear in the chamber above me
The patter of little feet,
The sound of a door that is opened,
And voices soft and sweet.

From my study I see in the lamplight,
Descending the broad hall stair,
Grave Alice, and laughing Allegra,
And Edith with golden hair.

A whisper, and then a silence:
Yet I know by their merry eyes
They are plotting and planning together
To take me by surprise.

A sudden rush from the stairway,
A sudden raid from the hall!
By three doors left unguarded
They enter my castle wall!

They climb up into my turret
O'er the arms and back of my chair;
If I try to escape, they surround me;
They seem to be everywhere.

They almost devour me with kisses,
Their arms about me entwine,
Till I think of the Bishop of Bingen
In his Mouse-Tower on the Rhine!

Do you think, O blue-eyed banditti,
Because you have scaled the wall,
Such an old mustache as I am
Is not a match for you all!

I have you fast in my fortress,
And will not let you depart,
But put you down into the dungeon
In the round-tower of my heart.

And there will I keep you forever,
Yes, forever and a day,
Till the walls shall crumble to ruin,
And moulder in dust away!

1859 1859

ENCELADUS

UNDER Mount Etna he lies,
It is slumber, it is not death;
For he struggles at times to arise,
And above him the lurid skies
Are hot with his fiery breath.

The crags are piled on his breast,
The earth is heaped on his head;
But the groans of his wild unrest,
Though smothered and half suppressed,
Are heard, and he is not dead.

And the nations far away
Are watching with eager eyes;
They talk together and say,
"Tomorrow, perhaps today,
Enceladus will arise!"

And the old gods, the austere
Oppressors in their strength,
Stand aghast and white with fear
At the ominous sounds they hear,
And tremble, and mutter, "At length!"

Ah me! for the land that is sown
With the harvest of despair!
Where the burning cinders, blown
From the lips of the overthrown
Enceladus, fill the air;

Where ashes are heaped in drifts
Over vineyard and field and town,
Whenever he starts and lifts
His head through the blackened rifts
Of the crags that keep him down.

See, see! the red light shines!
'Tis the glare of his awful eyes!
And the storm-wind shouts through the pines
Of Alps and of Apennines,
"Enceladus, arise!"

1859 1859

SNOW-FLAKES

OUT of the bosom of the Air,
Out of the cloud-folds of her garment shaken,
Over the woodlands brown and bare,
Over the harvest-fields forsaken,
Silent, and soft, and slow
Descends the snow.

Even as our cloudy fancies take
Suddenly shape in some divine expression,
Even as the troubled heart doth make
In the white countenance confession,
The troubled sky reveals
The grief it feels.

This is the poem of the air,
Slowly in silent syllables recorded;
This is the secret of despair,
Long in its cloudy bosom hoarded,
Now whispered and revealed
To wood and field.

1859 1859

THE CUMBERLAND

AT anchor in Hampton Roads we lay,
On board of the Cumberland, sloop-of-war;
And at times from the fortress across the bay
The alarum of drums swept past,
Or a bugle blast
From the camp on the shore.

Then far away to the south uprose
A little feather of snow-white smoke,
And we knew that the iron ship of our foes
Was steadily steering its course
To try the force
Of our ribs of oak.

Down upon us heavily runs,
Silent and sullen, the floating fort;
Then comes a puff of smoke from her guns,
And leaps the terrible death,
With fiery breath,
From each open port.

We are not idle, but send her straight
Defiance back in a full broadside!
As hail rebounds from a roof of slate,
Rebounds our heavier hail
From each iron scale
Of the monster's hide.

"Strike your flag!" the rebel cries,
In his arrogant old plantation strain.
"Never!" our gallant Morris replies;
"It is better to sink than to yield!"
And the whole air pealed
With the cheers of our men.

Then, like a kraken huge and black,
She crushed our ribs in her iron grasp!
Down went the Cumberland all a wrack,
With a sudden shudder of death,
And the cannon's breath
For her dying gasp.

Next morn, as the sun rose over the bay,
Still floated our flag at the mainmast head.
Lord, how beautiful was Thy day!
Every waft of the air
Was a whisper of prayer,
Or a dirge for the dead.

Ho! brave hearts that went down in the seas!
Ye are at peace in the troubled stream;
Ho! brave land! with hearts like these,
Thy flag, that is rent in twain,
Shall be one again,
And without a seam!

1862 1862

THE FALCON OF SER FEDERIGO

One summer morning, when the sun was hot,
Weary with labor in his garden-plot,
On a rude bench beneath his cottage eaves,
Ser Federigo sat among the leaves
Of a huge vine, that, with its arms outspread,
Hung its delicious clusters overhead.
Below him, through the lovely valley, flowed
The river Arno, like a winding road,
And from its banks were lifted high in air
The spires and roofs of Florence called the Fair;
To him a marble tomb, that rose above
His wasted fortunes and his buried love.
For there, in banquet and in tournament,
His wealth had lavished been, his substance spent,
To woo and lose, since ill his wooing sped,
Monna Giovanna, who his rival wed,
Yet ever in his fancy reigned supreme,
The ideal woman of a young man's dream.

Then he withdrew, in poverty and pain,
To this small farm, the last of his domain,
His only comfort and his only care
To prune his vines, and plant the fig and pear;
His only forester and only guest
His falcon, faithful to him, when the rest,
Whose willing hands had found so light of yore
The brazen knocker of his palace door,
Had now no strength to lift the wooden latch,
That entrance gave beneath a roof of thatch.
Companion of his solitary ways,
Purveyor of his feasts on holidays,
On him this melancholy man bestowed
The love with which his nature overflowed.

And so the empty-handed years went round,
Vacant, though voiceful with prophetic sound,
And so, that summer morn, he sat and mused
With folded, patient hands, as he was used,
And dreamily before his half-closed sight
Floated the vision of his lost delight.
Beside him, motionless, the drowsy bird
Dreamed of the chase, and in his slumber heard
The sudden, scythe-like sweep of wings, that dare
The headlong plunge through eddying gulfs of air,
Then, starting broad awake upon his perch,
Tinkled his bells, like mass-bells in a church,
And, looking at his master, seemed to say,
"Ser Federigo, shall we hunt today?"

Ser Federigo thought not of the chase;
The tender vision of her lovely face,
I will not say he seems to see, he sees
In the leaf-shadows of the trellises,
Herself, yet not herself; a lovely child
With flowing tresses, and eyes wide and wild,
Coming undaunted up the garden walk,
And looking not at him, but at the hawk.
"Beautiful falcon!" said he, "would that I
Might hold thee on my wrist, or see thee fly!"
The voice was hers, and made strange echoes start
Through all the haunted chambers of his heart,
As an æolian harp through gusty doors
Of some old ruin its wild music pours.

"Who is thy mother, my fair boy?" he said,
His hand laid softly on that shining head.

"Monna Giovanna. Will you let me stay
A little while, and with your falcon play?
We live there, just beyond your garden wall,
In the great house behind the poplars tall."

So he spake on: and Federigo heard
As from afar each softly uttered word,
And drifted onward through the golden gleams
And shadows of the misty sea of dreams,
As mariners becalmed through vapors drift,
And feel the sea beneath them sink and lift,
And hear far off the mournful breakers roar,
And voices calling faintly from the shore!
Then, waking from his pleasant reveries,
He took the little boy upon his knees,
And told him stories of his gallant bird,
Till in their friendship he became a third.

Monna Giovanna, widowed in her prime,
Had come with friends to pass the summer time
In her grand villa, half-way up the hill,
O'erlooking Florence, but retired and still;
With iron gates, that opened through long lines
Of sacred ilex and centennial pines,
And terraced gardens, and broad steps of stone,
And sylvan deities, with moss o'ergrown,
And fountains palpitating in the heat,
And all Val d'Arno stretched beneath its feet.
Here in seclusion, as a widow may,
The lovely lady whiled the hours away,
Pacing in sable robes the statued hall,
Herself the stateliest statue among all,
And seeing more and more, with secret joy,
Her husband risen and living in her boy,
Till the lost sense of life returned again,
Not as delight, but as relief from pain.
Meanwhile the boy, rejoicing in his strength,
Stormed down the terraces from length to length;
The screaming peacock chased in hot pursuit,
And climbed the garden trellises for fruit.
But his chief pastime was to watch the flight
Of a gerfalcon, soaring into sight,
Beyond the trees that fringed the garden wall,
Then downward stooping at some distant call;
And as he gazed full often wondered he
Who might the master of the falcon be,
Until that happy morning, when he found
Master and falcon in the cottage ground.

And now a shadow and a terror fell
On the great house, as if a passing-bell
Tolled from the tower, and filled each spacious room
With secret awe and preternatural gloom;
The petted boy grew ill, and day by day
Pined with mysterious malady away.
The mother's heart would not be comforted;
Her darling seemed to her already dead,
And often, sitting by the sufferer's side,
"What can I do to comfort thee?" she cried.
At first the silent lips made no reply,
But, moved at length by her importunate cry,
"Give me," he answered, with imploring tone,
"Ser Federigo's falcon for my own!"

No answer could the astonished mother make;
How could she ask, e'en for her darling's sake,
Such favor at a luckless lover's hand,
Well knowing that to ask was to command?
Well knowing, what all falconers confessed,
In all the land that falcon was the best,
The master's pride and passion and delight,
And the sole pursuivant of this poor knight.
But yet, for her child's sake, she could no less
Than give assent, to soothe his restlessness,
So promised, and then promising to keep
Her promise sacred, saw him fall asleep.

The morrow was a bright September morn;
The earth was beautiful as if new-born;
There was that nameless splendor everywhere,
That wild exhilaration in the air,
Which makes the passers in the city street
Congratulate each other as they meet.
Two lovely ladies, clothed in cloak and hood,
Passed through the garden gate into the wood,
Under the lustrous leaves, and through the sheen
Of dewy sunshine showering down between.
The one, close-hooded, had the attractive grace
Which sorrow sometimes lends a woman's face;
Her dark eyes moistened with the mists that roll
From the gulf-stream of passion in the soul;

The other with her hood thrown back, her hair
Making a golden glory in the air,
Her cheeks suffused with an auroral blush,
Her young heart singing louder than the thrush.
So walked, that morn, through mingled light and shade,
Each by the other's presence lovelier made,
Monna Giovanna and her bosom friend,
Intent upon their errand and its end.

They found Ser Federigo at his toil,
Like banished Adam, delving in the soil;
And when he looked and these fair women spied,
The garden suddenly was glorified;
His long-lost Eden was restored again,
And the strange river winding through the plain
No longer was the Arno to his eyes,
But the Euphrates watering Paradise!

Monna Giovanna raised her stately head,
And with fair words of salutation said:
"Ser Federigo, we come here as friends,
Hoping in this to make some poor amends
For past unkindness. I who ne'er before
Would even cross the threshold of your door,
I who in happier days such pride maintained,
Refused your banquets, and your gifts disdained,
This morning come, a self-invited guest,
To put your generous nature to the test,
And breakfast with you under your own vine."
To which he answered: "Poor desert of mine,
Not your unkindness call it, for if aught
Is good in me of feeling or of thought,
From you it comes, and this last grace outweighs
All sorrows, all regrets of other days."

And after further compliment and talk,
Among the asters in the garden walk
He left his guests; and to his cottage turned,
And as he entered for a moment yearned
For the lost splendors of the days of old,
The ruby glass, the silver and the gold,
And felt how piercing is the sting of pride,
By want embittered and intensified.
He looked about him for some means or way
To keep this unexpected holiday;
Searched every cupboard, and then searched again,
Summoned the maid, who came, but came in vain;
"The Signor did not hunt today," she said,
"There's nothing in the house but wine and bread."
Then suddenly the drowsy falcon shook
His little bells, with that sagacious look,
Which said, as plain as language to the ear,
"If anything is wanting, I am here!"

Yes, everything is wanting, gallant bird!
The master seized thee without further word.
Like thine own lure, he whirled thee round; ah me!
The pomp and flutter of brave falconry,
The bells, the jesses, the bright scarlet hood,
The flight and the pursuit o'er field and wood,
All these forevermore are ended now;
No longer victor, but the victim thou!

Then on the board a snow-white cloth he spread,
Laid on its wooden dish the loaf of bread,
Brought purple grapes with autumn sunshine hot,
The fragrant peach, the juicy bergamot;
Then in the midst a flask of wine he placed,
And with autumnal flowers the banquet graced.
Ser Federigo, would not these suffice
Without thy falcon stuffed with cloves and spice?

When all was ready, and the courtly dame
With her companion to the cottage came,
Upon Ser Federigo's brain there fell
The wild enchantment of a magic spell!
The room they entered, mean and low and small,
Was changed into a sumptuous banquet-hall,
With fanfares by aerial trumpets blown;
The rustic chair she sat on was a throne;
He ate celestial food, and a divine
Flavor was given to his country wine,
And the poor falcon, fragrant with his spice,
A peacock was, or bird of paradise!

When the repast was ended, they arose
And passed again into the garden-close.
Then said the lady, "Far too well I know,

Remembering still the days of long ago,
Though you betray it not, with what surprise
You see me here in this familiar wise.
You have no children, and you cannot guess
What anguish, what unspeakable distress
A mother feels, whose child is lying ill,
Nor how her heart anticipates his will.
And yet for this, you see me lay aside
All womanly reserve and check of pride,
And ask the thing most precious in your sight,
Your falcon, your sole comfort and delight,
Which if you find it in your heart to give,
My poor, unhappy boy perchance may live."

Ser Federigo listens, and replies,
With tears of love and pity in his eyes:
"Alas, dear lady! there can be no task
So sweet to me as giving when you ask.
One little hour ago, if I had known
This wish of yours, it would have been my
    own.
But thinking in what manner I could best
Do honor to the presence of my guest,
I deemed that nothing worthier could be
Than what most dear and precious was to me;
And so my gallant falcon breathed his last
To furnish forth this morning our repast."

In mute contrition, mingled with dismay,
The gentle lady turned her eyes away,
Grieving that he such sacrifice should make,
And kill his falcon for a woman's sake,
Yet feeling in her heart a woman's pride,
That nothing she could ask for was denied;
Then took her leave, and passed out at the
    gate
With footstep slow and soul disconsolate.

Three days went by, and lo! a passing-bell
Tolled from the little chapel in the dell;
Ten strokes Ser Federigo heard, and said,
Breathing a prayer, "Alas! her child is dead!"
Three months went by; and lo! a merrier chime
Rang from the chapel bells at Christmas-time;
The cottage was deserted, and no more
Ser Federigo sat beside its door,
But now, with servitors to do his will,
In the grand villa, half-way up the hill,
Sat at the Christmas feast, and at his side
Monna Giovanna, his beloved bride,
Never so beautiful, so kind, so fair,
Enthroned once more in the old rustic chair,
High-perched upon the back of which there
    stood
The image of a falcon carved in wood,
And underneath the inscription, with a date,
"All things come round to him who will but
    wait."

1863 1863

WEARINESS

O LITTLE feet! that such long years
Must wander on through hopes and fears,
  Must ache and bleed beneath your load;
I, nearer to the wayside inn
Where toil shall cease and rest begin,
  Am weary, thinking of your road!

O little hands! that, weak or strong,
Have still to serve or rule so long,
  Have still so long to give or ask;
I, who so much with book and pen
Have toiled among my fellow-men,
  Am weary, thinking of your task.

O little hearts! that throb and beat
With such impatient, feverish heat,
  Such limitless and strong desires;
Mine, that so long has glowed and burned,
With passions into ashes turned,
  Now covers and conceals its fires.

O little souls! as pure and white
And crystalline as rays of light
  Direct from heaven, their source divine;
Refracted through the mist of years,
How red my setting sun appears,
  How lurid looks this soul of mine!

1863? 1863

HAWTHORNE

How beautiful it was, that one bright day
  In the long week of rain!
Though all its splendor could not chase
    away
  The omnipresent pain.

The lovely town was white with apple-blooms,
  And the great elms o'erhead
Dark shadows wove on their aerial looms
  Shot through with golden thread.

Across the meadows, by the gray old manse,
The historic river flowed:
I was as one who wanders in a trance,
Unconscious of his road.

The faces of familiar friends seemed strange;
Their voices I could hear,
And yet the words they uttered seemed to change
Their meaning to my ear.

For the one face I looked for was not there,
The one low voice was mute;
Only an unseen presence filled the air,
And baffled my pursuit.

Now I look back, and meadow, manse, and stream
Dimly my thought defines;
I only see—a dream within a dream—
The hill-top hearsed with pines.

I only hear above his place of rest
Their tender undertone,
The infinite longings of a troubled breast,
The voice so like his own.

There in seclusion and remote from men
The wizard hand lies cold,
Which at its topmost speed let fall the pen,
And left the tale half told.

Ah! who shall lift that wand of magic power,
And the lost clew regain?
The unfinished window in Aladdin's tower
Unfinished must remain!

1864 1864

DIVINA COMMEDIA

I

Oft have I seen at some cathedral door
A laborer, pausing in the dust and heat,
Lay down his burden, and with reverent feet
Enter, and cross himself, and on the floor
Kneel to repeat his paternoster o'er;
Far off the noises of the world retreat;
The loud vociferations of the street
Become an undistinguishable roar.
So, as I enter here from day to day,
And leave my burden at this minster gate,
Kneeling in prayer, and not ashamed to pray,
The tumult of the time disconsolate
To inarticulate murmurs dies away,
While the eternal ages watch and wait.

1864 1864

II

How strange the sculptures that adorn these towers!
This crowd of statues, in whose folded sleeves
Birds build their nests; while canopied with leaves
Parvis and portal bloom like trellised bowers,
And the vast minster seems a cross of flowers!
But fiends and dragons on the gargoyled eaves
Watch the dead Christ between the living thieves,
And, underneath, the traitor Judas lowers!
Ah! from what agonies of heart and brain,
What exultations trampling on despair,
What tenderness, what tears, what hate of wrong,
What passionate outcry of a soul in pain,
Uprose this poem of the earth and air,
This mediæval miracle of song!

1864 1866

III

I enter, and I see thee in the gloom
Of the long aisles, O poet saturnine!
And strive to make my steps keep pace with thine.
The air is filled with some unknown perfume;
The congregation of the dead make room
For thee to pass; the votive tapers shine;
Like rooks that haunt Ravenna's groves of pine
The hovering echoes fly from tomb to tomb.
From the confessionals I hear arise
Rehearsals of forgotten tragedies,
And lamentations from the crypts below;
And then a voice celestial that begins
With the pathetic words, "Although your sins
As scarlet be," and ends with "as the snow."

1865 1866

IV

With snow-white veil and garments as of flame,
She stands before thee, who so long ago
Filled thy young heart with passion and the woe
From which thy song and all its splendors came;
And while with stern rebuke she speaks thy name,
The ice about thy heart melts as the snow
On mountain heights, and in swift overflow
Comes gushing from thy lips in sobs of shame.
Thou makest full confession; and a gleam,
As of the dawn on some dark forest cast,
Seems on thy lifted forehead to increase;
Lethe and Eunoë—the remembered dream
And the forgotten sorrow—bring at last
That perfect pardon which is perfect peace.

1867 1867

V

I lift mine eyes, and all the windows blaze
With forms of Saints and holy men who died,
Here martyred and hereafter glorified;
And the great Rose upon its leaves displays
Christ's Triumph, and the angelic roundelays,
With splendor upon splendor multiplied;
And Beatrice again at Dante's side
No more rebukes, but smiles her words of praise.
And then the organ sounds, and unseen choirs
Sing the old Latin hymns of peace and love
And benedictions of the Holy Ghost;
And the melodious bells among the spires
O'er all the house-tops and through heaven above
Proclaim the elevation of the Host!

1866 1866

VI

O star of morning and of liberty!
O bringer of the light, whose splendor shines
Above the darkness of the Apennines,
Forerunner of the day that is to be!
The voices of the city and the sea,
The voices of the mountains and the pines,
Repeat thy song, till the familiar lines
Are footpaths for the thought of Italy!
Thy flame is blown abroad from all the heights,
Through all the nations, and a sound is heard,
As of a mighty wind, and men devout,
Strangers of Rome, and the new proselytes,
In their own language hear thy wondrous word,
And many are amazed and many doubt.

1866 1866

KILLED AT THE FORD

He is dead, the beautiful youth,
The heart of honor, the tongue of truth,
He, the life and light of us all,
Whose voice was blithe as a bugle-call,
Whom all eyes followed with one consent,
The cheer of whose laugh, and whose pleasant word,
Hushed all murmurs of discontent.

Only last night, as we rode along,
Down the dark of the mountain gap,
To visit the picket-guard at the ford,
Little dreaming of any mishap,
He was humming the words of some old song:
"Two red roses he had on his cap
And another he bore at the point of his sword."

Sudden and swift a whistling ball
Came out of a wood, and the voice was still;
Something I heard in the darkness fall,
And for a moment my blood grew chill;
I spake in a whisper, as he who speaks
In a room where some one is lying dead;
But he made no answer to what I said.

We lifted him up to his saddle again,
And through the mire and the mist and the rain
Carried him back to the silent camp,
And laid him as if asleep on his bed;
And I saw by the light of the surgeon's lamp
Two white roses upon his cheeks,
And one, just over his heart, blood-red!

And I saw in a vision how far and fleet
That fatal bullet went speeding forth,
Till it reached a town in the distant North,
Till it reached a house in a sunny street,
Till it reached a heart that ceased to beat

Without a murmur, without a cry;
And a bell was tolled, in that far-off town,
For one who had passed from cross to crown,
And the neighbors wondered that she should die.

1866 1866

GIOTTO'S TOWER

How many lives, made beautiful and sweet
By self-devotion and by self-restraint,
Whose pleasure is to run without complaint
On unknown errands of the Paraclete,
Wanting the reverence of unshodden feet,
Fail of the nimbus which the artists paint
Around the shining forehead of the saint,
And are in their completeness incomplete!
In the old Tuscan town stands Giotto's tower,
The lily of Florence blossoming in stone,—
A vision, a delight, and a desire,—
The builder's perfect and centennial flower,
That in the night of ages bloomed alone,
But wanting still the glory of the spire.

1866 1866

EMMA AND EGINHARD

When Alcuin taught the sons of Charlemagne,
In the free schools of Aix, how kings should reign,
And with them taught the children of the poor
How subjects should be patient and endure,
He touched the lips of some, as best befit,
With honey from the hives of Holy Writ;
Others intoxicated with the wine
Of ancient history, sweet but less divine;
Some with the wholesome fruits of grammar fed;
Others with mysteries of the stars o'erhead,
That hang suspended in the vaulted sky
Like lamps in some fair palace vast and high.

In sooth, it was a pleasant sight to see
That Saxon monk, with hood and rosary,
With inkhorn at his belt, and pen and book,
And mingled love and reverence in his look,
Or hear the cloister and the court repeat
The measured footfalls of his sandaled feet,
Or watch him with the pupils of his school,
Gentle of speech, but absolute of rule.

Among them, always earliest in his place,
Was Eginhard, a youth of Frankish race,
Whose face was bright with flashes that forerun
The splendors of a yet unrisen sun.
To him all things were possible, and seemed
Not what he had accomplished, but had dreamed,
And what were tasks to others were his play,
The pastime of an idle holiday.

Smaragdo, Abbot of St. Michael's, said,
With many a shrug and shaking of the head,
Surely some demon must possess the lad,
Who showed more wit than ever schoolboy had,
And learned his Trivium thus without the rod;
But Alcuin said it was the grace of God.

Thus he grew up, in Logic point-device,
Perfect in Grammar, and in Rhetoric nice;
Science of Numbers, Geometric art,
And lore of Stars, and Music knew by heart;
A Minnesinger, long before the times
Of those who sang their love in Suabian rhymes.

The Emperor, when he heard this good report
Of Eginhard much buzzed about the court,
Said to himself, "This stripling seems to be
Purposely sent into the world for me;
He shall become my scribe, and shall be schooled
In all the arts whereby the world is ruled."
Thus did the gentle Eginhard attain
To honor in the court of Charlemagne;
Became the sovereign's favorite, his right hand,
So that his fame was great in all the land,
And all men loved him for his modest grace
And comeliness of figure and of face.
An inmate of the palace, yet recluse,
A man of books, yet sacred from abuse
Among the armèd knights with spur on heel,
The tramp of horses and the clang of steel;
And as the Emperor promised he was schooled
In all the arts by which the world is ruled.
But the one art supreme, whose law is fate,
The Emperor never dreamed of till too late.

Home from her convent to the palace came
The lovely Princess Emma, whose sweet name,

Whispered by seneschal or sung by bard,
Had often touched the soul of Eginhard.
He saw her from his window, as in state
She came, by knights attended through the gate;
He saw her at the banquet of that day,
Fresh as the morn, and beautiful as May;
He saw her in the garden, as she strayed
Among the flowers of summer with her maid,
And said to him, "O Eginhard, disclose
The meaning and the mystery of the rose;"
And trembling he made answer: "In good sooth,
Its mystery is love, its meaning youth!"

How can I tell the signals and the signs
By which one heart another heart divines?
How can I tell the many thousand ways
By which it keeps the secret it betrays?

O mystery of love! O strange romance!
Among the Peers and Paladins of France,
Shining in steel, and prancing on gay steeds,
Noble by birth, yet nobler by great deeds,
The Princess Emma had no words nor looks
But for this clerk, this man of thought and books.

The summer passed, the autumn came; the stalks
Of lilies blackened in the garden walks;
The leaves fell, russet-golden and blood-red,
Love-letters, thought the poet fancy-led,
Or Jove descending in a shower of gold
Into the lap of Danaë of old;
For poets cherish many a strange conceit,
And love transmutes all nature by its heat.

No more the garden lessons, nor the dark
And hurried meetings in the twilight park;
But now the studious lamp, and the delights
Of firesides in the silent winter nights,
And watching from his window hour by hour
The light that burned in Princess Emma's tower.

At length one night, while musing by the fire,
O'ercome at last by his insane desire,—
For what will reckless love not do and dare?—
He crossed the court, and climbed the winding stair,
With some feigned message in the Emperor's name;
But when he to the lady's presence came
He knelt down at her feet, until she laid
Her hand upon him, like a naked blade,
And whispered in his ear: "Arise, Sir Knight,
To my heart's level, O my heart's delight."

And there he lingered till the crowing cock,
The Alectryon of the farmyard and the flock,
Sang his aubade with lusty voice and clear,
To tell the sleeping world that dawn was near.
And then they parted; but at parting, lo!
They saw the palace courtyard white with snow,
And, placid as a nun, the moon on high
Gazing from cloudy cloisters of the sky.
"Alas!" he said, "how hide the fatal line
Of footprints leading from thy door to mine,
And none returning!" Ah, he little knew
What woman's wit, when put to proof, can do!

That night the Emperor, sleepless with the cares
And troubles that attend on state affairs,
Had risen before the dawn, and musing gazed
Into the silent night, as one amazed
To see the calm that reigned o'er all supreme,
When his own reign was but a troubled dream.
The moon lit up the gables capped with snow,
And the white roofs, and half the court below,
And he beheld a form, that seemed to cower
Beneath a burden, come from Emma's tower,
A woman, who upon her shoulders bore
Clerk Eginhard to his own private door,
And then returned in haste, but still essayed
To tread the footprints she herself had made;
And as she passed across the lighted space,
The Emperor saw his daughter Emma's face!

He started not; he did not speak or moan,
But seemed as one who hath been turned to stone;
And stood there like a statue, nor awoke
Out of his trance of pain, till morning broke,
Till the stars faded, and the moon went down,
And o'er the towers and steeples of the town
Came the gray daylight; then the sun, who took
The empire of the world with sovereign look,
Suffusing with a soft and golden glow
All the dead landscape in its shroud of snow,

Touching with flame the tapering chapel spires,
Windows and roofs, and smoke of household fires,
And kindling park and palace as he came;
The stork's nest on the chimney seemed in flame.
And thus he stood till Eginhard appeared,
Demure and modest with his comely beard
And flowing flaxen tresses, come to ask,
As was his wont, the day's appointed task.

The Emperor looked upon him with a smile,
And gently said: "My son, wait yet a while;
This hour my council meets upon some great
And very urgent business of the state.
Come back within the hour. On thy return
The work appointed for thee shalt thou learn."

Having dismissed this gallant Troubadour,
He summoned straight his council, and secure
And steadfast in his purpose, from the throne
All the adventure of the night made known;
Then asked for sentence; and with eager breath
Some answered banishment, and others death.

Then spake the king: "Your sentence is not mine;
Life is the gift of God, and is divine;
Nor from these palace walls shall one depart
Who carries such a secret in his heart;
My better judgment points another way.
Good Alcuin, I remember how one day
When my Pepino asked you, 'What are men?'
You wrote upon his tablets with your pen,
'Guests of the grave and travellers that pass!'
This being true of all men, we, alas!
Being all fashioned of the selfsame dust,
Let us be merciful as well as just;
This passing traveller, who hath stolen away
The brightest jewel of my crown today,
Shall of himself the precious gem restore;
By giving it, I make it mine once more.
Over those fatal footprints I will throw
My ermine mantle like another snow."

Then Eginhard was summoned to the hall,
And entered, and in presence of them all,
The Emperor said: "My son, for thou to me
Hast been a son, and evermore shalt be,
Long hast thou served thy sovereign, and thy zeal
Pleads to me with importunate appeal,
While I have been forgetful to requite
Thy service and affection as was right.
But now the hour is come, when I, thy Lord,
Will crown thy love with such supreme reward,
A gift so precious kings have striven in vain
To win it from the hands of Charlemagne."

Then sprang the portals of the chamber wide,
And Princess Emma entered, in the pride
Of birth and beauty, that in part o'ercame
The conscious terror and the blush of shame.
And the good Emperor rose up from his throne,
And taking her white hand within his own
Placed it in Eginhard's, and said: "My son,
This is the gift thy constant zeal hath won;
Thus I repay the royal debt I owe,
And cover up the footprints in the snow."

1872 1873

THE MONK OF CASAL-MAGGIORE

Once on a time, some centuries ago,
  In the hot sunshine two Franciscan friars
Wended their weary way with footsteps slow
  Back to their convent, whose white walls and spires
Gleamed on the hillside like a patch of snow;
  Covered with dust they were, and torn by briers,
And bore like sumpter-mules upon their backs
The badge of poverty, their beggar's sacks.

The first was Brother Anthony, a spare
  And silent man, with pallid cheeks and thin,
Much given to vigils, penance, fasting, prayer,
  Solemn and gray, and worn with discipline,
As if his body but white ashes were,
  Heaped on the living coals that glowed within;
A simple monk, like many of his day,
Whose instinct was to listen and obey.

A different man was Brother Timothy,
  Of larger mould and of a coarser paste;
A rubicund and stalwart monk was he,
  Broad in the shoulders, broader in the waist,
Who often filled the dull refectory
  With noise by which the convent was disgraced,

But to the mass-book gave but little heed,
By reason he had never learned to read.

Now, as they passed the outskirts of a wood,
They saw, with mingled pleasure and surprise,
Fast tethered to a tree an ass, that stood
Lazily winking his large, limpid eyes.
The farmer Gilbert, of that neighborhood,
His owner was, who, looking for supplies
Of fagots, deeper in the wood had strayed,
Leaving his beast to ponder in the shade.

As soon as Brother Timothy espied
The patient animal, he said: "Good-lack!
Thus for our needs doth Providence provide;
We'll lay our wallets on the creature's back."
This being done, he leisurely untied
From head and neck the halter of the jack,
And put it round his own, and to the tree
Stood tethered fast as if the ass were he.

And, bursting forth into a merry laugh,
He cried to Brother Anthony: "Away!
And drive the ass before you with your staff;
And when you reach the convent you may say
You left me at a farm, half tired and half
Ill with a fever, for a night and day,
And that the farmer lent this ass to bear
Our wallets, that are heavy with good fare."

Now Brother Anthony, who knew the pranks
Of Brother Timothy, would not persuade
Or reason with him on his quirks and cranks,
But, being obedient, silently obeyed;
And, smiting with his staff the ass's flanks,
Drove him before him over hill and glade,
Safe with his provend to the convent gate,
Leaving poor Brother Timothy to his fate.

Then Gilbert, laden with fagots for his fire,
Forth issued from the wood, and stood aghast
To see the ponderous body of the friar
Standing where he had left his donkey last.
Trembling he stood, and dared not venture nigher,
But stared, and gaped, and crossed himself full fast;
For, being credulous and of little wit,
He thought it was some demon from the pit.

While speechless and bewildered thus he gazed,
And dropped his load of fagots on the ground,
Quoth Brother Timothy: "Be not amazed
That where you left a donkey should be found
A poor Franciscan friar, half-starved and crazed,
Standing demure and with a halter bound;
But set me free, and hear the piteous story
Of Brother Timothy of Casal-Maggiore.

"I am a sinful man, although you see
I wear the consecrated cowl and cape;
You never owned an ass, but you owned me,
Changed and transformed from my own natural shape
All for the deadly sin of gluttony,
From which I could not otherwise escape,
Than by this penance, dieting on grass,
And being worked and beaten as an ass.

"Think of the ignominy I endured;
Think of the miserable life I led,
The toil and blows to which I was inured,
My wretched lodging in a windy shed,
My scanty fare so grudgingly procured,
The damp and musty straw that formed my bed!
But, having done this penance for my sins,
My life as man and monk again begins."

The simple Gilbert, hearing words like these,
Was conscience-stricken, and fell down apace
Before the friar upon his bended knees,
And with a suppliant voice implored his grace;
And the good monk, now very much at ease,
Granted him pardon with a smiling face,
Nor could refuse to be that night his guest,
It being late, and he in need of rest.

Upon a hillside, where the olive thrives,
With figures painted on its whitewashed walls,
The cottage stood; and near the humming hives
Made murmurs as of far-off waterfalls;
A place where those who love secluded lives
Might live content, and, free from noise and brawls,

Like Claudian's Old Man of Verona here
Measure by fruits the slow-revolving year.

And, coming to this cottage of content,
They found his children, and the buxom wench
His wife, Dame Cicely, and his father, bent
With years and labor, seated on a bench,
Repeating over some obscure event
In the old wars of Milanese and French;
All welcomed the Franciscan, with a sense
Of sacred awe and humble reverence.

When Gilbert told them what had come to pass,
How beyond question, cavil, or surmise,
Good Brother Timothy had been their ass,
You should have seen the wonder in their eyes;
You should have heard them cry, "Alas! alas!"
Have heard their lamentations and their sighs!
For all believed the story, and began
To see a saint in this afflicted man.

Forthwith there was prepared a grand repast,
To satisfy the craving of the friar
After so rigid and prolonged a fast;
The bustling housewife stirred the kitchen fire;
Then her two barnyard fowls, her best and last,
Were put to death, at her express desire,
And served up with a salad in a bowl,
And flasks of country wine to crown the whole.

It would not be believed should I repeat
How hungry Brother Timothy appeared;
It was a pleasure but to see him eat,
His white teeth flashing through his russet beard,
His face aglow and flushed with wine and meat,
His roguish eyes that rolled and laughed and leered!
Lord! how he drank the blood-red country wine
As if the village vintage were divine!

And all the while he talked without surcease,
And told his merry tales with jovial glee
That never flagged, but rather did increase,
And laughed aloud as if insane were he,
And wagged his red beard, matted like a fleece,
And cast such glances at Dame Cicely
That Gilbert now grew angry with his guest,
And thus in words his rising wrath expressed.

"Good father," said he, "easily we see
How needful in some persons, and how right,
Mortification of the flesh may be.
The indulgence you have given it tonight,
After long penance, clearly proves to me
Your strength against temptation is but slight,
And shows the dreadful peril you are in
Of a relapse into your deadly sin.

"Tomorrow morning, with the rising sun,
Go back unto your convent, nor refrain
From fasting and from scourging, for you run
Great danger to become an ass again,
Since monkish flesh and asinine are one;
Therefore be wise, nor longer here remain,
Unless you wish the scourge should be applied
By other hands, that will not spare your hide."

When this the monk had heard, his color fled
And then returned, like lightning in the air,
Till he was all one blush from foot to head,
And even the bald spot in his russet hair
Turned from its usual pallor to bright red!
The old man was asleep upon his chair.
Then all retired, and sank into the deep
And helpless imbecility of sleep.

They slept until the dawn of day drew near,
Till the cock should have crowed, but did not crow,
For they had slain the shining chanticleer
And eaten him for supper, as you know.
The monk was up betimes and of good cheer,
And, having breakfasted, made haste to go,
As if he heard the distant matin bell,
And had but little time to say farewell.

Fresh was the morning as the breath of kine;
Odors of herbs commingled with the sweet
Balsamic exhalations of the pine;
A haze was in the air presaging heat;
Uprose the sun above the Apennine,
And all the misty valleys at its feet
Were full of the delirious song of birds,
Voices of men, and bells, and low of herds.

All this to Brother Timothy was naught;
He did not care for scenery, nor here
His busy fancy found the thing it sought;
But when he saw the convent walls appear,
And smoke from kitchen chimneys upward caught
And whirled aloft into the atmosphere,
He quickened his slow footsteps, like a beast
That scents the stable a league off at least.

And as he entered through the convent gate
He saw there in the court the ass, who stood
Twirling his ears about, and seemed to wait,
Just as he found him waiting in the wood;
And told the Prior that, to alleviate
The daily labors of the brotherhood,
The owner, being a man of means and thrift,
Bestowed him on the convent as a gift.

And thereupon the Prior for many days
Revolved this serious matter in his mind,
And turned it over many different ways,
Hoping that some safe issue he might find;
But stood in fear of what the world would say,
If he accepted presents of this kind,
Employing beasts of burden for the packs
That lazy monks should carry on their backs.

Then, to avoid all scandal of the sort,
And stop the mouth of cavil, he decreed
That he would cut the tedious matter short,
And sell the ass with all convenient speed,
Thus saving the expense of his support,
And hoarding something for a time of need.
So he dispatched him to the neighboring Fair,
And freed himself from cumber and from care.

It happened now by chance, as some might say,
Others perhaps would call it destiny,
Gilbert was at the Fair; and heard a bray,
And nearer came, and saw that it was he,
And whispered in his ear, "Ah, lackaday!
Good father, the rebellious flesh, I see,
Has changed you back into an ass again,
And all my admonitions were in vain."

The ass, who felt this breathing in his ear,
Did not turn round to look, but shook his head,
As if he were not pleased these words to hear,
And contradicted all that had been said.
And this made Gilbert cry in voice more clear,
"I know you well; your hair is russet-red;
Do not deny it; for you are the same
Franciscan friar, and Timothy by name."

The ass, though now the secret had come out,
Was obstinate, and shook his head again;
Until a crowd was gathered round about
To hear this dialogue between the twain;
And raised their voices in a noisy shout
When Gilbert tried to make the matter plain,
And flouted him and mocked him all day long
With laughter and with jibes and scraps of song.

"If this be Brother Timothy," they cried,
"Buy him, and feed him on the tenderest grass;
Thou canst not do too much for one so tried
As to be twice transformed into an ass."
So simple Gilbert bought him, and untied
His halter, and o'er mountain and morass
He led him homeward, talking as he went
Of good behavior and a mind content.

The children saw them coming, and advanced,
Shouting with joy, and hung about his neck,—
Not Gilbert's, but the ass's,—round him danced,
And wove green garlands wherewithal to deck
His sacred person; for again it chanced
Their childish feelings, without rein or check,
Could not discriminate in any way
A donkey from a friar of Orders Gray.

"O Brother Timothy," the children said,
"You have come back to us just as before;
We were afraid, and thought that you were dead,
And we should never see you any more."
And then they kissed the white star on his head,
That like a birth-mark or a badge he wore,
And patted him upon the neck and face,
And said a thousand things with childish grace.

Thenceforward and forever he was known
As Brother Timothy, and led alway
A life of luxury, till he had grown
Ungrateful, being stuffed with corn and hay,
And very vicious. Then in angry tone,
Rousing himself, poor Gilbert said one day,

"When simple kindness is misunderstood
A little flagellation may do good."

His many vices need not here be told;
Among them was a habit that he had
Of flinging up his heels at young and old,
Breaking his halter, running off like mad
O'er pasture-lands and meadow, wood and wold,
And other misdemeanors quite as bad;
But worst of all was breaking from his shed
At night, and ravaging the cabbage-bed.

So Brother Timothy went back once more
To his old life of labor and distress;
Was beaten worse than he had been before;
And now, instead of comfort and caress,
Came labors manifold and trials sore;
And as his toils increased his food grew less,
Until at last the great consoler, Death,
Ended his many sufferings with his breath.

Great was the lamentation when he died;
And mainly that he died impenitent;
Dame Cicely bewailed, the children cried,
The old man still remembered the event
In the French war, and Gilbert magnified
His many virtues, as he came and went,
And said: "Heaven pardon Brother Timothy,
And keep us from the sin of gluttony."

1873 1873

CHAUCER

Petrarchan sonnet

An old man in a lodge within a park;
The chamber walls depicted all around
With portraitures of huntsman, hawk, and hound,
And the hurt deer. He listeneth to the lark,
Whose song comes with the sunshine through the dark
Of painted glass in leaden lattice bound;
He listeneth and he laugheth at the sound,
Then writeth in a book like any clerk.
He is the poet of the dawn, who wrote
The Canterbury Tales, and his old age
Made beautiful with song; and as I read
I hear the crowing cock, I hear the note
Of lark and linnet, and from every page
Rise odors of ploughed field or flowery mead.

1873 1875

SHAKESPEARE

A vision as of crowded city streets,
With human life in endless overflow;
Thunder of thoroughfares; trumpets that blow
To battle; clamor, in obscure retreats,
Of sailors landed from their anchored fleets;
Tolling of bells in turrets, and below
Voices of children, and bright flowers that throw
O'er garden walls their intermingled sweets!
This vision comes to me when I unfold
The volume of the Poet paramount,
Whom all the Muses loved, not one alone;—
Into his hands they put the lyre of gold,
And, crowned with sacred laurel at their fount,
Placed him as Musagetes on their throne.

1873 1875

MILTON

I pace the sounding sea-beach and behold
How the voluminous billows roll and run,
Upheaving and subsiding, while the sun
Shines through their sheeted emerald far unrolled,
And the ninth wave, slow gathering fold by fold
All its loose-flowing garments into one,
Plunges upon the shore, and floods the dun
Pale reach of sands, and changes them to gold.
So in majestic cadence rise and fall
The mighty undulations of thy song,
O sightless bard, England's Mæonides!
And ever and anon, high over all
Uplifted, a ninth wave superb and strong,
Floods all the soul with its melodious seas.

1873 1875

KEATS

The young Endymion sleeps Endymion's sleep;
The shepherd-boy whose tale was left half told!
The solemn grove uplifts its shield of gold
To the red rising moon, and loud and deep

The nightingale is singing from the steep;
It is midsummer, but the air is cold;
Can it be death? Alas, beside the fold
A shepherd's pipe lies shattered near his sheep.
Lo! in the moonlight gleams a marble white,
On which I read: "Here lieth one whose name
Was writ in water." And was this the meed
Of his sweet singing? Rather let me write:
"The smoking flax before it burst to flame
Was quenched by death, and broken the bruised reed."

1873 1875

CHARLES SUMNER

GARLANDS upon his grave,
And flowers upon his hearse,
And to the tender heart and brave
The tribute of this verse.

His was the troubled life,
The conflict and the pain,
The grief, the bitterness of strife,
The honor without stain.

Like Winkelried, he took
Into his manly breast
The sheaf of hostile spears, and broke
A path for the oppressed.

Then from the fatal field
Upon a nation's heart
Borne like a warrior on his shield!—
So should the brave depart.

Death takes us by surprise,
And stays our hurrying feet;
The great design unfinished lies,
Our lives are incomplete.

But in the dark unknown
Perfect their circles seem,
Even as a bridge's arch of stone
Is rounded in the stream.

Alike are life and death,
When life in death survives,
And the uninterrupted breath
Inspires a thousand lives.

Were a star quenched on high,
For ages would its light,
Still travelling downward from the sky,
Shine on our mortal sight.

So when a great man dies,
For years beyond our ken,
The light he leaves behind him lies
Upon the paths of men.

1874 1875

MORITURI SALUTAMUS

POEM FOR THE FIFTIETH ANNIVERSARY OF THE CLASS OF 1825 IN BOWDOIN COLLEGE

Tempora labuntur, tacitisque senescimus annis,
Et fugiunt freno non remorante dies.

OVID, *Fastorum*, Lib. vi.

"O CÆSAR, we who are about to die
Salute you!" was the gladiators' cry
In the arena, standing face to face
With death and with the Roman populace.

O ye familiar scenes,—ye groves of pine,
That once were mine and are no longer mine,—
Thou river, widening through the meadows green
To the vast sea, so near and yet unseen,—
Ye halls, in whose seclusion and repose
Phantoms of fame, like exhalations, rose
And vanished,—we who are about to die
Salute you; earth and air and sea and sky,
And the Imperial Sun that scatters down
His sovereign splendors upon grove and town.

Ye do not answer us! ye do not hear!
We are forgotten; and in your austere
And calm indifference, ye little care
Whether we come or go, or whence or where.
What passing generations fill these halls,
What passing voices echo from these walls,
Ye heed not; we are only as the blast,
A moment heard, and then forever past.

Not so the teachers who in earlier days
Led our bewildered feet through learning's maze;
They answer us—alas! what have I said?
What greetings come there from the voiceless dead?
What salutation, welcome, or reply?
What pressure from the hands that lifeless lie?
They are no longer here; they all are gone
Into the land of shadows,—all save one.

Honor and reverence, and the good repute
That follows faithful service as its fruit,
Be unto him, whom living we salute.

The great Italian poet, when he made
His dreadful journey to the realms of shade,
Met there the old instructor of his youth,
And cried in tones of pity and of ruth:
"Oh, never from the memory of my heart
Your dear, paternal image shall depart,
Who while on earth, ere yet by death surprised,
Taught me how mortals are immortalized;
How grateful am I for that patient care
All my life long my language shall declare."

Today we make the poet's words our own,
And utter them in plaintive undertone;
Nor to the living only be they said,
But to the other living called the dead,
Whose dear, paternal images appear
Not wrapped in gloom, but robed in sunshine here;
Whose simple lives, complete and without flaw,
Were part and parcel of great Nature's law;
Who said not to their Lord, as if afraid,
"Here is thy talent in a napkin laid,"
But labored in their sphere, as men who live
In the delight that work alone can give.
Peace be to them; eternal peace and rest,
And the fulfilment of the great behest:
"Ye have been faithful over a few things,
Over ten cities shall ye reign as kings."

And ye who fill the places we once filled,
And follow in the furrows that we tilled,
Young men, whose generous hearts are beating high,
We who are old, and are about to die,
Salute you; hail you; take your hands in ours,
And crown you with our welcome as with flowers!

How beautiful is youth! how bright it gleams
With its illusions, aspirations, dreams!
Book of Beginnings, Story without End,
Each maid a heroine, and each man a friend!
Aladdin's Lamp, and Fortunatus' Purse,
That holds the treasures of the universe!
All possibilities are in its hands,
No danger daunts it, and no foe withstands;
In its sublime audacity of faith,
"Be thou removed!" it to the mountain saith,
And with ambitious feet, secure and proud,
Ascends the ladder leaning on the cloud!

As ancient Priam at the Scæan gate
Sat on the walls of Troy in regal state
With the old men, too old and weak to fight,
Chirping like grasshoppers in their delight
To see the embattled hosts, with spear and shield,
Of Trojans and Achaians in the field;
So from the snowy summits of our years
We see you in the plain, as each appears,
And question of you; asking, "Who is he
That towers above the others? Which may be
Atreides, Menelaus, Odysseus,
Ajax the great, or bold Idomeneus?"

Let him not boast who puts his armor on
As he who puts it off, the battle done.
Study yourselves; and most of all note well
Wherein kind Nature meant you to excel.
Not every blossom ripens into fruit;
Minerva, the inventress of the flute,
Flung it aside, when she her face surveyed
Distorted in a fountain as she played;
The unlucky Marsyas found it, and his fate
Was one to make the bravest hesitate.

Write on your doors the saying wise and old,
"Be bold! be bold!" and everywhere, "Be bold;
Be not too bold!" Yet better the excess
Than the defect; better the more than less;
Better like Hector in the field to die,
Than like a perfumed Paris turn and fly.

And now, my classmates; ye remaining few
That number not the half of those we knew,
Ye, against whose familiar names not yet
The fatal asterisk of death is set,
Ye I salute! The horologe of Time
Strikes the half-century with a solemn chime,
And summons us together once again,
The joy of meeting not unmixed with pain.

Where are the others? Voices from the deep
Caverns of darkness answer me: "They sleep!"
I name no names; instinctively I feel
Each at some well-remembered grave will kneel,

And from the inscription wipe the weeds and moss,
For every heart best knoweth its own loss.
I see their scattered gravestones gleaming white
Through the pale dusk of the impending night;
O'er all alike the impartial sunset throws
Its golden lilies mingled with the rose;
We give to each a tender thought, and pass
Out of the graveyards with their tangled grass,
Unto these scenes frequented by our feet
When we were young, and life was fresh and sweet.

What shall I say to you? What can I say
Better than silence is? When I survey
This throng of faces turned to meet my own,
Friendly and fair, and yet to me unknown,
Transformed the very landscape seems to be;
It is the same, yet not the same to me.
So many memories crowd upon my brain,
So many ghosts are in the wooded plain,
I fain would steal away, with noiseless tread,
As from a house where some one lieth dead.

I cannot go;—I pause;—I hesitate;
My feet reluctant linger at the gate;
As one who struggles in a troubled dream
To speak and cannot, to myself I seem.

Vanish the dream! Vanish the idle fears!
Vanish the rolling mists of fifty years!
Whatever time or space may intervene,
I will not be a stranger in this scene.
Here every doubt, all indecision, ends;
Hail, my companions, comrades, classmates, friends!

Ah me! the fifty years since last we met
Seem to me fifty folios bound and set
By Time, the great transcriber, on his shelves,
Wherein are written the histories of ourselves.
What tragedies, what comedies, are there;
What joy and grief, what rapture and despair!
What chronicles of triumph and defeat,
Of struggle, and temptation, and retreat!
What records of regrets, and doubts, and fears!
What pages blotted, blistered by our tears!
What lovely landscapes on the margin shine,
What sweet, angelic faces, what divine
And holy images of love and trust,
Undimmed by age, unsoiled by damp or dust!

Whose hand shall dare to open and explore
These volumes, closed and clasped forever-more?
Not mine. With reverential feet I pass;
I hear a voice that cries, "Alas! alas!
Whatever hath been written shall remain,
Nor be erased nor written o'er again;
The unwritten only still belongs to thee:
Take heed, and ponder well what that shall be."

As children frightened by a thunder-cloud
Are reassured if some one reads aloud
A tale of wonder, with enchantment fraught,
Or wild adventure, that diverts their thought,
Let me endeavor with a tale to chase
The gathering shadows of the time and place,
And banish what we all too deeply feel
Wholly to say, or wholly to conceal.

In mediæval Rome, I know not where,
There stood an image with its arm in air,
And on its lifted finger, shining clear,
A golden ring with the device, "Strike here!"
Greatly the people wondered, though none guessed
The meaning that these words but half ex-pressed,
Until a learned clerk, who at noonday
With downcast eyes was passing on his way,
Paused, and observed the spot, and marked it well,
Whereon the shadow of the finger fell;
And, coming back at midnight, delved, and found
A secret stairway leading underground.
Down this he passed into a spacious hall,
Lit by a flaming jewel on the wall;
And opposite, in threatening attitude,
With bow and shaft a brazen statue stood.
Upon its forehead, like a coronet,
Were these mysterious words of menace set:
"That which I am, I am; my fatal aim
None can escape, not even yon luminous flame!"

Midway the hall was a fair table placed,
With cloth of gold, and golden cups enchased
With rubies, and the plates and knives were gold,

And gold the bread and viands manifold.
Around it, silent, motionless, and sad,
Were seated gallant knights in armor clad,
And ladies beautiful with plume and zone,
But they were stone, their hearts within were stone;
And the vast hall was filled in every part
With silent crowds, stony in face and heart.

Long at the scene, bewildered and amazed,
The trembling clerk in speechless wonder gazed;
Then from the table, by his greed made bold,
He seized a goblet and a knife of gold,
And suddenly from their seats the guests upsprang,
The vaulted ceiling with loud clamors rang,
The archer sped his arrow, at their call,
Shattering the lambent jewel on the wall,
And all was dark around and overhead;—
Stark on the floor the luckless clerk lay dead!

The writer of this legend then records
Its ghostly application in these words:
The image is the Adversary old,
Whose beckoning finger points to realms of gold;
Our lusts and passions are the downward stair
That leads the soul from a diviner air;
The archer, Death; the flaming jewel, Life;
Terrestrial goods, the goblet and the knife;
The knights and ladies, all whose flesh and bone
By avarice have been hardened into stone;
The clerk, the scholar whom the love of pelf
Tempts from his books and from his nobler self.

The scholar and the world! The endless strife,
The discord in the harmonies of life!
The love of learning, the sequestered nooks,
And all the sweet serenity of books;
The market-place, the eager love of gain,
Whose aim is vanity, and whose end is pain!

But why, you ask me, should this tale be told
To men grown old, or who are growing old?
It is too late! Ah, nothing is too late
Till the tired heart shall cease to palpitate.
Cato learned Greek at eighty; Sophocles
Wrote his grand Œdipus, and Simonides
Bore off the prize of verse from his compeers,
When each had numbered more than fourscore years,
And Theophrastus, at fourscore and ten,
Had but begun his "Characters of Men."
Chaucer, at Woodstock with the nightingales,
At sixty wrote the Canterbury Tales;
Goethe at Weimar, toiling to the last,
Completed Faust when eighty years were past.
These are indeed exceptions; but they show
How far the gulf-stream of our youth may flow
Into the arctic regions of our lives,
Where little else than life itself survives.

As the barometer foretells the storm
While still the skies are clear, the weather warm,
So something in us, as old age draws near,
Betrays the pressure of the atmosphere.
The nimble mercury, ere we are aware,
Descends the elastic ladder of the air;
The telltale blood in artery and vein
Sinks from its higher levels in the brain;
Whatever poet, orator, or sage
May say of it, old age is still old age.
It is the waning, not the crescent moon;
The dusk of evening, not the blaze of noon;
It is not strength, but weakness; not desire,
But its surcease; not the fierce heat of fire,
The burning and consuming element,
But that of ashes and of embers spent,
In which some living sparks we still discern,
Enough to warm, but not enough to burn.

What then? Shall we sit idly down and say
The night hath come; it is no longer day?
The night hath not yet come; we are not quite
Cut off from labor by the failing light;
Something remains for us to do or dare;
Even the oldest tree some fruit may bear;
Not Œdipus Coloneus, or Greek Ode,
Or tales of pilgrims that one morning rode
Out of the gateway of the Tabard Inn,
But other something, would we but begin;
For age is opportunity no less
Than youth itself, though in another dress,
And as the evening twilight fades away
The sky is filled with stars, invisible by day.

1874 1875

THREE FRIENDS OF MINE

I

When I remember them, those friends of mine,
Who are no longer here, the noble three,
Who half my life were more than friends to me,
And whose discourse was like a generous wine,
I most of all remember the divine
Something, that shone in them, and made us see
The archetypal man, and what might be
The amplitude of Nature's first design.
In vain I stretch my hands to clasp their hands;
I cannot find them. Nothing now is left
But a majestic memory. They meanwhile
Wander together in Elysian lands,
Perchance remembering me, who am bereft
Of their dear presence, and, remembering, smile.

II

In Attica thy birthplace should have been,
On the Ionian Isles, or where the seas
Encircle in their arms the Cyclades,
So wholly Greek wast thou in thy serene
And childlike joy of life, O Philhellene!
Around thee would have swarmed the Attic bees;
Homer had been thy friend, or Socrates,
And Plato welcomed thee to his demesne.
For thee old legends breathed historic breath;
Thou sawest Poseidon in the purple sea,
And in the sunset Jason's fleece of gold!
Oh, what hadst thou to do with cruel Death,
Who wast so full of life, or Death with thee,
That thou shouldst die before thou hadst grown old!

III

I stand again on the familiar shore,
And hear the waves of the distracted sea
Piteously calling and lamenting thee,
And waiting restless at thy cottage door.
The rocks, the sea-weed on the ocean floor,
The willows in the meadow, and the free
Wild winds of the Atlantic welcome me;
Then why shouldst thou be dead, and come no more?
Ah, why shouldst thou be dead, when common men
Are busy with their trivial affairs,
Having and holding? Why, when thou hadst read
Nature's mysterious manuscript, and then
Wast ready to reveal the truth it bears,
Why art thou silent? Why shouldst thou be dead?

IV

River, that stealest with such silent pace
Around the City of the Dead, where lies
A friend who bore thy name, and whom these eyes
Shall see no more in his accustomed place,
Linger and fold him in thy soft embrace,
And say good night, for now the western skies
Are red with sunset, and gray mists arise
Like damps that gather on a dead man's face.
Good night! good night! as we so oft have said
Beneath this roof at midnight, in the days
That are no more, and shall no more return.
Thou hast but taken thy lamp and gone to bed;
I stay a little longer, as one stays
To cover up the embers that still burn.

V

The doors are all wide open; at the gate
The blossomed lilacs counterfeit a blaze,
And seem to warm the air; a dreamy haze
Hangs o'er the Brighton meadows like a fate,
And on their margin, with sea-tides elate,
The flooded Charles, as in the happier days,
Writes the last letter of his name, and stays
His restless steps, as if compelled to wait.
I also wait; but they will come no more,
Those friends of mine, whose presence satisfied
The thirst and hunger of my heart. Ah me!
They have forgotten the pathway to my door!
Something is gone from nature since they died,
And summer is not summer, nor can be.

1874 1875

THE SOUND OF THE SEA

The sea awoke at midnight from its sleep,
And round the pebbly beaches far and wide
I heard the first wave of the rising tide
Rush onward with uninterrupted sweep;
A voice out of the silence of the deep,
A sound mysteriously multiplied
As of a cataract from the mountain's side,
Or roar of winds upon a wooded steep.
So comes to us at times, from the unknown
And inaccessible solitudes of being,
The rushing of the sea-tides of the soul;
And inspirations, that we deem our own,
Are some divine foreshadowing and fore-seeing
Of things beyond our reason or control.

1874 1875

A DUTCH PICTURE

Simon Danz has come home again,
From cruising about with his buccaneers;
He has singed the beard of the King of Spain,
And carried away the Dean of Jaen
And sold him in Algiers.

In his house by the Maese, with its roof of tiles,
And weathercocks flying aloft in air,
There are silver tankards of antique styles,
Plunder of convent and castle, and piles
Of carpets rich and rare.

In his tulip-garden there by the town,
Overlooking the sluggish stream,
With his Moorish cap and dressing-gown,
The old sea-captain, hale and brown,
Walks in a waking dream.

A smile in his gray mustachio lurks
Whenever he thinks of the King of Spain,
And the listed tulips look like Turks,
And the silent gardener as he works
Is changed to the Dean of Jaen.

The windmills on the outermost
Verge of the landscape in the haze,
To him are towers on the Spanish coast,
With whiskered sentinels at their post,
Though this is the river Maese.

But when the winter rains begin,
He sits and smokes by the blazing brands,
And old seafaring men come in,
Goat-bearded, gray, and with double chin,
And rings upon their hands.

They sit there in the shadow and shine
Of the flickering fire of the winter night;
Figures in color and design
Like those by Rembrandt of the Rhine,
Half darkness and half light.

And they talk of ventures lost or won,
And their talk is ever and ever the same,
While they drink the red wine of Tarragon,
From the cellars of some Spanish Don,
Or convent set on flame.

Restless at times with heavy strides
He paces his parlor to and fro;
He is like a ship that at anchor rides,
And swings with the rising and falling tides,
And tugs at her anchor-tow.

Voices mysterious far and near,
Sound of the wind and sound of the sea,
Are calling and whispering in his ear,
"Simon Danz! Why stayest thou here?
Come forth and follow me!"

So he thinks he shall take to the sea again
For one more cruise with his buccaneers,
To singe the beard of the King of Spain,
And capture another Dean of Jaen,
And sell him in Algiers.

1876 1878

NATURE

As a fond mother, when the day is o'er,
Leads by the hand her little child to bed,
Half willing, half reluctant to be led,
And leave his broken playthings on the floor,
Still gazing at them through the open door,
Nor wholly reassured and comforted
By promises of others in their stead,
Which, though more splendid, may not please him more;
So Nature deals with us, and takes away
Our playthings one by one, and by the hand

Leads us to rest so gently, that we go
Scarce knowing if we wish to go or stay,
Being too full of sleep to understand
How far the unknown transcends the what we know.

1876 1878

IN THE CHURCHYARD AT TARRYTOWN

Here lies the gentle humorist, who died
In the bright Indian Summer of his fame!
A simple stone, with but a date and name,
Marks his secluded resting-place beside
The river that he loved and glorified.
Here in the autumn of his days he came,
But the dry leaves of life were all aflame
With tints that brightened and were multiplied.
How sweet a life was his; how sweet a death!
Living, to wing with mirth the weary hours,
Or with romantic tales the heart to cheer;
Dying, to leave a memory like the breath
Of summers full of sunshine and of showers,
A grief and gladness in the atmosphere.

1876 1877

VENICE

White swan of cities, slumbering in thy nest
So wonderfully built among the reeds
Of the lagoon, that fences thee and feeds,
As sayeth thy old historian and thy guest!
White water-lily, cradled and caressed
By ocean streams, and from the silt and weeds
Lifting thy golden filaments and seeds,
Thy sun-illumined spires, thy crown and crest!
White phantom city, whose untrodden streets
Are rivers, and whose pavements are the shifting
Shadows of palaces and strips of sky;
I wait to see thee vanish like the fleets
Seen in mirage, or towers of cloud uplifting
In air their unsubstantial masonry.

1876 1878

THE POETS

O ye dead Poets, who are living still
Immortal in your verse, though life be fled,
And ye, O living Poets, who are dead
Though ye are living, if neglect can kill,
Tell me if in the darkest hours of ill,
With drops of anguish falling fast and red
From the sharp crown of thorns upon your head,
Ye were not glad your errand to fulfil?
Yes; for the gift and ministry of Song
Have something in them so divinely sweet,
It can assuage the bitterness of wrong;
Not in the clamor of the crowded street,
Not in the shouts and plaudits of the throng,
But in ourselves, are triumph and defeat.

1876 1878

VICTOR AND VANQUISHED

As one who long hath fled with panting breath
Before his foe, bleeding and near to fall,
I turn and set my back against the wall,
And look thee in the face, triumphant Death.
I call for aid, and no one answereth;
I am alone with thee, who conquerest all;
Yet me thy threatening form doth not appall,
For thou art but a phantom and a wraith.
Wounded and weak, sword broken at the hilt,
With armor shattered, and without a shield,
I stand unmoved; do with me what thou wilt;
I can resist no more, but will not yield.
This is no tournament where cowards tilt;
The vanquished here is victor of the field.

1876 1882

WAPENTAKE

TO ALFRED TENNYSON

Poet! I come to touch thy lance with mine;
Not as a knight, who on the listed field
Of tourney touched his adversary's shield
In token of defiance, but in sign
Of homage to the mastery, which is thine,
In English song; nor will I keep concealed,

And voiceless as a rivulet frost-congealed,
My admiration for thy verse divine.
Not of the howling dervishes of song,
Who craze the brain with their delirious dance,
Art thou, O sweet historian of the heart!
Therefore to thee the laurel-leaves belong,
To thee our love and our allegiance,
For thy allegiance to the poet's art.

1877 1877

THE CROSS OF SNOW

In the long, sleepless watches of the night,
A gentle face—the face of one long dead—
Looks at me from the wall, where round its head
The night-lamp casts a halo of pale light.
Here in this room she died; and soul more white
Never through martyrdom of fire was led
To its repose; nor can in books be read
The legend of a life more benedight.
There is a mountain in the distant West
That, sun-defying, in its deep ravines
Displays a cross of snow upon its side.
Such is the cross I wear upon my breast
These eighteen years, through all the changing scenes
And seasons, changeless since the day she died.

1879 1886

JUGURTHA

How cold are thy baths, Apollo!
Cried the African monarch, the splendid,
As down to his death in the hollow
Dark dungeons of Rome he descended,
Uncrowned, unthroned, unattended;
How cold are thy baths, Apollo!

How cold are thy baths, Apollo!
Cried the Poet, unknown, unbefriended,
As the vision, that lured him to follow,
With the mist and the darkness blended,
And the dream of his life was ended;
How cold are thy baths, Apollo!

1879 1880

THE TIDE RISES, THE TIDE FALLS

The tide rises, the tide falls,
The twilight darkens, the curlew calls;
Along the sea-sands damp and brown
The traveller hastens toward the town,
And the tide rises, the tide falls.

Darkness settles on roofs and walls,
But the sea in the darkness calls and calls;
The little waves, with their soft, white hands,
Efface the footprints in the sands,
And the tide rises, the tide falls.

The morning breaks; the steeds in their stalls
Stamp and neigh, as the hostler calls;
The day returns, but nevermore
Returns the traveller to the shore,
And the tide rises, the tide falls.

1879 1880

L'ENVOI: THE POET AND HIS SONGS

As the birds come in the Spring,
We know not from where;
As the stars come at evening
From depths of the air;

As the rain comes from the cloud,
And the brook from the ground;
As suddenly, low or loud,
Out of silence a sound;

As the grape comes to the vine,
The fruit to the tree;
As the wind comes to the pine,
And the tide to the sea;

As come the white sails of ships
O'er the ocean's verge;
As comes the smile to the lips,
The foam to the surge;

So come to the Poet his songs,
All hitherward blown
From the misty realm, that belongs
To the vast Unknown.

His, and not his, are the lays
He sings; and their fame
Is his, and not his; and the praise
And the pride of a name.

For voices pursue him by day,
  And haunt him by night,
And he listens, and needs must obey,
  When the Angel says, "Write!"

1880

THE BELLS OF SAN BLAS

What say the Bells of San Blas
To the ships that southward pass
  From the harbor of Mazatlan?
To them it is nothing more
Than the sound of surf on the shore,—
  Nothing more to master or man.

But to me, a dreamer of dreams,
To whom what is and what seems
  Are often one and the same,—
The Bells of San Blas to me
Have a strange, wild melody,
  And are something more than a name.

For bells are the voice of the church;
They have tones that touch and search
  The hearts of young and old;
One sound to all, yet each
Lends a meaning to their speech,
  And the meaning is manifold.

They are a voice of the Past,
Of an age that is fading fast,
  Of a power austere and grand;
When the flag of Spain unfurled
Its folds o'er this western world,
  And the Priest was lord of the land.

The chapel that once looked down
On the little seaport town
  Has crumbled into the dust;
And on oaken beams below
The bells swing to and fro,
  And are green with mould and rust.

"Is, then, the old faith dead,"
They say, "and in its stead
  Is some new faith proclaimed,
That we are forced to remain
Naked to sun and rain,
  Unsheltered and ashamed?

"Once in our tower aloof
We rang over wall and roof
  Our warnings and our complaints;
And round about us there
The white doves filled the air,
  Like the white souls of the saints.

"The saints! Ah, have they grown
Forgetful of their own?
  Are they asleep, or dead,
That open to the sky
Their ruined Missions lie,
  No longer tenanted?

"Oh, bring us back once more
The vanished days of yore,
  When the world with faith was filled;
Bring back the fervid zeal,
The hearts of fire and steel,
  The hands that believe and build.

"Then from our tower again
We will send over land and main
  Our voices of command,
Like exiled kings who return
To their thrones, and the people learn
  That the Priest is lord of the land!"

O Bells of San Blas, in vain
Ye call back the Past again!
  The Past is deaf to your prayer;
Out of the shadows of night
The world rolls into light;
  It is daybreak everywhere.

1882 1882

OUR NATIVE WRITERS

To an American there is something endearing in the very sound, Our Native Writers. Like the music of our native tongue, when heard in a foreign land, they have power to kindle up within him the tender memory of his home and fireside; and more than this, they foretell that whatever is noble and attractive in our national character will one day be associated with the sweet magic of Poetry. Is, then, our land to be indeed the land of song? Will it one day be rich in romantic associations? Will poetry, that hallows every scene,—that renders every spot classical,—and pours out on all things the soul of its enthusiasm, breathe over it that enchantment, which lives in the isles of Greece, and is more than life amid the "woods, that wave o'er Delphi's steep"? Yes! —and palms are to be won by our native writers!—by those that have been nursed and brought up with us in the civil and religious freedom of our country. Already has a voice been lifted up in this land,—already a spirit and a love of literature are springing up in the shadow of our free political institutions.

But as yet we can boast of nothing farther than a first beginning of a national literature: a literature associated and linked in with the grand and beautiful scenery of our country,—with our institutions, our manners, our customs,—in a word, with all that has helped to form whatever there is peculiar to us, and to the land in which we live. We cannot yet throw off our literary allegiance to Old England, we cannot yet remove from our shelves every book which is not strictly and truly American. English literature is a great and glorious monument, built up by the master-spirits of old time, that had no peers, and rising bright and beautiful until its summit is hid in the mists of antiquity.

Of the many causes which have hitherto retarded the growth of polite literature in our country, I have not time to say much. The greatest, which now exists, is doubtless the want of that exclusive attention, which eminence in any profession so imperiously demands. Ours is an age and a country of great minds, though perhaps not of great endeavors. Poetry with us has never yet been anything but a pastime. The fault, however, is not so much that of our writers as of the prevalent modes of thinking which characterize our country and our times. We are a plain people, that have had nothing to do with the mere pleasures and luxuries of life; and hence there has sprung up within us a quick-sightedness to the failings of literary men, and an aversion to everything that is not practical, operative, and thoroughgoing. But if we would ever have a national literature, our native writers must be patronized. Whatever there may be in letters, over which time shall have no power, must be "born of great endeavors," and those endeavors are the offspring of liberal patronage. Putting off, then, what Shakespeare calls "the visage of the times,"—we must become hearty wellwishers to our native authors:—and with them there must be a deep and thorough conviction of the glory of their calling,—an utter abandonment of everything else,—and a noble self-devotion to the cause of literature. We have indeed much to hope from these things;—for our hearts are already growing warm towards literary adventurers, and a generous spirit has gone abroad in our land, which shall liberalize and enlighten.

In the vanity of scholarship, England has reproached us that we have no finished scholars. But there is reason for believing that men of mere learning—men of sober research and studied correctness—do not give to a nation its great name. Our very poverty in this respect will have a tendency to give a national character to our literature. Our writers will not be constantly toiling and panting after classical allusions to the Vale of Tempe and the Etrurian river, nor to the Roman fountains shall—

"The emulous nations of the West repair
To kindle their quenched urns, and drink fresh
spirit there."

We are thus thrown upon ourselves: and thus shall our native hills become renowned in song, like those of Greece and Italy. Every rock shall become a chronicle of storied allusions; and the tomb of the Indian prophet be as hallowed as the sepulchres of ancient kings, or the damp vault and perpetual lamp of the Saracen monarch.

Having briefly mentioned one circumstance

which is retarding us in the way of our literary prosperity, I shall now mention one from which we may hope a happy and glorious issue: It is the influence of natural scenery in forming the poetical character. Genius, to be sure, must be born with a man; and it is its high prerogative to be free, limitless, irresponsible. Yet how is it molded by the plastic hand of Nature! how are its attributes shaped and modulated, when a genius like Canova's failed in the bust of the Corsican, and amid the splendor of the French metropolis languished for the sunny skies and vine-clad hills of Italy? Men may talk of sitting down in the calm and quiet of their libraries, and of forgetting, in the eloquent companionship of books, all the vain cares that beset them in the crowded thoroughfares of life; but, after all, there is nothing which so frees us from the turbulent ambition and bustle of the world, nothing which so fills the mind with great and glowing conceptions, and at the same time so warms the heart with love and tenderness, as a frequent and close communion with natural scenery. The scenery of our own country, too, so rich as it is in everything beautiful and magnificent, and so full of quiet loveliness or of sublime and solitary awe, has for our eyes enchantment, for our ears an impressive and unutterable eloquence. Its language is in high mountains, and in the pleasant valleys scooped out between them, in the garniture which the fields put on, and in the blue lake asleep in the hollow of the hills. There is an inspiration, too, in the rich sky that "brightens and purples" o'er our earth, when lighted up with the splendor of morning, or when the garment of the clouds comes over the setting sun.

Our poetry is not in books alone. It is in the hearts of those men, whose love for the world's gain,—for its business and its holiday,—has grown cold within them, and who have found there that sweet sentiment and pure devotion of feeling can spring up and live in the shadow of a low and quiet life, and amid those that have no splendor in their joys, and no parade in their griefs.

Thus shall the mind take color from things around us,—from them shall there be a genuine birth of enthusiasm,—a rich development of poetic feeling, that shall break forth in song. Though the works of art must grow old and perish away from the earth, the forms of nature shall keep forever their power over the human mind, and have their influence upon the literature of a people.

We may rejoice, then, in the hope of beauty and sublimity in our national literature, for no people are richer than we are in the treasures of nature. And well may each of us feel a glorious and high-minded pride in saying, as he looks on the hills and vales,—on the woods and waters of New England,—

"This is my own, my native land."

1825

From KAVANAGH

[AN AMERICAN LITERATURE]

Meanwhile, things had gone on very quietly and monotonously in Mr. Churchill's family. Only one event, and that a mysterious one, had disturbed its serenity. It was the sudden disappearance of Lucy, the pretty orphan girl; and as the booted centipede, who had so much excited Mr. Churchill's curiosity, disappeared at the same time, there was little doubt that they had gone away together. But whither gone, and wherefore, remained a mystery.

Mr. Churchill, also, had had his profile, and those of his wife and children, taken, in a very humble style, by Mr. Bantam, whose advertisement he had noticed on his way to school nearly a year before. His own was considered the best, as a work of art. The face was cut out entirely; the color of the coat velvet; the shirt-collar very high and white; and the top of his head ornamented with a crest of hair turning up in front, though his own turned down,—which slight deviation from nature was explained and justified by the painter as a license allowable in art.

One evening, as he was sitting down to begin for at least the hundredth time the great Romance,—subject of so many resolves and so much remorse, so often determined upon but never begun,—a loud knock at the street-door, which stood wide open, announced a visitor. Unluckily, the study-door was likewise open; and consequently, being in full view, he found it impossible to refuse himself;

nor, in fact, would have done so, had all the doors been shut and bolted,—the art of refusing one's self being at that time but imperfectly understood at Fairmeadow. Accordingly, the visitor was shown in.

He announced himself as Mr. Hathaway. Passing through the village, he could not deny himself the pleasure of calling on Mr. Churchill, whom he knew by his writings in the periodicals, though not personally. He wished, moreover, to secure the coöperation of one already so favorably known to the literary world in a new magazine he was about to establish in order to raise the character of American literature, which, in his opinion, the existing reviews and magazines had entirely failed to accomplish. A daily increasing want of something better was felt by the public; and the time had come for the establishment of such a periodical as he proposed. After explaining in a rather florid and exuberant manner his plans and prospects, he entered more at large into the subject of American literature, which it was his design to foster and patronize.

"I think, Mr. Churchill," said he, "that we want a national literature commensurate with our mountains and rivers,—commensurate with Niagara and the Alleghanies, and the Great Lakes."

"Oh!"

"We want a national epic that shall correspond to the size of the country; that shall be to all other epics what Banvard's Panorama of the Mississippi is to all other paintings,—the largest in the world."

"Ah!"

"We want a national drama in which scope enough shall be given to our gigantic ideas and to the unparalleled activity and progress of our people!"

"Of course."

"In a word, we want a national literature altogether shaggy and unshorn, that shall shake the earth, like a herd of buffaloes thundering over the prairies."

"Precisely," interrupted Mr. Churchill; "but excuse me!—are you not confounding things that have no analogy? Great has a very different meaning when applied to a river and when applied to a literature. Large and shallow may perhaps be applied to both. Literature is rather an image of the spiritual world, than of the physical, is it not?—of the internal, rather than the external. Mountains, lakes, and rivers are, after all, only its scenery and decorations, not its substance and essence. A man will not necessarily be a great poet because he lives near a great mountain. Nor, being a poet, will he necessarily write better poems than another, because he lives nearer Niagara."

"But, Mr. Churchill, you do not certainly mean to deny the influence of scenery on the mind?"

"No, only to deny that it can create genius. At best, it can only develop it. Switzerland has produced no extraordinary poet; nor, as far as I know, have the Andes, or the Himalaya Mountains, or the Mountains of the Moon in Africa."

"But, at all events," urged Mr. Hathaway, "let us have our literature national. If it is not national, it is nothing."

"On the contrary, it may be a great deal. Nationality is a good thing to a certain extent, but universality is better. All that is best in the great poets of all countries is not what is national in them, but what is universal. Their roots are in their native soil; but their branches wave in the unpatriotic air, that speaks the same language unto all men, and their leaves shine with the illimitable light that pervades all lands. Let us throw all the windows open; let us admit the light and air on all sides; that we may look toward the four corners of the heavens, and not always in the same direction."

"But you admit nationality to be a good thing?"

"Yes, if not carried too far; still, I confess, it rather limits one's views of truth. I prefer what is natural. Mere nationality is often ridiculous. Every one smiles when he hears the Icelandic proverb, 'Iceland is the best land the sun shines upon.' Let us be natural, and we shall be national enough. Besides, our literature can be strictly national only so far as our character and modes of thought differ from those of other nations. Now, as we are very like the English,—are, in fact, English under a different sky,—I do not see how our literature can be very different from theirs. Westward from hand to hand we pass the lighted torch, but it was lighted at the old domestic fireside of England."

"Then you think our literature is never to be anything but an imitation of the English?"

"Not at all. It is not an imitation, but, as some one has said, a continuation."

"It seems to me that you take a very narrow view of the subject."

"On the contrary, a very broad one. No literature is complete until the language in which it is written is dead. We may well be proud of our task and of our position. Let us see if we can build in any way worthy of our forefathers."

"But I insist on originality."

"Yes, but without spasms and convulsions. Authors must not, like Chinese soldiers, expect to win victories by turning somersets in the air."

"Well, really, the prospect from your point of view is not very brilliant. Pray, what do you think of our national literature?"

"Simply, that a national literature is not the growth of a day. Centuries must contribute their dew and sunshine to it. Our own is growing slowly but surely, striking its roots downward and its branches upward, as is natural; and I do not wish, for the sake of what some people call originality, to invert it, and try to make it grow with its roots in the air. And as for having it so savage and wild as you want it, I have only to say, that all literature, as well as all art, is the result of culture and intellectual refinement."

"Ah! we do not want art and refinement; we want genius,—untutored, wild, original, free."

"But if this genius is to find any expression it must employ art, for art is the external expression of our thoughts. Many have genius, but, wanting art, are forever dumb. The two must go together to form the great poet, painter, or sculptor."

"In that sense, very well."

"I was about to say also that I thought our literature would finally not be wanting in a kind of universality. As the blood of all nations is mingling with our own, so will their thoughts and feelings finally mingle in our literature. We shall draw from the Germans, tenderness; from the Spaniards, passion; from the French, vivacity, to mingle more and more with our English solid sense. And this will give us universality, so much to be desired."

1848 1849

JAMES RUSSELL LOWELL

TO THE SPIRIT OF KEATS

Great soul, thou sittest with me in my room,
Uplifting me with thy vast, quiet eyes,
On whose full orbs, with kindly lustre, lies
The twilight warmth of ruddy ember-gloom:
Thy clear, strong tones will oft bring sudden bloom
Of hope secure, to him who lonely cries,
Wrestling with the young poet's agonies,
Neglect and scorn, which seem a certain doom:
Yes! the few words which, like great thunder-drops,
Thy large heart down to earth shook doubtfully,
Thrilled by the inward lightning of its might,
Serene and pure, like gushing joy of light,
Shall track the eternal chords of Destiny,
After the moon-led pulse of ocean stops.

1841 1842

"GREAT TRUTHS ARE PORTIONS OF THE SOUL OF MAN"

Great Truths are portions of the soul of man;
Great souls are portions of Eternity;
Each drop of blood that e'er through true heart ran
With lofty message, ran for thee and me;
For God's law, since the starry song began,
Hath been, and still forevermore must be,
That every deed which shall outlast Time's span
Must spur the soul to be erect and free;
Slave is no word of deathless lineage sprung;
Too many noble souls have thought and died,
Too many mighty poets lived and sung,
And our good Saxon, from lips purified
With martyr-fire, throughout the world hath rung
Too long to have God's holy cause denied.

1841 1842

"I ASK NOT FOR THOSE THOUGHTS, THAT SUDDEN LEAP"

I ask not for those thoughts, that sudden leap
From being's sea, like the isle-seeming Kraken,
With whose great rise the ocean all is shaken
And a heart-tremble quivers through the deep;
Give me that growth which some perchance deem sleep,
Wherewith the steadfast coral-stems uprise,
Which, by the toil of gathering energies,
Their upward way into clear sunshine keep,
Until, by Heaven's sweetest influences,
Slowly and slowly spreads a speck of green
Into a pleasant island in the seas,
Where, 'mid tall palms, the cane-roofed home is seen,
And wearied men shall sit at sunset's hour,
Hearing the leaves and loving God's dear power.

1841 1843

"MY LOVE, I HAVE NO FEAR THAT THOU SHOULDST DIE"

My Love, I have no fear that thou shouldst die;
Albeit I ask no fairer life than this,
Whose numbering-clock is still thy gentle kiss,
While Time and Peace with hands enlockèd fly;
Yet care I not where in Eternity
We live and love, well knowing that there is
No backward step for those who feel the bliss
Of Faith as their most lofty yearnings high:
Love hath so purified my being's core,
Meseems I scarcely should be startled, even,
To find, some morn, that thou hadst gone before;
Since, with thy love, this knowledge too was given,

Which each calm day doth strengthen more
  and more,
That they who love are but one step from
  Heaven.

1841 1843

"BELOVED, IN THE NOISY CITY HERE"

Beloved, in the noisy city here,
The thought of thee can make all turmoil
  cease;
Around my spirit, folds thy spirit clear
Its still, soft arms, and circles it with peace;
There is no room for any doubt or fear
In souls so overfilled with love's increase,
There is no memory of the bygone year
But growth in heart's and spirit's perfect ease:
How hath our love, half nebulous at first,
Rounded itself into a full-orbed sun!
How have our lives and wills (as haply erst
They were, ere this forgetfulness begun)
Through all their earthly distances outburst,
And melted, like two rays of light in one!

1842 1843

"OUR LOVE IS NOT A FADING EARTHLY FLOWER"

Our love is not a fading earthly flower:
Its wingèd seed dropped down from Paradise,
And, nursed by day and night, by sun and
  shower,
Doth momently to fresher beauty rise:
To us the leafless autumn is not bare,
Nor winter's rattling boughs lack lusty green.
Our summer hearts make summer's fulness,
  where
No leaf, or bud, or blossom may be seen:
For nature's life in love's deep life doth lie,
Love,—whose forgetfulness is beauty's death,
Whose mystic key these cells of Thou and I
Into the infinite freedom openeth,
And makes the body's dark and narrow grate
The wide-flung leaves of Heaven's own
  palace-gate.

1842 1843

SONG

O moonlight deep and tender,
  A year and more agone,
Your mist of golden splendor
  Round my betrothal shone!

O elm-leaves dark and dewy,
  The very same ye seem,
The low wind trembles through ye,
  Ye murmur in my dream!

O river, dim with distance,
  Flow thus forever by,
A part of my existence
  Within your heart doth lie!

O stars, ye saw our meeting,
  Two beings and one soul,
Two hearts so madly beating
  To mingle and be whole!

O happy night, deliver
  Her kisses back to me,
Or keep them all, and give her
  A blissful dream of me!

1842 1843

THE SHEPHERD OF KING ADMETUS

There came a youth upon the earth,
  Some thousand years ago,
Whose slender hands were nothing worth,
Whether to plough, or reap, or sow.

Upon an empty tortoise-shell
  He stretched some chords, and drew
Music that made men's bosoms swell
Fearless, or brimmed their eyes with dew.

Then King Admetus, one who had
  Pure taste by right divine,
Decreed his singing not too bad
To hear between the cups of wine:

And so, well pleased with being soothed
  Into a sweet half-sleep,
Three times his kingly beard he smoothed,
And made him viceroy o'er his sheep.

His words were simple words enough,
  And yet he used them so,
That what in other mouths was rough
In his seemed musical and low.

Men called him but a shiftless youth,
  In whom no good they saw;
And yet, unwittingly, in truth,
They made his careless words their law.

They knew not how he learned at all,
For idly, hour by hour,
He sat and watched the dead leaves fall,
Or mused upon a common flower.

It seemed the loveliness of things
Did teach him all their use,
For, in mere weeds, and stones, and springs,
He found a healing power profuse.

Men granted that his speech was wise,
But, when a glance they caught
Of his slim grace and woman's eyes,
They laughed, and called him good-for-naught.

Yet after he was dead and gone,
And e'en his memory dim,
Earth seemed more sweet to live upon,
More full of love, because of him.

And day by day more holy grew
Each spot where he had trod,
Till after-poets only knew
Their first-born brother as a god.

1842

AN INCIDENT IN A RAILROAD CAR

He spoke of Burns: men rude and rough
Pressed round to hear the praise of one
Whose heart was made of manly, simple stuff,
As homespun as their own.

And, when he read, they forward leaned,
Drinking, with thirsty hearts and ears,
His brook-like songs whom glory never weaned
From humble smiles and tears.

Slowly there grew a tender awe,
Sun-like, o'er faces brown and hard,
As if in him who read they felt and saw
Some presence of the bard.

It was a sight for sin and wrong
And slavish tyranny to see,
A sight to make our faith more pure and strong
In high humanity.

I thought, these men will carry hence
Promptings their former life above,
And something of a finer reverence
For beauty, truth, and love.

God scatters love on every side
Freely among his children all,
And always hearts are lying open wide,
Wherein some grains may fall.

There is no wind but soweth seeds
Of a more true and open life,
Which burst, unlooked for, into high-souled deeds,
With wayside beauty rife.

We find within these souls of ours
Some wild germs of a higher birth,
Which in the poet's tropic heart bear flowers
Whose fragrance fills the earth.

Within the hearts of all men lie
These promises of wider bliss,
Which blossom into hopes that cannot die,
In sunny hours like this.

All that hath been majestical
In life or death, since time began,
Is native in the simple heart of all,
The angel heart of man.

And thus, among the untaught poor,
Great deeds and feelings find a home,
That cast in shadow all the golden lore
Of classic Greece and Rome.

O mighty brother-soul of man,
Where'er thou art, in low or high,
Thy skyey arches with exulting span
O'er-roof infinity!

All thoughts that mold the age begin
Deep down within the primitive soul,
And from the many slowly upward win
To one who grasps the whole:

In his wide brain the feeling deep
That struggled on the many's tongue
Swells to a tide of thought, whose surges leap
O'er the weak thrones of wrong.

All thought begins in feeling,—wide
In the great mass its base is hid,
And, narrowing up to thought, stands glorified,
A moveless pyramid.

Nor is he far astray, who deems
That every hope, which rises and grows broad
In the world's heart, by ordered impulse streams
From the great heart of God.

God wills, man hopes: in common souls
Hope is but vague and undefined,
Till from the poet's tongue the message rolls
A blessing to his kind.

Never did Poesy appear
So full of heaven to me, as when
I saw how it would pierce through pride and fear
To the lives of coarsest men.

It may be glorious to write
Thoughts that shall glad the two or three
High souls, like those far stars that come in sight
Once in a century;—

But better far it is to speak
One simple word, which now and then
Shall waken their free nature in the weak
And friendless sons of men;

To write some earnest verse or line,
Which, seeking not the praise of art,
Shall make a clearer faith and manhood shine
In the untutored heart.

He who doth this, in verse or prose,
May be forgotten in his day,
But surely shall be crowned at last with those
Who live and speak for aye.

1842 1842

STANZAS ON FREEDOM

Men! whose boast it is that ye
Come of fathers brave and free,
If there breathe on earth a slave,
Are ye truly free and brave?
If ye do not feel the chain,
When it works a brother's pain,
Are ye not base slaves indeed,
Slaves unworthy to be freed?

Women! who shall one day bear
Sons to breathe New England air,
If ye hear, without a blush,
Deeds to make the roused blood rush
Like red lava through your veins,
For your sisters now in chains,—
Answer! are ye fit to be
Mothers of the brave and free?

Is true Freedom but to break
Fetters for our own dear sake,
And, with leathern hearts, forget
That we owe mankind a debt?
No! true freedom is to share
All the chains our brothers wear,
And, with heart and hand, to be
Earnest to make others free!

They are slaves who fear to speak
For the fallen and the weak;
They are slaves who will not choose
Hatred, scoffing, and abuse,
Rather than in silence shrink
From the truth they needs must think;
They are slaves who dare not be
In the right with two or three.

1843 1843

WENDELL PHILLIPS

He stood upon the world's broad threshold; wide
The din of battle and of slaughter rose;
He saw God stand upon the weaker side,
That sank in seeming loss before its foes:
Many there were who made great haste and sold
Unto the cunning enemy their swords,
He scorned their gifts of fame, and power, and gold,
And, underneath their soft and flowery words,
Heard the cold serpent hiss; therefore he went
And humbly joined him to the weaker part,
Fanatic named, and fool, yet well content
So he could be the nearer to God's heart,
And feel its solemn pulses sending blood
Through all the widespread veins of endless good.

1843

RHŒCUS

God sends his teachers unto every age,
To every clime, and every race of men,
With revelations fitted to their growth

And shape of mind, nor gives the realm of Truth
Into the selfish rule of one sole race:
Therefore each form of worship that hath swayed
The life of man, and given it to grasp
The master-key of knowledge, reverence,
Infolds some germs of goodness and of right;
Else never had the eager soul, which loathes
The slothful down of pampered ignorance,
Found in it even a moment's fitful rest.

There is an instinct in the human heart
Which makes that all the fables it hath coined,
To justify the reign of its belief
And strengthen it by beauty's right divine,
Veil in their inner cells a mystic gift,
Which, like the hazel twig, in faithful hands,
Points surely to the hidden springs of truth.
For, as in nature naught is made in vain,
But all things have within their hull of use
A wisdom and a meaning which may speak
Of spiritual secrets to the ear
Of spirit; so, in whatsoe'er the heart
Hath fashioned for a solace to itself,
To make its inspirations suit its creed,
And from the niggard hands of falsehood wring
Its needful food of truth, there ever is
A sympathy with Nature, which reveals,
Not less than her own works, pure gleams of light
And earnest parables of inward lore.
Hear now this fairy legend of old Greece,
As full of gracious youth, and beauty still
As the immortal freshness of that grace
Carved for all ages on some Attic frieze.

A youth named Rhœcus, wandering in the wood,
Saw an old oak just trembling to its fall,
And, feeling pity of so fair a tree,
He propped its gray trunk with admiring care,
And with a thoughtless footstep loitered on.
But, as he turned, he heard a voice behind
That murmured "Rhœcus!" 'Twas as if the leaves,
Stirred by a passing breath, had murmured it,
And, while he paused bewildered, yet again
It murmured "Rhœcus!" softer than a breeze.
He started and beheld with dizzy eyes
What seemed the substance of a happy dream
Stand there before him, spreading a warm glow
Within the green glooms of the shadowy oak.
It seemed a woman's shape, yet far too fair
To be a woman, and with eyes too meek
For any that were wont to mate with gods.
All naked like a goddess stood she there,
And like a goddess all too beautiful
To feel the guilt-born earthliness of shame.
"Rhœcus, I am the Dryad of this tree,"
Thus she began, dropping her low-toned words
Serene, and full, and clear, as drops of dew,
"And with it I am doomed to live and die;
The rain and sunshine are my caterers,
Nor have I other bliss than simple life;
Now ask me what thou wilt, that I can give,
And with a thankful joy it shall be thine."

Then Rhœcus, with a flutter at the heart,
Yet by the prompting of such beauty bold,
Answered: "What is there that can satisfy
The endless craving of the soul but love?
Give me thy love, or but the hope of that
Which must be evermore my nature's goal."
After a little pause she said again,
But with a glimpse of sadness in her tone,
"I give it, Rhœcus, though a perilous gift;
An hour before the sunset meet me here."
And straightway there was nothing he could see
But the green glooms beneath the shadowy oak,
And not a sound came to his straining ears
But the low trickling rustle of the leaves,
And far away upon an emerald slope
The falter of an idle shepherd's pipe.

Now, in those days of simpleness and faith,
Men did not think that happy things were dreams
Because they overstepped the narrow bourn
Of likelihood, but reverently deemed
Nothing too wondrous or too beautiful
To be the guerdon of a daring heart.
So Rhœcus made no doubt that he was blest,
And all along unto the city's gate
Earth seemed to spring beneath him as he walked,

The clear, broad sky looked bluer than its wont,
And he could scarce believe he had not wings,
Such sunshine seemed to glitter through his veins
Instead of blood, so light he felt and strange.

Young Rhœcus had a faithful heart enough,
But one that in the present dwelt too much,
And, taking with blithe welcome whatsoe'er
Chance gave of joy, was wholly bound in that,
Like the contented peasant of a vale,
Deemed it the world, and never looked beyond.
So, haply meeting in the afternoon
Some comrades who were playing at the dice,
He joined them, and forgot all else beside.

The dice were rattling at the merriest,
And Rhœcus, who had met but sorry luck,
Just laughed in triumph at a happy throw,
When through the room there hummed a yellow bee
That buzzed about his ear with down-dropped legs
As if to light. And Rhœcus laughed and said,
Feeling how red and flushed he was with loss,
"By Venus! does he take me for a rose?"
And brushed him off with rough, impatient hand.
But still the bee came back, and thrice again
Rhœcus did beat him off with growing wrath.
Then through the window flew the wounded bee,
And Rhœcus, tracking him with angry eyes,
Saw a sharp mountain-peak of Thessaly
Against the red disk of the setting sun,—
And instantly the blood sank from his heart,
As if its very walls had caved away.
Without a word he turned, and, rushing forth,
Ran madly through the city and the gate,
And o'er the plain, which now the wood's long shade,
By the low sun thrown forward broad and dim,
Darkened wellnigh unto the city's wall.

Quite spent and out of breath he reached the tree,
And, listening fearfully, he heard once more
The low voice murmur "Rhœcus!" close at hand:
Whereat he looked around him, but could see
Naught but the deepening glooms beneath the oak.
Then sighed the voice, "O Rhœcus! nevermore
Shalt thou behold me or by day or night,
Me, who would fain have blessed thee with a love
More ripe and bounteous than ever yet
Filled up with nectar any mortal heart:
But thou didst scorn my humble messenger,
And sent'st him back to me with bruisèd wings.
We spirits only show to gentle eyes,
We ever ask an undivided love,
And he who scorns the least of Nature's works
Is thenceforth exiled and shut out from all.
Farewell! for thou canst never see me more."

Then Rhœcus beat his breast, and groaned aloud,
And cried, "Be pitiful! forgive me yet
This once, and I shall never need it more!"
"Alas!" the voice returned, "'tis thou art blind,
Not I unmerciful; I can forgive,
But have no skill to heal thy spirit's eyes;
Only the soul hath power o'er itself."
With that again there murmured "Nevermore!"
And Rhœcus after heard no other sound,
Except the rattling of the oak's crisp leaves,
Like the long surf upon a distant shore,
Raking the sea-worn pebbles up and down.
The night had gathered round him: o'er the plain
The city sparkled with its thousand lights,
And sounds of revel fell upon his ear
Harshly and like a curse; above, the sky,
With all its bright sublimity of stars,
Deepened, and on his forehead smote the breeze:
Beauty was all around him and delight,
But from that eve he was alone on earth.

1843

COLUMBUS

The cordage creaks and rattles in the wind,
With whims of sudden hush; the reeling sea
Now thumps like solid rock beneath the stern,

Now leaps with clumsy wrath, strikes short, and falling,
Crumbled to whispery foam, slips rustling down
The broad backs of the waves, which jostle and crowd
To fling themselves upon that unknown shore,
Their used familiar since the dawn of time,
Whither this foredoomed life is guided on
To sway on triumph's hushed, aspiring poise
One glittering moment, then to break fulfilled.

How lonely is the sea's perpetual swing,
The melancholy wash of endless waves,
The sigh of some grim monster undescried,
Fear-painted on the canvas of the dark,
Shifting on his uneasy pillow of brine!
Yet night brings more companions than the day
To this drear waste; new constellations burn,
And fairer stars, with whose calm height my soul
Finds nearer sympathy than with my herd
Of earthen souls, whose vision's scanty ring
Makes me its prisoner to beat my wings
Against the cold bars of their unbelief,
Knowing in vain my own free heaven beyond.
O God! this world, so crammed with eager life,
That comes and goes and wanders back to silence
Like the idle wind, which yet man's shaping mind
Can make his drudge to swell the longing sails
Of highest endeavor,—this mad, unthrift world,
Which, every hour, throws life enough away
To make her deserts kind and hospitable,
Lets her great destinies be waved aside
By smooth, lip-reverent, formal infidels,
Who weigh the God they not believe with gold,
And find no spot in Judas, save that he,
Driving a duller bargain than he ought,
Saddled his guild with too cheap precedent.
O Faith! if thou art strong, thine opposite
Is mighty also, and the dull fool's sneer
Hath ofttimes shot chill palsy through the arm
Just lifted to achieve its crowning deed,
And made the firm-based heart, that would have quailed
The rack or fagot, shudder like a leaf
Wrinkled with frost, and loose upon its stem.
The wicked and the weak, by some dark law,
Have a strange power to shut and rivet down
Their own horizon round us, to unwing
Our heaven-aspiring visions, and to blur
With surly clouds the Future's gleaming peaks,
Far seen across the brine of thankless years.
If the chosen soul could never be alone
In deep mid-silence, open-doored to God,
No greatness ever had been dreamed or done;
Among dull hearts a prophet never grew;
The nurse of full-grown souls is solitude.

The old world is effete; there man with man
Jostles, and, in the brawl for means to live,
Life is trod underfoot,—Life, the one block
Of marble that's vouchsafed wherefrom to carve
Our great thoughts, white and godlike, to shine down
The future, Life, the irredeemable block,
Which one o'er-hasty chisel-dint oft mars,
Scanting our room to cut the features out
Of our full hope, so forcing us to crown
With a mean head the perfect limbs, or leave
The god's face glowing o'er a satyr's trunk,
Failure's brief epitaph.

Yes, Europe's world
Reels on to judgment; there the common need,
Losing God's sacred use, to be a bond
'Twixt Me and Thee, sets each one scowlingly
O'er his own selfish hoard at bay; no state,
Knit strongly with eternal fibres up
Of all men's separate and united weals,
Self-poised and sole as stars, yet one as light,
Holds up a shape of large Humanity
To which by natural instinct every man
Pays loyalty exulting, by which all
Mould their own lives, and feel their pulses filled
With the red, fiery blood of the general life,
Making them mighty in peace, as now in war
They are, even in the flush of victory, weak,
Conquering that manhood which should them subdue.

And what gift bring I to this untried world?
Shall the same tragedy be played anew,
And the same lurid curtain drop at last
On one dread desolation, one fierce crash
Of that recoil which on its makers God
Lets Ignorance and Sin and Hunger make,
Early or late? Or shall that commonwealth
Whose potent unity and concentric force
Can draw these scattered joints and parts of men
Into a whole ideal man once more,
Which sucks not from its limbs the life away,
But sends it flood-tide and creates itself
Over again in every citizen,
Be there built up? For me, I have no choice;
I might turn back to other destinies,
For one sincere key opes all Fortune's doors;
But whoso answers not God's earliest call
Forfeits or dulls that faculty supreme
Of lying open to his genius
Which makes the wise heart certain of its ends.

Here am I; for what end God knows, not I;
Westward still points the inexorable soul:
Here am I, with no friend but the sad sea,
The beating heart of this great enterprise,
Which, without me, would stiffen in swift death;
This have I mused on, since mine eye could first
Among the stars distinguish and with joy
Rest on that God-fed Pharos of the north,
On some blue promontory of heaven lighted
That juts far out into the upper sea;
To this one hope my heart hath clung for years,
As would a foundling to the talisman
Hung round his neck by hands he knew not whose;
A poor, vile thing and dross to all beside,
Yet he therein can feel a virtue left
By the sad pressure of a mother's hand,
And unto him it still is tremulous
With palpitating haste and wet with tears,
The key to him of hope and humanness,
The coarse shell of life's pearl, Expectancy.
This hope hath been to me for love and fame,
Hath made me wholly lonely on the earth,
Building me up as in a thick-ribbed tower,
Wherewith enwalled my watching spirit burned,
Conquering its little island from the Dark,
Sole as a scholar's lamp, and heard men's steps,
In the far hurry of the outward world,
Pass dimly forth and back, sounds heard in dream.
As Ganymede by the eagle was snatched up
From the gross sod to be Jove's cup-bearer,
So was I lifted by my great design:
And who hath trod Olympus, from his eye
Fades not that broader outlook of the gods;
His life's low valleys overbrow earth's clouds,
And that Olympian spectre of the past
Looms towering up in sovereign memory,
Beckoning his soul from meaner heights of doom.
Had but the shadow of the Thunderer's bird,
Flashing athwart my spirit, made of me
A swift-betraying vision's Ganymede,
Yet to have greatly dreamed precludes low ends;
Great days have ever such a morning-red,
On such a base great futures are built up,
And aspiration, though not put in act,
Comes back to ask its plighted troth again,
Still watches round its grave the unlaid ghost
Of a dead virtue, and makes other hopes,
Save that implacable one, seem thin and bleak
As shadows of bare trees upon the snow,
Bound freezing there by the unpitying moon.

While other youths perplexed their mandolins,
Praying that Thetis would her fingers twine
In the loose glories of her lover's hair,
And wile another kiss to keep back day,
I, stretched beneath the many-centuried shade
Of some writhed oak, the wood's Laocoön,
Did of my hope a dryad mistress make,
Whom I would woo to meet me privily,
Or underneath the stars, or when the moon
Flecked all the forest floor with scattered pearls.
O days whose memory tames to fawning down
The surly fell of Ocean's bristled neck!

I know not when this hope enthralled me first,
But from my boyhood up I loved to hear
The tall pine-forests of the Apennine
Murmur their hoary legends of the sea,

Which hearing, I in vision clear beheld
The sudden dark of tropic night shut down
O'er the huge whisper of great watery wastes,
The while a pair of herons trailingly
Flapped inland, where some league-wide river hurled
The yellow spoil of unconjectured realms
Far through a gulf's green silence, never scarred
By any but the North-wind's hurrying keels.
And not the pines alone; all sights and sounds
To my world-seeking heart paid fealty,
And catered for it as the Cretan bees
Brought honey to the baby Jupiter,
Who in his soft hand crushed a violet,
Godlike foremusing the rough thunder's gripe;
Then did I entertain the poet's song,
My great Idea's guest, and, passing o'er
That iron bridge the Tuscan built to hell,
I heard Ulysses tell of mountain-chains
Whose adamantine links, his manacles,
The western main shook growling, and still gnawed.
I brooded on the wise Athenian's tale
Of happy Atlantis, and heard Björne's keel
Crunch the gray pebbles of the Vinland shore:
I listened, musing, to the prophecy
Of Nero's tutor-victim; lo, the birds
Sing darkling, conscious of the climbing dawn.
And I believed the poets; it is they
Who utter wisdom from the central deep,
And, listening to the inner flow of things,
Speak to the age out of eternity.

Ah me! old hermits sought for solitude
In caves and desert places of the earth,
Where their own heart-beat was the only stir
Of living thing that comforted the year;
But the bald pillar-top of Simeon,
In midnight's blankest waste, were populous,
Matched with the isolation drear and deep
Of him who pines among the swarm of men,
At once a new thought's king and prisoner,
Feeling the truer life within his life,
The fountain of his spirit's prophecy,
Sinking away and wasting, drop by drop,
In the ungrateful sands of sceptic ears.
He in the palace-aisles of untrod woods
Doth walk a king; for him the pent-up cell
Widens beyond the circles of the stars,
And all the sceptred spirits of the past
Come thronging in to greet him as their peer;
But in the market-place's glare and throng
He sits apart, an exile, and his brow
Aches with the mocking memory of its crown.
Yet to the spirit select there is no choice;
He cannot say, This will I do, or that,
For the cheap means putting Heaven's ends in pawn,
And bartering his bleak rocks, the freehold stern
Of destiny's first-born, for smoother fields
That yield no crop of self-denying will;
A hand is stretched to him from out the dark,
Which grasping without question, he is led
Where there is work that he must do for God.
The trial still is the strength's complement,
And the uncertain, dizzy path that scales
The sheer heights of supremest purposes
Is steeper to the angel than the child.
Chances have laws as fixed as planets have,
And disappointment's dry and bitter root,
Envy's harsh berries, and the choking pool
Of the world's scorn, are the right mother-milk
To the tough hearts that pioneer their kind,
And break a pathway to those unknown realms
That in the earth's broad shadow lie enthralled;
Endurance is the crowning quality,
And patience all the passion of great hearts;
These are their stay, and when the leaden world
Sets its hard face against their fateful thought,
And brute strength, like the Gaulish conqueror,
Clangs his huge glaive down in the other scale,
The inspired soul but flings his patience in,
And slowly that outweighs the ponderous globe,—
One faith against a whole earth's unbelief,
One soul against the flesh of all mankind.

Thus ever seems it when my soul can hear
The voice that errs not; then my triumph gleams,
O'er the blank ocean beckoning, and all night
My heart flies on before me as I sail;
Far on I see my lifelong enterprise,
That rose like Ganges 'mid the freezing snows
Of a world's solitude, sweep broadening down,

And, gathering to itself a thousand streams,
Grow sacred ere it mingle with the sea;
I see the ungated wall of chaos old,
With blocks Cyclopean hewn of solid night,
Fade like a wreath of unreturning mist
Before the irreversible feet of light;—
And lo, with what clear omen in the east
On day's gray threshold stands the eager dawn,
Like young Leander rosy from the sea
Glowing at Hero's lattice!

One day more
These muttering shoalbrains leave the helm to me:
God, let me not in their dull ooze be stranded;
Let not this one frail bark, to hollow which
I have dug out the pith and sinewy heart
Of my aspiring life's fair trunk, be so
Cast up to warp and blacken in the sun,
Just as the opposing wind 'gins whistle off
His cheek-swollen pack, and from the leaning mast
Fortune's full sail strains forward!

One poor day!—
Remember whose and not how short it is!
It is God's day, it is Columbus's.
A lavish day! One day, with life and heart,
Is more than time enough to find a world.

1844 1847

THE PRESENT CRISIS

When a deed is done for Freedom, through the broad earth's aching breast
Runs a thrill of joy prophetic, trembling on from east to west,
And the slave, where'er he cowers, feels the soul within him climb
To the awful verge of manhood, as the energy sublime
Of a century bursts full-blossomed on the thorny stem of Time.

Through the walls of hut and palace shoots the instantaneous throe,
When the travail of the Ages wrings earth's systems to and fro;
At the birth of each new Era, with a recognizing start,
Nation wildly looks at nation, standing with mute lips apart,
And glad Truth's yet mightier man-child leaps beneath the Future's heart.

So the Evil's triumph sendeth, with a terror and a chill,
Under continent to continent, the sense of coming ill,
And the slave, where'er he cowers, feels his sympathies with God
In hot tear-drops ebbing earthward, to be drunk up by the sod,
Till a corpse crawls round unburied, delving in the nobler clod.

For mankind are one in spirit, and an instinct bears along,
Round the earth's electric circle, the swift flash of right or wrong;
Whether conscious or unconscious, yet Humanity's vast frame
Through its ocean-sundered fibres feels the gush of joy or shame;—
In the gain or loss of one race all the rest have equal claim.

Once to every man and nation comes the moment to decide,
In the strife of Truth with Falsehood, for the good or evil side;
Some great cause, God's new Messiah, offering each the bloom or blight,
Parts the goats upon the left hand, and the sheep upon the right,
And the choice goes by forever 'twixt that darkness and that light.

Hast thou chosen, O my people, on whose party thou shalt stand,
Ere the Doom from its worn sandals shakes the dust against our land?
Though the cause of Evil prosper, yet 'tis Truth alone is strong,
And, albeit she wander outcast now, I see around her throng
Troops of beautiful, tall angels, to enshield her from all wrong.

Backward look across the ages and the beacon-moments see,
That, like peaks of some sunk continent, jut through Oblivion's sea;

Not an ear in court or market for the low foreboding cry
Of those Crises, God's stern winnowers, from whose feet earth's chaff must fly;
Never shows the choice momentous till the judgment hath passed by.

Careless seems the great Avenger; history's pages but record
One death-grapple in the darkness 'twixt old systems and the Word;
Truth forever on the scaffold, Wrong forever on the throne,—
Yet that scaffold sways the future, and, behind the dim unknown,
Standeth God within the shadow, keeping watch above his own.

We see dimly in the Present what is small and what is great,
Slow of faith how weak an arm may turn the iron helm of fate,
But the soul is still oracular; amid the market's din,
List the ominous stern whisper from the Delphic cave within,—
"They enslave their children's children who make compromise with sin."

Slavery, the earth-born Cyclops, fellest of the giant brood,
Sons of brutish Force and Darkness, who have drenched the earth with blood,
Famished in his self-made desert, blinded by our purer day,
Gropes in yet unblasted regions for his miserable prey;—
Shall we guide his gory fingers where our helpless children play?

Then to side with Truth is noble when we share her wretched crust,
Ere her cause bring fame and profit, and 'tis prosperous to be just;
Then it is the brave man chooses, while the coward stands aside,
Doubting in his abject spirit, till his Lord is crucified,
And the multitude make virtue of the faith they had denied.

Count me o'er earth's chosen heroes,—they were souls that stood alone,
While the men they agonized for hurled the contumelious stone,
Stood serene, and down the future saw the golden beam incline
To the side of perfect justice, mastered by their faith divine,
By one man's plain truth to manhood and to God's supreme design.

By the light of burning heretics Christ's bleeding feet I track,
Toiling up new Calvaries ever with the cross that turns not back,
And these mounts of anguish number how each generation learned
One new word of that grand *Credo* which in prophet-hearts hath burned
Since the first man stood God-conquered with his face to heaven upturned.

For Humanity sweeps onward: where today the martyr stands,
On the morrow crouches Judas with the silver in his hands;
Far in front the cross stands ready and the crackling fagots burn,
While the hooting mob of yesterday in silent awe return
To glean up the scattered ashes into History's golden urn.

'Tis as easy to be heroes as to sit the idle slaves
Of a legendary virtue carved upon our fathers' graves,
Worshippers of light ancestral make the present light a crime;—
Was the Mayflower launched by cowards, steered by men behind their time?
Turn those tracks toward Past or Future, that make Plymouth Rock sublime?

They were men of present valor, stalwart old iconoclasts,
Unconvinced by axe or gibbet that all virtue was the Past's;
But we make their truth our falsehood, thinking that hath made us free,
Hoarding it in mouldy parchments, while our tender spirits flee
The rude grasp of that great Impulse which drove them across the sea.

They have rights who dare maintain them; we are traitors to our sires,
Smothering in their holy ashes Freedom's new-lit altar-fires;
Shall we make their creed our jailer? Shall we, in our haste to slay,
From the tombs of the old prophets steal the funeral lamps away
To light up the martyr-fagots round the prophets of today?

New occasions teach new duties; Time makes ancient good uncouth;
They must upward still, and onward, who would keep abreast of Truth;
Lo, before us gleam her camp-fires! we ourselves must Pilgrims be,
Launch our Mayflower, and steer boldly through the desperate winter sea,
Nor attempt the Future's portal with the Past's blood-rusted key.

1844 1845

A CONTRAST

Thy love thou sentest oft to me,
And still as oft I thrust it back;
Thy messengers I could not see
In those who everything did lack,
The poor, the outcast and the black.

Pride held his hand before mine eyes,
The world with flattery stuffed mine ears;
I looked to see a monarch's guise,
Nor dreamed thy love would knock for years,
Poor, naked, fettered, full of tears.

Yet, when I sent my love to thee,
Thou with a smile didst take it in,
And entertain'dst it royally,
Though grimed with earth, with hunger thin,
And leprous with the taint of sin.

Now every day thy love I meet,
As o'er the earth it wanders wide,
With weary step and bleeding feet,
Still knocking at the heart of pride
And offering grace, though still denied.

1845

TO THE DANDELION

Dear common flower, that grow'st beside the way,
Fringing the dusty road with harmless gold,
First pledge of blithesome May,
Which children pluck, and full of pride uphold,
High-hearted buccaneers, o'erjoyed that they
An Eldorado in the grass have found,
Which not the rich earth's ample round
May match in wealth, thou art more dear to me
Than all the prouder summer-blooms may be.

Gold such as thine ne'er drew the Spanish prow
Through the primeval hush of Indian seas,
Nor wrinkled the lean brow
Of age, to rob the lover's heart of ease;
'Tis the Spring's largess, which she scatters now
To rich and poor alike, with lavish hand,
Though most hearts never understand
To take it at God's value, but pass by
The offered wealth with unrewarded eye.

Thou art my tropics and mine Italy;
To look at thee unlocks a warmer clime;
The eyes thou givest me
Are in the heart, and heed not space or time:
Not in mid June the golden-cuirassed bee
Feels a more summer-like warm ravishment
In the white lily's breezy tent,
His fragrant Sybaris, than I, when first
From the dark green thy yellow circles burst.

Then think I of deep shadows on the grass,
Of meadows where in sun the cattle graze,
Where, as the breezes pass,
The gleaming rushes lean a thousand ways,
Of leaves that slumber in a cloudy mass,
Or whiten in the wind, of waters blue
That from the distance sparkle through
Some woodland gap, and of a sky above,
Where one white cloud like a stray lamb doth move.

My childhood's earliest thoughts are linked
with thee;
The sight of thee calls back the robin's song,
Who, from the dark old tree
Beside the door, sang clearly all day long,
And I, secure in childish piety,
Listened as if I heard an angel sing
With news from heaven, which he could
bring
Fresh every day to my untainted ears
When birds and flowers and I were happy
peers.

How like a prodigal doth nature seem,
When thou, for all thy gold, so common art!
Thou teachest me to deem
More sacredly of every human heart,
Since each reflects in joy its scanty gleam
Of heaven, and could some wondrous secret
show,
Did we but pay the love we owe,
And with a child's undoubting wisdom look
On all these living pages of God's book.

1844? 1845

THE BIGLOW PAPERS

FIRST SERIES

No. I

A LETTER

FROM MR. EZEKIEL BIGLOW OF JAALAM TO THE HON. JOSEPH T. BUCKINGHAM, EDITOR OF THE BOSTON COURIER, INCLOSING A POEM OF HIS SON, MR. HOSEA BIGLOW

JAYLEM, june 1846.

MISTER EDDYTER,—Our Hosea wuz down to Boston last week, and he see a cruetin Sarjunt a struttin round as popler as a hen with 1 chicking, with 2 fellers a drummin and fifin arter him like all nater. the sarjunt he thout Hosea hed n't gut his i teeth cut cos he looked a kindo 's though he 'd jest com down, so he cal'lated to hook him in, but Hosy wood n't take none o' his sarse for all he hed much as 20 Rooster's tales stuck onto his hat and eenamost enuf brass a bobbin up and down on his shoulders and figureed onto his coat and trousis, let alone wut nater hed sot in his featers, to make a 6 pounder out on.

wal, Hosea he com home considerabal riled, and arter I'd gone to bed I heern Him a thrashin round like a short-tailed Bull in flitime. The old Woman ses she to me ses she, Zekle, ses she, our Hosee 's gut the chollery or suthin anuther ses she, don't you Bee skeered, ses I, he 's oney amakin pottery ses i, he 's ollers on hand at that ere busynes like Da & martin, and shure enuf, cum mornin, Hosy he cum down stares full chizzle, hare on eend and cote tales flyin, and sot rite of to go reed his varses to Parson Wilbur bein he haint aney grate shows o' book larnin himself, bimeby he cum back and sed the parson wuz dreffle tickled with 'em as i hoop you will Be, and said they wuz True grit.

Hosea ses taint hardly fair to call 'em hisn now, cos the parson kind o' slicked off sum o' the last varses, but he told Hosee he did n't want to put his ore in to tetch to the Rest on 'em, bein they wuz verry well As thay wuz, and then Hosy ses he sed suthin a nuther about Simplex Mundishes or sum sech feller, but I guess Hosea kind o' did n't hear him, for I never hearn o' nobody o' that name in this villadge, and I 've lived here man and boy 76 year cum next tater diggin, and thair aint no wheres a kitting spryer 'n I be.

If you print 'em I wish you 'd jest let folks know who hosy's father is, cos my ant Keziah used to say it 's nater to be curus ses she, she aint livin though and he 's a likely kind o' lad.

EZEKIEL BIGLOW.

THRASH away, you 'll *hev* to rattle
On them kittle-drums o' yourn,—
'T aint a knowin' kind o' cattle
Thet is ketched with moldy corn;
Put in stiff, you fifer feller,
Let folks see how spry you be,—
Guess you 'll toot till you are yeller
'Fore you git ahold o' me!

Thet air flag 's a leetle rotten,
Hope it aint your Sunday's best;—
Fact! it takes a sight o' cotton
To stuff out a soger's chest:
Sence we farmers hev to pay fer 't,
Ef you must wear humps like these,

S'posin' you should try salt hay fer 't,
It would du ez slick ez grease.

'T would n't suit them Southun fellers,
They 're a dreffle graspin' set,
We must ollers blow the bellers
Wen they want their irons het;
May be it 's all right ez preachin',
But *my* narves it kind o' grates,
Wen I see the overreachin'
O' them nigger-drivin' States.

Them thet rule us, them slave-traders,
Haint they cut a thunderin' swarth
(Helped by Yankee renegaders),
Thru the vartu o' the North!
We begin to think it 's nater
To take sarse an' not be riled;—
Who 'd expect to see a tater
All on eend at bein' biled?

Ez fer war, I call it murder,—
There you hev it plain an' flat;
I don't want to go no furder
Than my Testyment fer that;
God hez sed so plump an' fairly,
It 's ez long ez it is broad,
An' you 've gut to git up airly
Ef you want to take in God.

'T aint your eppyletts an' feathers
Make the thing a grain more right;
'T aint afollerin' your bell-wethers
Will excuse ye in His sight;
Ef you take a sword an' dror it,
An' go stick a feller thru,
Guv'ment aint to answer for it,
God 'll send the bill to you.

Wut 's the use o' meetin'-goin'
Every Sabbath, wet or dry,
Ef it 's right to go amowin'
Feller-men like oats an' rye?
I dunno but wut it 's pooty
Trainin' round in bobtail coats,—
But it 's curus Christian dooty
This 'ere cuttin' folks's throats.

They may talk o' Freedom's airy
Tell they 're pupple in the face,—
It 's a grand gret cemetary
Fer the barthrights of our race;
They jest want this Californy
So 's to lug new slave-States in
To abuse ye, an' to scorn ye,
An' to plunder ye like sin.

Aint it cute to see a Yankee
Take sech everlastin' pains,
All to get the Devil's thankee
Helpin' on 'em weld their chains?
Wy, it 's jest ez clear ez figgers,
Clear ez one an' one make two,
Chaps thet make black slaves o' niggers
Want to make wite slaves o' you.

Tell ye jest the eend I 've come to
Arter cipherin' plaguy smart,
An' it makes a handy sum, tu,
Any gump could larn by heart;
Laborin' man an' laborin' woman
Hev one glory an' one shame.
Ev'y thin' thet 's done inhuman
Injers all on 'em the same.

'T aint by turnin' out to hack folks
You 're agoin' to git your right,
Nor by lookin' down on black folks
Coz you 're put upon by wite;
Slavery aint o' nary color,
'T aint the hide thet makes it wus,
All it keers fer in a feller
'S jest to make him fill its pus.

Want to tackle *me* in, du ye?
I expect you 'll hev to wait;
Wen cold lead puts daylight thru ye
You 'll begin to kal'late;
S'pose the crows wun't fall to pickin'
All the carkiss from your bones,
Coz you helped to give a lickin'
To them poor half-Spanish drones?

Jest go home an' ask our Nancy
Wether I 'd be sech a goose
Ez to jine ye,—guess you 'd fancy
The etarnal bung wuz loose!
She wants me fer home consumption,
Let alone the hay 's to mow,—
Ef you 're arter folks o' gumption,
You 've a darned long row to hoe.

Take them editors thet 's crowin'
Like a cockerel three months old,—
Don't ketch any on 'em goin',
Though they *be* so blasted bold;

Aint they a prime lot o' fellers?
'Fore they think on 't guess they 'll sprout
(Like a peach thet 's got the yellers),
With the meanness bustin' out.

Wal, go 'long to help 'em stealin'
Bigger pens to cram with slaves,
Help the men thet 's ollers dealin'
Insults on your fathers' graves;
Help the strong to grind the feeble,
Help the many agin the few,
Help the men thet call your people
Witewashed slaves an' peddlin' crew!

Massachusetts, God forgive her,
She 's akneelin' with the rest,
She, thet ough' to ha' clung ferever
In her grand old eagle-nest;
She thet ough' to stand so fearless
W'ile the wracks are round her hurled,
Holdin' up a beacon peerless
To the oppressed of all the world!

Ha'n't they sold your colored seamen?
Ha'n't they made your env'ys w'iz?
Wut 'll make ye act like freemen?
Wut 'll git your dander riz?
Come, I 'll tell ye wut I 'm thinkin'
Is our dooty in this fix,
They 'd ha' done 't ez quick ez winkin'
In the days o' seventy-six.

Clang the bells in every steeple,
Call all true men to disown
The tradoocers of our people,
The enslavers o' their own;
Let our dear old Bay State proudly
Put the trumpet to her mouth,
Let her ring this messidge loudly
In the ears of all the South:—

"I 'll return ye good fer evil
Much ez we frail mortils can,
But I wun't go help the Devil
Makin' man the cus o' man;
Call me coward, call me traiter,
Jest ez suits your mean idees,—
Here I stand a tyrant-hater,
An' the friend o' God an' Peace!"

Ef I 'd *my* way I hed ruther
We should go to work an' part,
They take one way, we take t' other,
Guess it would n't break my heart;
Man hed ough' to put asunder
Them thet God has noways jined;
An' I should n't gretly wonder
Ef there 's thousands o' my mind.

June 17, 1846

[The first recruiting sergeant on record I conceive to have been that individual who is mentioned in the Book of Job as *going to and fro in the earth, and walking up and down in it.* Bishop Latimer will have him to have been a bishop, but to me that other calling would appear more congenial. The sect of Cainites is not yet extinct, who esteemed the first-born of Adam to be the most worthy, not only because of that privilege of primogeniture, but inasmuch as he was able to overcome and slay his younger brother. That was a wise saying of the famous Marquis Pescara to the Papal Legate, that *it was impossible for men to serve Mars and Christ at the same time.* Yet in time past the profession of arms was judged to be κατ' ἐξοχήν that of a gentleman, nor does this opinion want for strenuous upholders even in our day. Must we suppose, then, that the profession of Christianity was only intended for losels, or, at best, to afford an opening for plebeian ambition? Or shall we hold with that nicely metaphysical Pomeranian, Captain Vratz, who was Count Königsmark's chief instrument in the murder of Mr. Thynne, that the Scheme of Salvation has been arranged with an especial eye to the necessities of the upper classes, and that "God would consider *a gentleman* and deal with him suitably to the condition and profession he had placed him in"? It may be said of us all, *Exemplo plus quam ratione vivimus.*—H. W.]

No. V

THE DEBATE IN THE SENNIT

SOT TO A NUSRY RHYME

[The incident which gave rise to the debate satirized in the following verses was the unsuccessful attempt of Drayton and Sayres to give freedom to seventy men and women, fellow-beings and fellow-Christians. Had Tripoli, instead of Washington, been the scene of this undertaking, the unhappy leaders in it would have been as secure of the theoretic as they now are of the practical part of martyrdom. I question whether the Dey of Tripoli is blessed with a District Attorney so benighted as ours at the seat of government. Very fitly is he named Key, who would allow himself to be made the instrument of locking the door of hope against sufferers in such a cause. Not all the waters of the ocean can cleanse the vile smutch of the jailer's fingers from off that little Key. *Ahenea clavis*, a brazen Key indeed!

Mr. Calhoun, who is made the chief speaker in this burlesque, seems to think that the light of the nineteenth century is to be put out as soon as he tinkles his little cow-bell curfew. Whenever slavery is touched, he sets up his scarecrow of dissolving the Union. This may do for the North, but I should conjecture that something more than a pumpkin-lantern is required to scare manifest and irretrievable Destiny out of her path. Mr. Calhoun cannot let go the apron-string of the Past. The Past is a good nurse, but we must be weaned from her sooner or later, even though, like Plotinus, we should run home from school to ask the breast, after we are tolerably well-grown youths. It will not do for us to hide our faces in her lap, whenever the strange Future holds out her arms and asks us to come to her.

But we are all alike. We have all heard it said, often enough, that little boys must not play with fire; and yet, if the matches be taken away from us, and put out of reach upon the shelf, we must needs get into our little corner, and scowl and stamp and threaten the dire revenge of going to bed without our supper. The world shall stop till we get our dangerous plaything again. Dame Earth, meanwhile, who has more than enough household matters to mind, goes bustling hither and thither as a hiss or a sputter tells her that this or that kettle of hers is boiling over, and before bedtime we are glad to eat our porridge cold, and gulp down our dignity along with it.

Mr. Calhoun has somehow acquired the name of a great statesman, and, if it be great statesmanship to put lance in rest and run a tilt at the Spirit of the Age with the certainty of being next moment hurled neck and heels into the dust amid universal laughter, he deserves the title. He is the Sir Kay of our modern chivalry. He should remember the old Scandinavian mythus. Thor was the strongest of gods, but he could not wrestle with Time, nor so much as lift up a fold of the great snake which bound the universe together; and when he smote the Earth, though with his terrible mallet, it was but as if a leaf had fallen. Yet all the while it seemed to Thor that he had only been wrestling with an old woman, striving to lift a cat, and striking a stupid giant on the head.

And in old times, doubtless, the giants *were* stupid, and there was no better sport for the Sir Launcelots and Sir Gawains than to go about cutting off their great blundering heads with enchanted swords. But things have wonderfully changed. It is the giants, nowadays, that have the science and the intelligence, while the chivalrous Don Quixotes of Conservatism still cumber themselves with the clumsy armor of a bygone age. On whirls the restless globe through unsounded time, with its cities and its silences, its births and funerals, half light, half shade, but never wholly dark, and sure to swing round into the happy morning at last. With an involuntary smile, one sees Mr. Calhoun letting slip his pack-thread cable with a crooked pin at the end of it to anchor South Carolina upon the bank and shoal of the Past.—H. W.]

TO MR. BUCKENAM

MR. EDITER, As i wuz kinder prunin round in a little nussry sot out a year or 2 a go, the Dbait in the sennit cum inter my mine An so i took & Sot it to wut I call a nussry rime. I hev made sum onnable Gentlemun speak thut dident speak in a Kind uv Poetikul lie sense the seeson is dreffle backerd up This way

ewers as ushul

HOSEA BIGLOW.

"HERE we stan' on the Constitution, by thunder!
It 's a fact o' wich ther 's bushils o' proofs;
Fer how could we trample on 't so, I wonder,
Ef 't worn't thet it 's ollers under our hoofs?"
Sez John C. Calhoun, sez he;
"Human rights haint no more
Right to come on this floor,
No more'n the man in the moon," sez he.

"The North haint no kind o' bisness with nothin',
An' you 've no idee how much bother it saves;
We aint none riled by their frettin' an' frothin',
We 're *used* to layin' the string on our slaves,"
Sez John C. Calhoun, sez he;—
Sez Mister Foote,
"I should like to shoot
The holl gang, by the gret horn spoon!" sez he.

"Freedom's Keystone is Slavery, thet ther 's no doubt on,
It 's sutthin' thet 's—wha' d 'ye call it?—divine,—
An' the slaves thet we ollers *make* the most out on
Air them north o' Mason an' Dixon's line,"

Sez John C. Calhoun, sez he;—
"Fer all thet," sez Mangum,
"'T would be better to hang 'em,
An' so git red on 'em soon," sez he.

"The mass ough' to labor an' we lay on soffies,
Thet 's the reason I want to spread Freedom's aree;
It puts all the cunninest on us in office,
An' reelises our Maker's orig'nal idee,"
Sez John C. Calhoun, sez he;—
"Thet 's ez plain," sez Cass,
"Ez thet some one 's an ass,
It 's ez clear ez the sun is at noon," sez he.

"Now don't go to say I 'm the friend of oppression,
But keep all your spare breath fer coolin' your broth,
Fer I ollers hev strove (at least thet 's my impression)
To make cussed free with the rights o' the North,"
Sez John C. Calhoun, sez he;—
"Yes," sez Davis o' Miss.,
"The perfection o' bliss
Is in skinnin' thet same old coon," sez he.

"Slavery 's a thing thet depends on complexion,
It 's God's law thet fetters on black skins don't chafe;
Ef brains wuz to settle it (horrid reflection!)
Wich of our onnable body 'd be safe?"
Sez John C. Calhoun, sez he;—
Sez Mister Hannegan,
Afore he began agin,
"Thet exception is quite oppertoon," sez he.

"Gen'nle Cass, Sir, you need n't be twitchin' your collar,
Your merit 's quite clear by the dut on your knees,
At the North we don't make no distinctions o' color;
You can all take a lick at our shoes wen you please,"
Sez John C. Calhoun, sez he;—
Sez Mister Jarnagin,
"They wun't hev to larn agin,
They all on 'em know the old toon," sez he.

"The slavery question aint no ways bewilderin',
North an' South hev one int'rest, it 's plain to a glance;
No'thern men, like us patriarchs, don't sell their childrin,
But they *du* sell themselves, ef they git a good chance,"
Sez John C. Calhoun, sez he;—
Sez Atherton here,
"This is gittin' severe,
I wish I could dive like a loon," sez he.

"It 'll break up the Union, this talk about freedom,
An' your fact'ry gals (soon ez we split) 'll make head,
An' gittin' some Miss chief or other to lead 'em,
'll go to work raisin' permiscoous Ned,"
Sez John C. Calhoun, sez he;—
"Yes, the North," sez Colquitt,
"Ef we Southerners all quit,
Would go down like a busted balloon," sez he.

"Jest look wut is doin', wut annyky 's brewin'
In the beautiful clime o' the olive an' vine,
All the wise aristoxy 's atumblin' to ruin,
An' the sankylots drorin' an' drinkin' their wine,"
Sez John C. Calhoun, sez he;—
"Yes," sez Johnson, "in France
They 're beginnin' to dance
Beëlzebub's own rigadoon," sez he.

"The South's safe enough, it don't feel a mite skeery,
Our slaves in their darkness an' dut air tu blest
Not to welcome with proud hallylugers the ery
Wen our eagle kicks yourn from the naytional nest,"
Sez John C. Calhoun, sez he;—
"Oh," sez Westcott o' Florida,
"Wut treason is horrider
Then our priv'leges tryin' to proon?" sez he.

"It 's 'coz they 're so happy, thet, wen crazy sarpints
Stick their nose in our bizness, we git so darned riled;

We think it 's our dooty to give pooty sharp
hints,
Thet the last crumb of Edin on airth sha' n't
be spiled,"
Sez John C. Calhoun, sez he;—
"Ah," sez Dixon H. Lewis,
"It perfectly true is
Thet slavery's airth's grettest boon," sez
he.

[It was said of old time, that riches have wings; and, though this be not applicable in a literal strictness to the wealth of our patriarchal brethren of the South, yet it is clear that their possessions have legs, and an unaccountable propensity for using them in a northerly direction. I marvel that the grand jury of Washington did not find a true bill against the North Star for aiding and abetting Drayton and Sayres. It would have been quite of a piece with the intelligence displayed by the South on other questions connected with slavery. I think that no ship of state was ever freighted with a more veritable Jonah than this same domestic institution of ours. Mephistopheles himself could not feign so bitterly, so satirically sad a sight as this of three millions of human beings crushed beyond help or hope by this one mighty argument,—*Our fathers knew no better!* Nevertheless, it is the unavoidable destiny of Jonahs to be cast overboard sooner or later. Or shall we try the experiment of hiding our Jonah in a safe place, that none may lay hands on him to make jetsam of him? Let us, then, with equal forethought and wisdom, lash ourselves to the anchor, and await, in pious confidence, the certain result. Perhaps our suspicious passenger is no Jonah after all, being black. For it is well known that a superintending Providence made a kind of sandwich of Ham and his descendants, to be devoured by the Caucasian race.

In God's name, let all, who hear nearer and nearer the hungry moan of the storm and the growl of the breakers, speak out! But, alas! we have no right to interfere. If a man pluck an apple of mine, he shall be in danger of the justice; but if he steal my brother, I must be silent. Who says this? Our Constitution, consecrated by the callous consuetude of sixty years, and grasped in triumphant argument by the left hand of him whose right hand clutches the clotted slave-whip. Justice, venerable with the undethronable majesty of countless æons, says,—SPEAK! The Past, wise with the sorrows and desolations of ages, from amid her shattered fanes and wolf-housing palaces, echoes,—SPEAK! Nature, through her thousand trumpets of freedom, her stars, her sunrises, her seas, her winds, her cataracts, her mountains blue with cloudy pines, blows jubilant encouragement, and cries,—SPEAK! From the soul's trembling abysses the still, small voice not vaguely murmurs,—SPEAK! But, alas! the Constitution and the Honorable Mr. Bagowind, M. C., say—BE DUMB!

It occurs to me to suggest, as a topic of inquiry in this connection, whether, on that momentous occasion when the goats and the sheep shall be parted, the Constitution and the Honorable Mr. Bagowind, M. C., will be expected to take their places on the left as our hircine vicars.

Quid sum miser tunc dicturus?
Quem patronum rogaturus?

There is a point where toleration sinks into sheer baseness and poltroonery. The toleration of the worst leads us to look on what is barely better as good enough, and to worship what is only moderately good. Woe to that man, or that nation, to whom mediocrity has become an ideal!

Has our experiment of self-government succeeded, if it barely manage to *rub and go?* Here, now, is a piece of barbarism which Christ and the nineteenth century say shall cease, and which Messrs. Smith, Brown, and others say shall *not* cease. I would by no means deny the eminent respectability of these gentlemen, but I confess, that, in such a wrestling-match, I cannot help having my fears for them. *Discite justitiam, moniti, et non temnere divos.*—H. W.]

1848

From No. VI

THE PIOUS EDITOR'S CREED

I DU believe in Freedom's cause,
Ez fur away ez Payris is;
I love to see her stick her claws
In them infarnal Phayrisees;
It 's wal enough agin a king
To dror resolves an' triggers,—
But libbaty 's a kind o' thing
Thet don't agree with niggers.

I du believe the people want
A tax on teas an' coffees,
Thet nothin' aint extravygunt,—
Purvidin' I 'm in office;
Fer I hev loved my country sence
My eye-teeth filled their sockets,
An' Uncle Sam I reverence,
Partic'larly his pockets.

I du believe in *any* plan
O' levyin' the texes,
Ez long ez, like a lumberman,
I git jest wut I axes;
I go free-trade thru thick an' thin,
Because it kind o' rouses
The folks to vote,—an' keeps us in
Our quiet custom-houses.

I du believe it 's wise an' good
  To sen' out furrin missions,
Thet is, on sartin understood
  An' orthydox conditions;—
I mean nine thousan' dolls. per ann.,
  Nine thousan' more fer outfit,
An' me to recommend a man
  The place 'ould jest about fit.

I du believe in special ways
  O' prayin' an' convartin';
The bread comes back in many days,
  An' buttered, tu, fer sartin;
I mean in preyin' till one busts
  On wut the party chooses,
An' in convartin' public trusts
  To very privit uses.

I du believe hard coin the stuff
  Fer 'lectioneers to spout on;
The people 's ollers soft enough
  To make hard money out on;
Dear Uncle Sam pervides fer his,
  An' gives a good-sized junk to all,—
I don't care *how* hard money is,
  Ez long ez mine 's paid punctooal.

I du believe with all my soul
  In the gret Press's freedom,
To pint the people to the goal
  An' in the traces lead 'em;
Palsied the arm thet forges yokes
  At my fat contracts squintin',
An' withered be the nose thet pokes
  Inter the gov'ment printin'!

I du believe thet I should give
  Wut 's his'n unto Cæsar,
Fer it 's by him I move an' live,
  Frum him my bread an' cheese air;
I du believe thet all o' me
  Doth bear his superscription,—
Will, conscience, honor, honesty,
  An' things o' thet description.

I du believe in prayer an' praise
  To him thet hez the grantin'
O' jobs,—in every thin' thet pays,
  But most of all in Cantin';
This doth my cup with marcies fill,
  This lays all thought o' sin to rest,
I *don't* believe in princerple,
  But oh, I *du* in interest.

I du believe in bein' this
  Or thet, ez it may happen
One way or t' other hendiest is
  To ketch the people nappin';
It aint by princerples nor men
  My preudunt course is steadied,—
I scent wich pays the best, an' then
  Go into it baldheaded.

I du believe thet holdin' slaves
  Comes nat'ral to a Presidunt,
Let 'lone the rowdedow it saves
  To hev a wal-broke precedunt;
Fer any office, small or gret,
  I could n't ax with no face,
'uthout I 'd ben, thru dry an' wet,
  Th' unrizzest kind o' doughface.

I du believe wutever trash
  'll keep the people in blindness,
Thet we the Mexicuns can thrash
  Right inter brotherly kindness,
Thet bombshells, grape, an' powder 'n' ball
  Air good-will's strongest magnets,
Thet peace, to make it stick at all,
  Must be druv in with bagnets.

In short, I firmly du believe
  In Humbug generally,
Fer it 's a thing thet I perceive
  To hev a solid vally;
This heth my faithful shepherd ben,
  In pasturs sweet heth led me,
An' this 'll keep the people green
  To feed ez they hev fed me.

May 4, 1848

From No. VII

A LETTER

FROM A CANDIDATE FOR THE PRESIDENCY IN ANSWER TO SUTTIN QUESTIONS PROPOSED BY MR. HOSEA BIGLOW, INCLOSED IN A NOTE FROM MR. BIGLOW TO S. H. GAY, ESQ., EDITOR OF THE NATIONAL ANTI-SLAVERY STANDARD.

Dear Sir,—You wish to know my notions
  On sartin pints thet rile the land;
There 's nothin' thet my natur so shuns
  Ez bein' mum or underhand;

I'm a straight-spoken kind o' creetur
  Thet blurts right out wut 's in his head,
An' ef I 've one pecooler feetur,
  It is a nose thet wunt be led.

So, to begin at the beginnin'
  An' come direcly to the pint,
I think the country's underpinnin'
  Is some consid'ble out o' jint;
I aint agoin' to try your patience
  By tellin' who done this or thet,
I don't make no insinooations,
  I jest let on I smell a rat.

Thet is, I mean, it seems to me so,
  But, ef the public think I 'm wrong,
I wunt deny but wut I be so,—
  An', fact, it don't smell very strong;
My mind 's tu fair to lose its balance
  An' say wich party hez most sense;
There may be folks o' greater talence
  Thet can't set stiddier on the fence.

I 'm an eclectic; ez to choosin'
  'Twixt this an' thet, I 'm plaguy lawth;
I leave a side thet looks like losin',
  But (wile there's doubt) I stick to both;
I stan' upon the Constitution,
  Ez preudunt statesmun say, who 've planned
A way to git the most profusion 31
  O' chances ez to *ware* they 'll stand.

Ez fer the war, I go agin it,—
  I mean to say I kind o' du,—
Thet is, I mean thet, bein' in it,
  The best way wuz to fight it thru;
Not but wut abstract war is horrid,
  I sign to thet with all my heart,—
But civlyzation *doos* git forrid
  Sometimes upon a powder-cart.

About thet darned Proviso matter
  I never hed a grain o' doubt,
Nor I aint one my sense to scatter
  So 'st no one could n't pick it out;
My love fer North an' South is equil,
  So I 'll jest answer plump an' frank,
No matter wut may be the sequil,—
  Yes, Sir, I *am* agin a Bank.

Ez to the answerin' o' questions,
  I 'm an off ox at bein' druv,
Though I aint one thet ary test shuns
  'll give our folks a helpin' shove;
Kind o' permiscous I go it
  Fer the holl country, an' the ground
I take, ez nigh ez I can show it,
  Is pooty gen'ally all round.

I don't appruve o' givin' pledges;
  You 'd ough' to leave a feller free,
An' not go knockin' out the wedges
  To ketch his fingers in the tree;
Pledges air awfle breachy cattle
  Thet preudunt farmers don't turn out,—
Ez long 'z the people git their rattle,
  Wut is there fer 'm to grout about?

Ez to the slaves, there 's no confusion
  In *my* idees consarnin' them,—
I think they air an Institution,
  A sort of—yes, jest so,—ahem:
Do *I* own any? Of my merit
  On thet pint you yourself may jedge;
All is, I never drink no sperit,
  Nor I haint never signed no pledge.

Ez to my princerples, I glory
  In hevin' nothin' o' the sort;
I aint a Wig, I aint a Tory,
  I 'm jest a canderdate, in short;
Thet 's fair an' square an' parpendicler,
  But, ef the Public cares a fig
To hev me an' thin' in particler,
  Wy, I 'm a kind o' peri-Wig.

P. S.

Ez we 're a sort o' privateerin',
  O' course, you know, it 's sheer an' sheer,
An' there is sutthin' wuth your hearin'
  I 'll mention in *your* privit ear;
Ef you git *me* inside the White House,
  Your head with ile I 'll kin' o' 'nint
By gittin' *you* inside the Light-house
  Down to the eend o' Jaalam Pint.

An' ez the North hez took to brustlin'
  At bein' scrouged frum off the roost,
I 'll tell ye wut 'll save all tusslin'
  An' give our side a harnsome boost,—
Tell 'em thet on the Slavery question
  I'm RIGHT, although to speak I 'm lawth;
This gives you a safe pint to rest on,
  An' leaves me frontin' South by North.

AN INDIAN-SUMMER REVERIE

WHAT visionary tints the year puts on,
When falling leaves falter through motionless air
Or humbly cling and shiver to be gone!
How shimmer the low flats and pastures bare,
As with her nectar Hebe Autumn fills
The bowl between me and those distant hills,
And smiles and shakes abroad her misty, tremulous hair!

No more the landscape holds its wealth apart,
Making me poorer in my poverty,
But mingles with my senses and my heart;
My own projected spirit seems to me
In her own reverie the world to steep;
'Tis she that waves to sympathetic sleep,
Moving, as she is moved, each field and hill and tree.

How fuse and mix, with what unfelt degrees,
Clasped by the faint horizon's languid arms,
Each into each, the hazy distances!
The softened season all the landscape charms;
Those hills, my native village that embay,
In waves of dreamier purple roll away,
And floating in mirage seem all the glimmering farms.

Far distant sounds the hidden chickadee
Close at my side; far distant sound the leaves;
The fields seem fields of dream, where Memory
Wanders like gleaning Ruth; and as the sheaves
Of wheat and barley wavered in the eye
Of Boaz as the maiden's glow went by,
So tremble and seem remote all things the sense receives.

The cock's shrill trump that tells of scattered corn,
Passed breezily on by all his flapping mates,
Faint and more faint, from barn to barn is borne,
Southward, perhaps to far Magellan's Straits;
Dimly I catch the throb of distant flails;
Silently overhead the hen-hawk sails,
With watchful, measuring eye, and for his quarry waits.

The sobered robin, hunger-silent now,
Seeks cedar-berries blue, his autumn cheer;
The chipmunk, on the shingly shagbark's bough
Now saws, now lists with downward eye and ear,
Then drops his nut, and, cheeping, with a bound
Whisks to his winding fastness underground;
The clouds like swans drift down the streaming atmosphere.

O'er yon bare knoll the pointed cedar shadows
Drowse on the crisp, gray moss; the ploughman's call
Creeps faint as smoke from black, fresh-furrowed meadows;
The single crow a single caw lets fall;
And all around me every bush and tree
Says Autumn's here, and Winter soon will be,
Who snows his soft, white sleep and silence over all.

The birch, most shy and ladylike of trees,
Her poverty, as best she may, retrieves,
And hints at her foregone gentilities
With some saved relics of her wealth of leaves;
The swamp-oak, with his royal purple on,
Glares red as blood across the sinking sun,
As one who proudlier to a falling fortune cleaves.

He looks a sachem, in red blanket wrapt,
Who, 'mid some council of the sad-garbed whites,
Erect and stern, in his own memories lapt,
With distant eye broods over other sights,
Sees the hushed wood the city's flare replace,
The wounded turf heal o'er the railway's trace,
And roams the savage Past of his undwindled rights.

The red-oak, softer-grained, yields all for lost,
And, with his crumpled foliage stiff and dry,
After the first betrayal of the frost,
Rebuffs the kiss of the relenting sky;
The chestnuts, lavish of their long-hid gold,

To the faint Summer, beggared now and old,
Pour back the sunshine hoarded 'neath her favoring eye.

The ash her purple drops forgivingly
And sadly, breaking not the general hush;
The maple-swamps glow like a sunset sea,
Each leaf a ripple with its separate flush;
All round the wood's edge creeps the skirting blaze
Of bushes low, as when, on cloudy days,
Ere the rain fall, the cautious farmer burns his brush.

O'er yon low wall, which guards one unkempt zone,
Where vines and weeds and scrub-oaks intertwine
Safe from the plough, whose rough, discordant stone
Is massed to one soft gray by lichens fine,
The tangled blackberry, crossed and recrossed, weaves
A prickly network of ensanguined leaves;
Hard by, with coral beads, the prim black-alders shine.

Pillaring with flame this crumbling boundary,
Whose loose blocks topple 'neath the plough-boy's foot,
Who, with each sense shut fast except the eye,
Creeps close and scares the jay he hoped to shoot,
The woodbine up the elm's straight stem aspires,
Coiling it, harmless, with autumnal fires;
In the ivy's paler blaze the martyr oak stands mute.

Below, the Charles, a stripe of nether sky,
Now hid by rounded apple-trees between,
Whose gaps the misplaced sail sweeps bellying by,
Now flickering golden through a woodland screen,
Then spreading out, at his next turn beyond,
A silver circle like an inland pond—
Slips seaward silently through marshes purple and green.

Dear marshes! vain to him the gift of sight
Who cannot in their various incomes share,
From every season drawn, of shade and light,
Who sees in them but levels brown and bare;
Each change of storm or sunshine scatters free
On them its largess of variety,
For Nature with cheap means still works her wonders rare.

In Spring they lie one broad expanse of green,
O'er which the light winds run with glimmering feet:
Here, yellower stripes track out the creek unseen,
There, darker growths o'er hidden ditches meet;
And purpler stains show where the blossoms crowd,
As if the silent shadow of a cloud
Hung there becalmed, with the next breath to fleet.

All round, upon the river's slippery edge,
Witching to deeper calm the drowsy tide,
Whispers and leans the breeze-entangling sedge;
Through emerald glooms the lingering waters slide,
Or, sometimes wavering, throw back the sun,
And the stiff banks in eddies melt and run
Of dimpling light, and with the current seem to glide.

In Summer 'tis a blithesome sight to see,
As, step by step, with measured swing, they pass,
The wide-ranked mowers wading to the knee,
Their sharp scythes panting through the wiry grass;
Then, stretched beneath a rick's shade in a ring,
Their nooning take, while one begins to sing
A stave that droops and dies 'neath the close sky of brass.

Meanwhile that devil-may-care, the bobolink,
Remembering duty, in mid-quaver stops
Just ere he sweeps o'er rapture's tremulous brink,
And 'twixt the winrows most demurely drops,
A decorous bird of business, who provides
For his brown mate and fledglings six besides,
And looks from right to left, a farmer 'mid his crops.

Another change subdues them in the Fall,
But saddens not; they still show merrier tints,
Though sober russet seems to cover all;
When the first sunshine through their dewdrops glints,
Look how the yellow clearness, streamed across,
Redeems with rarer hues the season's loss,
As Dawn's feet there had touched and left their rosy prints.

Or come when sunset gives its freshened zest,
Lean o'er the bridge and let the ruddy thrill,
While the shorn sun swells down the hazy west,
Glow opposite;—the marshes drink their fill
And swoon with purple veins, then slowly fade
Through pink to brown, as eastward moves the shade,
Lengthening with stealthy creep, of Simond's darkening hill.

Later, and yet ere Winter wholly shuts,
Ere through the first dry snow the runner grates,
And the loath cart-wheel screams in slippery ruts,
While firmer ice the eager boy awaits,
Trying each buckle and strap beside the fire,
And until bedtime plays with his desire,
Twenty times putting on and off his new-bought skates;—

Then, every morn, the river's banks shine bright
With smooth plate-armor, treacherous and frail,
By the frost's clinking hammers forged at night,
'Gainst which the lances of the sun prevail,
Giving a pretty emblem of the day
When guiltier arms in light shall melt away,
And states shall move free-limbed, loosed from war's cramping mail.

And now those waterfalls the ebbing river
Twice every day creates on either side
Tinkle, as through their fresh-sparred grots they shiver
In grass-arched channels to the sun denied;
High flaps in sparkling blue the far-heard crow,
The silvered flats gleam frostily below,
Suddenly drops the gull and breaks the glassy tide.

But crowned in turn by vying seasons three,
Their winter halo hath a fuller ring;
This glory seems to rest immovably,—
The others were too fleet and vanishing;
When the hid tide is at its highest flow,
O'er marsh and stream one breathless trance of snow
With brooding fulness awes and hushes everything.

The sunshine seems blown off by the bleak wind,
As pale as formal candles lit by day;
Gropes to the sea the river dumb and blind;
The brown ricks, snow-thatched by the storm in play,
Show pearly breakers combing o'er their lee,
White crests as of some just enchanted sea,
Checked in their maddest leap and hanging poised midway.

But when the eastern blow, with rain aslant,
From mid-sea's prairies green and rolling plains
Drives in his wallowing herds of billows gaunt,
And the roused Charles remembers in his veins
Old Ocean's blood and snaps his gyves of frost,
That tyrannous silence on the shores is tost
In dreary wreck, and crumbling desolation reigns.

Edgewise or flat, in Druid-like device,
With leaden pools between or gullies bare,
The blocks lie strewn, a bleak Stonehenge of ice;
No life, no sound, to break the grim despair,
Save sullen plunge, as through the sedges stiff
Down crackles riverward some thaw-sapped cliff,
Or when the close-wedged fields of ice crunch here and there.

But let me turn from fancy-pictured scenes
To that whose pastoral calm before me lies:
Here nothing harsh or rugged intervenes;
The early evening with her misty dyes
Smooths off the ravelled edges of the nigh,
Relieves the distant with her cooler sky,
And tones the landscape down, and soothes the wearied eyes.

There gleams my native village, dear to me,
Though higher change's waves each day are seen,
Whelming fields famed in boyhood's history,
Sanding with houses the diminished green;
There, in red brick, which softening time defies,
Stand square and stiff the Muses' factories;—
How with my life knit up is every well-known scene!

Flow on, dear river! not alone you flow
To outward sight, and through your marshes wind;
Fed from the mystic springs of long-ago,
Your twin flows silent through my world of mind:
Grow dim, dear marshes, in the evening's gray!
Before my inner sight ye stretch away,
And will forever, though these fleshly eyes grow blind.

Beyond the hillock's house-bespotted swell,
Where Gothic chapels house the horse and chaise,
Where quiet cits in Grecian temples dwell,
Where Coptic tombs resound with prayer and praise,
Where dust and mud the equal year divide,
There gentle Allston lived, and wrought, and died,
Transfiguring street and shop with his illumined gaze.

Virgilium vidi tantum,—I have seen
But as a boy, who looks alike on all,
That misty hair, that fine Undine-like mien,
Tremulous as down to feeling's faintest call;—
Ah, dear old homestead! count it to thy fame
That thither many times the Painter came;—
One elm yet bears his name, a feathery tree and tall.

Swiftly the present fades in memory's glow,—
Our only sure possession is the past;
The village blacksmith died a month ago,
And dim to me the forge's roaring blast;
Soon fire-new mediævals we shall see
Oust the black smithy from its chestnut-tree,
And that hewn down, perhaps, the beehive green and vast.

How many times, prouder than king on throne,
Loosed from the village school-dame's A's and B's,
Panting have I the creaky bellows blown,
And watched the pent volcano's red increase,
Then paused to see the ponderous sledge, brought down
By that hard arm voluminous and brown,
From the white iron swarm its golden vanishing bees.

Dear native town! whose choking elms each year
With eddying dust before their time turn gray,
Pining for rain,—to me thy dust is dear;
It glorifies the eve of summer day,
And when the westering sun half sunken burns,
The mote-thick air to deepest orange turns,
The westward horseman rides through clouds of gold away,

So palpable, I've seen those unshorn few,
The six old willows at the causey's end
(Such trees Paul Potter never dreamed nor drew),
Through this dry mist their checkering shadows send,
Striped, here and there, with many a long-drawn thread,
Where streamed through leafy chinks the trembling red,
Past which, in one bright trail, the hangbird's flashes blend.

Yes, dearer far thy dust than all that e'er,
Beneath the awarded crown of victory,
Gilded the blown Olympic charioteer;
Though lightly prized the ribboned parchments three,
Yet *collegisse juvat*, I am glad
That here what colleging was mine I had,—
It linked another tie, dear native town, with thee!

Nearer art thou than simply native earth,
My dust with thine concedes a deeper tie;
A closer claim thy soil may well put forth,
Something of kindred more than sympathy;
For in thy bounds I reverently laid away
That blinding anguish of forsaken clay,
That title I seemed to have in earth and sea and sky,

That portion of my life more choice to me
(Though brief, yet in itself so round and whole)
Than all the imperfect residue can be;—
The Artist saw his statue of the soul
Was perfect; so, with one regretful stroke,
The earthen model into fragments broke,
And without her the impoverished seasons roll.

1846 1847

HEBE

I SAW the twinkle of white feet,
I saw the flash of robes descending;
Before her ran an influence fleet,
That bowed my heart like barley bending.

As, in bare fields, the searching bees
Pilot to blooms beyond our finding,
It led me on, by sweet degrees
Joy's simple honey-cells unbinding.

Those Graces were that seemed grim Fates;
With nearer love the sky leaned o'er me;
The long-sought Secret's golden gates
On musical hinges swung before me.

I saw the brimmed bowl in her grasp
Thrilling with godhood; like a lover
I sprang the proffered life to clasp;—
The beaker fell; the luck was over.

The Earth has drunk the vintage up;
What boots it patch the goblet's splinters?
Can Summer fill the icy cup,
Whose treacherous crystal is but Winter's?

O spendthrift haste! await the Gods;
The nectar crowns the lips of Patience;
Haste scatters on unthankful sods
The immortal gift in vain libations.

Coy Hebe flies from those that woo,
And shuns the hands would seize upon her;
Follow thy life, and she will sue
To pour for thee the cup of honor.

1847

THE VISION OF SIR LAUNFAL

PRELUDE TO PART FIRST

OVER his keys the musing organist,
Beginning doubtfully and far away,
First lets his fingers wander as they list,
And builds a bridge from Dreamland for his lay:
Then, as the touch of his loved instrument
Gives hope and fervor, nearer draws his theme,
First guessed by faint auroral flushes sent
Along the wavering vista of his dream.
Not only around our infancy
Doth heaven with all its splendors lie;
Daily, with souls that cringe and plot,
We Sinais climb and know it not.

Over our manhood bend the skies;
Against our fallen and traitor lives
The great winds utter prophecies;
With our faint hearts the mountain strives;
Its arms outstretched, the druid wood
Waits with its benedicite;
And to our age's drowsy blood
Still shouts the inspiring sea.

Earth gets its price for what Earth gives us;
The beggar is taxed for a corner to die in,
The priest hath his fee who comes and shrives us,
We bargain for the graves we lie in;
At the devil's booth are all things sold,
Each ounce of dross costs its ounce of gold;
For a cap and bells our lives we pay,
Bubbles we buy with a whole soul's tasking:
'Tis heaven alone that is given away,
'Tis only God may be had for the asking;
No price is set on the lavish summer;
June may be had by the poorest comer.

And what is so rare as a day in June?
Then, if ever, come perfect days;
Then Heaven tries earth if it be in tune,
And over it softly her warm ear lays;
Whether we look, or whether we listen,
We hear life murmur, or see it glisten;
Every clod feels a stir of might,
An instinct within it that reaches and towers,
And, groping blindly above it for light,
Climbs to a soul in grass and flowers;
The flush of life may well be seen
Thrilling back over hills and valleys;
The cowslip startles in meadows green,
The buttercup catches the sun in its chalice,
And there's never a leaf nor a blade too mean
To be some happy creature's palace;
The little bird sits at his door in the sun,
Atilt like a blossom among the leaves,
And lets his illumined being o'errun
With the deluge of summer it receives;
His mate feels the eggs beneath her wings,
And the heart in her dumb breast flutters and sings;
He sings to the wide world, and she to her nest,—
In the nice ear of Nature which song is the best?

Now is the high-tide of the year,
And whatever of life hath ebbed away
Comes flooding back with a ripply cheer,
Into every bare inlet and creek and bay;
Now the heart is so full that a drop overfills it,
We are happy now because God wills it;
No matter how barren the past may have been,
'Tis enough for us now that the leaves are green;
We sit in the warm shade and feel right well
How the sap creeps up and the blossoms swell;
We may shut our eyes, but we cannot help knowing
That skies are clear and grass is growing;
The breeze comes whispering in our ear,
That dandelions are blossoming near,
That maize has sprouted, that streams are flowing,
That the river is bluer than the sky,
That the robin is plastering his house hard by;
And if the breeze kept the good news back,
For other couriers we should not lack;
We could guess it all by yon heifer's lowing,—
And hark! how clear bold chanticleer,
Warmed with the new wine of the year,
Tells all in his lusty crowing!

Joy comes, grief goes, we know not how;
Everything is happy now,
Everything is upward striving;
'Tis as easy now for the heart to be true
As for grass to be green or skies to be blue,—
'Tis the natural way of living:
Who knows whither the clouds have fled?
In the unscarred heaven they leave no wake;
And the eyes forget the tears they have shed,
The heart forgets its sorrow and ache;
The soul partakes the season's youth,
And the sulphurous rifts of passion and woe
Lie deep 'neath a silence pure and smooth,
Like burnt-out craters healed with snow.
What wonder if Sir Launfal now
Remembered the keeping of his vow?

PART FIRST

I

"My golden spurs now bring to me,
And bring to me my richest mail,
For tomorrow I go over land and sea
In search of the Holy Grail;
Shall never a bed for me be spread,
Nor shall a pillow be under my head,
Till I begin my vow to keep;
Here on the rushes will I sleep,
And perchance there may come a vision true
Ere day create the world anew."

Slowly Sir Launfal's eyes grew dim,
Slumber fell like a cloud on him,
And into his soul the vision flew.

II

The crows flapped over by twos and threes,
In the pool drowsed the cattle up to their knees,
The little birds sang as if it were
The one day of summer in all the year,
And the very leaves seemed to sing on the trees:
The castle alone in the landscape lay
Like an outpost of winter, dull and gray:
'Twas the proudest hall in the North Countree,
And never its gates might opened be,
Save to lord or lady of high degree;
Summer besieged it on every side,
But the churlish stone her assaults defied;
She could not scale the chilly wall,
Though around it for leagues her pavilions tall
Stretched left and right,
Over the hills and out of sight;
Green and broad was every tent,
And out of each a murmur went
Till the breeze fell off at night.

III

The drawbridge dropped with a surly clang,
And through the dark arch a charger sprang,
Bearing Sir Launfal, the maiden knight,
In his gilded mail, that flamed so bright
It seemed the dark castle had gathered all
Those shafts the fierce sun had shot over its wall
In his siege of three hundred summers long,
And, binding them all in one blazing sheaf,
Had cast them forth: so, young and strong,
And lightsome as a locust-leaf,
Sir Launfal flashed forth in his maiden mail,
To seek in all climes for the Holy Grail.

IV

It was morning on hill and stream and tree,
And morning in the young knight's heart;
Only the castle moodily
Rebuffed the gifts of the sunshine free,
And gloomed by itself apart;
The season brimmed all other things up
Full as the rain fills the pitcher-plant's cup.

V

As Sir Launfal made morn through the darksome gate,
He was 'ware of a leper, crouched by the same,
Who begged with his hand and moaned as he sate;
And a loathing over Sir Launfal came;
The sunshine went out of his soul with a thrill,
The flesh 'neath his armor 'gan shrink and crawl,
And midway its leap his heart stood still
Like a frozen waterfall;
For this man, so foul and bent of stature,
Rasped harshly against his dainty nature,
And seemed the one blot on the summer morn,—
So he tossed him a piece of gold in scorn.

VI

The leper raised not the gold from the dust:
"Better to me the poor man's crust,
Better the blessing of the poor,
Though I turn me empty from his door;
That is no true alms which the hand can hold;
He gives only the worthless gold
Who gives from a sense of duty;
But he who gives but a slender mite,
And gives to that which is out of sight,
That thread of the all-sustaining Beauty
Which runs through all and doth all unite,—
The hand cannot clasp the whole of his alms,
The heart outstretches its eager palms,
For a god goes with it and makes it store
To the soul that was starving in darkness before."

PRELUDE TO PART SECOND

Down swept the chill wind from the mountain peak,
From the snow five thousand summers old;
On open wold and hilltop bleak
It had gathered all the cold,
And whirled it like sleet on the wanderer's cheek;
It carried a shiver everywhere
From the unleafed boughs and pastures bare;

The little brook heard it and built a roof
'Neath which he could house him, winter-proof;
All night by the white stars' frosty gleams
He groined his arches and matched his beams;
Slender and clear were his crystal spars
As the lashes of light that trim the stars:
He sculptured every summer delight
In his halls and chambers out of sight;
Sometimes his tinkling waters slipt
Down through a frost-leaved forest-crypt,
Long, sparkling aisles of steel-stemmed trees
Bending to counterfeit a breeze;
Sometimes the roof no fretwork knew
But silvery mosses that downward grew;
Sometimes it was carved in sharp relief
With quaint arabesques of ice-fern leaf;
Sometimes it was simply smooth and clear
For the gladness of heaven to shine through, and here
He had caught the nodding bulrush-tops
And hung them thickly with diamond drops,
That crystalled the beams of moon and sun,
And made a star of every one:
No mortal builder's most rare device
Could match this winter-palace of ice;
'Twas as if every image that mirrored lay
In his depths serene through the summer day,
Each fleeting shadow of earth and sky,
  Lest the happy model should be lost,
Had been mimicked in fairy masonry
  By the elfin builders of the frost.

Within the hall are song and laughter,
  The cheeks of Christmas glow red and jolly,
And sprouting is every corbel and rafter
  With lightsome green of ivy and holly;
Through the deep gulf of the chimney wide
Wallows the Yule-log's roaring tide;
The broad flame-pennons droop and flap
  And belly and tug as a flag in the wind;
Like a locust shrills the imprisoned sap,
  Hunted to death in its galleries blind;
And swift little troops of silent sparks,
  Now pausing, now scattering away as in fear,
Go threading the soot-forest's tangled darks
  Like herds of startled deer.

But the wind without was eager and sharp,
Of Sir Launfal's gray hair it makes a harp,
  And rattles and wrings
  The icy strings,
Singing, in dreary monotone,
A Christmas carol of its own,
Whose burden still, as he might guess,
Was "Shelterless, shelterless, shelterless!"
The voice of the seneschal flared like a torch
As he shouted the wanderer away from the porch,
And he sat in the gateway and saw all night
  The great hall-fire, so cheery and bold,
  Through the window-slits of the castle old,
Build out its piers of ruddy light
Against the drift of the cold.

PART SECOND

I

THERE was never a leaf on bush or tree,
The bare boughs rattled shudderingly;
The river was dumb and could not speak,
  For the weaver Winter its shroud had spun;
A single crow on the tree-top bleak
  From his shining feathers shed off the cold sun;
Again it was morning, but shrunk and cold,
As if her veins were sapless and old,
And she rose up decrepitly
For a last dim look at earth and sea.

II

Sir Launfal turned from his own hard gate,
For another heir in his earldom sate;
An old, bent man, worn out and frail,
He came back from seeking the Holy Grail;
Little he recked of his earldom's loss,
No more on his surcoat was blazoned the cross,
But deep in his soul the sign he wore,
The badge of the suffering and the poor.

III

Sir Launfal's raiment thin and spare
Was idle mail 'gainst the barbèd air,
For it was just at the Christmas time;
So he mused, as he sat, of a sunnier clime,
And sought for a shelter from cold and snow
In the light and warmth of long-ago;
He sees the snake-like caravan crawl
O'er the edge of the desert, black and small,

Then nearer and nearer, till, one by one,
He can count the camels in the sun,
As over the red-hot sands they pass
To where, in its slender necklace of grass,
The little spring laughed and leapt in the shade,
And with its own self like an infant played,
And waved its signal of palms.

IV

"For Christ's sweet sake, I beg an alms;"
The happy camels may reach the spring,
But Sir Launfal sees only the grewsome thing,
The leper, lank as the rain-blanched bone,
That cowers beside him, a thing as lone
And white as the ice-isles of Northern seas
In the desolate horror of his disease.

V

And Sir Launfal said, "I behold in thee
An image of Him who died on the tree;
Thou also hast had thy crown of thorns,
Thou also hast had the world's buffets and scorns,
And to thy life were not denied
The wounds in the hands and feet and side:
Mild Mary's Son, acknowledge me;
Behold, through him, I give to thee!"

VI

Then the soul of the leper stood up in his eyes
And looked at Sir Launfal, and straightway he
Remembered in what a haughtier guise
He had flung an alms to leprosie,
When he girt his young life up in gilded mail
And set forth in search of the Holy Grail.
The heart within him was ashes and dust;
He parted in twain his single crust,
He broke the ice on the streamlet's brink,
And gave the leper to eat and drink,
'Twas a mouldy crust of coarse brown bread,
'Twas water out of a wooden bowl,—
Yet with fine wheaten bread was the leper fed,
And 'twas red wine he drank with his thirsty soul.

VII

As Sir Launfal mused with a downcast face,
A light shone round about the place;
The leper no longer crouched at his side,
But stood before him glorified,
Shining and tall and fair and straight
As the pillar that stood by the Beautiful Gate,—
Himself the Gate whereby men can
Enter the temple of God in Man.

VIII

His words were shed softer than leaves from the pine,
And they fell on Sir Launfal as snows on the brine,
That mingle their softness and quiet in one
With the shaggy unrest they float down upon;
And the voice that was softer than silence said,
"Lo, it is I, be not afraid!
In many climes, without avail,
Thou hast spent thy life for the Holy Grail;
Behold, it is here,—this cup which thou
Didst fill at the streamlet for me but now;
This crust is my body broken for thee,
This water his blood that died on the tree;
The Holy Supper is kept, indeed,
In whatso we share with another's need;
Not what we give, but what we share,
For the gift without the giver is bare;
Who gives himself with his alms feeds three,
Himself, his hungering neighbor, and me."

IX

Sir Launfal awoke as from a swound:
"The Grail in my castle here is found!
Hang my idle armor up on the wall,
Let it be the spider's banquet-hall;
He must be fenced with stronger mail
Who would seek and find the Holy Grail."

X

The castle gate stands open now,
And the wanderer is welcome to the hall
As the hangbird is to the elm-tree bough;
No longer scowl the turrets tall,
The Summer's long siege at last is o'er;
When the first poor outcast went in at the door,
She entered with him in disguise,
And mastered the fortress by surprise;
There is no spot she loves so well on ground,

She lingers and smiles there the whole year
round;
The meanest serf on Sir Launfal's land
Has hall and bower at his command;
And there's no poor man in the North
Countree
But is lord of the earldom as much as he.

1848 1848

A FABLE FOR CRITICS

Reader! walk up at once (it will soon be too late),
and buy at a perfectly ruinous rate

A FABLE FOR CRITICS:

OR, BETTER,

(I LIKE, AS A THING THAT THE READER'S FIRST FANCY MAY STRIKE, AN OLD-FASHIONED TITLE-PAGE, SUCH AS PRESENTS A TABULAR VIEW OF THE VOLUME'S CONTENTS),

A GLANCE AT A FEW OF OUR LITERARY PROGENIES

(MRS. MALAPROP'S WORD)

FROM THE TUB OF DIOGENES;

A VOCAL AND MUSICAL MEDLEY,

THAT IS,

A SERIES OF JOKES

By A Wonderful Quiz,

WHO ACCOMPANIES HIMSELF WITH A RUB-A-DUB-DUB, FULL OF SPIRIT AND GRACE, ON THE TOP OF THE TUB.

Set forth in October, the 31st day,
In the year '48, G. P. Putnam, Broadway.

It being the commonest mode of procedure, I
premise a few candid remarks

To the Reader:—

This trifle, begun to please only myself and my own private fancy, was laid on the shelf. But some friends, who had seen it, induced me, by dint of saying they liked it, to put it in print. That is, having come to that very conclusion, I asked their advice when 'twould make no confusion. For though (in the gentlest of ways) they had hinted it was scarce worth the while, I should doubtless have printed it.

I began it, intending a Fable, a frail, slender thing, rhyme-ywinged, with a sting in its tail. But, by addings and alterings not previously planned, digressions chance-hatched, like birds' eggs in the sand, and dawdlings to suit every whimsey's demand (always freeing the bird which I held in my hand, for the two perched, perhaps out of reach, in the tree),—it grew by degrees to the size which you see. I was like the old woman that carried the calf, and my neighbors, like hers, no doubt, wonder and laugh; and when, my strained arms with their grown burthen full, I call it my Fable, they call it a bull.

Having scrawled at full gallop (as far as that goes) in a style that is neither good verse nor bad prose, and being a person whom nobody knows, some people will say I am rather more free with my readers than it is becoming to be, that I seem to expect them to wait on my leisure in following wherever I wander at pleasure, that, in short, I take more than a young author's lawful ease, and laugh in a queer way so like Mephistopheles, that the Public will doubt, as they grope through my rhythm, if in truth I am making fun *of* them or *with* them.

So the excellent Public is hereby assured that the sale of my book is already secured. For there is not a poet throughout the whole land but will purchase a copy or two out of hand, in the fond expectation of being amused in it, by seeing his betters cut up and abused in it. Now, I find, by a pretty exact calculation, there are something like ten thousand bards in the nation, of that special variety whom the Review and Magazine critics call *lofty* and *true*, and about thirty thousand (*this* tribe is increasing) of the kinds who are termed *full of promise* and *pleasing*. The Public will see by a glance at this schedule, that they cannot expect me to be over-sedulous about courting *them*, since it seems I have got enough fuel made sure of for boiling my pot.

As for such of our poets as find not their names mentioned once in my pages, with praises or blames, let them SEND IN THEIR CARDS, without further DELAY, to my friend

G. P. PUTNAM, Esquire, in Broadway, where a LIST will be kept with the strictest regard to the day and the hour of receiving the card. Then, taking them up as I chance to have time (that is, if their names can be twisted in rhyme), I will honestly give each his PROPER POSITION, at the rate of ONE AUTHOR to each NEW EDITION. Thus a PREMIUM is offered sufficiently HIGH (as the magazines say when they tell their best lie) to induce bards to CLUB their resources and buy the balance of every edition, until they have all of them fairly been run through the mill.

One word to such readers (judicious and wise) as read books with something behind the mere eyes, of whom in the country, perhaps, there are two, including myself, gentle reader, and you. All the characters sketched in this slight *jeu d'esprit*, though, it may be, they seem, here and there, rather free, and drawn from a somewhat too cynical standpoint, are *meant* to be faithful, for that is the grand point, and none but an owl would feel sore at a rub from a jester who tells you, without any subterfuge, that he sits in Diogenes' tub.

PHŒBUS, sitting one day in a laurel-tree's shade,
Was reminded of Daphne, of whom it was made,
For the god being one day too warm in his wooing,
She took to the tree to escape his pursuing;
Be the cause what it might, from his offers she shrunk,
And, Ginevra-like, shut herself up in a trunk;
And, though 'twas a step into which he had driven her,
He somehow or other had never forgiven her;
Her memory he nursed as a kind of a tonic,
Something bitter to chew when he'd play the Byronic,
And I can't count the obstinate nymphs that he brought over
By a strange kind of smile he put on when he thought of her.
"My case is like Dido's," he sometimes remarked;
"When I last saw my love, she was fairly embarked
In a laurel, as *she* thought—but (ah, how Fate mocks!)
She has found it by this time a very bad box;
Let hunters from me take this saw when they need it,—
You're not always sure of your game when you've treed it.
Just conceive such a change taking place in one's mistress!
What romance would be left?—who can flatter or kiss trees?
And, for mercy's sake, how could one keep up a dialogue
With a dull wooden thing that will live and will die a log,—
Not to say that the thought would forever intrude
That you've less chance to win her the more she is wood?
Ah! it went to my heart, and the memory still grieves,
To see those loved graces all taking their leaves;
Those charms beyond speech, so enchanting but now,
As they left me forever, each making its bough!
If her tongue *had* a tang sometimes more than was right,
Her new bark is worse than ten times her old bite."

. . . .

Apollo looked up, hearing footsteps approaching,
And slipped out of sight the new rhymes he was broaching,—
"Good day, Mr. D—, I'm happy to meet
With a scholar so ripe, and a critic so neat,
Who through Grub Street the soul of a gentleman carries;
What news from that suburb of London and Paris
Which latterly makes such shrill claims to monopolize
The credit of being the New World's metropolis?"

"Why, nothing of consequence, save this attack
On my friend there, behind, by some pitiful hack,

Who thinks every national author a poor one,
That isn't a copy of something that's foreign,
And assaults the American Dick—"
"Nay, 'tis clear
That your Damon there's fond of a flea in his ear,
And, if no one else furnished them gratis, on tick
He would buy some himself, just to hear the old click;
Why, I honestly think, if some fool in Japan
Should turn up his nose at the 'Poems on Man'
(Which contain many verses as fine, by the bye,
As any that lately came under my eye),
Your friend there by some inward instinct would know it,
Would get it translated, reprinted, and show it;
As a man might take off a high stock to exhibit
The autograph round his own neck of the gibbet;
Nor would let it rest so, but fire column after column,
Signed Cato, or Brutus, or something as solemn,
By way of displaying his critical crosses,
And tweaking that poor transatlantic proboscis,
His broadsides resulting (this last there's no doubt of)
In successively sinking the craft they're fired out of.
Now nobody knows when an author is hit,
If he have not a public hysterical fit;
Let him only keep close in his snug garret's dim ether,
And nobody'd think of his foes—or of him either;
If an author have any least fibre of worth in him,
Abuse would but tickle the organ of mirth in him;
All the critics on earth cannot crush with their ban
One word that's in tune with the nature of man."

. . . .

"But stay, here comes Tityrus Griswold, and leads on
The flocks whom he first plucks alive, and then feeds on,—
A loud-cackling swarm, in whose feathers warm drest,
He goes for as perfect a—swan as the rest.

"There comes Emerson first, whose rich words, every one,
Are like gold nails in temples to hang trophies on,
Whose prose is grand verse, while his verse, the Lord knows,
Is some of it pr—No, 'tis not even prose;
I'm speaking of metres; some poems have welled
From those rare depths of soul that have ne'er been excelled;
They're not epics, but that doesn't matter a pin,
In creating, the only hard thing's to begin;
A grass-blade's no easier to make than an oak;
If you've once found the way, you've achieved the grand stroke;
In the worst of his poems are mines of rich matter,
But thrown in a heap with a crash and a clatter;
Now it is not one thing nor another alone
Makes a poem, but rather the general tone,
The something pervading, uniting the whole,
The before unconceived, unconceivable soul,
So that just in removing this trifle or that, you
Take away, as it were, a chief limb of the statue;
Roots, wood, bark, and leaves singly perfect may be,
But, clapt hodge-podge together, they don't make a tree.

"But, to come back to Emerson (whom, by the way,
I believe we left waiting),—his is, we may say,
A Greek head on right Yankee shoulders, whose range
Has Olympus for one pole, for t'other the Exchange;
He seems, to my thinking (although I'm afraid

The comparison must, long ere this, have been made),
A Plotinus-Montaigne, where the Egyptian's gold mist
And the Gascon's shrewd wit cheek-by-jowl coexist;
All admire, and yet scarcely six converts he's got
To I don't (nor they either) exactly know what;
For though he builds glorious temples, 'tis odd
He leaves never a doorway to get in a god.
'Tis refreshing to old-fashioned people like me
To meet such a primitive Pagan as he,
In whose mind all creation is duly respected
As parts of himself—just a little projected;
And who's willing to worship the stars and the sun,
A convert to—nothing but Emerson.
So perfect a balance there is in his head,
That he talks of things sometimes as if they were dead;
Life, nature, love, God, and affairs of that sort,
He looks at as merely ideas; in short,
As if they were fossils stuck round in a cabinet,
Of such vast extent that our earth's a mere dab in it;
Composed just as he is inclined to conjecture her,
Namely, one part pure earth, ninety-nine parts pure lecturer;
You are filled with delight at his clear demonstration,
Each figure, word, gesture, just fits the occasion,
With the quiet precision of science he'll sort 'em,
But you can't help suspecting the whole a *post mortem.*

"There are persons, mole-blind to the soul's make and style,
Who insist on a likeness 'twixt him and Carlyle;
To compare him with Plato would be vastly fairer,
Carlyle's the more burly, but E. is the rarer;
He sees fewer objects, but clearlier, truelier,
If C.'s as original, E.'s more peculiar;
That he's more of a man you might say of the one,
Of the other he's more of an Emerson;
C.'s the Titan, as shaggy of mind as of limb,—
E. the clear-eyed Olympian, rapid and slim;
The one's two thirds Norseman, the other half Greek,
Where the one's most abounding, the other's to seek;
C.'s generals require to be seen in the mass,—
E.'s specialties gain if enlarged by the glass;
C. gives nature and God his own fits of the blues,
And rims common-sense things with mystical hues,—
E. sits in a mystery calm and intense,
And looks coolly around him with sharp common-sense;
C. shows you how every-day matters unite
With the dim transdiurnal recesses of night,—
While E., in a plain, preternatural way,
Makes mysteries matters of mere every day;
C. draws all his characters quite *à la* Fuseli,—
Not sketching their bundles of muscles and thews illy,
He paints with a brush so untamed and profuse
They seem nothing but bundles of muscles and thews;
E. is rather like Flaxman, lines strait and severe,
And a colorless outline, but full, round, and clear;—
To the men he thinks worthy he frankly accords
The design of a white marble statue in words.
C. labors to get at the centre, and then
Take a reckoning from there of his actions and men;
E. calmly assumes the said centre as granted,
And, given himself, has whatever is wanted.

"He has imitators in scores, who omit
No part of the man but his wisdom and wit,—
Who go carefully o'er the sky-blue of his brain,
And when he has skimmed it once, skim it again;
If at all they resemble him, you may be sure it is

Because their shoals mirror his mists and obscurities,
As a mud-puddle seems deep as heaven for a minute,
While a cloud that floats o'er is reflected within it.

"There comes ——, for instance; to see him's rare sport,
Tread in Emerson's tracks with legs painfully short;
How he jumps, how he strains, and gets red in the face,
To keep step with the mystagogue's natural pace!
He follows as close as a stick to a rocket,
His fingers exploring the prophet's each pocket.
Fie, for shame, brother bard; with good fruit of your own,
Can't you let Neighbor Emerson's orchards alone?
Besides, 'tis no use, you'll not find e'en a core,—
—— has picked up all the windfalls before.
They might strip every tree, and E. never would catch 'em,
His Hesperides have no rude dragon to watch 'em;
When they send him a dishful, and ask him to try 'em,
He never suspects how the sly rogues came by 'em;
He wonders why 'tis there are none such his trees on,
And thinks 'em the best he has tasted this season.

. . . .

"There is Bryant, as quiet, as cool, and as dignified,
As a smooth, silent iceberg, that never is ignified,
Save when by reflection 'tis kindled o' nights
With a semblance of flame by the chill Northern Lights.
He may rank (Griswold says so) first bard of your nation
(There's no doubt that he stands in supreme iceolation),
Your topmost Parnassus he may set his heel on,
But no warm applauses come, peal following peal on,—
He's too smooth and too polished to hang any zeal on:
Unqualified merits, I'll grant, if you choose, he has 'em,
But he lacks the one merit of kindling enthusiasm;
If he stir you at all, it is just, on my soul,
Like being stirred up with the very North Pole.

"He is very nice reading in summer, but *inter*
Nos, we don't want *extra* freezing in winter;
Take him up in the depth of July, my advice is,
When you feel an Egyptian devotion to ices.
But, deduct all you can, there's enough that's right good in him,
He has a true soul for field, river, and wood in him;
And his heart, in the midst of brick walls, or where'er it is,
Glows, softens, and thrills with the tenderest charities—
To you mortals that delve in this trade-ridden planet?
No, to old Berkshire's hills, with their limestone and granite.
If you're one who *in loco* (add *foco* here) *desipis*,
You will get of his outermost heart (as I guess) a piece;
But you'd get deeper down if you came as a precipice,
And would break the last seal of its inwardest fountain,
If you only could palm yourself off for a mountain.
Mr. Quivis, or somebody quite as discerning,
Some scholar who's hourly expecting his learning,
Calls B. the American Wordsworth; but Wordsworth
May be rated at more than your whole tuneful herd's worth.
No, don't be absurd, he's an excellent Bryant;
But, my friends, you'll endanger the life of your client,
By attempting to stretch him up into a giant:

If you choose to compare him, I think there are two per-
-sons fit for a parallel—Thomson and Cowper;[1]
I don't mean exactly,—there's something of each,
There's T.'s love of nature, C.'s penchant to preach;
Just mix up their minds so that C.'s spice of craziness
Shall balance and neutralize T.'s turn for laziness,
And it gives you a brain cool, quite frictionless, quiet,
Whose internal police nips the buds of all riot,—
A brain like a permanent strait-jacket put on
The heart that strives vainly to burst off a button,—
A brain which, without being slow or mechanic,
Does more than a larger less drilled, more volcanic;
He's a Cowper condensed, with no craziness bitten,
And the advantage that Wordsworth before him had written.

"But, my dear little bardlings, don't prick up your ears
Nor suppose I would rank you and Bryant as peers;
If I call him an iceberg, I don't mean to say
There is nothing in that which is grand in its way;
He is almost the one of your poets that knows
How much grace, strength, and dignity lie in Repose;
If he sometimes fall short, he is too wise to mar
His thought's modest fulness by going too far;
'Twould be well if your authors should all make a trial
Of what virtue there is in severe self-denial,
And measure their writings by Hesiod's staff,
Which teaches that all has less value than half.

"There is Whittier, whose swelling and vehement heart
Strains the strait-breasted drab of the Quaker apart,
And reveals the live Man, still supreme and erect,
Underneath the bemummying wrappers of sect;
There was ne'er a man born who had more of the swing
Of the true lyric bard and all that kind of thing;
And his failures arise (though he seem not to know it)
From the very same cause that has made him a poet,—
A fervor of mind which knows no separation
'Twixt simple excitement and pure inspiration,
As my Pythoness erst sometimes erred from not knowing
If 'twere I or mere wind through her tripod was blowing;
Let his mind once get head in its favorite direction
And the torrent of verse bursts the dams of reflection,
While, borne with the rush of the metre along,
The poet may chance to go right or go wrong,
Content with the whirl and delirium of song;
Then his grammar's not always correct, nor his rhymes,
And he's prone to repeat his own lyrics sometimes,
Not his best, though, for those are struck off at white-heats
When the heart in his breast like a trip-hammer beats,
And can ne'er be repeated again any more
Than they could have been carefully plotted before:
Like old what's-his-name there at the battle of Hastings
(Who, however, gave more than mere rhythmical bastings),
Our Quaker leads off metaphorical fights

[1] To demonstrate quickly and easily how per-
-versely absurd 'tis to sound this name *Cowper*,
As people in general call him named *super*,
I remark that he rhymes it himself with horse-trooper. [*Lowell's* [redacted]]

For reform and whatever they call human
rights,
Both singing and striking in front of the war,
And hitting his foes with the mallet of Thor;
Anne haec, one exclaims, on beholding his
knocks,
Vestis filii tui, O leather-clad Fox?
Can that be thy son, in the battle's mid din,
Preaching brotherly love and then driving
it in
To the brain of the tough old Goliath of sin,
With the smoothest of pebbles from Castaly's
spring
Impressed on his hard moral sense with a
sling?

"All honor and praise to the right-hearted
bard
Who was true to The Voice when such service
was hard,
Who himself was so free he dared sing for the
slave
When to look but a protest in silence was
brave;
All honor and praise to the women and men
Who spoke out for the dumb and the down-
trodden then!
It needs not to name them, already for each
I see History preparing the statue and niche;
They were harsh, but shall *you* be so shocked
at hard words
Who have beaten your pruning-hooks up into
swords,
Whose rewards and hurrahs men are surer to
gain
By the reaping of men and of women than
grain?
Why should *you* stand aghast at their fierce
wordy war, if
You scalp one another for Bank or for Tariff?
Your calling them cut-throats and knaves all
day long
Doesn't prove that the use of hard language is
wrong;
While the World's heart beats quicker to
think of such men
As signed Tyranny's doom with a bloody
steel-pen,
While on Fourth-of-Julys beardless orators
fright one
With hints at Harmodius and Aristogeiton,
You need not look shy at your sisters and
brothers
Who stab with sharp words for the freedom
of others;—
No, a wreath, twine a wreath for the loyal
and true
Who, for sake of the many, dared stand with
the few,
Not of blood-spattered laurel for enemies
braved,
But of broad, peaceful oak-leaves for citizens
saved!

. . . .

"There is Hawthorne, with genius so shrink-
ing and rare
That you hardly at first see the strength that
is there;
A frame so robust, with a nature so sweet,
So earnest, so graceful, so lithe and so fleet,
Is worth a descent from Olympus to meet;
'Tis as if a rough oak that for ages had stood,
With his gnarled bony branches like ribs of
the wood,
Should bloom, after cycles of struggle and
scathe,
With a single anemone trembly and rathe;
His strength is so tender, his wildness so
meek,
That a suitable parallel sets one to seek,—
He's a John Bunyan Fouqué, a Puritan Tieck;
When Nature was shaping him, clay was not
granted
For making so full-sized a man as she wanted,
So, to fill out her model, a little she spared
From some finer-grained stuff for a woman
prepared,
And she could not have hit a more excellent
plan
For making him fully and perfectly man.

. . . .

"Here's Cooper, who's written six volumes
to show
He's as good as a lord: well, let's grant that
he's so;
If a person prefer that description of praise,
Why, a coronet's certainly cheaper than bays;
But he need take no pains to convince us he's
not
(As his enemies say) the American Scott.

Choose any twelve men, and let C. read aloud
That one of his novels of which he's most proud,
And I'd lay any bet that, without ever quitting
Their box, they'd be all, to a man, for acquitting.
He has drawn you one character, though, that is new,
One wildflower he's plucked that is wet with the dew
Of this fresh Western world, and, the thing not to mince,
He has done naught but copy it ill ever since;
His Indians, with proper respect be it said,
Are just Natty Bumppo, daubed over with red,
And his very Long Toms are the same useful Nat,
Rigged up in duck pants and a sou'wester hat
(Though once in a Coffin, a good chance was found
To have slipped the old fellow away underground).
All his other men-figures are clothes upon sticks,
The *dernière chemise* of a man in a fix
(As a captain besieged, when his garrison's small,
Sets up caps upon poles to be seen o'er the wall);
And the women he draws from one model don't vary,
All sappy as maples and flat as a prairie.
When a character's wanted, he goes to the task
As a cooper would do in composing a cask;
He picks out the staves, of their qualities heedful,
Just hoops them together as tight as is needful,
And, if the best fortune should crown the attempt, he
Has made at the most something wooden and empty.

"Don't suppose I would underrate Cooper's abilities;
If I thought you'd do that, I should feel very ill at ease;
The men who have given to *one* character life
And objective existence are not very rife;
You may number them all, both prose-writers and singers,
Without overrunning the bounds of your fingers,
And Natty won't go to oblivion quicker
Than Adams the parson or Primrose the vicar.

"There is one thing in Cooper I like, too, and that is
That on manners he lectures his countrymen gratis;
Not precisely so either, because, for a rarity,
He is paid for his tickets in unpopularity.
Now he may overcharge his American pictures,
But you'll grant there's a good deal of truth in his strictures;
And I honor the man who is willing to sink
Half his present repute for the freedom to think,
And, when he has thought, be his cause strong or weak,
Will risk t'other half for the freedom to speak,
Caring naught for what vengeance the mob has in store,
Let that mob be the upper ten thousand or lower.

"There are truths you Americans need to be told,
And it never'll refute them to swagger and scold;
John Bull, looking o'er the Atlantic, in choler
At your aptness for trade, says you worship the dollar;
But to scorn such eye-dollar-try's what very few do,
And John goes to that church as often as you do.
No matter what John says, don't try to outcrow him,
'Tis enough to go quietly on and outgrow him;
Like most fathers, Bull hates to see Number One
Displacing himself in the mind of his son,
And detests the same faults in himself he'd neglected
When he sees them again in his child's glass reflected;

To love one another you're too like by half;
If he is a bull, you're a pretty stout calf,
And tear your own pasture for naught but to show
What a nice pair of horns you're beginning to grow.

"There are one or two things I should just like to hint,
For you don't often get the truth told you in print;
The most of you (this is what strikes all beholders)
Have a mental and physical stoop in the shoulders;
Though you ought to be free as the winds and the waves,
You've the gait and the manners of runaway slaves;
Though you brag of your New World, you don't half believe in it;
And as much of the Old as is possible weave in it;
Your goddess of freedom, a tight, buxom girl,
With lips like a cherry and teeth like a pearl,
With eyes bold as Herë's, and hair floating free,
And full of the sun as the spray of the sea,
Who can sing at a husking or romp at a shearing,
Who can trip through the forests alone without fearing,
Who can drive home the cows with a song through the grass,
Keeps glancing aside into Europe's cracked glass,
Hides her red hands in gloves, pinches up her lithe waist,
And makes herself wretched with transmarine taste;
She loses her fresh country charm when she takes
Any mirror except her own rivers and lakes.

"You steal Englishmen's books and think Englishmen's thought,
With their salt on her tail your wild eagle is caught;
Your literature suits its each whisper and motion
To what will be thought of it over the ocean;
The cast clothes of Europe your statesmanship tries
And mumbles again the old blarneys and lies;—
Forget Europe wholly, your veins throb with blood,
To which the dull current in hers is but mud:
Let her sneer, let her say your experiment fails,
In her voice there's a tremble e'en now while she rails,
And your shore will soon be in the nature of things
Covered thick with gilt drift-wood of castaway kings,
Where alone, as it were in a Longfellow's Waif,
Her fugitive pieces will find themselves safe.
O my friends, thank your god, if you have one, that he
'Twixt the Old World and you set the gulf of a sea;
Be strong-backed, brown-handed, upright as your pines,
By the scale of a hemisphere shape your designs,
Be true to yourselves and this new nineteenth age,
As a statue by Powers, or a picture by Page,
Plough, sail, forge, build, carve, paint, make all over new,
To your own New-World instincts contrive to be true,
Keep your ears open wide to the Future's first call,
Be whatever you will, but yourselves first of all,
Stand fronting the dawn on Toil's heaven-scaling peaks,
And become my new race of more practical Greeks."

. . . .

Here Miranda came up, and said, "Phœbus! you know
That the Infinite Soul has its infinite woe,
As I ought to know, having lived cheek by jowl,
Since the day I was born, with the Infinite Soul;
I myself introduced, I myself, I alone,

To my Land's better life authors solely my own,
Who the sad heart of earth on their shoulders have taken,
Whose works sound a depth by Life's quiet unshaken,
Such as Shakespeare, for instance, the Bible, and Bacon,
Not to mention my own works; Time's nadir is fleet,
And, as for myself, I'm quite out of conceit"—

"Quite out of conceit! I'm enchanted to hear it,"
Cried Apollo aside. "Who'd have thought she was near it?
To be sure, one is apt to exhaust those commodities
One uses too fast, yet in this case as odd it is
As if Neptune should say to his turbots and whitings,
'I'm as much out of salt as Miranda's own writings'
(Which, as she in her own happy manner has said,
Sound a depth, for 'tis one of the functions of lead).
She often has asked me if I could not find
A place somewhere near me that suited her mind;
I know but a single one vacant, which she,
With her rare talent that way, would fit to a T.
And it would not imply any pause or cessation
In the work she esteems her peculiar vocation,—
She may enter on duty today, if she chooses,
And remain Tiring-woman for life to the Muses."

. . . .

"There comes Poe, with his raven, like Barnaby Rudge,
Three fifths of him genius and two fifths sheer fudge,
Who talks like a book of iambs and pentameters,
In a way to make people of common sense damn metres,
Who has written some things quite the best of their kind,
But the heart somehow seems all squeezed out by the mind,
Who— But hey-day! What's this? Messieurs Mathews and Poe,
You mustn't fling mud-balls at Longfellow so,
Does it make a man worse that his character's such
As to make his friends love him (as you think) too much?
Why, there is not a bard at this moment alive
More willing than he that his fellows should thrive;
While you are abusing him thus, even now
He would help either one of you out of a slough;
You may say that he's smooth and all that till you're hoarse,
But remember that elegance also is force;
After polishing granite as much as you will,
The heart keeps its tough old persistency still;
Deduct all you can, *that* still keeps you at bay;
Why, he'll live till men weary of Collins and Gray.
I'm not over-fond of Greek metres in English,
To me rhyme's a gain, so it be not too jinglish,
And your modern hexameter verses are no more
Like Greek ones than sleek Mr. Pope is like Homer;
As the roar of the sea to the coo of a pigeon is,
So, compared to your moderns, sounds old Melesigenes;
I may be too partial, the reason, perhaps, o't is
That I've heard the old blind man recite his own rhapsodies,
And my ear with that music impregnate may be,
Like the poor exiled shell with the soul of the sea,
Or as one can't bear Strauss when his nature is cloven
To its deeps within deeps by the stroke of Beethoven;
But, set that aside, and 'tis truth that I speak,
Had Theocritus written in English, not Greek,

I believe that his exquisite sense would scarce change a line
In that rare, tender, virgin-like pastoral Evangeline.
That's not ancient nor modern, its place is apart
Where time has no sway, in the realm of pure Art,
'Tis a shrine of retreat from Earth's hubbub and strife
As quiet and chaste as the author's own life.

. . . .

"What! Irving? thrice welcome, warm heart and fine brain,
You bring back the happiest spirit from Spain,
And the gravest sweet humor, that ever were there
Since Cervantes met death in his gentle despair;
Nay, don't be embarrassed, nor look so beseeching,
I sha'n't run directly against my own preaching,
And, having just laughed at their Raphaels and Dantes,
Go to setting you up beside matchless Cervantes;
But allow me to speak what I honestly feel,—
To a true poet-heart add the fun of Dick Steele,
Throw in all of Addison, *minus* the chill,
With the whole of that partnership's stock and good-will,
Mix well, and while stirring, hum o'er, as a spell,
The fine *old* English Gentleman, simmer it well,
Sweeten just to your own private liking, then strain,
That only the finest and clearest remain,
Let it stand out of doors till a soul it receives
From the warm lazy sun loitering down through green leaves,
And you'll find a choice nature, not wholly deserving
A name either English or Yankee,—just Irving."

. . . .

Here, "Forgive me, Apollo," I cried, "while I pour
My heart out to my birthplace: O loved more and more
Dear Baystate, from whose rocky bosom thy sons
Should suck milk, strong-will-giving, brave, such as runs
In the veins of old Graylock—who is it that dares
Call thee pedler, a soul wrapped in bank-books and shares?
It is false! She's a Poet! I see, as I write,
Along the far railroad the steam-snake glide white,
The cataract-throb of her mill-hearts I hear,
The swift strokes of trip-hammers weary my ear,
Sledges ring upon anvils, through logs the saw screams,
Blocks swing to their place, beetles drive home the beams:—
It is songs such as these that she croons to the din
Of her fast-flying shuttles, year out and year in,
While from earth's farthest corner there comes not a breeze
But wafts her the buzz of her gold-gleaning bees:
What though those horn hands have as yet found small time
For painting and sculpture and music and rhyme?
These will come in due order; the need that pressed sorest
Was to vanquish the seasons, the ocean, the forest,
To bridle and harness the rivers, the steam,
Making those whirl her mill-wheels, this tug in her team,
To vassalize old tyrant Winter, and make
Him delve surlily for her on river and lake;—
When this New World was parted, she strove not to shirk
Her lot in the heirdom, the tough, silent Work,
The hero-share ever from Herakles down
To Odin, the Earth's iron sceptre and crown:
Yes, thou dear, noble Mother! if ever men's praise

Could be claimed for creating heroical lays,
Thou hast won it; if ever the laurel divine
Crowned the Maker and Builder, that glory is thine!
Thy songs are right epic, they tell how this rude
Rock-rib of our earth here was tamed and subdued;
Thou hast written them plain on the face of the planet
In brave, deathless letters of iron and granite;
Thou hast printed them deep for all time; they are set
From the same runic type-fount and alphabet
With thy stout Berkshire hills and the arms of thy Bay,—
They are staves from the burly old Mayflower lay.
If the drones of the Old World, in querulous ease,
Ask thy Art and thy Letters, point proudly to these,
Or, if they deny these are Letters and Art,
Toil on with the same old invincible heart;
Thou art rearing the pedestal broad-based and grand
Whereon the fair shapes of the Artist shall stand,
And creating, through labors undaunted and long,
The theme for all Sculpture and Painting and Song!

"But my good mother Baystate wants no praise of mine,
She learned from *her* mother a precept divine
About something that butters no parsnips, her *forte*
In another direction lies, work is her sport
(Though she'll curtsey and set her cap straight, that she will,
If you talk about Plymouth and red Bunker's hill).
Dear, notable goodwife! by this time of night,
Her hearth is swept neatly, her fire burning bright,
And she sits in a chair (of home plan and make) rocking,
Musing much, all the while, as she darns on a stocking,
Whether turkeys will come pretty high next Thanksgiving,
Whether flour'll be so dear, for, as sure as she's living,
She will use rye-and-injun then, whether the pig
By this time ain't got pretty tolerable big,
And whether to sell it outright will be best,
Or to smoke hams and shoulders and salt down the rest,—
At this minute, she'd swop all my verses, ah, cruel!
For the last patent stove that is saving of fuel;
So I'll just let Apollo go on, for his phiz
Shows I've kept him awaiting too long as it is."

"If our friend, there, who seems a reporter, is done
With his burst of emotion, why, *I* will go on,"
Said Apollo; some smiled, and, indeed, I must own
There was something sarcastic, perhaps, in his tone:

"There's Holmes, who is matchless among you for wit;
A Leyden-jar always full-charged, from which flit
The electrical tingles of hit after hit;
In long poems 'tis painful sometimes, and invites
A thought of the way the new Telegraph writes,
Which pricks down its little sharp sentences spitefully
As if you got more than you'd title to rightfully,
And you find yourself hoping its wild father Lightning
Would flame in for a second and give you a fright'ning.
He has perfect sway of what I call a sham metre,
But many admire it, the English pentameter,
And Campbell, I think, wrote most commonly worse,
With less nerve, swing, and fire in the same kind of verse,
Nor e'er achieved aught in't so worthy of praise
As the tribute of Holmes to the grand *Marseillaise.*

You went crazy last year over Bulwer's New
Timon;—
Why, if B., to the day of his dying, should rhyme on,
Heaping verses on verses and tomes upon tomes,
He could ne'er reach the best point and vigor of Holmes.
His are just the fine hands, too, to weave you a lyric
Full of fancy, fun, feeling, or spiced with satiric
In a measure so kindly you doubt if the toes
That are trodden upon are your own or your foes'.

"There is Lowell, who's striving Parnassus to climb
With a whole bale of *isms* tied together with rhyme,
He might get on alone, spite of brambles and boulders,
But he can't with that bundle he has on his shoulders,
The top of the hill he will ne'er come nigh reaching
Till he learns the distinction 'twixt singing and preaching;
His lyre has some chords that would ring pretty well,
But he'd rather by half make a drum of the shell,
And rattle away till he's old as Methusalem,
At the head of a march to the last new Jerusalem."

. . . .

Here Miranda came up and began, "As to that—"
Apollo at once seized his gloves, cane, and hat,
And, seeing the place getting rapidly cleared,
I too snatched my notes and forthwith disappeared.

1847–48 1848

SHE CAME AND WENT

As a twig trembles, which a bird
Lights on to sing, then leaves unbent,
So is my memory thrilled and stirred;—
I only know she came and went.

As clasps some lake, by gusts unriven,
The blue dome's measureless content,
So my soul held that moment's heaven;—
I only know she came and went.

As, at one bound, our swift spring heaps
The orchards full of bloom and scent,
So clove her May my wintry sleeps;—
I only know she came and went.

An angel stood and met my gaze,
Through the low doorway of my tent;
The tent is struck, the vision stays;—
I only know she came and went.

Oh, when the room grows slowly dim,
And life's last oil is nearly spent,
One gush of light these eyes will brim,
Only to think she came and went.

1847? 1849

ODE TO HAPPINESS

Spirit, that rarely comest now
And only to contrast my gloom,
Like rainbow-feathered birds that bloom
A moment on some autumn bough
That, with the spurn of their farewell,
Sheds its last leaves,—thou once didst dwell
With me year-long, and make intense
To boyhood's wisely vacant days
Their fleet but all-sufficing grace
Of trustful inexperience,
While soul could still transfigure sense,
And thrill, as with love's first caress,
At life's mere unexpectedness.
Days when my blood would leap and run
As full of sunshine as a breeze,
Or spray tossed up by Summer seas
That doubts if it be sea or sun!
Days that flew swiftly like the band
That played in Grecian games at strife,
And passed from eager hand to hand
The onward-dancing torch of life!

Wing-footed! thou abid'st with him
Who asks it not; but he who hath
Watched o'er the waves thy waning path,
Shall nevermore behold returning
Thy high-heaped canvas shoreward yearning!

Thou first reveal'st to us thy face
Turned o'er the shoulder's parting grace,
  A moment glimpsed, then seen no more,—
Thou whose swift footsteps we can trace
  Away from every mortal door!

Nymph of the unreturning feet,
  How may I win thee back? But no,
  I do thee wrong to call thee so;
'Tis I am changed, not thou art fleet:
The man thy presence feels again,
Not in the blood, but in the brain,
Spirit, that lov'st the upper air
Serene and passionless and rare,
  Such as on mountain heights we find
  And wide-viewed uplands of the mind;
Or such as scorns to coil and sing
Round any but the eagle's wing
  Of souls that with long upward beat
  Have won an undisturbed retreat
Where, poised like wingëd victories,
They mirror in relentless eyes
  The life broad-basking 'neath their feet,—
Man ever with his Now at strife,
  Pained with first gasps of earthly air,
  Then praying Death the last to spare,
Still fearful of the ampler life.

Not unto them dost thou consent
  Who, passionless, can lead at ease
A life of unalloyed content,
  A life like that of land-locked seas,
That feel no elemental gush
Of tidal forces, no fierce rush
  Of storm deep-grasping scarcely spent
  'Twixt continent and continent.
Such quiet souls have never known
  Thy truer inspiration, thou
  Who lov'st to feel upon thy brow
Spray from the plunging vessel thrown
  Grazing the tusked lee shore, the cliff
That o'er the abrupt gorge holds its breath,
  Where the frail hair-breadth of an *if*
Is all that sunders life and death:
These, too, are cared-for, and round these
Bends her mild crook thy sister Peace;
  These in unvexed dependence lie,
  Each 'neath his strip of household sky;
O'er these clouds wander, and the blue
Hangs motionless the whole day through;
  Stars rise for them, and moons grow large
  And lessen in such tranquil wise
  As joys and sorrows do that rise
  Within their nature's sheltered marge;
Their hours into each other flit
  Like the leaf-shadows of the vine
And fig-tree under which they sit,
  And their still lives to heaven incline
With an unconscious habitude,
  Unhistoried as smokes that rise
From happy hearths and sight elude
  In kindred blue of morning skies.

Wayward! when once we feel thy lack,
'Tis worse than vain to woo thee back!
  Yet there is one who seems to be
Thine elder sister, in whose eyes
A faint far northern light will rise
  Sometimes, and bring a dream of thee;
She is not that for which youth hoped,
  But she hath blessings all her own,
Thoughts pure as lilies newly oped,
  And faith to sorrow given alone;
Almost I deem that it is thou
Come back with graver matron brow,
  With deepened eyes and bated breath,
  Like one that somewhere hath met Death.
But "No," she answers, "I am she 101
Whom the gods love, Tranquillity;
  That other whom you seek forlorn
  Half earthly was; but I am born
Of the immortals, and our race
Wear still some sadness on our face:
  He wins me late, but keeps me long,
Who, dowered with every gift of passion,
In that fierce flame can forge and fashion
  Of sin and self the anchor strong;
Can thence compel the driving force
Of daily life's mechanic course,
Nor less the nobler energies
Of needful toil and culture wise;
Whose soul is worth the tempter's lure
Who can renounce, and yet endure,
To him I come, not lightly wooed,
But won by silent fortitude."

1854? 1861

THE WASHERS OF THE SHROUD

OCTOBER, 1861

ALONG a river-side, I know not where,
I walked one night in mystery of dream;
A chill creeps curdling yet beneath my hair,

To think what chanced me by the pallid gleam
Of a moon-wraith that waned through haunted air.

Pale fireflies pulsed within the meadow-mist
Their halos, wavering thistle downs of light;
The loon, that seemed to mock some goblin tryst,
Laughed; and the echoes, huddling in affright,
Like Odin's hounds, fled baying down the night.

Then all was silent, till there smote my ear
A movement in the stream that checked my breath:
Was it the slow plash of a wading deer?
But something said, "This water is of Death!
The Sisters wash a shroud,—ill thing to hear!"

I, looking then, beheld the ancient Three
Known to the Greek's and to the Northman's creed,
That sit in shadow of the mystic Tree,
Still crooning, as they weave their endless brede,
One song: "Time was, Time is, and Time shall be."

No wrinkled crones were they, as I had deemed,
But fair as yesterday, today, tomorrow,
To mourner, lover, poet, ever seemed;
Something too high for joy, too deep for sorrow,
Thrilled in their tones, and from their faces gleamed.

"Still men and nations reap as they have strawn,"
So sang they, working at their task the while;
"The fatal raiment must be cleansed ere dawn:
For Austria? Italy? the Sea-Queen's isle?
O'er what quenched grandeur must our shroud be drawn?

"Or is it for a younger, fairer corse,
That gathered States like children round his knees,
That tamed the wave to be his posting horse,
Feller of forests, linker of the seas,
Bridge-builder, hammerer, youngest son of Thor's?

"What make we, murmur'st thou? and what are we?
When empires must be wound, we bring the shroud,
The time-old web of the implacable Three:
Is it too coarse for him, the young and proud?
Earth's mightiest deigned to wear it,—why not he?"

"Is there no hope?" I moaned, "so strong, so fair!
Our Fowler whose proud bird would brook erewhile
No rival's swoop in all our western air!
Gather the ravens, then, in funeral file
For him, life's morn yet golden in his hair?

"Leave me not hopeless, ye unpitying dames!
I see, half seeing. Tell me, ye who scanned
The stars, Earth's elders, still must noblest aims
Be traced upon oblivious ocean-sands?
Must Hesper join the wailing ghosts of names?"

"When grass-blades stiffen with red battle-dew,
Ye deem we choose the victor and the slain:
Say, choose we them that shall be leal and true
To the heart's longing, the high faith of brain?
Yet there the victory lies, if ye but knew.

"Three roots bear up Dominion: Knowledge, Will,—
These twain are strong, but stronger yet the third,—
Obedience,—'tis the great tap-root that still,
Knit round the rock of Duty, is not stirred,
Though Heaven-loosed tempests spend their utmost skill.

"Is the doom sealed for Hesper? 'Tis not we
Denounce it, but the Law before all time:
The brave makes danger opportunity;
The waverer, paltering with the chance sublime,
Dwarfs it to peril: which shall Hesper be?

"Hath he let vultures climb his eagle's seat
To make Jove's bolts purveyors of their maw?
Hath he the Many's plaudits found more sweet

Than Wisdom? held Opinion's wind for Law?
Then let him hearken for the doomster's feet!

"Rough are the steps, slow-hewn in flintiest rock,
States climb to power by; slippery those with gold
Down which they stumble to eternal mock:
No chafferer's hand shall long the sceptre hold,
Who, given a Fate to shape, would sell the block.

"We sing old Sagas, songs of weal and woe,
Mystic because too cheaply understood;
Dark sayings are not ours; men hear and know,
See Evil weak, see strength alone in Good,
Yet hope to stem God's fire with walls of tow.

"Time Was unlocks the riddle of Time Is,
That offers choice of glory or of gloom;
The solver makes Time Shall Be surely his.
But hasten, Sisters! for even now the tomb
Grates its slow hinge and calls from the abyss."

"But not for him," I cried, "not yet for him,
Whose large horizon, westering, star by star
Wins from the void to where on Ocean's rim
The sunset shuts the world with golden bar,
Not yet his thews shall fail, his eye grow dim!

"His shall be larger manhood, saved for those
That walked unblenching through the trial-fires;
Not suffering, but faint heart, is worst of woes,
And he no base-born son of craven sires,
Whose eye need blench confronted with his foes.

"Tears may be ours, but proud, for those who win
Death's royal purple in the foeman's lines;
Peace, too, brings tears; and 'mid the battle-din,
The wiser ear some text of God divines,
For the sheathed blade may rust with darker sin.

"God, give us peace! not such as lulls to sleep,
But sword on thigh, and brow with purpose knit!
And let our Ship of State to harbor sweep,
Her ports all up, her battle-lanterns lit,
And her leashed thunders gathering for their leap!"

So cried I with clenched hands and passionate pain,
Thinking of dear ones by Potomac's side;
Again the loon laughed mocking, and again
The echoes bayed far down the night and died,
While waking I recalled my wandering brain.

1861 1861

THE BIGLOW PAPERS

SECOND SERIES

From No. II

JONATHAN TO JOHN

It don't seem hardly right, John,
When both my hands was full,
To stump me to a fight, John,—
Your cousin, tu, John Bull!
Ole Uncle S. sez he, "I guess
We know it now," sez he,
"The lion's paw is all the law,
Accordin' to J. B.,
Thet 's fit for you an' me!"

You wonder why we 're hot, John?
Your mark wuz on the guns,
The neutral guns, thet shot, John,
Our brothers an' our sons:
Ole Uncle S. sez he, "I guess
There 's human blood," sez he,
"By fits an' starts, in Yankee hearts,
Though 't may surprise J. B.
More 'n it would you an' me."

Ef *I* turned mad dogs loose, John,
On *your* front-parlor stairs,
Would it jest meet your views, John,
To wait an' sue their heirs?
Ole Uncle S. sez he, "I guess,
I on'y guess," sez he,
"Thet ef Vattel on *his* toes fell,
'T would kind o' rile J. B.,
Ez wal ez you an' me!"

Who made the law thet hurts, John,
Heads I win,—ditto tails?
"*J. B.*" was on his shirts, John,
Onless my memory fails.

Ole Uncle S. sez he, "I guess
(I 'm good at thet)," sez he,
"Thet sauce for goose ain't *jest* the juice
For ganders with J. B.,
No more 'n with you or me!"

When your rights was our wrongs, John,
You did n't stop for fuss,—
Britanny's trident prongs, John,
Was good 'nough law for us.
Ole Uncle S. sez he, "I guess,
Though physic 's good," sez he,
"It does n't foller thet he can swaller
Prescriptions signed 'J. B.,'
Put up by you an' me!"

We own the ocean, tu, John:
You mus' n' take it hard,
Ef we can't think with you, John,
It 's jest your own back-yard.
Ole Uncle S. sez he, "I guess,
Ef *thet* 's his claim," sez he,
"The fencin'-stuff 'll cost enough
To bust up friend J. B.,
Ez wal ez you an' me!"

Why talk so dreffle big, John,
Of honor when it meant
You did n't care a fig, John,
But jest for *ten per cent?*
Ole Uncle S. sez he, "I guess
He 's like the rest," sez he:
"When all is done, it 's number one
Thet 's nearest to J. B.,
Ez wal ez t' you an' me!"

We give the critters back, John,
Cos Abram thought 't was right;
It warn't your bullyin' clack, John,
Provokin' us to fight.
Ole Uncle S. sez he, "I guess
We 've a hard row," sez he,
"To hoe jest now; but thet, somehow,
May happen to J. B.,
Ez wal ez you an' me!"

We ain't so weak an' poor, John,
With twenty million people,
An' close to every door, John,
A school-house an' a steeple.
Ole Uncle S. sez he, "I guess,
It is a fact," sez he,
"The surest plan to make a Man
Is, think him so, J. B.,
Ez much ez you or me!"

Our folks believe in Law, John;
An' it 's for her sake, now,
They 've left the axe an' saw, John,
The anvil an' the plough.
Ole Uncle S. sez he, "I guess,
Ef 't warn't for law," sez he,
"There 'd be one shindy from here to Indy;
An' thet don't suit J. B.
(When 't ain't 'twixt you an' me!)"

We know we 've got a cause, John,
Thet 's honest, just, an' true;
We thought 't would win applause, John,
Ef nowheres else, from you.
Ole Uncle S. sez he, "I guess
His love of right," sez he,
"Hangs by a rotten fibre o' cotton:
There 's natur' in J. B.,
Ez wal 'z in you an' me!"

The South says, "*Poor folks down!*" John,
An' "*All men up!*" say we,—
White, yaller, black, an' brown, John:
Now which is your idee?
Ole Uncle S. sez he, "I guess,
John preaches wal," sez he;
"But, sermon thru, an' come to *du*,
Why, there 's the old J. B.
A-crowdin' you an' me!"

Shall it be love, or hate, John?
It 's you thet 's to decide;
Ain't *your* bonds held by Fate, John,
Like all the world's beside?
Ole Uncle S. sez he, "I guess
Wise men forgive," sez he,
"But not forgit; an' some time yit
Thet truth may strike J. B.,
Ez wal ez you an' me!"

God means to make this land, John,
Clear thru, from sea to sea,
Believe an' understand, John,
The *wuth* o' bein' free.
Ole Uncle S. sez he, "I guess,
God's price is high," sez he;

"But nothin' else than wut He sells
Wears long, an' thet J. B.
May larn, like you an' me!"

December, 1861 February, 1862

From No. IV

A MESSAGE OF JEFF DAVIS IN SECRET SESSION

Conjecturally reported by H. Biglow

TO THE EDITORS OF THE ATLANTIC MONTHLY

I sent you a messige, my friens, t' other day,
To tell you I' d nothin' pertickler to say:
't wuz the day our new nation gut kin' o' still-born,
So 't wuz my pleasant dooty t' acknowledge the corn,
An' I see clearly then, ef I did n't before,
Thet the *augur* in inauguration means *bore.*
I need n't tell *you* thet my messige wuz written
To diffuse correc' notions in France an' Gret Britten,
An' agin to impress on the poppylar mind
The comfort an' wisdom o' goin' it blind,—
To say thet I did n't abate not a hooter
O' my faith in a happy an' glorious futur',
Ez rich in each soshle an' p'litickle blessin'
Ez them thet we now hed the joy o' possessin',
With a people united, an' longin' to die
For wut *we* call their country, without askin' why,
An' all the gret things we concluded to slope for
Ez much within reach now ez ever—to hope for.
We 've gut all the ellerments, this very hour,
Thet make up a fus'-class, self-governin' power:
We 've a war, an' a debt, an' a flag; an' ef this
Ain't to be inderpendunt, why, wut on airth is?
An' nothin' now henders our takin' our station
Ez the freest, enlightenedest, civerlized nation,
Built up on our bran'-new politickle thesis
Thet a Gov'ment's fust right is to tumble to pieces,—
I say nothin' henders our takin' our place
Ez the very fus'-best o' the whole human race,
A spittin' tobacker ez proud ez you please
On Victory's bes' carpets, or loafin' at ease
In the Tool'ries front-parlor, discussin' affairs
With our heels on the backs o' Napoleon's new chairs,
An' princes a-mixin' our cocktails an' slings,—
Excep', wal, excep' jest a very few things,
Sech ez navies an' armies an' wherewith to pay,
An' gittin' our sogers to run t' other way,
An' not be too over-pertickler in tryin'
To hunt up the very las' ditches to die in.

Ther' are critters so base thet they want it explained
Jes' wut is the totle amount thet we 've gained,
Ez ef we could maysure stupenjious events
By the low Yankee stan'ard o' dollars an' cents:
They seem to forgit, thet, sence last year revolved,
We 've succeeded in gittin' seceshed an' dissolved,
An' thet no one can't hope to git thru dissolootion
'thout some kin' o' strain on the best Constitootion.
Who asks for a prospec' more flettrin' an' bright,
When from here clean to Texas it 's all one free fight?
Hain't we rescued from Seward the gret leadin' featurs
Thet makes it wuth while to be reasonin' creaturs?
Hain't we saved Habus Coppers, improved it in fact,
By suspendin' the Unionists 'stid o' the Act?
Ain't the laws free to all? Where on airth else d' ye see
Every freeman improvin' his own rope an' tree?
Ain't our piety sech (in our speeches an' messiges)
Ez t' astonish ourselves in the bes'-composed pessiges,
An' to make folks thet knowed us in th' ole state o' things
Think convarsion ez easy ez drinkin' gin-slings?

It 's ne'ssary to take a good confident tone
With the public; but here, jest amongst us, I own

Things look blacker 'n thunder. Ther' 's no use denyin'
We 're clean out o' money, an' 'most out o' lyin';
Two things a young nation can't mennage without,
Ef she wants to look wal at her fust comin' out;
For the fust supplies physickle strength, while the second
Gives a morril edvantage thet 's hard to be reckoned:
For this latter I 'm willin' to du wut I can;
For the former you 'll hev to consult on a plan,—
Though our *fust* want (an' this pint I want your best views on)
Is plausible paper to print I. O. U.s on.
Some gennlemen think it would cure all our cankers
In the way o' finance, ef we jes' hanged the bankers;
An' I own the proposle 'ud square with my views,
Ef their lives wuz n't all thet we 'd left 'em to lose.
Some say thet more confidence might be inspired,
Ef we voted our cities an' towns to be fired,—
A plan thet 'ud suttenly tax our endurance,
Coz 't would be our own bills we should git for th' insurance;
But cinders, no metter how sacred we think 'em,
Might n't strike furrin minds ez good sources of income,
Nor the people, perhaps, would n't like the eclaw
O' bein' all turned into paytriots by law.
Some want we should buy all the cotton an' burn it,
On a pledge, when we 've gut thru the war, to return it,—
Then to take the proceeds an' hold *them* ez security
For an issue o' bonds to be met at maturity
With an issue o' notes to be paid in hard cash
On the fus' Monday follerin' the 'tarnal All-smash:
This hez a safe air, an', once hold o' the gold,
'ud leave our vile plunderers out in the cold,
An' *might* temp' John Bull, ef it warn't for the dip he
Once gut from the banks o' my own Massissippi.
Some think we could make, by arrangin' the figgers,
A hendy home-currency out of our niggers;
But it wun't du to lean much on ary sech staff,
For they 're gittin' tu current a'ready, by half.

One gennleman says, ef we lef' our loan out
Where Floyd could git hold on 't *he* 'd take it, no doubt;
But 't ain't jes' the takin', though 't hez a good look,
We mus' git sunthin' out on it arter it 's took,
An' we need now more 'n ever, with sorrer I own,
Thet some one another should let us a loan,
Sence a soger wun't fight, on'y jes' while he draws his
Pay down on the nail, for the best of all causes,
'thout askin' to know wut the quarrel 's about,—
An' once come to thet, why, our game is played out.
It 's ez true ez though I should n't never hev said it,
Thet a hitch hez took place in our system o' credit;
I swear it 's all right in my speeches an' messiges,
But ther' 's idees afloat, ez ther' is about sessiges:
Folks wun't take a bond ez a basis to trade on,
Without nosin' round to find out wut it 's made on,
An' the thought more an' more thru the public min' crosses
Thet our Treshry hez gut 'mos' too many dead hosses.
Wut 's called credit, you see, is some like a balloon,
Thet looks while it 's up' most ez harnsome 'z a moon,
But once git a leak in 't, an' wut looked so grand
Caves righ' down in a jiffy ez flat ez your hand.
Now the world is a dreffle mean place, for our sins,

Where ther' ollus is critters about with long pins
A-prickin' the bubbles we 've blowed with sech care,
An' provin' ther' 's nothin' inside but bad air:
They 're all Stuart Millses, poor-white trash, an' sneaks,
Without no more chivverlry 'n Choctaws or Creeks,
Who think a real gennleman's promise to pay
Is meant to be took in trade's ornery way:
Them fellers an' I could n' never agree;
They 're the nateral foes o' the Southun Idee;
I 'd gladly take all of our other resks on me
To be red o' this low-lived politikle 'con'my!

Now a dastardly notion is gittin' about
Thet our bladder is bust an' the gas oozin' out,
An' onless we can mennage in some way to stop it,
Why, the thing 's a gone coon, an' we might ez wal drop it.
Brag works wal at fust, but it ain't jes' the thing
For a stiddy inves'ment the shiners to bring,
An' votin' we 're prosp'rous a hundred times over
Wun't change bein' starved into livin' in clover.
Manassas done sunthin' tow'rds drawin' the wool
O'er the green, antislavery eyes o' John Bull:
Oh, *warn't* it a godsend, jes' when sech tight fixes
Wuz crowdin' us mourners, to throw double-sixes!
I wuz tempted to think, an' it wuz n't no wonder,
Ther' wuz reely a Providence,—over or under,—
When, all packed for Nashville, I fust ascertained
From the papers up North wut a victory we 'd gained.
't wuz the time for diffusin' correc' views abroad
Of our union an' strength an' relyin' on God;
An', fact, when I 'd gut thru my fust big surprise,
I much ez half b'lieved in my own tallest lies,
An' conveyed the idee thet the whole Southun popperlace
Wuz Spartans all on the keen jump for Thermopperlies,
Thet set on the Lincolnites' bombs till they bust,
An' fight for the priv'lege o' dyin' the fust;
But Roanoke, Bufort, Millspring, an' the rest
Of our recent starn-foremost successes out West,
Hain't left us a foot for our swellin' to stand on,—
We 've showed *too* much o' wut Buregard calls *abandon*,
For all our Thermopperlies (an' it 's a marcy
We hain't hed no more) hev ben clean vicy-varsy,
An' wut Spartans wuz lef' when the battle wuz done
Wuz them thet wuz too unambitious to run.
Oh, ef we hed on'y jes' gut Reecognition,
Things now would ha' ben in a different position!
You 'd ha' hed all you wanted: the paper blockade
Smashed up into toothpicks; unlimited trade
In the one thing thet 's needfle, till niggers, I swow,
Hed ben thicker 'n provisional shin-plasters now;
Quinine by the ton 'ginst the shakes when they seize ye;
Nice paper to coin into C. S. A. specie;
The voice of the driver 'd be heerd in our land,
An' the univarse scringe, ef we lifted our hand:
Would n't *thet* be some like a fulfillin' the prophecies,
With all the fus' fem'lies in all the fust offices?
't wuz a beautiful dream, an' all sorrer is idle,—
But *ef* Lincoln *would* ha' hanged Mason an' Slidell!
For would n't the Yankees hev found they 'd ketched Tartars,
Ef they 'd raised two sech critters as them into martyrs?
Mason *wuz* F. F. V., though a cheap card to win on,
But t' other was jes' New York trash to begin on;
They ain't o' no good in Európean pellices,

But think wut a help they 'd ha' been on their gallowses!
They 'd ha' felt they wuz truly fulfillin' their mission,
An', oh, how dog-cheap we 'd ha' gut Ree-cognition!

But somehow another, wutever we 've tried,
Though the the'ry 's fust-rate, the facs *wun't* coincide:
Facs are contrary 'z mules, an' ez hard in the mouth,
An' they allus hev showed a mean spite to the South.
Sech bein' the case, we hed best look about
For some kin' o' way to slip *our* necks out:
Le' 's vote our las' dollar, ef one can be found,
(An', at any rate, votin' it hez a good sound,)—
Le' 's swear thet to arms all our people is flyin',
(The critters can't read, an' wun't know how we 're lyin',)—
Thet Toombs is advancin' to sack Cincinnater,
With a rovin' commission to pillage an' slahter,—
Thet we 've throwed to the winds all regard for wut 's lawfle,
An' gone in for sunthin' promiscu'sly awfle.
Ye see hitherto, it 's our own knaves an' fools
Thet we 've used, (those for whetstones, an' t' others ez tools,)
An' now our las' chance is in puttin' to test
The same kin' o' cattle up North an' out West,—
Your Belmonts, Vallandighams, Woodses, an' sech,
Poor shotes thet ye could n't persuade us to tech,
Not in ornery times, though we 're willin' to feed 'em
With a nod now an' then, when we happen to need 'em;
Why, for my part, I'd ruther shake hands with a nigger
Than with cusses that load an' don't darst dror a trigger;
They 're the wust wooden nutmegs the Yankees perdooce,
Shaky everywheres else, an' jes' sound on the goose;
They ain't wuth a cuss, an' I set nothin' by 'em,
But we 're in sech a fix thet I s'pose we mus' try 'em.
I— But, Gennlemen, here 's a despatch jes' come in
Which shows thet the tide 's begun turnin' agin',—
Gret Cornfedrit success! C'lumbus eevacooated!
I mus' run down an' hev the thing properly stated,
An' show wut a triumph it is, an' how lucky
To fin'lly git red o' thet cussed Kentucky,—
An' how, sence Fort Donelson, winnin' the day
Consists in triumphantly gittin' away.

1862

From No. VI
SUNTHIN' IN THE PASTORAL LINE

Once git a smell o' musk into a draw,
An' it clings hold like precerdents in law:
Your gra'ma'am put it there,—when, goodness knows,—
To jes' this-worldify her Sunday-clo'es;
But the old chist wun't sarve her gran'son's wife
(For, 'thout new funnitoor, wut good in life?),
An' so ole clawfoot, from the precinks dread
O' the spare chamber, slinks into the shed,
Where, dim with dust, it fust or last subsides
To holdin' seeds an' fifty things besides;
But better days stick fast in heart an' husk,
An' all you keep in 't gits a scent o' musk.

Jes' so with poets: wut they 've airly read
Gits kind o' worked into their heart an' head,
So 's 't they can't seem to write but jest on sheers
With furrin countries or played-out ideers,
Nor hev a feelin', ef it doos n't smack
O' wut some critter chose to feel 'way back:
This makes 'em talk o' daisies, larks, an' things,
Ez though we 'd nothin' here that blows an' sings
(Why, I 'd give more for one live bobolink
Than a square mile o' larks in printer's ink),—
This makes 'em think our fust o' May is May,
Which 't ain't, for all the almanicks can say.

O little city-gals, don't never go it
Blind on the word o' noospaper or poet!
They 're apt to puff, an' May-day seldom looks
Up in the country ez 't doos in books;
They 're no more like than hornets'-nests an' hives,
Or printed sarmons be to holy lives.
I, with my trouses perched on cowhide boots,
Tuggin' my foundered feet out by the roots,
Hev seen ye come to fling on April's hearse
Your muslin nosegays from the milliner's,
Puzzlin' to find dry ground your queen to choose,
An' dance your throats sore in morocker shoes:
I 've seen ye an' felt proud, thet, come wut would,
Our Pilgrim stock wuz pethed with hardihood.
Pleasure doos make us Yankees kind o' winch,
Ez though 't wuz sunthin' paid for by the inch;
But yit we du contrive to worry thru,
Ef Dooty tells us thet the thing 's to du,
An' kerry a hollerday, ef we set out,
Ez stiddily ez though 't wuz a redoubt.

I, country-born an' bred, know where to find
Some blooms thet make the season suit the mind,
An' seem to metch the doubtin' bluebird's notes,—
Half-vent'rin' liverworts in furry coats,
Bloodroots, whose rolled-up leaves ef you oncurl,
Each on 'em 's cradle to a baby-pearl,—
But these are jes' Spring's pickets; sure ez sin,
The rebble frosts 'll try to drive 'em in;
For half our May 's so awfully like May n't,
't would rile a Shaker or an evrige saint;
Though I own up I like our back'ard springs
Thet kind o' haggle with their greens an' things,
An' when you 'most give up, 'uthout more words
Toss the fields full o' blossoms, leaves, an' birds;
Thet 's Northun natur', slow an' apt to doubt,
But when it *doos* git stirred, ther' 's no gin-out!

Fust come the blackbirds clatt'rin' in tall trees,
An' settlin' things in windy Congresses,—
Queer politicians, though, for I 'll be skinned
Ef all on 'em don't head aginst the wind.
'fore long the trees begin to show belief,—
The maple crimsons to a coral-reef,
Then saffern swarms swing off from all the willers
So plump they look like yaller caterpillars,
Then gray hossches'nuts leetle hands unfold
Softer 'n a baby's be at three days old:
Thet 's robin-redbreast's almanick; he knows
Thet arter this ther' 's only blossom-snows;
So, choosin' out a handy crotch an' spouse,
He goes to plast'rin' his adobë house.

Then seems to come a hitch,—things lag behind,
Till some fine mornin' Spring makes up her mind,
An' ez, when snow-swelled rivers cresh their dams
Heaped-up with ice thet dovetails in an' jams,
A leak comes spirtin' thru some pin-hole cleft,
Grows stronger, fercer, tears out right an' left,
Then all the waters bow themselves an' come,
Suddin, in one gret slope o' shedderin' foam,
Jes' so our Spring gits everythin' in tune
An' gives one leap from Aperl into June:
Then all comes crowdin' in; afore you think,
Young oak-leaves mist the side-hill woods with pink;
The catbird in the laylock-bush is loud;
The orchards turn to heaps o' rosy cloud;
Red-cedars blossom tu, though few folks know it,
An' look all dipt in sunshine like a poet;
The lime-trees pile their solid stacks o' shade
An' drows'ly simmer with the bees' sweet trade;
In ellum-shrouds the flashin' hangbird clings
An' for the summer vy'ge his hammock slings;
All down the loose-walled lanes in archin' bowers
The barb'ry droops its strings o' golden flowers,
Whose shrinkin' hearts the school-gals love to try
With pins,—they 'll worry yourn so, boys, bimeby!
But I don't love your cat'logue style,—do you?—

Ez ef to sell off Natur' by vendoo;
One word with blood in 't 's twice ez good ez two:
'nuff sed, June's bridesman, poet o' the year,
Gladness on wings, the bobolink, is here;
Half-hid in tip-top apple-blooms he swings,
Or climbs aginst the breeze with quiverin' wings,
Or, givin' way to 't in a mock despair,
Runs down, a brook o' laughter, thru the air.

I ollus feel the sap start in my veins
In Spring, with curus heats an' prickly pains,
Thet drive me, when I git a chance, to walk
Off by myself to hev a privit talk
With a queer critter thet can't seem to 'gree
Along o' me like most folks,—Mister Me.
Ther' 's times when I 'm unsoshle ez a stone,
An' sort o' suffercate to be alone,—
I 'm crowded jes' to think thet folks are nigh,
An' can't bear nothin' closer than the sky;
Now the wind 's full ez shifty in the mind
Ez wut it is ou'-doors, ef I ain't blind,
An' sometimes, in the fairest sou'west weather,
My innard vane pints east for weeks together,
My natur' gits all goose-flesh, an' my sins
Come drizzlin' on my conscience sharp ez pins:
Wal, et sech times I jes' slip out o' sight
An' take it out in a fair stan'-up fight
With the one cuss I can't lay on the shelf,
The crook'dest stick in all the heap,—Myself.

'T wuz so las' Sabbath arter meetin'-time:
Findin' my feelin's would n't noways rhyme
With nobody's, but off the hendle flew
An' took things from an east-wind pint o' view,
I started off to lose me in the hills
Where the pines be, up back o' 'Siah's Mills:
Pines, ef you 're blue, are the best friends I know,
They mope an' sigh an' sheer your feelin's so,—
They hesh the ground beneath so, tu, I swan,
You half-forgit you 've gut a body on.
Ther' 's a small school'us' there where four roads meet,
The door-steps hollered out by little feet,
An' side-posts carved with names whose owners grew
To gret men, some on 'em, an' deacons, tu;
't ain't used no longer, coz the town hez gut
A high-school, where they teach the Lord knows wut:
Three-story larnin' 's pop'lar now; I guess
We thriv' ez wal on jes' two stories less,
For it strikes me ther' 's sech a thing ez sinnin'
By overloadin' children's underpinnin':
Wal, here it wuz I larned my A B C,
An' it 's a kind o' favorite spot with me.

We 're curus critters: Now ain't jes' the minute
Thet ever fits us easy while we 're in it;
Long ez 't wuz futur', 't would be perfect bliss,—
Soon ez it 's past, *thet* time 's wuth ten o' this;
An' yit there ain't a man thet need be told
Thet Now 's the only bird lays eggs o' gold.
A knee-high lad, I used to plot an' plan
An' think 't wuz life's cap-sheaf to be a man;
Now, gittin' gray, there 's nothin' I enjoy
Like dreamin' back along into a boy:
So the ole school'us' is a place I choose
Afore all others, ef I want to muse;
I set down where I used to set, an' git
My boyhood back, an' better things with it,—
Faith, Hope, an' sunthin', ef it is n't Cherrity,
It 's want o' guile, an' thet 's ez gret a rerrity,—
While Fancy's cushin', free to Prince and Clown,
Makes the hard bench ez soft ez milk-weed-down.

Now, 'fore I knowed, thet Sabbath arternoon
When I sot out to tramp myself in tune,
I found me in the school'us' on my seat,
Drummin' the march to No-wheres with my feet.
Thinkin' o' nothin', I 've heerd ole folks say
Is a hard kind o' dooty in its way:
It 's thinkin' everythin' you ever knew,
Or ever hearn, to make your feelin's blue.
I sot there tryin' thet on for a spell:
I thought o' the Rebellion, then o' Hell,
Which some folks tell ye now is jest a meterfor
(A the'ry, p'raps, it wun't *feel* none the better for);
I thought o' Reconstruction, wut we 'd win
Patchin' our patent self-blow-up agin:

I thought ef this 'ere milkin' o' the wits,
So much a month, warn't givin' Natur' fits,—
Ef folks warn't druv, findin' their own milk fail,
To work the cow thet hez an iron tail,
An' ef idees 'thout ripenin' in the pan
Would send up cream to humor ary man:
From this to thet I let my worryin' creep,
Till finally I must ha' fell asleep.

Our lives in sleep are some like streams thet glide
'twixt flesh an' sperrit boundin' on each side,
Where both shores' shadders kind o' mix an' mingle
In sunthin' thet ain't jes' like either single;
An' when you cast off moorin's from Today,
An' down towards Tomorrer drift away,
The imiges thet tengle on the stream
Make a new upside-down'ard world o' dream:
Sometimes they seem like sunrise-streaks an' warnin's
O' wut 'll be in Heaven on Sabbath-mornin's,
An', mixed right in ez ef jest out o' spite,
Sunthin' thet says your supper ain't gone right.
I 'm gret on dreams, an' often when I wake,
I 've lived so much it makes my mem'ry ache,
An' can't skurce take a cat-nap in my cheer
'thout hevin' 'em, some good, some bad, all queer.

Now I wuz settin' where I 'd ben, it seemed,
An' ain't sure yit whether I r'ally dreamed,
Nor, ef I did, how long I might ha' slep',
When I hearn some un stompin' up the step,
An' lookin' round, ef two an' two make four,
I see a Pilgrim Father in the door.
He wore a steeple-hat, tall boots, an' spurs
With rowels to 'em big ez ches'nut-burrs,
An' his gret sword behind him sloped away
Long 'z a man's speech thet dunno wut to say.—
"Ef your name 's Biglow, an' your given-name
Hosee," sez he, "it 's arter you I came;
I 'm your gret-gran'ther multiplied by three."—
"My *wut?*" sez I.—"Your gret-gret-gret," sez he:
"You would n't ha' never ben here but for me.
Two hundred an' three year ago this May
The ship I come in sailed up Boston Bay;
I 'd been a cunnle in our Civil War,—
But wut on airth hev *you* gut up one for?
Coz we du things in England, 't ain't for you
To git a notion you can du 'em tu:
I 'm told you write in public prints: ef true,
It 's nateral you should know a thing or two."—
"Thet air 's an argymunt I can't endorse,—
't would prove, coz you wear spurs, you kep' a horse:
For brains," sez I, "wutever you may think,
Ain't boun' to cash the drafs o' pen-an'-ink,—
Though mos' folks write ez ef they hoped jes' quickenin'
The churn would argoo skim-milk into thick-enin';
But skim-milk ain't a thing to change its view
O' wut it 's meant for more 'n a smoky flue.
But du pray tell me, 'fore we furder go,
How in all Natur' did you come to know
'bout our affairs," sez I, "in Kingdom-Come?"—
"Wal, I worked round at sperrit-rappin' some,
An' danced the tables till their legs wuz gone,
In hopes o' larnin' wut wuz goin' on,"
Sez he, "but mejums lie so like all-split
Thet I concluded it wuz best to quit.
But, come now, ef you wun't confess to knowin',
You 've some conjectures how the thing 's a-goin'."—
"Gran'ther," sez I, "a vane warn't never known
Nor asked to hev a jedgment of its own;
An' yit, ef 't ain't gut rusty in the jints,
It 's safe to trust its say on certin pints:
It knows the wind's opinions to a T,
An' the wind settles wut the weather 'll be."
"I never thought a scion of our stock
Could grow the wood to make a weathercock;
When I wuz younger 'n you, skurce more 'n a shaver,
No airthly wind," sez he, "could make me waver!"
(Ez he said this, he clinched his jaw an' fore-head,
Hitchin' his belt to bring his sword-hilt for-rard.)—

"Jes so it wuz with me," sez I, "I swow,
When *I* wuz younger 'n wut you see me now,—
Nothin' from Adam's fall to Huldy's bonnet,
Thet I warn't full-cocked with my jedgment on it;
But now I 'm gittin' on in life, I find
It 's a sight harder to make up my mind,—
Nor I don't often try tu, when events
Will du it for me free of all expense.
The moral question 's ollus plain enough,—
It 's jes' the human-natur' side thet 's tough;
Wut 's best to think may n't puzzle me nor you,—
The pinch comes in decidin' wut to *du;*
Ef you *read* History, all runs smooth ez grease,
Coz there the men ain't nothin' more 'n idees,—
But come to *make* it, ez we must today,
Th' idees hev arms an' legs an' stop the way:
It 's easy fixin' things in facts an' figgers,—
They can't resist, nor warn't brought up with niggers;
But come to try your the'ry on,—why, then
Your facts an' figgers change to ign'ant men
Actin' ez ugly—" —"Smite 'em hip an' thigh!"
Sez gran'ther, "and let every man-child die!
Oh for three weeks o' Crommle an' the Lord!
Up, Isr'el, to your tents an' grind the sword!"—
"Thet kind o' thing worked wal in ole Judee,
But you forgit how long it 's ben A. D.;
You think thet 's ellerkence,—I call it shoddy,
A thing," sez I, "wun't cover soul nor body;
I like the plain all-wool o' common-sense,
Thet warms ye now, an' will a twelvemonth hence.
You took to follerin' where the Prophets beckoned,
An', fust you knowed on, back come Charles the Second;
Now wut I want 's to hev all *we* gain stick,
An' not to start Millennium too quick;
We hain't to punish only, but to keep,
An' the cure 's gut to go a cent'ry deep."
"Wal, milk-an'-water ain't the best o' glue,"
Sez he, "an' so you 'll find afore you 're thru;
Ef reshness venters sunthin', shilly-shally
Loses ez often wut 's ten times the vally.
Thet exe of ourn, when Charles's neck gut split,
Opened a gap thet ain't bridged over yit:
Slav'ry 's your Charles, the Lord hez gin the exe—"
"Our Charles," sez I, "hez gut eight million necks.
The hardest question ain't the black man's right,
The trouble is to 'mancipate the white;
One 's chained in body an' can be sot free,
But t' other 's chained in soul to an idee:
It 's a long job, but we shall worry thru it;
Ef bagnets fail, the spellin'-book must du it."
"Hosee," sez he, "I think you 're goin to fail:
The rettlesnake ain't dangerous in the tail;
This 'ere rebellion 's nothing but the rettle,—
You 'll stomp on thet an' think you 've won the bettle;
It 's Slavery thet 's the fangs an' thinkin' head,
An' ef you want selvation, cresh it dead,—
An' cresh it suddin, or you 'll larn by waitin'
Thet Chance wun't stop to listen to debatin'!"—
"God's truth!" sez I,—"an' ef *I* held the club,
An' knowed jes' where to strike,—but there 's the rub!"—
"Strike soon," sez he, "or you 'll be deadly ailin',—
Folks thet 's afeared to fail are sure o' failin';
God hates your sneakin' creturs thet believe
He 'll settle things they run away an' leave!"
He brought his foot down fercely, ez he spoke,
An' give me sech a startle thet I woke.

1862

From No. VII

LATEST VIEWS OF MR. BIGLOW

Ef I a song or two could make
  Like rockets druv by their own burnin',
All leap an' light, to leave a wake
  Men's hearts an' faces skyward turnin'!—
But, it strikes me, 't ain't jest the time
  Fer stringin' words with settisfaction:
Wut 's wanted now 's the silent rhyme
  'Twixt upright Will an' downright Action.

Words, ef you keep 'em, pay their keep,
  But gabble 's the short cut to ruin;

It 's gratis (gals half-price), but cheap
At no rate, ef it henders doin';
Ther' 's nothin' wuss, 'less 't is to set
A martyr-prem'um upon jawrin':
Teapots git dangerous, ef you shet
Their lids down on 'em with Fort Warren.

'Bout long enough it 's ben discussed
Who sot the magazine afire,
An' whether, ef Bob Wickliffe bust,
'T would scare us more or blow us higher.
D' ye s'pose the Gret Foreseer's plan
Wuz settled fer him in town-meetin'?
Or thet ther' 'd ben no Fall o' Man,
Ef Adam 'd on'y bit a sweetin'?

Oh, Jon'than, ef you want to be
A rugged chap agin an' hearty,
Go fer wutever 'll hurt Jeff D.,
Nut wut 'll boost up ary party.
Here 's hell broke loose, an' we lay flat
With half the univarse a-singein',
Till Sen'tor This an' Gov'nor Thet
Stop squabblin' fer the garding-ingin.

It 's war we 're in, not politics;
It 's systems wrastlin' now, not parties;
An' victory in the eend 'll fix
Where longest will an' truest heart is.
An' wut 's the Guv'ment folks about?
Tryin' to hope ther' 's nothin' doin',
An' look ez though they did n't doubt
Sunthin' pertickler wuz a-brewin'.

Ther' 's critters yit thet talk an' act
Fer wut they call Conciliation;
They 'd hand a buff'lo-drove a tract
When they wuz madder than all Bashan.
Conciliate? it jest means *be kicked*,
No metter how they phrase an' tone it;
It means thet we 're to set down licked,
Thet we 're poor shotes an' glad to own it!

A war on tick 's ez dear 'z the deuce,
But it wun't leave no lastin' traces,
Ez 't would to make a sneakin' truce
Without no moral specie-basis:
Ef greenbacks ain't nut jest the cheese,
I guess ther' 's evils thet 's extremer,—
Fer instance,—shinplaster idees
Like them put out by Gov'nor Seymour.

Last year, the Nation, at a word,
When tremblin' Freedom cried to shield her,
Flamed weldin' into one keen sword
Waitin' an' longin' fer a wielder:
A splendid flash!—but how 'd the grasp
With sech a chance ez thet wuz tally?
Ther' warn't no meanin' in our clasp,—
Half this, half thet, all shilly-shally.

More men? More Man! It 's there we fail;
Weak plans grow weaker yit by lengthenin':
Wut use in addin' to the tail,
When it 's the head 's in need o' strengthenin'?
We wanted one thet felt all Chief
From roots o' hair to sole o' stockin',
Square-sot with thousan'-ton belief
In him an' us, ef earth went rockin'!

Ole Hick'ry would n't ha' stood see-saw
'Bout doin' things till they wuz done with,—
He 'd smashed the tables o' the Law
In time o' need to load his gun with;
He could n't see but jest one side,—
Ef his, 't wuz God's, an' thet wuz plenty;
An' so his "*Forrards!*" multiplied
An army's fightin' weight by twenty.

But this 'ere histin', creak, creak, creak,
Your cappen's heart up with a derrick,
This tryin' to coax a lightnin'-streak
Out of a half-discouraged hay-rick,
This hangin' on mont' arter mont'
Fer one sharp purpose 'mongst the twitter,—
I tell ye, it doos kind o' stunt
The peth and sperit of a critter.

In six months where 'll the People be,
Ef leaders look on revolution
Ez though it wuz a cup o' tea,—
Jest social el'ments in solution?
This weighin' things doos wal enough
When war cools down, an' comes to writin';
But while it 's makin', the true stuff
Is pison-mad, pig-headed fightin'.

Democ'acy gives every man
The right to be his own oppressor;
But a loose Gov'ment ain't the plan,
Helpless ez spilled beans on a dresser:

I tell ye one thing we might larn
From them smart critters, the Seceders,—
Ef bein' right 's the fust consarn,
The 'fore-the-fust 's cast-iron leaders.

But 'pears to me I see some signs
Thet we 're a-goin' to use our senses:
Jeff druv us into these hard lines,
An' ough' to bear his half th' expenses;
Slavery 's Secession's heart an' will,
South, North, East, West, where'er you find it,
An' ef it drors into War's mill,
D' ye say them thunder-stones sha'n't grind it?

D' ye s'pose, ef Jeff giv *him* a lick,
Ole Hick'ry 'd tried his head to sof'n
So 's 't would n't hurt thet ebony stick
Thet 's made our side see stars so of'n?
"No!" he 'd ha' thundered, "on your knees,
An' own one flag, one road to glory!
Soft-heartedness, in times like these,
Shows sof'ness in the upper story!"

An' why should we kick up a muss
About the Pres'dunt's proclamation?
It ain't a-goin' to lib'rate us,
Ef we don't like emancipation:
The right to be a cussed fool
Is safe from all devices human,
It 's common (ez a gin'l rule)
To every critter born o' woman.

So *we* 're all right, an' I, fer one,
Don't think our cause 'll lose in vally
By rammin' Scriptur in our gun,
An' gittin' Natur' fer an ally:
Thank God, say I, fer even a plan
To lift one human bein's level,
Give one more chance to make a man,
Or, anyhow, to spile a devil!

Not thet I 'm one thet much expec'
Millennium by express tomorrer;
They *will* miscarry,—I rec'lec'
Tu many on 'em, to my sorrer:
Men ain't made angels in a day,
No matter how you mould an' labor 'em,
Nor 'riginal ones, I guess, don't stay
With Abe so of'n ez with Abraham.

The'ry thinks Fact a pooty thing,
An' wants the banns read right ensuin';
But fact wun't noways wear the ring,
'Thout years o' settin' up an' wooin':
Though, arter all, Time's dial-plate
Marks cent'ries with the minute-finger,
An' Good can't never come tu late,
Though it doos seem to try an' linger.

An' come wut will, I think it 's grand
Abe 's gut his will et last bloom-furnaced
In trial-flames till it 'll stand
The strain o' bein' in deadly earnest:
Thet 's wut we want,—we want to know
The folks on our side hez the bravery
To b'lieve ez hard, come weal, come woe,
In Freedom ez Jeff doos in Slavery.

Set the two forces foot to foot,
An' every man knows who 'll be winner,
Whose faith in God hez ary root
Thet goes down deeper than his dinner:
Then 't will be felt from pole to pole,
Without no need o' proclamation,
Earth's biggest Country's gut her soul
An' risen up Earth's Greatest Nation!

1863

ODE RECITED AT THE HARVARD COMMEMORATION

JULY 21, 1865

I

WEAK-WINGED is song,
Nor aims at that clear-ethered height
Whither the brave deed climbs for light:
We seem to do them wrong,
Bringing our robin's-leaf to deck their hearse
Who in warm life-blood wrote their nobler verse,
Our trivial song to honor those who come
With ears attuned to strenuous trump and drum,
And shaped in squadron-strophes their desire,
Live battle-odes whose lines were steel and fire:
Yet sometimes feathered words are strong,
A gracious memory to buoy up and save
From Lethe's dreamless ooze, the common grave
Of the unventurous throng.

II

Today our Reverend Mother welcomes back
Her wisest Scholars, those who understood
The deeper teaching of her mystic tome,
And offered their fresh lives to make it good:
No lore of Greece or Rome,
No science peddling with the names of things,
Or reading stars to find inglorious fates,
Can lift our life with wings
Far from Death's idle gulf that for the many waits,
And lengthen out our dates
With that clear fame whose memory sings
In manly hearts to come, and nerves them and dilates:
Nor such thy teaching, Mother of us all!
Not such the trumpet-call
Of thy diviner mood,
That could thy sons entice
From happy homes and toils, the fruitful nest
Of those half-virtues which the world calls best,
Into War's tumult rude;
But rather far that stern device
The sponsors chose that round thy cradle stood
In the dim, unventured wood,
The VERITAS that lurks beneath
The letter's unprolific sheath,
Life of whate'er makes life worth living,
Seed-grain of high emprise, immortal food,
One heavenly thing whereof earth hath the giving.

III

Many loved Truth, and lavished life's best oil
Amid the dust of books to find her,
Content at last, for guerdon of their toil,
With the cast mantle she hath left behind her.
Many in sad faith sought for her,
Many with crossed hands sighed for her;
But these, our brothers, fought for her,
At life's dear peril wrought for her,
So loved her that they died for her,
Tasting the raptured fleetness
Of her divine completeness:
Their higher instinct knew
Those love her best who to themselves are true,
And what they dare to dream of, dare to do;
They followed her and found her
Where all may hope to find,
Not in the ashes of the burnt-out mind,
But beautiful, with danger's sweetness round her.
Where faith made whole with deed
Breathes its awakening breath
Into the lifeless creed,
They saw her plumed and mailed,
With sweet, stern face unveiled,
And all-repaying eyes, look proud on them in death.

IV

Our slender life runs rippling by, and glides
Into the silent hollow of the past;
What is there that abides
To make the next age better for the last?
Is earth too poor to give us
Something to live for here that shall outlive us?
Some more substantial boon
Than such as flows and ebbs with Fortune's fickle moon?
The little that we see
From doubt is never free;
The little that we do
Is but half-nobly true;
With our laborious hiving
What men call treasure, and the gods call dross,
Life seems a jest of Fate's contriving,
Only secure in every one's conniving,
A long account of nothings paid with loss,
Where we poor puppets, jerked by unseen wires,
After our little hour of strut and rave,
With all our pasteboard passions and desires,
Loves, hates, ambitions, and immortal fires,
Are tossed pell-mell together in the grave.
But stay! no age was e'er degenerate,
Unless men held it at too cheap a rate,
For in our likeness still we shape our fate.
Ah, there is something here
Unfathomed by the cynic's sneer,
Something that gives our feeble light
A high immunity from Night,
Something that leaps life's narrow bars

To claim its birthright with the hosts of heaven;
A seed of sunshine that can leaven
Our earthly dullness with the beams of stars,
And glorify our clay
With light from fountains elder than the Day;
A conscience more divine than we,
A gladness fed with secret tears,
A vexing, forward-reaching sense
Of some more noble permanence;
A light across the sea,
Which haunts the soul and will not let it be,
Still beaconing from the heights of undegenerate years.

V

Whither leads the path
To ampler fates that leads?
Not down through flowery meads,
To reap an aftermath
Of youth's vainglorious weeds,
But up the steep, amid the wrath
And shock of deadly-hostile creeds,
Where the world's best hope and stay
By battle's flashes gropes a desperate way,
And every turf the fierce foot clings to bleeds.
Peace hath her not ignoble wreath,
Ere yet the sharp, decisive word
Light the black lips of cannon, and the sword
Dreams in its easeful sheath;
But some day the live coal behind the thought,
Whether from Baäl's stone obscene,
Or from the shrine serene
Of God's pure altar brought,
Bursts up in flame; the war of tongue and pen
Learns with what deadly purpose it was fraught,
And, helpless in the fiery passion caught,
Shakes all the pillared state with shock of men:
Some day the soft Ideal that we wooed
Confronts us fiercely, foe-beset, pursued,
And cries reproachful: "Was it, then, my praise,
And not myself was loved? Prove now thy truth;
I claim of thee the promise of thy youth;
Give me thy life, or cower in empty phrase,
The victim of thy genius, not its mate!"
Life may be given in many ways,
And loyalty to Truth be sealed
As bravely in the closet as the field,
So bountiful is Fate;
But then to stand beside her,
When craven churls deride her,
To front a lie in arms and not to yield,
This shows, methinks, God's plan
And measure of a stalwart man,
Limbed like the old heroic breeds,
Who stands self-poised on manhood's solid earth,
Not forced to frame excuses for his birth,
Fed from within with all the strength he needs.

VI

Such was he, our Martyr-Chief,
Whom late the Nation he had led,
With ashes on her head,
Wept with the passion of an angry grief:
Forgive me, if from present things I turn
To speak what in my heart will beat and burn,
And hang my wreath on his world-honored urn.
Nature, they say, doth dote,
And cannot make a man
Save on some worn-out plan,
Repeating us by rote:
For him her Old-World moulds aside she threw,
And choosing sweet clay from the breast
Of the unexhausted West,
With stuff untainted shaped a hero new,
Wise, steadfast in the strength of God, and true.
How beautiful to see
Once more a shepherd of mankind indeed,
Who loved his charge, but never loved to lead;
One whose meek flock the people joyed to be,
Not lured by any cheat of birth,
But by his clear-grained human worth,
And brave old wisdom of sincerity!
They knew that outward grace is dust;
They could not choose but trust
In that sure-footed mind's unfaltering skill,
And supple-tempered will
That bent like perfect steel to spring again and thrust.
His was no lonely mountain-peak of mind,
Thrusting to thin air o'er our cloudy bars,

A sea-mark now, now lost in vapors blind;
Broad prairie rather, genial, level-lined,
Fruitful and friendly for all human kind,
Yet also nigh to heaven and loved of loftiest stars.
Nothing of Europe here,
Or, then, of Europe fronting mornward still,
Ere any names of Serf and Peer
Could Nature's equal scheme deface
And thwart her genial will;
Here was a type of the true elder race,
And one of Plutarch's men talked with us face to face.
I praise him not; it were too late;
And some innative weakness there must be
In him who condescends to victory
Such as the Present gives, and cannot wait,
Safe in himself as in a fate.
So always firmly he:
He knew to bide his time,
And can his fame abide,
Still patient in his simple faith sublime,
Till the wise years decide.
Great captains, with their guns and drums,
Disturb our judgment for the hour,
But at last silence comes;
These all are gone, and, standing like a tower,
Our children shall behold his fame.
The kindly-earnest, brave, foreseeing man,
Sagacious, patient, dreading praise, not blame,
New birth of our new soil, the first American.

VII

Long as man's hope insatiate can discern
Or only guess some more inspiring goal
Outside of Self, enduring as the pole,
Along whose course the flying axles burn
Of spirits bravely-pitched, earth's manlier brood;
Long as below we cannot find
The meed that stills the inexorable mind;
So long this faith to some ideal Good,
Under whatever mortal names it masks,
Freedom, Law, Country, this ethereal mood
That thanks the Fates for their severer tasks,
Feeling its challenged pulses leap,
While others skulk in subterfuges cheap,
And, set in Danger's van, has all the boon it asks,
Shall win man's praise and woman's love,
Shall be a wisdom that we set above
All other skills and gifts to culture dear,
A virtue round whose forehead we inwreathe
Laurels that with a living passion breathe
When other crowns grow, while we twine them, sear.
What brings us thronging these high rites to pay,
And seal these hours the noblest of our year,
Save that our brothers found this better way?

VIII

We sit here in the Promised Land
That flows with Freedom's honey and milk;
But 'twas they won it, sword in hand,
Making the nettle danger soft for us as silk.
We welcome back our bravest and our best;
Ah me! not all! some come not with the rest,
Who went forth brave and bright as any here!
I strive to mix some gladness with my strain,
But the sad strings complain,
And will not please the ear:
I sweep them for a pæan, but they wane
Again and yet again
Into a dirge, and die away, in pain.
In these brave ranks I only see the gaps,
Thinking of dear ones whom the dumb turf wraps,
Dark to the triumph which they died to gain:
Fitlier may others greet the living,
For me the past is unforgiving;
I with uncovered head
Salute the sacred dead,
Who went, and who return not.—Say not so!
'Tis not the grapes of Canaan that repay,
But the high faith that failed not by the way;
Virtue treads paths that end not in the grave;
No ban of endless night exiles the brave;
And to the saner mind
We rather seem the dead that stayed behind.
Blow, trumpets, all your exultations blow!
For never shall their aureoled presence lack:
I see them muster in a gleaming row,
With ever-youthful brows that nobler show;

We find in our dull road their shining track;
In every nobler mood
We feel the orient of their spirit glow,
Part of our life's unalterable good,
Of all our saintlier aspiration;
They come transfigured back,
Secure from change in their high-hearted ways,
Beautiful evermore, and with the rays
Of morn on their white Shields of Expectation!

IX

But is there hope to save
Even this ethereal essence from the grave?
What ever 'scaped Oblivion's subtle wrong
Save a few clarion names, or golden threads of song?
Before my musing eye
The mighty ones of old sweep by,
Disvoicèd now and insubstantial things,
As noisy once as we; poor ghosts of kings,
Shadows of empire wholly gone to dust,
And many races, nameless long ago,
To darkness driven by that imperious gust
Of ever-rushing Time that here doth blow:
O visionary world, condition strange,
Where naught abiding is but only Change,
Where the deep-bolted stars themselves still shift and range!
Shall we to more continuance make pretence?
Renown builds tombs; a life-estate is Wit;
And, bit by bit,
The cunning years steal all from us but woe;
Leaves are we, whose decays no harvest sow.
But, when we vanish hence,
Shall they lie forceless in the dark below,
Save to make green their little length of sods,
Or deepen pansies for a year or two,
Who now to us are shining-sweet as gods?
Was dying all they had the skill to do?
That were not fruitless: but the Soul resents
Such short-lived service, as if blind events
Ruled without her, or earth could so endure;
She claims a more divine investiture
Of longer tenure than Fame's airy rents;
Whate'er she touches doth her nature share;
Her inspiration haunts the ennobled air,
Gives eyes to mountains blind,
Ears to the deaf earth, voices to the wind,
And her clear trump sings succor everywhere
By lonely bivouacs to the wakeful mind;
For soul inherits all that soul could dare:
Yea, Manhood hath a wider span
And larger privilege of life than man.
The single deed, the private sacrifice,
So radiant now through proudly-hidden tears,
Is covered up erelong from mortal eyes
With thoughtless drift of the deciduous years;
But that high privilege that makes all men peers,
That leap of heart whereby a people rise
Up to a noble anger's height,
And, flamed on by the Fates, not shrink, but grow more bright,
That swift validity in noble veins,
Of choosing danger and disdaining shame,
Of being set on flame
By the pure fire that flies all contact base
But wraps its chosen with angelic might,
These are imperishable gains,
Sure as the sun, medicinal as light,
These hold great futures in their lusty reins
And certify to earth a new imperial race.

X

Who now shall sneer?
Who dare again to say we trace
Our lines to a plebeian race?
Roundhead and Cavalier!
Dumb are those names erewhile in battle loud;
Dream-footed as the shadow of a cloud,
They flit across the ear:
That is best blood that hath most iron in 't,
To edge resolve with, pouring without stint
For what makes manhood dear.
Tell us not of Plantagenets,
Hapsburgs, and Guelfs, whose thin bloods crawl
Down from some victor in a border-brawl!
How poor their outworn coronets,
Matched with one leaf of that plain civic wreath
Our brave for honor's blazon shall bequeath,
Through whose desert a rescued Nation sets

Her heel on treason, and the trumpet hears
Shout victory, tingling Europe's sullen ears
With vain resentments and more vain regrets!

XI

Not in anger, not in pride,
Pure from passion's mixture rude
Ever to base earth allied,
But with far-heard gratitude,
Still with heart and voice renewed,
To heroes living and dear martyrs dead,
The strain should close that consecrates our brave.
Lift the heart and lift the head!
Lofty be its mood and grave,
Not without a martial ring,
Not without a prouder tread
And a peal of exultation:
Little right has he to sing
Through whose heart in such an hour
Beats no march of conscious power,
Sweeps no tumult of elation!
'Tis no Man we celebrate,
By his country's victories great,
A hero half, and half the whim of Fate,
But the pith and marrow of a Nation
Drawing force from all her men,
Highest, humblest, weakest, all,
For her time of need, and then
Pulsing it again through them,
Till the basest can no longer cower,
Feeling his soul spring up divinely tall,
Touched but in passing by her mantle-hem.
Come back, then, noble pride, for 'tis her dower!
How could poet ever tower,
If his passions, hopes, and fears,
If his triumphs and his tears,
Kept not measure with his people?
Boom, cannon, boom to all the winds and waves!
Clash out, glad bells, from every rocking steeple!
Banners, advance with triumph, bend your staves!
And from every mountain-peak
Let beacon-fire to answering beacon speak,
Katahdin tell Monadnock, Whiteface he,
And so leap on in light from sea to sea,
Till the glad news be sent
Across a kindling continent,
Making earth feel more firm and air breathe braver:
"Be proud! for she is saved, and all have helped to save her!
She that lifts up the manhood of the poor,
She of the open soul and open door,
With room about her hearth for all mankind!
The fire is dreadful in her eyes no more;
From her bold front the helm she doth unbind,
Sends all her handmaid armies back to spin,
And bids her navies, that so lately hurled
Their crashing battle, hold their thunders in,
Swimming like birds of calm along the unharmful shore.
No challenge sends she to the elder world,
That looked askance and hated; a light scorn
Plays o'er her mouth, as round her mighty knees
She calls her children back, and waits the morn
Of nobler day, enthroned between her subject seas."

XII

Bow down, dear Land, for thou hast found release!
Thy God, in these distempered days,
Hath taught thee the sure wisdom of His ways,
And through thine enemies hath wrought thy peace!
Bow down in prayer and praise!
No poorest in thy borders but may now
Lift to the juster skies a man's enfranchised brow.
O Beautiful! my Country! ours once more!
Smoothing thy gold of war-dishevelled hair
O'er such sweet brows as never other wore,
And letting thy set lips,
Freed from wrath's pale eclipse,
The rosy edges of their smile lay bare,
What words divine of lover or of poet
Could tell our love and make thee know it,

Among the Nations bright beyond compare?
What were our lives without thee?
What all our lives to save thee?
We reck not what we gave thee;
We will not dare to doubt thee,
But ask whatever else, and we will dare!

1865 1865

THE CATHEDRAL

Far through the memory shines a happy day,
Cloudless of care, down-shod to every sense,
And simply perfect from its own resource,
As to a bee the new campanula's
Illuminate seclusion swung in air.
Such days are not the prey of setting suns,
Nor ever blurred with mist of after-thought;
Like words made magical by poets dead,
Wherein the music of all meaning is
The sense hath garnered or the soul divined,
They mingle with our life's ethereal part,
Sweetening and gathering sweetness evermore,
By Beauty's franchise disenthralled of time.

I can recall, nay, they are present still,
Parts of myself, the perfume of my mind,
Days that seem farther off than Homer's now
Ere yet the child had loudened to the boy,
And I, recluse from playmates, found perforce
Companionship in things that not denied
Nor granted wholly; as is Nature's wont,
Who, safe in uncontaminate reserve,
Lets us mistake our longing for her love,
And mocks with various echo of ourselves.

These first sweet frauds upon our consciousness,
That blend the sensual with its imaged world,
These virginal cognitions, gifts of morn,
Ere life grow noisy, and slower-footed thought
Can overtake the rapture of the sense,
To thrust between ourselves and what we feel,
Have something in them secretly divine.
Vainly the eye, once schooled to serve the brain,
With pains deliberate studies to renew
The ideal vision: second-thoughts are prose;
For Beauty's acme hath a term as brief
As the wave's poise before it break in pearl.
Our own breath dims the mirror of the sense,
Looking too long and closely: at a flash
We snatch the essential grace of meaning out,
And that first passion beggars all behind,
Heirs of a tamer transport prepossessed.
Who, seeing once, has truly seen again
The gray vague of unsympathizing sea
That dragged his Fancy from her moorings back
To shores inhospitable of eldest time,
Till blank foreboding of earth-gendered power,
Pitiless seignories in the elements,
Omnipotences blind that darkling smite,
Misgave him, and repaganized the world?
Yet, by some subtler touch of sympathy,
These primal apprehensions, dimly stirred,
Perplex the eye with pictures from within.
This hath made poets dream of lives foregone
In worlds fantastical, more fair than ours;
So Memory cheats us, glimpsing half-revealed.
Even as I write she tries her wonted spell
In that continuous redbreast boding rain:
The bird I hear sings not from yonder elm;
But the flown ecstasy my childhood heard
Is vocal in my mind, renewed by him,
Haply made sweeter by the accumulate thrill
That threads my undivided life and steals
A pathos from the years and graves between.

I know not how it is with other men,
Whom I but guess, deciphering myself;
For me, once felt is so felt nevermore.
The fleeting relish at sensation's brim
Had in it the best ferment of the wine.
One spring I knew as never any since:
All night the surges of the warm southwest
Boomed intermittent through the shuddering elms,
And brought a morning from the Gulf adrift,
Omnipotent with sunshine, whose quick charm
Startled with crocuses the sullen turf
And wiled the bluebird to his whiff of song:
One summer hour abides, what time I perched,
Dappled with noonday, under simmering leaves,
And pulled the pulpy oxhearts, while aloof
An oriole clattered and the robins shrilled,
Denouncing me an alien and a thief:
One morn of autumn lords it o'er the rest,
When in the lane I watched the ash-leaves fall,
Balancing softly earthward without wind,

Or twirling with directer impulse down
On those fallen yesterday, now barbed with frost,
While I grew pensive with the pensive year:
And once I learned how marvellous winter was,
When past the fence-rails, downy-gray with rime,
I creaked adventurous o'er the spangled crust
That made familiar fields seem far and strange
As those stark wastes that whiten endlessly
In ghastly solitude about the pole,
And gleam relentless to the unsetting sun:
Instant the candid chambers of my brain
Were painted with these sovran images;
And later visions seem but copies pale
From those unfading frescos of the past,
Which I, young savage, in my age of flint,
Gazed at, and dimly felt a power in me
Parted from Nature by the joy in her
That doubtfully revealed me to myself.
Thenceforward I must stand outside the gate;
And paradise was paradise the more,
Known once and barred against satiety.

What we call Nature, all outside ourselves,
Is but our own conceit of what we see,
Our own reaction upon what we feel;
The world 's a woman to our shifting mood,
Feeling with us, or making due pretence;
And therefore we the more persuade ourselves
To make all things our thought's confederates,
Conniving with us in whate'er we dream.
So when our Fancy seeks analogies,
Though she have hidden what she after finds,
She loves to cheat herself with feigned surprise.
I find my own complexion everywhere:
No rose, I doubt, was ever, like the first,
A marvel to the bush it dawned upon,
The rapture of its life made visible,
The mystery of its yearning realized,
As the first babe to the first woman born;
No falcon ever felt delight of wings
As when, an eyas, from the stolid cliff
Loosing himself, he followed his high heart
To swim on sunshine, masterless as wind;
And I believe the brown Earth takes delight
In the new snowdrop looking back at her,
To think that by some vernal alchemy
It could transmute her darkness into pearl;
What is the buxom peony after that,
With its coarse constancy of hoyden blush?
What the full summer to that wonder new?

But, if in nothing else, in us there is
A sense fastidious hardly reconciled
To the poor makeshifts of life's scenery,
Where the same slide must double all its parts,
Shoved in for Tarsus and hitched back for Tyre.
I blame not in the soul this daintiness,
Rasher of surfeit than a humming-bird,
In things indifferent by sense purveyed;
It argues her an immortality
And dateless incomes of experience,
This unthrift housekeeping that will not brook
A dish warmed-over at the feast of life,
And finds Twice stale, served with whatever sauce.
Nor matters much how it may go with me
Who dwell in Grub Street and am proud to drudge
Where men, my betters, wet their crust with tears:
Use can make sweet the peach's shady side,
That only by reflection tastes of sun.

But she, my Princess, who will sometimes deign
My garret to illumine till the walls,
Narrow and dingy, scrawled with hackneyed thought
(Poor Richard slowly elbowing Plato out),
Dilate and drape themselves with tapestries
Nausikaa might have stooped o'er, while, between,
Mirrors, effaced in their own clearness, send
Her only image on through deepening deeps
With endless repercussion of delight,—
Bringer of life, witching each sense to soul,
That sometimes almost gives me to believe
I might have been a poet, gives at least
A brain desaxonized, an ear that makes
Music where none is, and a keener pang
Of exquisite surmise outleaping thought,—
Her will I pamper in her luxury:
No crumpled rose-leaf of too careless choice
Shall bring a northern nightmare to her dreams,
Vexing with sense of exile; hers shall be

The invitiate firstlings of experience,
Vibrations felt but once and felt lifelong:
Oh, more than half-way turn that Grecian front
Upon me, while with self-rebuke I spell,
On the plain fillet that confines thy hair
In conscious bounds of seeming unconstraint,
The *Naught in overplus*, thy race's badge!

One feast for her I secretly designed
In that Old World so strangely beautiful
To us the disinherited of eld,—
A day at Chartres, with no soul beside
To roil with pedant prate my joy serene
And make the minster shy of confidence.
I went, and, with the Saxon's pious care,
First ordered dinner at the pea-green inn,
The flies and I its only customers.
Eluding these, I loitered through the town,
With hope to take my minster unawares
In its grave solitude of memory.
A pretty burgh, and such as Fancy loves
For bygone grandeurs, faintly rumorous now
Upon the mind's horizon, as of storm
Brooding its dreamy thunders far aloof,
That mingle with our mood, but not disturb.
Its once grim bulwarks, tamed to lovers' walks,
Look down unwatchful on the sliding Eure,
Whose listless leisure suits the quiet place,
Lisping among his shallows homelike sounds
At Concord and by Bankside heard before.
Chance led me to a public pleasure-ground,
Where I grew kindly with the merry groups,
And blessed the Frenchman for his simple art
Of being domestic in the light of day.
His language has no word, we growl, for Home;
But he can find a fireside in the sun,
Play with his child, make love, and shriek his mind,
By throngs of strangers undisprivacied.
He makes his life a public gallery,
Nor feels himself till what he feels comes back
In manifold reflection from without;
While we, each pore alert with consciousness,
Hide our best selves as we had stolen them,
And each bystander a detective were,
Keen-eyed for every chink of undisguise.

So, musing o'er the problem which was best,—
A life wide-windowed, shining all abroad,
Or curtains drawn to shield from sight profane
The rites we pay to the mysterious I,—
With outward senses furloughed and head bowed
I followed some fine instinct in my feet,
Till, to unbend me from the loom of thought,
Looking up suddenly, I found mine eyes
Confronted with the minster's vast repose.
Silent and gray as forest-leaguered cliff
Left inland by the ocean's slow retreat,
That hears afar the breeze-borne rote and longs,
Remembering shocks of surf that clomb and fell,
Spume-sliding down the baffled decuman,
It rose before me, patiently remote
From the great tides of life it breasted once,
Hearing the noise of men as in a dream.
I stood before the triple northern port,
Where dedicated shapes of saints and kings,
Stern faces bleared with immemorial watch,
Looked down benignly grave and seemed to say,
Ye come and go incessant; we remain
Safe in the hallowed quiets of the past;
Be reverent, ye who flit and are forgot,
Of faith so nobly realized as this.
I seem to have heard it said by learnëd folk
Who drench you with æsthetics till you feel
As if all beauty were a ghastly bore,
The faucet to let loose a wash of words,
That Gothic is not Grecian, therefore worse;
But, being convinced by much experiment
How little inventiveness there is in man,
Grave copier of copies, I give thanks
For a new relish, careless to inquire
My pleasure's pedigree, if so it please,
Nobly, I mean, nor renegade to art.
The Grecian gluts me with its perfectness,
Unanswerable as Euclid, self-contained,
The one thing finished in this hasty world,
Forever finished, though the barbarous pit,
Fanatical on hearsay, stamp and shout
As if a miracle could be encored.
But ah! this other, this that never ends,
Still climbing, luring fancy still to climb,
As full of morals half-divined as life,
Graceful, grotesque, with ever new surprise
Of hazardous caprices sure to please,
Heavy as nightmare, airy-light as fern,
Imagination's very self in stone!
With one long sigh of infinite release
From pedantries past, present, or to come,

I looked, and owned myself a happy Goth.
Your blood is mine, ye architects of dream,
Builders of aspiration incomplete,
So more consummate, souls self-confident,
Who felt your own thought worthy of record
In monumental pomp! No Grecian drop
Rebukes these veins that leap with kindred thrill,
After long exile, to the mother-tongue.

Ovid in Pontus, puling for his Rome
Of men invirile and disnatured dames
That poison sucked from the Attic bloom decayed,
Shrank with a shudder from the blue-eyed race
Whose force rough-handed should renew the world,
And from the dregs of Romulus express
Such wine as Dante poured, or he who blew
Roland's vain blast, or sang the Campeador
In verse that clanks like armor in the charge,—
Homeric juice, if brimmed in Odin's horn.
And they could build, if not the columned fane
That from the height gleamed seaward many-hued,
Something more friendly with their ruder skies:
The gray spire, molten now in driving mist,
Now lulled with the incommunicable blue;
The carvings touched to meanings new with snow,
Or commented with fleeting grace of shade;
The statues, motley as man's memory,
Partial as that, so mixed of true and false,
History and Legend meeting with a kiss
Across this bound-mark where their realms confine;
The painted windows, freaking gloom with glow,
Dusking the sunshine which they seem to cheer,
Meet symbol of the senses and the soul;
And the whole pile, grim with the Northman's thought
Of life and death, and doom, life's equal fee,—
These were before me: and I gazed abashed,
Child of an age that lectures, not creates,
Plastering our swallow-nests on the awful Past,
And twittering round the work of larger men,
As we had builded what we but deface.
Far up the great bells wallowed in delight,
Tossing their clangors o'er the heedless town,
To call the worshippers who never came,
Or women mostly, in loath twos and threes.
I entered, reverent of whatever shrine
Guards piety and solace for my kind
Or gives the soul a moment's truce of God,
And shared decorous in the ancient rite
My sterner fathers held idolatrous.
The service over, I was tranced in thought:
Solemn the deepening vaults, and most to me,
Fresh from the fragile realm of deal and paint,
Or brick mock-pious with a marble front;
Solemn the lift of high-embowered roof,
The clustered stems that spread in boughs disleaved,
Through which the organ blew a dream of storm,—
Though not more potent to sublime with awe
And shut the heart up in tranquillity,
Than aisles to me familiar that o'erarch
The conscious silences of brooding woods,
Centurial shadows, cloisters of the elk:
Yet here was sense of undefined regret,
Irreparable loss, uncertain what:
Was all this grandeur but anachronism,—
A shell divorced of its informing life,
Where the priest housed him like a hermit-crab,
An alien to that faith of elder days
That gathered round it this fair shape of stone?
Is old Religion but a spectre now,
Haunting the solitude of darkened minds,
Mocked out of memory by the sceptic day?
Is there no corner safe from peeping Doubt,
Since Gutenberg made thought cosmopolite
And stretched electric threads from mind to mind?
Nay, did Faith build this wonder? or did Fear,
That makes a fetish and misnames it God
(Blockish or metaphysic, matters not),
Contrive this coop to shut its tyrant in,
Appeased with playthings, that he might not harm?

I turned and saw a beldame on her knees;
With eyes astray, she told mechanic beads
Before some shrine of saintly womanhood,
Bribed intercessor with the far-off Judge:

Such my first thought, by kindlier soon rebuked,
Pleading for whatsoever touches life
With upward impulse: be He nowhere else,
God is in all that liberates and lifts,
In all that humbles, sweetens, and consoles:
Blessëd the natures shored on every side
With landmarks of hereditary thought!
Thrice happy they that wander not lifelong
Beyond near succor of the household faith,
The guarded fold that shelters, not confines!
Their steps find patience in familiar paths,
Printed with hope by loved feet gone before
Of parent, child, or lover, glorified
By simple magic of dividing Time.
My lids were moistened as the woman knelt,
And—was it will, or some vibration faint
Of sacred Nature, deeper than the will?—
My heart occultly felt itself in hers,
Through mutual intercession gently leagued.

Or was it not mere sympathy of brain?
A sweetness intellectually conceived
In simpler creeds to me impossible?
A juggle of that pity for ourselves
In others, which puts on such pretty masks
And snares self-love with bait of charity?
Something of all it might be, or of none:
Yet for a moment I was snatched away
And had the evidence of things not seen;
For one rapt moment; then it all came back,
This age that blots out life with question-marks,
This nineteenth century with its knife and glass
That make thought physical, and thrust far off
The Heaven, so neighborly with man of old,
To voids sparse-sown with alienated stars.

'Tis irrecoverable, that ancient faith,
Homely and wholesome, suited to the time,
With rod or candy for child-minded men:
No theologic tube, with lens on lens
Of syllogism transparent, brings it near,—
At best resolving some new nebula,
Or blurring some fixed-star of hope to mist.
Science was Faith once; Faith were Science now,
Would she but lay her bow and arrows by
And arm her with the weapons of the time.
Nothing that keeps thought out is safe from thought.
For there's no virgin-fort but self-respect,
And Truth defensive hath lost hold on God.
Shall we treat Him as if He were a child
That knew not His own purpose? nor dare trust
The Rock of Ages to their chemic tests,
Lest some day the all-sustaining base divine
Should fail from under us, dissolved in gas?
The armëd eye that with a glance discerns
In a dry blood-speck between ox and man,
Stares helpless at this miracle called life,
This shaping potency behind the egg,
This circulation swift of deity,
Where suns and systems inconspicuous float
As the poor blood-disks in our mortal veins.
Each age must worship its own thought of God,
More or less earthy, clarifying still
With subsidence continuous of the dregs;
Nor saint nor sage could fix immutably
The fluent image of the unstable Best,
Still changing in their very hands that wrought:
Today's eternal truth Tomorrow proved
Frail as frost-landscapes on a window-pane.
Meanwhile Thou smiledst, inaccessible,
At Thought's own substance made a cage for Thought,
And Truth locked fast with her own master-key;
Nor didst Thou reck what image man might make
Of his own shadow on the flowing world;
The climbing instinct was enough for Thee.
Or wast Thou, then, on ebbing tide that left
Strewn with dead miracle those eldest shores,
For men to dry, and dryly lecture on,
Thyself thenceforth incapable of flood?
Idle who hopes with prophets to be snatched
By virtue in their mantles left below;
Shall the soul live on other men's report,
Herself a pleasing fable of herself?
Man cannot be God's outlaw if he would,
Nor so abscond him in the caves of sense
But Nature still shall search some crevice out
With messages of splendor from that Source
Which, dive he, soar he, baffles still and lures.
This life were brutish did we not sometimes
Have intimation clear of wider scope,
Hints of occasion infinite, to keep
The soul alert with noble discontent

And onward yearnings of unstilled desire;
Fruitless, except we now and then divined
A mystery of Purpose, gleaming through
The secular confusions of the world,
Whose will we darkly accomplish, doing ours.
No man can think nor in himself perceive,
Sometimes at waking, in the street sometimes,
Or on the hillside, always unforewarned,
A grace of being, finer than himself,
That beckons and is gone,—a larger life
Upon his own impinging, with swift glimpse
Of spacious circles luminous with mind,
To which the ethereal substance of his own
Seems but gross cloud to make that visible,
Touched to a sudden glory round the edge.
Who that hath known these visitations fleet
Would strive to make them trite and ritual?
I, that still pray at morning and at eve,
Loving those roots that feed us from the past,
And prizing more than Plato things I learned
At that best academe, a mother's knee,
Thrice in my life perhaps have truly prayed,
Thrice, stirred below my conscious self, have felt
That perfect disenthralment which is God;
Nor know I which to hold worst enemy,—
Him who on speculation's windy waste
Would turn me loose, stript of the raiment warm
By Faith contrived against our nakedness,
Or him who, cruel-kind, would fain obscure,
With painted saints and paraphrase of God,
The soul's east-window of divine surprise.
Where others worship I but look and long;
For, though not recreant to my fathers' faith,
Its forms to me are weariness, and most
That drony vacuum of compulsory prayer,
Still pumping phrases for the Ineffable,
Though all the valves of memory gasp and wheeze.
Words that have drawn transcendent meanings up
From the best passion of all bygone time,
Steeped through with tears of triumph and remorse,
Sweet with all sainthood, cleansed in martyr-fires,
Can they, so consecrate and so inspired,
By repetition wane to vexing wind?
Alas! we cannot draw habitual breath
In the thin air of life's supremer heights,
We cannot make each meal a sacrament,
Nor with our tailors be disbodied souls,—
We men, too conscious of earth's comedy,
Who see two sides, with our posed selves debate,
And only for great stakes can be sublime!
Let us be thankful when, as I do here,
We can read Bethel on a pile of stones,
And, seeing where God *has* been, trust in Him.

Brave Peter Fischer there in Nuremberg,
Moulding Saint Sebald's miracles in bronze,
Put saint and stander-by in that quaint garb
Familiar to him in his daily walk,
Not doubting God could grant a miracle
Then and in Nuremberg, if so He would;
But never artist for three hundred years
Hath dared the contradiction ludicrous
Of supernatural in modern clothes.
Perhaps the deeper faith that is to come
Will see God rather in the strenuous doubt,
Than in the creed held as an infant's hand
Holds purposeless whatso is placed therein.

Say it is drift, not progress, none the less,
With the old sextant of the fathers' creed,
We shape our courses by new-risen stars,
And, still lip-loyal to what once was truth,
Smuggle new meanings under ancient names,
Unconscious perverts of the Jesuit, Time.
Change is the mask that all Continuance wears
To keep us youngsters harmlessly amused;
Meanwhile, some ailing or more watchful child,
Sitting apart, sees the old eyes gleam out,
Stern, and yet soft with humorous pity too.
Whilere, men burnt men for a doubtful point,
As if the mind were quenchable with fire,
And Faith danced round them with her war-paint on,
Devoutly savage as an Iroquois;
Now Calvin and Servetus at one board
Snuff in grave sympathy a milder roast,
And o'er their claret settle Comte unread.
Fagot and stake were desperately sincere:
Our cooler martyrdoms are done in types;
And flames that shine in controversial eyes
Burn out no brains but his who kindles them.
This is no age to get cathedrals built:
Did God, then, wait for one in Bethlehem?

Worst is not yet: lo, where his coming looms,
Of Earth's anarchic children latest born,
Democracy, a Titan who hath learned
To laugh at Jove's old-fashioned thunder-bolts,—
Could he not also forge them, if he would?
He, better skilled, with solvents merciless,
Loosened in air and borne on every wind,
Saps unperceived: the calm Olympian height
Of ancient order feels its bases yield,
And pale gods glance for help to gods as pale.
What will be left of good or worshipful,
Of spiritual secrets, mysteries,
Of fair Religion's guarded heritage,
Heirlooms of soul, passed downward unprofaned
From eldest Ind? This Western giant coarse,
Scorning refinements which he lacks himself,
Loves not nor heeds the ancestral hierarchies,
Each rank dependent on the next above
In orderly gradation fixed as fate.
King by mere manhood, nor allowing aught
Of holier unction than the sweat of toil;
In his own strength sufficient; called to solve,
On the rough edges of society,
Problems long sacred to the choicer few,
And improvise what elsewhere men receive
As gifts of Deity; tough foundling reared
Where every man's his own Melchisedek,
How make him reverent of a King of kings?
Or Judge self-made, executor of laws
By him not first discussed and voted on?
For him no tree of knowledge is forbid,
Or sweeter if forbid. How save the ark,
Or holy of holies, unprofaned a day
From his unscrupulous curiosity
That handles everything as if to buy,
Tossing aside what fabrics delicate
Suit not the rough-and-tumble of his ways?
What hope for those fine-nerved humanities
That made earth gracious once with gentler arts,
Now the rude hands have caught the trick of thought
And claim an equal suffrage with the brain?

The born disciple of an elder time,
(To me sufficient, friendlier than the new,)
Who in my blood feel motions of the Past,
I thank benignant Nature most for this,—
A force of sympathy, or call it lack
Of character firm-planted, loosing me
From the pent chamber of habitual self
To dwell enlarged in alien modes of thought,
Haply distasteful, wholesomer for that,
And through imagination to possess,
As they were mine, the lives of other men.
This growth original of virgin soil,
By fascination felt in opposites,
Pleases and shocks, entices and perturbs.
In this brown-fisted rough, this shirt-sleeved Cid,
This backwoods Charlemagne of empires new,
Whose blundering heel instinctively finds out
The goutier foot of speechless dignities,
Who, meeting Cæsar's self, would slap his back,
Call him "Old Horse," and challenge to a drink,
My lungs draw braver air, my breast dilates
With ampler manhood, and I front both worlds,
Of sense and spirit, as my natural fiefs,
To shape and then reshape them as I will.
It was the first man's charter; why not mine?
How forfeit? when deposed in other hands?

Thou shudder'st, Ovid? Dost in him forebode
A new avatar of the large-limbed Goth,
To break, or seem to break, tradition's clew,
And chase to dreamland back thy gods dethroned?
I think man's soul dwells nearer to the east,
Nearer to morning's fountains than the sun;
Herself the source whence all tradition sprang,
Herself at once both labyrinth and clew.
The miracle fades out of history,
But faith and wonder and the primal earth
Are born into the world with every child.
Shall this self-maker with the prying eyes,
This creature disenchanted of respect
By the New World's new fiend, Publicity,
Whose testing thumb leaves everywhere its smutch,
Not one day feel within himself the need
Of loyalty to better than himself,
That shall ennoble him with the upward look?
Shall he not catch the Voice that wanders earth,
With spiritual summons, dreamed or heard,
As sometimes, just ere sleep seals up the sense,

We hear our mother call from deeps of Time,
And, waking, find it vision,—none the less
The benediction bides, old skies return,
And that unreal thing, pre-eminent,
Makes air and dream of all we see and feel?
Shall he divine no strength unmade of votes,
Inward, impregnable, found soon as sought,
Not cognizable of sense, o'er sense supreme?
His holy places may not be of stone,
Nor made with hands, yet fairer far than aught
By artist feigned or pious ardor reared,
Fit altars for who guards inviolate
God's chosen seat, the sacred form of man.
Doubtless his church will be no hospital
For superannuate forms and mumping shams,
No parlor where men issue policies
Of life-assurance on the Eternal Mind,
Nor his religion but an ambulance
To fetch life's wounded and malingerers in,
Scorned by the strong; yet he, unconscious heir
To the influence sweet of Athens and of Rome,
And old Judæa's gift of secret fire,
Spite of himself shall surely learn to know
And worship some ideal of himself,
Some divine thing, large-hearted, brotherly,
Not nice in trifles, a soft creditor,
Pleased with his world, and hating only cant.
And, if his Church be doubtful, it is sure
That, in a world, made for whatever else,
Not made for mere enjoyment, in a world
Of toil but half-requited, or, at best,
Paid in some futile currency of breath,
A world of incompleteness, sorrow swift
And consolation laggard, whatsoe'er
The form of building or the creed professed,
The Cross, bold type of shame to homage turned,
Of an unfinished life that sways the world,
Shall tower as sovereign emblem over all.

The kobold Thought moves with us when we shift
Our dwelling to escape him; perched aloft
On the first load of household-stuff he went;
For, where the mind goes, goes old furniture.
I, who to Chartres came to feed my eye
And give to Fancy one clear holiday,
Scarce saw the minster for the thoughts it stirred
Buzzing o'er past and future with vain quest.
Here once there stood a homely wooden church,
Which slow devotion nobly changed for this
That echoes vaguely to my modern steps.
By suffrage universal it was built,
As practised then, for all the country came
From far as Rouen, to give votes for God,
Each vote a block of stone securely laid
Obedient to the master's deep-mused plan.
Will what our ballots rear, responsible
To no grave forethought, stand so long as this?
Delight like this the eye of after days
Brightening with pride that here, at least, were men
Who meant and did the noblest thing they knew?
Can our religion cope with deeds like this?
We, too, build Gothic contract-shams, because
Our deacons have discovered that it pays,
And pews sell better under vaulted roofs
Of plaster painted like an Indian squaw.
Shall not that Western Goth, of whom we spoke,
So fiercely practical, so keen of eye,
Find out, some day, that nothing pays but God,
Served whether on the smoke-shut battle-field,
In work obscure done honestly, or vote
For truth unpopular, or faith maintained
To ruinous convictions, or good deeds
Wrought for good's sake, mindless of heaven or hell?
Shall he not learn that all prosperity,
Whose bases stretch not deeper than the sense,
Is but a trick of this world's atmosphere,
A desert-born mirage of spire and dome,
Or find too late, the Past's long lesson missed,
That dust the prophets shake from off their feet
Grows heavy to drag down both tower and wall?
I know not; but, sustained by sure belief
That man still rises level with the height
Of noblest opportunities, or makes
Such, if the time supply not, I can wait.
I gaze round on the windows, pride of France,
Each the bright gift of some mechanic guild
Who loved their city and thought gold well spent
To make her beautiful with piety;

I pause, transfigured by some stripe of bloom,
And my mind throngs with shining auguries,
Circle on circle, bright as seraphim,
With golden trumpets, silent, that await
The signal to blow news of good to men.

Then the revulsion came that always comes
After these dizzy elations of the mind:
And with a passionate pang of doubt I cried,
"O mountain-born, sweet with snow-filtered air
From uncontaminate wells of ether drawn
And never-broken secrecies of sky,
Freedom, with anguish won, misprized till lost,
They keep thee not who from thy sacred eyes
Catch the consuming lust of sensual good
And the brute's license of unfettered will.
Far from the popular shout and venal breath
Of Cleon blowing the mob's baser mind
To bubbles of wind-piloted conceit,
Thou shrinkest, gathering up thy skirts, to hide
In fortresses of solitary thought
And private virtue strong in self-restraint.
Must we too forfeit thee misunderstood,
Content with names, nor inly wise to know
That best things perish of their own excess,
And quality o'er-driven becomes defect?
Nay, is it thou indeed that we have glimpsed,
Or rather such illusion as of old
Through Athens glided menadlike and Rome,
A shape of vapor, mother of vain dreams
And mutinous traditions, specious plea
Of the glaived tyrant and long-memoried priest?"

I walked forth saddened; for all thought is sad,
And leaves a bitterish savor in the brain,
Tonic, it may be, not delectable,
And turned, reluctant, for a parting look
At those old weather-pitted images
Of bygone struggle, now so sternly calm.
About their shoulders sparrows had built nests,
And fluttered, chirping, from gray perch to perch,
Now on a mitre poising, now a crown,
Irreverently happy. While I thought
How confident they were, what careless hearts
Flew on those lightsome wings and shared the sun,
A larger shadow crossed; and looking up,
I saw where, nesting in the hoary towers,
The sparrow-hawk slid forth on noiseless air,
With sidelong head that watched the joy below,
Grim Norman baron o'er this clan of Kelts.
Enduring Nature, force conservative,
Indifferent to our noisy whims! Men prate
Of all heads to an equal grade cashiered
On level with the dullest, and expect
(Sick of no worse distemper than themselves)
A wondrous cure-all in equality;
They reason that Tomorrow must be wise
Because Today was not, nor Yesterday,
As if good days were shapen of themselves,
Not of the very lifeblood of men's souls;
Meanwhile, long-suffering, imperturbable,
Thou quietly complet'st thy syllogism,
And from the premise sparrow here below
Draw'st sure conclusion of the hawk above,
Pleased with the soft-billed songster, pleased no less
With the fierce beak of natures aquiline.

Thou beautiful Old Time, now hid away
In the Past's valley of Avilion,
Haply, like Arthur, till thy wound be healed,
Then to reclaim the sword and crown again!
Thrice beautiful to us; perchance less fair
To who possessed thee, as a mountain seems
To dwellers round its bases but a heap
Of barren obstacle that lairs the storm
And the avalanche's silent bolt holds back
Leashed with a hair,—meanwhile some far-off clown,
Hereditary delver of the plain,
Sees it an unmoved vision of repose,
Nest of the morning, and conjectures there
The dance of streams to idle shepherds' pipes,
And fairer habitations softly hung
On breezy slopes, or hid in valleys cool,
For happier men. No mortal ever dreams
That the scant isthmus he encamps upon
Between two oceans, one, the Stormy, passed,
And one, the Peaceful, yet to venture on,
Has been that future whereto prophets yearned
For the fulfilment of Earth's cheated hope,
Shall be that past which nerveless poets moan
As the lost opportunity of song.

O Power, more near my life than life itself
(Or what seems life to us in sense immured),
Even as the roots, shut in the darksome earth,
Share in the tree-top's joyance, and conceive
Of sunshine and wide air and wingëd things
By sympathy of nature, so do I
Have evidence of Thee so far above,
Yet in and of me! Rather Thou the root
Invisibly sustaining, hid in light,
Not darkness, or in darkness made by us.
If sometimes I must hear good men debate
Of other witness of Thyself than Thou,
As if there needed any help of ours
To nurse Thy flickering life, that else must
    cease,
Blown out, as 'twere a candle, by men's breath,
My soul shall not be taken in their snare,
To change her inward surety for their doubt
Muffled from sight in formal robes of proof:
While she can only feel herself through Thee,
I fear not Thy withdrawal; more I fear,
Seeing, to know Thee not, hoodwinked with
    dreams
Of signs and wonders, while, unnoticed,
    Thou,
Walking Thy garden still, commun'st with
    men,
Missed in the commonplace of miracle.

1869 1869

AGASSIZ

Come
Dicesti *egli ebbe?* non viv' egli ancora?
Non fiere gli occhi suoi lo dolce lome?

I

1

The electric nerve, whose instantaneous thrill
Makes next-door gossips of the antipodes,
Confutes poor Hope's last fallacy of ease,—
The distance that divided her from ill:
Earth sentient seems again as when of old
    The horny foot of Pan
Stamped, and the conscious horror ran
Beneath men's feet through all her fibres cold:
Space's blue walls are mined; we feel the
    throe
From underground of our night-mantled foe:
    The flame-winged feet
Of Trade's new Mercury, that dry-shod run
Through briny abysses dreamless of the sun,
    Are mercilessly fleet,
  And at a bound annihilate
Ocean's prerogative of short reprieve;
    Surely ill news might wait,
And man be patient of delay to grieve:
    Letters have sympathies
  And tell-tale faces that reveal,
  To senses finer than the eyes,
Their errand's purport ere we break the seal;
They wind a sorrow round with circumstance
To stay its feet, nor all unwarned displace
The veil that darkened from our sidelong
    glance
    The inexorable face:
  But now Fate stuns as with a mace;
The savage of the skies, that men have caught
  And some scant use of language taught,
    Tells only what he must,—
The steel-cold fact in one laconic thrust.

2

So thought I, as, with vague, mechanic eyes,
I scanned the festering news we half despise
    Yet scramble for no less,
And read of public scandal, private fraud,
Crime flaunting scot-free while the mob ap-
    plaud,
Office made vile to bribe unworthiness,
  And all the unwholesome mess
The Land of Honest Abraham serves of late
  To teach the Old World how to wait,
    When suddenly,
As happens if the brain, from overweight
    Of blood, infect the eye,
Three tiny words grew lurid as I read,
And reeled commingling: *Agassiz is dead.*
As when, beneath the street's familiar jar,
An earthquake's alien omen rumbles far,
Men listen and forebode, I hung my head,
  And strove the present to recall,
As if the blow that stunned were yet to fall.

3

  Uprooted is our mountain oak,
That promised long security of shade
And brooding-place for many a wingèd
    thought;
  Not by Time's softly-cadenced stroke
With pauses of relenting pity stayed,
But ere a root seemed sapt, a bough decayed,

From sudden ambush by the whirlwind caught
And in his broad maturity betrayed!

4

Well might I, as of old, appeal to you,
O mountains, woods, and streams,
To help us mourn him, for ye loved him too;
But simpler moods befit our modern themes,
And no less perfect birth of nature can,
Though they yearn tow'rd him, sympathize with man,
Save as dumb fellow-prisoners through a wall;
Answer ye rather to my call,
Strong poets of a more unconscious day,
When Nature spake nor sought nice reasons why,
Too much for softer arts forgotten since
That teach our forthright tongue to lisp and mince,
And drown in music the heart's bitter cry!
Lead me some steps in your directer way,
Teach me those words that strike a solid root
Within the ears of men;
Ye chiefly, virile both to think and feel,
Deep-chested Chapman and firm-footed Ben,
For he was masculine from head to heel.
Nay, let himself stand undiminished by
With those clear parts of him that will not die.
Himself from out the recent dark I claim
To hear, and, if I flatter him, to blame;
To show himself, as still I seem to see,
A mortal, built upon the antique plan,
Brimful of lusty blood as ever ran,
And taking life as simply as a tree!
To claim my foiled good-by let him appear,
Large-limbed and human as I saw him near,
Loosed from the stiffening uniform of fame:
And let me treat him largely: I should fear
(If with too prying lens I chanced to err,
Mistaking catalogue for character,)
His wise forefinger raised in smiling blame.
Nor would I scant him with judicial breath
And turn mere critic in an epitaph;
I choose the wheat, incurious of the chaff
That swells fame living, chokes it after death,
And would but memorize the shining half
Of his large nature that was turned to me:
Fain had I joined with those that honored him
With eyes that darkened because his were dim,
And now been silent: but it might not be.

II

I

In some the genius is a thing apart,
A pillared hermit of the brain,
Hoarding with incommunicable art
Its intellectual gain;
Man's web of circumstance and fate
They from their perch of self observe,
Indifferent as the figures on a slate
Are to the planet's sun-swung curve
Whose bright returns they calculate;
Their nice adjustment, part to part,
Were shaken from its serviceable mood
By unpremeditated stirs of heart
Or jar of human neighborhood:
Some find their natural selves, and only then,
In furloughs of divine escape from men,
And when, by that brief ecstasy left bare,
Driven by some instinct of desire,
They wander worldward, 'tis to blink and stare,
Like wild things of the wood about a fire,
Dazed by the social glow they cannot share;
His nature brooked no lonely lair,
But basked and bourgeoned in copartnery,
Companionship, and open-windowed glee:
He knew, for he had tried,
Those speculative heights that lure
The unpractised foot, impatient of a guide,
Tow'rd ether too attenuately pure
For sweet unconscious breath, though dear to pride,
But better loved the foothold sure
Of paths that wind by old abodes of men
Who hope at last the churchyard's peace secure,
And follow time-worn rules, that them suffice,
Learned from their sires, traditionally wise,
Careful of honest custom's how and when;
His mind, too brave to look on Truth askance,
No more those habitudes of faith could share,
But, tinged with sweetness of the old Swiss manse,
Lingered around them still and fain would spare.
Patient to spy a sullen egg for weeks,
The enigma of creation to surprise,
His truer instinct sought the life that speaks

Without a mystery from kindly eyes;
In no self-spun cocoon of prudence wound,
He by the touch of men was best inspired,
And caught his native greatness at rebound
From generosities itself had fired;
Then how the heat through every fibre ran,
Felt in the gathering presence of the man,
While the apt word and gesture came un-
bid!
Virtues and faults it to one metal wrought,
Fined all his blood to thought,
And ran the molten man in all he said or
did.
All Tully's rules and all Quintilian's too
He by the light of listening faces knew,
And his rapt audience all unconscious lent
Their own roused force to make him elo-
quent;
Persuasion fondled in his look and tone;
Our speech (with strangers prudish) he could
bring
To find new charm in accents not her own;
Her coy constraints and icy hindrances
Melted upon his lips to natural ease,
As a brook's fetters swell the dance of spring.
Nor yet all sweetness: not in vain he wore,
Nor in the sheath of ceremony, controlled
By velvet courtesy or caution cold,
That sword of honest anger prized of old,
But, with two-handed wrath,
If baseness or pretension crossed his path,
Struck once nor needed to strike more.

2

His magic was not far to seek,—
He was so human! Whether strong or weak,
Far from his kind he neither sank nor soared,
But sate an equal guest at every board:
No beggar ever felt him condescend,
No prince presume; for still himself he bare
At manhood's simple level, and where'er
He met a stranger, there he left a friend.
How large an aspect! nobly unsevere,
With freshness round him of Olympian cheer,
Like visits of those earthly gods he came;
His look, wherever its good-fortune fell,
Doubled the feast without a miracle,
And on the hearthstone danced a happier
flame;
Philemon's crabbed vintage grew benign;
Amphitryon's gold-juice humanized to wine.

III

1

The garrulous memories
Gather again from all their far-flown nooks,
Singly at first, and then by twos and threes,
Then in a throng innumerable, as the rooks
Thicken their twilight files
Tow'rd Tintern's gray repose of roofless aisles:
Once more I see him at the table's head
When Saturday her monthly banquet spread
To scholars, poets, wits,
All choice, some famous, loving things, not
names,
And so without a twinge at others' fames;
Such company as wisest moods befits,
Yet with no pedant blindness to the worth
Of undeliberate mirth,
Natures benignly mixed of air and earth,
Now with the stars and now with equal zest
Tracing the eccentric orbit of a jest.

2

I see in vision the warm-lighted hall,
The living and the dead I see again,
And but my chair is empty; 'mid them all
'Tis I that seem the dead: they all remain
Immortal, changeless creatures of the brain:
Wellnigh I doubt which world is real most,
Of sense or spirit, to the truly sane;
In this abstraction it were light to deem
Myself the figment of some stronger dream;
They are the real things, and I the ghost
That glide unhindered through the solid door,
Vainly for recognition seek from chair to
chair,
And strive to speak and am but futile air,
As truly most of us are little more.

3

Him most I see whom we most dearly miss,
The latest parted thence,
His features poised in genial armistice
And armed neutrality of self-defence
Beneath the forehead's walled preëminence,
While Tyro, plucking facts with careless
reach,
Settles off-hand our human how and whence;
The long-trained veteran scarcely wincing
hears
The infallible strategy of volunteers

Making through Nature's walls its easy breach,
And seems to learn where he alone could teach.
Ample and ruddy, the board's end he fills
As he our fireside were, our light and heat,
Centre where minds diverse and various skills
Find their warm nook and stretch unhampered feet;
I see the firm benignity of face,
Wide-smiling champaign, without tameness sweet,
The mass Teutonic toned to Gallic grace,
The eyes whose sunshine runs before the lips
While Holmes's rockets curve their long ellipse,
And burst in seeds of fire that burst again
To drop in scintillating rain.

4

There too the face half-rustic, half-divine,
Self-poised, sagacious, freaked with humor fine,
Of him who taught us not to mow and mope
About our fancied selves, but seek our scope
In Nature's world and Man's, nor fade to hollow trope,
Content with our New World and timely bold
To challenge the o'ermastery of the Old;
Listening with eyes averse I see him sit
Pricked with the cider of the Judge's wit
(Ripe-hearted homebrew, fresh and fresh again),
While the wise nose's firm-built aquiline
Curves sharper to restrain
The merriment whose most unruly moods
Pass not the dumb laugh learned in listening woods
Of silence-shedding pine:
Hard by is he whose art's consoling spell
Hath given both worlds a whiff of asphodel,
His look still vernal 'mid the wintry ring
Of petals that remember, not foretell,
The paler primrose of a second spring.

5

And more there are: but other forms arise
And seen as clear, albeit with dimmer eyes:
First he from sympathy still held apart
By shrinking over-eagerness of heart,
Cloud charged with searching fire, whose shadow's sweep
Heightened mean things with sense of brooding ill,
And steeped in doom familiar field and hill,—
New England's poet, soul reserved and deep,
November nature with a name of May,
Whom high o'er Concord plains we laid to sleep,
While the orchards mocked us in their white array
And building robins wondered at our tears,
Snatched in his prime, the shape august
That should have stood unbent 'neath fourscore years,
The noble head, the eyes of furtive trust,
All gone to speechless dust.
And he our passing guest,
Shy nature, too, and stung with life's unrest,
Whom we too briefly had but could not hold,
Who brought ripe Oxford's culture to our board,
The Past's incalculable hoard,
Mellowed by scutcheoned panes in cloisters old,
Seclusions, ivy-hushed, and pavements sweet
With immemorial lisp of musing feet;
Young head time-tonsured smoother than a friar's,
Boy face, but grave with answerless desires,
Poet in all that poets have of best,
But foiled with riddles dark and cloudy aims,
Who now hath found sure rest,
Not by still Isis or historic Thames,
Nor by the Charles he tried to love with me,
But, not misplaced, by Arno's hallowed brim,
Nor scorned by Santa Croce's neighboring fames,
Haply not mindless, wheresoe'er he be,
Of violets that today I scattered over him.
He, too, is there,
After the good centurion fitly named,
Whom learning dulled not, nor convention tamed,

Shaking with burly mirth his hyacinthine hair,
Our hearty Grecian of Homeric ways,
Still found the surer friend where least he hoped the praise.

6

Yea truly, as the sallowing years
Fall from us faster, like frost-loosened leaves
Pushed by the misty touch of shortening days,
And that unwakened winter nears,
'Tis the void chair our surest guest receives,
'Tis lips long cold that give the warmest kiss,
'Tis the lost voice comes oftenest to our ears;
We count our rosary by the beads we miss:
To me, at least, it seemeth so,
An exile in the land once found divine,
While my starved fire burns low,
And homeless winds at the loose casement whine
Shrill ditties of the snow-roofed Apennine.

IV

1

Now forth into the darkness all are gone,
But memory, still unsated, follows on,
Retracing step by step our homeward walk,
With many a laugh among our serious talk,
Across the bridge where, on the dimpling tide,
The long red streamers from the windows glide,
Or the dim western moon
Rocks her skiff's image on the broad lagoon,
And Boston shows a soft Venetian side
In that Arcadian light when roof and tree,
Hard prose by daylight, dream in Italy;
Or haply in the sky's cold chambers wide
Shivered the winter stars, while all below,
As if an end were come of human ill,
The world was wrapt in innocence of snow
And the cast-iron bay was blind and still;
These were our poetry; in him perhaps
Science had barred the gate that lets in dream,
And he would rather count the perch and bream
Than with the current's idle fancy lapse;
And yet he had the poet's open eye
That takes a frank delight in all it sees,
Nor was earth voiceless, nor the mystic sky,
To him the life-long friend of fields and trees:
Then came the prose of the suburban street,
Its silence deepened by our echoing feet,
And converse such as rambling hazard finds;
Then he who many cities knew and many minds,
And men once world-noised, now mere Ossian forms
Of misty memory, bade them live anew
As when they shared earth's manifold delight,
In shape, in gait, in voice, in gesture true,
And, with an accent heightening as he warms,
Would stop forgetful of the shortening night,
Drop my confining arm, and pour profuse
Much worldly wisdom kept for others' use,
Not for his own, for he was rash and free,
His purse or knowledge all men's, like the sea.
Still can I hear his voice's shrilling might
(With pauses broken, while the fitful spark
He blew more hotly rounded on the dark
To hint his features with a Rembrandt light)
Call Oken back, or Humboldt, or Lamarck,
Or Cuvier's taller shade, and many more
Whom he had seen, or knew from others' sight,
And make them men to me as ne'er before:
Not seldom, as the undeadened fibre stirred
Of noble friendships knit beyond the sea,
German or French thrust by the lagging word,
For a good leash of mother-tongues had he.
At last, arrived at where our paths divide,
"Good night!" and, ere the distance grew too wide,
"Good night!" again; and now with cheated ear
I half hear his who mine shall never hear.

2

Sometimes it seemed as if New England air
For his large lungs too parsimonious were,
As if those empty rooms of dogma drear
Where the ghost shivers of a faith austere
Counting the horns o'er of the Beast,
Still scaring those whose faith in it is least,
As if those snaps o' th' moral atmosphere
That sharpen all the needles of the East,
Had been to him like death,
Accustomed to draw Europe's freer breath
In a more stable element;

Nay, even our landscape, half the year morose,
Our practical horizon grimly pent,
Our air, sincere of ceremonious haze,
Forcing hard outlines mercilessly close,
Our social monotone of level days,
  Might make our best seem banishment;
    But it was nothing so;
  Haply his instinct might divine,
Beneath our drift of puritanic snow,
  The marvel sensitive and fine
Of sanguinaria over-rash to blow
And trust its shyness to an air malign;
Well might he prize truth's warranty and pledge
In the grim outcrop of our granite edge,
Or Hebrew fervor flashing forth at need
In the gaunt sons of Calvin's iron breed,
As prompt to give as skilled to win and keep;
But, though such intuitions might not cheer,
Yet life was good to him, and, there or here,
With that sufficing joy, the day was never cheap;
Thereto his mind was its own ample sphere,
And, like those buildings great that through the year
Carry one temperature, his nature large
Made its own climate, nor could any marge
Traced by convention stay him from his bent:
He had a habitude of mountain air;
He brought wide outlook where he went,
  And could on sunny uplands dwell
Of prospect sweeter than the pastures fair
  High-hung of viny Neufchâtel;
    Nor, surely, did he miss
    Some pale, imaginary bliss
Of earlier sights whose inner landscape still was Swiss.

V

1

I cannot think he wished so soon to die
With all his senses full of eager heat,
And rosy years that stood expectant by
To buckle the winged sandals on their feet,
He that was friends with Earth, and all her sweet
Took with both hands unsparingly:
Truly this life is precious to the root,
And good the feel of grass beneath the foot;
To lie in buttercups and clover-bloom,
  Tenants in common with the bees,
And watch the white clouds drift through gulfs of trees,
Is better than long waiting in the tomb;
Only once more to feel the coming spring
As the birds feel it, when it bids them sing,
  Only once more to see the moon
Through leaf-fringed abbey-arches of the elms
  Curve her mild sickle in the West
Sweet with the breath of hay-cocks, were a boon
Worth any promise of soothsayer realms
Or casual hope of being elsewhere blest;
  To take December by the beard
And crush the creaking snow with springy foot,
While overhead the North's dumb streamers shoot,
Till Winter fawn upon the cheek endeared,
  Then the long evening-ends
  Lingered by cosy chimney-nooks,
With high companionship of books
  Or slippered talk of friends
  And sweet habitual looks,
Is better than to stop the ears with dust:
Too soon the spectre comes to say, "Thou must!"

2

When toil-crooked hands are crost upon the breast,
  They comfort us with sense of rest;
They must be glad to lie forever still;
  Their work is ended with their day;
Another fills their room; 'tis the World's ancient way,
  Whether for good or ill;
But the deft spinners of the brain,
Who love each added day and find it gain,
  Them overtakes the doom
To snap the half-grown flower upon the loom
(Trophy that was to be of life-long pain),
The thread no other skill can ever knit again.
  'Twas so with him, for he was glad to live,

'Twas doubly so, for he left work begun;
Could not this eagerness of Fate forgive
Till all the allotted flax were spun?
It matters not; for, go at night or noon,
A friend, whene'er he dies, has died too soon,
And, once we hear the hopeless *He is dead*,
So far as flesh hath knowledge, all is said.

VI

1

I seem to see the black procession go:
That crawling prose of death too well I know,
The vulgar paraphrase of glorious woe;
I see it wind through that unsightly grove,
Once beautiful, but long defaced
With granite permanence of cockney taste
And all those grim disfigurements we love:
There, then, we leave him: Him? such costly waste
Nature rebels at: and it is not true
Of those most precious parts of him we knew:
Could we be conscious but as dreamers be,
'Twere sweet to leave this shifting life of tents
Sunk in the changeless calm of Deity;
Nay, to be mingled with the elements,
The fellow-servant of creative powers,
Partaker in the solemn year's events,
To share the work of busy-fingered hours,
To be night's silent almoner of dew,
To rise again in plants and breathe and grow,
To stream as tides the ocean caverns through,
Or with the rapture of great winds to blow
About earth's shaken coignes, were not a fate
To leave us all-disconsolate;
Even endless slumber in the sweetening sod
Of charitable earth
That takes out all our mortal stains,
And makes us cleanlier neighbors of the clod,
Methinks were better worth
Than the poor fruit of most men's wakeful pains,
The heart's insatiable ache:
But such was not his faith,
Nor mine: it may be he had trod
Outside the plain old path of *God thus spake*,
But God to him was very God,
And not a visionary wraith
Skulking in murky corners of the mind,
And he was sure to be
Somehow, somewhere, imperishable as He,
Not with His essence mystically combined,
As some high spirits long, but whole and free,
A perfected and conscious Agassiz.
And such I figure him: the wise of old
Welcome and own him of their peaceful fold,
Not truly with the guild enrolled
Of him who seeking inward guessed
Diviner riddles than the rest,
And groping in the darks of thought
Touched the Great Hand and knew it not;
Rather he shares the daily light,
From reason's charier fountains won,
Of his great chief, the slow-paced Stagyrite,
And Cuvier clasps once more his long-lost son.

2

The shape erect is prone: forever stilled
The winning tongue; the forehead's high-piled heap,
A cairn which every science helped to build,
Unvalued will its golden secrets keep:
He knows at last if Life or Death be best:
Wherever he be flown, whatever vest
The being hath put on which lately here
So many-friended was, so full of cheer
To make men feel the Seeker's noble zest,
We have not lost him all; he is not gone
To the dumb herd of them that wholly die;
The beauty of his better self lives on
In minds he touched with fire, in many an eye
He trained to Truth's exact severity;
He was a Teacher: why be grieved for him
Whose living word still stimulates the air?
In endless file shall loving scholars come
The glow of his transmitted touch to share,
And trace his features with an eye less dim
Than ours whose sense familiar wont makes numb.

1874 1874

THREE MEMORIAL POEMS

"Coscienza fusca
O della propria o dell' altrui vergogna
Pur sentirà la tua parola brusca."

If I let fall a word of bitter mirth
When public shames more shameful pardon won,
Some have misjudged me, and my service done,

If small, yet faithful, deemed of little worth:
Through veins that drew their life from Western earth
Two hundred years and more my blood hath run
In no polluted course from sire to son;
And thus was I predestined ere my birth
To love the soil wherewith my fibres own
Instinctive sympathies; yet love it so
As honor would, nor lightly to dethrone
Judgment, the stamp of manhood, nor forego
The son's right to a mother dearer grown
With growing knowledge and more chaste than snow.

ODE

READ AT THE ONE HUNDREDTH ANNIVERSARY OF THE FIGHT AT CONCORD BRIDGE

19TH APRIL, 1875

I

WHO cometh over the hills,
Her garments with morning sweet,
The dance of a thousand rills
Making music before her feet?
Her presence freshens the air;
Sunshine steals light from her face;
The leaden footstep of Care
Leaps to the tune of her pace,
Fairness of all that is fair,
Grace at the heart of all grace,
Sweetener of hut and of hall,
Bringer of life out of naught,
Freedom, oh, fairest of all
The daughters of Time and Thought!

II

She cometh, cometh today:
Hark! hear ye not her tread,
Sending a thrill through your clay,
Under the sod there, ye dead,
Her nurslings and champions?
Do ye not hear, as she comes,
The bay of the deep-mouthed guns,
The gathering rote of the drums?
The bells that called ye to prayer,
How wildly they clamor on her,
Crying, "She cometh! prepare
Her to praise and her to honor,
That a hundred years ago
Scattered here in blood and tears
Potent seeds wherefrom should grow
Gladness for a hundred years!"

III

Tell me, young men, have ye seen
Creature of diviner mien
For true hearts to long and cry for,
Manly hearts to live and die for?
What hath she that others want?
Brows that all endearments haunt,
Eyes that make it sweet to dare,
Smiles that cheer untimely death,
Looks that fortify despair,
Tones more brave than trumpet's breath;
Tell me, maidens, have ye known
Household charm more sweetly rare,
Grace of woman ampler blown,
Modesty more debonair,
Younger heart with wit full grown?
Oh for an hour of my prime,
The pulse of my hotter years,
That I might praise her in rhyme
Would tingle your eyelids to tears,
Our sweetness, our strength, and our star,
Our hope, our joy, and our trust,
Who lifted us out of the dust,
And made us whatever we are!

IV

Whiter than moonshine upon snow
Her raiment is, but round the hem
Crimson stained; and, as to and fro
Her sandals flash, we see on them,
And on her instep veined with blue,
Flecks of crimson, on those fair feet,
High-arched, Diana-like, and fleet,
Fit for no grosser stain than dew:
Oh, call them rather chrisms than stains,
Sacred and from heroic veins!
For, in the glory-guarded pass,
Her haughty and far-shining head
She bowed to shrive Leonidas
With his imperishable dead;
Her, too, Morgarten saw,
Where the Swiss lion fleshed his icy paw;
She followed Cromwell's quenchless star
Where the grim Puritan tread
Shook Marston, Naseby, and Dunbar:
Yea, on her feet are dearer dyes
Yet fresh, not looked on with untearful eyes.

V

Our fathers found her in the woods
Where Nature meditates and broods,
The seeds of unexampled things
Which Time to consummation brings
Through life and death and man's unstable moods;
They met her here, not recognized,
A sylvan huntress clothed in furs,
To whose chaste wants her bow sufficed,
Nor dreamed what destinies were hers:
She taught them bee-like to create
Their simpler forms of Church and State;
She taught them to endue
The past with other functions than it knew,
And turn in channels strange the uncertain stream of Fate;
Better than all, she fenced them in their need
With iron-handed Duty's sternest creed,
'Gainst Self's lean wolf that ravens word and deed.

VI

Why cometh she hither today
To this low village of the plain
Far from the Present's loud highway,
From Trade's cool heart and seething brain?
Why cometh she? She was not far away.
Since the soul touched it, not in vain,
With pathos of immortal gain,
'Tis here her fondest memories stay.
She loves yon pine-bemurmured ridge
Where now our broad-browed poet sleeps,
Dear to both Englands; near him he
Who wore the ring of Canace;
But most her heart to rapture leaps
Where stood that era-parting bridge,
O'er which, with footfall still as dew,
The Old Time passed into the New;
Where, as your stealthy river creeps,
He whispers to his listening weeds
Tales of sublimest homespun deeds.
Here English law and English thought
'Gainst the self-will of England fought;
And here were men (coequal with their fate),
Who did great things, unconscious they were great.
They dreamed not what a die was cast
With that first answering shot; what then?
There was their duty; they were men
Schooled the soul's inward gospel to obey,
Though leading to the lion's den.
They felt the habit-hallowed world give way
Beneath their lives, and on went they,
Unhappy who was last.
When Buttrick gave the word,
That awful idol of the unchallenged Past,
Strong in their love, and in their lineage strong,
Fell crashing: if they heard it not,
Yet the earth heard,
Nor ever hath forgot,
As on from startled throne to throne,
Where Superstition sate or conscious Wrong,
A shudder ran of some dread birth unknown.
Thrice venerable spot!
River more fateful than the Rubicon!
O'er those red planks, to snatch her diadem,
Man's Hope, star-girdled, sprang with them,
And over ways untried the feet of Doom strode on.

VII

Think you these felt no charms
In their gray homesteads and embowered farms?
In household faces waiting at the door
Their evening step should lighten up no more?
In fields their boyish feet had known?
In trees their fathers' hands had set,
And which with them had grown,
Widening each year their leafy coronet?
Felt they no pang of passionate regret
For those unsolid goods that seem so much our own?
These things are dear to every man that lives,
And life prized more for what it lends than gives.
Yea, many a tie, through iteration sweet,
Strove to detain their fatal feet;
And yet the enduring half they chose,
Whose choice decides a man life's slave or king,
The invisible things of God before the seen and known:
Therefore their memory inspiration blows
With echoes gathering on from zone to zone;
For manhood is the one immortal thing
Beneath Time's changeful sky,

And, where it lightened once, from age to age,
Men come to learn, in grateful pilgrimage,
That length of days is knowing when to die.

VIII

What marvellous change of things and men!
She, a world-wandering orphan then,
So mighty now! Those are her streams
That whirl the myriad, myriad wheels
Of all that does, and all that dreams,
Of all that thinks, and all that feels,
Through spaces stretched from sea to sea;
By idle tongues and busy brains,
By who doth right, and who refrains,
Hers are our losses and our gains;
Our maker and our victim she.

IX

Maiden half mortal, half divine,
We triumphed in thy coming; to the brinks
Our hearts were filled with pride's tumultuous wine;
Better today who rather feels than thinks.
Yet will some graver thoughts intrude,
And cares of sterner mood;
They won thee: who shall keep thee? From the deeps
Where discrowned empires o'er their ruins brood,
And many a thwarted hope wrings its weak hands and weeps,
I hear the voice as of a mighty wind
From all heaven's caverns rushing unconfined,
"I, Freedom, dwell with Knowledge: I abide
With men whom dust of faction cannot blind
To the slow tracings of the Eternal Mind;
With men by culture trained and fortified,
Who bitter duty to sweet lusts prefer,
Fearless to counsel and obey.
Conscience my sceptre is, and law my sword,
Not to be drawn in passion or in play,
But terrible to punish and deter;
Implacable as God's word,
Like it, a shepherd's crook to them that blindly err.
Your firm-pulsed sires, my martyrs and my saints,
Offshoots of that one stock whose patient sense
Hath known to mingle flux with permanence,
Rated my chaste denials and restraints
Above the moment's dear-paid paradise:
Beware lest, shifting with Time's gradual creep,
The light that guided shine into your eyes.
The envious Powers of ill nor wink nor sleep:
Be therefore timely wise,
Nor laugh when this one steals, and that one lies,
As if your luck could cheat those sleepless spies,
Till the deaf Fury comes your house to sweep!"
I hear the voice, and unaffrighted bow;
Ye shall not be prophetic now,
Heralds of ill, that darkening fly
Between my vision and the rainbowed sky,
Or on the left your hoarse forebodings croak
From many a blasted bough
On Yggdrasil's storm-sinewed oak,
That once was green, Hope of the West, as thou:
Yet pardon if I tremble while I boast;
For I have loved as those who pardon most.

X

Away, ungrateful doubt, away!
At least she is our own today.
Break into rapture, my song,
Verses, leap forth in the sun,
Bearing the joyance along
Like a train of fire as ye run!
Pause not for choosing of words,
Let them but blossom and sing
Blithe as the orchards and birds
With the new coming of spring!
Dance in your jollity, bells;
Shout, cannon; cease not, ye drums;
Answer, ye hillside and dells;
Bow, all ye people! She comes,
Radiant, calm-fronted, as when
She hallowed that April day.
Stay with us! Yes, thou shalt stay,
Softener and strengthener of men,
Freedom, not won by the vain,
Not to be courted in play,
Not to be kept without pain.
Stay with us! Yes, thou wilt stay,
Handmaid and mistress of all,
Kindler of deed and of thought,
Thou that to hut and to hall

Equal deliverance brought!
Souls of her martyrs, draw near,
Touch our dull lips with your fire,
That we may praise without fear
Her our delight, our desire,
Our faith's inextinguishable star,
Our hope, our remembrance, our trust,
Our present, our past, our to be,
Who will mingle her life with our dust
And makes us deserve to be free!

1875 1875

UNDER THE OLD ELM

POEM READ AT CAMBRIDGE ON THE HUNDREDTH ANNIVERSARY OF WASHINGTON'S TAKING COMMAND OF THE AMERICAN ARMY, 3D JULY, 1775

I

1

WORDS pass as wind, but where great deeds were done
A power abides transfused from sire to son:
The boy feels deeper meanings thrill his ear,
That tingling through his pulse life-long shall run,
With sure impulsion to keep honor clear,
When, pointing down, his father whispers, "Here,
Here, where we stand, stood he, the purely great,
Whose soul no siren passion could unsphere,
Then nameless, now a power and mixed with fate."
Historic town, thou holdest sacred dust,
Once known to men as pious, learnèd, just,
And one memorial pile that dares to last;
But Memory greets with reverential kiss
No spot in all thy circuit sweet as this,
Touched by that modest glory as it past,
O'er which yon elm hath piously displayed
These hundred years its monumental shade.

2

Of our swift passage through this scenery
Of life and death, more durable than we,
What landmark so congenial as a tree
Repeating its green legend every spring,
And, with a yearly ring,
Recording the fair seasons as they flee,
Type of our brief but still-renewed mortality?
We fall as leaves: the immortal trunk remains,
Builded with costly juice of hearts and brains
Gone to the mould now, whither all that be
Vanish returnless, yet are procreant still
In human lives to come of good or ill,
And feed unseen the roots of Destiny.

II

1

Men's monuments, grown old, forget their names
They should eternize, but the place
Where shining souls have passed imbibes a grace
Beyond mere earth; some sweetness of their fames
Leaves in the soil its unextinguished trace,
Pungent, pathetic, sad with nobler aims,
That penetrates our lives and heightens them or shames.
This insubstantial world and fleet
Seems solid for a moment when we stand
On dust ennobled by heroic feet
Once mighty to sustain a tottering land,
And mighty still such burthen to upbear,
Nor doomed to tread the path of things that merely were:
Our sense, refined with virtue of the spot,
Across the mists of Lethe's sleepy stream
Recalls him, the sole chief without a blot,
No more a pallid image and a dream,
But as he dwelt with men decorously supreme.

2

Our grosser minds need this terrestrial hint
To raise long-buried days from tombs of print:
"Here stood he," softly we repeat,
And lo, the statue shrined and still
In that gray minster-front we call the Past,
Feels in its frozen veins our pulses thrill,
Breathes living air and mocks at Death's deceit.
It warms, it stirs, comes down to us at last,
Its features human with familiar light,
A man, beyond the historian's art to kill,
Or sculptor's to efface with patient chisel-blight.

3

Sure the dumb earth hath memory, nor for naught
Was Fancy given, on whose enchanted loom
Present and Past commingle, fruit and bloom
Of one fair bough, inseparably wrought
Into the seamless tapestry of thought.
So charmed, with undeluded eye we see
In history's fragmentary tale
Bright clues of continuity,
Learn that high natures over Time prevail,
And feel ourselves a link in that entail
That binds all ages past with all that are to be.

III

1

Beneath our consecrated elm
A century ago he stood,
Famed vaguely for that old fight in the wood
Whose red surge sought, but could not overwhelm
The life foredoomed to wield our rough-hewn helm:—
From colleges, where now the gown
To arms had yielded, from the town,
Our rude self-summoned levies flocked to see
The new-come chiefs and wonder which was he.
No need to question long; close-lipped and tall,
Long trained in murder-brooding forests lone
To bridle others' clamors and his own,
Firmly erect, he towered above them all,
The incarnate discipline that was to free
With iron curb that armed democracy.

2

A motley rout was that which came to stare,
In raiment tanned by years of sun and storm,
Of every shape that was not uniform,
Dotted with regimentals here and there;
An army all of captains, used to pray
And stiff in fight, but serious drill's despair,
Skilled to debate their orders, not obey;
Deacons were there, selectmen, men of note
In half-tamed hamlets ambushed round with woods,
Ready to settle Freewill by a vote,
But largely liberal to its private moods;
Prompt to assert by manners, voice, or pen,
Or ruder arms, their rights as Englishmen,
Nor much fastidious as to how and when:
Yet seasoned stuff and fittest to create
A thought-staid army or a lasting state:
Haughty they said he was, at first; severe;
But owned, as all men own, the steady hand
Upon the bridle, patient to command,
Prized, as all prize, the justice pure from fear,
And learned to honor first, then love him, then revere.
Such power there is in clear-eyed self-restraint
And purpose clean as light from every selfish taint.

3

Musing beneath the legendary tree,
The years between furl off: I seem to see
The sun-flecks, shaken the stirred foliage through,
Dapple with gold his sober buff and blue
And weave prophetic aureoles round the head
That shines our beacon now nor darkens with the dead.
O man of silent mood,
A stranger among strangers then,
How art thou since renowned the Great, the Good,
Familiar as the day in all the homes of men!
The wingèd years, that winnow praise to blame,
Blow many names out: they but fan and flame
The self-renewing splendors of thy fame.

IV

1

How many subtlest influences unite,
With spiritual touch of joy or pain,
Invisible as air and soft as light,
To body forth that image of the brain
We call our Country, visionary shape,
Loved more than woman, fuller of fire than wine,
Whose charm can none define,
Nor any, though he flee it, can escape!
All party-colored threads the weaver Time
Sets in his web, now trivial, now sublime,
All memories, all forebodings, hopes and fears,

Mountain and river, forest, prairie, sea,
A hill, a rock, a homestead, field, or tree,
The casual gleanings of unreckoned years,
Take goddess-shape at last and there is She,
Old at our birth, new as the springing hours,
Shrine of our weakness, fortress of our powers,
Consoler, kindler, peerless 'mid her peers,
A force that 'neath our conscious being stirs,
A life to give ours permanence, when we
Are borne to mingle our poor earth with hers,
And all this glowing world goes with us on
our biers.

2

Nations are long results, by ruder ways
Gathering the might that warrants length of
days;
They may be pieced of half-reluctant shares
Welded by hammer-strokes of broad-brained
kings,
Or from a doughty people grow, the heirs
Of wise traditions widening cautious rings;
At best they are computable things,
A strength behind us making us feel bold
In right, or, as may chance, in wrong;
Whose force by figures may be summed and
told,
So many soldiers, ships, and dollars strong,
And we but drops that bear compulsory part
In the dumb throb of a mechanic heart;
But Country is a shape of each man's mind
Sacred from definition, unconfined
By the cramped walls where daily drudgeries
grind;
An inward vision, yet an outward birth
Of sweet familiar heaven and earth;
A brooding Presence that stirs motions blind
Of wings within our embryo being's shell
That wait but her completer spell
To make us eagle-natured, fit to dare
Life's nobler spaces and untarnished air.

3

You, who hold dear this self-conceived ideal,
Whose faith and works alone can make it real,
Bring all your fairest gifts to deck her shrine
Who lifts our lives away from Thine and
Mine
And feeds the lamp of manhood more divine
With fragrant oils of quenchless constancy.
When all have done their utmost, surely he
Hath given the best who gives a character
Erect and constant, which nor any shock
Of loosened elements, nor the forceful sea
Of flowing or of ebbing fates, can stir
From its deep bases in the living rock
Of ancient manhood's sweet security:
And this he gave, serenely far from pride
As baseness, boon with prosperous stars allied,
Part of what nobler seed shall in our loins
abide.

4

No bond of men as common pride so strong,
In names time-filtered for the lips of song,
Still operant, with the primal Forces bound
Whose currents, on their spiritual round,
Transfuse our mortal will nor are gainsaid:
These are their arsenals, these the exhaustless
mines
That give a constant heart in great designs;
These are the stuff whereof such dreams are
made
As make heroic men: thus surely he
Still holds in place the massy blocks he laid
'Neath our new frame, enforcing soberly
The self-control that makes and keeps a people
free.

V

1

Oh, for a drop of that Cornelian ink
Which gave Agricola dateless length of days,
To celebrate him fitly, neither swerve
To phrase unkempt, nor pass discretion's
brink,
With him so statue-like in sad reserve,
So diffident to claim, so forward to deserve!
Nor need I shun due influence of his fame
Who, mortal among mortals, seemed as now
The equestrian shape with unimpassioned
brow,
That paces silent on through vistas of acclaim.

2

What figure more immovably august
Than that grave strength so patient and so
pure,
Calm in good fortune, when it wavered, sure,
That mind serene, impenetrably just,
Modelled on classic lines so simple they en-
dure?

That soul so softly radiant and so white
The track it left seems less of fire than light,
Cold but to such as love distemperature?
And if pure light, as some deem, be the force
That drives rejoicing planets on their course,
Why for his power benign seek an impurer source?
His was the true enthusiasm that burns long,
Domestically bright,
Fed from itself and shy of human sight,
The hidden force that makes a lifetime strong,
And not the short-lived fuel of a song.
Passionless, say you? What is passion for
But to sublime our natures and control
To front heroic toils with late return,
Or none, or such as shames the conqueror?
That fire was fed with substance of the soul
And not with holiday stubble, that could burn,
Unpraised of men who after bonfires run,
Through seven slow years of unadvancing war,
Equal when fields were lost or fields were won,
With breath of popular applause or blame,
Nor fanned nor damped, unquenchably the same,
Too inward to be reached by flaws of idle fame.

3

Soldier and statesman, rarest unison;
High-poised example of great duties done
Simply as breathing, a world's honors worn
As life's indifferent gifts to all men born;
Dumb for himself, unless it were to God,
But for his barefoot soldiers eloquent,
Tramping the snow to coral where they trod,
Held by his awe in hollow-eyed content;
Modest, yet firm as Nature's self; unblamed
Save by the men his nobler temper shamed;
Never seduced through show of present good
By other than unsetting lights to steer
New-trimmed in Heaven, nor than his steadfast mood
More steadfast, far from rashness as from fear;
Rigid, but with himself first, grasping still
In swerveless poise the wave-beat helm of will;
Not honored then or now because he wooed
The popular voice, but that he still withstood;
Broad-minded, higher-souled, there is but one,
Who was all this and ours, and all men's,
—WASHINGTON.

4

Minds strong by fits, irregularly great,
That flash and darken like revolving lights,
Catch more the vulgar eye unschooled to wait
On the long curve of patient days and nights
Rounding a whole life to the circle fair
Of orbed fulfilment; and this balanced soul,
So simple in its grandeur, coldly bare
Of draperies theatric, standing there
In perfect symmetry of self-control,
Seems not so great at first, but greater grows
Still as we look, and by experience learn
How grand this quiet is, how nobly stern
The discipline that wrought through lifelong throes
That energetic passion of repose.

5

A nature too decorous and severe,
Too self-respectful in its griefs and joys,
For ardent girls and boys
Who find no genius in a mind so clear
That its grave depths seem obvious and near,
Nor a soul great that made so little noise.
They feel no force in that calm-cadenced phrase,
The habitual full-dress of his well-bred mind,
That seems to pace the minuet's courtly maze
And tell of ampler leisures, roomier length of days.
His firm-based brain, to self so little kind
That no tumultuary blood could blind,
Formed to control men, not amaze,
Looms not like those that borrow height of haze:
It was a world of statelier movement then
Than this we fret in, he a denizen
Of that ideal Rome that made a man for men.

VI

1

The longer on this earth we live
And weigh the various qualities of men,
Seeing how most are fugitive,
Or fitful gifts, at best, of now and then,
Wind-wavered corpse-lights, daughters of the fen,
The more we feel the high stern-featured beauty

Of plain devotedness to duty,
Steadfast and still, nor paid with mortal praise,
But finding amplest recompense
For life's ungarlanded expense
In work done squarely and unwasted days.
For this we honor him, that he could know
How sweet the service and how free
Of her, God's eldest daughter here below,
And choose in meanest raiment which was she.

2

Placid completeness, life without a fall
From faith or highest aims, truth's breachless wall,
Surely if any fame can bear the touch,
His will say "Here!" at the last trumpet's call,
The unexpressive man whose life expressed so much.

VII

1

Never to see a nation born
Hath been given to mortal man,
Unless to those who, on that summer morn,
Gazed silent when the great Virginian
Unsheathed the sword whose fatal flash
Shot union through the incoherent clash
Of our loose atoms, crystallizing them
Around a single will's unpliant stem,
And making purpose of emotion rash.
Out of that scabbard sprang, as from its womb,
Nebulous at first but hardening to a star,
Through mutual share of sunburst and of gloom,
The common faith that made us what we are.

2

That lifted blade transformed our jangling clans,
Till then provincial, to Americans,
And made a unity of wildering plans;
Here was the doom fixed: here is marked the date
When this New World awoke to man's estate,
Burnt its last ship and ceased to look behind:
Nor thoughtless was the choice; no love or hate
Could from its poise move that deliberate mind,
Weighing between too early and too late
Those pitfalls of the man refused by Fate:
His was the impartial vision of the great
Who see not as they wish, but as they find.
He saw the dangers of defeat, nor less
The incomputable perils of success;
The sacred past thrown by, an empty rind;
The future, cloud-land, snare of prophets blind;
The waste of war, the ignominy of peace;
On either hand a sullen rear of woes,
Whose garnered lightnings none could guess,
Piling its thunder-heads and muttering "Cease!"
Yet drew not back his hand, but gravely chose
The seeming-desperate task whence our new nation rose.

3

A noble choice and of immortal seed!
Nor deem that acts heroic wait on chance
Or easy were as in a boy's romance;
The man's whole life preludes the single deed
That shall decide if his inheritance
Be with the sifted few of matchless breed,
Our race's sap and sustenance,
Or with the unmotived herd that only sleep and feed.
Choice seems a thing indifferent; thus or so,
What matters it? The Fates with mocking face
Look on inexorable, nor seem to know
Where the lot lurks that gives life's foremost place.
Yet Duty's leaden casket holds it still,
And but two ways are offered to our will,
Toil with rare triumph, ease with safe disgrace,
The problem still for us and all of human race.
He chose, as men choose, where most danger showed,
Nor ever faltered 'neath the load
Of petty cares, that gall great hearts the most,
But kept right on the strenuous up-hill road,
Strong to the end, above complaint or boast:
The popular tempest on his rock-mailed coast
Wasted its wind-borne spray,
The noisy marvel of a day;
His soul sate still in its unstormed abode.

VIII

Virginia gave us this imperial man
Cast in the massive mold
Of those high-statured ages old
Which into grander forms our mortal metal ran;
She gave us this unblemished gentleman:
What shall we give her back but love and praise
As in the dear old unestrangèd days
Before the inevitable wrong began?
Mother of States and undiminished men,
Thou gavest us a country, giving him,
And we owe alway what we owed thee then:
The boon thou wouldst have snatched from us again
Shines as before with no abatement dim.
A great man's memory is the only thing
With influence to outlast the present whim
And bind us as when here he knit our golden ring.
All of him that was subject to the hours
Lies in thy soil and makes it part of ours:
Across more recent graves,
Where unresentful Nature waves
Her pennons o'er the shot-ploughed sod,
Proclaiming the sweet Truce of God,
We from this consecrated plain stretch out
Our hands as free from afterthought or doubt
As here the united North
Poured her embrownèd manhood forth
In welcome of our savior and thy son.
Through battle we have better learned thy worth,
The long-breathed valor and undaunted will,
Which, like his own, the day's disaster done,
Could, safe in manhood, suffer and be still.
Both thine and ours the victory hardly won;
If ever with distempered voice or pen
We have misdeemed thee, here we take it back,
And for the dead of both don common black.
Be to us evermore as thou wast then,
As we forget thou hast not always been,
Mother of States and unpolluted men,
Virginia, fitly named from England's manly queen!

1875 1875

AN ODE

FOR THE FOURTH OF JULY, 1876

I

I

ENTRANCED I saw a vision in the cloud
That loitered dreaming in yon sunset sky,
Full of fair shapes, half creatures of the eye,
Half chance-evoked by the wind's fantasy
In golden mist, an ever-shifting crowd:
There, 'mid unreal forms that came and went
In air-spun robes, of evanescent dye,
A woman's semblance shone preëminent;
Not armed like Pallas, not like Hera proud,
But as on household diligence intent,
Beside her visionary wheel she bent
Like Aretë or Bertha, nor than they
Less queenly in her port: about her knee
Glad children clustered confident in play:
Placid her pose, the calm of energy;
And over her broad brow in many a round
(That loosened would have gilt her garment's hem),
Succinct, as toil prescribes, the hair was wound
In lustrous coils, a natural diadem.
The cloud changed shape, obsequious to the whim
Of some transmuting influence felt in me,
And, looking now, a wolf I seemed to see
Limned in that vapor, gaunt and hunger-bold,
Threatening her charge: resolve in every limb,
Erect she flamed in mail of sun-wove gold,
Penthesilea's self for battle dight;
One arm uplifted braced a flickering spear,
And one her adamantine shield made light;
Her face, helm-shadowed, grew a thing to fear,
And her fierce eyes, by danger challenged, took
Her trident-sceptred mother's dauntless look.
"I know thee now, O goddess-born!" I cried,
And turned with loftier brow and firmer stride;
For in that spectral cloud-work I had seen
Her image, bodied forth by love and pride,
The fearless, the benign, the mother-eyed,
The fairer world's toil-consecrated queen.

2

What shape by exile dreamed elates the mind
Like hers whose hand, a fortress of the poor,

No blood in vengeance spilt, though lawful, stains?
Who never turned a suppliant from her door?
Whose conquests are the gains of all mankind?
Today her thanks shall fly on every wind,
Unstinted, unrebuked, from shore to shore,
One love, one hope, and not a doubt behind!
Cannon to cannon shall repeat her praise,
Banner to banner flap it forth in flame;
Her children shall rise up to bless her name,
And wish her harmless length of days,
The mighty mother of a mighty brood,
Blessed in all tongues and dear to every blood,
The beautiful, the strong, and, best of all, the good.

3

Seven years long was the bow
Of battle bent, and the heightening
Storm-heaps convulsed with the throe
Of their uncontainable lightning;
Seven years long heard the sea
Crash of navies and wave-borne thunder;
Then drifted the cloud-rack a-lee,
And new stars were seen, a world's wonder;
Each by her sisters made bright,
All binding all to their stations,
Cluster of manifold light
Startling the old constellations:
Men looked up and grew pale:
Was it a comet or star,
Omen of blessing or bale,
Hung o'er the ocean afar?

4

Stormy the day of her birth:
Was she not born of the strong,
She, the last ripeness of earth,
Beautiful, prophesied long?
Stormy the days of her prime:
Hers are the pulses that beat
Higher for perils sublime,
Making them fawn at her feet.
Was she not born of the strong?
Was she not born of the wise?
Daring and counsel belong
Of right to her confident eyes:
Human and motherly they,
Careless of station or race:
Hearken! her children today
Shout for the joy of her face.

II

1

No praises of the past are hers,
No fanes by hallowing time caressed,
No broken arch that ministers
To Time's sad instinct in the breast:
She has not gathered from the years
Grandeur of tragedies and tears,
Nor from long leisure the unrest
That finds repose in forms of classic grace:
These may delight the coming race
Who haply shall not count it to our crime
That we who fain would sing are here before our time.
She also hath her monuments;
Not such as stand decrepitly resigned
To ruin-mark the path of dead events
That left no seed of better days behind,
The tourist's pensioners that show their scars
And maunder of forgotten wars;
She builds not on the ground, but in the mind,
Her open-hearted palaces
For larger-thoughted men with heaven and earth at ease:
Her march the plump mow marks, the sleepless wheel,
The golden sheaf, the self-swayed common-weal;
The happy homesteads hid in orchard trees
Whose sacrificial smokes through peaceful air
Rise lost in heaven, the household's silent prayer;
What architect hath bettered these?
With softened eye the westward traveller sees
A thousand miles of neighbors side by side,
Holding by toil-won titles fresh from God
The lands no serf or seigneur ever trod,
With manhood latent in the very sod,
Where the long billow of the wheatfield's tide
Flows to the sky across the prairie wide,
A sweeter vision than the castled Rhine,
Kindly with thoughts of Ruth and Bible-days benign.

2

O ancient commonwealths, that we revere
Haply because we could not know you near,
Your deeds like statues down the aisles of Time

Shine peerless in memorial calm sublime,
And Athens is a trumpet still, and Rome;
Yet which of your achievements is not foam
Weighed with this one of hers (below you far
In fame, and born beneath a milder star),
That to Earth's orphans, far as curves the dome
Of death-deaf sky, the bounteous West means
home,
With dear precedency of natural ties
That stretch from roof to roof and make men
gently wise?
And if the nobler passions wane,
Distorted to base use, if the near goal
Of insubstantial gain
Tempt from the proper race-course of the soul
That crowns their patient breath
Whose feet, song-sandalled, are too fleet for
Death,
Yet may she claim one privilege urbane
And haply first upon the civic roll,
That none can breathe her air nor grow hu-
mane.

3

Oh, better far the briefest hour
Of Athens self-consumed, whose plastic power
Hid Beauty safe from Death in words or stone;
Of Rome, fair quarry where those eagles
crowd
Whose fulgurous vans about the world had
blown
Triumphant storm and seeds of polity;
Of Venice, fading o'er her shipless sea,
Last iridescence of a sunset cloud;
Than this inert prosperity,
This bovine comfort in the sense alone!
Yet art came slowly even to such as those,
Whom no past genius cheated of their own
With prudence of o'ermastering precedent;
Petal by petal spreads the perfect rose,
Secure of the divine event;
And only children rend the bud half-blown
To forestall Nature in her calm intent:
Time hath a quiver full of purposes
Which miss not of their aim, to us unknown,
And brings about the impossible with ease:
Haply for us the ideal dawn shall break
From where in legend-tinted line
The peaks of Hellas drink the morning's wine,
To tremble on our lids with mystic sign
Till the drowsed ichor in our veins awake
And set our pulse in tune with moods divine:
Long the day lingered in its sea-fringed nest,
Then touched the Tuscan hills with golden
lance
And paused; then on to Spain and France
The splendor flew, and Albion's misty crest:
Shall Ocean bar him from his destined West?
Or are we, then, arrived too late,
Doomed with the rest to grope disconso-
late,
Foreclosed of Beauty by our modern date?

III

1

Poets, as their heads grow gray,
Look from too far behind the eyes,
Too long-experienced to be wise
In guileless youth's diviner way;
Life sings not now, but prophesies;
Time's shadows they no more behold,
But, under them, the riddle old
That mocks, bewilders, and defies:
In childhood's face the seed of shame,
In the green tree an ambushed flame,
In Phosphor a vaunt-guard of Night,
They, though against their will, divine,
And dread the care-dispelling wine
Stored from the Muse's vintage bright,
By age imbued with second-sight.
From Faith's own eyelids there peeps out,
Even as they look, the leer of doubt;
The festal wreath their fancy loads
With care that whispers and forebodes:
Nor this our triumph-day can blunt Megæra's
goads.

2

Murmur of many voices in the air
Denounces us degenerate,
Unfaithful guardians of a noble fate,
And prompts indifference or despair:
Is this the country that we dreamed in youth,
Where wisdom and not numbers should have
weight,
Seed-field of simpler manner, braver truth,
Where shams should cease to dominate
In household, church, and state?
Is this Atlantis? This the unpoisoned soil,
Sea-whelmed for ages and recovered late,
Where parasitic greed no more should coil

Round Freedom's stem to bend awry and blight
What grew so fair, sole plant of love and light?
Who sit where once in crowned seclusion sate
The long-proved athletes of debate
Trained from their youth, as none thinks needful now?
Is this debating club where boys dispute,
And wrangle o'er their stolen fruit,
The Senate, erewhile cloister of the few,
Where Clay once flashed and Webster's cloudy brow
Brooded those bolts of thought that all the horizon knew?

3

Oh, as this pensive moonlight blurs my pines,
Here while I sit and meditate these lines,
To gray-green dreams of what they are by day,
So would some light, not reason's sharp-edged ray,
Trance me in moonshine as before the flight
Of years had won me this unwelcome right
To see things as they are, or shall be soon,
In the frank prose of undissembling noon!

4

Back to my breast, ungrateful sigh!
Whoever fails, whoever errs,
The penalty be ours, not hers!
The present still seems vulgar, seen too nigh;
The golden age is still the age that's past:
I ask no drowsy opiate
To dull my vision of that only state
Founded on faith in man, and therefore sure to last.
For, O my country, touched by thee,
The gray hairs gather back their gold;
Thy thought sets all my pulses free;
The heart refuses to be old;
The love is all that I can see.
Not to thy natal-day belong
Time's prudent doubt or age's wrong,
But gifts of gratitude and song:
Unsummoned crowd the thankful words,
As sap in spring-time floods the tree,
Foreboding the return of birds,
For all that thou hast been to me!

IV

I

Flawless his heart and tempered to the core
Who, beckoned by the forward-leaning wave,
First left behind him the firm-footed shore,
And, urged by every nerve of sail and oar,
Steered for the Unknown which gods to mortals gave,
Of thought and action the mysterious door,
Bugbear of fools, a summons to the brave:
Strength found he in the unsympathizing sun,
And strange stars from beneath the horizon won,
And the dumb ocean pitilessly grave:
High-hearted surely he;
But bolder they who first off-cast
Their moorings from the habitable Past
And ventured chartless on the sea
Of storm-engendering Liberty:
For all earth's width of waters is a span,
And their convulsed existence mere repose,
Matched with the unstable heart of man,
Shoreless in wants, mist-girt in all it knows,
Open to every wind of sect or clan,
And sudden-passionate in ebbs and flows.

2

They steered by stars the elder shipmen knew,
And laid their courses where the currents draw
Of ancient wisdom channelled deep in law,
The undaunted few
Who changed the Old World for the New,
And more devoutly prized
Than all perfection theorized
The more imperfect that had roots and grew.
They founded deep and well,
Those danger-chosen chiefs of men
Who still believed in Heaven and Hell,
Nor hoped to find a spell,
In some fine flourish of a pen,
To make a better man
Than long-considering Nature will or can,
Secure against his own mistakes,
Content with what life gives or takes,
And acting still on some fore-ordered plan,
A cog of iron in an iron wheel,
Too nicely poised to think or feel,
Dumb motor in a clock-like commonweal.
They wasted not their brain in schemes

Of what man might be in some bubble-sphere,
As if he must be other than he seems
Because he was not what he should be here,
Postponing Time's slow proof to petulant
dreams:
Yet herein they were great
Beyond the incredulous lawgivers of yore,
And wiser than the wisdom of the shelf,
That they conceived a deeper-rooted state,
Of hardier growth, alive from rind to core,
By making man sole sponsor of himself.

3

God of our fathers, Thou who wast,
Art, and shalt be when those eye-wise who
flout
Thy secret presence shall be lost
In the great light that dazzles them to doubt,
We, sprung from loins of stalwart men
Whose strength was in their trust
That Thou wouldst make thy dwelling in their
dust
And walk with those a fellow-citizen
Who build a city of the just,
We, who believe Life's bases rest
Beyond the probe of chemic test,
Still, like our fathers, feel Thee near,
Sure that, while lasts the immutable decree,
The land to Human Nature dear
Shall not be unbeloved of Thee.

1876 1876

AUSPEX

My heart, I cannot still it,
Nest that had song-birds in it;
And when the last shall go,
The dreary days, to fill it,
Instead of lark or linnet,
Shall whirl dead leaves and snow.

Had they been swallows only,
Without the passion stronger
That skyward longs and sings,—
Woe's me, I shall be lonely
When I can feel no longer
The impatience of their wings!

A moment, sweet delusion,
Like birds the brown leaves hover;
But it will not be long
Before the wild confusion
Fall wavering down to cover
The poet and his song.

1878

TO WHITTIER

ON HIS SEVENTY-FIFTH BIRTHDAY

New England's poet, rich in love as years,
Her hills and valleys praise thee, her swift
brooks
Dance in thy verse; to her grave sylvan nooks
Thy steps allure us, which the wood-thrush
hears
As maids their lovers', and no treason fears;
Through thee her Merrimacs and Agiochooks
And many a name uncouth win gracious looks,
Sweetly familiar to both Englands' ears:

Peaceful by birthright as a virgin lake,
The lily's anchorage, which no eyes behold
Save those of stars, yet for thy brother's sake
That lay in bonds, thou blewst a blast as bold
As that wherewith the heart of Roland brake,
Far heard across the New World and the
Old.

1882 1882

TO HOLMES

ON HIS SEVENTY-FIFTH BIRTHDAY

Dear Wendell, why need count the years
Since first your genius made me thrill,
If what moved then to smiles or tears,
Or both contending, move me still?

What has the Calendar to do
With poets? What Time's fruitless tooth
With gay immortals such as you
Whose years but emphasize your youth?

One air gave both their lease of breath;
The same paths lured our boyish feet;
One earth will hold us safe in death
With dust of saints and scholars sweet.

Our legends from one source were drawn,
I scarce distinguish yours from mine,
And *don't* we make the Gentiles yawn
With "You remembers?" o'er our wine!

If I, with too senescent air,
  Invade your elder memory's pale,
You snub me with a pitying "Where
  Were you in the September Gale?"

Both stared entranced at Lafayette,
  Saw Jackson dubbed with LL. D.
What Cambridge saw not strikes us yet
  As scarcely worth one's while to see.

Ten years my senior, when my name
  In Harvard's entrance-book was writ,
Her halls still echoed with the fame
  Of you, her poet and her wit.

'Tis fifty years from then to now:
  But your Last Leaf renews its green,
Though, for the laurels on your brow
  (So thick they crowd), 'tis hardly seen.

The oriole's fledglings fifty times
  Have flown from our familiar elms;
As many poets with their rhymes
  Oblivion's darkling dust o'erwhelms.

The birds are hushed, the poets gone
  Where no harsh critic's lash can reach,
And still your wingèd brood sing on
  To all who love our English speech.

Nay, let the foolish records be
  That make believe you're seventy-five:
You're the old Wendell still to me,—
  And that's the youngest man alive.

The gray-blue eyes, I see them still,
  The gallant front with brown o'erhung,
The shape alert, the wit at will,
  The phrase that stuck, but never stung.

You keep your youth as yon Scotch firs,
  Whose gaunt line my horizon hems,
Though twilight all the lowland blurs,
  Hold sunset in their ruddy stems.

You with the elders? Yes, 'tis true,
  But in no sadly literal sense,
With elders and coevals too,
  Whose verb admits no preterite tense.

Master alike in speech and song
  Of fame's great antiseptic—Style,
You with the classic few belong
  Who tempered wisdom with a smile.

Outlive us all! Who else like you
  Could sift the seedcorn from our chaff,
And make us with the pen we knew
  Deathless at least in epitaph?

1884 1884

ENDYMION

A MYSTICAL COMMENT ON TITIAN'S "SACRED AND PROFANE LOVE"

I

My day began not till the twilight fell,
And, lo, in ether from heaven's sweetest well,
The New Moon swam divinely isolate
In maiden silence, she that makes my fate
Haply not knowing it, or only so
As I the secrets of my sheep may know;
Nor ask I more, entirely blest if she,
In letting me adore, ennoble me
To height of what the Gods meant making man,
As only she and her best beauty can.
Mine be the love that in itself can find
Seed of white thoughts, the lilies of the mind,
Seed of that glad surrender of the will
That finds in service self's true purpose still;
Love that in outward fairness sees the tent
Pitched for an inmate far more excellent;
Love with a light irradiate to the core,
Lit at her lamp, but fed from inborn store;
Love thrice-requited with the single joy
Of an immaculate vision naught could cloy,
Dearer because, so high beyond my scope,
My life grew rich with her, unbribed by hope
Of other guerdon save to think she knew
One grateful votary paid her all her due;
Happy if she, high-radiant there, resigned
To his sure trust her image in his mind.
O fairer even than Peace is when she comes
Hushing War's tumult, and retreating drums
Fade to a murmur like the sough of bees
Hidden among the noon-stilled linden-trees,
Bringer of quiet, thou that canst allay
The dust and din and travail of the day,
Strewer of Silence, Giver of the dew
That doth our pastures and our souls renew,
Still dwell remote, still on thy shoreless sea
Float unattained in silent empery,
Still light my thoughts, nor listen to a prayer
Would make thee less imperishably fair!

II

Can, then, my twofold nature find content
In vain conceits of airy blandishment?
Ask I no more? Since yesterday I task
My storm-strewn thoughts to tell me what I ask:
Faint premonitions of mutation strange
Steal o'er my perfect orb, and, with the change,
Myself am changed; the shadow of my earth
Darkens the disk of that celestial worth
Which only yesterday could still suffice
Upwards to waft my thoughts in sacrifice;
My heightened fancy with its touches warm
Moulds to a woman's that ideal form;
Nor yet a woman's wholly, but divine
With awe her purer essence bred in mine.
Was it long brooding on their own surmise,
Which, of the eyes engendered, fools the eyes,
Or have I seen through that translucent air
A Presence shaped in its seclusions bare,
My Goddess looking on me from above
As look our russet maidens when they love,
But high-uplifted o'er our human heat
And passion-paths too rough for her pearl feet?

Slowly the Shape took outline as I gazed
At her full-orbed or crescent, till, bedazed
With wonder-working light that subtly wrought
My brain to its own substance, steeping thought
In trances such as poppies give, I saw
Things shut from vision by sight's sober law,
Amorphous, changeful, but defined at last
Into the peerless Shape mine eyes hold fast.
This, too, at first I worshipt: soon, like wine,
Her eyes, in mine poured, frenzy-philtred mine;
Passion put Worship's priestly raiment on
And to the woman knelt, the Goddess gone.
Was I, then, more than mortal made? or she
Less than divine that she might mate with me?
If mortal merely, could my nature cope
With such o'ermastery of maddening hope?
If Goddess, could she feel the blissful woe
That women in their self-surrender know?

III

Long she abode aloof there in her heaven,
Far as the grape-bunch of the Pleiad seven
Beyond my madness' utmost leap; but here
Mine eyes have feigned of late her rapture near,
Moulded of mind-mist that broad day dispels,
Here in these shadowy woods and brook-lulled dells.

Have no heaven-habitants e'er felt a void
In hearts sublimed with ichor unalloyed?
E'er longed to mingle with a mortal fate
Intense with pathos of its briefer date?
Could she partake, and live, our human stains?
Even with the thought there tingles through my veins
Sense of unwarned renewal; I, the dead,
Receive and house again the ardor fled,
As once Alcestis; to the ruddy brim
Feel masculine virtue flooding every limb,
And life, like Spring returning, brings the key
That sets my senses from their winter free,
Dancing like naked fauns too glad for shame.
Her passion, purified to palest flame,
Can it thus kindle? Is her purpose this?
I will not argue, lest I lose a bliss
That makes me dream Tithonus' fortune mine
(Or what of it was palpably divine
Ere came the fruitlessly immortal gift);
I cannot curb my hope's imperious drift
That wings with fire my dull mortality;
Though fancy-forged, 'tis all I feel or see.

IV

My Goddess sinks; round Latmos' darkening brow
Trembles the parting of her presence now,
Faint as the perfume left upon the grass
By her limbs' pressure or her feet that pass
By me conjectured, but conjectured so
As things I touch far fainter substance show.
Was it mine eyes' imposture I have seen
Flit with the moonbeams on from shade to sheen
Through the wood-openings? Nay, I see her now
Out of her heaven new-lighted, from her brow
The hair breeze-scattered, like loose mists that blow

Across her crescent, goldening as they go
High-kirtled for the chase, and what was shown,
Of maiden rondure, like the rose half-blown.
If dream, turn real! If a vision, stay!
Take mortal shape, my philtre's spell obey!
If hags compel thee from thy secret sky
With gruesome incantations, why not I,
Whose only magic is that I distil
A potion, blent of passion, thought, and will,
Deeper in reach, in force of fate more rich,
Than e'er was juice wrung by Thessalian witch
From moon-enchanted herbs,—a potion brewed
Of my best life in each diviner mood?
Myself the elixir am, myself the bowl
Seething and mantling with my soul of soul.
Taste and be humanized: what though the cup,
With thy lips frenzied, shatter? Drink it up!
If but these arms may clasp, o'erquited so,
My world, thy heaven, all life means I shall know.

V

Sure she hath heard my prayer and granted half,
As Gods do who at mortal madness laugh.
Yet if life's solid things illusion seem,
Why may not substance wear the mask of dream?
In sleep she comes; she visits me in dreams,
And, as her image in a thousand streams,
So in my veins, that her obey, she sees,
Floating and flaming there, her images
Bear to my little world's remotest zone
Glad messages of her, and her alone.
With silence-sandalled Sleep she comes to me
(But softer-footed, sweeter-browed, than she),
In motion gracious as a seagull's wing,
And all her bright limbs, moving, seem to sing.
Let me believe so, then, if so I may
With the night's bounty feed my beggared day.
In dreams I see her lay the goddess down
With bow and quiver, and her crescent-crown
Flicker and fade away to dull eclipse
As down to mine she deigns her longed-for lips;
And as her neck my happy arms enfold,
Flooded and lustred with her loosened gold,
She whispers words each sweeter than a kiss:
Then, wakened with the shock of sudden bliss,
My arms are empty, my awakener fled,
And, silent in the silent sky o'erhead,
But coldly as on ice-plated snow, she gleams,
Herself the mother and the child of dreams.

VI

Gone is the time when phantasms could appease
My quest phantasmal and bring cheated ease;
When, if she glorified my dreams, I felt
Through all my limbs a change immortal melt
At touch of hers illuminate with soul.
Not long could I be stilled with Fancy's dole;
Too soon the mortal mixture in me caught
Red fire from her celestial flame, and fought
For tyrannous control in all my veins:
My fool's prayer was accepted; what remains?
Or was it some eidolon merely, sent
By her who rules the shades in banishment,
To mock me with her semblance? Were it thus,
How 'scape I shame, whose will was traitorous?
What shall compensate an ideal dimmed?
How blanch again my statue virgin-limbed,
Soiled with the incense-smoke her chosen priest
Poured more profusely as within decreased
The fire unearthly, fed with coals from far
Within the soul's shrine? Could my fallen star
Be set in heaven again by prayers and tears
And quenchless sacrifice of all my years,
How would the victim to the flamen leap,
And life for life's redemption paid hold cheap!

But what resource when she herself descends
From her blue throne, and o'er her vassal bends
That shape thrice-deified by love, those eyes
Wherein the Lethe of all others lies?
When my white queen of heaven's remoteness tires,
Herself against her other self conspires,
Takes woman's nature, walks in mortal ways,
And finds in my remorse her beauty's praise?
Yet all would I renounce to dream again

The dream in dreams fulfilled that made my pain,
My noble pain that heightened all my years
With crowns to win and prowess-breeding tears;
Nay, would that dream renounce once more to see
Her from her sky there looking down at me!

VII

Goddess, reclimb thy heaven, and be once more
An inaccessible splendor to adore,
A faith, a hope of such transcendent worth
As bred ennobling discontent with earth;
Give back the longing, back the elated mood
That, fed with thee, spurned every meaner good;
Give even the spur of impotent despair
That, without hope, still bade aspire and dare;
Give back the need to worship, that still pours
Down to the soul the virtue it adores!

Nay, brightest and most beautiful, deem naught
These frantic words, the reckless wind of thought:
Still stoop, still grant,—I live but in thy will;
Be what thou wilt, but be a woman still!
Vainly I cried, nor could myself believe
That what I prayed for I would fain receive.
My moon is set; my vision set with her;
No more can worship vain my pulses stir.
Goddess Triform, I own thy triple spell,
My heaven's queen,—queen, too, of my earth and hell!

1887 1888

THE FUNCTION OF THE POET

This was the concluding lecture in the course which Lowell read before the Lowell Institute in the winter of 1855. Doubtless Lowell never printed it because, as his genius matured, he felt that its assertions were too absolute, and that its style bore too many marks of haste in composition, and was too rhetorical for an essay to be read in print. How rapid was the growth of his intellectual judgment, and the broadening of his imaginative view, may be seen by comparing it with his essays on Swinburne, on Percival, and on Rousseau, published in 1866 and 1867—essays in which the topics of this lecture were touched upon anew, though not treated at large.

But the spirit of this lecture is so fine, its tone so full of the enthusiasm of youth, its conception of the poet so lofty, and the truths it contains so important, that it may well be prized as the expression of a genius which, if not yet mature, is already powerful, and aquiline alike in vision and in sweep of wing. It is not unworthy to stand with Sidney's and with Shelley's "Defence of Poesy," and it is fitted to warm and inspire the poetic heart of the youth of this generation, no less than of that to which it was first addressed. As a close to the lecture Lowell read his beautiful (then unpublished) poem "To the Muse."

Charles Eliot Norton

Whether, as some philosophers assume, we possess only the fragments of a great cycle of knowledge in whose centre stood the primeval man in friendly relation with the powers of the universe, and build our hovels out of the ruins of our ancestral palace; or whether, according to the development theory of others, we are rising gradually, and have come up out of an atom instead of descending from an Adam, so that the proudest pedigree might run up to a barnacle or a zoöphyte at last, are questions that will keep for a good many centuries yet. Confining myself to what little we can learn from history, we find tribes rising slowly out of barbarism to a higher or lower point of culture and civility, and everywhere the poet also is found, under one name or other, changing in certain outward respects, but essentially the same.

And however far we go back, we shall find this also—that the poet and the priest were united originally in the same person; which means that the poet was he who was conscious of the world of spirit as well as that of sense, and was the ambassador of the gods to men. This was his highest function, and hence his name of "seer." He was the discoverer and declarer of the perennial beneath the deciduous. His were the *epea pteroenta*, the true "winged words" that could fly down the unexplored future and carry the names of ancestral heroes, of the brave and wise and good. It was thus that the poet could reward virtue, and, by and by, as society grew more complex, could burn in the brand of shame. This is Homer's character of Demodocus, in the eighth book of the "Odyssey," "whom the Muse loved and gave the good and ill"—the gift of conferring good or evil immortality. The first histories were in verse; and sung as they were at feasts and gatherings of the people, they awoke in men the desire of fame, which is the first promoter of courage and self-trust, because it teaches men by degrees to appeal from the present to the future. We may fancy what the influence of the early epics was when they were recited to men who claimed the heroes celebrated in them for their ancestors, by what Bouchardon, the sculptor, said, only two centuries ago: "When I read Homer, I feel as if I were twenty feet high." Nor have poets lost their power over the future in modern times. Dante lifts up by the hair the face of some petty traitor, the Smith or Brown of some provincial Italian town, lets the fire of his Inferno glare upon it for a moment, and it is printed forever on the memory of mankind. The historians may iron out the shoulders of Richard the Third as smooth as they can, they will never get over the wrench that Shakespeare gave them.

The peculiarity of almost all early literature is that it seems to have a double meaning, that, underneath its natural, we find ourselves continually seeing or suspecting a supernatural meaning. In the older epics the characters seem to be half typical and only half historical. Thus did the early poets endeavor to make realities out of appearances; for, except a few typical men in whom certain ideas get embodied, the generations of mankind are mere apparitions who come out of the dark for a purposeless moment, and reënter the dark again after they have performed the nothing they came for.

Gradually, however, the poet as the "seer" became secondary to the "maker." His office became that of entertainer rather than teacher. But always something of the old tradition was kept alive. And if he has now come to be looked upon merely as the best expresser, the gift of seeing is implied as necessarily antecedent to that, and of seeing very deep, too. If any man would seem to have written without any conscious moral, that man is Shakespeare. But that must be a dull sense, indeed, which does not see through his tragic—yes, and his comic—masks awful eyes that flame with something intenser and deeper than a mere scenic meaning—a meaning out of the great deep that is behind and beyond all human and merely personal character. Nor was Shakespeare himself unconscious of his place as a teacher and profound moralist: witness that sonnet in which he bewails his having neglected sometimes the errand that was laid upon him:

> Alas, 'tis true I have gone here and there,
> And made myself a motley to the view,
> Gored mine own thoughts, sold cheap what is most dear,
> Made old offences of affections new;
> Most true it is that I have look'd on truth
> Askance and strangely;

the application of which is made clear by the next sonnet, in which he distinctly alludes to his profession.

There is this unmistakable stamp on all the great poets—that, however in little things they may fall below themselves, whenever there comes a great and noble thing to say, they say it greatly and nobly, and bear themselves most easily in the royalties of thought and language. There is not a mature play of Shakespeare's in which great ideas do not jut up in mountainous permanence, marking forever the boundary of provinces of thought, and known afar to many kindreds of men.

And it is for this kind of sight, which we call insight, and not for any faculty of observation and description, that we value the poet. It is in proportion as he has this that he is an adequate expresser, and not a juggler with words. It is by means of this that for every generation of man he plays the part of "namer." Before him, as before Adam, the creation passes to be named anew: first the material world; then the world of passions and emotions; then the world of ideas. But whenever a great imagination comes, however it may delight itself with imaging the outward beauty of things, however it may seem to flow thoughtlessly away in music like a brook, yet the shadow of heaven lies also in its depth beneath the shadow of earth. Continually the visible universe suggests the invisible. We are forever feeling this in Shakespeare. His imagination went down to the very bases of things, and while his characters are the most natural that poet ever created, they are also perfectly ideal, and are more truly the personifications of abstract thoughts and passions than those of any allegorical writer whatever.

Even in what seems so purely a picturesque poem as the "Iliad," we feel something of this. Beholding as Homer did, from the tower of contemplation, the eternal mutability and nothing permanent but change, he must look underneath the show for the reality. Great captains and conquerors came forth out of the eternal silence, entered it again with their trampling hosts, and shoutings, and trumpet-blasts, and were as utterly gone as those echoes of their deeds which he sang, and which faded with the last sound of his voice and the last tremble of his lyre. History relating outward events alone was an unmeaning gossip, with the world for a village. This life could only become other than phantasmagoric, could only become real, as it stood related to something that was higher and permanent. Hence the idea of Fate, of a higher power unseen—that shadow, as of an eagle circling to its swoop, which flits stealthily and swiftly across the windy plains of Troy. In the "Odyssey" we find pure allegory.

Now, under all these names—praiser, seer, soothsayer—we find the same idea lurking. The poet is he who can best see and best say what is ideal—what belongs to the world of soul and of beauty. Whether he celebrate the brave and good man, or the gods, or the beautiful as it appears in man or nature, something of a religious character still clings to him; he is the revealer of Deity. He may be unconscious of his mission; he may be false to it; but in proportion as he is a great poet, he rises to the level of it the more often. He does not always directly rebuke what is bad and base, but indirectly by making us feel what delight there is in the good and fair. If he besiege evil, it is with such beautiful engines of war (as Plutarch tells us of Demetrius) that the besieged themselves are charmed with them. Whoever reads the great poets cannot but be made better by it, for they always introduce him to a higher society, to a greater style of manners and of thinking. Whoever learns to love what is beautiful is made incapable of the low and mean and bad. If Plato excludes the poets from his Republic, it is expressly on the ground that they speak unworthy things of the gods; that is, that they have lost the secret of their art, and use artificial types instead of speaking the true universal language of imagination. He who translates the divine into the vulgar, the spiritual into the sensual, is the reverse of a poet.

The poet, under whatever name, always stands for the same thing—imagination. And imagination in its highest form gives him the power, as it were, of assuming the consciousness of whatever he speaks about, whether man or beast, or rock or tree. It is the ring of Canace, which whoso has on understands the language of all created things. And as regards expression, it seems to enable the poet to condense the whole of himself into a single word. Therefore, when a great poet has said a thing, it is finally and utterly expressed, and has as many meanings as there are men who read his verse. A great poet is something more than an interpreter between man and nature; he is also an interpreter between man and his own nature. It is he who gives us those key-words, the possession of which makes us masters of all the unsuspected treasure-caverns of thought, and feeling, and beauty which open under the dusty path of our daily life.

And it is not merely a dry lexicon that he compiles,—a thing which enables us to translate from one dead dialect into another as dead,—but all his verse is instinct with music, and his words open windows on every side to pictures of scenery and life. The difference between the dry fact and the poem is as great as that between reading the shipping news and seeing the actual coming and going of the crowd of stately ships,—"the city on the inconstant billows dancing,"—as there is between ten minutes of happiness and ten minutes by the clock. Everybody remembers the story of the little Montague who was stolen and sold to the chimney-sweep: how he could dimly remember lying in a beautiful chamber; how he carried with him in all his drudgery the vision of a fair, sad mother's face that sought him everywhere in vain; how he threw himself one day, all sooty as he was from his toil, on a rich bed and fell asleep, and how a kind person woke him, questioned him, pieced together his broken recollections for him, and so at last made the visions of the beautiful chamber and the fair, sad countenance real to him again. It seems to me that the offices that the poet does for us are typified in this nursery-tale. We all of us have our vague reminiscences of the stately home of our childhood,—for we are all of us poets and geniuses in our youth, while earth is all new to us, and the chalice of every buttercup is brimming with the wine of poesy,—and we all remember the beautiful, motherly countenance which nature bent over us there. But somehow we all get stolen away thence; life becomes to us a sooty taskmaster, and we crawl through dark passages without end—till suddenly the word of some poet redeems us, makes us know who we are, and of helpless orphans makes us the heirs to a great estate. It is to our true relations with the two great worlds of outward and inward nature that the poet reintroduces us.

But the imagination has a deeper use than merely to give poets a power of expression. It is the everlasting preserver of the world from blank materialism. It forever puts matter in the wrong, and compels it to show its title to existence. Wordsworth tells us that in his youth he was sometimes obliged to touch the walls to find if they were visionary or no, and such experiences are not uncommon with persons who converse much with their own thoughts. Dr. Johnson said that to kick one's foot against a stone was a sufficient confutation of Berkeley, and poor old Pyrrho has passed into a proverb because, denying the objectivity of matter, he was run over by a cart and killed. But all that he affirmed was that to the soul the cart was no more real than its own imaginative reproduction of it, and perhaps the shade of the philosopher ran up to the first of his deriders who crossed the Styx with a triumphant "I told you so! The cart did not run over *me*, for here I am without a bone broken."

And, in another sense also, do those poets who deal with human character, as all the greater do, continually suggest to us the purely phantasmal nature of life except as it is related to the world of ideas. For are not their personages more real than most of those in history? Is not Lear more authentic and permanent than Lord Raglan? Their realm is a purely spiritual one in which space and time and costume are nothing. What matters it that Shakespeare puts a seaport in Bohemia, and knew less geography than Tommy who goes to the district school? He understood eternal boundaries, such as are laid down on no chart, and are not defined by such transitory affairs as mountain chains, rivers, and seas.

No great movement of the human mind takes place without the concurrent beat of those two wings, the imagination and the understanding. It is by the understanding that we are enabled to make the most of this world, and to use the collected material of experience in its condensed form of practical wisdom; and it is the imagination which forever beckons toward that other world which is always future, and makes us discontented with this. The one rests upon experience; the other leans forward and listens after the *in*experienced, and shapes the features of that future with which it is forever in travail. The imagination might be defined as the common sense of the invisible world, as the understanding is of the visible; and as those are the finest individual characters in which the two moderate and rectify each other, so those are the finest eras where the same may be said of society. In the voyage of life, not only do we depend on the needle, true to its earthly instincts, but upon observation of the fixed stars, those beacons lighted upon the eternal promontories of heaven above the stirs and shiftings of our lower system.

But it seems to be thought that we have come upon the earth too late, that there has been a feast of imagination formerly, and all that is left for us is to steal the scraps. We hear that there is no poetry in railroads and steamboats and telegraphs, and especially none in Brother Jonathan. If this be true, so much the worse for him. But because *he* is a materialist shall there be no more poets? When we have said that we live in a materialistic age we have said something which meant more than we intended. If we say it in the way of blame, we have said a foolish thing, for probably one age is as good as another, and, at any rate, the worst is good enough company for us. The age of Shakespeare was richer than our own, only because it was lucky enough to have such a pair of eyes as his to see it, and such a gift of speech as his to report it. And so there is always room and occasion for the poet, who continues to be, just as he was in the early time, nothing more nor less than a "seer." He is always the man who is willing to take the age he lives in on trust, as the very best that ever was. Shakespeare did not sit down and cry for the water of Helicon to turn the wheels of his little private mill at the Bankside. He appears to have gone more quietly about his business than any other playwright in London, to have drawn off what water-power he needed from the great prosy current of affairs that flows alike for all and in spite of all, to have ground for the public what grist they wanted, coarse or fine, and it seems a mere piece of luck that the smooth stream of his activity reflected with such ravishing clearness every changing mood of heaven and earth, every stick and stone, every dog and clown and courtier that stood upon its brink. It is a curious illustration of the friendly manner in which Shakespeare received everything that came along,—of what a *present* man he was,—that in the very same year that the mulberry-tree was brought into England, he got one and planted it in his garden at Stratford.

It is perfectly true that this is a materialistic age, and for that very reason we want our poets all the more. We find that every generation contrives to catch its singing larks without the sky's falling. When the poet comes, he always turns out to be the man who discovers that the passing moment is the inspired one, and that the secret of poetry is not to have lived in Homer's day, or Dante's, but to be alive now. To be alive now, that is the great art and mystery. They are dead men who live in the past, and men yet unborn that live in the future. We are like Hans in Luck, forever exchanging the burdensome good we have for something else, till at last we come home empty-handed.

That pale-faced drudge of Time opposite me there, that weariless sexton whose callous hands bury our rosy hours in the irrevocable past, is even now reaching forward to a moment as rich in life, in character, and thought, as full of opportunity, as any since Adam. This little isthmus that we are now standing on is the point to which martyrs in their triumphant pain, prophets in their fervor, and poets in their ecstasy, looked forward as the golden future, as the land too good for them to behold with mortal eyes; it is the point toward which the faint-hearted and desponding hereafter will look back as the priceless past when there was still some good and virtue and opportunity left in the world.

The people who feel their own age prosaic are those who see only its costume. And that is what makes it prosaic—that we have not faith enough in ourselves to think our own clothes good enough to be presented to posterity in. The artists fancy that the court dress of posterity is that of Van Dyck's time, or Cæsar's. I have seen the model of a statue of Sir Robert Peel,—a statesman whose merit consisted in yielding gracefully to the present,—in which the sculptor had done his best to travesty the real man into a make-believe Roman. At the period when England produced its greatest poets, we find exactly the reverse of this, and we are thankful that the man who made the monument of Lord Bacon had genius to copy every button of his dress, everything down to the rosettes on his shoes, and then to write under his statue, "Thus sat Francis Bacon"—not "Cneius Pompeius"—"Viscount Verulam." Those men had faith even in their own shoe-strings.

After all, how is our poor scapegoat of a nineteenth century to blame? Why, for not being the seventeenth, to be sure! It is always raining opportunity, but it seems it was only the men two hundred years ago who were intelligent enough not to hold their cups bottom-up. We are like beggars who think if a piece of gold drop into their palm it must be counterfeit, and would rather change it for the smooth-worn piece of familiar copper. And so, as we stand in our mendicancy by the wayside, Time tosses carefully the great golden today into our hats, and we turn it over grumblingly and suspiciously, and are pleasantly surprised at finding that we can exchange it for beef and potatoes. Till Dante's time the

Italian poets thought no language good enough to put their nothings into but Latin,—and indeed a dead tongue was the best for dead thoughts,—but Dante found the common speech of Florence, in which men bargained and scolded and made love, good enough for him, and out of the world around him made a poem such as no Roman ever sang.

In our day, it is said despairingly, the understanding reigns triumphant: it is the age of common sense. If this be so, the wisest way would be to accept it manfully. But, after all, what is the meaning of it? Looking at the matter superficially, one would say that a striking difference between our science and that of the world's gray fathers is that there is every day less and less of the element of wonder in it. What they saw written in light upon the great arch of heaven, and, by a magnificent reach of sympathy, of which we are incapable, associated with the fall of monarchs and the fate of man, is for us only a professor, a piece of chalk, and a blackboard. The solemn and unapproachable skies we have vulgarized; we have peeped and botanized among the flowers of light, pulled off every petal, fumbled in every calyx, and reduced them to the bare stem of order and class. The stars can no longer maintain their divine reserves, but whenever there is a conjunction and congress of planets, every enterprising newspaper sends thither its special reporter with his telescope. Over those arcana of life where once a mysterious presence brooded, we behold scientific explorers skipping like so many incarnate notes of interrogation. We pry into the counsels of the great powers of nature, we keep our ears at the keyhole, and know everything that is going to happen. There is no longer any sacred inaccessibility, no longer any enchanting unexpectedness, and life turns to prose the moment there is nothing unattainable. It needs no more a voice out of the unknown proclaiming "Great Pan is dead!" We have found his tombstone, deciphered the arrowheaded inscription upon it, know his age to a day, and that he died universally regretted.

Formerly science was poetry. A mythology which broods over us in our cradle, which mingles with the lullaby of the nurse, which peoples the day with the possibility of divine encounters, and night with intimation of demonic ambushes, is something quite other, as the material for thought and poetry, from one that we take down from our bookshelves, as sapless as the shelf it stood on, as remote from all present sympathy with man or nature as a town history with its genealogies of Mr. Nobody's great-grandparents.

We have utilized everything. The Egyptians found a hint of the solar system in the concentric circles of the onion, and revered it as a symbol, while we respect it as a condiment in cookery, and can pass through all Weathersfield without a thought of the stars. Our world is a museum of natural history; that of our forefathers was a museum of supernatural history. And the rapidity with which the change has been going on is almost startling, when we consider that so modern and historical a personage as Queen Elizabeth was reigning at the time of the death of Dr. John Faustus, out of whose story the Teutonic imagination built up a mythus that may be set beside that of Prometheus.

Science, looked at scientifically, is bare and bleak enough. On those sublime heights the air is too thin for the lungs, and blinds the eyes. It is much better living down in the valleys, where one cannot see farther than the next farmhouse. Faith was never found in the bottom of a crucible, nor peace arrived at by analysis or synthesis. But all this is because science has become too grimly intellectual, has divorced itself from the moral and imaginative part of man. Our results are not arrived at in that spirit which led Kepler (who had his theory-traps set all along the tracks of the stars to catch a discovery) to say, "In my opinion the occasions of new discoveries have been no less wonderful than the discoveries themselves."

But we are led back continually to the fact that science cannot, if it would, disengage itself from human nature and from imagination. No two men have ever argued together without at least agreeing in this, that something more than proof is required to produce conviction, and that a logic which is capable of grinding the stubbornest facts to powder (as every man's *own* logic always is) is powerless against so delicate a structure as the brain.

Do what we will, we cannot contrive to bring together the yawning edges of proof and belief, to weld them into one. When Thor strikes Skrymir with his terrible hammer, the giant asks if a leaf has fallen. I need not appeal to the Thors of argument in the pulpit, the senate, and the mass-meeting, if they have not sometimes found the popular giant as provokingly insensible. The $\sqrt{-x}$ is nothing in comparison with the chance-caught smell of a single flower which by the magic of association recreates for us the unquestioning day of childhood. Demonstration may lead to the very gate of heaven, but there she makes us a civil bow, and leaves us to make our way back again to Faith, who has the key. That science which is of the intellect alone steps with indifferent foot upon the dead body of Belief, if only she may reach higher or see farther.

But we cannot get rid of our wonder—we who have brought down the wild lightning, from writing fiery doom upon the walls of heaven, to be our errand-boy and penny-postman. Wonder is crude imagination; and it is necessary to us, for man shall not live by bread alone, and exact knowledge is not enough. Do we get nearer the truth or farther from it that we have got a gas or an imponderable fluid instead of a spirit? We go on exorcising one thing after another, but what boots it? The evasive genius flits into something else, and defies us. The powers of the outer and inner world form hand in hand a magnetic circle for whose connection man is necessary. It is the imagination that takes his hand and clasps it with that other stretched to him in the dark, and for which he was vainly groping. It is that which renews the mystery in nature, makes it wonderful and beautiful again, and out of the gases of the man of science remakes the old spirit. But we seem to have created too many wonders to be capable of wondering any longer; as Coleridge said, when asked if he believed in ghosts, that he had seen too many of them. But nature all the more imperatively demands it, and science can at best but scotch it, not kill it. In this day of newspapers and electric telegraphs, in which common sense and ridicule can magnetize a whole continent between dinner and tea, we say that such a phenomenon as Mahomet were impossible, and behold Joe Smith and the State of Deseret! Turning over the yellow leaves of the same copy of "Webster on Witchcraft" which Cotton Mather studied, I thought, "Well, that goblin is laid at last!"—and while I mused the tables were turning, and the chairs beating the devil's tattoo all over Christendom. I have a neighbor who dug down through tough strata of clay to a spring pointed out by a witch-hazel rod in the hands of a seventh son's seventh son, and the water is the sweeter to him for the wonder that is mixed with it. After all, it seems that our scientific gas, be it never so brilliant, is not equal to the dingy old Aladdin's lamp.

It is impossible for men to live in the world without poetry of some sort or other. If they cannot get the best they will get some substitute for it, and thus seem to verify Saint Augustine's slur that it is wine of devils. The mind bound down too closely to what is practical either becomes inert, or revenges itself by rushing into the savage wilderness of "isms." The insincerity of our civilization has disgusted some persons so much that they have sought refuge in Indian wigwams and found refreshment in taking a scalp now and then. Nature insists above all things upon balance. She contrives to maintain a harmony between the material and spiritual, nor allows the cerebrum an expansion at the cost of the cerebellum. If the character, for example, run on one side into religious enthusiasm, it is not unlikely to develop on the other a counterpoise of worldly prudence. Thus the Shaker and the Moravian are noted for thrift, and mystics are not always the worst managers. Through all changes of condition and experience man continues to be a citizen of the world of idea as well as the world of fact, and the tax-gatherers of both are punctual.

And these antitheses which we meet with in individual character we cannot help seeing on the larger stage of the world also, a moral accompanying a material development. History, the great satirist, brings together Alexander and the blower of peas to hint to us that the tube of the one and the sword of the other were equally transitory; but meanwhile Aristotle was conquering kingdoms out of the unknown, and establishing a dynasty of thought from whose hand the sceptre has not yet passed. So there are Charles V, and Luther; the expansion of trade resulting from the Spanish and Portuguese discoveries, and the Elizabethan literature; the Puritans seeking spiritual El Dorados while so much valor and thought were spent in finding mineral ones. It seems to be the purpose of God that a certain amount of genius shall go to each generation, particular quantities being represented by individuals, and while no *one* is complete in himself, all collectively make up a whole ideal figure of a man. Nature is not like certain varieties of the apple that cannot bear two years in succession. It is only that her expansions are uniform in all directions, that in every age she completes her circle, and like a tree adds a ring to her growth be it thinner or thicker.

Every man is conscious that he leads two lives, the one trivial and ordinary, the other sacred and recluse; the one which he carries to the dinner-table and to his daily work, which grows old with his body and dies with it, the other that which is made up of the few inspiring moments of his higher aspiration and attainment, and in which his youth survives for him, his dreams, his unquenchable longings for something nobler than success. It is this life which the poets nourish for him, and sustain with their immortalizing nectar. Through them he feels once more the white innocence of his youth. His faith in something nobler than gold and iron and cotton comes back to him, not as an upbraiding ghost that wrings its pale hands and is gone, but beautiful and inspiring as a first love that recognizes nothing in him that is not high and noble. The poets are nature's perpetual pleaders, and protest with us against what is worldly. Out of their own undying youth they speak to ours. "Wretched is the man," says Goethe, "who has learned to despise the dreams of his youth!" It is from this misery that the imagination and the poets, who are its spokesmen, rescue us. The world goes to church, kneels to the eternal Purity, and then contrives to sneer at innocence and ignorance of evil by calling it green. Let every man thank God for what little there may be left in him of his vernal sweetness. Let him thank God if he have still the capacity for feeling an unmarketable enthusiasm, for that will make him worthy of the society of the noble dead, of the companionship of the poets. And let him love the poets for keeping youth young, woman womanly, and beauty beautiful.

There is as much poetry as ever in the world if we only knew how to find it out; and as much imagination, perhaps, only that it takes a more prosaic direction. Every man who meets with misfortune, who is stripped of material prosperity, finds that he has a little outlying mountain-farm of imagination, which did not appear in the schedule of his effects, on which his spirit is able to keep itself alive, though he never thought of it while he was fortunate. Job turns out to be a great poet as soon as his flocks and herds are taken away from him.

There is no reason why our continent should not sing as well as the rest. We have had the practical forced upon us by our position. We have had a whole hemisphere to clear up and put to rights. And we are descended from men who were hardened and stiffened by a downright wrestle with necessity. There was no chance for poetry among the Puritans. And yet if any people have a right to imagination, it should be the descendants of these very Puritans. They had enough of it, or they could never have conceived the great epic they did, whose books are States, and which is written on this continent from Maine to California.

But there seems to be another reason why we should not become a poetical people. Formerly the poet embodied the hopes and desires of men in visible types. He gave them the shoes of swiftness, the cap of invisibility and the purse of Fortunatus. These were once stories for grown men, and not for the nursery as now. We are apt ignorantly to wonder how our forefathers could find satisfaction in fiction the absurdity of which any of our primary-school children could demonstrate. But we forget that the world's gray fathers were children themselves, and that in their little world, with its circle of the black unknown all about it, the imagination was as active as it is with people in the dark. Look at a child's toys, and we shall understand the matter well enough. Imagination is the fairy godmother (every child has one still), at the wave of whose wand sticks become heroes, the closet in which she has been shut fifty times for being naughty is turned into a palace, and a bit of lath acquires all the potency of Excalibur.

But nowadays it is the understanding itself that has turned poet. In her railroads she has given us the shoes of swiftness. Fine-Ear herself could not hear so far as she, who in her magnetic telegraph can listen in Boston and hear what is going on in New Orleans. And what need of Aladdin's lamp when a man can build a palace with a patent pill? The office of the poet seems to be reversed, and he must give back these miracles of the understanding to poetry again, and find out what there is imaginative in steam and iron and telegraph-wires. After all, there is as much poetry in the iron horses that eat fire as in those of Diomed that fed on men. If you cut an apple across you may trace in it the lines of the blossom that the bee hummed around in May, and so the soul of poetry survives in things prosaic. Borrowing money on a bond does not seem the most promising subject in the world, but Shakespeare found the "Merchant of Venice" in it. Themes of song are waiting everywhere for the right man to sing them, like those enchanted swords which no one can pull out of the rock till the hero comes, and he finds no more trouble than in plucking a violet.

John Quincy Adams, making a speech at New Bedford, many years ago, reckoned the number of whaleships (if I remember rightly) that sailed out of that port, and, comparing it with some former period, took it as a type of American success. But, alas! it is with quite other oil that those far-shining lamps of a nation's true glory which burn forever must be filled. It is not by any amount of material splendor or prosperity, but only by moral greatness, by ideas, by works of imagination, that a race can conquer the future. No voice comes to us from the once mighty Assyria but the hoot of the owl that nests amid her crumbling palaces. Of Carthage, whose merchant-fleets once furled their sails in every port of the known world, nothing is left but the deeds of Hannibal. She lies dead on the shore of her once subject sea, and the wind of the desert only flings its handfuls of burial-sand upon her corpse. A fog can blot Holland or Switzerland out of existence. But how large is the space occupied in the maps of the soul by little Athens and powerless Italy! They were great by the soul, and their vital force is as indestructible as the soul.

Till America has learned to love art, not as an amusement, not as the mere ornament of her cities, not as a superstition of what is *comme il faut* for a great nation, but for its humanizing and ennobling energy, for its power of making men better by arousing in them a perception of their own instincts for what is beautiful, and therefore sacred and religious, and an eternal rebuke of the base and worldly, she will not have succeeded in that high sense which alone makes a nation out of a people, and raises it from a dead name to a living power. Were our little mother-island sunk beneath the sea, or, worse, were she conquered by Scythian barbarians, yet Shakespeare would be an immortal England, and would conquer countries, when the bones of her last sailor had kept their ghastly watch for ages in unhallowed ooze beside the quenched thunders of her navy.

Old Purchas in his "Pilgrims" tells of a sacred caste in India who, when they go out into the street, cry out, "Poo! Poo!" to warn all the world out of their way lest they should be defiled by something unclean. And it is just so that the understanding in its pride of success thinks to pooh-pooh all that it considers impractical and visionary. But whatever of life there is in man, except what comes of beef and pudding, is in the visionary and unpractical, and if it be not encouraged to find its activity or its solace in the production or enjoyment of art and beauty, if it be bewildered or thwarted by an outward profession of faith covering up a practical unbelief in anything higher and holier than the world of sense, it will find vent in such wretched holes and corners as table-tippings and mediums who sell news from heaven at a quarter of a dollar the item. Imagination cannot be banished out of the world. She may be made a kitchen-drudge, a Cinderella, but there are powers that watch over her. When her two proud sisters, the intellect and understanding, think her crouching over her ashes, she startles and charms by her splendid apparition, and Prince Soul will put up with no other bride.

The practical is a very good thing in its way—if it only be not another name for the worldly. To be absorbed in it is to eat of that insane root which the soldiers of Antonius found in their retreat from Parthia—which whoso tasted kept gathering sticks and stones as if they were some great matter till he died.

One is forced to listen, now and then, to a kind of talk which makes him feel as if this were the after-dinner time of the world, and mankind were doomed hereafter forever to that kind of contented materialism which comes to good stomachs with the nuts and raisins. The dozy old world has nothing to do now but stretch its legs under the mahogany, talk about stocks, and get rid of the hours as well as it can till bedtime. The centuries before us have drained the goblet of wisdom and beauty, and all we have left is to cast horoscopes in the dregs. But divine beauty, and the love of it, will never be without apostles and messengers on earth, till Time flings his hour-glass into the abyss as having no need to turn it longer to number the indistinguishable ages of Annihilation. It was a favorite speculation with the learned men of the sixteenth century that they had come upon the old age and decrepit second childhood of creation, and while they maundered, the soul of Shakespeare was just coming out of the eternal freshness of Deity, "trailing" such "clouds of glory" as would beggar a Platonic year of sunsets.

No; morning and the dewy prime are born into the earth again with every child. It is our fault if drought and dust usurp the noon. Every age says to her poets, like the mistress to her lover, "Tell me what I am like"; and, in proportion as it brings forth anything worth seeing, has need of seers and will have them. Our time is not an unpoetical one. We are in our heroic age, still face to face with the shaggy forces of unsubdued Nature, and we have our Theseuses and Perseuses, though they may be named Israel Putnam and Daniel Boone. It is nothing against us that we are a commercial people. Athens was a trading community; Dante and Titian were the growth of great marts, and England was already commercial when she produced Shakespeare.

This lesson I learn from the past: that grace and goodness, the fair, the noble, and the true, will never cease out of the world till the God from whom they emanate ceases out of it; that they manifest themselves in an eternal continuity of change to every generation of men, as new duties and occasions arise; that the sacred duty and noble office of the poet is to reveal and justify them to men; that so long as the soul endures, endures also the theme of new and unexampled song; that while there is grace in grace, love in love, and beauty in beauty, God will still send poets to find them and bear witness of them, and to hang their ideal portraitures in the gallery of memory. God with us is forever the mystical name of the hour that is passing. The lives of the great poets teach us that they were the men of their generation who felt most deeply the meaning of the present.

1855 1894

From THE LIFE AND LETTERS OF JAMES GATES PERCIVAL

[I. A NATIONAL LITERATURE]

. . . It had been resolved unanimously that we must and would have a national literature. England, France, Spain, Italy, each already had one, Germany was getting one made as fast as possible, and Ireland vowed that she once had one far surpassing them all. To be respectable, we must have one also, and that speedily. We forgot that artistic literature, the only literature possible under our modern conditions, thrives best in an air laden with tradition, in a soil mellow with immemorial culture, in the temperature steady yet stimulating of historic and national associations. We had none of these, but Sydney Smith's scornful question, "Who reads an American book?" tingled in our ears. Surely never was a young nation setting forth jauntily to seek its fortune so dumbfounded as Brother Jonathan when John Bull cried gruffly from the roadside, "Stand, and deliver a national literature!" After fumbling in his pockets, he was obliged to confess that he hadn't one about him at the moment, but vowed that he had left a first-rate one at home which he would have fetched along—only it was so everlasting heavy.

If the East should fail, as judged by European standards it seemed to have done, it was resolved that a poet should come out of the West, fashioned on a scale somewhat proportioned to our geographical pretensions. Our rivers, forests, mountains, cataracts, prairies, and inland seas were to find in him their antitype and voice. Shaggy he was to be, brown-fisted, careless of proprieties, unhampered by tradition, his Pegasus of the half-horse, half-alligator breed. By him at last the epos of the New World was to be fitly sung, the great tragi-comedy of democracy put upon the stage for all time. It was a cheap vision, for it cost no thought; and, like all judicious prophecy, it muffled itself from criticism in the loose drapery of its terms. Till the advent of this splendid apparition, who should dare affirm positively that he would never come? that, indeed, he was impossible? And yet his impossibility was demonstrable, nevertheless.

Supposing a great poet to be born in the West, though he would naturally levy upon what had always been familiar to his eyes for his images and illustrations, he would almost certainly look for his ideal somewhere outside of the life that lay immediately about him. Life in its large sense, and not as it is temporarily modified by manners or politics, is the only subject of the poet; and though its elements lie always close at hand, yet in its unity it seems always infinitely distant, and the difference of angle at which it is seen in India and in Minnesota is almost inappreciable. Moreover, a rooted discontent seems always to underlie all great poetry, if it be not even the motive of it. The Iliad and the Odyssey paint manners that are only here and there incidentally true to the actual, but which in their larger truth had either never existed or had long since passed away. Had Dante's scope been narrowed to contemporary Italy, the *Divina Commedia* would have been a picture-book merely. But his theme was Man, and the vision that inspired him was of an Italy that never was nor could be, his political theories as abstract as those of Plato or Spinoza. Shakespeare shows us less of the England that then was than any other considerable poet of his time. The struggle of Goethe's whole life was to emancipate himself from Germany, and fill his lungs for once with a more universal air.

Yet there is always a flavor of the climate in these rare fruits, some gift of the sun peculiar to the region that ripened them. If we are ever to have a national poet, let us hope that his nationality will be of this subtile essence, something that shall make him unspeakably nearer to us, while it does not provincialize him for the rest of mankind. The popular recipe for compounding him would give us, perhaps, the most sublimely furnished bore in human annals. The novel aspects of life under our novel conditions may give some freshness of color to our literature; but democracy itself, which many seem to regard as the necessary Lucina of some new poetic birth, is altogether too abstract an influence to serve for any such purpose. If any American author may be looked on as in some sort the result of our social and political ideal, it is Emerson, who, in his emancipation from the traditional, in the irresponsible freedom of his speculation, and in the absolute faith in the value of his own individuality, is certainly, to some extent, typical; but if ever author was inspired by the past, it is he, and he is as far as possible from the shaggy hero of prophecy. Of the sham-shaggy, who have tried the trick of Jacob upon us, we have had quite enough, and may safely doubt whether this satyr of masquerade is to be the representative singer. Were it so, it would not be greatly to the credit of democracy as an element of aesthetics. But we may safely hope for better things.

The themes of poetry have been pretty much the same from the first; and if a man should ever be born among us with a great imagination, and the gift of the right word,—for it is these and not sublime spaces, that make a poet,—he will be original rather in spite of democracy than in consequence of it, and will owe his inspiration quite as much to the accumulations of the Old World as to the promises of the New. But for a long while yet the proper conditions will be wanting, not, perhaps, for the birth of such a man, but for his development and culture. At present, with the largest reading population in the world, perhaps no country ever offered less encouragement to the higher forms of art or the more thorough achievements of scholarship. Even were it not so, it would be idle to expect us to produce any literature so peculiarly our own as was the natural growth of ages less communicative, less open to every breath of foreign influence. Literature tends more and more to become a vast commonwealth, with no dividing lines of nationality. . . .

[II. SENTIMENTALISM]

. . . If poetry, in Bacon's noble definition of it, "adapt the shows of things to the desires of the mind," sentimentalism is equally skilful in making realities shape themselves to the cravings of vanity. The theory that the poet is a being above the world and apart from it is true of him as an observer only who applies to the phenomena about him the test of a finer and more spiritual sense. That he is a creature divinely set apart from his fellow-men by a mental organization that makes them mutually unintelligible to each other is in flat contradiction with the lives of those poets universally acknowledged as greatest. Dante, Shakespeare, Cervantes, Calderon, Milton, Molière, Goethe,—in what conceivable sense is it true of them that they wanted the manly qualities which made them equal to the demands of the world in which they lived? That a poet should assume, as Victor Hugo used to do, that he is a reorganizer of the moral world, and that works cunningly adapted to the popular whim of the time form part of some mysterious system which is to give us a new heaven and a new earth, and to remodel laws of art which are as unchangeable as those of astronomy, can do no very great harm to any one but the author himself, who will thereby be led astray from his proper function, and from the only path to legitimate and lasting success. But when the theory is carried a step further, and we are asked to believe, as in Percival's case, that because a man can write verses, he is exempt from that inexorable logic of life and circumstances to which all other men are subjected, and to which it is wholesome for them that they should be, then it becomes mischievous, and calls for a protest from all those who have at heart the interests of good morals and healthy literature. It is the theory of idlers and *dilettanti*, of fribbles in morals and declaimers in verse, which a young man of real power may dally with during some fit of mental indigestion, but which when accepted by a mature man, and carried along through life, is a sure mark of feebleness and of insincere dealing with himself. Percival is a good example of a class of authors unhappily too numerous in these latter days. In Europe the natural growth of a world ill at ease with itself and still nervous with the frightful palpitation of the French Revolution, they are but feeble exotics in our healthier air. Without faith or hope, and deprived of that outward support in the habitual procession of events and in the authoritative limitations of thought which in ordinary times gives steadiness to feeble and timid intellects, they are turned inward, and are forced, like Hudibras's sword,

"To eat into themselves, for lack
Of other thing to hew and hack."

Compelled to find within them that stay which has hitherto been supplied by creeds and institutions, they learned to attribute to their own consciousness the grandeur which belongs of right only to the mind of the race, slowly endeavoring after an equilibrium between its desires and the external conditions under which they are attainable. Hence that exaggeration of the individual, and the depreciation of the social man, which has become the cant of modern literature. Abundance of such phenomena accompanied the rise of what was called Romanticism in Germany and France, reacting to some extent upon England, and consequently upon America. The smaller poets erected themselves into a kind of guild, to which all were admitted who gave proof of a certain feebleness of character which rendered them superior to their grosser fellow-men. It was a society of cripples undertaking to teach the new generation how to walk. . . . Percival belonged to this new order of bards, weak in the knees, and thinking it healthy exercise to climb the peaks of Dreamland. . . .

1867

From DANTE

[POETS AS TEACHERS]

No doubt it is primarily by his poetic qualities that a poet must be judged, for it is by these, if by anything, that he is to maintain his place in literature. And he must be judged by them absolutely, with reference, that is, to the highest standard, and not relatively to the fashions and opportunities of the age in which he lived. Yet these considerations must fairly enter into our decision of another side of the question, and one that has much to do with the true quality of the man, with his character as distinguished from his talent, and therefore with how much he will influence men as well as delight them. We may reckon up pretty exactly a man's advantages and defects as an artist; these he has in common with others, and they are to be measured by a recognized standard; but there is something in his *genius* that is incalculable. It would be hard to define the causes of the difference of impression made upon us respectively by two such men as Æschylus and Euripides, but we feel profoundly that the latter, though in some respects a better dramatist, was an infinitely lighter weight. Æschylus stirs something in us far deeper than the sources of mere pleasurable excitement. The man behind the verse is far greater than the verse itself, and the impulse he gives to what is deepest and most sacred in us, though we cannot always explain it, is none the less real and lasting. Some men always seem to remain outside their work; others make their individuality felt through every part of it; their very life vibrates in every verse, and we do not wonder that it has "made them lean for many years." The virtue that has gone out of them abides in what they do. The book such a man makes is indeed, as Milton called it, "the precious lifeblood of a master spirit." Theirs is a true immortality, for it is their soul, and not their talent, that survives in their work. Dante's concise forth-rightness of phrase, which to that of most other poets is as a stab [1] to a blow with a cudgel, the vigor of his thought, the beauty of his images, the refinement of his conception of spiritual things, are marvelous if we compare him with his age and its best achievement. But it is for his power of inspiring and sustaining, it is because they find in him a spur to noble aims, a secure refuge in that defeat which the present always seems, that they prize Dante who know and love him best. He is not merely a great poet, but an influence, part of the soul's resources in time of trouble. From him she learns that, "married to the truth, she is a mistress, but otherwise a slave shut out of all liberty." [1]

[1] To the "bestiality" of certain arguments Dante says, "one would wish to reply, not with words, but with a knife." (*Convito*, Tr. IV. c.14.)

All great poets have their message to deliver us, from something higher than they. We venture on no unworthy comparison between him who reveals to us the beauty of this world's love and the grandeur of this world's passion and him who shows that love of God is the fruit whereof all other loves are but the beautiful and fleeting blossom, that the passions are yet sublimer objects of contemplation, when, subdued by the will, they become patience in suffering and perseverance in the upward path. But we cannot help thinking that if Shakespeare be the most comprehensive intellect, so Dante is the highest spiritual nature that has expressed itself in rhythmical form. Had he merely made us feel how petty the ambitious sorrows, and vexations of earth appear when looked down on from the heights of our own character and the seclusion of our own genius, or from the region where we commune with God, he had done much:

> "I with my sight returned through one and all
> The sevenfold spheres, and I beheld this globe
> Such that I smiled at its ignoble semblance." [2]

But he has done far more; he has shown us the way by which that country far beyond the stars may be reached, may become the habitual dwelling-place and fortress of our nature, instead of being the object of its vague aspiration in moments of indolence. At the Round Table of King Arthur there was left always one seat empty for him who should accomplish the adventure of the Holy Grail. It was called the perilous seat because of the dangers he must encounter who would win it. In the company

[1] *Convito*, Tr. IV. c.2.

[2] *Paradiso*, XXII. 132–135; Ib., XXVII. 110.

of the epic poets there was a place left for whoever should embody the Christian idea of a triumphant life, outwardly all defeat, inwardly victorious, who should make us partakers of that cup of sorrow in which all are communicants with Christ. He who should do this would indeed achieve the perilous seat, for he must combine poesy with doctrine in such cunning wise that the one lose not its beauty nor the other its severity,—and Dante has done it. As he takes possession of it we seem to hear the cry he himself heard when Virgil rejoined the company of great singers,

"All honor to the loftiest of poets!"

1872

OLIVER WENDELL HOLMES

THE HEIGHT OF THE RIDICULOUS

I WROTE some lines once on a time
  In wondrous merry mood,
And thought, as usual, men would say
  They were exceeding good.

They were so queer, so very queer,
  I laughed as I would die;
Albeit, in the general way,
  A sober man am I.

I called my servant, and he came;
  How kind it was of him
To mind a slender man like me,
  He of the mighty limb!

"These to the printer," I exclaimed,
  And, in my humorous way,
I added (as a trifling jest),
  "There'll be the devil to pay."

He took the paper, and I watched,
  And saw him peep within;
At the first line he read, his face
  Was all upon the grin.

He read the next; the grin grew broad,
  And shot from ear to ear;
He read the third; a chuckling noise
  I now began to hear.

The fourth; he broke into a roar;
  The fifth; his waistband split;
The sixth; he burst five buttons off,
  And tumbled in a fit.

Ten days and nights, with sleepless eye,
  I watched that wretched man,
And since, I never dare to write
  As funny as I can.

1830

OLD IRONSIDES

AY, tear her tattered ensign down!
  Long has it waved on high,
And many an eye has danced to see
  That banner in the sky;
Beneath it rung the battle shout,
  And burst the cannon's roar;—
The meteor of the ocean air
  Shall sweep the clouds no more.

Her deck, once red with heroes' blood,
  Where knelt the vanquished foe,
When winds were hurrying o'er the flood,
  And waves were white below,
No more shall feel the victor's tread,
  Or know the conquered knee;—
The harpies of the shore shall pluck
  The eagle of the sea!

Oh, better that her shattered hulk
  Should sink beneath the wave;
Her thunders shook the mighty deep,
  And there should be her grave;
Nail to the mast her holy flag,
  Set every threadbare sail,
And give her to the god of storms,
  The lightning and the gale!

1830 1830

THE BALLAD OF THE OYSTERMAN

IT was a tall young oysterman lived by the river-side,
His shop was just upon the bank, his boat was on the tide;
The daughter of a fisherman, that was so straight and slim,
Lived over on the other bank, right opposite to him.

It was the pensive oysterman that saw a lovely maid,
Upon a moonlight evening, a-sitting in the shade;
He saw her wave her handkerchief, as much as if to say,
"I'm wide awake, young oysterman, and all the folks away."

Then up arose the oysterman, and to himself said he,
"I guess I'll leave the skiff at home, for fear that folks should see;

I read it in the story-book, that, for to kiss his dear,
Leander swam the Hellespont,—and I will swim this here."

And he has leaped into the waves, and crossed the shining stream,
And he has clambered up the bank, all in the moonlight gleam;
Oh there were kisses sweet as dew, and words as soft as rain,—
But they have heard her father's step, and in he leaps again!

Out spoke the ancient fisherman,—"Oh, what was that, my daughter?"
" 'Twas nothing but a pebble, sir, I threw into the water."
"And what is that, pray tell me, love, that paddles off so fast?"
"It's nothing but a porpoise, sir, that's been a-swimming past."

Out spoke the ancient fisherman,—"Now bring me my harpoon!
I'll get into my fishing-boat, and fix the fellow soon."
Down fell that pretty innocent, as falls a snow-white lamb,
Her hair drooped round her pallid cheeks, like seaweed on a clam.

Alas for those two loving ones! she waked not from her swound,
And he was taken with the cramp, and in the waves was drowned;
But Fate has metamorphosed them, in pity of their woe,
And now they keep an oyster-shop for mermaids down below.

1830

TO AN INSECT

I LOVE to hear thine earnest voice,
Wherever thou art hid,
Thou testy little dogmatist,
Thou pretty Katydid!
Thou mindest me of gentlefolks,—
Old gentlefolks are they,—
Thou say'st an undisputed thing
In such a solemn way.

Thou art a female, Katydid!
I know it by the trill
That quivers through thy piercing notes,
So petulant and shrill;
I think there is a knot of you
Beneath the hollow tree,—
A knot of spinster Katydids,—
Do Katydids drink tea?

Oh, tell me where did Katy live,
And what did Katy do?
And was she very fair and young,
And yet so wicked, too?
Did Katy love a naughty man,
Or kiss more cheeks than one?
I warrant Katy did no more
Than many a Kate has done.

Dear me! I'll tell you all about
My fuss with little Jane,
And Ann, with whom I used to walk
So often down the lane,
And all that tore their locks of black,
Or wet their eyes of blue,—
Pray tell me, sweetest Katydid,
What did poor Katy do?

Ah no! the living oak shall crash,
That stood for ages still,
The rock shall rend its mossy base
And thunder down the hill,
Before the little Katydid
Shall add one word, to tell
The mystic story of the maid
Whose name she knows so well.

Peace to the ever-murmuring race!
And when the latest one
Shall fold in death her feeble wings
Beneath the autumn sun,
Then shall she raise her fainting voice,
And lift her drooping lid,
And then the child of future years
Shall hear what Katy did.

1831

L'INCONNUE

Is thy name Mary, maiden fair?
Such should, methinks, its music be;
The sweetest name that mortals bear
Were best befitting thee;
And she to whom it once was given,
Was half of earth and half of heaven.

I hear thy voice, I see thy smile,
  I look upon thy folded hair;
Ah! while we dream not they beguile,
  Our hearts are in the snare;
And she who chains a wild bird's wing
Must start not if her captive sing.

So, lady, take the leaf that falls,
  To all but thee unseen, unknown:
When evening shades thy silent walls,
  Then read it all alone;
In stillness read, in darkness seal,
Forget, despise, but not reveal!

1831

MY AUNT

My aunt! my dear unmarried aunt!
  Long years have o'er her flown;
Yet still she strains the aching clasp
  That binds her virgin zone;
I know it hurts her,—though she looks
  As cheerful as she can;
Her waist is ampler than her life,
  For life is but a span.

My aunt! my poor deluded aunt!
  Her hair is almost gray;
Why will she train that winter curl
  In such a spring-like way?
How can she lay her glasses down,
  And say she reads as well,
When through a double convex lens
  She just makes out to spell?

Her father—grandpapa! forgive
  This erring lip its smiles—
Vowed she should make the finest girl
  Within a hundred miles;
He sent her to a stylish school;
  'T was in her thirteenth June;
And with her, as the rules required,
  "Two towels and a spoon."

They braced my aunt against a board,
  To make her straight and tall;
They laced her up, they starved her down,
  To make her light and small;
They pinched her feet, they singed her hair,
  They screwed it up with pins;—
Oh, never mortal suffered more
  In penance for her sins.

So, when my precious aunt was done,
  My grandsire brought her back
(By daylight, lest some rabid youth
  Might follow on the track);
"Ah!" said my grandsire, as he shook
  Some powder in his pan,
"What could this lovely creature do
  Against a desperate man!"

Alas! nor chariot, nor barouche,
  Nor bandit cavalcade,
Tore from the trembling father's arms
  His all-accomplished maid.
For her how happy had it been!
  And Heaven had spared to me
To see one sad, ungathered rose
  On my ancestral tree.

1831

Melville's Grandfather

THE LAST LEAF

I saw him once before,
As he passed by the door,
  And again
The pavement stones resound,
As he totters o'er the ground
  With his cane.

They say that in his prime,
Ere the pruning-knife of Time
  Cut him down,
Not a better man was found
By the Crier on his round
  Through the town.

But now he walks the streets,
And he looks at all he meets
  Sad and wan,
And he shakes his feeble head,
That it seems as if he said,
  "They are gone."

The mossy marbles rest
On the lips that he has prest
  In their bloom,
And the names he loved to hear
Have been carved for many a year
  On the tomb.

My grandmamma has said—
Poor old lady, she is dead
  Long ago—

That he had a Roman nose,
And his cheek was like a rose
In the snow;

But now his nose is thin,
And it rests upon his chin
Like a staff,
And a crook is in his back,
And a melancholy crack
In his laugh.

I know it is a sin
For me to sit and grin
At him here;
But the old three-cornered hat,
And the breeches, and all that,
Are so queer!

And if I should live to be
The last leaf upon the tree
In the spring,
Let them smile, as I do now,
At the old forsaken bough
Where I cling.

1831? 1833

POETRY

A METRICAL ESSAY, READ BEFORE THE PHI BETA KAPPA SOCIETY, HARVARD UNIVERSITY, AUGUST, 1836

TO CHARLES WENTWORTH UPHAM, THE FOLLOWING METRICAL ESSAY IS AFFECTIONATELY INSCRIBED.

This Academic Poem presents the simple and partial views of a young person trained after the schools of classical English verse as represented by Pope, Goldsmith, and Campbell, with whose lines his memory was early stocked. It will be observed that it deals chiefly with the constructive side of the poet's function. That which makes him a poet is not the power of writing melodious rhymes, it is not the possession of ordinary human sensibilities nor even of both these qualities in connection with each other. I should rather say, if I were now called upon to define it, it is the power of transfiguring the experiences and shows of life into an aspect which comes from his imagination and kindles that of others. Emotion is its stimulus and language furnishes its expression; but these are not all, as some might infer was the doctrine of the poem before the reader.

A common mistake made by young persons who suppose themselves to have the poetical gift is that their own spiritual exaltation finds a true expression in the conventional phrases which are borrowed from the voices of the singers whose inspiration they think they share.

Looking at this poem as an expression of some aspects of the *ars poetica*, with some passages which I can read even at this mature period of life without blushing for them, it may stand as the most serious representation of my early efforts. Intended as it was for public delivery, many of its paragraphs may betray the fact by their somewhat rhetorical and sonorous character.

SCENES of my youth! awake its slumbering fire!
Ye winds of Memory, sweep the silent lyre!
Ray of the past, if yet thou canst appear,
Break through the clouds of Fancy's waning year;
Chase from her breast the thin autumnal snow,
If leaf or blossom still is fresh below!

Long have I wandered; the returning tide
Brought back an exile to his cradle's side;
And as my bark her time-worn flag unrolled,
To greet the land-breeze with its faded fold,
So, in remembrance of my boyhood's time,
I lift these ensigns of neglected rhyme;
Oh, more than blest, that, all my wanderings through,
My anchor falls where first my pennons flew!

The morning light, which rains its quivering beams
Wide o'er the plains, the summits, and the streams,
In one broad blaze expands its golden glow
On all that answers to its glance below;
Yet, changed on earth, each far reflected ray
Braids with fresh hues the shining brow of day;
Now, clothed in blushes by the painted flowers,
Tracks on their cheeks the rosy-fingered hours;
Now, lost in shades, whose dark entangled leaves
Drip at the noontide from their pendent eaves,
Fades into gloom, or gleams in light again
From every dew-drop on the jewelled plain.

We, like the leaf, the summit, or the wave,
Reflect the light our common nature gave,
But every sunbeam, falling from her throne,
Wears on our hearts some coloring of our own:

Chilled in the slave, and burning in the free,
Like the sealed cavern by the sparkling sea;
Lost, like the lightning in the sullen clod,
Or shedding radiance, like the smiles of God;
Pure, pale in Virtue, as the star above,
Or quivering roseate on the leaves of Love;
Glaring like noontide, where it glows upon
Ambition's sands,—the desert in the sun,—
Or soft suffusing o'er the varied scene
Life's common coloring,—intellectual green.

Thus Heaven, repeating its material plan,
Arched over all the rainbow mind of man;
But he who, blind to universal laws,
Sees but effects, unconscious of their cause,—
Believes each image in itself is bright,
Not robed in drapery of reflected light,—
Is like the rustic who, amidst his toil,
Has found some crystal in his meagre soil,
And, lost in rapture, thinks for him alone
Earth worked her wonders on the sparkling stone,
Nor dreams that Nature, with as nice a line,
Carved countless angles through the boundless mine.

Thus err the many, who, entranced to find
Unwonted lustre in some clearer mind,
Believe that Genius sets the laws at naught
Which chain the pinions of our wildest thought;
Untaught to measure, with the eye of art,
The wandering fancy or the wayward heart;
Who match the little only with the less,
And gaze in rapture at its slight excess,
Proud of a pebble, as the brightest gem
Whose light might crown an emperor's diadem.

And, most of all, the pure ethereal fire
Which seems to radiate from the poet's lyre
Is to the world a mystery and a charm,
An Ægis wielded on a mortal's arm,
While Reason turns her dazzled eye away,
And bows her sceptre to her subject's sway;
And thus the poet, clothed with godlike state,
Usurped his Maker's title—to create;
He, whose thoughts differing not in shape, but dress,
What others feel more fitly can express,
Sits like the maniac on his fancied throne,
Peeps through the bars, and calls the world his own.

There breathes no being but has some pretence
To that fine instinct called poetic sense:
The rudest savage, roaming through the wild;
The simplest rustic, bending o'er his child;
The infant, listening to the warbling bird;
The mother, smiling at its half-formed word;
The boy uncaged, who tracks the fields at large;
The girl, turned matron to her babe-like charge;
The freeman, casting with unpurchased hand
The vote that shakes the turret of the land;
The slave, who, slumbering on his rusted chain,
Dreams of the palm-trees on his burning plain;
The hot-cheeked reveller, tossing down the wine,
To join the chorus pealing "Auld lang syne";
The gentle maid, whose azure eye grows dim,
While Heaven is listening to her evening hymn;
The jewelled beauty, when her steps draw near
The circling dance and dazzling chandelier;
E'en trembling age, when Spring's renewing air
Waves the thin ringlets of his silvered hair;—
All, all are glowing with the inward flame,
Whose wider halo wreathes the poet's name,
While, unembalmed, the silent dreamer dies,
His memory passing with his smiles and sighs!

If glorious visions, born for all mankind,
The bright auroras of our twilight mind;
If fancies, varying as the shapes that lie
Stained on the windows of the sunset sky;
If hopes, that beckon with delusive gleams,
Till the eye dances in the void of dreams;
If passions, following with the winds that urge
Earth's wildest wanderer to her farthest verge;—
If these on all some transient hours bestow
Of rapture tingling with its hectic glow,
Then all are poets; and if earth had rolled
Her myriad centuries, and her doom were told,
Each moaning billow of her shoreless wave
Would wail its requiem o'er a poet's grave!

If to embody in a breathing word
Tones that the spirit trembled when it heard;
To fix the image all unveiled and warm,
And carve in language its ethereal form,
So pure, so perfect, that the lines express
No meagre shrinking, no unlaced excess;
To feel that art, in living truth, has taught
Ourselves, reflected in the sculptured thought;—
If this alone bestow the right to claim
The deathless garland and the sacred name,
Then none are poets save the saints on high,
Whose harps can murmur all that words deny!

But though to none is granted to reveal
In perfect semblance all that each may feel,
As withered flowers recall forgotten love,
So, warmed to life, our faded passions move
In every line, where kindling fancy throws
The gleam of pleasures or the shade of woes.

When, schooled by time, the stately queen of art
Had smoothed the pathways leading to the heart,
Assumed her measured tread, her solemn tone,
And round her courts the clouds of fable thrown,
The wreaths of heaven descended on her shrine,
And wondering earth proclaimed the Muse divine.
Yet if her votaries had but dared profane
The mystic symbols of her sacred reign,
How had they smiled beneath the veil to find
What slender threads can chain the mighty mind!

Poets, like painters, their machinery claim,
And verse bestows the varnish and the frame;
Our grating English, whose Teutonic jar
Shakes the racked axle of Art's rattling car,
Fits like mosaic in the lines that gird
Fast in its place each many-angled word;
From Saxon lips Anacreon's numbers glide,
As once they melted on the Teian tide,
And, fresh transfused, the Iliad thrills again
From Albion's cliffs as o'er Achaia's plain!
The proud heroic, with its pulse-like beat,
Rings like the cymbals clashing as they meet;
The sweet Spenserian, gathering as it flows,
Sweeps gently onward to its dying close,
Where waves on waves in long succession pour,
Till the ninth billow melts along the shore;
The lonely spirit of the mournful lay,
Which lives immortal as the verse of Gray,
In sable plumage slowly drifts along,
On eagle pinion, through the air of song;
The glittering lyric bounds elastic by,
With flashing ringlets and exulting eye,
While every image, in her airy whirl,
Gleams like a diamond on a dancing girl!

Born with mankind, with man's expanded range
And varying fates the poet's numbers change;
Thus in his history may we hope to find
Some clearer epochs of the poet's mind,
As from the cradle of its birth we trace,
Slow wandering forth, the patriarchal race.

I

When the green earth, beneath the zephyr's wing,
Wears on her breast the varnished buds of Spring;
When the loosed current, as its folds uncoil,
Slides in the channels of the mellowed soil;
When the young hyacinth returns to seek
The air and sunshine with her emerald beak;
When the light snowdrops, starting from their cells,
Hang each pagoda with its silver bells;
When the frail willow twines her trailing bow
With pallid leaves that sweep the soil below;
When the broad elm, sole empress of the plain,
Whose circling shadow speaks a century's reign,
Wreathes in the clouds her regal diadem,—
A forest waving on a single stem;—
Then mark the poet; though to him unknown
The quaint-mouthed titles, such as scholars own,
See how his eye in ecstasy pursues
The steps of Nature tracked in radiant hues;
Nay, in thyself, whate'er may be thy fate,
Pallid with toil or surfeited with state,
Mark how thy fancies, with the vernal rose,
Awake, all sweetness, from their long repose;

Then turn to ponder o'er the classic page,
Traced with the idyls of a greener age,
And learn the instinct which arose to warm
Art's earliest essay and her simplest form.

To themes like these her narrow path confined
The first-born impulse moving in the mind;
In vales unshaken by the trumpet's sound,
Where peaceful Labor tills his fertile ground,
The silent changes of the rolling years,
Marked on the soil or dialled on the spheres,
The crested forests and the colored flowers,
The dewy grottos and the blushing bowers,—
These, and their guardians, who, with liquid names,
Strephons and Chloës, melt in mutual flames,
Woo the young Muses from their mountain shade,
To make Arcadias in the lonely glade.

Nor think they visit only with their smiles
The fabled valleys and Elysian isles;
He who is wearied of his village plain
May roam the Edens of the world in vain.
'Tis not the star-crowned cliff, the cataract's flow,
The softer foliage or the greener glow,
The lake of sapphire or the spar-hung cave,
The brighter sunset or the broader wave,
Can warm his heart whom every wind has blown
To every shore, forgetful of his own.

Home of our childhood! how affection clings
And hovers round thee with her seraph wings!
Dearer thy hills, though clad in autumn brown,
Than fairest summits which the cedars crown!
Sweeter the fragrance of thy summer breeze
Than all Arabia breathes along the seas!
The stranger's gale wafts home the exile's sigh,
For the heart's temple is its own blue sky!

Oh happiest they, whose early love unchanged,
Hopes undissolved, and friendship unestranged,
Tired of their wanderings, still can deign to see
Love, hopes, and friendship, centring all in thee!

And thou, my village! as again I tread
Amidst thy living and above thy dead;
Though some fair playmates guard with chaster fears
Their cheeks, grown holy with the lapse of years;
Though with the dust some reverend locks may blend,
Where life's last mile-stone marks the journey's end;
On every bud the changing year recalls,
The brightening glance of morning memory falls,
Still following onward as the months unclose
The balmy lilac or the bridal rose;
And still shall follow, till they sink once more
Beneath the snow-drifts of the frozen shore,
As when my bark, long tossing in the gale,
Furled in her port her tempest-rended sail!

What shall I give thee? Can a simple lay,
Flung on thy bosom like a girl's bouquet,
Do more than deck thee for an idle hour,
Then fall unheeded, fading like the flower?
Yet, when I trod, with footsteps wild and free,
The crackling leaves beneath yon linden-tree,
Panting from play or dripping from the stream,
How bright the visions of my boyish dream!
Or, modest Charles, along thy broken edge,
Black with soft ooze and fringed with arrowy sedge,
As once I wandered in the morning sun,
With reeking sandal and superfluous gun,
How oft, as Fancy whispered in the gale,
Thou wast the Avon of her flattering tale!
Ye hills, whose foliage, fretted on the skies,
Prints shadowy arches on their evening dyes,
How should my song with holiest charm invest
Each dark ravine and forest-lifting crest!
How clothe in beauty each familiar scene,
Till all was classic on my native green!

As the drained fountain, filled with autumn leaves,
The field swept naked of its garnered sheaves,
So wastes at noon the promise of our dawn,
The springs all choking, and the harvest gone.

Yet hear the lay of one whose natal star
Still seemed the brightest when it shone afar;

Whose cheek, grown pallid with ungracious toil,
Glows in the welcome of his parent soil;
And ask no garlands sought beyond the tide,
But take the leaflets gathered at your side.

II

But times were changed; the torch of terror came,
To light the summits with the beacon's flame;
The streams ran crimson, the tall mountain pines
Rose a new forest o'er embattled lines;
The bloodless sickle lent the warrior's steel,
The harvest bowed beneath his chariot wheel;
Where late the wood-dove sheltered her repose
The raven waited for the conflict's close;
The cuirassed sentry walked his sleepless round
Where Daphne smiled or Amaryllis frowned;
Where timid minstrels sung their blushing charms,
Some wild Tyrtæus called aloud, "To arms!"

When Glory wakes, when fiery spirits leap,
Roused by her accents from their tranquil sleep,
The ray that flashes from the soldier's crest
Lights, as it glances, in the poet's breast;—
Not in pale dreamers, whose fantastic lay
Toys with smooth trifles like a child at play,
But men, who act the passions they inspire,
Who wave the sabre as they sweep the lyre!

Ye mild enthusiasts, whose pacific frowns
Are lost like dew-drops caught in burning towns,
Pluck as ye will the radiant plumes of fame,
Break Cæsar's bust to make yourselves a name;
But if your country bares the avenger's blade
For wrongs unpunished or for debts unpaid,
When the roused nation bids her armies form,
And screams her eagle through the gathering storm,
When from your ports the bannered frigate rides,
Her black bows scowling to the crested tides,
Your hour has past; in vain your feeble cry
As the babe's wailings to the thundering sky!

Scourge of mankind! with all the dread array
That wraps in wrath thy desolating way,
As the wild tempest wakes the slumbering sea,
Thou only teachest all that man can be.
Alike thy tocsin has the power to charm
The toil-knit sinews of the rustic's arm,
Or swell the pulses in the poet's veins,
And bid the nations tremble at his strains.

The city slept beneath the moonbeam's glance,
Her white walls gleaming through the vines of France,
And all was hushed, save where the footsteps fell,
On some high tower, of midnight sentinel.
But one still watched; no self-encircled woes
Chased from his lids the angel of repose;
He watched, he wept, for thoughts of bitter years
Bowed his dark lashes, wet with burning tears:
His country's sufferings and her children's shame
Streamed o'er his memory like a forest's flame;
Each treasured insult, each remembered wrong,
Rolled through his heart and kindled into song.
His taper faded; and the morning gales
Swept through the world the war-song of Marseilles!

Now, while around the smiles of Peace expand,
And Plenty's wreaths festoon the laughing land;
While France ships outward her reluctant ore,
And half our navy basks upon the shore;
From ruder themes our meek-eyed Muses turn
To crown with roses their enamelled urn.

If e'er again return those awful days
Whose clouds were crimsoned with the beacon's blaze,
Whose grass was trampled by the soldier's heel,
Whose tides were reddened round the rushing keel,
God grant some lyre may wake a nobler strain
To rend the silence of our tented plain!

When Gallia's flag its triple fold displays,
Her marshalled legions peal the Marseillaise;
When round the German close the war-clouds dim,
Far through their shadows floats his battle-hymn;
When, crowned with joy, the camps of England ring,
A thousand voices shout, "God save the King!"
When victory follows with our eagle's glance,
Our nation's anthem pipes a country dance!

Some prouder Muse, when comes the hour at last,
May shake our hillsides with her bugle-blast;
Not ours the task; but since the lyric dress
Relieves the statelier with its sprightliness,
Hear an old song, which some, perchance, have seen
In stale gazette or cobwebbed magazine.
There was an hour when patriots dared profane
The mast that Britain strove to bow in vain;
And one, who listened to the tale of shame,
Whose heart still answered to that sacred name,
Whose eye still followed o'er his country's tides
Thy glorious flag, our brave Old Ironsides!
From yon lone attic, on a smiling morn,
Thus mocked the spoilers with his school-boy scorn.

III

When florid Peace resumed her golden reign,
And arts revived, and valleys bloomed again,
While War still panted on his broken blade,
Once more the Muse her heavenly wing essayed.
Rude was the song: some ballad, stern and wild,
Lulled the light slumbers of the soldier's child;
Or young romancer, with his threatening glance
And fearful fables of his bloodless lance,
Scared the soft fancy of the clinging girls,
Whose snowy fingers smoothed his raven curls.
But when long years the stately form had bent,
And faithless Memory her illusions lent,
So vast the outlines of Tradition grew
That History wondered at the shapes she drew,
And veiled at length their too ambitious hues
Beneath the pinions of the Epic Muse.

Far swept her wing; for stormier days had brought
With darker passions deeper tides of thought.
The camp's harsh tumult and the conflict's glow,
The thrill of triumph and the gasp of woe,
The tender parting and the glad return,
The festal banquet and the funeral urn,
And all the drama which at once uprears
Its spectral shadows through the clash of spears,
From camp and field to echoing verse transferred,
Swelled the proud song that listening nations heard.

Why floats the amaranth in eternal bloom
O'er Ilium's turrets and Achilles' tomb?
Why lingers fancy where the sunbeams smile
On Circe's gardens and Calypso's isle?
Why follows memory to the gate of Troy
Her plumed defender and his trembling boy?
Lo! the blind dreamer, kneeling on the sand
To trace these records with his doubtful hand;
In fabled tones his own emotion flows,
And other lips repeat his silent woes;
In Hector's infant see the babes that shun
Those deathlike eyes, unconscious of the sun,
Or in his hero hear himself implore,
"Give me to see, and Ajax asks no more!"

Thus live undying through the lapse of time
The solemn legends of the warrior's clime;
Like Egypt's pyramid or Pæstum's fane,
They stand the heralds of the voiceless plain.
Yet not like them, for Time, by slow degrees,
Saps the gray stone and wears the embroidered frieze,
And Isis sleeps beneath her subject Nile,
And crumbled Neptune strews his Dorian pile;

But Art's fair fabric, strengthening as it rears
Its laurelled columns through the mist of years,
As the blue arches of the bending skies
Still gird the torrent, following as it flies,
Spreads, with the surges bearing on mankind,
Its starred pavilion o'er the tides of mind!

In vain the patriot asks some lofty lay
To dress in state our wars of yesterday.
The classic days, those mothers of romance,
That roused a nation for a woman's glance;
The age of mystery, with its hoarded power,
That girt the tyrant in his storied tower,
Have passed and faded like a dream of youth,
And riper eras ask for history's truth.

On other shores, above their mouldering towns,
In sullen pomp the tall cathedral frowns,
Pride in its aisles and paupers at the door,
Which feeds the beggars whom it fleeced of yore.
Simple and frail, our lowly temples throw
Their slender shadows on the paths below;
Scarce steal the winds, that sweep his woodland tracks,
The larch's perfume from the settler's axe,
Ere, like a vision of the morning air,
His slight-framed steeple marks the house of prayer;
Its planks all reeking and its paint undried,
Its rafters sprouting on the shady side,
It sheds the raindrops from its shingled eaves
Ere its green brothers once have changed their leaves.

Yet Faith's pure hymn, beneath its shelter rude,
Breathes out as sweetly to the tangled wood
As where the rays through pictured glories pour
On marbled shaft and tessellated floor;—
Heaven asks no surplice round the heart that feels,
And all is holy where devotion kneels.

Thus on the soil the patriot's knee should bend
Which holds the dust once living to defend;
Where'er the hireling shrinks before the free,
Each pass becomes "a new Thermopylæ"!
Where'er the battles of the brave are won,
There every mountain "looks on Marathon"!

Our fathers live; they guard in glory still
The grass-grown bastions of the fortressed hill;
Still ring the echoes of the trampled gorge,
With *God and Freedom! England and Saint George!*
The royal cipher on the captured gun
Mocks the sharp night-dews and the blistering sun;
The red-cross banner shades its captor's bust,
Its folds still loaded with the conflict's dust;
The drum, suspended by its tattered marge,
Once rolled and rattled to the Hessian's charge;
The stars have floated from Britannia's mast,
The redcoat's trumpets blown the rebel's blast.

Point to the summits where the brave have bled,
Where every village claims its glorious dead;
Say, when their bosoms met the bayonet's shock,
Their only corselet was the rustic frock;
Say, when they mustered to the gathering horn,
The titled chieftain curled his lip in scorn,
Yet, when their leader bade his lines advance,
No musket wavered in the lion's glance;
Say, when they fainted in the forced retreat,
They tracked the snow-drifts with their bleeding feet,
Yet still their banners, tossing in the blast,
Bore *Ever Ready*, faithful to the last,
Through storm and battle, till they waved again
On Yorktown's hills and Saratoga's plain!

Then, if so fierce the insatiate patriot's flame,
Truth looks too pale and history seems too tame,
Bid him await some new Columbiad's page,
To gild the tablets of an iron age,
And save his tears, which yet may fall upon
Some fabled field, some fancied Washington!

IV

But once again, from their Æolian cave,
The winds of Genius wandered on the wave.
Tired of the scenes the timid pencil drew,
Sick of the notes the sounding clarion blew,

Sated with heroes who had worn so long
The shadowy plumage of historic song,
The new-born poet left the beaten course,
To track the passions to their living source.

Then rose the Drama;—and the world admired
Her varied page with deeper thought inspired:
Bound to no clime, for Passion's throb is one
In Greenland's twilight or in India's sun;
Born for no age, for all the thoughts that roll
In the dark vortex of the stormy soul,
Unchained in song, no freezing years can tame;
God gave them birth, and man is still the same.

So full on life her magic mirror shone,
Her sister Arts paid tribute to her throne;
One reared her temple, one her canvas warmed,
And Music thrilled, while Eloquence informed.
The weary rustic left his stinted task
For smiles and tears, the dagger and the mask;
The sage, turned scholar, half forgot his lore,
To be the woman he despised before.
O'er sense and thought she threw her golden chain,
And Time, the anarch, spares her deathless reign.

Thus lives Medea, in our tamer age,
As when her buskin pressed the Grecian stage;
Not in the cells where frigid learning delves
In Aldine folios mouldering on their shelves,
But breathing, burning in the glittering throng,
Whose thousand bravoes roll untired along,
Circling and spreading through the gilded halls,
From London's galleries to San Carlo's walls!

Thus shall he live whose more than mortal name
Mocks with its ray the pallid torch of Fame;
So proudly lifted that it seems afar
No earthly Pharos, but a heavenly star,
Who, unconfined to Art's diurnal bound,
Girds her whole zodiac in his flaming round,
And leads the passions, like the orb that guides,
From pole to pole, the palpitating tides!

V

Though round the Muse the robe of song is thrown,
Think not the poet lives in verse alone.
Long ere the chisel of the sculptor taught
The lifeless stone to mock the living thought;
Long ere the painter bade the canvas glow
With every line the forms of beauty know;
Long ere the iris of the Muses threw
On every leaf its own celestial hue,
In fable's dress the breath of genius poured,
And warmed the shapes that later times adored.

Untaught by Science how to forge the keys
That loose the gates of Nature's mysteries;
Unschooled by Faith, who, with her angel tread,
Leads through the labyrinth with a single thread,
His fancy, hovering round her guarded tower,
Rained through its bars like Danae's golden shower.

He spoke; the sea-nymph answered from her cave:
He called; the naiad left her mountain wave:
He dreamed of beauty; lo, amidst his dream,
Narcissus, mirrored in the breathless stream;
And night's chaste empress, in her bridal play,
Laughed through the foliage where Endymion lay;
And ocean dimpled, as the languid swell
Kissed the red lip of Cytherea's shell:
Of power,—Bellona swept the crimson field,
And blue-eyed Pallas shook her Gorgon shield;
O'er the hushed waves their mightier monarch drove,
And Ida trembled to the tread of Jove!

So every grace that plastic language knows
To nameless poets its perfection owes.
The rough-hewn words to simplest thoughts confined
Were cut and polished in their nicer mind;
Caught on their edge, imagination's ray
Splits into rainbows, shooting far away;—
From sense to soul, from soul to sense, it flies,
And through all nature links analogies;
He who reads right will rarely look upon
A better poet than his lexicon!

There is a race which cold, ungenial skies
Breed from decay, as fungous growths arise;
Though dying fast, yet springing fast again,
Which still usurps an unsubstantial reign,
With frames too languid for the charms of sense,
And minds worn down with action too intense;
Tired of a world whose joys they never knew,
Themselves deceived, yet thinking all untrue;
Scarce men without, and less than girls within,
Sick of their life before its cares begin;—
The dull disease, which drains their feeble hearts,
To life's decay some hectic thrills imparts,
And lends a force which, like the maniac's power,
Pays with blank years the frenzy of an hour.

And this is Genius! Say, does Heaven degrade
The manly frame, for health, for action made?
Break down the sinews, rack the brow with pains,
Blanch the bright cheek and drain the purple veins,
To clothe the mind with more extended sway,
Thus faintly struggling in degenerate clay?

No! gentle maid, too ready to admire,
Though false its notes, the pale enthusiast's lyre;
If this be genius, though its bitter springs
Glowed like the morn beneath Aurora's wings,
Seek not the source whose sullen bosom feeds
But fruitless flowers and dark, envenomed weeds.

But, if so bright the dear illusion seems,
Thou wouldst be partner of thy poet's dreams,
And hang in rapture on his bloodless charms,
Or die, like Raphael, in his angel arms,
Go and enjoy thy blessed lot,—to share
In Cowper's gloom or Chatterton's despair!

Not such were they whom, wandering o'er the waves,
I looked to meet, but only found their graves;
If friendship's smile, the better part of fame,
Should lend my song the only wreath I claim,
Whose voice would greet me with a sweeter tone,
Whose living hand more kindly press my own,
Than theirs,—could Memory, as her silent tread
Prints the pale flowers that blossom o'er the dead,
Those breathless lips, now closed in peace, restore,
Or wake those pulses hushed to beat no more?

Thou calm, chaste scholar! I can see thee now,
The first young laurels on thy pallid brow,
O'er thy slight figure floating lightly down
In graceful folds the academic gown,
On thy curled lip the classic lines that taught
How nice the mind that sculptured them with thought,
And triumph glistening in the clear blue eye,
Too bright to live,—but oh, too fair to die!

And thou, dear friend, whom Science still deplores,
And Love still mourns, on ocean-severed shores,
Though the bleak forest twice has bowed with snow
Since thou wast laid its budding leaves below,
Thine image mingles with my closing strain,
As when we wandered by the turbid Seine,
Both blessed with hopes, which revelled, bright and free,
On all we longed or all we dreamed to be;
To thee the amaranth and the cypress fell,—
And I was spared to breathe this last farewell!

But lived there one in unremembered days,
Or lives there still, who spurns the poet's bays,
Whose fingers, dewy from Castalia's springs,
Rest on the lyre, yet scorn to touch the strings?
Who shakes the senate with the silver tone
The groves of Pindus might have sighed to own?
Have such e'er been? Remember Canning's name!
Do such still live? Let "Alaric's Dirge" proclaim!

Immortal Art! where'er the rounded sky
Bends o'er the cradle where thy children lie,

Their home is earth, their herald every tongue
Whose accents echo to the voice that sung.
One leap of Ocean scatters on the sand
The quarried bulwarks of the loosening land;
One thrill of earth dissolves a century's toil
Strewed like the leaves that vanish in the soil;
One hill o'erflows, and cities sink below,
Their marbles splintering in the lava's glow;
But one sweet tone, scarce whispered to the air,
From shore to shore the blasts of ages bear;
One humble name, which oft, perchance, has borne
The tyrant's mockery and the courtier's scorn,
Towers o'er the dust of earth's forgotten graves,
As once, emerging through the waste of waves,
The rocky Titan, round whose shattered spear
Coiled the last whirlpool of the drowning sphere!

1836

LA GRISETTE

Ah, Clemence! when I saw thee last
  Trip down the Rue de Seine,
And turning, when thy form had past,
  I said, "We meet again,"—
I dreamed not in that idle glance
  Thy latest image came,
And only left to memory's trance
  A shadow and a name.

The few strange words my lips had taught
  Thy timid voice to speak,
Their gentler signs, which often brought
  Fresh roses to thy cheek,
The trailing of thy long loose hair
  Bent o'er my couch of pain,
All, all returned, more sweet, more fair;
  Oh, had we met again!

I walked where saint and virgin keep
  The vigil lights of Heaven,
I knew that thou hadst woes to weep,
  And sins to be forgiven;
I watched where Genevieve was laid,
  I knelt by Mary's shrine,
Beside me low, soft voices prayed;
  Alas! but where was thine?

And when the morning sun was bright,
  When wind and wave were calm,
And flamed, in thousand-tinted light,
  The rose of Notre Dame,
I wandered through the haunts of men,
  From Boulevard to Quai,
Till, frowning o'er Saint Etienne,
  The Pantheon's shadow lay.

In vain, in vain; we meet no more,
  Nor dream what fates befall;
And long upon the stranger's shore
  My voice on thee may call,
When years have clothed the line in moss
  That tells thy name and days,
And withered, on thy simple cross,
  The wreaths of Père-la-Chaise!

1836

ON LENDING A PUNCH-BOWL

This ancient silver bowl of mine, it tells of good old times,
Of joyous days and jolly nights, and merry Christmas chimes;
They were a free and jovial race, but honest, brave, and true,
Who dipped their ladle in the punch when this old bowl was new.

A Spanish galleon brought the bar,—so runs the ancient tale;
'Twas hammered by an Antwerp smith, whose arm was like a flail;
And now and then between the strokes, for fear his strength should fail,
He wiped his brow and quaffed a cup of good old Flemish ale.

'Twas purchased by an English squire to please his loving dame,
Who saw the cherubs, and conceived a longing for the same;
And oft as on the ancient stock another twig was found,
'Twas filled with caudle spiced and hot, and handed smoking round.

But, changing hands, it reached at length a Puritan divine,
Who used to follow Timothy, and take a little wine,

But hated punch and prelacy; and so it was, perhaps,
He went to Leyden, where he found conventicles and schnapps.

And then, of course, you know what's next: it left the Dutchman's shore
With those that in the Mayflower came,—a hundred souls and more,—
Along with all the furniture, to fill their new abodes,—
To judge by what is still on hand, at least a hundred loads.

'Twas on a dreary winter's eve, the night was closing dim,
When brave Miles Standish took the bowl, and filled it to the brim;
The little Captain stood and stirred the posset with his sword,
And all his sturdy men-at-arms were ranged about the board.

He poured the fiery Hollands in,—the man that never feared,—
He took a long and solemn draught, and wiped his yellow beard;
And one by one the musketeers—the men that fought and prayed—
All drank as 'twere their mother's milk, and not a man afraid.

That night, affrighted from his nest, the screaming eagle flew,
He heard the Pequot's ringing whoop, the soldier's wild halloo;
And there the sachem learned the rule he taught to kith and kin:
"Run from the white man when you find he smells of Hollands gin!"

A hundred years, and fifty more, had spread their leaves and snows,
A thousand rubs had flattened down each little cherub's nose,
When once again the bowl was filled, but not in mirth or joy,—
'Twas mingled by a mother's hand to cheer her parting boy.

"Drink, John," she said, "'twill do you good,—poor child, you'll never bear
This working in the dismal trench, out in the midnight air;
And if—God bless me!—you were hurt, 'twould keep away the chill."
So John *did* drink,—and well he wrought that night at Bunker's Hill!

I tell you, there was generous warmth in good old English cheer;
I tell you, 'twas a pleasant thought to bring its symbol here.
'Tis but the fool that loves excess; hast thou a drunken soul?
Thy bane is in thy shallow skull, not in my silver bowl!

I love the memory of the past,—its pressed yet fragrant flowers,—
The moss that clothes its broken walls, the ivy on its towers;
Nay, this poor bauble it bequeathed,—my eyes grow moist and dim,
To think of all the vanished joys that danced around its brim.

Then fill a fair and honest cup, and bear it straight to me;
The goblet hallows all it holds, whate'er the liquid be;
And may the cherubs on its face protect me from the sin
That dooms one to those dreadful words,—
"My dear, where *have* you been?"

1848

THE STETHOSCOPE SONG

A PROFESSIONAL BALLAD

THERE was a young man in Boston town,
He bought him a stethoscope nice and new,
All mounted and finished and polished down,
With an ivory cap and a stopper too.

It happened a spider within did crawl,
And spun him a web of ample size,
Wherein there chanced one day to fall
A couple of very imprudent flies.

The first was a bottle-fly, big and blue,
The second was smaller, and thin and long;
So there was a concert between the two,
Like an octave flute and a tavern gong.

Now being from Paris but recently,
This fine young man would show his skill;
And so they gave him, his hand to try,
A hospital patient extremely ill.

Some said that his *liver* was short of *bile*,
And some that his *heart* was over size,
While some kept arguing, all the while,
He was crammed with *tubercles* up to his eyes.

This fine young man then up stepped he,
And all the doctors made a pause;
Said he, The man must die, you see,
By the fifty-seventh of Louis's laws.

But since the case is a desperate one,
To explore his chest it may be well;
For if he should die and it were not done,
You know the *autopsy* would not tell.

Then out his stethoscope he took,
And on it placed his curious ear;
Mon Dieu! said he, with a knowing look,
Why, here is a sound that's mighty queer!

The *bourdonnement* is very clear,—
Amphoric buzzing, as I'm alive!
Five doctors took their turn to hear;
Amphoric buzzing, said all the five.

There's *empyema* beyond a doubt;
We'll plunge a *trocar* in his side.
The diagnosis was made out,—
They tapped the patient; so he died.

Now such as hate new-fashioned toys
Began to look extremely glum;
They said that *rattles* were made for boys,
And vowed that his *buzzing* was all a hum.

There was an old lady had long been sick,
And what was the matter none did know:
Her pulse was slow, though her tongue was quick;
To her this knowing youth must go.

So there the nice old lady sat,
With phials and boxes all in a row;
She asked the young doctor what he was at,
To thump her and tumble her ruffles so.

Now, when the stethoscope came out,
The flies began to buzz and whiz:
Oh, ho! the matter is clear, no doubt;
An *aneurism* there plainly is.

The *bruit de râpe* and the *bruit de scie*
And the *bruit de diable* are all combined;
How happy Bouillaud would be,
If he a case like this could find!

Now, when the neighboring doctors found
A case so rare had been descried,
They every day her ribs did pound
In squads of twenty; so she died.

Then six young damsels, slight and frail,
Received this kind young doctor's cares;
They all were getting slim and pale,
And short of breath on mounting stairs.

They all made rhymes with "sighs" and "skies,"
And loathed their puddings and buttered rolls,
And dieted, much to their friends' surprise,
On pickles and pencils and chalk and coals.

So fast their little hearts did bound,
The frightened insects buzzed the more;
So over all their chests he found
The *râle sifflant* and the *râle sonore*.

He shook his head. There's grave disease,—
I greatly fear you all must die;
A slight *post-mortem*, if you please,
Surviving friends would gratify.

The six young damsels wept aloud,
Which so prevailed on six young men
That each his honest love avowed,
Whereat they all got well again.

This poor young man was all aghast;
The price of stethoscopes came down;
And so he was reduced at last
To practise in a country town.

The doctors being very sore,
A stethoscope they did devise
That had a rammer to clear the bore,
With a knob at the end to kill the flies.

Now use your ears, all you that can,
But don't forget to mind your eyes,
Or you may be cheated, like this young man,
By a couple of silly, abnormal flies.

1848

THE STATESMAN'S SECRET

Who of all statesmen is his country's pride,
Her councils' prompter and her leaders' guide?
He speaks; the nation holds its breath to hear;
He nods, and shakes the sunset hemisphere.
Born where the primal fount of Nature springs
By the rude cradles of her throneless kings,
In his proud eye her royal signet flames,
By his own lips her Monarch she proclaims.
Why name his countless triumphs, whom to meet
Is to be famous, envied in defeat?
The keen debaters, trained to brawls and strife,
Who fire one shot, and finish with the knife,
Tried him but once, and, cowering in their shame,
Ground their hacked blades to strike at meaner game.
The lordly chief, his party's central stay,
Whose lightest word a hundred votes obey,
Found a new listener seated at his side,
Looked in his eye, and felt himself defied,
Flung his rash gauntlet on the startled floor,
Met the all-conquering, fought,—and ruled no more.
See where he moves, what eager crowds attend!
What shouts of thronging multitudes ascend!
If this is life,—to mark with every hour
The purple deepening in his robes of power,
To see the painted fruits of honor fall
Thick at his feet, and choose among them all,
To hear the sounds that shape his spreading name
Peal through the myriad organ-stops of fame,
Stamp the lone isle that spots the seaman's chart,
And crown the pillared glory of the mart,
To count as peers the few supremely wise
Who mark their planet in the angels' eyes,—
If this is life—
What savage man is he
Who strides alone beside the sounding sea?
Alone he wanders by the murmuring shore,
His thoughts as restless as the waves that roar;
Looks on the sullen sky as stormy-browed
As on the waves yon tempest-brooding cloud,
Heaves from his aching breast a wailing sigh,
Sad as the gust that sweeps the clouded sky.
Ask him his griefs; what midnight demons plough
The lines of torture on his lofty brow;
Unlock those marble lips, and bid them speak
The mystery freezing in his bloodless cheek.
His secret? Hid beneath a flimsy word;
One foolish whisper that ambition heard;
And thus it spake: "Behold yon gilded chair,
The world's one vacant throne,—thy place is there!"
Ah, fatal dream! What warning spectres meet
In ghastly circle round its shadowy seat!
Yet still the Tempter murmurs in his ear
The maddening taunt he cannot choose but hear:
"Meanest of slaves, by gods and men accurst,
He who is second when he might be first!
Climb with bold front the ladder's topmost round,
Or chain thy creeping footsteps to the ground!"
Illustrious Dupe! Have those majestic eyes
Lost their proud fire for such a vulgar prize?
Art thou the last of all mankind to know
That party-fights are won by aiming low?
Thou, stamped by Nature with her royal sign,
That party-hirelings hate a look like thine?
Shake from thy sense the wild delusive dream!
Without the purple, art thou not supreme?
And soothed by love unbought, thy heart shall own
A nation's homage nobler than its throne!

1850? 1861

NON-RESISTANCE

Perhaps too far in these considerate days
Has patience carried her submissive ways;
Wisdom has taught us to be calm and meek,
To take one blow, and turn the other cheek;
It is not written what a man shall do
If the rude caitiff smite the other too!

Land of our fathers, in thine hour of need
God help thee, guarded by the passive creed!

As the lone pilgrim trusts to beads and cowl,
When through the forest rings the gray wolf's
howl;
As the deep galleon trusts her gilded prow
When the black corsair slants athwart her bow;
As the poor pheasant, with his peaceful mien,
Trusts to his feathers, shining golden-green,
When the dark plumage with the crimson beak
Has rustled shadowy from its splintered
peak,—
So trust thy friends, whose babbling tongues
would charm
The lifted saber from thy foeman's arm,
Thy torches ready for the answering peal
From bellowing fort and thunder-freighted keel!

1850

AFTER A LECTURE ON WORDSWORTH

Come, spread your wings, as I spread mine,
And leave the crowded hall
For where the eyes of twilight shine
O'er evening's western wall.

These are the pleasant Berkshire hills,
Each with its leafy crown;
Hark! from their sides a thousand rills
Come singing sweetly down.

A thousand rills; they leap and shine,
Strained through the shadowy nooks,
Till, clasped in many a gathering twine,
They swell a hundred brooks.

A hundred brooks, and still they run
With ripple, shade, and gleam,
Till, clustering all their braids in one,
They flow a single stream.

A bracelet spun from mountain mist,
A silvery sash unwound,
With ox-bow curve and sinuous twist
It writhes to reach the Sound.

This is my bark,—a pygmy's ship;
Beneath a child it rolls;
Fear not,—one body makes it dip,
But not a thousand souls.

Float we the grassy banks between;
Without an oar we glide;
The meadows, drest in living green,
Unroll on either side.

Come, take the book we love so well,
And let us read and dream
We see whate'er its pages tell,
And sail an English stream.

Up to the clouds the lark has sprung,
Still trilling as he flies;
The linnet sings as there he sung;
The unseen cuckoo cries,

And daisies strew the banks along,
And yellow kingcups shine,
With cowslips, and a primrose throng,
And humble celandine.

Ah foolish dream! when Nature nursed
Her daughter in the West,
The fount was drained that opened first;
She bared her other breast.

On the young planet's orient shore
Her morning hand she tried;
Then turned the broad medallion o'er
And stamped the sunset side.

Take what she gives, her pine's tall stem,
Her elm with hanging spray;
She wears her mountain diadem
Still in her own proud way.

Look on the forests' ancient kings,
The hemlock's towering pride:
Yon trunk had thrice a hundred rings,
And fell before it died.

Nor think that Nature saves her bloom
And slights our grassy plain;
For she wears her court costume,—
Look on its broidered train;

The lily with the sprinkled dots,
Brands of the noontide beam;
The cardinal, and the blood-red spots,
Its double in the stream,

As if some wounded eagle's breast,
Slow throbbing o'er the plain,
Had left its airy path impressed
In drops of scarlet rain.

And hark! and hark! the woodland rings;
There thrilled the thrush's soul;
And look! that flash of flamy wings,—
The fire-plumed oriole!

Above, the hen-hawk swims and swoops,
  Flung from the bright, blue sky;
Below, the robin hops, and whoops
  His piercing Indian cry.

Beauty runs virgin in the woods
  Robed in her rustic green,
And oft a longing thought intrudes,
  As if we might have seen

Her every finger's every joint
  Ringed with some golden line,
Poet whom Nature did anoint!
  Had our wild home been thine.

Yet think not so; Old England's blood
  Runs warm in English veins;
But wafted o'er the icy flood
  Its better life remains:

Our children know each wildwood smell,
  The bayberry and the fern,
The man who does not know them well
  Is all too old to learn.

Be patient! On the breathing page
  Still pants our hurried past;
Pilgrim and soldier, saint and sage,—
  The poet comes the last!

Though still the lark-voiced matins ring
  The world has known so long;
The wood-thrush of the West shall sing
  Earth's last sweet even-song!

1853 1855

AFTER A LECTURE ON SHELLEY

ONE broad, white sail in Spezzia's treacherous bay;
  On comes the blast; too daring bark, beware!
The cloud has clasped her; lo! it melts away;
  The wide, waste waters, but no sail is there.

Morning: a woman looking on the sea;
  Midnight: with lamps the long veranda burns;
Come, wandering sail, they watch, they burn for thee!
  Suns come and go, alas! no bark returns.

And feet are thronging on the pebbly sands,
  And torches flaring in the weedy caves,
Where'er the waters lay with icy hands
  The shapes uplifted from their coral graves.

Vainly they seek; the idle quest is o'er;
  The coarse, dark women, with their hanging locks,
And lean, wild children gather from the shore
  To the black hovels bedded in the rocks.

But Love still prayed, with agonizing wail,
  "One, one last look, ye heaving waters, yield!"
Till Ocean, clashing in his jointed mail,
  Raised the pale burden on his level shield.

Slow from the shore the sullen waves retire;
  His form a nobler element shall claim;
Nature baptized him in ethereal fire,
  And Death shall crown him with a wreath of flame.

Fade, mortal semblance, never to return;
  Swift is the change within thy crimson shroud;
Seal the white ashes in the peaceful urn;
  All else has risen in yon silvery cloud.

Sleep where thy gentle Adonais lies,
  Whose open page lay on thy dying heart,
Both in the smile of those blue-vaulted skies,
  Earth's fairest dome of all divinest art.

Breathe for his wandering soul one passing sigh,
  O happier Christian, while thine eye grows dim,—
In all the mansions of the house on high,
  Say not that Mercy has not one for him!

1853 1861

FOR THE MEETING OF THE BURNS CLUB

1856

THE mountains glitter in the snow
  A thousand leagues asunder;
Yet here, amid the banquet's glow,
  I hear their voice of thunder;

Each giant's ice-bound goblet clinks;
A flowing stream is summoned;
Wachusett to Ben Nevis drinks;
Monadnock to Ben Lomond!

Though years have clipped the eagle's plume
That crowned the chieftain's bonnet,
The sun still sees the heather bloom,
The silver mists lie on it;
With tartan kilt and philibeg,
What stride was ever bolder
Than his who showed the naked leg
Beneath the plaided shoulder?

The echoes sleep on Cheviot's hills,
That heard the bugles blowing
When down their sides the crimson rills
With mingled blood were flowing;
The hunts where gallant hearts were game,
The slashing on the border,
The raid that swooped with sword and flame,
Give place to "law and order."

Not while the rocking steeples reel
With midnight tocsins ringing,
Not while the crashing war-notes peal,
God sets his poets singing;
The bird is silent in the night,
Or shrieks a cry of warning
While fluttering round the beacon-light,—
But hear him greet the morning!

The lark of Scotia's morning sky!
Whose voice may sing his praises?
With Heaven's own sunlight in his eye,
He walked among the daisies,
Till through the cloud of fortune's wrong
He soared to fields of glory;
But left his land her sweetest song
And earth her saddest story.

'Tis not the forts the builder piles
That chain the earth together;
The wedded crowns, the sister isles,
Would laugh at such a tether;
The kindling thought, the throbbing words,
That set the pulses beating,
Are stronger than the myriad swords
Of mighty armies meeting.

Thus while within the banquet glows,
Without, the wild winds whistle,
We drink a triple health,—the Rose,
The Shamrock, and the Thistle!
Their blended hues shall never fade
Till War has hushed his cannon,—
Close-twined as ocean-currents braid
The Thames, the Clyde, the Shannon!

1859

LATTER-DAY WARNINGS

When legislators keep the law,
When banks dispense with bolts and locks,
When berries—whortle, rasp, and straw—
Grow bigger *downwards* through the box,—

When he that selleth house or land
Shows leak in roof or flaw in right,
When haberdashers choose the stand
Whose window hath the broadest light,—

When preachers tell us all they think,
And party leaders all they mean,—
When what we pay for, that we drink,
From real grape and coffee-bean,—

When lawyers take what they would give,
And doctors give what they would take,—
When city fathers eat to live,
Save when they fast for conscience' sake,—

When one that hath a horse on sale
Shall bring his merit to the proof,
Without a lie for every nail
That holds the iron on the hoof,—

When in the usual place for rips
Our gloves are stitched with special care,
And guarded well the whalebone tips
Where first umbrellas need repair,—

When Cuba's weeds have quite forgot
The power of suction to resist,
And claret-bottles harbor not
Such dimples as would hold your fist,—

When publishers no longer steal,
And pay for what they stole before,—
When the first locomotive's wheel
Rolls through the Hoosac Tunnel's bore;—

Till then let Cumming blaze away,
And Miller's saints blow up the globe;
But when you see that blessed day,
Then order your ascension robe!

1857

THE CHAMBERED NAUTILUS

This is the ship of pearl, which, poets feign,
Sails the unshadowed main,—
The venturous bark that flings
On the sweet summer wind its purpled wings
In gulfs enchanted, where the Siren sings,
And coral reefs lie bare,
Where the cold sea-maids rise to sun their streaming hair.

Its webs of living gauze no more unfurl;
Wrecked is the ship of pearl!
And every chambered cell,
Where its dim dreaming life was wont to dwell,
As the frail tenant shaped his growing shell,
Before thee lies revealed,—
Its irised ceiling rent, its sunless crypt unsealed!

Year after year beheld the silent toil
That spread his lustrous coil;
Still, as the spiral grew,
He left the past year's dwelling for the new,
Stole with soft step its shining archway through,
Built up its idle door,
Stretched in his last-found home, and knew the old no more.

Thanks for the heavenly message brought by thee,
Child of the wandering sea,
Cast from her lap, forlorn!
From thy dead lips a clearer note is born
Than ever Triton blew from wreathèd horn!
While on mine ear it rings,
Through the deep caves of thought I hear a voice that sings:—

Build thee more stately mansions, O my soul,
As the swift seasons roll!
Leave thy low-vaulted past!
Let each new temple, nobler than the last,
Shut thee from heaven with a dome more vast,
Till thou at length art free,
Leaving thine outgrown shell by life's unresting sea!

1858

THE LIVING TEMPLE

Not in the world of light alone,
Where God has built his blazing throne,
Nor yet alone in earth below,
With belted seas that come and go,
And endless isles of sunlit green,
Is all thy Maker's glory seen:
Look in upon thy wondrous frame,—
Eternal wisdom still the same!

The smooth, soft air with pulse-like waves
Flows murmuring through its hidden caves,
Whose streams of brightening purple rush,
Fired with a new and livelier blush,
While all their burden of decay
The ebbing current steals away,
And red with Nature's flame they start
From the warm fountains of the heart.

No rest that throbbing slave may ask,
Forever quivering o'er his task,
While far and wide a crimson jet
Leaps forth to fill the woven net
Which in unnumbered crossing tides
The flood of burning life divides,
Then, kindling each decaying part,
Creeps back to find the throbbing heart.

But warmed with that unchanging flame
Behold the outward moving frame,
Its living marbles jointed strong
With glistening band and silvery thong,
And linked to reason's guiding reins
By myriad rings in trembling chains,
Each graven with the threaded zone
Which claims it as the master's own.

See how yon beam of seeming white
Is braided out of seven-hued light,
Yet in those lucid globes no ray
By any chance shall break astray.
Hark how the rolling surge of sound,
Arches and spirals circling round,
Wakes the hushed spirit through thine ear
With music it is heaven to hear.

Then mark the cloven sphere that holds
All thought in its mysterious folds;
That feels sensation's faintest thrill,
And flashes forth the sovereign will;

Think on the stormy world that dwells
Locked in its dim and clustering cells!
The lightning gleams of power it sheds
Along its hollow glassy threads!

O Father! grant thy love divine
To make these mystic temples thine!
When wasting age and wearying strife
Have sapped the leaning walls of life,
When darkness gathers over all,
And the last tottering pillars fall,
Take the poor dust thy mercy warms,
And mould it into heavenly forms!

1858

THE DEACON'S MASTERPIECE

OR, THE WONDERFUL "ONE-HOSS SHAY"

A LOGICAL STORY

Have you heard of the wonderful one-hoss shay,
That was built in such a logical way
It ran a hundred years to a day,
And then, of a sudden, it—ah, but stay,
I'll tell you what happened without delay,
Scaring the parson into fits,
Frightening people out of their wits,—
Have you ever heard of that, I say?

Seventeen hundred and fifty-five.
Georgius Secundus was then alive,—
Snuffy old drone from the German hive.
That was the year when Lisbon-town
Saw the earth open and gulp her down,
And Braddock's army was done so brown,
Left without a scalp to its crown.
It was on the terrible Earthquake-day
That the Deacon finished the one-hoss shay.

Now in building of chaises, I tell you what,
There is always *somewhere* a weakest spot,—
In hub, tire, felloe, in spring or thill,
In panel, or crossbar, or floor, or sill,
In screw, bolt, thoroughbrace,—lurking still,
Find it somewhere you must and will,—
Above or below, or within or without,—
And that's the reason, beyond a doubt,
That a chaise *breaks down*, but doesn't *wear out*.

But the Deacon swore (as deacons do,
With an "I dew vum," or an "I tell *yeou*")
He would build one shay to beat the taown
'N' the keounty 'n' all the kentry raoun';
It should be so built that it *could n'* break daown:
"Fur," said the Deacon, "'t 's mighty plain
Thut the weakes' place mus' stan' the strain;
'N' the way t' fix it, uz I maintain,
Is only jest
T' make that place uz strong uz the rest."

So the Deacon inquired of the village folk
Where he could find the strongest oak,
That couldn't be split nor bent nor broke,—
That was for spokes and floor and sills;
He sent for lancewood to make the thills;
The crossbars were ash, from the straightest trees,
The panels of white-wood, that cuts like cheese,
But lasts like iron for things like these;
The hubs of logs from the "Settler's ellum,"—
Last of its timber,—they couldn't sell 'em,
Never an axe had seen their chips,
And the wedges flew from between their lips,
Their blunt ends frizzled like celery-tips;
Step and prop-iron, bolt and screw,
Spring, tire, axle, and linchpin too,
Steel of the finest, bright and blue;
Thoroughbrace bison-skin, thick and wide;
Boot, top, dasher, from tough old hide
Found in the pit when the tanner died.
That was the way he "put her through."
"There!" said the Deacon, "naow she 'll dew!"

Do! I tell you, I rather guess
She was a wonder, and nothing less!
Colts grew horses, beards turned gray,
Deacon and deaconess dropped away,
Children and grandchildren—where were they?
But there stood the stout old one-hoss shay
As fresh as on Lisbon-earthquake-day!

Eighteen hundred;—it came and found
The Deacon's masterpiece strong and sound.
Eighteen hundred increased by ten;—
"Hahnsum kerridge" they called it then.
Eighteen hundred and twenty came;—
Running as usual; much the same.
Thirty and forty at last arrive,
And then come fifty, and FIFTY-FIVE.

Little of all we value here
Wakes on the morn of its hundredth year
Without both feeling and looking queer.
In fact, there's nothing that keeps its youth,
So far as I know, but a tree and truth.
(This is a moral that runs at large;
Take it.—You're welcome.—No extra charge.)

First of November,—the earthquake-day,—
There are traces of age in the one-hoss shay,
A general flavor of mild decay,
But nothing local, as one may say.
There couldn't be,—for the Deacon's art
Had made it so like in every part
That there wasn't a chance for one to start.
For the wheels were just as strong as the thills,
And the floor was just as strong as the sills,
And the panels just as strong as the floor,
And the whipple-tree neither less nor more,
And the back crossbar as strong as the fore,
And spring and axle and hub *encore*.
And yet, *as a whole*, it is past a doubt
In another hour it will be *worn out!*

First of November, 'Fifty-five!
This morning the parson takes a drive.
Now, small boys, get out of the way!
Here comes the wonderful one-hoss shay,
Drawn by a rat-tailed, ewe-necked bay.
"Huddup!" said the parson.—Off went they.
The parson was working his Sunday's text,—
Had got to *fifthly*, and stopped perplexed
At what the—Moses—was coming next.
All at once the horse stood still,
Close by the meet'n'-house on the hill.
First a shiver, and then a thrill,
Then something decidedly like a spill,—
And the parson was sitting upon a rock,
At half past nine by the meet'n'-house clock,—
Just the hour of the Earthquake shock!
What do you think the parson found,
When he got up and stared around?
The poor old chaise in a heap or mound,
As if it had been to the mill and ground!
You see, of course, if you're not a dunce,
How it went to pieces all at once,—
All at once, and nothing first,—
Just as bubbles do when they burst.

End of the wonderful one-hoss shay.
Logic is logic. That's all I say.

1858

CONTENTMENT

"Man wants but little here below."

Little I ask; my wants are few;
  I only wish a hut of stone
(A *very plain* brown stone will do)
  That I may call my own;—
And close at hand is such a one,
In yonder street that fronts the sun.

Plain food is quite enough for me;
  Three courses are as good as ten;—
If Nature can subsist on three,
  Thank Heaven for three. Amen!
I always thought cold victual nice;—
My *choice* would be vanilla-ice.

I care not much for gold or land;—
  Give me a mortgage here and there,—
Some good bank-stock, some note of hand,
  Or trifling railroad share,—
I only ask that Fortune send
A *little* more than I shall spend.

Honors are silly toys, I know,
  And titles are but empty names;
I would, *perhaps*, be Plenipo,—
  But only near St. James;
I'm very sure I should not care
To fill our Gubernator's chair.

Jewels are baubles; 'tis a sin
  To care for such unfruitful things;—
One good-sized diamond in a pin,—
  Some, *not so large*, in rings,—
A ruby, and a pearl, or so,
Will do for me;—I laugh at show.

My dame should dress in cheap attire
  (Good, heavy silks are never dear);—
I own perhaps I *might* desire
  Some shawls of true Cashmere,—
Some marrowy crapes of China silk,
Like wrinkled skins on scalded milk.

I would not have the horse I drive
  So fast that folks must stop and stare;
An easy gait—two forty-five—
  Suits me; I do not care;—
Perhaps, for just a *single spurt*,
Some seconds less would do no hurt.

Of pictures, I should like to own
  Titians and Raphaels three or four,—
I love so much their style and tone,
  One Turner, and no more
(A landscape,—foreground golden dirt,—
The sunshine painted with a squirt).

Of books but few,—some fifty score
  For daily use, and bound for wear;
The rest upon an upper floor;—
  Some *little* luxury *there*
Of red morocco's gilded gleam
And vellum rich as country cream.

Busts, cameos, gems,—such things as these,
  Which others often show for pride,
I value for their power to please,
  And selfish churls deride;—
One Stradivarius, I confess,
Two Meerschaums, I would fain possess.

Wealth's wasteful tricks I will not learn,
  Nor ape the glittering upstart fool;—
Shall not carved tables serve my turn,
  But *all* must be of buhl?
Give grasping pomp its double share,—
I ask but *one* recumbent chair.

Thus humble let me live and die,
  Nor long for Midas' golden touch;
If Heaven more generous gifts deny,
  I shall not miss them *much*,—
Too grateful for the blessing lent
Of simple tastes and mind content!

1858

THE VOICELESS

We count the broken lyres that rest
  Where the sweet wailing singers slumber,
But o'er their silent sister's breast
  The wild-flowers who will stoop to number?
A few can touch the magic string,
  And noisy Fame is proud to win them:—
Alas for those that never sing,
  But die with all their music in them!

Nay, grieve not for the dead alone
  Whose song has told their hearts' sad story,—
Weep for the voiceless, who have known
  The cross without the crown of glory!
Not where Leucadian breezes sweep
  O'er Sappho's memory-haunted billow,
But where the glistening night-dews weep
  On nameless sorrow's churchyard pillow.

O hearts that break and give no sign
  Save whitening lip and fading tresses,
Till Death pours out his longed-for wine
  Slow-dropped from Misery's crushing presses,—
If singing breath or echoing chord
  To every hidden pang were given,
What endless melodies were poured,
  As sad as earth, as sweet as heaven!

1858

THE BOYS

Has there any old fellow got mixed with the boys?
If there has, take him out, without making a noise.
Hang the Almanac's cheat and the Catalogue's spite!
Old Time is a liar! We're twenty tonight!

We're twenty! We're twenty! Who says we are more?
He's tipsy,—young jackanapes!—show him the door!
"Gray temples at twenty?"—Yes! *white* if we please;
Where the snow-flakes fall thickest there's nothing can freeze!

Was it snowing I spoke of? Excuse the mistake!
Look close,—you will see not a sign of a flake!
We want some new garlands for those we have shed,—
And these are white roses in place of the red.

We've a trick, we young fellows, you may have been told,
Of talking (in public) as if we were old:—
That boy we call "Doctor," and this we call "Judge";
It's a neat little fiction,—of course it's all fudge.

That fellow's the "Speaker,"—the one on the right;
"Mr. Mayor," my young one, how are you tonight?
That's our "Member of Congress," we say when we chaff;
There's the "Reverend" What's his name?—don't make me laugh.

That boy with the grave mathematical look
Made believe he had written a wonderful book,
And the ROYAL SOCIETY thought it was *true!*
So they chose him right in; a good joke it was, too!

There's a boy, we pretend, with a three-decker brain,
That could harness a team with a logical chain;
When he spoke for our manhood in syllabled fire,
We called him "The Justice," but now he's "The Squire."

And there's a nice youngster of excellent pith,—
Fate tried to conceal him by naming him Smith;
But he shouted a song for the brave and the free,—
Just read on his medal, "My country," "of thee!"

You hear that boy laughing?—You think he's all fun;
But the angels laugh, too, at the good he has done;
The children laugh loud as they troop to his call,
And the poor man that knows him laughs loudest of all!

Yes, we're boys,—always playing with tongue or with pen,—
And I sometimes have asked,—Shall we ever be men?
Shall we always be youthful, and laughing, and gay,
Till the last dear companion drops smiling away?

Then here's to our boyhood, its gold and its gray!
The stars of its winter, the dews of its May!
And when we have done with our life-lasting toys,
Dear Father, take care of thy children, THE BOYS!

1859 1859

THE TWO STREAMS

BEHOLD the rocky wall
That down its sloping sides
Pours the swift rain-drops, blending, as they fall,
In rushing river-tides!

Yon stream, whose sources run
Turned by a pebble's edge,
Is Athabasca, rolling toward the sun
Through the cleft mountain-ledge.

The slender rill had strayed,
But for the slanting stone,
To evening's ocean, with the tangled braid
Of foam-flecked Oregon.

So from the heights of Will
Life's parting stream descends,
And, as a moment turns its slender rill,
Each widening torrent bends,—

From the same cradle's side,
From the same mother's knee,—
One to long darkness and the frozen tide,
One to the Peaceful Sea!

1859

AT A MEETING OF FRIENDS

AUGUST 29, 1859

I REMEMBER—why, yes! God bless me! and was it so long ago?
I fear I'm growing forgetful, as old folks do, you know;
It must have been in 'forty—I would say 'thirty-nine—
We talked this matter over, I and a friend of mine.

He said, "Well now, old fellow, I'm thinking that you and I,
If we act like other people, shall be older by and by;

What though the bright blue ocean is smooth as a pond can be,
There is always a line of breakers to fringe the broadest sea.

"We're taking it mighty easy, but that is nothing strange,
For up to the age of thirty we spend our years like change;
But creeping up towards the forties, as fast as the old years fill,
And Time steps in for payment, we seem to change a bill."

"I know it," I said, "old fellow; you speak the solemn truth;
A man can't live to a hundred and likewise keep his youth;
But what if the ten years coming shall silver-streak my hair,
You know I shall then be forty; of course I shall not care.

"At forty a man grows heavy and tired of fun and noise;
Leaves dress to the five-and-twenties and love to the silly boys;
No foppish tricks at forty, no pinching of waists and toes,
But high-low shoes and flannels and good thick worsted hose."

But one fine August morning I found myself awake:
My birthday:—By Jove, I'm forty! Yes, forty and no mistake!
Why, this is the very milestone, I think I used to hold,
That when a fellow had come to, a fellow would then be old!

But that is the young folks' nonsense; they're full of their foolish stuff;
A man's in his prime at forty,—I see *that* plain enough;
At *fifty* a man *is* wrinkled, and *may be* bald or gray;
I call men old at fifty, in spite of all they say.

At last comes another August with mist and rain and shine;
Its mornings are slowly counted and creep to twenty-nine,
And when on the western summits the fading light appears,
It touches with rosy fingers the last of my fifty years.

There have been both men and women whose hearts were firm and bold,
But there never was one of fifty that loved to say "I'm old";
So any elderly person that strives to shirk his years,
Make him stand up at a table and try him by his peers.

Now here I stand at fifty, my jury gathered round;
Sprinkled with dust of silver, but not yet silver-crowned,
Ready to meet your verdict, waiting to hear it told;
Guilty of fifty summers; speak! Is the verdict *old?*

No! say that his hearing fails him; say that his sight grows dim;
Say that he's getting wrinkled and weak in back and limb,
Losing his wits and temper, but pleading, to make amends,
The youth of his fifty summers he finds in his twenty friends.

1859 1859

HYMN OF TRUST

O Love Divine, that stooped to share
Our sharpest pang, our bitterest tear,
On Thee we cast each earth-born care,
We smile at pain while Thou art near!

Though long the weary way we tread,
And sorrow crown each lingering year,
No path we shun, no darkness dread,
Our hearts still whispering, Thou art near!

When drooping pleasure turns to grief,
And trembling faith is changed to fear,
The murmuring wind, the quivering leaf,
Shall softly tell us, Thou art near!

On Thee we fling our burdening woe,
O Love Divine, forever dear,
Content to suffer while we know,
Living and dying, Thou art near!

1859

A SUN-DAY HYMN

Lord of all being! throned afar,
Thy glory flames from sun and star;
Centre and soul of every sphere,
Yet to each loving heart how near!

Sun of our life, thy quickening ray
Sheds on our path the glow of day;
Star of our hope, thy softened light
Cheers the long watches of the night.

Our midnight is thy smile withdrawn;
Our noontide is thy gracious dawn;
Our rainbow arch thy mercy's sign;
All, save the clouds of sin, are thine!

Lord of all life, below, above,
Whose light is truth, whose warmth is love,
Before thy ever-blazing throne
We ask no lustre of our own.

Grant us thy truth to make us free,
And kindling hearts that burn for thee,
Till all thy living altars claim
One holy light, one heavenly flame!

1859

BROTHER JONATHAN'S LAMENT FOR SISTER CAROLINE

MARCH 25, 1861

She has gone,—she has left us in passion and pride,—
Our stormy-browed sister, so long at our side!
She has torn her own star from our firmament's glow,
And turned on her brother the face of a foe!

Oh, Caroline, Caroline, child of the sun,
We can never forget that our hearts have been one,—
Our foreheads both sprinkled in Liberty's name,
From the fountain of blood with the finger of flame!

You were always too ready to fire at a touch;
But we said, "She is hasty,—she does not mean much."
We have scowled, when you uttered some turbulent threat;
But Friendship still whispered, "Forgive and forget!"

Has our love all died out? Have its altars grown cold?
Has the curse come at last which the fathers foretold?
Then Nature must teach us the strength of the chain
That her petulant children would sever in vain.

They may fight till the buzzards are gorged with their spoil,
Till the harvest grows black as it rots in the soil,
Till the wolves and the catamounts troop from their caves,
And the shark tracks the pirate, the lord of the waves:

In vain is the strife! When its fury is past,
Their fortunes must flow in one channel at last,
As the torrents that rush from the mountains of snow
Roll mingled in peace through the valleys below.

Our Union is river, lake, ocean, and sky:
Man breaks not the medal, when God cuts the die!
Though darkened with sulphur, though cloven with steel,
The blue arch will brighten, the waters will heal!

Oh, Caroline, Caroline, child of the sun,
There are battles with Fate that can never be won!
The star-flowering banner must never be furled,
For its blossoms of light are the hope of the world!

Go, then, our rash sister! afar and aloof,
Run wild in the sunshine away from our roof;
But when your heart aches and your feet have grown sore,
Remember the pathway that leads to our door!

1861 1861

PROLOGUE TO "SONGS IN MANY KEYS"

THE piping of our slender, peaceful reeds
Whispers uncared for while the trumpets bray;
Song is thin air; our hearts' exulting play
Beats time but to the tread of marching deeds,
Following the mighty van that Freedom leads,
Her glorious standard flaming to the day!
The crimsoned pavement where a hero bleeds
Breathes nobler lessons than the poet's lay.
Strong arms, broad breasts, brave hearts, are better worth
Than strains that sing the ravished echoes dumb.
Hark! 'tis the loud reverberating drum
Rolls o'er the prairied West, the rock-bound North:
The myriad-handed Future stretches forth
Its shadowy palms. Behold, we come,—we come!

Turn o'er these idle leaves. Such toys as these
Were not unsought for, as, in languid dreams,
We lay beside our lotus-feeding streams,
And nursed our fancies in forgetful ease.
It matters little if they pall or please,
Dropping untimely, while the sudden gleams
Glare from the mustering clouds whose blackness seems
Too swollen to hold its lightning from the trees.
Yet, in some lull of passion, when at last
These calm revolving moons that come and go—
Turning our months to years, they creep so slow—
Have brought us rest, the not unwelcome past
May flutter to thee through these leaflets, cast
On the wild winds that all around us blow.

1861 1861

UNION AND LIBERTY

FLAG of the heroes who left us their glory,
Borne through their battle-fields' thunder and flame,
Blazoned in song and illumined in story,
Wave o'er us all who inherit their fame!
Up with our banner bright,
Sprinkled with starry light,
Spread its fair emblems from mountain to shore,
While through the sounding sky
Loud rings the Nation's cry,—
UNION AND LIBERTY! ONE EVERMORE!

Light of our firmament, guide of our Nation,
Pride of her children, and honored afar,
Let the wide beams of thy full constellation
Scatter each cloud that would darken a star!
Up with our banner bright, etc.

Empire unsceptred! what foe shall assail thee,
Bearing the standard of Liberty's van?
Think not the God of thy fathers shall fail thee,
Striving with men for the birthright of man!
Up with our banner bright, etc.

Yet if, by madness and treachery blighted,
Dawns the dark hour when the sword thou must draw,
Then with the arms of thy millions united,
Smite the bold traitors to Freedom and Law!
Up with our banner bright, etc.

Lord of the Universe! shield us and guide us,
Trusting Thee always, through shadow and sun!
Thou hast united us, who shall divide us?
Keep us, oh keep us the MANY IN ONE!
Up with our banner bright,
Sprinkled with starry light,
Spread its fair emblems from mountain to shore,
While through the sounding sky
Loud rings the Nation's cry,—
UNION AND LIBERTY! ONE EVERMORE!

1861 1861

TO MY READERS

NAY, blame me not; I might have spared
Your patience many a trivial verse,
Yet these my earlier welcome shared,
So, let the better shield the worse.

And some might say, "Those ruder songs
Had freshness which the new have lost;
To spring the opening leaf belongs,
The chestnut-burs await the frost."

When those I wrote, my locks were brown,
When these I write—ah, well-a-day!
The autumn thistle's silvery down
Is not the purple bloom of May!

Go, little book, whose pages hold
Those garnered years in loving trust;
How long before your blue and gold
Shall fade and whiten in the dust?

O sexton of the alcoved tomb,
Where souls in leathern cerements lie,
Tell me each living poet's doom!
How long before his book shall die?

It matters little, soon or late,
A day, a month, a year, an age,—
I read oblivion in its date,
And Finis on its title-page.

Before we sighed, our griefs were told;
Before we smiled, our joys were sung;
And all our passions shaped of old
In accents lost to mortal tongue.

In vain a fresher mould we seek,—
Can all the varied phrases tell
That Babel's wandering children speak
How thrushes sing or lilacs smell?

Caged in the poet's lonely heart,
Love wastes unheard its tenderest tone;
The soul that sings must dwell apart,
Its inward melodies unknown.

Deal gently with us, ye who read!
Our largest hope is unfulfilled,—
The promise still outruns the deed,—
The tower, but not the spire, we build.

Our whitest pearl we never find;
Our ripest fruit we never reach;
The flowering moments of the mind
Drop half their petals in our speech.

These are my blossoms; if they wear
One streak of morn or evening's glow,
Accept them; but to me more fair
The buds of song that never blow.

1862 *1862*

VOYAGE OF THE GOOD SHIP UNION

1862

'Tis midnight: through my troubled dream
Loud wails the tempest's cry;
Before the gale, with tattered sail,
A ship goes plunging by.
What name? Where bound?—The rocks around
Repeat the loud halloo.
—The good ship Union, Southward bound:
God help her and her crew!

And is the old flag flying still
That o'er your fathers flew,
With bands of white and rosy light,
And field of starry blue?
—Ay! look aloft! its folds full oft
Have braved the roaring blast,
And still shall fly when from the sky
This black typhoon has past!

Speak, pilot of the storm-tost bark!
May I thy peril share?
—O landsman, there are fearful seas
The brave alone may dare!
—Nay, ruler of the rebel deep,
What matters wind or wave?
The rocks that wreck your reeling deck
Will leave me naught to save!

O landsman, art thou false or true?
What sign hast thou to show?
—The crimson stains from loyal veins
That hold my heart-blood's flow!
—Enough! what more shall honor claim?
I know the sacred sign;
Above thy head our flag shall spread,
Our ocean path be thine!

The bark sails on; the Pilgrim's Cape
Lies low along her lee,
Whose headland crooks its anchor-flukes
To lock the shore and sea.
No treason here! it cost too dear
To win this barren realm!
And true and free the hands must be
That hold the whaler's helm!

Still on! Manhattan's narrowing bay
No rebel cruiser scars;

Her waters feel no pirate's keel
  That flaunts the fallen stars!
—But watch the light on yonder height,—
  Ay, pilot, have a care!
Some lingering cloud in mist may shroud
  The capes of Delaware!

Say, pilot, what this fort may be,
  Whose sentinels look down
From moated walls that show the sea
  Their deep embrasures' frown?
The Rebel host claims all the coast,
  But these are friends, we know,
Whose footprints spoil the "sacred soil,"
  And this is?—Fort Monroe!

The breakers roar,—how bears the shore?
  —The traitorous wreckers' hands
Have quenched the blaze that poured its rays
  Along the Hatteras sands.
—Ha! say not so! I see its glow!
  Again the shoals display
The beacon light that shines by night,
  The Union Stars by day!

The good ship flies to milder skies,
  The wave more gently flows,
The softening breeze wafts o'er the seas
  The breath of Beaufort's rose.
What fold is this the sweet winds kiss,
  Fair-striped and many-starred,
Whose shadow palls these orphaned walls,
  The twins of Beauregard?

What! heard you not Port Royal's doom?
  How the black war-ships came
And turned the Beaufort roses' bloom
  To redder wreaths of flame?
How from Rebellion's broken reed
  We saw his emblem fall,
As soon his cursèd poison-weed
  Shall drop from Sumter's wall?

On! on! Pulaski's iron hail
  Falls harmless on Tybee!
The good ship feels the freshening gales,
  She strikes the open sea;
She rounds the point, she threads the keys
  That guard the Land of Flowers,
And rides at last where firm and fast
  Her own Gibraltar towers!

The good ship Union's voyage is o'er,
  At anchor safe she swings,
And loud and clear with cheer on cheer
  Her joyous welcome rings:
Hurrah! Hurrah! it shakes the wave,
  It thunders on the shore,—
One flag, one land, one heart, one hand,
  One Nation, evermore!

1862 1862

BRYANT'S SEVENTIETH BIRTHDAY

NOVEMBER 3, 1864

O EVEN-HANDED Nature! we confess
This life that men so honor, love, and bless
Has filled thine olden measure. Not the less

We count the precious seasons that remain;
Strike not the level of the golden grain,
But heap it high with years, that earth may
  gain

What heaven can lose,—for heaven is rich in
  song:
Do not all poets, dying, still prolong
Their broken chants amid the seraph throng,

Where, blind no more, Ionia's bard is seen,
And England's heavenly minstrel sits between
The Mantuan and the wan-cheeked Floren-
  tine?

This was the first sweet singer in the cage
Of our close-woven life. A new-born age
Claims in his vesper song its heritage:

Spare us, oh spare us long our heart's desire!
Moloch, who calls our children through the
  fire,
Leaves us the gentle master of the lyre.

We count not on the dial of the sun
The hours, the minutes, that his sands have
  run;
Rather, as on those flowers that one by one

From earliest dawn their ordered bloom dis-
  play
Till evening's planet with her guiding ray
Leads in the blind old mother of the day,

We reckon by his songs, each song a flower,
The long, long daylight, numbering hour by hour,
Each breathing sweetness like a bridal bower.

His morning glory shall we e'er forget?
His noontide's full-blown lily coronet?
His evening primrose has not opened yet;

Nay, even if creeping Time should hide the skies
In midnight from his century-laden eyes,
Darkened like his who sang of Paradise,

Would not some hidden song-bud open bright
As the resplendent cactus of the night
That floods the gloom with fragrance and with light?

How can we praise the verse whose music flows
With solemn cadence and majestic close,
Pure as the dew that filters through the rose?

How shall we thank him that in evil days
He faltered never,—nor for blame, nor praise,
Nor hire, nor party, shamed his earlier lays?

But as his boyhood was of manliest hue,
So to his youth his manly years were true,
All dyed in royal purple through and through!

He for whose touch the lyre of Heaven is strung
Needs not the flattering toil of mortal tongue:
Let not the singer grieve to die unsung!

Marbles forget their message to mankind:
In his own verse the poet still we find,
In his own page his memory lives enshrined,

As in their amber sweets the smothered bees,—
As the fair cedar, fallen before the breeze,
Lies self-embalmed amidst the mouldering trees.

Poets, like youngest children, never grow
Out of their mother's fondness. Nature so
Holds their soft hands, and will not let them go,

Till at the last they track with even feet
Her rhythmic footsteps, and their pulses beat
Twinned with her pulses, and their lips repeat

The secrets she has told them, as their own:
Thus is the inmost soul of Nature known,
And the rapt minstrel shares her awful throne!

O lover of her mountains and her woods,
Her bridal chamber's leafy solitudes,
Where Love himself with tremulous step intrudes,

Her snows fall harmless on thy sacred fire:
Far be the day that claims thy sounding lyre
To join the music of the angel choir!

Yet, since life's amplest measure must be filled,
Since throbbing hearts must be forever stilled,
And all must fade that evening sunsets gild,

Grant, Father, ere he close the mortal eyes
That see a Nation's reeking sacrifice,
Its smoke may vanish from these blackened skies!

Then, when his summons comes, since come it must,
And, looking heavenward with unfaltering trust,
He wraps his drapery round him for the dust,

His last fond glance will show him o'er his head
The Northern fires beyond the zenith spread
In lambent glory, blue and white and red,—

The Southern cross without its bleeding load,
The milky way of peace all freshly strowed,
And every white-throned star fixed in its lost abode!

1864 1864

ALL HERE

It is not what we say or sing,
  That keeps our charm so long unbroken,
Though every lightest leaf we bring
  May touch the heart as friendship's token;
Not what we sing or what we say
  Can make us dearer to each other;
We love the singer and his lay,
  But love as well the silent brother.

Yet bring whate'er your garden grows,
  Thrice welcome to our smiles and praises;
Thanks for the myrtle and the rose,
  Thanks for the marigolds and daisies;

One flower ere long we all shall claim,
  Alas! unloved of Amaryllis—
Nature's last blossom—need I name
  The wreath of threescore's silver lilies?

How many, brothers, meet tonight
  Around our boyhood's covered embers?
Go read the treasured names aright
  The old triennial list remembers;
Though twenty wear the starry sign
  That tells a life has broke its tether,
The fifty-eight of 'twenty-nine—
  God bless The Boys!—are all together!

These come with joyous look and word,
  With friendly grasp and cheerful greeting,—
Those smile unseen, and move unheard,
  The angel guests of every meeting;
They cast no shadow in the flame
  That flushes from the gilded lustre,
But count us—we are still the same;
  One earthly band, one heavenly cluster!

Love dies not when he bows his head
  To pass beyond the narrow portals,—
The light these glowing moments shed
  Wakes from their sleep our lost immortals;
They come as in their joyous prime,
  Before their morning days were numbered,—
Death stays the envious hand of Time,—
  The eyes have not grown dim that slumbered!

The paths that loving souls have trod
  Arch o'er the dust where worldlings grovel
High as the zenith o'er the sod,—
  The cross above the sexton's shovel!
We rise beyond the realms of day;
  They seem to stoop from spheres of glory
With us one happy hour to stray,
  While youth comes back in song and story.

Ah! ours is friendship true as steel
  That war has tried in edge and temper;
It writes upon its sacred seal
  The priest's *ubique—omnes—semper!*
It lends the sky a fairer sun
  That cheers our lives with rays as steady
As if our footsteps had begun
  To print the golden streets already!

The tangling years have clinched its knot
  Too fast for mortal strength to sunder;
The lightning bolts of noon are shot;
  No fear of evening's idle thunder!
Too late! too late!—no graceless hand
  Shall stretch its cords in vain endeavor
To rive the close encircling band
  That made and keeps us one forever!

So when upon the fated scroll
  The falling stars have all descended,
And, blotted from the breathing roll,
  Our little page of life is ended,
We ask but one memorial line
  Traced on thy tablet, Gracious Mother:
"My children. Boys of '29.
  In pace. How they loved each other!"

1867 1867

BILL AND JOE

Come, dear old comrade, you and I
Will steal an hour from days gone by,
The shining days when life was new,
And all was bright with morning dew,
The lusty days of long ago,
When you were Bill and I was Joe.

Your name may flaunt a titled trail
Proud as a cockerel's rainbow tail,
And mine as brief appendix wear
As Tam O'Shanter's luckless mare;
Today, old friend, remember still
That I am Joe and you are Bill.

You've won the great world's envied prize,
And grand you look in people's eyes,
With H O N. and L L. D.
In big brave letters, fair to see,—
Your fist, old fellow! off they go!—
How are you, Bill? How are you, Joe?

You've worn the judge's ermined robe;
You've taught your name to half the globe;
You've sung mankind a deathless strain;
You've made the dead past live again:
The world may call you what it will,
But you and I are Joe and Bill.

The chaffing young folks stare and say
"See those old buffers, bent and gray,—

They talk like fellows in their teens!
Mad, poor old boys! That's what it means,"—
And shake their heads; they little know
The throbbing hearts of Bill and Joe!—

How Bill forgets his hour of pride,
While Joe sits smiling at his side;
How Joe, in spite of time's disguise,
Finds the old schoolmate in his eyes,—
Those calm, stern eyes that melt and fill
As Joe looks fondly up at Bill.

Ah, pensive scholar, what is fame?
A fitful tongue of leaping flame;
A giddy whirlwind's fickle gust,
That lifts a pinch of mortal dust;
A few swift years, and who can show
Which dust was Bill and which was Joe?

The weary idol takes his stand,
Holds out his bruised and aching hand,
While gaping thousands come and go,—
How vain it seems, this empty show!
Till all at once his pulses thrill;—
'Tis poor old Joe's "God bless you, Bill!"

And shall we breathe in happier spheres
The names that pleased our mortal ears;
In some sweet lull of harp and song
For earth-born spirits none too long,
Just whispering of the world below
Where this was Bill and that was Joe?

No matter; while our home is here
No sounding name is half so dear;
When fades at length our lingering day,
Who cares what pompous tombstones say?
Read on the hearts that love us still,
Hic jacet Joe. *Hic jacet* Bill.

1868 1868

DOROTHY Q.

A FAMILY PORTRAIT

GRANDMOTHER'S mother: her age, I guess,
Thirteen summers, or something less;
Girlish bust, but womanly air;
Smooth, square forehead with uprolled hair;
Lips that lover has never kissed;
Taper fingers and slender wrist;
Hanging sleeves of stiff brocade;
So they painted the little maid.

On her hand a parrot green
Sits unmoving and broods serene.
Hold up the canvas full in view,—
Look! there's a rent the light shines through,
Dark with a century's fringe of dust,—
That was a Red-Coat's rapier-thrust!
Such is the tale the lady old,
Dorothy's daughter's daughter, told.

Who the painter was none may tell,—
One whose best was not over well;
Hard and dry, it must be confessed,
Flat as a rose that has long been pressed;
Yet in her cheek the hues are bright,
Dainty colors of red and white,
And in her slender shape are seen
Hint and promise of stately mien.

Look not on her with eyes of scorn,—
Dorothy Q. was a lady born!
Ay! since the galloping Normans came,
England's annals have known her name;
And still to the three-hilled rebel town
Dear is that ancient name's renown,
For many a civic wreath they won,
The youthful sire and the gray-haired son.

O Damsel Dorothy! Dorothy Q.!
Strange is the gift that I owe to you;
Such a gift as never a king
Save to daughter or son might bring,—
All my tenure of heart and hand,
All my title to house and land;
Mother and sister and child and wife
And joy and sorrow and death and life!

What if a hundred years ago
Those close-shut lips had answered No,
When forth the tremulous question came
That cost the maiden her Norman name,
And under the folds that look so still
The bodice swelled with the bosom's thrill?
Should I be I, or would it be
One tenth another, to nine tenths me?

Soft is the breath of a maiden's YES:
Not the light gossamer stirs with less;
But never a cable that holds so fast
Through all the battles of wave and blast,
And never an echo of speech or song
That lives in the babbling air so long!

There were tones in the voice that whispered then
You may hear today in a hundred men.

O lady and lover, how faint and far
Your images hover,—and here we are,
Solid and stirring in flesh and bone,—
Edward's and Dorothy's—all their own,—
A goodly record for Time to show
Of a syllable spoken so long ago!—
Shall I bless you, Dorothy, or forgive
For the tender whisper that bade me live?

It shall be a blessing, my little maid!
I will heal the stab of the Red-Coat's blade,
And freshen the gold of the tarnished frame,
And gild with a rhyme your household name;
So you shall smile on us brave and bright
As first you greeted the morning's light,
And live untroubled by woes and fears
Through a second youth of a hundred years.

1871

WIND-CLOUDS AND STAR-DRIFTS

FROM THE YOUNG ASTRONOMER'S POEM

I

AMBITION

ANOTHER clouded night; the stars are hid,
The orb that waits my search is hid with them.
Patience! Why grudge an hour, a month, a year,
To plant my ladder and to gain the round
That leads my footsteps to the heaven of fame,
Where waits the wreath my sleepless midnights won?
Not the stained laurel such as heroes wear
That withers when some stronger conqueror's heel
Treads down their shrivelling trophies in the dust;
But the fair garland whose undying green
Not time can change, nor wrath of gods or men!

With quickened heart-beats I shall hear the tongues
That speak my praise; but better far the sense
That in the unshaped ages, buried deep
In the dark mines of unaccomplished time
Yet to be stamped with morning's royal die
And coined in golden days,—in those dim years
I shall be reckoned with the undying dead,
My name emblazoned on the fiery arch,
Unfading till the stars themselves shall fade.
Then, as they call the roll of shining worlds,
Sages of race unborn in accents new
Shall count me with the Olympian ones of old,
Whose glories kindle through the midnight sky:
Here glows the God of Battles; this recalls
The Lord of Ocean, and yon far-off sphere
The Sire of Him who gave his ancient name
To the dim planet with the wondrous rings;
Here flames the Queen of Beauty's silver lamp,
And there the moon-girt orb of mighty Jove;
But *this*, unseen through all earth's æons past,
A youth who watched beneath the western star
Sought in the darkness, found, and showed to men;
Linked with his name thenceforth and evermore!
So shall that name be syllabled anew
In all the tongues of all the tribes of men:
I that have been through immemorial years
Dust in the dust of my forgotten time
Shall live in accents shaped of blood-warm breath,
Yea, rise in mortal semblance, newly born
In shining stone, in undecaying bronze,
And stand on high, and look serenely down
On the new race that calls the earth its own.

Is this a cloud, that, blown athwart my soul,
Wears a false seeming of the pearly stain
Where worlds beyond the world their mingling rays
Blend in soft white,—a cloud that, born of earth,
Would cheat the soul that looks for light from heaven?
Must every coral-insect leave his sign
On each poor grain he lent to build the reef,
As Babel's builders stamped their sunburnt clay,
Or deem his patient service all in vain?
What if another sit beneath the shade
Of the broad elm I planted by the way,—

What if another heed the beacon light
I set upon the rock that wrecked my keel,—
Have I not done my task and served my kind?
Nay, rather act thy part, unnamed, unknown,
And let Fame blow her trumpet through the world
With noisy wind to swell a fool's renown,
Joined with some truth he stumbled blindly o'er,
Or coupled with some single shining deed
That in the great account of all his days
Will stand alone upon the bankrupt sheet
His pitying angel shows the clerk of Heaven.
The noblest service comes from nameless hands,
And the best servant does his work unseen.
Who found the seeds of fire and made them shoot,
Fed by his breath, in buds and flowers of flame?
Who forged in roaring flames the ponderous stone,
And shaped the moulded metal to his need?
Who gave the dragging car its rolling wheel,
And tamed the steed that whirls its circling round?
All these have left their work and not their names,—
Why should I murmur at a fate like theirs?
This is the heavenly light; the pearly stain
Was but a wind-cloud drifting o'er the stars!

II

REGRETS

Brief glimpses of the bright celestial spheres,
False lights, false shadows, vague, uncertain gleams,
Pale vaporous mists, wan streaks of lurid flame,
The climbing of the upward-sailing cloud,
The sinking of the downward-falling star,—
All these are pictures of the changing moods
Borne through the midnight stillness of my soul.

Here am I, bound upon this pillared rock,
Prey to the vulture of a vast desire
That feeds upon my life. I burst my bands
And steal a moment's freedom from the beak,
The clinging talons and the shadowing plumes;
Then comes the false enchantress, with her song;
"Thou wouldst not lay thy forehead in the dust
Like the base herd that feeds and breeds and dies!
Lo, the fair garlands that I weave for thee,
Unchanging as the belt Orion wears,
Bright as the jewels of the seven-starred Crown,
The spangled stream of Berenice's hair!"
And so she twines the fetters with the flowers
Around my yielding limbs, and the fierce bird
Stoops to his quarry,—then to feed his rage
Of ravening hunger I must drain my blood
And let the dew-drenched, poison-breeding night
Steal all the freshness from my fading cheek,
And leave its shadows round my caverned eyes.
All for a line in some unheeded scroll;
All for a stone that tells to gaping clowns,
"Here lies a restless wretch beneath a clod
Where squats the jealous nightmare men call Fame!"

I marvel not at him who scorns his kind
And thinks not sadly of the time foretold
When the old hulk we tread shall be a wreck,
A slag, a cinder drifting through the sky
Without its crew of fools! We live too long,
And even so are not content to die,
But load the mould that covers up our bones
With stones that stand like beggars by the road
And show death's grievous wound and ask for tears;
Write our great books to teach men who we are,
Sing our fine songs that tell in artful phrase
The secrets of our lives, and plead and pray
For alms of memory with the after time,
Those few swift seasons while the earth shall wear
Its leafy summers, ere its core grows cold
And the moist life of all that breathes shall die;
Or as the new-born seer, perchance more wise,
Would have us deem, before its growing mass,
Pelted with star-dust, stoned with meteor-balls,
Heats like a hammered anvil, till at last

Man and his works and all that stirred itself
Of its own motion, in the fiery glow
Turns to a flaming vapor, and our orb
Shines a new sun for earths that shall be born.

I am as old as Egypt to myself,
Brother to them that squared the pyramids
By the same stars I watch. I read the page
Where every letter is a glittering world,
With them who looked from Shinar's clay-built towers,
Ere yet the wanderer of the Midland sea
Had missed the fallen sister of the seven.
I dwell in spaces vague, remote, unknown,
Save to the silent few, who, leaving earth,
Quit all communion with their living time.
I lose myself in that ethereal void,
Till I have tired my wings and long to fill
My breast with denser air, to stand, to walk
With eyes not raised above my fellow-men.
Sick of my unwalled, solitary realm,
I ask to change the myriad lifeless worlds
I visit as mine own for one poor patch
Of this dull spheroid and a little breath
To shape in word or deed to serve my kind.
Was ever giant's dungeon dug so deep,
Was ever tyrant's fetter forged so strong,
Was e'er such deadly poison in the draught
The false wife mingles for the trusting fool,
As he whose willing victim is himself,
Digs, forges, mingles, for his captive soul?

III

SYMPATHIES

The snows that glittered on the disk of Mars
Have melted, and the planet's fiery orb
Rolls in the crimson summer of its year;
But what to me the summer or the snow
Of worlds that throb with life in forms unknown,
If life indeed be theirs; I heed not these.
My heart is simply human; all my care
For them whose dust is fashioned like mine own;
These ache with cold and hunger, live in pain,
And shake with fear of worlds more full of woe;
There may be others worthier of my love,
But such I know not save through these I know.

There are two veils of language, hid beneath
Whose sheltering folds, we dare to be ourselves;
And not that other self which nods and smiles
And babbles in our name; the one is Prayer,
Lending its licensed freedom to the tongue
That tells our sorrows and our sins to Heaven;
The other, Verse, that throws its spangled web
Around our naked speech and makes it bold.
I, whose best prayer is silence; sitting dumb
In the great temple where I nightly serve
Him who is throned in light, have dared to claim
The poet's franchise, though I may not hope
To wear his garland; hear me while I tell
My story in such form as poets use,
But breathed in fitful whispers, as the wind
Sighs and then slumbers, wakes and sighs again.

Thou Vision, floating in the breathless air
Between me and the fairest of the stars,
I tell my lonely thoughts as unto thee.
Look not for marvels of the scholar's pen
In my rude measure; I can only show
A slender-margined, unillumined page,
And trust its meaning to the flattering eye
That reads it in the gracious light of love.
Ah, wouldst thou clothe thyself in breathing shape
And nestle at my side, my voice should lend
Whate'er my verse may lack of tender rhythm
To make thee listen.
I have stood entranced
When, with her fingers wandering o'er the keys,
The white enchantress with the golden hair
Breathed all her soul through some unvalued rhyme;
Some flower of song that long had lost its bloom;
Lo! its dead summer kindled as she sang!
The sweet contralto, like the ringdove's coo,
Thrilled it with brooding, fond, caressing tones,
And the pale minstrel's passion lived again,
Tearful and trembling as a dewy rose
The wind has shaken till it fills the air
With light and fragrance. Such the wondrous charm

A song can borrow when the bosom throbs
That lends it breath.
So from the poet's lips
His verse sounds doubly sweet, for none like him
Feels every cadence of its wave-like flow;
He lives the passion over, while he reads,
That shook him as he sang his lofty strain,
And pours his life through each resounding line,
As ocean, when the stormy winds are hushed,
Still rolls and thunders through his billowy caves.

IV

MASTER AND SCHOLAR

Let me retrace the record of the years
That made me what I am. A man most wise,
But overworn with toil and bent with age,
Sought me to be his scholar,—me, run wild
From books and teachers,—kindled in my soul
The love of knowledge; led me to his tower,
Showed me the wonders of the midnight realm
His hollow sceptre ruled, or seemed to rule,
Taught me the mighty secrets of the spheres,
Trained me to find the glimmering specks of light
Beyond the unaided sense, and on my chart
To string them one by one, in order due,
As on a rosary a saint his beads.
I was his only scholar; I became
The echo to his thought; whate'er he knew
Was mine for asking; so from year to year
We wrought together, till there came a time
When I, the learner, was the master half
Of the twinned being in the dome-crowned tower.

Minds roll in paths like planets; they revolve,
This in a larger, that a narrower ring,
But round they come at last to that same phase,
That selfsame light and shade they showed before.
I learned his annual and his monthly tale,
His weekly axiom and his daily phrase,
I felt them coming in the laden air,
And watched them laboring up to vocal breath,
Even as the first-born at his father's board
Knows ere he speaks the too familiar jest
Is on its way, by some mysterious sign
Forewarned, the click before the striking bell.

He shrivelled as I spread my growing leaves,
Till trust and reverence changed to pitying care;
He lived for me in what he once had been,
But I for him, a shadow, a defence,
The guardian of his fame, his guide, his staff,
Leaned on so long he fell if left alone.
I was his eye, his ear, his cunning hand,
Love was my spur and longing after fame,
But his the goading thorn of sleepless age
That sees its shortening span, its lengthening shades,
That clutches what it may with eager grasp,
And drops at last with empty, outstretched hands.
All this he dreamed not. He would sit him down
Thinking to work his problems as of old,
And find the star he thought so plain a blur,
The columned figures labyrinthine wilds
Without my comment, blind and senseless scrawls
That vexed him with their riddles; he would strive
And struggle for a while, and then his eye
Would lose its light, and over all his mind
The cold gray mist would settle; and erelong
The darkness fell, and I was left alone.

V

ALONE

Alone! no climber of an Alpine cliff,
No Arctic venturer on the waveless sea,
Feels the dread stillness round him as it chills
The heart of him who leaves the slumbering earth
To watch the silent worlds that crowd the sky.

Alone! And as the shepherd leaves his flock
To feed upon the hillside, he meanwhile
Finds converse in the warblings of the pipe
Himself has fashioned for his vacant hour,
So have I grown companion to myself,
And to the wandering spirits of the air

That smile and whisper round us in our dreams.
Thus have I learned to search if I may know
The whence and why of all beneath the stars
And all beyond them, and to weigh my life
As in a balance,—poising good and ill
Against each other,—asking of the Power
That flung me forth among the whirling worlds,
If I am heir to any inborn right,
Or only as an atom of the dust 289
That every wind may blow where'er it will.

VI

QUESTIONING

I AM not humble; I was shown my place,
Clad in such robes as Nature had at hand;
Took what she gave, not chose; I know no shame,
No fear for being simply what I am.
I am not proud, I hold my every breath
At Nature's mercy. I am as a babe
Borne in a giant's arms, he knows not where;
Each several heart-beat, counted like the coin
A miser reckons, is a special gift
As from an unseen hand; if that withhold 300
Its bounty for a moment, I am left
A clod upon the earth to which I fall.

Something I find in me that well might claim
The love of beings in a sphere above
This doubtful twilight world of right and wrong;
Something that shows me of the selfsame clay
That creeps or swims or flies in humblest form.
Had I been asked, before I left my bed
Of shapeless dust, what clothing I would wear,
I would have said, More angel and less worm;
But for their sake who are even such as I,
Of the same mingled blood, I would not choose 312
To hate that meaner portion of myself
Which makes me brother to the least of men.

I dare not be a coward with my lips
Who dare to question all things in my soul;
Some men may find their wisdom on their knees,
Some prone and groveling in the dust like slaves;
Let the meek glowworm glisten in the dew;
I ask to lift my taper to the sky
As they who hold their lamps above their heads, 321
Trusting the larger currents up aloft,
Rather than crossing eddies round their breast,
Threatening with every puff the flickering blaze.

My life shall be a challenge, not a truce!
This is my homage to the mightier powers,
To ask my boldest question, undismayed
By muttered threats that some hysteric sense
Of wrong or insult will convulse the throne
Where wisdom reigns supreme; and if I err,
They all must err who have to feel their way
As bats that fly at noon; for what are we 332
But creatures of the night, dragged forth by day,
Who needs must stumble, and with stammering steps
Spell out their paths in syllables of pain?

Thou wilt not hold in scorn the child who dares
Look up to Thee, the Father,—dares to ask
More than thy wisdom answers. From thy hand
The worlds were cast; yet every leaflet claims
From that same hand its little shining sphere
Of star-lit dew; thine image, the great sun, 341
Girt with his mantle of tempestuous flame,
Glares in mid-heaven; but to his noon-tide blaze
The slender violet lifts its lidless eye,
And from his splendor steals its fairest hue,
Its sweetest perfume from his scorching fire.

VII

WORSHIP

FROM my lone turret as I look around
O'er the green meadows to the ring of blue,
From slope, from summit, and from half-hid vale
The sky is stabbed with dagger-pointed spires,
Their gilded symbols whirling in the wind, 351
Their brazen tongues proclaiming to the world,
"Here truth is sold, the only genuine ware;
See that it has our trade-mark! You will buy

Poison instead of food across the way,
The lies of——" this or that, each several name
The standard's blazon and the battle-cry
Of some true-gospel faction, and again
The token of the Beast to all beside.
And grouped round each I see a huddling crowd
Alike in all things save the words they use;
In love, in longing, hate and fear the same.

Whom do we trust and serve? We speak of one
And bow to many; Athens still would find
The shrines of all she worshipped safe within
Our tall barbarian temples, and the thrones
That crowned Olympus mighty as of old.
The god of music rules the Sabbath choir;
The lyric muse must leave the sacred nine
To help us please the dilettante's ear;
Plutus limps homeward with us, as we leave
The portals of the temple where we knelt
And listened while the god of eloquence
(Hermes of ancient days, but now disguised
In sable vestments) with that other god
Somnus, the son of Erebus and Nox,
Fights in unequal contest for our souls;
The dreadful sovereign of the underworld
Still shakes his sceptre at us, and we hear
The baying of the triple-throated hound;
Eros is young as ever, and as fair
The lovely Goddess born of ocean's foam.

These be thy gods, O Israel! Who is he,
The one ye name and tell us that ye serve,
Whom ye would call me from my lonely tower
To worship with the many-headed throng?
Is it the God that walked in Eden's grove
In the cool hour to seek our guilty sire?
The God who dealt with Abraham as the sons
Of that old patriarch deal with other men?
The jealous God of Moses, one who feels
An image as an insult, and is wroth
With him who made it and his child unborn?
The God who plagued his people for the sin
Of their adulterous king, beloved of him,—
The same who offers to a chosen few
The right to praise him in eternal song
While a vast shrieking world of endless woe
Blends its dread chorus with their rapturous hymn?
Is this the God ye mean, or is it he
Who heeds the sparrow's fall, whose loving heart
Is as the pitying father's to his child,
Whose lesson to his children is "Forgive,"
Whose plea for all, "They know not what they do"?

VIII

MANHOOD

I CLAIM the right of knowing whom I serve,
Else is my service idle; He that asks
My homage asks it from a reasoning soul.
To crawl is not to worship; we have learned
A drill of eyelids, bended neck and knee,
Hanging our prayers on hinges, till we ape
The flexures of the many-jointed worm.
Asia has taught her Allahs and salaams
To the world's children,—we have grown to men!
We who have rolled the sphere beneath our feet
To find a virgin forest, as we lay
The beams of our rude temple, first of all
Must frame its doorway high enough for man
To pass unstooping; knowing as we do
That He who shaped us last of living forms
Has long enough been served by creeping things,
Reptiles that left their footprints in the sand
Of old sea-margins that have turned to stone,
And men who learned their ritual; we demand
To know Him first, then trust Him and then love
When we have found Him worthy of our love,
Tried by our own poor hearts and not before;
He must be truer than the truest friend,
He must be tenderer than a woman's love,
A father better than the best of sires;
Kinder than she who bore us, though we sin
Oftener than did the brother we are told
We—poor ill-tempered mortals—must forgive,
Though seven times sinning threescore times and ten.

This is the new world's gospel: Be ye men!
Try well the legends of the children's time;
Ye are the chosen people, God has led

Your steps across the desert of the deep
As now across the desert of the shore;
Mountains are cleft before you as the sea
Before the wandering tribe of Israel's sons;
Still onward rolls the thunderous caravan,
Its coming printed on the western sky,
A cloud by day, by night a pillared flame;
Your prophets are a hundred unto one
Of them of old who cried, "Thus saith the Lord";
They told of cities that should fall in heaps,
But yours of mightier cities that shall rise
Where yet the lonely fishers spread their nets,
Where hides the fox and hoots the midnight owl;
The tree of knowledge in your garden grows
Not single, but at every humble door;
Its branches lend you their immortal food,
That fills you with the sense of what ye are,
No servants of an altar hewed and carved
From senseless stone by craft of human hands,
Rabbi, or dervish, brahmin, bishop, bonze,
But masters of the charm with which they work
To keep your hands from that forbidden tree!

Ye that have tasted that divinest fruit,
Look on this world of yours with opened eyes!
Ye are as gods! Nay, makers of your gods,—
Each day ye break an image in your shrine
And plant a fairer image where it stood:
Where is the Moloch of your fathers' creed,
Whose fires of torment burned for span-long babes?
Fit object for a tender mother's love!
Why not? It was a bargain duly made
For these same infants through the surety's act
Intrusted with their all for earth and heaven,
By Him who chose their guardian, knowing well
His fitness for the task,—this, even this,
Was the true doctrine only yesterday
As thoughts are reckoned,—and today you hear
In words that sound as if from human tongues
Those monstrous, uncouth horrors of the past
That blot the blue of heaven and shame the earth
As would the saurians of the age of slime,
Awakening from their stony sepulchres
And wallowing hateful in the eye of day!

IX

RIGHTS

WHAT am I but the creature Thou hast made?
What have I save the blessings Thou hast lent?
What hope I but thy mercy and thy love?
Who but myself shall cloud my soul with fear?
Whose hand protect me from myself but thine?

I claim the rights of weakness, I, the babe,
Call on my sire to shield me from the ills
That still beset my path, not trying me
With snares beyond my wisdom or my strength,
He knowing I shall use them to my harm,
And find a tenfold misery in the sense
That in my childlike folly I have sprung
The trap upon myself as vermin use,
Drawn by the cunning bait to certain doom.
Who wrought the wondrous charm that leads us on
To sweet perdition, but the selfsame power
That set the fearful engine to destroy
His wretched offspring (as the Rabbis tell),
And hid its yawning jaws and treacherous springs
In such a show of innocent sweet flowers
It lured the sinless angels and they fell?

Ah! He who prayed the prayer of all mankind
Summed in those few brief words the mightiest plea
For erring souls before the courts of heaven,—
Save us from being tempted,—lest we fall!

If we are only as the potter's clay
Made to be fashioned as the artist wills,
And broken into shards if we offend
The eye of Him who made us, it is well;
Such love as the insensate lump of clay
That spins upon the swift-revolving wheel
Bears to the hand that shapes its growing form,—
Such love, no more, will be our hearts' return
To the great Master-workman for his care,—
Or would be, save that this, our breathing clay,
Is intertwined with fine innumerous threads
That make it conscious in its framer's hand;

And this He must remember who has filled
These vessels with the deadly draught of life,—
Life, that means death to all it claims. Our love
Must kindle in the ray that streams from heaven,
A faint reflection of the light divine;
The sun must warm the earth before the rose
Can show her inmost heart-leaves to the sun.

He yields some fraction of the Maker's right
Who gives the quivering nerve its sense of pain;
Is there not something in the pleading eye
Of the poor brute that suffers, which arraigns
The law that bids it suffer? Has it not
A claim for some remembrance in the book
That fills its pages with the idle words
Spoken of men? Or is it only clay,
Bleeding and aching in the potter's hand,
Yet all his own to treat it as He will
And when He will to cast it at his feet,
Shattered, dishonored, lost forevermore?
My dog loves me, but could he look beyond
His earthly master, would his love extend
To Him who— Hush! I will not doubt that He
Is better than our fears, and will not wrong
The least, the meanest of created things!

He would not trust me with the smallest orb
That circles through the sky; He would not give
A meteor to my guidance; would not leave
The coloring of a cloudlet to my hand;
He locks my beating heart beneath its bars
And keeps the key himself; He measures out
The draughts of vital breath that warm my blood,
Winds up the springs of instinct which uncoil,
Each in its season; ties me to my home,
My race, my time, my nation, and my creed
So closely that if I but slip my wrist
Out of the band that cuts it to the bone,
Men say, "He hath a devil"; He has lent
All that I hold in trust, as unto one
By reason of his weakness and his years
Not fit to hold the smallest shred in fee
Of those most common things he calls his own,—
And yet—my Rabbi tells me—He has left
The care of that to which a million worlds
Filled with unconscious life were less than naught,
Has left that mighty universe, the Soul,
To the weak guidance of our baby hands,
Let the foul fiends have access at their will,
Taking the shape of angels, to our hearts,—
Our hearts already poisoned through and through
With the fierce virus of ancestral sin;
Turned us adrift with our immortal charge,
To wreck ourselves in gulfs of endless woe.
If what my Rabbi tells me is the truth
Why did the choir of angels sing for joy?
Heaven must be compassed in a narrow space,
And offer more than room enough for all
That pass its portals; but the under-world,
The godless realm, the place where demons forge
Their fiery darts and adamantine chains,
Must swarm with ghosts that for a little while
Had worn the garb of flesh, and being heirs
Of all the dulness of their stolid sires,
And all the erring instincts of their tribe,
Nature's own teaching, rudiments of "sin,"
Fell headlong in the snare that could not fail
To trap the wretched creatures shaped of clay
And cursed with sense enough to lose their souls!

Brother, thy heart is troubled at my word;
Sister, I see the cloud is on thy brow.
He will not blame me, He who sends not peace,
But sends a sword, and bids us strike amain
At Error's gilded crest, where in the van
Of earth's great army, mingling with the best
And bravest of its leaders, shouting loud
The battle-cries that yesterday have led
The host of Truth to victory, but today
Are watchwords of the laggard and the slave,
He leads his dazzled cohorts. God has made
This world a strife of atoms and of spheres;
With every breath I sigh myself away
And take my tribute from the wandering wind
To fan the flame of life's consuming fire;
So, while my thought has life, it needs must burn,
And, burning, set the stubble-fields ablaze,
Where all the harvest long ago was reaped
And safely garnered in the ancient barns.
But still the gleaners, groping for their food,

Go blindly feeling through the close-shorn straw,
While the young reapers flash their glittering steel
Where later suns have ripened nobler grain!

X

TRUTHS

THE time is racked with birth-pangs; every hour
Brings forth some gasping truth, and truth newborn
Looks a misshapen and untimely growth,
The terror of the household and its shame,
A monster coiling in its nurse's lap
That some would strangle, some would only starve;
But still it breathes, and passed from hand to hand,
And suckled at a hundred half-clad breasts,
Comes slowly to its stature and its form,
Calms the rough ridges of its dragon-scales,
Changes to shining locks its snaky hair,
And moves transfigured into angel guise,
Welcomed by all that cursed its hour of birth,
And folded in the same encircling arms
That cast it like a serpent from their hold!

If thou wouldst live in honor, die in peace,
Have the fine words the marble-workers learn
To carve so well, upon thy funeral-stone,
And earn a fair obituary, dressed
In all the many-colored robes of praise,
Be deafer than the adder to the cry
Of that same foundling truth, until it grows
To seemly favor, and at length has won
The smiles of hard-mouthed men and light-lipped dames;
Then snatch it from its meagre nurse's breast,
Fold it in silk and give it food from gold;
So shalt thou share its glory when at last
It drops its mortal vesture, and, revealed
In all the splendor of its heavenly form,
Spreads on the startled air its mighty wings!

Alas! how much that seemed immortal truth
That heroes fought for, martyrs died to save,
Reveals its earth-born lineage, growing old
And limping in its march, its wings unplumed,
Its heavenly semblance faded like a dream!
Here in this painted casket, just unsealed,
Lies what was once a breathing shape like thine,
Once loved as thou art loved; there beamed the eyes
That looked on Memphis in its hour of pride,
That saw the walls of hundred-gated Thebes,
And all the mirrored glories of the Nile.
See how they toiled that all-consuming time
Might leave the frame immortal in its tomb;
Filled it with fragrant balms and odorous gums
That still diffuse their sweetness through the air,
And wound and wound with patient fold on fold
The flaxen bands thy hand has rudely torn!
Perchance thou yet canst see the faded stain
Of the sad mourner's tear.

XI

IDOLS

But what is this?
The sacred beetle, bound upon the breast
Of the blind heathen! Snatch the curious prize,
Give it a place among thy treasured spoils,
Fossil and relic,—corals, encrinites,
The fly in amber and the fish in stone,
The twisted circlet of Etruscan gold,
Medal, intaglio, poniard, poison-ring,—
Place for the Memphian beetle with thine hoard!

Ah! longer than thy creed has blest the world
This toy, thus ravished from thy brother's breast,
Was to the heart of Mizraim as divine,
As holy, as the symbol that we lay
On the still bosom of our white-robed dead,
And raised above their dust that all may know
Here sleeps an heir of glory. Loving friends,
With tears of trembling faith and choking sobs,
And prayers to those who judge of mortal deeds,
Wrapped this poor image in the cerement's fold
That Isis and Osiris, friends of man,
Might know their own and claim the ransomed soul.

An idol? Man was born to worship such!
An idol is an image of his thought;
Sometimes he carves it out of gleaming stone,
And sometimes moulds it out of glittering gold,
Or rounds it in a mighty frescoed dome,
Or lifts it heavenward in a lofty spire,
Or shapes it in a cunning frame of words,
Or pays his priest to make it day by day;
For sense must have its god as well as soul;
A newborn Dian calls for silver shrines,
And Egypt's holiest symbol is our own,
The sign we worship as did they of old
When Isis and Osiris ruled the world.

Let us be true to our most subtle selves,
We long to have our idols like the rest.
Think! when the men of Israel had their God
Encamped among them, talking with their chief,
Leading them in the pillar of the cloud
And watching o'er them in the shaft of fire,
They still must have an image; still they longed
For somewhat of substantial, solid form
Whereon to hang their garlands, and to fix
Their wandering thoughts and gain a stronger hold
For their uncertain faith, not yet assured
If those same meteors of the day and night
Were not mere exhalations of the soil.
  Are we less earthly than the chosen race?
Are we more neighbors of the living God
Than they who gathered manna every morn,
Reaping where none had sown, and heard the voice
Of him who met the Highest in the mount,
And brought them tables, graven with His hand?
Yet these must have their idol, brought their gold,
That star-browed Apis might be god again;
Yea, from their ears the women brake the rings
That lent such splendors to the gypsy brown
Of sunburnt cheeks,—what more could woman do
To show her pious zeal? They went astray,
But nature led them as it leads us all.
  We too, who mock at Israel's golden calf
And scoff at Egypt's sacred scarabee,
Would have our amulets to clasp and kiss,
And flood with rapturous tears, and bear with us
To be our dear companions in the dust;
Such magic works an image in our souls!

Man is an embryo; see at twenty years
His bones, the columns that uphold his frame
Not yet cemented, shaft and capital,
Mere fragments of the temple incomplete.
At twoscore, threescore, is he then full grown?
Nay, still a child, and as the little maids
Dress and undress their puppets, so he tries
To dress a lifeless creed, as if it lived,
And change its raiment when the world cries shame!
  We smile to see our little ones at play
So grave, so thoughtful, with maternal care
Nursing the wisps of rags they call their babes;—
Does He not smile who sees us with the toys
We call by sacred names, and idly feign
To be what we have called them? He is still
The Father of this helpless nursery-brood,
Whose second childhood joins so close its first,
That in the crowding, hurrying years between
We scarce have trained our senses to their task
Before the gathering mist has dimmed our eyes,
And with our hollowed palm we help our ear,
And trace with trembling hand our wrinkled names,
And then begin to tell our stories o'er,
And see—not hear—the whispering lips that say,
"You know——? Your father knew him.—This is he,
Tottering and leaning on the hireling's arm,"—
And so, at length, disrobed of all that clad
The simple life we share with weed and worm,
Go to our cradles, naked as we came.

XII

LOVE

WHAT if a soul redeemed, a spirit that loved
While yet on earth and was beloved in turn,
And still remembered every look and tone
Of that dear earthly sister who was left
Among the unwise virgins at the gate,—
Itself admitted with the bridegroom's train,—

What if this spirit redeemed, amid the host
Of chanting angels, in some transient lull
Of the eternal anthem, heard the cry
Of its lost darling, whom in evil hour
Some wilder pulse of nature led astray
And left an outcast in a world of fire,
Condemned to be the sport of cruel fiends,
Sleepless, unpitying, masters of the skill
To wring the maddest ecstasies of pain
From worn-out souls that only ask to die,—
Would it not long to leave the bliss of heaven,—
Bearing a little water in its hand
To moisten those poor lips that plead in vain
With Him we call our Father? Or is all
So changed in such as taste celestial joy
They hear unmoved the endless wail of woe;
The daughter in the same dear tones that hushed
Her cradle slumbers; she who once had held
A babe upon her bosom from its voice
Hoarse with its cry of anguish, yet the same?

No! not in ages when the Dreadful Bird
Stamped his huge footprints, and the Fearful Beast
Strode with the flesh about those fossil bones
We build to mimic life with pygmy hands,—
Not in those earliest days when men ran wild
And gashed each other with their knives of stone,
When their low foreheads bulged in ridgy brows
And their flat hands were callous in the palm
With walking in the fashion of their sires,
Grope as they might to find a cruel god
To work their will on such as human wrath
Had wrought its worst to torture, and had left
With rage unsated, white and stark and cold,
Could hate have shaped a demon more malign
Than him the dead men mummied in their creed
And taught their trembling children to adore!

Made in *his* image! Sweet and gracious souls
Dear to my heart by nature's fondest names,
Is not your memory still the precious mould
That lends its form to Him who hears my prayer?
Thus only I behold Him, like to them,
Long-suffering, gentle, ever slow to wrath,
If wrath it be that only wounds to heal,
Ready to meet the wanderer ere he reach
The door he seeks, forgetful of his sin,
Longing to clasp him in a father's arms,
And seal his pardon with a pitying tear!

Four gospels tell their story to mankind,
And none so full of soft, caressing words
That bring the Maid of Bethlehem and her Babe
Before our tear-dimmed eyes, as his who learned
In the meek service of his gracious art
The tones which, like the medicinal balms
That calm the sufferer's anguish, soothe our souls.
Oh that the loving woman, she who sat
So long a listener at her Master's feet,
Had left us Mary's Gospel,—all she heard
Too sweet, too subtle for the ear of man!
Mark how the tender-hearted mothers read
The messages of love between the lines
Of the same page that loads the bitter tongue
Of him who deals in terror as his trade
With threatening words of wrath that scorch like flame!

They tell of angels whispering round the bed
Of the sweet infant smiling in its dream,
Of lambs enfolded in the Shepherd's arms,
Of Him who blessed the children; of the land
Where crystal rivers feed unfading flowers,
Of cities golden-paved with streets of pearl,
Of the white robes the winged creatures wear,
The crowns and harps from whose melodious strings
One long, sweet anthem flows forevermore!
We too had human mothers, even as Thou,
Whom we have learned to worship as remote
From mortal kindred, wast a cradled babe.
The milk of woman filled our branching veins,
She lulled us with her tender nursery-song,
And folded round us her untiring arms,
While the first unremembered twilight year
Shaped us to conscious being; still we feel
Her pulses in our own,—too faintly feel;
Would that the heart of woman warmed our creeds!

Not from the sad-eyed hermit's lonely cell,
Not from the conclave where the holy men
Glare on each other, as with angry eyes

They battle for God's glory and their own,
Till, sick of wordy strife, a show of hands
Fixes the faith of ages yet unborn,—
Ah, not from these the listening soul can hear
The Father's voice that speaks itself divine!
Love must be still our Master; till we learn
What he can teach us of a woman's heart,
We know not His whose love embraces all.

1872

EPILOGUE TO THE BREAKFAST-TABLE SERIES

AUTOCRAT—PROFESSOR—POET

AT A BOOKSTORE

Anno Domini 1972

A CRAZY bookcase, placed before
A low-price dealer's open door;
Therein arrayed in broken rows
A ragged crew of rhyme and prose,
The homeless vagrants, waifs, and strays
Whose low estate this line betrays
(Set forth the lesser birds to lime)
YOUR CHOICE AMONG THESE BOOKS 1 DIME!

Ho! dealer; for its motto's sake
This scarecrow from the shelf I take;
Three starveling volumes bound in one,
Its covers warping in the sun.
Methinks it hath a musty smell,
I like its flavor none too well,
But Yorick's brain was far from dull,
Though Hamlet pah!'d, and dropped his skull.

Why, here comes rain! The sky grows dark,—
Was that the roll of thunder? Hark!
The shop affords a safe retreat,
A chair extends its welcome seat,
The tradesman has a civil look
(I've paid, impromptu, for my book),
The clouds portend a sudden shower,—
I'll read my purchase for an hour.

. . . .

What have I rescued from the shelf?
A Boswell, writing out himself!
For though he changes dress and name,
The man beneath is still the same,
Laughing or sad, by fits and starts,
One actor in a dozen parts,
And whatsoe'er the mask may be,
The voice assures us, *This is he.*

I say not this to cry him down;
I find my Shakespeare in his clown,
His rogues the selfsame parent own;
Nay! Satan talks in Milton's tone!
Where'er the ocean inlet strays,
The salt sea wave its source betrays;
Where'er the queen of summer blows,
She tells the zephyr, "I'm the rose!"

And his is not the playwright's page;
His table does not ape the stage;
What matter if the figures seen
Are only shadows on a screen,
He finds in them his lurking thought,
And on their lips the words he sought,
Like one who sits before the keys
And plays a tune himself to please.

And was he noted in his day?
Read, flattered, honored? Who shall say?
Poor wreck of time the wave has cast
To find a peaceful shore at last,
Once glorying in thy gilded name
And freighted deep with hopes of fame,
Thy leaf is moistened with a tear,
The first for many a long, long year!

For be it more or less of art
That veils the lowliest human heart
Where passion throbs, where friendship glows,
Where pity's tender tribute flows,
Where love has lit its fragrant fire,
And sorrow quenched its vain desire,
For me the altar is divine,
Its flame, its ashes,—all are mine!

And thou, my brother, as I look
And see thee pictured in thy book,
Thy years on every page confessed
In shadows lengthening from the west,
Thy glance that wanders, as it sought
Some freshly opening flower of thought,
Thy hopeful nature, light and free,
I start to find myself in thee!

. . . .

Come, vagrant, outcast, wretch forlorn
In leather jerkin stained and torn,
Whose talk has filled my idle hour
And made me half forget the shower,

I'll do at least as much for you,
Your coat I'll patch, your gilt renew,
Read you—perhaps—some other time.
Not bad, my bargain! Price one dime!

1872 1872

PROGRAMME

OCTOBER 7, 1874

READER—gentle—if so be
Such still live, and live for me,
Will it please you to be told
What my tenscore pages hold?

Here are verses that in spite
Of myself I needs must write,
Like the wine that oozes first
When the unsqueezed grapes have burst.

Here are angry lines, "too hard!"
Says the soldier, battle-scarred.
Could I smile his scars away
I would blot the bitter lay,

Written with a knitted brow,
Read with placid wonder now.
Throbbed such passion in my heart?
Did his wounds once really smart?

Here are varied strains that sing
All the changes life can bring,
Songs when joyous friends have met,
Songs the mourner's tears have wet.

See the banquet's dead bouquet,
Fair and fragrant in its day;
Do they read the selfsame lines,—
He that fasts and he that dines?

Year by year, like milestones placed,
Mark the record Friendship traced.
Prisoned in the walls of time
Life has notched itself in rhyme:

As its seasons slid along,
Every year a notch of song,
From the June of long ago,
When the rose was full in blow,

Till the scarlet sage has come
And the cold chrysanthemum.
Read, but not to praise or blame;
Are not all our hearts the same?

For the rest, they take their chance,—
Some may pay a passing glance;
Others,—well, they served a turn,—
Wherefore written, would you learn?

Not for glory, not for pelf,
Not, be sure, to please myself,
Not for any meaner ends,—
Always "by request of friends."

Here's the cousin of a king,—
Would I do the civil thing?
Here's the first-born of a queen:
Here's a slant-eyed Mandarin.

Would I polish off Japan?
Would I greet this famous man,
Prince or Prelate, Sheik or Shah?—
Figaro çi and Figaro là!
Would I just this once comply?—
So they teased and teased till I
(Be the truth at once confessed)
Wavered—yielded—did my best.

Turn my pages,—never mind
If you like not all you find;
Think not all the grains are gold
Sacramento's sand-banks hold.

Every kernel has its shell,
Every chime its harshest bell,
Every face its weariest look,
Every shelf its emptiest book,

Every field its leanest sheaf,
Every book its dullest leaf,
Every leaf its weakest line,—
Shall it not be so with mine?

Best for worst shall make amends,
Find us, keep us, leave us friends
Till, perchance, we meet again.
Benedicite.—Amen!

1874 1874

FOR WHITTIER'S SEVENTIETH BIRTHDAY

DECEMBER 17, 1877

I BELIEVE that the copies of verses I've spun,
Like Scheherezade's tales, are a thousand and one;
You remember the story,—those mornings in bed,—
'Twas the turn of a copper,—a tale or a head.

A doom like Scheherezade's falls upon me
In a mandate as stern as the Sultan's decree:
I'm a florist in verse, and what *would* people say
If I came to a banquet without my bouquet?

It is trying, no doubt, when the company knows
Just the look and the smell of each lily and rose,
The green of each leaf in the sprigs that I bring,
And the shape of the bunch and the knot of the string.

Yes,—"the style is the man," and the nib of one's pen
Makes the same mark at twenty, and three-score and ten;
It is so in all matters, if truth may be told;
Let one look at the cast, he can tell you the mould.

How we all know each other! no use in disguise;
Through the holes in the mask comes the flash of the eyes;
We can tell by his—somewhat—each one of our tribe,
As we know the old hat which we cannot describe.

Though in Hebrew, in Sanscrit, in Choctaw you write,
Sweet singer who gave us the "Voices of Night,"
Though in buskin or slipper your song may be shod,
Or the velvety verse that Evangeline trod,

We shall say, "You can't cheat us,—we know it is you,"
There is one voice like that, but there cannot be two,
Maëstro, whose chant like the dulcimer rings:
And the woods will be hushed while the nightingale sings.

And he, so serene, so majestic, so true,
Whose temple hypæthral the planets shine through,
Let us catch but five words from that mystical pen,
We should know our one sage from all children of men.

And he whose bright image no distance can dim,
Through a hundred disguises we can't mistake him,
Whose play is all earnest, whose wit is the edge
(With a beetle behind) of a sham-splitting wedge.

Do you know whom we send you, Hidalgos of Spain?
Do you know your old friends when you see them again?
Hosea was Sancho! you Dons of Madrid,
But Sancho that wielded the lance of the Cid!

And the wood-thrush of Essex,—you know whom I mean,
Whose song echoes round us while he sits unseen,
Whose heart-throbs of verse through our memories thrill
Like a breath from the wood, like a breeze from the hill,

So fervid, so simple, so loving, so pure,
We hear but one strain and our verdict is sure,—
Thee cannot elude us,—no further we search,—
'Tis Holy George Herbert cut loose from his church!

We think it the voice of a seraph that sings,—
Alas! we remember that angels have wings,—
What story is this of the day of his birth?
Let him live to a hundred! we want him on earth!

One life has been paid him (in gold) by the sun;
One account has been squared and another begun;
But he never will die if he lingers below
Till we've paid him in love half the balance we owe!

1877 1877

TWO SONNETS: HARVARD

"CHRISTO ET ECCLESIÆ." 1700

To God's annointed and his chosen flock:
So ran the phrase the black-robed conclave chose
To guard the sacred cloisters that arose
Like David's altar on Moriah's rock.
Unshaken still those ancient arches mock
The ram's-horn summons of the windy foes
Who stand like Joshua's army while it blows
And wait to see them toppling with the shock.
Christ and the Church. *Their* church, whose narrow door
Shut out the many, who if over bold
Like hunted wolves were driven from the fold,
Bruised with the flails these godly zealot's bore,
Mindful that Israel's altar stood of old
Where echoed once Araunah's threshing-floor.

1643 "VERITAS." 1878

Truth: So the frontlet's older legend ran,
On the brief record's opening page displayed;
Not yet those clear-eyed scholars were afraid
Lest the fair fruit that wrought the woe of man
By far Euphrates—where our sire began
His search for truth, and, seeking, was betrayed—
Might work new treason in their forest shade,
Doubling the curse that brought life's shortened span.
Nurse of the future, daughter of the past,
That stern phylactery best becomes thee now:
Lift to the morning star thy marble brow!
Cast thy brave truth on every warring blast!
Stretch thy white hand to that forbidden bough,
And let thine earliest symbol be thy last!

1878 1878

THE SILENT MELODY

"Bring me my broken harp," he said;
"We both are wrecks,—but as ye will,—
Though all its ringing tones have fled,
Their echoes linger round it still;
It had some golden strings, I know,
But that was long—how long!—ago.

"I cannot see its tarnished gold,
I cannot hear its vanished tone,
Scarce can my trembling fingers hold
The pillared frame so long their own;
We both are wrecks,—awhile ago
It had some silver strings, I know,

"But on them Time too long has played
The solemn strain that knows no change,
And where of old my fingers strayed
The chords they find are new and strange,—
Yes! iron strings,—I know,—I know,—
We both are wrecks of long ago.

"We both are wrecks,—a shattered pair,—
Strange to ourselves in time's disguise . . .
What say ye to the lovesick air
That brought the tears from Marian's eyes?
Ay! trust me,—under breasts of snow
Hearts could be melted long ago!

"Or will ye hear the storm-song's crash
That from his dreams the soldier woke,
And bade him face the lightning flash
When battle's cloud in thunder broke? . . .
Wrecks,—nought but wrecks!—the time was when
We two were worth a thousand men!"

And so the broken harp they bring
With pitying smiles that none could blame;
Alas! there's not a single string
Of all that filled the tarnished frame!
But see! like children overjoyed,
His fingers rambling through the void!

"I clasp thee! Ay . . . mine ancient lyre . . .
Nay, guide my wandering fingers. . . . There!
They love to dally with the wire
As Isaac played with Esau's hair. . . .
Hush! ye shall hear the famous tune
That Marian called the Breath of June!"

And so they softly gather round:
Rapt in his tuneful trance he seems:
His fingers move: but not a sound!
A silence like the song of dreams. . . .
"There! ye have heard the air," he cries,
"That brought the tears from Marian's eyes!"

Ah, smile not at his fond conceit,
Nor deem his fancy wrought in vain;
To him the unreal sounds are sweet,—

No discord mars the silent strain
Scored on life's latest, starlit page—
The voiceless melody of age.

Sweet are the lips of all that sing,
When Nature's music breathes unsought,
But never yet could voice or string
So truly shape our tenderest thought
As when by life's decaying fire
Our fingers sweep the stringless lyre!

1878

THE IRON GATE

WHERE is this patriarch you are kindly greeting?
Not unfamiliar to my ear his name,
Nor yet unknown to many a joyous meeting
In days long vanished,—is he still the same,

Or changed by years, forgotten and forgetting,
Dull-eared, dim-sighted, slow of speech and thought,
Still o'er the sad, degenerate present fretting,
Where all goes wrong, and nothing as it ought?

Old age, the graybeard! Well, indeed, I know him,—
Shrunk, tottering, bent, of aches and ills the prey;
In sermon, story, fable, picture, poem,
Oft have I met him from my earliest day:

In my old Æsop, toiling with his bundle,—
His load of sticks,—politely asking Death,
Who comes when called for,—would he lug or trundle
His fagot for him?—he was scant of breath.

And sad "Ecclesiastes, or the Preacher,"—
Has he not stamped the image on my soul,
In that last chapter, where the worn-out Teacher
Sighs o'er the loosened cord, the broken bowl?

Yes, long, indeed, I've known him at a distance,
And now my lifted door-latch shows him here;
I take his shrivelled hand without resistance,
And find him smiling as his step draws near.

What though of gilded baubles he bereaves us,
Dear to the heart of youth, to manhood's prime;
Think of the calm he brings, the wealth he leaves us,
The hoarded spoils, the legacies of time!

Altars once flaming, still with incense fragrant,
Passion's uneasy nurslings rocked asleep,
Hope's anchor faster, wild desire less vagrant,
Life's flow less noisy, but the stream how deep!

Still as the silver cord gets worn and slender,
Its lightened task-work tugs with lessening strain,
Hands get more helpful, voices, grown more tender,
Soothe with their softened tones the slumberous brain.

Youth longs and manhood strives, but age remembers,
Sits by the raked-up ashes of the past,
Spreads its thin hands above the whitening embers
That warm its creeping life-blood till the last.

Dear to its heart is every loving token
That comes unbidden ere its pulse grows cold,
Ere the last lingering ties of life are broken,
Its labors ended and its story told.

Ah, while around us rosy youth rejoices,
For us the sorrow-laden breezes sigh,
And through the chorus of its jocund voices
Throbs the sharp note of misery's hopeless cry.

As on the gauzy wings of fancy flying
From some far orb I track our watery sphere,
Home of the struggling, suffering, doubting, dying,
The silvered globule seems a glistening tear.

But Nature lends her mirror of illusion
To win from saddening scenes our age-dimmed eyes,
And misty day-dreams blend in sweet confusion
The wintry landscape and the summer skies.

So when the iron portal shuts behind us,
And life forgets us in its noise and whirl,
Visions that shunned the glaring noonday find us,
And glimmering starlight shows the gates of pearl.

I come not here your morning hour to sadden,
A limping pilgrim, leaning on his staff,—
I, who have never deemed it sin to gladden
This vale of sorrows with a wholesome laugh.

If word of mine another's gloom has brightened,
Through my dumb lips the heaven-sent message came;
If hand of mine another's task has lightened,
It felt the guidance that it dares not claim.

But, O my gentle sisters, O my brothers,
These thick-sown snow-flakes hint of toil's release;
These feebler pulses bid me leave to others
The tasks once welcome; evening asks for peace.

Time claims his tribute; silence now is golden;
Let me not vex the too long suffering lyre;
Though to your love untiring still beholden,
The curfew tells me—cover up the fire.

And now with grateful smile and accents cheerful,
And warmer heart than look or word can tell,
In simplest phrase—these traitorous eyes are tearful—
Thanks, Brothers, Sisters,—Children,—and farewell!

1879 1880

AT THE SATURDAY CLUB

THIS is our place of meeting; opposite
That towered and pillared building: look at it;
King's Chapel in the Second George's day,
Rebellion stole its regal name away,—
Stone Chapel sounded better; but at last
The poisoned name of our provincial past
Had lost its ancient venom; then once more
Stone Chapel was King's Chapel as before.
(So let rechristened North Street, when it can,
Bring back the days of Marlborough and Queen Anne!)
Next the old church your wandering eye will meet—
A granite pile that stares upon the street—
Our civic temple; slanderous tongues have said
Its shape was modelled from St. Botolph's head,
Lofty, but narrow; jealous passers-by
Say Boston always held her head too high.
Turn half-way round, and let your look survey
The white façade that gleams across the way,—
The many-windowed building, tall and wide,
The palace-inn that shows its northern side
In grateful shadow when the sunbeams beat
The granite wall in summer's scorching heat.
This is the place; whether its name you spell
Tavern, or caravansera, or hotel.
Would I could steal its echoes! you should find
Such store of vanished pleasures brought to mind:
Such feasts! the laughs of many a jocund hour
That shook the mortar from King George's tower;
Such guests! What famous names its record boasts,
Whose owners wander in the mob of ghosts!
Such stories! Every beam and plank is filled
With juicy wit the joyous talkers spilled,
Ready to ooze, as once the mountain pine
The floors are laid with oozed its turpentine!

A month had flitted since The Club had met;
The day came round; I found the table set,
The waiters lounging round the marble stairs,
Empty as yet the double row of chairs.
I was a full half hour before the rest,
Alone, the banquet-chamber's single guest.
So from the table's side a chair I took,
And having neither company nor book
To keep me waking, by degrees there crept
A torpor over me,—in short, I slept.
Loosed from its chain, along the wreck-strown track
Of the dead years my soul goes travelling back;

My ghosts take on their robes of flesh; it seems
Dreaming is life; nay, life less life than dreams,
So real are the shapes that meet my eyes.
They bring no sense of wonder, no surprise,
No hint of other than an earth-born source;
All seems plain daylight, everything of course.
How dim the colors are, how poor and faint
This palette of weak words with which I paint!
Here sit my friends; if I could fix them so
As to my eyes they seem, my page would glow
Like a queen's missal, warm as if the brush
Of Titian or Velasquez brought the flush
Of life into their features. *Ay de mi!*
If syllables were pigments, you should see
Such breathing portraitures as never man
Found in the Pitti or the Vatican.

Here sits our POET, Laureate, if you will.
Long has he worn the wreath, and wears it still.
Dead? Nay, not so; and yet they say his bust
Looks down on marbles covering royal dust,
Kings by the Grace of God, or Nature's grace;
Dead! No! Alive! I see him in his place,
Full-featured, with the bloom that heaven denies
Her children, pinched by cold New England skies,
Too often, while the nursery's happier few
Win from a summer cloud its roseate hue.
Kind, soft-voiced, gentle, in his eye there shines
The ray serene that filled Evangeline's.
Modest he seems, not shy; content to wait
Amid the noisy clamor of debate
The looked-for moment when a peaceful word
Smooths the rough ripples louder tongues have stirred.
In every tone I mark his tender grace
And all his poems hinted in his face;
What tranquil joy his friendly presence gives!
How could I think him dead? He lives! He lives!

There, at the table's further end I see
In his old place our Poet's *vis-à-vis*,
The great PROFESSOR, strong, broad-shouldered, square,
In life's rich noontide, joyous, debonair.
His social hour no leaden care alloys,
His laugh rings loud and mirthful as a boy's,—
That lusty laugh the Puritan forgot,—
What ear has heard it and remembers not?
How often, halting at some wide crevasse
Amid the windings of his Alpine pass,
High up the cliffs, the climbing mountaineer,
Listening the far-off avalanche to hear,
Silent, and leaning on his steel-shod staff,
Has heard that cheery voice, that ringing laugh,
From the rude cabin whose nomadic walls
Creep with the moving glacier as it crawls!
How does vast Nature lead her living train
In ordered sequence through that spacious brain,
As in the primal hour when Adam named
The new-born tribes that young creation claimed!—
How will her realm be darkened, losing thee,
Her darling, whom we call *our* AGASSIZ!

But who is he whose massive frame belies
The maiden shyness of his downcast eyes?
Who broods in silence till, by questions pressed,
Some answer struggles from his laboring breast?
An artist Nature meant to dwell apart,
Locked in his studio with a human heart,
Tracking its caverned passions to their lair,
And all its throbbing mysteries laying bare.
Count it no marvel that he broods alone
Over the heart he studies,—'tis his own;
So in his page, whatever shape it wear,
The Essex wizard's shadowed self is there,—
The great ROMANCER, hid beneath his veil
Like the stern preacher of his sombre tale;
Virile in strength, yet bashful as a girl,
Prouder than Hester, sensitive as Pearl.

From his mild throng of worshippers released,
Our Concord Delphi sends its chosen priest,
Prophet or poet, mystic, sage, or seer,
By every title always welcome here.
Why that ethereal spirit's frame describe?
You know the race-marks of the Brahmin tribe,—
The spare, slight form, the sloping shoulder's droop,
The calm, scholastic mien, the clerkly stoop,

The lines of thought the sharpened features wear,
Carved by the edge of keen New England air.
  List! for he speaks! As when a king would choose
The jewels for his bride, he might refuse
This diamond for its flaw,—find that less bright
Than those, its fellows, and a pearl less white
Than fits her snowy neck, and yet at last,
The fairest gems are chosen, and made fast
In golden fetters; so, with light delays
He seeks the fittest word to fill his phrase;
Nor vain nor idle his fastidious quest,
His chosen word is sure to prove the best.
  Where in the realm of thought, whose air is song,
Does he, the Buddha of the West, belong?
He seems a wingèd Franklin, sweetly wise,
Born to unlock the secrets of the skies;
And which the nobler calling,—if 'tis fair
Terrestrial with celestial to compare,—
To guide the storm-cloud's elemental flame,
Or walk the chambers whence the lightning came,
Amidst the sources of its subtile fire,
And steal their effluence for his lips and lyre?
  If lost at times in vague aërial flights,
None treads with firmer footstep when he lights;
A soaring nature, ballasted with sense,
Wisdom without her wrinkles or pretence,
In every Bible he has faith to read,
And every altar helps to shape his creed.
Ask you what name this prisoned spirit bears
While with ourselves this fleeting breath it shares?
Till angels greet him with a sweeter one
In heaven, on earth we call him EMERSON.

  I start; I wake; the vision is withdrawn;
Its figures fading like the stars at dawn;
Crossed from the roll of life their cherished names,
And memory's pictures fading in their frames;
Yet life is lovelier for these transient gleams
Of buried friendships; blest is he who dreams!

1884

THE LYRE OF ANACREON

THE minstrel of the classic lay
  Of love and wine who sings
Still found the fingers run astray
  That touched the rebel strings.

Of Cadmus he would fain have sung,
  Of Atreus and his line;
But all the jocund echoes rung
  With songs of love and wine.

Ah, brothers! I would fain have caught
  Some fresher fancy's gleam;
My truant accents find, unsought,
  The old familiar theme.

Love, Love! but not the sportive child
  With shaft and twanging bow,
Whose random arrows drove us wild
  Some threescore years ago;

Not Eros, with his joyous laugh,
  The urchin blind and bare,
But Love, with spectacles and staff,
  And scanty, silvered hair.

Our heads with frosted locks are white,
  Our roofs are thatched with snow,
But red, in chilling winter's spite,
  Our hearts and hearthstones glow.

Our old acquaintance, Time, drops in,
  And while the running sands
Their golden thread unheeded spin,
  He warms his frozen hands.

Stay, wingèd hours, too swift, too sweet,
  And waft this message o'er
To all we miss, from all we meet
  On life's fast-crumbling shore:

Say that, to old affection true,
  We hug the narrowing chain
That binds our hearts,—alas, how few
  The links that yet remain!

The fatal touch awaits them all
  That turns the rocks to dust;
From year to year they break and fall,—
  They break, but never rust.

Say if one note of happier strain
  This worn-out harp afford,—
One throb that trembles, not in vain,—
  Their memory lent its chord.

Say that when Fancy closed her wings
  And Passion quenched his fire,
Love, Love, still echoed from the strings
  As from Anacreon's lyre!

1885 1888

AFTER THE CURFEW

The Play is over. While the light
  Yet lingers in the darkening hall,
I come to say a last Good-night
  Before the final *Exeunt all.*

We gathered once, a joyous throng:
  The jovial toasts went gayly round;
With jest, and laugh, and shout, and song,
  We made the floors and walls resound.

We come with feeble steps and slow,
  A little band of four or five,
Left from the wrecks of long ago,
  Still pleased to find ourselves alive.

Alive! How living, too, are they
  Whose memories it is ours to share!
Spread the long table's full array,—
  There sits a ghost in every chair!

One breathing form no more, alas!
  Amid our slender group we see;
With him we still remained "The Class,"—
  Without his presence what are we?

The hand we ever loved to clasp,—
  That tireless hand which knew no rest,—
Loosed from affection's clinging grasp,
  Lies nerveless on the peaceful breast.

The beaming eye, the cheering voice,
  That lent to life a generous glow,
Whose every meaning said "Rejoice,"
  We see, we hear, no more below.

The air seems darkened by his loss,
  Earth's shadowed features look less fair,
And heavier weighs the daily cross
  His willing shoulders helped us bear.

Why mourn that we, the favored few
  Whom grasping Time so long has spared
Life's sweet illusions to pursue,
  The common lot of age have shared?

In every pulse of Friendship's heart
  There breeds unfelt a throb of pain,—
One hour must rend its links apart,
  Though years on years have forged the chain.

So ends "The Boys,"—a lifelong play.
  We too must hear the Prompter's call
To fairer scenes and brighter day:
  Farewell! I let the curtain fall.

1889 1889

INVITÂ MINERVÂ

Vex not the Muse with idle prayers,—
  She will not hear thy call;
She steals upon thee unawares,
  Or seeks thee not at all.

Soft as the moonbeams when they sought
  Endymion's fragrant bower,
She parts the whispering leaves of thought
  To show her full-blown flower.

For thee her wooing hour has passed,
  The singing birds have flown,
And winter comes with icy blast
  To chill thy buds unblown.

Yet, though the woods no longer thrill
  As once their arches rung,
Sweet echoes hover round thee still
  Of songs thy summer sung.

Live in thy past; await no more
  The rush of heaven-sent wings;
Earth still has music left in store
  While Memory sighs and sings.

1890

JAMES RUSSELL LOWELL

1819–1891

Thou shouldst have sung the swan-song for the choir
  That filled our groves with music till the day
Lit the last hilltop with its reddening fire,
  And evening listened for thy lingering lay.

But thou hast found thy voice in realms afar
Where strains celestial blend their notes with thine;
Some cloudless sphere beneath a happier star
Welcomes the bright-winged spirit we resign.

How Nature mourns thee in the still retreat
Where passed in peace thy love-enchanted hours!
Where shall she find an eye like thine to greet
Spring's earliest footprints on her opening flowers?

Have the pale wayside weeds no fond regret
For him who read the secrets they enfold?
Shall the proud spangles of the field forget
The verse that lent new glory to their gold?

And ye whose carols wooed his infant ear,
Whose chants with answering woodnotes he repaid,
Have ye no song his spirit still may hear
From Elmwood's vaults of overarching shade?

Friends of his studious hours, who thronged to teach
The deep-read scholar all your varied lore,
Shall he no longer seek your shelves to reach
The treasure missing from his world-wide store?

This singer whom we long have held so dear
Was Nature's darling, shapely, strong, and fair;
Of keenest wit, of judgment crystal-clear,
Easy of converse, courteous, debonair,

Fit for the loftiest or the lowliest lot,
Self-poised, imperial, yet of simplest ways;
At home alike in castle or in cot,
True to his aim, let others blame or praise.

Freedom he found an heirloom from his sires;
Song, letters, statecraft, shared his years in turn;
All went to feed the nation's altar-fires
Whose mourning children wreathe his funeral urn.

He loved New England,—people, language, soil,
Unweaned by exile from her arid breast.
Farewell awhile, white-handed son of toil,
Go with her brown-armed laborers to thy rest.

Peace to thy slumber in the forest shade!
Poet and patriot, every gift was thine;
Thy name shall live while summers bloom and fade,
And grateful Memory guard thy leafy shrine!

1891 1891

[HOLMES'S POETIC THEORY]

[I. TALENT AND GENIUS]

Poets are never young, in one sense. Their delicate ear hears the far-off whispers of eternity, which coarser souls must travel towards for scores of years before their dull sense is touched by them. A moment's insight is sometimes worth a life's experience. . . .

. . . Talent is a docile creature. It bows its head meekly while the world slips the collar over it. It backs into the shafts like a lamb. It draws its load cheerfully, and is patient of the bit and of the whip. But genius is always impatient of its harness; its wild blood makes it hard to train.

Talent seems, at first, in one sense, higher than genius,—namely, that it is more uniformly and absolutely submitted to the will, and therefore more distinctly human in its character. Genius, on the other hand, is much more like those instincts which govern the admirable movements of the lower creatures, and therefore seems to have something of the lower or animal character. A goose flies by a chart which the Royal Geographical Society could not mend. A poet, like the goose, sails without visible landmarks to unexplored regions of truth, which philosophy has yet to lay down on its atlas. The philosopher gets his track by observation; the poet trusts to his inner sense, and makes the straighter and swifter line.

And yet, to look at it in another light, is not even the lowest instinct more truly divine than any volunteer human act done by the suggestion of reason? What is a bee's architecture but an *un*obstructed divine thought?—what is a builder's approximate rule but an obstructed thought of the Creator, a mutilated and imperfect copy of some absolute rule Divine Wisdom has established, transmitted through a human soul as an image through beclouded glass?

Talent is a very common family-trait; genius belongs rather to individuals;—just as you find one giant or one dwarf in a family, but rarely a whole brood of either. Talent is often to be envied, and genius very commonly to be pitied. It stands twice the chance of the other of dying in hospital, in jail, in debt, in bad repute. It is a perpetual insult to mediocrity; its every word is a trespass against somebody's vested ideas,—blasphemy against somebody's *O'm*, or intangible private truth.

—What is the use of my weighing out antitheses in this way, like a rhetorical grocer?—You know twenty men of talent, who are making their way in the world; you may, perhaps, know one man of genius, and very likely do not want to know any more. For a divine instinct, such as drives the goose southward and the poet heavenward, is a hard thing to manage, and proves too strong for many whom it possesses. It must have been a terrible thing to have a friend like Chatterton or Burns. . . .

(From *The Professor at the Breakfast-Table*, pp. 239–241.)

[II. THE PERSONAL ELEMENT]

I shall say many things which an uncharitable reader might find fault with as personal. I should not dare to call myself a poet if I did not; for if there is anything that gives one a title to that name, it is that his inner nature is naked and is not ashamed. But there are many such things I shall put in words, not because they are personal, but because they are human, and are born of just such experiences as those who hear or read what I say are like to have had in greater or less measure. I find myself so much like other people that I often wonder at the coincidence. It was only the other day that I sent out a copy of verses about my great-grandmother's picture, and I was surprised to find how many other people had portraits of their great-grandmothers or other progenitors, about which they felt as I did about mine, and for whom I had spoken, thinking I was speaking for myself only. And so I am not afraid to talk very freely with you, my precious reader or listener. You, too, Beloved, were born somewhere and remember your birthplace or your early home; for you some house is haunted by recollections; to some roof you have bid farewell. Your hand is upon mine, then, as I guide my pen. Your heart frames the responses to the litany of my remembrance. . . .

(From *The Poet at the Breakfast-Table*, p. 11.)

[III. THE MATERIAL OF POETRY]

Take the poet. On the one hand, I believe that a person with the poetical faculty finds material everywhere. The grandest objects of sense and thought are common to all climates and civilizations. The sky, the woods, the waters, the storms, life, death, love, the hope and vision of eternity,—these are images which write themselves in poetry in every soul which has anything of the divine gift.

On the other hand, there is such a thing as a lean, impoverished life, in distinction from a rich and suggestive one. Which our common New England life might be considered, I will not decide. But there are some things I think the poet misses in our western Eden. I trust it is not unpatriotic to mention them in this point of view as they come before us in so many other aspects.

There is no sufficient flavor of humanity in the soil out of which we grow. At Cantabridge, near the sea, I have once or twice picked up an Indian arrowhead in a fresh furrow. At Canoe Meadow, in the Berkshire Mountains, I have found Indian arrowheads. So everywhere Indian arrowheads. Whether a hundred or a thousand years old, who knows? who cares? There is no history to the red race,—there is hardly an individual in it;—a few instincts on legs and holding a tomahawk—there is the Indian of all time. The story of one red ant is the story of all red ants. So, the poet, in trying to wing his way back through the life that has kindled, flitted, and faded along our watercourses and on our southern hillsides for unknown generations, finds nothing to breathe or fly in; he meets

"A vast vacuity! all unawares,
Fluttering his pennons vain, plumb down he drops
Ten thousand fathom deep."

But think of the Old World,—that part of it which is the seat of ancient civilization! The stakes of the Britons' stockades are still standing in the bed of the Thames. The ploughman turns up an old Saxon's bones, and beneath them is a tessellated pavement of the time of the Caesars. In Italy, the works of mediæval Art seem to be of yesterday,—Rome, under her kings, is but an intruding new-comer, as we contemplate her in the shadow of the Cyclopean walls of Fiesole or Volterra. It makes a man human to live on these old humanized soils. He cannot help marching in step with his kind in the rear of such a procession. They say a dead man's hand cures swellings, if laid on them. There is nothing like the dead cold hand of the Past to take down our tumid egotism and lead us into the solemn flow of the life of our race. Rousseau came out of one of his sad self-torturing fits, as he cast his eye on the arches of the old Roman aqueduct, the Pont du Gard.

I am far from denying that there is an attraction in a thriving railroad village. The new "dépôt," the smartly-painted pine houses, the spacious brick hotel, the white meeting-houses, and the row of youthful and leggy trees before it, *are* exhilarating. They speak of progress, and the time when there shall be a city, with His Honor the Mayor, in the place of their trim but transient architectural growths. Pardon me, if I prefer the pyramids. They seem to me crystals formed from a stronger solution of humanity than the steeple of the new meeting-house. I may be wrong, but the Tiber has a voice for me, as it whispers to the piers of the Pons Ælius, even more full of meaning than my well-beloved Charles eddying round the piles of West Boston Bridge.

Then, again, we Yankees are a kind of gypsies,—a mechanical and migratory race. A poet wants a home. He can dispense with an apple-parer and a reaping-machine. I feel this more for others than for myself, for the home of my birth and childhood has been as yet exempted from the change which has invaded almost everything around it. . .

Our hearts are held down to our homes by innumerable fibres, trivial as that I have just recalled; but Gulliver was fixed to the soil, you remember, by pinning his head a hair at a time. Even a stone with a whitish band crossing it, belonging to the pavement of the back-yard, insisted on becoming one of the talismans of memory. This intussusception of the ideas of inanimate objects, and their faithful storing away among the sentiments, are curiously prefigured in the material structure of the thinking centre itself. . . .

(From *The Professor at the Breakfast-Table*, pp. 244–247.)

[IV. REALISM]

We got talking on the subject of *realism*, of which so much has been said of late.

It seems to me, I said, that the great additions which have been made by realism to the territory of literature consist largely in swampy, malarious, ill-smelling patches of soil which had previously been left to reptiles and vermin. It is perfectly easy to be original by violating the laws of decency and the canons of good taste. The general consent of civilized people was supposed to have banished certain subjects from the conversation of well-bred people and the pages of respectable literature. There is no subject, or hardly any, which may not be treated of at the proper time, in the proper place, by the fitting person, for the right kind of listener or reader. But when the poet or the story-teller invades the province of the man of science, he is on dangerous ground. I need say nothing of the blunders he is pretty sure to make. The imaginative writer is after effects. The scientific man is after truth. Science is decent, modest; does not try to startle, but to instruct. The same scenes and objects which outrage every sense of delicacy in the story-teller's highly colored paragraphs can be read without giving offence in the chaste language of the physiologist or the physician.

There is a very celebrated novel, "Madame Bovary," the work of Flaubert, which is noted for having been the subject of prosecution as an immoral work. That it has a serious lesson there is no doubt, if one will drink down to the bottom of the cup. But the honey of sensuous description is spread so deeply over the surface of the goblet that a large proportion of its readers never think of its holding anything else. All the phases of unhallowed passion are described in full detail. That is what the book is bought and read for, by the great majority of its purchasers, as all but simpletons very well know. That is what makes it sell and brought it into the courts of justice. This book is famous for its realism; in fact, it is recognized as one of the earliest and most brilliant examples of that modern style of novel which, beginning where Balzac left off, attempted to do for literature what the photograph has done for art. For those who take the trouble to drink out of the cup below the rim of honey, there is a scene where realism is carried to its extreme,—surpassed in horror by no writer, unless it be the one whose name must be looked for at the bottom of the alphabet, as if its natural place were as low down in the dregs of realism as it could find itself. This is the death-bed scene, where Madame Bovary expires in convulsions. The author must have visited the hospitals for the purpose of watching the terrible agonies he was to depict, tramping from one bed to another until he reached the one where the cries and contortions were the most frightful. Such a scene he has reproduced. No hospital physician would have pictured the struggle in such colors. In the same way, that other realist, M. Zola, has painted a patient suffering from delirium tremens, the disease known to common speech as "the horrors." In describing this case he does all that language can do to make it more horrible than the reality. He gives us, not realism, but super-realism, if such a term does not contradict itself.

In this matter of the literal reproduction of sights and scenes which our natural instinct and our better informed taste and judgment teach us to avoid, art has been far in advance of literature. It is three hundred years since Joseph Ribera, more commonly known as Spagnoletto, was born in the province Valencia, in Spain. We had the misfortune of seeing a painting of his in a collection belonging to one of the French princes, and exhibited at the Art Museum. It was that of a man performing upon himself the operation known to the Japanese as hara-kiri. Many persons who looked upon this revolting picture will never get rid of its remembrance, and will regret the day when their eyes fell upon it. I should share the offence of the painter if I ventured to describe it. Ribera was fond of depicting just such odious and frightful subjects. "Saint Lawrence writhing on his gridiron, Saint Sebastian full of arrows, were equally a source of delight to him. Even in subjects which had no such elements of horror he finds the materials for the delectation of his ferocious pencil; he makes up for the defect by rendering with a brutal realism deformity and ugliness."

The first great mistake made by the ultra-realists, like Flaubert and Zola, is, as I have said, their ignoring the line of distinction between imaginative art and science. We can find realism enough in books of anatomy, surgery, and medicine. In studying the human figure, we want to see it clothed with its natural integuments. It is well for the artist to study the *écorché* in the dissecting-room, but we do not want the Apollo or the Venus to leave their skins behind them when they go into the gallery for exhibition. Lancisi's figures show us how the great statues look when divested of their natural covering. It is instructive, but useful chiefly as a means to aid in the true artistic reproduction of nature. When hospitals are invaded by the novelist, he should learn something from the physician as well as from the patients. Science delineates in monochrome. She never uses high tints and strontian lights to astonish lookers-on. Such scenes as Flaubert and Zola describe would be reproduced in their essential characters, but not dressed up in picturesque phrases. That is the first stumbling-block in the way of the reader of such realistic stories as those to which I have referred. There are subjects which must be investigated by scientific men which most educated persons would be glad to know nothing about. When a realistic writer like Zola surprises his reader into a kind of knowledge he never thought of wishing for, he sometimes harms him more than he has any idea of doing. He wants to produce a sensation, and he leaves a permanent disgust not to be got rid of. Who does not remember odious images that can never be washed out of the consciousness which they have stained? A man's vocabulary is terribly retentive of evil words, and the images they present cling to his memory and will not loose their hold. One who has had the mischance to soil his mind by reading certain poems of Swift will never cleanse it to its original whiteness. Expressions and thoughts of a certain character stain the fibre of the thinking organ, and in some degree affect the hue of every idea that passes through the discolored tissues.

This is the gravest accusation to bring against realism, old or recent, whether in the brutal paintings of Spagnoletto or in the unclean revelations of Zola. Leave the description of the drains and cesspools to the hygienic specialist, the painful facts of disease to the physician, the details of the laundry to the washerwoman. If we are to have realism in its tedious descriptions of unimportant particulars, let it be of particulars which do not excite disgust. Such is the description of the vegetables in Zola's "Ventre de Paris," where, if one wishes to see the apotheosis of turnips, beets, and cabbages, he can find them glorified as supremely as if they had been symbols of so many deities; their forms, their colors, their expression, worked upon until they seem as if they were made to be looked at and worshipped rather than to be boiled and eaten.

I am pleased to find a French critic of M. Flaubert expressing ideas with which many of my own entirely coincide. "The great mistake of the realists," he says, "is that they profess to tell the truth because they tell everything. This puerile hunting after details, this cold and cynical inventory of all the wretched conditions in the midst of which poor humanity vegetates, not only do not help us to understand it better, but, on the contrary, the effect on the spectators is a kind of dazzled confusion mingled with fatigue and disgust. The material truthfulness to which the school of M. Flaubert more especially pretends misses its aim in going beyond it. Truth is lost in its own excess."

I return to my thoughts on the relations of imaginative art in all its forms with science. The subject which in the hands of the scientific student is handled decorously,—reverently, we might almost say,—becomes repulsive, shameful, and debasing in the unscrupulous manipulations of the low-bred man of letters.

I confess that I am a little jealous of certain tendencies in our own American literature, which led one of the severest and most outspoken of our satirical fellow-countrymen, no longer living, to be called to account for it, to say, in a moment of bitterness, that the mission of America was to vulgarize mankind. I myself have sometimes wondered at the pleasure some Old World critics have professed to find in the most lawless freaks of the New World literature. I have questioned whether their delight was not like that of the Spartans in the drunken antics of their Helots. But I suppose I belong to another age, and must not attempt to judge the present by my old-fashioned standards. . . .

(From *Over the Teacups*, pp. 105–110.)

[V. POETIC CONCEPTION]

A lyric conception—my friend, the Poet, said—hits me like a bullet in the forehead. I have often had the blood drop from my cheeks when it struck, and felt that I turned as white as death. Then comes a creeping as of centipedes running down the spine,—then a gasp and a great jump of the heart,—then a sudden flush and a beating in the vessels of the head,—then a long sigh,—and the poem is written.

It is an impromptu, I suppose, then, if you write it so suddenly,—I replied.

No,—said he,—far from it. I said written, but I did not say *copied.* Every such poem has a soul and a body, and it is the body of it, or the copy, that men read and publishers pay for. The soul of it is born in an instant in the poet's soul. It comes to him a thought, tangled in the meshes of a few sweet words,—

words that have loved each other from the cradle of the language, but have never been wedded until now. Whether it will ever fully embody itself in a bridal train of a dozen stanzas or not is uncertain; but it exists potentially from the instant that the poet turns pale with it. It is enough to stun and scare anybody, to have a hot thought come crashing into his brain, and ploughing up those parallel ruts where the wagon trains of common ideas were jogging along in their regular sequences of association. No wonder the ancient made the poetical impulse wholly external. Μῆνιν ἄειδε Θεά. Goddess,—Muse,—divine afflatus,—something outside always. *I* never wrote any verses worth reading. I can't. I'm too stupid. If I ever copied any that were worth reading, I was only a medium.

. . . Does a poet love the verses written through him, do you think, Sir?—said the divinity-student.

So long as they are warm from his mind,—carry any of his animal heat about them, *I know* he loves them,—I answered. When they have had time to cool, he is more indifferent.

A good deal as it is with buckwheat cakes,—said the young fellow whom they call John.

The last words, only, reached the ear of the economically organized female in black bombazine.—Buckwheat is skerce and high,—she remarked. [Must be a poor relation sponging on our landlady—pays nothing,—so she must stand by the guns and be ready to repel boarders.]

I liked the turn the conversation had taken, for I had some things I wanted to say, and so, after waiting a minute, I began again.—I don't think the poems I read you sometimes can be fairly appreciated, given to you as they are in the green state.

—You don't know what I mean by the *green state?* Well, then, I will tell you. Certain things are good for nothing until they have been kept a long while; and some are good for nothing until they have been long kept and *used.* Of the first, wine is the illustrious and immortal example. Of those which must be kept and used I will name three,—meerschaum pipes, violins, and poems. The meerschaum is but a poor affair until it has burned a thousand offerings to the cloud-compelling deities. It comes to us without complexion or flavor,—born of the sea-foam, like Aphrodite, but colorless as *pallida Mors* herself. The fire is lighted in its central shrine, and gradually the juices which the broad leaves of the Great Vegetable had sucked up from an acre and curdled into a drachm are diffused through its thirsting pores. First a discoloration, then a stain, and at last a rich, glowing, umber tint spreading over the whole surface. Nature true to her old brown autumnal hue, you see,—as true in the fire of the meerschaum as in the sunshine of October! And then the cumulative wealth of its fragrant reminiscences! he who inhales its vapors takes a thousand whiffs in a single breath; and one cannot touch it without awakening the old joys that hang around it as the smell of flowers clings to the dresses of the daughters of the house of Farina! . . .

Violins, too,—the sweet old Amati!—the divine Stradivarius! Played on by ancient *maestros* until the bow-hand lost its power and the flying fingers stiffened. Bequeathed to the passionate young enthusiast, who made it whisper his hidden love, and cry his inarticulate longings, and scream his untold agonies, and wail his monotonous despair. Passed from his dying hand to the cold *virtuoso,* who let it slumber in its case for a generation, till, when his hoard was broken up, it came forth once more and rode the stormy symphonies of royal orchestras, beneath the rushing bow of their lord and leader. Into lonely prisons with improvident artists; into convents from which arose, day and night, the holy hymns with which its tones were blended; and back again to orgies in which it learned to howl and laugh as if a legion of devils were shut up in it; then again to the gentle *dilettante* who calmed it down with easy melodies until it answered him softly as in the days of the old *maestros.* And so given into our hands, its pores all full of music; stained, like the meerschaum, through and through, with the concentrated hue and sweetness of all the harmonies which have kindled and faded on its strings.

Now I tell you a poem must be kept *and used,* like a meerschaum, or a violin. A poem is just as porous as the meerschaum;—the more porous it is, the better. I mean to say that a genuine poem is capable of absorbing an indefinite amount of the essence of our own humanity,—its tenderness, its heroism, its regrets, its aspirations, so as to be gradually stained through with a divine secondary color derived from ourselves. So you see it must take time to bring the sentiment of a poem into harmony with our nature, by staining ourselves through every thought and image our being can penetrate.

Then again as to the mere music of a new poem, why, who can expect anything more from that than from the music of a violin fresh from the maker's hands? Now you know very well that there are no less than fifty-eight different pieces in a violin. These pieces are strangers to each other, and it takes a century, more or less, to make them thoroughly acquainted. At last they learn to vibrate in harmony and the instrument becomes an organic whole, as if it were a great seed-capsule which had grown from a garden-bed in Cremona, or elsewhere. Besides, the wood is juicy and full of sap for fifty years or so, but at the end of fifty or a hundred more gets tolerably dry and comparatively resonant.

Don't you see that all this is just as true of a poem? Counting each word as a piece, there are more pieces in an average copy of verses than in a violin. The poet has forced all these words together, and fastened them, and they don't understand it at first. But let the poem be repeated aloud and murmured over in the mind's muffled whisper often enough, and at length the parts become knit together in such absolute solidarity that you could not change a syllable without the whole world's crying out against you for meddling with the harmonious fabric. Observe, too, how the drying process takes place in the stuff of a poem just as in that of a violin. Here is a Tyrolese fiddle that is just coming to its hundredth birthday, —(Pedro Klauss, Tyroli, fecit, 1760),—the sap is pretty well out of it. And here is the song of an old poet whom Neæra cheated:—

"Nox erat, et cœlo fulgebat Luna sereno
  Inter minora sidera,
Cum tu magnorum numen læsura deorum
  In verba jurabas mea."

Don't you perceive the sonorousness of these old dead Latin phrases? Now I tell you that every word fresh from the dictionary brings with it a certain succulence; and though I cannot expect the sheets of the "Pactolian," in which, as I told you, I sometimes print my verses, to get so dry as the crisp papyrus that held those words of Horatius Flaccus, yet you may be sure, that, while the sheets are damp, and while the lines hold their sap, you can't fairly judge of my performances, and that, if made of the true stuff, they will ring better after a while.

(From *The Autocrat of the Breakfast-Table*, pp. 98–105.)

EMILY DICKINSON[1]

[THERE'S A CERTAIN SLANT OF LIGHT]

THERE'S a certain slant of light,
On winter afternoons,
That oppresses, like the weight
Of cathedral tunes.

Heavenly hurt it gives us;
We can find no scar,
But internal difference
Where the meanings are.

None may teach it anything,
'Tis the seal, despair,—
An imperial affliction
Sent us of the air.

When it comes, the landscape listens,
Shadows hold their breath;
When it goes, 'tis like the distance
On the look of death.

[I'LL TELL YOU HOW THE SUN ROSE]

I'LL tell you how the sun rose,—
A ribbon at a time.
The steeples swam in amethyst,
The news like squirrels ran.

The hills untied their bonnets,
The bobolinks begun.
Then I said softly to myself,
"That must have been the sun!"

. . . .

But how he set, I know not.
There seemed a purple stile
Which little yellow boys and girls
Were climbing all the while

Till when they reached the other side,
A dominie in gray
Put gently up the evening bars,
And led the flock away.

[I LIKE TO SEE IT LAP THE MILES]

I LIKE to see it lap the miles,
And lick the valleys up,
And stop to feed itself at tanks;
And then, prodigious, step

Around a pile of mountains,
And, supercilious, peer
In shanties by the sides of roads;
And then a quarry pare

To fit its sides, and crawl between,
Complaining all the while
In horrid, hooting stanza;
Then chase itself down hill

And neigh like Boanerges;
Then, punctual as a star,
Stop—docile and omnipotent—
At its own stable door.

[APPARENTLY WITH NO SURPRISE]

APPARENTLY with no surprise
To any happy flower,
The frost beheads it at its play
In accidental power.

The blond assassin passes on,
The sun proceeds unmoved
To measure off another day
For an approving God.

[IF I SHOULDN'T BE ALIVE]

IF I shouldn't be alive
When the robins come,
Give the one in red cravat
A memorial crumb.

If I couldn't thank you,
Being just asleep,
You will know I'm trying
With my granite lip!

[1] The selections from Emily Dickinson are reprinted from *The Poems of Emily Dickinson*, Centenary Edition, edited by Martha Dickinson Bianchi and Alfred Leete Hampson, by permission of Little, Brown & Company, publishers.

[TO HEAR AN ORIOLE SING]

To hear an oriole sing
May be a common thing,
Or only a divine.

It is not of the bird
Who sings the same, unheard,
As unto crowd.

The fashion of the ear
Attireth that it hear
In dun or fair.

So whether it be rune,
Or whether it be none,
Is of within;

The "tune is in the tree,"
The sceptic showeth me;
"No, sir! In thee!"

[WHERE SHIPS OF PURPLE]

Where ships of purple gently toss
On seas of daffodil,
Fantastic sailors mingle,
And then—the wharf is still.

[I GOT SO I COULD HEAR HIS NAME]

I got so I could hear his name
Without—
Tremendous gain!—
That stop-sensation in my soul,
And thunder in the room.

I got so I could walk across
That angle in the floor
Where he turned—so—and I turned how—
And all our sinew tore.

I got so I could stir the box
In which his letters grew—
Without that forcing in my breath
As staples driven through.

Could dimly recollect a Grace—
I think they called it "God,"
Renowned to ease extremity
When formula had failed—

And shape my hands petition's way—
Tho' ignorant of word
That Ordination utters—
My business with the cloud.

If any Power behind it be
Not subject to despair,
To care in some remoter way
For so minute affair
As misery—
Itself too vast for interrupting more,
Supremer than—
Superior to—

[HEART, WE WILL FORGET HIM!]

Heart, we will forget him!
You and I, to-night!
You may forget the warmth he gave,
I will forget the light.

When you have done, pray tell me,
That I my thoughts may dim;
Haste! lest while you're lagging,
I may remember him!

[OF ALL THE SOULS]

Of all the souls that stand create
I have elected one.
When sense from spirit flies away,
And subterfuge is done;

When that which is and that which was
Apart, intrinsic, stand,
And this brief tragedy of flesh
Is shifted like a sand;

When figures show their royal front
And mists are carved away,—
Behold the atom I preferred
To all the lists of clay!

[A WIFE AT DAYBREAK]

A wife at daybreak I shall be;
Sunrise, hast thou a flag for me?
At midnight I am yet a maid—
How short it takes to make it bride!
Then, Midnight, I have passed from thee
Unto the East and Victory.

Midnight, "Good night!"
I hear them call.
The Angels bustle in the hall,
Softly my Future climbs the stair,
I fumble at my childhood's prayer—
So soon to be a child no more!
Eternity, I'm coming, Sir,—
Master, I've seen that face before.

[AFTER GREAT PAIN]

After great pain a formal feeling comes—
The nerves sit ceremonious like tombs;
The stiff Heart questions—was it He that bore?
And yesterday—or centuries before?

The feet mechanical
Go round a wooden way
Of ground or air or Ought, regardless grown,
A quartz contentment like a stone.

This is the hour of lead
Remembered if outlived,
As freezing persons recollect the snow—
First chill, then stupor, then the letting go.

[THEY SAY THAT "TIME ASSUAGES"]

They say that "time assuages,"—
Time never did assuage;
An actual suffering strengthens,
As sinews do, with age.

Time is a test of trouble,
But not a remedy.
If such it prove, it prove too
There was no malady.

[TO FIGHT ALOUD]

To fight aloud is very brave,
But gallanter, I know,
Who charge within the bosom,
The cavalry of woe.

Who win, and nations do not see,
Who fall, and none observe,
Whose dying eyes no country
Regards with patriot love.

We trust, in plumed procession,
For such the angels go,
Rank after rank, with even feet
And uniforms of snow.

[TITLE DIVINE]

Title divine is mine
The Wife without
The Sign.
Acute degree
Conferred on me—
Empress of Calvary.
Royal all but the
Crown—
Betrothed, without the swoon
God gives us women
When two hold
Garnet to garnet,
Gold to gold—
Born—Bridalled—
Shrouded—
In a day
Tri-Victory—
"My Husband"
Women say
Stroking the melody,
Is this the way?

[TRIUMPH]

A triumph may be of several kinds.
There's triumph in the room
When that old imperator, Death,
By faith is overcome.

There's triumph of the finer mind
When truth, affronted long,
Advances calm to her supreme,
Her God her only throng.

A triumph when temptation's bribe
Is slowly handed back,
One eye upon the heaven renounced
And one upon the rack.

Severer triumph, by himself
Experienced, who can pass
Acquitted from that naked bar,
Jehovah's countenance!

[GROWTH OF MAN]

Growth of Man like growth of Nature
Gravitates within,
Atmosphere and sun confirm it
But it stirs alone.

Each its difficult ideal
Must achieve itself,
Through the solitary prowess
Of a silent life.

Effort is the sole condition,
Patience of itself—
Patience of opposing forces,
And distinct belief.

Looking on is the department
Of its audience,
But transaction is assisted
By no countenance.

[WHAT SOFT, CHERUBIC CREATURES]

WHAT soft, cherubic creatures
These gentlewomen are!
One would as soon assault a plush
Or violate a star.

Such dimity convictions,
A horror so refined
Of freckled human nature,
Of Deity ashamed,—

It's such a common glory,
A fisherman's degree!
Redemption, brittle lady,
Be so ashamed of thee.

[READ, SWEET, HOW OTHERS STROVE]

READ, sweet, how others strove,
Till we are stouter;
What they renounced,
Till we are less afraid;
How many times they bore
The faithful witness,
Till we are helped,
As if a kingdom cared!

Read then of faith
That shone above the fagot;
Clear strains of hymn
The river could not drown;
Brave names of men
And celestial women,
Passed out of record
Into renown!

[THE GLEAM OF AN HEROIC ACT]

THE gleam of an heroic act,
Such strange illumination—
The Possible's slow fuse is lit
By the Imagination!

[SUPERIORITY TO FATE]

SUPERIORITY to fate
Is difficult to learn.
'Tis not conferred by any,
But possible to earn

A pittance at a time,
Until, to her surprise,
The soul with strict economy
Subsists till Paradise.

[ON THE BLEAKNESS OF MY LOT]

ON the bleakness of my lot
Bloom I strove to raise.
Late, my acre of a rock
Yielded grape and maize.

Soil of flint if steadfast tilled
Will reward the hand;
Seed of palm by Lybian sun
Fructified in sand.

['TIS LITTLE I COULD CARE]

'TIS little I could care for pearls
Who own the ample sea;
Or brooches, when the Emperor
With rubies pelteth me;

Or gold, who am the Prince of Mines;
Or diamonds, when I see
A diadem to fit a dome
Continual crowning me.

[RENUNCIATION]

RENUNCIATION
Is a piercing virtue,
The letting go
A presence for an expectation—
Not now.

The putting out of eyes
Just sunrise,
Lest Day Day's great progenitor
Out-show.

Renunciation is the choosing
Against itself,
Itself to justify
Unto itself;

When larger function
Make that appear
Smaller, that sated vision
Here.

[HE PREACHED UPON "BREADTH"]

He preached upon "breadth" till it argued him narrow,—
The broad are too broad to define;
And of "truth" until it proclaimed him a liar,—
The truth never flaunted a sign.

Simplicity fled from his counterfeit presence
As gold the pyrites would shun.
What confusion would cover the innocent Jesus
To meet so enabled a man!

[ARCTURUS]

Arcturus is his other name,—
I'd rather call him star!
It's so unkind of science
To go and interfere!

I pull a flower from the woods,—
A monster with a glass
Computes the stamens in a breath,
And has her in a class.

Whereas I took the butterfly
Aforetime in my hat,
He sits erect in cabinets,
The clover-bells forgot.

What once was heaven, is zenith now.
Where I proposed to go
When time's brief masquerade was done,
Is mapped, and charted too!

What if the poles should frisk about
And stand upon their heads!
I hope I'm ready for the worst,
Whatever prank betides!

Perhaps the kingdom of Heaven's changed!
I hope the children there
Won't be new-fashioned when I come,
And laugh at me, and stare!

I hope the father in the skies
Will lift his little girl,—
Old-fashioned, naughty, everything,—
Over the stile of pearl!

[AT LEAST TO PRAY IS LEFT]

At least to pray is left, is left.
O Jesus! in the air
I know not which thy chamber is,—
I'm knocking everywhere.

Thou stirrest earthquake in the South,
And maelstrom in the sea;
Say, Jesus Christ of Nazareth,
Hast thou no arm for me?

[I STEPPED FROM PLANK TO PLANK]

I stepped from plank to plank
So slow and cautiously;
The stars about my head I felt,
About my feet the sea.

I knew not but the next
Would be my final inch,—
This gave me that precarious gait
Some call experience.

[I NEVER SAW A MOOR]

I never saw a moor,
I never saw the sea;
Yet know I how the heather looks,
And what a wave must be.

I never spoke with God,
Nor visited in heaven;
Yet certain am I of the spot
As if the chart were given.

[MY LIFE CLOSED TWICE]

My life closed twice before its close;
It yet remains to see
If Immortality unveil
A third event to me,

So huge, so hopeless to conceive,
As these that twice befell.
Parting is all we know of heaven,
And all we need of hell.

[THE SOUL'S SUPERIOR INSTANTS]

THE Soul's superior instants
Occur to Her alone,
When friend and earth's occasion
Have infinite withdrawn.

Or she, Herself, ascended
To too remote a height,
For lower recognition
Than Her Omnipotent.

This mortal abolition
Is seldom, but as fair
As Apparition—subject
To autocratic air.

Eternity's disclosure
To favorites, a few,
Of the Colossal substance
Of immortality.

[I DID NOT REACH THEE]

I DID not reach thee,
But my feet slip nearer every day;
Three Rivers and a Hill to cross,
One Desert and a Sea—
I shall not count the journey one
When I am telling thee.

Two deserts—but the year is cold
So that will help the sand—
One desert crossed, the second one
Will feel as cool as land.
Sahara is too little price
To pay for thy Right hand!

The sea comes last. Step merry, feet!
So short have we to go
To play together we are prone,
But we must labor now,
The last shall be the lightest load
That we have had to draw.

The Sun goes crooked—that is night—
Before he makes the bend
We must have passed the middle sea,
Almost we wish the end
Were further off—too great it seems
So near the Whole to stand.

We step like plush, we stand like snow—
The waters murmur now,
Three rivers and the hill are passed,
Two deserts and the sea!
Now Death usurps my premium
And gets the look at Thee.

[THIS WORLD IS NOT CONCLUSION]

THIS world is not conclusion;
A sequel stands beyond,
Invisible, as music,
But positive, as sound.
It beckons and it baffles;
Philosophies don't know,
And through a riddle, at the last,
Sagacity must go.
To guess it puzzles scholars;
To gain it, men have shown
Contempt of generations,
And crucifixion known.

[WHO HAS NOT FOUND]

WHO has not found the heaven below
Will fail of it above.
God's residence is next to mine,
His furniture is love.

[I DIED FOR BEAUTY]

I DIED for beauty, but was scarce
Adjusted in the tomb,
When one who died for truth was lain
In an adjoining room.

He questioned softly why I failed?
"For beauty," I replied.
"And I for truth,—the two are one;
We brethren are," he said.

And so, as kinsmen met a night,
We talked between the rooms,
Until the moss had reached our lips,
And covered up our names.

[THIS WAS A POET]

THIS was a Poet—it is that
Distills amazing sense
From ordinary meanings,
And attars so immense

From the familiar species
That perished by the door,
We wonder it was not ourselves
Arrested it before.

Of pictures the discloser
The Poet, it is he,
Entitles us by contrast
To ceaseless poverty.

Of portion so unconscious
The robbing could not harm,
Himself, to him, a fortune
Exterior to Time.

[UNTO MY BOOKS]

Unto my books so good to turn
Far ends of tired days;
It half endears the abstinence,
And pain is missed in praise.

As flavors cheer retarded guests
With banquetings to be,
So spices stimulate the time
Till my small library.

It may be wilderness without,
Far feet of failing men,
But holiday excludes the night,
And it is bells within.

I thank these kinsmen of the shelf;
Their countenances bland
Enamour in prospective,
And satisfy, obtained.

[PUBLICATION]

Publication is the auction
Of the mind of man,
Poverty be justifying
For so foul a thing.

Possibly,—but we would rather
From our garret go
White unto the White Creator,
Than invest our snow.

Thought belongs to Him who gave it—
Then to him who bear
Its corporeal illustration.
Sell the Royal air
In the parcel,—be the merchant
Of the Heavenly Grace,
But reduce no human spirit
To disgrace of price!

[TO TELL THE BEAUTY WOULD DECREASE]

To tell the beauty would decrease,
To state the Spell demean,
There is a syllableless sea
Of which it is the sign.

My will endeavours for its word
And fails, but entertains
A rapture as of legacies—
Of introspective mines.

[I RECKON, WHEN I COUNT AT ALL]

I reckon, when I count at all,
First Poets—then the Sun—
Then Summer—then the Heaven of God—
And then the list is done.
But looking back—the first so seems
To comprehend the whole—
The others look a needless show,
So I write Poets—All.
This summer lasts a solid year,
They can afford a sun
The East would deem extravagant,
And if the final Heaven
Be beautiful as they disclose
To those who trust in them,
It is too difficult a grace
To justify the dream.

SIDNEY LANIER

NIGHT AND DAY

The innocent, sweet Day is dead.
Dark Night hath slain her in her bed.
O, Moors are as fierce to kill as to wed!
—Put out the light, said he.

A sweeter light than ever rayed
From star of heaven or eye of maid
Has vanished in the unknown Shade.
—She's dead, she's dead, said he.

Now, in a wild, sad after-mood
The tawny Night sits still to brood
Upon the dawn-time when he wooed.
—I would she lived, said he.

Star-memories of happier times,
Of loving deeds and lovers' rhymes,
Throng forth in silvery pantomimes.
—Come back, O Day! said he.

1866 1884

THE RAVEN DAYS

Our hearths are gone out and our hearts are broken,
And but the ghosts of homes to us remain,
And ghastly eyes and hollow sighs give token
From friend to friend of an unspoken pain.

O Raven days, dark Raven days of sorrow,
Bring to us in your whetted ivory beaks
Some sign out of the far land of To-morrow,
Some strip of sea-green dawn, some orange streaks.

Ye float in dusky files, forever croaking.
Ye chill our manhood with your dreary shade.
Dumb in the dark, not even God invoking,
We lie in chains, too weak to be afraid.

O Raven days, dark Raven days of sorrow,
Will ever any warm light come again?
Will ever the lit mountains of To-morrow
Begin to gleam athwart the mournful plain?

1868 1868

RESURRECTION

Sometimes in morning sunlights by the river
Where in the early fall long grasses wave,
Light winds from over the moorland sink and shiver
And sigh as if just blown across a grave.

And then I pause and listen to this sighing.
I look with strange eyes on the well-known stream.
I hear wild birth-cries uttered by the dying.
I know men waking who appear to dream.

Then from the water-lilies slow uprises
The still vast face of all the life I know,
Changed now, and full of wonders and surprises,
With fire in eyes that once were glazed with snow.

Fair now the brows old Pain had erewhile wrinkled,
And peace and strength about the calm mouth dwell.
Clean of the ashes that Repentance sprinkled,
The meek head poises like a flower-bell.

All the old scars of wanton wars are vanished;
And what blue bruises grappling Sense had left
And sad remains of redder stains are banished,
And the dim blotch of heart-committed theft.

O still vast vision of transfigured features
Unvisited by secret crimes or dooms,
Remain, remain amid these water-creatures,
Stand, shine among yon water-lily blooms.

For eighteen centuries ripple down the river,
And windy times the stalks of empires wave,
—Let the winds come from the moor and sigh and shiver,
Fain, fain am I, O Christ, to pass the grave.

1868 1868

MAY THE MAIDEN

Song for "The Jacquerie"

May the maiden,
Violet-laden
Out of the violet sea,
Comes and hovers
Over lovers,
Over thee, Marie, and me,
Over me and thee.

Day the stately,
Sunken lately
Into the violet sea,
Backward hovers
Over lovers,
Over thee, Marie, and me,
Over me and thee.

Night the holy,
Sailing slowly
Over the violet sea,
Stars uncovers
Over lovers,
Stars for thee, Marie, and me,
Stars for me and thee.

1868

THAR'S MORE IN THE MAN THAN THAR IS IN THE LAND

I knowed a man, which he lived in Jones,
Which Jones is a county of red hills and stones,
And he lived pretty much by gittin' of loans,
And his mules was nuthin' but skin and bones,
And his hogs was flat as his corn-bread pones,
And he had 'bout a thousand acres o' land.

This man—which his name it was also Jones—
He swore that he'd leave them old red hills and stones,
Fur he couldn't make nuthin' but yallerish cotton,
And little o' *that*, and his fences was rotten,
And what little corn he had, *hit* was boughten
And dinged ef a livin' was in the land.

And the longer he swore the madder he got,
And he riz and he walked to the stable lot,
And he hollered to Tom to come thar and hitch
Fur to emigrate somewhar whar land was rich,
And to quit raisin' cock-burrs, thistles and sich,
And a wastin' ther time on the cussed land.

So him and Tom they hitched up the mules,
Pertestin' that folks was mighty big fools
That 'ud stay in Georgy ther lifetime out,
Jest scratchin' a livin' when all of 'em mought
Git places in Texas whar cotton would sprout
By the time you could plant it in the land.

And he driv by a house whar a man named Brown
Was a livin', not fur from the edge o' town,
And he bantered Brown fur to buy his place,
And said that bein' as money was skace,
And bein' as sheriffs was hard to face,
Two dollars an acre would git the land.

They closed at a dollar and fifty cents,
And Jones he bought him a waggin and tents,
And loaded his corn, and his wimmin, and truck,
And moved to Texas, which it tuck
His entire pile, with the best of luck,
To git thar and git him a little land.

But Brown moved out on the old Jones' farm,
And he rolled up his breeches and bared his arm,
And he picked all the rocks from off'n the groun',
And he rooted it up and he plowed it down,
Then he sowed his corn and his wheat in the land.

Five years glid by, and Brown, one day
(Which he'd got so fat that he wouldn't weigh),
Was a settin' down, sorter lazily,
To the bulliest dinner you ever see,
When one o' the children jumped on his knee
And says, "Yan's Jones, which you bought his land."

And thar was Jones, standin' out at the fence,
And he hadn't no waggin, nor mules, nor tents,
Fur he had left Texas afoot and cum
To Georgy to see if he couldn't git sum
Employment, and he was a lookin' as hum-
Ble as ef he had never owned any land.

But Brown he axed him in, and he sot
Him down to his vittles smokin' hot,
And when he had filled hisself and the floor
Brown looked at him sharp and riz and swore
That, "whether men's land was rich or poor
Thar was more in the *man* than thar was in the *land*."

1866 1869?, 1884

IN ABSENCE

I

The storm that snapped our fate's one ship in twain
Hath blown my half o' the wreck from thine apart.
O Love! O Love! across the gray-waved main
To thee-ward strain my eyes, my arms, my heart.
I ask my God if e'en in His sweet place,
Where, by one waving of a wistful wing,
My soul could straightway tremble face to face
With thee, with thee, across the stellar ring—
Yea, where thine absence I could ne'er bewail
Longer than lasts that little blank of bliss
When lips draw back, with recent pressure pale,
To round and redden for another kiss—
Would not my lonesome heart still sigh for thee
What time the drear kiss-intervals must be?

II

So do the mottled formulas of Sense
Glide snakewise through our dreams of Aftertime;
So errors breed in reeds and grasses dense
That bank our singing rivulets of rhyme.
By Sense rule Space and Time; but in God's Land
Their intervals are not, save such as lie
Betwixt successive tones in concords bland
Whose loving distance makes the harmony.
Ah, there shall never come 'twixt me and thee
Gross dissonances of the mile, the year;
But in the multichords of ecstasy
Our souls shall mingle, yet be featured clear,
And absence, wrought to intervals divine,
Shall part, yet link, thy nature's tone and mine.

III

Look down the shining peaks of all my days
Base-hidden in the valleys of deep night,
So shalt thou see the heights and depths of praise
My love would render unto love's delight;
For I would make each day an Alp sublime
Of passionate snow, white-hot yet icy-clear,
—One crystal of the true-loves of all time
Spiring the world's prismatic atmosphere;
And I would make each night an awful vale
Deep as thy soul, obscure as modesty,
With every star in heaven trembling pale
O'er sweet profounds where only Love can see.
Oh, runs not thus the lesson thou hast taught?—
When life's all love, 'tis life: aught else, 'tis naught.

IV

Let no man say, *He at his lady's feet*
Lays worship that to Heaven alone belongs;
Yea, swings the incense that for God is meet
In flippant censers of light lover's songs.
Who says it, knows not God, nor love, nor thee;
For love is large as is yon heavenly dome:
In love's great blue, each passion is full free
To fly his favorite flight and build his home.
Did e'er a lark with skyward-pointing beak
Stab by mischance a level-flying dove?
Wife-love flies level, his dear mate to seek:
God-love darts straight into the skies above.
Crossing, the windage of each other's wings
But speeds them both upon their journeyings.

1874 1875

THE SYMPHONY

"O Trade! O Trade! would thou wert dead!
The Time needs heart—'tis tired of head:
We're all for love," the violins said.
"Of what avail the rigorous tale
Of bill for coin and box for bale?

Grant thee, O Trade! thine uttermost hope:
Level red gold with blue sky-slope,
And base it deep as devils grope:
When all's done, what hast thou won
Of the only sweet that's under the sun?
Ay, canst thou buy a single sigh
Of true love's least, least ecstasy?"
Then, with a bridegroom's heart-beats trembling,
All the mightier strings assembling
Ranged them on the violins' side
As when the bridegroom leads the bride,
And, heart in voice, together cried:
"Yea, what avail the endless tale
Of gain by cunning and plus by sale?
Look up the land, look down the land
The poor, the poor, the poor, they stand
Wedged by the pressing of Trade's hand
Against an inward-opening door
That pressure tightens evermore:
They sigh a monstrous foul-air sigh
For the outside leagues of liberty,
Where Art, sweet lark, translates the sky
Into a heavenly melody.
'Each day, all day' (these poor folks say),
'In the same old year-long, drear-long way,
We weave in the mills and heave in the kilns,
We sieve mine-meshes under the hills,
And thieve much gold from the Devil's bank tills,
To relieve, O God, what manner of ills?—
The beasts, they hunger, and eat, and die;
And so do we, and the world's a sty;
Hush, fellow-swine: why nuzzle and cry?
Swinehood hath no remedy
Say many men, and hasten by,
Clamping the nose and blinking the eye.
But who said once, in the lordly tone,
Man shall not live by bread alone
But all that cometh from the Throne?
Hath God said so?
But Trade saith *No:*
And the kilns and the curt-tongued mills say *Go!*
There's plenty that can, if you can't: we know.
Move out, if you think you're underpaid.
The poor are prolific; we're not afraid;
Trade is trade.'"
Thereat this passionate protesting
Meekly changed, and softened till
It sank to sad requesting
And suggesting sadder still:
"And oh, if men might some time see
How piteous-false the poor decree
That trade no more than trade must be!
Does business mean, *Die, you—live, I?*
Then 'Trade is trade' but sings a lie:
'Tis only war grown miserly.
If business is battle, name it so:
War-crimes less will shame it so,
And widows less will blame it so.
Alas, for the poor to have some part
In yon sweet living lands of Art,
Makes problem not for head, but heart.
Vainly might Plato's brain revolve it:
Plainly the heart of a child could solve it."

And then, as when from words that seem but rude
We pass to silent pain that sits abrood
Back in our heart's great dark and solitude,
So sank the strings to gentle throbbing
Of long chords change-marked with sobbing—
Motherly sobbing, not distinctlier heard
Than half wing-openings of the sleeping bird,
Some dream of danger to her young hath stirred.
Then stirring and demurring ceased, and lo!
Every least ripple of the strings' song-flow
Died to a level with each level bow 79
And made a great chord tranquil-surfaced so,
As a brook beneath his curving bank doth go
To linger in the sacred dark and green
Where many boughs the still pool overlean
And many leaves make shadow with their sheen.
But presently
A velvet flute-note fell down pleasantly
Upon the bosom of that harmony,
And sailed and sailed incessantly,
As if a petal from a wild-rose blown
Had fluttered down upon that pool of tone
And boatwise dropped o' the convex side
And floated down the glassy tide
And clarified and glorified
The solemn spaces where the shadows bide.
From the warm concave of that fluted note
Somewhat, half song, half odor, forth did float,
As if a rose might somehow be a throat:
"When Nature from her far-off glen

Flutes her soft messages to men,
The flute can say them o'er again;
Yea, Nature, singing sweet and lone,
Breathes through life's strident polyphone
The flute-voice in the world of tone.
Sweet friends,
Man's love ascends
To finer and diviner ends
Than man's mere thought e'er comprehends
For I, e'en I,
As here I lie,
A petal on a harmony,
Demand of Science whence and why
Man's tender pain, man's inward cry,
When he doth gaze on earth and sky?
I am not overbold:
I hold
Full powers from Nature manifold.
I speak for each no-tonguéd tree
That, spring by spring, doth nobler be,
And dumbly and most wistfully
His mighty prayerful arms outspreads
Above men's oft-unheeding heads,
And his big blessing downward sheds.
I speak for all-shaped blooms and leaves,
Lichens on stones and moss on eaves,
Grasses and grains in ranks and sheaves;
Broad-fronded ferns and keen-leaved canes,
And briery mazes bounding lanes,
And marsh-plants, thirsty-cupped for rains,
And milky stems and sugary veins;
For every long-armed woman-vine
That round a piteous tree doth twine;
For passionate odors, and divine
Pistils, and petals crystalline;
All purities of shady springs,
All shynesses of film-winged things
That fly from tree-trunks and bark-rings;
All modesties of mountain-fawns
That leap to covert from wild lawns,
And tremble if the day but dawns;
All sparklings of small beady eyes
Of birds, and sidelong glances wise
Wherewith the jay hints tragedies;
All piquancies of prickly burs,
And smoothnesses of downs and furs
Of eiders and of minevers;
All limpid honeys that do lie
At stamen-bases, nor deny
The humming-birds' fine roguery,
Bee-thighs, nor any butterfly;
All gracious curves of slender wings,
Bark-mottlings, fibre-spiralings,
Fern-wavings and leaf-flickerings;
Each dial-marked leaf and flower-bell
Wherewith in every lonesome dell
Time to himself his hours doth tell;
All tree-sounds, rustlings of pine-cones,
Wind-sighings, doves' melodious moans,
And night's unearthly under-tones;
All placid lakes and waveless deeps,
All cool reposing mountain-steeps,
Vale-calms and tranquil lotos-sleeps;—
Yea, all fair forms, and sounds, and lights,
And warmths, and mysteries, and mights,
Of Nature's utmost depths and heights,
—These doth my timid tongue present,
Their mouthpiece and leal instrument
And servant, all love-eloquent.
I heard, when '*All for love*' the violins cried:
So, Nature calls through all her system wide,
Give me thy love, O man, so long denied.
Much time is run, and man hath changed his ways,
Since Nature, in the antique fable-days,
Was hid from man's true love by proxy fays,
False fauns and rascal gods that stole her praise.
The nymphs, cold creatures of man's colder brain,
Chilled Nature's streams till man's warm heart was fain
Never to lave its love in them again.
Later, a sweet Voice *Love thy neighbor* said;
Then first the bounds of neighborhood outspread
Beyond all confines of old ethnic dread.
Vainly the Jew might wag his covenant head:
'*All men are neighbors,*' so the sweet Voice said.
So, when man's arms had circled all man's race,
The liberal compass of his warm embrace
Stretched bigger yet in the dark bounds of space;
With hands a-grope he felt smooth Nature's grace,
Drew her to breast and kissed her sweetheart face:
Yea man found neighbors in great hills and trees
And streams and clouds and suns and birds and bees,
And throbbed with neighbor-loves in loving these.

But oh, the poor! the poor! the poor!
That stand by the inward-opening door
Trade's hand doth tighten ever more,
And sigh their monstrous foul-air sigh
For the outside hills of liberty,
Where Nature spreads her wild blue sky
For Art to make into melody!
Thou Trade! thou king of the modern days!
  Change thy ways,
  Change thy ways;
Let the sweaty laborers file
  A little while,
  A little while,
Where Art and Nature sing and smile.
Trade! is thy heart all dead, all dead?
And hast thou nothing but a head?
I'm all for heart," the flute-voice said,
And into sudden silence fled,
Like as a blush that while 'tis red
Dies to a still, still white instead.

Thereto a thrilling calm succeeds,
Till presently the silence breeds
A little breeze among the reeds
That seems to blow by sea-marsh weeds:
Then from the gentle stir and fret
Sings out the melting clarionet,
Like as a lady sings while yet
Her eyes with salty tears are wet.
"O Trade! O Trade!" the Lady said,
"I too will wish thee utterly dead
If all thy heart is in thy head.
For O my God! and O my God!
What shameful ways have women trod
At beckoning of Trade's golden rod!
Alas when sighs are traders' lies,
And heart's-ease eyes and violet eyes
  Are merchandise!
O purchased lips that kiss with pain!
O cheeks coin-spotted with smirch and stain!
O trafficked hearts that break in twain!
—And yet what wonder at my sisters' crime?
So hath Trade withered up Love's sinewy prime,
Men love not women as in olden time.
Ah, not in these cold merchantable days
Deem men their life an opal gray, where plays
The one red Sweet of gracious ladies'-praise.
Now, comes a suitor with sharp prying eye—
Says, *Here, you Lady, if you'll sell, I'll buy:*
Come, heart for heart—a trade? What! weeping? why?
Shame on such wooers' dapper mercery!
I would my lover kneeling at my feet
In humble manliness should cry, *O sweet!*
I know not if thy heart my heart will greet:
I ask not if thy love my love can meet:
Whate'er thy worshipful soft tongue shall say,
I'll kiss thine answer, be it yea or nay:
I do but know I love thee, and I pray
To be thy knight until my dying day.
Woe him that cunning trades in hearts contrives!
Base love good women to base loving drives.
If men loved larger, larger were our lives;
And wooed they nobler, won they nobler wives."

There thrust the bold straightforward horn
To battle for that lady lorn,
With heartsome voice of mellow scorn,
Like any knight in knighthood's morn.
  "Now comfort thee," said he,
  "Fair Lady.
For God shall right thy grievous wrong,
And man shall sing thee a true-love song,
Voiced in act his whole life long,
  Yea, all thy sweet life long,
  Fair Lady.
Where's he that craftily hath said,
The day of chivalry is dead?
I'll prove that lie upon his head,
  Or I will die instead,
  Fair Lady.
Is Honor gone into his grave?
Hath Faith become a caitiff knave,
And Selfhood turned into a slave
  To work in Mammon's cave,
  Fair Lady?
Will Truth's long blade ne'er gleam again?
Hath Giant Trade in dungeons slain
All great contempts of mean-got gain
  And hates of inward stain,
  Fair Lady?
For aye shall name and fame be sold,
And place be hugged for the sake of gold,
And smirch-robed Justice feebly scold
  At Crime all money-bold,
  Fair Lady?
Shall self-wrapt husbands aye forget
Kiss-pardons for the daily fret

Wherewith sweet wifely eyes are wet—
Blind to lips kiss-wise set—
Fair Lady?
Shall lovers higgle, heart for heart,
Till wooing grows a trading mart
Where much for little, and all for part,
Make love a cheapening art,
Fair Lady?
Shall woman scorch for a single sin
That her betrayer may revel in,
And she be burnt, and he but grin
When that the flames begin,
Fair Lady?
Shall ne'er prevail the woman's plea,
We maids would far, far whiter be
If that our eyes might sometimes see
Men maids in purity,
Fair Lady?
Shall Trade aye salve his conscience-aches
With jibes at Chivalry's old mistakes—
The wars that o'erhot knighthood makes
For Christ's and ladies' sakes,
Fair Lady?
Now by each knight that e'er hath prayed
To fight like a man and love like a maid,
Since Pembroke's life, as Pembroke's blade,
I' the scabbard, death, was laid,
Fair Lady,
I dare avouch my faith is bright
That God doth right and God hath might.
Nor time hath changed His hair to white,
Nor His dear love to spite,
Fair Lady.
I doubt no doubts: I strive, and shrive my clay,
And fight my fight in the patient modern way
For true love and for thee—ah me! and pray
To be thy knight until my dying day,
Fair Lady."
Made end that knightly horn, and spurred away
Into the thick of the melodious fray.

And then the hautboy played and smiled,
And sang like any large-eyed child,
Cool-hearted and all undefiled.
"Huge Trade!" he said,
"Would thou wouldst lift me on thy head
And run where'er my finger led!
Once said a Man—and wise was He—
Never shalt thou the heavens see,
Save as a little child thou be."
Then o'er sea-lashings of commingling tunes
The ancient wise bassoons,
Like weird
Gray-beard
Old harpers sitting on the high sea-dunes,
Chanted runes:
"Bright-waved gain, gray-waved loss,
The sea of all doth lash and toss,
One wave forward and one across:
But now 'twas trough, now 'tis crest,
And worst doth foam and flash to best,
And curst to blest.

Life! Life! thou sea-fugue, writ from east to west,
Love, Love alone can pore
On thy dissolving score
Of harsh half-phrasings,
Blotted ere writ,
And double erasings
Of chords most fit.
Yea, Love, sole music-master blest,
May read thy weltering palimpsest.
To follow Time's dying melodies through,
And never to lose the old in the new,
And ever to solve the discords true—
Love alone can do.
And ever Love hears the poor-folks' crying,
And ever Love hears the women's sighing,
And ever sweet knighthood's death-defying,
And ever wise childhood's deep implying,
But never a trader's glozing and lying.

And yet shall Love himself be heard,
Though long deferred, though long deferred:
O'er the modern waste a dove hath whirred:
Music is Love in search of a word."

1875

CORN

TODAY the woods are trembling through and through
With shimmering forms, that flash before my view,
Then melt in green as dawn-stars melt in blue.
The leaves that wave against my cheek caress
Like women's hands; the embracing boughs express
A subtlety of mighty tenderness;
The copse-depths into little noises start,
That sound anon like beatings of a heart,

Anon like talk 'twixt lips not far apart.
The beech dreams balm, as a dreamer hums a song;
Through that vague wafture, expirations strong
Throb from young hickories breathing deep and long
With stress and urgence bold of prisoned spring
And ecstasy of burgeoning.
Now, since the dew-plashed road of morn is dry,
Forth venture odors of more quality
And heavenlier giving. Like Jove's locks awry,
Long muscadines
Rich-wreathe the spacious foreheads of great pines,
And breathe ambrosial passion from their vines.
I pray with mosses, ferns and flowers shy
That hide like gentle nuns from human eye
To lift adoring perfumes to the sky.
I hear faint bridal-sighs of brown and green
Dying to silent hints of kisses keen
As far lights fringe into a pleasant sheen.
I start at fragmentary whispers, blown
From undertalks of leafy souls unknown,
Vague purports sweet, of inarticulate tone.
Dreaming of gods, men, nuns and brides, between
Old companies of oaks that inward lean
To join their radiant amplitudes of green
I slowly move, with ranging looks that pass
Up from the matted miracles of grass
Into yon veined complex of space
Where sky and leafage interlace
So close, the heaven of blue is seen
Inwoven with a heaven of green.

I wander to the zigzag-cornered fence
Where sassafras, intrenched in brambles dense,
Contests with stolid vehemence
The march of culture, setting limb and thorn
As pikes against the army of the corn.

There, while I pause, my fieldward-faring eyes
Take harvests, where the stately corn-ranks rise,
Of inward dignities
And large benignities and insights wise,
Graces and modest majesties.
Thus, without theft, I reap another's field;
Thus, without tilth, I house a wondrous yield,
And heap my heart with quintuple crops concealed.

Look, out of line one tall corn-captain stands
Advanced beyond the foremost of his bands,
And waves his blades upon the very edge
And hottest thicket of the battling hedge.
Thou lustrous stalk, that ne'er mayst walk nor talk,
Still shalt thou type the poet-soul sublime
That leads the vanward of his timid time
And sings up cowards with commanding rhyme—
Soul calm, like thee, yet fain, like thee, to grow
By double increment, above, below;
Soul homely, as thou art, yet rich in grace like thee,
Teaching the yeomen selfless chivalry
That moves in gentle curves of courtesy;
Soul filled like thy long veins with sweetness tense,
By every godlike sense
Transmuted from the four wild elements.
Drawn to high plans,
Thou lift'st more stature than a mortal man's,
Yet ever piercest downward in the mould
And keepest hold
Upon the reverend and steadfast earth
That gave thee birth;
Yea, standest smiling in thy future grave,
Serene and brave,
With unremitting breath
Inhaling life from death,
Thine epitaph writ fair in fruitage eloquent,
Thyself thy monument.

As poets should,
Thou hast built up thy hardihood
With universal food,
Drawn in select proportion fair
From honest mould and vagabond air;
From darkness of the dreadful night,
And joyful light;
From antique ashes, whose departed flame
In thee has finer life and longer fame;
From wounds and balms,
From storms and calms,

From potsherds and dry bones
And ruin-stones.
Into thy vigorous substance thou hast wrought
Whate'er the hand of Circumstance hath brought;
Yea, into cool solacing green hast spun
White radiance hot from out the sun.
So thou dost mutually leaven
Strength of earth with grace of heaven;
So thou dost marry new and old
Into a one of higher mould;
So thou dost reconcile the hot and cold,
The dark and bright,
And many a heart-perplexing opposite,
And so,
Akin by blood to high and low,
Fitly thou playest out thy poet's part,
Richly expending thy much-bruiséd heart
In equal care to nourish lord in hall
Or beast in stall:
Thou took'st from all that thou mightst give to all.

O steadfast dweller on the selfsame spot
Where thou wast born, that still repinest not—
Type of the home-fond heart, the happy lot!—
Deeply thy mild content rebukes the land
Whose flimsy homes, built on the shifting sand
Of trade, for ever rise and fall
With alternation whimsical,
Enduring scarce a day,
Then swept away
By swift engulfments of incalculable tides
Whereon capricious Commerce rides.
Look, thou substantial spirit of content!
Across this little vale, thy continent,
To where, beyond the mouldering mill,
Yon old deserted Georgian hill
Bares to the sun his piteous aged crest
And seamy breast,
By restless-hearted children left to lie
Untended there beneath the heedless sky,
As barbarous folk expose their old to die.
Upon that generous-rounding side,
With gullies scarified
Where keen Neglect his lash hath plied,
Dwelt one I knew of old, who played at toil,
And gave to coquette Cotton soul and soil.
Scorning the slow reward of patient grain,
He sowed his heart with hopes of swifter gain,
Then sat him down and waited for the rain.
He sailed in borrowed ships of usury—
A foolish Jason on a treacherous sea,
Seeking the Fleece and finding misery.
Lulled by smooth-rippling loans, in idle trance
He lay, content that unthrift Circumstance
Should plough for him the stony field of Chance.
Yea, gathering crops whose worth no man might tell,
He staked his life on games of Buy-and-Sell,
And turned each field into a gambler's hell.
Aye, as each year began,
My farmer to the neighboring city ran;
Passed with a mournful anxious face
Into the banker's inner place;
Parleyed, excused, pleaded for longer grace;
Railed at the drought, the worm, the rust, the grass;
Protested ne'er again 'twould come to pass;
With many an *oh* and *if* and *but alas*
Parried or swallowed searching questions rude,
And kissed the dust to soften Dives's mood.
At last, small loans by pledges great renewed,
He issues smiling from the fatal door,
And buys with lavish hand his yearly store
Till his small borrowings will yield no more.
Aye, as each year declined,
With bitter heart and ever-brooding mind
He mourned his fate unkind.
In dust, in rain, with might and main,
He nursed his cotton, cursed his grain,
Fretted for news that made him fret again,
Snatched at each telegram of Future Sale,
And thrilled with Bulls' or Bears' alternate wail—
In hope or fear alike for ever pale.
And thus from year to year, through hope and fear,
With many a curse and many a secret tear,
Striving in vain his cloud of debt to clear,
At last
He woke to find his foolish dreaming past,
And all his best-of-life the easy prey
Of squandering scamps and quacks that lined his way
With vile array,
From rascal statesman down to petty knave;

Himself, at best, for all his bragging brave,
A gamester's catspaw and a banker's slave.
Then, worn and gray, and sick with deep unrest,
He fled away into the oblivious West,
Unmourned, unblest.

Old hill! old hill! thou gashed and hairy Lear
Whom the divine Cordelia of the year,
E'en pitying Spring, will vainly strive to cheer—
King, that no subject man nor beast may own,
Discrowned, undaughtered and alone—
Yet shall the great God turn thy fate,
And bring thee back into thy monarch state
And majesty immaculate.
Lo, through hot waverings of the August morn,
Thou givest from thy vasty sides forlorn
Visions of golden treasuries of corn—
Ripe largesse lingering for some bolder heart
That manfully shall take thy part,
And tend thee,
And defend thee,
With antique sinew and with modern art.

1874 1875

ACKNOWLEDGMENT

I

O AGE that half believ'st thou half believ'st,
Half doubt'st the substance of thine own half doubt,
And, half perceiving that thou half perceiv'st,
Stand'st at thy temple door, heart in, head out!
Lo! while thy heart's within, helping the choir,
Without, thine eyes range up and down the time,
Blinking at o'er-bright science, smit with desire
To see and not to see. Hence, crime on crime.
Yea, if the Christ (called thine) now paced yon street,
Thy halfness hot with His rebuke would swell;
Legions of scribes would rise and run and beat
His fair intolerable Wholeness twice to hell.
Nay (so, dear Heart, thou whisperest in my soul),
'Tis a half time, yet Time will make it whole.

II

Now at thy soft recalling voice I rise
Where thought is lord o'er Time's complete estate,
Like as a dove from out the gray sedge flies
To tree-tops green where cooes his heavenly mate.
From these clear coverts high and cool I see
How every time with every time is knit,
And each to all is mortised cunningly,
And none is sole or whole, yet all are fit.
Thus, if this Age but as a comma show
'Twixt weightier clauses of large-worded years,
My calmer soul scorns not the mark: I know
This crooked point Time's complex sentence clears.
Yet more I learn while, Friend! I sit by thee:
Who sees all time, sees all eternity.

III

If I do ask, How God can dumbness keep
While Sin creeps grinning through His house of Time,
Stabbing His saintliest children in their sleep,
And staining holy walls with clots of crime?—
Or, How may He whose wish but names a fact
Refuse what miser's-scanting of supply
Would richly glut each void where man hath lacked
Of grace or bread?—or, How may Power deny
Wholeness to th' almost-folk that hurt our hope—
These heart-break Hamlets who so barely fail
In life or art that but a hair's more scope
Had set them fair on heights they ne'er may scale?—
Somehow by thee, dear Love, I win content:
Thy Perfect stops th' Imperfect's argument.

IV

By the more height of thy sweet stature grown,
Twice-eyed with thy gray vision set in mine,
I ken far lands to wifeless men unknown,
I compass stars for one-sexed eyes too fine.
No text on sea-horizons cloudily writ,
No maxim vaguely starred in fields or skies,
But this wise thou-in-me deciphers it:
Oh, thou'rt the Height of heights, the Eye of eyes.
Not hardest Fortune's most unbounded stress
Can blind my soul nor hurl it from on high,
Possessing thee, the self of loftiness,
And very light that Light discovers by.
Howe'er thou turn'st, wrong Earth! still Love's in sight:
For we are taller than the breadth of night.

1874–5 1876

ROSE–MORALS

I. RED

WOULD that my songs might be
What roses make by day and night—
Distillments of my clod of misery
Into delight.

Soul, could'st thou bare thy breast
As yon red rose, and dare the day,
All clean, and large, and calm with velvet rest?
Say yea—say yea!

Ah, dear my Rose, good-bye;
The wind is up; so; drift away.
That songs from me as leaves from thee may fly,
I strive, I pray.

II. WHITE

Soul, get thee to the heart
Of yonder tuberose: hide thee there—
There breathe the meditations of thine art
Suffused with prayer.

Of spirit grave yet light,
How fervent fragrances uprise
Pure-born from these most rich and yet most white
Virginities!
Mulched with unsavory death,
Grow, Soul! unto such white estate,
That virginal-prayerful art shall be thy breath,
Thy work, thy fate.

1875–76 1876

PSALM OF THE WEST

LAND of the willful gospel, thou worst and thou best;
Tall Adam of lands, new-made of the dust of the West;
Thou wroughtest alone in the Garden of God, unblest
Till He fashioned lithe Freedom to lie for thine Eve on thy breast—
Till out of thy heart's dear neighborhood, out of thy side,
He fashioned an intimate Sweet one and brought thee a Bride.
Cry hail! nor bewail that the wound of her coming was wide.
Lo, Freedom reached forth where the world as an apple hung red;
Let us taste the whole radiant round of it, gayly she said:
If we die, at the worst we shall lie as the first of the dead.
Knowledge of Good and of Ill, O Land! she hath given thee;
Perilous godhoods of choosing have rent thee and riven thee;
Will's high adoring to Ill's low exploring hath driven thee—
Freedom, thy Wife, hath uplifted thy life and clean shriven thee!
Her shalt thou clasp for a balm to the scars of thy breast,
Her shalt thou kiss for a calm to thy wars of unrest,
Her shalt extol in the psalm of the soul of the West.
For Weakness, in freedom, grows stronger than Strength with a chain;
And Error, in freedom, will come to lamenting his stain,
Till freely repenting he whiten his spirit again;
And Friendship, in freedom, will blot out the bounding of race;

And straight Law, in freedom, will curve to the rounding of grace;
And Fashion, in freedom, will die of the lie in her face;
And Desire flame white on the sense as a fire on a height,
And Sex flame white in the soul as a star in the night,
And Marriage plight sense unto soul as the two-colored light
Of the fire and the star shines one with a duplicate might;
And Science be known as the sense making love to the All,
And Art be known as the soul making love to the All,
And Love be known as the marriage of man with the All—
Till Science to knowing the Highest shall lovingly turn,
Till Art to loving the Highest shall consciously burn,
Till Science to Art as a man to a woman shall yearn,
—Then morn!
When Faith from the wedding of Knowing and Loving shall purely be born,
And the Child shall smile in the West, and the West to the East give morn,
And the Time in that ultimate Prime shall forget old regretting and scorn,
Yea, the stream of the light shall give off in a shimmer the dream of the night forlorn.

Once on a time a soul
Too full of his dole
In a querulous dream went crying from pole to pole—
Went sobbing and crying
For ever a sorrowful song of living and dying,
How *life was the dropping and death the drying*
Of a Tear that fell in a day when God was sighing.
And ever Time tossed him bitterly to and fro
As a shuttle inlaying a perilous warp of woe
In the woof of things from terminal snow to snow,
Till, lo!
Rest.

And he sank on the grass of the earth as a lark on its nest,
And he lay in the midst of the way from the east to the west.
Then the East came out from the east and the West from the west,
And, behold! in the gravid deeps of the lower dark,
While, above, the wind was fanning the dawn as a spark,
The East and the West took form as the wings of a lark.
One wing was feathered with facts of the uttermost Past,
And one with the dreams of a prophet; and both sailed fast
And met where the sorrowful Soul on the earth was cast.
Then a Voice said: *Thine, if thou lovest enough to use;*
But another: *To fly and to sing is pain: refuse!*
Then the Soul said: *Come, O my wings! I cannot but choose.*
And the Soul was a-tremble like as a new-born thing,
Till the spark of the dawn wrought a conscience in heart as in wing,
Saying, *Thou art the lark of the dawn; it is time to sing.*

Then that artist began in a lark's low circling to pass;
And first he sang at the height of the top of the grass
A song of the herds that are born and die in the mass.
And next he sang a celestial-passionate round
At the height of the lips of a woman above the ground,
How *Love was a fair true Lady, and Death a wild hound,*
And she called, and he licked her hand and with girdle was bound.
And then with a universe-love he was hot in the wings,
And the sun stretched beams to the worlds as the shining strings
Of the large hid harp that sounds when an all-lover sings;
And the sky's blue traction prevailed o'er the earth's in might,

And the passion of flight grew mad with the glory of height
And the uttering of song was like to the giving of light;
And he learned that hearing and seeing wrought nothing alone,
And that music on earth much light upon Heaven had thrown,
And he melted-in silvery sunshine with silvery tone;
And the spirals of music e'er higher and higher he wound
Till the luminous cinctures of melody up from the ground
Arose as the shaft of a tapering tower of sound—
Arose for an unstricken full-finished Babel of sound.
But God was not angry, nor ever confused his tongue,
For not out of selfish nor impudent travail was wrung
The song of all men and all things that the all-lover sung.
Then he paused at the top of his tower of song on high,
And the voice of the God of the artist from far in the sky
Said, *Son, look down: I will cause that a Time gone by*
Shall pass, and reveal his heart to thy loving eye.

Far spread, below,
The sea that fast hath locked in his loose flow
All secrets of Atlantis' drownèd woe
Lay bound about with night on every hand,
Save down the eastern brink a shining band
Of day made out a little way from land.
Then from that shore the wind upbore a cry:
Thou Sea, thou Sea of Darkness! why, oh why
Dost waste thy West in unthrift mystery?
But ever the idiot sea-mouths foam and fill,
And never a wave doth good for man or ill,
And Blank is king, and Nothing hath his will;
And like as grim-beaked pelicans level file
Across the sunset toward their nightly isle
On solemn wings that wave but seldomwhile,
So leanly sails the day behind the day
To where the Past's lone Rock o'erglooms the spray,
And down its mortal fissures sinks away.

Master, Master, break this ban:
The wave lacks Thee.
Oh, is it not to widen man
Stretches the sea?
Oh, must the sea-bird's idle van
Alone be free?

Into the Sea of the Dark doth creep
Björne's pallid sail,
As the face of a walker in his sleep,
Set rigid and most pale,
About the night doth peer and peep
In a dream of an ancient tale.

Lo, here is made a hasty cry:
Land, land, upon the west!—
God save such land! Go by, go by:
Here may no mortal rest,
Where this waste hell of state doth lie
And grind the glacier's breast.

The sail goeth limp: hey, flap and strain!
Round eastward slanteth the mast;
As the sleep-walker waked with pain,
White-clothed in the midnight blast,
Doth stare and quake, and stride again
To houseward all aghast.

Yet as, *A ghost!* his household cry:
He hath followed a ghost in flight.
Let us see the ghost—his household fly
With lamps to search the night—
So Norsemen's sails run out and try
The Sea of the Dark with light.

Stout Are Marson, southward whirled
From out the tempest's hand,
Doth skip the sloping of the world
To Huitramannaland,
Where Georgia's oaks with moss-beards curled
Wave by the shining strand,

And sway in sighs from Florida's Spring
Or Carolina's Palm—
What time the mocking-bird doth bring
The woods his artist's-balm,

Singing the Song of Everything
Consummate-sweet and calm—

Land of large merciful-hearted skies,
Big bounties, rich increase,
Green rests for Trade's blood-shotten eyes,
For o'er-beat brains surcease,
For Love the dear woods' sympathies,
For Grief the wise woods' peace,
For Need rich givings of hid powers
In hills and vales quick-won,
For Greed large exemplary flowers
That ne'er have toiled nor spun,
For Heat fair-tempered winds and showers,
For Cold the neighbor sun.

Land where the Spirits of June-Heat
From out their forest-maze
Stray forth at eve with loitering feet,
And fervent hymns upraise
In bland accord and passion sweet
Along the Southern ways:—

"O Darkness, tawny Twin whose Twin hath ceased,
Thou Odor from the day-flower's crushing born,
Thou visible Sigh out of the mournful East,
That cannot see her lord again till morn:
O Leaves, with hollow palms uplifted high
To catch the stars' most sacred rain of light:
O pallid Lily-petals fain to die
Soul-stung by subtle passion of the night:
O short-breath'd Winds beneath the gracious moon
Running mild errands for mild violets,
Or carrying sighs from the red lips of June
What wavering way the odor-current sets:
O Stars wreathed vinewise round yon heavenly dells,
Or thrust from out the sky in curving sprays,
Or whorled, or looped with pendent flower-bells,
Or bramble-tangled in a brilliant maze,
Or lying like young lilies in a lake
About the great white Lily of the moon,
Or drifting white from where in heaven shake
Star-portraitures of apple trees in June,
Or lapp'd as leaves of a great rose of stars,
Or shyly clambering up cloud-lattices,
Or trampled pale in the red path of Mars,
Or trim-set quaint in gardeners'-fantasies:
O long June Night-sounds crooned among the leaves;
O whispered confidence of Dark and Green;
O murmurs in old moss about old eaves;
O tinklings floating over water-sheen."

Then Leif, bold son of Eric the Red,
To the South of the West doth flee—
Past slaty Helluland is sped,
Past Markland's woody lea,
Till round about fair Vinland's head,
Where Taunton helps the sea,

The Norseman calls, the anchor falls,
The mariners hurry a-strand:
They wassail with fore-drunken skals
Where prophet wild grapes stand;
They lift the Leifsbooth's hasty walls
They stride about the land—

New England, thee! whose ne'er-spent wine
As blood doth stretch each vein,
And urge thee, sinewed like thy vine,
Through peril and all pain
To grasp Endeavor's towering Pine,
And, once ahold, remain—

Land where the strenuous-handed Wind
With sarcasm of a friend
Doth smite the man would lag behind
To frontward of his end;
Yea, where the taunting fall and grind
Of Nature's Ill doth send

Such mortal challenge of a clown
Rude-thrust upon the soul,
That men but smile where mountains frown
Or scowling waters roll,
And Nature's front of battle down
Do hurl from pole to pole.

Now long the Sea of Darkness glimmers low
With sails from Northland flickering to and
fro—
Thorwald, Karlsefne, and those twin heirs of
woe,
Hellboge and Finnge, in treasonable bed
Slain by the ill-born child of Eric Red,
Freydisa false. Till, as much time is fled,
Once more the vacant airs with darkness fill,
Once more the wave doth never good nor ill,
And Blank is king, and Nothing works his will;
And leanly sails the day behind the day
To where the Past's lone Rock o'erglooms
the spray,
And down its mortal fissures sinks away,
As when the grim-beaked pelicans level file
Across the sunset to their seaward isle
On solemn wings that wave but seldomwhile.

Master, Master, poets sing;
The Time calls Thee;
Yon Sea binds hard on everything
Man longs to be:
Oh, shall the sea-bird's aimless wing
Alone move free?

Santa Maria, well thou tremblest down the
wave,
Thy *Pinta* far abow, thy *Niña* nigh astern:
Columbus stands in the night alone, and, passing grave,
Yearns o'er the sea as tones o'er under-
silence yearn.
Heartens his heart as friend befriends his friend
less brave,
Makes burn the faiths that cool, and cools
the doubts that burn:—

I

"'Twixt this and dawn, three hours my soul
will smite
With prickly seconds, or less tolerably
With dull-blade minutes flatwise slap-
ping me.
Wait, Heart! Time moves.—Thou lithe
young Western Night,
Just-crownèd king, slow riding to thy right,
Would God that I might straddle mutiny
Calm as thou sitt'st yon never-managed
sea,
Balk'st with his balking, fliest with his flight,
Giv'st supple to his rearings and his falls,
Nor dropp'st one coronal star about thy
brow
Whilst ever dayward thou art steadfast
drawn!
Yea, would I rode these mad contentious
brawls
No damage taking from their If and How,
Nor no result save galloping to my
Dawn!

II

"My Dawn? my Dawn? How if it never
break?
How if this West by other Wests is pieced,
And these by vacant Wests on Wests in-
creased—
One Pain of Space, with hollow ache on ache
Throbbing and ceasing not for Christ's own
sake?—
Big perilous theorem, hard for king and
priest:
*Pursue the West but long enough, 'tis
East!*
Oh, if this watery world no turning take!
Oh, if for all my logic, all my dreams,
Provings of that which is by that which
seems,
Fears, hopes, chills, heats, hastes, patiences,
droughts, tears,
Wife-grievings, slights on love, embezzled
years,
Hates, treaties, scorns, upliftings, loss and
gain,—
This earth, no sphere, be all one sickening
plane!

III

"Or, haply, how if this contrarious West,
That me by turns hath starved, by turns
hath fed,
Embraced, disgraced, beat back, solicited,
Have no fixed heart of Law within his breast,
Or with some different rhythm doth e'er
contest
Nature in the East? Why, 'tis but three
weeks fled
I saw my Judas needle shake his head
And flout the Pole that, east, he Lord con-
fessed!
God! if this West should own some other
Pole,

And with his tangled ways perplex my soul
Until the maze grow mortal, and I die
Where distraught Nature clean hath gone astray,
On earth some other wit than Time's at play,
Some other God than mine above the sky!

IV

"Now speaks mine other heart with cheerier seeming:
Ho, Admiral! o'er-defalking to thy crew
Against thyself, thyself far overfew
To front yon multitudes of rebel scheming?
Come, ye wild twenty years of heavenly dreaming!
Come, ye wild weeks since first this canvas drew
Out of vexed Palos ere the dawn was blue,
O'er milky waves about the bows full-creaming!
Come set me round with many faithful spears
Of confident remembrance—how I crushed
Cat-lived rebellions, pitfalled treasons, hushed
Scared husbands' heart-break cries on distant wives,
Make cowards blush at whining for their lives,
Watered my parching souls, and dried their tears.

V

"Ere we Gomera cleared, a coward cried,
Turn, turn: here be three caravels ahead,
From Portugal, to take us: we are dead!
Hold Westward, pilot, calmly I replied.
So when the last land down the horizon died,
Go back, go back! they prayed: *our hearts are lead.*—
Friends, we are bound into the West, I said.
Then passed the wreck of a mast upon our side.
See (so they wept) *God's Warning! Admiral, turn!*—
Steersman, I said, *hold straight into the West.*
Then down the night we saw the meteor burn.
So do the very heavens in fire protest:
Good Admiral, put about! O Spain, dear Spain!—
Hold straight into the West, I said again.

VI

"Next drive we o'er the slimy-weeded sea.
Lo! herebeneath (another coward cries)
The cursèd land of sunk Atlantis lies:
This slime will suck us down—turn while thou'rt free!—
But no! I said, *Freedom bears West for me!*
Yet when the long-time stagnant winds arise,
And day by day the keel to westward flies,
My Good my people's Ill doth come to be:
Ever the winds into the West do blow;
Never a ship, once turned, might homeward go;
Meanwhile we speed into the lonesome main.
For Christ's sake, parley, Admiral! Turn, before
We sail outside all bounds of help from pain!—
Our help is in the West, I said once more.

VII

"So when there came a mighty cry of *Land!*
And we clomb up and saw, and shouted strong
Salve Regina! all the ropes along,
But knew at morn how that a counterfeit band
Of level clouds had aped a silver strand;
So when we heard the orchard-bird's small song,
And all the people cried, *A hellish throng*
To tempt us onward by the Devil planned,
Yea, all from hell—keen heron, fresh green weeds,
Pelican, tunny-fish, fair tapering reeds,
Lie-telling lands that ever shine and die
In clouds of nothing round the empty sky.
Tired Admiral, get thee from this hell, and rest!—
Steersman, I said, *hold straight into the West.*

VIII

"I marvel how mine eye, ranging the Night,
From its big circling ever absently
Returns, thou large low Star, to fix on thee.

Maria! Star? No star: a Light, a Light!
Wouldst leap ashore, Heart? Yonder burns
—a Light.
Pedro Gutierrez, wake! come up to me.
I prithee stand and gaze about the sea:
What seest? *Admiral, like as land—a Light!*
Well! Sanchez of Segovia, come and try:
What seest? *Admiral, naught but sea and sky!*
Well! But *I* saw It. Wait! the Pinta's gun!
Why, look, 'tis dawn, the land is clear:
'tis done!
Two dawns do break at once from Time's
full hand—
God's, East—mine, West: good friends, behold my Land!"

Master, Master! faster fly
Now the hurrying seasons by;
Now the Sea of Darkness wide
Rolls in light from side to side;
Mark, slow drifting to the West
Down the trough and up the crest,
Yonder piteous heartsease petal
Many-motioned rise and settle—
Petal cast a-sea from land
By the awkward-fingered Hand
That, mistaking Nature's course,
Tears the love it fain would force—
Petal calm of heartsease flower
Smiling sweet on tempest sour,
Smiling where by crest and trough
Heartache Winds at heartsease scoff,
Breathing mild perfumes of prayer
'Twixt the scolding sea and air.

Mayflower, piteous Heartsease Petal!
Suavely down the sea-troughs settle,
Gravely breathe perfumes of prayer
'Twixt the scolding sea and air,
Bravely up the sea-hills rise—
Sea-hills slant thee toward the skies.
Master, hold disaster off
From the crest and from the trough;
Heartsease, on the heartache sea
God, thy God, will pilot thee.

Mayflower, Ship of Faith's best Hope!
Thou art sure if all men grope;
Mayflower, Ship of Hope's best Faith!
All is true the great God saith;
Mayflower, Ship of Charity!
Love is Lord of land and sea.
Oh, with love and love's best care
Thy large godly freightage bear—
Godly Hearts that, Grails of gold,
Still the blood of Faith do hold.

Now bold Massachusetts clear
Cuts the rounding of the sphere.
Out the anchor, sail no more,
Lay us by the Future's shore—
Not the shore we sought, 'tis true,
But the time is come to do.
Leap, dear Standish, leap and wade;
Bradford, Hopkins, Tilley, wade:
Leap and wade ashore and kneel—
God be praised that steered the keel!
Home is good and soft is rest,
Even in this jagged West:
Freedom lives, and Right shall stand;
Blood of Faith is in the land.

Then in what time the primal icy years
Scraped slowly o'er the Puritans' hopes and
fears,
Like as great glaciers built of frozen tears,
The Voice from far within the secret sky
Said, *Blood of Faith ye have? So; let us try.*
And presently
The anxious-masted ships that westward
fare,
Cargo'd with trouble and a-list with care,
Their outraged decks hot back to England
bear,
Then come again with stowage of worse
weight,
Battle, and tyrannous Tax, and Wrong, and
Hate,
And all bad items of Death's perilous freight.

O'er Cambridge set the yeomen's mark:
Climb, patriot, through the April dark.
O lanthorn! kindle fast thy light,
Thou budding star in the April night,
For never a star more news hath told,
Or later flame in heaven shall hold.
Ay, lanthorn on the North Church tower,
When that thy church hath had her hour,
Still from the top of Reverence high
Shalt thou illume Fame's ampler sky;
For, statured large o'er town and tree,
Time's tallest Figure stands by thee,
And, dim as now thy wick may shine
The Future lights his lamp at thine.

Now haste thee while the way is clear,
Paul Revere!
Haste, Dawes! but haste thou not, O Sun!
To Lexington.

Then Devens looked and saw the light:
He got him forth into the night,
And watched alone on the river-shore,
And marked the British ferrying o'er.

John Parker! rub thine eyes and yawn:
But one o'clock and yet 'tis Dawn!
Quick, rub thine eyes and draw thy hose:
The Morning comes ere darkness goes.
Have forth and call the yeomen out,
For somewhere, somewhere close about
Full soon a Thing must come to be
Thine honest eyes shall stare to see—
Full soon before thy patriot eyes
Freedom from out of a Wound shall rise.

Then haste ye, Prescott and Revere!
Bring all the men of Lincoln here;
Let Chelmsford, Littleton, Carlisle,
Let Acton, Bedford, hither file—
Oh hither file, and plainly see
Out of a wound leap Liberty.
Say, Woodman April! all in green,
Say, Robin April! hast thou seen
In all thy travel round the earth
Ever a morn of calmer birth?
But Morning's eye alone serene
Can gaze across yon village-green
To where the trooping British run
Through Lexington.

Good men in fustian, stand ye still;
The men in red come o'er the hill.
Lay down your arms, damned Rebels! cry
The men in red full haughtily.
But never a grounding gun is heard;
The men in fustian stand unstirred;
Dead calm, save maybe a wise bluebird
Puts in his little heavenly word.
O men in red! if ye but knew
The half as much as bluebirds do,
Now in this little tender calm
Each hand would out, and every palm
With patriot palm strike brotherhood's stroke
Or ere these lines of battle broke.

O men in red! if ye but knew
The least of the all that bluebirds do,
Now in this little godly calm
Yon voice might sing the Future's Psalm—
The Psalm of Love with the brotherly eyes
Who pardons and is very wise—
Yon voice that shouts, high-hoarse with ire,
Fire!
The red-coats fire, the homespuns fall:
The homespuns' anxious voices call,
Brother, art hurt? and *Where hit, John?*
And, *Wipe this blood*, and *Men, come on*,
And, *Neighbor, do but lift my head*,
And *Who is wounded? Who is dead?*
Seven are killed. My God! my God!
Seven lie dead on the village sod.
Two Harringtons, Parker, Hadley, Brown,
Monroe and Porter,—these are down.
Nay, look! Stout Harrington not yet dead!
He crooks his elbow, lifts his head.
He lies at the step of his own house-door;
He crawls and makes a path of gore.
The wife from the window hath seen, and rushed;
He hath reached the step, but the blood hath gushed;
He hath crawled to the step of his own house-door,
But his head hath dropped: he will crawl no more.
Clasp, Wife, and kiss, and lift the head:
Harrington lies at his doorstep dead.

But, O ye Six that round him lay
And bloodied up that April day!
As Harrington fell, ye likewise fell—
At the door of the House wherein ye dwell;
As Harrington came, ye likewise came
And died at the door of your House of Fame.

Go by, old Field of Freedom's hopes and fears;
Go by, old Field of Brothers' hate and tears:
Behold! yon home of Brothers' Love appears
Set in the burnished silver of July,
On Schuylkill wrought as in old broidery
Clasped hands upon a shining baldric lie,
New Hampshire, Georgia, and the mighty ten

That lie between, have heard the huge-nibbed pen
Of Jefferson tell the rights of man to men.
They sit in the reverend Hall: *Shall we declare?*
Floats round about the anxious-quivering air
'Twixt narrow Schuylkill and broad Delaware.
Already, Land! thou *hast* declared: 'tis done.
Ran ever clearer speech than that did run
When the sweet Seven died at Lexington?
Canst legibler write than Concord's large-stroked Act,
Or when at Bunker Hill the clubbed guns cracked?
Hast ink more true than blood, or pen than fact?
Nay, as the poet mad with heavenly fires
Flings men his song white-hot, then back retires,
Cools heart, broods o'er the song again, inquires,
Why did I this, why that? and slowly draws
From Art's unconscious act Art's conscious laws;
So, Freedom, writ, declares her writing's cause.
All question vain, all chill foreboding vain.
Adams, ablaze with faith, is hot and fain;
And he, straight-fibred Soul of mighty grain,
Deep-rooted Washington, afire, serene—
Tall Bush that burns, yet keeps its substance green—
Sends daily word, of import calm yet keen,
Warm from the front of battle, till the fire
Wraps opposition in and flames yet higher,
And Doubt's thin tissues flash where Hope's aspire;
And, *Ay, declare*, and ever strenuous *Ay*
Falls from the Twelve, and Time and Nature cry
Consent with kindred burnings of July;
And delegate Dead from each past age and race,
Viewless to man, in large procession pace
Downward athwart each set and steadfast face,
Responding *Ay* in many tongues; and lo!
Manhood and Faith and Self and Love and Woe
And Art and Brotherhood and Learning go
Rearward the files of dead, and softly say
Their saintly *Ay*, and softly pass away
By airy exits of that ample day.
Now fall the chill reactionary snows
Of man's defect, and every wind that blows
Keeps back the Spring of Freedom's perfect Rose.
Now naked feet with crimson fleck the ways,
And Heaven is stained with flags that mutinies raise,
And Arnold-spotted move the creeping days.
Long do the eyes that look from Heaven see
Time smoke, as in the spring the mulberry tree,
With buds of battles opening fitfully,
Till Yorktown's winking vapors slowly fade,
And Time's full top casts down a pleasant shade
Where Freedom lies unarmed and unafraid.

Master, ever faster fly
Now the vivid seasons by;
Now the glittering Western land
Twins the day-lit Eastern Strand;
Now white Freedom's sea-bird wing
Roams the Sea of Everything;
Now the freemen to and fro
Bind the tyrant sand and snow,
Snatching Death's hot bolt ere hurled,
Flash new Life about the world,
Sun the secrets of the hills,
Shame the gods' slow-grinding mills,
Prison Yesterday in Print,
Read Tomorrow's weather-hint,
Haste before the halting Time,
Try new virtue and new crime,
Mould new faiths, devise new creeds,
Run each road that frontward leads,
Driven by an Onward-ache,
Scorning souls that circles make.
Now, O Sin! O Love's lost Shame!
Burns the land with redder flame:
North in line and South in line

Yell the charge and spring the mine.
Heartstrong South would have his way,
Headstrong North hath said him nay:
O strong Heart, strong Brain, beware!
Hear a Song from out the air:

I

"Lists all white and blue in the skies;
And the people hurried amain
To the Tournament under the ladies' eyes
Where jousted Heart and Brain.

II

"*Blow, herald, blow!* There entered Heart,
A youth in crimson and gold.
Blow, herald, blow! Brain stood apart,
Steel-armored, glittering, cold.

III

"Heart's palfrey caracoled gayly round,
Heart tra-li-raed merrily;
But Brain sat still, with never a sound—
Full cynical-calm was he.

IV

"Heart's helmet-crest bore favors three
From his lady's white hand caught;
Brain's casque was bare as Fact—not he
Or favor gave or sought.

V

"*Blow, herald, blow!* Heart shot a glance
To catch his lady's eye;
But Brain looked straight a-front, his lance
To aim more faithfully.

VI

"They charged, they struck; both fell, both bled;
Brain rose again, ungloved;
Heart fainting smiled, and softly said,
My love to my Beloved."

Heart and Brain! no more be twain;
Throb and think, one flesh again!
Lo! they weep, they turn, they run;
Lo! they kiss: Love, thou art one!

Now the Land, with drying tears,
Counts him up his flocks of years,
"See," he says, "my substance grows;
Hundred-flocked my Herdsman goes,
Hundred-flocked my Herdsman stands
On the Past's broad meadow-lands,
Come from where ye mildly graze,
Black herds, white herds, nights and days.
Drive them homeward, Herdsman Time,
From the meadows of the Prime:
I will feast my house, and rest.
Neighbor East, come over West;
Pledge me in good wine and words
While I count my hundred herds,
Sum the substance of my Past
From the first unto the last,
Chanting o'er the generous brim
Cloudy memories yet more dim,
Ghostly rhymes of Norsemen pale
Staring by old Björne's sail,
Strains more noble of that night
Worn Columbus saw his Light,
Psalms of still more heavenly tone,
How the Mayflower tossed alone,
Olden tale and later song
Of the Patriot's love and wrong,
Grandsire's ballad, nurse's hymn—
Chanting o'er the sparkling brim
Till I shall from first to last
Sum the substance of my Past."

Then called the Artist's God from in the sky:
"This Time shall show by dream and mystery
The heart of all his matter to thine eye.
Son, study stars by looking down in streams,
Interpret that which is by that which seems,
And tell thy dreams in words which are but dreams."

I

The Master with His lucent hand
Pinched up the atom hills and plains
O'er all the moiety of land
The ocean-bounded West contains:
The dust lay dead upon the calm
And mighty middle of His palm.

II

And lo! He wrought full tenderly,
And lo! He wrought with love and might,
And lo! He wrought a thing to see
Was marvel in His people's sight:
He wrought His image dead and small,
A nothing fashioned like an All.

III

Then breathed He softly on the dead:
"Live Self!—thou part, yet none, of Me;
Dust for humility," He said,
"And my warm breath for Charity.
Behold my latest work, thou Earth!
The Self of Man is taking birth."

IV

Then, Land, tall Adam of the West,
Thou stood'st upon the springy sod,
Thy large eye ranging self-possest,
Thy limbs the limbs of God's young god,
Thy Passion murmuring *I will*—
Lord of the Lordship Good-and-Ill.

V

O manful arms, of supple size
To clasp a world or a waist as well!
O manful eyes, to front the skies
Or look much pity down on hell!
O manful tongue, to work and sing,
And soothe a child and dare a king!

VI

O wonder! Now thou sleep'st in pain,
Like as some dream thy soul did grieve:
God wounds thee, heals thee whole again,
And calls thee trembling to thine Eve.
Wide-armed, thou dropp'st on knightly knee:
Dear Love, Dear Freedom, go with me!

VII

Then all the beasts before thee passed—
Beast War, Oppression, Murder, Lust,
False Art, False Faith, slow skulking last—
And out of Time's thick-rising dust
Thy Lord said, "Name them, tame them, Son;
Nor rest, nor rest, till thou hast done."

VIII

Ah, name thou false, or tame thou wrong,
At heart let no man fear for thee:
Thy Past sings ever Freedom's Song,
Thy Future's voice sounds wondrous free;
And Freedom is more large than Crime,
And Error is more small than Time.

IX

Come, thou whole Self of Latter Man!
Come o'er thy realm of Good-and-Ill,
And do, thou Self that say'st *I can*,
And love, thou Self that say'st *I will;*
And prove and know Time's worst and best,
Thou tall young Adam of the West!

1876 1876

EVENING SONG

Look off, dear Love, across the sallow sands,
And mark yon meeting of the sun and sea,
How long they kiss in sight of all the lands.
Ah! longer, longer, we.

Now in the sea's red vintage melts the sun,
As Egypt's pearl dissolved in rosy wine,
And Cleopatra night drinks all. 'Tis done,
Love, lay thine hand in mine.

Come forth, sweet stars, and comfort heaven's heart;
Glimmer, ye waves, round else unlighted sands.
O night! divorce our sun and sky apart,
Never our lips, our hands.

1876 1877

THE STIRRUP-CUP

Death, thou'rt a cordial old and rare:
Look how compounded, with what care!
Time got his wrinkles reaping thee
Sweet herbs from all antiquity.

David to thy distillage went,
Keats, and Gotama excellent,
Omar Khayyam, and Chaucer bright,
And Shakspere for a king-delight.

Then, Time, let not a drop be spilt:
Hand me the cup whene'er thou wilt;
'Tis thy rich stirrup-cup to me;
I'll drink it down right smilingly.

1877 1877

A SONG OF ETERNITY IN TIME

Once, at night, in the manor wood
My Love and I long silent stood,
Amazed that any heavens could
Decree to part us, bitterly repining.

My Love, in aimless love and grief,
Reached forth and drew aside a leaf
That just above us played the thief
And stole our starlight that for us was shining.

A star that had remarked her pain
Shone straightway down that leafy lane,
And wrought his image, mirror-plain,
Within a tear that on her lash hung gleaming.
"Thus Time," I cried, "is but a tear
Some one hath wept 'twixt hope and fear,
Yet in his little lucent sphere
Our star of stars, Eternity, is beaming."

1867–79 1881

SONG OF THE CHATTAHOOCHEE

Out of the hills of Habersham,
Down the valleys of Hall,
I hurry amain to reach the plain,
Run the rapid and leap the fall,
Split at the rock and together again,
Accept my bed, or narrow or wide,
And flee from folly on every side
With a lover's pain to attain the plain
Far from the hills of Habersham,
Far from the valleys of Hall.

All down the hills of Habersham,
All through the valleys of Hall,
The rushes cried *Abide, abide,*
The willful waterweeds held me thrall,
The laving laurel turned my tide,
The ferns and the fondling grass said *Stay,*
The dewberry dipped for to work delay,
And the little reeds sighed *Abide, abide,*
Here in the hills of Habersham,
Here in the valleys of Hall.

High o'er the hills of Habersham,
Veiling the valleys of Hall,
The hickory told me manifold
Fair tales of shade, the poplar tall
Wrought me her shadowy self to hold,
The chestnut, the oak, the walnut, the pine,
Overleaning, with flickering meaning and sign,
Said, *Pass not, so cold, these manifold*
Deep shades of the hills of Habersham,
These glades in the valleys of Hall.

And oft in the hills of Habersham,
And oft in the valleys of Hall,
The white quartz shone, and the smooth brook-stone
Did bar me of passage with friendly brawl,
And many a luminous jewel lone
—Crystals clear or a-cloud with mist,
Ruby, garnet and amethyst—
Made lures with the lights of streaming stone
In the clefts of the hills of Habersham,
In the beds of the valleys of Hall.

But oh, not the hills of Habersham,
And oh, not the valleys of Hall
Avail: I am fain for to water the plain.
Downward the voices of Duty call—
Downward, to toil and be mixed with the main,
The dry fields burn, and the mills are to turn,
And a myriad flowers mortally yearn,
And the lordly main from beyond the plain
Calls o'er the hills of Habersham,
Calls through the valleys of Hall.

1877? 1883

THE REVENGE OF HAMISH

It was three slim does and a ten-tined buck in the bracken lay;
And all of a sudden the sinister smell of a man,
Awaft on a wind-shift, wavered and ran
Down the hill-side and sifted along through the bracken and passed that way.

Then Nan got a-tremble at nostril; she was the daintiest doe;
In the print of her velvet flank on the velvet fern
She reared, and rounded her ears in turn.
Then the buck leapt up, and his head as a king's to a crown did go

Full high in the breeze, and he stood as if Death had the form of a deer;
And the two slim does long lazily stretching arose,
For their day-dream slowlier came to a close,
Till they woke and were still, breath-bound with waiting and wonder and fear.

Then Alan the huntsman sprang over the hillock, the hounds shot by,
The does and the ten-tined buck made a marvellous bound,
The hounds swept after with never a sound,
But Alan loud winded his horn in sign that the quarry was nigh.

For at dawn of that day proud Maclean of Lochbuy to the hunt had waxed wild,
And he cursed at old Alan till Alan fared off with the hounds
For to drive him the deer to the lower glen-grounds:
"I will kill a red deer," quoth Maclean, "in the sight of the wife and the child."

So gayly he paced with the wife and the child to his chosen stand;
But he hurried tall Hamish the henchman ahead: "Go turn,"—
Cried Maclean—"if the deer seek to cross to the burn,
Do thou turn them to me: nor fail, lest thy back be red as thy hand."

Now hard-fortuned Hamish, half blown of his breath with the height of the hill,
Was white in the face when the ten-tined buck and the does
Drew leaping to burn-ward; huskily rose
His shouts, and his nether lip twitched, and his legs were o'er-weak for his will.

So the deer darted lightly by Hamish and bounded away to the burn.
But Maclean never bating his watch tarried waiting below
Still Hamish hung heavy with fear for to go
All the space of an hour; then he went, and his face was greenish and stern,

And his eye sat back in the socket, and shrunken the eyeballs shone,
As withdrawn from a vision of deeds it were shame to see.
"Now, now, grim henchman, what is't with thee?"
Brake Maclean, and his wrath rose red as a beacon the wind hath upblown.

"Three does and a ten-tined buck made out," spoke Hamish, full mild,
"And I ran for to turn, but my breath it was blown, and they passed;
I was weak, for ye called ere I broke me my fast."
Cried Maclean: "Now a ten-tined buck in the sight of the wife and the child

I had killed if the gluttonous kern had not wrought me a snail's own wrong!"
Then he sounded, and down came kinsmen and clansmen all:
"Ten blows, for ten tine, on his back let fall,
And reckon no stroke if the blood follow not at the bite of thong!"

So Hamish made bare, and took him his strokes; at the last he smiled.
"Now I'll to the burn," quoth Maclean, "for it still may be,
If a slimmer-paunched henchman will hurry with me,
I shall kill me the ten-tined buck for a gift to the wife and the child!"

Then the clansmen departed, by this path and that; and over the hill
Sped Maclean with an outward wrath for an inward shame;
And that place of the lashing full quiet became;
And the wife and the child stood sad; and bloody-backed Hamish sat still.

But look! red Hamish has risen; quick about and about turns he.
"There is none betwixt me and the crag-top!" he screams under breath.
Then, livid as Lazarus lately from death,
He snatches the child from the mother, and clambers the crag toward the sea.

Now the mother drops breath; she is dumb, and her heart goes dead for a space,
Till the motherhood, mistress of death, shrieks, shrieks through the glen,
And that place of the lashing is live with men,
And Maclean, and the gillie that told him, dash up in a desperate race.

Not a breath's time for asking; an eye-glance reveals all the tale untold.
They follow mad Hamish afar up the crag toward the sea,
And the lady cries: "Clansmen, run for a fee!—
Yon castle and lands to the two first hands that shall hook him and hold

Fast Hamish back from the brink!"—and ever she flies up the steep,
And the clansmen pant, and they sweat, and they jostle and strain.
But, mother, 'tis vain; but, father, 'tis vain;
Stern Hamish stands bold on the brink, and dangles the child o'er the deep.

Now a faintness falls on the men that run, and they all stand still.
And the wife prays Hamish as if he were God, on her knees,
Crying: "Hamish! O Hamish! but please, but please
For to spare him!" and Hamish still dangles the child, with a wavering will.

On a sudden he turns; with a sea-hawk scream, and a gibe, and a song,
Cries: "So; I will spare ye the child if, in sight of ye all,
Ten blows on Maclean's bare back shall fall,
And ye reckon no stroke if the blood follow not at the bite of the thong!"

Then Maclean he set hardly his tooth to his lip that his tooth was red,
Breathed short for a space, said: "Nay, but it never shall be!
Let me hurl off the damnable hound in the sea!"
But the wife: "Can Hamish go fish us the child from the sea, if dead?

Say yea!—Let them lash *me*, Hamish?"—"Nay!"—"Husband, the lashing will heal;
But, oh, who will heal me the bonny sweet bairn in his grave?
Could ye cure me my heart with the death of a knave?
Quick! Love! I will bare thee—so—kneel!"
Then Maclean 'gan slowly to kneel

With never a word, till presently downward he jerked to the earth.
Then the henchman—he that smote Hamish—would tremble and lag;
"Strike, hard!" quoth Hamish, full stern, from the crag;
Then he struck him, and "One!" sang Hamish, and danced with the child in his mirth.

And no man spake beside Hamish; he counted each stroke with a song.
When the last stroke fell, then he moved him a pace down the height,
And he held forth the child in the heart-aching sight
Of the mother, and looked all pitiful grave, as repenting a wrong.

And there as the motherly arms stretched out with the thanksgiving prayer—
And there as the mother crept up with a fearful swift pace,
Till her finger nigh felt of the bairnie's face—
In a flash fierce Hamish turned round and lifted the child in the air,

And sprang with the child in his arms from the horrible height in the sea,
Shrill screeching, "Revenge!" in the wind-rush; and pallid Maclean,
Age-feeble with anger and impotent pain,
Crawled up on the crag, and lay flat, and locked hold of dead roots of a tree—

And gazed hungrily o'er, and the blood from his back drip-dripped in the brine,
And a sea-hawk flung down a skeleton fish as he flew,
And the mother stared white on the waste of blue,
And the wind drove a cloud to seaward, and the sun began to shine.

1878 1878

THE HARLEQUIN OF DREAMS

Swift, through some trap mine eyes have never found
Dim-panelled in the painted scene of Sleep,
Thou, giant Harlequin of Dreams, dost leap
Upon my spirit's stage. Then Sight and Sound,

Then Space and Time, then Language, Mete and Bound,
And all familiar Forms that firmly keep
Man's reason in the road, change faces, peep
Betwixt the legs and mock the daily round.
Yet thou canst more than mock: sometimes my tears
At midnight break through bounden lids—a sign
Thou hast a heart: and oft thy little leaven
Of dream-taught wisdom works me bettered years.
In one night witch, saint, trickster, fool divine,
I think thou'rt Jester at the Court of Heaven!

1878 1878

REMONSTRANCE

"Opinion, let me alone: I am not thine.
Prim Creed, with categoric point, forbear
To feature me my Lord by rule and line.
Thou canst not measure Mistress Nature's hair,
Not one sweet inch: nay, if thy sight is sharp,
Would'st count the strings upon an angel's harp?
Forbear, forbear.

"Oh let me love my Lord more fathom deep
Than there is line to sound with: let me love
My fellow not as men that mandates keep:
Yea, all that's lovable, below, above,
That let me love by heart, by heart, because
(Free from the penal pressure of the laws)
I find it fair.

"The tears I weep by day and bitter night,
Opinion! for thy sole salt vintage fall.
—As morn by morn I rise with fresh delight,
Time through my casement cheerily doth call
'Nature is new, 'tis birthday every day,
Come feast with me, let no man say me nay,
Whate'er befall.'

"So fare I forth to feast: I sit beside
Some brother bright: but, ere good-morrow's passed,
Burly Opinion wedging in hath cried
'Thou shalt not sit by us, to break thy fast,
Save to our Rubric thou subscribe and swear—
Religion hath blue eyes and yellow hair:
She's Saxon, all.'

"Then, hard a-hungered for my brother's grace
Till well-nigh fain to swear his folly's true,
In sad dissent I turn my longing face
To him that sits on the left: 'Brother,—with you?'
—'Nay, not with me, save thou subscribe and swear
Religion hath black eyes and raven hair:
Nought else is true.'

"Debarred of banquets that my heart could make
With every man on every day of life,
I homeward turn, my fires of pain to slake
In deep endearments of a worshipped wife.
'I love thee well, dear Love,' quoth she, 'and yet
Would that thy creed with mine completely met,
As one, not two.'

"Assassin! Thief! Opinion, 'tis thy work.
By Church, by throne, by hearth, by every good
That's in the Town of Time, I see thee lurk,
And e'er some shadow stays where thou hast stood.
Thou hand'st sweet Socrates his hemlock sour;
Thou sav'st Barabbas in that hideous hour,
And stabb'st the good

"Deliverer Christ; thou rack'st the souls of men;
Thou tossest girls to lions and boys to flames;
Thou hew'st Crusader down by Saracen;
Thou buildest closets full of secret shames;
Indifferent cruel, thou dost blow the blaze
Round Ridley or Servetus; all thy days
Smell scorched; I would

"—Thou base-born Accident of time and place—
Bigot Pretender unto Judgment's throne—
Bastard, that claimest with a cunning face

Those rights the true, true Son of Man doth own
By Love's authority—thou Rebel cold
At head of civil wars and quarrels old—
Thou Knife on a throne—

"I would thou left'st me free, to live with love,
And faith, that through the love of love doth find
My Lord's dear presence in the stars above,
The clods below, the flesh without, the mind
Within, the bread, the tear, the smile.
Opinion, damned Intriguer, gray with guile,
Let me alone."

1878–9 1883

THE CRYSTAL

At midnight, death's and truth's unlocking time,
When far within the spirit's hearing rolls
The great soft rumble of the course of things—
A bulk of silence in a mask of sound,—
When darkness clears our vision that by day
Is sun-blind, and the soul's a ravening owl
For truth and flitteth here and there about
Low-lying woody tracts of time and oft
Is minded for to sit upon a bough,
Dry-dead and sharp, of some long-stricken tree
And muse in that gaunt place,—'twas then my heart,
Deep in the meditative dark, cried out:

"Ye companies of governor-spirits grave,
Bards, and old bringers-down of flaming news
From steep-wall'd heavens, holy malcontents,
Sweet seers, and stellar visionaries, all
That brood about the skies of poesy,
Full bright ye shine, insuperable stars;
Yet, if a man look hard upon you, none
With total lustre blazeth, no, not one
But hath some heinous freckle of the flesh
Upon his shining cheek, not one but winks
His ray, opaqued with intermittent mist
Of defect; yea, you masters all must ask
Some sweet forgiveness, which we leap to give,
We lovers of you, heavenly-glad to meet
Your largesse so with love, and interplight
Your geniuses with our mortalities.

Thus unto thee, O sweetest Shakspere sole,
A hundred hurts a day I do forgive
('Tis little, but, enchantment! 'tis for thee):
Small curious quibble; Juliet's prurient pun
In the poor, pale face of Romeo's fancied death;
Cold rant of Richard; Henry's fustian roar
Which frights away that sleep he invocates;
Wronged Valentine's unnatural haste to yield;
Too-silly shifts of maids that mask as men
In faint disguises that could ne'er disguise—
Viola, Julia, Portia, Rosalind;
Fatigues most drear, and needless overtax
Of speech obscure that had as lief be plain;
Last I forgive (with more delight, because
'Tis more to do) the labored-lewd discourse
That e'en thy young invention's youngest heir
Besmirched the world with.

Father Homer, thee,
Thee also I forgive thy sandy wastes
Of prose and catalogue, thy drear harangues
That tease the patience of the centuries,
Thy sleazy scrap of story,—but a rogue's
Rape of a light-o'-love,—too soiled a patch
To broider with the gods.

Thee, Socrates,
Thou dear and very strong one, I forgive
Thy year-worn cloak, thine iron stringencies
That were but dandy upside-down, thy words
Of truth that, mildlier spoke, had mainlier wrought.

So, Buddha, beautiful! I pardon thee
That all the All thou hadst for needy man
Was Nothing, and thy Best of being was
But not to be.

Worn Dante, I forgive
The implacable hates that in thy horrid hells
Or burn or freeze thy fellows, never loosed
By death, nor time, nor love.

And I forgive
Thee, Milton, those thy comic-dreadful wars
Where, armed with gross and inconclusive steel,
Immortals smite immortals mortalwise
And fill all heaven with folly.

Also thee,
Brave Æschylus, thee I forgive, for that
Thine eye, by bare bright justice basilisked,
Turned not, nor ever learned to look where Love
Stands shining.

So, unto thee, Lucretius mine
(For oh, what heart hath loved thee like to this
That's now complaining?), freely I forgive
Thy logic poor, thine error rich, thine earth
Whose graves eat souls and all.

Yea, all you hearts
Of beauty, and sweet righteous lovers large:
Aurelius fine, oft superfine; mild Saint
A Kempis, overmild; Epictetus,
Whiles low in thought, still with old slavery tinct;
Rapt Behmen, rapt too far; high Swedenborg,
O'ertoppling; Langley, that with but a touch
Of art hadst sung Piers Plowman to the top
Of English songs, whereof 'tis dearest, now,
And most adorable; Cædmon, in the morn
A-calling angels with the cow-herd's call
That late brought up the cattle; Emerson,
Most wise, that yet, in finding Wisdom, lost
Thy Self, sometimes; tense Keats, with angels' nerves
Where men's were better; Tennyson, largest voice
Since Milton, yet some register of wit
Wanting;—all, all, I pardon, ere 'tis asked,
Your more or less, your little mole that marks
You brother and your kinship seals to man.

But Thee, but Thee, O sovereign Seer of time,
But Thee, O poets' Poet, Wisdom's Tongue,
But Thee, O man's best Man, O love's best Love,
O perfect life in perfect labor writ,
O all men's Comrade, Servant, King, or Priest,—
What *if* or *yet*, what mole, what flaw, what lapse,
What least defect or shadow of defect,
What rumor, tattled by an enemy,
Of inference loose, what lack of grace
Even in torture's grasp, or sleep's, or death's,—
Oh, what amiss may I forgive in Thee,
Jesus, good Paragon, thou Crystal Christ?"

1880 1880

HYMNS OF THE MARSHES

I

SUNRISE

In my sleep I was fain of their fellowship, fain
Of the live-oak, the marsh, and the main.
The little green leaves would not let me alone in my sleep;
Up-breathed from the marshes, a message of range and of sweep,
Interwoven with waftures of wild sea-liberties, drifting,
Came through the lapped leaves sifting, sifting,
Came to the gates of sleep.
Then my thoughts, in the dark of the dungeon-keep
Of the Castle of Captives hid in the City of Sleep,
Upstarted, by twos and by threes assembling:
The gates of sleep fell a-trembling
Like as the lips of a lady that forth falter *yes*,
Shaken with happiness:
The gates of sleep stood wide.

I have waked, I have come, my beloved! I might not abide:
I have come ere the dawn, O beloved, my love-oaks, to hide
In your gospelling glooms,—to be
As a lover in heaven, the marsh my marsh and the sea my sea.

Tell me, sweet burly-bark'd, man-bodied Tree
That mine arms in the dark are embracing, dost know
From what fount are these tears at thy feet which flow?
They rise not from reason, but deeper inconsequent deeps.
Reason's not one that weeps.
What logic of greeting lies
Betwixt dear over-beautiful trees and the rain of the eyes?

O cunning green leaves, little masters! like as ye gloss
All the dull-tissued dark with your luminous darks that emboss
The vague blackness of night into pattern and plan,
So,
(But would I could know, but would I could know,)
With your question embroid'ring the dark of the question of man,—
So, with your silences purfling this silence of man
While his cry to the dead for some knowledge is under the ban,
Under the ban,—
So, ye have wrought me
Designs on the night of our knowledge,—yea, ye have taught me,
So,
That haply we know somewhat more than we know.

Ye lispers, whisperers, singers in storms,
Ye consciences murmuring faiths under forms,
Ye ministers meet for each passion that grieves,
Friendly, sisterly, sweetheart leaves,
Oh, rain me down from your darks that contain me
Wisdoms ye winnow from winds that pain me,—
Sift down tremors of sweet-within-sweet
That advise me of more than they bring,—repeat
Me the woods-smell that swiftly but now brought breath
From the heaven-side bank of the river of death,—
Teach me the terms of silence,—preach me
The passion of patience,—sift me,—impeach me,—
And there, oh there
As ye hang with your myriad palms upturned in the air,
Pray me a myriad prayer.

My gossip, the owl,—is it thou
That out of the leaves of the low-hanging bough,
As I pass to the beach, art stirred?
Dumb woods, have ye uttered a bird?

* * *

Reverend Marsh, low-couched along the sea,
Old chemist, rapt in alchemy,
Distilling silence,—lo,
That which our father-age had died to know—
The menstruum that dissolves all matter—thou
Hast found it: for this silence, filling now
The globéd clarity of receiving space,
This solves us all: man, matter, doubt, disgrace,
Death, love, sin, sanity,
Must in yon silence' clear solution lie.
Too clear! That crystal nothing who'll peruse?
The blackest night could bring us brighter news.
Yet precious qualities of silence haunt
Round these vast margins, ministrant.
Oh, if thy soul's at latter gasp for space,
With trying to breathe no bigger than thy race
Just to be fellow'd, when that thou hast found
No man with room, or grace enough of bound
To entertain that New thou tell'st, thou art,—
'Tis here, 'tis here thou canst unhand thy heart
And breathe it free, and breathe it free,
By rangy marsh, in lone sea-liberty.

The tide's at full: the marsh with flooded streams
Glimmers, a limpid labyrinth of dreams.
Each winding creek in grave entrancement lies
A rhapsody of morning-stars. The skies
Shine scant with one forked galaxy,—
The marsh brags ten: looped on his breast they lie.

Oh, what if a sound should be made!
Oh, what if a bound should be laid
To this bow-and-string tension of beauty and silence a-spring,—
To the bend of beauty the bow, or the hold of silence the string!
I fear me, I fear me yon dome of diaphanous gleam
Will break as a bubble o'er-blown in a dream,—
Yon dome of too-tenuous tissues of space and of night,
Over-weighted with stars, over-freighted with light,
Over-sated with beauty and silence, will seem
But a bubble that broke in a dream,
If a bound of degree to this grace be laid,
Or a sound or a motion made.

But no: it is made: list! somewhere,—mystery, where?
In the leaves? in the air?
In my heart? is a motion made:
'Tis a motion of dawn, like a flicker of shade on shade.
In the leaves 'tis palpable: low multitudinous stirring
Upwinds through the woods; the little ones, softly conferring,
Have settled my lord's to be looked for; so; they are still;
But the air and my heart and the earth are a-thrill,—
And look where the wild duck sails round the bend of the river,—
And look where a passionate shiver
Expectant is bending the blades
Of the marsh-grass in serial shimmers and shades,—
And invisible wings, fast fleeting, fast fleeting,
Are beating
The dark overhead as my heart beats,—and steady and free
Is the ebb-tide flowing from marsh to sea—
(Run home, little streams,
With your lapfulls of stars and dreams),—
And a sailor unseen is hoisting a-peak,
For list, down the inshore curve of the creek
How merrily flutters the sail,—
And lo, in the East! Will the East unveil?
The East is unveiled, the East hath confessed
A flush: 'tis dead; 'tis alive: 'tis dead, ere the West
Was aware of it: nay, 'tis abiding, 'tis unwithdrawn:
Have a care, sweet Heaven! 'Tis Dawn.

Now a dream of a flame through that dream of a flush is up rolled:
To the zenith ascending, a dome of undazzling gold
Is builded, in shape as a bee-hive, from out of the sea:
The hive is of gold undazzling, but oh, the Bee,
The star-fed Bee, the build-fire Bee,
Of dazzling gold is the great Sun-Bee
That shall flash from the hive-hole over the sea.

Yet now the dew-drop, now the morning gray,
Shall live their little lucid sober day
Ere with the sun their souls exhale away.
Now in each pettiest personal sphere of dew
The summ'd morn shines complete as in the blue
Big dew-drop of all heaven: with these lit shrines
O'er-silvered to the farthest sea-confines,
The sacramental marsh one pious plain
Of worship lies. Peace to the ante-reign
Of Mary Morning, blissful mother mild,
Minded of nought but peace, and of a child.

Not slower than Majesty moves, for a mean and a measure
Of motion,—not faster than dateless Olympian leisure
Might pace with unblown ample garments from pleasure to pleasure,—
The wave-serrate sea-rim sinks unjarring, unreeling,
Forever revealing, revealing, revealing,
Edgewise, bladewise, halfwise, wholewise,—'tis done!
Good-morrow, lord Sun!
With several voice, with ascription one,
The woods and the marsh and the sea and my soul

Unto thee, whence the glittering stream of all morrows doth roll,
Cry good and past-good and most heavenly morrow, lord Sun.

O Artisan born in the purple,—Workman Heat,—
Parter of passionate atoms that travail to meet
And be mixed in the death-cold oneness,—innermost Guest
At the marriage of elements,—fellow of publicans,—blest
King in the blouse of flame, that loiterest o'er
The idle skies yet laborest fast evermore,—
Thou, in the fine forge-thunder, thou, in the beat
Of the heart of a man, thou Motive,—Laborer Heat:
Yea, Artist, thou, of whose art yon sea's all news,
With his inshore greens and manifold mid-sea blues,
Pearl-glint, shell-tint, ancientest perfectest hues
Ever shaming the maidens,—lily and rose
Confess thee, and each mild flame that glows
In the clarified virginal bosoms of stones that shine,
It is thine, it is thine:

Thou chemist of storms, whether driving the winds a-swirl
Or a-flicker the subtiler essences polar that whirl
In the magnet earth,—yea, thou with a storm for a heart,
Rent with debate, many-spotted with question, part
From part oft sundered, yet ever a globéd light,
Yet ever the artist, ever more large and bright
Than the eye of a man may avail of:—manifold One,
I must pass from thy face, I must pass from the face of the Sun:
Old Want is awake and agog, every wrinkle a-frown;
The worker must pass to his work in the terrible town:
But I fear not, nay, and I fear not the thing to be done;
I am strong with the strength of my lord the Sun:
How dark, how dark soever the race that must needs be run,
I am lit with the Sun.

Oh, never the mast-high run of the seas
Of traffic shall hide thee,
Never the hell-colored smoke of the factories
Hide thee,
Never the reek of the time's fen-politics
Hide thee,
And ever my heart through the night shall with knowledge abide thee,
And ever by day shall my spirit, as one that hath tried thee,
Labor, at leisure, in art,—till yonder beside thee
My soul shall float, friend Sun,
The day being done.

1880 1882

II

INDIVIDUALITY

Sail on, sail on, fair cousin Cloud:
Oh loiter hither from the sea.
Still-eyed and shadow-brow'd,
Steal off from yon far-drifting crowd,
And come and brood upon the marsh with me.

Yon laboring low horizon-smoke,
Yon stringent sail, toil not for thee
Nor me; did heaven's stroke
The whole deep with drown'd commerce choke,
No pitiless tease of risk or bottomry
Would to thy rainy office close
Thy will, or lock mine eyes from tears,
Part wept for traders'-woes,
Part for that ventures mean as those
In issue bind such sovereign hopes and fears.

—Lo, Cloud, thy downward countenance stares
Blank on the blank-faced marsh, and thou
Mindest of dark affairs;
Thy substance seems a warp of cares;
Like late wounds run the wrinkles on thy brow.

Well may'st thou pause, and gloom, and stare,
A visible conscience: I arraign
Thee, criminal Cloud, of rare
Contempts on Mercy, Right, and Prayer,—
Of murders, arsons, thefts,—of nameless stain

(Yet though life's logic grow as gray
As thou, my soul's not in eclipse.)
Cold Cloud, but yesterday
Thy lightning slew a child at play,
And then a priest with prayers upon his lips

For his enemies, and then a bright
Lady that did but ope the door
Upon the storming night
To let a beggar in,—strange spite,—
And then thy sulky rain refused to pour

Till thy quick torch a barn had burned
Where twelve months' store of victual lay,
A widow's sons had earned;
Which done, thy floods with winds returned,—
The river raped their little herd away.

What myriad righteous errands high
Thy flames *might* run on! In that hour
Thou slewest the child, oh why
Not rather slay Calamity,
Breeder of Pain and Doubt, infernal Power?

Or why not plunge thy blades about
Some maggot politician throng
Swarming to parcel out
The body of a land, and rout
The maw-conventicle, and ungorge Wrong?

What the cloud doeth
The Lord knoweth,
The cloud knoweth not.
What the artist doeth,
The Lord knoweth;
Knoweth the artist not?

Well-answered!—O dear artists, ye
—Whether in forms of curve or hue
Or tone your gospels be—
Say wrong *This work is not of me,*
But God: it is not true, it is not true.

Awful is Art because 'tis free.
The artist trembles o'er his plan
Where men his Self must see.
Who made a song or picture, he
Did it, and not another, God nor man.

My Lord is large, my Lord is strong:
Giving, He gave: my me is mine.
How poor, how strange, how wrong,
To dream He wrote the little song
I made to Him with love's unforced design!

Oh, not as clouds dim laws have plann'd
To strike down Good and fight for Ill,—
Oh, not as harps that stand
In the wind and sound the wind's command:
Each artist—gift of terror!—owns his will.

For thee, Cloud,—if thou spend thine all
Upon the South's o'er-brimming sea
That needs thee not; or crawl
To the dry provinces, and fall
Till every convert clod shall give to thee

Green worship; if thou grow or fade,
Bring on delight or misery,
Fly east or west, be made
Snow, hail, rain, wind, grass, rose, light, shade;
What matters it to thee? There is no thee.

Pass, kinsman Cloud, now fair and mild:
Discharge the will that's not thine own.
I work in freedom wild,
But work, as plays a little child,
Sure of the Father, Self, and Love, alone.

1878–9 1882

III

MARSH SONG—AT SUNSET

OVER the monstrous shambling sea,
Over the Caliban sea,
Bright Ariel-cloud, thou lingerest:
Oh wait, oh wait, in the warm red West,—
Thy Prospero I'll be.

Over the humped and fishy sea,
Over the Caliban sea
O cloud in the West, like a thought in the heart
Of pardon, loose thy wing, and start,
And do a grace for me.

Over the huge and huddling sea,
Over the Caliban sea,
Bring hither my brother Antonio,—Man,—
My injurer: night breaks the ban:
Brother, I pardon thee.

1879–80 1882

IV

THE MARSHES OF GLYNN

Glooms of the live-oaks, beautiful-braided and woven
With intricate shades of the vines that myriad-cloven
Clamber the forks of the multiform boughs,—
Emerald twilights,—
Virginal shy lights,
Wrought of the leaves to allure to the whisper of vows,
When lovers pace timidly down through the green colonnades
Of the dim sweet woods, of the dear dark woods,
Of the heavenly woods and glades,
That run to the radiant marginal sand-beach within
The wide sea-marshes of Glynn;—

Beautiful glooms, soft dusks in the noon-day fire,—
Wildwood privacies, closets of lone desire,
Chamber from chamber parted with wavering arras of leaves,—
Cells for the passionate pleasure of prayer to the soul that grieves,
Pure with a sense of the passing of saints through the wood,
Cool for the dutiful weighing of ill with good;—

O braided dusks of the oak and woven shades of the vine,
While the riotous noon-day sun of the June-day long did shine
Ye held me fast in your heart and I held you fast in mine;
But now when the noon is no more, and riot is rest,
And the sun is a-wait at the ponderous gate of the West,
And the slant yellow beam down the wood-aisle doth seem
Like a lane into heaven that leads from a dream,—
Ay, now, when my soul all day hath drunken the soul of the oak,
And my heart is at ease from men, and the wearisome sound of the stroke
Of the scythe of time and the trowel of trade is low,
And belief overmasters doubt, and I know that I know,
And my spirit is grown to a lordly great compass within,
That the length and the breadth and the sweep of the marshes of Glynn
Will work me no fear like the fear they have wrought me of yore
When length was fatigue, and when breadth was but bitterness sore,
And when terror and shrinking and dreary unnamable pain
Drew over me out of the merciless miles of the plain,—

Oh, now, unafraid, I am fain to face
The vast sweet visage of space.
To the edge of the wood I am drawn, I am drawn,
Where the gray beach glimmering runs, as a belt of the dawn,
For a mete and a mark
To the forest-dark:—
So:
Affable live-oak, leaning low,—
Thus—with your favor—soft, with a reverent hand,
(Not lightly touching your person, Lord of the land!)
Bending your beauty aside, with a step I stand
On the firm-packed sand,
Free
By a world of marsh that borders a world of sea.
Sinuous southward and sinuous northward the shimmering band
Of the sand-beach fastens the fringe of the marsh to the folds of the land.
Inward and outward to northward and southward the beach-lines linger and curl
As a silver-wrought garment that clings to and follows the firm sweet limbs of a girl.
Vanishing, swerving, evermore curving again into sight,
Softly the sand-beach wavers away to a dim gray looping of light.
And what if behind me to westward the wall of the woods stands high?

The world lies east: how ample, the marsh and the sea and the sky!
A league and a league of marsh-grass, waist-high, broad in the blade,
Green, and all of a height, and unflecked with a light or a shade,
Stretch leisurely off, in a pleasant plain,
To the terminal blue of the main.

Oh, what is abroad in the marsh and the terminal sea?
Somehow my soul seems suddenly free
From the weighing of fate and the sad discussion of sin,
By the length and the breadth and the sweep of the marshes of Glynn.

Ye marshes, how candid and simple and nothing-withholding and free
Ye publish yourselves to the sky and offer yourselves to the sea!
Tolerant plains, that suffer the sea and the rains and the sun,
Ye spread and span like the catholic man who hath mightily won
God out of knowledge and good out of infinite pain
And sight out of blindness and purity out of a stain.

As the marsh-hen secretly builds on the watery sod,
Behold I will build me a nest on the greatness of God:
I will fly in the greatness of God as the marsh-hen flies
In the freedom that fills all the space 'twixt the marsh and the skies:
By so many roots as the marsh-grass sends in the sod
I will heartily lay me a-hold on the greatness of God:
Oh, like to the greatness of God is the greatness within
The range of the marshes, the liberal marshes of Glynn.

And the sea lends large, as the marsh: lo, out of his plenty the sea
Pours fast: full soon the time of the flood-tide must be:
Look how the grace of the sea doth go
About and about through the intricate channels that flow
Here and there,
Everywhere,
Till his waters have flooded the uttermost creeks and the low-lying lanes,
And the marsh is meshed with a million veins,
That like as with rosy and silvery essences flow
In the rose-and-silver evening glow.
Farewell, my lord Sun!
The creeks overflow: a thousand rivulets run
'Twixt the roots of the sod; the blades of the marsh-grass stir;
Passeth a hurrying sound of wings that westward whirr;
Passeth, and all is still; and the currents cease to run;
And the sea and the marsh are one.

How still the plains of the waters be!
The tide is in his ecstasy.
The tide is at his highest height:
And it is night.

And now from the Vast of the Lord will the waters of sleep
Roll in on the souls of men,
But who will reveal to our waking ken
The forms that swim and the shapes that creep
Under the waters of sleep?
And I would I could know what swimmeth below when the tide comes in
On the length and the breadth of the marvellous marshes of Glynn.

1878 1879

A BALLAD OF TREES AND THE MASTER

INTO the woods my Master went,
Clean forspent, forspent.
Into the woods my Master came,
Forspent with love and shame.
But the olives they were not blind to Him,
The little gray leaves were kind to Him:
The thorn-tree had a mind to Him
When into the woods He came.

Out of the woods my Master went,
And He was well content.
Out of the woods my Master came,
Content with death and shame.
When Death and Shame would woo Him last,
From under the trees they drew Him last:
'Twas on a tree they slew Him—last
When out of the woods He came.

1880 1880

From MUSIC AND POETRY

The hearer of the Seventh Symphony last night and, it may be added, of the descriptive piece called "The Calm of the Sea" will find himself at the verge of a whole new field of appreciation for those pieces if he will remember that the same era which produces Maillet, Darwin, Spencer, Huxley and Tyndall has produced also Beethoven in music and the landscape school in painting. For these three phenomena—the modern scientist, the musician, and the landscape painter—are merely three developments in different directions, of one mighty impulse which under-runs them all. This impulse is that direct sympathy with physical nature which the man of today possesses, and which the man of old did not possess. The Greeks had an intermediate set of beings between him and his mother earth. . . . We are under no such necessity. Our Darwin boldly takes hold of nature as if it were a rose, pulls it to pieces, puts it under the microscope, and reports to us without fear or favor. Beethoven, on the other hand, approaching the same good Nature—from a different direction, with different motives,—and looking upon it with the artist's—not the scientist's—eye, finds it a beautiful whole: he does not analyze, but, pursuing the synthetic process, shows it to us as a perfect rose, reporting his observations to us in terms of harmony. (Pp. 70–71.)

From THE SCIENCE OF ENGLISH VERSE

That all worthy poets belong substantially to the school of David, that it is the poet's business to keep the line of men touching shoulders with each other, that the poet is in charge of all learning to convert it into wisdom, and that therefore a treatise on the poet's method is in its last result a sort of disciplinary preparation and *magister choralis* for the congregation as well as for the preacher of the future,—these will not be regarded merely visionary propositions, and perhaps will be here accepted at least as giving a final unity to the principles now to be set forth. (P. iv f.)

In short, when we hear verse, we *hear* a set of relations between sounds; when we silently read verse, we *see* that which brings to us a set of relations between sounds; when we imagine verse, we *imagine* a set of relations between sounds. (P. 23.)

The study of verse must therefore begin with the study of sounds.

Sounds may be studied with reference to four and only four, particulars. We may observe—

(1) How long a sound lasts (*duration*);
(2) How loud a sound is (*intensity*);
(3) How shrill—that is, how high, as to bass or treble—a sound is (*pitch*);
and
(4) Of what sounds a given sound is composed—for, as in studying colors we find purple composed of red and violet, and the like, so many sounds have been discovered to be made up of other sounds (*tone-color*). (P. 24.)

It will presently be found that the sound-relations which constitute music are the same with those which constitute verse, and that the main distinction between music and verse is, when stated with scientific precision, the difference between the scale of tones used in music and the scale of tones used by the human speaking-voice. (P. 35.)

The art of verse, then, as well as the art of music,—the two species of the genus art of sound,—includes all the three great classes of phenomena summed up under the terms rhythm, tune, and tone-color. We will presently find many problems solved by the full recognition of this fact that there is absolutely no difference between the sound-relations used in music and those used in verse. (P. 48.)

The science of verse, then, observes and classifies all the phenomena of rhythm, of tune, and of tone-color, so far as they can be exhibited to the ear directly by spoken words,—or to the ear, through the eye, by written or printed signs of spoken words,—or to the mind by the conception of spoken words; and,

The science of *English* verse observes and classifies these phenomena so far as they can be indicated through the medium of spoken English words. (P. 58.)

Time is the essential basis of rhythm. "Accent" can effect nothing, except in arranging materials already rhythmical through some temporal recurrence. Possessing a series of sounds temporally equal or temporally proportionate, we can group them into various orders of larger and larger groups, as we shall presently see, by means of accent; but the primordial temporalness is always necessary. (P. 65.)

The great underlying principle, however, of all Shakspere's applications of his technic in practice was a superb confidence in the common rhythmic perception of men and a clear insight into the rhythmic habit of familiar English utterance. This method of working with a constant inward reference to the great average and sum of men, and with an absolute reliance upon their final perception, is the secret of that infinitely-varied rhythm which we find plashing through all the later blank verse of Shakspere; and one of the most frequent means by which he effected these variations without either impairing the type of the verse or straining the habit of utterance out of its familiar course was the artful transference into verse of the actual use which English-speaking people make of the rhythmic accent in their current discourse.

Perhaps every one has observed that particularly in Shakspere's later plays he seems absolutely careless as to what kind of word the rhythmic accent may fall on. Sometimes it is on the article *the*, sometimes the preposition *of*, sometimes the conjunction *and*, sometimes the unaccented syllable of a two-sound word as *quickéns* instead of *quíckens*, and so on.

This apparent carelessness is really perfect art. It is the consummate management of dramatic dialogue in blank verse, by which the wilder rhythmic patterns of ordinary current discourse are woven along through the regular strands of the orderly typic lines. (P. 213.)

But rhythm not only thus appears as perhaps the widest artistic instinct in man: it would seem to be a universal principle throughout nature. Perhaps every one, in these days, is more or less familiar with the complete way in which modern physical science has reduced all that enormous and complex mass of phenomena which we call physical nature to a series of motions. Older conceptions of substance as opposed to form have resolved themselves into the general conception of force producing motion in certain modes. It would seem that the general primordial mode of all these motions which we assemble under the general term "nature" is rhythm. The essential principle of rhythm—the student must have observed—is recurrence at an interval of time which furnishes a unit of measure by which all the times marked-off by the recurrences may be coördinated. Mr. Herbert Spencer claims to have observed such a prevalence of this rhythmic periodicity throughout nature as to convince him that it is universal: and states that this belief is shared by Mr. Tyndall. It would indeed seem that every thing moves to measure (ῥυθμὸς). The spiral distribution of the remote nebulae hints at rhythmic motion: the variable stars brighten and pale at rhythmic intervals; planet, satellite, comet, revolve and return in proportionate periods; the seasons, the magnetic variations, the sun-spots, come and go, orderly; the great tides in the sea, the great trade-winds in the air, flow by rhythmic rule; the terrible sawyer in the Mississippi marks a vertical rhythmus, the sweet long grasses in running brooks a horizontal one; the lungs of the man, the heart of the beast, the cilia of the animalcule, play to and fro with rhythmic systole and diastole. (P. 247 f.)

One of the most striking similes in all literature involves this rhythmic idea. Edgar Poe, in his fantastic *Eureka*, after having detailed the process of the primal diffusion of matter in space, the aggregation of atoms into worlds, the revolution of these worlds for a time, their necessary return after that time into the central sun, and the then necessary re-diffusion of the atoms into space, again to aggregate into worlds, to fall into the central sun, and to be again re-diffused—ever contracting, ever expanding—closes his raptus of thought with declaring that this prodigious process is nothing more than the rhythmic beating of the heart of God. (P. 249.)

And there is yet a more general view of the rhythmic principle which hints that this proportion in which the worlds move and by which "things stand to be good or beautiful" is due to antagonism. Mr. Herbert Spencer has formulated the proposition that where opposing forces act, rhythm appears, and has traced the rhythmic motions of nature to the antagonistic forces there found, such as the two motions which carry the earth towards, and away from, the sun and so result in the periodicity of the earth's progress, and others.

Perhaps this view may be made, without strain, to bind together even facts so remote from each other as the physical and the moral. When we compare what one may call the literal rhythm which rules throughout physical nature, with that metaphorical rhythm or proportion which governs good behavior as well as good art; when we find that opposition in the physical world results in rhythm, and that so opposition in the moral world—the fret, the sting, the thwart, the irreconcilable me as against all other me's, the awful struggle for existence, the desperate friction of individualities, the no of death to all requests—may also result in rhythm; when we perceive that through all those immeasurable agitations which constitute both moral and physical nature this beautiful and orderly principle of rhythm thus swings to and fro like the shuttle of a loom and weaves a definite and comprehensible pattern into the otherwise chaotic fabric of things: we may be able to see dimly into that old Orphic saying of the seer, "The father of metre is rhythm, and the father of rhythm is God." (P. 250.)

And this sketch of the colors of English verse may now be closed with the statement, already partly anticipated in several other connections, that the matters herein treated are only in the nature of hints leading to the widest possible views of poetic form, and by no means laws. For the artist in verse there is no law: the perception and love of beauty constitute the whole outfit; and what is herein set forth is to be taken merely as enlarging that perception and exalting that love. In all cases, the appeal is to the ear; but the ear should, for that purpose, be educated up to the highest possible plane of culture. With this sort of ear understood, one may say that King James has summed up the whole matter in his homely Scotch words: "Zour eare maun be the onely iudge, as of all the other parts of *Flowing*," (that is, of *rhythmic movement*) "the verie twichestane quhairof is musique." (P. 315.)

From LETTERS OF LANIER

[*To* GIBSON PEACOCK]

Baltimore, Dec. 21, 1878

I saw your notice of the "Masque of Poets." The truth is, it is a distressing, an aggravated, yea, an intolerable collection of mediocrity and mere cleverness. Some of the pieces come so near being good that one is ready to tear one's hair and to beat somebody with a stick from pure exasperation that such narrow misses should after all come to no better net result—in the way of art—than so many complete failures. I could find only four poems in the book. As for Guy Vernon, one marvels that a man with any poetic feeling could make so many stanzas of so trivial a thing. It does not even sparkle enough to redeem it as *vers de société*. This is the kind of poetry that is technically called culture-poetry; yet it is in reality the product of a *want* of culture. If these gentlemen and ladies would read the old English poetry—I mean the poetry before Chaucer, the genuine Anglish utterances, from Cædmon in the seventh century to Langland in the fourteenth—they could never be content to put forth these little diffuse prettinesses and dandy kickshaws of verse. . . .

[*To* Gibson Peacock]

Baltimore, June 1, 1880

I've just read your notice of "The Science of English Verse," and cannot help sending a line to say how much it pleases me. It seems a model of the way in which a newspaper should deal with a work of this sort which in the nature of things cannot be fairly described without more space than any ordinary journal can allow.

I was all the more pleased because I had just read a long notice sent me by the ——'s "critic," which, with the best intentions in the world, surely capped the climax of silly misrepresentation. It is perfectly sober to say that if this "critic" had represented Professor Huxley's late treatise on the Crayfish as a cookery-book containing new and ingenious methods of preparing shellfish for the table, and had proceeded to object earnestly that the book was a dangerous one, as stimulating over-nicety in eating,—he would have been every whit as near the truth. Indeed, on thinking of it, I find this is a perfect parallel; for he objected to "The Science of Verse" on the ground that it had "a tendency . . . to exaggerate . . . the undue attention already given to . . . the pretty fripperies of ingenious verse-making!" If the book has one tendency beyond another in this respect, it surely is, as you sensibly say in your last paragraph but one, to make real artists out of those who study it, and to warn off all scribblers from this holy and arduous ground.

But this is the least offence. Although three of the very mottoes on the Titlepage (namely, those of Sir Philip Sidney, of King James, and of Dante) set up the sharpest distinction between Verse and Poetry,—between mere Technic and Inspiration,—and although the Preface presents an ideal of the *poet's* (as distinct from the *versifier's*) mission which culminates in declaring the likeness of all worthy poets to David (who wrote much poetry, but *no verse*),—while, further, the very first ten lines of Chapter I carry on this distinction to what one would think a point infinitely beyond mistake,—in spite of all, the "critic" gravely makes, and as gravely discusses, the assertion that "in Mr. Lanier's book . . . *poetry* . . . is a mere matter of pleasing sounds and pleasing arrangements of sounds!"

This would be a curiosity of woodenness, if it were not still obscured by another assertion: that this "Science of Verse" originates in "a suggestion" made by Edgar Poe as to the "division into long and short syllables,"—which suggestion, he says, "is the key to Mr. Lanier's system"!

It would be quite as accurate to say that Professor Huxley's argument from the transition forms of the horse in proof of the evolution of species was suggested by King Richard the Third's exclamation of "A horse! a horse! my kingdom for a horse!"

The Easter-card with the lovely design of Corn has been in my work-room's most prominent niche, and is the constant admiration of my visitors, who always quickly recognize its propriety. Tell Maria—between two kisses—that nothing but outrageous absorption could have made me fail so long to acknowledge what has given us all so much pleasure.

—But this letter will make you perspire, with the very sight of its five pages: and so, God bless you.

Your friend, Sidney L.

[*To* His Wife]

September, 1871

And to-night I come out of what might have been heaven. . . .

'Twas opening night of Theo. Thomas' orchestra, at Central Park Garden, and I could not resist the temptation to go and bathe in the sweet amber seas of the music of this fine orchestra, and so I went, and tugged me through a vast crowd, and, after standing some while, found a seat, and the *bâton* tapped and waved, and I plunged into the sea, and lay and floated. Ah! the dear flutes and oboes and horns drifted me hither and thither, and the great violins and small violins swayed me upon waves, and overflowed me with strong lavations, and sprinkled glistening foam in my face, and in among the clarinetti, as among waving water-lilies with flexile stems, I pushed my easy way, and so, even lying in the music-waters, I floated and flowed, my soul utterly bent and prostrate . . .

[*To* MR. HAYNE]

Marietta, Ga., May 26, 1873

My Dear Mr. Hayne: The gracious odor of your "violets" has reached into my soul, and I have been loth to send them back to you. Stanza No. III is unalloyedly delicious; and the closing line,—

> "Breathing of heart-break and sad death of love,"—

is simply ravishing. This sings itself over and over in my heart; and this:—

> "Some with raised brows, and eyes of constancy
> Fixed with fond meanings on a goal above."

What a tender music these two lines make! Are you, by the way, a musician? Strange, that I have never before asked this question,—when so much of my own life consists of music. I don't know that I've ever told you, that whatever turn I have for art, is purely musical; poetry being, with me, a mere tangent into which I shoot sometimes. I could play passably on several instruments before I could write legibly; and since then, the very deepest of my life has been filled with music, which I have studied and cultivated far more than poetry. I only mention this in order that you may understand the delight your poetry gives me. It is so rarely *musical*, so melodiously pure and silvery in flow: it occupies in poetry the place of Mendelssohn in music, or of Franz Abt or of Schubert. It is, in this respect, simply unique in modern poetry: William Morris comes nearest to it, but Morris lives too closely within hearing of Tennyson to write unbroken music: for Tennyson (let me not blaspheme against the Gods!) is not a musical, tho' in other respects (particularly in that of phrase-making) a very wonderful writer. . . .

[*To* BAYARD TAYLOR]

March 20, 1876

. . . Now it seems to me . . . that every poem, from a sonnet to Macbeth, has substantially these elements,—(1) a Hero, (2) a Plot, and (3) a Crisis; and that its perfection as a work of art will consist in the simplicity and the completeness with which the first is involved in the second and illustrated in the third. In the case of a short poem the Hero is the central Idea, whatever that may be; the plot is whatever is said about that idea, its details all converging, both in tone and in general direction, thereupon: and the crisis is the unity of impression sealed or confirmed or climaxed by the last connected sentence, or sentiment, or verse, of the poem. Of course I mean that this is the most general expression of the artistic plan of a poem: it is the system of verses, which may be infinitely varied, but to which all variations may be finally referred. I do not think that there is, as you feared, any necessary reason why a poem so constructed should present "a too-conscious air of design"; that is a matter which will depend solely upon the genuineness of the inspiration and the consummate command of his resources by the artist.

Is not this framework essentially that of every work of any art? Does not every painting, every statue, every architectural design owe whatever it has of artistic perfection to the nearness with which it may approach the fundamental scheme of a Ruling Idea (or Hero), a Plot (or involution of the Ruling Idea in complexities related to or clustering about it), and a Dénouement or Impression-as-a-whole? . . .

From POEM OUTLINES

The Church is too hot, and Nothing is too cold. I find my proper Temperature in Art. Art offers to me a method of adoring the sweet master Jesus Christ, the beautiful souled One, without the straitness of a Creed which confines my genuflexions, a Church which confines my limbs, and without the vacuity of the doubt which numbs them. An unspeakable gain has come to me in simply turning a certain phrase the other way: the beauty of holiness becomes a new and wonderful saying to me when I figure it to myself in reverse as the holiness of beauty. This is like opening a window of dark stained glass, and letting in a flood of white light. I thus keep upon the walls of my soul a church-wall rubric which has been somewhat clouded by the expiring breaths of creeds dying their natural death. For in art there is no doubt. My heart beat all last night without my supervision: for I was asleep; my heart did not doubt a throb; I left it beating when I slept, I found it beating when I awoke; it is thus with art: it beats in my sleep. A holy tune was in my soul when I fell asleep; it was going when I awoke. This melody is always moving along in the background of my spirit. If I wish to compose, I abstract my attention from the thoughts which occupy the front of the stage, the *dramatis personæ* of the moment, and fix myself upon the deeper scene in the rear. (Pp. 104–105.)

It is now time that one should arise in the world and cry out that Art was made for man and not man for art: that government is made for man and not man for government: that religion is made for man and not man for religion: that trade is made for man and not man for trade. This is essentially the utterance of Christ in declaring that the Sabbath was made for man and not man for the Sabbath. (P. 106.)

From THE ENGLISH NOVEL

Indeed we may say that he who has not yet perceived how artistic beauty and moral beauty are convergent lines which run back into a common ideal origin, and who therefore is not afire with moral beauty just as with artistic beauty—that he, in short, who has not come to that stage of quiet and eternal frenzy in which the beauty of holiness and the holiness of beauty mean one thing, burn as one fire, shine as one light, within him;—he is not yet the great artist. Here it is most instructive to note how fine and beautiful souls of time appear after awhile to lose all sense of distinction between these terms, Beauty, Truth, Love, Wisdom, Goodness, and the like. (P. 273.)

WALT WHITMAN

SONG OF MYSELF

1

I CELEBRATE myself, and sing myself,
And what I assume you shall assume,
For every atom belonging to me as good belongs to you.

I loafe and invite my soul,
I lean and loafe at my ease observing a spear of summer grass.

My tongue, every atom of my blood, form'd from this soil, this air,
Born here of parents born here from parents the same, and their parents the same,
I, now thirty-seven years old in perfect health begin,
Hoping to cease not till death.

Creed and schools in abeyance,
Retiring back a while sufficed at what they are, but never forgotten,
I harbor for good or bad, I permit to speak at every hazard,
Nature without check with original energy.

2

Houses and rooms are full of perfumes, the shelves are crowded with perfumes,
I breathe the fragrance myself and know it and like it,
The distillation would intoxicate me also, but I shall not let it.

The atmosphere is not a perfume, it has no taste of the distillation, it is odorless,
It is for my mouth forever, I am in love with it,
I will go to the bank by the wood and become undisguised and naked,
I am mad for it to be in contact with me.

The smoke of my own breath,
Echoes, ripples, buzz'd whispers, love-root, silk-thread, crotch and vine,
My respiration and inspiration, the beating of my heart, the passing of blood and air through my lungs,
The sniff of green leaves and dry leaves, and of the shore and dark-color'd sea-rocks, and of hay in the barn,
The sound of the belch'd words of my voice loos'd to the eddies of the wind,
A few light kisses, a few embraces, a reaching around of arms,
The play of shine and shade on the trees as the supple boughs wag,
The delight alone or in the rush of the streets, or along the fields and hill-sides,
The feeling of health, the full-noon trill, the song of me rising from bed and meeting the sun.

Have you reckon'd a thousand acres much? have you reckon'd the earth much?
Have you practis'd so long to learn to read?
Have you felt so proud to get at the meaning of poems?

Stop this day and night with me and you shall possess the origin of all poems,
You shall possess the good of the earth and sun, (there are millions of suns left,)
You shall no longer take things at second or third hand, nor look through the eyes of the dead, nor feed on the spectres in books,
You shall not look through my eyes either, nor take things from me,
You shall listen to all sides and filter them from your self.

3

I have heard what the talkers were talking, the talk of the beginning and the end,
But I do not talk of the beginning or the end.

There was never any more inception than there is now,
Nor any more youth or age than there is now,
And will never be any more perfection than there is now,
Nor any more heaven or hell than there is now.

Urge and urge and urge,
Always the procreant urge of the world.

Out of the dimness opposite equals advance, always substance and increase, always sex,
Always a knit of identity, always distinction, always a breed of life.

To elaborate is no avail, learn'd and unlearn'd feel that it is so.

Sure as the most certain sure, plumb in the uprights, well entretied, braced in the beams,
Stout as a horse, affectionate, haughty, electrical,
I and this mystery here we stand.

Clear and sweet is my soul, and clear and sweet is all that is not my soul.

Lack one lacks both, and the unseen is proved by the seen,
Till that becomes unseen and receives proof in its turn.

Showing the best and dividing it from the worst age vexes age,
Knowing the perfect fitness and equanimity of things, while they discuss I am silent, and go bathe and admire myself.

Welcome is every organ and attribute of me, and of any man hearty and clean,
Not an inch nor a particle of an inch is vile, and none shall be less familiar than the rest.

I am satisfied—I see, dance, laugh, sing;
As the hugging and loving bed-fellow sleeps at my side through the night, and withdraws at the peep of the day with stealthy tread,
Leaving me baskets cover'd with white towels swelling the house with their plenty,
Shall I postpone my acceptation and realization and scream at my eyes,
That they turn from gazing after and down the road,
And forthwith cipher and show me to a cent,
Exactly the value of one and exactly the value of two, and which is ahead?

4

Trippers and askers surround me,
People I meet, the effect upon me of my early life or the ward and city I live in, or the nation,
The latest dates, discoveries, inventions, societies, authors old and new,
My dinner, dress, associates, looks, compliments, dues,
The real or fancied indifference of some man or woman I love,
The sickness of one of my folks or of myself, or ill-doing or loss or lack of money, or depressions or exaltations,
Battles, the horrors of fratricidal war, the fever of doubtful news, the fitful events;
These come to me days and nights and go from me again,
But they are not the Me myself.

Apart from the pulling and hauling stands what I am,
Stands amused, complacent, compassionating, idle, unitary,
Looks down, is erect, or bends an arm on an impalpable certain rest,
Looking with side-curved head curious what will come next,
Both in and out of the game and watching and wondering at it.

Backward I see in my own days where I sweated through fog with linguists and contenders,
I have no mockings or arguments, I witness and wait.

5

I believe in you my soul, the other I am must not abase itself to you,
And you must not be abased to the other.

Loafe with me on the grass, loose the stop from your throat,
Not words, not music or rhyme I want, not custom or lecture, not even the best,
Only the lull I like, the hum of your valvéd voice.

I mind how once we lay such a transparent summer morning,

How you settled your head athwart my hips
and gently turn'd over upon me,
And parted the shirt from my bosom-bone,
and plunged your tongue to my bare-stript heart,
And reach'd till you felt my beard, and reach'd
till you held my feet.

Swiftly arose and spread around me the peace
and knowledge that pass all the argument
of the earth,
And I know that the hand of God is the promise of my own,
And I know that the spirit of God is the brother
of my own,
And that all the men ever born are also my
brothers, and the women my sisters and
lovers,
And that a kelson of the creation is love,
And limitless are leaves stiff or drooping in
the fields,
And brown ants in the little wells beneath
them,
And mossy scabs of the worm fence, heap'd
stones, elder, mullein and poke-weed.

6

A child said *What is the grass?* fetching it to
me with full hands;
How could I answer the child? I do not know
what it is any more than he.

I guess it must be the flag of my disposition,
out of hopeful green stuff woven.

Or I guess it is the handkerchief of the Lord,
A scented gift and remembrancer designedly
dropt,
Bearing the owner's name someway in the
corners, that we may see and remark, and
say *Whose?*

Or I guess the grass is itself a child, the produced babe of the vegetation.

Or I guess it is a uniform hieroglyphic,
And it means, Sprouting alike in broad zones
and narrow zones,
Growing among black folks as among white,
Kanuck, Tuckahoe, Congressman, Cuff, I
give them the same, I receive them the
same.

And now it seems to me the beautiful uncut
hair of graves.

Tenderly will I use you curling grass,
It may be you transpire from the breasts of
young men,
It may be if I had known them I would have
loved them,
It may be you are from old people, or from
offspring taken soon out of their mothers'
laps,
And here you are the mothers' laps.

This grass is very dark to be from the white
heads of old mothers,
Darker than the colorless beards of old men,
Dark to come from under the faint red roofs
of mouths.

O I perceive after all so many uttering tongues,
And I perceive they do not come from the
roofs of mouths for nothing.

I wish I could translate the hints about the
dead young men and women,
And the hints about old men and mothers,
and the offspring taken soon out of their
laps.

What do you think has become of the young
and old men?
And what do you think has become of the
women and children?

They are alive and well somewhere,
The smallest sprout shows there is really no
death,
And if ever there was it led forward life, and
does not wait at the end to arrest it,
And ceas'd the moment life appear'd.

All goes onward and outward, nothing collapses,
And to die is different from what any one
supposed, and luckier.

7

Has any one supposed it lucky to be born?
I hasten to inform him or her it is just as
lucky to die, and I know it.

I pass death with the dying and birth with the
new-wash'd babe, and am not contain'd
between my hat and boots,

And peruse manifold objects, no two alike and every one good,
The earth good and the stars good, and their adjuncts all good.

I am not an earth nor an adjunct of an earth,
I am the mate and companion of people, all just as immortal and fathomless as myself,
(They do not know how immortal, but I know.)

Every kind for itself and its own, for me mine male and female,
For me those that have been boys and that love women,
For me the man that is proud and feels how it stings to be slighted,
For me the sweet-heart and the old maid, for me mothers and the mothers of mothers,
For me lips that have smiled, eyes that have shed tears,
For me children and the begetters of children.

Undrape! you are not guilty to me, nor stale nor discarded,
I see through the broadcloth and gingham whether or no,
And am around, tenacious, acquisitive, tireless, and cannot be shaken away.

8

The little one sleeps in its cradle,
I lift the gauze and look a long time, and silently brush away flies with my hand.

The youngster and the red-faced girl turn aside up the bushy hill,
I peeringly view them from the top.

The suicide sprawls on the bloody floor of the bedroom,
I witness the corpse with its dabbled hair, I note where the pistol has fallen.

The blab of the pave, tires of carts, sluff of boot-soles, talk of the promenaders,
The heavy omnibus, the driver with his interrogating thumb, the clank of the shod horses on the granite floor,
The snow-sleighs, clinking, shouted jokes, pelts of snow-balls,
The hurrahs for popular favorites, the fury of rous'd mobs,
The flap of the curtain'd litter, a sick man inside borne to the hospital,
The meeting of enemies, the sudden oath, the blows and fall,
The excited crowd, the policeman with his star quickly working his passage to the centre of the crowd,
The impassive stones that receive and return so many echoes,
What groans of over-fed or half-starv'd who fall sunstruck or in fits,
What exclamations of women taken suddenly who hurry home and give birth to babes,
What living and buried speech is always vibrating here, what howls restrain'd by decorum,
Arrests of criminals, slights, adulterous offers made, acceptances, rejections with convex lips,
I mind them or the show or resonance of them—I come and I depart.

9

The big doors of the country barn stand open and ready,
The dried grass of the harvest-time loads the slow-drawn wagon,
The clear light plays on the brown gray and green intertinged,
The armfuls are pack'd to the sagging mow.

I am there, I help, I came stretch'd atop of the load,
I felt its soft jolts, one leg reclined on the other,
I jump from the cross-beams and seize the clover and timothy,
And roll head over heels and tangle my hair full of wisps.

10

Alone far in the wilds and mountains I hunt,
Wandering amazed at my own lightness and glee,
In the late afternoon choosing a safe spot to pass the night,
Kindling a fire and broiling the fresh-kill'd game,
Falling asleep on the gather'd leaves with my dog and gun by my side.

The Yankee clipper is under her sky-sails, she cuts the sparkle and scud,

My eyes settle the land, I bend at her prow or shout joyously from the deck.

The boatmen and clam-diggers arose early and stopt for me,
I tuck'd my trowser-ends in my boots and went and had a good time;
You should have been with us that day round the chowder-kettle.

I saw the marriage of the trapper in the open air in the far west, the bride was a red girl,
Her father and his friends sat near cross-legged and dumbly smoking, they had moccasins to their feet and large thick blankets hanging from their shoulders,
On a bank lounged the trapper, he was drest mostly in skins, his luxuriant beard and curls protected his neck, he held his bride by the hand,
She had long eyelashes, her head was bare, her coarse straight locks descended upon her voluptuous limbs and reach'd to her feet.

The runaway slave came to my house and stopt outside,
I heard his motions crackling the twigs of the woodpile,
Through the swung half-door of the kitchen I saw him limpsy and weak,
And went where he sat on a log and led him in and assured him,
And brought water and fill'd a tub for his sweated body and bruis'd feet,
And gave him a room that enter'd from my own, and gave him some coarse clean clothes,
And remember perfectly well his revolving eyes and his awkwardness,
And remember putting plasters on the galls of his neck and ankles;
He staid with me a week before he was recuperated and pass'd north,
I had him sit next me at table, my fire-lock lean'd in the corner.

11

Twenty-eight young men bathe by the shore,
Twenty-eight young men and all so friendly;
Twenty-eight years of womanly life and all so lonesome.

She owns the fine house by the rise of the bank,
She hides handsome and richly drest aft the blinds of the window.

Which of the young men does she like the best?
Ah the homeliest of them *is* beautiful to her.

Where are you off to, lady? for I see you,
You splash in the water there, yet stay stock still in your room.

Dancing and laughing along the beach came the twenty-ninth bather,
The rest did not see her, but she saw them and loved them.

The beards of the young men glisten'd with wet, it ran from their long hair,
Little streams pass'd all over their bodies.

An unseen hand also pass'd over their bodies,
It descended tremblingly from their temples and ribs.

The young men float on their backs, their white bellies bulge to the sun, they do not ask who seizes fast to them,
They do not know who puffs and declines with pendant and bending arch,
They do not think whom they souse with spray.

12

The butcher-boy puts off his killing-clothes, or sharpens his knife at the stall in the market,
I loiter enjoying his repartee and his shuffle and break-down.

Blacksmiths, with grimed and hairy chests environ the anvil,
Each has his main-sledge, they are all out, there is a great heat in the fire.

From the cinder-strew'd threshold I follow their movements,
The lithe sheer of their waists plays even with their massive arms,
Overhand the hammers swing, overhand so slow, overhand so sure,
They do not hasten, each man hits in his place.

13

The negro holds firmly the reins of his four horses, the block swags underneath on its tied-over chain,
The negro that drives the long dray of the stone-yard, steady and tall he stands pois'd on one leg on the string-piece,
His blue shirt exposes his ample neck and breast and loosens over his hip-band,
His glance is calm and commanding, he tosses the slouch of his hat away from his forehead,
The sun falls on his crispy hair and mustache, falls on the black of his polish'd and perfect limbs.

I behold the picturesque giant and love him, and I do not stop there,
I go with the team also.

In me the caresser of life wherever moving, backward as well as forward sluing,
To niches aside and junior bending, not a person or object missing,
Absorbing all to myself and for this song.

Oxen that rattle the yoke and chain or halt in the leafy shade, what is that you express in your eyes?
It seems to me more than all the print I have read in my life.

My tread scares the wood-drake and wood-duck on my distant and day-long ramble,
They rise together, they slowly circle around.

I believe in those wing'd purposes,
And acknowledge red, yellow, white, playing within me,
And consider green and violet and the tufted crown intentional,
And do not call the tortoise unworthy because she is not something else,
And the jay in the woods never studied the gamut, yet trills pretty well to me,
And the look of the bay mare shames silliness out of me.

14

The wild gander leads his flock through the cool night,
Ya-honk he says, and sounds it down to me like an invitation,
The pert may suppose it meaningless, but I listening close,
Find its purpose and place up there toward the wintry sky.

The sharp-hoof'd moose of the north, the cat on the house-sill, the chickadee, the prairie-dog,
The litter of the grunting sow as they tug at her teats,
The brood of the turkey-hen and she with her half-spread wings,
I see in them and myself the same old law.

The press of my foot to the earth springs a hundred affections,
They scorn the best I can do to relate them.

I am enamour'd of growing out-doors,
Of men that live among cattle or taste of the ocean or woods,
Of the builders and steerers of ships and the wielders of axes and mauls, and the drivers of horses,
I can eat and sleep with them week in and week out.

What is commonest, cheapest, nearest, easiest, is Me,
Me going in for my chances, spending for vast returns,
Adorning myself to bestow myself on the first that will take me,
Not asking the sky to come down to my good will,
Scattering it freely forever.

15

The pure contralto sings in the organ loft,
The carpenter dresses his plank, the tongue of his foreplane whistles its wild ascending lisp,
The married and unmarried children ride home to their Thanksgiving dinner,
The pilot seizes the king-pin, he heaves down with a strong arm,
The mate stands braced in the whale-boat, lance and harpoon are ready,
The duck-shooter walks by silent and cautious stretches,
The deacons are ordain'd with cross'd hands at the altar,

The spinning-girl retreats and advances to the hum of the big wheel,
The farmer stops by the bars as he walks on a First-day loafe and looks at the oats and rye,
The lunatic is carried at last to the asylum a confirm'd case,
(He will never sleep any more as he did in the cot in his mother's bed-room;)
The jour printer with gray head and gaunt jaws works at his case,
He turns his quid of tobacco while his eyes blurr with the manuscript;
The malform'd limbs are tied to the surgeon's table,
What is removed drops horribly in a pail;
The quadroon girl is sold at the auction-stand, the drunkard nods by the bar-room stove,
The machinist rolls up his sleeves, the police-man travels his beat, the gate-keeper marks who pass,
The young fellow drives the express-wagon, (I love him, though I do not know him;)
The half-breed straps on his light boots to compete in the race,
The western turkey-shooting draws old and young, some lean on their rifles, some sit on logs,
Out from the crowd steps the marksman, takes his position, levels his piece;
The groups of newly-come immigrants cover the wharf or levee,
As the woolly-pates hoe in the sugar-field, the overseer views them from his saddle,
The bugle calls in the ball-room, the gentle-men run for their partners, the dancers bow to each other,
The youth lies awake in the cedar-roof'd gar-ret and harks to the musical rain,
The Wolverine sets traps on the creek that helps fill the Huron,
The squaw wrapt in her yellow-hemm'd cloth is offering moccasins and bead-bags for sale,
The connoisseur peers along the exhibition-gallery with half-shut eyes bent sideways,
As the deck-hands make fast the steamboat the plank is thrown for the shore-going pas-sengers,
The young sister holds out the skein while the elder sister winds it off in a ball, and stops now and then for the knots,
The one-year wife is recovering and happy having a week ago borne her first child,
The clean-hair'd Yankee girl works with her sewing-machine or in the factory or mill,
The paving-man leans on his two-handed rammer, the reporter's lead flies swiftly over the note-book, the sign-painter is lettering with blue and gold,
The canal boy trots on the tow-path, the book-keeper counts at his desk, the shoemaker waxes his thread,
The conductor beats time for the band and all the performers follow him,
The child is baptized, the convert is making his first professions,
The regatta is spread on the bay, the race is begun, (how the white sails sparkle!)
The drover watching his drove sings out to them that would stray,
The pedler sweats with his pack on his back, (the purchaser higgling about the odd cent;)
The bride unrumples her white dress, the minute-hand of the clock moves slowly,
The opium-eater reclines with rigid head and just-open'd lips,
The prostitute draggles her shawl, her bonnet bobs on her tipsy and pimpled neck,
The crowd laugh at her blackguard oaths, the men jeer and wink to each other,
(Miserable! I do not laugh at your oaths nor jeer you;)
The President holding a cabinet council is surrounded by the great Secretaries,
On the piazza walk three matrons stately and friendly with twined arms,
The crew of the fish-smack pack repeated layers of halibut in the hold,
The Missourian crosses the plains toting his wares and his cattle,
As the fare-collector goes through the train he gives notice by the jingling of loose change,
The floor-men are laying the floor, the tinners are tinning the roof, the masons are calling for mortar,
In single file each shouldering his hod pass onward the laborers;
Seasons pursuing each other the indescribable

crowd is gather'd, it is the fourth of Seventh-month, (what salutes of cannon and small arms!)
Seasons pursuing each other the plougher ploughs, the mower mows, and the winter-grain falls in the ground;
Off on the lakes the pike-fisher watches and waits by the hole in the frozen surface,
The stumps stand thick round the clearing, the squatter strikes deep with his axe,
Flatboatmen make fast towards dusk near the cotton-wood or pecan-trees,
Coon-seekers go through the regions of the Red river or through those drain'd by the Tennessee, or through those of the Arkansas,
Torches shine in the dark that hangs on the Chattahooche or Altamahaw,
Patriarchs sit at supper with sons and grand-sons and great-grandsons around them,
In walls of adobie, in canvas tents, rest hunters and trappers after their day's sport,
The city sleeps and the country sleeps,
The living sleep for their time, the dead sleep for their time,
The old husband sleeps by his wife and the young husband sleeps by his wife;
And these tend inward to me, and I tend outward to them,
And such as it is to be of these more or less I am,
And of these one and all I weave the song of myself.

16

I am of old and young, of the foolish as much as the wise,
Regardless of others, ever regardful of others,
Maternal as well as paternal, a child as well as a man,
Stuff'd with the stuff that is coarse and stuff'd with the stuff that is fine,
One of the Nation of many nations, the smallest the same and the largest the same,
A Southerner soon as a Northerner, a planter nonchalant and hospitable down by the Oconee I live,
A Yankee bound my own way ready for trade, my joints the limberest joints on earth and the sternest joints on earth,
A Kentuckian walking the vale of the Elkhorn in my deer-skin leggings, a Louisianian or Georgian,
A boatman over lakes or bays or along coasts, a Hoosier, Badger, Buckeye;
At home on Kanadian snow-shoes or up in the bush, or with fishermen off Newfoundland,
At home in the fleet of ice-boats, sailing with the rest and tacking,
At home on the hills of Vermont or in the woods of Maine, or the Texan ranch,
Comrade of Californians, comrade of free North-Westerners, (loving their big proportions,)
Comrade of raftsmen and coalmen, comrade of all who shake hands and welcome to drink and meat,
A learner with the simplest, a teacher of the thoughtfullest,
A novice beginning yet experient of myriads of seasons,
Of every hue and caste am I, of every rank and religion,
A farmer, mechanic, artist, gentleman, sailor, quaker,
Prisoner, fancy-man, rowdy, lawyer, physician, priest.

I resist any thing better than my own diversity,
Breathe the air but leave plenty after me,
And am not stuck up, and am in my place.

(The moth and the fish-eggs are in their place,
The bright suns I see and the dark suns I cannot see are in their place,
The palpable is in its place and the impalpable is in its place.)

17

These are really the thoughts of all men in all ages and lands, they are not original with me,
If they are not yours as much as mine they are nothing, or next to nothing,
If they are not the riddle and the untying of the riddle they are nothing,
If they are not just as close as they are distant they are nothing.

This is the grass that grows wherever the land is and the water is,
This is the common air that bathes the globe.

18

With music strong I come, with my cornets and my drums,
I play not marches for accepted victors only, I play marches for conquer'd and slain persons.

Have you heard that it was good to gain the day?
I also say it is good to fall, battles are lost in the same spirit in which they are won.

I beat and pound for the dead,
I blow through my embouchures my loudest and gayest for them.

Vivas to those who have fail'd!
And to those whose war-vessels sank in the sea!
And to those themselves who sank in the sea!
And to all generals that lost engagements, and all overcome heroes!
And the numberless unknown heroes equal to the greatest heroes known!

19

This is the meal equally set, this the meat for natural hunger,
It is for the wicked just the same as the righteous, I make appointments with all,
I will not have a single person slighted or left away,
The kept-woman, sponger, thief, are hereby invited,
The heavy-lipp'd slave is invited, the venerealee is invited;
There shall be no difference between them and the rest.

This is the press of a bashful hand, this the float and odor of hair,
This the touch of my lips to yours, this the murmur of yearning,
This the far-off depth and height reflecting my own face,
This the thoughtful merge of myself, and the outlet again.

Do you guess I have some intricate purpose?
Well I have, for the Fourth-month showers have, and the mica on the side of a rock has.

Do you take it I would astonish?
Does the daylight astonish? does the early redstart twittering through the woods?
Do I astonish more than they?

This hour I tell things in confidence,
I might not tell everybody, but I will tell you.

20

Who goes there? hankering, gross, mystical, nude;
How is it I extract strength from the beef I eat?

What is a man anyhow? what am I? what are you?

All I mark as my own you shall offset it with your own,
Else it were time lost listening to me.

I do not snivel that snivel the world over,
That months are vacuums and the ground but wallow and filth.

Whimpering and truckling fold with powders for invalids, conformity goes to the fourth-remov'd,
I wear my hat as I please indoors or out.

Why should I pray? why should I venerate and be ceremonious?

Having pried through the strata, analyzed to a hair, counsel'd with doctors and calculated close,
I find no sweeter fat than sticks to my own bones.

In all people I see myself, none more and not one a barley-corn less,
And the good or bad I say of myself I say of them.

I know I am solid and sound,
To me the converging objects of the universe perpetually flow,
All are written to me, and I must get what the writing means.

I know I am deathless,
I know this orbit of mine cannot be swept by a carpenter's compass,
I know I shall not pass like a child's carlacue cut with a burnt stick at night.

I know I am august,
I do not trouble my spirit to vindicate itself or be understood,
I see that the elementary laws never apologize,
(I reckon I behave no prouder than the level I plant my house by, after all.)

I exist as I am, that is enough,
If no other in the world be aware I sit content,
And if each and all be aware I sit content.

One world is aware and by far the largest to me, and that is myself,
And whether I come to my own to-day or in ten thousand or ten million years,
I can cheerfully take it now, or with equal cheerfulness I can wait.

My foothold is tenon'd and mortis'd in granite,
I laugh at what you call dissolution,
And I know the amplitude of time.

21

I am the poet of the Body and I am the poet of the Soul,
The pleasures of heaven are with me and the pains of hell are with me,
The first I graft and increase upon myself, the latter I translate into a new tongue.

I am the poet of the woman the same as the man,
And I say it is as great to be a woman as to be a man,
And I say there is nothing greater than the mother of men.

I chant the chant of dilation or pride,
We have had ducking and deprecating about enough,
I show that size is only development.

Have you outstript the rest? are you the President?
It is a trifle, they will more than arrive there every one, and still pass on.

I am he that walks with the tender and growing night,
I call to the earth and sea half-held by the night.

Press close bare-bosom'd night—press close magnetic nourishing night!
Night of south winds—night of the large few stars!
Still nodding night—mad naked summer night.

Smile O voluptuous cool-breath'd earth!
Earth of the slumbering and liquid trees!
Earth of departed sunset—earth of the mountains misty-topt!
Earth of the vitreous pour of the full moon just tinged with blue!
Earth of shine and dark mottling the tide of the river!
Earth of the limpid gray of clouds brighter and clearer for my sake!
Far-swooping elbow'd earth—rich apple-blossom'd earth!
Smile, for your lover comes.

Prodigal, you have given me love—therefore I to you give love!
O unspeakable passionate love.

22

You sea! I resign myself to you also—I guess what you mean,
I behold from the beach your crooked inviting fingers,
I believe you refuse to go back without feeling of me,
We must have a turn together, I undress, hurry me out of sight of the land,
Cushion me soft, rock me in billowy drowse,
Dash me with amorous wet, I can repay you.

Sea of stretch'd ground-swells,
Sea breathing broad and convulsive breaths,
Sea of the brine of life and of unshovell'd yet always-ready graves,
Howler and scooper of storms, capricious and dainty sea,
I am integral with you, I too am of one phase and of all phases.

Partaker of influx and efflux I, extoller of hate and conciliation,
Extoller of amies and those that sleep in each others' arms.

I am he attesting sympathy,
(Shall I make my list of things in the house and skip the house that supports them?)

I am not the poet of goodness only, I do not decline to be the poet of wickedness also.

What blurt is this about virtue and about vice?
Evil propels me and reform of evil propels me, I stand indifferent,
My gait is no fault-finder's or rejecter's gait,
I moisten the roots of all that has grown.

Did you fear some scrofula out of the unflagging pregnancy?
Did you guess the celestial laws are yet to be work'd over and rectified?

I find one side a balance and the antipodal side a balance,
Soft doctrine as steady help as stable doctrine,
Thoughts and deeds of the present our rouse and early start.

This minute that comes to me over the past decillions,
There is no better than it and now.

What behaved well in the past or behaves well to-day is not such a wonder,
The wonder is always and always how there can be a mean man or an infidel.

23

Endless unfolding of words of ages!
And mine a word of the modern, the word En-Masse.

A word of the faith that never balks,
Here or henceforward it is all the same to me, I accept Time absolutely.

It alone is without flaw, it alone rounds and completes all,
That mystic baffling wonder alone completes all.

I accept Reality and dare not question it,
Materialism first and last imbuing.

Hurrah for positive science! long live exact demonstration!
Fetch stonecrop mixt with cedar and branches of lilac,
This is the lexicographer, this the chemist, this made a grammar of the old cartouches,
These mariners put the ship through dangerous unknown seas,
This is the geologist, this works with the scalpel, and this is a mathematician.

Gentlemen, to you the first honors always!
Your facts are useful, and yet they are not my dwelling,
I but enter by them to an area of my dwelling.

Less the reminders of properties told my words,
And more the reminders they of life untold, and of freedom and extrication,
And make short account of neuters and geldings, and favor men and women fully equipt,
And beat the gong of revolt, and stop with fugitives and them that plot and conspire.

24

Walt Whitman, a kosmos, of Manhattan the son,
Turbulent, fleshy, sensual, eating, drinking and breeding,
No sentimentalist, no stander above men and women or apart from them,
No more modest than immodest.

Unscrew the locks from the doors!
Unscrew the doors themselves from their jambs!

Whoever degrades another degrades me,
And whatever is done or said returns at last to me.

Through me the afflatus surging and surging, through me the current and index.

I speak the pass-word primeval, I give the sign of democracy,
By God! I will accept nothing which all cannot have their counterpart of on the same terms.

Through me many long dumb voices,
Voices of the interminable generations of prisoners and slaves,
Voices of the diseas'd and despairing and of thieves and dwarfs,
Voices of cycles of preparation and accretion,
And of the threads that connect the stars, and of wombs and of the father-stuff,
And of the rights of them the others are down upon,

Of the deform'd, trivial, flat, foolish, despised,
Fog in the air, beetles rolling balls of dung.

Through me forbidden voices,
Voices of sexes and lusts, voices veil'd and I remove the veil,
Voices indecent by me clarified and transfigur'd.

I do not press my fingers across my mouth,
I keep as delicate around the bowels as around the head and heart,
Copulation is no more rank to me than death is.

I believe in the flesh and the appetites,
Seeing, hearing, feeling, are miracles, and each part and tag of me is a miracle.

Divine am I inside and out, and I make holy whatever I touch or am touch'd from,
The scent of these arm-pits aroma finer than prayer,
This head more than churches, bibles, and all the creeds.

If I worship one thing more than another it shall be the spread of my own body, or any part of it,
Translucent mould of me it shall be you!
Shaded ledges and rests it shall be you!
Firm masculine colter it shall be you!
Whatever goes to the tilth of me it shall be you!
You my rich blood! your milky stream pale strippings of my life!
Breast that presses against other breasts it shall be you!
My brain it shall be your occult convolutions!
Root of wash'd sweet-flag! timorous pond-snipe! nest of guarded duplicate eggs, it shall be you!
Mix'd tussled hay of head, beard, brawn, it shall be you!
Trickling sap of maple, fibre of manly wheat, it shall be you!
Sun so generous it shall be you!
Vapors lighting and shading my face it shall be you!
You sweaty brooks and dews it shall be you!
Winds whose soft-tickling genitals rub against me it shall be you!
Broad muscular fields, branches of live oak, loving lounger in my winding paths, it shall be you!
Hands I have taken, face I have kiss'd, mortal I have ever touch'd, it shall be you.

I dote on myself, there is that lot of me and all so luscious,
Each moment and whatever happens thrills me with joy,
I cannot tell how my ankles bend, nor whence the cause of my faintest wish,
Nor the cause of the friendship I emit, nor the cause of the friendship I take again.

That I walk up my stoop, I pause to consider if it really be,
A morning-glory at my window satisfies me more than the metaphysics of books.

To behold the day-break!
The little light fades the immense and diaphanous shadows,
The air tastes good to my palate.

Hefts of the moving world at innocent gambols silently rising, freshly exuding,
Scooting obliquely high and low.

Something I cannot see puts upward libidinous prongs,
Seas of bright juice suffuse heaven.

The earth by the sky staid with, the daily close of their junction,
The heav'd challenge from the east that moment over my head,
The mocking taunt, See then whether you shall be master!

25

Dazzling and tremendous how quick the sun-rise would kill me,
If I could not now and always send sun-rise out of me.

We also ascend dazzling and tremendous as the sun,
We found our own O my soul in the calm and cool of the daybreak.

My voice goes after what my eyes cannot reach,
With the twirl of my tongue I encompass worlds and volumes of worlds.

Speech is the twin of my vision, it is unequal to measure itself,
It provokes me forever, it says sarcastically,
Walt you contain enough, why don't you let it out then?

Come now I will not be tantalized, you conceive too much of articulation,
Do you not know O speech how the buds beneath you are folded?
Waiting in gloom, protected by frost,
The dirt receding before my prophetical screams,
I underlying causes to balance them at last,
My knowledge my live parts, it keeping tally with the meaning of all things,
Happiness, (which whoever hears me let him or her set out in search of this day.)

My final merit I refuse you, I refuse putting from me what I really am,
Encompass worlds, but never try to encompass me,
I crowd your sleekest and best by simply looking toward you.

Writing and talk do not prove me,
I carry the plenum of proof and every thing else in my face,
With the hush of my lips I wholly confound the skeptic.

26

Now I will do nothing but listen,
To accrue what I hear into this song, to let sounds contribute toward it.

I hear bravuras of birds, bustle of growing wheat, gossip of flames, clack of sticks cooking my meals,
I hear the sound I love, the sound of the human voice,
I hear all sounds running together, combined, fused or following,
Sounds of the city and sounds out of the city, sounds of the day and night,
Talkative young ones to those that like them, the loud laugh of work-people at their meals,
The angry base of disjointed friendship, the faint tones of the sick,
The judge with hands tight to the desk, his pallid lips pronouncing a death-sentence,
The heave'e'yo of stevedores unlading ships by the wharves, the refrain of the anchor-lifters,
The ring of alarm-bells, the cry of fire, the whirr of swift-streaking engines and hose-carts with premonitory tinkles and color'd lights,
The steam-whistle, the solid roll of the train of approaching cars,
The slow march play'd at the head of the association marching two and two,
(They go to guard some corpse, the flag-tops are draped with black muslin.)

I hear the violoncello, ('tis the young man's heart's complaint,)
I hear the key'd cornet, it glides quickly in through my ears,
It shakes mad-sweet pangs through my belly and breast.

I hear the chorus, it is a grand opera,
Ah this indeed is music—this suits me.

A tenor large and fresh as the creation fills me,
The orbic flex of his mouth is pouring and filling me full.

I hear the train'd soprano (what work with hers is this?)
The orchestra whirls me wider than Uranus flies,
It wrenches such ardors from me I did not know I possess'd them,
It sails me, I dab with bare feet, they are lick'd by the indolent waves,
I am cut by bitter and angry hail, I lose my breath,
Steep'd amid honey'd morphine, my windpipe throttled in fakes of death,
At length let up again to feel the puzzle of puzzles,
And that we call Being.

27

To be in any form, what is that?
(Round and round we go, all of us, and ever come back thither,)
If nothing lay more develop'd the quahaug in its callous shell were enough.

Mine is no callous shell,
I have instant conductors all over me whether I pass or stop,
They seize every object and lead it harmlessly through me.

I merely stir, press, feel with my fingers, and am happy,
To touch my person to some one else's is about as much as I can stand.

28

Is this then a touch? quivering me to a new identity,
Flames and ether making a rush for my veins,
Treacherous tip of me reaching and crowding to help them,
My flesh and blood playing out lightning to strike what is hardly different from myself,
On all sides prurient provokers stiffening my limbs,
Straining the udder of my heart for its withheld drip,
Behaving licentious toward me, taking no denial,
Depriving me of my best as for a purpose,
Unbuttoning my clothes, holding me by the bare waist,
Deluding my confusion with the calm of the sunlight and pasture-fields,
Immodestly sliding the fellow-senses away,
They bribed to swap off with touch and go and graze at the edges of me,
No consideration, no regard for my draining strength or my anger,
Fetching the rest of the herd around to enjoy them a while,
Then all uniting to stand on a headland and worry me.

The sentries desert every other part of me,
They have left me helpless to a red marauder,
They all come to the headland to witness and assist against me.

I am given up by traitors,
I talk wildly, I have lost my wits, I and nobody else am the greatest traitor,
I went myself first to the headland, my own hands carried me there.

You villain touch! what are you doing? my breath is tight in its throat,
Unclench your floodgates, you are too much for me.

29

Blind loving wrestling touch, sheath'd hooded sharp-tooth'd touch!
Did it make you ache so, leaving me?

Parting track'd by arriving, perpetual payment of perpetual loan,
Rich showering rain, and recompense richer afterward.

Sprouts take and accumulate, stand by the curb prolific and vital,
Landscapes projected masculine, full-sized and golden.

30

All truths wait in all things,
They neither hasten their own delivery nor resist it,
They do not need the obstetric forceps of the surgeon,
The insignificant is as big to me as any,
(What is less or more than a touch?)

Logic and sermons never convince,
The damp of the night drives deeper into my soul.

(Only what proves itself to every man and woman is so,
Only what nobody denies is so.)

A minute and a drop of me settle my brain,
I believe the soggy clods shall become lovers and lamps,
And a compend of compends is the meat of a man or woman,
And a summit and flower there is the feeling they have for each other,
And they are to branch boundlessly out of that lesson until it becomes omnific,
And until one and all shall delight us, and we them.

31

I believe a leaf of grass is no less than the journey-work of the stars,
And the pismire is equally perfect, and a grain of sand, and the egg of the wren,

And the tree-toad is a chef-d'œuvre for the highest,
And the running blackberry would adorn the parlors of heaven,
And the narrowest hinge in my hand puts to scorn all machinery,
And the cow crunching with depress'd head surpasses any statue,
And a mouse is miracle enough to stagger sextillions of infidels.

I find I incorporate gneiss, coal, long-threaded moss, fruits, grains, esculent roots,
And am stucco'd with quadrupeds and birds all over,
And have distanced what is behind me for good reasons,
But call any thing back again when I desire it.

In vain the speeding or shyness,
In vain the plutonic rocks send their old heat against my approach,
In vain the mastodon retreats beneath its own powder'd bones,
In vain objects stand leagues off and assume manifold shapes,
In vain the ocean settling in hollows and the great monsters lying low,
In vain the buzzard houses herself with the sky,
In vain the snake slides through the creepers and logs,
In vain the elk takes to the inner passes of the woods,
In vain the razor-bill'd auk sails far north to Labrador,
I follow quickly, I ascend to the nest in the fissure of the cliff.

32

I think I could turn and live with animals, they're so placid and self-contain'd,
I stand and look at them long and long.

They do not sweat and whine about their condition,
They do not lie awake in the dark and weep for their sins,
They do not make me sick discussing their duty to God,
Not one is dissatisfied, not one is demented with the mania of owning things,
Not one kneels to another, nor to his kind that lived thousands of years ago,
Not one is respectable or unhappy over the whole earth.

So they show their relations to me and I accept them,
They bring me tokens of myself, they evince them plainly in their possession.

I wonder where they get those tokens,
Did I pass that way huge times ago and negligently drop them?

Myself moving forward then and now and forever,
Gathering and showing more always and with velocity,
Infinite and omnigenous, and the like of these among them,
Not too exclusive toward the reachers of my remembrancers,
Picking out here one that I love, and now go with him on brotherly terms.

A gigantic beauty of a stallion, fresh and responsive to my caresses,
Head high in the forehead, wide between the ears,
Limbs glossy and supple, tail dusting the ground,
Eyes full of sparkling wickedness, ears finely cut, flexibly moving.

His nostrils dilate as my heels embrace him,
His well-built limbs tremble with pleasure as we race around and return.

I but use you a minute, then I resign you, stallion,
Why do I need your paces when I myself out-gallop them?
Even as I stand or sit passing faster than you.

33

Space and Time! now I see it is true, what I guess'd at,
What I guess'd when I loaf'd on the grass,
What I guess'd while I lay alone in my bed,
And again as I walk'd the beach under the paling stars of the morning.

My ties and ballasts leave me, my elbows rest in sea-gaps,

I skirt sierras, my palms cover continents,
I am afoot with my vision.

By the city's quadrangular houses—in log huts, camping with lumbermen,
Along the ruts of the turnpike, along the dry gulch and rivulet bed,
Weeding my onion-patch or hoeing rows of carrots and parsnips, crossing savannas, trailing in forests,
Prospecting, gold-digging, girdling the trees of a new purchase,
Scorch'd ankle-deep by the hot sand, hauling my boat down the shallow river,
Where the panther walks to and fro on a limb overhead, where the buck turns furiously at the hunter,
Where the rattlesnake suns his flabby length on a rock, where the otter is feeding on fish,
Where the alligator in his tough pimples sleeps by the bayou,
Where the black bear is searching for roots or honey, where the beaver pats the mud with his paddle-shaped tail;
Over the growing sugar, over the yellow-flower'd cotton plant, over the rice in its low moist field,
Over the sharp-peak'd farm house, with its scallop'd scum and slender shoots from the gutters,
Over the western persimmon, over the long-leav'd corn, over the delicate blue-flower flax,
Over the white and brown buckwheat, a hummer and buzzer there with the rest,
Over the dusky green of the rye as it ripples and shades in the breeze;
Scaling mountains, pulling myself cautiously up, holding on by low scragged limbs,
Walking the path worn in the grass and beat through the leaves of the brush,
Where the quail is whistling betwixt the woods and the wheat-lot,
Where the bat flies in the Seventh-month eve, where the great gold-bug drops through the dark,
Where the brook puts out of the roots of the old tree and flows to the meadow,
Where cattle stand and shake away flies with the tremulous shuddering of their hides,
Where the cheese-cloth hangs in the kitchen, where andirons straddle the hearth-slab, where cobwebs fall in festoons from the rafters;
Where trip-hammers crash, where the press is whirling its cylinders,
Wherever the human heart beats with terrible throes under its ribs,
Where the pear-shaped balloon is floating aloft, (floating in it myself and looking composedly down,)
Where the life-car is drawn on the slip-noose, where the heat hatches pale-green eggs in the dented sand,
Where the she-whale swims with her calf and never forsakes it,
Where the steam-ship trails hind-ways its long pennant of smoke,
Where the fin of the shark cuts like a black chip out of the water,
Where the half-burn'd brig is riding on unknown currents,
Where shells grow to her slimy deck, where the dead are corrupting below;
Where the dense-starr'd flag is borne at the head of the regiments,
Approaching Manhattan up by the long-stretching island,
Under Niagara, the cataract falling like a veil over my countenance,
Upon a door-step, upon the horse-block of hard wood outside,
Upon the race-course, or enjoying picnics or jigs or a good game of base-ball,
At he-festivals, with blackguard gibes, ironical license, bull-dances, drinking, laughter,
At the cider-mill tasting the sweets of the brown mash, sucking the juice through a straw,
At apple-peelings wanting kisses for all the red fruit I find,
At musters, beach-parties, friendly bees, huskings, house-raisings;
Where the mocking-bird sounds his delicious gurgles, cackles, screams, weeps,
Where the hay-rick stands in the barn-yard, where the dry-stalks are scatter'd, where the brood-cow waits in the hovel,
Where the bull advances to do his masculine work, where the stud to the mare, where the cock is treading the hen,

Where the heifers browse, where geese nip their food with short jerks,
Where sun-down shadows lengthen over the limitless and lonesome prairie,
Where herds of buffalo make a crawling spread of the square miles far and near,
Where the humming-bird shimmers, where the neck of the long-lived swan is curving and winding,
Where the laughing-gull scoots by the shore, where she laughs her near-human laugh,
Where bee-hives range on a gray bench in the garden half hid by the high weeds,
Where band-neck'd partridges roost in a ring on the ground with their heads out,
Where burial coaches enter the arch'd gates of a cemetery,
Where winter wolves bark amid wastes of snow and icicled trees,
Where the yellow-crown'd heron comes to the edge of the marsh at night and feeds upon small crabs,
Where the splash of swimmers and divers cools the warm noon,
Where the katy-did works her chromatic reed on the walnut-tree over the well,
Through patches of citrons and cucumbers with silver-wired leaves,
Through the salt-lick or orange glade, or under conical firs,
Through the gymnasium, through the curtain'd saloon, through the office or public hall;
Pleas'd with the native and pleas'd with the foreign, pleas'd with the new and old,
Pleas'd with the homely woman as well as the handsome,
Pleas'd with the quakeress as she puts off her bonnet and talks melodiously,
Pleas'd with the tune of the choir of the whitewash'd church,
Pleas'd with the earnest words of the sweating Methodist preacher, impress'd seriously at the camp-meeting;
Looking in at the shop-windows of Broadway the whole forenoon, flatting the flesh of my nose on the thick plate-glass,
Wandering the same afternoon with my face turn'd up to the clouds, or down a lane or along the beach,
My right and left arms round the sides of two friends, and I in the middle;
Coming home with the silent and dark-cheek'd bush-boy, (behind me he rides at the drape of the day,)
Far from the settlements studying the print of animals' feet, or the moccasin print,
By the cot in the hospital reaching lemonade to a feverish patient,
Nigh the coffin'd corpse when all is still, examining with a candle;
Voyaging to every port to dicker and adventure,
Hurrying with the modern crowd as eager and fickle as any,
Hot toward one I hate, ready in my madness to knife him,
Solitary at midnight in my back yard, my thoughts gone from me a long while,
Walking the old hills of Judæa with the beautiful gentle God by my side,
Speeding through space, speeding through heaven and the stars,
Speeding amid the seven satellites and the broad ring, and the diameter of eighty thousand miles,
Speeding with tail'd meteors, throwing fireballs like the rest,
Carrying the crescent child that carries its own full mother in its belly,
Storming, enjoying, planning, loving, cautioning,
Backing and filling, appearing and disappearing,
I tread day and night such roads.

I visit the orchards of spheres and look at the product,
And look at quintillions ripen'd and look at quintillions green.

I fly those flights of a fluid and swallowing soul,
My course runs below the soundings of plummets.

I help myself to material and immaterial,
No guard can shut me off, no law prevent me.

I anchor my ship for a little while only,
My messengers continually cruise away or bring their returns to me.

I go hunting polar furs and the seal, leaping chasms with a pike-pointed staff, clinging to topples of brittle and blue.

I ascend to the foretruck,
I take my place late at night in the crow's-nest,
We sail the arctic sea, it is plenty light enough,
Through the clear atmosphere I stretch around on the wonderful beauty,
The enormous masses of ice pass me and I pass them, the scenery is plain in all directions,
The white-topt mountains show in the distance, I fling out my fancies toward them,
We are approaching some great battle-field in which we are soon to be engaged,
We pass the colossal outposts of the encampment, we pass with still feet and caution,
Or we are entering by the suburbs some vast and ruin'd city,
The blocks and fallen architecture more than all the living cities of the globe.

I am a free companion, I bivouac by invading watchfires,
I turn the bridegroom out of bed and stay with the bride myself,
I tighten her all night to my thighs and lips.

My voice is the wife's voice, the screech by the rail of the stairs,
They fetch my man's body up dripping and drown'd.

I understand the large hearts of heroes,
The courage of present times and all times,
How the skipper saw the crowded and rudderless wreck of the steam-ship, and Death chasing it up and down the storm,
How he knuckled tight and gave not back an inch, and was faithful of days and faithful of nights,
And chalk'd in large letters on a board, *Be of good cheer, we will not desert you;*
How he follow'd with them and tack'd with them three days and would not give it up,
How he saved the drifting company at last,
How the lank loose-gown'd women look'd when boated from the side of their prepared graves,
How the silent old-faced infants and the lifted sick, and the sharp-lipp'd unshaved men;

All this I swallow, it tastes good, I like it well, it becomes mine,
I am the man, I suffer'd, I was there.

The disdain and calmness of martyrs,
The mother of old, condemn'd for a witch, burnt with dry wood, her children gazing on,
The hounded slave that flags in the race, leans by the fence, blowing, cover'd with sweat,
The twinges that sting like needles his legs and neck, the murderous buckshot and the bullets,
All these I feel or am.

I am the hounded slave, I wince at the bite of the dogs,
Hell and despair are upon me, crack and again crack the marksmen,
I clutch the rails of the fence, my gore dribs, thinn'd with the ooze of my skin,
I fall on the weeds and stones,
The riders spur their unwilling horses, haul close,
Taunt my dizzy ears and beat me violently over the head with whip-stocks.

Agonies are one of my changes of garments,
I do not ask the wounded person how he feels, I myself become the wounded person,
My hurts turn livid upon me as I lean on a cane and observe.

I am the mash'd fireman with breast-bone broken,
Tumbling walls buried me in their debris,
Heat and smoke I inspired, I heard the yelling shouts of my comrades,
I heard the distant click of their picks and shovels,
They have clear'd the beams away, they tenderly lift me forth.

I lie in the night air in my red shirt, the pervading hush is for my sake,
Painless after all I lie exhausted but not so unhappy,
White and beautiful are the faces around me, the heads are bared of their fire-caps,
The kneeling crowd fades with the light of the torches.

Distant and dead resuscitate,
They show as the dial or move as the hands of me, I am the clock myself.

I am an old artillerist, I tell of my fort's bombardment,
I am there again.

Again the long roll of the drummers,
Again the attacking cannon, mortars,
Again to my listening ears the cannon responsive.

I take part, I see and hear the whole,
The cries, curses, roar, the plaudits for well-aim'd shots,
The ambulanza slowly passing trailing its red drip,
Workmen searching after damages, making indispensable repairs,
The fall of grenades through the rent roof, the fan-shaped explosion,
The whizz of limbs, heads, stone, wood, iron, high in the air.

Again gurgles the mouth of my dying general, he furiously waves with his hand,
He gasps through the clot *Mind not me—mind—the entrenchments.*

34

Now I tell what I knew in Texas in my early youth,
(I tell not the fall of Alamo,
Not one escaped to tell the fall of Alamo,
The hundred and fifty are dumb yet at Alamo,)
'Tis the tale of the murder in cold blood of four hundred and twelve young men.

Retreating they had form'd in a hollow square with their baggage for breastworks,
Nine hundred lives out of the surrounding enemy's, nine times their number, was the price they took in advance,
Their colonel was wounded and their ammunition gone,
They treated for an honorable capitulation, receiv'd writing and seal, gave up their arms and march'd back prisoners of war.
They were the glory of the race of rangers,
Matchless with horse, rifle, song, supper, courtship,
Large, turbulent, generous, handsome, proud, and affectionate,
Bearded, sunburnt, drest in the free costume of hunters,
Not a single one over thirty years of age.
The second First-day morning they were brought out in squads and massacred, it was beautiful early summer,
The work commenced about five o'clock and was over by eight.

None obey'd the command to kneel,
Some made a mad and helpless rush, some stood stark and straight,
A few fell at once, shot in the temple or heart, the living and dead lay together,
The maim'd and mangled dug in the dirt, the new-comers saw them there,
Some half-kill'd attempted to crawl away,
These were despatch'd with bayonets or batter'd with the blunts of muskets,
A youth not seventeen years old seiz'd his assassin till two more came to release him,
The three were all torn and cover'd with the boy's blood.

At eleven o'clock began the burning of the bodies;
That is the tale of the murder of the four hundred and twelve young men.

35

Would you hear of an old-time sea-fight?
Would you learn who won by the light of the moon and stars?
List to the yarn, as my grandmother's father the sailor told it to me.

Our foe was no skulk in his ship I tell you, (said he,)
His was the surly English pluck, and there is no tougher or truer, and never was, and never will be;
Along the lower'd eve he came horribly raking us.

We closed with him, the yards entangled, the cannon touch'd,
My captain lash'd fast with his own hands.

We had receiv'd some eighteen pound shots under the water,

On our lower-gun-deck two large pieces had burst at the first fire, killing all around and blowing up overhead.

Fighting at sun-down, fighting at dark,
Ten o'clock at night, the full moon well up, our leaks on the gain, and five feet of water reported,
The master-at-arms loosing the prisoners confined in the afterhold to give them a chance for themselves.

The transit to and from the magazine is now stopt by the sentinels,
They see so many strange faces they do not know whom to trust.

Our frigate takes fire,
The other asks if we demand quarter?
If our colors are struck and the fighting done?

Now I laugh content, for I hear the voice of my little captain,
We have not struck, he composedly cries, *we have just begun our part of the fighting*.

Only three guns are in use,
One is directed by the captain himself against the enemy's main-mast,
Two well serv'd with grape and canister silence his musketry and clear his decks.

The tops alone second the fire of this little battery, especially the main-top,
They hold out bravely during the whole of the action.

Not a moment's cease,
The leaks gain fast on the pumps, the fire eats toward the powder-magazine.

One of the pumps has been shot away, it is generally thought we are sinking.

Serene stands the little captain,
He is not hurried, his voice is neither high nor low,
His eyes give more light to us than our battle-lanterns.

Toward twelve there in the beams of the moon they surrender to us.

36

Stretch'd and still lies the midnight,
Two great hulls motionless on the breast of the darkness,
Our vessel riddled and slowly sinking, preparations to pass to the one we have conquer'd,
The captain on the quarter-deck coldly giving his orders through a countenance white as a sheet,
Near by the corpse of the child that serv'd in the cabin,
The dead face of an old salt with long white hair and carefully curl'd whiskers,
The flames spite of all that can be done flickering aloft and below,
The husky voices of the two or three officers yet fit for duty,
Formless stacks of bodies and bodies by themselves, dabs of flesh upon the masts and spars,
Cut of cordage, dangle of rigging, slight shock of the soothe of waves,
Black and impassive guns, litter of powder-parcels, strong scent,
A few large stars overhead, silent and mournful shining,
Delicate sniffs of sea-breeze, smells of sedgy grass and fields by the shore, death-messages given in charge to survivors,
The hiss of the surgeon's knife, the gnawing teeth of his saw,
Wheeze, cluck, swash of falling blood, short wild scream, and long, dull, tapering groan,
These so, these irretrievable.

37

You laggards there on guard! look to your arms!
In at the conquer'd doors they crowd! I am possess'd!
Embody all presences outlaw'd or suffering,
See myself in prison shaped like another man,
And feel the dull unintermitted pain.

For me the keepers of convicts shoulder their carbines and keep watch,
It is I let out in the morning and barr'd at night.

Not a mutineer walks handcuff'd to jail but I am handcuff'd to him and walk by his side,
(I am less the jolly one there, and more the silent one with sweat on my twitching lips.)

Not a youngster is taken for larceny but I go up too, and am tried and sentenced.
Not a cholera patient lies at the last gasp but I also lie at the last gasp,
My face is ash-color'd, my sinews gnarl, away from me people retreat.

Askers embody themselves in me and I am embodied in them,
I project my hat, sit shame-faced, and beg.

38

Enough! enough! enough!
Somehow I have been stunn'd. Stand back!
Give me a little time beyond my cuff'd head, slumbers, dreams, gaping,
I discover myself on the verge of a usual mistake.

That I could forget the mockers and insults!
That I could forget the trickling tears and the blows of the bludgeons and hammers!
That I could look with a separate look on my own crucifixion and bloody crowning!

I remember now,
I resume the overstaid fraction,
The grave of rock multiplies what has been confided to it, or to any graves,
Corpses rise, gashes heal, fastenings roll from me.

I troop forth replenish'd with supreme power, one of an average unending procession,
Inland and sea-coast we go, and pass all boundary lines,
Our swift ordinances on their way over the whole earth,
The blossoms we wear in our hats the growth of thousands of years.

Eleves, I salute you! come forward!
Continue your annotations, continue your questionings.

39

The friendly and flowing savage, who is he?
Is he waiting for civilization, or past it and mastering it?

Is he some Southwesterner rais'd out-doors? is he Kanadian?
Is he from the Mississippi country? Iowa, Oregon, California?
The mountains? prairie-life, bush-life? or sailor from the sea?

Wherever he goes men and women accept and desire him,
They desire he should like them, touch them, speak to them, stay with them.

Behavior lawless as snow-flakes, words simple as grass, uncomb'd head, laughter, and naiveté,
Slow-stepping feet, common features, common modes and emanations,
They descend in new forms from the tips of his fingers,
They are wafted with the odor of his body or breath, they fly out of the glance of his eyes.

40

Flaunt of the sunshine I need not your bask—lie over!
You light surfaces only, I force surfaces and depths also.

Earth! you seem to look for something at my hands,
Say, old top-knot, what do you want?

Man or woman, I might tell how I like you, but cannot,
And might tell what it is in me and what it is in you, but cannot,
And might tell that pining I have, that pulse of my nights and days.

Behold, I do not give lectures or a little charity,
When I give I give myself.

You there, impotent, loose in the knees,
Open your scarf'd chops till I blow grit within you,
Spread your palms and lift the flaps of your pockets,
I am not to be denied, I compel, I have stores plenty and to spare,
And any thing I have I bestow.

I do not ask who you are, that is not important to me,

You can do nothing and be nothing but what I will infold you.

To cotton-field drudge or cleaner of privies I lean,
On his right cheek I put the family kiss,
And in my soul I swear I never will deny him.

On women fit for conception I start bigger and nimbler babes,
(This day I am jetting the stuff of far more arrogant republics.)

To any one dying, thither I speed and twist the knob of the door,
Turn the bed-clothes toward the foot of the bed,
Let the physician and the priest go home.

I seize the descending man and raise him with resistless will,
O despairer, here is my neck,
By God, you shall not go down! hang your whole weight upon me.

I dilate you with tremendous breath, I buoy you up,
Every room of the house do I fill with an arm'd force,
Lovers of me, bafflers of graves.

Sleep—I and they keep guard all night,
Not doubt, not disease shall dare to lay finger upon you,
I have embraced you, and henceforth possess you to myself,
And when you rise in the morning you will find what I tell you is so.

41

I am he bringing help for the sick as they pant on their backs,
And for strong upright men I bring yet more needed help.

I heard what was said of the universe,
Heard it and heard it of several thousand years;
It is middling well as far as it goes—but is that all?

Magnifying and applying come I,
Outbidding at the start the old cautious hucksters,
Taking myself the exact dimensions of Jehovah,
Lithographing Kronos, Zeus his son, and Hercules his grandson,
Buying drafts of Osiris, Isis, Belus, Brahma, Buddha,
In my portfolio placing Manito loose, Allah on a leaf, the crucifix engraved,
With Odin and the hideous-faced Mexitli and every idol and image,
Taking them all for what they are worth and not a cent more,
Admitting they were alive and did the work of their days,
(They bore mites as for unfledg'd birds who have now to rise and fly and sing for themselves,)
Accepting the rough deific sketches to fill out better in myself, bestowing them freely on each man and woman I see,
Discovering as much or more in a framer framing a house,
Putting higher claims for him there with his roll'd-up sleeves driving the mallet and chisel,
Not objecting to special revelations, considering a curl of smoke or a hair on the back of my hand just as curious as any revelation,
Lads ahold of fire-engines and hook-and-ladder ropes no less to me than the gods of the antique wars,
Minding their voices peal through the crash of destruction,
Their brawny limbs passing safe over charr'd laths, their white foreheads whole and unhurt out of the flames;
By the mechanic's wife with her babe at her nipple interceding for every person born,
Three scythes at harvest whizzing in a row from three lusty angels with shirts bagg'd out at their waists,
The snag-tooth'd hostler with red hair redeeming sins past and to come,
Selling all he possesses, traveling on foot to fee lawyers for his brother and sit by him while he is tried for forgery;
What was strewn in the amplest strewing the square rod about me, and not filling the square rod then,

The bull and the bug never worshipp'd half enough,
Dung and dirt more admirable than was dream'd,
The supernatural of no account, myself waiting my time to be one of the supremes,
The day getting ready for me when I shall do as much good as the best, and be as prodigious;
By my life-lumps! becoming already a creator,
Putting myself here and now to the ambush'd womb of the shadows.

42

A call in the midst of the crowd,
My own voice, orotund sweeping and final.

Come my children,
Come my boys and girls, my women, household and intimates,
Now the performer launches his nerve, he has pass'd his prelude on the reeds within.

Easily written loose-finger'd chords—I feel the thrum of your climax and close.

My head slues round on my neck,
Music rolls, but not from the organ,
Folks are around me, but they are no household of mine.

Ever the hard unsunk ground,
Ever the eaters and drinkers, ever the upward and downward sun, ever the air and the ceaseless tides,
Ever myself and my neighbors, refreshing, wicked, real,
Ever the old inexplicable query, ever that thorn'd thumb, that breath of itches and thirsts,
Ever the vexer's *hoot! hoot!* till we find where the sly one hides and bring him forth,
Ever love, ever the sobbing liquid of life,
Ever the bandage under the chin, ever the trestles of death.

Here and there with dimes on the eyes walking,
To feed the greed of the belly the brains liberally spooning,
Tickets buying, taking, selling, but in to the feast never once going,
Many sweating, ploughing, thrashing, and then the chaff for payment receiving,
A few idly owning, and they the wheat continually claiming.

This is the city and I am one of the citizens,
Whatever interests the rest interests me, politics, wars, markets, newspapers, schools,
The mayor and councils, banks, tariffs, steamships, factories, stocks, stores, real estate and personal estate.

The little plentiful manikins skipping around in collars and tail'd coats,
I am aware who they are, (they are positively not worms or fleas,)
I acknowledge the duplicates of myself, the weakest and shallowest is deathless with me,
What I do and say the same waits for them,
Every thought that flounders in me the same flounders in them.

I know perfectly well my own egotism,
Know my omnivorous lines and must not write any less,
And would fetch you whoever you are flush with myself.

Not words of routine this song of mine,
But abruptly to question, to leap beyond yet nearer bring;
This printed and bound book—but the printer and the printing-office boy?
The well-taken photographs—but your wife or friend close and solid in your arms?
The black ship mail'd with iron, her mighty guns in her turrets—but the pluck of the captain and engineers?
In the houses the dishes and fare and furniture—but the host and hostess, and the look out of their eyes?
The sky up there—yet here or next door, or across the way?
The saints and sages in history—but you yourself?
Sermons, creeds, theology—but the fathomless human brain,
And what is reason? and what is love? and what is life?

43

I do not despise you priests, all time, the world over,
My faith is the greatest of faiths and the least of faiths,
Enclosing worship ancient and modern and all between ancient and modern,
Believing I shall come again upon the earth after five thousand years,
Waiting responses from oracles, honoring the gods, saluting the sun,
Making a fetich of the first rock or stump, powowing with sticks in the circle of obis,
Helping the llama or brahmin as he trims the lamps of the idols,
Dancing yet through the streets in a phallic procession, rapt and austere in the woods a gymnosophist,
Drinking mead from the skull-cup, to Shastas and Vedas admirant, minding the Koran,
Walking the teokallis, spotted with gore from the stone and knife, beating the serpent-skin drum,
Accepting the Gospels, accepting him that was crucified, knowing assuredly that he is divine,
To the mass kneeling or the puritan's prayer rising, or sitting patiently in a pew,
Ranting and frothing in my insane crisis, or waiting dead-like till my spirit arouses me,
Looking forth on pavement and land, or outside of pavement and land,
Belonging to the winders of the circuit of circuits.

One of that centripetal and centrifugal gang I turn and talk like a man leaving charges before a journey.

Down-hearted doubters dull and excluded,
Frivolous, sullen, moping, angry, affected, disheartend'd, atheistical,
I know every one of you, I know the sea of torment, doubt, despair and unbelief.

How the flukes splash!
How they contort rapid as lightning, with spasms and spouts of blood!

Be at peace bloody flukes of doubters and sullen mopers,
I take my place among you as much as among any,
The past is the push of you, me, all, precisely the same,
And what is yet untried and afterward is for you, me, all, precisely the same.

I do not know what is untried and afterward,
But I know it will in its turn prove sufficient, and cannot fail.

Each who passes is consider'd, each who stops is consider'd, not a single one can it fail.

It cannot fail the young man who died and was buried,
Nor the young woman who died and was put by his side,
Nor the little child that peep'd in at the door, and then drew back and was never seen again,
Nor the old man who has lived without purpose, and feels it with bitterness worse than gall,
Nor him in the poor-house tubercled by rum and the bad disorder,
Nor the numberless slaughter'd and wreck'd, nor the brutish koboo call'd the ordure of humanity,
Nor the sacs merely floating with open mouths for food to slip in,
Nor any thing in the earth, or down in the oldest graves of the earth,
Nor any thing in the myriads of spheres, nor the myriads of myriads that inhabit them,
Nor the present, nor the least wisp that is known.

44

It is time to explain myself—let us stand up.

What is known I strip away,
I launch all men and women forward with me into the Unknown.

The clock indicates the moment—but what does eternity indicate?

We have thus far exhausted trillions of winters and summers,
There are trillions ahead, and trillions ahead of them.

Births have brought us richness and variety,
And other births will bring us richness and
variety.

I do not call one greater and one smaller,
That which fills its period and place is equal to
any.

Were mankind murderous or jealous upon
you, my brother, my sister?
I am sorry for you, they are not murderous or
jealous upon me,
All has been gentle with me, I keep no account
with lamentation,
(What have I to do with lamentation?)

I am an acme of things accomplish'd, and I an
encloser of things to be.

My feet strike an apex of the apices of the stairs,
On every step bunches of ages, and larger
bunches between the steps,
All below duly travel'd, and still I mount and
mount.

Rise after rise bow the phantoms behind me,
Afar down I see the huge first Nothing, I know
I was even there,
I waited unseen and always, and slept through
the lethargic mist,
And took my time, and took no hurt from
the fetid carbon.

Long I was hugg'd close—long and long.

Immense have been the preparations for me,
Faithful and friendly the arms that have help'd
me.

Cycles ferried my cradle, rowing and rowing
like cheerful boatmen,
For room to me stars kept aside in their own
rings,
They sent influences to look after what was to
hold me.

Before I was born out of my mother generations guided me,
My embryo has never been torpid, nothing
could overlay it.

For it the nebula cohered to an orb,
The long slow strata piled to rest it on,
Vast vegetables gave it sustenance,
Monstrous sauroids transported it in their
mouths and deposited it with care.

All forces have been steadily employ'd to
complete and delight me,
Now on this spot I stand with my robust soul.

45

O span of youth! ever-push'd elasticity!
O manhood, balanced, florid and full.

My lovers suffocate me,
Crowding my lips, thick in the pores of my
skin,
Jostling me through streets and public halls,
coming naked to me at night,
Crying by day *Ahoy!* from the rocks of the
river, swinging and chirping over my
head,
Calling my name from flower-beds, vines,
tangled underbrush,
Lighting on every moment of my life,
Bussing my body with soft balsamic busses,
Noiselessly passing handfuls out of their hearts
and giving them to be mine.

Old age superbly rising! O welcome, ineffable
grace of dying days!

Every condition promulges not only itself, it
promulges what grows after and out of
itself,
And the dark hush promulges as much as any.

I open my scuttle at night and see the far-
sprinkled systems,
And all I see multiplied as high as I can cipher
edge but the rim of the farther systems.

Wider and wider they spread, expanding, always expanding,
Outward and outward and forever outward.

My sun has his sun and round him obediently
wheels,
He joins with his partners a group of superior
circuit,
And greater sets follow, making specks of the
greatest inside them.

There is no stoppage and never can be stoppage,
If I, you, and the worlds, and all beneath or
upon their surfaces, were this moment
reduced back to a pallid float, it would
not avail in the long run,

We should surely bring up again where we now stand,
And surely go as much farther, and then farther and farther.

A few quadrillions of eras, a few octillions of cubic leagues, do not hazard the span or make it impatient,
They are but parts, any thing is but a part.

See ever so far, there is limitless space outside of that,
Count ever so much, there is limitless time around that.

My rendezvous is appointed, it is certain,
The Lord will be there and wait till I come on perfect terms,
The great Camerado, the lover true for whom I pine will be there.

46

I know I have the best of time and space, and was never measured and never will be measured.

I tramp a perpetual journey, (come listen all!)
My signs are a rain-proof coat, good shoes, and a staff cut from the woods,
No friend of mine takes his ease in my chair,
I have no chair, no church, no philosophy,
I lead no man to a dinner-table, library, exchange,
But each man and each woman of you I lead upon a knoll,
My left hand hooking you round the waist,
My right hand pointing to landscapes of continents and the public road.

Not I, not any one else can travel that road for you,
You must travel it for yourself.

It is not far, it is within reach,
Perhaps you have been on it since you were born and did not know,
Perhaps it is everywhere on water and on land.

Shoulder your duds dear son, and I will mine, and let us hasten forth,
Wonderful cities and free nations we shall fetch as we go.

If you tire, give me both burdens, and rest the chuff of your hand on my hip,
And in due time you shall repay the same service to me,
For after we start we never lie by again.

This day before dawn I ascended a hill and look'd at the crowded heaven,
And I said to my spirit *When we become the enfolders of those orbs, and the pleasure and knowledge of every thing in them, shall we be fill'd and satisfied then?*
And my spirit said *No, we but level that lift to pass and continue beyond.*

You are also asking me questions and I hear you,
I answer that I cannot answer, you must find out for yourself.

Sit a while dear son,
Here are biscuits to eat and here is milk to drink,
But as soon as you sleep and renew yourself in sweet clothes, I kiss you with a good-by kiss and open the gate for your egress hence.

Long enough have you dream'd contemptible dreams,
Now I wash the gum from your eyes,
You must habit yourself to the dazzle of the light and of every moment of your life.

Long have you timidly waded holding a plank by the shore,
Now I will you to be a bold swimmer,
To jump off in the midst of the sea, rise again, nod to me, shout, and laughingly dash with your hair.

47

I am the teacher of athletes,
He that by me spreads a wider breast than my own proves the width of my own,
He most honors my style who learns under it to destroy the teacher.

The boy I love, the same becomes a man not through derived power, but in his own right,
Wicked rather than virtuous out of conformity or fear,
Fond of his sweetheart, relishing well his steak,

Unrequited love or a slight cutting him worse than sharp steel cuts,
First-rate to ride, to fight, to hit the bull's eye, to sail a skiff, to sing a song or play on the banjo,
Preferring scars and the beard and faces pitted with small-pox over all latherers,
And those well-tann'd to those that keep out of the sun.

I teach straying from me, yet who can stray from me?
I follow you whoever you are from the present hour,
My words itch at your ears till you understand them.

I do not say these things for a dollar or to fill up the time while I wait for a boat,
(It is you talking just as much as myself, I act as the tongue of you,
Tied in your mouth, in mine it begins to be loosen'd.)

I swear I will never again mention love or death inside a house,
And I swear I will never translate myself at all, only to him or her who privately stays with me in the open air.

If you would understand me go to the heights or water-shore,
The nearest gnat is an explanation, and a drop or motion of waves a key,
The maul, the oar, the hand-saw, second my words.

No shutter'd room or school can commune with me,
But roughs and little children better than they.

The young mechanic is closest to me, he knows me well,
The woodman that takes his axe and jug with him shall take me with him all day,
The farm-boy ploughing in the field feels good at the sound of my voice,
In vessels that sail my words sail, I go with fishermen and seamen and love them.

The soldier camp'd or upon the march is mine,
On the night ere the pending battle many seek me, and I do not fail them,
On that solemn night (it may be their last) those that know me seek me.
My face rubs to the hunter's face when he lies down alone in his blanket,
The driver thinking of me does not mind the jolt of his wagon,
The young mother and old mother comprehend me,
The girl and the wife rest the needle a moment and forget where they are,
They and all would resume what I have told them.

48

I have said that the soul is not more than the body,
And I have said that the body is not more than the soul,
And nothing, not God, is greater to one than one's self is,
And whoever walks a furlong without sympathy walks to his own funeral drest in his shroud,
And I or you pocketless of a dime may purchase the pick of the earth,
And to glance with an eye or show a bean in its pod confounds the learning of all times,
And there is no trade or employment but the young man following it may become a hero,
And there is no object so soft but it makes a hub for the wheel'd universe,
And I say to any man or woman, Let your soul stand cool and composed before a million universes.

And I say to mankind, Be not curious about God,
For I who am curious about each am not curious about God,
(No array of terms can say how much I am at peace about God and about death.)

I hear and behold God in every object, yet understand God not in the least,
Nor do I understand who there can be more wonderful than myself.

Why should I wish to see God better than this day?

I see something of God each hour of the twenty-four, and each moment then,
In the faces of men and women I see God, and in my own face in the glass,
I find letters from God dropt in the street, and every one is sign'd by God's name,
And I leave them where they are, for I know that wheresoe'er I go,
Others will punctually come for ever and ever.

49

And as to you Death, and you bitter hug of mortality, it is idle to try to alarm me.

To his work without flinching the accoucheur comes,
I see the elder-hand pressing receiving supporting,
I recline by the sills of the exquisite flexible doors,
And mark the outlet, and mark the relief and escape.

And as to you Corpse I think you are good manure, but that does not offend me,
I smell the white roses sweet-scented and growing,
I reach to the leafy lips, I reach to the polish'd breasts of melons.

And as to you Life I reckon you are the leavings of many deaths,
(No doubt I have died myself ten thousand times before.)

I hear you whispering there O stars of heaven,
O suns—O grass of graves—O perpetual transfers and promotions,
If you do not say any thing how can I say any thing?

Of the turbid pool that lies in the autumn forest,
Of the moon that descends the steeps of the soughing twilight,
Toss, sparkles of day and dusk—toss on the black stems that decay in the muck,
Toss to the moaning gibberish of the dry limbs.

I ascend from the moon, I ascend from the night,
I perceive that the ghastly glimmer is noonday sunbeams reflected,
And debouch to the steady and central from the offspring great or small.

50

There is that in me—I do not know what it is—but I know it is in me.

Wrench'd and sweaty—calm and cool then my body becomes,
I sleep—I sleep long.

I do not know it—it is without name—it is a word unsaid,
It is not in any dictionary, utterance, symbol.

Something it swings on more than the earth I swing on,
To it the creation is the friend whose embracing awakes me.

Perhaps I might tell more. Outlines! I plead for my brothers and sisters.

Do you see O my brothers and sisters?
It is not chaos or death—it is form, union, plan—it is eternal life—it is Happiness.

51

The past and present wilt—I have fill'd them, emptied them,
And proceed to fill my next fold of the future.

Listener up there! what have you to confide to me?
Look in my face while I snuff the sidle of evening,
(Talk honestly, no one else hears you, and I stay only a minute longer.)

Do I contradict myself?
Very well then I contradict myself,
(I am large, I contain multitudes.)

I concentrate toward them that are nigh, I wait on the door-slab.

Who has done his day's work? who will soonest be through with his supper?
Who wishes to walk with me?

Will you speak before I am gone? will you prove already too late?

52

The spotted hawk swoops by and accuses me, he complains of my gab and my loitering.

I too am not a bit tamed, I too am untranslatable,
I sound my barbaric yawp over the roofs of the world.

The last scud of day holds back for me,
It flings my likeness after the rest and true as any on the shadow'd wilds,
It coaxes me to the vapor and the dusk.

I depart as air, I shake my white locks at the runaway sun,
I effuse my flesh in eddies, and drift it in lacy jags.

I bequeath myself to the dirt to grow from the grass I love,
If you want me again look for me under your boot-soles.

You will hardly know who I am or what I mean,
But I shall be good health to you nevertheless,
And filter and fibre your blood.

Failing to fetch me at first keep encouraged,
Missing me one place search another,
I stop somewhere waiting for you.

1855

CROSSING BROOKLYN FERRY

1

FLOOD-TIDE below me! I see you face to face!
Clouds of the west—sun there half an hour high—I see you also face to face.

Crowds of men and women attired in the usual costumes, how curious you are to me!
On the ferry-boats the hundreds and hundreds that cross, returning home, are more curious to me than you suppose,
And you that shall cross from shore to shore years hence are more to me, and more in my meditations, than you might suppose.

2

The impalpable sustenance of me from all things at all hours of the day,
The simple, compact, well-join'd scheme, myself disintegrated, every one disintegrated yet part of the scheme,
The similitudes of the past and those of the future,
The glories strung like beads on my smallest sights and hearings, on the walk in the street and the passage over the river,
The current rushing so swiftly and swimming with me far away,
The others that are to follow me, the ties between me and them,
The certainty of others, the life, love, sight, hearing of others.

Others will enter the gates of the ferry and cross from shore to shore,
Others will watch the run of the flood-tide,
Others will see the shipping of Manhattan north and west, and the heights of Brooklyn to the south and east,
Others will see the islands large and small;
Fifty years hence, others will see them as they cross, the sun half an hour high,
A hundred years hence, or ever so many hundred years hence, others will see them,
Will enjoy the sunset, the pouring-in of the flood-tide, the falling-back to the sea of the ebb-tide.

3

It avails not, time nor place—distance avails not,
I am with you, you men and women of a generation, or ever so many generations hence,
Just as you feel when you look on the river and sky, so I felt,
Just as any of you is one of a living crowd, I was one of a crowd,
Just as you are refresh'd by the gladness of the river and the bright flow, I was refresh'd,
Just as you stand and lean on the rail, yet hurry with the swift current, I stood yet was hurried,

Just as you look on the numberless masts of ships and the thick-stemm'd pipes of steamboats, I look'd.

I too many and many a time cross'd the river of old,
Watched the Twelfth-month sea-gulls, saw them high in the air floating with motionless wings, oscillating their bodies,
Saw how the glistening yellow lit up parts of their bodies and left the rest in strong shadow,
Saw the slow-wheeling circles and the gradual edging toward the south,
Saw the reflection of the summer sky in the water,
Had my eyes dazzled by the shimmering track of beams,
Look'd at the fine centrifugal spokes of light round the shape of my head in the sunlit water,
Look'd on the haze on the hills southward and south-westward,
Look'd on the vapor as it flew in fleeces tinged with violet,
Look'd toward the lower bay to notice the vessels arriving,
Saw their approach, saw aboard those that were near me,
Saw the white sails of schooners and sloops, saw the ships at anchor,
The sailors at work in the rigging or out astride the spars,
The round masts, the swinging motion of the hulls, the slender serpentine pennants,
The large and small steamers in motion, the pilots in their pilot-houses,
The white wake left by the passage, the quick tremulous whirl of the wheels,
The flags of all nations, the falling of them at sunset,
The scallop-edged waves in the twilight, the ladled cups, the frolicsome crests and glistening,
The stretch afar growing dimmer and dimmer, the gray walls of the granite storehouses by the docks,
On the river the shadowy group, the big steam-tug closely flank'd on each side by the barges, the hay-boat, the belated lighter,
On the neighboring shore, the fires from the foundry chimneys burning high and glaringly into the night,
Casting their flicker of black contrasted with wild red and yellow light over the tops of houses, and down into the clefts of streets.

4

These and all else were to me the same as they are to you,
I loved well those cities, loved well the stately and rapid river,
The men and women I saw were all near to me,
Others the same—others who look back on me because I look'd forward to them,
(The time will come, though I stop here today and to-night.)

5

What is it then between us?
What is the count of the scores or hundreds of years between us?

Whatever it is, it avails not—distance avails not, and place avails not,
I too lived, Brooklyn of ample hills was mine,
I too walk'd the streets of Manhattan island, and bathed in the waters around it,
I too felt the curious abrupt questionings stir within me,
In the day among crowds of people sometimes they came upon me,
In my walks home late at night or as I lay in my bed they came upon me,
I too had been struck from the float forever held in solution,
I too had receiv'd identity by my body,
That I was I knew was of my body, and what I should be I knew I should be of my body.

6

It is not upon you alone the dark patches fall,
The dark threw its patches down upon me also,
The best I had done seem'd to me blank and suspicious,
My great thoughts as I supposed them, were they not in reality meagre?
Nor is it you alone who know what it is to be evil,

I am he who knew what it was to be evil,
I too knitted the old knot of contrariety,
Blabb'd, blush'd, resented, lied, stole, grudg'd,
Had guile, anger, lust, hot wishes I dared not speak,
Was wayward, vain, greedy, shallow, sly, cowardly, malignant,
The wolf, the snake, the hog, not wanting in me,
The cheating look, the frivolous word, the adulterous wish, not wanting,
Refusals, hates, postponements, meanness, laziness, none of these wanting,
Was one with the rest, the days and haps of the rest,
Was call'd by my nighest name by clear loud voices of young men as they saw me approaching or passing,
Felt their arms on my neck as I stood, or the negligent leaning of their flesh against me as I sat,
Saw many I loved in the street or ferry-boat or public assembly, yet never told them a word,
Lived the same life with the rest, the same old laughing, gnawing, sleeping,
Play'd the part that still looks back on the actor or actress,
The same old rôle, the rôle that is what we make it, as great as we like,
Or as small as we like, or both great and small.

7

Closer yet I approach you,
What thought you have of me now, I had as much of you—I laid in my stores in advance,
I consider'd long and seriously of you before you were born.

Who was to know what should come home to me?
Who knows but I am enjoying this?
Who knows, for all the distance, but I am as good as looking at you now, for all you cannot see me?

8

Ah, what can ever be more stately and admirable to me than mast-hemm'd Manhattan?
River and sunset and scallop-edg'd waves of flood-tide?
The sea-gulls oscillating their bodies, the hay-boat in the twilight, and the belated lighter?

What gods can exceed these that clasp me by the hand, and with voices I love call me promptly and loudly by my nighest name as I approach?
What is more subtle than this which ties me to the woman or man that looks in my face?
Which fuses me into you now, and pours my meaning into you?

We understand then do we not?
What I promis'd without mentioning it, have you not accepted?
What the study could not teach—what the preaching could not accomplish is accomplish'd, is it not?

9

Flow on, river! flow with the flood-tide, and ebb with the ebb-tide!
Frolic on, crested and scallop-edg'd waves!
Gorgeous clouds of the sunset! drench with your splendor me, or the men and women generations after me!
Cross from shore to shore, countless crowds of passengers!
Stand up, tall masts of Mannahatta! stand up, beautiful hills of Brooklyn!
Throb, baffled and curious brain! throw out questions and answers!
Suspend here and everywhere, eternal float of solution!
Gaze, loving and thirsting eyes, in the house or street or public assembly!
Sound out, voices of young men! loudly and musically call me by my nighest name!
Live, old life! play the part that looks back on the actor or actress!
Play the old rôle, the rôle that is great or small according as one makes it!
Consider, you who peruse me, whether I may not in unknown ways be looking upon you;
Be firm, rail over the river, to support those who lean idly, yet haste with the hasting current;

Fly on, sea-birds! fly sideways, or wheel in large circles high in the air;
Receive the summer sky, you water, and faithfully hold it till all downcast eyes have time to take it from you!
Diverge, fine spokes of light, from the shape of my head, or any one's head, in the sunlit water!
Come on, ships from the lower bay! pass up or down, white-sail'd schooners, sloops, lighters!
Flaunt away, flags of all nations! be duly lower'd at sunset!
Burn high your fires, foundry chimneys! cast black shadows at nightfall! cast red and yellow light over the tops of the houses!
Appearances, now or henceforth, indicate what you are,
You necessary film, continue to envelop the soul,
About my body for me, and your body for you, be hung our divinest aromas,
Thrive, cities—bring your freight, bring your shows, ample and sufficient rivers,
Expand, being than which none else is perhaps more spiritual,
Keep your places, objects than which none else is more lasting.

You have waited, you always wait, you dumb, beautiful ministers,
We receive you with free sense at last, and are insatiate henceforward,
Not you any more shall be able to foil us, or withhold yourselves from us,
We use you, and do not cast you aside—we plant you permanently within us,
We fathom you not—we love you—there is perfection in you also,
You furnish your parts toward eternity,
Great or small, you furnish your parts toward the soul.

1856

SONG OF THE OPEN ROAD

1

Afoot and light-hearted I take to the open road,
Healthy, free, the world before me,
The long brown path before me leading wherever I choose.

Henceforth I ask not good-fortune, I myself am good-fortune,
Henceforth I whimper no more, postpone no more, need nothing,
Done with indoor complaints, libraries, querulous criticisms,
Strong and content I travel the open road.

The earth, that is sufficient,
I do not want the constellations any nearer,
I know they are very well where they are,
I know they suffice for those who belong to them.

(Still here I carry my old delicious burdens,
I carry them, men and women, I carry them with me wherever I go,
I swear it is impossible for me to get rid of them,
I am fill'd with them, and I will fill them in return.)

2

You road I enter upon and look around, I believe you are not all that is here,
I believe that much unseen is also here.

Here the profound lesson of reception, nor preference nor denial,
The black with his woolly head, the felon, the diseas'd, the illiterate person, are not denied;
The birth, the hasting after the physician, the beggar's tramp, the drunkard's stagger, the laughing party of mechanics,
The escaped youth, the rich person's carriage, the fop, the eloping couple,
The early market-man, the hearse, the moving of furniture into the town, the return back from the town,
They pass, I also pass, any thing passes, none can be interdicted,
None but are accepted, none but shall be dear to me.

3

You air that serves me with breath to speak!
You objects that call from diffusion my meanings and give them shape!
You light that wraps me and all things in delicate equable showers!

You paths worn in the irregular hollows by the roadsides!
I believe you are latent with unseen existences, you are so dear to me.

You flagg'd walks of the cities! you strong curbs at the edges!
You ferries! you planks and posts of wharves! you timber-lined sides! you distant ships!
You rows of houses! you window-pierc'd façades! you roofs!
You porches and entrances! you copings and iron guards!
You windows whose transparent shells might expose so much!
You doors and ascending steps! you arches!
You gray stones of interminable pavements! you trodden crossings!
From all that has touch'd you I believe you have imparted to yourselves, and now would impart the same secretly to me,
From the living and the dead you have peopled your impassive surfaces, and the spirits thereof would be evident and amicable with me.

4

The earth expanding right hand and left hand,
The picture alive, every part in its best light,
The music falling in where it is wanted, and stopping where it is not wanted,
The cheerful voice of the public road, the gay fresh sentiment of the road.

O highway I travel, do you say to me *Do not leave me?*
Do you say *Venture not—if you leave me you are lost?*
Do you say *I am already prepared, I am well-beaten and undenied, adhere to me?*

O public road, I say back I am not afraid to leave you, yet I love you,
You express me better than I can express myself,
You shall be more to me than my poem.

I think heroic deeds were all conceiv'd in the open air, and all free poems also,
I think I could stop here myself and do miracles,
I think whatever I shall meet on the road I shall like, and whoever beholds me shall like me,
I think whoever I see must be happy.

5

From this hour I ordain myself loos'd of limits and imaginary lines,
Going where I list, my own master total and absolute,
Listening to others, considering well what they say,
Pausing, searching, receiving, contemplating,
Gently, but with undeniable will, divesting myself of the holds that would hold me.

I inhale great draughts of space,
The east and the west are mine, and the north and the south are mine.

I am larger, better than I thought,
I did not know I held so much goodness.

All seems beautiful to me,
I can repeat over to men and women You have done such good to me I would do the same to you,
I will recruit for myself and you as I go,
I will scatter myself among men and women as I go,
I will toss a new gladness and roughness among them,
Whoever denies me it shall not trouble me,
Whoever accepts me he or she shall be blessed and shall bless me.

6

Now if a thousand perfect men were to appear it would not amaze me,
Now if a thousand beautiful forms of women appear'd it would not astonish me.

Now I see the secret of the making of the best persons,
It is to grow in the open air and to eat and sleep with the earth.

Here a great personal deed has room,
(Such a deed seizes upon the hearts of the whole race of men,
Its effusion of strength and will overwhelms law and mocks all authority and all argument against it.)

Here is the test of wisdom,
Wisdom is not finally tested in schools,
Wisdom cannot be pass'd from one having it to another not having it,
Wisdom is of the soul, is not susceptible of proof, is its own proof,
Applies to all stages and objects and qualities and is content,
Is the certainty of the reality and immortality of things, and the excellence of things;
Something there is in the float of the sight of things that provokes it out of the soul.

Now I re-examine philosophies and religions,
They may prove well in lecture-rooms, yet not prove at all under the spacious clouds and along the landscape and flowing currents.

Here is realization,
Here is a man tallied—he realizes here what he has in him,
The past, the future, majesty, love—if they are vacant of you, you are vacant of them.

Only the kernel of every object nourishes;
Where is he who tears off the husks for you and me?
Where is he that undoes stratagems and envelopes for you and me?

Here is adhesiveness, it is not previously fashion'd, it is apropos;
Do you know what it is as you pass to be loved by strangers?
Do you know the talk of those turning eye-balls?

7

Here is the efflux of the soul,
The efflux of the soul comes from within through embower'd gates, ever provoking questions,
These yearnings why are they? these thoughts in the darkness why are they?
Why are there men and women that while they are nigh me the sunlight expands my blood?
Why when they leave me do my pennants of joy sink flat and lank?
Why are there trees I never walk under but large and melodious thoughts descend upon me?
(I think they hang there winter and summer on those trees and always drop fruit as I pass;)
What is it I interchange so suddenly with strangers?
What with some driver as I ride on the seat by his side?
What with some fisherman drawing his seine by the shore as I walk by and pause?
What gives me to be free to a woman's and man's good-will? what gives them to be free to mine?

8

The efflux of the soul is happiness, here is happiness,
I think it pervades the open air, waiting at all times,
Now it flows unto us, we are rightly charged.

Here rises the fluid and attaching character,
The fluid and attaching character is the freshness and sweetness of man and woman,
(The herbs of the morning sprout no fresher and sweeter every day out of the roots of themselves, than it sprouts fresh and sweet continually out of itself.)
Toward the fluid and attaching character exudes the sweat of the love of young and old,
From it falls distill'd the charm that mocks beauty and attainments,
Toward it heaves the shuddering longing ache of contact.

9

Allons! whoever you are come travel with me!
Traveling with me you find what never tires.

The earth never tires,
The earth is rude, silent, incomprehensible at first, Nature is rude and incomprehensible at first,
Be not discouraged, keep on, there are divine things well envelop'd,
I swear to you there are divine things more beautiful than words can tell.

Allons! we must not stop here,
However sweet these laid-up stores, however convenient this dwelling we cannot remain here,

However shelter'd this port and however calm these waters we must not anchor here,
However welcome the hospitality that surrounds us we are permitted to receive it but a little while.

10

Allons! the inducements shall be greater,
We will sail pathless and wild seas,
We will go where winds blow, waves dash, and the Yankee clipper speeds by under full sail.

Allons! with power, liberty, the earth, the elements,
Health, defiance, gayety, self-esteem, curiosity;
Allons! from all formules!
From your formules, O bat-eyed and materialistic priests.

The stale cadaver blocks up the passage—the burial waits no longer.

Allons! yet take warning!
He traveling with me needs the best blood, thews, endurance,
None may come to the trial till he or she bring courage and health,
Come not here if you have already spent the best of yourself,
Only those may come who come in sweet and determin'd bodies,
No diseas'd person, no rum-drinker or venereal taint is permitted here.
(I and mine do not convince by arguments, similes, rhymes,
We convince by our presence.)

11

Listen! I will be honest with you,
I do not offer the old smooth prizes, but offer rough new prizes,
These are the days that must happen to you:
You shall not heap up what is call'd riches,
You shall scatter with lavish hand all that you earn or achieve,
You but arrive at the city to which you were destin'd, you hardly settle yourself to satisfaction before you are call'd by an irresistible call to depart,
You shall be treated to the ironical smiles and mockings of those who remain behind you,
What beckonings of love you receive you shall only answer with passionate kisses of parting,
You shall not allow the hold of those who spread their reach'd hands toward you.

12

Allons! after the great Companions, and to belong to them!
They too are on the road—they are the swift and majestic men—they are the greatest women,
Enjoyers of calms of seas and storms of seas,
Sailors of many a ship, walkers of many a mile of land,
Habitués of many distant countries, habitués of far-distant dwellings,
Trusters of men and women, observers of cities, solitary toilers,
Pausers and contemplators of tufts, blossoms, shells of the shore,
Dancers at wedding-dances, kissers of brides, tender helpers of children, bearers of children,
Soldiers of revolts, standers by gaping graves, lowerers-down of coffins,
Journeyers over consecutive seasons, over the years, the curious years each emerging from that which preceded it,
Journeyers as with companions, namely their own diverse phases,
Forth-steppers from the latent unrealized baby-days,
Journeyers gayly with their own youth, journeyers with their bearded and well-grain'd manhood,
Journeyers with their womanhood, ample, unsurpass'd, content,
Journeyers with their own sublime old age of manhood or womanhood,
Old age, calm, expanded, broad with the haughty breadth of the universe,
Old age, flowing free with the delicious near-by freedom of death.

13

Allons! to that which is endless as it was beginningless,
To undergo much, tramps of days, rests of nights,

To merge all in the travel they tend to, and the days and nights they tend to,
Again to merge them in the start of superior journeys,
To see nothing anywhere but what you may reach it and pass it,
To conceive no time, however distant, but what you may reach it and pass it,
To look up or down no road but it stretches and waits for you, however long but it stretches and waits for you,
To see no being, not God's or any, but you also go thither,
To see no possession but you may possess it, enjoying all without labor or purchase, abstracting the feast yet not abstracting one particle of it,
To take the best of the farmer's farm and the rich man's elegant villa, and the chaste blessings of the well-married couple, and the fruits of orchards and flowers of gardens,
To take to your use out of the compact cities as you pass through,
To carry buildings and streets with you afterward wherever you go,
To gather the minds of men out of their brains as you encounter them, to gather the love out of their hearts,
To take your lovers on the road with you, for all that you leave them behind you,
To know the universe itself as a road, as many roads, as roads for traveling souls.

All parts away for the progress of souls,
All religion, all solid things, arts, governments—all that was or is apparent upon this globe or any globe, falls into niches and corners before the procession of souls along the grand roads of the universe.

Of the progress of the souls of men and women along the grand roads of the universe, all other progress is the needed emblem and sustenance.

Forever alive, forever forward,
Stately, solemn, sad, withdrawn, baffled, mad, turbulent, feeble, dissatisfied,
Desperate, proud, fond, sick, accepted by men, rejected by men,
They go! they go! I know that they go, but I know not where they go,
But I know that they go toward the best—toward something great.

Whoever you are, come forth! or man or woman come forth!
You must not stay sleeping and dallying there in the house, though you built it, or though it has been built for you.

Out of the dark confinement! out from behind the screen!
It is useless to protest, I know all and expose it.

Behold through you as bad as the rest,
Through the laughter, dancing, dining, supping, of people,
Inside of dresses and ornaments, inside of those wash'd and trimm'd faces,
Behold a secret silent loathing and despair.

No husband, no wife, no friend, trusted to hear the confession,
Another self, a duplicate of every one, skulking and hiding it goes,
Formless and wordless through the streets of the cities, polite and bland in the parlors,
In the cars of railroads, in steamboats, in the public assembly,
Home to the houses of men and women, at the table, in the bedroom, everywhere,
Smartly attired, countenance smiling, form upright, death under the breast-bones, hell under the skull-bones,
Under the broadcloth and gloves, under the ribbons and artificial flowers,
Keeping fair with the customs, speaking not a syllable of itself,
Speaking of any thing else but never of itself.

14

Allons! through struggles and wars!
The goal that was named cannot be countermanded.

Have the past struggles succeeded?
What has succeeded? yourself? your nation? Nature?
Now understand me well—it is provided in the essence of things that from any fruition of success, no matter what, shall come

forth something to make a greater struggle necessary.

My call is the call of battle, I nourish active rebellion,
He going with me must go well arm'd,
He going with me goes often with spare diet, poverty, angry enemies, desertions.

15

Allons! the road is before us!
It is safe—I have tried it—my own feet have tried it well—be not detain'd!
Let the paper remain on the desk unwritten, and the book on the shelf unopen'd!
Let the tools remain in the workshop! let the money remain unearn'd!
Let the school stand! mind not the cry of the teacher!
Let the preacher preach in his pulpit! let the lawyer plead in the court, and the judge expound the law.

Camerado, I give you my hand!
I give you my love more precious than money,
I give you myself before preaching or law;
Will you give me yourself? will you come travel with me?
Shall we stick by each other as long as we live?

1856

MIRACLES

WHY, who makes much of a miracle?
As to me I know of nothing else but miracles,
Whether I walk the streets of Manhattan,
Or dart my sight over the roofs of houses toward the sky,
Or wade with naked feet along the beach just in the edge of the water,
Or stand under trees in the woods,
Or talk by day with any one I love, or sleep in the bed at night with any one I love,
Or sit at table at dinner with the rest,
Or look at strangers opposite me riding in the car,
Or watch honey-bees busy around the hive of a summer forenoon,
Or animals feeding in the fields,
Or birds, or the wonderfulness of insects in the air,
Or the wonderfulness of the sundown, or of stars shining so quiet and bright,
Or the exquisite delicate thin curve of the new moon in spring;
These with the rest, one and all, are to me miracles,
The whole referring, yet each distinct and in its place.

To me every hour of the light and dark is a miracle,
Every cubic inch of space is a miracle,
Every square yard of the surface of the earth is spread with the same,
Every foot of the interior swarms with the same.
To me the sea is a continual miracle,
The fishes that swim—the rocks—the motion of the waves—the ships with men in them,
What stranger miracles are there?

1856

ASSURANCES

I NEED no assurances, I am a man who is pre-occupied of his own soul;
I do not doubt that from under the feet and beside the hands and face I am cognizant of, are now looking faces I am not cognizant of, calm and actual faces,
I do not doubt but the majesty and beauty of the world are latent in any iota of the world,
I do not doubt I am limitless, and that the universes are limitless, in vain I try to think how limitless,
I do not doubt that the orbs and the systems of orbs play their swift sports through the air on purpose, and that I shall one day be eligible to do as much as they, and more than they,
I do not doubt that temporary affairs keep on and on millions of years,
I do not doubt interiors have their interiors, and exteriors have their exteriors, and that the eyesight has another eyesight, and the hearing another hearing, and the voice another voice,
I do not doubt that the passionately-wept deaths of young men are provided for, and that the deaths of young women and

the deaths of little children are provided for,
(Did you think Life was so well provided for, and Death, the purport of all Life, is not well provided for?)
I do not doubt that wrecks at sea, no matter what the horrors of them, no matter whose wife, child, husband, father, lover, has gone down, are provided for, to the minutest points,
I do not doubt that whatever can possibly happen anywhere at any time, is provided for in the inherences of things,
I do not think Life provides for all and for Time and Space, but I believe Heavenly Death provides for all.

1856

OUT OF THE CRADLE ENDLESSLY ROCKING

OUT of the cradle endlessly rocking,
Out of the mocking-bird's throat, the musical shuttle,
Out of the Ninth-month midnight,
Over the sterile sands and the fields beyond where the child leaving his bed wander'd alone, bareheaded, barefoot,
Down from the shower'd halo,
Up from the mystic play of shadows twining and twisting as if they were alive,
Out from the patches of briers and blackberries,
From the memories of the bird that chanted to me,
From your memories sad brother, from the fitful risings and fallings I heard,
From under that yellow half-moon late-risen and swollen as if with tears,
From those beginning notes of yearning and love there in the mist,
From the thousand responses of my heart never to cease,
From the myriad thence-arous'd words,
From the word stronger and more delicious than any,
From such as now they start the scene revisiting,
As a flock, twittering, rising, or overhead passing,
Borne hither, ere all eludes me, hurriedly,
A man, yet by these tears a little boy again,
Throwing myself on the sand, confronting the waves,
I, chanter of pains and joys, uniter of here and hereafter,
Taking all hints to use them, but swiftly leaping beyond them,
A reminiscence sing.

Once Paumanok,
When the lilac-scent was in the air and Fifth-month grass was growing,
Up this seashore in some briers,
Two feather'd guests from Alabama, two together,
And their nest, and four light-green eggs spotted with brown,
And every day the he-bird to and fro near at hand,
And every day the she-bird crouch'd on her nest, silent, with bright eyes,
And every day I, a curious boy, never too close, never disturbing them,
Cautiously peering, absorbing, translating.

Shine! shine! shine!
Pour down your warmth, great sun!
While we bask, we two together.

Two together!
Winds blow south, or winds blow north,
Day come white, or night come black,
Home, or rivers and mountains from home,
Singing all time, minding no time,
While we two keep together.

Till of a sudden,
May-be kill'd, unknown to her mate,
One forenoon the she-bird crouch'd not on the nest,
Nor return'd that afternoon, nor the next,
Nor ever appear'd again.

And thenceforward all summer in the sound of the sea,
And at night under the full of the moon in calmer weather,
Over the hoarse surging of the sea,
Or flitting from brier to brier by day,
I saw, I heard at intervals the remaining one, the he-bird,
The solitary guest from Alabama.

Blow! blow! blow!
Blow up sea-winds along Paumanok's shore;
I wait and I wait till you blow my mate to me.

Yes, when the stars glisten'd,
All night long on the prong of a moss-scallop'd stake,
Down almost amid the slapping waves,
Sat the lone singer wonderful causing tears.

He call'd on his mate,
He pour'd forth the meanings which I of all men know.

Yes my brother I know,
The rest might not, but I have treasur'd every note,
For more than once dimly down to the beach gliding,
Silent, avoiding the moonbeams, blending myself with the shadows,
Recalling now the obscure shapes, the echoes, the sounds and sights after their sorts,
The white arms out in the breakers tirelessly tossing,
I, with bare feet, a child, the wind wafting my hair,
Listen'd long and long.

Listen'd to keep, to sing, now translating the notes,
Following you my brother.

Soothe! soothe! soothe!
Close on its wave soothes the wave behind,
And again another behind embracing and lapping, every one close,
But my love soothes not me, not me.

Low hangs the moon, it rose late,
It is lagging—O I think it is heavy with love, with love.

O madly the sea pushes upon the land,
With love, with love.

O night! do I not see my love fluttering out among the breakers?
What is that little black thing I see there in the white?

Loud! loud! loud!
Loud I call to you, my love!
High and clear I shoot my voice over the waves,
Surely you must know who is here, is here,
You must know who I am, my love.

Low-hanging moon!
What is that dusky spot in your brown yellow?
O it is the shape, the shape of my mate!
O moon do not keep her from me any longer.

Land! land! O land!
Whichever way I turn, O I think you could give me my mate back again if you only would,
For I am almost sure I see her dimly whichever way I look.

O rising stars!
Perhaps the one I want so much will rise, will rise with some of you.

O throat! O trembling throat!
Sound clearer through the atmosphere!
Pierce the woods, the earth,
Somewhere listening to catch you must be the one I want.

Shake out carols!
Solitary here, the night's carols!
Carols of lonesome love! death's carols!
Carols under that lagging, yellow, waning moon!
O under that moon where she droops almost down into the sea!
O reckless despairing carols.

But soft! sink low!
Soft, let me just murmur,
And do you wait a moment you husky-nois'd sea,
For somewhere I believe I heard my mate responding to me,
So faint, I must be still, be still to listen,
But not altogether still, for then she might not come immediately to me.

Hither my love!
Here I am! here!
With this just-sustain'd note I announce myself to you,
This gentle call is for you my love, for you.

Do not be decoy'd elsewhere,
That is the whistle of the wind, it is not my voice,
That is the fluttering, the fluttering of the spray,
Those are the shadows of leaves.

O darkness! O in vain!
O I am very sick and sorrowful.

O brown halo in the sky near the moon, drooping upon the sea!
O troubled reflection in the sea!
O throat! O throbbing heart!
And I singing uselessly, uselessly all the night.

O past! O happy life! O songs of joy!
In the air, in the woods, over fields,
Loved! loved! loved! loved! loved!
But my mate no more, no more with me!
We two together no more.

The aria sinking,
All else continuing, the stars shining,
The winds blowing, the notes of the bird continuous echoing,
With angry moans the fierce old mother incessantly moaning,
On the sands of Paumanok's shore gray and rustling,
The yellow half-moon enlarged, sagging down, drooping, the face of the sea almost touching,
The boy ecstatic, with his bare feet the waves, with his hair the atmosphere dallying,
The love in the heart long pent, now loose, now at last tumultuously bursting,
The aria's meaning, the ears, the soul, swiftly depositing,
The strange tears down the cheeks coursing,
The colloquy there, the trio, each uttering,
The undertone, the savage old mother incessantly crying,
To the boy's soul's questions sullenly timing, some drown'd secret hissing,
To the outsetting bard.

Demon or bird! (said the boy's soul,)
Is it indeed toward your mate you sing? or is it really to me?
For I, that was a child, my tongue's use sleeping, now I have heard you,
Now in a moment I know what I am for, I awake,
And already a thousand singers, a thousand songs, clearer, louder and more sorrowful than yours,
A thousand warbling echoes have started to life within me, never to die.

O you singer solitary, singing by yourself, projecting me,
O solitary me listening, never more shall I cease perpetuating you,
Never more shall I escape, never more the reverberations,
Never more the cries of unsatisfied love be absent from me,
Never again leave me to be the peaceful child I was before what there in the night,
By the sea under the yellow and sagging moon,
The messenger there arous'd, the fire, the sweet hell within,
The unknown want, the destiny of me.

O give me the clew! (it lurks in the night here somewhere,)
O if I am to have so much, let me have more!

A word then, (for I will conquer it,)
The word final, superior to all,
Subtle, sent up—what is it?—I listen;
Are you whispering it, and have been all the time, you sea-waves?
Is that it from your liquid rims and wet sands?

Whereto answering, the sea,
Delaying not, hurrying not,
Whisper'd me through the night, and very plainly before daybreak,
Lisp'd to me the low and delicious word death,
And again death, death, death, death,
Hissing melodious, neither like the bird nor like my arous'd child's heart,
But edging near as privately for me rustling at my feet,
Creeping thence steadily up to my ears and laving me softly all over,
Death, death, death, death, death.

Which I do not forget,
But fuse the song of my dusky demon and brother,
That he sang to me in the moonlight on Paumanok's gray beach,
With the thousand responsive songs at random,
My own songs awaked from that hour,
And with them the key, the word up from the waves,
The word of the sweetest song and all songs,
That strong and delicious word which, creeping to my feet,

(Or like some old crone rocking the cradle, swathed in sweet garments, bending aside,)
The sea whisper'd me.

1859

FACING WEST FROM CALIFORNIA'S SHORES

FACING west from California's shores,
Inquiring, tireless, seeking what is yet unfound,
I, a child, very old, over waves, towards the house of maternity, the land of migrations, look afar,
Look off the shores of my Western sea, the circle almost circled;
For starting westward from Hindustan, from the vales of Kashmere,
From Asia, from the north, from the God, the sage, and the hero,
From the south, from the flowery peninsulas and the spice islands,
Long having wander'd since, round the earth having wander'd,
Now I face home again, very pleas'd and joyous,
(But where is what I started for so long ago?
And why is it yet unfound?)

1860

FOR YOU O DEMOCRACY

COME, I will make the continent indissoluble,
I will make the most splendid race the sun ever shone upon,
I will make divine magnetic lands,
With the love of comrades,
With the life-long love of comrades.

I will plant companionship thick as trees along all the rivers of America, and along the shores of the great lakes, and all over the prairies,
I will make inseparable cities with their arms about each other's necks,
By the love of comrades,
By the manly love of comrades.

For you these from me, O Democracy, to serve you ma femme!
For you, for you I am trilling these songs.

1860

RECORDERS AGES HENCE

RECORDERS ages hence,
Come, I will take you down underneath this impassive exterior, I will tell you what to say of me,
Publish my name and hang up my picture as that of the tenderest lover,
The friend the lover's portrait, of whom his friend his lover was fondest,
Who was not proud of his songs, but of the measureless ocean of love within him, and freely pour'd it forth,
Who often walk'd lonesome walks thinking of his dear friends, his lovers,
Who pensive away from one he lov'd often lay sleepless and dissatisfied at night,
Who knew too well the sick, sick dread lest the one he lov'd might secretly be indifferent to him,
Whose happiest days were far away through fields, in woods, on hills, he and another wandering hand in hand, they twain apart from other men,
Who oft as he saunter'd the streets curv'd with his arm the shoulder of his friend, while the arm of his friend rested upon him also.

1860

I SAW IN LOUISIANA A LIVE-OAK GROWING

I SAW in Louisiana a live-oak growing,
All alone stood it and the moss hung down from the branches,
Without any companion it grew there uttering joyous leaves of dark green,
And its look, rude, unbending, lusty, made me think of myself,
But I wonder'd how it could utter joyous leaves standing alone there without its friend near, for I knew I could not,
And I broke off a twig with a certain number of leaves upon it, and twined around it a little moss,
And brought it away, and I have placed it in sight in my room,
It is not needed to remind me as of my own dear friends,
(For I believe lately I think of little else than of them,)

Yet it remains to me a curious token, it makes me think of manly love;
For all that, and though the live-oak glistens there in Louisiana solitary in a wide flat space,
Uttering joyous leaves all its life without a friend a lover near,
I know very well I could not.

1860

I HEAR IT WAS CHARGED AGAINST ME

I HEAR it was charged against me that I sought to destroy institutions,
But really I am neither for nor against institutions,
(What indeed have I in common with them? or what with the destruction of them?)
Only I will establish in the Mannahatta and in every city of these States inland and seaboard,
And in the fields and woods, and above every keel little or large that dents the water,
Without edifices or rules or trustees or any argument,
The institution of the dear love of comrades.

1860

I HEAR AMERICA SINGING

I HEAR America singing, the varied carols I hear,
Those of mechanics, each one singing his as it should be blithe and strong,
The carpenter singing his as he measures his plank or beam,
The mason singing his as he makes ready for work, or leaves off work,
The boatman singing what belongs to him in his boat, the deck-hand singing on the steamboat deck,
The shoemaker singing as he sits on his bench, the hatter singing as he stands,
The wood-cutter's song, the ploughboy's on his way in the morning, or at noon intermission or at sundown,
The delicious singing of the mother, or of the young wife at work, or of the girl sewing or washing,
Each singing what belongs to him or her and to none else,
The day what belongs to the day—at night the party of young fellows, robust, friendly,
Singing with open mouths their strong melodious songs.

1860

GIVE ME THE SPLENDID SILENT SUN

I

GIVE me the splendid silent sun with all his beams full-dazzling,
Give me juicy autumnal fruit ripe and red from the orchard,
Give me a field where the unmow'd grass grows,
Give me an arbor, give me the trellis'd grape,
Give me fresh corn and wheat, give me serene-moving animals teaching content,
Give me nights perfectly quiet as on high plateaus west of the Mississippi, and I looking up at the stars,
Give me odorous at sunrise a garden of beautiful flowers where I can walk undisturb'd,
Give me for marriage a sweet-breath'd woman of whom I should never tire,
Give me a perfect child, give me away aside from the noise of the world a rural domestic life,
Give me to warble spontaneous songs recluse by myself, for my own ears only,
Give me solitude, give me Nature, give me again O Nature your primal sanities!

These demanding to have them (tired with ceaseless excitement, and rack'd by the war-strife),
These to procure incessantly asking, rising in cries from my heart,
While yet incessantly asking still I adhere to my city,
Day upon day and year upon year O city, walking your streets,
Where you hold me enchain'd a certain time refusing to give me up,
Yet giving to make me glutted, enrich'd of soul, you give me forever faces;
(Oh I see what I sought to escape, confronting, reversing my cries,

I see my own soul trampling down what it
ask'd for.)

2

Keep your splendid silent sun,
Keep your woods O Nature, and the quiet places by the woods,
Keep your fields of clover and timothy, and your corn-fields and orchards,
Keep the blossoming buckwheat fields where the Ninth-month bees hum;
Give me faces and streets—give me these phantoms incessant and endless along the trottoirs!
Give me interminable eyes—give me women—give me comrades and lovers by the thousand!
Let me see new ones every day—let me hold new ones by the hand every day!
Give me such shows—give me the streets of Manhattan!
Give me Broadway, with the soldiers marching—give me the sound of the trumpets and drums!
(The soldiers in companies or regiments—some starting away, flush'd and reckless,
Some, their time up, returning with thinn'd ranks, young, yet very old, worn, marching, noticing nothing;)
Give me the shores and wharves heavy-fringed with black ships!
O such for me! O an intense life, full to repletion and varied!
The life of the theatre, bar-room, huge hotel, for me!
The saloon of the steamer! the crowded excursion for me! the torchlight procession!
The dense brigade bound for the war, with high piled military wagons following;
People, endless, streaming, with strong voices, passions, pageants,
Manhattan streets with their powerful throbs, with beating drums as now,
The endless and noisy chorus, the rustle and clank of muskets (even the sight of the wounded),
Manhattan crowds, with their turbulent musical chorus!
Manhattan faces and eyes forever for me.

1865

LONG, TOO LONG AMERICA

Long, too long America,
Traveling roads all even and peaceful you learn'd from joys and prosperity only,
But now, ah now, to learn from crises of anguish, advancing, grappling with direst fate and recoiling not,
And now to conceive and show to the world what your children en-masse really are,
(For who except myself has yet conceiv'd what your children en-masse really are?)

1865

PIONEERS! O PIONEERS!

Come my tan-faced children,
Follow well in order, get your weapons ready,
Have you your pistols? have you your sharp-edged axes?
Pioneers! O pioneers!

For we cannot tarry here,
We must march my darlings, we must bear the brunt of danger,
We the youthful sinewy races, all the rest on us depend,
Pioneers! O pioneers!

O you youths, Western youths,
So impatient, full of action, full of manly pride and friendship,
Plain I see you Western youths, see you tramping with the foremost,
Pioneers! O pioneers!

Have the elder races halted?
Do they droop and end their lesson, wearied over there beyond the seas?
We take up the task eternal, and the burden and the lesson,
Pioneers! O pioneers!

All the past we leave behind,
We debouch upon a newer mightier world, varied world,
Fresh and strong the world we seize, world of labor and the march,
Pioneers! O pioneers!

We detachments steady throwing,
Down the edges, through the passes, up the mountains steep,

Conquering, holding, daring, venturing as we go the unknown ways,
Pioneers! O pioneers!

We primeval forests felling,
We the rivers stemming, vexing we and piercing deep the mines within,
We the surface broad surveying, we the virgin soil upheaving,
Pioneers! O pioneers!

Colorado men are we,
From the peaks gigantic, from the great sierras and the high plateaus,
From the mine and from the gully, from the hunting trail we come,
Pioneers! O pioneers!

From Nebraska, from Arkansas,
Central inland race are we, from Missouri, with the continental blood intervein'd,
All the hands of comrades clasping, all the Southern, all the Northern,
Pioneers! O pioneers!

O resistless restless race!
O beloved race in all! O my breast aches with tender love for all!
O I mourn and yet exult, I am rapt with love for all,
Pioneers! O pioneers!

Raise the mighty mother mistress,
Waving high the delicate mistress, over all the starry mistress, (bend your heads all,)
Raise the fang'd and warlike mistress, stern, impassive, weapon'd mistress,
Pioneers! O pioneers!

See my children, resolute children,
By those swarms upon our rear we must never yield or falter,
Ages back in ghostly millions frowning there behind us urging,
Pioneers! O pioneers!

On and on the compact ranks,
With accessions ever waiting, with the places of the dead quickly fill'd,
Through the battle, through defeat, moving yet and never stopping,
Pioneers! O pioneers!

O to die advancing on!
Are there some of us to droop and die? has the hour come?
Then upon the march we fittest die, soon and sure the gap is fill'd,
Pioneers! O pioneers!

All the pulses of the world,
Falling in they beat for us, with the Western movement beat,
Holding single or together, steady moving to the front, all for us,
Pioneers! O pioneers!

Life's involv'd and varied pageants,
All the forms and shows, all the workmen at their work,
All the seamen and the landsmen, all the masters with their slaves,
Pioneers! O pioneers!

All the hapless silent lovers,
All the prisoners in the prisons, all the righteous and the wicked,
All the joyous, all the sorrowing, all the living, all the dying,
Pioneers! O pioneers!

I too with my soul and body,
We, a curious trio, picking, wandering on our way,
Through these shores amid the shadows, with the apparitions pressing,
Pioneers! O pioneers!

Lo, the darting bowling orb!
Lo, the brother orbs around, all the clustering suns and planets,
All the dazzling days, all the mystic nights with dreams,
Pioneers! O pioneers!

These are of us, they are with us,
All for primal needed work, while the followers there in embryo wait behind,
We to-day's procession heading, we the route for travel clearing,
Pioneers! O pioneers!

O you daughters of the West!
O you young and elder daughters! O you mothers and you wives!

Never must you be divided, in our ranks you move united,
Pioneers! O pioneers!

Minstrels latent on the prairies!
(Shrouded bards of other lands, you may rest, you have done your work,)
Soon I hear you coming warbling, soon you rise and tramp amid us,
Pioneers! O pioneers!

Not for delectations sweet,
Not the cushion and the slipper, not the peaceful and the studious,
Not the riches safe and palling, not for us the tame enjoyment,
Pioneers! O pioneers!

Do the feasters gluttonous feast?
Do the corpulent sleepers sleep? have they lock'd and bolted doors?
Still be ours the diet hard, and the blanket on the ground,
Pioneers! O pioneers!

Has the night descended?
Was the road of late so toilsome? did we stop discouraged nodding on our way?
Yet a passing hour I yield you in your tracks to pause oblivious,
Pioneers! O pioneers!

Till with sound of trumpet,
Far, far off the daybreak call—hark! how loud and clear I hear it wind,
Swift! to the head of the army!—swift! spring to your places,
Pioneers! O pioneers!

1865

WHEN I HEARD THE LEARN'D ASTRONOMER

When I heard the learn'd astronomer,
When the proofs, the figures, were ranged in columns before me,
When I was shown the charts and diagrams, to add, divide, and measure them,
When I sitting heard the astronomer where he lectured with much applause in the lecture-room,
How soon unaccountable I became tired and sick,
Till rising and gliding out I wander'd off by myself,
In the mystical moist night-air, and from time to time,
Look'd up in perfect silence at the stars.

1865

OUT OF THE ROLLING OCEAN THE CROWD

Out of the rolling ocean the crowd came a drop gently to me,
Whispering *I love you, before long I die,*
I have travel'd a long way merely to look on you to touch you,
For I could not die till I once look'd on you,
For I fear'd I might afterward lose you.

Now we have met, we have look'd, we are safe,
Return in peace to the ocean my love,
I too am part of that ocean my love, we are not so much separated,
Behold the great rondure, the cohesion of all, how perfect!
But as for me, for you, the irresistible sea is to separate us,
As for an hour carrying us diverse, yet cannot carry us diverse forever;
Be not impatient—a little space—know you I salute the air, the ocean and the land,
Every day at sundown for your dear sake my love.

1865

FROM PAUMANOK STARTING I FLY LIKE A BIRD

From Paumanok starting I fly like a bird,
Around and around to soar to sing the idea of all,
To the north betaking myself to sing their arctic songs,
To Kanada till I absorb Kanada in myself, to Michigan then,
To Wisconsin, Iowa, Minnesota, to sing their songs, (they are inimitable;)
Then to Ohio and Indiana to sing theirs, to Missouri and Kansas and Arkansas to sing theirs,
To Tennessee and Kentucky, to the Carolinas and Georgia to sing theirs,

To Texas and so along up toward California, to roam accepted everywhere;
To sing first, (to the tap of the war-drum if need be,)
The idea of all, of the Western world one and inseparable,
And then the song of each member of these States.

1865

RISE O DAYS FROM YOUR FATHOMLESS DEEPS

1

Rise O days from your fathomless deeps, till you loftier, fiercer sweep,
Long for my soul hungering gymnastic I devour'd what the earth gave me,
Long I roam'd the woods of the north, long I watch'd Niagara pouring,
I travel'd the prairies over and slept on their breast, I cross'd the Nevadas, I cross'd the plateaus,
I ascended the towering rocks along the Pacific, I sail'd out to sea,
I sail'd through the storm, I was refresh'd by the storm,
I watch'd with joy the threatening maws of the waves,
I mark'd the white combs where they career'd so high, curling over,
I heard the wind piping, I saw the black clouds,
Saw from below what arose and mounted, (O superb! O wild as my heart, and powerful!)
Heard the continuous thunder as it bellow'd after the lightning,
Noted the slender and jagged threads of lightning as sudden and fast amid the din they chased each other across the sky;
These, and such as these, I, elate, saw—saw with wonder, yet pensive and masterful,
All the menacing might of the globe uprisen around me,
Yet there with my soul I fed, I fed content, supercilious.

2

'Twas well, O soul—'twas a good preparation you gave me,
Now we advance our latent and ampler hunger to fill,
Now we go forth to receive what the earth and the sea never gave us,
Not through the mighty woods we go, but through the mightier cities,
Something for us is pouring now more than Niagara pouring,
Torrents of men, (sources and rills of the Northwest are you indeed inexhaustible?)
What, to pavements and homesteads here, what were those storms of the mountains and sea?
What, to passions I witness around me to-day? was the sea risen?
Was the wind piping the pipe of death under the black clouds?
Lo! from deeps more unfathomable, something more deadly and savage,
Manhattan rising, advancing with menacing front—Cincinnati, Chicago, unchain'd;
What was that swell I saw on the ocean? behold what comes here,
How it climbs with daring feet and hands—how it dashes!
How the true thunder bellows after the lightning—how bright the flashes of lightning!
How Democracy with desperate vengeful port strides on, shown through the dark by those flashes of lightning!
(Yet a mournful wail and low sob I fancied I heard through the dark,
In a lull of the deafening confusion.)

3

Thunder on! stride on, Democracy! strike with vengeful stroke!
And do you rise higher than ever yet O days, O cities!
Crash heavier, heavier yet O storms! you have done me good,
My soul prepared in the mountains absorbs your immortal strong nutriment,
Long had I walk'd my cities, my country roads through farms, only half satisfied,
One doubt nauseous undulating like a snake, crawl'd on the ground before me,
Continually preceding my steps, turning upon me oft, ironically hissing low;
The cities I loved so well I abandon'd and left, I sped to the certainties suitable to me,

Hungering, hungering, hungering, for primal energies and Nature's dauntlessness,
I refresh'd myself with it only, I could relish it only,
I waited the bursting forth of the pent fire—on the water and air I waited long;
But now I no longer wait, I am fully satisfied, I am glutted,
I have witness'd the true lightning, I have witness'd my cities electric,
I have lived to behold man burst forth and warlike America rise,
Hence I will seek no more the food of the northern solitary wilds,
No more the mountains roam or sail the stormy sea.

1865

COME UP FROM THE FIELDS FATHER

COME up from the fields father, here's a letter from our Pete,
And come to the front door mother, here's a letter from thy dear son.

Lo, 'tis autumn,
Lo, where the trees, deeper green, yellower and redder,
Cool and sweeten Ohio's villages with leaves fluttering in the moderate wind,
Where apples ripe in the orchards hang and grapes on the trellis'd vines,
(Smell you the smell of the grapes on the vines?
Smell you the buckwheat where the bees were lately buzzing?)

Above all, lo, the sky so calm, so transparent after the rain, and with wondrous clouds,
Below too, all calm, all vital and beautiful, and the farm prospers well.

Down in the fields all prospers well,
But now from the fields come father, come at the daughter's call,
And come to the entry mother, to the front door come right away.

Fast as she can she hurries, something ominous, her steps trembling,
She does not tarry to smooth her hair nor adjust her cap.

Open the envelope quickly,
O this is not our son's writing, yet his name is sign'd,
O a strange hand writes for our dear son, O stricken mother's soul!
All swims before her eyes, flashes with black, she catches the main words only,
Sentences broken, *gunshot wound in the breast, cavalry skirmish, taken to hospital,*
At present low, but will soon be better.

Ah now the single figure to me,
Amid all teeming and wealthy Ohio with all its cities and farms,
Sickly white in the face and dull in the head, very faint,
By the jamb of a door leans.

Grieve not so, dear mother, (the just-grown daughter speaks through her sobs,
The little sisters huddle around speechless and dismay'd,)
See, dearest mother, the letter says Pete will soon be better.

Alas poor boy, he will never be better, (nor may-be needs to be better, that brave and simple soul,)
While they stand at home at the door he is dead already,
The only son is dead.

But the mother needs to be better,
She with thin form presently drest in black,
By day her meals untouch'd, then at night fitfully sleeping, often waking,
In the midnight waking, weeping, longing with one deep longing,
O that she might withdraw unnoticed, silent from life escape and withdraw,
To follow, to seek, to be with her dear dead son.

1865

CAVALRY CROSSING A FORD

A LINE in long array where they wind betwixt green islands,
They take a serpentine course, their arms flash in the sun—hark to the musical clank,
Behold the silvery river, in it the splashing horses loitering stop to drink,

Behold the brown-faced men, each group, each person a picture, the negligent rest on the saddles,
Some emerge on the opposite bank, others are just entering the ford—while,
Scarlet and blue and snowy white,
The guidon flags flutter gayly in the wind.

1865

THE WOUND-DRESSER

1

An old man bending I come among new faces,
Years looking backward resuming in answer to children,
Come tell us old man, as from young men and maidens that love me,
(Arous'd and angry, I'd thought to beat the alarum, and urge relentless war,
But soon my fingers fail'd me, my face droop'd and I resign'd myself,
To sit by the wounded and soothe them, or silently watch the dead;)
Years hence of these scenes, of these furious passions, these chances,
Of unsurpass'd heroes, (was one side so brave? the other was equally brave;)
Now be witness again, paint the mightiest armies of earth,
Of those armies so rapid so wondrous what saw you to tell us?
What stays with you latest and deepest? of curious panics,
Of hard-fought engagements or sieges tremendous what deepest remains?

2

O maidens and young men I love and that love me,
What you ask of my days those the strangest and sudden your talking recalls,
Soldier alert I arrive after a long march cover'd with sweat and dust,
In the nick of time I come, plunge in the fight, loudly shout in the rush of successful charge,
Enter the captur'd works—yet lo, like a swift-running river they fade,
Pass and are gone they fade—I dwell not on soldiers' perils or soldiers' joys,
(Both I remember well—many the hardships, few the joys, yet I was content.)

But in silence, in dreams' projections,
While the world of gain and appearance and mirth goes on,
So soon what is over forgotten, and waves wash the imprints off the sand,
With hinged knees returning I enter the doors, (while for you up there,
Whoever you are, follow without noise and be of strong heart.)

Bearing the bandages, water and sponge,
Straight and swift to my wounded I go,
Where they lie on the ground after the battle brought in,
Where their priceless blood reddens the grass the ground,
Or to the rows of the hospital tent, or under the roof'd hospital,
To the long rows of cots up and down each side I return,
To each and all one after another I draw near, not one do I miss,
An attendant follows holding a tray, he carries a refuse pail,
Soon to be filled with clotted rags and blood, emptied, and fill'd again.

I onward go, I stop,
With hinged knees and steady hand to dress wounds,
I am firm with each, the pangs are sharp yet unavoidable,
One turns to me his appealing eyes—poor boy! I never knew you,
Yet I think I could not refuse this moment to die for you, if that would save you.

3

On, on I go, (open doors of time! open hospital doors!)
The crush'd head I dress, (poor crazed hand tear not the bandage away,)
The neck of the cavalry-man with the bullet through and through I examine,
Hard the breathing rattles, quite glazed already the eye, yet life struggles hard,
(Come sweet death! be persuaded O beautiful death!
In mercy come quickly.)

From the stump of the arm, the amputated hand,
I undo the clotted lint, remove the slough, wash off the matter and blood,
Back on his pillow the soldier bends with curv'd neck and side-falling head,
His eyes are closed, his face is pale, he dares not look on the bloody stump,
And has not yet look'd on it.

I dress a wound in the side, deep, deep,
But a day or two more, for see the frame all wasted and sinking,
And the yellow-blue countenance see.

I dress the perforated shoulder, the foot with the bullet-wound,
Cleanse the one with a gnawing and putrid gangrene, so sickening, so offensive,
While the attendant stands behind aside me holding the tray and pail.

I am faithful, I do not give out,
The fractur'd thigh, the knee, the wound in the abdomen,
These and more I dress with impassive hand, (yet deep in my breast a fire, a burning flame.)

4

Thus in silence in dreams' projections,
Returning, resuming, I thread my way through the hospitals,
The hurt and wounded I pacify with soothing hand,
I sit by the restless all the dark night, some are so young,
Some suffer so much, I recall the experience sweet and sad,
(Many a soldier's loving arms about this neck have cross'd and rested,
Many a soldier's kiss dwells on these bearded lips.)

1865

OVER THE CARNAGE ROSE PROPHETIC A VOICE

Over the carnage rose prophetic a voice,
Be not dishearten'd, affection shall solve the problems of freedom yet,
Those who love each other shall become invincible,
They shall yet make Columbia victorious.

Sons of the Mother of All, you shall yet be victorious,
You shall yet laugh to scorn the attacks of all the remainder of the earth.

No danger shall balk Columbia's lovers,
If need be a thousand shall sternly immolate themselves for one.

One from Massachusetts shall be a Missourian's comrade,
From Maine and from hot Carolina, and another an Oregonese, shall be friends triune,
More precious to each other than all the riches of the earth.

To Michigan, Florida perfumes shall tenderly come,
Not the perfumes of flowers, but sweeter, and wafted beyond death.

It shall be customary in the houses and streets to see manly affection,
The most dauntless and rude shall touch face to face lightly,
The dependence of Liberty shall be lovers,
The continuance of Equality shall be comrades.

These shall tie you and band you stronger than hoops of iron,
I, ecstatic, O partners! O lands! with the love of lovers tie you.

(Were you looking to be held together by lawyers?
Or by an agreement on a paper? or by arms?
Nay, nor the world, nor any living thing, will so cohere.)

1865

TURN O LIBERTAD

Turn O Libertad, for the war is over,
From it and all henceforth expanding, doubting no more, resolute, sweeping the world,
Turn from lands retrospective recording proofs of the past,
From the singers that sing the trailing glories of the past,
From the chants of the feudal world, the triumphs of kings, slavery, caste,

Turn to the world, the triumphs reserv'd and to come—give up that backward world,
Leave to the singers of hitherto, give them the trailing past,
But what remains remains for singers for you—wars to come are for you,
(Lo, how the wars of the past have duly inured to you, and the wars of the present also inure;)
Then turn, and be not alarm'd O Libertad—turn your undying face,
To where the future, greater than all the past,
Is swiftly, surely preparing for you.

1865

THICK-SPRINKLED BUNTING

THICK-SPRINKLED bunting! flag of stars!
Long yet your road, fateful flag—long yet your road, and lined with bloody death,
For the prize I see at issue at last is the world,
All its ships and shores I see interwoven with your threads greedy banner;
Dream'd again the flags of kings, highest borne, to flaunt unrival'd?
O hasten flag of man—O with sure and steady step, passing highest flags of kings,
Walk supreme to the heavens mighty symbol—run up above them all,
Flag of stars! thick-sprinkled bunting!

1865

YEARS OF THE MODERN

YEARS of the modern! years of the unperform'd!
Your horizon rises, I see it parting away for more august dramas,
I see not America only, not only Liberty's nation but other nations preparing,
I see tremendous entrances and exits, new combinations, the solidarity of races,
I see that force advancing with irresistible power on the world's stage,
(Have the old forces, the old wars, played their parts? are the acts suitable to them closed?)
I see Freedom, completely arm'd and victorious and very haughty, with Law on one side and Peace on the other,
A stupendous trio all issuing forth against the idea of caste;
What historic denouements are these we so rapidly approach?
I see men marching and countermarching by swift millions,
I see the frontiers and boundaries of the old aristocracies broken,
I see the landmarks of European kings removed,
I see this day the People beginning their landmarks, (all others give way;)
Never were such sharp questions ask'd as this day,
Never was average man, his soul, more energetic, more like a God,
Lo, how he urges and urges, leaving the masses no rest!
His daring foot is on land and sea everywhere, he colonizes the Pacific, the archipelagoes,
With the steamship, the electric telegraph, the newspaper, the wholesale engines of war,
With these and the world-spreading factories he interlinks all geography, all lands;
What whispers are these O lands, running ahead of you, passing under the seas?
Are all nations communing? is there going to be but one heart to the globe?
Is humanity forming en-masse? for lo, tyrants tremble, crowns grow dim,
The earth, restive, confronts a new era, perhaps a general divine war,
No one knows what will happen next, such portents fill the days and nights;
Years prophetical! the space ahead as I walk, as I vainly try to pierce it, is full of phantoms,
Unborn deeds, things soon to be, project their shapes around me,
This incredible rush and heat, this strange ecstatic fever of dreams O years!
Your dreams O years, how they penetrate through me! (I know not whether I sleep or wake;)
The perform'd America and Europe grow dim, retiring in shadow behind me,
The unperform'd, more gigantic than ever, advance, advance upon me.

1865

ASHES OF SOLDIERS

Ashes of soldiers South or North,
As I muse retrospective murmuring a chant in thought,
The war resumes, again to my sense your shapes,
And again the advance of the armies.

Noiseless as mists and vapors,
From their graves in the trenches ascending,
From cemeteries all through Virginia and Tennessee,
From every point of the compass out of the countless graves,
In wafted clouds, in myriads large, or squads of twos or threes or single ones they come,
And silently gather round me.

Now sound no note O trumpeters,
Not at the head of my cavalry parading on spirited horses,
With sabres drawn and glistening, and carbines by their thighs, (ah my brave horsemen!
My handsome tan-faced horsemen! what life, what joy and pride,
With all the perils were yours.)

Nor you drummers, neither at reveillé at dawn,
Nor the long roll alarming the camp, nor even the muffled beat for a burial,
Nothing from you this time O drummers bearing my warlike drums.

But aside from these and the marts of wealth and the crowded promenade,
Admitting around me comrades close unseen by the rest and voiceless,
The slain elate and alive again, the dust and debris alive,
I chant this chant of my silent soul in the name of all dead soldiers.

Faces so pale with wondrous eyes, very dear, gather closer yet,
Draw close, but speak not.

Phantoms of countless lost,
Invisible to the rest henceforth become my companions,
Follow me ever—desert me not while I live.

Sweet are the blooming cheeks of the living—sweet are the musical voices sounding,
But sweet, ah sweet, are the dead with their silent eyes.

Dearest comrades, all is over and long gone,
But love is not over—and what love, O comrades!
Perfume from battle-fields rising, up from the fœtor arising.

Perfume therefore my chant, O love, immortal love,
Give me to bathe the memories of all dead soldiers,
Shroud them, embalm them, cover them all over with tender pride.

Perfume all—make all wholesome,
Make these ashes to nourish and blossom,
O love, solve all, fructify all with the last chemistry.

Give me exhaustless, make me a fountain,
That I exhale love from me wherever I go like a moist perennial dew,
For the ashes of all dead soldiers South or North.

1865

WHEN LILACS LAST IN THE DOORYARD BLOOM'D

1

When lilacs last in the dooryard bloom'd,
And the great star early droop'd in the western sky in the night,
I mourn'd, and yet shall mourn with ever-returning spring.

Ever-returning spring, trinity sure to me you bring,
Lilac blooming perennial and drooping star in the west,
And thought of him I love.

2

O powerful western fallen star!
O shades of night—O moody, tearful night!
O great star disappear'd—O the black murk that hides the star!
O cruel hands that hold me powerless—O helpless soul of me!
O harsh surrounding cloud that will not free my soul.

3

In the dooryard fronting an old farm-house near the whitewash'd palings,
Stands the lilac-bush tall-growing with heart-shaped leaves of rich green,
With many a pointed blossom rising delicate, with the perfume strong I love,
With every leaf a miracle—and from this bush in the dooryard,
With delicate-color'd blossoms and heart-shaped leaves of rich green,
A sprig with its flower I break.

4

In the swamp in secluded recesses,
A shy and hidden bird is warbling a song.

Solitary the thrush,
The hermit withdrawn to himself, avoiding the settlements,
Sings by himself a song.

Song of the bleeding throat,
Death's outlet song of life, (for well dear brother I know,
If thou wast not granted to sing thou would'st surely die.)

5

Over the breast of the spring, the land, amid cities,
Amid lanes and through old woods, where lately the violets peep'd from the ground, spotting the gray debris,
Amid the grass in the fields each side of the lanes, passing the endless grass,
Passing the yellow-spear'd wheat, every grain from its shroud in the dark-brown fields uprisen,
Passing the apple-tree blows of white and pink in the orchards,
Carrying a corpse to where it shall rest in the grave,
Night and day journeys a coffin.

6

Coffin that passes through lanes and streets,
Through day and night with the great cloud darkening the land,
With the pomp of the inloop'd flags with the cities draped in black,
With the show of the States themselves as of crape-veil'd women standing,
With processions long and winding and the flambeaus of the night,
With the countless torches lit, with the silent sea of faces and the unbared heads,
With the waiting depot, the arriving coffin, and the sombre faces,
With dirges through the night, with the thousand voices rising strong and solemn,
With all the mournful voices of the dirges pour'd around the coffin,
The dim-lit churches and the shuddering organs—where amid these you journey,
With the tolling tolling bells' perpetual clang,
Here, coffin that slowly passes,
I give you my sprig of lilac.

7

(Nor for you, for one alone,
Blossoms and branches green to coffins all I bring,
For fresh as the morning, thus would I chant a song for you O sane and sacred death.

All over bouquets of roses,
O death, I cover you over with roses and early lilies,
But mostly and now the lilac that blooms the first,
Copious I break, I break the sprigs from the bushes,
With loaded arms I come, pouring for you,
For you and the coffins all of you O death.)

8

O western orb sailing the heaven,
Now I know what you must have meant as a month since I walk'd,
As I walk'd in silence the transparent shadowy night,
As I saw you had something to tell as you bent to me night after night,
As you droop'd from the sky low down as if to my side, (while the other stars all look'd on,)
As we wander'd together the solemn night, (for something I know not what kept me from sleep,)
As the night advanced, and I saw on the rim of the west how full you were of woe,

As I stood on the rising ground in the breeze in the cool transparent night,
As I watch'd where you pass'd and was lost in the netherward black of the night,
As my soul in its trouble dissatisfied sank, as where you sad orb,
Concluded, dropt in the night, and was gone.

9

Sing on there in the swamp,
O singer bashful and tender, I hear your notes, I hear your call,
I hear, I come presently, I understand you,
But a moment I linger, for the lustrous star has detain'd me,
The star my departing comrade holds and detains me.

10

O how shall I warble myself for the dead one there I loved?
And how shall I deck my song for the large sweet soul that has gone?
And what shall my perfume be for the grave of him I love?

Sea-winds blown from east and west,
Blown from the Eastern sea and blown from the Western sea, till there on the prairies meeting,
These and with these and the breath of my chant,
I'll perfume the grave of him I love.

11

O what shall I hang on the chamber walls?
And what shall the pictures be that I hang on the walls,
To adorn the burial-house of him I love?
Pictures of growing spring and farms and homes,
With the Fourth-month eve at sundown, and the gray smoke lucid and bright,
With floods of the yellow gold of the gorgeous, indolent, sinking sun, burning, expanding the air,
With the fresh sweet herbage under foot, and the pale green leaves of the trees prolific,
In the distance the flowing glaze, the breast of the river, with a wind-dapple here and there,
With ranging hills on the banks, with many a line against the sky, and shadows,
And the city at hand with dwellings so dense, and stacks of chimneys,
And all the scenes of life and the workshops, and the workmen homeward returning.

12

Lo, body and soul—this land,
My own Manhattan with spires, and the sparkling and hurrying tides, and the ships,
The varied and ample land, the South and the North in the light, Ohio's shores and flashing Missouri,
And ever the far-spreading prairies cover'd with grass and corn.

Lo, the most excellent sun so calm and haughty,
The violet and purple morn with just-felt breezes,
The gentle soft-born measureless light,
The miracle spreading bathing all, the fulfill'd noon,
The coming eve delicious, the welcome night and the stars,
Over my cities shining all, enveloping man and land.

13

Sing on, sing on you gray-brown bird,
Sing from the swamps, the recesses, pour your chant from the bushes,
Limitless out of the dusk, out of the cedars and pines.

Sing on dearest brother, warble your reedy song,
Loud human song, with voice of uttermost woe.

O liquid and free and tender!
O wild and loose to my soul—O wondrous singer!
You only I hear—yet the star holds me, (but will soon depart,)
Yet the lilac with mastering odor holds me.

14

Now while I sat in the day and look'd forth,
In the close of the day with its light and the

fields of spring, and the farmers preparing their crops,
In the large unconscious scenery of my land with its lakes and forests,
In the heavenly aerial beauty, (after the perturb'd winds and the storms,)
Under the arching heavens of the afternoon swift passing, and the voices of children and women,
The many-moving sea-tides, and I saw the ships how they sail'd,
And the summer approaching with richness, and the fields all busy with labor,
And the infinite separate houses, how they all went on, each with its meals and minutia of daily usages,
And the streets how their throbbings throbb'd, and the cities pent—lo, then and there,
Falling upon them all and among them all, enveloping me with the rest,
Appear'd the cloud, appear'd the long black trail,
And I knew death, its thought, and the sacred knowledge of death.

Then with the knowledge of death as walking one side of me,
And the thought of death close-walking the other side of me,
And I in the middle as with companions, and as holding the hands of companions,
I fled forth to the hiding receiving night that talks not,
Down to the shores of the water, the path by the swamp in the dimness,
To the solemn shadowy cedars and ghostly pines so still.

And the singer so shy to the rest receiv'd me,
The gray-brown bird I know receiv'd us comrades three,
And he sang the carol of death, and a verse for him I love.

From deep secluded recesses,
From the fragrant cedars and the ghostly pines so still,
Came the carol of the bird.

And the charm of the carol rapt me,
As I held as if by their hands my comrades in the night,
And the voice of my spirit tallied the song of the bird.

Come lovely and soothing death,
Undulate round the world, serenely arriving, arriving,
In the day, in the night, to all, to each,
Sooner or later delicate death.

Prais'd be the fathomless universe,
For life and joy, and for objects and knowledge curious,
And for love, sweet love—but praise! praise! praise!
For the sure-enwinding arms of cool-enfolding death.

Dark mother always gliding near with soft feet,
Have none chanted for thee a chant of fullest welcome?
Then I chant it for thee, I glorify thee above all,
I bring thee a song that when thou must indeed come, come unfalteringly.

Approach strong deliveress,
When it is so, when thou hast taken them I joyously sing the dead,
Lost in the loving floating ocean of thee,
Laved in the flood of thy bliss O death.

From me to thee glad serenades,
Dances for thee I propose saluting thee, adornments and feastings for thee,
And the sights of the open landscape and the high-spread sky are fitting,
And life and the fields, and the huge and thoughtful night.

The night in silence under many a star,
The ocean shore and the husky whispering wave whose voice I know,
And the soul turning to thee O vast and well-veil'd death,
And the body gratefully nestling close to thee.

Over the tree-tops I float thee a song,
Over the rising and sinking waves, over the myriad fields and the prairies wide,
Over the dense-pack'd cities all and the teeming wharves and ways,
I float this carol with joy, with joy to thee O death.

15

To the tally of my soul,
Loud and strong kept up the gray-brown bird,
With pure deliberate notes spreading filling the night.

Loud in the pines and cedars dim,
Clear in the freshness moist and the swamp-perfume,
And I with my comrades there in the night.

While my sight that was bound in my eyes unclosed,
As to long panoramas of visions.

And I saw askant the armies,
I saw as in noiseless dreams hundreds of battle-flags,
Borne through the smoke of the battles and pierc'd with missiles I saw them,
And carried hither and yon through the smoke, and torn and bloody,
And at last but a few shreds left on the staffs, (and all in silence,)
And the staffs all splinter'd and broken.

I saw battle-corpses, myriads of them,
And the white skeletons of young men, I saw them,
I saw the debris and debris of all the slain soldiers of the war,
But I saw they were not as was thought,
They themselves were fully at rest, they suffer'd not,
The living remain'd and suffer'd, the mother suffer'd,
And the wife and the child and the musing comrade suffer'd,
And the armies that remain'd suffer'd.

16

Passing the visions, passing the night,
Passing, unloosing the hold of my comrades' hands,
Passing the song of the hermit bird and the tallying song of my soul,
Victorious song, death's outlet song, yet varying ever-altering song,
As low and wailing, yet clear the notes, rising and falling, flooding the night,
Sadly sinking and fainting, as warning and warning, and yet again bursting with joy,
Covering the earth and filling the spread of the heaven,
As that powerful psalm in the night I heard from recesses,
Passing, I leave thee lilac with heart-shaped leaves,
I leave thee there in the door-yard, blooming, returning with spring.

I cease from my song for thee,
From my gaze on thee in the west, fronting the west, communing with thee,
O comrade lustrous with silver face in the night.

Yet each to keep and all, retrievements out of the night,
The song, the wondrous chant of the gray-brown bird,
And the tallying chant, the echo arous'd in my soul,
With the lustrous and drooping star with the countenance full of woe,
With the holders holding my hand nearing the call of the bird,
Comrades mine and I in the midst, and their memory ever to keep, for the dead I loved so well,
For the sweetest, wisest soul of all my days and lands—and this for his dear sake,
Lilac and star and bird twined with the chant of my soul,
There in the fragrant pines and the cedars dusk and dim.

1865 1865–6

O CAPTAIN! MY CAPTAIN!

O Captain! my Captain! our fearful trip is done,
The ship has weather'd every rack, the prize we sought is won,
The port is near, the bells I hear, the people all exulting,
While follow eyes the steady keel, the vessel grim and daring;
But O heart! heart! heart!
O the bleeding drops of red,
Where on the deck my Captain lies,
Fallen cold and dead.

O Captain! my Captain! rise up and hear the bells;
Rise up—for you the flag is flung—for you the bugle trills,
For you bouquets and ribbon'd wreaths—for you the shores a-crowding,
For you they call, the swaying mass, their eager faces turning;
    Here Captain! dear father!
      This arm beneath your head!
        It is some dream that on the deck,
          You've fallen cold and dead.

My Captain does not answer, his lips are pale and still,
My father does not feel my arm, he has no pulse nor will,
The ship is anchor'd safe and sound, its voyage closed and done,
From fearful trip the victor ship comes in with object won;
    Exult O shores, and ring O bells!
      But I with mournful tread,
        Walk the deck my Captain lies,
          Fallen cold and dead.

1865 1865–6; 1871

CHANTING THE SQUARE DEIFIC

1

CHANTING the square deific, out of the One advancing, out of the sides,
Out of the old and new, out of the square entirely divine,
Solid, four-sided, (all the sides needed,) from this side Jehovah am I,
Old Brahm I, and I Saturnius am;
Not Time affects me—I am Time, old, modern as any,
Unpersuadable, relentless, executing righteous judgments,
As the Earth, the Father, the brown old Kronos, with laws,
Aged beyond computation, yet ever new, ever with those mighty laws rolling,
Relentless I forgive no man—whoever sins dies—I will have that man's life;
Therefore let none expect mercy—have the seasons, gravitation, the appointed days, mercy? no more have I,
But as the seasons and gravitation, and as all the appointed days that forgive not,
I dispense from this side judgments inexorable without the least remorse.

2

Consolator most mild, the promis'd one advancing,
With gentle hand extended, the mightier God am I,
Foretold by prophets and poets in their most rapt prophecies and poems,
From this side, lo! the Lord Christ gazes—lo! Hermes I—lo! mine is Hercules' face,
All sorrow, labor, suffering, I, tallying it, absorb in myself,
Many times have I been rejected, taunted, put in prison, and crucified, and many times shall be again,
All the world have I given up for my dear brothers' and sisters' sake, for the soul's sake,
Wending my way through the homes of men, rich or poor, with the kiss of affection,
For I am affection, I am the cheer-bringing God, with hope and all-enclosing charity,
With indulgent words as to children, with fresh and sane words, mine only,
Young and strong I pass knowing well I am destin'd myself to an early death;
But my charity has no death—my wisdom dies not, neither early nor late,
And my sweet love bequeath'd here and elsewhere never dies.

3

Aloof, dissatisfied, plotting revolt,
Comrade of criminals, brother of slaves,
Crafty, despised, a drudge, ignorant,
With sudra face and worn brow, black, but in the depths of my heart, proud as any,
Lifted now and always against whoever scorning assumes to rule me,
Morose, full of guile, full of reminiscences, brooding, with many wiles,
(Though it was thought I was baffled and dispel'd, and my wiles done, but that will never be,)
Defiant, I, Satan, still live, still utter words, in new lands duly appearing, (and old ones also,)
Permanent here from my side, warlike, equal with any, real as any,

Nor time nor change shall ever change me or my words.

4

Santa Spirita, breather, life,
Beyond the light, lighter than light,
Beyond the flames of hell, joyous, leaping easily above hell,
Beyond Paradise, perfumed solely with mine own perfume,
Including all life on earth, touching, including God, including Saviour and Satan,
Ethereal, pervading all, (for without me what were all? what were God?)
Essence of forms, life of the real identities, permanent, positive, (namely the unseen,)
Life of the great round world, the sun and stars, and of man, I, the general soul,
Here the square finishing, the solid, I the most solid,
Breathe my breath also through these songs.

1865–6

ONE'S-SELF I SING

One's-self I sing, a simple separate person,
Yet utter the word Democratic, the word En-Masse.

Of physiology from top to toe I sing,
Not physiognomy alone nor brain alone is worthy for the Muse, I say the Form complete is worthier far,
The Female equally with the Male I sing.

Of Life immense in passion, pulse, and power,
Cheerful, for freest action form'd under the laws divine,
The Modern Man I sing.

1867

WHISPERS OF HEAVENLY DEATH

Whispers of heavenly death murmur'd I hear,
Labial gossip of night, sibilant chorals,
Footsteps gently ascending, mystical breezes wafted soft and low,
Ripples of unseen rivers, tides of a current flowing, forever flowing,
(Or is it the plashing of tears? the measureless waters of human tears?)

I see, just see skyward, great cloud-masses,
Mournfully slowly they roll, silently swelling and mixing,
With at times a half-dimm'd sadden'd far-off star,
Appearing and disappearing.

(Some parturition rather, some solemn immortal birth;
On the frontiers to eyes impenetrable,
Some soul is passing over.)

1868

PROUD MUSIC OF THE STORM

1

Proud music of the storm,
Blast that careers so free, whistling across the prairies,
Strong hum of forest tree-tops—wind of the mountains,
Personified dim shapes—you hidden orchestras,
You serenades of phantoms with instruments alert,
Blending with Nature's rhythmus all the tongues of nations;
You chords left as by vast composers—you choruses,
You formless, free, religious dances—you from the Orient,
You undertone of rivers, roar of pouring cataracts,
You sounds from distant guns with galloping cavalry,
Echoes of camps with all the different bugle-calls,
Trooping tumultuous, filling the midnight late, bending me powerless,
Entering my lonesome slumber-chamber, why have you seiz'd me?

2

Come forward O my soul, and let the rest retire,
Listen, lose not, it is toward thee they tend,
Parting the midnight, entering my slumber-chamber,
For thee they sing and dance O soul.

A festival song,
The duet of the bridegroom and the bride, a marriage-march,

With lips of love, and hearts of lovers fill'd to the brim with love,
The red-flush'd cheeks and perfumes, the cortege swarming full of friendly faces young and old,
To flutes' clear notes and sounding harps' cantabile.

Now loud approaching drums,
Victoria! see'st thou in powder-smoke the banners torn but flying? the rout of the baffled?
Hearest those shouts of a conquering army?

(Ah soul, the sobs of women, the wounded groaning in agony,
The hiss and crackle of flames, the blacken'd ruins, the embers of cities,
The dirge and desolation of mankind.)

Now airs antique and mediæval fill me,
I see and hear old harpers with their harps at Welsh festivals,
I hear the minnesingers singing their lays of love,
I hear the minstrels, gleemen, troubadours, of the middle ages.

Now the great organ sounds,
Tremulous, while underneath, (as the hid footholds of the earth,
On which arising rest, and leaping forth depend,
All shapes of beauty, grace and strength, all hues we know,
Green blades of grass and warbling birds, children that gambol and play, the clouds of heaven above,)
The strong base stands, and its pulsations intermits not,
Bathing, supporting, merging all the rest, maternity of all the rest,
And with it every instrument in multitudes,
The players playing, all the world's musicians,
The solemn hymns and masses rousing adoration,
All passionate heart-chants, sorrowful appeals,
The measureless sweet vocalists of ages,
And for their solvent setting earth's own diapason,
Of winds and woods and mighty ocean waves,
A new composite orchestra, binder of years and climes, ten-fold renewer,
As of the far-back days the poets tell, the Paradiso,
The straying thence, the separation long, but now the wandering done,
The journey done, the journeyman come home,
And man and art with Nature fused again.

Tutti! for earth and heaven;
(The Almighty leader now for once has signal'd with his wand.)
The manly strophe of the husbands of the world,
And all the wives responding.

The tongues of violins,
(I think O tongues ye tell this heart, that cannot tell itself,
This brooding yearning heart, that cannot tell itself.)

3

Ah from a little child,
Thou knowest soul how to me all sounds became music,
My mother's voice in lullaby or hymn,
(The voice, O tender voices, memory's loving voices,
Last miracle of all, O dearest mother's, sister's, voices;)
The rain, the growing corn, the breeze among the long-leav'd corn,
The measur'd sea-surf beating on the sand,
The twittering bird, the hawk's sharp scream,
The wild-fowl's notes at night as flying low migrating north or south,
The psalm in the country church or mid the clustering trees, the open air camp-meeting,
The fiddler in the tavern, the glee, the long-strung sailor-song,
The lowing cattle, bleating sheep, the crowing cock at dawn.

All songs of current lands come sounding round me,
The German airs of friendship, wine and love,
Irish ballads, merry jigs and dances, English warbles,
Chansons of France, Scotch tunes, and o'er the rest,
Italia's peerless compositions.

Across the stage with pallor on her face, yet lurid passion,
Stalks Norma brandishing the dagger in her hand.

I see poor crazed Lucia's eyes' unnatural gleam,
Her hair down her back falls loose and dishevel'd.

I see where Ernani walking the bridal garden,
Amid the scent of night-roses, radiant, holding his bride by the hand,
Hears the infernal call, the death-pledge of the horn.

To crossing swords and gray hairs bared to heaven,
The clear electric base and baritone of the world,
The trombone duo, Libertad forever!

From Spanish chestnut trees' dense shade,
By old and heavy convent walls a wailing song,
Song of lost love, the torch of youth and life quench'd in despair,
Song of the dying swan, Fernando's heart is breaking.

Awaking from her woes at last retriev'd Amina sings,
Copious as stars and glad as morning light the torrents of her joy.

(The teeming lady comes,
The lustrous orb, Venus contralto, the blooming mother,
Sister of loftiest gods, Alboni's self I hear.)

4

I hear those odes, symphonies, operas,
I hear in the *William Tell* the music of an arous'd and angry people,
I hear Meyerbeer's *Huguenots*, the *Prophet*, or *Robert*,
Gounod's *Faust*, or Mozart's *Don Juan*.

I hear the dance-music of all nations,
The waltz, some delicious measure, lapsing, bathing me in bliss,
The bolero to tinkling guitars and clattering castanets.

I see religious dances old and new,
I hear the sound of the Hebrew lyre,
I see the crusaders marching bearing the cross on high, to the martial clang of cymbals,
I hear dervishes monotonously chanting, interspers'd with frantic shouts, as they spin around turning always towards Mecca,
I see the rapt religious dances of the Persians and the Arabs,
Again, at Eleusis, home of Ceres, I see the modern Greeks dancing,
I hear them clapping their hands as they bend their bodies,
I hear the metrical shuffling of their feet.

I see again the wild old Corybantian dance, the performers wounding each other,
I see the Roman youth to the shrill sound of flageolets throwing and catching their weapons,
As they fall on their knees and rise again.

I hear from the Mussulman mosque the muezzin calling,
I see the worshippers within, nor form nor sermon, argument nor word,
But silent, strange, devout, rais'd, glowing heads, ecstatic faces.

I hear the Egyptian harp of many strings,
The primitive chants of the Nile boatmen,
The sacred imperial hymns of China,
To the delicate sounds of the king, (the stricken wood and stone,)
Or to Hindu flutes and the fretting twang of the vina,
A band of bayaderes.

5

Now Asia, Africa leave me, Europe seizing inflates me,
To organs huge and bands I hear as from vast concourses of voices,
Luther's strong hymn *Eine feste Burg ist unser Gott*,
Rossini's *Stabat Mater dolorosa*,
Or floating in some high cathedral dim with gorgeous color'd windows,
The passionate *Agnus Dei* or *Gloria in Excelsis*.

Composers! mighty maestros!
And you, sweet singers of old lands, soprani, tenori, bassi!

To you a new bard caroling in the West,
Obeisant sends his love.

(Such led to thee O soul,
All senses, shows and objects, lead to thee,
But now it seems to me sound leads o'er all the rest.)

I hear the annual singing of the children in St. Paul's cathedral,
Or, under the high roof of some colossal hall, the symphonies, oratorios of Beethoven, Handel, or Haydn,
The *Creation* in billows of godhood laves me.

Give me to hold all sounds, (I madly struggling cry,)
Fill me with all the voices of the universe,
Endow me with their throbbings, Nature's also,
The tempests, waters, winds, operas and chants, marches and dances,
Utter, pour in, for I would take them all!

6

Then I woke softly,
And pausing, questioning awhile the music of my dream,
And questioning all those reminiscences, the tempest in its fury,
And all the songs of sopranos and tenors,
And those rapt oriental dances of religious fervor,
And the sweet varied instruments, and the diapason of organs,
And all the artless plaints of love and grief and death,
I said to my silent curious soul out of the bed of the slumber-chamber,
Come, for I have found the clew I sought so long,
Let us go forth refresh'd amid the day,
Cheerfully tallying life, walking the world, the real,
Nourish'd henceforth by our celestial dream.

And I said, moreover,
Haply what thou hast heard O soul was not the sound of winds,
Nor dream of raging storm, nor sea-hawk's flapping wings nor harsh scream,
Nor vocalism of sun-bright Italy,
Nor German organ majestic, nor vast concourse of voices, nor layers of harmonies,
Nor strophes of husbands and wives, nor sound of marching soldiers,
Nor flutes, nor harps, nor the bugle-calls of camps,
But to a new rhythmus fitted for thee,
Poems bridging the way from Life to Death, vaguely wafted in night air, uncaught, unwritten,
Which let us go forth in the bold day and write.

1869

PASSAGE TO INDIA

1

SINGING my days,
Singing the great achievements of the present,
Singing the strong light works of engineers,
Our modern wonders, (the antique ponderous Seven outvied,)
In the Old World the east the Suez canal,
The New by its mighty railroad spann'd,
The seas inlaid with eloquent gentle wires;
Yet first to sound, and ever sound, the cry with thee O soul,
The Past! the Past! the Past!

The Past—the dark unfathom'd retrospect!
The teeming gulf—the sleepers and the shadows!
The past—the infinite greatness of the past!
For what is the present after all but a growth out of the past?
(As a projectile form'd, impell'd, passing a certain line, still keeps on,
So the present, utterly form'd, impell'd by the past.)

2

Passage O soul to India!
Eclaircise the myths Asiatic, the primitive fables.

Not you alone proud truths of the world,
Nor you alone ye facts of modern science,
But myths and fables of eld, Asia's, Africa's fables,
The far-darting beams of the spirit, the unloos'd dreams,
The deep diving bibles and legends,

The daring plots of the poets, the elder religions;
O you temples fairer than lilies pour'd over by the rising sun!
O you fables spurning the known, eluding the hold of the known, mounting to heaven!
You lofty and dazzling towers, pinnacled, red as roses, burnish'd with gold!
Towers of fables immortal fashion'd from mortal dreams!
You too I welcome and fully the same as the rest!
You too with joy I sing.

Passage to India!
Lo, soul, seest thou not God's purpose from the first?
The earth to be spann'd, connected by network,
The races, neighbors, to marry and be given in marriage,
The oceans to be cross'd, the distant brought near,
The lands to be welded together.

A worship new I sing,
You captains, voyagers, explorers, yours,
You engineers, you architects, machinists, yours,
You, not for trade or transportation only,
But in God's name, and for thy sake O soul.

3

Passage to India!
Lo soul for thee of tableaus twain,
I see in one the Suez canal initiated, open'd,
I see the procession of steamships, the Empress Eugenie's leading the van,
I mark from on deck the strange landscape, the pure sky, the level sand in the distance,
I pass swiftly the picturesque groups, the workmen gather'd,
The gigantic dredging machines.

In one again, different, (yet thine, all thine, O soul, the same,)
I see over my own continent the Pacific railroad surmounting every barrier,
I see continual trains of cars winding along the Platte carrying freight and passengers,
I hear the locomotives rushing and roaring, and the shrill steam-whistle,
I hear the echoes reverberate through the grandest scenery in the world,
I cross the Laramie plains, I note the rocks in grotesque shapes, the buttes,
I see the plentiful larkspur and wild onions, the barren, colorless, sage-deserts,
I see in glimpses afar or towering immediately above me the great mountains, I see the Wind river and the Wahsatch mountains,
I see the Monument mountain and the Eagle's Nest, I pass the Promontory, I ascend the Nevadas,
I scan the noble Elk mountain and wind around its base,
I see the Humboldt range, I thread the valley and cross the river,
I see the clear waters of lake Tahoe, I see forests of majestic pines,

Or crossing the great desert, the alkaline plains, I behold enchanting mirages of waters and meadows,
Marking through these and after all, in duplicate slender lines,
Bridging the three or four thousand miles of land travel,
Tying the Eastern to the Western sea,
The road between Europe and Asia.

(Ah Genoese thy dream! thy dream!
Centuries after thou art laid in thy grave,
The shore thou foundest verifies thy dream.)

4

Passage to India!
Struggles of many a captain, tales of many a sailor dead,
Over my mood stealing and spreading they come,
Like clouds and cloudlets in the unreach'd sky.

Along all history, down the slopes,
As a rivulet running, sinking now, and now again to the surface rising,
A ceaseless thought, a varied train—lo, soul, to thee, thy sight, they rise,
The plans, the voyages again, the expeditions;
Again Vasco da Gama sails forth,
Again the knowledge gain'd, the mariner's compass,

Lands found and nations born, thou born America,
For purpose vast, man's long probation fill'd,
Thou rondure of the world at last accomplish'd.

5

O vast Rondure, swimming in space,
Cover'd all over with visible power and beauty,
Alternate light and day and the teeming spiritual darkness,
Unspeakable high processions of sun and moon and countless stars above,
Below, the manifold grass and waters, animals, mountains, trees,
With inscrutable purpose, some hidden prophetic intention,
Now first it seems my thought begins to span thee.

Down from the gardens of Asia descending radiating,
Adam and Eve appear, then their myriad progeny after them,
Wandering, yearning, curious, with restless explorations,
With questionings, baffled, formless, feverish, with never-happy hearts,
With that sad incessant refrain, *Wherefore unsatisfied soul?* and *Whither O mocking life?*

Ah who shall soothe these feverish children?
Who justify these restless explorations?
Who speak the secret of impassive earth?
Who bind it to us? what is this separate Nature so unnatural?
What is this earth to our affections? (unloving earth, without a throb to answer ours,
Cold earth, the place of graves.)

Yet soul be sure the first intent remains, and shall be carried out,
Perhaps even now the time has arrived.

After the seas are all cross'd, (as they seem already cross'd,)
After the great captains and engineers have accomplish'd their work,
After the noble inventors, after the scientists, the chemist, the geologist, ethnologist,
Finally shall come the poet worthy that name,
The true son of God shall come singing his songs.

Then not your deeds only O voyagers, O scientists and inventors shall be justified,
All these hearts as of fretted children shall be sooth'd,
All affection shall be fully responded to, the secret shall be told,
All these separations and gaps shall be taken up and hook'd and link'd together,
The whole earth, this cold, impassive, voiceless earth, shall be completely justified,
Trinitas divine shall be gloriously accomplish'd and compacted by the true son of God, the poet,
(He shall indeed pass the straits and conquer the mountains,
He shall double the cape of Good Hope to some purpose,)
Nature and Man shall be disjoin'd and diffused no more,
The true son of God shall absolutely fuse them.

6

Year at whose wide-flung door I sing!
Year of the purpose accomplish'd!
Year of the marriage of continents, climates and oceans!
(No mere doge of Venice now wedding the Adriatic,)
I see O year in you the vast terraqueous globe given and giving all,
Europe to Asia, Africa join'd, and they to the New World,
The lands, geographies, dancing before you, holding a festival garland,
As brides and bridegrooms hand in hand.

Passage to India!
Cooling airs from Caucasus far, soothing cradle of man,
The river Euphrates flowing, the past lit up again.

Lo soul, the retrospect brought forward,
The old, most populous, wealthiest of earth's lands,
The streams of the Indus and the Ganges and their many affluents,

(I my shores of America walking to-day behold, resuming all,)
The tale of Alexander on his warlike marches suddenly dying,
On one side China and on the other side Persia and Arabia,
To the south the great seas and the bay of Bengal,
The flowing literatures, tremendous epics, religions, castes,
Old occult Brahma interminably far back, the tender and junior Buddha,
Central and southern empires and all their belongings, possessors,
The wars of Tamerlane, the reign of Aurungzebe,
The traders, rulers, explorers, Moslems, Venetians, Byzantium, the Arabs, Portuguese,
The first travelers famous yet, Marco Polo, Batouta the Moor,
Doubts to be solv'd, the map incognita, blanks to be fill'd,
The foot of man unstay'd, the hands never at rest,
Thyself O soul that will not brook a challenge.

The mediæval navigators rise before me,
The world of 1492, with its awaken'd enterprise,
Something swelling in humanity now like the sap of the earth in spring,
The sunset splendor of chivalry declining.

And who art thou sad shade?
Gigantic, visionary, thyself a visionary,
With majestic limbs and pious beaming eyes,
Spreading around with every look of thine a golden world,
Enhuing it with gorgeous hues.

As the chief histrion,
Down to the footlights walks in some great scena,
Dominating the rest I see the Admiral himself,
(History's type of courage, action, faith,)
Behold him sail from Palos leading his little fleet,
His voyage behold, his return, his great fame,
His misfortunes, calumniators, behold him a prisoner, chain'd,
Behold his dejection, poverty, death.

(Curious in time I stand, noting the efforts of heroes,
Is the deferment long? bitter the slander, poverty, death?
Lies the seed unreck'd for centuries in the ground? lo, to God's due occasion,
Uprising in the night, it sprouts, blooms,
And fills the earth with use and beauty.)

7

Passage indeed O soul to primal thought,
Not lands and seas alone, thy own clear freshness,
The young maturity of brood and bloom,
To realms of budding bibles.

O soul, repressless, I with thee and thou with me,
Thy circumnavigation of the world begin,
Of man, the voyage of his mind's return,
To reason's early paradise,
Back, back to wisdom's birth, to innocent intuitions,
Again with fair creation.

8

O we can wait no longer,
We too take ship O soul,
Joyous we too launch out on trackless seas,
Fearless for unknown shores on waves of ecstasy to sail,
Amid the wafting winds, (thou pressing me to thee, I thee to me, O soul,)
Caroling free, singing our song of God,
Chanting our chant of pleasant exploration.

With laugh and many a kiss,
(Let others deprecate, let others weep for sin, remorse, humiliation,)
O soul thou pleasest me, I thee.

Ah more than any priest O soul we too believe in God,
But with the mystery of God we dare not dally.

O soul thou pleasest me, I thee,
Sailing these seas or on the hills, or waking in the night,
Thoughts, silent thoughts, of Time and Space and Death, like waters flowing,
Bear me indeed as through the regions infinite,

Whose air I breathe, whose ripples hear, lave me all over,
Bathe me O God in thee, mounting to thee,
I and my soul to range in range of thee.

O thou transcendent,
Nameless, the fibre and the breath,
Light of the light, shedding forth universes, thou centre of them,
Thou mightier centre of the true, the good, the loving,
Thou moral, spiritual fountain—affection's source—thou reservoir,
(O pensive soul of me—O thirst unsatisfied—waitest not there?
Waitest not haply for us somewhere there the Comrade perfect?)
Thou pulse—thou motive of the stars, suns, systems,
That, circling, move in order, safe, harmonious,
Athwart the shapeless vastnesses of space,
How should I think, how breathe a single breath, how speak, if, out of myself,
I could not launch, to those, superior universes?

Swiftly I shrivel at the thought of God,
At Nature and its wonders, Time and Space and Death,
But that I, turning, call to thee O soul, thou actual Me,
And lo, thou gently masterest the orbs,
Thou matest Time, smilest content at Death,
And fillest, swellest full the vastnesses of Space.

Greater than stars or suns,
Bounding O soul thou journeyest forth;
What love than thine and ours could wider amplify?
What aspirations, wishes, outvie thine and ours O soul?
What dreams of the ideal? what plans of purity, perfection, strength?
What cheerful willingness for others' sake to give up all?
For others' sake to suffer all?

Reckoning ahead O soul, when thou, the time achiev'd,
The seas all cross'd, weather'd the capes, the voyage done,
Surrounded, copest, frontest God, yieldest, the aim attain'd,
As filled with friendship, love complete, the Elder Brother found,
The Younger melts in fondness in his arms.

9

Passage to more than India!
Are thy wings plumed indeed for such far flights?
O soul, voyagest thou indeed on voyages like those?
Disportest thou on waters such as those?
Soundest below the Sanscrit and the Vedas?
Then have thy bent unleash'd.

Passage to you, your shores, ye aged fierce enigmas!
Passage to you, to mastership of you, ye strangling problems!
You, strew'd with the wrecks of skeletons, that, living, never reach'd you.

Passage to more than India!
O secret of the earth and sky!
Of you O waters of the sea! O winding creeks and rivers!
Of you O woods and fields! of you strong mountains of my land!
Of you O prairies! of you gray rocks!
O morning red! O clouds! O rain and snows!
O day and night, passage to you!

O sun and moon and all you stars! Sirius and Jupiter!
Passage to you!

Passage, immediate passage! the blood burns in my veins!
Away O soul! hoist instantly the anchor!
Cut the hawsers—haul out—shake out every sail!
Have we not stood here like trees in the ground long enough?
Have we not grovel'd here long enough, eating and drinking like mere brutes?
Have we not darken'd and dazed ourselves with books long enough?

Sail forth—steer for the deep waters only,
Reckless O soul, exploring, I with thee, and thou with me,

For we are bound where mariner has not yet dared to go,
And we will risk the ship, ourselves and all.

O my brave soul!
O farther farther sail!
O daring joy, but safe! are they not all the seas of God?
O farther, farther, farther sail!

1869 1871

THE BASE OF ALL METAPHYSICS

AND now gentlemen,
A word I give to remain in your memories and minds,
As base and finalè too for all metaphysics.

(So to the students the old professor,
At the close of his crowded course.)

Having studied the new and antique, the Greek and Germanic systems,
Kant having studied and stated, Fichte and Schelling and Hegel,
Stated the lore of Plato, and Socrates greater than Plato,
And greater than Socrates sought and stated, Christ divine having studied long,
I see reminiscent to-day those Greek and Germanic systems,
See the philosophies all, Christian churches and tenets see,
Yet underneath Socrates clearly see, and underneath Christ the divine I see,
The dear love of man for his comrade, the attraction of friend to friend,
Of the well-married husband and wife, of children and parents,
Of city for city and land for land.

1871

THOU MOTHER WITH THY EQUAL BROOD

I

THOU Mother with thy equal brood,
Thou varied chain of different States, yet one identity only,
A special song before I go I'd sing o'er all the rest,
For thee, the future.

I'd sow a seed for thee of endless Nationality,
I'd fashion thy ensemble including body and soul,
I'd show away ahead thy real Union, and how it may be accomplish'd.

The paths to the house I seek to make,
But leave to those to come the house itself.

Belief I sing, and preparation;
As Life and Nature are not great with reference to the present only,
But greater still from what is yet to come,
Out of that formula for thee I sing.

2

As a strong bird on pinions free,
Joyous, the amplest spaces heavenward cleaving,
Such be the thought I'd think of thee America,
Such be the recitative I'd bring for thee.

The conceits of the poets of other lands I'd bring thee not,
Nor the compliments that have served their turn so long,
Nor rhyme, nor the classics, nor perfume of foreign court or indoor library;
But an odor I'd bring as from forests of pine in Maine, or breath of an Illinois prairie,
With open airs of Virginia or Georgia or Tennessee, or from Texas uplands, or Florida's glades,
Or the Saguenay's black stream, or the wide blue spread of Huron,
With presentment of Yellowstone's scenes, or Yosemite,
And murmuring under, pervading all, I'd bring the rustling sea-sound,
That endlessly sounds from the two Great Seas of the world.

And for thy subtler sense subtler refrains dread Mother,
Preludes of intellect tallying these and thee, mind-formulas fitted for thee, real and sane and large as these and thee,
Thou! mounting higher, diving deeper than we knew, thou transcendental Union!
By thee fact to be justified, blended with thought,

Thought of man justified, blended with God,
Through thy idea, lo, the immortal reality!
Through thy reality, lo, the immortal idea!

3

Brain of the New World, what a task is thine
To formulate the Modern—out of the peerless grandeur of the modern,
Out of thyself, comprising science, to recast poems, churches, art,
(Recast, may-be discard them, end them—may-be their work is done, who knows?)
By vision, hand, conception, on the background of the mighty past, the dead,
To limn with absolute faith the mighty living present.

And yet thou living present brain, heir of the dead, the Old World brain,
Thou that lay folded like an unborn babe within its folds so long,
Thou carefully prepared by it so long—haply thou but unfoldest it, only maturest it,
It to eventuate in thee—the essence of the by-gone time contain'd in thee,
Its poems, churches, arts, unwitting to themselves, destined with reference to thee;
Thou but the apples, long, long, long a-growing,
The fruit of all the Old ripening to-day in thee.

4

Sail, sail thy best, ship of Democracy,
Of value is thy freight, 'tis not the Present only,
The Past is also stored in thee,
Thou holdest not the venture of thyself alone, not of the Western continent alone,
Earth's *résumé* entire floats on thy keel O ship, is steadied by thy spars,
With thee Time voyages in trust, the antecedent nations sink or swim with thee,
With all their ancient struggles, martyrs, heroes, epics, wars, thou bear'st the other continents,
Theirs, theirs as much as thine, the destination-port triumphant;
Steer then with good strong hand and wary eye O helmsman, thou carriest great companions,
Venerable priestly Asia sails this day with thee,
And royal feudal Europe sails with thee.

5

Beautiful world of new superber birth that rises to my eyes,
Like a limitless golden cloud filling the western sky,
Emblem of general maternity lifted above all,
Sacred shape of the bearer of daughters and sons,
Out of thy teeming womb thy giant babes in ceaseless procession issuing,
Acceding from such gestation, taking and giving continual strength and life,
World of the real—world of the twain in one,
World of the soul, born by the world of the real alone, led to identity, body, by it alone,
Yet in beginning only, incalculable masses of composite precious materials,
By history's cycles forwarded, by every nation, language, hither sent,
Ready, collected here, a freer, vast, electric world, to be constructed here,
(The true New World, the world of orbic science, morals, literatures to come,)
Thou wonder world yet undefined, unform'd, neither do I define thee,
How can I pierce the impenetrable blank of the future?
I feel thy ominous greatness evil as well as good,
I watch thee advancing, absorbing the present, transcending the past,
I see thy light lighting, and thy shadow shadowing, as if the entire globe,
But I do not undertake to define thee, hardly to comprehend thee,
I but thee name, thee prophesy, as now,
I merely thee ejaculate!
Thee in thy future,
Thee in thy only permanent life, career, thy own unloosen'd mind, thy soaring spirit,
Thee as another equally needed sun, radiant, ablaze, swift-moving, fructifying all,
Thee risen in potent cheerfulness and joy, in endless great hilarity,

Scattering for good the cloud that hung so long, that weigh'd so long upon the mind of man,
The doubt, suspicion, dread, of gradual, certain decadence of man;
Thee in thy larger, saner brood of female, male—thee in thy athletes, moral, spiritual, South, North, West, East,
(To thy immortal breasts, Mother of All, thy every daughter, son, endear'd alike, forever equal,)
Thee in thy own musicians, singers, artists, unborn yet, but certain,
Thee in thy moral wealth and civilization, (until which thy proudest material civilization must remain in vain,)
Thee in thy all-supplying, all-enclosing worship—thee in no single bible, saviour, merely,
Thy saviours countless, latent within thyself, thy bibles incessant within thyself, equal to any, divine as any,
(Thy soaring course thee formulating, not in thy two great wars, nor in thy century's visible growth,
But far more in these leaves and chants; thy chants, great Mother!)
Thee in an education grown of thee, in teachers, studies, students, born of thee,
Thee in thy democratic fêtes en-masse, thy high original festivals, operas, lecturers, preachers,
Thee in thy ultimata, (the preparations only now completed, the edifice on sure foundations tied,)
Thee in thy pinnacles, intellect, thought, thy topmost rational joys, thy love and godlike aspiration,
In thy resplendent coming literati, thy full-lung'd orators, thy sacerdotal bards, kosmic savans,
These! these in thee, (certain to come,) to-day I prophesy.

6

Land tolerating all, accepting all, not for the good alone, all good for thee,
Land in the realms of God to be a realm unto thyself,
Under the rule of God to be a rule unto thyself.
(Lo, where arise three peerless stars,
To be thy natal stars my country, Ensemble, Evolution, Freedom,
Set in the sky of Law.)
Land of unprecedented faith, God's faith,
Thy soil, thy very subsoil, all upheav'd,
The general inner earth so long so sedulously draped over, now hence for what it is boldly laid bare,
Open'd by thee to heaven's light for benefit or bale.

Not for success alone,
Not to fair-sail unintermitted always,
The storm shall dash thy face, the murk of war and worse than war shall cover thee all over,
(Wert capable of war, its tug and trials? be capable of peace its trials,
For the tug and mortal strain of nations come at last in prosperous peace, not war;)
In many a smiling mask death shall approach beguiling thee, thou in disease shalt swelter,
The livid cancer spread its hideous claws, clinging upon thy breasts, seeking to strike thee deep within,
Consumption of the worst, moral consumption, shall rouge thy face with hectic,
But thou shalt face thy fortunes, thy diseases, and surmount them all,
Whatever they are to-day and whatever through time they may be,
They each and all shall lift and pass away and cease from thee,
While thou, Time's spirals rounding, out of thyself, thyself still extricating, fusing,
Equable, natural, mystical Union thou, (the mortal with immortal blent,)
Shalt soar toward the fulfilment of the future, the spirit of the body and the mind,
The soul, its destinies.

The soul, its destinies, the real real,
(Purport of all these apparitions of the real;)
In thee America, the soul, its destinies,
Thou globe of globes! thou wonder nebulous!
By many a throe of heat and cold convuls'd, (by these thyself solidifying,)
Thou mental, moral orb—thou New, indeed new, Spiritual World!

The Present holds thee not—for such vast growth as thine,
For such unparallel'd flight as thine, such brood as thine,
The FUTURE only holds thee and can hold thee.

1872

THE MYSTIC TRUMPETER

1

HARK, some wild trumpeter, some strange musician,
Hovering unseen in air, vibrates capricious tunes to-night.
I hear thee trumpeter, listening alert I catch thy notes,
Now pouring, whirling like a tempest round me,
Now low, subdued, now in the distance lost.

2

Come nearer bodiless one, haply in thee resounds
Some dead composer, haply thy pensive life
Was fill'd with aspirations high, unform'd ideals,
Waves, oceans musical, chaotically surging,
That now ecstatic ghost, close to me bending, thy cornet echoing, pealing,
Gives out to no one's ears but mine, but freely gives to mine,
That I may thee translate.

3

Blow trumpeter free and clear, I follow thee,
While at thy liquid prelude, glad, serene,
The fretting world, the streets, the noisy hours of day withdraw,
A holy calm descends like dew upon me,
I walk in cool refreshing night the walks of Paradise,
I scent the grass, the moist air and the roses;
Thy song expands my numb'd imbonded spirit, thou freest, launchest me,
Floating and basking upon heaven's lake.

4

Blow again trumpeter! and for my sensuous eyes,
Bring the old pageants, show the feudal world.

What charm thy music works! thou makest pass before me,
Ladies and cavaliers long dead, barons are in their castle halls, the troubadours are singing,
Arm'd knights go forth to redress wrongs, some in quest of the holy Graal;
I see the tournament, I see the contestants incased in heavy armor seated on stately champing horses,
I hear the shouts, the sounds of blows and smiting steel;
I see the Crusaders' tumultuous armies—hark, how the cymbals clang,
Lo, where the monks walk in advance, bearing the cross on high.

5

Blow again trumpeter! and for thy theme,
Take now the enclosing theme of all, the solvent and the setting,
Love, that is pulse of all, the sustenance and the pang,
The heart of man and woman all for love,
No other theme but love—knitting, enclosing, all-diffusing love.

O how the immortal phantoms crowd around me!
I see the vast alembic ever working, I see and know the flames that heat the world,
The glow, the blush, the beating hearts of lovers,
So blissful happy some, and some so silent, dark, and nigh to death;
Love, that is all the earth to lovers—love, that mocks time and space,
Love, that is day and night—love, that is sun and moon and stars,
Love, that is crimson, sumptuous, sick with perfume,
No other words but words of love, no other thought but love.

6

Blow again trumpeter—conjure war's alarums.
Swift to thy spell a shuddering hum like distant thunder rolls,
Lo, where the arm'd men hasten—lo, mid the clouds of dust the glint of bayonets,
I see the grime-faced cannoneers, I mark the

rosy flash amid the smoke, I hear the cracking of the guns;
Nor war alone—thy fearful music-song, wild player, brings every sight of fear,
The deeds of ruthless brigands, rapine, murder—I hear the cries for help!
I see ships foundering at sea, I behold on deck and below deck the terrible tableaus.

7

O trumpeter, methinks I am myself the instrument thou playest,
Thou melt'st my heart, my brain—thou movest, drawest, changest them at will;
And now thy sullen notes send darkness through me,
Thou takest away all cheering light, all hope,
I see the enslaved, the overthrown, the hurt, the opprest of the whole earth,
I feel the measureless shame and humiliation of my race, it becomes all mine,
Mine too the revenges of humanity, the wrongs of ages, baffled feuds and hatreds,
Utter defeat upon me weighs—all lost—the foe victorious,
(Yet 'mid the ruins Pride colossal stands unshaken to the last,
Endurance, resolution to the last.)

8

Now trumpeter for thy close,
Vouchsafe a higher strain than any yet,
Sing to my soul, renew its languishing faith and hope,
Rouse up my slow belief, give me some vision of the future,
Give me for once its prophecy and joy.

O glad, exulting, culminating song!
A vigor more than earth's is in thy notes,
Marches of victory—man disenthral'd—the conqueror at last,
Hymns to the universal God from universal man—all joy!
A reborn race appears—a perfect world, all joy!
Women and men in wisdom innocence and health—all joy!
Riotous laughing bacchanals fill'd with joy!
War, sorrow, suffering gone—the rank earth purged—nothing but joy left!
The ocean fill'd with joy—the atmosphere all joy!
Joy! joy! in freedom, worship, love! joy in the ecstasy of life!
Enough to merely be! enough to breathe!
Joy! joy! all over joy!

1872

TO A LOCOMOTIVE IN WINTER

THEE for my recitative,
Thee in the driving storm even as now, the snow, the winter-day declining,
Thee in thy panoply, thy measur'd dual throbbing and thy beat convulsive,
Thy black cylindric body, golden brass and silvery steel,
Thy ponderous side-bars, parallel and connecting rods, gyrating, shuttling at thy sides,
Thy metrical, now swelling pant and roar, now tapering in the distance,
Thy great protruding head-light fix'd in front,
Thy long, pale, floating vapor-pennants, tinged with delicate purple,
The dense and murky clouds out-belching from thy smokestack,
Thy knitted frame, thy springs and valves, the tremulous twinkle of thy wheels,
Thy train of cars behind, obedient, merrily following,
Through gale or calm, now swift, now slack, yet steadily careering;
Type of the modern—emblem of motion and power—pulse of the continent,
For once come serve the Muse and merge in verse, even as here I see thee,
With storm and buffeting gusts of wind and falling snow,
By day thy warning ringing bell to sound its notes,
By night thy silent signal lamps to swing.

Fierce-throated beauty!
Roll through my chant with all thy lawless music, thy swinging lamps at night,
Thy madly-whistled laughter, echoing, rumbling like an earthquake, rousing all,
Law of thyself complete, thine own track firmly holding,

(No sweetness debonair of tearful harp or glib
piano thine,)
Thy trills of shrieks by rocks and hills return'd,
Launch'd o'er the prairies wide, across the
lakes,
To the free skies unpent and glad and strong.

1876

SPIRIT THAT FORM'D THIS SCENE

Written in Platte Cañon, Colorado

Spirit that form'd this scene,
These tumbled rock-piles grim and red,
These reckless heaven-ambitious peaks,
These gorges, turbulent-clear streams, this
naked freshness,
These formless wild arrays, for reasons of their
own,
I know thee, savage spirit—we have com-
muned together,
Mine too such wild arrays, for reasons of their
own;
Was't charged against my chants they had for-
gotten art?
To fuse within themselves its rules precise and
delicatesse?
The lyrist's measur'd beat, the wrought-out
temple's grace—column and polish'd arch
forgot?
But thou that revelest here—spirit that form'd
this scene,
They have remember'd thee.

1879 1881

ROAMING IN THOUGHT

(*After reading* HEGEL)

ROAMING in thought over the Universe, I saw
the little that is Good steadily hastening
towards immortality,
And the vast all that is call'd Evil I saw hastening to merge itself and become lost and
dead.

1881

WITH HUSKY-HAUGHTY LIPS O SEA!

WITH husky-haughty lips, O sea!
Where day and night I wend thy surf-beat
shore,
Imaging to my sense thy varied strange suggestions,
(I see and plainly list thy talk and conference
here,)
Thy troops of white-maned racers racing to
the goal,
Thy ample, smiling face, dash'd with the
sparkling dimples of the sun,
Thy brooding scowl and murk—thy unloos'd
hurricanes,
Thy unsubduedness, caprices, wilfulness;
Great as thou art above the rest, thy many
tears—a lack from all eternity in thy con-
tent,
(Naught but the greatest struggles, wrongs,
defeats, could make thee greatest—no less
could make thee,)
Thy lonely state—something thou ever seek'st
and seek'st, yet never gain'st,
Surely some right withheld—some voice, in
huge monotonous rage, of freedom-lover
pent,
Some vast heart, like a planet's, chain'd and
chafing in those breakers,
By lengthen'd swell, and spasm, and panting
breath,
And rhythmic rasping of thy sands and waves,
And serpent hiss, and savage peals of laughter,
And undertones of distant lion roar,
(Sounding, appealing to the sky's deaf ear—
but now, rapport for once,
A phantom in the night thy confidant for
once,)
The first and last confession of the globe,
Outsurging, muttering from thy soul's abysms,
The tale of cosmic elemental passion,
Thou tellest to a kindred soul.

1884

GOOD-BYE MY FANCY!

GOOD-BYE my Fancy!
Farewell dear mate, dear love!
I'm going away, I know not where,
Or to what fortune, or whether I may ever see
you again,
So Good-bye my Fancy.

Now for my last—let me look back a moment;
The slower fainter ticking of the clock is in me,
Exit, nightfall, and soon the heart-thud stop-
ping.

Long have we lived, joy'd, caress'd together;
Delightful!—now separation—Good-bye my Fancy.

Yet let me not be too hasty,
Long indeed have we lived, slept, filter'd, become really blended into one;
Then if we die we die together (yes, we'll remain one),
If we go anywhere we'll go together to meet what happens,
May-be we'll be better off and blither, and learn something,
May-be it is yourself now really ushering me to the true songs, (who knows?)
May-be it is you the mortal knob really undoing, turning—so now finally,
Good-bye—and hail! my Fancy.

1891–92

PREFACE TO 1855 EDITION OF "LEAVES OF GRASS"

AMERICA does not repel the past or what it has produced under its forms or amid other politics or the idea of castes or the old religions . . . accepts the lesson with calmness . . . is not so impatient as has been supposed that the slough still sticks to opinions and manners and literature while the life which served its requirements has passed into the new life of the new forms . . . perceives that the corpse is slowly borne from the eating and sleeping rooms of the house . . . perceives that it waits a little while in the door . . . that it was fittest for its days . . . that its action has descended to the stalwart and wellshaped heir who approaches . . . and that he shall be fittest for his days.

The Americans of all nations at any time upon the earth have probably the fullest poetical nature. The United States themselves are essentially the greatest poem. In the history of the earth hitherto the largest and most stirring appear tame and orderly to their ampler largeness and stir. Here at last is something in the doings of man that corresponds with the broadcast doings of the day and night. Here is not merely a nation but a teeming nation of nations. Here is action untied from strings necessarily blind to particulars and details magnificently moving in vast masses. Here is the hospitality which forever indicates heroes. . . . Here are the roughs and beards and space and ruggedness and nonchalance that the soul loves. Here the performance disdaining the trivial unapproached in the tremendous audacity of its crowds and groupings and the push of its perspective spreads with crampless and flowing breadth and showers its prolific and splendid extravagance. One sees it must indeed own the riches of the summer and winter, and need never be bankrupt while corn grows from the ground or the orchards drop apples or the bays contain fish or men beget children upon women.

Other states indicate themselves in their deputies . . . but the genius of the United States is not best or most in its executives or legislatures, nor in its ambassadors or authors or colleges or churches or parlors, nor even in its newspapers or inventors . . . but always most in the common people. Their manners, speech, dress, friendships—the freshness and candor of their physiognomy—the picturesque looseness of their carriage . . . their deathless attachment to freedom—their aversion to anything indecorous or soft or mean—the practical acknowledgment of the citizens of one state by the citizens of all other states—the fierceness of their roused resentment—their curiosity and welcome of novelty—their self-esteem and wonderful sympathy—their susceptibility to a slight—the air they have of persons who never knew how it felt to stand in the presence of superiors—the fluency of their speech—their delight in music, the sure symptom of manly tenderness and native elegance of soul . . . their good temper and openhandedness—the terrible significance of their elections—the President's taking off his hat to them not they to him—these too are unrhymed poetry. It awaits the gigantic and generous treatment worthy of it.

The largeness of nature or the nation were monstrous without a corresponding largeness and generosity of the spirit of the citizen. Not nature nor swarming states nor streets and steamships nor prosperous business nor farms nor capital nor learning may suffice for the ideal of man . . . nor suffice the poet. No reminiscences may suffice either. A live nation can always cut a deep mark and can have the best authority the cheapest . . . namely from its own soul. This is the sum of the profitable uses of individuals or states and of present action and grandeur and of the subjects of poets.—As if it were necessary to trot back generation after generation to the eastern records! As if the beauty and sacredness of the demonstrable must fall behind that of the mythical! As if men do not make their mark out of any times! As if the opening of the western continent by discovery and what has transpired since in North and South America were less than the small theatre of the antique or the aimless sleepwalking of the middle ages! The pride of the United States leaves the wealth and finesse of the cities and all returns of commerce and agriculture and all the magnitude of geography or shows of exterior victory to enjoy the breed of fullsized men or one fullsized man unconquerable and simple.

The American poets are to enclose old and new for America is the race of races. Of them a bard is to be commensurate with a people. To him the other continents arrive as contributions . . . he gives them reception for their sake and his own sake. His spirit responds to his country's spirit . . . he incarnates its geography and natural life and rivers and lakes. Mississippi with annual freshets and changing chutes, Missouri and Columbia and Ohio and Saint Lawrence with the falls and beautiful masculine Hudson, do not embouchure where they spend themselves more than they embouchure into him. The blue breadth over the inland sea of Virginia and Maryland and the sea off Massachusetts and Maine and over Manhattan bay and over Champlain and Erie and over Ontario and Huron and Michigan and Superior, and over the Texan and Mexican and Floridian and Cuban seas and over the seas off California and Oregon, is not tallied by the blue breadth of the waters below more than the breadth of above and below is tallied by him. When the long Atlantic coast stretches longer and the Pacific coast stretches longer he easily stretches with them north or south. He spans between them also from east to west and reflects what is between them. On him rise solid growths that offset the growths of pine and cedar and hemlock and liveoak and locust and chestnut and cypress and hickory and limetree and cottonwood and tuliptree and cactus and wildvine and tamarind and persimmon . . . and tangles as tangled as any canebreak or swamp . . . and forests coated with transparent ice and icicles hanging from the boughs and crackling in the wind . . . and sides and peaks of mountains . . . and pasturage sweet and free as savannah or upland or prairie . . . with flights and songs and screams that answer those of the wildpigeon and highhold and orchard-oriole and coot and surfduck and redshouldered-hawk and fish-hawk and white-ibis and indian-hen and cat-owl and water-pheasant and qua-bird and piedsheldrake and blackbird and mockingbird and buzzard and condor and night-heron and eagle. To him the hereditary countenance descends both mother's and father's. To him enter the essences of the real things and past and present events—of the enormous diversity of temperature and agriculture and mines—the tribes of red aborigines—the weatherbeaten vessels entering new ports or making landings on rocky coasts—the first settlements north or south—the rapid stature and muscle—the haughty defiance of '76, and the war and peace and formation of the constitution . . . the union always surrounded by blatherers and always calm and impregnable—the perpetual coming of immigrants—the wharf-hem'd cities and superior marine—the unsurveyed interior—the loghouses and clearings and wild animals and hunters and trappers . . . the free commerce—the fisheries and whaling and golddigging—the endless gestation of new states—the convening of Congress every December, the members duly coming up from all climates and the uttermost parts . . . the noble character of the young mechanics and of all free American workmen and workwomen . . . the general ardor and friendliness and enterprise—the perfect equality of the female with the male . . . the large amativeness—the fluid movement of the population—the factories and mercantile life and labor-saving machinery—the Yankee swap—the New-York firemen and the target excursion—the southern plantation life—the character of the northeast and of the northwest and southwest—slavery and the tremulous spreading of hands to protect it, and the stern opposition to it which shall never cease till it ceases or the speaking of tongues and the moving of lips cease. For such the expression of the American poet is to be transcendent and new. It is to be indirect and not direct or descriptive or epic. Its quality goes through these to much more. Let the age and wars of other nations be chanted and their eras and characters be illustrated and that finish the verse. Not so the great psalm of the republic. Here the theme is creative and has vista. Here comes one among the well-beloved stonecutters and plans with decision and science and sees the solid and beautiful forms of the future where there are now no solid forms.

Of all nations the United States with veins full of poetical stuff most need poets and will doubtless have the greatest and use them the greatest. Their Presidents shall not be their common referee so much as their poets shall. Of all mankind the great poet is the equable man. Not in him but off from him things are grotesque or eccentric or fail of their sanity. Nothing out of its place is good and nothing in its place is bad. He bestows on every object or quality its fit proportions neither more nor less. He is the arbiter of the diverse and he is the key. He is the equalizer of his age and land . . . he supplies what wants supplying and checks what wants checking. If peace is the routine out of him speaks the spirit of peace, large, rich, thrifty, building vast and populous cities, encouraging agriculture and the arts and commerce—lighting the study of man, the soul, immortality—federal, state or municipal government, marriage, health, free trade, intertravel by land and sea . . . nothing too close, nothing too far off . . . the stars not too far off. In war he is the most deadly force of the war. Who recruits him recruits horse and foot . . . he fetches parks of artillery the best that engineer ever knew. If the time becomes slothful and heavy he knows how to arouse it . . . he can make every word he speaks draw blood. Whatever stagnates in the flat of custom or obedience or legislation he never stagnates. Obedience does not master him, he masters it. High up out of reach he stands turning a concentrated light . . . he turns the pivot with his finger . . . he baffles the swiftest runners as he stands and easily overtakes and envelops them. The time straying toward infidelity and confections and persiflage he withholds by his steady faith . . . he spreads out his dishes . . . he offers the sweet firmfibred meat that grows men and women. His brain is the ultimate brain. He is no arguer . . . he is judgment. He judges not as the judge judges but as the sun falling around a helpless thing. As he sees the farthest he has the most faith. His thoughts are the hymns of the praise of things. In the talk on the soul and eternity and God off of his equal plane he is silent. He sees eternity less like a play with a prologue and denouement . . . he sees eternity in men and women . . . he does not see men and women as dreams or dots. Faith is the antiseptic of the soul . . . it pervades the common people and preserves them . . . they never give up believing and expecting and trusting. There is that indescribable freshness and unconsciousness about an illiterate person that humbles and mocks the power of the noblest expressive genius. The poet sees for a certainty how one not a great artist may be just as sacred and perfect as the greatest artist. . . . The power to destroy or remould is freely used by him but never the power of attack. What is past is past. If he does not expose superior models and prove himself by every step he takes he is not what is wanted. The presence of the greatest poet conquers . . . not parleying or struggling or any prepared attempts. Now he has passed that way see after him! there is not left any vestige of despair or misanthropy or cunning or exclusiveness or the ignominy of a nativity or color or delusion of hell or the necessity of hell . . . and no man thenceforward shall be degraded for ignorance or weakness or sin.

The greatest poet hardly knows pettiness or triviality. If he breathes into any thing that was before thought small it dilates with the grandeur and life of the universe. He is a seer . . . he is individual . . . he is complete in himself . . . the others are as good as he, only he sees it and they do not. He is not one of the chorus . . . he does not stop for any regulations . . . he is the president of regulation. What the eyesight does to the rest he does to the rest. Who knows the curious mystery of the eyesight? The other senses corroborate themselves, but this is removed from any proof but its own and foreruns the identities of the spiritual world. A single glance of it mocks all the investigations of man and all the instruments and books of the earth and all reasoning. What is marvelous? what is unlikely? what is impossible or baseless or vague? after you have once just opened the space of a peachpit and given audience to far and near and to the sunset and had all things enter with electric swiftness softly and duly without confusion or jostling or jam.

The land and sea, the animals fishes and birds, the sky of heaven and the orbs, the forests mountains and rivers, are not small themes . . . but folks expect of the poet to indicate more than the beauty and dignity which always attach to dumb real objects . . . they expect him to indicate the path between reality and their souls. Men and women perceive the beauty well enough . . . probably as well as he. The passionate tenacity of hunters, woodmen, early risers, cultivators of gardens and orchards and fields, the love of healthy women for the manly form, seafaring persons, drivers of horses, the passion for light and the open air, all is an old varied sign of the unfailing perception of beauty and of a residence of the poetic in outdoor people. They can never be assisted by poets to perceive . . . some may but they never can. The poetic quality is not marshalled in rhyme or uniformity or abstract addresses to things nor in melancholy complaints or good precepts, but is the life of these and much else and is in the soul. The profit of rhyme is that it drops seeds of a sweeter and more luxuriant rhyme, and of uniformity that it conveys itself into its own roots in the ground out of sight. The rhyme and uniformity of perfect poems show the free growth of metrical laws and bud from them as unerringly and loosely as lilacs or roses on a bush, and take shapes as compact as the shapes of chestnuts and oranges and melons and pears, and shed the perfume impalpable to form. The fluency and ornaments of the finest poems or music or orations or recitations are not independent but dependent. All beauty comes from beautiful blood and a beautiful brain. If the greatnesses are in conjunction in a man or woman it is enough . . . the fact will prevail through the universe . . . but the gaggery and gilt of a million years will not prevail. Who troubles himself about his ornaments or fluency is lost. This is what you shall do: Love the earth and sun and the animals, despise riches, give alms to every one that asks, stand up for the stupid and crazy, devote your income and labor to others, hate tyrants, argue not concerning God, have patience and indulgence toward the people, take off your hat to nothing known or unknown or to any man or number of men, go freely with powerful uneducated persons and with the young and with the mothers of families, read these leaves in the open air every season of every year of your life, re-examine all you have been told at school or church or in any book, dismiss whatever insults your own soul, and your very flesh shall be a great poem and have the richest fluency not only in its words but in the silent lines of its lips and face and between the lashes of your eyes and in every motion and joint of your body. . . . The poet shall not spend his time in unneeded work. He shall know that the ground is always ready plowed and manured . . . others may not know it but he shall. He shall go directly to the creation. His trust shall master the trust of everything he touches . . . and shall master all attachment.

The known universe has one complete lover and that is the greatest poet. He consumes an eternal passion and is indifferent which chance happens and which possible contingency of fortune or misfortune and persuades daily and hourly his delicious pay. What balks or breaks others is fuel for his burning progress to contact and amorous joy. Other proportions of the reception of pleasure dwindle to nothing to his proportions. All expected from heaven or from the highest he is rapport with in the sight of the daybreak or a scene of the winter-woods or the presence of children playing or with his arm round the neck of a man or woman. His love above all love has leisure and expanse . . . he leaves room ahead of himself. He is no irresolute or suspicious lover . . . he is sure . . . he scorns intervals. His experience and the showers and thrills are not for nothing. Nothing can jar him . . . suffering and darkness cannot—death and fear cannot. To him complaint and jealousy and envy are corpses buried and rotten in the earth . . . he saw them buried. The sea is not surer of the shore or the shore of the sea than he is of the fruition of his love and of all perfection and beauty.

The fruition of beauty is no chance of hit or miss . . . it is inevitable as life . . . it is exact and plumb as gravitation. From the eyesight proceeds another eyesight and from the hearing proceeds another hearing and from the voice proceeds another voice eternally curious of the harmony of things with man. To these respond perfections not only in the committees that were supposed to stand for the rest but in the rest themselves just the same. These understand the law of perfection in masses and floods . . . that its finish is to each for itself and onward from itself . . . that it is profuse and impartial . . . that there is not a minute of the light or dark nor an acre of the earth or sea without it—nor any direction of the sky nor any trade or employment nor any turn of events. This is the reason that about the proper expression of beauty there is precision and balance . . . one part does not need to be thrust above another. The best singer is not the one who has the most lithe and powerful organ . . . the pleasure of poems is not in them that take the handsomest measure and similes and sound.

Without effort and without exposing in the least how it is done the greatest poet brings the spirit of any or all events and passions and scenes and persons some more and some less to bear on your individual character as you hear or read. To do this well is to compete with the laws that pursue and follow time. What is the purpose must surely be there and the clue of it must be there . . . and the faintest indication is the indication of the best and then becomes the clearest indication. Past and present and future are not disjoined but joined. The greatest poet forms the consistence of what is to be from what has been and is. He drags the dead out of their coffins and stands them again on their feet . . . he says to the past, Rise and walk before me that I may realize you. He learns the lesson . . . he places himself where the future becomes present. The greatest poet does not only dazzle his rays over character and scenes and passions . . . he finally ascends and finishes all . . . he exhibits the pinnacles that no man can tell what they are for or what is beyond . . . he glows a moment on the extremest verge. He is most wonderful in his last half-hidden smile or frown . . . by that flash of the moment of parting the one that sees it shall be encouraged or terrified afterwards for many years. The greatest poet does not moralize or make applications of morals . . . he knows the soul. The soul has that measureless pride which consists in never acknowledging any lessons but its own. But it has sympathy as measureless as its pride and the one balances the other and neither can stretch too far while it stretches in company with the other. The inmost secrets of art sleep with the twain. The greatest poet has lain close betwixt both and they are vital in his style and thoughts.

The art of art, the glory of expression and the sunshine of the light of letters is simplicity. Nothing is better than simplicity . . . nothing can make up for excess or for the lack of definiteness. To carry on the heave of impulse and pierce intellectual depths and give all subjects their articulations are powers neither common nor very uncommon. But to speak in literature with the perfect rectitude and insouciance of the movements of animals and the unimpeachableness of the sentiment of trees in the woods and grass by the roadside is the flawless triumph of art. If you have looked on him who has achieved it you have looked on one of the masters of the artists of all nations and times. You shall not contemplate the flight of the graygull over the bay or the mettlesome action of the blood horse or the tall leaning of sunflowers on their stalk or the appearance of the sun journeying through heaven or the appearance of the moon afterward with any more satisfaction than you shall contemplate him. The greatest poet has less a marked style and is more the channel of thoughts and things without increase or diminution, and is the free channel of himself. He swears to his art, I will not be meddlesome, I will not have in my writing any elegance or effect or originality to hang in the way between me and the rest like curtains. I will have nothing hang in the way, not the richest curtains. What I tell I tell for precisely what it is. Let who may exalt or startle or fascinate or sooth I will have purposes as health or heat or snow has and be as regardless of observation. What I experience or portray shall go from my composition without a shred of my composition. You shall stand by my side and look in the mirror with me.

The old red blood and stainless gentility of great poets will be proved by their unconstraint. A heroic person walks at his ease through and out of that custom or precedent or authority that suits him not. Of the traits of the brotherhood of writers savans musicians inventors and artists nothing is finer than silent defiance advancing from new free forms. In the need of poems philosophy politics mechanism science behaviour, the craft of art, and appropriate native grand-opera, shipcraft, or any craft, he is greatest forever and forever who contributes the greatest original practical example. The cleanest expression is that which finds no sphere worthy of itself and makes one.

The messages of great poets to each man and woman are, Come to us on equal terms, Only then can you understand us, We are no better than you, What we enclose you enclose, What we enjoy you may enjoy. Did you suppose there could be only one Supreme? We affirm there can be unnumbered Supremes, and that one does not countervail another any more than one eyesight countervails another . . . and that men can be good or grand only of the consciousness of their supremacy within them. What do you think is the grandeur of storms and dismemberments and the deadliest battles and wrecks and the wildest fury of the elements and the power of the sea and the motion of nature and of the throes of human desires and dignity and hate and love? It is that something in the soul which says, Rage on, Whirl on, I tread master here and everywhere, Master of the spasms of the sky and of the shatter of the sea, Master of nature and passion and death, And of all terror and all pain.

The American bards shall be marked for generosity and affection and for encouraging competitors. . . . They shall be kosmos . . . without monopoly or secresy . . . glad to pass any thing to any one . . . hungry for equals night and day. They shall not be careful of riches and privilege . . . they shall be riches and privilege . . . they shall perceive who the most affluent man is. The most affluent man is he that confronts all the shows he sees by equivalents out of the stronger wealth of himself. The American bard shall delineate no class of persons nor one or two out of the strata of interests nor love most nor truth most nor the soul most nor the body most . . . and not be for the eastern states more than the western or the northern states more than the southern.

Exact science and its practical movements are no checks on the greatest poet but always his encouragement and support. The outset and remembrance are there . . . there are the arms that lifted him first and brace him best . . . there he returns after all his goings and comings. The sailor and traveler . . . the anatomist chemist astronomer geologist phrenologist spiritualist mathematician historian and lexicographer are not poets, but they are the lawgivers of poets and their construction underlies the structure of every perfect poem. No matter what rises or is uttered they sent the seed of the conception of it . . . of them and by them stand the visible proofs of souls . . . always of their fatherstuff must be begotten the sinewy races of bards. If there shall be love and content between the father and the son and if the greatness of the son is the exuding of the greatness of the father there shall be love between the poet and the man of demonstrable science. In the beauty of poems are the tuft and final applause of science.

Great is the faith of the flush of knowledge and of the investigation of the depths of qualities and things. Cleaving and circling here swells the soul of the poet yet is president of itself always. The depths are fathomless and therefore calm. The innocence and nakedness are resumed . . . they are neither modest nor immodest. The whole theory of the special and supernatural and all that was twined with it or educed out of it departs as a dream. What has ever happened . . . what happens and whatever may or shall happen, the vital laws enclose all . . . they are sufficient for any case and for all cases . . . none to be hurried or retarded . . . any miracle of affairs or persons inadmissible in the vast clear scheme where every motion and every spear of grass and the frames and spirits of men and women and all that concerns them are unspeakably perfect miracles all referring to all and each distinct and in its place. It is also not consistent with the reality of the soul to admit that there is anything in the known universe more divine than men and women.

Men and women and the earth and all upon it are simply to be taken as they are, and the investigation of their past and present and future shall be unintermitted and shall be done with perfect candor. Upon this basis philosophy speculates ever looking toward the poet, ever regarding the eternal tendencies of all toward happiness never inconsistent with what is clear to the senses and to the soul. For the eternal tendencies of all toward happiness make the only point of sane philosophy. Whatever comprehends less than that . . . whatever is less than the laws of light and of astronomical motion . . . or less than the laws that follow the thief the liar the glutton and the drunkard through this life and doubtless afterward . . . or less than vast stretches of time or the slow formation of density or the patient upheaving of strata—is of no account. Whatever would put God in a poem or system of philosophy as contending against some being or influence is also of no account. Sanity and ensemble characterise the great master . . . spoilt in one principle all is spoilt. The great master has nothing to do with miracles. He sees health for himself in being one of the mass . . . he sees the hiatus in singular eminence. To the perfect shape comes common ground. To be under the general law is great for that is to correspond with it. The master knows that he is unspeakably great and that all are unspeakably great . . . that nothing for instance is greater than to conceive children and bring them up well . . . that to be is just as great as to perceive or tell.

In the make of the great masters the idea of political liberty is indispensable. Liberty takes the adherence of heroes wherever men and women exist . . . but never takes any adherence or welcome from the rest more than from poets. They are the voice and exposition of liberty. They out of ages are worthy the grand idea . . . to them it is confided and they must sustain it. Nothing has precedence of it and nothing can warp or degrade it. The attitude of great poets is to cheer up slaves and horrify despots. The turn of their necks, the sound of their feet, the motions of their wrists, are full of hazard to the one and hope to the other. Come nigh them awhile and though they neither speak or advise you shall learn the faithful American lesson. Liberty is poorly served by men whose good intent is quelled from one failure or two failures or any number of failures, or from the casual indifference or ingratitude of the people, or from the sharp show of the tushes of power, or the bringing to bear soldiers and cannon or any penal statutes. Liberty relies upon itself, invites no one, promises nothing, sits in calmness and light, is positive and composed, and knows no discouragement. The battle rages with many a loud alarm and frequent advance and retreat . . . the enemy triumphs . . . the prison, the handcuffs, the iron necklace and anklet, the scaffold, garrote and leadballs do their work . . . the cause is asleep . . . the strong throats are choked with their own blood . . . the young men drop their eyelashes toward the ground when they pass each other . . . and is liberty gone out of that place? No never. When liberty goes it is not the first to go nor the second or third to go . . . it waits for all the rest to go . . . it is the last. . . . When the memories of the old martyrs are faded utterly away . . . when the large names of patriots are laughed at in the public halls from the lips of the orators . . . when the boys are no more christened after the same but christened after tyrants and traitors instead . . . when the laws of the free are grudgingly permitted and laws for informers and bloodmoney are sweet to the taste of the people . . . when I and you walk abroad upon the earth stung with compassion at the sight of numberless brothers answering our equal friendship and calling no man master—and when we are elated with noble joy at the sight of slaves . . . when the soul retires in the cool communion of the night and surveys its experience and has much extasy over the word and deed that put back a helpless innocent person into the gripe of the gripers or into any cruel inferiority . . . when those in all parts of these states who could easier realize the true American character but do not yet—when the swarms of cringers, suckers, doughfaces, lice of politics, planners of sly involutions for their own preferment to city offices or state legislatures or the judiciary or congress or the presidency, obtain a response of love and natural deference from the people whether they get the offices or no . . . when it is better to be a bound booby and rogue in office at a high salary than the poorest free mechanic or farmer with his hat unmoved from his head and firm eyes and a candid and generous heart . . . and when servility by town or state or the federal government or any oppression on a large scale or small scale can be tried on without its own punishment following duly after in exact proportion against the smallest chance of escape . . . or rather when all life and all the souls of men and women are discharged from any part of the earth—then only shall the instinct of liberty be discharged from that part of the earth.

As the attributes of the poets of the kosmos concentre in the real body and soul and in the pleasure of things they possess the superiority of genuineness over all fiction and romance. As they emit themselves facts are showered over with light . . . the daylight is lit with more volatile light . . . also the deep between the setting and rising sun goes deeper many fold. Each precise object or condition or combination or process exhibits a beauty . . . the multiplication table its—old age its—the carpenter's trade its—the grand-opera its . . . the hugehulled cleanshaped New-York clipper at sea under steam or full sail gleams with unmatched beauty . . . the American circles and large harmonies of government gleam with theirs . . . and the commonest definite intentions and actions with theirs. The poets of the kosmos advance through all interpositions and coverings and turmoils and stratagems to first principles. They are of use . . . they dissolve poverty from its need and riches from its conceit. You large proprietor they say shall not realize or perceive more than any one else. The owner of the library is not he who holds a legal title to it having bought and paid for it. Any one and every one is owner of the library who can read the same through all the varieties of tongues and subjects and styles, and in whom they enter with ease and take residence and force toward paternity and maternity, and make supple and powerful and rich and large. . . . These American states strong and healthy and accomplished shall receive no pleasure from violations of natural models and must not permit them. In paintings or mouldings or carvings in mineral or wood, or in the illustrations of books or newspapers, or in any comic or tragic prints, or in the patterns of woven stuffs or any thing to beautify rooms or furniture or costumes, or to put upon cornices or monuments or on the prows or sterns of ships, or to put anywhere before the human eye indoors or out, that which distorts honest shapes or which creates unearthly beings or places or contingencies is a nuisance and revolt. Of the human form especially it is so great it must never be made ridiculous. Of ornaments to a work nothing outre can be allowed . . . but those ornaments can be allowed that conform to the perfect facts of the open air and that flow out of the nature of the work and come irrepressibly from it and are necessary to the completion of the work. Most works are most beautiful without ornament. . . . Exaggerations will be revenged in human physiology. Clean and vigorous children are jetted and conceived only in those communities where the models of natural forms are public every day. . . . Great genius and the people of these states must never be demeaned to romances. As soon as histories are properly told there is no more need of romances.

The great poets are also to be known by the absence in them of tricks and by the justification of perfect personal candor. Then folks echo a new cheap joy and a divine voice leaping from their brains: How beautiful is candor! All faults may be forgiven of him who has perfect candor. Henceforth let no man of us lie, for we have seen that openness wins the inner and outer world and that there is no single exception, and that never since our earth gathered itself in a mass have deceit or subterfuge or prevarication attracted its smallest particle or the faintest tinge of a shade—and that through the enveloping wealth and rank of a state or the whole republic of states a sneak or sly person shall be discovered and despised

. . . and that the soul has never been once fooled and never can be fooled . . . and thrift without the loving nod of the soul is only a fœtid puff . . . and there never grew up in any of the continents of the globe nor upon any planet or satellite or star, nor upon the asteroids, nor in any part of ethereal space, nor in the midst of density, nor under the fluid wet of the sea, nor in that condition which precedes the birth of babes, nor at any time during the changes of life, nor in that condition that follows what we term death, nor in any stretch of abeyance or action afterward of vitality, nor in any process of formation or reformation anywhere, a being whose instinct hated the truth.

Extreme caution or prudence, the soundest organic health, large hope and comparison and fondness for women and children, large alimentiveness and destructiveness and causality, with a perfect sense of the oneness of nature and the propriety of the same spirit applied to human affairs . . . these are called up of the float of the brain of the world to be parts of the greatest poet from his birth out of his mother's womb and from her birth out of her mother's. Caution seldom goes far enough. It has been thought that the prudent citizen was the citizen who applied himself to solid gains and did well for himself and his family and completed a lawful life without debt or crime. The greatest poet sees and admits these economies as he sees the economies of food and sleep, but has higher notions of prudence than to think he gives much when he gives a few slight attentions at the latch of the gate. The premises of the prudence of life are not the hospitality of it or the ripeness and harvest of it. Beyond the independence of a little sum laid aside for burial-money, and of a few clap-boards around and shingles overhead on a lot of American soil owned, and the easy dollars that supply the year's plain clothing and meals, the melancholy prudence of the abandonment of such a great being as a man is to the toss and pallor of years of moneymaking with all their scorching days and icy nights and all their stifling deceits and underhanded dodgings, or infinitesimals of parlors, or shameless stuffing while others starve . . . and all the loss of the bloom and odor of the earth and of the flowers and atmosphere and of the sea and of the true taste of the women and men you pass or have to do with in youth or middle age, and the issuing sickness and desperate revolt at the close of a life without elevation or naivete, and the ghastly chatter of a death without serenity or majesty, is the great fraud upon modern civilization and forethought, blotching the surface and system which civilization undeniably drafts, and moistening with tears the immense features it spreads and spreads with such velocity before the reached kisses of the soul. . . . Still the right explanation remains to be made about prudence. The prudence of the mere wealth and respectability of the most esteemed life appears too faint for the eye to observe at all when little and large alike drop quietly aside at the thought of the prudence suitable for immortality. What is wisdom that fills the thinness of a year or seventy or eighty years to wisdom spaced out by ages and coming back at a certain time with strong reinforcements and rich presents and the clear faces of wedding-guests as far as you can look in every direction running gaily toward you? Only the soul is of itself . . . all else has reference to what ensues. All that a person does or thinks is of consequence. Not a move can a man or woman make that affects him or her in a day or a month or any part of the direct lifetime or the hour of death but the same affects him or her onward afterward through the indirect lifetime. The indirect is always as great and real as the direct. The spirit receives from the body just as much as it gives to the body. Not one name of word or deed . . . not of venereal sores or discolorations . . . not the privacy of the onanist . . . not of the putrid veins of gluttons or rum-drinkers . . . not peculation or cunning or betrayal or murder . . . no serpentine poison of those that seduce women . . . not the foolish yielding of women . . . not prostitution . . . not of any depravity of young men . . . not of the attainment of gain by discreditable means . . . not any nastiness of appetite . . . not any harshness of officers to men or judges to prisoners or fathers to sons or sons to fathers or husbands to wives or bosses to their boys . . . not of greedy looks or malignant wishes . . . nor any of the wiles practised by people upon themselves . . . ever is or ever can be stamped on the programme but it is duly realized and returned, and that returned in further performances . . . and they returned again. Nor can the push of charity or personal force ever be any thing else than the profoundest reason, whether it brings arguments to hand or no. No specification is necessary . . . to add or subtract or divide is in vain. Little or big, learned or unlearned, white or black, legal or illegal, sick or well, from the first inspiration down the windpipe to the last expiration out of it, all that a male or female does that is vigorous and benevolent and clean is so much sure profit to him or her in the unshakable order of the universe and through the whole scope of it forever. If the savage or felon is wise it is well . . . if the greatest poet or savan is wise it is simply the same . . . if the President or chief justice is wise it is the same . . . if the young mechanic or farmer is wise it is no more or less . . . if the prostitute is wise it is no more nor less. The interest will come round . . . all will come round. All the best actions of war and peace . . . all help given to relatives and strangers and the poor and old and sorrowful and young children and widows and the sick, and to all shunned persons . . . all furtherance of fugitives and of the escape of slaves . . . all the self-denial that stood steady and aloof on wrecks and saw others take the seats of the boats . . . all offering of substance or life for the good old cause, or for a friend's sake or opinion's sake . . . all pains of enthusiasts scoffed at by their neighbors . . . all the vast sweet love and precious suffering of mothers . . . all honest men baffled in strifes recorded or unrecorded . . . all the grandeur and good of the few ancient nations whose fragments of annals we inherit . . . and all the good of the hundreds of far mightier and more ancient nations unknown to us by name or date or location . . . all that was ever manfully begun, whether it succeeded or not . . . all that has at any time been well suggested out of the divine heart of man or by the divinity of his mouth or by the shaping of his great hands . . . and all that is well thought or done this day on any part of the surface of the globe . . . or on any of the wandering stars or fixed stars by those there as we are here . . . or that is henceforth to be well thought or done by you whoever you are, or by any one—these singly and wholly inured at their time and inure now and will inure always to the identities from which they sprung or shall spring. . . . Did you guess any of them lived only its moment? The world does not so exist . . . no parts palpable or impalpable so exist . . . no result exists now without being from its long antecedent result, and that from its antecedent, and so backward without the farthest mentionable spot coming a bit nearer to the beginning than any other spot. . . . Whatever satisfies the soul is truth. The prudence of the greatest poet answers at last the craving and glut of the soul, is not contemptuous of less ways of prudence if they conform to its ways, puts off nothing, permits no let-up for its own case or any case, has no particular sabbath or judgment-day, divides not the living from the dead or the righteous from the unrighteous, is satisfied with the present, matches every thought or act by its correlative, knows no possible forgiveness or deputed atonement . . . knows that the young man who composedly periled his life and lost it has done exceeding well for himself, while the man who has not periled his life and retains it to old age in riches and ease has perhaps achieved nothing for himself worth mentioning . . . and that only that person has no great prudence to learn who has learnt to prefer real longlived things, and favors body and soul the same, and perceives the indirect assuredly following the direct, and what evil or good he does leaping onward and waiting to meet him again—and who in his spirit in any emergency whatever neither hurries or avoids death.

The direct trial of him who would be the greatest poet is today. If he does not flood himself with the immediate age as with vast oceanic tides . . . and if he does not attract his own land body and soul to himself and hang on its neck with incomparable love and plunge his semitic muscle into its merits and demerits . . . and if he be not himself the age transfigured . . . and if to him is not opened the eternity which gives similitude to all periods and locations and processes and animate and inanimate forms, and which is the bond of time, and rises up from its inconceivable vagueness and infiniteness in the swimming shape of today, and is held by the ductile anchors of life, and makes the present spot the passage from what was to what shall be, and commits itself to the representation of this wave of an hour and this one of the sixty beautiful children of the wave—let him merge in the general run and wait his development. . . . Still the final test of poems or any character or work remains. The prescient poet projects himself centuries ahead and judges performer or performance after the changes of time. Does it live through them? Does it still hold on untired? Will the same style and the direction of genius to similar points be satisfactory now? Has no new discovery in science or arrival at superior planes of thought and judgment and behaviour fixed him or his so that either can be looked down upon? Have the marches of tens and hundreds and thousands of years made willing detours to the right hand and the left hand for his sake? Is he beloved long and long after he is buried? Does the young man think often of him? and the young woman think often of him? and do the middleaged and the old think of him?

A great poem is for ages and ages in common and for all degrees and complexions and all departments and sects and for a woman as much as a man and a man as much as a woman. A great poem is no finish to a man or woman but rather a beginning. Has any one fancied he could sit at last under some due authority and rest satisfied with explanations and realize and be content and full? To no such terminus does the greatest poet bring . . . he brings neither cessation or sheltered fatness and ease. The touch of him tells in action. Whom he takes he takes with firm sure grasp into live regions previously unattained . . . thenceforward is no rest . . . they see the space and ineffable sheen that turn the old spots and lights into dead vacuums. The companion of him beholds the birth and progress of stars and learns one of the meanings. Now there shall be a man cohered out of tumult and chaos . . . the elder encourages the younger and shows him how . . . they two shall launch off fearlessly together till the new world fits an orbit for itself and looks unabashed on the lesser orbits of the stars and sweeps through the ceaseless rings and shall never be quiet again.

There will soon be no more priests. Their work is done. They may wait awhile . . . perhaps a generation or two . . . dropping off by degrees. A superior breed shall take their place . . . the gangs of kosmos and prophets en masse shall take their place. A new order shall arise and they shall be the priests of man, and every man shall be his own priest. The churches built under their umbrage shall be the churches of men and women. Through the divinity of themselves shall the kosmos and the new breed of poets be interpreters of men and women and of all events and things. They shall find their inspiration in real objects today, symptoms of the past and future. . . . They shall not deign to defend immortality or God or the perfection of things or liberty or the exquisite beauty and reality of the soul. They shall arise in America and be responded to from the remainder of the earth.

The English language befriends the grand American expression . . . it is brawny enough and limber and full enough. On the tough stock of a race who through all change of circumstances was never without the idea of political liberty, which is the animus of all liberty, it has attracted the terms of daintier and gayer and subtler and more elegant tongues. It is the powerful language of resistance . . . it is the dialect of common sense. It is the speech of the proud and melancholy races and of all who aspire. It is the chosen tongue to express growth faith self-esteem freedom justice equality friendliness amplitude prudence decision and courage. It is the medium that shall well nigh express the inexpressible.

No great literature nor any like style of behaviour or oratory or social intercourse or household arrangements or public institutions or the treatment by bosses of employed people, nor executive detail or detail of the army or navy, nor spirit of legislation or courts or police or tuition or architecture or songs or amusements or the costumes of young men, can long elude the jealous and passionate instinct of American standards. Whether or no the sign appears from the mouths of the people, it throbs a live interrogation in every freeman's and freewoman's heart after that which passes by or this built to remain. Is it uniform with my country? Are its disposals without ignominious distinctions? Is it for the evergrowing communes of brothers and lovers, large, well-united, proud beyond the old models, generous beyond all models? Is it something grown fresh out of the fields or drawn from the sea for use to me today here? I know that what answers for me an American must answer for any individual or nation that serves for a part of my materials. Does this answer? or is it without reference to universal needs? or sprung of the needs of the less developed society of special ranks? or old needs of pleasure overlaid by modern science and forms? Does this acknowledge liberty with audible and absolute acknowledgement, and set slavery at naught for life and death? Will it help breed one goodshaped and wellhung man, and a woman to be his perfect and independent mate? Does it improve manners? Is it for the nursing of the young of the republic? Does it solve readily with the sweet milk of the nipples of the breasts of the mother of many children? Has it too the old ever-fresh forbearance and impartiality? Does it look with the same love on the last born and those hardening toward stature, and on the errant, and on those who disdain all strength of assault outside of their own?

The poems distilled from other poems will probably pass away. The coward will surely pass away. The expectation of the vital and great can only be satisfied by the demeanor of the vital and great. The swarms of the polished deprecating and reflectors and the polite float off and leave no remembrance. America prepares with composure and goodwill for the visitors that have sent word. It is not intellect that is to be their warrant and welcome. The talented, the artist, the ingenious, the editor, the statesman, the erudite . . . they are not unappreciated . . . they fall in their place and do their work. The soul of the nation also does its work. No disguise can pass on it . . . no disguise can conceal from it. It rejects none, it permits all. Only toward as good as itself and toward the like of itself will it advance half-way. An individual is as superb as a nation when he has the qualities which make a superb nation. The soul of the largest and wealthiest and proudest nation may well go half-way to meet that of its poets. The signs are effectual. There is no fear of mistake. If the one is true the other is true. The proof of a poet is that his country absorbs him as affectionately as he has absorbed it.

VACHEL LINDSAY[1]

A GOSPEL OF BEAUTY

(I recited these three poems more than any others in my mendicant preaching tour through the West. Taken as a triad, they hold in solution my theory of American civilization.)

I. THE PROUD FARMER

(In memory of E. S. Frazee, Rush County, Indiana.)

INTO the acres of the newborn state
He poured his strength, and plowed his ancient name,
And, when the traders followed him, he stood
Towering above their furtive souls and tame.

That brow without a stain, that fearless eye
Oft left the passing stranger wondering
To find such knighthood in the sprawling land,
To see a democrat well-nigh a king.

He lived with liberal hand, with guests from far,
With talk and joke and fellowship to spare,—
Watching the wide world's life from sun to sun,
Lining his walls with books from everywhere.

He read by night, he built his world by day.
The farm and house of God to him were one.
For forty years he preached and plowed and wrought—
A statesman in the fields, who bent to none.

His plowmen-neighbors were as lords to him.
His was an ironside, democratic pride.
He served a rigid Christ, but served him well—
And, for a lifetime, saved the countryside.

Here lie the dead, who gave the church their best
Under his fiery preaching of the word.
They sleep with him beneath the ragged grass . . .
The village withers, by his voice unstirred.

And tho' his tribe be scattered to the wind
From the Atlantic to the China Sea,
Yet do they think of that bright lamp he burned
Of family worth and proud integrity.

And many a sturdy grandchild hears his name
In reverence spoken, till he feels akin
To all the lion-eyed who build the world—
And lion-dreams begin to burn within.

II. THE ILLINOIS VILLAGE

O YOU who lose the art of hope,
Whose temples seem to shrine a lie,
Whose sidewalks are but stones of fear,
Who weep that Liberty must die,
Turn to the little prairie towns,
Your higher hope shall yet begin.
On every side awaits you there
Some gate where glory enters in.
Yet when I see the flocks of girls,
Watching the Sunday train go through
(As though the whole wide world went by)
With eyes that long to travel too,
I sigh, despite my soul made glad
By cloudy dresses and brown hair,
Sigh for the sweet life wrenched and torn
By thundering commerce, fierce and bare.
Nymphs of the wheat these girls should be:
Kings of the grove, their lovers, strong.
Why are they not inspired, aflame?
This beauty calls for valiant song—
For men to carve these fairy-forms
And faces in a fountain-frieze;
Dancers that own immortal hours;
Painters that work upon their knees;
Maids, lovers, friends, so deep in life,

[1] All the selections from Vachel Lindsay, with the exception of "The Voyage," are reprinted from his *Collected Poems* (revised and illustrated edition, 1925), by permission of The Macmillan Company, publishers. "The Voyage" is reprinted from *Every Soul Is a Circus* (copyright, 1929), by permission of The Macmillan Company, publishers.

So deep in love and poet's deeds,
The railroad is a thing disowned,
The city but a field of weeds.

Who can pass a village church
By night in these clean prairie lands
Without a touch of Spirit-power?
So white and fixed and cool it stands—
A thing from some strange fairy-town,
A pious amaranthine flower,
Unsullied by the winds, as pure
As jade or marble, wrought this hour:—
Rural in form, foursquare and plain,
And yet our sister, the new moon,
Makes it a praying wizard's dream.
The trees that watch at dusty noon
Breaking its sharpest lines, veil not
The whiteness it reflects from God,
Flashing like Spring on many an eye,
Making clean flesh, that once was clod.

Who can pass a district school
Without the hope that there may wait
Some baby-heart the books shall flame
With zeal to make his playmates great,
To make the whole wide village gleam
A strangely carved celestial gem,
Eternal in its beauty-light,
The Artist's town of Bethlehem!

III. ON THE BUILDING OF SPRINGFIELD

Let not our town be large, remembering
That little Athens was the Muses' home,
That Oxford rules the heart of London still,
That Florence gave the Renaissance to Rome.

Record it for the grandson of your son—
A city is not builded in a day:
Our little town cannot complete her soul
Till countless generations pass away.

Now let each child be joined as to a church
To her perpetual hopes, each man ordained:
Let every street be made a reverent aisle
Where Music grows and Beauty is unchained.

Let Science and Machinery and Trade
Be slaves of her, and make her all in all,
Building against our blatant, restless time
An unseen, skilful, medieval wall.

Let every citizen be rich toward God.
Let Christ the beggar, teach divinity.
Let no man rule who holds his money dear.
Let this, our city, be our luxury.

We should build parks that students from afar
Would choose to starve in, rather than go
home,
Fair little squares, with Phidian ornament,
Food for the spirit, milk and honeycomb.

Songs shall be sung by us in that good day,
Songs we have written, blood within the
rhyme
Beating, as when Old England still was glad,—
The purple, rich Elizabethan time.

. . . .

Say, is my prophecy too fair and far?
I only know, unless her faith be high,
The soul of this, our Nineveh, is doomed,
Our little Babylon will surely die.

Some city on the breast of Illinois
No wiser and no better at the start
By faith shall rise redeemed, by faith shall rise
Bearing the western glory in her heart.

The genius of the Maple, Elm and Oak,
The secret hidden in each grain of corn,
The glory that the prairie angels sing
At night when sons of Life and Love are born,

Born but to struggle, squalid and alone,
Broken and wandering in their early years.
When will they make our dusty streets their
goal,
Within our attics hide their sacred tears?

When will they start our vulgar blood athrill
With living language, words that set us
free?
When will they make a path of beauty clear
Between our riches and our liberty?

We must have many Lincoln-hearted men.
A city is not builded in a day.
And they must do their work, and come and
go,
While countless generations pass away.

1908

QUEEN MAB IN THE VILLAGE

Once I loved a fairy,
Queen Mab it was. Her voice
Was like a little Fountain
That bids the birds rejoice.
Her face was wise and solemn,
Her hair was brown and fine.
Her dress was pansy velvet,
A butterfly design.

To see her hover round me
Or walk the hills of air,
Awakened love's deep pulses
And boyhood's first despair;
A passion like a sword-blade
That pierced me through and through:
Her fingers healed the sorrow
Her whisper would renew.
We sighed and reigned and feasted
Within a hollow tree,
We vowed our love was boundless,
Eternal as the sea.
She banished from her kingdom
The mortal boy I grew—
So tall and crude and noisy,
I killed grasshoppers too.
I threw big rocks at pigeons,
I plucked and tore apart
The weeping, wailing daisies,
And broke my lady's heart.
At length I grew to manhood,
I scarcely could believe
I ever loved the lady,
Or caused her court to grieve,
Until a dream came to me
One bleak first night of Spring
Ere tides of apple blossoms
Rolled in o'er everything,
While rain and sleet and snowbanks
Were still a-vexing men,
Ere Robin and his comrades
Were nesting once again.

I saw Mab's Book of Judgment—
Its clasps were iron and stone,
Its leaves were mammoth ivory,
Its boards were mammoth bone,—
Hid in her seaside mountains,
Forgotten or unkept,
Beneath its mighty covers
Her wrath against me slept.
And deeply I repented
Of brash and boyish crime,
Of murder of things lovely
Now and in olden time.
I cursed my vain ambition,
My would-be worldly days,
And craved the paths of wonder,
Of dewy dawns and fays.
I cried, "Our love was boundless,
Eternal as the sea,
O Queen, reverse the sentence,
Come back and master me!"

The book was by the cliff-side
Upon its edge upright.
I laid me by it softly,
And wept throughout the night.
And there at dawn I saw it,
No book now, but a door,
Upon its panels written,
"Judgment is no more."
The bolt flew back with thunder,
I saw within that place
A mermaid wrapped in seaweed
With Mab's immortal face,
Yet grown now to a woman,
A woman to the knee.
She cried, she clasped me fondly,
We soon were in the sea.

Ah, she was wise and subtle,
And gay and strong and sleek,
We chained the wicked swordfish,
We played at hide and seek.
We floated on the water,
We heard the dawn-wind sing,
I made from ocean-wonders,
Her bridal wreath and ring.
All mortal girls were shadows,
All earth-life but a mist,
When deep beneath the maelstrom,
The mermaid's heart I kissed.

I woke beside the church-door
Of our small inland town,
Bowing to a maiden
In a pansy-velvet gown,
Who had not heard of fairies,
Yet seemed of love to dream.
We planned an earthly cottage
Beside an earthly stream.

Our wedding long is over,
With toil the years fill up,
Yet in the evening silence,
We drink a deep-sea cup.
Nothing the fay remembers,
Yet when she turns to me,
We meet beneath the whirlpool,
We swim the golden sea.

1912

THE WEDDING OF THE ROSE AND THE LOTUS

The wide Pacific waters
And the Atlantic meet.
With cries of joy they mingle,
In tides of love they greet.
Above the drownèd ages
A wind of wooing blows:—
The red rose woos the lotus,
The lotus woos the rose . . .

The lotus conquered Egypt.
The rose was loved in Rome.
Great India crowned the lotus:
(Britain the rose's home).
Old China crowned the lotus,
They crowned it in Japan.
But Christendom adored the rose
Ere Christendom began . . .

The lotus speaks of slumber:
The rose is as a dart.
The lotus is Nirvana:
The rose is Mary's heart.
The rose is deathless, restless,
The splendor of our pain:
The flush and fire of labor
That builds, not all in vain. . . .

The genius of the lotus
Shall heal earth's too-much fret.
The rose, in blinding glory,
Shall waken Asia yet.
Hail to their loves, ye peoples!
Behold, a world-wind blows,
That aids the ivory lotus
To wed the red, red rose!

1912

THE KING OF YELLOW BUTTERFLIES

(A Poem Game)

The King of Yellow Butterflies,
The King of Yellow Butterflies,
The King of Yellow Butterflies,
Now orders forth his men.
He says "The time is almost here
When violets bloom again."
Adown the road the fickle rout
Goes flashing proud and bold,
Adown the road the fickle rout
Goes flashing proud and bold,
Adown the road the fickle rout
Goes flashing proud and bold,
They shiver by the shallow pools,
They shiver by the shallow pools,
They shiver by the shallow pools,
And whimper of the cold.
They drink and drink. A frail pretense!
They love to pose and preen.
Each pool is but a looking glass,
Where their sweet wings are seen.
Each pool is but a looking glass,
Where their sweet wings are seen.
Each pool is but a looking glass,
Where their sweet wings are seen.
Gentlemen adventurers! Gypsies every whit!
They live on what they steal. Their wings
By briars are frayed a bit.
Their loves are light. They have no house.
And if it rains today,
They'll climb into your cattle-shed,
They'll climb into your cattle-shed,
They'll climb into your cattle-shed,
And hide them in the hay,
And hide them in the hay,
And hide them in the hay,
And hide them in the hay.

1912, 1923

GENERAL WILLIAM BOOTH ENTERS INTO HEAVEN

(To be sung to the tune of "The Blood of the Lamb" with indicated instrument.)

I

(*Bass drum beaten loudly.*)

Booth led boldly with his big bass drum—
(Are you washed in the blood of the Lamb?)

The Saints smiled gravely and they said:
"He's come."
(Are you washed in the blood of the Lamb?)
Walking lepers followed, rank on rank,
Lurching bravos from the ditches dank,
Drabs from the alleyways and drug fiends pale—
Minds still passion-ridden, soul-powers frail:—
Vermin-eaten saints with moldy breath,
Unwashed legions with the ways of Death—
(Are you washed in the blood of the Lamb?)

(*Banjos.*)

Every slum had sent its half-a-score
The round world over. (Booth had groaned for more.)
Every banner that the wide world flies
Bloomed with glory and transcendent dyes.
Big-voiced lasses made their banjos bang,
Tranced, fanatical they shrieked and sang:—
"Are you washed in the blood of the Lamb?"
Hallelujah! It was queer to see
Bull-necked convicts with that land make free.
Loons with trumpets blowed a blare, blare, blare
On, on upward through the golden air!
(Are you washed in the blood of the Lamb?)

II

(*Bass drum slower and softer.*)

Booth died blind and still by faith he trod,
Eyes still dazzled by the ways of God.
Booth led boldly, and he looked the chief
Eagle countenance in sharp relief,
Beard a-flying, air of high command
Unabated in that holy land.

(*Sweet flute music.*)

Jesus came from out the court-house door,
Stretched his hands above the passing poor.
Booth saw not, but led his queer ones there
Round and round the mighty court-house square.
Then, in an instant all that blear review
Marched on spotless, clad in raiment new.
The lame were straightened, withered limbs uncurled
And blind eyes opened on a new, sweet world.

(*Bass drum louder.*)

Drabs and vixens in a flash made whole!
Gone was the weasel-head, the snout, the jowl!
Sages and sibyls now, and athletes clean,
Rulers of empires, and of forests green!

(*Grand chorus of all instruments. Tambourines to the foreground.*)

The hosts were sandalled, and their wings were fire!
(Are you washed in the blood of the Lamb?)
But their noise played havoc with the angel-choir.
(Are you washed in the blood of the Lamb?)
Oh, shout Salvation! It was good to see
Kings and Princes by the Lamb set free.
The banjos rattled and the tambourines
Jing-jing-jingled in the hands of Queens.

(*Reverently sung, no instruments.*)

And when Booth halted by the curb for prayer
He saw his Master thro' the flag-filled air.
Christ came gently with a robe and crown
For Booth the soldier, while the throng knelt down.
He saw King Jesus. They were face to face,
And he knelt a-weeping in that holy place.
Are you washed in the blood of the Lamb?

1913

A NET TO SNARE THE MOONLIGHT

(*What the Man of Faith Said*)

THE dew, the rain and moonlight
All prove our Father's mind.
The dew, the rain and moonlight
Descend to bless mankind.

Come, let us see that all men
Have land to catch the rain,
Have grass to snare the spheres of dew,
And fields spread for the grain.

Yea, we would give to each poor man
Ripe wheat and poppies red,—
A peaceful place at evening
With the stars just overhead:

A net to snare the moonlight,
A sod spread to the sun,
A place of toil by daytime,
Of dreams when toil is done.

1913

ABRAHAM LINCOLN WALKS AT MIDNIGHT

(In Springfield, Illinois)

It is portentous, and a thing of state
That here at midnight, in our little town
A mourning figure walks, and will not rest,
Near the old court-house pacing up and down.

Or by his homestead, or in shadowed yards,
He lingers where his children used to play,
Or through the market, on the well-worn stones
He stalks until the dawn-stars burn away.

A bronzed, lank man! His suit of ancient black,
A famous high top-hat and plain worn shawl
Make him the quaint great figure that men love,
The prairie-lawyer, master of us all.

He cannot sleep upon his hillside now.
He is among us:—as in times before!
And we who toss and lie awake for long
Breathe deep, and start, to see him pass the door.

His head is bowed. He thinks on men and kings.
Yea, when the sick world cries, how can he sleep?
Too many peasants fight, they know not why,
Too many homesteads in black terror weep.

The sins of all the war-lords burn his heart.
He sees the dreadnaughts scouring every main
He carries on his shawl-wrapped shoulders now
The bitterness, the folly and the pain.

He cannot rest until a spirit-dawn
Shall come;—the shining hope of Europe free:
The league of sober folk, the Workers' Earth,
Bringing long peace to Cornland, Alp and Sea.

It breaks his heart that kings must murder still,
That all his hours of travail here for men
Seem yet in vain. And who will bring white peace
That he may sleep upon his hill again?

1914

THE SANTA-FÉ TRAIL (A HUMORESQUE)

(I asked the old negro: "What is that bird that sings so well?" He answered: "That is the Rachel-Jane." "Hasn't it another name—lark, or thrush, or the like?" "No. Jus' Rachel-Jane.")

I. IN WHICH A RACING AUTO COMES FROM THE EAST

To be sung delicately, to an improvised tune.

This is the order of the music of the morning:—
First, from the far East comes but a crooning.
The crooning turns to a sunrise singing.
Hark to the *calm*-horn, *balm*-horn, *psalm*-horn.
Hark to the *faint*-horn, *quaint*-horn, *saint*-horn . . .

To be sung or read with great speed.

Hark to the *pace*-horn, *chase*-horn, *race*-horn.
And the holy veil of the dawn has gone.
Swiftly the brazen car comes on.
It burns in the East as the sunrise burns.
I see great flashes where the far trail turns.
Its eyes are lamps like the eyes of dragons.
It drinks gasoline from big red flagons.
Butting through the delicate mists of the morning,
It comes like lightning, goes past roaring.

It will hail all the windmills, taunting, ringing,
Dodge the cyclones,
Count the milestones,
On through the ranges the prairie-dog tills—
Scooting past the cattle on the thousand hills. . . .
Ho for the tear-horn, scare-horn, dare-horn,
Ho for the *gay*-horn, *bark*-horn, *bay*-horn.
Ho for Kansas, land that restores us
When houses choke us, and great books bore us!
Sunrise Kansas, harvesters' Kansas,
A million men have found you before us.
A million men have found you before us.

To be read or sung in a rolling bass, with some deliberation.

II. IN WHICH MANY AUTOS PASS WESTWARD

In an even, deliberate, narrative manner.

I want live things in their pride to remain.
I will not kill one grasshopper vain
Though he eats a hole in my shirt like a door.
I let him out, give him one chance more.
Perhaps, while he gnaws my hat in his whim,
Grasshopper lyrics occur to him.

I am a tramp by the long trail's border,
Given to squalor, rags and disorder.
I nap and amble and yawn and look,
Write fool-thoughts in my grubby book,
Recite to the children, explore at my ease,
Work when I work, beg when I please,
Give crank-drawings, that make folks stare
To the half-grown boys in the sunset glare,
And get me a place to sleep in the hay
At the end of a live-and-let-live day.

I find in the stubble of the new-cut weeds
A whisper and a feasting, all one needs:
The whisper of the strawberries, white and red
Here where the new-cut weeds lie dead.

But I would not walk all alone till I die
Without some life-drunk horns going by.
And up round this apple-earth they come
Blasting the whispers of the morning dumb:—
Cars in a plain realistic row.
And fair dreams fade
When the raw horns blow.

On each snapping pennant
A big black name:—
The careering city
Whence each car came.
They tour from Memphis, Atlanta, Savannah,
Tallahassee and Texarkana.
They tour from St. Louis, Columbus, Manistee,

They tour from Peoria, Davenport, Kankakee.
Like a train-caller in a Union Depot.
Cars from Concord, Niagara, Boston,
Cars from Topeka, Emporia, and Austin.
Cars from Chicago, Hannibal, Cairo.
Cars from Alton, Oswego, Toledo.
Cars from Buffalo, Kokomo, Delphi,
Cars from Lodi, Carmi, Loami.
Ho for Kansas, land that restores us
When houses choke us, and great books bore us!
While I watch the highroad
And look at the sky,
While I watch the clouds in amazing grandeur
Roll their legions without rain
Over the blistering Kansas plain—
While I sit by the milestone
And watch the sky,
The United States
Goes by.

To be given very harshly, with a snapping explosiveness.
Listen to the iron-horns, ripping, racking.
Listen to the quack-horns, slack and clacking.
Way down the road, trilling like a toad,
Here comes the *dice*-horn, here comes the *vice*-horn,
Here comes the *snarl*-horn, *brawl*-horn, *lewd*-horn,
Followed by the *prude*-horn, bleak and squeaking:—
(Some of them from Kansas, some of them from Kansas.)
Here comes the *hod*-horn, *plod*-horn, *sod*-horn,
Nevermore-to-*roam*-horn, *loam*-horn, *home*-horn.
(Some of them from Kansas, some of them from Kansas.)

To be read or sung, well-nigh in a whisper.
Far away the Rachel-Jane
Not defeated by the horns
Sings amid a hedge of thorns:—
"Love and life,
Eternal youth—
Sweet, sweet, sweet, sweet,
Dew and glory,
Love and truth,
Sweet, sweet, sweet, sweet."

Louder and louder, faster and faster.
WHILE SMOKE-BLACK FREIGHTS ON THE DOUBLE-TRACKED RAILROAD,
DRIVEN AS THOUGH BY THE FOUL FIEND'S OX-GOAD,
SCREAMING TO THE WEST COAST, SCREAMING TO THE EAST,
CARRY OFF A HARVEST, BRING BACK A FEAST,
AND HARVESTING MACHINERY AND HARNESS FOR THE BEAST,
THE HAND-CARS WHIZ, AND RATTLE ON THE RAILS,
THE SUNLIGHT FLASHES ON THE TIN DINNER-PAILS.

In a rolling bass, with increasing deliberation.
And then, in an instant, ye modern men,
Behold the procession once again,
The United States goes by!

With a snapping explosiveness.
Listen to the iron-horns, ripping, racking,
Listen to the *wise*-horn, desperate-to-*advise* horn,
Listen to the *fast*-horn, *kill*-horn, *blast*-horn. . .

Far away the Rachel-Jane
Not defeated by the horns
Sings amid a hedge of thorns:—
"Love and life,
Eternal youth,
Sweet, sweet, sweet, sweet,
Dew and glory,
Love and truth.
Sweet, sweet, sweet, sweet."

To be sung or read well-nigh in a whisper.

The mufflers open on a score of cars
With wonderful thunder,
CRACK, CRACK, CRACK,
CRACK-CRACK, CRACK-CRACK,
CRACK, CRACK, CRACK,
Listen to the gold-horn . . .
Old-horn . . .
Cold horn . . .
And all of the tunes, till the night comes down
On hay-stack, and ant-hill, and wind-bitten town.

To be bawled in the beginning with a snapping explosiveness ending in a languorous chant.

Then far in the west, as in the beginning,
Dim in the distance, sweet in retreating,
Hark to the faint-horn, quaint-horn, saint-horn,
Hark to the calm-horn, balm-horn, psalm-horn. . . .

To be sung to exactly the same whispered tune as the first five lines.

They are hunting the goals that they understand:—
San Francisco and the brown sea-sand.
My goal is the mystery the beggars win.
I am caught in the web the night-winds spin.
The edge of the wheat-ridge speaks to me.
I talk with the leaves of the mulberry tree.
And now I hear, as I sit all alone
In the dusk, by another big Santa-Fé stone,
The souls of the tall corn gathering round
And the gay little souls of the grass in the ground.
Listen to the tale the cottonwood tells.
Listen to the windmills, singing o'er the wells.
Listen to the whistling flutes without price
Of myriad prophets out of paradise.
Harken to the wonder
That the night-air carries. . . .
Listen . . . to . . . the . . . whisper . . .
Of . . . the . . . prairie . . . fairies

This section beginning sonorously, ending in a languorous whisper.

Singing o'er the fairy plain:—
"Sweet, sweet, sweet, sweet.
Love and glory,
Stars and rain,
Sweet, sweet, sweet, sweet. . . ."

To the same whispered tune as the Rachel-Jane song—but very slowly.

1914

THE SHIELD OF FAITH

THE full moon is the Shield of Faith:
  As long as it shall rise,
I know that Mystery comes again,
  That Wonder never dies.

I know that Shadow has its place,
  That Noon is not our goal,
That Heaven has non-official hours
  To soothe and mend the soul;

That witchcraft can be angel-craft
  And wizard deeds sublime;
That utmost darkness bears a flower,
  Though long the budding-time.

1914

THE CHINESE NIGHTINGALE

A SONG IN CHINESE TAPESTRIES

"How, how," he said. "Friend Chang," I said,
"San Francisco sleeps as the dead—
Ended license, lust and play:
Why do you iron the night away?
Your big clock speaks with a deadly sound,
With a tick and a wail till dawn comes round.
While the monster shadows glower and creep,
What can be better for man than sleep?"

"I will tell you a secret," Chang replied;
"My breast with vision is satisfied,
And I see green trees and fluttering wings,
And my deathless bird from Shanghai sings."
Then he lit five firecrackers in a pan.
"Pop, pop," said the firecrackers, "cra-cra-crack."
He lit a joss stick long and black.
Then the proud gray joss in the corner stirred;
On his wrist appeared a gray small bird,
And this was the song of the gray small bird:
"Where is the princess, loved forever,
Who made Chang first of the kings of men?"

And the joss in the corner stirred again;
And the carved dog, curled in his arms, awoke,
Barked forth a smoke-cloud that whirled and broke.
It piled in a maze round the ironing-place,
And there on the snowy table wide
Stood a Chinese lady of high degree,
With a scornful, witching, tea-rose face. . . .
Yet she put away all form and pride,
And laid her glimmering veil aside
With a childlike smile for Chang and for me.

The walls fell back, night was aflower,
The table gleamed in a moonlit bower,
While Chang, with a countenance carved of stone,
Ironed and ironed, all alone.
And thus she sang to the busy man Chang:
"Have you forgotten . . .
Deep in the ages, long, long ago,
I was your sweetheart, there on the sand—
Storm-worn beach of the Chinese land?
We sold our grain in the peacock town—
Built on the edge of the sea-sands brown—
Built on the edge of the sea-sands brown. . . .

When all the world was drinking blood
From the skulls of men and bulls
And all the world had swords and clubs of stone,
We drank our tea in China beneath the sacred spice-trees,
And heard the curled waves of the harbor moan.
And this gray bird, in Love's first spring,
With a bright-bronze breast and a bronze-brown wing,
Captured the world with his carolling.
Do you remember, ages after,
At last the world we were born to own?
You were the heir of the yellow throne—
The world was the field of the Chinese man
And we were the pride of the Sons of Han?
We copied deep books and we carved in jade,
And wove blue silks in the mulberry shade. . . ."

"I remember, I remember
That Spring came on forever,
That Spring came on forever,"
Said the Chinese nightingale.

My heart was filled with marvel and dream,
Though I saw the western street-lamps gleam,
Though dawn was bringing the western day,
Though Chang was a laundryman ironing away. . . .
Mingled there with the streets and alleys,

The railroad-yard and the clock-tower bright,
Demon clouds crossed ancient valleys;
Across wide lotus-ponds of light
I marked a giant firefly's flight.

And the lady, rosy-red,
Flourished her fan, her shimmering fan,
Stretched her hand toward Chang, and said:
"Do you remember,
Ages after,
Our palace of heart-red stone?
Do you remember
The little doll-faced children
With their lanterns full of moon-fire,
That came from all the empire
Honoring the throne?—
The loveliest fête and carnival
Our world had ever known?
The sages sat about us
With their heads bowed in their beards,
With proper meditation on the sight.
Confucius was not born;
We lived in those great days
Confucius later said were lived aright. . . .
And this gray bird, on that day of spring,
With a bright-bronze breast, and a bronze-brown wing,
Captured the world with his carolling.
Late at night his tune was spent.
Peasants,
Sages,
Children,
Homeward went,
And then the bronze bird sang for you and me.
We walked alone. Our hearts were high and free.
I had a silvery name, I had a silvery name,
I had a silvery name—do you remember
The name you cried beside the tumbling sea?"

Chang turned not to the lady slim—
He bent to his work, ironing away;
But she was arch, and knowing and glowing,
For the bird on his shoulder spoke for him.

"Darling . . . darling . . . darling . . . darling . . ."
Said the Chinese nightingale.

The great gray joss on the rustic shelf,
Rakish and shrewd, with his collar awry,
Sang impolitely, as though by himself,
Drowning with his bellowing the nightingale's cry:
"Back through a hundred, hundred years
Hear the waves as they climb the piers,
Hear the howl of the silver seas,
Hear the thunder.
Hear the gongs of holy China,
How the waves and tunes combine
In a rhythmic clashing wonder,
Incantation old and fine:
'Dragons, dragons, Chinese dragons,
Red firecrackers, and green firecrackers
And dragons, dragons, Chinese dragons.'"
Then the lady, rosy-red,
Turned to her lover Chang and said:
"Dare you forget that turquoise dawn
When we stood in our mist-hung velvet lawn,
And worked a spell this great joss taught,
Till a God of the Dragons was charmed and caught?
From the flag high over our palace home
He flew to our feet in rainbow-foam—
A king of beauty and tempest and thunder
Panting to tear our sorrows asunder.
A dragon of fair adventure and wonder.
We mounted the back of that royal slave
With thoughts of desire that were noble and grave.
We swam down the shore to the dragon-mountains,
We whirled to the peaks and the fiery fountains.
To our secret ivory house we were borne.
We looked down the wonderful wing-filled regions
Where the dragons darted in glimmering legions.
Right by my breast the nightingale sang;
The old rhymes rang in the sunlit mist
That we this hour regain—
Song-fire for the brain.
When my hands and my hair and my feet you kissed,
When you cried for your heart's new pain,
What was my name in the dragon-mist,
In the rings of rainbowed rain?"

"Sorrow and love, glory and love,"
Said the Chinese nightingale,
"Sorrow and love, glory and love,"
Said the Chinese nightingale.

And now the joss broke in with his song:
"Dying ember, bird of Chang,
Soul of Chang, do you remember?—
Ere you returned to the shining harbor
There were pirates by ten thousand
Descended on the town
In vessels mountain-high and red and brown,
Moon-ships that climbed the storms and cut the skies.
On their prows were painted terrible bright eyes.
But I was then a wizard and a scholar and a priest;
I stood upon the sand;
With lifted hand I looked upon them
And sunk their vessels with my wizard eyes,
And the stately lacquer-gate made safe again.
Deep, deep below the bay, the seaweed and the spray,
Embalmed in amber every pirate lies,
Embalmed in amber every pirate lies."

Then this did the noble lady say:
"Bird, do you dream of our home-coming day
When you flew like a courier on before
From the dragon-peak to our palace door,
And we drove the steed in your singing path—
The ramping dragon of laughter and wrath:
And found our city all aglow,
And knighted this joss that decked it so?
There were golden fishes in the purple river
And silver fishes and rainbow fishes.
There were golden junks in the laughing river,
And silver junks and rainbow junks:
There were golden lilies by the bay and river,
And silver lilies and tiger-lilies,
And tinkling wind-bells in the gardens of the town
By the black-lacquer gate
Where walked in state
The kind king Chang
And his sweetheart mate. . . .
With his flag-born dragon
And his crown of pearl . . . and . . . jade,
And his nightingale reigning in the mulberry shade,
And sailors and soldiers on the sea-sands brown,
And priests who bowed them down to your song—
By the city called Han, the peacock town,
By the city called Han, the nightingale town,
The nightingale town."

Then sang the bird, so strangely gay,
Fluttering, fluttering, ghostly and gray,
A vague, unravelling, final tune,
Like a long unwinding silk cocoon;
Sang as though for the soul of him
Who ironed away in that bower dim:—
"I have forgotten
Your dragons great,
Merry and mad and friendly and bold.
Dim is your proud lost palace gate.
I vaguely know
There were heroes of old,
Troubles more than the heart could hold,
There were wolves in the woods
Yet lambs in the fold,
Nests in the top of the almond tree. . . .
The evergreen tree . . . and the mulberry tree . . .
Life and hurry and joy forgotten,
Years on years I but half-remember. . . .
Man is a torch, then ashes soon,
May and June, then dead December,
Dead December, then again June.
Who shall end my dream's confusion?
Life is a loom, weaving illusion . . .
I remember, I remember
There were ghostly veils and laces . . .
In the shadowy bowery places . . .
With lovers' ardent faces
Bending to one another,
Speaking each his part.
They infinitely echo
In the red cave of my heart.
'Sweetheart, sweetheart, sweetheart,'
They said to one another.
They spoke, I think, of perils past.
They spoke, I think, of peace at last.
One thing I remember:
Spring came on forever,
Spring came on forever,"
Said the Chinese nightingale.

1915

THE GHOST OF THE BUFFALOES

Last night at black midnight I woke with a cry,
The windows were shaking, there was thunder on high,
The floor was atremble, the door was ajar,
White fires, crimson fires, shone from afar.
I rushed to the dooryard. The city was gone.
My home was a hut without orchard or lawn.
It was mud-smear and logs near a whispering stream,
Nothing else built by man could I see in my dream . . .
Then . . .
Ghost-kings came headlong, row upon row,
Gods of the Indians, torches aglow.

They mounted the bear and the elk and the deer,
And eagles gigantic, aged and sere,
They rode long-horn cattle, they cried "A-la-la."
They lifted the knife, the bow, and the spear,
They lifted ghost-torches from dead fires below,
The midnight made grand with the cry "A-la-la."
The midnight made grand with a red-god charge,
A red-god show,
A red-god show,
"A-la-la, a-la-la, a-la-la, a-la-la."

With bodies like bronze, and terrible eyes
Came the rank and the file, with catamount cries,
Gibbering, yipping, with hollow-skull clacks,
Riding white bronchos with skeleton backs,
Scalp-hunters, beaded and spangled and bad,
Naked and lustful and foaming and mad,
Flashing primeval demoniac scorn,
Blood-thirst and pomp amid darkness reborn.
Power and glory that sleep in the grass
While the winds and the snows and the great rains pass.
They crossed the gray river, thousands abreast,
They rode in infinite lines to the west,
Tide upon tide of strange fury and foam,
Spirits and wraiths, the blue was their home,
The sky was their goal where the star-flags were furled,
And on past those far golden splendors they whirled.
They burned to dim meteors, lost in the deep.
And I turned in dazed wonder, thinking of sleep.

And the wind crept by
Alone, unkempt, unsatisfied,
The wind cried and cried—
Muttered of massacres long past,
Buffaloes in shambles vast . . .
An owl said: "Hark, what is a-wing?"
I heard a cricket carolling,
I heard a cricket carolling,
I heard a cricket carolling.

Then . . .
Snuffing the lightning that crashed from on high
Rose royal old buffaloes, row upon row.
The lords of the prairie came galloping by.
And I cried in my heart "A-la-la, a-la-la,
A red-god show,
A red-god show,
A-la-la, a-la-la, a-la-la, a-la-la."

Buffaloes, buffaloes, thousands abreast,
A scourge and amazement, they swept to the west.
With black bobbing noses, with red rolling tongues,
Coughing forth steam from their leather-wrapped lungs,
Cows with their calves, bulls big and vain,
Goring the laggards, shaking the mane,
Stamping flint feet, flashing moon eyes.
Pompous and owlish, shaggy and wise.
Like sea-cliffs and caves resounded their ranks
With shoulders like waves, and undulant flanks.
Tide upon tide of strange fury and foam,
Spirits and wraiths, the blue was their home,
The sky was their goal where the star-flags are furled,
And on past those far golden splendors they whirled.
They burned to dim meteors, lost in the deep,
And I turned in dazed wonder, thinking of sleep.

I heard a cricket's cymbals play,
A scarecrow lightly flapped his rags,
And a pan that hung by his shoulder rang,
Rattled and thumped in a listless way,
And now the wind in the chimney sang,
The wind in the chimney,
The wind in the chimney,
The wind in the chimney,
Seemed to say:—
"Dream, boy, dream,
If you anywise can.
To dream is the work
Of beast or man.
Life is the west-going dream-storms' breath,
Life is a dream, the sigh of the skies,
The breath of the stars, that nod on their pillows
With their golden hair mussed over their eyes."
The locust played on his musical wing,
Sang to his mate of love's delight.
I heard the whippoorwill's soft fret.
I heard a cricket carolling,
I heard a cricket carolling,
I heard a cricket say: "Good-night, good-night,
Good-night, good-night, . . . good-night."

. . . . . .

1917

IN PRAISE OF JOHNNY APPLESEED [1]

(Born 1775; died 1847)

I. OVER THE APPALACHIAN BARRICADE

To be read like old leaves on the elm tree of Time, Sifting soft winds with sentence and rhyme.

In the days of President Washington,
The glory of the nations,
Dust and ashes,
Snow and sleet,
And hay and oats and wheat,
Blew west,
Crossed the Appalachians,
Found the glades of rotting leaves, the soft deer-pastures,
The farms of the far-off future
In the forest.
Colts jumped the fence,
Snorting, ramping, snapping, sniffing,
With gastronomic calculations,
Crossed the Appalachians,
The east walls of our citadel,
And turned to gold-horned unicorns,
Feasting in the dim, volunteer farms of the forest.
Stripedest, kickingest kittens escaped,
Caterwauling "Yankee Doodle Dandy,"
Renounced their poor relations,
Crossed the Appalachians,
And turned to tiny tigers
In the humorous forest.
Chickens escaped
From farmyard congregations,
Crossed the Appalachians,
And turned to amber trumpets
On the ramparts of our Hoosiers' nest and citadel,

[1] The best account of John Chapman's career, under the name "Johnny Appleseed," is to be found in *Harper's Monthly Magazine*, November, 1871. [*Lindsay's note.*]

Millennial heralds
Of the foggy mazy forest.
Pigs broke loose, scrambled west,
Scorned their loathsome stations,
Crossed the Appalachians,
Turned to roaming, foaming wild boars
Of the forest.
The smallest, blindest puppies toddled west
While their eyes were coming open,
And, with misty observations,
Crossed the Appalachians,
Barked, barked, barked
At the glow-worms and the marsh lights and the lightning-bugs
And turned to ravening wolves
Of the forest.
Crazy parrots and canaries flew west,
Drunk on May-time revelations,
Crossed the Appalachians,
And turned to delirious, flower-dressed fairies
Of the lazy forest.
Haughtiest swans and peacocks swept west,
And, despite soft derivations,
Crossed the Appalachians,
And turned to blazing warrior souls
Of the forest,
Singing the ways
Of the Ancient of Days.
And the "Old Continentals
In their ragged regimentals,"
With bard's imaginations,
Crossed the Appalachians.
And
A boy
Blew west,
And with prayers and incantations,
And with "Yankee Doodle Dandy,"
Crossed the Appalachians,
And was "young John Chapman,"
Then
"Johnny Appleseed, Johnny Appleseed,"
Chief of the fastnesses, dappled and vast,
In a pack on his back,
In a deer-hide sack,
The beautiful orchards of the past,
The ghosts of all the forests and the groves—
In that pack on his back,
In that talisman sack,
Tomorrow's peaches, pears, and cherries,
Tomorrow's grapes and red raspberries,
Seeds and tree-souls, precious things,
Feathered with microscopic wings,

All the outdoors the child heart knows,
And the apple, green, red, and white,
Sun of his day and his night—
The apple allied to the thorn,
Child of the rose.
Porches untrod of forest houses
All before him, all day long,
"Yankee Doodle" his marching song;
And the evening breeze
Joined his psalms of praise
As he sang the ways
Of the Ancient of Days.
Leaving behind august Virginia,
Proud Massachusetts, and proud Maine,
Planting the trees that would march and train
On, in his name to the great Pacific,
Like Birnam wood to Dunsinane,
Johnny Appleseed swept on,
Every shackle gone,
Loving every sloshy brake,
Loving every skunk and snake,
Loving every leathery weed,
Johnny Appleseed, Johnny Appleseed,
Master and ruler of the unicorn-ramping forest,
The tiger-mewing forest,
The rooster-trumpeting, boar-foaming, wolf-ravening forest,
The spirit-haunted forest, fairy-enchanted,
Stupendous and endless,
Searching its perilous ways
In the name of the Ancient of Days.

II. THE INDIANS WORSHIP HIM, BUT HE HURRIES ON

Painted kings in the midst of the clearing
Heard him asking his friends the eagles
To guard each planted seed and seedling.
Then he was a god, to the red man's dreaming;
Then the chiefs brought treasures grotesque and fair,—
Magical trinkets and pipes and guns,
Beads and furs from their medicine-lair,—
Stuck holy feathers in his hair.
Hailed him with austere delight.
The orchard god was their guest through the night.

While the late snow blew from bleak Lake Erie,
Scourging rock and river reed,
All night long they made great medicine
For Jonathan Chapman,
Johnny Appleseed,
Johnny Appleseed;
And as though his heart were a wind-blown wheat-sheaf,

As though his heart were a new built nest,
As though their heaven house were his breast,
In swept the snowbirds singing glory.
And I hear his bird heart beat its story,
Hear yet how the ghost of the forest shivers,
Hear yet the cry of the gray, old orchards,
Dim and decaying by the rivers,
And the timid wings of the bird-ghosts beating,
And the ghosts of the tom-toms beating, beating.

But he left their wigwams and their love.
By the hour of dawn he was proud and stark,
Kissed the Indian babes with a sigh,
Went forth to live on roots and bark,
Sleep in the trees, while the years howled by.
Calling the catamounts by name,
And buffalo bulls no hand could tame.
Slaying never a living creature,
Joining the birds in every game,
With the gorgeous turkey gobblers mocking,
With the lean-necked eagles boxing and shouting;
Sticking their feathers in his hair,—
Turkey feathers,
Eagle feathers,
Trading hearts with all beasts and weathers
He swept on, winged and wonder-crested,
Bare-armed, barefooted, and bare-breasted.
The maples, shedding their spinning seeds,
Called to his appleseeds in the ground,
Vast chestnut-trees, with their butterfly nations,
Called to his seeds without a sound.
And the chipmunk turned a "summerset."
And the foxes danced the Virginia reel;
Hawthorn and crab-thorn bent, rain-wet,
And dropped their flowers in his night-black hair;
And the soft fawns stopped for his perorations
And his black eyes shone through the forest-gleam,
And he plunged young hands into new-turned earth,
And prayed dear orchard boughs into birth;
And he ran with the rabbit and slept with the stream,
And he ran with the rabbit and slept with the stream,
And he ran with the rabbit and slept with the stream.
And so for us he made great medicine,
And so for us he made great medicine,
And so for us he made great medicine,
In the days of President Washington.

While you read, hear the hoof-beats of deer in the snow. And see, by their track, bleeding footprints we know.

While you read, see conventions of deer go by. The bucks toss their horns, the fuzzy fawns fly.

III. JOHNNY APPLESEED'S OLD AGE

Long, long after,
When settlers put up beam and rafter,
They asked of the birds: "Who gave this fruit?

Who watched this fence till the seeds took root?
Who gave these boughs?" They asked the sky,
And there was no reply.
But the robin might have said,
"To the farthest West he has followed the sun,
His life and his empire just begun."
Self-scourged, like a monk, with a throne for wages,
Stripped, like the iron-souled Hindu sages,
Draped like a statue, in strings like a scarecrow,
His helmet-hat an old tin pan,
But worn in the love of the heart of man,
More sane than the helm of Tamerlane!
Hairy Ainu, wild man of Borneo, Robinson Crusoe—Johnny Appleseed!
And the robin might have said,
"Sowing, he goes to the far, new West,
With the apple, the sun of his burning breast—
The apple allied to the thorn,
Child of the rose."

To be read like faint hoof-beats of fawns long gone From respectable pasture, and park and lawn, And heart-beats of fawns that are coming again When the forest, once more, is the master of men.

Washington buried in Virginia,
Jackson buried in Tennessee,
Young Lincoln, brooding in Illinois,
And Johnny Appleseed, priestly and free,
Knotted and gnarled, past seventy years,
Still planted on in the woods alone.
Ohio and young Indiana—
These were his wide altar-stone,
Where still he burnt out flesh and bone.
Twenty days ahead of the Indian, twenty years ahead of the white man,
At last the Indian overtook him, at last the Indian hurried past him;
At last the white man overtook him, at last the white man hurried past him;
At last his own trees overtook him, at last his own trees hurried past him.
Many cats were tame again,
Many ponies tame again,
Many pigs were tame again,
Many canaries tame again;
And the real frontier was his sunburnt breast.
From the fiery core of that apple, the earth,
Sprang apple-amaranths divine.
Love's orchards climbed to the heavens of the West.
And snowed the earthly sod with flowers.
Farm hands from the terraces of the blest
Danced on the mists with their ladies fine;
And Johnny Appleseed laughed with his dreams,
And swam once more the ice-cold streams.
And the doves of the spirit swept through the hours,
With doom-calls, love-calls, death-calls, dream-calls;
And Johnny Appleseed, all that year,
Lifted his hands to the farm-filled sky,
To the apple-harvesters busy on high;
And so once more his youth began,

And so for us he made great medicine—
Johnny Appleseed, medicine-man.
Then
The sun was his turned-up broken barrel,
Out of which his juicy apples rolled,
Down the repeated terraces,
Thumping across the gold,
An angel in each apple that touched the forest mold,
A ballot-box in each apple,
A state capital in each apple,
Great high schools, great colleges,
All America in each apple,
Each red, rich, round, and bouncing moon
That touched the forest mold.
Like scrolls and rolled-up flags of silk,
He saw the fruits unfold,
And all our expectations in one wild-flower written dream.
Confusion, and death-sweetness, and a thicket of crab-thorns!
Heart of a hundred midnights, heart of the merciful morns.
Heaven's boughs bent down with their alchemy,
Perfumed airs, and thoughts of wonder.
And the dew on the grass and his own cold tears
Were one in brooding mystery,
Though death's loud thunder came upon him,
Though death's loud thunder struck him down—
The boughs and the proud thoughts swept through the thunder,
Till he saw our wide nation, each State a flower,
Each petal a park for holy feet,
With wild fawns merry on every street,
With wild fawns merry on every street,
The vista of ten thousand years, flower-lighted and complete.

And there stood by his side, as he died:
Buddha, St. Francis; no others could praise him.
They were there, in the name of the Ancient of Days.

Hear the lazy weeds murmuring, bays and rivers whispering,
From Michigan to Texas, California to Maine;
Listen to the eagles screaming, calling,
"Johnny Appleseed, Johnny Appleseed,"
There by the doors of old Fort Wayne.

In the four-poster bed Johnny Appleseed built,
Autumn rains were the curtains, autumn leaves were the quilt.
He laid him down sweetly, and slept through the night,
Like a stone washed white,
There by the doors of old Fort Wayne.

1921

AN ARGUMENT

I. THE VOICE OF THE MAN IMPATIENT WITH VISIONS AND UTOPIAS

We find your soft Utopias as white
As new-cut bread, and dull as life in cells,
O scribes who dare forget how wild we are,
How human breasts adore alarum bells.
You house us in a hive of prigs and saints
Communal, frugal, clean and chaste by law.
I'd rather brood in bloody Elsinore
Or be Lear's fool, straw-crowned amid the straw.
Promise us all our share in Agincourt
Say that our clerks shall venture scorns and death,
That future ant-hills will not be too good
For Henry Fifth, or Hotspur, or Macbeth.
Promise that through tomorrow's spirit-war
Man's deathless soul will hack and hew its way,
Each flaunting Caesar climbing to his fate
Scorning the utmost steps of yesterday.
Never a shallow jester any more!
Let not Jack Falstaff spill the ale in vain.
Let Touchstone set the fashions for the wise,
And Ariel wreak his fancies through the rain.

II. THE RHYMER'S REPLY: INCENSE AND SPLENDOR

Incense and Splendor haunt me as I go. 21
Though my good works have been, alas, too few,
Though I do naught, High Heaven comes down to me,
And future ages pass in tall review.
I see the years to come as armies vast,
Stalking tremendous through the fields of time.
Man is unborn. Tomorrow he is born,
Flame-like to hover o'er the moil and grime,
Striving, aspiring till the shame is gone,
Sowing a million flowers where now we mourn—
Laying new, precious pavements with a song,
Founding new shrines the good streets to adorn.
I have seen lovers by those new-built walls
Clothed like the dawn in orange, gold and red.
Eyes flashing forth the glory-light of love
Under the wreath that crowned each royal head.
Life was made greater by their sweetheart prayers.
Passion was turned to civic strength that day—
Piling the marbles, making fairer domes
With zeal that else had burned bright youth away.
I have seen priestesses of life go by,
Gliding in samite through the incense-sea—
Innocent children marching with them there,
Singing in flowered robes, "The earth so free":
While on the fair, deep-carved unfinished towers
Sentinels watched in armor, night and day—
Guarding the brazier-fires of hope and dream—
Wild was their peace, and dawn-bright their array!

1923?

THE UNPARDONABLE SIN

This is the sin against the Holy Ghost:—
To speak of bloody power as right divine,
And call on God to guard each vile chief's house,
And for such chiefs, turn men to wolves and swine:—

To go forth killing in White Mercy's name,
Making the trenches stink with spattered brains,
Tearing the nerves and arteries apart,
Sowing with flesh the unreaped golden plains.

In any Church's name, to sack fair towns,
And turn each home into a screaming sty,
To make the little children fugitive,
And have their mothers for a quick death cry,—

This is the sin against the Holy Ghost:
This is the sin no purging can atone:—
To send forth rapine in the name of Christ:—
To set the face, and make the heart a stone.

1923?

ALADDIN AND THE JINN

"Bring me soft song," said Aladdin.
"This tailor-shop sings not at all.
Chant me a word of the twilight,

Of roses that mourn in the fall.
Bring me a song like hashish
That will comfort the stale and the sad,
For I would be mending my spirit,
Forgetting these days that are bad,
Forgetting companions too shallow,
Their quarrels and arguments thin,
Forgetting the shouting Muezzin:"
"I AM YOUR SLAVE," said the Jinn.

"Bring me old wines," said Aladdin.
"I have been a starved pauper too long.
Serve them in vessels of jade and of shell,
Serve them with fruit and with song:—
Wines of pre-Adamite Sultans
Digged from beneath the black seas:—
New-gathered dew from the heavens
Dripped down from Heaven's sweet trees,
Cups from the angels' pale tables
That will make me both handsome and wise,
For I have beheld her, the princess,
Firelight and starlight her eyes.
Pauper I am, I would woo her.
And—let me drink wine, to begin,
Though the Koran expressly forbids it."
"I AM YOUR SLAVE," said the Jinn.

"Plan me a dome," said Aladdin,
"That is drawn like the dawn of the MOON,
When the sphere seems to rest on the mountains,
Half-hidden, yet full-risen soon.
Build me a dome," said Aladdin,
"That shall cause all young lovers to sigh,
The fullness of life and of beauty,
Peace beyond peace to the eye—
A palace of foam and of opal,
Pure moonlight without and within,
Where I may enthrone my sweet lady."
"I AM YOUR SLAVE," said the Jinn.

1923?

THE VOYAGE

(Written for Ted Shawn)

SEE my mast, a pen!
What are my sails?
Many crescent moons.
What is my sea?
A bottle of ink.
Where do I go?
To heaven again.
What do I eat?
The Amaranth flower
While the winds through the jungles
Swing old tunes.
I eat that flower with ivory spoons.
While the winds, through the jungles
Swing old tunes.
The songs the angels used to sing
When Heaven was not old autumn, but spring,
The old sweet songs of Heaven
And spring.

1929

EDWIN ARLINGTON ROBINSON

CREDO [1]

I CANNOT find my way: there is no star
In all the shrouded heavens anywhere;
And there is not a whisper in the air
Of any living voice but one so far
That I can hear it only as a bar
Of lost, imperial music, played when fair
And angel fingers wove, and unaware,
Dead leaves to garlands where no roses are.

No, there is not a glimmer, nor a call,
For one that welcomes, welcomes when he fears,
The black and awful chaos of the night;
For through it all—above, beyond it all—
I know the far-sent message of the years,
I feel the coming glory of the Light.

1897

CALVARY

FRIENDLESS and faint, with martyred steps and slow,
Faint for the flesh, but for the spirit free,
Stung by the mob that came to see the show,
The Master toiled along to Calvary;
We gibed him, as he went, with houndish glee,
Till his dimmed eyes for us did overflow;
We cursed his vengeless hands thrice wretchedly,—
And this was nineteen hundred years ago.

But after nineteen hundred years the shame
Still clings, and we have not made good the loss
That outraged faith has entered in his name.
Ah, when shall come love's courage to be strong!
Tell me, O Lord—tell me, O Lord, how long
Are we to keep Christ writhing on the cross!

1897

[1] This poem and the five immediately following are reprinted from *The Children of the Night* (1897) by Edwin Arlington Robinson, by permission of Charles Scribner's Sons, publishers.

GEORGE CRABBE

GIVE him the darkest inch your shelf allows,
Hide him in lonely garrets, if you will,—
But his hard, human pulse is throbbing still
With the sure strength that fearless truth endows.
In spite of all fine science disavows,
Of his plain excellence and stubborn skill
There yet remains what fashion cannot kill,
Though years have thinned the laurel from his brows.

Whether or not we read him, we can feel
From time to time the vigor of his name
Against us like a finger for the shame
And emptiness of what our souls reveal
In books that are as altars where we kneel
To consecrate the flicker, not the flame.

1897

ZOLA

BECAUSE he puts the compromising chart
Of hell before your eyes, you are afraid;
Because he counts the price that you have paid
For innocence, and counts it from the start,
You loathe him. But he sees the human heart
Of God meanwhile, and in His hand was weighed
Your squeamish and emasculate crusade
Against the grim dominion of his art.

Never until we conquer the uncouth
Connivings of our shamed indifference
(We call it Christian faith) are we to scan
The racked and shrieking hideousness of Truth
To find, in hate's polluted self-defence
Throbbing, the pulse, the divine heart of man.

1897

SONNET

OH for a poet—for a beacon bright
To rift this changeless glimmer of dead gray;
To spirit back the Muses, long astray,
And flush Parnassus with a newer light;

To put these little sonnet-men to flight
Who fashion, in a shrewd mechanic way,
Songs without souls, that flicker for a day,
To vanish in irrevocable night.

What does it mean, this barren age of ours?
Here are the men, the women, and the flowers,
The seasons, and the sunset, as before.
What does it mean? Shall there not one arise
To wrench one banner from the western skies,
And mark it with his name forevermore?

1897

RICHARD CORY

Whenever Richard Cory went down town,
We people on the pavement looked at him:
He was a gentleman from sole to crown,
Clean favored, and imperially slim.

And he was always quietly arrayed,
And he was always human when he talked;
But still he fluttered pulses when he said,
"Good-morning," and he glittered when he walked.

And he was rich—yes, richer than a king—
And admirably schooled in every grace:
In fine, we thought that he was everything
To make us wish that we were in his place.

So on we worked, and waited for the light,
And went without the meat, and cursed the bread;
And Richard Cory, one calm summer night,
Went home and put a bullet through his head.

1897

MINIVER CHEEVY[1]

Miniver Cheevy, child of scorn,
Grew lean while he assailed the seasons;
He wept that he was ever born,
And he had reasons.

Miniver loved the days of old
When swords were bright and steeds were prancing;
The vision of a warrior bold
Would set him dancing.

Miniver sighed for what was not,
And dreamed, and rested from his labors;
He dreamed of Thebes and Camelot,
And Priam's neighbors.

Miniver mourned the ripe renown
That made so many a name so fragrant;
He mourned Romance, now on the town,
And Art, a vagrant.

Miniver loved the Medici,
Albeit he had never seen one;
He would have sinned incessantly
Could he have been one.

Miniver cursed the commonplace
And eyed a khaki suit with loathing;
He missed the mediæval grace
Of iron clothing.

Miniver scorned the gold he sought,
But sore annoyed was he without it;
Miniver thought, and thought, and thought,
And thought about it.

Miniver Cheevy, born too late,
Scratched his head and kept on thinking;
Miniver coughed, and called it fate,
And kept on drinking.

1907

HOW ANNANDALE WENT OUT

"They called it Annandale—and I was there
To flourish, to find words, and to attend:
Liar, physician, hypocrite, and friend,
I watched him; and the sight was not so fair
As one or two that I have seen elsewhere:
An apparatus not for me to mend—
A wreck, with hell between him and the end,
Remained of Annandale; and I was there.

"I knew the ruin as I knew the man;
So put the two together, if you can,
Remembering the worst you know of me.
Now view yourself as I was, on the spot—
With a slight kind of engine. Do you see?
Like this . . . You wouldn't hang me? I thought not."

1910

[1] This and the following poem are reprinted from *The Town Down the River* (1910) by Edwin Arlington Robinson, by permission of Charles Scribner's Sons, publishers.

FLAMMONDE [1]

The man Flammonde, from God knows where,
With firm address and foreign air,
With news of nations in his talk
And something royal in his walk,
With glint of iron in his eyes,
But never doubt, nor yet surprise,
Appeared, and stayed, and held his head
As one by kings accredited.

Erect, with his alert repose
About him, and about his clothes,
He pictured all tradition hears
Of what we owe to fifty years.
His cleansing heritage of taste
Paraded neither want nor waste;
And what he needed for his fee
To live, he borrowed graciously.

He never told us what he was,
Or what mischance, or other cause,
Had banished him from better days
To play the Prince of Castaways.
Meanwhile he played surpassing well
A part, for most, unplayable;
In fine, one pauses, half afraid
To say for certain that he played.

For that, one may as well forego
Conviction as to yes or no;
Nor can I say just how intense
Would then have been the difference
To several, who, having striven
In vain to get what he was given,
Would see the stranger taken on
By friends not easy to be won.

Moreover, many a malcontent
He soothed and found munificent;
His courtesy beguiled and foiled
Suspicion that his years were soiled;
His mien distinguished any crowd,
His credit strengthened when he bowed;
And women, young and old, were fond
Of looking at the man Flammonde.

There was a woman in our town
On whom the fashion was to frown;
But while our talk renewed the tinge
Of a long-faded scarlet fringe,
The man Flammonde saw none of that,
And what he saw we wondered at—
That none of us, in her distress,
Could hide or find our littleness.

There was a boy that all agreed
Had shut within him the rare seed
Of learning. We could understand,
But none of us could lift a hand.
The man Flammonde appraised the youth,
And told a few of us the truth;
And thereby, for a little gold,
A flowered future was unrolled.

There were two citizens who fought
For years and years, and over nought;
They made life awkward for their friends,
And shortened their own dividends.
The man Flammonde said what was wrong
Should be made right; nor was it long
Before they were again in line,
And had each other in to dine.

And these I mention are but four
Of many out of many more.
So much for them. But what of him—
So firm in every look and limb?
What small satanic sort of kink
Was in his brain? What broken link
Withheld him from the destinies
That came so near to being his?

What was he, when we came to sift
His meaning, and to note the drift
Of incommunicable ways
That make us ponder while we praise?
Why was it that his charm revealed
Somehow the surface of a shield?
What was it that we never caught?
What was he, and what was he not?

How much it was of him we met
We cannot ever know; nor yet
Shall all he gave us quite atone
For what was his, and his alone;
Nor need we now, since he knew best,
Nourish an ethical unrest:

[1] This poem and the seven poems that follow are all reprinted from *Collected Poems* (1930) by Edwin Arlington Robinson, by permission of The Macmillan Company, publishers.

Rarely at once will nature give
The power to be Flammonde and live.

We cannot know how much we learn
From those who never will return,
Until a flash of unforeseen
Remembrance falls on what has been.
We've each a darkening hill to climb;
And this is why, from time to time
In Tilbury Town, we look beyond
Horizons for the man Flammonde.

1915

THE MAN AGAINST THE SKY

BETWEEN me and the sunset, like a dome
Against the glory of a world on fire,
Now burned a sudden hill,
Bleak, round, and high, by flame-lit height made higher,
With nothing on it for the flame to kill
Save one who moved and was alone up there
To loom before the chaos and the glare
As if he were the last god going home
Unto his last desire.

Dark, marvelous, and inscrutable he moved on
Till down the fiery distance he was gone,
Like one of those eternal, remote things
That range across a man's imaginings
When a sure music fills him and he knows
What he may say thereafter to few men,—
The touch of ages having wrought
An echo and a glimpse of what he thought
A phantom or a legend until then;
For whether lighted over ways that save,
Or lured from all repose,
If he go on too far to find a grave,
Mostly alone he goes.

Even he, who stood where I had found him,
On high with fire all round him,
Who moved along the molten west,
And over the round hill's crest
That seemed half ready with him to go down,
Flame-bitten and flame-cleft,
As if there were to be no last thing left
Of a nameless unimaginable town,—
Even he who climbed and vanished may have taken
Down to the perils of a depth not known,
From death defended though by men forsaken,
The bread that every man must eat alone;
He may have walked while others hardly dared
Look on to see him stand where many fell;
And upward out of that, as out of hell,
He may have sung and striven
To mount where more of him shall yet be given,
Bereft of all retreat,
To sevenfold heat,—
As on a day when three in Dura shared
The furnace, and were spared
For glory by that king of Babylon
Who made himself so great that God, who heard,
Covered him with long feathers, like a bird.

Again, he may have gone down easily,
By comfortable altitudes, and found,
As always, underneath him solid ground
Whereon to be sufficient and to stand
Possessed already of the promised land,
Far stretched, and fair to see:
A good sight, verily,
And one to make the eyes of her who bore him
Shine glad with hidden tears.
Why question of his ease of who before him,
In one place or another where they left
Their names as far behind them as their bones,
And yet by dint of slaughter toil and theft,
And shrewdly sharpened stones,
Carved hard the way for his ascendency
Through deserts of lost years?
Why trouble him now who sees and hears
No more than what his innocence requires,
And therefore to no other height aspires
Than one at which he neither quails nor tires?
He may do more by seeing what he sees
Than others eager for iniquities;
He may, by seeing all things for the best,
Incite futurity to do the rest.

Or with an even likelihood,
He may have met with atrabilious eyes
The fires of time on equal terms and passed
Indifferently down, until at last
His only kind of grandeur would have been,
Apparently, in being seen.

He may have had for evil or for good
No argument; he may have had no care
For what without himself went anywhere
To failure or to glory, and least of all
For such a stale, flamboyant miracle;
He may have been the prophet of an art
Immovable to old idolatries;
He may have been a player without a part,
Annoyed that even the sun should have the skies
For such a flaming way to advertise;
He may have been a painter sick at heart
With Nature's toiling for a new surprise;
He may have been a cynic, who now, for all
Of anything divine that his effete
Negation may have tasted,
Saw truth in his own image, rather small,
Forbore to fever the ephemeral,
Found any barren height a good retreat
From any swarming street,
And in the sun saw power superbly wasted:
And when the primitive old-fashioned stars
Came out again to shine on joys and wars
More primitive, and all arrayed for doom,
He may have proved a world a sorry thing
In his imagining,
And life a lighted highway to the tomb.

Or, mounting with infirm unsearching tread,
His hopes to chaos led,
He may have stumbled up there from the past,
And with an aching strangeness viewed the last
Abysmal conflagration of his dreams,—
A flame where nothing seems
To burn but flame itself, by nothing fed;
And while it all went out,
Not even the faint anodyne of doubt
May then have eased a painful going down
From pictured heights of power and lost renown,
Revealed at length to his outlived endeavor
Remote and unapproachable forever;
And at his heart there may have gnawed
Sick memories of a dead faith foiled and flawed
And long dishonored by the living death
Assigned alike by chance
To brutes and hierophants;
And anguish fallen on those he loved around him
May once have dealt the last blow to confound him,
And so have left him as death leaves a child,
Who sees it all too near;
And he who knows no young way to forget
May struggle to the tomb unreconciled.
Whatever suns may rise or set
There may be nothing kinder for him here
Than shafts and agonies;
And under these
He may cry out and stay on horribly;
Or, seeing in death too small a thing to fear,
He may go forward like a stoic Roman
Where pangs and terrors in his pathway lie,—
Or, seizing the swift logic of a woman,
Curse God and die.

Or maybe there, like many another one
Who might have stood aloft and looked ahead,
Black-drawn against wild red,
He may have built, unawed by fiery gules
That in him no commotion stirred,
A living reason out of molecules
Why molecules occurred,
And one for smiling when he might have sighed
Had he seen far enough,
And in the same inevitable stuff
Discovered an odd reason too for pride
In being what he must have been by laws
Infrangible and for no kind of cause.
Deterred by no confusion or surprise
He may have seen with his mechanic eyes
A world without a meaning, and had room,
Alone amid magnificence and doom,
To build himself an airy monument
That should, or fail him in his vague intent,
Outlast an accidental universe—
To call it nothing worse—
Or, by the burrowing guile
Of Time disintegrated and effaced,
Like once-remembered mighty trees go down
To ruin, of which by man may now be traced
No part sufficient even to be rotten,
And in the book of things that are forgotten
Is entered as a thing not quite worth while.
He may have been so great
That satraps would have shivered at his frown,
And all he prized alive may rule a state
No larger than a grave that holds a clown;

He may have been a master of his fate,
And of his atoms,—ready as another
In his emergence to exonerate
His father and his mother;
He may have been a captain of a host,
Self-eloquent and ripe for prodigies,
Doomed here to swell by dangerous degrees,
And then give up the ghost.
Nahum's great grasshoppers were such as these,
Sun-scattered and soon lost.

Whatever the dark road he may have taken,
This man who stood on high
And faced alone the sky,
Whatever drove or lured or guided him,—
A vision answering a faith unshaken,
An easy trust assumed of easy trials,
A sick negation born of weak denials,
A crazed abhorrence of an old condition,
A blind attendance on a brief ambition,—
Whatever stayed him or derided him,
His way was even as ours;
And we, with all our wounds and all our powers,
Must each await alone at his own height
Another darkness or another light;
And there, of our poor self dominion reft,
If inference and reason shun
Hell, Heaven, and Oblivion,
May thwarted will (perforce precarious,
But for our conservation better thus)
Have no misgiving left
Of doing yet what here we leave undone?
Or if unto the last of these we cleave,
Believing or protesting we believe
In such an idle and ephemeral
Florescence of the diabolical,—
If, robbed of two fond old enormities,
Our being had no onward auguries,
What then were this great love of ours to say
For launching other lives to voyage again
A little farther into time and pain,
A little faster in a futile chase
For a kingdom and a power and a Race
That would have still in sight
A manifest end of ashes and eternal night?
Is this the music of the toys we shake
So loud,—as if there might be no mistake
Somewhere in our indomitable will?
Are we no greater than the noise we make
Along one blind atomic pilgrimage
Whereon by crass chance billeted we go
Because our brains and bones and cartilage
Will have it so?
If this we say, then let us all be still
About our share in it, and live and die
More quietly thereby.

Where was he going, this man against the sky?
You know not, nor do I.
But this we know, if we know anything:
That we may laugh and fight and sing
And of our transience here make offering
To an orient Word that will not be erased,
Or, save in incommunicable gleams
Too permanent for dreams,
Be found or known.
No tonic and ambitious irritant
Of increase or of want
Has made an otherwise insensate waste
Of ages overthrown
A ruthless, veiled, implacable foretaste
Of other ages that are still to be
Depleted and rewarded variously
Because a few, by fate's economy,
Shall seem to move the world the way it goes;
No soft evangel of equality,
Safe-cradled in a communal repose
That huddles into death and may at last
Be covered well with equatorial snows—
And all for what, the devil only knows—
Will aggregate an inkling to confirm
The credit of a sage or of a worm,
Or tell us why one man in five
Should have a care to stay alive
While in his heart he feels no violence
Laid on his humor and intelligence
When infant Science makes a pleasant face
And waves again that hollow toy, the Race;
No planetary trap where souls are wrought
For nothing but the sake of being caught
And sent again to nothing will attune
Itself to any key of any reason
Why man should hunger through another season
To find out why 'twere better late than soon
To go away and let the sun and moon
And all the silly stars illuminate
A place for creeping things,
And those that root and trumpet and have wings,

And herd and ruminate,
Or dive and flash and poise in rivers and seas,
Or by their loyal tails in lofty trees
Hang screeching lewd victorious derision
Of man's immortal vision.
Shall we, because Eternity records
Too vast an answer for the time-born words
We spell, whereof so many are dead that once
In our capricious lexicons
Were so alive and final, hear no more
The Word itself, the living word
That none alive has ever heard
Or ever spelt,
And few have ever felt
Without the fears and old surrenderings
And terrors that began
When Death let fall a feather from his wings
And humbled the first man?
Because the weight of our humility,
Wherefrom we gain
A little wisdom and much pain,
Falls here too sore and there too tedious,
Are we in anguish or complacency,
Not looking far enough ahead
To see by what mad couriers we are led
Along the roads of the ridiculous,
To pity ourselves and laugh at faith
And while we curse life bear it?
And if we see the soul's dead end in death,
Are we to fear it?
What folly is here that has not yet a name
Unless we say outright that we are liars?
What have we seen beyond our sunset fires
That lights again the way by which we came?
Why pay we such a price, and one we give
So clamoringly, for each racked empty day
That leads one more last human hope away,
As quiet fiends would lead past our crazed eyes
Our children to an unseen sacrifice?
If after all that we have lived and thought,
All comes to Nought,—
If there be nothing after Now,
And we be nothing anyhow,
And we know that,—why live?
'Twere sure but weaklings' vain distress
To suffer dungeons where so many doors
Will open on the cold eternal shores
That look sheer down
To the dark tideless floods of Nothingness
Where all who know may drown.

1916

BEN JONSON ENTERTAINS A MAN FROM STRATFORD

You are a friend then, as I make it out,
Of our man Shakespeare, who alone of us
Will put an ass's head in Fairyland
As he would add a shilling to more shillings,
All most harmonious,—and out of his
Miraculous inviolable increase
Fills Ilion, Rome, or any town you like
Of olden time with timeless Englishmen;
And I must wonder what you think of him—
All you down there where your small Avon flows
By Stratford, and where you're an Alderman.
Some, for a guess, would have him riding back
To be a farrier there, or say a dyer;
Or maybe one of your adept surveyors;
Or like enough the wizard of all tanners.
Not you—no fear of that; for I discern
In you a kindling of the flame that saves—
The nimble element, the true caloric;
I see it, and was told of it, moreover,
By our discriminate friend himself, no other.
Had you been one of the sad average,
As he would have it,—meaning, as I take it,
The sinew and the solvent of our Island,
You'd not be buying beer for this Terpander's
Approved and estimated friend Ben Jonson;
He'd never foist it as a part of his
Contingent entertainment of a townsman
While he goes off rehearsing, as he must,
If he shall ever be the Duke of Stratford.
And my words are no shadow on your town—
Far from it; for one town's as like another
As all are unlike London. Oh, he knows it,—
And there's the Stratford in him; he denies it,
And there's the Shakespeare in him. So, God help him!
I tell him he needs Greek; but neither God
Nor Greek will help him. Nothing will help that man.
You see the fates have given him so much,
He must have all or perish,—or look out
Of London, where he sees too many lords.
They're part of half what ails him: I suppose
There's nothing fouler down among the demons

Than what it is he feels when he remembers
The dust and sweat and ointment of his calling
With his lords looking on and laughing at him.
King as he is, he can't be king *de facto*,
And that's as well, because he wouldn't like it;
He'd frame a lower rating of men then
Than he has now; and after that would come
An abdication or an apoplexy.
He can't be king, not even king of Stratford,—
Though half the world, if not the whole of it,
May crown him with a crown that fits no king
Save Lord Apollo's homesick emissary:
Not there on Avon, or on any stream
Where Naiads and their white arms are no more,
Shall he find home again. It's all too bad.
But there's a comfort, for he'll have that House—
The best you ever saw; and he'll be there
Anon, as you're an Alderman. Good God!
He makes me lie awake o'nights and laugh.

And you have known him from his origin,
You tell me; and a most uncommon urchin
He must have been to the few seeing ones—
A trifle terrifying, I dare say,
Discovering a world with his man's eyes,
Quite as another lad might see some finches,
If he looked hard and had an eye for nature.
But this one had his eyes and their foretelling,
And he had you to fare with, and what else?
He must have had a father and a mother—
In fact I've heard him say so—and a dog,
As a boy should, I venture; and the dog,
Most likely, was the only man who knew him.
A dog, for all I know, is what he needs
As much as anything right here today,
To counsel him about his disillusions,
Old aches, and parturitions of what's coming,—
A dog of orders, an emeritus,
To wag his tail at him when he comes home,
And then to put his paws up on his knees
And say, "For God's sake, what's it all about?"

I don't know whether he needs a dog or not—
Or what he needs. I tell him he needs Greek;
I'll talk of rules and Aristotle with him,
And if his tongue's at home he'll say to that,
"I have your word that Aristotle knows,
And you mine that I don't know Aristotle."
He's all at odds with all the unities,
And what's yet worse, it doesn't seem to matter;
He treads along through Time's old wilderness
As if the tramp of all the centuries
Had left no roads—and there are none, for him;
He doesn't see them, even with those eyes,—
And that's a pity, or I say it is.
Accordingly we have him as we have him—
Going his way, the way that he goes best,
A pleasant animal with no great noise
Or nonsense anywhere to set him off—
Save only divers and inclement devils
Have made of late his heart their dwelling place.
A flame half ready to fly out sometimes
At some annoyance may be fanned up in him,
But soon it falls, and when it falls goes out;
He knows how little room there is in there
For crude and futile animosities,
And how much for the joy of being whole,
And how much for long sorrow and old pain.
On our side there are some who may be given
To grow old wondering what he thinks of us
And some above us, who are, in his eyes,
Above himself,—and that's quite right and English.
Yet here we smile, or disappoint the gods
Who made it so: the gods have always eyes
To see men scratch; and they see one down here
Who itches, manor-bitten to the bone,
Albeit he knows himself—yes, yes, he knows—
The lord of more than England and of more
Than all the seas of England in all time
Shall ever wash. D'ye wonder that I laugh?
He sees me, and he doesn't seem to care;
And why the devil should he? I can't tell you.

I'll meet him out alone of a bright Sunday,
Trim, rather spruce, and quite the gentleman.
"What ho, my lord!" say I. He doesn't hear me;
Wherefore I have to pause and look at him.
He's not enormous, but one looks at him.

A little on the round if you insist,
For now, God save the mark, he's growing old;
He's five and forty, and to hear him talk
These days you'd call him eighty; then you'd add
More years to that. He's old enough to be
The father of a world, and so he is.
"Ben, you're a scholar, what's the time of day?"
Says he; and there shines out of him again
An aged light that has no age or station—
The mystery that's his—a mischievous
Half-mad serenity that laughs at fame
For being won so easy, and at friends
Who laugh at him for what he wants the most,
And for his dukedom down in Warwickshire;—
By which you see we're all a little jealous. . . .
Poor Greene! I fear the color of his name
Was even as that of his ascending soul;
And he was one where there are many others,—
Some scrivening to the end against their fate,
Their puppets all in ink and all to die there;
And some with hands that once would shade an eye
That scanned Euripides and Æschylus
Will reach by this time for a pot-house mop
To slush their first and last of royalties.
Poor devils! and they all play to his hand;
For so it was in Athens and old Rome.
But that's not here or there; I've wandered off.
Greene does it, or I'm careful. Where's that boy?

Yes, he'll go back to Stratford. And we'll miss him?
Dear sir, there'll be no London here without him.
We'll all be riding, one of these fine days,
Down there to see him—and his wife won't like us;
And then we'll think of what he never said
Of women—which, if taken all in all
With what he did say, would buy many horses.
Though nowadays he's not so much for women:
"So few of them," he says, "are worth the guessing."
But there's a worm at work when he says that,
And while he says it one feels in the air
A deal of circumambient hocus-pocus.
They've had him dancing till his toes were tender,
And he can feel 'em now, come chilly rains.
There's no long cry for going into it,
However, and we don't know much about it.
But you in Stratford, like most here in London,
Have more now in the *Sonnets* than you paid for;
He's put one there with all her poison on,
To make a singing fiction of a shadow
That's in his life a fact, and always will be.
But she's no care of ours, though Time, I fear,
Will have a more reverberant ado
About her than about another one
Who seems to have decoyed him, married him,
And sent him scuttling on his way to London,—
With much already learned, and more to learn,
And more to follow. Lord! how I see him now,
Pretending, maybe trying, to be like us.
Whatever he may have meant, we never had him;
He failed us, or escaped, or what you will,—
And there was that about him (God knows what,—
We'd flayed another had he tried it on us)
That made as many of us as had wits
More fond of all his easy distances
Than one another's noise and clap-your-shoulder.
But think you not, my friend, he'd never talk!
Talk? He was eldritch at it; and we listened—
Thereby acquiring much we knew before
About ourselves, and hitherto had held
Irrelevant, or not prime to the purpose.
And there were some, of course, and there be now,
Disordered and reduced amazedly
To resignation by the mystic seal
Of young finality the gods had laid
On everything that made him a young demon;
And one or two shot looks at him already
As he had been their executioner;

And once or twice he was, not knowing it,—
Or knowing, being sorry for poor clay
And saying nothing. . . . Yet, for all his engines,
You'll meet a thousand of an afternoon
Who strut and sun themselves and see around 'em
A world made out of more that has a reason
Than his, I swear, that he sees here today;
Though he may scarcely give a Fool an exit
But we mark how he sees in everything
A law that, given we flout it once too often,
Brings fire and iron down on our naked heads.
To me it looks as if the power that made him,
For fear of giving all things to one creature,
Left out the first,—faith, innocence, illusion,
Whatever 'tis that keeps us out o' Bedlam,—
And thereby, for his too consuming vision,
Empowered him out of nature; though to see him,
You'd never guess what's going on inside him.
He'll break out some day like a keg of ale
With too much independent frenzy in it;
And all for cellaring what he knows won't keep,
And what he'd best forget—but that he can't.
You'll have it, and have more than I'm foretelling;
And there'll be such a roaring at the Globe
As never stunned the bleeding gladiators.
He'll have to change the color of its hair
A bit, for now he calls it Cleopatra.
Black hair would never do for Cleopatra.
But you and I are not yet two old women,
And you're a man of office. What he does
Is more to you than how it is he does it,—
And that's what the Lord God has never told him.
They work together, and the Devil helps 'em;
They do it of a morning, or if not,
They do it of a night; in which event
He's peevish of a morning. He seems old;
He's not the proper stomach or the sleep—
And they're two sovran agents to conserve him
Against the fiery art that has no mercy
But what's in that prodigious grand new House.
I gather something happening in his boyhood
Fulfilled him with a boy's determination
To make all Stratford 'ware of him. Well, well,
I hope at last he'll have his joy of it,
And all his pigs and sheep and bellowing beeves,
And frogs and owls and unicorns, moreover,
Be less than hell to his attendant ears.
Oh, past a doubt we'll all go down to see him.

He may be wise. With London two days off,
Down there some wind of heaven may yet revive him;
But there's no quickening breath from anywhere
Shall make of him again the poised young faun
From Warwickshire, who'd made, it seems, already
A legend of himself before I came
To blink before the last of his first lightning.
Whatever there be, there'll be no more of that;
The coming on of his old monster Time
Has made him a still man; and he has dreams
Were fair to think on once, and all found hollow.
He knows how much of what men paint themselves
Would blister in the light of what they are;
He sees how much of what was great now shares
An eminence transformed and ordinary;
He knows too much of what the world has hushed
In others, to be loud now for himself;
He knows now at what height low enemies
May reach his heart, and high friends let him fall;
But what not even such as he may know
Bedevils him the worst: his lark may sing
At heaven's gate how he will, and for as long
As joy may listen, but *he* sees no gate,
Save one whereat the spent clay waits a little
Before the churchyard has it, and the worm.
Not long ago, late in an afternoon,
I came on him unseen down Lambeth way,
And on my life I was afear'd of him:
He gloomed and mumbled like a soul from Tophet,
His hands behind him and his head bent solemn.
"What is it now," said I,—"another woman?"

That made him sorry for me, and he smiled.
"No, Ben," he mused; "it's Nothing. It's all Nothing.
We come, we go; and when we're done, we're done.
Spiders and flies—we're mostly one or t'other—
We come, we go; and when we're done, we're done."
"By God, you sing that song as if you knew it!"
Said I, by way of cheering him; "what ails ye?"
"I think I must have come down here to think,"
Says he to that, and pulls his little beard;
"Your fly will serve as well as anybody,
And what's his hour? He flies, and flies, and flies,
And in his fly's mind has a brave appearance;
And then your spider gets him in her net,
And eats him out, and hangs him up to dry.
That's Nature, the kind mother of us all.
And then your slattern housemaid swings her broom,
And where's your spider? And that's Nature, also.
It's Nature, and it's Nothing. It's all Nothing.
It's all a world where bugs and emperors
Go singularly back to the same dust,
Each in his time; and the old, ordered stars
That sang together, Ben, will sing the same
Old stave tomorrow."
When he talks like that,
There's nothing for a human man to do
But lead him to some grateful nook like this
Where we be now, and there to make him drink.
He'll drink, for love of me, and then be sick;
A sad sign always in a man of parts,
And always very ominous. The great
Should be as large in liquor as in love,—
And our great friend is not so large in either:
One disaffects him, and the other fails him;
Whatso he drinks that has an antic in it,
He's wondering what's to pay in his insides;
And while his eyes are on the Cyprian
He's fribbling all the time with that damned House.
We laugh here at his thrift, but after all
It may be thrift that saves him from the devil;
God gave it, anyhow,—and we'll suppose
He knew the compound of his handiwork.
Today the clouds are with him, but anon
He'll out of 'em enough to shake the tree
Of life itself and bring down fruit unheard-of,—
And, throwing in the bruised and whole together,
Prepare a wine to make us drunk with wonder;
And if he live, there'll be a sunset spell
Thrown over him as over a glassed lake
That yesterday was all a black wild water.

God send he live to give us, if no more,
What now's a-rampage in him, and exhibit,
With a decent half-allegiance to the ages
An earnest of at least a casual eye
Turned once on what he owes to Gutenberg,
And to the fealty of more centuries
Than are as yet a picture in our vision.
"There's time enough,—I'll do it when I'm old,
And we're immortal men," he says to that;
And then he says to me, "Ben, what's 'immortal'?
Think you by any force of ordination
It may be nothing of a sort more noisy
Than a small oblivion of component ashes
That of a dream-addicted world was once
A moving atomy much like your friend here?"
Nothing will help that man. To make him laugh,
I said then he was a mad mountebank,—
And by the Lord I nearer made him cry.
I could have eat an eft then, on my knees,
Tail, claws, and all of him; for I had stung
The king of men, who had no sting for me,
And I had hurt him in his memories;
And I say now, as I shall say again,
I love the man this side idolatry.

He'll do it when he's old, he says. I wonder.
He may not be so ancient as all that.
For such as he, the thing that is to do
Will do itself,—but there's a reckoning;
The sessions that are now too much his own,
The roiling inward of a stilled outside,
The churning out of all those blood-fed lines,
The nights of many schemes and little sleep,

The full brain hammered hot with too much
thinking,
The vexed heart over-worn with too much
aching,—
This weary jangling of conjoined affairs
Made out of elements that have no end.
And all confused at once, I understand,
Is not what makes a man to live forever.
O no, not now! He'll not be going now:
There'll be time yet for God knows what
explosions
Before he goes. He'll stay awhile. Just
wait:
Just wait a year or two for Cleopatra,
For she's to be a balsam and a comfort;
And that's not all a jape of mine now, either.
For granted once the old way of Apollo
Sings in a man, he may then, if he's able,
Strike unafraid whatever strings he will
Upon the last and wildest of new lyres;
Nor out of his new magic, though it hymn
The shrieks of dungeoned hell, shall he create
A madness or a gloom to shut quite out
A cleaving daylight, and a last great calm
Triumphant over shipwreck and all storms.
He might have given Aristotle creeps,
But surely would have given him his *katharsis*.

He'll not be going yet. There's too much yet
Unsung within the man. But when he goes,
I'd stake ye coin o' the realm his only care
For a phantom world he sounded and found
wanting
Will be a portion here, a portion there,
Of this or that thing or some other thing
That has a patent and intrinsical
Equivalence in those egregious shillings.
And yet he knows, God help him! Tell me,
now,
If ever there was anything let loose
On earth by gods or devils heretofore
Like this mad, careful, proud, indifferent
Shakespeare!
Where was it, if it ever was? By heaven,
'Twas never yet in Rhodes or Pergamon—
In Thebes or Nineveh, a thing like this!
No thing like this was ever out of England;
And that he knows. I wonder if he cares.
Perhaps he does. . . . O Lord, that House in
Stratford!

1916

THE MILL

The miller's wife had waited long,
The tea was cold, the fire was dead;
And there might yet be nothing wrong
In how he went and what he said:
"There are no millers any more,"
Was all that she had heard him say;
And he had lingered at the door
So long that it seemed yesterday.

Sick with a fear that had no form
She knew that she was there at last;
And in the mill there was a warm
And mealy fragrance of the past.
What else there was would only seem
To say again what he had meant;
And what was hanging from a beam
Would not have heeded where she went.

And if she thought it followed her,
She may have reasoned in the dark
That one way of the few there were
Would hide her and would leave no mark:
Black water, smooth above the weir
Like starry velvet in the night,
Though ruffled once, would soon appear
The same as ever to the sight.

1920

MR. FLOOD'S PARTY

Old Eben Flood, climbing alone one night
Over the hill between the town below
And the forsaken upland hermitage
That held as much as he should ever know
On earth again of home, paused warily.
The road was his with not a native near;
And Eben, having leisure, said aloud,
For no man else in Tilbury Town to hear:

"Well, Mr. Flood, we have the harvest moon
Again, and we may not have many more;
The bird is on the wing, the poet says,
And you and I have said it here before.
Drink to the bird." He raised up to the light
The jug that he had gone so far to fill,
And answered huskily: "Well, Mr. Flood,
Since you propose it, I believe I will."

Alone, as if enduring to the end
A valiant armor of scarred hopes outworn,
He stood there in the middle of the road

Like Roland's ghost winding a silent horn.
Below him, in the town among the trees,
Where friends of other days had honored him,
A phantom salutation of the dead
Rang thinly till old Eben's eyes were dim.

Then, as a mother lays her sleeping child
Down tenderly, fearing it may awake,
He set the jug down slowly at his feet
With trembling care, knowing that most things break;
And only when assured that on firm earth
It stood, as the uncertain lives of men
Assuredly did not, he paced away,
And with his hand extended paused again:

"Well, Mr. Flood, we have not met like this
In a long time; and many a change has come
To both of us, I fear, since last it was
We had a drop together. Welcome home!"
Convivially returning with himself,
Again he raised the jug up to the light;
And with an acquiescent quaver said:
"Well, Mr. Flood, if you insist, I might.

"Only a very little, Mr. Flood—
For auld lang syne. No more, sir; that will do."
So, for the time, apparently it did,
And Eben evidently thought so too;
For soon amid the silver loneliness
Of night he lifted up his voice and sang,
Secure, with only two moons listening,
Until the whole harmonious landscape rang—

"For auld lang syne." The weary throat gave out,
The last word wavered, and the song was done.
He raised again the jug regretfully
And shook his head, and was again alone.
There was not much that was ahead of him,
And there was nothing in the town below—
Where strangers would have shut the many doors
That many friends had opened long ago.

1920

A CHRISTMAS SONNET

For One in Doubt

While you that in your sorrow disavow
Service and hope, see love and brotherhood
Far off as ever, it will do no good
For you to wear his thorns upon your brow
For doubt of him. And should you question how
To serve him best, he might say, if he could,
"Whether or not the cross was made of wood
Whereon you nailed me, is no matter now."

Though other saviors have in older lore
A Legend, and for older gods have died—
Though death may wear the crown it always wore
And ignorance be still the sword of pride—
Something is here that was not here before,
And strangely has not yet been crucified.

1925

DEMOS AND DIONYSUS

DIONYSUS

Good morning, Demos.

DEMOS

I thought you were dead.

DIONYSUS

If you look too assuredly for death
To consummate your preference and desire,
Sometime you may endure, to your surprise,
The pang of an especial disappointment.
Why such a fever of unfriendliness?
And why, again, so brief a courtesy?

DEMOS

There was no courtesy. Had I the power
To crown my will with its accomplishment,
The crowning would be brief enough, God knows.

DIONYSUS

And you would then be king.

DEMOS

Say as you like,
Your words are of a measure with your works.

DIONYSUS

If you assume with me too large a license,
How do you know that you may not be seized
With one of my more celebrated frenzies
And eat yourself alive? If you do that,
Who then shall be the king that shall inherit
The realm that is your envy and the dream
Of your immoderate magnificence?

DEMOS

There are to be no kings where I shall reign.

DIONYSUS

Not so? Then how are you to do your reigning?
I'm asking only as an eager child
Might ask as much of an impatient father.
We'll say a patient and unusual child,
Not listening always for a sudden answer.

DEMOS

Your days are as the pages of a book,
And one where Finis waits for no long reading.

DIONYSUS

You are somewhat irrelevant, and too hasty,
But that's to be forgiven of a king.
The king can do no wrong. As for my book
Where Finis waits, how far along are you
In reading it, and thereby in absorbing
The indemnifying gist of what it means?

DEMOS

I have read far enough to find in it
No sure indemnity save one of grief,
And one of death.

DIONYSUS

Nothing of life at all?

DEMOS

Nothing of life to me.

DIONYSUS

How came you then
So neutrally and unecstatically
At one time to be born?

DEMOS

I do not see
More than some words in that.

DIONYSUS

I know you don't,
The book of what you do not see, my friend,
Would have no Finis in it. Your dim faith—
Your faith in something somewhere out of nothing—
And your industrious malevolence
Against yourself and the divine escape
That makes a wine of water when it will—
Or not, if it will not—may soon or late
Consume your folly to a long fatigue,
And to an angry death. You measure me
By something in a flagon or a glass—
And we're away from that. Leaving aside
The lesser and the larger mysteries,
By what obscured immeasurable means
Are you to have in your attractive prison
The music of the world and of the stars
Without me, or to make of love and art
The better part—without me? Do you know?

DEMOS

I do not see the prison.

DIONYSUS

But you will;
And having filled it you may blow it up
In the necessity of desperation.

DEMOS

I do not know your language; and far less
Do I concede with you in love and art
The better part.

DIONYSUS

And that you never will.

DEMOS

I hope not.

DIONYSUS

All your hope will come to pass,
If you achieve your way. You stamp your coin
Of words too small to compass their design,
Or to authenticate their currency.

DEMOS

Yet somehow they are current.

DIONYSUS

So they are;
And so are the uncounted flying seeds
Of death for you to breathe and eat and drink,
Never aware of their ascendency
Till you are down where they're devouring you
And you are groaning to be rid of them.

DEMOS

There are physicians.

DIONYSUS

There are not so many
That you may trust them for immunity
From your disease, or pay them for a cure
With your ingenious coin. Under your sway
They would all be as easily indisposed
As you are now, and at as blind a loss
To say what ailed them. Given release enough,
They might arrive, in a combined rebellion,
At some unethical unanimity
As to the poison most expedient
For the accomplishment of your transition,
But they would never cure you otherwise;
And they will never make you less the monster
That you would be, and may be—for a time.
There are futilities and enormities
That must be loved and honored and obeyed
Before they are found out. If you be one,
Or other, or both, as I believe you are,
God help the credulous and expectant slaves
Of your unconscionable supremacy.

DEMOS

They are expectant, certainly, and wisely;
My argument enfolds them and assures them.

DIONYSUS

And obfuscates their proper sight of you.
In your forensic you are not unlike
The pleasant and efficient octopus,
Who inks the sea around him with a cloud
That hides his most essential devilishness,
Leaving his undulating tentacles
To writhe and shoot and strangle as they may.

DEMOS

By turning your two eyes to land again
You may regard some hundred million souls
Or more that are awaiting my tuition—
Where Reason and Equality, like strong twins,
Will soon be brother giants, overseeing
Incessantly the welfare of them all.
A little strangling will be good for them, 109
And they will have no courage to complain.

DIONYSUS

They will not have their souls by then. By then,
You and your twins—both illegitimate,
And the most credible liars ever conceived—
Will have reduced their souls to common fuel,
And their obedient selves to poor machines
That ultimately will disintegrate,
Leaving you outcast and discredited,
A king of ruins; though you are not yet worse
Than a malignant and a specious warning—
Albeit you may attain to your desire
If it be fate that you shall be the scourge
Of a slave-ridden state for long enough
To prove and alienate your demonship
Till you are done with. In the mixed meantime,
A thousand men, had they the will to speak,
Might shred your folly to its least of words
And thereby have the ruin less methodized
If not forestalled and thwarted. You may smile
Till you may be as far from recognition
As from a reason why a man should live,
But you will be no lovelier then for that
Than you are now. Why do you wet your lips
With your mendacious tongue, and rub your hands?

DEMOS

Why do I smile? Why do I rub my hands?
Because your thousand men will never speak.
I have you there, my master. Some will curse
Among themselves a little; some will grunt;
Others will shrug their unoffending shoulders
At my offensive name; others will stretch
Themselves, and in the refuge of a yawn
Will say they have enough to last their time
And that the future must attend itself—
As you foresee it will. They are all safe,
And comfortably gagged. They will not speak–
Or not more than a few—and fewer still
Will act; and those who do may do no more
Than a few shipwrecked generals on an island
Might do if they were all to draw their swords
At once, and then make faces and throw stones
At my perfidious and indifferent image.
I fear, my master, you are left behind.
One of these days, the world will be a hive—
The veritable asylum you deplore
So vainly now. Then every little bee
Will have his little task, and having done it,
His time to play. So all will be in order,
And the souring hopes of individuals
To be some day themselves, though God knows how,
Will all be sweetened with synthetic honey.

The waste of excellence that you call art
Will be a thing remembered as a toy
Dug somewhere from forgotten history;
And this infirmity that you name love
Will be subdued to studious procreation.

DIONYSUS

Of what?

DEMOS

Why, of Reason and Equality.

DIONYSUS

Your twins again. With you for the king-bee,
And with an army of converted drones
Stinging your hive to order, as you say,
Where then would be the purpose or the need
Of any such hive? Were it not better now,
Beforehand, to forestall monotony
And servitude with one complete carouse,
Capped with a competent oblivion—
Or with a prayer at least for such an end?
If in the sorry picture that you flaunt
Before me as your ultimate panorama
Of an invertebrate futility
You see no reason to be sick at heart,—
I do. I see a reason to shed tears.
What will be left in your millennium
When self and soul are gone and all subdued
Insensibly?

DEMOS

Self and soul will not be missed,
Having been rather too much in the way,
And too long, for the good of the machine,
In which I see an end and a beginning.
Men have been playing heretofore too much
With feeling and with unprofitable fancy.

DIONYSUS

I see an end, but not yet the beginning.
Feeling and fancy? What do you know of them?

DEMOS

Enough to say that in the kingdom coming—
O yes, I shall be king—they shall be whipped
And rationed into reason. Where a few
That are peculiar would precede the many,
Measures are always waiting.

DIONYSUS

If there be not
A few that are peculiar in your world,
Your world will be a more peculiar place
Than all your nightmares have inhabited;
And howsoever you compel your zeal
To swallow your deceit, I'll apprehend
Their presence even in your machinery.
Something will break if they are not subdued.

DEMOS

They will be ground to death if they are there,
And in the way.

DIONYSUS

And if the machine breaks
In breaking them, who patches the machine?
You and your amiable automatons
Will have no more the feeling or the fancy
To prove or guess what ails it.

DEMOS

The machine,
Once running, will run always. As for you,
You will be driven off somewhere from the world,
And in some hell of exile and remembrance
Will see how it all goes, and how securely
The mechanistic hive subdues itself
To system and to order—and to Reason.

DIONYSUS

And to Equality. How do you know today
That I may not return again from hell—
Acceptably, perchance—and bring some honey?

DEMOS

Your sort of honey will have no taste then
For palates that are duly neutralized;
And all its evil sweet and stickiness
Will be a freight for you to ferry back
To the same place where you discovered it.

DIONYSUS

Why do you so invidiously insist
That I shall go so far—or that my honey
Is half so evil or so inimical
As that of your abject anticipation?

DEMOS

Abject? I do not wholly see it so.

DIONYSUS

It must have been the milder side of me
That held a lodging for so mild a word.
While I consider the compliant slaves
That you would have subdued to your machine,
I beg your mechanistic leave to shudder,
For your "subdued" pursues me.

DEMOS

As in due time
It will for certain seize you and arraign you
For what you are.

DIONYSUS

Would that it might do so!
Yet that's the one of all things onerous
And easy that will not be done for me.
Simplicity was not my father's name,
Nor was it ever mine; yet I'm unfeigned
To see, for those who may. My mother died
Because she would see God. I did not die.
Was it not strange that I should be twice born
For nothing, if I be what you make of me—
A lord of life that has no worthier fate
Than one of hell, with death and evil honey
For my companionship and consolation?

DEMOS

I have not made of you a lord of life;
And as for recommending hell and honey,
There may be one for you without the other.
We shall have neither here.

DIONYSUS

I'm of a mind
To prophesy that you may have the one
And hunger for the other, till presently
You shall have both again, as you do now.
My way would not be yours; and my machine
Would have a more forbearing alternation
Attending a less dread beneficence.

DEMOS

What do you mean by that?

DIONYSUS

I mean as much
As an observing child might understand
Who grows to see between him and another
A living difference and an impetus
To breathe and be himself. I mean, also,
An increment of reason not like yours,
Which is the crucifixion of all reason,
But one that quickens in the seed of truth
And is the flower of truth—not always fair,
Yet always to be found if you will see it.
There *is* a Demos, and you know his name
By force of easy stealing; yet his face
Would be one of a melancholy stranger
To you if he saw yours. I know his face,
And why he keeps it hidden until the wreck
Of your invention shall betray itself
As a monstrosity beyond repair,
And only by slow toil to be removed.
I mean that all your frantic insolence
Of hate and of denatured eagerness
To build in air a solid monument
From the wrong end will end in a collapse,
With you beneath it bellowing for relief
Not interested or available.
I mean that of all noxious tyrannies
Potential in imaginable folly,
The tyrant of the most intolerable
And unenduring will obscure himself
With much the same suave and benevolent mask
As this that you are wearing now to cover
The guile you dare not show to your disciples.
I mean that your delirious clumsy leap
From reason to the folly you call reason
Will only make of you and of your dupes
A dislocated and unlovely mess
For undertakers, who are not yet born
To view the coming ruin that is to be
Their occupation and emolument—
If your delusion for a time prevail,
As like enough it will. I mean, also,
That after suffering time has had enough
Of you and of your sterile dispensation,
Some wholesome fire of thought and competence
Will make of what is left a cannistered
Memorial of unlovely orts and ashes,
To be a warning and a wonderment
Where you shall plot no more. I mean a world
Fit for a self-defending human race
To recognize, and finally to live in.

DEMOS

I'll put the clamps on harder, just for that,
And let you see what Reason really is,
In fact and action. We have had too much
Of the insurgent individual

With his free fancy and free this and that,
And his ingenuous right to be himself.
What right has anyone now to be himself,
Since I am here to fix him in his place
And hold him there? And as for your fit world,
I'll have it all alike and of a piece—
Punctual, accurate, tamed and uniform,
And equal. Then romance and love and art
And ecstasy will be remembrances
Of man's young weakness on his way to reason.
When my world's once in order, you shall see.

DIONYSUS

I may, but God forbid the sight of it.
I'd rather stay in hell, which you imply
To be preparing for me.

DEMOS

I approve
Unspeakably of such a preference
On your part. Go at once, for all I care,
And stay.

DIONYSUS

I may go somewhere, for a while,
But I am one of those who have perforce
To live and to return. Should there be need
Of me, I may remain; and you may find
One day a merry welcome waiting you
In the same place where you say I belong:
Take off your mask and find another name,
Or I'll be sure you will. Good morning, Demos.

DEMOS

Good morning, Dionysus. Wait and see.

1925

From TRISTRAM

III

Lost in a gulf of time where time was lost,
And heedless of a light queen's light last words
That were to be remembered, he saw now
Before him in the gloom a ghostly ship
Cleaving a way to Cornwall silently
From Ireland, with himself on board and one
That with her eyes told him intolerably
How little of his blind self a crowded youth,
With a sight error-flecked and pleasure-flawed,
Had made him see till on that silent voyage
There was no more to see than faith betrayed,
Or life disowned. The sorrow in his name
Came out, and he was Tristram, born for sorrow
Of an unguarded and forgotten mother,
Who may have seen as those who are to die
Are like to see. A king's son, he had given
Himself in honor unto another king
For gratitude, not knowing what he had given,
Or seeing what he had done. Now he could see,
And there was no need left of a ship's ghost,
Or ghost of anything else than life before him,
To make him feel, though he might not yet hear it,
The nearness of a doom that was descending
Upon him, and anon should hold him fast—
If he were not already held fast enough
To please the will of fate.

"Brangwaine!" he said,
Turning and trembling. For a softer voice
Than Morgan's now had spoken; a truer voice,
Which had not come alone to plead with him
In the King's name for courtesy.

"Sir Tristram! . . ."
Brangwaine began, and ended. Then she seized
His hands and held them quickly to her lips
In fealty that he felt was his for ever.
"Brangwaine, for this you make a friend of me
Until I die. If there were more for one
To say . . ." He said no more, for some one else
Than Brangwaine was above him on the stairs.
Coming down slowly and without a sound
She moved, and like a shadow saying nothing
Said nothing while she came. Isolt of Ireland,
With all her dark young majesty unshaken
By grief and shame and fear that made her shake
Till to go further would have been to fall,
Came nearer still to him and still said nothing,
Till terror born of passion became passion
Reborn of terror while his lips and hers
Put speech out like a flame put out by fire.
The music poured unheard, Brangwaine had vanished,
And there were these two in the world alone,
Under the cloudy light of a cold moon

That glimmered now as cold on Brittany
As on Cornwall.
Time was aware of them,
And would beat soon upon his empty bell
Release from such a fettered ecstasy
As fate would not endure. But until then
There was no room for time between their souls
And bodies, or between their silences,
Which were for them no less than heaven and hell,
Fused cruelly out of older silences
That once a word from either might have ended,
And so annihilated into life
Instead of death—could her pride then have spoken,
And his duped eyes have seen, before his oath
Was given to make them see. But silences
By time are slain, and death, or more than death,
May come when silence dies. At last Isolt
Released herself enough to look at him,
With a world burning for him in her eyes,
And two worlds crumbling for him in her words:
"What have I done to you, Tristram!" she said;
"What have you done to me! What have we done
To Fate, that she should hate us and destroy us,
Waiting for us to speak. What have we done
So false or foul as to be burned alive
And then be buried alive—as we shall be—
As I shall be!"
He gazed upon a face
Where all there was of beauty and of love
That was alive for him, and not for him,
Was his while it was there. "I shall have burned
And buried us both," he said. "Your pride would not
Have healed my blindness then, even had you prayed
For God to let you speak. When a man sues
The fairest of all women for her love,
He does not cleave the skull first of her kinsman
To mark himself a man. That was my way;
And it was not the wisest—if your eyes
Had any truth in them for a long time.
Your pride would not have let me tell them more—
Had you prayed God, I say."

"I did do that,
Tristram, but he was then too far from heaven
To hear so little a thing as I was praying
For you on earth. You had not seen my eyes
Before you fought with Morhaus; and for that,
There was your side and ours. All history sings
Of two sides, and will do so till all men
Are quiet; and then there will be no men left
Or women alive to hear them. It was long
Before I learned so little as that; and you
It was who taught me while I nursed and healed
Your wound, only to see you go away."

"And once having seen me go away from you,
You saw me coming back to you again,
Cheerful and healed, as Mark's ambassador.
Would God foresee such folly alive as that
In anything he had made, and still make more?
If so, his ways are darker than divines
Have drawn them for our best bewilderments.
Be it so or not, my share in this is clear.
I have prepared a way for us to take,
Because a king was not so much a devil
When I was young as not to be a friend,
An uncle, and an easy counsellor.
Later, when love was yet no more for me
Then a gay folly glancing everywhere
For triumph easier sometimes than defeat,
Having made sure that I was blind enough,
He sealed me with an oath to make you his
Before I had my eyes, or my heart woke
From pleasure in a dream of other faces
That now are nothing else than silly skulls
Covered with skin and hair. The right was his
To make of me a shining knight at arms,
By fortune may be not the least adept
And emulous. But God! for seizing you,
And having you here tonight, and all his life
Having you here, by the blind means of me,
I could tear all the cords out of his neck
To make a rope, and hang the rest of him.
Isolt, forgive me! This is only sound
That I am making with a tongue gone mad
That you should be so near me as to hear me
Saying how far away you are to go

When you go back to him, driven by—me!
A fool may die with no great noise or loss;
And whether a fool should always live or not . . ."

Isolt, almost as with a frightened leap
Muffled his mouth with hers in a long kiss,
Blending in their catastrophe two fires
That made one fire. When she could look at him
Again, her tears, unwilling still to flow,
Made of her eyes two shining lakes of pain
With moonlight living in them; and she said,
"There is no time for you to tell me this;
And you are younger than time says you are,
Or you would not be losing it, saying over
All that I know too well, or for my sake
Giving yourself these names that are worth nothing.
It was our curse that you were not to see
Until you saw too late. No scourge of names
That you may lay for me upon yourself
Will have more consequence for me, or you,
Than beating with a leaf would have on horses;
So give yourself no more of them tonight.
The King says you are coming back with me.
How can you come? And how can you not come!
It will be cruel enough for me without you,
But with you there alive in the same walls
I shall be hardly worthy of life tonight
If I stay there alive—although I shall,
For this may not be all. This thing has come
For us, and you are not to see the end
Through any such fog of honor and self-hate
As you may seek to throw around yourself
For being yourself. Had you been someone else,
You might have been one like your cousin Andred,
Who looks at me as if he were a snake
That has heard something. Had you been someone else,
You might have been like Modred, or like Mark.
God—you like Mark! You might have been a slave.
We cannot say what either of us had been
Had we been something else. All we can say
Is that this thing has come to us tonight.
You can do nothing more unless you kill him.
And that would be the end of you and me.
Time on our side, this may not be the end."

"I might have been a slave, by you unseen,"
He answered, "and you still Isolt of Ireland,
To me unknown. That would have been for you
The better way. But that was not the way."

"No it was not," she said, trying to smile;
And weary then for trying, held him closer.
"But I can feel the hands of time on me,
And they will soon be tearing me away.
Tristram, say to me once before I go,
What you believe and what you see for us
Before you. Are you sure that a word given
Is always worth more than a world forsaken?
Who knows there may not be a lonely place
In heaven for souls that are ashamed and sorry
For fearing hell?"

"It is not hell tonight,
Isolt," he said, "or any beyond the grave,
That I fear most for you or for myself.
Fate has adjusted and made sure of that
Where we are now—though we see not the end,
And time be on our side. Praise God for time,
And for such hope of what may come of it
As time like this may grant. I could be strong,
But to be over-strong now at this hour
Would only be destruction. The King's ways
Are not those of one man against another,
And you must live, and I must live—for you.
If there were not an army of guards below us
To bring you back to fruitless ignominy,
There would soon be an end of this offense
To God and the long insult of this marriage.
But to be twice a fool is not the least
Insane of ways to cure a first affliction.
God!—is it so—that you are going back
To be up there with him—with Mark—to-night?
Before you came, I had been staring down
On those eternal rocks and the white foam
Around them; and I thought how sound and long
A sleep would soon begin for us down there
If we were there together—before you came.

That was a fancy, born of circumstance,
And I was only visioning some such thing
As that. The moon may have been part of it.
I think there was a demon born with me
And in the malediction of my name,
And that his work is to make others suffer—
Which is the worst of burdens for a man
Whose death tonight were nothing, could the death
Of one be the best end of this for two."

"If that was to be said," Isolt replied,
"It will at least not have to be said over.
For since the death of one would only give
The other a twofold weight of wretchedness
To bear, why do you pour these frozen words
On one who cannot be so confident
As you that we may not be nearer life,
Even here tonight, than we are near to death?
I must know more than you have told me yet
Before I see, so clearly as you see it,
The sword that must for ever be between us.
Something in you was always in my father:
A darkness always was around my father,
Since my first eyes remembered him. He saw
Nothing, but he would see the shadow of it
Before he saw the color or shape it had,
Or where the sun was. Tristram, fair things yet
Will have a shadow black as night before them,
And soon will have a shadow black as night
Behind them. And all this may be a shadow,
Sometime, that we may live to see behind us—
Wishing that we had not been all so sure
Tonight that it was always to be night."

"Your father may have fancied where the sun was
When first he saw the shadow of King Mark
Coming with mine before me. You are brave
Tonight, my love. A bravery like yours now
Would be the summons for a mightier love
Than mine, if there were room for such a love
Among things hidden in the hearts of men.
Isolt! Isolt! . . ."

Out of her struggling eyes
There were tears flowing, and withheld in his,
Tears were a veil of pity and desperation
Through which he saw the dim face of Isolt
Before him like a phantom in a mist—
Till to be sure that she was not a phantom,
He clutched and held her fast against his heart,
And through the cloak she wore felt the warm life
Within her trembling to the life in him,
And to the sorrow and the passion there
That would be always there. "Isolt! Isolt!"
Was all the language there was left in him
And she was all that was left anywhere—
She that would soon be so much worse than gone
That if he must have seen her lying still,
Dead where she was, he could have said that fate
Was merciful at least to one of them.
He would have worn through life a living crown
Of death, for memory more to be desired
Than any furtive and forsworn desire,
Or shattered oath of his to serve a King,
His mother's brother, without wilful stain,
Was like to be with all else it might be.
So Tristram, in so far as there was reason
Left in him, would have reasoned—when Isolt
Drew his face down to hers with all her strength
Or so it seemed, and kissed his eyes and cheeks
And mouth until there was no reason left
In life but love—love that was not to be,
Save as a wrenching and a separation
Past reason or reprieve. If she forgot
For long enough to smile at him through tears,
He may have read it as a sign that God
Was watching her and all might yet be well;
And if he knew that all might not be well,
Some God might still be watching over her,
With no more power than theirs now against Rome,
Or the pernicious valor of sure ruin,
Or against fate, that like an unseen ogre
Made hungry sport of these two there alone
Above the moaning wash of Cornish water,
Cold upon Cornish rocks.

"No bravery, love,"
She said, "or surely none like mine, would hide,
Among things in my heart that are not hidden,

A love larger than all time and all places,
And stronger beyond knowledge than all numbers
Around us that can only make us dead
When they are done with us. Tristram, believe
That if I die my love will not be dead,
As I believe that yours will not be dead.
If in some after time your will may be
To slay it for the sake of a new face,
It will not die. Whatever you do to it,
It will not die. We cannot make it die,
We are not mighty enough to sentence love
Stronger than death to die, though we may die.
I do not think there is much love like ours
Here in this life, or that too much of it
Would make poor men and women who go alone
Into their graves without it more content,
Or more by common sorrow to be envied
Than they are now. This may be true, or not.
Perhaps I am not old enough to know—
Not having lived always, nor having seen
Much else than everything disorderly
Deformed to order into a small court,
Where love was most a lie. Might not the world,
If we could sift it into a small picture,
Be more like that than it would be like—this?
No, there is not much like this in the world—
And there may not be this!"

Tristram could see
Deep in the dark wet splendor of her eyes,
A terror that he knew was more for him
Than for herself. "You are still brave enough,"
He said, "and you might look to me for strength,
If I were a magician and a wizard,
To vanquish the invincible. Destruction
Of such a sort as one here among hundreds
Might wreak upon himself would be a pastime,
If ruin of him would make you free again
Without him."

"I would not be free without him,"
Isolt said, as if angry: "And you know
That I should not be free if I were free
Without him. Say no more about destruction
Till we see more, who are not yet destroyed.
O God, if only one of us had spoken—
When there was all that time!"

"You mean by that,
If only I had spoken," Tristram said;
And he could say no more till her quick lips
That clung to his again would let him speak.
"You mean, if only I had been awake
In paradise, instead of asleep there,
No jealous angel with a burning sword
Would have had power enough to drive me out,
Though God himself had sent him."

Isolt smiled,
As with a willing pity, and closed her eyes
To keep more tears from coming out of them;
And for a time nothing was to be heard
Except the pounding of two hearts in prison,
The torture of a doom-begotten music
Above them, and the wash of a cold foam
Below them on those cold eternal rocks
Where Tristram and Isolt had yesterday
Come to be wrecked together. When her eyes
Opened again, he saw there, watching him,
An aching light of memory; and his heart
Beat harder for remembering the same light
That he had seen before in the same eyes.

"Alone once in the moonlight on that ship,"
She said, still watching him and clinging warm
Against him, "I believed that you would speak,
For I could hear your silence like a song
Out of the sea. I stood by the ship's rail,
Looking away into the night, with only
You and the ocean and the moon and stars
There with me. I was not seeing where I looked,
For I had waited too long for your step
Behind me to care then if the ship sailed
Or sank, so long as one true word of yours
Went wheresoever the ship went with me.
If these eyes, that were looking off so far
Over the foam, found anything there that night
Worth looking at, they have forgotten it;
And if my ears heard even the waves that night,
Or if my cheeks felt even the wind that night,
They have forgotten waves and wind together,
Remembering only there was you somewhere
On the same ship where I was, all alone

As I was, and alive. When you did come,
At last, and were there with me, and still silent,
You had already made yourself in vain
The loyal counterfeit of someone else
That never was, and I hope never shall be,
To make me sure there was no love for me
To find in you, where love was all I found.
You had not quite the will or quite the wish,
Knowing King Mark, not to reveal yourself,
When revelation was no more the need
Of my far larger need than revelation.
There was enough revealed, but nothing told.
Since I dare say to you how sure I am
Of the one thing that's left me to be sure of,
Know me and love me as I was that night,
As I am now, and as I shall be always—
All yours; and all this means for you and me
Is no small care for you. If you had spoken
There on that ship what most was in your heart
To say—if you had held me close—like this—
If you had kissed me then—like this—I wonder
If there would have been kings and crowns enough
In Cornwall or in England or elsewhere
To make the crowns of all kings everywhere
Shine with a light that would have let me see
No king but you and no crown but our love.
Tristram, believe, whatever the rest may be,
This is all yours—for God to weigh at last,
And as he will. And if it be found wanting,
He will not find what's left so ordinary
As not to say of it, 'This was Isolt—
Isolt who was all love.' He made her so,
And some time he may tell her why it is
So many that are on earth are there to suffer.
I say this now, for time will not wait always,
And we shall not be here when we are old—
If time can see us old. I had not thought
Of that; and will not think of it again.
There must be women who are made for love,
And of it, and are mostly pride and fire
Without it. There would not be much else left
Of them without it than sold animals
That might as well be driven and eating grass
As weaving, riding, hunting, and being queens,
Or not being queens. But when two loves like ours
Wear down the wall of time dividing them,
Two oceans come together and flow over
Time and his evil work. It was too long,
That wall, but there is nothing left of it,
And there is only love where the wall was.
And while you love me you will not forget
That you are all there is in my life now
That I would live for longer. And since nothing
Is left to me but to be sure of nothing
That you have not been sure of and been told,
You can believe me, though you cannot save me.
No, there is only one way to do that. . . .
If I were sure this was to be the end,
I should make this the end . . . Tristram! Tristram!
With you in the same house!"

"Do not say that."
He shook, and held her face away from him,
Gazing upon it as a man condemned
To darkness might have gazed for the last time
At all there was of life that he should see
Before his eyes were blinded by white irons.
"Tell me to throw myself over this wall,
Down upon those dead rocks, and I will do it.
Tell me to fall down now upon the point
Of this too restive sword, and you will see
How brief a sting death has. Tell me to drink
Tonight the most efficient mortal poison,
And of all drink that may be poured tomorrow
None shall be poured for me. But do not say,
Or make me say, where I shall be tonight.
All I can say is, I shall not be here.
Something within me is too near to breaking,
And it is not my heart. That will not break,
Nor shall a madness that is in me now
Break time in two—time that is on our side.
Yet I would see as little of Mark tonight
As may be well for my forgetfulness.
That was the best for me to say to you,
And now it has been said. I shall not kill him."

She trembled in his arms, and with a cry
Of stricken love gave all there was of her
That she could give to him in one more kiss
In which the world was melted and was nothing
For them but love—until another cry,
From Brangwaine, all forgotten in the garden,

Made the world firm again. He leapt away,
Leaving Isolt bewildered and heart-sick
With fear for him, and for she knew not what,
And lastly for herself. But soon she felt
A noise that was like one of shadows fighting.
Then she saw Tristram, who was bringing with him
A choking load that he dragged after him;
And then she could see Brangwaine, white as death
Behind those two. And while she saw them there,
She could hear music from those walls above her,
And waves foaming on the cold rocks below.
When Tristram spoke, his words came hoarse and few.
"I knew the vermin I should find," he said,
And said no more. He muttered and hurled something
Away from him against the parapet,
Hearing the sound that a skull makes on stone;
And without looking one way or another,
He stood there for a time like a man struck
By doom to an ungovernable silence,
Breathing above the crumpled shape of Andred.

1927

NOTES

CHRONOLOGICAL, BIBLIOGRAPHICAL, CRITICAL

PHILIP FRENEAU

CHRONOLOGY

1752 Born in New York, in home of refinement and culture.

1767 His preparation received from private tutors, he entered the sophomore class of the College of New Jersey, where he was a classmate of James Madison.

1771 Collaborated with H. H. Brackenridge in the poem, "The Rising Glory of America," which was read by latter at graduating exercises of his class.

1772 Taught school for short while, and thoroughly disliked it.

1775 Published eight pamphlets satirizing British, among them *General Gage's Soliloquy* and *General Gage's Confession*.

1775–78 Secretary in home of prominent planter of Vera Cruz. Wrote "Santa Cruz," "The Jamaica Funeral," and "The House of Night." On his return trip was captured and released by British.

1780 On voyage between the Azores and New York, his ship was captured by the British and he was placed first on a prison ship, and then on a hospital ship. "The British Prison Ship" (1781) describes these experiences.

1781–84 Employed in Philadelphia Post Office. Satires against Loyalists published in *Freeman's Journal*. The poems of this period won him the title, "The Poet of the American Revolution."

1786 *Poems of Philip Freneau written chiefly during the late war.* (Philadelphia.)

1784–89 Sailed as master of brig, was shipwrecked, survived a hurricane, wrote hurricane lyric. Period ended by his marriage to Eleanor Forman, 1789.

1788 *Miscellaneous Works of Mr. Philip Freneau Containing His Essays, and Additional Poems.* (Philadelphia.)

1791 Accepted Jefferson's offer of position as translating clerk for Department of State at $250 a year. Moved to Philadelphia and started the *National Gazette*, which supported the Democrats and attacked Fenno's Federalist *Gazette of the United States;* as editor of the *National Gazette* he won from Jefferson the statement that he "saved our Constitution, which was galloping fast into monarchy."

1793 *National Gazette* suspended, partly for lack of funds. Resigned from government position when Jefferson retired.

1795 *Poems Written between the Years 1768 and 1794, by Philip Freneau of New Jersey.* (Monmouth, N. J.)

1795–97 Edited papers; *Jersey Chronicle* (1795–96), New York *Time-Piece* (1797).

1799 *Letters on Various Interesting and Important Subjects; Many of Which Have Appeared in the Aurora.* (Philadelphia.)

1803–07 Went to sea, urged by poverty.

1809 *Poems Written and Published during the American Revolutionary War.* (2 vols. Philadelphia. Ran to three editions in 1809.)

1815 *A Collection of Poems, on American Affairs . . . Written between the Year 1797 and the Present Time.* (2 vols. New York.)

1832 Lost his way while returning home in a blizzard, and died.

BIBLIOGRAPHY

I. Bibliography

Paltsits, V. C. *A Bibliography of the Separate and Collected Works of Philip Freneau.* New York: 1903.

[See also Pattee and Marble below.]

II. Text

Clark, Harry H. (ed.) *Poems of Freneau.* New York: 1929. (Selections, edited with an introduction.)

Smith, John Russell (ed.) *Poems on various Subjects, but chiefly illustrative of the Events and Actors in the American War of Independence.* By Philip Freneau. Reprinted from the rare edition printed at Philadelphia in 1786. With a Preface. London: 1861.

Duyckinck, Evert A. (ed.) *Poems relating to the American Revolution.* By Philip Freneau. With an introductory memoir and notes. New York: 1865.

Heartman, C. F. (ed.) *Unpublished Freneauana.* New York: 1918. (Letters.)

Pattee, Fred Lewis (ed.) *Poems of Philip Freneau, Poet of the American Revolution.* Princeton: 1902–1907. 3 vols. (Lists 119 poems omitted, but the most complete edition. Especially valuable for notes on place and date of first publication of most of the poems. The Introduction of 112 pages is the most reliable biography. The bibliography, Vol. III, pp. 407–417, aims "to correct a few omissions and errors" in Mr. Paltsits' *Bibliography*.)

[See Freneau's individual volumes listed under Chronology above.]

III. Biography and Criticism

Ainsworth, E. G. "An American Translator of Ariosto: Philip Freneau," *American Literature*, IV, 393–395 (Jan., 1933).

Allen, Gay W. "Freneau," in *American Prosody*. New York: 1935, pp. 1–22. (A scholarly survey.)

Austin, M. S. *Philip Freneau, The Poet of the Revolution. A History of His Life and Times*. Edited by Helen Kearny Vreeland. New York: 1901. (Eulogistic and unscholarly.)

Beatty, J. M., Jr. "Churchill and Freneau," *American Literature*, II, 121–130 (May, 1930). (Mr. Beatty finds an influence of Churchill in Freneau's "Discovery," "American Liberty," "The Midnight Consultations," "MacSwiggen," and "America Independent.")

Benson, Adolph B. "The Misconception in Philip Freneau's 'Scandinavian War Song,'" *Journal of English and Germanic Philology*, XXVIII, 111–116.

Bleyer, Willard G. *History of American Journalism*. Boston: 1927, pp. 109–111.

Bowers, C. G. *Jefferson and Hamilton: The Struggle for Democracy in America*. Boston: 1925. (Vivid account of the conflict in which Freneau took part. Consult index.)

Brenner, Rica. *Twelve American Poets before 1900*. New York: 1933, pp. 3–23.

Calverton, V. F. "Philip Freneau: An Apostle of Freedom," *Modern Monthly*, VII, 533–546 (Oct., 1933). (Appreciation of his radicalism.)

Clark, H. H. "Literary Influences on Philip Freneau," *Studies in Philology*, XXII, 1–33 (Jan., 1925).

—— "What Made Freneau the Father of American Poetry?" *Studies in Philology*, XXVI, 1–22 (Jan., 1929).

—— (ed.) *Poems of Freneau*. American Authors Series. New York: 1929. (Introduction, pp. xiii–lviii, discusses Freneau as poet of American independence, journalist of Jeffersonian and French democracy, apostle of religion of nature and humanity; and "Father of American Poetry." Considers scientific deism as the core of his thought.)

—— "What Made Freneau the Father of American Prose?" *Transactions of the Wisconsin Academy of Sciences, Arts, and Letters*, XXV, 39–50 (May, 1930).

De Lancey, E. F. "Philip Freneau, the Huguenot Patriot-Poet of the Revolution, and His Poetry," *Proceedings of the Huguenot Society of America*. Vol. II, No. 2, 1891.

Farley, F. E. "The Dying Indian," in *Anniversary Papers by the Colleagues and Pupils of George Lyman Kittredge*. Boston: 1913, pp. 251–260. (Deals with Freneau's Indian poems.)

Forman, S. E. "The Political Activities of Philip Freneau," *Johns Hopkins University Studies in Historical and Political Science*, Series XX, Nos. 9–10. Baltimore: 1902. (Extended scholarly survey.)

Gummere, R. M. "Apollo on Locust Street," *Pennsylvania Magazine of History*, LXVI, 68–92. (Treats Freneau's debt to the ancient classics, pp. 88–92.)

Grundy, J. Owen. "Philip Freneau, Jersey Patriot and Poet of the Revolution," *Proceedings of the New Jersey Historical Society*, N. S. XIV, 481–488 (Oct., 1929). (Appreciation.)

Holliday, Carl. *Wit and Humor of Colonial Days*. Philadelphia: 1912, pp. 170–198. (Discursive.)

Hustvedt, S. B. "Philippic Freneau," *American Speech*, IV, 1–18 (Oct., 1928). (On vocabulary.)

Keiser, A. *The Indian in American Literature*. New York: 1933, pp. 21–32. (Good analysis.)

Kreymborg, A. *Our Singing Strength*. New York: 1929, pp. 21–26. (Impressionistic.)

Marble, Mrs. A. R. *Heralds of American Literature*. Chicago: 1907, pp. 61–106, and Bibliography, pp. 327–333. (A good study.)

More, P. E. "Philip Freneau," in *Shelburne Essays*. Fifth Series. New York: 1908.

Otis, W. B. *American Verse, 1625–1807*. New York: 1909. (See index and pp. 182–194. Appreciative survey.)

Parrington, V. L. *The Colonial Mind, 1620–1800*. New York: 1927, pp. 368–381. (Stimulating account of Freneau's liberal humanitarianism. See also Forman, above.)

Pattee, F. L. *Poems of Philip Freneau, Poet of the American Revolution*. Vol. I, Introduction. Princeton: 1902.

—— "Philip Freneau as Postal Clerk," *American Literature*, IV, 61–62 (Mar., 1932).

—— "The Modernness of Philip Freneau," in *Sidelights on American Literature*. New York: 1922, pp. 250–292. (Readable and general.)

Patterson, S. W. *The Spirit of the American Revolution as Revealed in the Poetry of the Period*. Boston: [1915]. (Pedestrian.)

Payne, G. H. *History of Journalism in the United States*. New York: 1920, pp. 160–166.

Smith, F. "Philip Freneau and 'The Time-Piece and Literary Companion,'" *American Literature*, IV, 270–287 (Nov., 1932). (Scholarly.)

Tyler, M. C. *The Literary History of the American Revolution, 1763–1783*. 2 vols. New York: 1897. Vol. I, pp. 171–183, 415–425; Vol. II, 426–476. (Descriptive and appreciative; by a master of the whole period.)

Woodbury, Margaret. "Public Opinion in Philadelphia, 1789–1801," *Smith College Studies in History*, V, 1–138 (Oct. 1919–Jan. 1920.) (An exhaustive study. Pp. 5, 10, 12, 20–24, and 35 deal with Freneau.)

NOTES

"If scientific deism determined Freneau's treatment of indigenous American nature, if the consequent sensuousness accounts for the aesthetic quality of his poetry, it must be pointed out that his naturalism is distinctively of the eighteenth century transitional sort. His work falls between two eras, the neoclassic and the romantic, the age of Pope and the age of Wordsworth, and it partakes of the character of each. His genius and individuality were not so great as to prevent him, chameleon-like, from taking protective coloring against his changing age; this fact, however, renders his works valuable as a cross-section of the complex age of transition in American letters. This transitional position helps to account for the absence in Freneau of what Emerson called 'a foolish consistency.' He is unconsciously a bundle of apparent contradictions. He is both a bitter satirist, 'full of invective and loaded with spleen,' and a sentimentalist who laments popular indifference toward the 'plaintive elegy' and 'lyric ode.' Idolizing 'thrice happy Dryden,' 'god-like Addison,' and 'heav'nly Pope,' he leads the revolt against their themes and diction. An ardent student of the classics, he rebukes 'the Student of the Dead Languages' for wasting time on the 'antique gibberish' of 'Latin lore and heathen Greek.' Glorifier of the 'gen'rous soul' of the benevolent and noble red man, he attacks his vices. His ferocious hatreds are equaled only by his humanitarian sympathies, his humor only by his pensive melancholy. The poet of Reason, he grieves that he dwells

> 'Where rigid *Reason* reigns alone,
> Where lovely *Fancy* has no sway.'

An ardent apostle, as we have seen, of natural goodness and human perfectibility, he is the author of the apparently contradictory poems on 'The Projectors' and 'The Millennium.' And finally, he is the poet of deistic optimism—'all, all is right'—as well as the poet of transience and death. His eighteenth century tastes are more striking when one recalls that he outlived but never referred to Byron, Shelley, Keats, and Hazlitt, and that Hawthorne, Whittier, Poe, as well as Tennyson and Carlyle, were all writing at his death. The parallels to his nascent romanticism appear in precursors such as Parnell, Shenstone, Thomson, Blair, Young, Collins, Gray, the Wartons, Beattie, Cowper, Crabbe, Goldsmith, Beckford, Blake, and Burns. If on the political side his closest parallel is Shelley, that is because both poets drew from eighteenth century naturalism their major doctrines such as faith in natural goodness, the perfectibility of man, the sovereignty of reason, universal benevolence, and the dependence of evil on social institutions."—Harry Hayden Clark, Introduction to *Poems of Freneau*, pp. l–li.

Page 1. THE POWER OF FANCY

Freneau's glorification of Fancy as a "vagrant restless thing," undisciplined to seek the normal and representative but rather a means of escape to the distant, the strange, and the glamorous, parallels the tendencies of those who heralded the Romantic era. Advanced students will be interested in the fact that parts of this poem are strikingly parallel to and perhaps based upon Joseph Warton's "Ode to Fancy" (1746). See H. H. Clark's study of "Literary Influences on Philip Freneau," *Studies in Philology*, XXII, 1–33 (Jan., 1925). Note that Freneau has been reading Milton and Ossian. Freneau's friend Jefferson and other contemporaries also admired Ossian; see "The Vogue of Ossian in America" by F. I. Carpenter, *American Literature*, II, 405–417 (Jan., 1931). Note also, in this early poem, that lines 11–20 express the current view of scientific deists that physical nature rather than the Bible is a divine revelation. For a detailed analysis of Freneau's versification see Gay W. Allen's *American Prosody*, pp. 1–21.

Page 2. THE RISING GLORY OF AMERICA

This was originally a commencement poem (Princeton, 1771) written in collaboration with H. H. Brackenridge, Freneau's classmate and the author of *Modern Chivalry*. F. L. Pattee (*Poems of Philip Freneau*, I, xxi), says that "in 1786 Freneau isolated his own portion for publication in the first edition of his works." The present text is taken from this first edition. Note the ardent Americanism, the belief in natural goodness, and the millennial utopianism. The poem also illustrates Freneau's competent use of blank verse at a time when the heroic couplet was fashionable.

Page 22. THE HOUSE OF NIGHT

One of the most original and romantic poems of early American literature, this poem in its Gothic horror is part of the natural reaction against the earlier rationality, convention, restraint, and unimaginativeness—the manifestation in aesthetic terms of the spirit of independence then dominating politics. Of various analogues, of especial interest is "The Induction" contributed in 1563 by Sir Thomas Sackville (co-author of the Senecan *Gorboduc*) to *The Mirror for Magistrates*. See Oral Coad on "The Gothic Element in American Literature before 1835" (*Journal of English and Germanic Philology*, XXIV, 72–93), where many parallels in contemporary painting are also cited. Compare the treatment of horror in Brockden Brown, Whittier (*Legends of New England*, 1831), Poe, and Hawthorne. Although the poem was printed in *The United States Magazine*, Aug., 1779, the only complete version is that of the edition of 1786, from which this text is taken.

Page 31. THE BEAUTIES OF SANTA CRUZ

This poem was written in 1776, on the island of Santa Cruz. "My agreeable residence at this place for above two years, off and on during the wars in America, renders the idea of it all too pleasing, and makes me feel much the same anxiety at a distance from it as Adam did after he was banished from the bowers of Eden." (Quoted by Pattee, *Poems*, etc., I, xxvii, from *The United States Magazine*, Feb., 1779.) The poem and his idyllic escape from the Revolution illustrate that the so-called "Poet of the Revolution" had a lyric and sensuous devotion to poetry and to natural beauty which for a time made him indifferent to the struggle for independence. Oliver Elton (*A Survey of English Literature*, New York, 1920, I, 9–10) has defined romanticism as "the convalescence of the feeling for beauty . . . This feeling is enriched from three separate but meeting sources. First of all, the *senses of the artist are regenerated;* this is at the bottom of everything. Secondly, his renewed perceptions of the face of living nature are attended by a *vision of humanity*, a new passion and humour, the expression of which is brought under the law of beauty. Thirdly, this new knowledge and self-knowledge are read in the light of *new ideas;* philosophical conceptions and visions invade literary art, and are brought under its law." Note in this poem of 1776 the multitude of sense-appeals, and compare with Keats's much later development of this side of romanticism. The three developments noted by Professor Elton should be kept in mind throughout the reading of Freneau; to what extent were his humanitarianism and his sensuousness derivations from his philosophical outlook—his scientific deism—expressed in part in "The Power of Fancy" (ll. 17–20), "On the Universality and Other Attributes of the God of Nature," "On the Religion of Nature," "Reflections on the Gradual Progress of Nations from Democratic States to Despotic Empires," "On the Abuse of Human Power," "The Pictures of Columbus," and elsewhere?

Page 39. TO THE MEMORY OF THE BRAVE AMERICANS

Freneau rendered great service as the poet of American independence in the Revolution and the War of 1812 by writing poems ridiculing and attacking the enemy, celebrating American victories, and glorifying the dead. It is said that the poems were sometimes posted to be read by the disheartened soldiers. While many of the attacks in verse are coarse and frontal, hardly meriting the term satire, many of the elegies, such as the one "To the Memory of the Brave Americans" who fell at Eutaw Springs, have a tender and lyric beauty reminiscent of Collins's "Ode Written in the Beginning of the Year 1746."

Page 44. BARNEY'S INVITATION

In this poem and in "The Hurricane" one finds illustrated Freneau's typical late eighteenth century transitional treatment of the sea, which he was among the first to introduce into American poetry. He shares the earlier view of the sea as a commercial highway and a savage destroyer. And yet he also foreshadows Cooper's manly delight in realistic naval details; and his treatment of the vaster and more terrifying aspects of the sea as well as his view of the sea as a refuge from an unkind society, foreshadow Byron and Masefield. Compare Freneau's sea poems with those of Longfellow and Whitman.

Page 49. THE DYING INDIAN: TOMO-CHEQUI

In this poem, in parts of "Pictures of Columbus," and in many other poems, Freneau stresses the romantic picturesqueness of the noble savage who is regarded as benevolent and as untainted by the evil which is attributed to civilization. In other poems, however, such as "The Indian Convert," the Indian is viewed not through primitivistic but through realistic eyes as barbarous and cruel. This bifurcated attitude toward the Indian is characteristic of Freneau's transitional position. For the backgrounds see F. E. Farley in *Anniversary Papers by the Colleagues and Pupils of George Lyman Kittredge*, pp. 251–260 (Boston, 1913); Benjamin Bissell, *The American Indian in English Literature of the Eighteenth Century*, Yale Studies in English, LXVIII (New Haven, 1925); Hoxie Fairchild, *The Noble Savage; A Study in Romantic Naturalism* (New York, 1928); A. Keiser, *The Indian in American Literature* (New York, 1933).

Page 52. ON THE SLEEP OF PLANTS

This poem illustrates Freneau's belief, shared with Erasmus Darwin, whom he admitted imitating (C. F. Heartman's *Unpublished Freneauana*, New York, 1918), in the kinship of man and nature. Compare Freneau's view of 1790 that the plant

"enjoys her little span
With *Reason*, only less complete
Than that which makes the boast of *man*,"

with Wordsworth's view eight years *later*, in "Lines Written in Early Spring," that

"every flower
Enjoys the air it breathes."

If Freneau seems at times to anticipate the views of the English romanticists, or at least to be philosophically parallel to them, the fact is perhaps explained by his having been influenced by the same currents of thought which influenced them. This is especially true as regards the political thought of Freneau and Shelley.

TO THE PUBLIC

This poem appeared in the first number of Freneau's *National Gazette* (Oct. 31, 1791), a militantly Jeffersonian paper attacking Fenno's Federalistic *Gazette of the United States*. On the history and backgrounds of this journalistic conflict see studies cited in Bibliography above by Forman, Woodbury, and Payne.

TO MY BOOK

When this poem was first published in the *National Gazette,* August 4, 1792, a note called attention to the following attack: "'The National Gazette is the vehicle of party spleen and opposition to the great principles of order, virtue, and religion.' Gaz. U. States." It should be noted then that in ll. 12–16 Freneau is quoting his opponents' words — in paraphrase — and ridiculing them.

Page 53. ON MR. PAINE'S *RIGHTS OF MAN*

Thomas Paine (1737–1809) wrote *Rights of Man* (1791–1792) as a democratic defense of the French Revolution in answer to Edmund Burke's hostile *Reflections on the French Revolution* (1790). In these two important books one has embodied respectively the radical and the conservative patterns of ideas which divided contemporaries. On Paine see M. D. Conway's *The Life of Thomas* Paine (New York, 1892) and H. H. Clark's "Toward a Reinterpretation of Thomas Paine," *American Literature,* V, 133–145 (May, 1933). Freneau helped to broadcast Paine's political and religious ideas, which radiate from scientific deism as a core, and which are very similar to his own.

Page 54. ON THE DEATH OF A REPUBLICAN PRINTER

This poem on a printer who had broadcast democratic ideas in the West, and "Crispin's Answer," together with many other poems such as that "On the Emigration to America and Peopling the Western Country," illustrate Freneau's devotion to the frontier as the home of democracy. It should be noted that Freneau became the spokesman of the dissenting, deistic, agrarian, anti-capitalistic, anti-British, optimistic frontier, that he welcomed foreigners escaping from European despotism, and that as an exponent of French philosophical and political views he helped to bring about that union of physical and philosophical conditions which has inspired much that is distinctive in American democracy. On the backgrounds see F. J. Turner, *The Frontier in American History* (New York, 1921); F. L. Paxson, *History of the American Frontier* (Boston, 1924); and Lucy Hazard, *The Frontier in American Literature* (New York, 1927).

Page 55. ON THE ANNIVERSARY OF THE STORMING OF THE BASTILLE

With some half-dozen other poems of Freneau's on the French Revolution and its devotion to liberty, fraternity, and equality, this illustrates the manner in which, with his heroes Jefferson and Thomas Paine, Freneau sympathized with French liberalism and helped as the journalist of Jeffersonian and French democracy to popularize French thought in America. S. E. Forman concludes in his extensive study of "The Political Activities of Philip Freneau" that "Freneau's paper [*The National Gazette*] did much to give a French coloring to our political philosophy. The doctrines of liberty, fraternity, equality, of equal rights to all and special privilege to none, were unwelcome to many minds in Freneau's day, yet this was the keynote of all Freneau's writings. The editor of the National Gazette was the schoolmaster who drilled Jeffersonian or French democracy into the minds—willing or unwilling—of the American people." (*Johns Hopkins University Studies in Historical and Political Science,* Series XX, Nos. 9–10, 1902.) Howard Mumford Jones's *America and French Culture* (Chapel Hill, N. C., 1927) is a monumental study of French influence, which was strongest about 1793 in Philadelphia where Freneau's office on High Street was the headquarters for those who sympathized with the French philosophy. For general backgrounds see Edward Dowden's *The French Revolution and English Literature* (New York, 1897); C. D. Hazen's *Contemporary Opinion* [in America] *of the French Revolution* (Baltimore, 1897); Charles Cestre's *La Révolution Française et les Poètes Anglaises, 1789–1809* (Dijon, 1905); A. E. Hancock's *The French Revolution and the English Poets* (New York, 1899).

Page 57. ON THE RELIGION OF NATURE

In this and the two preceding poems, as well as in "The Power of Fancy" Freneau expresses a religious view which is classified as deism. He revolted from the Calvinistic belief in the Trinity, in a fickle and capricious divine intervention, in the divinity of Christ, in the Bible as the revelation of God, in total depravity, the elect, and predestination. He believed in one God, a Creator, who had established in the creation (nature), which was his only revelation, immutable laws with which he was powerless to interfere; he believed that men shared the cosmic harmony which Newton had found in nature, that man was naturally altruistic (see "Reflections," ll. 63–67), that man had freedom of the will, and that evil had resulted mainly from social institutions. It should be noted that to Freneau, as to Pope and Paine, nature meant Newtonian law and order, and progress involved the recovery of this eternal, uniformitarian law and order obscured by artificial or corrupt institutions. Freneau had read earlier deists such as Alexander Pope (see his *Essay on Man,* 1734), and he was familiar with American deists such as Franklin and Paine. For the backgrounds see Leslie Stephen's *History of English Thought in the Eighteenth Century* (London, 1902); I. W. Riley's *American Philosophy: The Early Schools* (New York, 1907); and G. A. Koch's *Republican Religion: The American Revolution and the Cult of Reason* (New York, 1933). The student should consider carefully the extent to which the turn from Puritanism to Deism involved a change in fundamental assumptions which influenced the political, religious, social, economic, educational, and literary life of the nation. He should consider, also, the extent to which the deistic view of one deity revealed in harmonious and immutable laws of nature paved the way for Emerson's belief in the Over-Soul as "the law alive and beautiful."

ADVICE TO AUTHORS

A Note on Freneau's Poetic Theories

It is hoped that the student will begin his study of these American poets by trying to read and interpret them sympathetically in the light of what they themselves aimed to do. It is essential, therefore, that each poet's literary theories should be understood as a guide to an understanding of his practice.

Freneau's literary theories await exhaustive study. From scattered sources we can suggest here, however, a few of his main theories. The extent to which these were nourished by those of other literary masters may be studied in part in the light of what is known of his reading; see bibliography under Pattee, Beatty, and Clark. In keeping with his general transitional character, his poetic theories are transitional, partly neo-classical and partly romantic, and they embody in part the parallel English conflict in aesthetic theories and the intermingling of uniformitarianism (cf. Pope), aesthetic primitivism, and the cult of the unique, strange, and national (cf. parts of Edward Young, Addison, Goldsmith, and Hugh Blair). Expositions of the theories of Freneau's English contemporaries will be found analyzed in A. Bosker's *Literary Criticism in the Age of Johnson* (1930).

First as an apostle of deism, which is the core of his thought, he appeals to the universal light of nature which he regarded as guiding all men without respect to nationality or culture. He also resembles the theorists of the Age of Pope in his love of satire for practical purposes. "To My Book" boasts a poetry "applied" to "the people's, to Freedom's side," and "hostile to garter, ribbon, crown, and star," to "every claim of well-born wights." He glories in the ability to further the cause of freedom by creating satirical poems

"So full of invective, and loaded with spleen,
So sneeringly smart, and so hellishly keen."

He reminds readers that his lines, "Occasioned by a Legislation Bill Proposing a Tax upon Newspapers" (1791), "did some good" in the revolutionary hour of need, and he proceeds to satirize attempts to limit newspapers to "courtly stuff" (cf. Fenno, editor of *The Gazette of the United States*), to prevent "the common herd" from viewing "the state machine" from "behind the scene." "To the Public," which ushered in *The National Gazette* (Oct. 31, 1791), promises to please both "the grave and the gay" by truth concisely presented with reference to contemporary political affairs:

"With a code of new doctrines the universe rings,
And *Paine* is addressing strange sermons to kings."

And Freneau heralded the newspaper *The Time-Piece*, of which he was editor, by a statement of his literary aims in "Prefatory Lines to a Periodical Publication" (Mar. 13, 1791): not without "the pepper of satire," he is forever prepared "in the service of freedom," confident that "the trade of an author importance may claim" since European tyranny falls before enlightenment; in order, then, to advance "a new system of things," he adapts his "style . . . to the taste of the day."

Second, Freneau read and has much in common with aesthetic primitivists and emotional lyrists such as the Wartons, Akenside, and Goldsmith. When his satirical bitterness and vindictiveness reaps its reward, he is prone to deplore his countrymen's lack of appreciation as in "To Zoilus" and "To an Author" (1788). In the latter the satirist and rationalist bemoans the fact that "an age employed in edging steel / Can no poetic raptures feel," that he dwells "where rigid Reason reigns alone, / Where lovely Fancy has no sway," aided by "magic forms," solitude, leisure, and shaded streams. "A Satire in Answer to a Hostile Attack" (1775) abuses his critics, but expresses his decision to descend to the sea "with weary steps" to seek romantic and "distant isles" wherein to "court in softer shades the unwilling muse." "To Sylvius: On the Folly of Writing Poetry" (1788) pities the neglect, poverty, and woes of "the scribbling tribe," since he thinks even Chaucer, Spenser, and Shakespeare are forgotten by a philistine age. Hurt by the critic's conceit and the merchant's indifference, he urges escape to Neptune where poets may "ease the aching heart." His "Power of Fancy," which cites Ossian, has interesting parallels to Joseph Warton's "Ode to Fancy" (1746), and is in the verse form of Milton's "Il Penseroso," suggests his delight in the fickleness and caprice of fancy as related to the strange in nature.

In the third place, Freneau is one of our earliest advocates of an anti-European and anti-traditional Americanism and nationalistic uniqueness. It should be noted that while the struggle for our political independence undoubtedly reinforced this trend in Freneau, it was a trend in line with that of English theorists expressed *before* the Revolution, and may have been suggested by their stress on differences between nations (cf. Goldsmith, *The Citizen of the World*) and by their advocacy that a poet treat local themes. Freneau's nationalism in "The Rising Glory of America" (1775) is reiterated in the same year in "A Satire in Answer to a Hostile Attack" (originally entitled "MacSwiggen"):

"Blessed be our western world—its scenes conspire
To raise a poet's fancy and his fire,
Lo, blue-topt mountains to the skies ascend!
Lo, shady forests to the breezes bend!
See mighty streams meandering to the main!
See lambs and lambkins sport on every plain!
The spotted herds in flowery meadows see!"

Thus, partly, perhaps, through the European deistic faith that nature is a divine revelation, Freneau turns from those who would "prove from scripture what it never meant" to find "charms in all that nature yields" in America:

"All that we see, about, abroad,
What is it all, but nature's God?"

In "Literary Importation" (1788) he exclaims,

"Can we never be thought to have learning or grace
Unless it be brought from that horrible place
Where tyranny reigns . . ."

"Advice to Authors" (1788) suggests primitivistic theorists such as Edward Young (*Conjectures on Original Composition*, 1759) in its anti-traditional insistence that "a mere scholar and an original author are two animals as different from each other as a fresh and salt water sailor [*sic*], that the "original author" does not write consciously in the light of literary precedent but "he knows not how" and in the light of an "impelling flame of inspiration." He says "sprightliness of fancy and elevation of soul . . . alone constitute an author," and he attacks patronage and urges "independence of spirit" and "a decent pride." The essay is mainly, however, a plea for literary nationalism: "our own natural manufactures ought to be primarily attended to and encouraged," and a tax levied on imported authors.

Concurrently with this anti-traditionalism and this shrill nationalism, Freneau increasingly advocated in practice and theory a simple, concrete, genuine diction, a revolt against what Wordsworth called "the gaudy and inane phraseology" of Pope. Freneau's "Epistle from Dr. Franklin (deceased) to his Poetical Panegyrists, on some of their Absurd Compliments" (1790) attacks the pathetic fallacy and the common grandiloquent manner illustrated in poets saying "nature wept" for the deceased, that the snow was his "winding sheet."

"Poets, I pray you . . .
That reason should your pens direct,
Or else you pay me no respect.

Let reason be your constant rule,
And Nature, trust me, is no fool."

WILLIAM CULLEN BRYANT

CHRONOLOGY

1794 Born, Cummington, Mass., Nov. 3. Father a physician and a strong Federalist.

1808 Published *The Embargo*, a satire attacking Jefferson.

1810–11 Studied at Williams College.

1811 First draft of "Thanatopsis."

1811–14 Studied law.

1815–16 Admitted to the bar; practised law in Plainfield.

1816–25 Practiced law in Great Barrington, Mass., and held various town offices.

1816 Published "Early American Verse," attacking its imitativeness.

1817 Published "Thanatopsis," in *North American Review*.

1821 Married Frances Fairchild. Delivered *The Ages* as Phi Beta Kappa poem at Harvard. Published *Poems*.

1824–25 Wrote many poems for the *United States Literary Gazette* of Boston.

1825 Gave up law and moved to New York, becoming joint editor of the *New-York Review*.

1826–27 Became joint editor of the *United States Review*. Delivered his *Lectures on Poetry* before the Athenæum Society.

1829–78 After serving as assistant editor of the *New York Evening Post* in 1827–28, Bryant became its editor-in-chief, assisted by John Bigelow and Parke Godwin. Bryant's editorship, in which he urged free trade and abolition, brought him a considerable fortune. He made *The Post* the greatest American newspaper of the time.

1832 His *Poems* published in New York, and (under Irving's editorship) in London. Visited Illinois. Wrote short stories.

1834–36 First of Bryant's six trips to Europe.

1842 *The Fountain and Other Poems*.

1843 Residence at Roslyn, Long Island.

1844 *The White-Footed Deer and Other Poems*.

1845 To Europe.

1849 To Europe, the trip resulting in *Letters of a Traveller*, 1850.

1852 *A Discourse on the Life and Genius of James Fenimore Cooper*.

1852–53 To Europe and the Near East.

1855 Helped form the Republican Party, of which he became an influential member.

1857–58 To Europe. Had a Unitarian clergyman baptize him in Naples. Trip resulted in a second series of *Letters of a Traveller*, 1859.

1859–65 As journalist and poet Bryant offered powerful support of the Union and the Civil War. He had presided at Lincoln's address in Cooper Union, New York, in 1859.

1864 Published *Thirty Poems* and (privately) *Hymns*.

1866 Death of Mrs. Bryant.

1866–67 To Europe. Began translating Homer to divert mind from sorrow. Widely popular as an orator on literary and civic affairs.

1869 Eulogy of Fitz-Greene Halleck, a fellow poet. Published *Letters from the East*, based on his travels.

1870 Published *The Iliad of Homer*, a translation in blank verse.

1871–72 *The Odyssey of Homer*. Edited *A Library of Poetry and Song*, with an introduction on "Poets and Poetry of the English Language." Speech at Williams College attacking Darwinism.

1878 Address on Mazzini. Died in New York, June 12.

BIBLIOGRAPHY

I. Bibliography

Sturges, H. C. *Chronologies of the Life and Writings of William Cullen Bryant, with a Bibliography of His Works in Prose and Verse*. New York. 1903. Also in *Poetical Works*. Roslyn Edition. New York: 1903. (This is the most complete bibliography, giving the individual poems in the supposed order of composition, the most important editions, and the separate publications in verse and prose. It contains some errors, however, which have been corrected by A. H. Herrick and by Tremaine McDowell (see below).

Pang, C. M. *The Cambridge History of American Literature*. New York: 1917. I, 517–521. (The brief list of critical items about Bryant does not extend beyond 1911.)

Herrick, A. H. "The Chronology of a Group of Poems by W. C. Bryant," *Modern Language Notes*, XXXII, 180–182 (March, 1917). (Corrects errors in the dates of seven poems as given by Sturges and Godwin.)

McDowell, Tremaine. *William Cullen Bryant*. American Writers Series. New York: 1935. (The footnotes and the notes contain much fresh information regarding the dates of the first publication of Bryant's poems. The selected bibliography, pp. lxxiii–lxxxii, lists all important studies of Bryant to the present and contains descriptive and judicial comments on each item, by the recognized authority on the subject.)

II. Text

The Poetical Works of William Cullen Bryant. New York: 1876. (Since this edition was the last which Bryant supervised, it is the best source for the text of his poems.)

The Poetical Works of William Cullen Bryant. New York: 1883. 2 vols. (These constitute vols. 3 and 4 of *The Life and Writings of William Cullen Bryant*. Parke Godwin, the editor, added to the poems in the earlier volumes a number of translations, hymns, and some previously unpublished poems. Godwin made some unwarranted but slight textual changes. Helpful notes.)

Prose Writings of William Cullen Bryant. New York: 1884. 2 vols. (These constitute vols. 5 and 6 of *The Life and Writings*, edited by Godwin, who made slight changes in the prose.)

The Early Poems of William Cullen Bryant. New York: 1893. (Contains no poems not in Godwin's *Biography of William Cullen Bryant* or in the *Poetical Works*, edited by Godwin. See McDowell's "The Juvenile Verse of William Cullen Bryant," in Bibliography below.)

The Poetical Works of William Cullen Bryant. New York: 1903. Roslyn Edition. (Contains more poems than any other one volume, but without Godwin's notes. Contains also R. H. Stoddard's "Memoir" and H. C. Sturges's "Chronologies.")

William Cullen Bryant, ed. by Tremaine McDowell. American Writers Series. New York: 1935. (Contains "twelve uncollected pieces of prose, four uncollected poems, and seven unpublished poems.")

(Bryant's volumes of travel and translation will be found listed in the Chronology, above.)

III. Biography and Criticism

Allen, G. W. *American Prosody.* New York: 1935, pp. 27–55. (Detailed scholarly survey of Bryant's metrical practice in the light of his poetic theories. Indispensable.)

Bailey, E. J. "Bryant," in *Religious Thought in the Greater American Poets.* Boston: 1922, pp. 10–31. (A competent but somewhat verbose survey, dealing with the four sources of Bryant's religious belief—the Bible, inward promptings, nature, and history—and his view of God, the Holy Ghost, Christ, life, death, and immortality. Although not a Trinitarian, Bryant was strongly influenced by the broad tradition of dualistic Christianity.)

Banks, L. A. *The Religious Life of Famous Americans.* New York: 1904, pp. 211–220. (Describes Bryant's religious practices, with a few anecdotes.)

Bartlett, D. W. "Bryant," in *Modern Agitators.* New York: 1855 pp., 183–192. (Shows that contemporaries recognized Bryant as an influential reformer.)

Bigelow, John. *William Cullen Bryant.* American Men of Letters Series. Boston: 1890. (One of the standard biographies, this is especially valuable because Bigelow, Bryant's associate on the *Post*, draws upon personal memories in treating Bryant's editorial and political activities. See especially pp. 70–116 and 200–257. Ch. VII, pp. 117–175, deals with "The Poet.")

Bradley, W. A. *William Cullen Bryant.* English Men of Letters Series. New York: 1905. (Although Bradley may emphasize a bit disproportionately Bryant's debt to the Christian [Puritan] and the classical traditions, the debt is important. This book contains much judicious criticism of a general sort. The biographical facts are drawn from Godwin and Bigelow.)

Brenner, Rica. "William Cullen Bryant," in *Twelve American Poets before 1900.* New York: 1933, pp. 23–47. (Sympathetic appreciation, mostly biographical, with a few scattered comments on religious, political, and literary theories; brief treatment of Bryant as a poet of "over-emphasized" intellectual appeal and of nature, with the conclusion that he "was essentially an ethical poet.")

Bryant Centennial. Cummington, August the Sixteenth, 1894. Springfield, Mass.: [1894?]. (Eulogies and reminiscences.)

Bryant Festival at "The Century." New York: 1865. (Praise by contemporary writers.)

Cairns, W. B. *British Criticisms of American Writings, 1815–1833.* Madison, Wis.: 1922, pp. 158–164, and *passim.* (A valuable guide to, and summary of, early English reactions to Bryant, with extensive quotations. See also Moulton and MacDowell, below.)

Charvat, William. *Origins of American Critical Thought, 1810–1835.* Philadelphia: 1935. (Although only two or three pages of this dissertation are devoted to Bryant, it contains much valuable background material and emphasizes the influence in America of the Scotch critics Kames and Blair.)

Collins, J. C. "Poetry and Poets of America," in *Studies in Poetry and Criticism.* London: 1905, pp. 1–77. (A distinguished English critic renders a notable tribute to Bryant for his treatment of nature and his originality.)

Cheney, J. V. "William Cullen Bryant," in *That Dome in Air.* Chicago: 1895, pp. 127–143. (Conventional stress on Bryant's coldness and narrowness. Says Bryant is a painter of nature but a priest of morals, that he relied not on inspiration or passion but on meditation. Discursive.)

Curtis, G. W. *The Life, Character, and Writings of William Cullen Bryant.* New York: [1879]. (A memorial tribute based on personal acquaintance.)

Foerster, Norman. "Bryant," in *Nature in American Literature.* New York: 1923, pp. 1–19. (The most detailed analysis of Bryant's treatment of various aspects of nature. Shows how Bryant differs from romantic pantheists. "His God is not in the landscape, nor in the creative mind of the poet . . . More distinctly than any other of the greater American poets, Bryant brings into our literature the Puritan spirit" [pp. 17–19]. Judicious.)

Glicksberg, C. I. "William Cullen Bryant and Fanny Wright," *American Literature*, VI, 427–432 (Jan., 1935). (Prints for the first time Bryant's clever satiric "Ode to Miss Frances

Wright," with his editorial comment in the *Post* [Jan. 10, 1829]. In condemning Miss Wright's feminism and her assaults on revealed religion, Bryant shows that he was not as "liberal" as some have thought.)

—— "Bryant and the *United States Review*," *New England Quarterly*, VII, 687–701 (Dec., 1934). (Identifies two literary notices by Bryant in this *Review*, of which he was joint editor in 1826–1827.)

—— "William Cullen Bryant and Communism," *Modern Monthly*, VIII, 353–359 (July, 1934). (Bryant was not a communist, but a sensible liberal. Mr. Glicksberg holds that Bryant was not a utopian, and that he distrusted panaceas.)

—— "William Cullen Bryant, a Reinterpretation," *Revue Anglo-Américaine*, XI, 495–504 (August, 1934). (Although Bryant "was not at one with himself" because of the conflict "between life in the city and life in the country, between journalism and poetry, between Nature and politics," this unresolved conflict made his life "more rounded and fruitful" than generally supposed and resulted in his transferring to journalism a poetic idealism which rendered him an influential "fighter in the great cause of human freedom." A stimulating general discussion.)

—— "Bryant, the Poet of Humor," *Americana*, XXIX, 364–374 (July, 1935). (Some of Bryant's poems in the *Post* are identified, and extracts from two unpublished letters by Charles Sedgwick to Bryant are printed.)

Godwin, Parke. *A Biography of William Cullen Bryant, with Extracts from His Private Correspondence*. New York: 1883. 2 vols. (Published as the first two volumes of the *Life and Writings*. The most complete and fundamental biography, with many hitherto unpublished letters and poems. Godwin was associated with Bryant on the *Post* and became his son-in-law. Supplemented by various articles by McDowell—see below.)

Gourmont, Rémy de. *Deux Poètes de la Nature: Bryant et Emerson*. Paris: 1925, pp. 25–50. (Contains a stimulating discussion of Bryant's concern with death.)

Herrick, A. H. "William Cullen Bryants Beziehungen zur Deutschen Dichtung," *Modern Language Notes*, XXXII, 344–351 (June, 1917). (A scholarly assembly of references showing Bryant's considerable debt to and interest in German culture.)

Herrick, M. T. "Rhetoric and Poetry in Bryant," *American Literature*, VII, 188–194 (May, 1935). (A scholarly discussion showing that in theory and practice Bryant, in accord with his age, favored eloquence that was rhetorical, although he surpassed his age in distinguishing somewhat between rhetoric and pure poetry as simple, sensuous, and passionate. See also Charvat and Allen.)

Hervey, J. L. "Bryant and 'The New Poetry,'" *Dial*, LIX, 92–93 (Aug. 15, 1915); "A Few Facts about Bryant," *ibid.*, 361–363 (Oct. 28, 1915); and "Some Further Remarks about Bryant," *ibid.*, 555–557 (Dec. 9, 1915). (Vigorous replies to Miss Harriet Monroe's disparagement of Bryant—see below.)

Irving, Washington. Preface to Bryant's *Poems* (London: 1832), pp. iii–vi. (Praise of Bryant's writings as "essentially American" and as distinguished for "a purity of morals, an elevation and refinement of thought, and a terseness and elegance of diction." Reprinted in McDowell's *Bryant*, pp. 375–376.)

Johnson, W. F. "Thanatopsis, Old and New," *North American Review*, CCXXIV, 566–572 (Nov., 1927). (A comparison of the original and subsequent versions of "Thanatopsis," with discussion of the revisions. See also Van Doren, below.)

Kreymborg, Alfred. "Forefather Bryant," in *Our Singing Strength*. New York: 1929, pp. 27–40. (A somewhat unsympathetic essay, partly biographical and partly impressionistic.)

Leonard, W. E. "Bryant," in *Cambridge History of American Literature*. New York: 1917. I, 260–278. (The best brief interpretation and criticism of Bryant's mind and art.)

Lewis, C. T. "Mr. Bryant's Translation of The Iliad," *North American Review*, CXII, 328–370 (April, 1871). (A judicious article concluding that Bryant's translation is the best available. Shows Bryant's deep understanding of the classical tradition.)

McDowell, Tremaine. "The Ancestry of William Cullen Bryant," *Americana*, XXII, 408–420 (Oct., 1928).

—— "Cullen Bryant Prepares for College," *South Atlantic Quarterly*, XXX, 125–133 (April, 1931).

—— "Cullen Bryant at Williams College," *New England Quarterly*, I, 443–466 (Oct., 1928).

—— "William Cullen Bryant and Yale," *New England Quarterly*, III, 706–716 (Oct., 1930). (A scholarly article, printing some hitherto unpublished early letters.)

—— "The Juvenile Verse of William Cullen Bryant," *Studies in Philology*, XXVI, 96–116 (Jan., 1929). (An important scholarly contribution, printing some hitherto unpublished verse and discussing Bryant's treatment of five themes from 1803 to 1809—Religion, Satire, Pastoralism, Federalistic Politics, and the Classics.)

—— "Bryant and *The North American Review*," *American Literature*, I, 14–26 (March, 1929). (A scholarly survey, showing that by publishing his early verse and prose and encouraging him, the editors of the *Review* kept young Bryant within the field of *belles-lettres* during the critical period from 1816 to 1821, and "made it certain that, during the half-century which followed, the man Bryant would never again consider desertion of the muse.")

—— *Bryant*. New York: 1935. (The closely-documented introduction, pp. xiii–lxviii, offers the best available analysis of the development of Bryant's political, religious, social, and literary theories considered in their genetic interrelations. Stress is laid on Bryant's liberalism. He is regarded as having evolved from Federalism, Calvinism, and Classicism to Democracy, Unitarianism, and Romanticism. An appendix, pp. 363–388, reprints extracts from thirteen contemporary reviews and essays, enabling one to trace the growth of his reputation from 1808 to 1864. There is also a full list, pp. 359–362, of literary articles and addresses by Bryant, many of which are uncollected.)

Monroe, Harriet. "Aere Perennius," *Poetry*, VI, 197–200 (July, 1915). (An attack on Bryant, replied to by J. L. Hervey [see above], to whom Miss Monroe replied in "Bryant and the New Poetry," *Dial*, LIX, 314–315 [Oct. 14, 1915] and "William Cullen Bryant Again," *ibid.*, 479–480 [Nov. 25, 1915].)

Moulton, C. W. (editor). *Library of Literary Criticism of English and American Authors*. New York: 1910. VII, 109–128. (A convenient assembly of critical comments enabling one to trace Bryant's later reputation as a poet. See Cairns and McDowell, above.)

Nevins, Allan. *The Evening Post: A Century of Journalism*. New York: 1922. (The most extensive account of Bryant's journalistic work and his championship of abolition, Unionism and other liberal ideals. By one of the leading historical authorities on that period.)

Otto, Walther. *William Cullen Bryants Poetische Werke und Übersetzungen*. Leipzig: 1903. (Although this is somewhat superficial, it is of interest because of its concern with Bryant in relation to European literatures.)

Parrington, V. L. "William Cullen Bryant, Puritan Liberal," in *The Romantic Revolution in America*. New York: 1927, pp. 238–246. (A stimulating account of Bryant's very influential political work as a journalist, with perhaps excessive stress on his liberalism, although Parrington admits "Bryant was never a Jeffersonian, perhaps not even a Jacksonian." An "economic" interpretation.)

Pattee, F. L. "The Centenary of Bryant's Poetry," in *Side-Lights on American Literature*. New York: 1922, pp. 293–326. Reprinted with slight changes in Pattee's *The First Century of American Literature*. New York: 1935, pp. 299–313. (A well-written discursive essay, generally judicious. If Bryant was influenced by Wordsworth, he was tempered by New England Puritanism. "His ideal is the Puritan one of self-realization, self-improvement, self-salvation . . . He was not of the nineteenth century at all.")

Phelps, W. L. "Bryant," in *Howells, James, Bryant and other Essays*. New York: 1924, pp. 1–30.

Poe, E. A. Review of Bryant's *Poems* (New York: 1836), *Southern Literary Messenger*, III, 41–49 (Jan., 1837); "A Notice of William Cullen Bryant," *Burton's Gentleman's Magazine*, VI, 203–205 (May, 1840); review of Bryant's *Complete Poetical Works* (1846), *Godey's Magazine and Lady's Book*, XXXII, 182–186 (April, 1846). These three articles are found in *The Complete Works of Edgar Allen Poe* (New York: 1902, Monticello Edition), IX, 268–305; X, 85–91; XIII, 125–141. (The first is enthusiastic in its praise of Bryant, the second regards him as correct, and the third is lukewarm.)

Russell, J. A. "The Romantic Indian in Bryant's Poetry," *Education*, XLVIII, 642–649 (June, 1928). (A brief survey, concluding that "in the main he had the romantic rather than the realistic conception of the aborigine.")

Schick, J. S. "William Cullen Bryant and Théophile Gautier," *Modern Language Journal*, XVII, 260–267 (Jan., 1933). (Shows similarities between Bryant's "The Poet" and Gautier's "L'Art.")

Sedgwick, H. D., Jr. "Bryant's Permanent Contribution to Literature," *Atlantic Monthly*, LXXIX, 539–549 (April, 1897). (A severely judicial essay.)

Stedman, E. C. "Mr. Bryant's 'Thirty Poems,'" *Round Table*, I, 73–74 (Jan. 16, 1864). This review was included in *Genius and Other Essays*. New York: 1911, pp. 111–124. (In this same volume, pp. 125–140, Stedman also discussed Bryant's "Homer.")

—— "William Cullen Bryant," in *Poets of America*. Boston: 1885, pp. 62–94. (A judicious and comprehensive critique, considering in general terms both Bryant's journalism and his poetry. Stedman finds him deficient, as a poet, in passion, humor, and individuality, and he concludes that his distinctive power lay in "the *elemental quality* of his song" [p. 81].)

Stewart, George, Jr. *Evenings in the Library*. St. John, N.B.: 1878, pp. 161–193.

Strong, A. H. "William Cullen Bryant," in *American Poets and Their Theology*. Philadelphia: 1916, pp. 3–48. (Somewhat piously verbose, but valuable. Presents evidence to show that, although Bryant may have believed in Christ's divinity rather than his absolute deity, he never completely outgrew his early Puritanism. Unlike the pantheists, he "never confounded" God and nature. Unlike the humanitarians who traced evil to institutions, Bryant traced it to the "sinfulness" of the individual. See also Bailey, McDowell, Foerster, Bradley, and Voigt.)

Van Doren, Carl. "The Growth of 'Thanatopsis,'" *Nation*, CI, 432–433 (Oct. 7, 1915). (Shows that while Bryant had originally spoken in his own person a subjective dread, he revised the poem so as to have the sentiments put into the mouth of nature, giving them a classical objectivity "as pagan as Lucretius." See also McDowell's *Bryant*, pp. xxv ff. and 389–391.)

Voigt, G. P. "Bryant," in *The Religious and Ethical Element in the Major American Poets.* Bulletin of the Graduate School of the University of South Carolina, No. I, June 1, 1925, pp. 13–27. (Concludes that Bryant was "not only an earnest Christian but a faithful churchman as well; that while he passed from the stern sublimity of a Puritan atmosphere into the catholicity and tolerance of Unitarianism, he retained his Calvinistic faith in the sovereignty of a just God and in the redemptive work of a Divine Christ, along with his vivid sense of Death as the gateway to eternity; that while anything but a bigot he was none the less devout; that his keen sense of justice, his passion for freedom and righteousness, and his confidence in the power of love and brotherhood, made him a crusader against wrong, an apostle of holiness, and a prophet of universal peace.")

Wilkinson, W. C. *A Free Lance in the Field of Life and Letters.* New York: 1874, pp. 184–254. (A sharply trenchant critique, considering not only Bryant's ideas but his metrics and his translation of the *Iliad* in relation to other translations. Interesting insistence upon Bryant's classical qualities, such as simplicity and repose, by a distinguished classical scholar.)

Wilson, J. G. "William Cullen Bryant," in *Bryant and His Friends.* New York: 1886, pp. 11–127. (A Boswellian assembly of interesting anecdotes, brought together by one of Bryant's intimate friends.)

NOTES

ROMANTICISM

Since American poets from Bryant to Whitman lived during the period of European romanticism and are roughly classified as romanticists, it may be of interest to ascertain to what extent each one embodies the elements of romanticism as set forth in the generally accepted definition by Dr. Paul Kaufman, who says that by romance "we mean either the temper or the expression in literature of some form of idealization, of departure from the commonplace and portrayal of the exceptional, the marvelous, the mysterious; of life conceived in high colors and in more striking aspects. This we mean when we characterize the American drama and prose fiction during the period in question as romantic. But the romantic movement in Europe expresses far more than this quality; and no simple formula will comprehend its varied impulses. Let us say that it includes a recovery of the past as an effort to broaden emotional and imaginative outlooks; the revolt against tradition and authority in whatever area of human concern; humanitarian sympathy including new interests in humble life and assertion of individual rights; a fresh perception of nature; the renascence of wonder; and in general an ascendancy of feeling and imagination. And all these we may properly apply in testing American literature. To these we may add what we may call a patriotic romanticism, expressing itself in declarations of literary independence, which began during the Revolution, and also deliberately expressing American scenes and themes, in which latter respect it bears striking parallel to the first stages of German romanticism."—*The Reinterpretation of American Literature* (ed. Norman Foerster). New York: 1928, pp. 120–121.

On English backgrounds see Ernest Bernbaum's *Guide through the Romantic Movement* (New York: 1930). What elements of current English romanticism did American poets accept? What factors modified this movement in America?

THE GROWTH OF BRYANT'S MIND

Tremaine McDowell concludes, as a result of his extensive studies, that the key to an understanding of the development of Bryant's mind is his gradual turn from his native Federalism, Calvinism, and Classicism to his later Democracy, Unitarianism, and Romanticism, and his successful achieving of a "final mediation" between these two sets of formative factors. (See Introduction to *Bryant*, in American Writers Series.) One of the chief problems or difficulties in the accurate interpretation of Bryant is that of paying due regard to *both* the conservative *and* the radical aspects of his thought. It should also be noted that besides being a poet Bryant was (1) a literary critic or theorizer and (2) an editor devoted to social and political justice, and that a knowledge of these interests helps one to place his poetry in its proper contexture of his complete pattern of thought.

Page 61. THANATOPSIS

Bryant described his reading before writing this poem as follows: "About this time my father brought home, I think from one of his visits to Boston, the 'Remains of Henry Kirke White,' which had been re-published in this country. I read the poems with great eagerness, and so often that I had committed several of them to memory, particularly the ode to the Rosemary. The melancholy tone which prevails in them deepened the interest with which I read them, for about that time I had, as young poets are apt to have, a liking for poetry of a querulous caste. I remember reading, at this time, that remarkable poem, Blair's 'Grave,' and dwelling with great pleasure upon its finer passages. I had the opportunity of comparing it with a poem on a kindred subject, also in blank verse, that of Bishop Porteus on 'Death,' and of observing how much the verse of the obscure Scottish minister excelled in originality of thought and vigor of expression that of the English prelate. In my father's library I found a small, thin volume of the miscellaneous poems of Southey, to which he had not called my attention, containing some of the finest of Southey's shorter poems. I read it greedily. Cowper's poems had been in my hands from an early age, and I now passed from his shorter poems, which are generally mere rhymed prose, to his 'Task,' the finer passages of which supplied a form of blank verse that captivated my admiration."—Parke Godwin, *Biography*, I, 37.

Thanatopsis was written in September or October of 1811, when he was sixteen, but it was not published until 1817. For details of publication see McDowell, "Bryant and *The North American Review*," *American Literature*, I, 14–26 (March, 1929).

In 1821, when the poem was first printed in book form, Bryant added an introduction and a conclusion. Whereas the early manuscript version of the poem had put the discussion of death into the mouth of Bryant's own "better genius," making the poem subjective, he now arranged the introduction so as to put the discussion into the mouth of Nature. On the revisions, see C. Van Doren, "The Growth of 'Thanatopsis,'" *Nation*, CI, 432–33 (Oct. 7, 1915).

Some critics have tended to regard the poem as an expression of the general spirit of Puritanism—see W. A. Bradley, p. 33, who quotes G. W. Curtis to the same effect; and N. Foerster, *Nature in American Literature*, p. 16. Other critics, however, have tended to regard the poem as the expression of a "remarkable liberalism"—see McDowell, *Bryant*, pp. xxv ff., and 391; and Van Doren, above, who finds the poem "as pagan as Lucretius."

For detailed analysis of the excellences of the blank verse in this poem—the run-on lines, the long breath-sweeps, and the attainment of variety by the occasional substitution of "Trisyllabic Feet in Iambic Measure" in accordance with Bryant's essay by that title (*Prose Writings*, I, 57–67)—see G. W. Allen, *American Prosody*, pp. 31–35.

Page 62. INSCRIPTION FOR THE ENTRANCE TO A WOOD

McDowell suggests (*op. cit.*, p. 393) that Bryant may have had in mind, in writing this poem, Southey's "Inscriptions" such as "For a Tablet on the Bank of a Stream" and "In a Forest." He calls attention to ll. 6–10 as compared with Wordsworth's "Lines Composed a Few Miles above Tintern Abbey," ll. 22–30, and Bryant's ll. 26–28 as compared with Wordwsorth's "Lines Written in Early Spring," ll. 11–12.

Bryant said that as a boy he had been so imbued with Calvinism that he had "supposed it to be the accepted belief of the religious world." For a characterization of seven of his early Calvinistic poems, see McDowell, "The Juvenile Verse of William Cullen Bryant." In the present "Inscription," note that Bryant thinks that, following "the primal curse" (l. 11), "the world is full of guilt and misery," although nature's calm may bring "a balm" to man's "sick heart."

From the artistic standpoint, note Bryant's skill in focusing descriptive details so as to produce a harmonized unity of mood.

TO A WATERFOWL

In the winter of 1815 Bryant journeyed from his birthplace to Plainfield, where he hoped to make a living as a lawyer. He later recalled, according to Godwin (*Biography*, I, 143–144), that as he walked over the hills, he felt "very forlorn and desolate indeed, not knowing what was to become of him in the big world, which grew bigger as he ascended, and yet darker with the coming on of night. The sun had already set, leaving behind it one of those brilliant seas of chrysolite and opal which often flood the New England skies; and, while he was looking upon the rosy splendor with rapt admiration, a solitary bird made wing along the illuminated horizon. He watched the lone wanderer until it was lost in the distance, asking himself whither it had come and to what far home it was flying. When he went to the house where he was to stop for the night, his mind was still full of what he had seen and felt, and he wrote these lines."

Matthew Arnold is reported to have said that he regarded "To a Waterfowl" as the finest short poem in the language. W. A. Bradley (*Bryant*, pp. 48–49) writes:

"'The Waterfowl' is a great poem, the finest expression, as we have said, of Bryant's genius. It combines that power of imaginative description which Bryant had been cultivating during the preceding months, with an intensity of emotional feeling that is very rarely felt in his poetry and is never again fused so completely with the objects that inspired it. The main criticism that has been passed upon the poem is that it is marred by didacticism. . . . But in 'The Waterfowl' the moral idea is the central inspiration. The bird presented itself at first sight to Bryant as a symbol of his own destiny, and this thought underlies the piece through the entire course of its development. Not unless we deny the existence of moral emotions and of their right to expression in poetry, can any fault be found with 'The Waterfowl,' which is an elevated and passionate utterance of man's most profound religious faith and hope in divine guidance."

Page 63. GREEN RIVER and A WINTER PIECE

Note in these two poems Bryant's retreat to the tonic and "quiet haunts" of nature when the "ills of life had chafed" his spirit. In the latter poem, written forty-five years before Whittier's "Snow-Bound," note the rich, colorful description, and the harmony of mood.

Page 65. "OH FAIREST OF THE RURAL MAIDS"

This is one of four poems Bryant addressed to Frances Fairchild, who became his wife. The poem was highly praised by Edgar Allan Poe in 1837 as "a gem, of which we cannot sufficiently express our admiration." He delighted in its "rich simplicity . . . of design and execution," which he found "strikingly perceptible in the opening and concluding lines, and in *expression* throughout. But there is," he said, "a far higher and more strictly *ideal* beauty, which it is less easy to analyze. The original conception is of the very loftiest order of true Poesy." Poe thought that the image in lines 13–14 "is one which, . . . for appropriateness, completeness, and every perfect beauty of which imagery is susceptible, has never been surpassed." Cf. Wordsworth's "Three Years She Grew."

Page 65. HYMN TO DEATH

Just as Wordsworth's brother John died while the "Ode on Intimations of Immortality" was in process of composition, so Bryant's father died just after the poet had written the first 133 lines of this "Hymn" with its "praises" of death's "nobler triumphs" as deliverer and avenger, always "on virtue's side" as "the great reformer of the world." After the news of his father's death, Bryant wrote lines 134–168 to repudiate the earlier praise of death, now regarded as "an idle revery," and to express his grief for the one who taught him in youth "the art of verse." Note that he questions death's justice (ll. 160–165), yet is confident of immortality, of a "happier life" that shall "waken" his father's "insensible dust."

Page 67. THE AGES

"The Ages" was delivered August 30, 1821, in the Old Congregational Church at Cambridge at the invitation of the Phi Beta Kappa Society of Harvard College. It was published with other poems by Bryant in a small pamphlet of 44 pages in the same year, and copied in a selection of American poetry published by Allman in London in 1822. *Blackwood's* (June, 1822, pp. 684 ff.) contained a favorable criticism.

Poe criticized "The Ages" as developing "the one improper theme of its author. The design is, 'from a survey of the past ages of the world, and of the successive advances of mankind in knowledge and virtue, to justify and confirm the hopes of the philanthropist for the future destinies of the human race.' All this would have been more rationally, because more effectually, accomplished in prose. Dismissing it as a poem (which in its general tendency it is not), one might commend the force of its argumentation but for the radical error of deducing a hope of progression from the cycles of physical nature.

"The sixth stanza is a specimen of noble versification (within the narrow limits of the iambic pentameter) . . .

"The cadences here at 'page,' 'swarms,' and 'surge,' cannot be surpassed. There are comparatively few consonants. Liquids and the softer vowels abound and the partial line after the pause at 'surge,' with the stately march of the succeeding Alexandrine, is one of the finest conceivable *finales*.

"The poem, in general, has unity, completeness. Its tone of calm, elevated and hopeful contemplation is well sustained throughout."—Poe, *Works*, ed. Stedman and Woodberry, VI, 112–113.

Bryant wrote one other poem in Spenserian stanzas, "After the Tempest" (1824), which is also interesting as having anticipated in its fifth stanza the passage in Tennyson's "Locksley Hall" beginning, "For I looked into the future. . . ."

Page 73. THE INDIAN GIRL'S LAMENT

Although Bryant, like Freneau, occasionally portrays a cruel Indian (see "The Prairies," l. 59), this poem on the Indian girl's lament for her deceased lover is essentially typical of his dozen poems on the Indian in its wistful sentimentality and picturesque fancifulness. It has been suggested that his supposed Indians were "merely the conventional heroes and heroines of romance, employed not to reveal Indian character but to act in familiar tragic episodes dear to all sentimentalists." (For discussion see McDowell, *Bryant*, pp. xlv ff.; A. Keiser, *The Indian in American Literature* (New York: 1933), pp. 178 ff.; and J. A. Russell, as noted in Bibliography, above.) Yet Bryant does not seriously accept the current romantic primitivistic faith in the natural goodness of the Indian discussed in H. N. Fairchild's *The Noble Savage* (New York: 1928).

Page 74. MUTATION

This sonnet of 1824, one of ten published by Bryant, is in the Spenserian form (i.e., ababbcbccdcdee) and "is probably the best sonnet he ever wrote," in the opinion of G. W. Allen, who surveys Bryant's pioneer work in America in this form. (See *American Prosody*, pp. 44–45.)

Page 75. "I BROKE THE SPELL THAT HELD ME LONG"

After Bryant's marriage in 1821 and resultant responsibilities, he tried to turn away from poetry to the law. But flowers, streams, stars, and sun taught him that "these and poetry are one" (l. 16), that nature is the concrete symbol by which the poet bodies forth his thought. In the second of his "Lectures on Poetry" (*Prose Writings*, I, 19), he says: "Among the most remarkable of the influences of poetry is the exhibition of those analogies and correspondences which it beholds between the things of the moral and of the natural world. I refer to its adorning and illustrating each by the other—infusing a moral sentiment into natural objects, and bringing images of visible beauty and majesty to heighten the effect of moral sentiment. Thus it binds into one all the passages of human life and connects all the varieties of human feeling with the works of creation." On Bryant's knowledge and his use of various aspects of nature in his art, see his essay "Our Native Fruits and Flowers" (*Prose Writings*, II, 194–202), and N. Foerster's analysis in *Nature in American Literature*, pp. 1–19. This poem shows that at a crucial stage in Bryant's career nature did much to make him a poet.

A FOREST HYMN

Bryant told R. H. Dana, according to the latter, that on his first reading of the *Lyrical Ballads*, by Wordsworth and Coleridge, "a thousand springs seemed to gush up at once into my heart and the face of Nature, of a sudden, to change into a strange freshness and life" (R. H. Dana's *Poems and Prose Writings*. Boston: 1833, p. 148). In "A Forest Hymn," the notion (ll. 63–66) that the "forest flower" is "an emanation of the indwelling Life" of the universe approaches the pantheism of Wordsworth's "Lines Composed a Few Miles above Tintern Abbey" (ll. 92–102), where he sees God, man, and nature "interfused." It should be noted, however, that Bryant even in this same poem believes in a personal Creator who "hath reared these venerable columns" (l. 25), and that whereas Wordsworth thinks that nature is all beneficent, that "Nature never did betray/The heart that loved her," Bryant, like the Puritan Edwards, accepts a personal Creator not only of Love but of Wrath, who "dost scare the world with tempests" and "thunderbolts," and who "drowns the villages" (ll. 102 ff.). For full discussion see N. Foerster, *op. cit.* It is important to note that, while Bryant accepted many of the more picturesque and superficial aspects of current Romanticism, he tempered its excesses with a partial allegiance to the two older traditions—Classicism and Christianity.

"A Forest Hymn" was praised by Poe for its "great rhythmical beauty."

Page 78. THE AFRICAN CHIEF

Note that, in this tragic story of the African chief who became "crazed in brain" and died as a result of becoming a "Christian's slave," Bryant indicates as early as 1825 the sympathy for the slaves which was to make him one of the most vigorous of the Abolitionists and Unionists. Compare this poem with Longfellow's "The Slave's Dream" (p. 295). Bryant left the following note on his poem: "The story of the African chief, related in this ballad, may be found in the 'African Repository' for April, 1825. The subject of it was a warrior of majestic stature, the brother of Yarradee, king of the Solima nation. He had been taken in battle, and was brought in chains for sale to the Rio Pongas, where he was exhibited in the market-place, his ankles still adorned with massy rings of gold which he wore when captured. The refusal of his captors to listen to his offers of ransom drove him mad, and he died a maniac."

On Bryant's many poems and editorials directed against slavery, see McDowell, *Bryant*, pp. xx ff., and 308 ff., as well as Allan Nevins, *The Evening Post*, pp. 145 ff. Like Lowell and Thoreau, he opposed the war with Mexico for the extension of slavery, and in 1848 he turned from the Democratic party to the radical "Barnburners" and the Free Soil party, and finally to the Republican party. As editor he attacked the Fugitive Slave Law as "the most ruffianly act ever authorized by a deliberate assembly" (quoted in Nevins, p. 246). He celebrated "The Death of Slavery" in a swelling poem by that title, comparable to Whittier's "Laus Deo."

Like Lowell, Bryant was less interested, however, in sentimental pity for the slave than in the preservation of the Union. Compare his cogent editorial, "Peaceable Secession an Absurdity" (*The Post*, Nov. 12, 1860; reprinted in McDowell, pp. 327–331), with Lowell's "E Pluribus Unum" (Lowell's *Writings*, V, 45–74).

Page 83. EARTH

In describing Italian scenery in 1834, Bryant wrote: "The grander features of the landscape . . . are beyond the power of man to injure: the towering mountain summits, the bare walls and peaks of rock piercing the sky, which, with the deep, irregular valleys, betoken, more than anything I have seen in America, an upheaving and engulfing of the original crust of this world." Says W. A. Bradley (*Bryant*, pp. 142–143): "Such traits of elemental and chaotic grandeur made always a powerful appeal to Bryant's imagination. These vast upheavals symbolized for him the stormy history of the human race and awakened a vein of profound and gloomy reflection. The mood found expression in that sombre and powerful poem, 'Earth,' which he wrote in 1834, at Pisa, and in which the following passage [ll. 12–18], describing the voices of the earth to which he listens, lying, at midnight, under a sky black with clouds, is perhaps more impressive than anything he had written since 'Thanatopsis.' . . . This is a style of writing in which Bryant has never been excelled or perhaps even equalled. No poet has ever given so well as he an imaginative sense of immensity, and of the mystery of the infinite in nature."

Page 85. THE ANTIQUITY OF FREEDOM

It should be noted that Bryant's characterization of freedom as "armed to the teeth," as "twin-born with man," and as destined to "wax stronger with the years" if proper vigilance be maintained, shows his kinship, when this poem is interpreted in the light of his prose utterances, with spokesmen of freedom such as Milton and Emerson and Lowell, with men who sought to make man not masterless but self-mastered. Bryant no doubt turned from some of the more extreme Federalistic views of his "Embargo" days, but he was always realistic enough to recognize "the frauds of men" in a world "full of guilt and misery"; he did not, like the radicals such as Paine, believe that men are naturally altruistic and that evil is caused and cured by institutions. If socialism involves the increasing interference by government with private enterprise, and the multiplication of outward coercion, Bryant places himself at the opposite pole as a political theorist. Bryant's fellow-editor and son-in-law, who shared his belief in free trade, summed up his view as follows: Government ought "to maintain the conditions of universal liberty or the equilibrium and harmony of the social forces so that the energies of the individual may the most freely act and expand, according to his own judgment, his own capacities, his own views of the duties and destinies of man here upon earth. It must not undertake directly any enterprises of its own—religious, intellectual, artistic, or economical—but it must secure a perfectly safe and open field to every kind of enterprise and to every one of its members" (Godwin, *Biography*, I, 254). It is important, when Bryant is spoken of as a liberal defender of freedom, to understand precisely what he meant by freedom.

Page 86. "OH MOTHER OF A MIGHTY RACE"

Although Bryant is usually associated with the urban capitalism of New York, he occasionally glorified the democratic spirit of the American frontier —in this poem doing so at the expense of feudalistic Europe from which he had recently returned. See also his poems, "The Prairies," "The Hunter of the West," "The Hunter of the Prairies," and "The Song of the Sower," celebrating agriculture as the basis of all life. The half-petulant attitude of the poem here reprinted is hardly typical, however, of his view of the question of primitivism versus literary tradition. His lifelong interest in books was crowned by his successful attempt in old age to make Homer available for his countrymen. For a more realistic view of the sordid and unpleasant aspects of frontier life, see his "Illinois Fifty Years Ago" (*Prose Writings*, II, 19 ff.). The subject is ably discussed in McDowell's *Bryant*, pp. xlvii–xlix. It will be recalled that in the "Hymn of the City" Bryant finds God revealed not only in the country but in the city.

Page 87. ITALY

Bryant was interested throughout life in the struggle for freedom not only in America but in Europe. Besides the "Italy" see also his poems, "Spain" (1822), "Romero" (1829), "The Song of the Greek Amazon" (1824), and "The Greek Partisan" (1825), as well as his addresses on "Italian Unity" (1871, in *Prose Writings*, II, 274–277) and "Mazzini" (1878, *ibid.*, II, 343–346). It will be recalled that he vigorously advocated free trade and that he was much interested in the international aspects of commerce. On Bryant's liking for the language, the literature, and the colorful and romantic in the life of France, Italy, and Spain (which he expressed long before Irving), see McDowell, *Bryant*, pp. liii–liv. He not only wrote much on foreign nations, but he made many translations, preceding by many years both Irving and Longfellow as an interpreter to America of European romance.

Page 88. THE POET

In "A Fable for Critics" (p. 468, l. 186) Lowell emphasized Bryant's "iceolation." The striking contrast between this charge and Bryant's demand in "The Poet" for emotional warmth and "words of flame" that will "touch the heart or fire the blood at will," is perhaps explained by the fact that Lowell was writing of Bryant in 1848 before he was so profoundly stirred by the great human issues of the Civil War as illustrated in such poems as "Our Country's Call" and "The Death of Lincoln."

ll. 37–42. Cf. Wordsworth's "The Daffodils," where the poet writes of aspects of nature as "They flash upon that inward eye."

THE FLOOD OF YEARS

Like Emerson and Whittier, Bryant is devoted not only to what he calls "the circle of eternal change/Which is the life of nature," but to the changeless life of the spirit. He recognized both Variety and Unity, and the transience of the first and the permanence of the second. In this poem, the "sturdy swain," the artisan, the student, the revellers, the armed men, "the steed and rider," "the funeral train," the "loud-voiced orator," the "kneeling crowd," the sculptor, the painter, the poet, the two lovers, the aged man, even "massive palaces" and "populous realms,"—all these varieties of temporal life—are "engulfed and lost" in "the never-ending Flood of Years," by the march of time. The Past is "a waste of waters weltering over graves," and the present and the future must be the prey of change. Yet, with Bryant's respect for human tradition, for "what the wise and good have said," he believes in the permanence of everything in history that "was good,/ Noble and truly great." (Cf. Bryant's poem, "The Past," p. 78.) He seems to believe in a personal immortality in which "hands are clasped/ In joy unspeakable." He is confident that beyond "the eternal Change" of temporal nature there is a spiritual and "everlasting Concord." Compare the view of Wordsworth after he had grown conservative and Christian—his faith in

"Authentic tidings of invisible things;
Of ebb and flow, and ever-during power;
And central peace, subsisting at the heart
Of endless agitation." (*Excursion*, IV, 1144 ff.)

Page 90. BRYANT'S POETIC THEORIES

See the selections here reprinted from "Early American Verse," "Lectures on Poetry," and "Introduction to a Library of Poetry and Song." See also notes above on "I Broke the Spell That Held Me Long" and "The Poet."

Although Bryant wrote a great deal on literary theory and was our first important literary critic, there is no extended scholarly interpretation of this phase of his work. Besides the passages here reprinted, one finds among his criticism essays on Shakespeare ("On Writing Tragedy"), Moriscan Romances, the Provençal poets, Cowley, German literature, Scott, Burns, Goethe, Schiller, the Bible, the poems of Henry Pickering, *Percy's Masque* by Hillhouse, "American Society as a Field for Fiction," "Recent Poetry," Percival, Oldham, Franklin, three long memorial addresses on his friends Irving, Halleck, and Cooper, the well-known introduction to the *Library of Poetry and Song* surveying the history of poetry, the revolutionary essay "On Trisyllabic Feet in Iambic Measure," and many others. Much of his critical prose remains uncollected in the files of the *Evening Post* and elsewhere. (On Bryant's literary judgments see Allan Nevins's *The Evening Post*, pp. 216–224.) "Early American Verse" first appeared in the *North American Review*, July, 1818. "Lectures on Poetry" were delivered before the New York Athenaeum in April, 1825, and published from notes in Bryant's *Prose* in 1884. Of the lectures here omitted, No. II is "On the Value and Uses of Poetry" as it influences and uplifts (*a*) the imagination, (*b*) the passions, and (*c*) the intellect, and No. III is "On Poetry in Its Relation to Our Age and Country," an answer to the argument that contemporary America could not produce true poetry. Analysis of Bryant's literary theories may be found in McDowell's *Bryant* (pp. lvi–lxiii) and in Charvat's *The Origins of Critical Thought, 1810–1835*. See also W. E. Sedgwick, "The Materials for an American Literature: A Critical Problem of the Early Nineteenth Century," *Harvard Studies and Notes in Philology and Literature*, XVII, 141–162 (1935).

As a literary theorist Bryant advocated (1) avoiding "a sickly and affected imitation of the peculiar manner of some of the late popular (neoclassic) poets of England"; (2) avoiding "striking novelties of expression" and "subtilties of thought, remote from the common apprehension"; (3) a preference for "a luminous style," one of "the most important requisites for a great poet"; (4) a balanced harmony of emotion, understanding, and imagination; (5) going directly to nature for imagery as a means of bodying forth ideas; (6) the guidance of literary tradition, and discriminating study of the merits and demerits of other poets; (7) the short lyric, "poems of a moderate length" (anticipating Poe); (8) a revolt against "the precepts of Lord Kames and other writers, who framed their rules of versification chiefly from the writings of Pope," in favor of the substitution of trisyllabic feet in iambic measure to obtain "more varied pauses and a greater license of prosody," "an ancient birthright of the poets [such as Spenser, Milton, and Cowley] which ought not to be given up"; (9) selection in the interest of elevation and ethical beauty; (10) a concern with the elemental and the universal, arrived at through the particular purged of its singularities. *To what extent did Bryant practice these theories?*

JOHN GREENLEAF WHITTIER

CHRONOLOGY

1807 Born in Haverhill, Mass., December 17, son of a poor Quaker farmer.

1821 Became an enthusiastic reader of Burns's poetry.

1826 Garrison, abolitionist, published Whittier's first poem in a local newspaper.

1827–28 At Haverhill Academy, supporting himself by making shoes.

1829–32 Editor of various newspapers—*American Manufacturer* (Boston), 1829; *Haverhill Gazette*, 1830; *Essex Gazette* (Haverhill), 1830; *New England Review* (Hartford), 1830–32.

1825–35 Wrote a number of romantic poems such as "The Demon's Cave" and "The Fire Ship," suggesting Byron, Scott, Burns, and Coleridge.

1831 *Legends of New England*. Sketches and poems based mainly on local scenes viewed through romantic eyes.

1833 *Justice and Expediency*. Went to the Anti-Slavery Convention in Philadelphia. Wrote anti-slavery poems for *New England Magazine* and *Liberator*.

1835–36 Member of the Massachusetts legislature.

1838–40 Edited *Pennsylvania Freeman* (Philadelphia). His office burned by mob.

1843 *Lays of My Home and Other Poems*.

1844–45 Editor of *Middlesex Standard;* stayed in Lowell six months; wrote *The Stranger in Lowell* (prose).

1846 *Voices of Freedom*.

1849 *Poems* (collected edition).

1850 *Songs of Labor and Other Poems*. Also *Old Portraits and Modern Sketches*. Declines nomination as State Senator on coalition ticket.

1854 *Literary Recreations and Miscellanies*.

1856 *The Panorama and Other Poems*.

1857 Began his contributions to the *Atlantic Monthly* with "The Gift of Tritemus" in the first number.

1863 "Barbara Frietchie" in *Atlantic* for October, and included in *In War Time and Other Poems*.

1866 *Snow-Bound*. LL.D. from Harvard.

1867 *The Tent on the Beach and Other Poems*. Becomes comparatively well-to-do.

1868 *Among the Hills and Other Poems*.

1872 "The Pennsylvania Pilgrim" (considered by Whittier his best poem).

1874 *Hazel Blossoms*.

1876 Although he kept his house in Amesbury, he spent most of his time in Danvers, Mass.

1878 *The Vision of Echard and Other Poems*.

1887 Eightieth birthday celebrated widely throughout the country.

1892 Died in New Hampshire, September 7.

BIBLIOGRAPHY

I. Bibliography

Bierstadt, E. H. "A Bibliography of the Original Editions of the Works of John Greenleaf Whittier," *Book Buyer*, N.S. xii, May–October, 1895.

Carter, G. F. "Some Little Known Whittierana," *Literary Collector*, VII, 169–172 (April, 1904).

Ristine, F. H. *The Cambridge History of American Literature*. New York: 1918. II, 436–451. (This bibliography is the most complete now available, but it will be superseded by the exhaustive bibliography of Whittier now being prepared by T. F. Currier.)

"The John Greenleaf Whittier Centenary Exhibition at the Essex Institute, Dec. 17, 1907–Jan. 31, 1908," *Essex Institute Historical Collections*, April, 1908, pp. 123–146.

The Stephen H. Wakeman Collection. 1924. (Whittier Nos. 1076–1279.) (See also Mordell and Pray below.)

II. Text

Albree, J. (ed.) *Whittier Correspondence from the Oak Knoll Collection, 1830–92*. Salem: 1911.

Pickard, S. T. *Whittier as a Politician*. Illustrated by his letters to Professor Elizur Wright, Jr., now first published. Boston: 1900. (These fifty-three pages of letters by Whittier, with Pickard's editorial comment, furnish valuable evidence of Whittier's activities as an abolitionist and astutely practical politician.)

Pray, Frances M. *A Study of Whittier's Apprenticeship as a Poet: Dealing with Poems Written between 1825 and 1835 not available in the Poet's Collected Works*. Bristol, N. H.: 1930. (Prints 109 early poems. Of these ten, signed "Ichabod," are probably not by Whittier—see Mordell, *Quaker Militant*, p. 18. A list of uncollected poems prior to 1835 is printed on pages 247–262. The introduction of about 100 pages surveys [up to 1835] general influences on Whittier, his poems inspired by reading, his poems on social and political subjects, his reflective poems, love poems, and poems on New England and its past.)

Scudder, H. E. (ed.). *The Complete Poetical Works of John Greenleaf Whittier*. Cambridge Edition. Boston: 1894. (The indispensable one-volume edition of the authorized text. The head notes are useful, as well as the notes at the back of the book. The poems follow Whittier's own topical arrangement, but the valuable "List of Mr. Whittier's Poems Arranged Chronologically" furnishes the basis for the study of the growth of his mind. The many early poems not retained by Whittier may be located through the work of Miss Pray and T. F. Currier.)

Tapley, Harriet S. (ed.) "John Greenleaf Whittier Manuscripts. The Oak Knoll Collection," *Essex Institute Historical Collections*, LXVII, 113–118 (April, 1931). (Includes 135 letters written to Mrs. Grantham, 13 unpublished poems written between 1824–1825, some manuscripts of his published works, some "jottings" on situations appropriate for verse, some publishers' proof sheets, more than 100 letters to other people, and more than 800 letters from other people to Whittier. Only a few of the letters by Whittier were published by Albree in 1911.)

The Writings of John Greenleaf Whittier. Riverside Edition. 7 vols. Boston: 1888–1889. (The standard edition, including his prose.)

III. Biography and Criticism

Allen, Gay W. *American Prosody*. New York: 1935. (Pp. 127–153 contain a detailed and comprehensive analysis of Whittier's handling of various meters and stanzas. Authoritative.)

Bailey, E. J. *Religious Thought in the Greater American Poets*. Boston: 1922. (The chapter on Whittier, pp. 70–107, presents convincing evidence to show that Emerson and Whittier "were in agreement upon a striking number of fundamental beliefs," although the latter was more mystical and more sharply dualistic. Important. See also A. H. Strong, below.)

Bartlett, David [Vaudewater Golden]. *Modern Agitators*. New York: 1855, pp. 240–265. (This account, by a contemporary of the abolition period, concludes, "We know of no man more worthy of the name of agitator.")

Brenner, Rica. *Twelve American Poets before 1900*. New York: 1933, pp. 109–142. (More of an appreciative biographical "consideration of Whittier the man than of Whittier the poet." Neglects his thought and his art.)

Carpenter, G. R. *John Greenleaf Whittier*. American Men of Letters Series. Boston: 1903. (Probably the best general life, although the much more partisan work of Mordell has superseded it in some matters of fact. Pp. 255–295 deal judiciously with Whittier as "Poet, 1860–1892.")

Chrisman, L. H. "The Spiritual Message of Whittier," in *John Ruskin, Preacher, and Other Essays*. New York: 1921, pp. 56–75. (An appreciative interpretation showing Whittier's emphasis on spirituality rather than on dogma, on elements common to all sects, and on the need of translating creeds into deeds.)

Christy, A. "Orientalism in New England: Whittier," *American Literature*, I, 372–392 (Jan., 1930). (A scholarly survey of Whittier's poems having a "definite literary model or text taken from the English translation of Oriental scriptures." Concludes, p. 392, "He was a humanitarian . . . who took from the stream of Oriental influence which entered the thought-life of his time the ethical and moral principles with which he sympathized. But he never relinquished the Christian spectacles through which he read.")

Currier, T. F. "Whittier and the *New England Weekly Review*," *New England Quarterly*, VI, 589–597 (Sept., 1933). (A scholarly survey of his editorship, during 1830 and 1831, in which he developed "his political attitude,—opposed to the administration of Jackson and favorable to the candidacy of Henry Clay.")

—— "Whittier and the Amesbury-Salisbury Strike," *New England Quarterly*, VIII, 105–112 (March, 1935). (A rare pamphlet shows that Whittier interested himself in the mill strike of 1852.)

Eastburn, Iola K. *Whittier's Relation to German Life and Thought*. Philadelphia: 1915. (A University of Pennsylvania thesis, carefully documented, showing that Whittier was considerably influenced by German pietistic thought and political liberalism.)

Felton, C. C. Review of "Mogg Megone," *North American Review*, XLIV, 547–549 (Apr., 1837). (Sees "distinguished power" and "considerable defects." Sensible, constructive criticism, urging Whittier to avoid revolting themes, careless structure, and lack of finish.)

Fields, Mrs. J. T. *Whittier: Notes of his Life and Friendships*. New York: 1893. (Interesting and valuable; based on personal knowledge.)

Flower, B. O. *Whittier: Prophet, Seer, and Man*. Boston: 1896. (Appreciative but superficial.)

Foerster, N. *Nature in American Literature*. New York: 1923, pp. 20–36. (The attractively written chapter on Whittier not only surveys thoroughly the aspects of nature which interested him but also his religious dualism, his subordination of the changing life of nature to the changeless life of the spirit. Authoritative.)

Gosse, Edmund. "A Visit to Whittier," in *Portraits and Sketches*. London: 1912, pp. 137–147.

Hawkins, Rev. Chauncey. *The Mind of Whittier*. New York: 1904. (Discursive, didactic, and somewhat confused. Cites much relevant evidence, but without dates, titles, or page references. Tends to place disproportionate stress on Whittier's outward humanitarianism.)

Hawley, C. A. "Whittier and Iowa," *Iowa Journal of History and Politics*, XXXIV, 115–143 (April, 1936). (An important study based on much fresh evidence showing Whittier's keen interest in the Quakers and abolitionists of Iowa as well as his successful editorial work in having Iowa's pro-slavery Senator A. C. Dodge defeated in 1855.)

[Hawthorne, Nathaniel.] Review of *Supernaturalism in New England*, *Literary World*, I, 247–248 (April 17, 1847). (Unsigned, but now known to have been by Hawthorne. Urged Whittier to leave off reform activities and devote his great ability to purely literary pursuits.)

Hearn, Lafcadio. "A Note on Whittier," in Hearn's *Complete Lectures on Poets* (edited by Tanabé, Ochiai, and Nishizaki). Tokyo, Japan: 1934, pp. 777–800. (Stresses his peculiar national flavor, and his skill in ballads and narratives. "Whittier was a true artist in this sense,—that beauty, moral beauty, was always beauty for him, no matter where it came from" [p. 787]. While Tennyson as a storyteller relied on art, Whittier relied on an appeal to feeling and leaves a deeper impression.)

Higginson, T. W. *John Greenleaf Whittier*. New York: 1902. (Discursive sympathetic account by a fellow abolitionist and friend.)

Howe, W. D. "Whittier," in *American Writers on American Literature* (edited by John Macy). New York: 1931, pp. 125–134. (A charmingly written and discriminating survey, concluding that "Whittier's chief claim to lasting distinction as a poet must rest with his narrative verse." Among his deficiencies Howe mentions "a diffuseness, a lack of technical skill, a frequent use of poor rhymes and formless stanzas, an affection for moral tags.")

Hurd, H. E. "Paradoxes in the Life and Poetry of John Greenleaf Whittier," *Poetry Review* (London), XVII, 261–267 (1926). ("He was a man of limited culture . . . yet he captured the affections of all truly educated men"; in "violating the conventions of versification, Whittier became a great poet"; he "was an ardent lover who never married"; he "spiritualized the hard life that crushed him"; he was a dreamer who was a practical schemer; he was a "prophet of peace," yet he "sharpened the swords of the North"; and he was "without a pulpit," yet he was "a powerful preacher." The paradoxes are more startling than they would have been had the approach been that of the genetic historian.)

Independent, XLIV, pp. 1286 and 1289 (Sept. 15, 1892.) (A Whittier number.)

Kennedy, W. S. *John G. Whittier: His Life, Genius and Writings*. Boston: 1882. (The first book to be published about Whittier, who was displeased with it because it treated his religious views as naïve and out of touch with modern science.)

—— *John Greenleaf Whittier, the Poet of Freedom*. American Reformers Series. New York: 1892. (Contains the best account of Whittier's abolition interests prior to Mordell's book.)

Kreymborg, A. *Our Singing Strength*. New York: 1929, pp. 84–96. ("A Rustic Quaker Goes to War." Appreciative, especially of "Snow-Bound," which is analyzed with reference to "its fidelity to Whittier's life and environment and to the spontaneity of the language . . . The poem is finely wrought, the plot well sustained, and the successive stanzas dovetail without apparent effort.")

Lawton, W. C. "Whittier, the Quaker Laureate of Puritanism," in *The New England Poets*. New York: 1898, pp. 155–194. (Claims that Whittier's limitations and undoubted blemishes "endear him the more to his fellow-provincials. We love him as the Scots do Burns, because he is just his faulty, glorious self!" [p. 162]. A richly appreciative essay by one who had a deep knowledge of the New England character.)

Lewis, Georgianna K. *John Greenleaf Whittier: His Life and Work*. London: 1913. (Discursive.)

Linton, W. J. *Life of John Greenleaf Whittier*. London: 1893. (In the Great Writers Series.)

Literary World, Dec. 1, 1877. (A Whittier number, with many tributes.)

Lowell, James Russell. Review of the 1849 edition of Whittier's *Poems*, *National Anti-Slavery Standard*, Dec. 21, 1848.

—— Reviews of *In War Time*, *Home Ballads*, and *Snow-Bound*, conveniently reprinted in Lowell's *The Function of the Poet and Other Essays* (ed. A. Mordell). Boston: 1920, pp. 127–140. (Judicious appreciation. "Mr. Whittier is, on the whole, the most American of our poets. . . . 'Skipper Ireson's Ride' we hold to be by long odds the best of modern ballads." Lowell mentions Whittier's "too great tendency to metaphysics and morals" and his faulty rhymes.)

Macy, John. *The Spirit of American Literature*. New York: 1913, pp. 111–122. (Discursive. "Spontaneity, sincerity, passion, these are his high gifts; they triumph over all his verbal difficulties.")

Mordell, Albert. *Quaker Militant: John Greenleaf Whittier*. Boston: 1933. (Supersedes other biographies in the fullness of its facts, especially those relating to Whittier's political liberalism; but these facts are subjected to a highly partisan and often unconvincing interpretation in the light of both Freudian and socialistic assumptions. Contains a detailed Chronology [pp. 323–332], and a valuable Bibliography [pp. 333–343] which supplements Ristine, above.)

More, P. E. "Whittier the Poet," in *Shelburne Essays*, Third Series. New York: 1906, pp. 28–53. (A general but charming interpretation and appreciation. "What he needed above everything else, what his surroundings were least able to give him, was a canon of taste, which would have driven him to stiffen his work, to purge away the flaccid and set the genuinely poetical in stronger relief—a purely literary canon which would have offset the moralist and reformer in him" [p. 35]. He is the poet of the American people because he united the "ideal of home" and the "homely comforts of the spirit." Follows Whittier himself in regarding "The Pennsylvania Pilgrim" as his best poem.)

Murray, A. T. *A Selection of Religious Poems by John Greenleaf Whittier with an Interpretative Essay*. Philadelphia: 1934. (The introductory essay, pp. 5–48, is sensibly appreciative.)

Parrington, V. L. "John G. Whittier, Puritan Quaker," in *The Romantic Revolution in America*. New York: 1927, pp. 361–370. ("Compared with Whitman he is only a minor figure . . . His economics, like his democracy, was of a bygone time." Although unsympathetic, this essay is stimulating and well-written. Concludes Whittier "reveals no sympathy with agrarianism," that he favored "the developing industrialism of Massachusetts," and that "he was conscience rather than intellect." Errs in saying [p. 366]: "Rousseau and Tom Paine and Jefferson, with whom he certainly would have sympathized, he seems not to have been acquainted with." Whittier cited each.)

Payne, W. M. "Whittier," in *Cambridge History of American Literature*. New York: 1918. II, 42–54. (An admirable, judicious estimate, although brief and general.)

Perry, Bliss. "Whittier for Today," *Atlantic Monthly*, C, 851–859 (Dec., 1907), and in *Park Street Papers*. Boston: 1908. ("Controversy made him a poet, and his pictures of the hearth and home and countryside confirmed his fame; his human sympathy still brings his verse into touch with the vital political and social issues; but his abiding claim upon the remembrance of his countrymen may yet be found to lie in the wistful tenderness, the childlike simplicity, with which he turned to the other world." An excellent essay. The description of the New England of today as compared with that of Whittier's time is particularly choice.)

—— "John Greenleaf Whittier," in *The Early Years of the Saturday Club, 1855–1870*, edited by E. W. Emerson. Boston: 1918, pp. 188–196.

Pickard, S. T. *Life and Letters of John Greenleaf Whittier*. 2 vols. Boston: 1894. (The official biography, by the husband of Whittier's niece. Although eulogistic and not distinguished for interpretative or critical acumen, this remains the primary source book for the basic evidence.)

—— *Whittier-Land*. Boston: 1904. (Contains considerable material by Whittier, including a number of poems not previously collected, but most interesting for the additions which it makes to the *Life and Letters*.)

[Review.] "Whittier in Prose" (on *The Stranger in Lowell*), *United States Magazine and Democratic Review*, XVII, 115–126 (August, 1845). (Calls attention to Whittier's little known powers as a writer of prose.)

Russell, J. A. "The Aboriginal Element in Whittier's Writings," *Granite Monthly*, LX, 217–223 (April–May, 1928). (A survey of his view of the Indian.)

Sanborn, F. B. "Whittier as Man, Poet, and Reformer," *Bibliotheca Sacra*, LXV, 193–213 (April, 1908). (The title is misleading, for this excellent essay is devoted mainly to Whittier's political interests.)

Scott, W. T. "Poetry in American: a New Consideration of Whittier's Verse," *New England Quarterly*, VII, 258–275 (June, 1934). (An appraisal which endeavors to consider both merits and demerits.)

Stedman, E. C. *Poets of America*. Boston: 1885, pp. 95–132. ("Of all our poets he is the most natural balladist" [p. 112]. This essay is inadequate in its disregard of the genetic approach. Concludes correctly that it is the poetry "written from 1860 onward, that has secured him a more than local reputation." In general this essay is comprehensive in dealing with the many aspects of Whittier's work, and it is one of the best of the general critiques.)

Stevens, J. S. *Whittier's Use of the Bible*. University of Maine Studies, Second Series, No. 16. Orono, Maine: 1930. (The mass of evidence showing the influence of the Bible on Whittier's art here presented has been much supplemented by G. W. Allen's review, *American Literature*, III, 109–110.)

Stewart, George, Jr. *Essays from Reviews*. First Series. Quebec: 1892, pp. 139–171. See also Stewart's *Evenings in the Library*.

Stoddard, R. H. "John Greenleaf Whittier," *Scribner's Monthly*, XVIII, 569–583 (August, 1879). (An able essay.)

Strong, A. H. "Whittier," in *American Poets and Their Theology*. Philadelphia: 1916, pp. 105–158. (A bit verbose and didactic, but important in showing Whittier's divergence from romantic exponents of pantheism and natural goodness. Strong concludes, "Of all our American poets Whittier is the most sane and true, because at the basis of his poetry there is genuine conviction of sin. . . . He was not so far away from Calvinism as he thought" [pp. 137, 145]. See also E. D. Snyder, "Whittier's Religious Poetry," *Friends Quarterly Examiner*, April, 1934.)

Taylor, E. E. *John Greenleaf Whittier: Poet, Reformer, Mystic*. London: 1913.

Thayer, W. S. "John Greenleaf Whittier and His Writings," *North American Review*, LXXIX, 31–53 (July, 1854).

Underwood, F. H. *John Greenleaf Whittier: a Biography*. Boston: 1883. (Although eulogistic, this biography is valuable because Underwood obtained directly from Whittier much of his information. The book is especially useful in its data regarding the time and place of the first publication of many of the poems.)

Wendell, Barrett. "John Greenleaf Whittier," in *Stelligeri and Other Essays Concerning America*. New York: 1893, pp. 149–201. (Although this essay fails to take sufficient cognizance of Whittier's changes of view as his mind developed, it is one of the most penetrating interpretations of Whittier with reference to the religious spirit of New England. Wendell concludes that Whittier's "chance of survival is better than that of any other contemporary American man of letters.")

Whipple, E. P. "Poets and Poetry of America," in *Essays and Reviews*. 2 vols. Boston: 1850. I,

31–80. (The estimate of Whittier, particularly pp. 68–71, did much to raise his standing as a poet at a time when abolitionist activities had beclouded his literary fame. Whipple's article first appeared as a review of Griswold's *Poets and Poetry of America* in the *North American Review*, LVIII, 1–39 [Jan., 1844].)

Williams, C. B. *The Historicity of Whittier's Leaves from Margaret Smith's Journal.* 1933. (A valuable doctoral dissertation available in manuscript at the Library of the University of Chicago. Successive chapters treat the *Journal's* relation to Whittier's career, its historical and literary background, its historical material as adapted by Whittier, its significance as a medium for his ideas, and its historical phases considered as literature. Whittier emerges as a militant Quaker endeavoring to steer a middle course between contemporary Puritan and Anglican interpreters who were making extravagant claims for the early Puritans on one side and vilifying them on the other. Much fresh information on his view of the Indians, of witchcraft, and of religious persecution. Exhaustively documented, this dissertation casts a flood of light on the whole subject of Whittier's reading and his treatment of the New England past and its conflicting traditions.)

Woodberry, G. E. "John Greenleaf Whittier," in *Makers of Literature.* New York: 1900, pp. 302–323. (A fresh and judicious appreciation by a discriminating critic. Stresses nation-wide appeal and the manner in which his Quakerism inspired his work.)

NOTES

GENERAL

A new full-length interpretation of Whittier, based on new evidence supplied by T. F. Currier, Frances M. Pray, Albert Mordell, Nelson Adkins, and others, is badly needed. Although it may be that certain ideas are never entirely absent from Whittier's work, an attentive reading of the complete literary record in the order of its creation suggests that the growth of Whittier's mind and art can be best interpreted if we begin with the hypothesis that he developed through three phases of interest. Up to 1833 he was chiefly interested, as a *fanciful romanticist* and apostle of Scott-like localism, in the lurid, the strange, the sensational, or the dreamy; from 1833 to about 1859 he was chiefly interested as a *political liberal* in emancipation, sympathy, and social reform to be effected by outward means; and from about 1859 to his death he transcended his earlier interests by including them in a more comprehensive philosophy, in a *religious humanism* chiefly concerned with helping the individual to find spiritual peace through self-conquest, through a reliance on the fact that man is endowed with the power of bringing his conduct, through free-will and self-discipline, into fruitful harmony with Divine Law revealed to him intuitively through the Inner Light of aspiration shining amidst the dark impulses of the natural man. It is important to remember that these interests are by no means mutually exclusive; if one can find traces of *all* these interests in each year of his articulate life, however, it can be shown, I think, that his *chief* interests for the periods mentioned were those just defined. As a whole, his life is an interesting illustration of experimentation, of growth, and consequently it can be adequately interpreted and viewed in proper perspective only by means of the genetic approach.

"He was not a minor poet, nor altogether a provincial one. In spite of his intellectual deficiencies and his trivial technical faults, he is a poet of a high order, because he effectively dealt with important themes. His intensity of emotion, his universality of appeal, and his natural gift of expression enhance the value of his poetry. Of course, he ranks far below Milton and Shelley, but he should be placed with them among the poets of liberty. He was not a mere sectarian poet, like Bernard Barton, nor a poet of a class only, like Ebenezer Elliott. He stood out as a poet of nature, as a balladist, as a singer of home affections, as a recorder of old legends, as a poet of reform, as a religious poet, as a composer of hymns, as a writer of elegies, but, above all, as a champion of liberty; he takes his position on a higher plane than poets with more limited ranges and less intensity—poets like Bryant, Lowell, Holmes, Longfellow, and Poe. His messages of the antislavery days are vital for all time, because liberty always remains an ideal for which to fight, because oppression with the sanction of the law still exists, because modern capitalist is old slaveholder writ large. As long as social injustice and wage-slavery last, Whittier's poems of freedom will find responsive chords in human hearts. He is one of the great New England literary quartette—he ranks with Emerson, Hawthorne, and Thoreau. He is one of the few prophets in American literature."—Albert Mordell, *Quaker Militant: John Greenleaf Whittier*, pp. 320–321.

Page 105. THE DEMON'S CAVE

This poem was first published in the *New England Review*, July 25, 1831. It is included to represent a great number of Whittier's poems prior to 1832 which may be conveniently studied in Miss Pray's collection (see Bibliography). It should be noted that he combines an actual local setting (the cave is in Chester, New Hampshire) with Gothic horror "to romance dear" (cf. l. 56, "phantoms of murdered men"). This accords with his literary theory expressed in the Preface to *Legends of New England* (1831)—see p. 185, above. Perhaps he was following Scott and Byron in part. See Carpenter, *Whittier*, pp. 96–99. The *Legends* contained nine prose tales whose titles alone indicate the quest of the fanciful, the strange, the weird, and the horrible: "The Midnight Attack"; "The Rattlesnake Hunter"; "The Haunted House"; "The Pow-wow"; "The Human Sacrifice"; "A Night Among Wolves"; "The Mother's Revenge." Of his early Gothic or morbid tales, "The Opium Eater" (1833) is the only one he preserved. These tales should not be regarded as subjective confessions, for the poverty-stricken young Whittier was merely trying to meet the demands of the time as amply illustrated in the magazines of a period devoted to the Gothic and the strange. Consult Oral Coad's "The Gothic Element in American Literature before 1835," *Journal of English and Germanic Philology*, XXIV, 72–93 (1925).

TO WILLIAM LLOYD GARRISON

The ardent abolitionist and humanitarian, Garrison, later editor of *The Liberator* (see F. L. Mott, *A History of American Magazines*, index), met Whittier and encouraged him to write poetry and to join the abolition cause after the poet's sister had sent him one of Whittier's poems for his Newburyport *Free Press* in 1826. (See Carpenter, pp. 36–40, and index, and *William L. Garrison: The Story of His Life*, by his sons, I, 67 ff.) On March 22nd, 1833, Garrison wrote Whittier: "My brother, there are upwards of two million of our countrymen who are doomed to the most horrible servitude which ever cursed our race and blackened the page of history. . . . This, then, is a time for the philanthropist . . . Whittier, enlist!" In June, 1833, Whittier published his prose piece, *Justice and Expediency*, which alienated many of his friends and enrolled him definitely with the abolitionists. Although he later differed strongly from Garrison, who advocated disunion, Whittier paid him high tribute—see his essay on Garrison, written in 1879 (*Works*, VII, 189–192).

Page 106. TO ——, WITH A COPY OF WOOLMAN'S JOURNAL

It should be noted that Whittier during this period and later was influenced not only by contemporary humanitarians such as Garrison, but by the doctrines of equality and brotherly charity implicit in his ancestral Quaker faith. John Woolman, whose *Journal* (1774) Whittier later edited in 1871 with a long and reverent introduction (Whittier's *Works*, VII, 315–359), had left touching testimony of his charity of heart in his writings entitled *The Keeping of Negroes* (1754–62), and *On Labour, Schools, and the Right Use of the Lord's Outward Gifts* (1768). (See Muriel Kent, "John Woolman: Mystic and Reformer," *Hibbert Journal*, XXVI, 302–313 [Jan., 1928].) Note in this poem Whittier's insistence, following Woolman, upon faith's being applied in "works of love and duty," upon the need of inward wrestling "with familiar evil" and "assailing every form of wrong," upon the superiority of the Inner Light to "the pride of reason," and upon the fact that "a soul-sufficing answer" to man's deepest questions is to be sought not in outward "Nature's many voices" but "within." Note, then, that Whittier's interest in abolition was grounded not only on sentimental pity and current humanitarianism but upon the earlier tradition of Christian charity and the inviolable sanctity and spiritual equality of all human souls before God. In his first abolition pamphlet, he mentioned, as a practical man, "Expediency" and economic arguments, but chiefly he exalted the "Justice" taught him mystically by the Inner Light. In *What Is Slavery?* (*Works*, VII, 100–107) he defined it as "the transformation of sentient immortal beings into 'chattels personal.' . . . The voice of God condemns it in the deep places of the human heart." To him the abolition crusade was a "Moral Warfare," as elaborated in his great poem by that title (1847): he fought with weapons supernatural—with "The Light, and Truth, and Love of Heaven." These weapons he took from the armory of the pacifist Quakers, especially from John Woolman.

Page 108. HAMPTON BEACH

In this nature poem, somewhat marred by its moralizing conclusion (ll. 36 ff.), note that, characteristically, Whittier does not enumerate features of the landscape (as Scott did) but that he presents the luminous impression the scene makes on his mind. For full discussion, see N. Foerster, in Bibliography, above.

Page 109. CASSANDRA SOUTHWICK

Whittier prefaced this poem with the following note: "In 1658 two young persons, son and daughter of Lawrence Southwick of Salem, who had himself been imprisoned and deprived of nearly all his property for having entertained Quakers at his house, were fined for non-attendance at church. They being unable to pay the fine, the General Court issued an order empowering 'The Treasurer of the County to sell the said persons to any of the English nation of *Virginia* or *Barbadoes*, to answer said fines.' An attempt was made to carry this order into execution, but no shipmaster was found willing to convey them to the West Indies."

This is one of Whittier's best ballads, a form in which he is especially distinguished. The humble Quaker colonial, Cassandra, tells in dramatic-monologue manner of her sacrifices and of how she has resisted the temptation to surrender her Quaker ideals to obtain release from the intolerant Puritans' prison. Mordell thinks, "Whittier made her the symbol of his own inner trials, for he too had shut himself out of the light of this glorious world. He too had made sacrifices—his literary and political career; he too had let love and wealth pass him by; truly he was also in prison" (*Quaker*

Militant, p. 130). Whittier attacked the New England Puritans' intolerance of Quakers (see his controversial letters on the subject, Pickard's *Life*, II, 775–785); but he thought of the great Puritan Revolution of the seventeenth century as "the golden age of England" (*Works*, VI, 35), and he testified that the Puritan liberal, "blind Milton, approaches nearly to my conception of a true hero" (Whittier's *Stranger in Lowell*, 1845, p. 154). He read and re-read Milton's prose defenses of liberty, and said, "My whole life has felt the influence of his writings" (quoted by Annie Fields, *Authors and Friends*, 1924, p. 292).

Note in this poem especially the ringing dramatic quality of the Captain's refusal to carry Cassandra to slavery (ll. 108 ff.). This ringing quality is accentuated by the measure, the iambic hexameter and heptameter rhyming in couplets.

Page 112. MEMORIES

Whittier placed this beautiful and touching poem at the head of the group he entitled "Subjective and Reminiscent" in his collected works. On Whittier's love for Mary Emerson Smith, the girl referred to in this poem of broken hopes, see Mordell, *Quaker Militant*, pp. 39–53. Note that in part Whittier's sacrifice was caused by his allegiance to his Quakerism (ll. 55–63).

Page 113. EGO

A "sad and sombre gift," this poem is Whittier's *apologia pro vita sua*, recording his state of mind regarding his important transition from his earlier devotion to romance to a devotion to political reform. He recognizes that he is now "banished . . . from Fashion's sphere" and the society he early loved, because he chose to attack wrong "through the harsh trumpet of Reform" (l. 22 and l. 42). Note that his sacrifice for "suffering human-kind" is partly inspired by his devotion to spiritual as opposed to temporal values.

Page 115. MASSACHUSETTS TO VIRGINIA

This poem was read at the Essex County Convention in Ipswich on January 2, 1843, and it is said to have electrified the audience. Mordell (p. 145) quotes W. F. Channing as saying of Whittier: "His anti-slavery songs were stronger than the laws, and moulded the future more than anything else in contemporaneous literature, within my knowledge, either in this country or Europe." It should be noted that beside his appeal to divine justice and to expediency and to humanitarian pity, Whittier as abolitionist developed a logical argument designed to show that the Southerners were inconsistent and "False to their fathers' memory, false to the faith they loved" (l. 30)—that is, they had betrayed the humanitarian ideal of liberty of which Virginians such as Patrick Henry and Jefferson were exponents and for which North and South fought England. This effective argument is developed at length in Whittier's prose piece, "Democracy and Slavery," 1843 (*Works*, VII, 108–114), in which he pays glowing tribute to a Southerner, "the great leader of American Democracy, Thomas Jefferson, . . . an ultra-abolitionist." It should be noted that Whittier paid his allegiance not so much to the traditionalistic Constitution of the Federalists as to the doctrines of *a priori* natural rights, "the great principles enunciated in the revolutionary declaration" of Independence, according to which "all men are created equal, endowed with rights inalienable" (*Works*, VII, 100–101). In summary, then, Whittier's crusade for the liberty of the slaves may be attributed to (1) current humanitarian philanthropy represented by Garrison; (2) the Quaker faith in the equality and sanctity of all human souls; (3) Puritan liberalism as represented by Milton and the seventeenth-century idealists on whom Whittier wrote many essays (*Works*, VI, 9–103); (4) the natural-rights tradition associated with revolutionary America and France as represented by Jefferson and others; and (5) by his own Yankee sense of practical expediency (see his argument that "free labor . . . is more productive, and more advantageous to the planter than slave labor" (*Works*, VIII, 34–47). On backgrounds, see A. B. Hart, *Slavery and Abolition, 1831–1841* (New York: 1906); A. C. Cole, *The Irrepressible Conflict, 1850–1865* (New York: 1934), with a valuable bibliography on all phases of the period; R. G. Gettell, *History of American Political Thought* (New York: 1928), pp. 279–312; Lorenzo D. Turner, *Anti-Slavery Sentiment in America Prior to 1865* (Washington, D. C.: 1929); and E. D. Adams, *The Power of Ideals in American History* (New Haven: 1913), chapter II. It is desirable to study the arguments of the Northern abolitionists such as Bryant, Whittier, Emerson, and Lowell in the light of *Pro-Slavery Thought in the Old South* (Chapel Hill, N. C.: 1935), a scholarly study by W. S. Jenkins. For sympathetic presentations of the Southern view see also V. L. Parrington on "The Mind of the South," in *The Romantic Revolution*, pp. 1–136, and E. W. Parks's introduction (pp. l–cxlviii) and annotated bibliography in *Southern Poets* (New York: 1936).

Page 117. SONGS OF LABOR: DEDICATION

(See note dealing with Whittier's poetic theories, p. 815, below.)

Pages 118 and 119. THE SHOEMAKERS and THE HUSKERS

No American poet has so successfully represented the healthy delight in labor. Whittier never sentimentalized the horror of doing an honest day's work; he glorified the humble and the commonplace without condescension or primitivistic implications. It is probably true that Whittier has been much more widely read by the "common people" than has Walt Whitman, although the latter is supposed by intellectuals to be distinctive in his democratic appeal.

Page 120. THE REFORMER

This is one of the most iconoclastic of Whittier's poems. It presents the symbol of "a Strong One" smiting down the shrines dear to the Church, Wealth, Fraud, Sloth, Art, Reverence, Custom, and "Young Romance" (ll. 1–24). Yet Whittier, the optimist, concludes that "the Waster seemed the Builder too," that "life shall on and upward go." Note that in his radical attack on "the outworn rite, the old abuse,/ The pious fraud," in his faith that the decay of the old will lead to a "fresher life" in the future, Whittier draws on what "the Indian seer" wisely taught. On this subject see Arthur Christy's "Orientalism in New England: Whittier," *American Literature*, I, 372–392 (Jan., 1930).

Page 122. PROEM

In this modest poem, introducing his first volume of collected poems, Whittier gives an accurate description of his work during the period just prior to 1847. He loves the "old melodious lays" of Spenser and Sidney; yet he tries to emulate their notes in vain. The lack in his poems of "rounded art" and "mystic beauty, dreamy grace," is a result in part, he suggests, of "the rigor of a frozen clime," of his "untaught ear," and of the demands of hurried Labor and Duty. He is unable to reveal as a seer the profounder "secrets of the heart and mind" or to treat the extremes of "a more intense despair or brighter hope." He therefore takes as his subject "our common world of joy and woe" and strives to atone for his artistic shortcomings by his humanitarian liberalism, by "an earnest sense of human right and weal," a "hate of tyranny intense," and a sympathy for his "brother's pain and sorrow." If he cannot equal "mighty Milton's gift divine" or "Marvell's wit and graceful song," his love of Freedom is "as deep and strong as theirs," and he lays his poems at the shrine of Freedom. Cf. Whittier's somewhat similar "Songs of Labor: Dedication" (pp. 117–118, above), and see note on his poetic theories, below.

BARCLAY OF URY

Whittier's own experience may have helped to inspire the impassioned sympathy of this excellent ballad-tribute to a Quaker who incurred social ostracism and abuse by following the divine Inner Light.

Whittier's note on the subject of this poem: "Among the earliest converts to the doctrines of Friends in Scotland was Barclay of Ury, an old and distinguished soldier, who had fought under Gustavus Adolphus, in Germany. As a Quaker, he became the object of persecution and abuse at the hands of the magistrates and the populace. None bore the indignities of the mob with greater patience and nobleness of soul than this once proud gentleman and soldier. One of his friends, on an occasion of uncommon rudeness, lamented that he should be treated so harshly in his old age who had been so honored before. 'I find more satisfaction,' said Barclay, 'as well as honor, in being thus insulted for my religious principles, than when, a few years ago, it was usual for the magistrates, as I passed the city of Aberdeen, to meet me on the road and conduct me to public entertainment in their hall, and then escort me out again, to gain my favor.'"

Page 124. WHAT THE VOICE SAID

When Whittier invokes God to smite others such as the slaveholders, he hears a voice saying, "Art thou free from sin?" Within each of us are "all germs of evil" (l. 25). Note the gradual turning away from attacking others and outward laws to the question of evil within the individual.

Page 125. MY SOUL AND I

Although uninspired and pedestrian in form, this poem is significant in defining the human aspects of Whittier's religion, his distaste for other-worldliness, and the way in which in this period religion meant to him not so much self-reform as outward service to others. Christian charity mingled with current humanitarianism, giving his religion a worldly cast. He concludes that "heaven and hell . . ./ Are now and here," and the past and the future "are one,/ And both are now." (Cf. Emerson's view, p. 218, above, ll. 323–34, that "Past, Present, Future shoot/ Triple blossoms from one root.") Whittier concludes his essay on Richard Baxter (about 1847) with a censure, because in the presence of temporal suffering "he made no efforts to remove its political or social causes" (which Whittier in this humanitarian period implies are outward and institutional). "Baxter overlooked the evils and oppressions which were around him, and forgot the necessities and duties of the world of time and sense in his earnest aspirations towards the world of spirits . . . God is best served through His suffering children, and . . . love and reverence for visible humanity is an indispensable condition of the appropriate worship of the Unseen God" (*Works*, VI, 182–183).

Page 127. WORSHIP

This poem, like the above, disparages older religious usages and interprets religion almost exclusively in terms of charity or outward service: the "holier worship" is that which "feeds the widow and the fatherless" (ll. 42–44). Cf. Emerson, advocate of self-reliance as opposed to humanitarianism: "He that feeds men serveth few;/ He serves all who dares be true" (p. 219, above, ll. 412–413). Cf. Whittier's views in this period with those in Lowell's *Vision of Sir Launfal* (p. 463, above, ll. 315 ff.).

Page 128. THE POOR VOTER ON ELECTION DAY

Whittier is confident that "simple manhood" by means of the equal vote is able to redress wrongs. Cf. his poem "Democracy." Note that in "The Problem" (1877), pp. 183–184, above, he had apparently grown skeptical of such remedies: "Solution there is none/ Save in the Golden Rule of Christ."

ICHABOD

G. R. Carpenter remarks that the title, a Hebrew word meaning "inglorious," was probably suggested to Whittier by Lowell's sentence in the *National Anti-Slavery Standard* for July 2, 1846: "Shall not the Recording Angel write *Ichabod* after the name of this man in the great book of Doom?"

"This poem," Whittier wrote, "was the outcome of the surprise and grief and forecast of evil consequences which I felt on reading the seventh of March speech of Daniel Webster in support of the 'compromise' and the Fugitive Slave Law. No partisan or personal enmity dictated it. On the contrary my admiration of the splendid personality and intellectual power of the great Senator was never stronger than when I laid down his speech, and, in one of the saddest moments of my life, penned my protest. I saw, as I wrote, with painful clearness its sure results,—the Slave Power arrogant and defiant, strengthened and encouraged to carry out its scheme for the extension of its baleful system, or the dissolution of the Union, the guaranties of personal liberty in the free States broken down, and the whole country made the hunting-ground of slave-catchers. In the horror of such a vision, so soon fearfully fulfilled, if one spoke at all, he could only speak in tones of stern and sorrowful rebuke.

"But death softens all resentments, and the consciousness of a common inheritance of frailty and weakness modifies the severity of judgment. Years after, in *The Lost Occasion*, I gave utterance to an almost universal regret that the great statesman did not live to see the flag which he loved trampled under the feet of Slavery, and, in view of this desecration, make his last days glorious in defence of 'Liberty and Union, one and inseparable.'"

Garrison, Phillips, Lowell, and Emerson also attacked Webster as a traitor to the ideal of liberty, as a "lost leader." On Oct. 4, 1850, Whittier wrote a letter declining nomination by the united Democrats and Free Soilers as State Senator because he would not swear to obey laws which included the Fugitive Slave Law (see the letter in Mordell, p. 158). It should be remembered that while Webster thought it wisest to compromise on slavery to save the Union, Whittier was willing to have the Union dissolved ("A Word for the Hour," *Poetical Works*, Cambridge Edition, p. 333) rather than to tolerate the Fugitive Slave Law.

Whatever one thinks of the political issues involved, it is true that Whittier's verses "are, in their awful scorn, the most powerful he ever wrote" (Carpenter, p. 222). W. C. Lawton (*New England Poets*, p. 181) finds the culminating lines, 31–32, Dantesque, citing the *Inferno*, XXXIII, 121–135. Whittier's stern indignation has burned away the diffuse elements which marred so many of his poems.

Page 129. WORDSWORTH

Note that Whittier regards Wordsworth's as "the sweetest lays" in English. His influence may have reinforced that of Burns in turning Whittier gradually away from the "strife of sect and party noise" (l. 14) to the "simple joys" and "common forms" of nature. Whittier's "The Trailing Arbutus" and "A Mystery" are clearly Wordsworthian in spirit. See Whittier's Preface to *Songs of Three Centuries* (1876), and Annabel Newton's *Wordsworth in Early American Criticism* (Chicago: 1928).

A SABBATH SCENE

This is one of Whittier's most violent abolition poems. It was written with the hope of preventing the passage of Clay's Fugitive Slave Bill, supported by Webster. The reverent Quaker later said, "We believe in the Scriptures because they repeat the warnings and admonitions and promises of the indwelling Light" (quoted, Bailey, p. 78). But here, angered by the clergymen's use of the Scripture to support slavery, he says he would prefer to hear "the written Word/ Interpreted by Nature" (l. 100), which he usually disparaged as a guide. Cf. "A Pastoral Letter" and "Official Piety."

One of Whittier's typical editorials of the time, quoted by Mordell (*Quaker Militant*, pp. 135–136), begins: "Men who maintain the doctrine that slaveholding is a divine institution, and consistent with the holy attributes of Deity, have no more claim to the character of Christian than the worshippers of the Scandinavian Odin, or the devotees of Brahma and Vishnu. The Deity which they profess to worship, and on whose altars, reared with the unpaid toil and cemented with the blood of human victims, they offer the fruits of robbery and tithe the gains of oppression, is not the God of the Bible. . . . The Priesthood of the god of Slavery stand up in Northern pulpits, and lift in mockery of prayer to the Father of Mercies hands red and reeking with the blood of human sacrifices offered to their own horrible idol."

For backgrounds, see C. L. Shanks, "The Biblical Anti-Slavery Argument of the Decade

1830–1840," *Journal of Negro History*, XVI, 132–157 (April, 1931).

Page 131. THE PEACE OF EUROPE

This ironical poem illustrates the fact that Whittier's political liberalism embraced a keen interest in struggles for freedom and peace in other countries. For illustrations of this point, see the following poems in the Cambridge Edition: "Bolivar" (1830), "Isabella of Austria" (1831), "The World's Convention" (1839), "Follen" (1842), "The Peace Convention at Brussels" (1848), "To Pius IX" (1849), "Kossuth" (1851), "The Conquest of Finland" (1856), "The New Exodus" (1856), "Freedom in Brazil" (1867), and "Garibaldi" (1869).

Page 133. FIRST-DAY THOUGHTS

Note that the Quaker reads in his own heart "a still diviner law/ Than Israel's leader on his tables saw." In 1870, when the Darwinian cult of the survival of the fittest was lending in the popular mind a philosophic sanction to ruthless competition in the exploitation of our vast frontier resources in the West and in business, resulting in a period of gross materialism, Whittier wrote: "The hour is coming when, under the searching eye of philosophy and the terrible analysis of science, the letter and the outward evidence will not altogether avail us; when the surest dependence must be upon the Light of Christ within, disclosing the law and the prophets in our own souls, and confirming the truth of outward Scripture by inward experience" (*Works*, VII, 313—see the whole statement of his faith, pp. 305–314). The point is, that just as the Inner Light (individual aspirations toward perfection) confirmed for Whittier the Bible (socially mediated tradition), so this tradition, this body of other men's aspirations and judgments, tended to correct and interpret and test his own individual aspiration. Whittier's creed embraced both introspective richness and respect for tradition; they reinforced each other. He was liberal in recognizing that the Scriptures "are *a* rule, not *the* rule of faith and practice . . . the reason of our obedience to which is mainly that we find in them the eternal precepts of the Divine spirit declared and repeated, to which our conscience bears witness." Cf. Emerson's doctrine that one can recognize great poetry because "the great poet makes *us* feel our *own* wealth," and *we* are "born into the great, the universal mind" (Emerson's *Works*, II, 289, 296. Italics are the editor's).

MAUD MULLER

This has been one of the most popular of all American poems, and it has been widely parodied. It is noteworthy that in this humanitarian period even Whittier's poems dealing with love embody attacks on social institutions—in this case the Judge's worship of wealth and social position. See Mordell (*Quaker Militant*, p. 177) for a development of the idea that the poem symbolized Whittier's "own tragedy" in being rejected by Mary Emerson Smith on account of his poverty and social inferiority. Although the couplet near the end, riming "pen" and "been," has been much ridiculed, it gives the particular story a universal tone—the pathos of unfulfilled hopes.

Whittier's note on the source of "Maud Muller" reads as follows: " . . . The poem had no real foundation in fact, though a hint of it may have been found in recalling an incident, trivial in itself, of a journey on the picturesque Maine seaboard with my sister some years before it was written. We had stopped to rest our tired horse under the shade of an apple-tree, and refresh him with water from a little brook which rippled through the stone wall across the road. A very beautiful young girl in scantest summer attire was at work in the hay-field, and as we talked with her we noticed that she strove to hide her bare feet by raking hay over them, blushing as she did so, through the tan of her cheek and neck."

Page 135. BURNS

"One day," wrote Whittier, "we had a call from a 'pawky auld carle' of a wandering Scotchman. To him I owe my first introduction to the songs of Burns. After eating his bread and cheese and drinking his mug of cider he gave us Bonny Doon, Highland Mary, and Auld Lang Syne. He had a rich, full voice, and entered heartily into the spirit of his lyrics." Elsewhere Whittier wrote: "When I was fourteen years old, my first school-master, Joshua Coffin, the able, eccentric historian of Newbury, brought with him to our house a volume of Burns's poems, from which he read, greatly to my delight. I begged him to leave the book with me, and set myself at once to the task of mastering the glossary of the Scottish dialect at its close. This was about the first poetry I had ever read (with the exception of that of the Bible, of which I was a close student), and it had a lasting influence upon me. I began to make rhymes myself, and to imagine stories and adventures."

It was Burns who taught Whittier to see, he says, "through all familiar things/ The romance underlying" (ll. 61–62). B. O. Flower (*Whittier*, p. 160) quotes the poet as having said of Burns: "He was the first poet I read, and he will be the last. . . . I read Burns every moment I had to spare. And this was one great result to me of my communion with him: I found that the things out of which poems came were not, as I had always imagined, somewhere away off in a world and life lying outside the edge of our own New England sky—they were right here about my feet and among the people I knew."

Burns and Whittier derived from the same sort of humble parentage and were reared in the same sort of countryside. They had many other things in common, besides writing about the same themes. Yet Burns, with all his lovable genius, admitted himself to be "a poor, damned, incautious, duped, unfortunate fool; the sport, the miserable victim of rebellious pride, hypochondriac imaginations, agonizing sensibilities, and bedlam passions." He died an ignoble death as a rake and a drunkard who had taught himself to laugh at his confessed wrongdoing. Whittier probably comes nearest of all the writers in English in the nineteenth century to being a saint. It is interesting to speculate on the extent to which this difference was a result of the fact that in America the individualism of Romanticism was tempered by the more immediate influence of the Puritan spirit, of which Quakerism is one aspect.

It should be noted that Whittier not only read much more than is generally recognized, but that he wrote a considerable number of essays, long and short, on authors and books—on Bunyan, Thomas Ellwell, Baxter, Andrew Marvell, Robert Dinsmore, Placido the slave poet, Dora Greenwell, Carlyle, Woolman, Lydia Child, Macaulay, Longfellow, Holmes, C. B. Brown, Bayard Taylor, E. P. Whipple, and on nineteenth-century poets (see his preface to *Songs of Three Centuries*).

Page 136. THE RENDITION

Note that the forcible return by Massachusetts of the slave Anthony Burns, in accordance with the Fugitive Slave Law, "an unloosed maniac," made the most localistic of American poets substitute a "deep disgust" for "all love of home, all pride of place." (Whitman's "A Boston Ballad" deals with the same episode.) But when a plan was formed to rescue Burns by force, Whittier wrote (June 29, 1854), "I would die rather than aid in that wicked law; but I deplore all forcible resistance to it." Cf. Thoreau's essay on "Civil Disobedience."

Page 137. ARISEN AT LAST

Whittier's note: "On the passage of the bill to protect the rights and liberties of the people of the State against the Fugitive Slave Act." He rejoices that Massachusetts has subordinated interest in "trade and gain" to the ideal of the sanctity of the individual soul safeguarded by "a Christian State." Ll. 27–30 refer to Whittier's idol, Milton. Cf. Whittier's yearning (*Works*, VII, 209) for "the coming of that time when Milton's definition of a true commonwealth shall be no longer a prophecy, but the description of an existing fact,—'a huge Christian personage, a mighty growth and stature of an honest man, moved by the purpose of a love of God and of mankind.'" For other references to Milton as the ideal liberal see Whittier's *The Stranger in Lowell*, p. 154; Pickard's *Life*, II, 587, 727, 781; Mordell's *Quaker Militant*, pp. 133–149; Carpenter's *Life*, 173; and Whittier's *Works*, IV, 22, 34, 127; VI, 87, 103, 215, 361–362; VII, 209, 278–279, 385.

FOR RIGHTEOUSNESS' SAKE

Note Whittier's humanitarian indictment of his age as "deaf to moaning want." Apostle of brotherhood, he "gives thanks to God" because his "friends under arrest for treason against the slave power" have given vent to "the holy rage" with which the early Christian prophets attacked the "decent seemings" of their materialistic age. He relies on the "appeal of Truth to Time."

THE LAST WALK IN AUTUMN

Mordell concludes (*Quaker Militant*, p. 178) that the humanitarian "work of Whittier as the poet of freedom and the singer of the oppressed really ended with his fiftieth year" (1857). He did not abandon his earlier interest in outward reform and liberty—in fact he was always proud of it; but he gradually transcended this interest by including it in a much more comprehensive reading of life which involved not only outward reform but inward reform beginning with the individual, in whom he found "all germs of evil." He came to emphasize self-development in the midst of one's native environment and normal family relations.

"The Last Walk in Autumn" (1857) marks the beginning of Whittier's trend in this direction. In youth (cf. "The Demon's Cave") he had celebrated legends of his own locality; but whereas his interest then had been in the sensational, the lurid, and the weird, he now dealt with the quiet, the normal, and the typical (cf. "Snow-Bound"), the environment being subordinated as a frame to his pictures of humanity, of serene inward self-development. Like Burke, his mind proceeded from "kin to kind"; like the reminiscent Wordsworth, he thought "the child is father of the man." Hence he grows increasingly introspective and gradually deals more and more with the development of his own mind in its native natural and human setting.

ll. 57–88. With this idea that the fancy or imagination can find the universal and sublime in the immediate particulars of daily life, compare his poem "To——" (Cambridge Edition, p. 188) developing the idea that "The Beauty which old Greece or Rome/ Sung, painted, wrought, lies close at home," and is discoverable by the imaginative "eye and ear/ In all our daily walks." Cf. Emerson's "Written in Naples," and his conclusion in *Nature* (*Works*, I, 74) that "The invariable mark of wisdom is to see the miraculous in the common." The idea had also been foreshadowed in Whittier's "Burns" (1854), and is of course an outgrowth of his early advocacy of localism—see his preface to *Poems of J. G. C. Brainard* (1832, quoted by Carpenter, pp. 86–87) and his essay on Dinsmore, pp. 185–187, above.

ll. 89–136. Note that Whittier enjoys not only nature but the "goodly company" of wise men, and their books, "the good, the beautiful, the brave" (the Platonic Emerson, ll. 105–112, the "troubadour" Bayard Taylor, ll. 113–120, and the Christ-like statesman Charles Sumner, ll. 121–128).

ll. 145–176. He who had been in youth "a dreamer wild" now thinks it is "Better to stem with heart and hand/ The roaring tide of life," to do and to know, to help safeguard New England's "freeman's vote," her "equal village schools," her religious freedom, and her laborers' right to their reward.

ll. 177 ff. Chiefly, however, he glorifies the "sweet homes" of New England, and he says he designs his songs for "a place at home and hearth," confident that out of "the baffling present" will come victory through God and the "old home-bred virtues."

Page 141. SKIPPER IRESON'S RIDE

This poem further illustrates Whittier's trend toward combining his earlier localism with a psychological analysis of the individual's inward life. Local and realistic is the story of the hard-hearted skipper who deserted his sinking ship and who was tarred and feathered by "the women o' Morble'ead," the wives of the drowned crew. But the key to the ballad is not in the melodramatic outward details, but in the conscience-stricken Skipper's inward spiritual torture and the women's resultant awe:

"'What is the shame that clothes the skin
To the nameless horror that lives within?' . . .

"Then the wife of the skipper lost at sea
Said, 'God has touched him! why should we!'"

It is true, of course, that the ballad is technically skilful in the vigorous sweep of the verse and refrain which keeps before us the righteous indignation of the bereaved women. But the dramatic climax of this moving story surely depends primarily on Whittier's recognition of the dual conflict within the heart of man.

Whittier wrote Lowell, editor of the *Atlantic Monthly*, "I send for December (I hope in season) a bit of a Yankee ballad, the spirit of which pleases me more than the execution. Will it do? Look at it, and use the freedom of an old friend towards it and the author. The incident occurred sometime in the last century. The refrain is the actual song of the women on this march. To relish it, one must understand the peculiar tone and dialect of the ancient Marbleheaders." Lowell replied (Nov. 4, 1857): "I thank you heartily for the ballad, which will go into the next number. I like it all the better for its provincialism—in all fine pears, you know, we can taste the old *pucker*. I know the story well. I am familiar with Marblehead and its dialect, and as the burthen is intentionally provincial I have taken the liberty to print it in such a way as shall give the peculiar accent thus:—

'Cap'n Ireson for his horrd horrt
Was torred and feathered and corried in a corrt.'

That's the way I've always 'horrd it'—only it began, 'Old Flud Ireson.' What a good name Ireson (son of wrath) is for the hero of such a history!" (Quoted in Pickard's *Life*, II, 406–407.)

Mr. Samuel Roads, Jr., in his *History of Marblehead*, published in 1879, tried to show that Captain Ireson was not responsible for the abandonment of the disabled ship. In a letter to Mr. Roads, Whittier said:

"I have now no doubt that thy version of Skipper Ireson's ride is the correct one. My verse was founded solely on a fragment of rhyme which I heard from one of my early schoolmates, a native of Marblehead. I supposed the story to which it referred dated back at least a century. I knew nothing of the participators, and the narrative of the ballad was pure fancy. I am glad for the sake of truth and justice that the real facts are given in thy book. I certainly would not knowingly do injustice to any one, dead or living."

Page 142. TELLING THE BEES

Whittier's note: "A remarkable custom, brought from the Old Country, formerly prevailed in the rural districts of New England. On the death of a member of the family, the bees were at once informed of the event, and their hives dressed in mourning. This ceremonial was supposed to be necessary to prevent the swarms from leaving their hives and seeking a new home."

This poem, like "Skipper Ireson's Ride," combines localism (a faithful, almost Wordsworthian, description of the Fernside farm) and psychological drama. The lover passing by, seeing the chore-girl covering the bees, thinks his Mary's grandsire is dead, and is stunned to hear that "Mistress Mary is dead and gone!"

THE OVER-HEART

Compare and contrast with Emerson's essay, "The Over-Soul," embodying his transcendental faith.

The religious distinctions between Quakerism and Transcendentalism deserve careful study. To what extent is the following statement true? "Whittier was indeed a Quaker of the olden time. The inner light upon which he depended was a very different light from that which was recognized by Emerson. Emerson's light was the light of nature; Whittier's was the light of Christ. Emerson regarded the fixed successions of the physical world as the primitive reality; Whittier thought conscience and heart of more importance than all the paraphernalia of planets and of suns. Emerson was influenced by the materialistic philosophy of the English deists, and by the Unitarian reaction from the older Calvinistic theology [and also by Plato and Kant who stressed a reality transcending that of physical nature?]; Whittier drew his inspiration and his doctrine from deep personal experience of sin and of redemption, and from sympathetic observation of the sorrow and guilt of humanity. In short, Emerson began with nature; Whittier began with man. Emerson interpreted man by nature; Whittier interpreted nature by man. For this reason there is a prevailing ethical element in Whittier's poetry, which Emerson's almost wholly lacks; the keynote of Whittier's is compassion, while that of Emerson is speculation; Emerson's intuitions are the uncertain utterances of his own imperfect moral being; Whittier's inner light is that of an indwelling and personal God."—A. H. Strong, *American Poets and Their Theology*, pp. 114–115.

There is certainly an element of truth in the above comparison. But does it sufficiently take into account Emerson's indebtedness to such influences as Platonism, Orientalism, and Kantean transcendentalism, which stressed a reality transcending that of physical nature? On the other hand, it should be recalled that Emerson himself said, "I am more of a Quaker than anything else." (See Emerson's *Works*, Centenary Edition, VIII, 431; 307–310; XI, 4; XI, 488; XI, 415; XI, 107; IV, 183; II, 318; III, 432–433; IV, 139–140—on Quakeristic inner light as the inner check; II, 335 and 497 ff.; III, 397; III, 493; *Journals*, II, 358; III, 258, 398–399, 426; VI, 280.)

l. 6. *Indian mystics*. See Christy's study of Oriental influence (Bibliography), and compare with his conclusions regarding Emerson in *The Orient in American Transcendentalism* (1932), pp. 61–185.

ll. 23–26. Note that although Whittier's God is synonymous with Love, "The earthquake and the storm are God's,/ And good and evil interflow." Cf. Bryant's "The Forest Hymn," p. 76, l. 102 ff., and Milton's *Paradise Lost*, I, 366, where he says evil exists "through God's high sufferance for the trial of man."

Page 143. MY PLAYMATE

Mordell, (*op. cit.*, pp. 39 and 208) claims that the girl referred to was Mary Emerson Smith, whom Whittier loved as a young man.

"Tennyson said justly to Mrs. Maria S. Porter, 'It ("My Playmate") is a perfect poem; in some of his descriptions of scenery and wild flowers, he would rank with Wordsworth.' . . . Note that in the whole sixteen verses the great majority of the words are monosyllables; observe how the veeries sing themselves into the line; and how the moaning of the sea of change rushes out and prolongs itself until the revery is passed, and the same sea sweeps in and ends the dream as absolutely as that one whirling cloud of disastrous air, from the St. Pierre volcano, ended every breath of mortal life for thirty-six thousand human beings. See, again, how in the fourth verse, out of twenty-six words, every one is made monosyllabic in order that the one word 'bashful' may linger and be effective; and see how in the sixth the one long word in the whole poem 'uneventful' multiplies indefinitely those bereft and solitary years. Did Whittier plan those effects deliberately? Probably not, but they are there; and the most exquisite combination of sounds in Tennyson or in Mrs. Browning's 'Sonnets from the Portuguese,' can only equal them."—T. W. Higginson, *John Greenleaf Whittier*, pp. 141–142.

Page 144. THE SHADOW AND THE LIGHT

This is Whittier's most extended discussion of the central problem of religion—the problem of reconciling the existence of evil in the world with the existence of a deity who is at once all-good and all-powerful, and hence responsible for all things. Note that the Quaker draws upon St. Augustine.

For full discussion see studies listed in Bibliography, above, under Bailey, Murray, and Strong.

Page 145. THE WAITING

Cf. Milton's "On His Blindness," ending "They also serve who only stand and wait." Although as a Quaker Whittier could take no active part in the Civil War, it should be noted that he saw himself as helping to speed "troop after troop" of soldiers with his prayers. Cf. the following poem, ll. 9–16, where he recognizes "the awful beauty of self-sacrifice" in a war for a righteous cause.

Page 146. AMY WENTWORTH

Lines 1–79 show Whittier as a literary theorist, laying aside "the harsh trumpet of Reform" (cf. "Ego," p. 113, above), turning to "milder keys" and "household melodies" to "relieve the storm-stunned ear" and to hold the "vantage ground of light." Here he begins a trend which is to culminate in "Snow-Bound" and "The Pennsylvania Pilgrim." Note that Whittier is guided in part by the remembrance that "through the war-march of the Puritan/ The silver stream of Marvell's music ran" (ll. 37–38). Cf. his eloquent essay on Andrew Marvell (*Works*, VI, 87–103), friend of Milton and defender of English liberty, whose almost Wordsworthian poems on hill and grove and trees and birds and "trout stream" Whittier loved. The "simple legend" which the Quaker poet times "to the sound of wind in the woods" deals with the love of a high-born colonial maid for a brave but humble sailor, with the democratic triumph over caste of love's "own sweet will."

Page 147. ANDREW RYKMAN'S PRAYER

Whittier wrote that he had "bestowed much thought" on this poem, and that he regarded it as "in some respects the best thing I have ever written" (Pickard, *Life*, II, 449). Fields, editor of the *Atlantic*, to whom Whittier had sent the poem in November, 1862, suggested some changes, and the poet replied, December 2, as follows: "I return Mr. Rykman. I know that 'pearl' and 'marl' do not jingle together well—but the lines have a meaning in them, and if the reader will roll his r's a little they will do. I add a verse at the tail of it. John de Labadie [cf. l. 204] was a devout 'come-outer' in Holland two centuries ago . . . Abraham's message is a great improvement in point of style. It's conclusion is really noble."

It should be noted that Whittier modestly refracts his own creed dramatically through the prayer of Rykman. He turns away from the turmoil of war in the outward world of change where "all things flow and fluctuate"—from "this whirl of swooning trance"—to the changeless realm of spiritual "permanence" (ll. 83–91); and, "evil-stained," he recognizes that God alone can bring peace to "the dual heart of man" torn between "soul and sense." This growth of perspective, based on Whittier's quickened consciousness of a dualism between change and changelessness and between good and evil within the heart of the individual, appears concurrently in Whittier's prose of this period. "In the chaos of civil strife," he says (*Works*, VII, 303–304) in 1863, "and the shadow of mourning which rests over the land, the contemplation of 'things unseen which are eternal' might not be unwelcome; . . . when the foundations of human confidence are shaken, and the trust in man proves vain, there might be glad listeners to a voice calling from the outward and the temporal to the inward and the spiritual; from the troubles and perplexities of time, to the eternal quietness which God giveth."

Page 150. BRYANT ON HIS BIRTHDAY

With Whittier's growing emphasis on the inward life and the organic relation between the poet's character and his poetic creation, it is fitting that he should find Bryant's life his "noblest strain, / His manhood better than his verse!"

l. 8. Refers to Wordsworth.

THE VANISHERS

In writing Fields regarding this poem, September 27, 1864, Whittier said: "If thee have read Schoolcraft thee will remember what he says of the Puck-wud-jinnies, or 'Little Vanishers.' The legend is very beautiful, and I hope I have done it justice in some sort" (Pickard, *Life*, II, 481). This poem of immortality, based on the sweet Indian legend of the shades of the departed guiding the living to the Sunset Land of Souls, was also inspired by the death of Whittier's beloved sister Elizabeth twenty-four days before he sent the poem to Fields. Doubtless her death had helped to suggest to the reformer that there are sorrows which cannot be cured by legislation. Wordsworth's parallel turn from humanitarianism to centrality, from the temporal to the spiritual (cf. "Ode on Intimations of Immortality"), had been encouraged by the death of his brother John. Note that whereas Whittier's earlier poems involving Indian themes (cf. "Mogg Megone") had emphasized outward melodramatic aspects, he is now concerned with the Indians' spiritual legends. On backgrounds see J. A. Russell, "The Aboriginal Element in Whittier's Writings," *Granite Monthly*, LX, 217–223. Some measure of his development is found in his wish to "kill Mogg Megone over again" (Pickard, *Life*, II, 393).

LAUS DEO!

"The poem 'Laus Deo!' was suggested to Mr. Whittier as he sat in the Friends' meeting-house in Amesbury, and listened to the bells and the cannon which were proclaiming the passage of the constitutional amendment abolishing slavery, in 1865. . . . When he returned to his home, he recited these passages, which had not yet been committed to paper, to the family sitting in the 'garden room.' . . . 'It wrote itself [he told Lucy Larcom later] or rather sang itself, while the bells rang'" (Pickard's *Life*, II, 488–489).

See also Whittier's "Hymn for the Celebration of Emancipation at Newburyport."

Page 151. THE ETERNAL GOODNESS

This is probably the best and most widely known of Whittier's hymns. Note his tactful expression of indifference to "iron creeds" and "logic linked and strong"—referring, perhaps, to Calvinism. (Cf. Holmes's "The Deacon's Masterpiece.") And note Whittier's final dependence upon unreasoned faith in God's all-seeing "love and care." Another of his famous hymns is that part of "The Brewing of Soma" which begins, "Dear Lord and Father of mankind."

Page 152. OUR MASTER

Five familiar hymns have been taken from this poem. They begin respectively with stanzas one, seven, sixteen, twenty-four, and thirty-five.

ll. 139–40. It should be noted that Whittier's increasing concern with the inward life in accordance with Christian teaching did not render him indifferent to helping others, for that teaching included charity of heart as one of its triune virtues. Compare and contrast Christian charity and humanitarianism.

Page 154. SNOW-BOUND

"The inmates of the family at the Whittier homestead who are referred to in the poem were my father, mother, my brother and two sisters, and my uncle and aunt, both unmarried. In addition, there was the district school master, who boarded with us. The 'not unfeared, half-welcome guest' was Harriet Livermore, daughter of Judge Livermore, of New Hampshire, a young woman of fine natural ability, enthusiastic, eccentric, with slight control over her violent temper, which sometimes made her religious profession doubtful. She was equally ready to exhort in school-house prayer-meetings and dance in a Washington ball-room, while her father was a member of congress. She early embraced the doctrine of the Second Advent, and felt it her duty to proclaim the Lord's speedy coming. With this message she crossed the Atlantic and spent the greater part of a long life in travelling over Europe and Asia. She lived some time with Lady Hester Stanhope, a woman as fantastic and mentally strained as herself, on the slope of Mt. Lebanon, but finally quarrelled with her in regard to two white horses with red marks on their backs which suggested the idea of saddles, on which her titled hostess expected to ride into Jerusalem with the Lord. A friend of mine found her, when quite an old woman, wandering in Syria with a tribe of Arabs, who with the Oriental notion that madness is inspiration, accepted her as their prophetess and leader. At the time referred to in *Snow-Bound* she was boarding at the Rocks Village, about two miles from us.

"In my boyhood, in our lonely farm-house, we had scanty sources of information; few books and only a small weekly newspaper. Our only annual was the Almanac. Under such circumstances story-telling was a necessary resource in the long winter evenings. My father when a young man had traversed the wilderness to Canada, and could tell us of his adventures with Indians and wild beasts, and of his sojourn in the French villages. My uncle was ready with his record of hunting and fishing and, it must be confessed, with stories, which he at least half believed, of witchcraft and apparitions. My mother, who was born in the Indian-haunted region of Somersworth, New Hampshire, between Dover and Portsmouth, told us of the inroads of the savages, and the narrow escape of her ancestors. She described strange people who lived on the Piscataqua and Cocheco, among whom was Bantam the sorcerer. I have in my possession the wizard's 'conjuring book,' which he solemnly opened when consulted. It is a copy of Cornelius Agrippa's *Magic*, printed in 1651, dedicated to Dr. Robert Child, who, like Michael Scott, had learned

'the art of glammorie
In Padua beyond the sea,'

and who is famous in the annals of Massachusetts, where he was at one time a resident, as the first man who dared petition the General Court for liberty of conscience. The full title of the book is *Three Books of Occult Philosophy, by Henry Cornelius Agrippa, Knight, Doctor of both Laws, Counsellor to Cæsar's Sacred Majesty and Judge of the Prerogative Court.*" [*Whittier's note.*]

This poem is discussed in Pickard's *Life*, I, 27–36, and II, 494–500; and in *Whittier-Land*, pp. 12, 24, 39, 74.

It should be noted that, as G. R. Carpenter has said, although the poem is based on reminiscences which are personal, Whittier has stressed the aspects of his life which were representative and typical. Much as he loved nature, he has subordinated nature here to human character. In re-living "the winter joys his boyhood knew," Whittier wrote in a mood of wistful and reverential piety shared by most thoughtful people who recall the simplicity and serenity of an earlier day. The poem should be compared with "The Cotter's Saturday Night" by Burns. Whittier presents a representative portrait of simple, brave, sturdy country-folk rare in human history. "What makes them what they are," says Barrett Wendell, "is that they are still lords of themselves and of the soil they till. Simple with all the simplicity of hereditary farming folk, they are at the same time gentle with the unconscious grace of people who are aware of no earthly superiors. This is the phase of human nature that Whittier knew first and best. This is what he assumed and believed that all mankind might be. Very surely, too, this is the stuff of which any sound democracy must be made" (*Stelligeri*, p. 169). Compare "Among the Hills," lines 100–105, for Whittier's ideal of American life. His respect for sturdy and cultured rusticity should not be confused with Rousseauistic primitivism. The evenness, which sometimes approaches monotony, of the four-stress couplets (Whittier's favorite form) is well suited to the subject.

Many critics admit that Whittier is admirable as a reformer and moralist, but question whether as an artist in words he ever achieved what Arnold defined as the "grand style"—a style which "arises in poetry, *when a noble nature, poetically gifted, treats with simplicity or with severity a serious subject*, . . . saying a thing with a kind of intense compression, or in an allusive, brief, almost haughty way, as if the poet's mind were charged with so many and such grave matters, that he would not deign to treat any one of them explicitly" ("On Translating Homer: Last Words"). It is true that such passages are not continuous in Whittier's work (or in that of other nineteenth-century poets in England and America), but Barrett Wendell has called attention to the greatness of certain passages in "Snow-Bound" (in addition to those noted below, see ll. 155–174; 374–375; 418–422). The following lines on the dead are perhaps typical and they do not accord ill with Arnold's definition of the "grand style":

"Their written words we linger o'er
But *in the sun they cast no shade,*
No voice is heard, no sign is made . . ." (ll. 196 ff.)

"How many a poor one's blessing went
With thee *beneath the low green tent*
Whose curtain never outward swings!" (ll. 389 ff.)

". . . Where cool and long the shadows grow,
I walk to meet *the night that soon*
Shall shape and shadow overflow . . ." (ll. 429 ff.)

l. 215. Whittier explained that this line was in Sarah Wentworth Morton's poem, "The African

Chief," which appeared in Bingham's *The American Preceptor,* a schoolbook. Note that the antislavery sentiment seems dragged in.

l. 286. "Sewel's ancient tome" refers to William Sewel's *History of the Christian People Called Quakers,* a book which emphasizes the persecutions of the Quakers in England and America. It is interesting to note the books with which Whittier was familiar as a boy. On the backgrounds of the tastes of his sect, see Luella Wright's scholarly book, *The Literary Life of the Early Friends, 1650–1725* (New York: 1932).

l. 289. Refers to Thomas Chalkley (1675–1741), an eccentric Quaker preacher who visited America.

l. 307. Cf. Pickard's *Life,* I, 32–33, and Whittier's *Works,* V, 320–325 ("The Fish I Didn't Catch").

l. 392. Whittier's sister Elizabeth, who died in 1864, was his constant companion. See Pickard, *Life,* I, 29–31, and Whittier's poems "To My Sister" and "The Last Eve of Summer."

ll. 510–578. Cf. Whittier's prefatory note, above. In this sharp characterization he refers to Harriet Livermore, of Haverhill, who later crossed the sea to dwell at the foot of Mt. Lebanon with Lady Hester Stanhope, the "crazy queen" to whom the poet refers, l. 555. On Lady Stanhope, see Kinglake's *Eothen,* ch. VIII, cited by Whittier. He wrote Fields that his characterization of Harriet Livermore "is as near the life as I can give it." Note that this character does much to give color to the somewhat gray poem, and to throw the other characters into relief by contrast.

l. 683. Thomas Ellwood (1639–1713), an English Quaker, wrote a "drab" epic on King David entitled *Davideis.* He was a friend of Milton and suggested that he write *Paradise Regained.* See Whittier's long essay on Ellwood (*Works,* VI, 37–68), showing his full knowledge of and admiration for the seventeenth-century liberals, especially John Milton. To Whittier these were "Brave men and faithful! . . . Ye maintained the austere dignity of virtue, and, with King and Church and Parliament arrayed against you, vindicated the Rights of Conscience, at the cost of home, fortune, and life. English liberty owes more to your unyielding firmness than to the blows stricken for her at Worcester and Naseby" (*ibid.,* pp. 57–58). Consider the influence on the young Whittier of Ellwood's liberal spirit in his poetry ("a single book was all we had"), read repeatedly by the family fireside.

Alfred Kreymborg (*Our Singing Strength,* p. 89) concludes that "Whittier's masterpiece, autobiographical throughout, might serve, had he written nothing else, as the narrative of his whole life, ideals and environment. The poem is finely wrought, the plot well sustained, and the successive stanzas dovetail without apparent effort." The crown of Whittier's work, his most popular poem, and probably much more typically American than anything Whitman ever wrote, "Snow-Bound" interweaves into its themes most of Whittier's life-long interests—his devotion to a locality, to antislavery and labor reform, to nature and to sincere and simple rustic characters, to books, to the "subjective and reminiscent," and to religion. With the over-wrought melodramatic early poems, such as "The Demon's Cave" and "The Fire-Ship," compare this poem's placid fidelity and justice of details, and its quiet and wholesome presentation of the universal through the particular. Paul Elmer More (*Shelburne Essays,* XI, p. 21) speaks of early New England literature revealing a majority of households "in which the tenderness to every duty, the sense of due subordination, the competence of training, the repose of a clear conscience, must have evoked an atmosphere of serene and equitable joy. The very discipline of the passions, the renunciation of the wider sweep of human experience, would put a stamp of sacredness on those chaster pleasures which knit a family together in contented unison. In a way all of New England may be said to have been snow-bound, in creed as well as in climate, but in the shelter of the hearth there was warmth for the body and there was comfort for the soul. Whittier was recalling a true incident of his childhood, and was writing also an allegory of New England's inner life, when he described that night of storm and snow."

Page 162. ABRAHAM DAVENPORT

Whittier's note: "The famous Dark Day of New England, May 19, 1780, was a physical puzzle for many years to our ancestors, but its occurrence brought something more than philosophical speculation into the minds of those who passed through it. The incident of Colonel Abraham Davenport's sturdy protest is a matter of history." Note, again, that while Whittier deals with a local story, it is but the basis for a spiritual symbol of an import universal. The poem has a vibrant simplicity and terseness which places it among Whittier's better works.

Page 163. THE MEETING

ll. 59 ff. Note that while as a youthful radical Whittier tended to see the cause and cure of evil in outward institutions, he now concentrates first on the inward life of the individual. In the Self is "the origin . . . of sin"; to be saved "is only this,—Salvation from our selfishness" (l. 222). Yet, in accordance with the doctrine of Christian charity of heart, he condemns a monastic solitude and a quest of "the selfish good" (l. 53), and he finds that Christ "lives today" in the spiritual help we render the poor, the blind, "the bound and suffering of our kind" (ll. 240 ff.).

ll. 63 ff. Much as Greenleaf Whittier loved nature—he once presented a green leaf to someone as a substitute for his visiting card!—he increasingly insisted that, rather than revealing, nature "hides the Giver in the given," and offers us only "perpetual riddles of surprise" (l. 76 and l. 71). Cf. Emerson (*Works*, III, 193 ff.) on "a slight treachery and derision" in the natural universe, whose "secret is untold . . . But if, instead of identifying ourselves with the work [nature], we feel that the soul of the Workman streams through us, we shall find the peace of the morning dwelling first in our hearts . . ."

ll. 147 ff. With Whittier's view of the "old-time faith" and "cramping bounds of creeds," and his insistence that "God is near us now as then," compare Emerson's "Divinity School Address" (*Works*, I, 134): "Men have come to speak of the revelation as somewhat long ago given and done, as if God were dead." Cf. also Emerson's opening sentences in *Nature* (1836).

Page 165. AMONG THE HILLS

This poem, originally called "A Summer Idyl," was planned as a companion piece to "Snow-Bound, a Winter Idyl." It is less artistic than "Snow-Bound," partly because the story of the wooing of the cultured city girl by the uncouth farmer does not ring quite true and is told to prove a thesis. Yet the poem has many excellent passages, and it is especially interesting as embodying Whittier's mature social philosophy. He recognizes that farm life is often "hard and colorless" (ll. 45–98), that it has its share of

"Shrill, querulous women, sour and sullen men,"

and it is clear that if he had wished he could have written like Crabbe, or Hamlin Garland, or Edith Wharton in *Ethan Frome*. With his later philosophy of centrality, he knows that no environment can make bad people good. If he himself likes country life, it is only as the setting for spiritual self-conquest. He is not a primitivist whose love of nature involves a hatred of books and a socially-mediated tradition; the whole point of the poem's story is that the farmer can fulfill his true potentialities only "with beauty, art, taste, culture, books" (l. 102). Indeed, Parrington, the champion of philosophic agrarianism, goes so far as to say that the folk-poet of New England "reveals no sympathy with agrarianism," and that he was rather proud of the "developing industrialism" (*The Romantic Revolution*, p. 366). Whittier was broad enough to respect honest labor in all fields, but his later emphasis was not on the field but on the individual. He sought not to breed class-hate and class-war but to unite "culture's charm and labor's strength" (l. 495).

It should be noted that in Whittier's warmly sensuous description of nature in the first thirty-three lines—including the "drowsy smell of flowers" and the "symphony of peace"—he comes closer, perhaps, than in any of his other work, to the sensuous magic of John Keats.

Page 171. THE PENNSYLVANIA PILGRIM

"On the 24th of May [1872] Mr. Whittier wrote to James R. Osgood: 'I am half inclined to think it would be best to print my poem, a part of which I showed thee, in a volume by itself. It contains about five hundred lines, divided into verses of three lines, and with the introduction and notes will make nearly fifty pages, or about the size of "Snow-Bound." I have added a good deal to it and, I think, made it a better poem. I think honestly it is as good as (if not better than) any long poem I have written.' . . . Sixteen stanzas of this poem, descriptive of the 'Quaker Meeting,' were published in the *Independent*, in June, 1872" (S. T. Pickard, *Life*, II, 575–576). A little later he wrote to Celia Thaxter of "The Pennsylvania Pilgrim," "It is as long as 'Snow-Bound,' and better, but nobody will find it out." Paul Elmer More, one of the most distinguished of modern critics, agrees with Whittier's judgment of this poem, written "in the full maturity of his powers," and concludes that in this "exquisite idyl . . . all the better elements of his genius are displayed . . . in opulent freedom" (*Shelburne Essays*, Third Series, pp. 48, 50). More especially praises Whittier's ability to deal with the life of the spirit in concrete and homely terms. F. H. Underwood (*Whittier*, pp. 274–275) remarks of the poem, "Pastorius and his beautiful wife, their charming home, gardens, and vineyard, and their fine old-time manners are depicted in tender if sober colors. The quiet of the scene becomes contagious, and the reader, harassed by the bustle and worry of modern life, slips back in imagination into those pastoral times, and gains rest and refreshment of soul. It is a story to be read under apple-blossoms, while bees are filling the air with a drowsy hum, and the landscape lies in dream-like repose. The Friends alone among moderns appear to know the blessedness of calm souls."

If Whittier developed through three phases—romantic localism; humanitarianism; and religious humanism—all three phases are distinguishable in "The Pennsylvania Pilgrim." The groundwork of the poem is localistic. He calls the poem "a study of the life and times of the Pennsylvania colonist,—a simple picture of a noteworthy man and his locality." The story of this poem, based on local fact, is

"A truer idyl than the bards have told
Of Arno's banks or Arcady of old" (ll. 555–556).

Second, the poem illustrates the fact that the mature Whittier transcended his earlier humanitarianism by *including* it in a larger philosophy. For "The Pennsylvania Pilgrim" is devoted in part to showing an example of the way in which Quaker influence "has been felt through two centuries in the amelioration of penal severities, the abolition of slavery, the reform of the erring, the relief of the poor and suffering,—felt, in brief, in every step of human progress." And third, finding the universal in localistic particulars, Whittier, the Quaker, embodies in this poem such elements of religious humanism as the essential inwardness of sin; the dualism between outward nature and "the Spirit's law, the Inward Rule and Guide," "the soul's communion with the Eternal Mind"; the stress on Christian charity even if outward reform is partial and ephemeral without inward reform; centrality and immanence—"Within himself he found the law of right"; a reliance on tradition properly interpreted—Pastorius "read his Bible by the Inward Light"; a respect for the guidance of exalted human lives; stress on a free-willed obedience to divine law; and the resultant "calm and measureless content."

Page 183. A MYSTERY

This poem and "The Trailing Arbutus" (p. 184) show how beautifully Whittier could follow in the path of Wordsworth when he chose to do so.

THE PROBLEM

This poem, embodying Whittier's mature attitude toward problems of social reform, tends to make his readers take sides in accordance with their social and political philosophies. Radicals such as Mordell (*Quaker Militant*, 258) claim that in this poem Whittier "virtually deserted the cause of liberty" because he finally denominated agitators for labor reform by merely mechanical means as "demagogues" offering "vain and evil counsels" (l. 9). More sympathetic readers are likely to think that, while Whittier stood for Christian charity, he sees social problems in increasing perspective in tracking suffering to the lack of self-conquest on the part of the individual. Here he says that neither class alone—Capital or Labor—has a monopoly on virtue, that each needs the other and that there is no solution "save in the Golden Rule of Christ alone"—save in each individual's imposing self-discipline and restraint. The ex-radical, who had been so fiery in blaming laws and institutions as a young man, wrote in 1889: "There is very little of actual suffering which may not be traced to intemperance, idleness, and utter lack of economy, wasteful and careless of the future when wages are good. We need the gospel of Poor Richard's Almanac sadly" (Pickard's *Life*, II, 742). In *Poor Richard* the New-England-born Franklin, who acknowledged that the Puritan Cotton Mather had "an influence on my conduct through life" (*Writings*, ed. Smyth, IX, 208), concluded that we are taxed "four times as much by our Folly [as by government]; and from these taxes the Commissioners cannot ease or deliver us" (*ibid.*, III, 409).

Page 185. WHITTIER'S POETIC THEORIES

Whittier's first book, *Legends of New England*, appeared in Hartford, Conn., 1831. The selection from the opening of the essay on "Robert Dinsmore" (of Windham, N. H.) appears to have been begun early in 1828 (see Pickard's *Life*, I, 66) although the reference to "The Biglow Papers" shows that it must have been revised after 1846. "The Beautiful" has been located by F. H. Ristine in a volume called *Voices of the True-Hearted* (Philadelphia, 1846), pp. 177–178, and it is probable that it was first published in 1844.

The development of Whittier's literary theory is a rich field for investigation, and it has been almost untouched. Only broad outlines can be suggested here. (See the notes, above, on "Ego," "Dedication, Songs of Labor," "Proem," "Wordsworth," "Burns," and "The Last Walk in Autumn.") Following the general growth of his mind indicated earlier, his literary theory evolved through three phases. First, until about 1833, he advocated either romance—fanciful, dreamy, or Gothic—or nationalistic localism (see the first two selections here printed and his preface to the *Literary Remains of John G. C. Brainard*, Hartford, 1832), although one can trace beginnings of his next phase (see Pickard's *Life*, I, 67 and 71). Whittier later characterized himself, in turning from his first to his second poetic ideal, held from about 1833 to 1858, as follows:

> "[He was] a dreamer born,
>   Who, with a mission to fulfil,
> Had left the Muses' haunt to turn
>   The crank of an opinion-mill,
> Making his rustic reed of song
> A weapon in the war with wrong."

Although he admits that "beauty is its own excuse" ("Dedication, Songs of Labor," 1850), he says that, recognizing his own limitations, he will use poetry as propaganda to further "human right and weal" ("Proem"), and "a manlier spirit of content" with "life's common things." "Ego" records his turning from his earlier "Fairy-land" to "pour the fiery breath of storm / Through the harsh trumpet of Reform." His attitude is represented in a letter to a friend in 1838 in which he said he admired her poems because "to their intrinsic beauty is added the holier aim of Philanthropy" (Mordell, *Quaker Militant*, p. 110). "I would rather have the memory," he said, "of a Howard, a Wilberforce, and a Clarkson [English reformers] than the undying fame of a Byron [whom he had earlier imitated]" (Pickard, *Life*, I, 71). "Burns" had awakened him, he says, from idyllic or lurid dreams to the superiority of "simple truth of fact and feeling." Third, from 1858 on, he develops the view presaged in the essay on "The Beautiful" in 1846, according to which beauty is not a matter of romantic escape or nationalistic peculiarities but a spiritual quality, a timeless and placeless "beauty of holiness." In "The Tent on the Beach" (1867) Whittier has one of the characters say:

"Art no other sanction needs
Than beauty for its own fair sake.
It grinds not in the mill of use,
Nor asks for leave, nor begs excuse;
It makes the flexile laws it deigns to own,
And gives its atmosphere its color and its tone."

Ultimately, then, Whittier comes to adopt Emerson's organic theory of poetic creation; he had prefaced "The Beautiful" with a statement by Emerson regarding beauty, and in this essay he develops the idea that the highest beauty is the inward beauty of holiness. In 1884 Whittier said, "I regard Emerson [who had said, "Beauty is the mark God sets upon virtue"] as foremost in the rank of American poets; he has written better than any of us" (Pickard, *Life*, II, 696). Much as he loved the beauties of nature, he finally came to regard them, as Emerson did, as "outward types and signs / Of the eternal beauty which fulfils / The one great purpose of creation, Love" ("Among the Hills," 1868). And in "An Artist of the Beautiful" (1885) he concluded that

"Beauty is goodness; ugliness is sin."

RALPH WALDO EMERSON

CHRONOLOGY

1803 Born, Boston, Mass., May 25, son of a Unitarian clergyman.

1817–21 After poverty-stricken youth and preparation at Boston Latin School, graduated from Harvard College. Began keeping a Journal in 1820.

1825 After trying school-teaching, studied for ministry.

1826–27 Went to Florida for his health.

1829 Became associate pastor of Second Church of Boston. Married Ellen Tucker, who died in 1831.

1832 Became indifferent to rites such as the Lord's Supper, and resigned pastorate.

1832–33 Went to Italy, France, and England, finding his heroes—Landor, Coleridge, Wordsworth, and Carlyle—"deficient in insight into religious truth."

1834 Made ancestral Concord, Mass., his home.

1835 Married Lydia Jackson.

1836 *Nature*, the core of most of the doctrines he later developed. Attacked traditionalism in religion and defended immanence. His son Waldo born.

1837 "The American Scholar," read before the Harvard society of Phi Beta Kappa.

1838 "Divinity School Address" at Harvard caused "tempest in a tea-pot" because of his doctrine of a deity depersonalized and immutable, an ever-present beneficent law.

1840–44 Wrote for *The Dial*, the organ of Transcendentalism. Emerson was editor 1842–1844, after Margaret Fuller.

1841 *Essays, First Series.*

1842 His son Waldo died.

1844 *Essays, Second Series.*

1847 *Poems.* Second visit to Europe.

1847–48 Delivered lectures on "Representative Men" in Europe, renewing friendship with Carlyle with whom he corresponded from 1834 to 1878. This *Correspondence* was published in 1883.

1849 *Nature, Addresses and Lectures* collected and published.

1850 *Representative Men* published.

1855 Championed abolition and woman's suffrage.

1856 *English Traits.*

1857 Began writing for *Atlantic Monthly* under Lowell's editorship, continuing his lyceum lecturing. With Lowell, Holmes, Longfellow, Hawthorne, Motley, Agassiz, organized the Saturday Club.

1860 *The Conduct of Life* (essays), including "Fate" and "Illusions."

1867 *May-Day and Other Pieces*, his second volume of poems.

1868–70 Lectured at Harvard on "Natural History of the Intellect."

1870 *Society and Solitude.* Mellow essays such as "Works and Days."

1871 Visited California.

1872 Mind began to fail. Third trip to Europe; visited Egypt.

1873 ff. Venerated as a sage.

1875 *Letters and Social Aims.*

1876 Made his last entry in the Journal.

1882 Died in Concord, April 27.

BIBLIOGRAPHY

I. Bibliography

Cooke, G. W. *A Bibliography of Ralph Waldo Emerson.* Boston: 1908. (Exhaustive up to its date. Pp. 205–309 list studies about Emerson.)

Steeves, H. R. Bibliography of Emerson in *The Cambridge History of American Literature.* New York: 1917. I, 551–566. ("It includes in particular all the publications of importance which have appeared [up to 1917] since Mr. Cooke's volume.")

II. Text

Complete Writings, ed. by J. E. Cabot. Riverside Edition. Boston: 1884–1893. 14 vols.; Riverside popular edition. Boston: 1926. Vols. 13 and 14 contain Cabot's *Memoir.*

Complete Works of Ralph Waldo Emerson. Centenary Edition. Boston: 1903–1904. 12 vols. (Ed. by Emerson's son, with a valuable biographical introduction and detailed notes. The standard edition.)

Hale, E. E. *Ralph Waldo Emerson: Together with Two Early Essays of Emerson.* Boston: 1904. (The two essays are "The Character of Socrates," 1820, and "The Present State of Ethical Philosophy," 1821, with an address on Emerson by Hale, pp. 9–53.)

Correspondence between Ralph Waldo Emerson and Herman Grimm, ed. by F. W. Holls. Boston: 1903. Originally published in the *Atlantic Monthly*, XCI, 467–479 (April, 1903).

Emerson's Journals, ed. by Edward Emerson and Waldo Emerson Forbes. Boston: 1909–14. 10 vols.

Uncollected Lectures of Ralph Waldo Emerson, ed. by Clarence Gohdes. New York: 1932.

Uncollected Writings, Essays, Addresses, Poems, Reviews and Letters by Ralph Waldo Emerson, ed. by C. C. Biglow. New York: 1912.

The Heart of Emerson's Journals, ed. by Bliss Perry. Boston: 1926.

The Correspondence of Thomas Carlyle and Ralph Waldo Emerson, 1834–1872, ed. by C. E. Norton. Revised edition, Boston: 1888. 2 vols.

A Correspondence between John Sterling and Ralph Waldo Emerson, ed. by E. W. Emerson. Boston: 1897.

"The Emerson-Thoreau Correspondence," ed. by F. B. Sanborn, *Atlantic Monthly*, LXIX, 577–596, 736–753 (May and June, 1892).

Letters from Ralph Waldo Emerson to a Friend, 1838–1853 [Samuel Gray Ward], ed. by C. E. Norton. Boston: 1899.

"Early Letters of Emerson," ed. by Mary Withington, *Century Magazine*, o.s. XXVI, 454–458 (July, 1883).

Emerson-Clough Letters, ed. by H. F. Lowry and R. L. Rusk. Cleveland: 1934. (Sixteen hitherto unpublished letters by Emerson.)

(Professor R. L. Rusk is preparing several volumes of Emerson's unpublished letters for the Columbia University Press.)

III. Biography and Criticism

Allen, G. W. *American Prosody*. New York: 1935, pp. 91–121. (A scholarly survey of Emerson's meters and stanzas in the light of his prosodic and poetic theories. Shows that "many of Emerson's first drafts of his poems are actually what we today call 'free verse.'" And concludes that his "technique places greater importance on images, cadenced phrases, and rhetoric than on rimes and meters.")

Arnold, Matthew. "Emerson," in *Discourses in America*. London: 1885, pp. 138–207. (Among judicial essays, this has been one of the most influential. "We have not in Emerson a great poet, a great writer, a great philosophy-maker." He is rather "the friend and aider of those who would live in the spirit." "Emerson's *Essays* are, I think, the most important work done in prose" in the nineteenth century. "His work is more important than Carlyle's" [pp. 178–179, 196]. Denies that his poetry is simple, or sensuous, or impassioned.)

Bailey, E. J. *Religious Thought in the Greater American Poets*. Boston: 1922, pp. 47–69. (A readable essay tracing the development of Emerson's religious ideas through his poetry, which Mr. Bailey regards [p. 49] as a better source for such a study than Emerson's less autobiographical prose. Slights his attitude toward evil. See Jorgenson, below.)

Beach, J. W. "Emerson and Evolution," *University of Toronto Quarterly*, III, 474–497 (July, 1934). (A discriminating study, tracing in the light of Emerson's reading in "a succession of second-rate, popular, and more or less dubious authorities" his "transition from the scale-of-being phase . . . to the strictly evolutionary phase" of thought, at which Mr. Beach thinks he did not arrive until about 1844.)

Brittin, N. A. "Emerson and the Metaphysical Poets," *American Literature*, VIII, 1–21 (March, 1936). (Shows resemblance of passages in Emerson's poetry to passages in Donne and Cowley and especially to passages in Herbert and Marvell.)

Brooks, Van Wyck. *The Life of Emerson*. New York: 1932. (Readable, with flashes of intuition, but lacking in scholarly precision and documentation.)

Brownell, W. C. "Emerson," in *American Prose Masters*. New York: 1909, pp. 131–204. (An austere evaluation by a distinguished critic. Section VII deals with Emerson's poetry, regarded as inferior to the essays, of which it is "a kind of intimate reverberation." Brownell, following Arnold, regards his poetry as over-intellectual, as "without distinction . . . in imaginative construction, in concrete imagery, in sensuousness or in sentiment.")

Bruel, Andrée. *Emerson et Thoreau*. Paris: 1929. (A valuable analysis of their relationship and of their common interest in natural law and human liberty. Admirably documented.)

Cabot, J. E. *A Memoir of Ralph Waldo Emerson*. Boston: 1887. 2 vols. (The official biography, containing the basic materials.)

Canby, H. S. "Emerson," in *Classic Americans*. New York: 1931, pp. 143–183. (A thoughtful and discriminating essay. Mr. Canby thinks Emerson's debt to European culture has been over-emphasized, and he interprets him interestingly as "a New Englander in the stream of time, and an intuitive mind reflecting upon the triple impact of Puritan moralism, experimental science, and the industrialism that was about to determine an epoch in all Western culture" [p. 143]. Concludes that "the merits of Emerson's poetry are prose merits.")

Carpenter, F. I. *Emerson and Asia*. Cambridge, Mass.: 1930. (Considers Emerson's debt to Orientalism and to Neo-Platonism. Reviewed in *University of California Chronicle*, XXXII, 498–500 [Oct., 1930] and [adversely] in *Modern Philology*, XXVIII, 245–248 [Nov., 1930]. See also Carpenter's comprehensive Introduction to *Emerson* [1934] in American Writers Series, emphasizing Emerson's modernity.)

Cestre, Charles. "Le Romantisme d'Emerson," *Revue Anglo-Américaine*, VII, 1–18; 113–131 (Oct., Dec., 1929). (One of the ablest of many attempts to present romantic individualism, optimism, expansiveness, and Americanism as fundamental in Emerson, who is viewed as the father of Whitman. An interesting interpretation by one of the greatest living French critics; may be supplemented by interpretations emphasizing Emerson's dualistic and conservative elements. See Harrison and Foerster, below.)

Chapman, J. J. "Emerson," in *Emerson and Other Essays*. New York: 1898, pp. 3–108. (A judicious critique emphasizing Emerson's heroic role in preaching a sound self-development and individualism as opposed to all tyranny, including that of the opinion of the masses. Finds his poetry has "too much thought," too little music.)

Christy, Arthur. *The Orient in American Transcendentalism: A Study of Emerson, Thoreau, and Alcott.* New York: 1932, pp. 61–183. (An elaborately documented analysis of Emerson's debt to Oriental religions.)

Clark, H. H. "Emerson and Science," *Philological Quarterly*, X, 225–260 (July, 1931). (Attempts to show that Emerson's interest in astronomy and evolution "helped to motivate, during his formative years up to 1838, his turn against ecclesiasticism and an antiquarian devotion to the past, and concurrently, his turn toward a faith in a relatively depersonalized Over-Soul, perhaps best defined as a 'beneficent tendency' or 'conscious,' 'animated law.'")

Conway, M. D. *Emerson at Home and Abroad.* Boston: 1882. (Based on personal knowledge. Somewhat grandiloquent.)

Davis, Ada E. "Emerson's Thoughts on Education," *Education*, XLV, 353–372 (Feb., 1925). (An able, well-documented, brief survey, concluding [p. 371]: "He believes in education, not in the limited sense of systems and schools acting upon the mass of society, nor in intellectual culture per se though he values this highly, but in an education which embraces all experience, all phases of thinking, feeling, and acting, which discovers man to himself and reveals his union with God and the universe." In view of Emerson's great exaltation of the potency of ideas and of the scholar, this study is important.)

Dugard, Marie. *Ralph Waldo Emerson, sa vie et son œuvre.* Paris: 1907. (An appreciative, generally judicious, scholarly dissertation. The chapters are: I, "L'homme"; II, "Les idées générales"; III, "La vie individuelle"; IV, "La vie domestique"; V, "La société et les questions qui s'y rattachent" [an important chapter, pp. 241–309]; VI, "La vie religieuse"; VII, "Du génie d'Emerson et de son influence.")

Emerson, E. W. *Emerson in Concord; A Memoir.* Boston: 1888. (By Emerson's son. A valuable supplement to Cabot.)

Ferguson, J. De L. *American Literature in Spain.* New York: 1916, pp. 157–170. (A Columbia University dissertation containing a detailed survey of Emerson's vogue in Spain.)

Firkins, O. W. *Ralph Waldo Emerson.* Boston: 1915. (A brilliant book, especially in the critical chapters such as Chapter VI, "Emerson as Poet," pp. 274–296. Trenchant and judicious.)

Foerster, Norman. "Emerson," in *Nature in American Literature.* New York: 1923, pp. 37–68. (A well-written and acute survey of "the natural influences on his life, the knowledge of the facts of nature revealed in his poetry, and his eager response—the response of a true poet—to the provocation of her loveliness and mystery." Concludes that ultimately Emerson, "true descendant of the Puritans," agreed with Milton in relying not on nature or the "law for thing" but on the "law for man" and the moral sentiment.)

——"Emerson," in *American Criticism.* Boston: 1928, pp. 52–110. (A remarkably acute and cogent exposition and criticism of Emerson's literary creed [summarized, p. 59], of his view of art as organic expression, his doctrine of inspiration, his distinction between genius and talent, his debt to and kinship with the Greek tradition, his view of the unity and parity of Beauty, Truth and Goodness and of the inter-penetration of æstheticism and ethicism. Concludes that "the main current of Emerson's mind was not the romantic but the classic [p. 84]." Reinforces J. S. Harrison and counterbalances the conventional interpretation of Emerson as primarily a romanticist. See also J. T. Flanagan, "Emerson as a Critic of Fiction," *Philological Quarterly*, XV, 30–45 [Jan., 1936].)

Frothingham, O. B. *Transcendentalism in New England: A History.* New York: 1876, pp. 218–248. (Somewhat discursive and old-fashioned, but based on personal knowledge.)

Garnett, Richard. *Life of Ralph Waldo Emerson.* Great Writers Series. London: 1888. (Judicious for its day, but now mostly superseded by more specialized studies.)

Gay, R. M. *Emerson: A Study of the Poet as Seer.* New York: 1928. (A good readable "narrative and interpretation." The author says he has "eschewed criticism.")

Goddard, H. C. *Studies in New England Transcendentalism.* New York: 1908. (The standard study of the subject. Pp. 113–183 deal with "Transcendentalism and Practical Life." See also Mr. Goddard's essay on "Transcendentalism" in *The Cambridge History of American Literature*, I, 326–348, with bibliography, pp. 546–551.)

Gohdes, C. L. F. *The Periodicals of American Transcendentalism.* Durham, N. C.: 1931. (A valuable scholarly study of the diffusion of the transcendental spirit and of Emerson's relation to *The Western Messenger* and *The Dial*, *The Boston Quarterly Review*, *The Present*, *The Harbinger*, *The Spirit of the Age*, *Æsthetic Papers*, *The Massachusetts Quarterly Review*, the Cincinnati *Dial*, *The Radical*, and *The Index*. There is no bibliography, but the work is admirably footnoted. G. W. Cooke's two-volume *Historical and Biographical Introduction to Accompany The Dial* [1902] supplements the scanty treatment here by Mr. Gohdes.)

Gorely, Jean. "Emerson's Theory of Poetry," *Poetry Review*, XXII, 263–273 (July–Aug., 1931). (An interesting brief study, emphasizing the idea that to Emerson poetry is the result of mystical inspiration, and that "poetry is spiritual and forms a link between the visible and invisible worlds.")

Gray, H. D. *Emerson: A Statement of New England Transcendentalism as Expressed in the Philosophy of Its Chief Exponent.* Stanford, California: 1917. (A closely documented dissertation which attempts to show that the "distinctive contribution to philosophy" of the Transcendentalists consisted in the fact that "they took as a test of idealism its practicability . . . The Transcendentalism of these men was a Pragmatic Mysticism" [p. 14]. Claims that "no revision of the original thesis [completed in 1909] has been made necessary" [p. 5] by the publication of the ten volumes of *Journals*. Besides thoughtful chapters on Emerson's philosophy, religion and ethics, pp. 80–94 deal with his "Contribution to Sociology," and pp. 95–104 deal with his "Esthetics." Of considerable importance.)

Harrison, J. S. *The Teachers of Emerson.* New York: 1910. (Although this book neglects many other factors, it is peculiarly acute in dealing in detail with Emerson's profound debt to dualistic Platonism and Neo-Platonism, with some reference to Bacon and Coleridge. One of the most important interpretations of a major influence; to be balanced by studies of other influences by Canby, Beach, Clark, Gray, Goddard, Marchand, Thompson, and Ustick.)

Hill, A. S. "The Influence of Emerson," *Studies and Notes in Philology and Literature,* V, 23–40 (1897). (A general discussion. Does not consider exhaustively Emerson's specific influence on individuals.)

Hill, J. A. *Emerson and His Philosophy.* London: 1919.

Holmes, O. W. *Ralph Waldo Emerson.* American Men of Letters Series. Boston: 1885. (Mainly of value for the personalia. Holmes the rationalist lacked sympathy with transcendentalism, but paid tribute to Emerson's Yankee shrewdness and practicality.)

Hotson, Clarence. "Emerson and Swedenborg," *New-Church Messenger,* CXL, 274–277 (Oct. 1, 1930). (Claims that Emerson's somewhat unsympathetic essay on Swedenborg is "unscholarly, inaccurate, inconsistent, illogical, irresponsible, and quite unreliable." Dr. Hotson, a militant defender of Swedenborg, has published more than a dozen articles based on his Harvard dissertation, *Emerson and Swedenborg* [1929]; these will be found listed in *American Literature,* IV, 427 [Jan., 1933].)

Hubbell, G. S. *A Concordance to the Poems of Ralph Waldo Emerson.* New York: 1932.

James, Henry. "Emerson," in *Partial Portraits.* London: 1888, pp. 1–33. (A stimulating and appreciative essay by a distinguished novelist and critic who in many ways drew upon and continued the Emersonian tradition. "No one," James concludes, "has had so steady and constant, and above all so natural, a vision of what we require and what we are capable of in the way of aspiration and independence. With Emerson it is ever the special capacity for moral experience—always that and only that." He knew that "the prized was within" [p. 9].)

Jorgenson, C. E. "Emerson's Paradise under the Shadow of Swords," *Philological Quarterly,* XI, 274–292 (July, 1932). (Since it has been conventional to imagine that the great weakness of Emerson consisted in his blindness to sin and evil, this exhaustive assembly and interpretation of a mass of evidence which practically refutes this charge is of great importance. Mr. Jorgenson concludes, "Emerson's attitude toward evil has been shown to resemble essentially that of Milton" [p. 292], whom Emerson so devoutly admired.)

Keller, Hans. *Emerson in Frankreich Wirkungen und Parallelen.* Giessen: 1932. (A thorough dissertation.)

Kreymborg, Alfred. "The Intoxicated Emerson," in *Our Singing Strength.* New York: 1929, pp. 67–83. (Although a bit jaunty, this well-supported appreciation by a contemporary poet is a welcome counterbalance to the views of those who allowed some of Emerson's minor lapses in technicalities to overshadow all the merits of his poems. Finds his verse "compact of richer tones and a deeper passion than is the verse of either Bryant or Poe. . . . Fire abounds all through Emerson." He was "the harbinger of the general Revolution beginning with Whitman." See Noyes, below.)

Lowell, J. R. "Emerson, the Lecturer," in *My Study Windows.* Boston: 1871, pp. 375–384. (One of the best-known and most lyrical of the records of the impression Emerson made on an intelligent listener. "There is no man living to whom, as a writer, so many of us feel and thankfully acknowledge so great an indebtedness for ennobling impulses. . . . Though he writes in prose, he is essentially a poet. . . . To him more than to all other causes together did the young martyrs of our civil war owe the sustaining strength of thoughtful heroism that is so touching in every record of their lives.")

Marchand, Ernest. "Emerson and the Frontier," *American Literature,* III, 149–174 (May, 1931). (A spirited and scholarly survey of Emerson's reactions, in his readings and travels, to the western frontier, showing that the influence of the optimistic romantic individualism of European culture synchronized in his mind with the influence of the American frontier—its democracy, individualism, and optimism. A concrete and important study, which helps to counterbalance many one-sided studies which ignore American influences and derive Emerson entirely from European books. Besides Canby, above, see also H. H. Hoeltje, "Emerson in Iowa," *Iowa Journal of History and Politics,* pp. 236–276 [April, 1927] and "Emerson in Minnesota," *Minnesota History,* II, 145–159; and Willard Thorp, "Emerson on Tour," *Quarterly Journal of Speech*, XVI, 19–34 [Feb., 1930], which is especially interesting for its demonstration of the way in which newspaper reports of Emerson's lectures in the East and in the West differed in attitude and manner.)

McQuiston, Raymer. "The Relation of Ralph Waldo Emerson to Public Affairs," *Bulletin of the University of Kansas*, XXIV, No. 8, Humanistic Studies, III, No. 1, April, 1923, pp. 1–63. (Although brief, this is thus far the best treatment of Emerson's political views in English. It shows that, unlike the mature Lowell, Emerson subordinated the question of preserving the Union to the abolition question. See also Dorothy L. Werner, *The Idea of Union in American Verse* [Philadelphia: 1932], index, for analysis of Emerson's poems on this subject. See also Odell, below.)

Mead, E. D. *The Influence of Emerson*. Boston: 1903. (After a chapter on Emerson's philosophy [pp. 3–90], the book deals with his relation to Theodore Parker [pp. 91–156] and to Carlyle [pp. 157–304]. Not so much a comprehensive factual exposition, precise and objective, as a moralistic exhortation.)

Michaud, Régis. *L'Esthétique d'Emerson*. Paris: 1927. (An elaborate study of Emerson's thought in terms of genius, art, and history. See also Michaud's *La Pensée Américaine: Autour D'Emerson*. Paris: 1924. Chapter III, pp. 65–95, is entitled "Emerson et l'esthetique du Paysage.")

—— *Emerson: the Enraptured Yankee*, tr. by George Boas. New York: 1930. (A rhapsodic, readable book of slight value to the serious student in quest of precise information or dispassionate, measured judgment.)

Moore, J. B. "Emerson on Wordsworth," *Publications of the Modern Language Association*, XLI, 179–192 (March, 1926). (Important. See also F. T. Thompson.)

More, P. E. "Emerson" in *The Cambridge History of American Literature*. New York: 1917. I, 349–362. (Reprinted in *Shelburne Essays*, Eleventh Series. Boston: 1921, pp. 67–94. Although brief and without much documentation, this is a generally judicious critique, concluding that Emerson's philosophy is "a kind of reconciled dualism." More's conventional view that Emerson tends to disregard "the darker facts of human nature" [p. 361] may be modified by the evidence assembled by Jorgenson—see above. See also More's well-written essay, "The Influence of Emerson," in *Shelburne Essays*, First Series [Boston: 1904], pp. 71–84.)

Noyes, Alfred. "The Poetry of Emerson," in *Some Aspects of Modern Poetry*. New York: 1924, pp. 65–80. (A distinguished English poet deplores the fact that we have under-valued our "greatest poet, . . . both in the depth of his thought and in the subtlety of his music" [p. 65]. He finds Emerson "a far subtler musician in verse than Poe," and suggests that in his use of the "subtly displaced accent" Emerson anticipated the methods of modern poets. Special praise is given "The Humble-Bee," "Bacchus," and "Threnody." A significant essay.)

Odell, A. T. *La Doctrine Sociale d'Emerson*. Paris: 1931. (A dissertation of importance. Includes analysis of his view of reform [pp. 40–85], of the professions [pp. 86–105], of economic life [pp. 106–115], of the state [pp. 116–138], and of slavery and abolition [pp. 139–201]. Concludes that during 1821–1824 he was chauvinistic, while from 1824 to 1836 he exalted the individual above the masses; during 1836–1846 he formulated his abstract theory in more detail, being cool to reform; after 1846, in his maturity, Emerson studied the actual life of the nation in the light of his abstract theory, lecturing on abolition questions and the War and discussing many aspects of political and social affairs. The periods are not mutually exclusive, but the classification is suggestive. There is no translation. See also McQuiston and Marchand, above.)

Parrington, V. L. "Emerson, Transcendental Critic," in *The Romantic Revolution in America*. New York: 1927, pp. 386–399. (Stimulating but questionable. For example: "The apotheosis of individualism—such in briefest terms was the gospel of Emerson . . . It was the same revolutionary conception . . . that Rousseau had come upon" [p. 390]. Actually the individualism preached by these men was very different: Rousseau boasted, "I am like no one I have seen"; Emerson advocated a self-reliance which he defined [*Works*, X, 65] as "a self-trust which is a trust in God himself," God being "the Universal Mind" [*Journals*, IV, 61]. Thus one stood for idiosyncracy and the other universality.)

Perry, Bliss. *Emerson Today*. Princeton: 1931. (Graceful public lectures. Chap. I surveys "the general drift of studies of Emerson"; chap. II surveys his worldly career; chap. III is entitled "The Mystic and the Poet"; and in chap. IV, "Revaluations," Perry concludes that a summary "of Emerson's faith seems far more typical of the current thought of the day [1931] than it did at the beginning of the century" [p. 121]. The discussion of Emerson's poetry [pp. 76–97] is charming and discriminating. See also Perry's very ably written essays on "The American Scholar" and on "Emerson's *Journals*" in his book, *The Praise of Folly* [Boston: 1923], pp. 81–113.)

Pettigrew, R. C. "Emerson and Milton," *American Literature*, III, 45–59 (March, 1931). (An important scholarly analysis of all Emerson's references to Milton, showing that "in æsthetic *theory* . . . Milton and Emerson are of the same school," and that Emerson's distinctively ethical "criticism of no other poet yields for us material so richly illustrative of his own literary prepossessions." See also Foerster, Jorgenson, and Sutcliffe.)

Robertson, J. M. "Emerson," in *Modern Humanists*. London: 1891, pp. 112–136. (A militant rationalist attacks Emerson's reliance on intuition, his complacent inconsistencies, and his disregard for the continuity of argument and literary form. Praises his criticism of politics. A stimulating general essay.)

Russell, Phillips. *Emerson: the Wisest American*. New York: 1929. (Readable, but journalistic.)

Sakmann, Paul. *Emerson's Geisteswelt*. Stuttgart: 1927. (One of the ablest of the comprehensive interpretations of Emerson's philosophy. Unfortunately, there is no translation.)

Sanborn, F. B. (ed.). *The Genius and Character of Emerson*. Boston: 1885. (Contains sixteen essays by various acquaintances such as Alcott, Julian Hawthorne, Elizabeth Peabody, Julia Ward Howe, and W. T. Harris.)

Santayana, George. "Emerson," in *Interpretations of Poetry and Religion*. New York: 1900, pp. 217–233. (Discursive reflections by a distinguished philosopher. Emerson "was not primarily a philosopher, but a Puritan mystic with a poetic fancy and a gift for observation and epigram" [p. 230].)

Scudder, Townsend, III. "Emerson's British Lecture Tour, 1847–1848," *American Literature*, VII, 15–36; 166–180 (March and May, 1935). (Exhaustive scholarly analyses of the preparations for the tour, the nature of Emerson's audiences, his manner of lecturing, and the reception of the lectures, especially as revealed in English periodicals. See also Scudder's "Emerson in London and the London Lectures," *American Literature*, VIII, 22–36 [March, 1936], and "A Chronological List of Emerson's Lectures on His British Tour of 1847–1848," *Publications of the Modern Language Association*, LI, 243–248 [March, 1936].)

Sherman, S. P. "The Emersonian Liberation," in *Americans*. New York: 1924, pp. 63–121. (Well-written and generally judicious discussions of Emerson's influence, his religion, philosophy, morals, politics, and literature and art, a section being devoted to each of these topics. Finds his philosophy "a fairly clean-cut dualism." One of the best of the recent brief comprehensive essays.)

Silver, R. G. "Emerson as Abolitionist," *New England Quarterly*, VI, 154–158 (March, 1933). (Gives a report of a speech by Emerson from the files of the *Liberator*.)

Stedman, E. C. "Emerson," in *Poets of America*. Boston: 1885, pp. 133–179. (A reasonably judicious and comprehensive essay, based on the idea that Emerson's "peculiar beauties and deficiencies" as a poet are explained by the fact that he often found himself in a state "of indecision *between the methods of philosophy and art*" [p. 134].)

Stephen, Leslie. "Emerson," in *Studies of a Biographer*. London: 1902. IV, 121–155. (A graceful and incisive essay by a great philosophical critic in a fireside mood.)

Strong, A. H. "Emerson," in *American Poets and Their Theology*. Philadelphia: 1916, pp. 51–103. (A didactic, hostile study from the admittedly Calvinistic angle. It certainly overstates the case in claiming that Emerson led people to pantheism [p. 57] and that he had "no sense of sin" [p. 66]. Yet parts of the essay are stimulating, even in their exaggeration, as in the statement that "his optimism is a pantheistic denial of any moral evil." Actually, Emerson said "Pantheism leads to Atheism" [*Journals*, II, 178], and that "The dualism is ever present, though variously denominated" [*ibid.*, III, 377]. See dualistic interpretations by Harrison, Firkins, Foerster, Sutcliffe, Sherman, and Jorgenson.)

Sutcliffe, E. G. *Emerson's Theories of Literary Expression*. Urbana, Ill.: 1923. (Next to Foerster's study, this is the best, as it is by far the longest and most documented, study of the subject. Originally a dissertation supervised in part by Stuart P. Sherman. The study is developed in terms of Emerson's view of the relation of fact and symbol, considered in the light of his dualistic philosophy of the Many and the One and of the complicated literary influences, classical and romantic, which helped to mold that philosophy. See also Sutcliffe's article on "Whitman, Emerson, and the New Poetry," *New Republic*, XIX, 114–116 [May 24, 1919].)

Thompson, F. T. "Emerson and Carlyle," *Studies in Philology*, XXIV, 438–453 (July, 1927). (An acute, scholarly study, concluding that Carlyle's influence on Emerson was strong only from 1830 to 1833 [p. 453], that he brought "to Emerson the full force of the Sturm und Drang period of Germany" [p. 444] in his criticism, and that, while Carlyle found Emerson inadequate in being too abstractly idealistic, Emerson increasingly found Carlyle too worldly, and consequently "turned to Coleridge rather than to Carlyle [after 1833] as an interpreter of Transcendental philosophy" [p. 453].)

—— "Emerson's Indebtedness to Coleridge," *Studies in Philology*, XXIII, 55–76 (Jan., 1926). (An able philosophic attempt to unravel and distinguish the proportions of the very complicated diverse influences of Plato, Kant, Carlyle, and Coleridge. Concludes that after 1833 Coleridge, as philosopher, psychologist, and literary critic, showed Emerson how to reconcile Platonism and Transcendentalism and how to use as criteria the triple distinctions between the Understanding and the Reason, the Fancy and Imagination, and

Talent and Genius, criteria which were to enable Emerson to appreciate Wordsworth.)

——"Emerson's Theory and Practice of Poetry," *Publications of the Modern Language Association*, XLIII, 1170–1184 (Dec., 1928). (Traces in closely documented form the development of Emerson's appreciation of Wordsworth's poetry, especially his *Ode on the Intimations of Immortality*, an appreciation made possible by his acceptance of Coleridge's distinction between Fancy and Imagination. Thompson concludes that "these two forces, Wordsworth's poetry and Coleridge's criticism . . . furnished him [Emerson] with a theory of poetry and helped to shape the form and content of his verse" [p. 1184]. These three valuable studies by Thompson are based on a dissertation directed by Norman Foerster.)

Ustick, W. L. "Emerson's Debt to Montaigne," *Washington University Studies*, Humanistic Series (1921), IX, 4th series, No. 2, 245–262. (A well-considered study of an interesting influence.)

Van Doren, Mark. "Emerson," in *Dictionary of American Biography*. New York: 1931. Vol. VI, 132–141. (Succinct, up-to-date, and authoritative.)

Wahr, F. B. *Emerson and Goethe*. Ann Arbor, Mich.: 1915. (A scholarly and judicious little book, especially interesting in its comparison of Emerson and Goethe as "The Idealist and the Realist" [pp. 119–149]. Concludes that because "The New England Transcendental revolt remained rooted in the Puritanic tradition" [p. 119], Emerson could understand Goethe only imperfectly.)

Woodberry, G. E. *Ralph Waldo Emerson*. English Men of Letters Series. New York: 1907. (Although Woodberry admitted, "I have little intellectual sympathy with him in any way" [p. 176], this admirably written survey contains much discriminating criticism. The poems are discussed in pp. 158–177.)

Woodbury, C. J. *Talks with Ralph Waldo Emerson*. New York: 1890.

Zink, Harriet R. "Emerson's Use of the Bible," *University of Nebraska Studies in Language, Literature, and Criticism*, No. 14. Lincoln, Neb.: 1935. (An exhaustive assembly of evidence to show Emerson's great knowledge of the Bible and the Christian tradition. Scholars have yet to interpret and appraise proportionately, however, the extent to which Christian ideas, whether Puritan, Unitarian, or Quaker, entered into the main pattern of Emerson's ideas, genetically considered, and modified ideas of classical and of romantic derivation.)

NOTE: A number of valuable but unpublished doctoral dissertations on Emerson, available in manuscript at various university libraries, will be found listed in *American Literature*, IV, 427–429 (Jan., 1933).

NOTES

FORMATIVE FACTORS IN EMERSON'S WORK

Many extreme and one-sided interpretations have been made of Emerson's teaching through a failure to recognize the great variety of influences of which his teaching is the synthesis. While ultimately genius is of course inexplicable, one may say that Emerson's genius was fostered by influences among which the following should be especially considered:

A. European culture:

1. Oriental mysticism (see Bibliography under Carpenter and Christy).
2. Platonism and Neo-Platonism (see Bibliography under Harrison).
3. The Renaissance: Montaigne and Shakespeare (see Bibliography under Ustick).
4. Seventeenth-century English religious writers: Milton, Herbert, etc. (see Bibliography under Pettigrew and Brittin).
5. Deism and Quakerism.
6. English romanticism: Coleridge, Carlyle, Wordsworth (see Bibliography under Thompson).
7. German romanticism (see Bibliography under Goddard, Frothingham, and Wahr).
8. Science (see Bibliography under Beach and Clark).

B. American environment:

1. The inherited moral earnestness of Puritanism. (There is no scholarly study of Emerson's relation to Puritanism; for backgrounds, however, consult H. W. Schneider, *The Puritan Mind* [New York, 1930]. Lowell, in his essay on Thoreau, remarked that "the Puritanism that made New England what it is . . . found its voice in Emerson.")
2. American political life and affairs: democracy, abolition, the Civil War, reform (see Bibliography under McQuiston and Odell).
3. The frontier spirit (see Bibliography under Marchand and Hoeltze).
4. Concord and its intellectual citizens in the mid-nineteenth century: Thoreau, Margaret Fuller, Alcott, Cranch, Jones Very, Hawthorne, Channing, not to mention Bostonians such as Lowell, Longfellow, Holmes, and others (see Bibliography under Cabot, Gohdes, Russell; E. W. Emerson's *The Early Years of the Saturday Club* [1918]; and *Dictionary of American Biography*).
5. Unitarianism (see Bibliography under Cooke).
6. The lyceum system (see *The American Lyceum System* [*Old South Leaflets*, No. 139]; H. B. Adams, "Educational Extension in the United States" [U. S. Commissioner of Education, Report for 1899–1900,

I, 284–299]; Genevieve Bergstresser, *The Influence of the American Lyceum Movement upon the Cultural Development of the United States, 1828–1861* [manuscript dissertation, University of Iowa, 1925]).

TRANSCENDENTALISM

Broadly speaking, transcendentalism was a reaction against the teachings of John Locke which had dominated most thinking during the revolutionary period before Emerson wrote. Locke's *Essay concerning Human Understanding* (1690) argued that men have no innate ideas, that men are essentially the product of their sensuous environment. (This doctrine came to be developed so as to encourage revolutionists and humanitarians to seek perfection through legislative modification of the environment rather than through the self-reform of individuals.) It has become conventional to trace transcendentalism to a German philosopher, Immanuel Kant. His *Critique of Pure Reason* (1781) taught that time and space are not external realities but creations of the mind; and his *Critique of Practical Reason* (1788) went further, in contrast to Locke, and asserted that the ideas of the deity, of freedom, and of immortality, are *intuitions* native to the individual man, and constitute the highest reality. "I call all knowledge *transcendental*," said Kant, "which is concerned, not with objects, but with our mode of knowing objects so far as this is possible *a priori*." In general, then, transcendentalism is a mystical and individualistic philosophy which exalted the authority of those intuitions which transcend both the experience of the senses and pedestrian logical argument. Locke's practical, worldly "understanding" was subordinated to the "Reason," that intuitive perception of occasional aspirations within the individual to approximate what generations of men have called god-like. Englishmen such as Carlyle, the later Coleridge, and DeQuincey disseminated German transcendentalism in England, and the first two especially served as the intermediate source of much of Emerson's knowledge of this philosophy. He also regarded Wordsworth's transcendental "Ode on Intimations of Immortality," with its "obstinate questionings of sense and outward things," as "the high water mark which the intellect has reached in this age" (Emerson's *Works*, V, 298; VIII, 346). (See Melvin Rader's "The Transcendentalism of William Wordsworth," *Modern Philology*, XXVI, 169–190, and the studies in the Bibliography by F. T. Thompson on Emerson's debt to Carlyle, Coleridge, and Wordsworth.)

Emerson helped to found the Transcendental Club in 1836 in which he and his friends such as Alcott, Margaret Fuller, F. H. Hedge, Jones Very, Thoreau, and many others met to discuss the "new ideas." He himself in his essay "The Transcendentalist" defined transcendentalism as "Idealism as it appears in 1842" (*Works*, I, 330), meaning that ideas, things of the mind and spirit, are more real and important than the reports of the five senses. Since this doctrine is sometimes thought of as incomprehensible and excessively mystical, it may help to elucidate it if we take an illustration which Emerson himself might have chosen. A concrete phenomenon such as an apple falling from a tree is sensuously real; but surely this physical apple, soon to decay, is far less real than the law of gravity which it obeys, for that is universal and it operates in all times and places. Yet we cannot touch, taste, or smell this invisible law: it is an abstraction, and was discovered by means of a hypothesis existing first in the mind of Newton. "The sensual man," Emerson says, "conforms thoughts to things; the poet conforms things to his thoughts" (*Works*, I, 52). Now Emerson believed that physical nature and the mind of man both reveal divine laws, that they are both revelations of God. According to the doctrine of analogy which he seems to have found in people as different as Bacon, Swedenborg, and Wordsworth, Emerson held that "the laws of moral nature answer to those of matter as face to face in a glass" (*Works*, I, 33). Just as there are physical laws, so there are moral laws, and just as one acquires health by obeying (rather than violating) the laws of health, so one acquires spiritual health by obeying these moral laws which are the supreme reality. These laws are revealed to us by analogy in physical nature; they are better revealed to us in the history and literature of mankind, illustrating the moral identity of all men at their best; and these laws may be best of all revealed to each of us immediately through our intermittent consciousness of a striving toward perfection. This doctrine of the potential indwelling of divinity in the individual man, as opposed to a revelation of God's will long ago and subject to ecclesiastical interpretation, is the core of Emerson's teaching. While occasionally he seems to approach the doctrine of the goodness of the natural man popularized by revolutionists such as the rationalistic Tom Paine and Jefferson, it should be noted that, unlike them, he is not rationalistic but mystical, and that while they, following disciples of Locke, sought salvation in a legislative modification of the outward environment of the community, Emerson was indifferent to outward reforms and exalted first of all the inward self-reform of the individual. (See Jorgenson's study of Emerson's full recognition of the inwardness of evil.) As a transcendentalist Emerson did not deny the existence of matter, as sometimes imagined; he simply held that, relatively speaking, matter is less real, first, than the universal physical laws which govern it, and second, it is less real than the moral laws which these physical laws symbolize. Just as in obeying the laws of health we avail ourselves of beneficent forces, so in obeying spiritual laws man avails himself of a vast reservoir of spiritual power which transcends his understanding.

Emerson himself recognized transcendentalism as embodying "the very oldest of thoughts," and recent scholarship (as the foregoing list of formative factors and the Bibliography suggest) has tended to see the source of these "thoughts," once attributed mainly to German thinkers, in many diverse traditions. Emerson seems to have found them, in part, in the religions of the ancient East (see Christy and Carpenter), in the Platonic and Neo-Platonic doctrine of the One and the Many (see J. S. Harrison), and in the Quaker doctrine of the illumination of the Holy Spirit. As Marchand has shown, the American frontier taught Emerson part of the lessons of self-reliance, equality, and optimism which have been attributed exclusively to transcendentalism. Scientific doctrines of the unity of law and the variety of its manifestation, of immanence (evolution) and immutability (astronomy), conditioned his rejection of ecclesiasticism and his definition of God as "Conscious Law" (see Clark). And finally, Emerson's transcendentalism may be defined as European "romanticism on Puritan ground," to quote his friend Cabot (*Memoir*, I, 248). The transplantation of romantic doctrines to the American *milieu* gave them a distinctive flavor, conditioned in Emerson's case by his ancient Puritan heritage. It is not fanciful, perhaps, to think that his transcendentalism is not without debt to his ancestral Puritan habits of mind in its intense passion for "the good life"; in its emphasis on self-discipline and its ascetic attitude toward "the flesh"; in its introspectiveness and its allegiance to what the Puritan Edwards called "A Divine and Supernatural Light, immediately imparted to the soul by the spirit of God"; and in its relatively anti-traditional doctrine of the rightful duty of free inquiry and of the priesthood of all believers—in its consecrated individualism. "Self-reliance," as Emerson defines it, "the height and perfection of man is reliance on God" (*Works*, XI, 236; X, 65–66). Thus transcendentalism tempered by Puritanism served as the basis of the high democracy which Emerson preached in his twenty-odd essays dealing with our political destiny. For democracy, he said, "has its root in the sacred truth that every man hath in him the Divine Reason, or that, though few men since the creation of the world live according to the dictates of Reason, yet all men are created capable of so doing. That is the equality and the only equality of all men" (*Journals*, III, 390).

According to C. E. Norton, Emerson's friend, "The essence of his spiritual teaching seems to me to be comprised in three fundamental articles,—first, that of the Unity of Being in God and Man; second, that of the creation of the visible, material world by Mind, and of its being the symbol of the spiritual world; and third, that of the identity and universality of moral law in the spiritual and material universe. These truths are for him the basis of life, the substance of religion, and the meaning of the universe" (*Emerson's Centenary in Concord*. Cambridge: 1903, p. 49).

(For detailed scholarly discussions of transcendentalism, consult in Bibliography, besides studies already indicated, those by Goddard, Gray, Sakmann, Frothingham, and Gohdes. Among contemporary discussions, see James Murdock's "American Transcendentalism," 1842, available in H. G. Townsend's *Philosophical Ideas in the United States*, New York, 1934, pp. 253–265, and Theodore Parker's *Transcendentalism*, 1876.)

EMERSON'S POETRY

Most critics agree as to Emerson's defects, among which are faulty versification and rhyme, want of organization or a structural sense of the whole, and a sustained power of clear and concrete development of thought. On the other hand it is urged that he intentionally roughened his lines to give them vigor, and that he has a distinctive structural method—he builds up a poem by piling image on image, often one to the line, the lines being held together by their parallel thoughts. According to Firkins, "Emerson's rhythm had two forms, expressive of two aspects of his contrasted nature: a noble and weighty blank verse in which his philosophic breadth and tranquillity found fit and high embodiment, and an airy, springing, buoyant lyricism, in which freedom and rapture are the dominating notes." Firkins lists the distinctive qualities of his verse, finding two conspicuous: "the tingling, outleaping spontaneity, remarkable in a nature which seemed calm and measured to the superficial eye and which arraigned itself for sluggishness and hesitation; and the aromatic warmth and pungency, noteworthy in a character which was wont to deplore its want of hearty animal life, of soundness and exuberance of constitution." Many acute critics, such as Alfred Noyes, regard Emerson as our "greatest poet, . . . both in the depth of his thought and in the subtlety of his music." His poetic practice should be correlated with his poetic theory; see essay, "The Poet," p. 230, above, and the note upon it, below.

Page 191. GOOD-BYE

Emerson sent this poem to James Freeman Clarke's *Western Messenger*, where it appeared in April, 1839. He wrote Clarke that these verses "were written sixteen years ago, when I kept school in Boston, and lived in a corner of Roxbury called Canterbury. They have a slight misanthropy, a deeper shade than belongs to me . . ." (See *Works*, IX, 403, and Cabot, *Memoir*, pp. 84–85.) In this poem, says Norman Foerster (*Nature in American Literature*, p. 43), "at the threshold of manhood, we have virtually everything that characterizes his poetry of nature: the preference of solitude to society; the self-reliant rejection of traditionalism; the happy confidence in a revelation here and now; the feeling that in nature, rightly studied, he may come to know what spirit is; the very setting itself, with its pines and evening star."

THOUGHT

"The capital secret of the preacher's profession," according to Emerson, "is to convert life into truth." For the development of the idea that "these five words define Emerson's own work in the world with precision," see Brownell's *American Prose Masters* (ed. Sherman, pp. 114–126). Brownell regards Emerson's work as a "deification of the intellect," and thinks he treats moral and related questions "without reference to any criterion but that of reason."

THE RHODORA

Written in 1834, and first published in the *Western Messenger*, July, 1839. Since many modernists disparage the New England writers because they think these writers placed the claims of didactic moralizing above the claims of beauty, it should be noted that Emerson, the greatest of New England writers, says here that "Beauty is its own excuse for being," and elsewhere that "We call the Beautiful the highest, because it appears to us the golden mean, escaping the dowdiness of the good and the heartlessness of the true" (*Works*, I, 355). The passage should be read, however, in the light of his complete æsthetic theory if one would understand its full meaning. A student of Plato, he worshipped "an interchangeable Truth, Beauty, and Goodness, each wholly interfused in the other" (*ibid.*, XII, 330). He acknowledged a physical beauty, and an intellectual beauty, and a spiritual beauty, the richest beauty being that which appealed not to one but to *all* of man's interests. Hence the highest beauty must include the spiritual and moral, "the beauty of holiness," which is in his eyes an organic by-product of harmonious living: "Beauty is the mark God sets upon virtue" (*ibid.*, I, 19). In the light of this harmonious synthesis of "the eternal trinity of Truth, Goodness, and Beauty, each in its perfection including the three" (*ibid.*, I, 354), "The Rhodora" can scarcely be interpreted as a defense of poetry or beauty totally divorced from ethics, nor can Emerson be said to be oblivious of the high claims of beauty in its more profound implications. See the note below on the essay, "The Poet," and see Foerster's study listed in Bibliography, above.

Page 192. EACH AND ALL

First published in the *Western Messenger*, Feb., 1839. For some of the physical experiences out of which this poem grew, the walk by the seashore and the talk of the shells which lost their beauty when separated from sea and sky, as well as the shepherd in his red cloak, see *Journals*, III, p. 298, for May 16, and p. 373, for November, 1834. The philosophic theme, dealing with "unity and variety," doubtless owes something to Emerson's study of Plato as suggested in the essay on this greatest of his *Representative Men.* (See J. S. Harrison's *The Teachers of Emerson.*) It is possible that Emerson, who had been reading Coleridge's *The Friend* just before writing this poem, may have found the following passage suggestive: "It is the idea alone of the common centre, of the universal law, by which all power manifests itself in opposite yet interdependent forces . . . which enlightening inquiry, multiplying experiment, and at once inspiring humility and perseverance will lead him to comprehend gradually and progressively the relation of each to the other, of each to all, and of all to each" (Coleridge's *Complete Works*, ed. Shedd, II, 462). See also F. T. Thompson's "Emerson's Indebtedness to Coleridge."

NATURE

These lines preface the second edition (1849) of Emerson's first book, *Nature* (1836), which is the hub from which the spokes of many of his theories radiate. In his unpublished lecture on the "Humanity of Science" (1836), he speaks of Lamarck, one of the heralds of evolution, as "finding a monad of organic life common to every animal, and becoming a worm, a mastiff, or a man, according to circumstances. He says to the caterpillar, How dost thou, brother? Please God, you shall yet be a philosopher." In Emerson's *Journal* for 1849 he quotes Stallo as follows: "The development of all individual forms will be spiral." For discussion of Emerson's knowledge of and debt to science, consult (in Bibliography) Beach and Clark. W. T. Harris thought that the idea of this poem was found in Plotinus. It is interesting to observe that the book *Nature* is itself constructed on a sort of scale-of-being spiral plan. After the introductory portions, it rises from discussion of physical "Commodity" through "Beauty" (physical, intellectual, spiritual), "Language," "Discipline," to "Idealism" and "Spirit"—to the dualistic doctrine of "the eternal distinction between the soul and the world"—with a peroration on "Prospects."

Page 193. THE HUMBLE-BEE

In this poem and in "The Snow-Storm" (p. 204, above) note Emerson's delight in nature and the skill with which he creates the illusion of both Spring and Winter. Compare his appeals to the senses with those of Keats.

THE POET

Emerson's son says (*Works*, IX, 500–501) that this uncompleted poem, begun as early as 1838, was first entitled "The Discontented Poet, a Masque," since in its earlier form it embodied Emerson's impressions of his discouraging struggle to write poetry measuring up to his high ideal of the poet's office. Eventually, as he began to succeed, he changed the title and omitted lines which seemed to him morbid. O. W. Holmes cited the poem, along with "May-Day" and "Threnody," as representing Emerson's poetic genius at its best.

Since the poem is somewhat difficult, a brief summary may not be amiss as a means of suggesting the sequence of Emerson's thought:

ll. 1–26. Although the poet was "born and nourished in miracles," his early work was "unregarded" and met with a "jeer"; but after the "noisy scorn" of "idle clowns," he was enabled to make his "wingèd words" steer "right to the heaven."

ll. 27–50. "A Brother of the world," the poet wore the Times "as his clothing-weeds" and touched the full circumference of all life's experiences, whether painful or fortunate.

ll. 50–72. The wide-roving poet "through man and woman and sea and star" in all times and lands "Saw musical order and pairing rhymes," saw the apparent particulars of life as illustrating the unity and universality of divinely ordered law. (Cf. "The Sphinx.")

ll. 73–90. The poet overheard the gods talk in nature, perceived underlying laws, and he "Seeks how he may fitly tell / The heart-o'erlading miracle."

ll. 91–249. Biding his time, confident of "the coming light," the poet watched the "enormous galaxy" of the stars, symbols of "an animated law" or the over-soul which is God. He "Thanked Nature for each stroke she dealt," and asked only to feel. Yet he was handicapped by an ineffectual "wandering will," and he prayed the "dear stars" to "clothe these hands with power / In just proportion," to give him means of expressing his intuitions.

ll. 250 ff. The chorus of spirits, suppliants of the divine law, replies to his entreaty that "soul's desire is means enow," that they will never depart from him, and that man is potentially able to avail himself of divine inspiration constantly: he has only to serve the divine law. (Cf. the opening lines of the book *Nature* [1836] and "The Divinity School Address" [1838] on his characteristic idea of the need of supplanting the ecclesiastical view of revelation as long past with the view that the immediate intuitions of the purified individual are a divine revelation here and now. The poem should also be read in connection with other expressions of Emerson's poetic theory in "Merlin," "Art," and the essay on "The Poet.")

Page 196. URIEL

This fable, describing how the advent of a new truth shocked the gods, should be read in the light of Emerson's "Divinity School Address" (1838) wherein he attacked traditionalism in religion and defended the doctrine of immanence or a depersonalized deity of animated law. See note by Emerson's son (*Works*, IX, 408–409). In *Paradise Lost* Uriel is the radiant archangel of the Sun.

Page 197. THE PROBLEM

The germ of this poem is found in Emerson's *Journals* (V, 29–30), August 28, 1838: "It is very grateful to my feelings to go into a Roman Cathedral, yet I look as my countrymen do at the Roman priesthood. It is very grateful to me to go into an English Church and hear the liturgy read. Yet nothing would induce me to be the English priest. I find an unpleasant dilemma in this nearer home. I dislike to be a clergyman and refuse to be one. Yet how rich a music would be to me a holy clergyman in my town. It seems to me he cannot be a man, quite and whole; yet how plain is the need of one, and how high, yes, highest, is the function. Here is division of labor that I like not. A man must sacrifice his manhood for the social good. Something is wrong, I see not what."

l. 10. Cf. *Works*, II, 108.

ll. 46 ff. The thought, that art, like successful living, is a result of harmonizing one's spirit with the "animated law" divine, is expanded in Emerson's essays on "The Over-Soul" (*Works*, II, 265–297) and on "Art" (*ibid.*, II, 349–369). F. I. Carpenter (*Emerson and Asia*, 87–89) thinks that the doctrine of ll. 39 ff., that the artist should not imitate nature but find inspiration in "Thought's interior sphere," was found by Emerson in Plotinus, whom Emerson quoted in 1837 (*Journals*, IV, 218–221) to the same effect.

l. 68. In his *Journals* Emerson speaks of Jeremy Taylor (1613–1667), the author of *Holy Living and Holy Dying*, as "a Christian Plato."

Page 198. ART

These lines prefaced Emerson's essay on "Art" (*Works*, II, 351–369), in the light of which the poem should be interpreted. Emerson says that commonplace reality—"barrows, trays, and pans" —are proper materials for the artist, provided these particulars are used as symbols of the universal. In this essay he says that the "creative impulse" behind art is "the inlet of that higher illumination which teaches to convey a larger sense by simpler symbols," that the "artist must employ the symbols in use in his day and nation"; but the chief interest should be not in the symbol but in the idea symbolized. (For discussion see E. G. Sutcliffe's chapters on "The Symbol" and "The Fact and the Symbol," in *Emerson's Theories of Literary Expression*, pp. 17–106.) With Emerson's pervading idea, alluded to in line 20, that art and literature should cheer, compare Poe's idea that beauty is inseparably associated with melancholy. Note that Emerson looks upon art as cheering chiefly by enabling us to "live on even terms with Time" (l. 26), to see troubles in perspective—"to believe what the years and the centuries say, against the hours" (*Works*, IV, 185).

Page 199. PRUDENCE

These lines preface Emerson's essay on "Prudence" (*Works*, II, 221–241), in which he shows that his idealism was not inconsistent with an almost Franklin-like practicality and respect for mundane obligations. "Prudence," he says, "is the virtue of the senses." It is the "law of shows," and worldly success depends upon obeying these worldly laws, just as spiritual success depends on obeying spiritual laws. Indeed, physical well-being he regards as essential to spiritual development. "Thus truth, frankness, courage, love, humility and all the virtues range themselves on the side of prudence, or the art of securing a present well-being."

HEROISM

These lines preface Emerson's essay on "Heroism" (*Works*, II, 245–264), inculcating the doctrine of social solidarity and subordination. Emerson says, "Self-trust is the essence of heroism. It is the state of the soul at war, and its ultimate objects are the last defiance of falsehood and wrong, and the power to bear all that can be inflicted by evil agents." In this essay he pays high tribute to one of his masters, the classical Plutarch, whom he regarded as Heroism's "Doctor and historian."

SPIRITUAL LAWS

In the essay on "Spiritual Laws" (*Works*, II, 131–166), which these lines preface, the so-called radical writes: "A higher law than that of our will regulates events . . . By contenting ourselves with obedience we become divine . . . We need only obey . . . Virtue is adherence in action to the nature of things . . . The object of the man, the aim of these moments, is . . . to suffer the law to traverse his whole being without obstruction . . ."

WOODNOTES

Kreymborg (*Our Singing Strength*, p. 77) concludes, "'Woodnotes I and II' are among the longest and most sustained of Emerson's ecstatic hymns. They are a survey of all he felt, thought and believed . . ."

ll. 30 ff. Probably refer to Thoreau.

ll. 137–138. This romantic doctrine of nature's benevolence is hardly characteristic of Emerson. For his Darwinian doctrine of "a certain ferocity in nature," see *Works*, II, 249, and VI, 6–7.

l. 440. *conscious Law is King of kings*. (Cf. the definition in "The Over-Soul," *Works*, II, 270 f.: God is "Highest Law . . . All reform aims . . . to engage us to obey.") This is one of Emerson's best definitions of the Over-Soul: "conscious Law" or divine immanence in immutable but beneficent physical and spiritual law. The first concept was probably reinforced in his mind by his interest in early doctrines of evolution; the second, by his interest in astronomy. Of course there were countless other influences, many of which have been listed at the beginning of these notes. With this definition of the deity as "conscious Law," compare his dualistic statement which climaxes "New England Reformers," where he says the great man "shall not take counsel of flesh and blood [variety, or the senses], but shall rely on the Law alive and beautiful which works over our hands and under our feet. Pitiless, it avails itself of our success when we obey it, and of our ruin when we contravene it" (*Works*, III, 283).

Page 204. THE SPHINX

First published in the *Dial*, Jan., 1841. "Mr. Emerson wrote in his note-book in 1859: 'I have often been asked the meaning of the 'Sphinx.' It is this,—The perception of identity unites all things and explains one by another, and the most rare and strange is equally facile as the most common. But if the mind live only in particulars, and see only differences (wanting the power to see the whole—all in each), then the world addresses to this mind a question it cannot answer, and each new fact tears it in pieces, and it is vanquished by the distracting variety'" (*Works*, IX, p. 412). See also Thoreau's *Writings* (Walden ed., 1906), VII, 229–237, for his interpretation of "The Sphinx."

Page 206. GRACE

As the author of the essay on "Self-Reliance," Emerson is often regarded as an apostle of an idiosyncratic individualism and as a utopian optimist scornful of conventional restraints and oblivious of sin. As a matter of fact, since to him "God is the Universal Mind" (*Journals*, IV, 61), and since by self-reliance he means "a self-trust which is a trust in God himself" (*Works*, X, 65 f.), it should be obvious that the practice of his theory of self-reliance would make men like rather than unlike each other, would make them aim not at being queer and eccentric and different but at imitating a standard of excellence which would be universal. The poem "Grace" is one of many evidences that Emerson did not ignore "the depths of sin" in the human heart and the practical value of conventional restraints such as "example, custom, fear, occasion slow." For the contemporary view of Emerson's inadequate recognition of evil, see C. E. Norton, *Letters* (Boston: 1913), I, 504 ff.; this view must be considerably corrected in the light of the evidence of Emerson's view of evil exhaustively assembled and ably interpreted by C. E. Jorgenson in "Emerson's Paradise under the Shadow of Swords." See also G. R. Elliott's "On Emerson's 'Grace' and 'Self-Reliance,'" *New England Quarterly*, II, 93–104 (Jan., 1929).

THRENODY

This great elegy (on the death of Emerson's five-year-old son Waldo) should be compared with other great elegies, such as Milton's "Lycidas," Shelley's "Adonais," Tennyson's *In Memoriam*, and Arnold's "Thyrsis." What was the reaction of each to death, and what specific consolation did each express?

On Emerson's great love for his "sweet and wonderful boy," see Cabot's *Memoir* (II, 481–489); the *Correspondence of Emerson and Carlyle* (I, 358–360); and Emerson's *Journals* (VI, 150 ff. [Jan. 28, 1842]). "Threnody" should be compared with Emerson's essay on "Immortality." Lines 1–175 embody his lament; lines 176–289, his consolation. The key to the latter is perhaps line 245—"And many-seeming life is one"—which becomes more clear when read with reference to his Platonic theory of the Many and the One, of the life of the changing senses finding meaning only in the life of the changeless world of spiritual value, the One. Elsewhere he spoke of the death of the individual, starkly pent in "figure, bone and lineament," as analogous to a bottle of water broken in the sea—"lost in God, in Godhead found."

Page 209. POLITICS

This poem prefaces Emerson's essay on "Politics" (1844; *Works*, III, 199–221), which should be read in this connection. See also his essay on "Napoleon," as "the incarnate Democrat," in *Representative Men* (*ibid.*, IV, 223–258); his many essays and speeches on political questions in *Miscellanies* (*ibid.*, XI), and his essays on "New England Reformers" (*ibid.*, 249–285), "Man the Reformer," "Lecture on the Times," "The Conservative" (*ibid.*, I, 227–326), and "The Young American" (*ibid.*, I, 363–395). Emerson was interested especially in three phases of our political life: the abolition of slavery, the preservation of the Union, and social reform. In general he looked forward to the progressive substitution of inner control for governmental control, and he thought that contemporary reformers laid disproportionate stress on external reforms and neglected inner or self-reform. For interpretations of Emerson's political views see Bibliography under Odell, McQuiston, Marchand.

Page 210. THE DAY'S RATION

This poem illustrates the ecstasy with which Emerson lived, and his sense of the magnitude of life's blessings compared with the limited time available for enjoying them. The idea is amplified in *Works*, IV, 184.

BACCHUS

This poem shows the influence of both Hafiz (see F. I. Carpenter, *Emerson and Asia*, pp. 163, 169, 188 f.) and of Proclus and the Neoplatonists (see J. S. Harrison, *The Teachers of Emerson*, pp. 275 ff.). Emerson's son thought the section on "Idealism" in *Nature* (1836) gives the "key" to this poem "on the inspiration which Nature gives, when seen as not final, but a symbol of the Universal Mind" (*Works*, IX, 443). According to Alfred Kreymborg (*Our Singing Strength*, pp. 78–79), "There is physical gusto in the deep-bellied rhythms of the poem to Bacchus . . . there is no poet among us whose drunken poems equal Emerson's. He was not in love with forms or exhibitions, but with the whole of life. The most prevalent note, no matter what the theme or occasion, is saturated with intoxication. Not even the canny philosopher could restrain the seer and bard, nor the demands of traditional poetry hem in the free rhythm of their speech. Emerson's poetry was the first rebellion against British poetry, and the harbinger of the general Revolution beginning with Whitman."

Page 211. ODE INSCRIBED TO W. H. CHANNING

William Henry Channing, a nephew of the elder William Ellery Channing, the famous champion of Unitarianism, was himself a Unitarian minister of Boston and an ardent humanitarian, and was associated with many experiments in social reform, notably that at Brook Farm.

This poem is especially interesting as the embodiment of Emerson's view of contemporary devotion to reforms to be effected by outward means. He here says that he is loath to decline a friend's request, but that he cannot leave his quest of truth for the "statesman's rant." Since the age and country are in bondage to materialism (l. 50), outward changes will be of slight avail until individuals, white as well as black, learn through self-discipline to free themselves from slavery to the "law for thing" which "doth the man unking." The central basis of Emerson's attitude is found in the following idea developed in "New England Reformers" (*Works*, III, 261): "The criticism and attack on institutions, which we have witnessed, has made one thing plain, that society gains nothing whilst a man, not himself renovated, attempts to renovate things around him: he has become tediously good in some particular but negligent or narrow in the rest; and hypocrisy and vanity are often the disgusting result." (Hawthorne developed the same general view in the character of the humanitarian Hollingsworth in *The Blithedale Romance*.) Emerson said in 1852, "I have quite other slaves to free than those negroes, to wit, imprisoned spirits, imprisoned thoughts . . . which, important to the republic of man, have no watchman, or lover, or defender, but I" (*Journals*, VIII, 316). Eventually, however, as in Emerson's address on John Brown and elsewhere, he spoke out vigorously against slavery, and Lowell testified that his teachings were a powerful inspiration to the Northern soldiers of the Civil War. Perhaps the rather unfeeling view of abolition in this *Ode* should be balanced against the much more sympathetic view in Emerson's "Boston Hymn" (1863), which is as near to humanitarianism as he ever came. See also Emerson's somewhat humanitarian poem, the "Chartist's Complaint" (*Poems*, Centenary Edition, p. 232). For full discussion of the development of Emerson's attitude toward abolition and toward outward reform in general see McQuiston; Odell; W. M. Slater ("Emerson's Views of Society and Reform," *International Journal of Ethics*, XIII, 414–21, July, 1903); Van Wyck Brooks ("Emerson and the Reformers," *Harper's Magazine*, CLIV, 114–119, Dec., 1926).

Page 212. MERLIN

Compare this finished version with that first written in Emerson's Journal and printed in *Poems*, Centenary Edition, p. 441. The first draft, as G. W. Allen remarks, "not only illustrates but even expresses a free-verse theory," indifferent to rhymes and meters. What concessions did Emerson make to conventional taste in "polishing" the poem for publication?

"Merlin" expresses many of the ideals which Emerson would set for the true poet. Thus the poet's is "no jingling serenader's art"; he must "smite the chords rudely and hard" to appeal to the "mystic springs" of "manly hearts." His quest should not involve "the coil of rhythm and number" but lofty spirituality. He is to dispense joy—not melancholy (cf. Poe). He must not sing when uninspired: let him await the open hours "when the God's will sallies free." Since "balance-loving Nature / Made all things in pairs," the idealism of the poet "modulates" worldly affairs, idealism and practicality reinforcing each other. Compare this poem with Emerson's essays, "The Poet" and "Compensation."

Page 213. THE WORLD-SOUL

Although "politics are base" and "trade and the streets ensnare us" and the present is generally corrupt, Emerson holds that the ultimately-beneficent "Destiny never swerves," and that if it "kills the cripple and the sick," he will "from the wrecks and sediment / The fairer world complete." The "Dæmon" (l. 77) is the spirit of fate. Compare the poem with Emerson's essays on "Fate," and "Power." The poem, celebrating Emerson's favorite doctrine of immutable law and optimism, is essentially in accord with the conclusion of the essay on "Montaigne" (*Works*, IV, 185–186): "Through the years and the centuries, through evil agents, through toys and atoms, a great and beneficent tendency irresistibly streams."

G. W. Allen (*American Prosody*, p. 114) says: "'The World-Soul' has a much more elaborate and consistent construction than most of Emerson's poems. Yet it is significant that the eight-line stanza has only two rimes, four of the eight lines being without rime. The scheme is *abcbdefe*." He calls attention to "the constant shifting of stresses and the use of parallelism," especially in the first stanza, "where it is combined with reiteration, which controls the rhythm."

Page 215. INITIAL, DÆMONIC, AND CELESTIAL LOVE

The present version is that embodying Emerson's revision of 1876. The theme, the ascent from physical love to intellectual love, to spiritual love, should be compared with that of Emerson's "Hermione" and of his essay on "Love." The poem is based on Plato's *Banquet*, whose teaching, Emerson says (in "Plato," *Works*, IV, 70), is "that the love of the sexes is initial, and symbolizes at a distance the passion of the soul for that immense lake of beauty it exists to seek. This faith in the Divinity is never out of mind, and constitutes the ground of all his dogmas. Body cannot teach wisdom;—God only." See also *Works*, IV, 127, and Harrison's *Teachers of Emerson*.

ll. 323–24. Compare these lines with the conclusion of his essay on "History": "Let it suffice that in the light of these two facts, namely, that the Mind is One, and that nature [the Many, Variety] is its correlative, history is to be read and written" (*Works*, II, 38). In keeping with Emerson's pervasive dualism, he recognizes that the external customs, manners, and superficial aspects of successive ages differ, but he insists on seeking the qualities common to all ages which constitute the moral identity of Past, Present, and Future. This is the key to his much-discussed view of tradition. He scorned only the antiquarian worship of the past as something totally foreign to the present; he held that the "books are the best type of the influence of the past," and that they are "the best of things, well used" ("The American Scholar"). He himself, of course, read very widely, as anyone can see who glances at the indexes of his *Works* and his *Journals*. He advocated, however, "creative reading," in the faith that, genius being not something peculiar but "a larger imbibing of the common heart," a proper reading of a "great poet makes *us* feel our *own* wealth" and enables *us* to be "born into the great, the universal mind" (*Works*, II, 289; 296).

Page 219. ALPHONSO OF CASTILE

This king, traditionally accepted as wise, urged that "nine in ten" should be killed in order that the "remnant decimal" might "in schemes of broader scope engage." Is this puzzling poem merely a skilfully versified story without serious intent, or does it accord with Emerson's stern view of the ultimate beneficence of nature in creating an aristocracy by killing "the cripple and the sick" (cf. "The World-Soul," l. 91)?

Page 220. DAYS

First published in the *Atlantic Monthly*, Nov., 1857, this poem was regarded by Emerson as his best poetic treatment of a theme more fully developed in the essay "Works and Days" (*Works*, VII, 155–185) involving his dualistic outlook. Lowell thought this poem "as limpid and complete as a Greek epigram" (Scudder's *Lowell*, I, 414). O. W. Firkins (*Emerson*, p. 282) thought the parable-loving Emerson was most successful in "Days": "Here all conditions meet, apt parable, interesting story, picture, drama, vivid culmination, compression into eleven beautiful lines."

Page 221. WEALTH

These lines preface Emerson's essay on "Wealth" (*Works*, VI, 83–127), in which the idealist shows considerable respect for property. "Wealth has its source in applications of mind to nature . . . I have never seen a man as rich as all men ought to be, or with an adequate command of nature. The pulpit and the press have many commonplaces denouncing the thirst for wealth; but if men should take these moralists at their word and leave off aiming to be rich, the moralists would rush to rekindle at all hazards this love of power in the people, lest civilization should be undone. . . . Property is an intellectual production. The game requires coolness, right reasoning, promptness and patience in the players. . . . Wealth brings with it its own checks and balances. The basis of political economy is non-interference. The only safe rule is found in the self-adjusting meter of demand and supply. Do not legislate. Meddle, and you snap the sinews with your sumptuary laws. . . . Open the doors of opportunity to talent and virtue and they will do themselves justice, and property will not be in bad hands." (With this *laissez-faire* doctrine based on optimism regarding human nature compare the socialistic doctrine.) For full discussion of Emerson's economic theories, see also "Wealth" in *English Traits* (*Works*, V, 153–171); and works listed in Bibliography by McQuiston (pp. 23–26), Odell (pp. 106–116), and Marchand.

Page 222. VOLUNTARIES

This stirring poem, of which lines 71–74 have become classic, is a dirge for Colonel Robert Gould Shaw who was killed with many of the members of one of the first enlisted colored regiments in the Civil War.

l. 30. *Lured by "Union" as the bribe.* Cf. Emerson's poem "Webster," p. 191, above. Unlike Lowell, Emerson set abolition above the Union. See McQuiston, pp. 50 ff.

ll. 35 ff. Emerson pays tribute to the Negroes who fought for freedom, and to the "generous chief" who led them at the call of heroic duty.

l. 121. The word "these" refers to "Eternal Rights" (l. 109) which Emerson viewed as directing the outcome of the War.

Page 224. MAY-DAY

This ode, which Kreymborg (*op. cit.*, p. 83) calls a "bacchanalian symphony irresistible in its drunken joy" in nature, was built up of lines which go back as far as the Journal of 1845. The present text is that approved by Emerson's son in 1883 and represents a slight rearrangement of an earlier version. On ll. 79–82, see *ante* the note on "Nature" involving evolution. Notice, especially in the first twenty-two lines, the variety of Emerson's appeals to the senses of sight, hearing, touch, etc., and note, especially in ll. 366 and 496, that the Transcendentalist recognizes and is grateful for nature's power to soothe man's cares. Emerson's belief in a divine "beneficent tendency" (*Works*, IV, 186) appears in the final dozen lines, where nature is regarded as a mask, a symbol, of "Nature's king, . . . Lifting Better up to Best." It should be remembered, however, that this delight in nature's pleasanter aspects and this ultimate optimism were not inconsistent with a realistic recognition of a "treachery" and a "ferocity" in nature. See Emerson's essay on "Nature" (*Works*, III, 169–196, especially pp. 190–193), and his essay on "Fate" (*Works*, VI, 3–49). In the latter (pp. 6–8), he shows that he had heard of Winter as well as Spring, that he understood Darwin's evolutionary doctrine of the "struggle for existence" as part of nature. "Nature," Emerson says, "is no sentimentalist,—does not cosset or pamper us. . . . The cold, inconsiderate of persons, tingles your blood, benumbs your feet, freezes a man like an apple. The diseases, the elements, fortune, gravity, lightning, respect no persons. The way of Providence is a little rude. The habit of snake and spider, the snap of the tiger and other leapers and bloody jumpers, the crackle of the bones of his prey in the coil of the anaconda,—these are in the system, and our habits are like theirs. . . . The forms of the shark, the *labrus*, the jaw of the sea-wolf paved with crushing teeth, the weapons of the grampus, and other warriors hidden in the sea, are hints of ferocity in the interiors of nature. Let us not deny it up and down." On this subject see the full discussion in Foerster's essay on Emerson in *Nature in American Literature*. Cf. also Emerson's dualistic severing of the "law for thing" from the "law for man," and his recognition that the "law for thing . . . runs wild / And doth the man unking." An interesting question to consider is the extent to which Emerson himself depended not upon a revelation in outward nature but upon a revelation in man's inward impulses toward perfection as revealed in the great books of the world, the books embodying "our universal humanity" and demonstrating that potentially in all ages "the mind is One" (*Works*, II, 38). On the other hand, what reasoning led him to say in an early essay that "the ancient precept, 'Know thyself' [thy humanity], and the modern precept, 'Study nature,' become at last one maxim" (*Works*, I, 87)?

Page 230. THE POET: EMERSON'S POETIC THEORIES

The most important studies of this subject are those by Foerster and Sutcliffe, listed in the Bibliography. For special phases of the subject consult also Allen, Brownell, Carpenter (pp. 86–94), DeMille, Flanagan (under Foerster), Gorely, Gray (pp. 94–104), Gohdes, Harrison, Pettigrew, and Thompson. In this volume see also the poems "The Rhodora" (p. 191), "The Apology" (p. 192), "Merlin" (p. 212), "The Test" (p. 222), and "The Poet" (p. 230); and see in Emerson's *Essays* those on "Beauty" (also the section on "Beauty" in *Nature*), "Art," "Books," "The American Scholar," and "Poetry and Imagination."

In the essay "The Poet" Emerson discusses three main topics, as indicated by the sign-posts at the end of the first paragraph: (a) "the nature and functions of the Poet, or man of Beauty" (to the first paragraph, p. 233); (b) "the means and materials he uses" (from p. 233 to p. 239, col. 2, l. 30); (c) "the general aspect of art in the present time" (to the conclusion).

Page 231.

col. 2, ll. 1–5. This doctrine of the unity and parity of beauty, truth, and goodness is fundamental to an understanding of Emerson. Cf. *Works*, I, 19–24: "Beauty is the mark God sets upon virtue," and compare the doctrine of the beauty of holiness, beauty as the by-product of right living and spiritual health, of which Milton, Spenser, and Plato were spokesmen. Emerson regarded Beauty, Truth, and Goodness as "interchangeable." See *Works*, XII, 330; VII, 48; X, 55; I, 355; *Journals*, III, 35, and 200. To what extent did Poe connect beauty and goodness? Compare and contrast his views with Emerson's.

Page 232.

col. 1, ll. 30 ff. *it is not metres, but a metre-making argument that makes a poem.* Emerson revolts from the tendency to make the argument secondary and finish primary. He believes that the poetic process is organic, that from the intuitive thought will proceed the appropriate form. This theory, involving indifference to form, undoubtedly explains in part the relative lack of sequence and architectonic structure in some of Emerson's writings.

Page 233.

col. 2. Variety and Unity, and nature as a symbol. Consult J. S. Harrison for a penetrating and full discussion of Emerson's theory with reference to the classical doctrine of the Many and the One, and see Emerson's essay on "Plato" (*Works*, IV, 47–54) for Emerson's acceptance of this dualistic philosophy. He urges the use of images drawn from common nature, but these images (Variety) are to be so focused as to symbolize universal spiritual truths common to all men (Unity). For further discussion, see Sutcliffe, pp. 17–106.

Page 235.

col. 2, l. 16. *Language is fossil poetry.* See Emerson's amplification of this view in the section on "Language" in *Nature* (*Works*, I, 25–35), where he says that "Words are signs of natural facts," "Particular natural facts are symbols of particular spiritual facts," and "Nature is the symbol of spirit."

Page 236.

col. 1, ll. 48 ff. Cf. Emerson's essay on "Intellect" (*Works*, II, 336–337): "The imaginative vocabulary . . . does not flow from experience only or mainly, but from a richer source. Not by any conscious imitation of particular forms are the grand strokes of the painter executed, but by repairing to the fountain-head of all forms in his mind." Has this doctrine more in common with that of Plato and Plotinus, or with that of modern Pragmatists to whom some critics have related Emerson? Compare Emerson's view of imagination with that of Wordsworth (*Prelude*, XIII, ll. 300–311), who identifies imagination and spiritual insight. "Imagination," says Emerson (*Works*, I, 52), "may be defined to be the use which Reason makes of the material world." For full discussion see F. T. Thompson and N. Foerster.

Page 237.

ll. 51 f. *The sublime vision comes to the pure and simple soul in a clean and chaste body.* Although Emerson appears at times to advocate a capricious romantic emotionalism, he does in fact exalt restraint. "The teachings of the high Spirit," he said, "are abstemious, and, in regard to particulars, negative. . . . The Hindoos have denominated the Supreme Being, the 'Internal Check'" (*Works*, IV, 139–140). "Genius is always ascetic, and piety, and love. Appetite shows to the finer souls as a disease, and they find beauty in rites and bounds that resist it" (*ibid.*, II, 231). "Dante was free imagination,—all wings—yet he wrote like Euclid."

Page 239.

col. 2, ll. 30 ff. With his desire that the immediate environment and time should be used by a poet, one can understand Emerson's initial responsiveness to Whitman. It should be noted, however, that according to Emerson's doctrine the American scene (Variety) is to be used to symbolize the Unity of mankind's spiritual heritage, their moral identity in all times and lands, whereas Whitman advocated an anti-traditional literature based on the democratic frontier and on evolutionary science, a literature devoted to our nationalistic uniqueness. Compare and contrast the literary theories of these two poets, including their attitude toward restraint.

Emerson's poetic theories may be briefly summarized as follows:

1. True poetry results from the poet's obeying and being in ethical harmony with divine law: he thus becomes a medium for divine truth, which is universal; genius is not eccentric but "a larger imbibing of the common heart," an "influx of the Divine mind into our mind."
2. "The creation of beauty is Art," but since the highest beauty "is the mark God sets upon virtue," art, including poetry, involves right living and spiritual health. Beauty, Truth, and Goodness are one, and poetry and ethics cannot be divorced.
3. "The expression is organic" not only with character but with thought. It is "not metres, but metre-making argument, that makes a poem,—a thought so passionate and alive, that . . . it has an architecture of its own." Attend to the thought, and the form of expression will take care of itself.
4. The poet does not imitate nature, the life of the senses, but an ideal divinely-inspired concept in his mind. Yet concrete facts are symbols of spiritual ideas, and the former help the poet to body forth the latter. He may use nature, including the immediate and familiar American scene, an aspect of the Platonic Many, but only as a *means*, as a symbol, to focus attention upon the Unity of our common humanity and the universal moral law transcending the bounds of nationality, of time and space.
5. The poet is guided and inspired not only by the influx of divinity into his own individual mind and by his own yearnings for perfection, but by the literature of the past in so far as it illustrates the fact that throughout history "the mind is One," that Past, Present, and Future are "triple blossoms from one root." Other poets reveal to him his own wealth, his own kinship with those who have been media of the over-soul.
6. The poet should be a liberator and consoler. He frees us from bondage to matter by showing us that our distinctively human destiny is spiritual. He consoles us by teaching us to see particulars, including individual cases of suffering, in perspective; he teaches us to see "the permanent in the mutable and fleeting," to "believe what the years and the centuries say, against the hours."
7. While poetry helps us to realize our complete humanity, to obey the "law for man" as opposed to the "law for thing," in proportion as we achieve this end we have less need for poetry, for if one achieved complete harmony with the Over-Soul his own life would itself constitute a poem.

EDGAR ALLAN POE

CHRONOLOGY

1809 Born in Boston, son of actor and actress, January 19.
1811 Parents died. Poe adopted by Mr. John Allan of Richmond, Virginia.
1815–20 Schooling in England.
1824 Tragic death of Jane Stith Stanard, mother of a schoolmate, the "Helen" of his famous poem.
1826 Attended University of Virginia. Left after one term, heavily in debt.
1827 Quarreled with Allan, went to Boston. *Tamerlane and Other Poems.*
1827–29 In army. Allan secured a discharge for him.
1829 *Al Aaraaf, Tamerlane, and Minor Poems,* his second volume.
1830–31 At West Point. Dismissed for disobedience.
1831 *Poems.*
1831–35 Baltimore.
1833 Prize from a Baltimore paper for "MS. Found in a Bottle," a short story.
1835–37 Richmond. Began to write for *Southern Literary Messenger,* as assistant editor.
1836 Married Virginia Clemm, his thirteen-year-old cousin.
1837 Went with wife and mother-in-law to New York, where he earned a scanty living, chiefly doing hack work.
1838–44 Philadelphia.
1838 "Ligeia" appeared in Baltimore *Museum.*
1839 Associate editor of *Burton's Gentleman's Magazine.* Contributed, among other things, "The Fall of the House of Usher."
1840 *Tales of the Grotesque and Arabesque.*
1841–42 Edited *Graham's Magazine,* contributed "The Murders of the Rue Morgue."
1843 "The Gold Bug."
1844 New York. Connected with *Evening Mirror.*
1845 Publication of "The Raven" made him famous. Editor of the *Broadway Journal,* engaged in "Longfellow war." *Tales. The Raven and Other Poems.*
1847 Wife died. Poverty. "Ulalume."
1848 *Eureka: A Prose Poem.*
1849 Died in Baltimore, October 7.

BIBLIOGRAPHY

I. Bibliography

Cambridge History of American Literature, II, 452–468. (An excellent bibliography, but includes items only to 1918.)

Campbell, Killis. "The Poe Canon," in *The Mind of Poe.* Cambridge: 1933, pp. 187–238. Also "Gleanings in the Bibliography of Poe," *Modern Language Notes,* XXXII, 267–272 (May, 1917); *Poe's Short Stories* (New York: 1927), pp. xxix–xxxvi; "Recent Books about Poe," *Studies in Philology,* XXIV, 474–479 (July, 1927).

Engel, C. E. "L'état des travaux sur Edgar Allan Poe en France," *Modern Philology,* XXIX, 482–485.

Heartman, C. F., and Rede, Kenneth. *A Census of First Editions and Source Materials by Edgar Allan Poe in American Collections.* 2 vols. Metuchen, N. J.: 1932. (Vol. I includes "A Bibliographical Check List of First Editions"; Vol. II, "Edgar Allan Poe's Contribution to Annuals and Periodicals: a Check List.")

Robertson, J. W. *A Bibliography of the Writings of Edgar A. Poe.* San Francisco: 1934. 2 vols. (Chronological list, 1827–1850. The latest bibliography, including many obscure items. David Randall's review, *Publishers' Weekly,* CXXV, 1540–1543 [Apr. 21, 1934] is valuable for the inaccuracies it corrects in Robertson.)

II. Text

Campbell, Killis (ed.) *The Poems of Edgar Allan Poe.* Boston: 1917. (Indispensable. Contains scholarly notes of great value.)

Griswold, R. W. (ed.) *The Works of the Late Edgar Allan Poe.* New York: 1849–1856, 1858, etc. 4 vols.

Harrison, J. A. (ed.) *The Complete Works of Edgar Allan Poe.* New York: 1902. 17 vols. (The Virginia Edition. By all odds the best edition.)

—— *Last Letters of Edgar Allan Poe to Sarah Helen Whitman.* New York: 1909.

Ingram, J. H. (ed.) *The Works of Edgar Allan Poe.* 4 vols. Edinburgh: 1874–1875.

Mabbott, T. O. (ed.) *Politian, an Unfinished Tragedy.* Richmond: 1923. (With useful notes, presenting some new information.)

Richardson, C. F. (ed.) *The Complete Works of Edgar Allan Poe.* New York: 1902. 10 vols.

Spannuth, J. E., and Mabbott, T. O. (eds.) *Doings in Gotham, as described in a Series of Letters to the Editors of the Columbia Spy;* together with various Editorial Comments and Criticisms by Poe; also a Poem entitled "New Year's Address of the Carriers of the Columbia Spy." Now first collected by Jacob E. Spannuth; with a Preface, Introduction and Comments by T. O. Mabbott. Pottsville, Pa.: 1929.

Stanard, Mary N. (ed.) *Edgar Allan Poe Letters Till Now Unpublished, in the Valentine Museum, Richmond, Virginia.* Philadelphia: 1925. (With introduction and commentary.)

Stedman, E. C., and Woodberry, G. E. (eds.) *The Works of Edgar Allan Poe.* Chicago: 1894–1895; New York: 1914. 10 vols. (The critical introductions are good, as well as most of the texts;

but not all of Poe's works are included, nor are the dates and sources of text always indicated.)

Stoddard, R. H. (ed.) *The Works of Edgar Allan Poe.* New York: 1884, 1894. 6 vols. (Superseded by the editions of Harrison, and of Stedman and Woodberry.)

Whitty, J. H. (ed.) *The Complete Poems of Edgar Allan Poe.* Boston: 1911. Second edition, revised and enlarged, 1917. (Excellent text and bibliography.)

Wilson, J. S. (ed.) "The Letters of Edgar A. Poe to George W. Eveleth," *Alumni Bulletin*, University of Virginia, Jan., 1924, pp. 34–59.

Woodberry, G. E. (ed.) "The Poe-Chivers Papers," *Century Magazine*, XLIII, 435–447 (Jan., 1903), 545–558 (Feb. 1903).

III. Biography and Criticism

Allen, G. W. "Edgar Allan Poe," in *American Prosody.* New York: 1935, pp. 56–90. (An authoritative survey of Poe's meters and stanzas, in the light of his prosodic theory as set forth in "The Rationale of Verse." Illustrates precisely how he used rhyme, alliteration, reiterations, imagery, and meter to produce novel moods of beauty in sound, his emphasis being on music.)

Allen, Hervey. *Israfel: The Life and Times of Edgar Allan Poe.* New York: 1926. Revised edition in one vol., 1934. (The most elaborate biography. Valuable in showing in detail Poe's indebtedness to his environment, notably in Philadelphia. Devotes considerable attention to his breakdown "due to his unhappy youth and heredity and the stimulants [opium] which he used." Killis Campbell concludes, "Mr. Allen is always readable, but he is also very prolix, and he is not a very careful scholar—by no means so careful as was Professor Woodberry.")

Alterton, Margaret. *Origins of Poe's Critical Theory,* University of Iowa Humanistic Studies, II, No. 3, 1925. (A scholarly genetic study of the sources, in Poe's reading, of his central criterion of unity and its corollaries, with emphasis on his indebtedness to Newtonian astronomy. Some attention is devoted to his debt to the Greeks and to contemporaries such as the Germans and Coleridge. Of major importance.)

Alterton, Margaret, and Craig, Hardin. *Edgar Allan Poe.* New York: 1935. American Writers Series. (The elaborately documented introduction, pp. xiii–cxviii, is the most comprehensive study available of the growth of Poe's philosophic, literary, political, and social ideas in their genetic inter-relations. The interpretation endeavors to show that Poe's work has "a sometimes forgotten consistency, since he was able to see in all aspects of the material universe and of life the features of a single plan"—a view elaborated in *Eureka* and derived mainly from science.)

Bailey, E. J. "Poe," in *Religious Thought in the Great American Poets.* Boston: 1922, pp. 32–46. (This essay is by no means as incisive as the work of Alterton and Craig, partly because it ignores all of Poe's prose utterances which furnish the necessary key to an understanding of his ideas in his poetry. The evidence in the latter is assembled, however, and Mr. Bailey concludes: "Beyond these tenets of God and immortality—tenets which, as he phrases them, are far more pagan than Christian in character—the religion of Poe did not reach" [p. 45]. See also Forrest and Strong, below.)

Baldwin, Summerfield. "The Æsthetic Theory of Edgar Poe," *Sewanee Review,* XXVI, 210–221 (April–June, 1918). (A rich and thoughtful essay. Concludes that Poe's importance as critic lies in the fact that "he clearly foreshadowed, if he did not originate, the entire corpus of modern æsthetic theory." He furnished "a basis for relating and distinguishing literature and art"; he showed "the dual character of poetry" [involving illusion and imitation]; "he mediated between the Platonists and the Aristotelians"; and he showed us "the place of technique in the resources of creative genius" [pp. 210, 220].)

Belden, H. M. "Observation and Imagination in Coleridge and Poe: a Contrast," in *In Honor of the Ninetieth Birthday of Charles Frederick Johnson.* Hartford, Conn.: 1928. (Concludes that "the whole effect of Poe's work is merely fantastic," while Coleridge "speaks to the whole man," and that this contrast derives from the fact that "Coleridge drew the elements of his magic essentially from the raw material of experience, Poe sought his . . . in '*novel* combinations of *those combinations which our predecessors . . . have already set in order.*'" Coleridge not only excelled in concrete observation and imagery, but in contrast Poe is distinguished for "the lack of moral and social sensibility" [p. 134]. A scholarly analysis, somewhat unsympathetic to Poe; profitably counterbalanced by studies of Poe's religious and social interests by Campbell [*Mind of Poe*], Forrest, Canby, and Marchand.)

Bell, L. C. *Poe and Chivers.* Columbus, Ohio: 1931. (A sharp criticism of S. F. Damon's *Thomas Holley Chivers* [1930], attempting to show that Mr. Damon's view that Poe derived much of "The Raven" from Chivers's "Isadore" is unproved because he failed to establish the prior publication of the latter poem.)

Boynton, P. H. "Poe and Journalism," *English Journal,* XXI, 345–352 (May, 1932). (Poe strove for journalistic effects which now militate against his fame. See also Canby.)

Brownell, W. C. "Poe," in *American Prose Masters.* New York: 1909. (The topics treated are "Exotic Art," "Poetry," "Technic," "Lack of Substance," "Scenic Imagination," "Culture and Criticism," and "The Poe Legend." One of the most acute of many judicial critiques disparaging Poe as "exclusively an artist" whose writings "lack substance" and "correspondence with reality.")

Cairns, W. B. "Some Notes on Poe's 'Al Aaraaf,'" *Modern Philology*, XIII, 35–44 (May, 1915). (A scholarly study. See Stovall.)

Cambiaire, C. P. *The Influence of Edgar Allan Poe in France*. New York: 1927. (A useful scholarly study exhaustively surveying Poe's vogue in France not only among the Symbolists but among critics and detective story writers and others. Includes discussion of translations of Poe.)

Campbell, Killis. *The Mind of Poe and Other Studies*. Cambridge, Mass.: 1933. (This invaluable volume crowns the work of the man who has contributed most to our information regarding Poe. The collected essays include "The Mind of Poe" [pp. 3–33]; "Contemporary Opinion of Poe" [pp. 34–62]; "The Poe-Griswold Controversy" [pp. 63–98]; "The Backgrounds of Poe," showing how constantly he drew upon contemporary American life [pp. 99–125]; "Self-Revelation in Poe's Poems and Tales" [pp. 126–146]; "The Origins of Poe" [pp. 147–186]; and "The Poe Canon" [pp. 187–238]. See also Mr. Campbell's chapter on Poe in *The Cambridge History of American Literature*, II, 55–69; his introduction to *Poe's Tales* [1927]; his introduction and precious notes to *The Poems of Edgar Allan Poe* [1917]; "Marginalia on Longfellow, Lowell, and Poe," *Modern Language Notes*, XLII, 516–521; "Three Notes on Poe," *American Literature*, IV, 385–388; and his exhaustive study, "Poe's Reading," University of Texas *Studies in English*, V, 166–196, with "Poe's Reading: Addenda and Corrigenda," *ibid.*, VII, 175–180.)

Canby, H. S. "Poe," in *Classic Americans*. New York: 1931, pp. 263–307. (An incisive and fresh essay, stressing the influence of journalism on Poe and the manner in which he was enabled to give his neurotic materials artistic order by his interest in science and the cosmic order which he celebrated in *Eureka*. Follows Miss Alterton in her emphasis on science. See also Canby's study of Poe in *The Short Story in English* [New York: 1909], pp. 227–245, and in *A Study of the Short Story* [New York: 1913], pp. 30–38. Dr. Canby concludes in the latter that "the art of perfect tone, which had already been used in poetry" [p. 35] is one of the two elements which account for the success of Poe's short stories, the other element being perfect suspense.)

Chase, L. N. *Poe and his Poetry*. London: 1913.

Damon, S. F. *Thomas Holley Chivers, Friend of Poe*. New York: 1930. (Chiefly interesting to the student of Poe for its attempt to show that Poe derived important suggestions for many of his poems from Chivers, and especially that his "Crowning appropriation for 'The Raven' came . . . from [Chivers's] 'Isadore.' . . . Chivers's priority in these things—idea, meter, refrain, and something of the atmosphere—is unquestionable" [pp. 210–211]. See L. C. Bell, above; A. G. Newcomer, "The Poe-Chivers Tradition Reëxamined," *Sewanee Review*, XII, 20–35 [Jan., 1904]; and G. E. Woodberry's *Life of Poe*, II, 376–390.)

Darnell, F. M. "The Americanism of Edgar Allan Poe," *English Journal*, XVI, 185–192 (March, 1927).

De Mille, G. E. "Poe" in *Literary Criticism in America*. New York: 1931, pp. 86–117. (Finds that "Poe's greatest fault," his "hysterical admiration for second-rate writers," results from his "having almost no standards of comparison outside of his contemporaries" [pp. 95–96]. [But see J. P. Pritchard below.] The essay is mostly devoted to a readable general survey of Poe's theory of four forms—the novel, the drama, the short story, and the lyric poem. See also Foerster, Baldwin, Prescott, and Alterton.

Dudley, F. A. "Tintinnabulation: and a Source for Poe's 'The Bells,'" *American Literature*, IV, 296–300 (Nov., 1932).

Englekirk, J. E. *Edgar Allan Poe in Hispanic Literature*. New York: 1934. (An exhaustive and scholarly book. Pp. 466–474 are devoted to "Poe and the New Esthetics." Extensive bibliography.)

Ferguson, J. DeL. "Poe," in *American Literature in Spain*. New York: 1916, pp. 55–86. (A dissertation. Concludes, p. 86, that in Spain "Poe won no distinguished followers" but stimulated a "healthy reaction.")

Foerster, Norman. "Poe," in *American Criticism*. Boston: 1928, pp. 1–51. (One of the ablest attempts to present Poe's critical ideas in their precise logical articulation [summarized on p. 6] and to indicate their shortcomings. Concludes that, in contrast to the classicists, Poe exalts an imaginative ideality which in his actual practice is associated with indeterminate sensuous longing as illustrated in "The Island of the Fay" and "The Domain of Arnheim." "His vision oscillated . . . between the infernal and the Arcadian" [p. 50].)

Forrest, W. M. *Biblical Allusions in Poe*. New York: 1928. (Pp. 11–83 constitute an able and erudite discussion of Poe's general religious views, offering ample refutation to the popular notion that he was merely an artistic craftsman without interest in philosophic questions. Chapter VIII, pp. 101–129, on "Poetic Resemblances to the Bible," shows in detail how Poe "skillfully employed the methods of the biblical poets in making music through elaborate and varied repetitions of words, sentences, and stanzas." The Appendix, pp. 151–208, contains exhaustive lists of all Poe's allusions to the Bible. A valuable book, much broader in scope than its title suggests. Reviewed by Killis Campbell, in "Poe's Knowledge of the Bible," *Studies in Philology*, XXVII, 546–551 [July, 1930].)

Fruit, J. P. *The Mind and Art of Poe's Poetry*. New York: 1899. (One of the best of the early treatments of its subject.)

Greenlaw, Edwin. "Poe in the Light of Literary History," *Johns Hopkins Alumni Magazine*, XVIII, 273–290 (June, 1930). (A stimulating essay.)

Gruener, Gustav. "Poe's Knowledge of German," *Modern Philology*, II, 125–140 (June, 1904).

Harrison, J. A. *Life and Letters of Edgar Allan Poe*. 2 vols. New York: 1903. (One of the most sensible and reliable of the biographies. Also as Vols. I and XVII of *Complete Works*, Virginia Edition.)

Hungerford, Edward. "Poe and Phrenology," *American Literature*, II, 209–231 (Nov., 1930). (A readable and scholarly article, including a section showing how Poe "begins to build up his theory of poetry, employing for literary criticism the terminology of his newly discovered science" [p. 214 ff.].)

Hutcherson, D. "*The Philadelphia Saturday Museum* Text of Poe's Poems," *American Literature*, V, 36–48 (March, 1933).

Ingram, J. H. *Edgar Allan Poe: His Life, Letters, and Opinions*. London: 1880. 2 vols. (Widely influential.)

Jackson, D. K. *Poe and The Southern Literary Messenger*. Richmond: 1934. (A valuable book, showing how journalism conditioned Poe's work.)

Kent, C. W. "Poe the Poet," introduction to Vol. VII of the Virginia Edition of Poe's *Works*.

Kent, C. W. and Patton, J. S. (eds.) *The Book of the Poe Centenary*. Charlottesville, Va.: 1909.

Kreymborg, Alfred. "The Weary Wayworn Wanderer," in *Our Singing Strength*. New York: 1929, pp. 53–66. (A readable impressionistic survey, emphasizing the notion that Poe was a "man without a country," a "disembodied spirit"—a notion largely refuted by Campbell, Marchand, Canby, Varner, and others who have shown his lively interest in contemporary American life. Some of Kreymborg's criticisms of individual poems are stimulating.)

Lauvrière, Émile. *Edgar Poe, sa vie et son œuvre, étude de psychologie pathologique*. Paris: 1904. (Hardin Craig calls this "one of the best books of Poe criticism in French.")

—— *The Strange Life and Loves of Edgar Allan Poe*. Philadelphia: 1935. (Emphasizes pathological aspects. Readable.)

Lemonnier, Léon. *Edgar Poe et les poètes français*. Paris: 1932.

—— *Edgar Poe et la Critique française de 1845 à 1875*. Paris: 1928. (A closely documented dissertation. Treats French reactions to Poe as romantic hero, as romantic and as scientific storyteller, and [pp. 194–295] the French "Réaction du bon sens.")

Lowell, J. R. "Edgar Allan Poe," *Graham's Magazine*, XXVI, 49–53 (Feb., 1845). (See also Lowell's characterization of Poe in *A Fable for Critics*.)

Marchand, Ernest. "Poe as Social Critic," *American Literature*, VI, 28–43 (March, 1934). (A spirited and exhaustively documented refutation of the conventional notion of V. L. Parrington and others that Poe's "aloofness from his own Virginia world was complete. Aside from his art he had no philosophy and no programs and no causes" [Parrington's *Romantic Revolution*, p. 57]. After surveying Poe's "personal experience with the politics of the period," Marchand assembles convincing evidence of (1) his aristocratic individualism; (2) his vigorous interest in attacking current schemes of social reform, including abolition; (3) his distrust of progress *via* scientific inventions and industrialism; and (4) his constant and hostile criticism of democratic reliance on the rabble—ideas revealing "the influence of that Virginia world of which he is said never to have been aware." A paper of major importance. See also Campbell [*Mind of Poe*, "Backgrounds"], Canby, Jackson, Varner.)

Markham, Edwin. "Poe," in *American Writers on American Literature* (ed. by John Macy). New York: 1931, pp. 135–152. (An eloquent and fairly discriminating appreciation by a fellow poet.)

Mauclair, Camille. *Le génie d'Edgar Poe; la légende et la vérité; la pensée, l'influence en France*. Paris: 1925. (Informative. See also his article, "Edgar Allan Poe as Inspirer of Ideas," *Fortnightly Review*, CXX, 474–485 [Sept., 1923].)

Messac, Régis. *Influences françaises dans l'œuvre d'Edgar Poe*. Paris: 1929.

More, P. E. "The Origins of Hawthorne and Poe," in *Shelburne Essays*. First Series. New York: 1904, pp. 51–70. (See also More's "A Note on Poe's Method," *Studies in Philology*, XX, 302–309 [July, 1923].)

Moses, M. J. *The Literature of the South*. New York: 1910, pp. 246–291. (An able book, useful in placing Poe in relation to the literature of his section.)

Parks, E. W. "Introduction" [pp. xvii–cxxix] and annotated "Bibliography" [pp. cxxx–cxlviii], in *Southern Poets*. New York: 1936. (Especially useful for the backgrounds of social, political, and literary theory which conditioned Poe's work.)

Pattee, F. L. *Development of the American Short Story*. New York: 1923, pp. 115–144. (The standard book on its subject.)

—— *The First Century of American Literature: 1770–1870*. New York: 1935, 503–515. (Treats Poe in conjunction with his fellow "magazinists.")

Pattee, F. L. "Poe's 'Ulalume,'" in *Side-Lights on American Literature*. New York: 1922, pp. 327–342. (An ingenious interpretation of this difficult poem as a purely subjective confession. See note on "Ulalume," below.)

Pettigrew, R. C. "Poe's Rime," *American Literature*, IV, 151–159 (Jan., 1933). (An exhaustive tabulation of Poe's rhyme emphasizing its "fundamental poverty." "I doubt that any other important poet is so repetitive in his riming as Poe. This distressing limitation—which is only one more intimation that he could never have been more than a comparatively minor poet—is made all the more conspicuous by his essential emphasis on verbal melody in his rimes, which consequently force themselves upon our attention. Not only that, but almost all of his rimes are entirely too obvious—already too threadbare before he rendered them more so—to bear the merciless repetition to which he subjects them" [p. 156]. It should be noted, however, that repetition was in some measure part of Poe's art in dealing with melancholy moods—see Forrest and Smith.)

Phillips, Mary E. *Edgar Allan Poe—the Man*. Chicago: 1926. 2 vols. (One of the more important recent biographies based on independent research.)

Pope-Hennessey, Una. *Edgar Allan Poe (1809–1849): A Critical Biography*. London: 1934. (Although Killis Campbell [*American Literature*, VII, 220–224, May, 1935] finds a few errors of fact in this book, he concludes that it gives us "by far the fullest account we have of the ultimate origins of Poe's writings and [reveals] more new facts about Poe's best-known poems and tales, and is, on the whole, one of the best biographies we have.")

Pound, Louise. "On Poe's 'The City in the Sea,'" *American Literature*, VI, 22–27 (March, 1934). (Exhaustive; see note on that poem, below.)

Prescott, F. C. "Introduction" [pp. ix–li], in *Selections from the Critical Writings of Edgar Allan Poe*. New York: 1909. (Valuable. Closely documented, with detailed notes.)

Pritchard, J. P. "Aristotle's *Poetics* and Certain American Literary Critics," *Classical Weekly*, XXVII, 81–85, 89–93, 97–99 (Jan. 8, 15, 22, 1934). (Pp. 81–85 deal with Poe. A valuable closely-documented analysis, showing numerous parallels and concluding that the classical Aristotle "had a strong shaping influence upon his criticism." See also Pritchard's documented study of "Horace and Edgar Allan Poe," *Classical Weekly*, XXVI, 129–133 [March, 1933], which concludes that, except in the matter of an aversion to didacticism, "his theory [of poetry] is substantially that of Horace." On Poe and the classics, see also Emma K. Norman, "Poe's Knowledge of Latin," *American Literature*, VI, 72–77; J. J. Jones, "Poe's 'Nicéan Barks,'" *ibid.*, II, 433–438; and Killis Campbell, "Poe's Reading" [see Campbell above].)

Ransome, Arthur. *Edgar Allan Poe, A Critical Study*. London: 1912.

Rhea, R. L. "Some Observations on Poe's Origins," University of Texas *Studies in English*, X, 135–146 (1930).

Robertson, J. M. "Poe," in *New Essays toward a Critical Method*. London: 1897, pp. 55–130 and 331–378. (A sympathetic and sometimes incisive study, although Robertson misses the point of *Eureka*. Includes discussion of Poe's poetry, tales, æsthetics, criticism, and philosophy. Emphasizes his versatility and his masterful intellect undermined by emotional weaknesses and bad luck.)

Seylaz, Louis. *Edgar Poe et les premiers symbolistes français*. Lausanne: 1923. (A useful study. Note that, if Poe immediately after his death influenced French rather than American poets, later American poets were influenced by Poe *via* France: see René Taupin's scholarly book, *L'Influence du Symbolisme Français sur la Poésie Américaine [de 1910 à 1920]*. Paris: 1931.)

Smith, C. A. *Poe—How to Know Him*. Indianapolis: 1921. (An appreciative interpretation and defence, perhaps somewhat too enthusiastic. See also *Repetition and Parallelism in English Verse* [New York: 1894, pp. 44–56] in conjunction with Forrest's study of the Biblical influence on Poe, above.)

Stedman, E. C. "Poe," in *Poets of America*. Boston: 1885, pp. 225–272. (Revision and extension of the essay which first appeared in *Scribner's Monthly*, May, 1880. An intelligent, well-balanced general critique. See also *Life and Letters of Edmund Clarence Stedman* [New York: 1910, II, 209–239]; and the introductions to Poe's Tales, Literary Criticism, and Poems, in the Stedman and Woodberry edition of *The Works of Edgar Allan Poe*, I, 91–121; VI, xi–xxv; and X, xiii–xxxv.)

Stovall, Floyd. "An Interpretation of Poe's 'Al Aaraaf,'" University of Texas *Studies in English*, IX, 106–133 (see note on "Al Aaraaf," below); "Poe's Debt to Coleridge," *ibid.*, X, 70–127, an exhaustive study which furnishes a mass of evidence to support Woodberry's view that Coleridge was "the guiding genius of Poe's entire intellectual life"; "The Women of Poe's Poems and Tales," *ibid.*, V, 197–209; and "Poe as a Poet of Ideas," *ibid.*, XI, 56–62. (The latter study is of special importance in refuting the conventional notion that Poe divorced Beauty from Truth. Mr. Stovall, one of the most acute of Poe scholars, concludes: "With the transcendentalists, he held intuitive truth to be the highest and surest of all, and the most suitable for poetic treatment. In short, what Poe really believed was that poetry, like all the other arts, may depict or suggest truth, but may not preach or reason of it . . Poe conceived of beauty and truth as complementary aspects of harmony" [p. 57]. This well-documented view helps to supplement the interpretation of Alterton and Craig—see above.)

Strong, A. H. "Poe," in *American Poets and Their Theology*. Philadelphia: 1916, pp. 161–206. (To this militant Calvinist, Poe's *Eureka*, which celebrates divine immanence, is a product of atheism and materialism. As a counterbalance, see Forrest's chapters on Poe's "Spirituality," "Pantheism," and "Mysticism." On the other hand, Strong's essay contains many suggestive, if prejudiced, comments.)

Taylor, W. F. "Israfel in Motley: a Study of Poe's Humor," *Sewanee Review*, XLII, 330–340 (July–Sept., 1934). (An able study, concluding that the evidence "offers a most salutary corrective to the morbidly sentimental paintings evolved from the dubious moralism of a former generation, and the equally dubious amateur psychology of our own" [p. 340]. Supplemented by J. S Wilson's "The Devil was in It," *American Mercury*, XXIV, 215–220 [Oct., 1931], which shows that Poe began his work as a prose writer with satire of current tastes and manners, burlesquing writers such as Horace Smith and the animosities of editors, worship of false heroes, and various sorts of fraud and quackery.)

Trent, W. P. "The Centenary of Poe," in *Longfellow and Other Essays*. New York: 1910, pp. 213–244.

Wächtler, P. *Edgar Allan Poe und die deutsche Romantik*. Leipzig: 1911.

Werner, W. L. "Poe's Theories and Practice in Poetic Technique," *American Literature*, II, 157–165 (May, 1930). (A scholarly study of technicalities, to be supplemented by studies of Poe's general theories by Foerster, Alterton and Craig, Baldwin, De Mille, and Prescott. "In summary, Poe is careful in his arrangement of sounds though careless about rimes; unusual in preferring *n*-sounds to *r* and *l* to *s;* conservative in insisting on a strongly predominant beat with few variations; modern in opposing contractions, inversions, and archaisms; and unconventional in his habitual use of loose stanza arrangements" [p. 164]. See also G. W. Allen.)

Wilson, J. S. "Poe's Philosophy of Composition," *North American Review*, CCXXIII, 675–684 (Dec., 1926). (An able article, especially interesting in showing Poe's distinction between unity of structure in the finished writing and the unity of psychological effect a writer plans to make on the reader's mind, the latter sort of unity being what Poe especially sought. See also Wilson's able introduction to *Tales of Edgar Allan Poe* [New York: 1927, pp. v–xxi] and his article listed under Taylor above.)

—— "The Young Man Poe," *Virginia Quarterly Review*, II, 238–253 (April, 1926).

Wilt, Napier. "Poe's Attitude toward His Tales: A New Document," *Modern Philology*, XXV, 101–105 (Aug., 1927). (On the basis of a newly discovered Poe letter to T. W. White, Apr. 30, 1835, which Mr. Wilt prints, he concludes that "far from claiming any originality in the manufacture of the formula [underlying his tales], . . . Poe definitely states that it was arrived at from the study of tales found in popular magazines" [p. 102]. Mr. Wilt offers a timely warning against sentimental and subjective interpretations of Poe, "The greatest care should be used in reading into Poe's use of horrible and morbid situations and details a reflection of the horror and morbidness of his own mind" [p. 105]. It might have been added that Poe was at times, at least, equally objective in his attempt to supply current demands as regards poetry. "'The Raven' has had a great 'run,' Thomas," Poe wrote F. W. Thomas, May 4, 1845, "but I wrote it for the express purpose of running—just as I did the 'Gold-Bug,' you know. The bird beat the bug, though, all hollow" [*Letters*, Virginia Edition, XVII, 205].)

Woodberry, G. E. *Edgar Allan Poe*. American Men of Letters Series. Boston: 1885.

—— *The Life of Edgar Allan Poe, Personal and Literary, with His Chief Correspondence with Men of Letters*. Boston: 1909. 2 vols. (Although Woodberry was not always in sympathy with Poe, he is usually fair and this is generally regarded as the best literary biography of Poe.)

NOTES

SOME POE CONTROVERSIES

Since Poe has aroused more controversy than almost any other American author except Whitman, it is perhaps desirable to consider some of the conventional charges which have been made against him in the light of evidence assembled by recent scholarship. The most often repeated charges are as follows:

(1) Poe lived "out of time and out of space" without interest in the political and social life of his time. (For qualifications of this view see preceding Bibliography under Marchand, H. Allen, Alterton-Craig, and Canby.)

(2) Poe was morbid and inhuman as illustrated by his poems and tales of horror, which are regarded as subjective confessions. (For refutation of this view through a revelation of his sources and of the fact that he was consciously following for commercial reasons the vogue of certain types of writings popular in current magazines, see Bibliography under Damon, Campbell, and Wilt. For evidence that Poe had a sense of humor and was consciously ridiculing current horror stories in some of his writings which have been taken seriously, see Bibliography under Taylor and Wilson.)

(3) Poe in theory and practice stood for art for art's sake, and ruled Truth out of the writer's domain. (For qualifications see Bibliography under Stovall, Woodberry [*Life of Poe*], Alterton, and Alterton-Craig.)

(4) Poe was merely a literary technician, a "jingle-man," devoid of interest in ultimate questions of religion. (For refutation see Alterton, Alterton-Craig, Bailey, and Forrest.)

GENERAL

According to Killis Campbell, the chief authority on the subject:

"Poe's critical doctrines find their best exemplification in his own poems. He is, first of all, a poet of beauty, paying little heed to morality or to the life of his fellow-men. He is, in the second place, a master-craftsman, who has produced a dozen poems of a melody incomparable so far as the western world is concerned; and he has achieved an all but flawless construction of the whole in such poems as 'The Raven,' 'The Haunted Palace,' and 'The Conqueror Worm'; while in 'The Bells' he has performed a feat in onomatopœia quite unapproached before or since in the English language. He is, moreover, one of the most original of poets. And the best of his verse exhibits a spontaneity and finish and perfection of phrase, as well as, at times, a vividness of imagery, that it is difficult to match elsewhere in American poetry.

"But his poems of extraordinary worth are exceedingly few—scarcely above a score at most—in which must be included the earlier lines 'To Helen,' 'Israfel,' 'The City in the Sea,' 'The Sleeper,' 'The Haunted Palace,' 'Dream-Land,' 'The Raven,' 'Ulalume,' 'For Annie,' and 'Annabel Lee.' And most of his earlier verses are manifestly imitative, Byron and Moore and Coleridge and Shelley being his chief models; while much of his earlier work, including all of the volume of 1827, and some of his latest—notably the verses addressed to Mrs. Osgood and Mrs. Shew and Mrs. Lewis—are either fragmentary and 'incondite' or mere 'verses,' or both. It has been justly said that 'there is almost no poet between whose best and worst verse there is a wider disparity.' His range, too, is narrower than that of any other American poet of front rank. Consistently with one of his theories already adverted to, he wrote no long poem, save the juvenile 'Tamerlane' and 'Al Aaraaf,' both of them extremely crude performances (though 'Al Aaraaf' contains excellent passages and played a large part in his development as poet), and an abortive play, *Politian*, which he never saw fit to publish in its entirety; so that he lives as poet solely by reason of his lyrics. And within the realm of the lyric he confined himself to the narrowest range of ideas. Nature he employed merely as ornament or as symbol or to fill in the background; and nowhere in his poems does he deal with the life about him, except in so far as he writes of friends and kindred. His most constant theme—if we exclude the poet himself, for few writers have so constantly reflected themselves in their work—is either the death of a beautiful woman and the grief occasioned thereby, or the realm of shades—the spirit-world—a subject to which he was strongly attracted, especially in his middle years. Hence, although most European critics have accorded him first place among American poets, most American critics have hesitated to accept their verdict."—*Cambridge History of American Literature*, II, 65–66.

The text of Poe's poems as reprinted in this anthology is that of Killis Campbell's *The Poems of Edgar Allan Poe* (Boston, 1917), and is used with the courteous permission of the editor and of the publishers, Ginn and Company. The student is urged to acquaint himself with the elaborate and scholarly notes in Professor Campbell's edition, to which the present editor is gratefully indebted.

Page 243. TAMERLANE

This very early and immature poem, printed first in Poe's collection of 1827, is typical of the collection in its indebtedness to Byron. Cf. *The Giaour* (ll. 916 ff.) and *Manfred* (III, i, ll. 66–78) with "Tamerlane," ll. 1–12. Poe's love affair with Sarah Elmira Royster of Richmond may have been the basis of the romance woven into the plot.

Page 245. SONG

Refers to Miss Royster's marriage.

SONNET—TO SCIENCE

First appeared in *Al Aaraaf, Tamerlane, and Minor Poems* (1829). The poem is a protest against science, or philosophy, as preying upon poetry. Keats's *Lamia* had elaborated the theme that beauty flies "at the mere touch of cold philosophy" (cf. *Lamia*, ll. 1–6, with this sonnet, ll. 9–14). Poe developed the same idea, attacking Wordsworth, in his "Letter to B——," in which he says "learning has little to do with the imagination"; following Coleridge, he says that a poem "is opposed to a work of science by having, for its *immediate* object, pleasure, not truth." This was in 1831. In his later work, notably in *Eureka* (1848), he emphasized the dependence of poetry upon scientific concepts of the ordered harmony of the universe.

Page 246. AL AARAAF

First published in the volume of 1829, this poem is an obscure allegory, indebted in part to Milton and Moore, with the theme, according to Woodberry (*Life of Poe*, I, 61–62), that "beauty is the direct revelation of the divine to mankind, and the protection of the soul against sin." W. B. Cairns, "Some Notes on Poe's 'Al Aaraaf,'" (*Modern Philology*, XIII, 35–44 [May, 1915]), develops in part Woodberry's theory. See also "An Interpretation of Poe's 'Al Aaraaf,'" by F. Stovall, in the University of Texas *Studies in English*, X, 106–133 (1929). It is noteworthy that Professor Stovall presents evidence to show that "'Al Aaraaf' was written by Poe with the conscious purpose of presenting allegorically his theory of poetry, and that this theory, as then conceived, was substantially the same as later enunciated. . . We misjudge Poe when we class him as a worshipper of beauty for its own sake. On the contrary, he loved beauty as a revealer of truth beyond the scope of reason." See also the full notes in the Alterton-Craig *Poe*, pp. 479–490.

Page 250. ROMANCE

Poe regarded this poem as the "best thing" in every respect except "sound" in his 1829 volume; he was "certain" that lines 11–15 had "never been surpassed." (Letter to John Neal, quoted in Woodberry, *Life*, I, 369.) The poem was greatly enlarged in the 1831 version; but the added passages, which were personal and included a reference to Poe's drinking, were omitted in the 1845 version here reprinted.

Page 251. TO——("The bowers whereat . . .")

Campbell (*Poems of Poe*, pp. 148 and 194) and others have suggested that this poem refers to Miss Royster and her rejection of Poe.

TO——("I heed not that . . .")

Poe scholars have been unable to ascertain to whom this poem is addressed. Campbell (p. 196) suggests it is "barely possible that the lady referred to is Mrs. Clemm."

TO HELEN

Poe apparently approved Lowell's statement that this poem was written when the poet was only fourteen years old. But Campbell has pointed out that the poem was not printed until the 1831 edition appeared, and that if the poem had existed, Poe would hardly have omitted it from his editions of 1827 and 1829. The poem records Poe's sorrow at the death (April 28, 1824) of Mrs. Jane Stith Stanard of Richmond. Poe spoke of her as "the first purely ideal love of my soul."

Edwin Markham (see Bibliography) says, "Poe never surpassed the serene exaltation and divine poise of this poem. It shows his passion for a crystalline perfection. Save for a false rhyme and a dubious phrase or two, the poem is perfect, having the careless grace of a young lily swaying on the stem. In its wandering music and flower-like freshness of form, it stands with the deathless lyrics; with 'Tears, Idle Tears,' 'Rose Aylmer,' 'One Word Is Too Often Profaned.'" Lowell (Harrison edition of Poe, I, 367–383) praised it in much the same terms.

Many conjectures have been made as to the source of "Nicéan barks"; J. J. Jones ("Poe's 'Nicéan Barks,'" *American Literature*, II, 433–438), seems to have been most plausible in suggesting Catullus, nos. 4, 31, and 46, dealing with Catullus's journey to Nicea.

LENORE

For elaborate analysis of three stages in the development of this elegiac poem showing how Poe labored to attain the unity of effect he prized, see Campbell's *Poems of Poe*, pp. 68–72, giving various versions, and pp. 214–217. The present text is that of 1849 in the *Richmond Whig*, with minor corrections by Campbell.

To Poe beauty is inseparable from melancholy, and in "The Philosophy of Composition" and elsewhere he claimed that the death of a young and beautiful woman "is, unquestionably, the most poetical topic in the world." In discussing an elegiac poem by Amelia Welby (*Works*, ed. Harrison, XI, 277–8), Poe says: "When I say, then, that Mrs. Welby's stanzas are good among the class *passionate* (using the term commonly and falsely applied), I mean that her tone is properly subdued, and is not so much the tone of passion, as of a gentle and melancholy regret, interwoven with a pleasant sense of the natural loveliness surrounding the lost in the tomb, and a memory of her human beauty when alive.—Elegiac poems should either assume this character, or dwell purely on the beauty (moral or physical) of the departed—or, better still, utter the notes of triumph. I have endeavored to carry out this latter idea in some verses which I have called 'Lenore.'" It is unknown whether the poem commemorates Mrs. Stanard or Mrs. Allan.

l. 3. *Guy De Vere.* Campbell suggests that this name of the bereaved lover, introduced into the 1843 *Pioneer* version, was derived from Tennyson's "Lady Clara Vere de Vere."

ll. 8–12. The poem is semi-dramatic, and Poe reproaches the false friends who loved Lenore for her wealth. It is probable that the name Lenore, first used in the 1843 version of the poem, derived from Bürger, whose widely popular ballad "Lenore" contains some situations parallel to those of Poe's poem.

Page 252. ISRAFEL

This poem should be considered when Poe is charged with being a mere "jingle man" who cannot treat ideas in poetry. It contributes to our knowledge of his poetic theory, embodying and illustrating this theory in lines of the choicest melody. Campbell says (*Poems*, p. 203): "In *Israfel* Poe gives us, as in *Al Aaraaf*, a partial expression of his poetic creed. In *Al Aaraaf* he had sung of the 'holiness of beauty'; here he proclaims the belief that the true poet will write from his heart, that his numbers will be melodious, and that he will be informed with a superior wisdom. In the concluding stanza there is also the hint that the poet's success will be conditioned, to some extent, on his environment."

On the question of whether Chivers's "The Song of Seralim" is an imitation of Poe's "Israfel," see S. F. Damon (*Chivers*, pp. 87–90), who tries to acquit Chivers of the charge of direct imitation, and L. C. Bell (*Poe and Chivers*, pp. 16–39), who tries to show Chivers's "crowning appropriations of Poe's idea and language."

THE CITY IN THE SEA

After its appearance in the volume of 1831 under the title "The Doomed City," this poem was printed in the *Southern Literary Messenger* (August, 1836) as "The City of Sin." See Campbell's notes (pp. 207–210) on Poe's many versions of the poem, and on its relation to six other poems dealing with the "Spirits of the Dead." It should be noted that the poem does not involve all spirits, but only the spirits of the *sinful* dead. For an admirable scholarly discussion, see Louise Pound's "On Poe's 'The City in the Sea'" (*American Literature*, VI, 22–27). Compare ll. 30–41 and Byron's "Darkness." G. W. Allen (*American Prosody*, 66–67) points out that "The first lines of the 'City in the Sea' . . . are practically free stress, each line containing four accents but with the syllables ranging from seven to twelve . . . . As the poem progresses, it becomes more regular in rhythm, partly as the result of reiteration and alliteration."

Page 253. THE SLEEPER

The original version in the volume of 1831, entitled "Irene," was very different from the present version, which Campbell based on the 1845 Lorimer Graham copy. Poe wrote (*Letters*, ed. Harrison, 207), "In the higher qualities of poetry it ["The Sleeper"] is better than 'The Raven'; but there is not one man in a million who could be brought to agree with me in this opinion. 'The Raven,' of course, is far the better as a work of art; but in the true basis of all art, 'The Sleeper' is the superior. I wrote the latter when quite a boy." Note Poe's consummate skill, pointed out by G. W. Allen (*American Prosody*, p. 67), in using meter, alliteration, and vowel color in combination "to produce the mood of voluptuous drowsiness."

Page 255. THE HAUNTED PALACE

This poem appeared in the same year as an independent poem in the *Baltimore Museum* (April, 1839), and as one of Roderick Usher's "rhymed verbal improvisations" in the tale, "The Fall of the House of Usher," in *Burton's Gentleman's Magazine* (Sept., 1839). On Poe's charge that Longfellow drew upon this poem in his "The Beleaguered City," see Campbell, *Poems*, 237–238. The main question of interpretation of "The Haunted Palace" is this: is the poem exclusively an expression of Roderick Usher's neurasthenic personality, and hence to be considered as a dramatic utterance without reflection on Poe; or is the poem a subjective confession by Poe of his own dementia? He wrote that "by 'The Haunted Palace' I mean to imply a mind haunted by phantoms—a disordered brain" (*Letters*, 83–84). In "The Fall of the House of Usher," it should be noted that the "House" involves a series of symbols: the literal house that falls into the tarn; the family or line of Usher which perishes; the nerve-shattered body of Usher himself; his disordered mind—a haunted palace with its "red-litten windows."

Page 256. THE CONQUEROR WORM

It has been suggested that Poe was partly inspired to write this poem by a stanza by Spencer Wallis Cone quoted by Poe in a review in *Burton's Gentleman's Magazine* (June, 1840), which he characterized as breathing "the true soul of poetry." In "The Sleeper," "Silence," "The Premature Burial," and the impressive "Masque of the Red Death," Poe also deals with this theme of the "worm" as the conqueror. Since some critics have taken the poem as a subjective confession of Poe's "morbidity," it should be noted that Poe used the poem as a dramatic utterance in "Ligeia" (1845) in which the action of the story, in which the heroine returns from the dead, refutes the poem. Just after its recitation, Ligeia rises, saying (cf. Emerson, *Works*, I, 10), "O God! O Divine Father! . . . shall this conqueror be not once conquered? Are we not part and parcel in Thee?" In Poe's essay on Longfellow's *Ballads* (*Graham's Magazine*, April, 1842), the year before this poem, he had defined poetry as "a wild effort to reach the beauty above," an effort "inspired with a prescient ecstasy of the beauty beyond the grave . . ." (Alterton-Craig, *Poe*, p. 345). His views of immortality are fully discussed in *Eureka*. It will be noted that, as Kent said, the five stanzas of "The Conqueror Worm" correspond roughly to the five acts of a play. Woodberry (*Life of Poe*, II, 39, 174) called it a "fine poem," a "marvelous allegory." It should be interpreted, however, in the light of other expressions of Poe's religious views cited above.

SONNET—SILENCE

It should be noted that Poe not only accepted a dualism between selfishness and altruism within the individual, distrusting radical social thinkers who ignored it (see Marchand's "Poe as Social Critic") but that in this sonnet and elsewhere he accepts life's "twin entity" and the dualism of "body and soul." Campbell interprets the incorporate Silence as "the tyrant that rules in the nether world, in which the spirits of the unrighteous remain till the Day of Judgment."

Poe's belief in immortality is based, however,

not so much upon Christian mysticism as upon a religion rooted in science. In his long prose work *Eureka* he develops the Emersonian idea of "two classes of consciousness" in which "Nature and the God of Nature are distinct," although at death the animate Many become blended into the one, "all within the Spirit Divine." At the end of his review of Macaulay's essays (Alterton-Craig, *Poe*, p. 321) he says, "Indeed, to our mind, the *only* irrefutable argument in support of the soul's immortality—or, rather, the only conclusive proof of man's alternate dissolution and rejuvenescence *ad infinitum*—is to be found in analogies deduced from the modern established theory of the nebular cosmogony," a theory whose religious implications he discussed at length in *Eureka*. Here again we have evidence of the absurdity of the popular notion that Poe was utterly uninterested in religion and that he was a mere materialist.

Page 257. THE RAVEN

First published in the New York *Evening Mirror* (Jan. 29, 1845), and revised some sixteen times. See Poe's full commentary in "The Philosophy of Composition," the accuracy of which has been questioned in part because he does not mention his probable indebtedness to work by contemporaries such as Chivers's "Isadore," not to mention Elizabeth Barrett's "Lady Geraldine's Courtship," which he had previously reviewed. According to S. F. Damon (*Chivers*, p. 211), "Chivers's priority in these things—idea, meter, refrain, and something of the atmosphere—is unquestionable." If this is true, to what extent can the poem be regarded as an expression of Poe's subjective religious faith? C. A. Smith (*E. A. Poe: How to Know Him*, p. 221) says, "'The Raven' embodies not remorse but the universal protest of the soul against the denial of immortality. As Poe sometimes celebrates beauty *via* decay, so here he celebrates faith *via* doubt." Is the poem of interest chiefly as a personal religious utterance or as an experiment in poetic technique? See J. H. Ingram, *The Raven . . . with Literary and Historical Commentary* (London: 1885); H. E. Legler, *Poe's Raven: Its Origin and Genesis* (Wausau, Wis.: 1907); and especially the elaborate notes in Killis Campbell's *Poems of Poe* (pp. 246–259) and in the Alterton-Craig *Poe* (pp. 500–504).

It will be recalled that the theme of "The Raven," the grief occasioned by the death of a beautiful woman, is also dealt with in Poe's prose tales "Morella," "Berenice," and "Ligeia." In the latter especially, the idea is developed that man does not yield himself "unto death utterly, save only through the weakness of his feeble will." (See note on "The Conqueror Worm," above.) In *Eureka* Poe developed the idea that the universe emanates from an eternal Essence, and that it is being drawn back into the same Essence, that this process of emanation and absorption goes on continually. He says that "we shall lose our individual identity" through "the absorption by each individual intelligence of all other intelligences (that is, of the Universe) into its own. That God may become all and in all, each must become God" (Harrison ed. *Works*, XVI, 336). Cf. Emerson's "Threnody" ("The many-seeming life is one," etc.), and Whitman's "Song of Myself."

Page 260. ULALUME

First published in the *American Whig Review* (Dec., 1847). Poe's bride Virginia had died in January of the same year. F. L. Pattee ("Poe's 'Ulalume,'" in *Side-Lights on American Literature*, pp. 327–342) regards the poem as "a cry of utter despair from a man's inmost soul," torn between grief for the deceased Virginia and the flickering hope of happiness with Mrs. Shew. See the many differing interpretations of "Ulalume" cited in Campbell's *Poems of Poe*, pp. 269–272. The poem has some parallels to Henry Beck Hirst's *Endymion* and *Coming of the Mammoth*, which Poe reviewed (*Broadway Journal*, July 12, 1845). T. O. Mabbott ("The Astrological Symbolism of Poe's 'Ulalume,'" *Notes and Queries*, CLXI, 27) suggests that the astrological allusions here indicate a reference to Poe's amour with Mrs. Osgood. One is disposed to raise the question as to the validity of a strictly autobiographical interpretation of the poem when it is compared with Thomas Holley Chivers's "Nacoochee" (1837), the idea of which, says Damon (*Chivers*, pp. 214–215), "is taken over bodily into 'Ulalume.' . . . Chivers (as is made clear in the last stanzas) is mourning a lost beloved; Poe, his 'lost Ulalume.' Chivers's lost beloved, Nacoochee, symbolizes the soul and is actually named 'Psyche' in stanza xxviii; Poe also introduces 'Psyche my soul.' Chivers contrasts Dian (chastity) with Astarte (passion); so does Poe. Both poets introduce a vision of Astarte. Nacoochee fears Astarte and her powers; so does Poe's Psyche. Ostenee has no such fear; neither has Poe's hero. In both cases, Death seizes the lady as a result."

To what extent, in this and other poems of Poe, does the presence of sources, or at least striking parallels to other poems, make it legitimate to question whether (as in the case of Shakespeare and his sources) Poe was expressing fully his *own* ideas at the time? Or is the fact that he chose deliberately certain ideas of others for elaboration significant of his own state of mind? To what extent can the ideas in this and other poems be supported by parallels in his letters and other prose where he is unquestionably expressing his own mind?

Page 262. THE BELLS

This poem, which grew from 17 to 113 lines, was first published in the *Union Magazine* (Dec., 1849). Among various sources and analogues suggested are Chateaubriand's *Génie du Christianisme* (Paris,

1836, III, 43), and Dickens's *Chimes*. Ingram (*Life of Poe*, p. 361) cites Mrs. Shew as follows: "One day he came in," she records, "and said 'Marie Louise, I have to write a poem; I have no feeling, no sentiment, no inspiration.' His hostess persuaded him to have some tea. It was served in the conservatory, the windows of which were open, and admitted the sound of neighboring church bells. Mrs. Shew said, playfully, 'Here is paper'; but the poet, declining it, declared, 'I so dislike the noises of the bells tonight, I cannot write. I have no subject—I am exhausted.' The lady then took up the pen, and, pretending to mimic his style, wrote, '"The Bells," by E. A. Poe'; and then in pure sportiveness, 'The Bells, the little silver Bells,' Poe finishing off the stanza. She then suggested for the next verse, 'The heavy iron Bells'; and this Poe also extended into a stanza. He next copied out the complete poem, and headed it, 'By Mrs. M. L. Shew,' remarking that it was her poem, as she had suggested and composed so much of it." The poem has been attacked as a mere jingle devoid of ideas, but it should be noted that the four stanzas, dealing respectively with sleigh bells, wedding bells, alarum bells, and funeral bells, suggest the cycle of life, the method being analogous to that of Masefield in "Cargoes." Edwin Markham calls "The Bells" "the finest example in our language of the suggestive power of rhyme and of the echo of sound to sense." See also F. A. Dudley, "Tintinnabulation: and a Source of Poe's 'The Bells,'" (*American Literature*, IV, 296–300).

Page 263. ELDORADO

First printed in *Flag of Our Union* (April 21, 1849), and perhaps suggested by the gold rush of the Forty-Niners. It will be recalled that Poe defined the Poetic Principle as "strictly and simply the Human Aspiration for Supernal Beauty." Compare this poem representing Poe's ideality with such prose pieces as "The Island of the Fay," "The Domain of Arnheim," etc. Norman Foerster concludes that Poe's "aspiration for the infinite, or highest reality, turns out to be not merely the fascination of an unreal fairyland, a land of idle dreams; it reduces itself, at length, to an insatiable thirst for rather material luxury . . . For the rational principle in Poe, unaided by moral imagination, became the accomplice of the senses, or appetitive principle, and so enabled him to produce only an inferior range of harmonies—shuddering harmonies of the murky subconscious, and roseate harmonies of sensuous longing posing as spirituality. His vision oscillated not between the earthly and the supernal, but between the infernal and the Arcadian" (*American Criticism*, pp. 40, 50).

Page 265. ANNABEL LEE

This poem, embodying "the culmination of Poe's lyric style," was published in the New York *Tribune* on October 9, 1849, two days after Poe's death. Note Poe's subtle use here of parallelism, reiteration, internal rhyme, rhymes at irregular intervals, vowel melody, and consonant alliteration. Mr. G. W. Allen concludes (*American Prosody*, pp. 79–80): "The poem is, in practically every respect, the realization of Poe's ideal: a poem with sense wedded to sound, the result being primarily music; a poem of an unearthly mood or 'atmosphere' achieved by every sort of reiteration of which Poe was capable; and, above all, a poem which is suggestive rather than definite, beautifully unreal with its generalities." R. A. Law (*Journal of English and Germanic Philology*, XXI, 341 ff.) has suggested as a probable source "The Mourner," published in the Charleston *Courier* in 1807. As Miss Alterton noted, the thought of the poem represents Poe's final "serene triumph over his earlier sensationalism."

THE PHILOSOPHY OF COMPOSITION

First published in *Graham's Magazine*, April, 1846. "One does not have to believe in the literal truth of Poe's essay as a factual account of the production of the poem ["The Raven"] (although in a sense it may be that), but one must believe in its truth in a high sense as perfect exposition and interpretaton of the act of composition. This is equivalent to saying that 'The Philosophy of Composition' is one of the most masterly examples of literary criticism in the language. It takes rank with Coleridge's criticism of Wordsworth's poems in *Biographia Literaria*, DeQuincey's 'On the Knocking at the Gate in "Macbeth,"' and Swinburne's essay on the poet Collins. . . One may point out that the technical method of 'The Raven' differs in no particular from that of those tales in which a state of emotion has been regularized by the application of logic or reason, except of course in those technical elements which distinguish poetry from prose" (Alterton-Craig, *Poe*, cvii–cviii).

In Poe's quest of materials embodying the grotesque, the strange, the remote, the extravagant, the sensational, the morbid, the mysterious, or the horrible, he reveals his kinship with certain phases of contemporary romanticism. His special distinction lies in the fact that, given romantic or decadent materials, he was able to control and focus these materials by imposing on them a rational pattern and ordered form. At a time when many romanticists and transcendentalists were attacking rationalism and glorifying genius as a divine visitation whose workings were inscrutable and inexplicable, Poe stands apart as an exponent of rational processes and conscious craftsmanship.

Page 241. *From* EUREKA

First published, as a book, in 1848. In the preface Poe wrote: "To the few who love me and whom I love—to those who feel rather than to those who think—to the dreamers and those who put faith in dreams as the only realities—I offer this Book of Truths, not in its character of Truth-Teller, but for the Beauty that abounds in its Truth; constituting it true. To these I present the composition as an Art-Product alone:—let us say as a Romance; or, if I be not urging too lofty a claim, as a Poem.

"*What I here propound is true:*—therefore it cannot die:—or if by any means it be now trodden down so that it die, it will 'rise again to the Life Everlasting.'

"Nevertheless it is as a Poem only that I wish the work to be judged after I am dead."

Eureka was dedicated to Alexander von Humbolt, whose great scientific work, *Kosmos*, had begun to appear in 1845.

It will be noted that Poe's study of Newtonian astronomy, based on the laws of gravitation, gave him his magnificent vision of a universe of ordered harmony. The key lines in *Eureka* illustrate the manner in which he connected astronomical law and order and literary composition: "In the construction of *plot* . . . in fictitious literature, we should aim at so arranging the incidents that we shall not be able to determine, of any one of them, whether it depends from any one other or upholds it. In this sense, of course, *perfection* of *plot* is really, or practically, unattainable—but only because it is a finite intelligence that constructs. The plots of God are perfect. The Universe is the plot of God." See Miss Alterton's *Origins of Poe's Critical Theory* and the Introduction to the Alterton-Craig *Poe* (1935) for a detailed and masterly exposition of the manner in which Poe's theory and practice of composition, his quest of unity and totality of effect and of musical harmony, derive from the scientific principles elucidated in *Eureka*, which is a final summing up of his philosophy.

Page 275. THE POETIC PRINCIPLE

Originally delivered by Poe as a lecture in 1848–1849, "The Poetic Principle" was published posthumously in *Sartain's Union Magazine*, October, 1850. It is a summary of principles scattered throughout Poe's earlier essays, and hence the most important single comprehensive statement of his poetic theories. For full discussion see Bibliography under Allen, Alterton, Baldwin, De Mille, Foerster, Pettigrew, Prescott, Werner, and Wilson.

For Poe's further discussion of the question of the didactic, see *Works*, edited by Harrison, VII, xxxvii, xliii; IX, 305; X, 141; XI, 67–68, 79, 84, 244–254; XII, 33–34; XIII, 131. It should be noted that in "The Poetic Principle," while Poe opposed the excessive didacticism of his day and the notion that if the moral "lesson" of a poem were edifying its lack of intrinsic quality as a work of art should be disregarded, he readily admits that "It by no means follows . . . that . . . the precepts of Duty, or even the lessons of Truth, may not be introduced into a poem, and with advantage; for they may subserve, incidentally, in various ways, the general purposes of the work . . ." The climax of "The Poetic Principle" hardly supports the popular notion of Poe as a non-moral technician who would banish from the poet's domain all consideration of virtue. The poet, he concludes, finds beauty in nature but chiefly in human character, especially that of noble women. He "owns it in all noble thoughts—in all unworldly motives—in all holy impulses—in all chivalrous, generous, and self-sacrificing deeds." Do not such passages suggest that Poe is not so far from Emerson, and his doctrine of the beauty of virtue, as popularly supposed? (See note on "Al Aaraaf," above, and studies by Stovall.)

SUMMARY OF POE'S POETIC THEORIES

1. Poetry is the rhythmical creation of beauty, independent of either truth or goodness in the narrow sense, although beauty may lead one to divine truth and guard the soul against sin. (Cf. "Al Aaraaf".) The immediate object of a poem is "pleasure, not truth."
2. "Beauty of whatever kind, in its supreme development, invariably excites the sensitive soul to tears. Melancholy is thus the most legitimate of all the poetical tones" ("The Philosophy of Composition"). All details and imagery must harmonize so as to achieve a unity of effect on the mind of the reader—a hypnotic effect, preferably of melancholy.
3. In order to create this tone or mood, the poem must be of a length suitable for reading at one sitting. Poe believed that for securing this effect the length of a poem must be limited to about one hundred lines.
4. The first element of poetry is "the thirst for supernal Beauty—a beauty which is not afforded the soul by any existing collocation of earth's forms . . ." Poetry may be aided by reproducing sensuous forms and colors, "but this repetition is not Poesy . . . It is a wild effort to reach the beauty above," a beauty created by the imagination and not by the memory of sensuous experience.
5. "It is in Music, perhaps, that the soul most nearly attains that end upon which we have commented—the creation of supernal beauty." One should seek "a suggestive indefiniteness of meaning, with the view of bringing about a definiteness of vague and therefore spiritual *effect*." See also Poe's statement glorifying music quoted in Woodberry's *Life*, II, 90–95.
6. Technically, poetry depends not upon accent but only upon time or quantity. Each foot should be pronounceable in a period of time uniform with that of every other foot in the line, no matter how many syllables the foot contains. Unlike Bryant, Poe opposes substi-

tution of an anapest or a dactyl for an iamb or a trochee. There should be no contractions or elisions, no "harsh consonants," no rhymes which are identic, light, or inexact, no archaisms, contractions, or inversions.
7. In seeking musical harmony and a balanced inter-penetration of imagination and reason in "plot," one should take as his goal the harmoniously ordered cosmic system of the universe: "The plots of God are perfect. The Universe is the plot of God."

To what extent did Poe succeed in practicing these seven theories? Compare and contrast his theory and practice with those of Emerson and Lanier.

HENRY WADSWORTH LONGFELLOW

CHRONOLOGY

1807 Born in Portland, Maine, February 27.

1825 Graduated from Bowdoin College, many of his poems already having been published in magazines.

1826–29 Studied in France, Spain, Italy, Germany.

1829–35 Professor and librarian at Bowdoin. Married Mary Storer Potter, 1831.

1835–36 Accepted professorship of modern languages and belles-lettres at Harvard, and went abroad to improve his knowledge of German and Scandinavian. Wife died. *Outre-Mer* published.

1836 Began comfortable but busy period of college work and pleasant social life.

1839 *Hyperion* and *Voices of the Night* published.

1841 *Ballads and Other Poems.*

1842 Went to Europe. Formed friendship with Freiligrath. Visited Dickens and others in England. Wrote *Poems on Slavery* on trip home.

1843 Married Frances Elizabeth Appleton. *The Spanish Student.*

1845 *The Belfry of Bruges and Other Poems* (published Dec., 1845; dated 1846).

1847 *Evangeline.*

1849 *Kavanagh,* a novel.

1850 *The Seaside and the Fireside.*

1851 *The Golden Legend* (afterwards part II of *Christus*).

1854 Resigned professorship.

1855 *The Song of Hiawatha.*

1858 *The Courtship of Miles Standish and Other Poems.*

1861 Tragic death of his wife.

1863 *Tales of a Wayside Inn* (second and third parts published in 1872 and 1873 respectively). Finished translation of Dante's *Divine Comedy,* begun earlier: publication completed in 1867.

1866 *Flower-de-Luce* (dated 1867).

1868 *New England Tragedies* (afterwards part III of *Christus*).

1868–69 Toured Europe. Honorary degrees from Cambridge and Oxford.

1871 *The Divine Tragedy* (afterwards part I of *Christus*).

1872 *Christus, a Mystery* (made up of the three parts already listed, with additions of interludes and a finale). *Three Books of Song.*

1873 *Aftermath.*

1874 *The Hanging of the Crane.*

1875 *The Masque of Pandora, and Other Poems.*

1878 *Kéramos and Other Poems.*

1880 *Ultima Thule.*

1881 Suffered nervous prostration.

1882 Died in Cambridge, March 24. *In the Harbor* (part II of *Ultima Thule*).

1883 *Michael Angelo* published.

1884 Bust unveiled in Westminster Abbey—first American so honored.

BIBLIOGRAPHY

I. Bibliography

The Cambridge History of American Literature, II, 425–436. (The basic bibliography, prepared by H. W. L. Dana. Includes items about Longfellow prior to 1918.)

Chew, B. *The Longfellow Collectors' Hand-Book: A Bibliography of First Editions.* New York: 1885.

Livingston, L. S. *A Bibliography of the First Editions in Book Form of the Writings of Henry Wadsworth Longfellow.* New York: 1908.

II. Text

The Writings of Henry Wadsworth Longfellow, with Bibliographical and Critical Notes. Riverside Edition. Boston: 1886. 11 vols. (Poems, I–VI; Prose, VII–VIII; Divine Comedy, IX–XI. Vol. VII, pp. 409–410, lists 22 reviews and studies of literary topics which have never been collected and are available only in periodicals, such as the review of a new edition of Sidney's *Defence of Poetry* in the *North American Review,* XXXIV, 56–78 [Jan., 1832].)

Complete Works. Standard Library Edition. Boston: 1891. 14 vols. (Same as above, illustrated, with the addition of the three-volume *Life* by Samuel Longfellow.)

Complete Writings. Craigie Edition. Boston: 1904. 11 vols. (Same as the Riverside Edition, with illustrations added.)

Complete Poetical Works, ed. by H. E. Scudder. Cambridge Edition. Boston: 1903. (Reprinted at later dates. The best one-volume edition, with valuable headnotes, and with "A Chronological List of Mr. Longfellow's Poems" on pp. 676–679. There are other one-volume editions, the Household, the Cabinet, etc.)

Pettengill, R. W. (ed.). *Longfellow's Boyhood Poems; a Paper . . . together with the Text of Hitherto Uncollected Early Poems and Bibliography.* Saratoga Springs, N. Y.: 1925. (The "Paper" is by G. T. Little.)

III. Biography and Criticism

Allen, G. W. "Longfellow," in *American Prosody.* New York: 1935, pp. 154–192. (An authoritative and detailed survey of Longfellow's use of a wide variety of meters and stanzas. Concludes: "Longfellow's greatest contribution . . . was not specifically any new theory or practice but a general, broad, and deep influence toward the search for new forms, based on a wide acquaintance with the chief poetic techniques of the world" [p. 191].)

Appelmann, A. H. "Longfellow's *Poems on*

Slavery in Their Relationship to Freiligrath," *Modern Language Notes*, XXX, 101–102 (April, 1915).

—— "The Relation of Longfellow's *Evangeline* to Tegnér's *Frithiof's Saga*," *Publications of the Society for the Advancement of Scandinavian Study*, II, 165–180 (July, 1915).

Axon, W. E. A. "On the Sources of Longfellow's *Tales of a Wayside Inn*," *Royal Society of Literature Transactions*, III, 159–172 (London: 1911).

Bailey, E. J. "Longfellow," in *Religious Thought in the Greater American Poets*. Boston: 1922, pp. 108–136. (A thoughtful and appreciative essay, assembling much relevant evidence and concluding, "Apparently, without resort to any book, council, or creed, as a source of authority, he took his unquestioning stand upon the three important fundamental doctrines, the goodness of God, the divinity of Christ, and the immortality of the soul" [p. 116].)

Brenner, Rica. *Twelve American Poets before 1900*. New York: 1933, pp. 80–108. (A graceful essay, mostly biographical. Concludes Longfellow cannot be cast aside because historically he "introduced into American poetry a European attitude and atmosphere," breaking down provincialism, and because "the simpler things and the simple emotions of life endure.")

Campbell, Killis. "Marginalia on Longfellow, Lowell, and Poe," *Modern Language Notes*, XLII, 516–521 (Dec., 1927).

Carman, Bliss. "Longfellow," in *The Poetry of Life*. Boston: 1905, pp. 127–150. (A wise defence by a fellow poet.)

Carpenter, G. R. *Henry Wadsworth Longfellow*. Beacon Biographies Series. Boston: 1901. (Succinct and judicious.)

Chamberlin, W. A. "Longfellow's Attitude toward Goethe," *Modern Philology*, XVI, 57–76 (June, 1918). (A scholarly study. See also O. W. Long.)

Colton, Arthur. "Longfellow: An Essay in Reputations," *Bookman*, LXXVI, 128–133 (Feb., 1933). (A vigorous reappraisal, comparing Longfellow favorably with Keats as a master of narrative verse.)

Deiml, Otto. *Der Prosastil Henry Wadsworth Longfellows*. Erlangen: 1927.

Dunn, E. C. "Longfellow the Teacher," *North American Review*, CCXI, 259–265 (Feb., 1920).

Elliott, G. R. "The Gentle Shades of Longfellow," in *The Cycle of Modern Poetry*. Princeton, N. J.: 1929. (A Pater-like essay of exquisite æsthetic discrimination emphasizing the distinctive "shadowy loveliness" of Longfellow's best work which Elliott sees as partly the "ghostly offspring of the pioneer and the Puritan" traditions. "Longfellow had a wider experience of that life [of poetry], and a clearer gift in applying it, than anyone else so far in America" [p. 73].)

Fiske, C. F. "Mercerized Folklore," *Poet-Lore*, XXXI, 538–575 (Winter, 1920).

Ferguson, J. D. *American Literature in Spain*. New York: 1916. (Pp. 109–147 deal with Longfellow. A scholarly dissertation. See also Iris L. Whitman's valuable *Longfellow in Spain* [New York: 1927].)

Gavigan, W. V. "Longfellow and Catholicism," *Catholic World*, CXXXVIII, 42–50 (Oct., 1933). (An appreciative survey of relevant evidence, concluding that Longfellow "felt spiritually sympathetic to the Catholic Church." See also Richard P. Hickey, *Catholic Influence on Longfellow* [1928]; and A. C. Boggess, "The Old Testament in Longfellow's Poems," *Methodist Review*, CIII, 263–271 [March–April, 1920].)

Goggio, Emilio. "Italian Influence on Longfellow's Works," *Romanic Review*, XVI, 208–222 (July–Sept., 1925).

—— "The Sources of Longfellow's *Michael Angelo*," *Romanic Review*, XXV, 314–324 (Oct.–Dec., 1934). (A scholarly study of his debt to Vasari, Grimm, Cellini, Varchi, Condivi, Pignotti, and others.)

Gorman, H. S. *A Victorian American, Henry Wadsworth Longfellow*. New York: 1926. (Condescending and journalistic.)

Greenslet, Ferris (ed.). *The Sonnets of Henry Wadsworth Longfellow*. Boston: 1907. (Mr. Greenslet, an able critic, says, "his work in this kind is upon a more even and a higher level than any other similar body of sonnets that can readily be found." See also P. E. More, below.)

Hatfield, J. T. *New Light on Longfellow: with Special Reference to His Relations to Germany*. Boston: 1933. (A fresh and valuable book, showing the vigorous courage of the young Longfellow in introducing and advancing new subjects and teaching methods at Harvard, and the great influence of German literature upon his work.)

Hawthorne, Hildegarde. *The Poet of Craigie House: The Story of Henry Wadsworth Longfellow*. New York: 1936. (A lively and popular biography, by Hawthorne's granddaughter, written mainly for high-school students and based in part on unpublished material. Emphasizes colorful details, especially his courtships. L. R. Thompson [*American Literature*, VIII, 234–235] calls attention to many minor errors.)

Heywood, C. B. M. "Hiawatha at Cambridge," *London Mercury*, XXVII, 6–30 (Nov., 1932).

Higginson, T. W. *Old Cambridge*. Boston: 1900. (Pp. 111–144 interesting for testimony regarding Longfellow as a teacher. See also Hatfield and Dunn.)

—— *Henry Wadsworth Longfellow*. American Men of Letters Series. Boston: 1902. (A judicious general account, readable but discursive. Pp. 258–277 deal with "Longfellow as a Poet.")

Hill, M. G. "Some of Longfellow's Sources for the Second Part of *Evangeline*," *Publications of the*

Modern Language Association, XXXI, 161–180 (1916).

Howells, W. D. "The White Mr. Longfellow," in *Literary Friends and Acquaintance*. New York: 1900, pp. 178–211. (A discursive and charming personal record of intimacy with Longfellow. Emphasizes his gentleness, forbearance, and charity of heart. Considering the New England group, Howells concludes that Longfellow was "the finest artist of them all.")

—— "The Art of Longfellow," *North American Review*, CLXXXIV, 472–485 (March, 1907).

Hutton, R. H. "Longfellow," in *Criticisms on Contemporary Thought and Thinkers*. London: 1894. I, pp. 76–86.

Johnson, C. F. "Longfellow," in *Three Americans and Three Englishmen*. New York: 1886, pp. 213–245. (One of the best of the earlier judicial critiques.)

Johnson, C. L. "Longfellow in France," in Harvard University *Summaries of Theses*, 1933, pp. 311 ff. (This dissertation, available in manuscript at the Harvard Library, easily supersedes all other treatments of the subject.)

—— "Three Notes on Longfellow," *Harvard Studies and Notes in Philology and Literature*, XIV, 249–271 (1932).

Jones, H. M. "Longfellow," in *American Writers on American Literature*, ed. by John Macy. New York: 1931, pp. 105–124. (An admirable brief essay. Attributes part of Longfellow's weakness to European romanticism. Praises his narrative skill, his sonnets, and "Morituri Salutamus," finding the latter "no unworthy rival of 'Ulysses' and 'Rabbi Ben Ezra.'")

Keiser, Albert. "Hiawatha—The Dawn of Culture," in *The Indian in American Literature*. New York: 1933, pp. 189–208. (A readable and well-informed survey of *Hiawatha* in the light of all its sources. Finds it "unquestionably the longest successful poetic delineation of the American Indian thus far." See also Schramm, below.)

Kennedy, W. S. *Henry W. Longfellow: Biography, Anecdotes, Letters, Criticism*. Boston: 1882.

Kratz, F. *Das deutsche Element in den Werken H. W. Longfellows*. Wasserburg: 1901–2. 2 vols. (See also Paul Morin, Chamberlain, Long, and Hatfield.)

Kreymborg, Alfred. "The Fallen Prince of Popularity," in *Our Singing Strength*. New York: 1927, pp. 97–115. (Condescending and harsh. Conventional stress on Longfellow as bookish, didactic, and Victorian.)

Krumpelmann, J. T. "Longfellow's 'Golden Legend' and the 'Armer Heinrich' Theme in Modern German Literature," *Journal of English and Germanic Philology*, XXV, 173–192 (April, 1926). (A valuable study.)

Long, O. W. "Goethe and Longfellow," in *Literary Pioneers*. Cambridge: 1935, pp. 159–198. (A valuable survey, based on many unpublished manuscripts, of Longfellow's interest in Germany and German literature, with special stress on his reaction to and his teaching of Goethe. Finely documented.)

Longfellow, Samuel. *Life of Henry Wadsworth Longfellow, with Extracts from His Journals and Correspondence*. Boston: 1886. 2 vols. (The material in *Final Memorials*, 1887, was properly distributed and the resultant three-volume *Life*, as we now have it, appeared in 1891. Although not critical or incisive, this life is the standard source of information about Longfellow, and is especially valuable because of the extensive quotations from the Journals.)

Monroe, Harriet. "Poe and Longfellow," *Poetry*, XXIX, 266–274 (Feb., 1927).

More, P. E. "The Centenary of Longfellow," in *Shelburne Essays*. Fifth Series. New York: 1908, pp. 132–157. (A graceful and discriminating discussion, concluding that Longfellow's sonnets, especially those on Dante, entitle him to high rank among American poets.)

Morin, Paul. *Les Sources de l'Œuvre de Henry Wadsworth Longfellow*. Paris: 1913. (An extensive, elaborately documented dissertation which comprehensively surveys Longfellow's debt to a great variety of foreign literatures and illustrates his important role as the introducer to America of the romance of Europe.)

Norton, C. E. *Henry Wadsworth Longfellow: a Sketch of his Life . . . together with Longfellow's Chief Autobiographical Poems*. Boston: 1907. (By a close friend, associated with Longfellow in his work on Dante.)

Noyes, Alfred. "Longfellow and Modern Critics," in *Some Aspects of Modern Poetry*. New York: 1924, pp. 245–257. (An able defense by a poet from the æsthetic angle.)

Perry, Bliss. "The Centenary of Longfellow," in *Park Street Papers*. Boston: 1908, pp. 107–140. (A charmingly-written, judicious discussion, praising Longfellow's "fine dignity of the eighteenth century," and concluding that his reputation is safe with unsophisticated readers.)

Poe, E. A. "Hyperion," *Works*, Virginia Edition, X, 39–40; "Voices of the Night," *ibid.*, X, 71–80; "Ballads and Other Poems," *ibid.*, XI, 64–85; "Imitation," "Plagiarism," "Mr. Poe's Reply to Outis," "The Longfellow War," *ibid.*, XII, 41–106; "The Spanish Student," *ibid.*, XIII, 54–73. (Although Poe's criticism of Longfellow is unduly harsh and he overdoes his charges of plagiarism, it is incisive in its metrical and detailed analysis.)

Pritchard, J. P. "The Horatian Influence upon Longfellow," *American Literature*, IV, 22–38 (March, 1932). (A scholarly study, useful not only as a survey of Longfellow's knowledge of Horace and as a revelation of numerous parallel expressions of critical ideas but also as a study of Longfellow's literary theory. Concludes that "the ideas on life and letters which

Horace imparted to Longfellow as a youth exerted a governing influence upon him in later life, and molded for the better his literary work" [p. 38].)

Robertson, E. S. *Life of Henry Wadsworth Longfellow*. Great Writers Series. London: 1887. (A judicious general survey, emphasizing Longfellow's "artistic eclecticism.")

Saintsbury, George. "Longfellow," in *Prefaces and Essays*. London: 1933, pp. 324–344. (A judicious introductory essay by a distinguished English critic. See also his discussion of Longfellow in "American Poets and Prosodists," *History of English Prosody* [New York: 1910], III, 487–490.)

Schramm, W. L. "*Hiawatha* and Its Predecessors," *Philological Quarterly*, XI, 321–343 (Oct., 1932). (A scholarly examination of eleven Indian narrative poems published between 1790 and 1849 as they relate to *Hiawatha*. Concludes: "A little better material, much better selection, and a great deal of good craftsmanship—that is the secret of *Hiawatha*" [p. 343]. See Keiser above.)

Shepard, Odell. "Introduction" to *Longfellow*. American Writers Series. New York: 1934, pp. xi–lv. (Combines charm, sympathy, and critical discrimination.)

Smeaton, O. *Longfellow and His Poetry*. London: 1919. (A judicious English view.)

Stedman, E. C. "Longfellow," in *Poets of America*. Boston: 1885, pp. 180–224. (A judicious general survey of Longfellow's work, book by book. Concludes, considering Milton's criteria, that while Longfellow's poetry is simple, it is seldom genuinely sensuous and never passionate. "I see him, a silver-haired minstrel, touching melodious keys, playing and singing in the twilight, within sound of the rote of the sea.")

Steele, R. B. "The Poetry of Longfellow," *Sewanee Review*, XIII, 177–197 (April, 1905).

Strong, A. H. "Longfellow," in *American Poets and Their Theology*. Philadelphia: 1916, pp. 209–263. (Admittedly writing from the Calvinist angle, Mr. Strong concludes that Longfellow would have been a greater poet if he had rightly understood God's holiness, man's sin, and Christ's atonement [p. 261]. Seems to underrate Longfellow's sympathy with the Puritan tradition and the medieval Dante. Although partly biographical, the essay is useful in its assembly of evidence. See Bailey and Gavigan.)

Trent, W. P. "Longfellow," in *Longfellow and Other Essays*. New York: 1910, pp. 3–35. See also Trent's admirable chapter on Longfellow in *The Cambridge History of American Literature*, II, 32–41.

Underwood, F. H. *The Life of Henry Wadsworth Longfellow; with Critical and Descriptive Sketches of His Writings*. Boston: 1882.

Varnhagen, Hermann. *Longfellow's "Tales of a Wayside Inn" und ihre Quellen nebst Nachweisen und Untersuchungen über die vom Dichter bearbeiten Stoff*. Berlin: 1884. (A painstaking study of Longfellow's sources. For minor corrections see J. P. Worden, "Longfellow's Tales . . . and their Origin," *Anglia*, XXIII, 316–322 [1901]. See also Paul Morin.)

Werner, Dorothy L. *The Idea of Union in American Verse (1776–1876)*. Philadelphia: 1932. (See numerous references in index. A scholarly study.)

NOTES

GENERAL

According to W. P. Trent, Longfellow's function was three-fold: he was the "transmitter of Old World culture to the New, shaper into verse of aboriginal, colonial, and Revolutionary material, both legendary and historical, and lyric interpreter of the simple thoughts and feelings of an unsophisticated people. . . . Neither in . . . [his] earlier volumes, to which may be added *The Belfry of Bruges and Other Poems* (1846), nor in *Evangeline* (1847) and succeeding tales in verse, did Longfellow show himself to be a consummate metrical and verbal artist of the highest order or a poet of sustained imaginative flight; nor was he, in compensation, one of those writers who produce a strong effect through their subtle knowledge of human character or their exceptional ability to describe and interpret nature or their profound understanding of a country or a period. Yet even in these particulars he was capable of exhibiting distinguished merit—witness his command of the simpler rhythms, his wide-reaching metrical experimentation, his feeling for the sea, his sympathetic attitude toward the Middle Ages displayed in *The Golden Legend* (1851), his presentation of the larger natural features of America in *Evangeline*—and in his lyrical appeal, especially through his semi-didactic poems of reflection and sentiment, as well as in his general narrative power, he was during his life, and he still remains, unapproached by any other American poet." Trent concludes that Longfellow's reputation rests "in the main on his gifts as a story-teller in verse, on his power to transplant to American literature some of the colour and melody and romantic charm of the complex European literatures he had studied, and, more especially, on his skill in expressing in comparatively artless lyrics of sentiment and reflection homely and wholesome thoughts and feelings which he shared with his countrymen of all classes throughout a broad land the occupation of which proceeded apace during his own span of years."—*The Cambridge History of American Literature*, II, 32, 37, 41.

During recent years, following a period when it was fashionable to ridicule Longfellow, wise scholars and critics have tended to rest their claims regarding his intrinsic greatness as an artist on (a) his mastery of the *sonnet* form, (b) his introduction into American poetry of large *narrative* designs, and (c) his effective use of *imagery* to evoke the moods desired. (See especially studies by More, Greenslet, Jones, Colton, and Elliott listed in Bibliography.) Odell Shepard and others have demonstrated his historical significance in helping his countrymen make a desirable transition from Puritan didacticism to an enjoyment of literary art for its intrinsic beauty. He is akin to Poe and Lanier in his devotion to æsthetic craftsmanship.

Page 287. PRELUDE

This poem introduces *Voices of the Night* (1839), Longfellow's first collection of verse, and forms a very effective summary of the ideas upon which his poetic practice was based throughout his entire career.

Page 288. A PSALM OF LIFE

Longfellow's first wife had died while they were in Europe in 1835. He wrote this poem on July 26, 1838. "I kept it some time in manuscript," he said later, "unwilling to show it to any one, it being a voice from my inmost heart at a time when I was rallying from depression." While Longfellow has often been regarded as a "genteel" romanticist who sought to escape to German sentimental romance, it should be remembered that in his chapter entitled "Glimpses into Cloud-Land" in *Hyperion* he recognized the German romantic "poetic reverie" as "day-dreams only, as shadows, not substantial things," and he expressed ultimate "dislike" for this "New Philosophy." Possibly with Horace's "*carpe diem*" teaching in mind, Longfellow in this poem advocates that one should not dream but "act in the living Present," a theme of practical idealism common to most of his great poems. Cf. *Christus* and its moral that he only follows the Master's teaching who "*doeth* the will"; and also "Morituri Salutamus"—even in old age, "Something remains for us to do or dare." Whittier wrote of "A Psalm of Life": "These nine simple verses are worth more than all the dreams of Shelley, and Keats, and Wordsworth. They are alive and vigorous with the spirit of the day in which we live,—the moral steam-enginery of an age of action." From the standpoint of art, however, Longfellow probably errs here in didactically stating his idea in abstract terms rather than bodying it forth concretely in such a way that the poem may teach, like life, by indirection.

THE REAPER AND THE FLOWERS

This poem illustrates Longfellow's occasional tendency toward sentimentalism in treating themes requiring a greater graveness.

Page 289. THE LIGHT OF STARS

Note that in a romantic and pantheistic age celebrating the benevolence of nature Longfellow recognizes that "the cold light of stars" symbolizes the fact that nature will merely "smile upon my pain."

THE WRECK OF THE HESPERUS

This poem also illustrates Longfellow's recognition of the cruelty of nature. He wrote in his Journal on December 17, 1839: "News of shipwrecks horrible on the coast. Twenty bodies washed ashore near Gloucester, one lashed to a piece of wreck. There is a reef called Norman's Woe where many of these took place; among others the schooner Hesperus . . . I must write a ballad on this." Later, December 30, he added: "I sat till twelve o'clock by my fire, smoking, when suddenly it came into my head to write 'The Ballad of the Schooner Hesperus'; which I accordingly did . . . It hardly cost me an effort." Compare Longfellow's method in this ballad with that in "Sir Patrick Spens," especially in his lines 13–20.

Page 291. HYMN TO THE NIGHT

The motto, taken from the *Iliad*, is translated, "Welcome! Thrice prayed for!" Compare and contrast this poem with *Hymns to the Night*, by the German Novalis, mystic, dreamer, poet of the shades. According to Poe, "No poem ever opened with a beauty more august." Note Longfellow's recognition of the soothing power of nature without any pantheistic implications.

FOOTSTEPS OF ANGELS

This beautiful but somewhat sentimental poem refers (l. 13) to George W. Pierce, Longfellow's dear friend and brother-in-law who died in 1835, and (l. 21) to his first wife.

Page 292. THE BELEAGUERED CITY

For a discussion of Poe's charges that Longfellow plagiarized this poem from "The Haunted Palace" see K. Campbell, *Poems of Poe*, pp. 237–238. Longfellow's suggestion came, rather, from a footnote in Scott's *Border Minstrelsy:* "Similar to this was the *Nacht Lager*, or midnight camp, which seemed nightly to beleaguer the walls of Prague, but which disappeared at the recitation of the magical words, *Vezelé*, Vezelé, ho! ho! ho!" The poem is a somewhat prettified statement of Longfellow's characteristically Christian view of the inward heart of man as a "battle-ground" where good and evil are in constant conflict. He does not derive evil from institutions.

THE SKELETON IN ARMOR

"This ballad was suggested to me," Longfellow records, "while riding on the seashore at Newport. A year or two previous a skeleton had been dug up at Fall River, clad in broken and corroded armor; and the idea occurred to me of connecting it with the Round Tower at Newport, generally known hitherto as the Old Windmill, though now claimed by the Danes as a work of their early ancestors."

In the review of Longfellow (*Graham's Magazine*, April, 1842) in which Poe censured Longfellow on the charge that "didacticism is the prevalent tone of his song" and defined "the Poetry of words as the *Rhythmical Creation of Beauty* alone," Poe singled out Longfellow's "The Village Blacksmith," "The Wreck of the Hesperus," and "The Skeleton in Armor" as "thoroughly fulfilling" his non-didactic ideal. "In the 'Skeleton in Armor,' . . ." Poe writes, "we find the beauty of bold courage and self-confidence, of love and maiden devotion, of reckless adventure, and finally of life-contemning grief. Combined with all this, we have numerous points of beauty apparently insulated, but all aiding the main effect or impression. The heart is stirred, and the mind does not lament its mal-instruction. The metre is simple, sonorous, well-balanced and fully adapted to the subject. Upon the whole, there are few truer poems than this."

Page 295. EXCELSIOR

The motto on the shield of New York State is said to have suggested this poem to Longfellow. Compare this individualistic idea of striving upward toward perfection with the humanitarian idea of serving one's fellows embodied in Lanier's "Song of the Chattahoochee," p. 632, above.

THE SLAVE'S DREAM and THE WARNING

While abroad in 1842 on leave of absence from Harvard, Longfellow read Dickens's *American Notes* with its "grand chapter on slavery" and he associated with the ardent humanitarian in person. The poet had earlier read the Quaker Benjamin Lundy's *Genius of Universal Emancipation*, and he was urged to exert his influence against slavery by his close friend, Senator Charles Sumner. Longfellow described his stormy voyage home in a letter to Freiligrath: "I was not out of my berth more than twelve hours for the first twelve days. I was in the forward part of the vessel, where all the great waves struck and broke with voices of thunder. There, 'cribbed, cabined, and confined,' I passed fifteen days. During this time I wrote seven poems on Slavery; I meditated upon them in the stormy, sleepless nights, and wrote them down with a pencil in the morning. A small window in the side of the vessel admitted light into my berth, and there I lay on my back and soothed my soul with songs." Adding to the seven poems thus written an eighth, "The Warning," previously written, Longfellow published them in December, 1842, in a little book of thirty-one pages in glazed paper covers. Abolition was unpopular at this time among people of Longfellow's standing, and the publication of the book required courage. This fact, and the fact that the controversy had not in 1842 become as bitter as it became later, account in part for Longfellow's mildness. Partly because of his wide general popularity, the *Poems on Slavery* attracted great attention. To his father he wrote: "How do you like the Slavery Poems? I think they make an impression; I have received many letters about them, which I will send to you by the first good opportunity. Some persons regret that I should have written them, but for my own part I am glad of what I have done. My feelings prompted me, and my judgment approved, and still approves."

Page 297. MEZZO CAMMIN

Longfellow wrote this sonnet in 1842 in Marienberg, Germany, whither he had gone to improve his health (*Life*, I, 423). The "tower of song with lofty parapet" which he seeks to create probably refers to *Christus*, an outline of which has been found in his notebooks of this period. Note (l. 7) that he says his sorrow at the death of his first wife almost killed him and kept him from fulfilling his plans as a poet.

THE ARSENAL AT SPRINGFIELD

Longfellow's brother writes (*Life*, II, 2–3) that on their wedding journey when they visited the Arsenal at Springfield with Charles Sumner "Mrs. Longfellow pleased her husband by remarking how like an organ looked the ranged and shining gun-barrels which covered the walls from floor to ceiling, and suggesting what mournful music Death would bring from them. 'We grew quite warlike against war,' she wrote, 'and I urged H. to write a peace poem.' From this hint came 'The Arsenal at Springfield,' written some months later."

l. 19, *teocallis:* Mexican temples.

Page 298. NUREMBERG

On Longfellow's visit to Nuremberg which inspired this poem, see his letter of Sept. 24, 1842 to Freiligrath (*Life*, I, 436 f.). The poem illustrates Longfellow's skill in interpreting for his practical and untraveled countrymen the rich romance of the Old World, and in thus serving to effect a transition in America from the moralistic to the æsthetic taste. Stedman (*Poets of America*, pp. 181–182) illustrates the effect of such poems as follows: "Take the case of a child whose Sunday outlook was restricted, in a decaying Puritan village, to a wooden meeting-house of the old Congregational type. The interior—plain, colorless, rigid with dull white pews and dismal galleries—increased the spiritual starvation of a young nature unconsciously longing for color and variety. Many a child like this one, on a first holiday visit to the town, seeing the vine-grown walls, the roofs and arches, of a graceful Gothic church, has felt a sense of something rich and strange; and many, now no longer children, can remember that the impression upon entrance was such as the stateliest cathedral now could not renew. The columns and tinted walls, the ceiling of oak and blue, the windows of gules and azures and gold,—the service, moreover, with its chant and organ roll,—all this enraptured and possessed them. To the one relief hitherto afforded them, that of nature's picturesqueness,—which even Calvinism endured without compunction,—was added a new joy, a glimpse of the beauty and sanctity of human art. A similar delight awaited the first readers of Longfellow's prose (*Outre-Mer*, "a kind of Sketch-Book of scenes in France, Spain, and Italy," 1835, and *Hyperion*, 1839) and verse. Here was a painter and a romancer indeed, who had journeyed far and returned with gifts for all at home, and who promised often and again to

> '. . . sing a more wonderful song
> Or tell a more wonderful tale.'"

Page 299. SEAWEED

According to Odell Shepard, "In versification, verbal music, and imagery, the first four stanzas of this poem are among the finest things of Longfellow's accomplishment. To the taste of our day the final stanzas are worse than valueless. Longfellow's homiletic method is clearly illustrated here."

Page 300. THE DAY IS DONE

This poem, which is sometimes erroneously regarded as embodying Longfellow's ideal of the poet as a dreamer who would "banish the thoughts of day," was expressly written as a proem to a volume of minor poets he had edited, entitled *The Waif*. It should be noted that the poems he characterizes are intended simply for certain moods only; he does not confuse the "humbler poet" of whom he writes with "the grand old masters" or the "bards sublime."

Poe, who was usually a harsh critic of Longfellow, wrote of this poem in "The Poetic Principle": "With no great range of imagination, these lines have been justly admired for the delicacy of their expression. Some of the images are very effective. Nothing could be better than—

> '. . . The bards sublime,
> Whose distant footsteps echo
> Down the corridors of Time.'

The idea of the last quatrain [which Poe slightly misquotes] is also very effective. The poem, on the whole, however, is chiefly to be admired for the graceful *insouciance* of its metre, so well in accordance with the character of the sentiments, and especially for the *ease* of the general manner." Poe proceeds to praise the *tone* which he says "should always be that which the mass of mankind would adopt—and must perpetually vary, of course, with the occasion."

THE BRIDGE

Longfellow first entitled this poem "The Bridge over the Charles" (*Life*, II, 23). "I always stop on the bridge," he said. And on another occasion (*Life*, I, 289), "As I walked over the bridge, the rising moon shone through the misty air. The reflection of the stars in the dark water looked like sparks of fire. Stood still to hear the soft sound of the dissolving ice-cakes in the brine,—a low and musical sound, a gentle simmering like the foaming of champagne." The poem records Longfellow's retrospect of his sorrow following the death of his first wife, considered now from the vantage point of his present happiness with his second wife.

Page 301. AFTERNOON IN FEBRUARY

This poem illustrates the fact that Longfellow could approach the modern imagists in their evocation of moods when he chose.

Page 302. THE ARROW AND THE SONG

It has been pointed out that this poem, which Longfellow called "literally an improvisation," is related to a quatrain in Goethe's *Sprüche in Reimen*.

Page 303. TO THE DRIVING CLOUD

Longfellow "has written many poems like *A Dutch Picture* and *Kéramos*, which are almost unknown to the 'critics' and to the general public of the hour, and . . . the art in them is exquisite. The poem *To the Driving Cloud*, whatever may be the final judgment on the use of the hexameter in English, is the most majestic and gorgeous picture ever painted in literature of the tragic passing of the Red Man.

"There is the very touch of reality in that slow drifting to the west of the scanty smokes of his wigwams, while, night by night, the campfires of the newer races draw remorselessly nearer across the prairies."—Alfred Noyes, *Some Aspects of Modern Poetry*, pp. 247–248.

WANDERER'S NIGHT-SONGS

This translation illustrates the exquisite taste with which Longfellow made available to his countrymen many of the most beautiful lyrics of the European romanticists.

Page 304. THE BUILDERS

Although unduly didactic from the artistic standpoint, this poem illustrates Longfellow's belief in free-will and individual responsibility: "All are architects of fate." Cf. *Kavanagh* (*Works*, VIII, p. 412), where Longfellow censures the dilatory hero: "All his defects and mortifications he attributed to the outward circumstances of his life, the exigencies of his profession, the accidents of chance. But, in reality, they lay much deeper than this. They were within himself. He wanted the all-controlling, all-subduing will. He wanted the fixed purpose that sways and bends all circumstances to its uses, as the wind bends the reeds and rushes beneath it." (Contrast with Holmes's view of determinism, and also with Robinson's view of fate, especially in *Tristram.*) Longfellow himself, as a young man, stunned by the death of his first wife and addicted naturally to melancholy brooding of the German romantic sort, illustrated in his own life the power of the masterful will he here celebrates in his personal restraint, his productivity as a poet amid the distractions of his professorship in which he acted as an educational pathfinder, and in his gracious social life.

Page 305. THE BUILDING OF THE SHIP

The impassioned conclusion of this poem (beginning with l. 377, "Thou too, sail on, O Ship of State") and the history of its great influence in arousing vast audiences to support the Union, ought to be carefully studied by those who accept the contemporary notion that Longfellow was only concerned with escape to German romance and was totally indifferent to the plight of his country. This conclusion was substituted immediately for a much weaker conclusion, which is reprinted in the *Life*, III, 443–444. Longfellow records (*Life*, II, 172) being present Feb. 12, 1850, when the great actress, Fanny Kemble, "read [the poem] before the Mercantile Library Association, to an audience of more than three thousand, . . . standing out upon the platform, book in hand, trembling, palpitating, and weeping, and giving every word its true weight and emphasis." President Lincoln asked Noah Brooks to read the poem to him. The latter reported ("Lincoln's Imagination," *Scribner's Monthly*, August, 1879) that Lincoln's "eyes filled with tears, and his cheeks were wet. He did not speak for some minutes, but finally said, with simplicity: 'It is a wonderful gift to be able to stir men like that.'" In the midst of the profound agitation of the decade which led up to the Civil War the poem was recited on hundreds of stages and printed in hundreds of newspapers: its influence was enormous. In her book on *The Idea of Union in American Verse* (1932), Dorothy Werner shows that of "well over seven hundred" poems on the Union, "the most influential poem of the period, is, of course, Longfellow's *The Building of the Ship;* it was the model for most other Union poems" (p. 49).

The general idea of the poem may have been suggested to Longfellow by Schiller's *Das Lied von der Glocke,* but the figure of the ship was natural to one who had been reared in a seaport and who loved the sea and ships. G. W. Allen (*American Prosody*, 177–178) regards this poem as Longfellow's best ode. "It is different," he says, "from the other odes in several minor details. One is the use of an opening four-stress trochaic quatrain as a sort of 'text,' which is repeated as a refrain in the middle of the poem [ll. 196–199] . . . Where the lines are most irregular, with frequent initial trochaic feet (or 'clipped' iambs), the rhythm is as monotonous as most of Longfellow's other four-stress verse, though it has a certain vigor that the trochaic rhythms lack [cf. ll. 176–178] . . . Some lines are also onomatopoetic [cf. ll. 186–195] . . . One of the most effective passages is the freest in number of stresses and accentuation [cf. ll. 228–245] . . . Some of the lines are longer than those of Emerson's *Threnody*, but the poem is in the same tradition."

The full evidence regarding Longfellow's political and social ideas awaits exhaustive assembly and interpretation. Mention has been made of his slavery poems and of his deep interest in the work of his friend, Senator Charles Sumner. In general, like Lowell after 1850, Longfellow stood for abolition but thought the preservation of the Union much more important. In his interest in ordered liberty and in the rule of the best minds and in a generally paternalistic social system he is akin to Federalists such as John Adams, although he was not as trenchant a thinker or so keenly distrustful of the people. For a brief discussion, with references to most of the passages in which Longfellow discusses political matters, see Odell Shepard, *Longfellow*, pp. xix–xx.

Page 310. THE GOLDEN LEGEND

For full evidence on the genesis of this second part of Longfellow's trilogy of Christus, see his brother's "Introductory Note" to *Christus* (*Works*, V, 7–20), the notes (*ibid.*, pp. 441–455), and also the very detailed notes in the edition by S. Arthur Best. According to Longfellow's plan, *Christus* was to be a dramatic poem in three parts, the first dealing with "The Times of Christ," representing Hope, the second, dealing with "The Middle Ages," representing Faith, and the third, dealing with "The Present," representing Charity. According to his brother, no other work of the poet "so dominated his literary life . . . During those thirty-two years [1841–1873], which represent almost the whole of Mr. Longfellow's productive period, the subject of the trilogy seems never to have been long absent from his mind . . . He esteemed the work which he had undertaken as the really great work of his life." Thus in Longfellow's own eyes *Christus* occupies a position in the development of his mind and art comparable to that of *Paradise Lost* and *Paradise Regained* in the case of Milton, although of course Longfellow's execution of his aims was much less successful. But no one can do justice to Longfellow without studying this strangely neglected poem.

The core of "The Golden Legend" was admittedly taken from the story of *Der Arme Heinrich* as related by Hartmann von der Aue, a minnesinger of the twelfth century, and printed in Mailáth's *Altdeutsche Gedichte* (Stuttgart, 1809). On the poet's use of this source see Krumpelmann's scholarly study listed in the Bibliography. According to Longfellow, "The Miracle Play is founded on the Apocryphal Gospels of James and the Infancy of Christ."

As regards the main theme of "The Golden Legend," Longfellow said, "I have endeavored to show in it, among other things, that through the darkness and corruption of the Middle Ages ran a bright, deep stream of Faith, strong enough for all the exigencies of life and death. In order to do this, I had to introduce some portion of this darkness and corruption as a background" (*Works*, V, 12–13). Ruskin, who was something of a master of the medieval spirit, testified that "Longfellow, in his 'Golden Legend' has entered more closely into the temper of the monk, for good and for evil, than ever yet theological writer or historian, though they may have given their life's labor to the analysis" (*Modern Painters*, V, ch. 20). Indeed, the reader accustomed to Longfellow's tendency toward sentimentality and optimism is likely to be most surprised, in reading this poem for the first time, to note the almost Rabelaisian realism with which the poet presents the "darkness and corruption" of many of his characters, especially of the monks who "gave themselves up to all kinds of sin" (*Works*, V, 240). His brother says, however, that "he had been steeping his soul in Dante" (*ibid.*, V, 8), and it is therefore not surprising, perhaps, that in "The Golden Legend" he should have approached most nearly to adequate practice of his theory that the true poet must deal sternly with the conflict between good and evil within the individual (cf. *ibid.*, V, 252). It is also noteworthy that Longfellow, essentially a mystic, regards rationalism as a tool of Satan (*ibid.*, V, 277). In brief outline, the story concerns one Prince Henry, whose disease can be cured only by the life-blood of a maiden. Elsie, the heroine whom the poet characterized "as sweet as Imogen" (*ibid.*, V, 10), offers to sacrifice herself to save her Prince, but just before it was too late the selfish Prince recognizes the nobility of her unselfishness and the sinfulness of his self-centered life. As a result of saving her, he is miraculously restored to his youth, and they marry and live happily ever after. The Epilogue celebrates the "beauty of holiness, / Of self-forgetfulness, of lowliness!" Thus the theme supplements that of *Kavanagh* and its view that "the life of man consists not in seeing visions, and in dreaming dreams, but in active charity and willing service." What Longfellow's hero, Kavanagh, admired in Catholicism was "not its bigotry, and fanaticism, and intolerance; but its zeal, its self-devotion, its heavenly aspirations, its human sympathies, its endless deeds of charity" (*ibid.*, VIII, 355).

As to "The Golden Legend" from the artistic standpoint, W. P. Trent (*American Literature*, p. 404) says, "It has never ranked among Longfellow's popular works, yet it is inferior to none of them in charm and deserves ungrudging praise, if only for the sweetness of its versification and for its varied picturesqueness." According to G. W. Allen (*American Prosody*, p. 191), the poem "is interesting technically because of its use of the octosyllabic couplet (varied by alternate rime) for narrative and dramatic purposes, a practice unusual in English versification and an evident Goethean influence. Also this drama contains many other short-line (*i.e.*, dimeters, trimeters, etc.) speeches and lyrics, used in the *Faust* manner.

"Hence, it is evident that Longfellow's versification was profoundly influenced by the German . . ."

Page 368. THE ROPEWALK

Compare the vivid imagism in ll. 25–30 with similar themes in Sandburg who is popularly supposed to have been among those leading a revolt against Longfellowism. G. R. Elliott (*The Cycle of Modern Poetry*, pp. 69 ff.) has cited many passages in which Longfellow anticipated the modern poets who imagined they were pioneers in doing things the older poet could not do.

Page 369. THE SONG OF HIAWATHA

"This Indian Edda—if I may so call it—is founded on a tradition, prevalent among the North American Indians, of a personage of miraculous birth who was sent among them to clear their rivers, forests, and fishing-grounds, and to teach them the arts of peace. . . . Mr. Schoolcraft gives an account of him in his *Algic Researches* . . . and in his *History, Condition, and Prospects of the Indian Tribes of the United States* . . . may be found the Iroquois form of the tradition, derived from the verbal narrative of an Onondaga chief.

"Into this old tradition I have woven other curious Indian legends, drawn chiefly from the various and valuable writings of Mr. Schoolcraft . . . The scene of the poem is among the Ojibways on the southern shore of Lake Superior, in the region between the Pictured Rocks and the Grand Sable." (Longfellow's note.)

For *Hiawatha*, which was begun in June, 1854, and which runs to twenty-three parts, including the "Introduction," Longfellow adopted the unrhymed trochaic meter of *Kalevala*, the Finnish epic.

According to P. H. Boynton, *Hiawatha* is not only a picturesque children's story but an epic for grown-ups: "A peace is declared among the warring tribes; Hiawatha is sent by Mudjekeewis back to live and toil among his people; he is commended by Mondamin because he prays 'For advantage of the nations'; he fights the pestilence to save the people; he divides his trophies of battle with them; and he departs when the advent of the white man marks the doom of the Indian. And so the ordering of the parts is ethnic, tracing the Indian chronicle through the stages that all peoples have traversed, from the nomad life of hunting and fishing to primitive agriculture and community life; thus come song and festival, a common religion and a common fund of legend, and finally, in the tragic life of this people, come the decline of strength, in the death of Kwasind, the passing of song with Chibiabos, and the departure of national heroism as Hiawatha is lost to view

> 'In the glory of the sunset,
> In the purple mists of evening.'

It is no mean achievement to write a children's classic, but the enduring fact about *Hiawatha* is that it is a genuine epic as well."—*A History of American Literature*, 1919, pp. 274–276, Ginn and Company, publishers.

Consult studies by Schramm and Keiser.

Page 384. MY LOST YOUTH

For a scholarly study of the origin of this poem, with a reproduction of the original manuscript, see J. T. Hatfield, "Longfellow's Lapland Song," *Publications of the Modern Language Association*, XLV, 1188–1192.

"For perfect simplicity, for truth of quite unaffected feeling, for beauty and enchantment of the kind that can only be drawn up from the living wells of memory by a true poet, there is nothing very much better in our language than that exquisite poem 'My Lost Youth.' Here, in one poem, we have the most important part of his own historical background, and the best that he had to give the world in his art. It could have been written only by a man who loved nature intensely, whose whole being was suffused with the sunsets of that beautiful old New England town where his boyhood was passed, and was really haunted, as he wrote, by the verse of the Lapland song, into which he distilled the essence of all the poetry that he had made his own in Europe. Even in technique, the unrhymed line at the end of the stanza, at the time when it was written, had an entirely original effect, and is not without metrical suggestiveness at the present day. The sweetness and truth of the poem can hardly be praised too highly. Nothing is here exaggerated, wrenched, or over-stated. There is no false realism, dwelling on the insignificant or ugly for the mere sensation of it. It is an absolutely true impression of the past, idealized only by the harmony of nature and art and memory. The remembered town is no more than 'dear' and 'old' and 'beautiful.' The streets are merely 'pleasant'; and yet what a glamour is thrown over it all by the sheer longing of the heart. . . . Poetry of this kind does not die; and it will never be dislodged from the memory of the race."—Alfred Noyes, *Some Aspects of Modern Poetry*, pp. 256–257.

Page 386. THE COURTSHIP OF MILES STANDISH

In 1837 Longfellow, in his review of Hawthorne's *Twice-Told Tales* (*Works*, VII, 360–367), had praised his friend of college days for dealing with our American past. "This is the right material for story . . . The dreary old Puritanical times begin to look romantic in the distance." Elsewhere (*Life*, III, 412) Longfellow said, "The stern old puritanical character rises above the common level of life; it has a breezy air about its summits, but they are bleak and forbidding." Now, at the age of fifty, at the height of his poetic powers, Longfellow turned to write of his own ancestral past, for he was himself descended from Priscilla and John Alden, and of the customs and traditions of his people. William Bradford's *History of Plymouth Plantation*, published shortly before Longfellow set to work, was his main guide. In creating this sympathetic picture of Puritan times he also made use of Belknap's *American Biography*, C. W. Elliott's *History of New England*, Young's *Chronicles of the Pilgrims*, Banvard's *Plymouth and the Pilgrims*, Drake's *Nooks and Corners of the New England Coast*, and John Eliot's accounts of the Indians he sought to convert. The most memorable passage in the poem, Priscilla's "Why don't you speak for yourself, John?" is derived from oral tradition. The poem is generally regarded as superior to the much more sentimental *Evangeline* not only because of its artistic qualities but because of its salty humor and its more masculine tone. According to G. W. Allen (*American Prosody*, 183–184), "The greatest development in the versification of *The Courtship of Miles Standish* . . . is the use of initial reiteration of words and phrases, especially in couplet groups at frequent intervals . . . It is interesting to conjecture whether the biblical tone of much of this poem influenced the use of initial reiteration and parallelism." Many critics, such as Poe in "The Rationale of Verse," have attacked Longfellow's use of the hexameter, but the poem has been and is exceedingly popular. Although Longfellow was himself a Unitarian and disliked some of the Puritans' harsh theological beliefs (in Mr. Poindexter of *Kavanagh* and the Parson in "The Birds of Killingworth"), he had profound respect for their general ethical elevation and firmness of purpose, and many aspects of his own sterling character may be traced to the Puritan heritage which he treats in this poem with such sympathetic understanding.

"*Evangeline* and *The Courtship of Miles Standish* . . . are poems as soft and lovely as the paintings of the English landscape school," writes Howard Mumford Jones. "If we could but read these narratives for the first time, we should see, I think, how skillfully they are put together, with what deft devices the poet has knitted his plot, and how beautifully the descriptive passages are made to melt into the steady flow of the narrative—one of the most difficult feats in this kind of verse, as the relative failure of Keats in keeping his stories free of encumbrance sadly testifies. And I would particularly instance the genre paintings in both pieces—the village of Grand-Pré, for instance, as well known to most of us as *Vanity Fair*, or *David Copperfield*. Read again the opening passages of *The Courtship of Miles Standish*, and note how deftly the characters, the room, the situation are drawn—we have a complete comedy in a hundred lines. Or consider the wonderful vividness of this portrait of René Leblanc in *Evangeline;* the whole man and all his little history is made to appear before us. . . .

"How clearly a whole civilization rises up before us as we read! When our own writers of folk-novels tell us these things, we exclaim with pleasure, but when Longfellow paints pictures so exquisite, evokes with so much charm a past that has vanished, we smile because we have been told so often that he is the children's poet! I am inclined to believe that a proper appreciation of the merits of his narratives requires a riper wisdom than some of our critics yet possess.

"That there are defects in both poems is clear, but they are lost in the general excellence of the pathos of the one, the geniality of the other. Perhaps the greatest fault is a certain diffuseness; the last half of *Evangeline* could, perhaps, be more condensed; the fifth and sixth sections of *The Courtship of Miles Standish* scarcely advance the narrative."—*American Writers on American Literature*, ed. John Macy, pp. 119–120.

Page 408. SNOWFLAKES

"The lyric entitled 'Snowflakes' has a cadence of its own, and a delicacy—especially in its last two lines—that give the very sense of the troubled air and the illumination of the landscape, together with the intellectual and spiritual significance of its imagery. That the poem makes no use of merely poetic language is a merit, not a fault; that it is a subtle piece of imagery, rather than a mere representation, is a merit, not a fault; and the failure of the present generation of critics to observe these demonstrable facts, despite the common lip-worship which the hour pays both to the renunciation of merely æsthetic word-play and to 'images,' is curious . . . Here, at any rate, is poetry, and the word is exactly fitted to the inner and outer meanings of the poet. . . .

"While I am on the subject of conventionally unconventional criticism, it may be worth while pointing out that this beautiful measure is—so far as I know—unique in our language. . . . On the other hand, the majority of our 'unconventional' rebels use either forms that have been used scores of times, or write with a formlessness that, in the very nature of things, cannot be distinctive. They assume that Longfellow added nothing to the metrical range of English poetry, while it is, in fact, demonstrable that again and again he actually did the very thing which the 'rebels' utterly erroneously claim as their own achievement. Meter, cadence, imagery, all are here quite distinctive."—Alfred Noyes, *Some Aspects of Modern Poetry*, pp. 249–250.

Page 409. THE FALCON OF SER FEDERIGO

Perhaps with Boccaccio's *Decameron* and *The Canterbury Tales* in mind, Longfellow presented *Tales of a Wayside Inn* (1860–63) as stories, connected by a prelude, interludes, and an epilogue, told by a circle including a landlord, a student, a Sicilian, a Spanish Jew, a theologian, a poet, and a musician—identified with actual friends of his—who met at the Red Horse Tavern in Sudbury which is still standing. Detailed notes will be found in J. H. Castleman's edition of *Tales of a Wayside Inn*. On the sources see studies, listed in Bibliography, by Axon, Vanhagen, Warden, and Morin.

"The Falcon of Ser Federigo" is told by the student, following "Paul Revere's Ride" told by the landlord. According to the note in the Standard Library Edition (IV, 262), "The story is found in the *Decameron*, fifth day, ninth tale. As Boccaccio, however, was not the first to tell it, so Mr. Longfellow is not the only one after him to repeat it. So remote a source as *Pantschatantra* (Benfey, II, 247) contains it, and La Fontaine includes it in his *Contes et Nouvelles* under the title of *La Faucon*. Tennyson has treated the subject dramatically in *The Falcon*. See also Delisle de la Drévetière, who turned Boccaccio's story into a comedy in three acts." In the Interlude which follows this tale, when the theologian objects to "these old Italian tales" from Decameron as "a stagnant fen" where a "white lily" now and then blooms, the student expresses his thanks for the white lily and reminds us that "from these reservoirs" the imperial Shakespeare drew his Moor of Venice and Romeo and Juliet.

Page 412. WEARINESS

"There is no tenderer poem in the language than the exquisite lines to his children which he entitled 'Weariness.' . . . The poem has something of the classical perfection of Landor."—Alfred Noyes, *Some Aspects of Modern Poetry*, pp. 255–256.

Page 413. DIVINA COMMEDIA

Just as Bryant sought consolation following the death of his wife in translating the classical Homer, so Longfellow, following the death of his second wife in 1861, concentrated upon translating Dante, the "voice of ten silent centuries" of the Christian tradition. (He had conceived the translation in 1843, and he published it in 1867.) "In the completed form of his translation," says Odell Shepard, "a sonnet precedes and follows each of the three divisions. Each is subtly related to the position for which it is designed, in a manner not entirely different from Dante's own. Considered as a unit, the group stands high in Longfellow's work, revealing a depth and strength attributable to his bereavement and to the constant association with a supreme mind." For full discussion of Longfellow's debt to medieval Catholicism and his function in interpreting its beauty to his countrymen see studies in the Bibliography by Gavigan, Hickey, and Goggio. "All of his sonnets," says G. W. Allen (*American Prosody*, p. 189), "are in the Italian form (*abba abba cdcdcd*, or *cdecde*) .... Longfellow's sonnets are also typically Italian in the management of full stops and thought-groups. Each quatrain of the octave ends with either a period or a semicolon. Enjambment within the quatrain is used freely, but seldom does the fourth line run on into the fifth. The octave and sestet divisions are consistently observed." Longfellow is generally regarded as having written the greatest sonnets in American literature, although G. H. Boker (see his *Sonnets*, ed. E. S. Bradley, Philadelphia, 1929) occasionally approaches him. See L. G. Sterner, *The Sonnet in American Literature*, Philadelphia, 1930.

Page 415. EMMA AND EGINHARD

This un-Victorian story in *Tales of a Wayside Inn* is fittingly told by the student following the poet's story "Charlemagne." In Longfellow's diary for May 12th, 1872, we read (*Life*, III, 200), "Wrote a short poem on 'Charlemagne' from a story in an old Chronicle, *De Factis Caroli Magni*, quoted by Cantù, *Storia degli Italiani*, ii, 122. I first heard it from Charles Perkins in one of his lectures." Arthur Colton (see Bibliography) compares Longfellow's simple and lucid narrative art in *The Tales of a Wayside Inn* with what he calls the "stained-glass" narrative style of Keats in "The Eve of St. Agnes" and "Isabella." Alfred Kreymborg (in *Our Singing Strength*, p. 108) concludes that of all Longfellow's writings these *Tales* are "the poet's most enduring work."

Page 422. MORITURI SALUTAMUS

"And finally there is the one long poem of his [Longfellow's] in which he put such wisdom as had come to him in some seventy years of life— the 'Morituri Salutamus,' written for the fiftieth anniversary meeting of his college class. It is a simple, unpretentious piece, written for once in rhymed pentameter; into it he introduces the inevitable literary allusion without which, for him, no poem was quite complete—this time, a long story from the *Gesta Romanorum*. . . . This is surely no unworthy rival of 'Ulysses' and 'Rabbi Ben Ezra'; here is surely the philosophic temper for which, in some sense, poetry exists; and this ripe and Senecan wisdom, these easy and colloquial lines, apparently so effortless but withal so cunning —all this, I say, is the utterance of that riper Longfellow who has been so curiously ignored." —H. M. Jones, in *American Writers on American Literature* (ed. John Macy), pp. 122–124.

Page 426. THREE FRIENDS OF MINE

Sonnet II treats C. C. Felton, Longfellow's close friend, who, as Harvard's professor of Greek, must have done much to keep the poet in touch with the spirit of classicism. (See *Life*, III, 4, 7, 9. See also Pritchard's study of Longfellow's debt to Horace.) Sonnet III treats Agassiz, the master scientist, who was also Longfellow's frequent companion. Agassiz, a devout Catholic, did not accept Darwinism in so far as it militated against the older religions. Cf. Lowell's "Agassiz," Whittier's "The Prayer of Agassiz," and Holmes's "At the Saturday Club." Sonnet IV treats Charles Sumner, whom Longfellow first knew in 1836 as a lecturer at the Harvard Law School and who became a powerful senator opposed to slavery and disunion. Cf. also Longfellow's poem "Charles Sumner." He was especially dear to Longfellow, and through him the poet followed with keen interest the political questions of the day, while Sumner acknowledged Longfellow's inspiring influence on his appeal to the "higher law." Line 44, "The City of the Dead," refers to the Cemetery of Mount Auburn where Sumner, Agassiz, Lowell, Holmes, Willis, Prescott, Motley, Parkman, and Longfellow himself now lie buried.

Page 427. THE SOUND OF THE SEA

Note (ll. 9–14) that like the transcendentalists, Longfellow looked upon his inspirations as of divine origin and "beyond our reason or control."

A DUTCH PICTURE

Lines 11–15 and 26–30 compare favorably in their imagism with the work of Amy Lowell and those who supposed that "Imagism" was a revolt against Longfellow.

Page 428. THE POETS

Note that at a time when humanitarians regarded man as molded by society and social institutions, Longfellow, an exponent of centrality, insists upon self-conquest: "But in ourselves, are triumph and defeat."

SUMMARY OF LONGFELLOW'S POETIC THEORIES

Since no comprehensive assembly and interpretation of evidence bearing on Longfellow's literary theories is available, it may be worthwhile to summarize these theories in some detail here:

1. *Respect for criticism and tradition.* Although Longfellow disliked exclusively unsympathetic, destructive, and prematurely judicial criticism, he eagerly sought and respected competent, constructive, and severe criticism by his peers such as Lowell, Norton, and Felton (cf. the Dante Club, *Life*, III, 63 ff., and *ibid.*, I, 59; II, 86). He thought that "next to being a great poet is the power of understanding one" (*Works*, VIII, 81), and Whitman reported him as saying that "ere the New World can be worthily original, . . . she must be well saturated with the originality of others, and respectfully consider the heroes that lived before Agamemnon." (For studies of Longfellow's debt to other writers of the past in all lands see Bibliography under Morin, Pritchard, Chamberlain, Long, Gavigan, Goggio, Hatfield, Hill, Keiser, Schramm, Krumpelmann, and Varnhagen.)

2. *Sentimental escapism vs. artistic ethicism.* In youth especially Longfellow was "better pleased with those pieces which touch the feelings and improve the heart" (*Life*, I, 30), and he was addicted to "poetic reverie" which could "banish the thoughts of day." Ultimately, however, he expressed "dislike" for the German romantic "glimpses into cloudland" and recognized the results as "day dreams only, as shadows, not substantial things" (*Works*, VIII, 106–107). In "The Prelude" to *Voices of the Night* and in "Michael Angelo" he set himself the ideal of confronting resolutely, in artistic terms, the central fact of the conflict within the individual between good and evil.

3. *Out of the particular and the chaotic commonplace the shaping imagination selects the idealized universal.* In "Michael Angelo," in which his brother said he "was more distinctly declaring his artistic creed than in any other of his works" (*Works*, VI, 48), Longfellow says that, guided by an imagination which seeks the "shaped and perfect," the artist has only to "hew away" the idiosyncrasies that "imprison the lovely apparition" concealed in the particular and commonplace, "in every block of marble." The artist selects and re-creates, giving us an ideal beauty "more lovely than the real" although a part of the real (*Works*, VI, 167; III, 154). "The difficulty," he remarked with reference to writing "Evangeline," "is to select, to give unity to variety" (*Life*, II, 67), a view reminding us of Emerson's Platonic doctrine. He opposed rancid realism and Kodak writing. "The highest exercise of the imagination is not to devise what has no existence, but rather to perceive what really exists, though unseen by the outward eye—*not creation, but insight*" (*Final Memorials*, p. 378). Mere imitation of nature "is not enough. There are two great schools of art,—the imitative and the imaginative. The latter is the most noble and enduring" (*Works*, VIII, 122, also III, 233).

4. *Turn from nationalism to universalism.* In 1825, Longfellow says in his address on "Our Native Writers" (here reprinted, p. 431) that our "national literature" is to achieve sublimity because "no people are richer than we are in the treasures of nature." In 1832, in his review of a new edition of Sidney's *Defence of Poesy* (*North American Review*, XXXIV, 56–78), he is more idealistic, but he urges that our native poets "should be more original, and withal more national"—in fact, "as national as possible." In 1837, in his review of Hawthorne's *Twice-Told Tales* (*Works*, VII, 365 ff.), he praises that work for being "national in character," for dealing with the romantic American past: "This is the right material for poetry." In 1839, in "The Prelude" (see above, p. 287), he resolves to turn from nature and to find "the land of Song within." In 1849, in *Kavanagh* (Chapter XX, here reprinted, pp. 432–434), Longfellow finally comes to ridicule the ideal of a uniquely national literature based on nature, and he concludes, "Nationality is a good thing to a certain extent, but universality is better. All that is best in the great poets of all countries is not what is national in them, but what is universal."

5. *True art is from God and it should glorify God.* Like Milton, Longfellow thought that "all great achievements are the natural fruits of a great character" (*Works*, VI, 145; see also III, 267). The poet is a medium for the divine: his songs come to him miraculously out of "the Unknown" (*ibid.*, III, 257–258). "Glorious indeed is the world of God around us, but more glorious is the world of God *within us*. There lies the Land of Song" (*ibid.*, VIII, 64). There can be no true poetry without "the tragic element"; "There are dark abysses and yawning gulfs in the human heart. . . . These are the great themes of human thought; not green grass . . ." (*ibid.*, VII, 408; VIII, 64). Cf. Longfellow's nearly tragic theme in "The Golden Legend." In an "age of doubt and disbelief" (*ibid.*, VIII, 101) the poet is to inspire "faith in the Ideal" (*ibid.*, VI, 144). Longfellow agreed with Cowley that the communication of delight is "the main end of poetry" (*Life*, II, 87), but he thought the richest delight embraced not only man's body and mind but also his spirit. The highest beauty is the beauty of holiness. (Cf. Emerson.) That art

> "Which bears the consecration and the seal
> Of holiness upon it will prevail
> Over all others."

> "Art is the gift of God, and must be used
> Unto his glory. That art is highest
> Which aims at this." (*Works*, VI, 65–66.)

To what extent did Longfellow succeed in *practising* each of these theories or aims? Special attention should be given to "The Golden Legend," a part of the lofty *Christus*, which the poet regarded "as the really great work of his life" (*Works*, V, 8).

JAMES RUSSELL LOWELL

CHRONOLOGY

1819 Born in Cambridge, February 22.
1838 Could not read in person the class poem he had written for his graduation from Harvard, since he was rusticated to the care of a Concord minister for misdemeanors at college.
1840 Graduated from Harvard Law School.
1841 *A Year's Life and Other Poems.*
1843 Co-editor with Robert Carter of *The Pioneer: A Literary and Critical Magazine,* which was discontinued after three months.
1844 *Poems.* Married to Maria White, who was interested in poetry and the anti-slavery cause. Editorial writer for *Pennsylvania Freeman.*
1845 *Conversations on Some of the Old Poets.*
1845–48 Anti-slavery writing. Connected with the *National Anti-Slavery Standard;* corresponding editor, 1848.
1848 *Poems* (2 vols.). *A Fable for Critics. The Biglow Papers,* first series. *The Vision of Sir Launfal.*
1851–52 Traveled in Europe.
1853 Wife died.
1855 Smith professor of the French and Spanish languages and literatures and professor of belles-lettres at Harvard in succession to Longfellow.
1855–56 Studied in Germany and Italy.
1857 Editor of the *Atlantic Monthly.* Married Frances Dunlap.
1864 Associated with C. E. Norton as joint-editor of the *North American Review;* contributed vigorous prose pieces which appeared as *Political Essays,* 1888. *Fireside Travels.*
1865 *Ode Recited at the Harvard Commemoration.*
1867 *Biglow Papers,* second series. (These had previously appeared in *Atlantic Monthly,* 1862–65.)
1868 *Under the Willows.*
1870 *The Cathedral. Among My Books.*
1871 *My Study Windows.*
1872 Resigned professorship. Third visit to Europe.
1876 *Among My Books,* second series. Delegate to Republican Convention.
1877 *Three Memorial Poems.* Minister to Spain until 1880.
1880–85 Minister to England.
1884 "Democracy," address.
1885 Wife died. Diplomatic service ended.
1885–90 Four visits to England.
1886 *Democracy and Other Addresses.*
1888 *Heartsease and Rue.*
1891 Died at Cambridge, on August 12. *Latest Literary Essays and Addresses.*
1892 *The Old English Dramatists.*

BIBLIOGRAPHY

I. Bibliography

Campbell, Killis. "Bibliographical Notes on Lowell," *University of Texas Bulletin,* Studies in English, No. 4, pp. 115–119 (1924). (To Lowell's list of published writings, Mr. Campbell adds one poem ["Lover's Drink Song"] and four prose pieces. He gives the first place of publication of ten pieces and calls attention to variant versions of six pieces.)

Chamberlain, J. C., and Livingston, L. S. *First Editions of the Writings of James Russell Lowell.* New York: 1914. (A valuable list of items printed as individual volumes, as pamphlets, or in volumes such as annuals. Does not include items which appeared in magazines or newspapers.)

Cooke, G. W. *A Bibliography of James Russell Lowell.* Boston: 1906. (A masterly compilation, indispensable for all serious students because it gives the date and place of first publication of all Lowell's writings, a great many of which are not included in his collected works, and because it lists all notices and criticisms of his work by others to 1906.)

Joyce, H. E. "A Bibliographical Note on James Russell Lowell," *Modern Language Notes,* XXXV, 249–250 (April, 1920). (To the seven known poems by Lowell in *The Pioneer,* Joyce adds "The Poet and Apollo" in the January issue and the "Song" ["Oh Moonlight deep and tender"] in the February issue.)

Scudder, H. E. *James Russell Lowell: A Biography.* Boston: 1901, II, 421–447. (The pages indicated contain a chronological list of Lowell's writings, with date and place of first publication.)

II. Text

Writings. Riverside Edition. Boston: 1890. 11 vols. Prose, I–VII; Poems, VII–X; Latest Essays.

Writings. Standard Library Edition. Boston: 1891. 11 vols. (Printed from plates of the Riverside Edition, with contents of individual volumes unchanged. Scudder's *Life* in 2 vols. added in 1902.)

Complete Writings. Elmwood Edition. Boston: 1904. 16 vols. ("This edition varies from the Riverside Edition of 1890 in the retention of the original titles of the volumes of prose essays."—Publishers' note in Vol. I. Includes *Letters of Lowell* [3 vols.], and Scudder's *Life* [2 vols.].)

Complete Poetical Works. Household Edition. Boston: 1895.

Complete Poetical Works, ed. by H. E. Scudder. Cambridge Edition. Boston: 1897, 1917. (Especially valuable for headnotes, and for chronology of the poems, pp. 481–484.)

Early Prose Writings, with a prefatory note by Dr. Hale . . . and an introduction by Walter Littlefield. London: 1902.

The Function of the Poet and Other Essays, collected and edited by Albert Mordell. Boston: 1920. (Early essays and reviews throwing important light on the growth of Lowell's mind.)

The Round Table. Boston: 1913. (A title given by an anonymous editor to a collection of nine of Lowell's reviews not included in his collected works.)

Lectures on the English Poets. Cleveland: 1897. (The Rowfant Club here reprints from the Boston *Daily Advertiser* the Lowell Institute lectures given by Lowell in 1855.)

The Anti-Slavery Papers of James Russell Lowell. Boston: 1902. 2 vols. (According to the unsigned introduction, p. vi: "The two volumes contain more than fifty articles, the first five being contributed during 1844 to the 'Pennsylvania Freeman,' the rest, between 1845 and 1850, to the 'National Anti-Slavery Standard,' of which he was for two of these years titular associate editor." None of these papers are in Lowell's collected works. They are indispensable to any full and just estimate of the growth of his mind and his political influence.)

Impressions of Spain. Boston: 1899. Compiled from the *Diplomatic Correspondence*, by J. B. Gilder, with an Introduction by A. A. Adee.

Papers Relating to the Foreign Relations of the United States, 1877–1885. Washington, D. C. (Contains the record of his diplomatic career.)

Last Poems of James Russell Lowell, ed. by C. E. Norton. Boston: 1895. (Two of the ten poems appeared here for the first time.)

Letters of James Russell Lowell, ed. by C. E. Norton. New York: 1894. 2 vols. (Norton says, in his editorial note that he has tried to select letters which will give the work "an autobiographic character.")

Letters of James Russell Lowell, ed. by C. E. Norton. Boston: 1904. 3 vols. (Enlarged from the edition of 1894. Norton says in the first volume: "A number of letters, which have come to me since the original edition of this selection of Mr. Lowell's letters was published, are now included in their respective places in these volumes. They add nothing essential to the image of him presented in the former edition, but serve to fill up some minor parts of its outline with details which strengthen the likeness." It should be carefully noted that this three-volume edition supersedes the earlier two-volume edition, and is indispensable for any exhaustive scholarly interpretation of Lowell.)

New Letters of James Russell Lowell, ed. by M. A. DeW. Howe. New York: 1932. (These letters, many of them to Lowell's daughter, serve especially to reveal the more intimate and human aspects of the man, but they contribute little to a history of his ideas.)

[It should be noted that, in addition to 181 poems, a considerable body of Lowell's prose pieces remains uncollected. These may be located in the original magazines and newspapers by referring to G. W. Cooke's *Bibliography* and to notes by Campbell and Joyce, above.]

III. Biography and Criticism

Allen, G. W. "Lowell," in *American Prosody*. New York: 1935, pp. 244–270. (A comprehensive and scholarly survey of the meters and stanzaic forms used by Lowell. Finds that his versification introduced into American poetry a freedom involving "a more varied placing of accents and the combination of different kinds of feet to produce a suggestiveness of tone and cadence" tending toward "a greater emphasis of melody and harmony" [pp. 269–270].)

Bailey, E. J. "Lowell," in *Religious Thought in the Greater American Poets*. Boston: 1922, pp. 158–182. (A competent general survey. Concludes that Lowell's "attitude toward many important religious ideas may not unjustly be termed . . . nobly pagan," although he had a profound faith in God. "He could not bring himself to feel that the Church and the Bible speak with authority, yet he was far from sneering at the claims of the former or thrusting the latter aside as valueless" [p. 171]. See Shea, below.)

Brenner, Rica. "Lowell," in *Twelve American Poets before 1900*. New York: 1933, pp. 199–228. (Mostly biographical. Contains some unsympathetic "criticism of Lowell's technical skill and of his inability to meet completely the modern point of view" especially as regards his attitude toward science. He was "too many-sided a person to be a great poet.")

Brownell, W. C. "Lowell," in *American Prose Masters*. New York: 1909, pp. 271–335. (Probably the best of the general critiques on Lowell. The last section deals with his poetry. Brownell concludes that Lowell's poetry "constitutes, on the whole, the most admirable American contribution to the nature poetry of English literature," and that his *Commemoration Ode* "has the elevation of ecstasy and the splendor of the sublime.")

Campbell, Killis. "Lowell's Uncollected Poems," *Publications of the Modern Language Association*, XXXVIII, 933–937 (Dec., 1923). (A valuable study. Concludes that "Lowell acted wisely in rejecting" from his "final collective edition a total of 181 poems that had hitherto been published." Mr. Campbell thinks that the "sheer immaturity" and "diffuseness and an imperfect focus will sufficiently account for the discarding of most of the rejected longer poems of the early forties.")

—— "Three Notes on Lowell," *Modern Language Notes*, XXXVIII, 121–122 (Feb., 1923). (Identifies a sonnet by Lowell on Charles Dickens, an advance notice of *A Fable for Critics*, and finds Emersonian influence in "The Sphinx," "To Perdita, Singing," "Ode," "The Landlord," "Bibliolatres," and "The Fountain of Youth.")

Chapman, E. M. "The Biglow Papers Fifty Years After," *Yale Review*, N. S., VI, 120–134 (Oct., 1916). (An interesting appreciation, concluding that *The Biglow Papers* are "always humane, shrewd, and right-minded," that they represent "the complex and sometimes contradictory qualities of New England character," and that they are vitally alive today.)

Cheney, J. V. "Lowell," in *That Dome in Air*. Chicago: 1895, pp. 61–90. (A discursive critique. Finds Lowell inferior to Arnold, although the two sowed the same field. Emphasizes Lowell's deficiency in "primal power of construction," "minor points of technics," "music and passion.")

Chrisman, L. H. "Permanent Values in *The Biglow Papers*," in *John Ruskin, Preacher, and Other Essays*. New York: 1921, pp. 163–176. (Concludes that "no other writer has written in dialect lines so pathetically beautiful and enchantingly melodious" [p. 172], that "in the field of satire we have nothing better to show than Lowell's Biglow Papers" [p. 163], that often in a few sentences he packs "whole chapters of social psychology." An interesting and well-written appreciation.)

Clark, H. H. "Lowell's Criticism of Romantic Literature," *Publications of the Modern Language Association*, XLI, 209–228 (March, 1926). (Attempts to show that Lowell's judgments of the romanticists were based on well-considered philosophic and literary principles. Dissents from the view of J. J. Reilly that Lowell was merely an impressionist.)

—— "Lowell—Humanitarian, Nationalist, or Humanist?" *Studies in Philology*, XXVII, 411–441 (July, 1930). (Attempts to show the development of Lowell's mind through three different philosophies. Stresses the need of the genetic approach.)

The Critic, Feb. 23, 1889. (A special number celebrating Lowell's seventieth birthday. Of many tributes, that by J. H. Morse, picturing Lowell as a teacher, is especially interesting.)

Curtis, G. W. *James Russell Lowell*. New York: 1892. (A memorial address delivered at the Brooklyn Institute.)

DeMille, G. E. "Lowell," in *Literary Criticism in America*. New York: 1931, pp. 49–85. (A reasonably good, readable essay, somewhat unsympathetic to Lowell. Although Mr. DeMille admits that "Foerster has completely and finally demolished" Reilly's view that Lowell had no critical doctrines, he tends to emphasize what he regards as Lowell's inconsistencies and discursiveness.)

Eliot, C. W. "James Russell Lowell as a Professor," *Harvard Graduates' Magazine*, XXVII, 492–497 (June, 1919). (A charmingly written account. Says Lowell's greatest work as a teacher was done in his evening classes in his own library.)

Flower, B. O. "James Russell Lowell as a Poet of Freedom and Human Rights," *Arena*, XLI, 309–317 (March, 1909). (Lowell "justly holds a foremost place among the American poets of freedom and progress" [p. 310]. Emphasizes the influence of Maria White. Although somewhat vague and grandiloquent, the essay is interesting in showing the continuation of appreciation of Lowell as a radical.)

Foerster, Norman. "Lowell," in *Nature in American Literature*. New York: 1923, pp. 143–175. (An exhaustive survey of Lowell's treatment of various aspects of nature, followed by a penetrating analysis of his philosophic reaction to nature-philosophies. Concludes that in spite of "a confusion of mind and heart" colored by the time-spirit, Lowell increasingly came to see, "however fitfully, the futility of an humanitarianism divorced from both the discipline of humanism and the discipline of religion" [p. 175].)

—— "Lowell," in *American Criticism*. Boston: 1928, pp. 111–156. (A masterly assembly and analysis of the elements of Lowell's literary creed, which Foerster regards as "almost the unwritten constitution of the republic of letters" [p. 149]. Includes discriminating interpretation and appraisal of Lowell's view of the task of the critic, of the relation of form and the ideal, of imagination, and of the function of literature. This essay is hardly equalled in modern criticism of American writers for logical cogency and sustained acuteness.)

Fuess, C. M. "Some Forgotten Political Essays by Lowell," *Massachusetts Historical Society Proceedings*, LXII, 3–12 (Oct., 1928). (A description of uncollected essays in the *Atlantic* on "Mr. Buchanan's Administration," April, 1858; "The Pocket-Celebration of the Fourth," Aug., 1858, attacking Choate as a weak compromiser; and "A Sample of Consistency," Nov., 1858, attacking Cushing as a self-seeking traitor to the North.)

Grandgent, C. H. "From Franklin to Lowell. A Century of New England Pronunciation," *Publications of the Modern Language Association*, XIV, 207–239 (1899). (A scholarly article by a great philologist, especially interesting in its analysis of the linguistic aspects of *The Biglow Papers*.)

Grattan, C. H. "Lowell," *American Mercury*, II, 63–69 (May, 1924). (A good example of the bitter attacks made on Lowell by journalistic radicals during the nineteen-twenties. Based partly on a failure to recognize the extent to which Lowell's thought developed as he grew older.)

Greenslet, Ferris. *James Russell Lowell*. Boston: 1905. American Men of Letters Series. (A good brief biography. Chapter VII, pp. 245–265, deals with "Lowell's Poetry.")

Grubb, Edward. "The Socialism of James Russell Lowell," *New England Magazine*, N. S., VI, 676–678 (July, 1892). (An able article. Concludes, on the basis of convincing evidence, that Lowell was an adherent of socialism when the word is defined as "the practical application of Christianity to life" but that in the political sense of the word he was in no way a socialist.)

Hale, E. E., Jr. *James Russell Lowell and His Friends*. Boston: 1899. (Valuable for personal reminiscences.)

—— *James Russell Lowell*. Beacon Biographies Series. Boston: 1899. (Very brief.)

Hart, J. M. "James Russell Lowell," *Publications of the Modern Language Association*, VII, 25–31 (1892). (An obituary essay, paying tribute to Lowell as "a truly representative American scholar" worthy of serving "as our model" because "his culture was the broadest and richest that our people has yet exhibited." Lowell was the first president of the Association.)

Harte, Bret. "A Few Words about Mr. Lowell," *New Review*, V, 193–201 (Sept., 1891). (A sensitive and charming appreciation of Lowell's many-sided genius.)

Heil, J. A. "*Die Volkssprache im Nordosten der Vereinigten Staaten von Amerika, dargestellt auf Grund der Biglow Papers von James Russel Lowell*," in *Giessener Beiträge zur Erforschung der Sprache und Kultur Englands und Nordamerikas*. Breslau, 1927. III, No. 2, 205–311. (A. G. Kennedy, reviewing this work in *American Speech* [III, 426–427, June, 1928], concludes that Heil offers a careful study of the New England dialect by classification and comparison of sounds, inflections, and syntactical peculiarities, and that his comparisons with forms from Middle English lends dignity to Biglow's words as part of the historical development of the English language. Mr. Kennedy indicates frequent textual errors and misprints in Heil's work.)

Henry, H. T. "James Russell Lowell's Moral Intuitions," *Catholic Educational Review*, XXII, 6–17 (Jan., 1924).

—— "Religious Intimations in the Writings of James Russell Lowell," *Catholic Educational Review*, XXI, 398–408 (Sept., 1923).

—— "Music in Lowell's Prose and Verse," *Musical Quarterly*, XXIV, 546–572 (Oct., 1924). (An interesting survey of Lowell's allusions to music, concluding: "in no other writer of any generation who has not written professedly on musical topics, will so many musical ideas and expressions be found" [p. 572]. Shows that he thought a sense of harmony and a knowledge of music essential to a poet, and that as a critic he included musical harmony among his criteria in appraising the poetry of others. This preliminary study could be much further developed.)

Howe, M. A. DeW. "Lowell," in *Dictionary of American Biography*. New York: 1933, XI, 458–464. (The best brief, up-to-date biography.)

Howells, W. D. "Studies of Lowell," in *Literary Friends and Acquaintance*. New York: 1900, pp. 212–250. (Invaluable and charmingly written testimony by a friend regarding Lowell's tolerance, kindliness, and magnanimity toward a realist and a socialist. Probably the most vivid presentation available of Lowell in his habit as he lived. Howells was instrumental in having Hayes appoint Lowell minister to Spain, and he has many interesting comments on his political views. He concludes that, of all the great men of that period, "Lowell was of the richest nature I have known.")

Hudson, W. H. *Lowell and His Poetry*. London: 1914. (A discursive English view, dealing successively through Lowell's poetry with his love for Maria White, his nature interests, his patriotism, his academic interests, and his religion.)

James, Henry. "James Russell Lowell," in *Essays in London and Elsewhere*. New York: 1893, pp. 44–80. (A charming essay, by a friend, based partly on conversations with Lowell in London and emphasizing his passionate devotion to America and the republican ideal.)

Jameson, J. F. "Lowell and Public Affairs," *Review of Reviews*, IV, 287–291 (Oct., 1891). (A brief but very judicious survey of an important subject by a distinguished historian. Concludes that as a poet Lowell's "best inspiration was derived from passionate interest in public affairs," as illustrated in *The Biglow Papers* and the *Commemoration Ode*. Finds the former "the best political satires the present century has produced," being comparable to the work of Swift, Dryden, and Butler. "None has ever enjoyed a more brilliant reception" as ambassador to England. Pays high tribute to Lowell as representative of the idealistic man of thought "devoted to the good of the commonwealth," and deplores the growing divergence between traditional idealism and politics. This essay is followed by one by C. T. Winchester on "Lowell as a Man of Letters," one by R. D. Jones on "Lowell and the Public Schools," one by W. T. Stead on "Lowell's Message, and How It Helped Me," and one by Raymond Blathwayt on "A Last Interview.")

Jenkins, W. G. "Lowell's Criteria of Political Values," *New England Quarterly*, VII, 115–141 (March, 1934). (A carefully documented, comprehensive survey supplementing Jameson's study above. Concludes, "To realize the fact that Lowell's political thought was based on moral ideas is of prime importance. The progress in which he believed was a progress toward moral improvement. . . . Increasingly ever as he grew older did he refer to this past as a storehouse of experience and knowledge. Just here was the importance of the statesman as he saw it: he must know the value of the past and should be able to determine the general trend of his people and endeavor to direct opinion toward conformity with ethics" [pp. 140–141]. Although this study may not make quite enough allowance for Lowell's change of opinions as he grew older, it is of fundamental importance.)

Killheffer, Marie. "A Comparison of the Dialect of the 'Biglow Papers' with the Dialect of Four Yankee Plays," *American Speech*, III, 222–236 (Feb., 1928). (The plays are Royall Tyler's *The Contrast*, 1787, David Humphreys's *The Yankey in England*, 1815, Joseph Jones's *The People's Lawyer*, 1839, and Denman Thompson's *The Old Homestead*, 1886. Compared with these authors, Lowell used a higher percentage of low colloquials along with picturesque compounds and phrasings, and he approached dialect from a scientific angle, although he was more concerned with the written than with the spoken word. A scholarly study.)

Kreymborg, Alfred. "The Poet of Too Many Isms," in *Our Singing Strength*. New York: 1929, pp. 116–133. (An interesting impressionistic survey, somewhat condescending. Conventional stress on Lowell's eccentricities, versatility, and his inability to give his poems "the final finish to make them endure.")

Lange, Alexis F. "James Russell Lowell as a Critic," *California University Chronicle*, VIII, 352–364 (1906). (Deals with Lowell's canons of criticism. Thinks his qualifications as interpreter equal to those of Arnold. According to Lowell's "working creed for criticism," literature was purely an "expression of human experience" and "the books . . . always stood for the writers" [p. 355]. He did not neglect artistic form, but viewed it as organic, as "the living thought creating its embodiment" [p. 357]. See Foerster above.)

Lawton, W. C. *The New England Poets*. New York: 1898. (Commonplace.)

Literary World, XVI, 217–226 (June 27, 1885). (A "Lowell Number.")

Lockwood, Ferris. "Mr. Lowell on Art-Principles," *Scribner's Magazine*, XV, 186–189 (Feb., 1894). (A penetrating, succinct, and well-documented exposition of the basis of Lowell's poetry and criticism: his doctrine that the artist must select materials from actual life which are to be "ideally reproduced through the imagination," which not only shapes them into unity of design but inspires style, "a sense of indefinable completeness." Lockwood says these principles "come with especial authority from one who, while he will always stand in the front rank as a critic, was at the same time greater still as an artist" [p. 189].)

Lovett, R. M. "Lowell," in *American Writers on American Literature*, ed. by John Macy. New York: 1931, pp. 177–189. (A felicitous essay, with apt quotations, praising Lowell's early radicalism, and contrasting Concord to Cambridge culture at the expense of the latter. Mr. Lovett's view that Lowell "had no passion for ideas" [p. 186] in his criticism, that he was as critic "nearer to Charles Lamb than to Coleridge or Matthew Arnold" [p. 187], and that his later mature development represented merely a "stiffening of mind and hardening of heart" [p. 188] would seem to require much modification in the light of evidence presented by Foerster and others.)

Macy, John. "Lowell," in *The Spirit of American Literature*. New York: 1908. (A spirited and radical nationalist praises *The Biglow Papers* and Lowell's other early radical utterances, and thinks that after 1880 he became "a mere literary man" and "degenerated into a polite conservative statesman." Macy thinks the merits of his prose are "its humanity, audacity, colloquial ease"; its defects, "his amateurishness, capricious responsibility." He says of Lowell's nationalistic *Political Essays*, "no one of the time has left us a better volume of its kind.")

Mead, E. D. "Lowell's *Pioneer*," *New England Magazine*, N.S. V, 235–258 (Oct., 1891).

Mims, Edwin. "Lowell as a Citizen," *South Atlantic Quarterly*, I, 27–40 (Jan., 1902). (An intelligent and sympathetic essay. Unlike the radicals, Mr. Mims sees that one of Lowell's best qualities as a citizen was "his ability to change as conditions changed" [p. 36]. His political writings were not those "of an eager-hearted, narrow reformer, but of a wise, practical statesman—who seemed to have many of the qualities of his hero [Lincoln]—the 'good sense, the good humor, the sagacity, the large-mindedness, and the unselfish honesty'" [p. 36]. "It was his belief that in a democracy every man must do what he can to create right public sentiment" [p. 27].)

Moulton, C. W. *Library of Literary Criticism*. Buffalo: 1905. VIII, 17–42. (Useful assembly of excerpts from criticisms of Lowell enabling one to trace the history of his reputation.)

Nichols, E. J. "Identification of Characters in Lowell's 'A Fable for Critics,'" *American Literature*, IV, 191–194 (May, 1932). (Would substitute Thoreau and Channing for two blanks in "A Fable.")

Norton, C. E. "James Russell Lowell," *Harper's Magazine*, LXXXVI, 846–857 (May, 1893). (Written before Lowell's letters were published, this essay offered the sort of biographical sketch and character delineation that only an intimate friend could have provided.)

Palmer, Ray. "James Russell Lowell and Modern Literary Criticism," *International Review*, IV, 264–281 (March, 1877). (A review of Lowell's *Among My Books*, both series, this is by far the ablest of the early essays on Lowell as critic. In contrast to most contemporary critics, with whom Mr. Palmer compares Lowell, he finds him unique in his fruitful harmonizing of historical, interpretative, and judicial criticism. His essays contain "scholarly accuracy, . . . keenness of perception, . . . comprehensiveness of knowledge . . . esthetic culture, . . . impartial judgment, together with the power of expressing the nicest shades of thought" [p. 267]. He has "attained to a high ideal of what the work of criticism properly involves" [p. 269].)

Parrington, V. L. "Lowell, Cambridge Brahmin," in *The Romantic Revolution in America*. New York: 1927, pp. 460–472. (A prejudiced but stimulating interpretation by a radical economic determinist. Repeats the conventional charge that Lowell showed an "inveterate unwillingness to think. He never speculated widely or analyzed critically. Ideas, systems of thought, intellectual and social movements, he had no interest in; he was content to remain a bookish amateur in letters . . . History remained a blank to him" [p. 461]. For different views supported by evidence, see Foerster, Jenkins, Pritchard, and Clark.)

Parsons, E. S. "Lowell's Conception of Poetry," *Colorado College Publications*, Language Series, II, 67–84 (Sept., 1908). (An able and sympathetic interpretation, well buttressed by evidence.)

Perry, Bliss. "Lowell," in *The Praise of Folly and Other Papers*. Boston: 1923, pp. 130–150. (An appreciative survey, delightfully written. Emphasizes Lowell's distinction as "an inheritor and an enricher of the Great Tradition," devoted to "the common interests of all" and to "civic responsibility.")

Pettigrew, R. C. "Lowell's Criticism of Milton," *American Literature*, III, 457–464 (Jan., 1932). (A scholarly article, concluding that, while Lowell offers a "really excellent discussion of Milton's metrics," his utterances on Milton in general [Lowell's *Works*, IV, 58–117, and VII, 94–110] reveal him "as one whose critical powers are largely impressionistic," largely devoted in this case to kindling our enthusiasm.)

Phelps, W. L. "Lowell," in *Howells, James, Bryant, and Other Essays*. New York: 1924, pp. 96–122. (Discursive and appreciative.)

Poe, E. A. "Poems of Lowell," *Graham's Magazine*, XXIV, 142–143 (March, 1844); and "A Fable for Critics," *Southern Literary Messenger* (March, 1849). The first is reprinted in Poe's *Complete Works*, edited by J. A. Harrison, XI, 243–249; the second in *ibid.*, XIII, 165–175. (In the review mentioned, Poe praises "The Legend of Britanny" as one of our best poems. In the second he was prejudiced because Lowell was "one of the most rabid of the Abolitionist fanatics" and because he had characterized Poe as "two fifths sheer fudge." Attacks *A Fable* as "essentially 'loose'—ill-conceived and feebly executed as well in detail as in general," as wanting "artistic finish . . . especially in its versification," and as malevolent, especially toward Margaret Fuller. Yet he concludes that Lowell and Longfellow are "upon the whole, perhaps our best" poets. A very sharp and influential essay by a shrewd critic.)

Pollak, Gustav. "Lowell: Patriot and Cosmopolitan," in *International Perspective in Criticism: Goethe, Grillparzer, Sainte-Beuve, Lowell*. New York: 1914, pp. 58–83. (Compares the views of the four critics regarding the same authors. An important study, concluding that Lowell ranks favorably with the critics named and that "his outlook on life and literature was that of the serene philosopher and the cosmopolitan critic" [p. 59].)

——— "Lowell: Patriot and Cosmopolitan," in *International Minds and the Search for the Restful*. New York: 1919, pp. 68–80.

Pritchard, J. P. "Lowell's Debt to Horace's *Ars Poetica*," *American Literature*, III, 259–276 (November, 1931). (A valuable scholarly study casting much light on Lowell's literary theory and its kinship with that of classicism. Lowell referred intelligently to Horace's *Ars Poetica* throughout life. The two theorizers agreed that poetry should give profitable pleasure; that it springs from genius and careful study, from knowledge of men supplementing knowledge of books. They agreed that a poet should await inspiration; should select and combine materials to achieve unity of effect; should accept originality as a fresh vision of the familiar; should carefully attend to criticism and to execution. They agreed as to the need of attention to diction and metre and the need of guarding against the prosaic and the temptation to be unworthily popular for the moment by disregarding the rules based on the unity of memory and taste common to the centuries.)

——— "Aristotle's *Poetics* and Certain American Literary Critics," *Classical Weekly*, XXVII, 81–85; 89–93; 97–99 (1934). (The critics are Poe, Lowell, and Stedman. Lowell is treated in the issue for Jan. 15, 1934, pp. 89–93. An able classical scholar here gives a fine, documented analysis of Lowell's references and probable debt to Aristotle. Shows his deep interest and "first-hand information"; concludes that his critical position is "based largely upon his knowledge of the principles advocated by Aristotle in the *Poetics*, and his adherence to them." These two valuable studies by Pritchard supplement and reinforce the interpretation by Foerster noted above.)

Quayle, W. A. *Modern Poets and Christian Teaching: Lowell.* New York: 1906. (Somewhat vague and fanatical chapters on Lowell's relation to Christianity, the moral atmosphere, love, and humor shown in his work. The best chapter is XII, dealing with "The Cathedral." Concludes that Lowell "lacked the divine, contagious faith . . . and did not know that Christ was God" [p. 155]. See Bailey, Shea, and Strong.)

Reilly, J. J. *James Russell Lowell as a Critic.* New York: 1915. (An extensive, elaborately documented, but prejudiced book, with bibliography. Chapters on the man and writer; his range of knowledge; the breadth and limitations of his sympathy; relation to the judicial attitude; penetration; type of mind; the critic and his criticism. Concludes, "If Lowell is to survive, it must be frankly as an impressionist. For so far as criticism approaches a science, so far as it depends to any serious extent on ultimate principles, so far, in a word, as it is something more fundamental and abiding than the *ipse dixit* of an appreciator, Lowell is not a critic" [p. 214]. While Foerster is now generally regarded as having presented evidence of Lowell's advocacy and practice of judicial criticism which refutes Reilly's conclusion, this book nevertheless contains much that is of value along the way.)

Review of "The Biglow Papers," *New Englander*, o.s., VII, 63–72 (1849). (Appreciative. Says that twenty years hence the dialect will seem to readers "more expressive than the most courtly English.")

Rice, Wallace. "Lowell on Human Liberty," *Dial*, XXXIV, 14–16 (January 1, 1903). (An interesting review of Lowell's *Anti-Slavery Papers.* Concludes that "The theme of the collection is something greatly broader and deeper than the mere abolition of chattel slavery in the southern United States," that it can be applied to any nation in any age.)

Roberts, R. E. "James Russell Lowell: A British Estimate," *Living Age*, CCCI, 231–235 (April 26, 1919). (Reprinted from the London *Bookman*, LV, 185–187, March, 1919. An unbiased, sane and richly appreciative essay showing that the British loved Lowell chiefly because they thought him spiritually "healthy." Although much of Lowell's poetry was anti-British and democratic, this British critic says Lowell's place in British affections depends wholly on his poetry and its sense of brotherhood and political equality. Compares him to Dickens and Lamb in his humanity. Praises Lowell as a critic for his breadth of sympathy, quick insight, appreciation, commonsense, and generous enthusiasm for both beauty and honor.)

Robertson, J. M. "Lowell as a Critic," *North American Review*, CCIX, 246–262 (Feb., 1919). (Starts out to refute Reilly's conclusion that "Lowell is not 'a critic,'" then comes to a rather lame and partial agreement. Claims that criticism is also creation, that "Lowell 'creates' . . . getting his impressions less judicially, more spontaneously, trusting his 'intuitions' until further knowledge moves him tacitly to discard them" [p. 255]. "Impressionist and 'expressionist,' his function was to expatiate, not to compare notes, or to reason reciprocally" [p. 257]. A rather disappointing essay.)

Savage, Rev. M. J. "The Religion of Lowell's Poems," *Arena*, IX, 705–722 (May, 1894). (Appreciative but vague. Superseded by Bailey, Shea, Strong, and Voigt.)

Scudder, H. E. *James Russell Lowell: A Biography.* Boston: 1901. 2 vols. (This is the most extensive biography—a competent conservative work. For his political interests see especially "In the Anti-Slavery Ranks," I, 151–237; "Lowell and the War for the Union," II, 1–73; "Politics," II, 185–220; "The Spanish Mission," II, 221–258; "The English Mission," II, 259–321. Reviewed in *Atlantic Monthly*, LXXXIX, 253–264 [Feb., 1902].)

—— "Mr. Lowell as a Teacher," *Scribner's Magazine*, X, 645–649 (Nov., 1891). (See also Eliot and Wendell.)

Shea, L. M. *Lowell's Religious Outlook.* Washington, D. C.: 1926. (A scholarly dissertation done at The Catholic University of America and distinguished for precision, elaborate documentation, and detachment. Includes analysis of Lowell's view of God, providence, immortality, and science. The best treatment of the subject, although to be supplemented in parts by Bailey and Strong.)

Smalley, G. W. "Mr. Lowell in England," *Harper's*, XCII, 788–801 (April, 1896).

Smith, F. D. "Mr. Wilbur's Posthumous Macaronics," *Quarterly Journal of the University of North Dakota*, X, 436–443 (1920). (A scholarly analysis of No. VIII of the second series of *The Biglow Papers.*)

Stedman, E. C. "James Russell Lowell," in *Poets of America.* Boston: 1885, pp. 304–348. (A comprehensive general essay, considering Lowell as our "representative man of letters" devoted to culture, to idealism, to the republican idea, and to catholicity of taste. Finds that his "irregular ear" occasionally left "technical blemishes" in his poems, and that his fine passages are not infrequently marred by "odd conceits, mixed metaphors, and licenses . . ." Concludes that he is "a poet who is our most brilliant and learned critic, and . . . has given us our best native idyll, our best and most complete work in dialectic verse, and the noblest heroic ode that America has produced,—each and all ranking with the first of their kinds in English literature of the modern time" [pp. 347–348]. A judicious and influential essay.)

Strong, A. H. "James Russell Lowell," in *American Poets and Their Theology*. Philadelphia: 1916, pp. 265–317. (Although somewhat garrulous, didactic, and confessedly partisan, Strong's work is of value because he supports his conclusions with considerable evidence, and it serves as a partial supplement to "economic" interpretations. Views Lowell as distinctively our chief poetical moralist, whose ethics vitalized his patriotism and his criticism. As a Calvinist, Strong finds Lowell's chief "error" [p. 297] in his ignoring "man's sin and perversity" and his disregard for a miraculous revelation of a transcendent God. Attacks Lowell's humanistic idea in "The Cathedral" that each man is able to redeem himself in the light of divine perfection inwardly revealed, and that Christ is not divine but one of many admirable traditional guides. Yet Strong admits that "the good in his poetry rests on an inherited Christian faith." Probably in his later work on Puritanism and Dante Lowell recognized the conflict between good and evil within the individual much more than Strong indicates.)

Swift, Lindsay. "Our Literary Diplomats: Part IV," *Book-Buyer*, N.S., XXI, 90–98 (Sept., 1900). (A rather general and superficial review of Lowell's diplomatic career. Concludes that he "performed all of . . . [the] exactions according to his lights, which were excellent.")

Tandy, Jeannette. "The Biglow Papers," in *Crackerbox Philosophers in American Humor and Satire*. New York: 1925, pp. 43–64. (An admirable scholarly study. "Lowell's range and penetration in satirical portraiture are unsurpassed in America." Interesting proof that the supposed academic eastern snob was a pioneer and master in a field in which the West and South are popularly supposed to have had a monopoly—in the humorous and dialectical presentation of the common man.)

Taylor, Bayard. "Lowell," in *Critical Essays and Literary Notes*. New York: 1880, pp. 298–301. (Brief but discriminating appreciation by a fellow poet. "No one of our poets shows a richer or wider range of thought than Mr. Lowell: no one a greater variety of expression in verse." Yet he "seems hostile to that quality which compels each conception to shape itself into clear symmetry." Concludes that "The Cathedral" best represents Lowell's virtues and vices.)

Thayer, W. R. "James Russell Lowell as a Teacher: Recollections of His Last Pupil," *Scribner's Magazine*, LXVIII, 473–480 (Oct., 1920). (An interesting account of Lowell's methods as a teacher, by one of his former students.)

Thorndike, A. H. "Lowell," in *The Cambridge History of American Literature*. New York: 1918, II, 245–257. (A brief but judicious survey, emphasizing Lowell's great function as a critic in teaching "a new people to guide their steps by the great men and the great ideas of the past.")

Traill, H. D. "Mr. J. R. Lowell," *Fortnightly Review*, N.S., XXXVIII, 79–89 (July, 1885). (An amusing and excellent appreciation by a representative English critic. Discusses "the homage so effusively paid to him . . . by his English admirers," and concludes that "the contrast . . . between a somewhat far-fetched thought and its nobly simple expression . . . is the *ism* which really prevented him from scaling Parnassus" [p. 85–86].)

Traubel, H. L. "Lowell—Whitman: A Contrast," *Poet-Lore*, IV, 22–31 (Jan. 15, 1892). (An ardent champion of Whitman disparages Lowell as a critical and scholarly "conservator" who "ploughs along accomplished ways," while Whitman is a "creator" with "vital pluck out of nature's heart; . . . in his soul are illuminating fires, hot with the glow of immortal meaning." See also Portia Barker, "Walt Whitman and *The Atlantic Monthly*," *American Literature*, VI, 283–301, especially pp. 287–288.)

Underwood, F. H. *James Russell Lowell: A Biographical Sketch*. Boston: 1882.

—— *The Poet and the Man: Recollections and Appreciations of James Russell Lowell*. Boston: 1893.

Voigt, G. P. "Lowell," in *The Religious and Ethical Element in the Major American Poets*. Bulletin of the University of South Carolina, The Graduate School, June 1, 1925, pp. 100–123. (Generally judicious, especially in his recognition that Lowell "felt an increasingly strong inclination towards some of the doctrines of Calvinism" [p. 104], such as predestination, the sovereignty of God, and the moral earnestness of the Puritans, although he abandoned some of their other beliefs such as that in original sin. Supplements Bailey and Strong.)

Warren, Austin. "Lowell on Thoreau," *Studies in Philology*, XXVII, 442–461 (July, 1930). (An exhaustive and judicious study of the development of Lowell's hostile attitude towards Thoreau and a statement of the points at final issue between the two men. Throws important light on a transitional period in Lowell's critical thought and practice.)

Watson, William. "Lowell as a Critic," in *Excursions in Criticism*. London. 1893, pp. 89–96. (An appreciative and shrewd English view; brief and discursive. Lowell is America's "most brilliant 'all-around' literary representative." His critical prose is "the product of judgment aërated by wit." His "forte is profusion, and his foible prodigality"; his criticism is "delightfully fresh and tonic, with a certain saline shrewdness in it," and his direct method is "picturesque and robust.")

Wendell, Barrett. "Mr. Lowell as a Teacher," in *Stelligeri and Other Essays Concerning America*. New York: 1893, pp. 205–217. (Himself a great teacher, Wendell, one of Lowell's former students, charmingly describes his methods and concludes that he was "the most inspiring teacher I had ever had" [p. 217].)

Werner, Dorothy L. *The Idea of Union in American Verse (1776–1876)*. Philadelphia: 1932. (A dissertation done at the University of Pennsylvania. See index for many references to Lowell's political poems. A valuable compilation and discussion.)

Wilkinson, W. C. "Mr. Lowell's Poetry," "Mr. Lowell's 'Cathedral,'" and "Mr. Lowell's Prose," in *A Free Lance in the Field of Life and Letters*. New York: 1874, pp. 50–183. (Remarkably sharp judicial criticism, finely detailed, by a critic of classical bias. Thinks that "The Vision of Sir Launfal" shows Lowell's "most perfect felicity" [p. 64], and that "The Commemoration Ode" is among the few "greatest odes in the English language" [p. 67]. In general, however, Wilkinson censures Lowell's "*want of firm and harmonious tone*" [p. 113] as well as his "remarkable incoherencies and inconsistencies." Finds him "in the noblest sense conservative," and thinks that "Puritanism might almost have made Mr. Lowell a lesser Milton" [p. 89]. While Wilkinson attacks "The Cathedral" especially, he thinks that "Mr. Lowell is primarily a poet" [p. 150], and he belittles his criticism, especially on grammatical grounds. Each point is strikingly illustrated by quotations.)

Will, T. E. "A Poet of Freedom," *Arena*, XXXI, 262–271 (March, 1904).

Willson, Beckles. *America's Ambassadors to England (1785–1929)*. New York: 1929, pp. 374–388. (An excellent summary of Lowell's diplomatic career in England, with many sidelights upon the questions of international affairs during Lowell's term of office. Lowell was especially troubled by the attempts of Irishmen to secure release from English prisons by fraudulently claiming that they were American citizens entitled to the intervention of our minister.)

Woodberry, G. E. "James Russell Lowell," in *Authors at Home*, ed. by J. L. and J. B. Gilder. New York: 1889, pp. 229–235.

—— "James Russell Lowell," in *Makers of Literature*. New York: 1900, pp. 324–349. (An appreciative and generally judicious essay by a discriminating critic who continued in some measure the impressionistic aspect of Lowell's work.)

NOTES

GENERAL

"No doubt Lowell lacked the concentration and focus of form necessary for the highest effectiveness; no doubt one can quote sentences out of their context which savor of truisms; no doubt an age accustomed to the mask of pseudo-scientific terminology may mistake his simplicity of phrase for shallowness of thought; no doubt, beset as he was by contemporary conflicts between religion and science, ancients and moderns, aristocracy and democracy, Lowell did not succeed in bringing complete order out of chaos. Nevertheless, I believe that a close scrutiny will reveal a rather distinct pattern in Lowell's thought, which is not less interesting because he responded so fully as poet, essayist, humorist, editor, teacher, scholar, and diplomat, to the needs of the American people. If we watch intently the evolution of his mind, if we humbly submit ourselves to the chronological record, I cannot help thinking that we shall be able to distinguish the successive emergence of three general bases of hope: the *humanitarian hope* [up to 1850] of advancing mankind through emancipation, sympathy, and outward reform; the *nationalistic hope* [from 1850–1868] that the mutable Many might find worthy perpetuation in the immutable One, a coercive Union; and the *humanistic hope* [after 1868] that the individual might find happiness through self-perfection, through inner reform, guided by an imaginative synthesis of the human ideal embodied in the literary record of the experience of the race."—H. H. Clark, "Lowell—Humanitarian, Nationalist, or Humanist?" *Studies in Philology*, XXVII, 411–441 (July, 1930).

Page 435. TO THE SPIRIT OF KEATS

In writing of this sonnet to E. A. Duyckinck, December 5, 1841, Lowell spoke of Keats as "a poet whom I especially love and whom I consider to be one of the true old Titan brood." On Lowell's early interest in Keats, as well as in Tennyson and Spenser, see Scudder, *Biography*, I, 94–96. Keats is echoed in "Bobolink," "Ianthe," "Irene" (Lowell's tribute to Maria White, who became his bride), and "A Legend of Brittany" (cf. "Isabella, or the Pot of Basil"). Lowell's cool essay on Keats, now in his collected works, originally an introduction to an edition of *Keats's Poems* (Boston, 1854), shows that his early enthusiasm for the romanticist has become considerably tempered by critical judgment.

Thirty-five sonnets by Lowell were collected in his first book, *A Year's Life* (1841), but of these he preserved only two in later collections. On the relation of these to the history of the sonnet in America see L. G. Sterner's Introduction to *The Sonnet in American Literature* (Philadelphia, 1930), and F. W. Powell's *The Sonnet in American Magazines before 1860* (a dissertation of 1932, available in manuscript at the library of the University of Virginia).

Page 436. THE SHEPHERD OF KING ADMETUS

This is one of the many illustrations of the fact that Lowell could write simply and without the didactic "isms" which he recognized as his besetting sin. The primitivistic notion, however, that the mere "loveliness of things," of nature, taught the first poet all he knew, is typical of Lowell's general disregard of cultural tradition at this time.

Page 437. AN INCIDENT IN A RAILROAD CAR

Note Lowell's early faith in goodness of "the primitive soul" as the basis of democracy, and his view that "all thought begins in feeling."

Page 438. WENDELL PHILLIPS

On the work of this great abolitionist whom Lowell admired, especially during his early humanitarian period, see Carlos Martyn, *Wendell Phillips: the Agitator* (New York, 1890).

RHŒCUS

"This fairy legend of old Greece," telling the story of a mortal who lost his love because he wounded a bee, represents Lowell's early humanitarian view, especially in its moral:

"he who scorns the least of Nature's works
Is thenceforth exiled and shut out from all."

Cf. "The Ancient Mariner"—the episode of securing release from penance by blessing water-snakes, and the attendant moral in lines 614-617.

Page 440. COLUMBUS

This spirited dramatic monologue embodies Lowell's early anti-traditionalism ("Europe's world / Reels on to judgment") and his ardent humanitarian utopianism.

Page 444. THE PRESENT CRISIS

The "crisis" was the controversy regarding whether Texas should be annexed and the area of slavery extended. This poem probably represents the high-water mark in the sonorous and lofty expression of moral passion aimed at slavery. Lowell may have had the verse form of "Locksley Hall" in mind, although as a whole the poem has much greater intensity than Tennyson's has. A trumpet-call to fight wrong even if single-handed, the poem is built around the idea of progress ("Humanity sweeps onward") and the resultant conviction that the Past can teach us nothing but the necessity of revolt: "Time makes ancient good uncouth"; we must not "attempt the Future's portal with the Past's blood-rusted key." "For twenty years," says Greenslet (*Lowell*, p. 79), "the solemn monitory music of this poem never ceased to reëcho in public halls. In the Lowell Memorial Address which George William Curtis delivered before the Brooklyn Institute, February 22, 1892, he said in his heightened way of some passages of 'The Present Crisis': 'Wendell Phillips [the orator] winged with their music and tipped with their flame the darts of his fervid appeal and manly scorn. As he quoted them with suppressed emotion in his low, melodious, penetrating voice the white plume of the resistless Navarre of eloquence gained a loftier grace, that relentless sword of invective a more flashing edge.' And the stanza of 'The Present Crisis,' beginning, 'For humanity sweeps onward,' was made by Sumner the text and motif of that famous 'Crime against Speech' oration that provoked the assault of Preston Brooks."

Page 447. THE BIGLOW PAPERS

In Lowell's "Introduction" to the collected second series of *The Biglow Papers* (1862) he explained his aims in part as follows: "... When, more than twenty years ago, I wrote the first of the series, I had no definite plan and no intention of ever writing another. Thinking the Mexican war, as I think it still, a national crime committed in behoof of Slavery, our common sin, and wishing to put the feeling of those who thought as I did in a way that would tell, I imagined to myself such an upcountry man as I had often seen at antislavery gatherings, capable of district-school English, but always instinctively falling back into the natural stronghold of his homely dialect when heated to the point of self-forgetfulness. When I began to carry out my conception and to write in my assumed character, I found myself in a strait between two perils. On the one hand, I was in danger of being carried beyond the limit of my own opinions, or at least of that temper with which every man should speak his mind in print, and on the other I feared the risk of seeming to vulgarize a deep and sacred conviction. I needed on occasion to rise above the level of mere *patois*, and for this purpose conceived the Rev. Mr. Wilbur, who should express the more cautious element of the New England character and its pedantry, as Mr. Biglow should serve for its homely common-sense vivified and heated by conscience. The parson was to be the complement rather than the antithesis of his parishioner, and I felt or fancied a certain humorous element in the real identity of the two under a seeming incongruity. Mr. Wilbur's fondness for scraps of Latin, though drawn from the life, I adopted deliberately to heighten the contrast. Finding soon after that I needed some one as a mouthpiece of the mere drollery, for I conceive that true humor is never divorced from moral conviction, I invented Mr. Sawin for the clown of my little puppet-show. I meant to embody in him that half-conscious *unmorality* which I had noticed as the recoil in gross natures from a puritanism that still strove to keep in its creed the intense savor which had long gone out of its faith and life. In the three I thought I should find room enough to express, as it was my plan to do, the popular feeling and opinion of the time. For the names of two of my characters, since I have received some remonstrances from very worthy persons who happen to bear them, I would say that they were purely fortuitous, probably mere unconscious memories of signboards or directories. Mr. Sawin's sprang from the accident of a rhyme at the end of his first epistle, and I purposely christened him by the impossible surname of Birdofredum not more to stigmatize him as the incarnation of 'Manifest Destiny,' in other words, of national recklessness as to right and wrong, than to avoid the chance of wounding any private sensitiveness.

"The success of my experiment soon began not only to astonish me, but to make me feel the responsibility of knowing that I held in my hand a weapon instead of the mere fencing-stick I had supposed. Very far from being a popular author under my own name, so far, indeed, as to be almost unread, I found the verses of my pseudonym copied everywhere; I saw them pinned up in workshops; I heard them quoted and their authorship debated; I once even, when rumor had at length caught up my name in one of its eddies, had the satisfaction of overhearing it demonstrated, in the pauses of a concert, that *I* was utterly incompetent to have written anything of the kind. I had read too much not to know the utter worthlessness of contemporary reputation, especially as regards satire, but I knew also that by giving a certain amount of influence it also had its worth, if that influence were used on the right side. I had learned, too, that the first requisite of good writing is to have an earnest and definite purpose, whether æsthetic or moral, and that even good writing, to please long, must have more than an average amount either of imagination or common-sense. The first of these falls to the lot of scarcely one in several generations; the last is within the reach of many in every one that passes; and of this an author may fairly hope to become in part the mouthpiece. If I put on the cap and bells and made myself one of the court-fools of King Demos, it was less to make his majesty laugh than to win a passage to his royal ears for certain serious things which I had deeply at heart. I say this because there is no imputation that could be more galling to any man's self-respect than that of being a mere jester. I endeavored, by generalizing my satire, to give it what value I could beyond the passing moment and the immediate application. How far I have succeeded I cannot tell, but I have had better luck than I ever looked for in seeing my verses survive to pass beyond their nonage.

"In choosing the Yankee dialect, I did not act without forethought. It had long seemed to me that the great vice of American writing and speaking was a studied want of simplicity, that we were in danger of coming to look on our mother-tongue as a dead language, to be sought in the grammar and dictionary rather than in the heart, and that our only chance of escape was by seeking it at its living sources among those who were, as Scottowe says of Major-General Gibbons, 'divinely illiterate.' President Lincoln, the only really great public man whom these latter days have seen, was great also in this, that he was master—witness his speech at Gettysburg—of a truly masculine English, classic, because it was of no special period, and level at once to the highest and lowest of his countrymen. I learn from the highest authority that his favorite reading was in Shakespeare and Milton, to which, of course, the Bible should be added. But whoever should read the debates in Congress might fancy himself present at a meeting of the city council of some city of Southern Gaul in the decline of the Empire, where barbarians with a Latin varnish emulated each other in being more than Ciceronian. Whether it be want of culture, for the highest outcome of that is simplicity, or for whatever reason, it is certain that very few American writers or speakers wield their native language with the directness, precision, and force that are common as the day in the mother country. We use it like Scotsmen, not as if it belonged to us, but as if we wished to prove that we belonged to it, by showing our intimacy with its written rather than with its spoken dialect. And yet all the while our popular idiom is racy with life and vigor and originality, bucksome (as Milton used the word) to our new occasions, and proves itself no mere graft by sending up new suckers from the old root in spite of us. It is only from its roots in the living generations of men that a language can be reinforced with fresh vigor for its needs; what may be called a literate dialect grows ever more and more pedantic and foreign, till it becomes at last as unfitting a vehicle for living thought as monkish Latin. That we should all be made to talk like books is the danger with which we are threatened by the Universal Schoolmaster, who does his best to enslave the minds and memories of his victims to what he esteems the best models of English composition, that is to say, to the writers whose style is faultily correct and has no blood-warmth in it. No language after it has faded into *diction*, none that cannot suck up the feeding juices secreted for it in the rich mother-earth of common folk, can bring forth a sound and lusty book. True vigor and heartiness of phrase do not pass from page to page, but from man to man, where the brain is kindled and the lips suppled by downright living interests and by passion in its very throe. Language is the soil of thought, and our own especially is a rich leaf-mould, the slow deposit of ages, the shed foliage of feeling, fancy, and imagination, which has suffered an earth-change, that the vocal forest, as Howell called it, may clothe itself anew with living green. There is death in the dictionary; and, where language is too strictly limited by convention, the ground for expression to grow in is limited also; and we get a *potted* literature, Chinese dwarfs instead of healthy trees. . . .

"The quality of exaggeration has often been remarked on as typical of American character, and especially of American humor. In Dr. Petri's *Gedrängtes Handbuch der Fremdwörter*, we are told that the word *humbug* is commonly used for the exaggerations of the North-Americans. To be sure, one would be tempted to think the dream of Columbus half fulfilled, and that Europe had found in the West a nearer way to Orientalism, at least in diction. But it seems to me that a great deal of what is set down as mere extravagance is more fitly to be called intensity and picturesqueness, symptoms of the imaginative faculty in full health and strength, though producing, as yet, only the raw and formless material in which poetry is to work. By and by, perhaps, the world will see it fashioned into poem and picture, and Europe, which will be hard pushed for originality erelong, may have to thank us for a new sensation. The French continue to find Shakespeare exaggerated because he treated English just as our country-folk do when they speak of a 'steep price,' or say that they 'freeze to' a thing. The first postulate of an original literature is that a people should use their language instinctively and unconsciously, as if it were a lively part of their growth and personality, not as the mere torpid boon of education or inheritance."

In becoming "one of the court-fools of King Demos," Lowell said he had in mind "serious things." He used laughter as a weapon to modify public opinion of contemporary events. (These events, as they relate to *The Biglow Papers*, have been discussed in detail in notes—to which I am gratefully indebted—by F. B. Williams, printed in the Cambridge Edition of Lowell's *Poetical Works*, pp. 471–479.) As a satiric humorist Lowell carried on certain traditions embodied in earlier American humorists such as Seba Smith (author of Jack Downing's papers, collected as *My Thirty Years out of the Senate*) and Thomas Chandler Haliburton (Sam Slick). Hosea, like Downing and Slick, was a rustic and illiterate Yankee, who said wise and comical things in dialect about politics and who indulged in apt caricatures. Lowell himself refers in *The Biglow Papers*, First Series, No. VIII, to Enoch Timbertoes:

"'Then you call me "Timbertoes"—thet's wut the people likes,
Sutthin combinin' morril truth with phrases sech ez strikes.'"

(See Bibliography for scholarly studies of his relation to earlier humorists by Miss Jeanette Tandy, and of his use of the Yankee dialect by Grandgent, Heil, and Miss Killheffer.) It is interesting to notice that Lowell, who is popularly regarded today as a snobbish and academic Brahmin of "The Genteel Tradition," actually gave us one of our best and most sympathetic portraits of rustic common sense in Hosea Biglow. In general Lowell's shift from sentiment to humor as a weapon in his humanitarian campaign is an index to his broadening perspective and masculinity.

Satire of contemporary political events seldom outlives the memory of the events satirized, and the continued popularity of *The Biglow Papers* is probably accounted for in part by the fact that in them Lowell departed from most of his predecessors by creating three characters and arranging them so as to produce a credible piece of fiction. For example, Birdofredum Sawin, a study in degeneration and disillusionment, is thrown into relief, in his delightful rascality, by the pedantic Parson Wilbur. The chief character, however, is of course Hosea Biglow, the embodiment of "homely common-sense vivified and heated by conscience." Whereas Jack Downing was a politician, Hosea is a farmer, with a farmer's homely illustrations at the tip of his tongue. As W. D. Howells, the novelist, concluded (*Atlantic*, XIX, 123, Jan., 1867), "It is not as mere satire, however, that the *Biglow Papers* are to be valued. The First and Second Series form a creative fiction of unique excellence." J. R. Dennet (*Nation*, III, 387, Nov., 1866) agreed that Lowell's characters are "so life-like and, in the main, so true to nature—so good as individuals and as types that we know not where in literature to look for . . . others that excel them." Incidentally Lowell not only illustrated himself his theory that our literature should be vivid and homely and strongly flavored with the soil, but he also, as editor of the *Atlantic*, encouraged the writing of short stories which heralded the realistic movement in American fiction.

Page 447. A LETTER FROM MR. EZEKIEL BIGLOW OF JAALAM TO THE HON. JOSEPH T. BUCKINGHAM

It should be noted here that Lowell in this humanitarian period (1846) advocates through Hosea both pacifism (l. 33) and disunion (l. 154), attitudes which he reversed in his next period. Hosea, riled at the attempt to recruit soldiers for the Mexican War to extend slavery, is created by Lowell to express his own views as opposed to those of Birdofredum Sawin, who enlists and reports his gradual disillusionment regarding the glory of war as a result of his manifold sufferings, including the loss of a leg, an arm, four fingers, one eye, etc. (See *Biglow Papers*, Series One, Nos. II and VIII.) Note Hosea's absolute appeal to the religious conscience of the inheritors of Puritanism and his constant reference to details of the farmer's life. His rusticity is thrown into relief by Parson Wilbur's pedantic introductory letter and his postscript.

Page 449. THE DEBATE IN THE SENNIT

Captain Drayton and his mate Sayres tried, in April, 1848, to kidnap seventy-seven slaves from Washington. The slaves were recaptured and returned to the South, and Drayton and Sayres, barely escaping from a mob, were sentenced to long terms of imprisonment. When Senator Hale of New Hampshire introduced a resolution (April 20, 1848) suggesting sympathy with the slaves, Senator Calhoun said he "would as soon argue with a maniac from Bedlam" as with Mr. Hale, and rested the case on the Constitution, which, in safeguarding property, was interpreted as sanctioning the right to slaves. Henry S. Foote, Senator from Mississippi from 1847 to 1852, said that Mr. Hale was "as guilty as if he had committed highway robbery," and that he could not advance ten miles within the state of Mississippi before "he would grace one of the tallest trees of the forest with a rope around his neck, with the approbation of all honest and patriotic citizens." These expressions illustrate the heatedness with which the debate was then carried on in the Senate. (For Calhoun's views see his *Disquisition on Government* [1851], his *Discourse on the Constitution and the Government of the United States* [1851], F. Bancroft's *Calhoun and the South Carolina Nullification Movement* [Baltimore: 1928], and V. L. Parrington's *The Romantic Revolution* [New York: 1927, pp. 69–82]. Briefly, it may be said that Calhoun regarded the contract of the individual states in entering into the union as revocable when their interests were violated; Webster and Lincoln held this contract irrevocable, and the abolitionists did not admit that property could rightfully include a human being. The latter appealed to the "higher law"—the moral law—as opposed to the Constitution.)

Note Lowell's dire irony in setting the debate to a nursery rime, and his skill in making Calhoun's arguments seem ridiculous. See Lowell's similar method in "What Mr. Robinson Thinks," *Biglow Papers*, First Series, No. III.

During this humanitarian period when he scorned the past and traditional restraints such as checks and balances, Lowell regarded the Constitution as a "Sacred Parasol" to be interposed "wherever there seemed danger from the hostile incursions of Light" (Lowell's *Anti-Slavery Papers*, I, 85–92).

Page 452. THE PIOUS EDITOR'S CREED

This poem was occasioned by the fact that although Southerners, such as Senator Foote, glorified the revolution in France as marking the downfall of "the age of tyranny and slavery," the attorney for Drayton and Sayres who quoted these words in defence of his clients was silenced by the judge for trying to "endanger our institutions" with words which were "inflammatory."

Lowell himself wrote a great deal for anti-slavery journals, notably the *Anti-Slavery Standard*, and he exalted the journalist's responsibility and power.

Page 453. A LETTER FROM A CANDIDATE . . .

The colorless Zachary Taylor was nominated in 1848 for the presidency by the Whigs, who wished to draw votes from both North and South through an avoidance of any statement as to policy. Early in 1847, when the *Cincinnati Signal* inquired regarding Taylor's attitude toward the Wilmot Proviso, he stated his position in such a two-faced manner that he was interpreted as being on both sides at once. (This Proviso was a measure for excluding slavery from Texas which passed the House but not the Senate.) The refusal of the Whigs to make the Wilmot Proviso a campaign issue resulted in many voters deserting the Whigs for the Free-Soil Party, which eventually evolved into the Republican Party.

This is one of the most satisfying satires on fence-straddling and hypocrisy in the English language.

Page 459. THE VISION OF SIR LAUNFAL

Lowell's first mention of this poem is in a letter to Briggs, dated February 1, 1848, where he speaks of it as "a sort of story, and more likely to be popular than what I write generally. Maria thinks very highly of it." It was published first in book form Dec. 17, 1848, after *The Biglow Papers, First Series*, and in the same year as *Poems, Second Series* and *A Fable for Critics*. It was the work of this Annus Mirabilis which determined his recognition as poet, political satirist, humorist, and critic. Shortly after the publication of "The Vision of Sir Launfal," Lowell wrote Briggs: "I walked to Watertown [to the wedding of Mrs. Lowell's sister] over the snow with the new moon before me and a sky exactly like that in Page's evening landscape. Orion was rising behind me, and, as I stood on the hill just before you enter the village, the stillness of the fields around me was delicious, broken only by the tinkle of a little brook which runs too swiftly for Frost to catch it. My picture of the brook in 'Sir Launfal' was drawn from it. But why do I send you this description—like the bones of a chicken I had picked? Simply because I was so happy as I stood there, and felt so sure of doing something that would justify my friends. But why do I not say that I *have* done something? I believe I have done better than the world knows yet, but the past seems so little compared with the future. . . . I am the first poet who has endeavored to express the American Idea, and I shall be popular by and by."—Norton, *Letters*, I, 148.

According to H. E. Scudder (*Biography*, I, 268): "As Tennyson threw into his retelling of Arthurian romance a moral sense, so Lowell, also a moralist in his poetic apprehension, made a parable of his tale, and, in the broadest interpretation of democracy, sang of the levelling of all ranks in a common divine humanity. There is a subterranean passage connecting the 'Biglow Papers' with 'Sir Launfal'; it is the holy zeal which attacks slavery issuing in this fable of a beautiful charity, Christ in the guise of a beggar." Mr. Scudder thinks the invention may "have been suggested by Tennyson's 'Sir Galahad,' but the verses in the poem which linger longest in the mind are not those connected with the fable, but rather the full-throated burst of song in praise of June."

For an able analysis of the technique of the poem, see Allen's *American Prosody*, pp. 256–258. Mr. Allen shows that "No American poet had hitherto achieved more varied and subtle effects with meter, and indeed Lowell scarcely ever succeeded so well again himself." Beginning with the idea of a "musing organist" who "lets his fingers wander as they list," Lowell begins with iambic pentameter, turns to octosyllabic couplets, shifts to irregular four-stress verse with frequent trisyllabic substitutions, and in certain places varies from four to ten syllables to the line. Lowell used double rhyme more than any of his predecessors. Mr. Allen regards this poem as the chief illustration of Lowell's distinctive skill as a prosodist in introducing into American poetry a greater metrical freedom, melody, and harmony, secured chiefly by a more varied placing of accents and the combining of different kinds of feet to produce a suggestiveness of tone and cadence.

Page 464. A FABLE FOR CRITICS

Lowell's comment on his progress in composing this *Fable*, at first published anonymously, may be found in his letters of November 13, 1847, and March 26 and May 12, 1848. One of the earlier of our "surveys" of American literature, it illustrates his youthful contempt for tradition ("Forget Europe wholly") and also his gradual turn from sentimentalism to the critical temper which was to be developed so finely in his long series of mature critical essays. (On parallel contemporary "surveys" see E. C. Hassold, *American Literary History before the Civil War*, Chicago, 1935.) Many of Lowell's thumbnail sketches show surprising critical insight, and many of his conclusions have been supported by recent exhaustive studies.

ll. 73 ff., on Emerson. Note that, like Holmes (p. 592, above), Lowell emphasizes Emerson's balance, his union of idealism and practicality: he is "Plotinus-Montaigne." See Lowell's essay on "Emerson the Lecturer," and his comparison and contrast of Carlyle and Emerson in his essay on Thoreau, *Writings*, I, 363–368, where he emphasizes "the tendency of the one toward Authority and of the other toward Independency."

ll. 165 ff., on Thoreau. For a scholarly discussion of Lowell's failure to do Thoreau justice (especially in his essay on Thoreau in *Writings*, I, and in his essay on Thoreau's *Week* in Lowell's *The Round Table*), see Austin Warren's "Lowell on Thoreau," *Studies in Philology*, XXVII, 442–461 (July, 1930).

ll. 181 ff., on Bryant. In a letter of May 12, 1848, Lowell wrote of this passage: "Bryant is funny, and as fair as I could make it, immitigably just. Indeed I have endeavored to be so in all." The curious discrepancy between Lowell's view of Bryant's "iceolation" and Bryant's own glorification of poetic "fire" in his poem "The Poet" may be accounted for in part by the fact that Lowell wrote in 1848 before Bryant had been stirred by the issues leading to the Civil War, while Bryant's poem recorded his feeling in 1860.

ll. 242 ff., on Whittier. As fellow-abolitionists Lowell and Whittier always had cordial relations, and when Lowell founded the *Atlantic* he published many of Whittier's poems, often suggesting improvements in phrasing. See, for example, his suggestions regarding "Skipper Ireson's Ride," p. 809, above. Lowell's several sympathetic reviews of Whittier's poems will be found listed in the Whittier bibliography, p. 800, above. Lowell not only recognized Whittier's genius as a balladist of local themes but he saw that he transcended his Quaker sect in his broad humanity and his treatment of the universal aspects of man's destiny.

ll. 278–303. Note the manner in which this poem represents Lowell's first humanitarian period not only in its contempt for European traditionalism but in its high tribute to abolitionists.

ll. 304 ff., on Hawthorne. For an able elaboration of the view that Hawthorne is "a Puritan Tieck," an unstable compound of stern moralist and fantastic romanticist, see W. C. Brownell's essay in *American Prose Masters*. Lowell regarded Hawthorne as having "the rarest creative imagination of the century, the rarest in some ideal respects since Shakespeare" (*Writings*, I, 365). He planned to write the biography of Hawthorne for the American Men of Letters Series.

ll. 321 ff., on Cooper. Elsewhere (*Writings*, II, 5) Lowell wrote with reference to American life and our literature: "There was, indeed, one poetic side to the existence otherwise so narrow and practical; and to have conceived this, however partially, is the one original and American thing in Cooper. This diviner glimpse illumines the lives of our Daniel Boones, the man of civilization and old-world ideas confronted with our forest solitudes,—confronted, too, for the first time, with his real self, and so led gradually to disentangle the original substance of his manhood from the artificial results of culture. Here was our new Adam of the wilderness, forced to name anew, not the visible creation of God, but the invisible creation of man, in those forms that lie at the base of social institutions, so sensibly moulding personal character and controlling individual action. Here is the protagonist of our New World epic, a figure as poetic as that of Achilles, as ideally representative as that of Don Quixote, as romantic in its relation to our homespun and plebian myths as Arthur in his to the mailed and plumed cycle of chivalry." See the admirable essay in H. S. Canby's *Classic Americans*, pp. 97–142.

l. 361. *Than Adams the parson or Primrose the vicar.* The reference is to Parson Adams in Joseph Fielding's *Joseph Andrews* and to Oliver Goldsmith's Dr. Primrose in *The Vicar of Wakefield*—

two of the most memorably humanized characters of English fiction.

l. 367. *truth in his strictures*. In Cooper's *American Democrat* and other books of social criticism he attacked the uncouthness and lack of individuality and distinction in equalitarian democracy. His point of view was essentially Federalistic. For full discussion see R. E. Spiller's Introduction to *Cooper* in the American Writers Series.

ll. 374 ff. Note Lowell's ardent nationalism and his contempt for European traditionalism.

ll. 436 ff., on Miranda (Margaret Fuller). Lowell had been much hurt by Margaret Fuller's belittling of him in her essay "American Literature," and he was tempted to retaliate, although in a letter of May 12, 1848, he said, "With her I have been perfectly good-humored, but I have a fancy that what I say will stick uncomfortably. It will make you laugh." Margaret Fuller was an ardent Transcendentalist, an editor of *The Dial*, and a disseminator of German philosophy. See her *Memoirs* (edited by Emerson, Channing, and Clarke, 1852) and Helen N. McMaster's *Margaret Fuller as a Literary Critic* (Buffalo: 1928).

ll. 463 ff., on Poe. For a more extended discussion see Lowell's essay on Poe in *Graham's Magazine*, XXVI, 49–53 (Feb., 1845). Poe reviewed *The Fable*, attacking its abolitionism. In many ways Lowell and Poe were antithetical: contrast their critical creeds as summarized in Foerster's *American Criticism*.

ll. 596 ff., on Holmes. Although eventually Lowell and Holmes, colleagues on the Harvard faculty, were good friends, being the wits of The Saturday Club, Lowell had originally tried as a humanitarian to reprimand Holmes, ten years his senior, for his apparent indifference to reforms. See Holmes's reply (Morse's *Life and Letters*, I, 295–303) to a letter from Lowell defending himself against the latter's criticism of his indifference to (1) pacifism, (2) abolition, (3) temperance, (4) the poor, and (5) reform in general. It should be noted that Lowell's characterization in *A Fable* was written ten years before Holmes's *Autocrat*, which Lowell persuaded him to contribute serially to his newly founded *Atlantic Monthly* in 1857.

ll. 618 ff. On Lowell and his "whole bale of *isms*." This self-criticism illustrates that as early as 1848 Lowell had begun to see the poetic perils of the didactic humanitarianism to which he had been addicted. In 1849 he severed his connection with the *Anti-Slavery Standard*, for which he had written steadily in favor of abolitionism. In a letter of January 23, 1850, he summarizes his "mental and moral latitude and longitude," convinced that he is "farther eastward and nearer morning than ever hitherto." "I begin to feel that I must enter on a new year of my apprenticeship. My poems have thus far had a regular and natural sequence. First, Love and the mere happiness of existence beginning to be conscious of itself, then Freedom—both being the sides of Beauty presented to me—and now I am going to try more *wholly* after Beauty herself. Next, if I live, I shall try to present Life as I have seen it. In the 'Nooning' I shall not even glance towards Reform. . . . Certainly I shall not grind for any Philistines, whether Reformers or Conservatives. I find that Reform cannot take up the whole of me, and I am sure that eyes were given us to look about us with sometimes, and not to be always looking forward." Lowell was coming to see life in broader perspective and to be indifferent to fanaticism and propaganda and an intolerance of the past. Travel and extended reading were soon to give him a greater responsiveness to what was excellent in the culture of other times and lands. And the death of his wife and his children was about to suggest to the hitherto complacent reformer that before the most profound of human sufferings and sorrows merely outward legislative reform stands impotent.

Page 476. ODE TO HAPPINESS

This poem was not published until 1861 (*Atlantic Monthly*, VIII, 365 ff.), and should not be confused with Lowell's poem "Happiness" (*Atlantic*, I, 685, April, 1858). The "Ode to Happiness" occupies a place in Lowell's intellectual development somewhat analogous to that of the "Ode to Duty" in Wordsworth's development: both embody a recantation of the poets' earlier philosophy, and a turn toward conservatism. Lowell, following his disillusionment with outward reform and his grief at the death of his two daughters and his wife, is confident that, although the capricious "half-earthly" happiness of boyhood has fled, Tranquillity, her "elder sister, . . . born of the immortals," will come to him who matches impulse with control: passion and sin, regarded as of inward origin, are to be matched by "culture wise" and renunciation. The poem marks Lowell's turn from an outward environmentalism and a contempt for traditionalism toward a reverence for traditionalism and an insistence upon inward control and self-mastery.

Page 477. THE WASHERS OF THE SHROUD

This important poem, first published in the *Atlantic*, VIII, 641–643 (November, 1861), is comparable in its impassioned Unionism to Longfellow's "The Building of the Ship"—in fact both men use the same figure to represent the Union. Regarding the composition of this poem Lowell wrote his friend C. E. Norton (*Letters*, I, 318): "I had just two days allowed me by Fields for the November *Atlantic*, and I got it done. It had been in my head some time, and when you see it you will remember my having spoken to you about it. Indeed, I owe it to you, for the hint came from one of those books of Souvestre's you lent me —the Breton legends. The writing took hold of me enough to leave me tired out and to satisfy me entirely as to what was the original of my head and back pains. But whether it is good or not, I am not yet far enough off to say. But *do* like it, if you can. Fields says it is 'splendid,' with tears in his eyes—but then I read it to him, which is half the battle. I began it as a lyric, but it *would* be too aphoristic for that, and finally flatly refused to sing at any price. So I submitted, took to pentameters, and only hope the thoughts are good enough to be preserved in the ice of the colder and almost glacier-slow measure. I think I have done well—in some stanzas at least—and not wasted words."

This poem is much more philosophical than Longfellow's "The Building of the Ship," and its significance in the growth of Lowell's mind is thrown into sharper relief when we compare its ideas with his earlier democratic radicalism. First, the former pacifist who had said in 1846, "Ez fer war, I call it murder" (p. 448, col. 1, l. 33), now knows that "the sheathed blade may rust with darker sin" (p. 479, l. 100). This recoil from pacifism is also expressed in the "Commemoration Ode" (p. 492, col. 2, ll. 143 ff.), and in *The Biglow Papers*, Second Series (*Works*, VIII, 264). Second, the former equalitarian democrat who had sung of "levelling of all ranks in a common humanity" and who had tended to sentimentalize religion (cf. "Rhoecus" and "The Vision of Sir Launfal"), now sees temporal law as sanctioned by eternal law—like Emerson's Over-Soul—whose violation invites our destruction. Nerved by his Puritan heritage (cf. "New England Two Centuries Ago," *Works*, II, 1–76), Lowell concluded, "Every human government is bound to make its laws so far resemble His that they shall be uniform, certain, and unquestionable in their operation; and this it can do only by a timely show of power, and by an appeal to that authority which is of divine right, inasmuch as its office is to maintain that order which is the single attribute of the Infinite Reason" (*Works*, V, 74). This is the sublime mood, then, which inspired "The Washers of the Shroud" with its impassioned conviction that America's doom depends not on democratic voting, on "Opinion's wind," but on an intelligent and purposeful obedience to "the Law before all time":

"Three roots bear up Dominion: Knowledge, Will—
These twain are strong, but stronger yet the third,—
Obedience."

In the third place, the former radical who had urged revolt from the past, who had insisted that one cannot unlock "the Future's portal with the Past's blood-rusted key" (p. 446, col. 1, l. 90), now holds that "Time Was unlocks the riddle of Time Is" (l. 81), showing an increasing respect for tradition. For full discussion see Bibliography under Jenkins and Clark.

Page 479. JONATHAN TO JOHN

Parson Wilbur's letter introducing "Mason and Slidell: A Yankee Idyll" discusses the "idyll" as a form which involves rustic language and the description of real scenery and manners—illustrating Lowell's trend toward localism and nationalism in literary theory. This letter also contains a resentful discussion of England's tendency to favor the South in the Civil War, a tendency which culminated in England's preparation for war after the Unionist Captain Wilkes had removed from an English vessel Mason and Slidell who were going to England and France as commissioners to seek aid for the South. (For backgrounds see F. L. Owsley's *King Cotton Diplomacy*, Chicago, 1925, and L. M. Sears's *John Slidell*, Durham, N. C., 1925.) Note that Lowell's growing nationalism was accentuated by England's insolence at this time.

This letter by Parson Wilbur is followed by a poem, omitted here, describing Hosea Biglow's dream in which, while at the Concord Battle Ground, he overhears an argument between Concord Bridge (representing resentment against England) and the Bunker Hill Monument (representing those who urge tolerance toward England). The argument is followed by an eloquent prophecy of America's greatness.

The poem "Jonathan to John" is effective in its mingled expression of outraged feelings (ll. 11–13), disdainful ridicule (ll. 96–97) of England's self-interest, advocacy of America's forgiveness, and insistence on the righteousness of her cause. Cf. Holmes's earlier poem on the estrangement between the North and South, "Brother Jonathan's Lament for Sister Caroline," p. 568, below.

Page 481. A MESSAGE OF JEFF DAVIS IN SECRET SESSION

Mr. Wilbur's letter introducing this poem by Hosea Biglow was dated March 10, 1862. In this poem, an imaginary speech by the President of the Confederacy, Lowell satirizes the difficulty of the South in securing funds to preserve its status as a nation founded on the Secessionists' doctrine "Thet a Gov'ment's fust right is to tumble to pieces." Needless to say, he is grossly unfair to Davis in portraying him as an arch-hypocrite.

l. 92. *Once . . my own Massissippi.* The chances of Davis in securing recognition of his confederate nation in England were lessened by the fact that in the period of 1830–1840 he had strongly advocated the repudiation of Mississippi's debt which was mainly owed to England.

l. 155. *But Roanoke, Bufort, Millspring.* These were strategic points whose capture by the North early in 1862 deprived the South of Port Royal, South Carolina, one of its finest harbors.

l. 163. *Oh, ef we hed on'y jes' gut Reecognition.* It is said that only the timely news of the defeat of the South at Gettysburg prevented England from recognizing the independence of the Confederacy.

Compare and contrast this poem with Freneau's poems ridiculing the pretensions of England in the Revolution.

Page 484. SUNTHIN' IN THE PASTORAL LINE

Lines 1–107 illustrate the fact that, in keeping with Lowell's nationalism of this period, he opposed having poets draw on foreign countries (l. 16) in their use of nature. His practice of treating the flowers and birds of his native locality should be compared with the rich knowledge of nature which he reveals in his essay on "My Garden Acquaintance." (For full discussion see N. Foerster on Lowell in *Nature in American Literature.*) It will be recalled that this plea that our poets treat the American scene goes back at least as far as Freneau.

In Parson Wilbur's letter introducing this poem he had developed the idea that the New England Puritans "showed remarkable practical sagacity as statesmen and founders." In the poem Hosea dreams, while asleep in the schoolhouse, that a Pilgrim Father appeared and said that just as he had helped behead the tyrannical Charles I, so now Hosea, his descendant, must overthrow slavery as "the fangs an' thinkin' head" of tyranny. This portion of the poem should be read in the light of Lowell's essay "New England Two Centuries Ago," in which he traces his view of a coercive federated republic back to the Puritan tradition of civil liberty; conversely, in his essays on "Rebellion: Its Causes and Consequences" (1864) and "Rousseau and the Sentimentalists" (1867) he traces the doctrine of secession, which he identifies with anarchy, back to Jefferson, author of the Kentucky Resolutions (1799), and to Jefferson's "father," the French radical, Rousseau. Lowell says that the Puritans "knew that liberty in the hands of feeble-minded and unreasoning persons . . . means nothing less . . . than downright chaos." "Sober, earnest, and thoughtful men, it was no Utopia, no New Atlantis, no realization of a splendid dream, which they had at heart, but the establishment of the divine principle of Authority on the common interest and the common consent; the making, by a contribution from the free-will of all, a power which should curb and guide the free-will of each for the general good" (*Writings*, II, 9–10).

l. 303. *The trouble is to 'mancipate the white.* Cf. Emerson's "Ode, inscribed to W. H. Channing," p. 211, above.

Page 488. LATEST VIEWS OF MR. BIGLOW

With this poem Lowell announced the death of Parson Wilbur. The unfinished letter which the Parson left, dated Dec. 24, 1862, contained the following passage, expressing Lowell's own views at that time: "Though I believe Slavery to have been the cause of it [the war], by so thoroughly demoralizing Northern politicks for its own purposes as to give opportunity and hope to treason, yet I would not have our thought and purpose diverted from their true object,—the maintenance of the idea of Government. We are not merely suppressing an enormous riot, but contending for the possibility of permanent order coexisting with democratical fickleness; and while I would not superstitiously venerate form to the sacrifice of substance, neither would I forget that an adherence to precedent and prescription can alone give that continuity and coherence under a democratical constitution which are inherent in the person of a despotick monarch and the selfishness of an aristocratical class. *Stet pro ratione voluntas* is as dangerous in a majority as in a tyrant."

At this time Lincoln and his policies were meeting with strong opposition. Horatio Seymour (l. 56) had been elected governor of New York on the Democratic Party's platform which denounced practically all of Lincoln's measures. Seymour's influence is supposed to have been partly responsible for the Draft Riot which took place in New York in July, 1863. Although Lincoln's first inaugural address early in 1861 had disclaimed any intention of interfering with slavery in its original stronghold, he became convinced that the nation could not exist half slave and half free, and on September 22, 1862, he issued a proclamation (l. 122) giving warning that unless certain conditions were fulfilled he would emancipate all the slaves of the States in rebellion on the first day of the next year. In the ensuing election opposition to this policy was so strong that the Republicans were defeated in New York, Pennsylvania, Ohio, Indiana, and Illinois. However, the support of New England, the West, and the Border Slave States gave Lincoln a majority which enabled him to emancipate the slaves. In this great crisis Lowell's "pep-talk" denouncing "Conciliation" (l. 42) and demanding "pisonmad, pig-headed fightin'" (l. 96) in support of Lincoln's "grand" policy, was particularly timely and effective. The great popularity of *The Biglow Papers* and their demand for decisive action must have heartened Lincoln in those dark days when, as Lowell said, systems and not parties were wrestling (l. 34).

ll. 145–148. Note that Lowell's earlier a priori utopianism has given way to a more sober recognition of the necessity of taking into account not only theories but facts and concrete circumstances. Cf. also "Sunthin' in the Pastoral Line" (l. 274), where he says "Th' idees hev arms an' legs." Compare this realistic, practical view with that of Lowell's idol, Burke, who denounced the French Revolutionists because they were logical abstractionists who ignored expediency and historical relativism and circumstances.

Page 490. ODE RECITED AT THE HARVARD COMMEMORATION

Although this sublime "Ode" embodied thoughts which had been growing slowly but steadily in Lowell's mind, it is possible that he derived immediate inspiration for it from a poem read by George Henry Boker before the Phi Beta Kappa Society at Harvard University on July 20, 1865, as Dr. A. H. Quinn has suggested ("George Henry Boker—Playright and Patriot," *Scribner's Magazine*, LXXIII, 701 ff. [June, 1923]).

Since few casual readers grasp the full meaning of the poem, it may not be amiss to note here the sequence of thought in the successive stanzas:

I. Compared to verse written in life-blood, "weak-winged is song," yet "feathered words" may preserve the memory of heroic deeds.

II. The heroic deeds and the sacrifice of lives here commemorated were inspired by the passion for Truth for which Harvard stands.

III. Yet Truth not externalized, "made whole with deed," is futile. (Cf. Emerson on "Action" in "The American Scholar," and cf. Carlyle.)

IV. In a world of constant change, "What is there that abides . . . ?" (Cf. Lowell's earlier celebration of change, progress, and revolt from the past.) Yet the life of man sacrificed for an ideal gives our life of change and oblivion "a high immunity from Night," a "noble permanence" which "haunts the soul."

V. Peace is not ignoble, but man should be ready when his Ideal is "foe-beset" to "front a lie in arms and not to yield," whether in the closet or the field. (Cf. Lowell's earlier pacifism—"Ez fer war, I call it murder.")

VI. Lincoln exemplified the ideal of the courageous, self-poised warrior against falsehood, molded by "the unexhausted West," the American frontier, with "nothing of Europe here."

VII. As long as man is loyal to "some more inspiring goal / Outside of Self," to "some ideal Good"—"Freedom, Law, Country" —man shall reverence sacrifice for its preservation.

VIII. Let us salute and honor "the sacred dead" who are "secure from change in their high-hearted ways."

IX. In the face of Oblivion and Change, the "Soul resents / Such short-lived service" and claims "a more divine investiture" in "a new imperial race." (Cf. stanza IV.)

X. Nobler than Europe's feudal rewards is "that plain civic wreath" given the brave by "a rescued Nation" which sets "her heel on treason."

XI. "Lift the heart," for "'tis no Man we celebrate," but "the pith and marrow of a Nation." She is saved, and she "sends all her handmaid armies back to spin."

XII. He calls the country to "prayer and praise," for the preservation of the united nation.

Regarding the composition and form of this "Ode," Lowell wrote James B. Thayer: "But what I wished to say a word to you about (since you are so generous in your judgment) is the measures I have chosen in these [*Three Memorial Poems*] as well as the 'Commemoration Ode.' I am induced to this by reading in an article on Cowley copied into the *Living Age* from the *Cornhill* (and a very good article too, in the main) the following passage, 'As lately as our own day' (*my* ear would require '*So* lately as,' by the way) 'Mr. Lowell's "Commemoration Ode" is a specimen of the formless poem of unequal lines and broken stanzas supposed to be in the manner of Pindar, but truly the descendant of our royalist poet's "majestick numbers."' Now, whatever my other shortcomings (and they are plenty, as none knows better than I), want of reflection is not one of them. The poems were all intended for public recitation. That was the first thing to be considered. I suppose my ear (from long and painful practice on ΦΒΚ poems) has more technical experience in this than almost any. The least tedious measure is the rhymed heroic, but this, too, palls unless relieved by passages of wit or even mere fun. A long series of uniform stanzas (I am always speaking of public recitation) with regularly recurring rhymes produces somnolence among the men and a desperate resort to their fans on the part of the women. No method has yet been invented by which the train of thought or feeling can be shunted off from the epical to the lyrical track. My ears have been jolted often enough over the sleepers on such occasions to know that. I know *something* (of course an American can't know much) about Pindar. But *his* odes had the advantage of being chanted. Now, my problem was to contrive a measure which should not be tedious by uniformity, which should vary with varying moods, in which the transitions (including those of the voice) should be managed without jar. I at first thought of mixed rhymed and blank verses of unequal measures, like those in the choruses of *Samson Agonistes*, which are in the main masterly. Of course, Milton *deliberately* departed from that stricter form of the Greek Chorus to which it was bound quite as much (I suspect) by the law of its musical accompaniment as by any sense of symmetry. I wrote some stanzas of the 'Commemoration Ode' on this theory at first, leaving some verses without a rhyme to match. But my ear was better pleased when the rhyme, coming at a longer interval, as a far-off echo rather than instant reverberation, produced the same effect almost, and yet was grateful by unexpectedly recalling an association and faint reminiscence of consonance. I think I have succeeded pretty well, and if you try reading aloud I believe you would agree with me. The sentiment of the 'Concord Ode' demanded a larger proportion of lyrical movements, of course, than the others. Harmony, without sacrifice of melody, was what I had mainly in view."—Norton, *Letters*, II, 189–190.

Page 496. THE CATHEDRAL

The Cathedral, which first appeared in book form at Christmas, 1869, as well as in the *Atlantic* for January, 1870, was first entitled *A Day at Chartres*. Lowell described it to Howells as having "a bit of clean carving here and there, a solid buttress or two, and perhaps a gleam through painted glass . . ." (*Letters*, II, 35). Of the composition of the poem, Lowell said, "I wrote it in pencil, then copied it out in ink, and worked over it as I never worked over anything before. I may fairly say that there is not a word in it which I have not thought, not an objection which I did not foresee and maturely consider." "I hope it is good," he wrote Miss Norton, "for it fairly trussed me at last and bore me up as high as my poor lungs will bear into the heaven of invention. I was happy writing it, and so steeped in it that if I had written to you it would have been in blank verse. It is a kind of religious poem . . ." (*Letters*, II, 38). Ruskin wrote of it, "The main substance of the poem is most precious to me, and its separate lines sometimes unbetterable." According to H. E. Scudder (*Biography*, II, 141–142), "Lowell here builds upon the foundation of human life a fane of worship, and in the speculations which discriminate between the conventional and the free aspirations of the soul, constructs out of living stones a house of prayer. Nor is there absent that capricious mood which carved grotesques upon the under side of the benches at which worshippers kneeled, so that when the reader, borne along by the high thought, stumbles over such lines as

'Who, meeting Caesar's self, would slap his back,
Call him "Old Horse" and challenge to a drink,'

he may, if he will, console himself with the reflection that the most aspiring Gothic carries like grimacing touches within its majestic walls

'Imagination's very self in stone.'

That is the epithet Lowell bestows on Chartres Cathedral, and in the few spirited lines in which he contrasts the Greek with the Goth, and hints at the historic evolution of the latter, he is in a large way reflecting the native constitution of his own mind,

'Still climbing, luring fancy still to climb.'"

Devoted as Lowell was to the Greek tradition and to his native Puritanism, he confessed "a singular sympathy with what are known as the Middle Ages," finding it more difficult "to bridge over the gulf to Paganism." His study of the Middle Ages which crystallized in his great essay on Dante (*Works*, IV, 118–264) led him to recognize the values of Catholicism—"she has never lost sight of the truth" that man is "composed of the sum of flesh and spirit"; she is "the only church that has been loyal to the heart and soul of man, that has clung to her faith in the imagination," with a wholesome recognition of the perils of surrendering everything to "the iconoclast Understanding," the "blunder" of Protestantism. Nevertheless, in this scientific "age that blots out life with question marks," he confesses "'tis irrecoverable, that ancient faith," "its forms are weariness." Reluctantly, then, since "each age must worship its own thought of God," since the contemporary religion of nature has turned out to be "but our own conceit of what we see," Lowell takes refuge in the doctrine of immanence and he finds "inward surety" in faith in a depersonalized deity "so far above, yet in and of me," a deity revealed to the inward man in every impulse "that liberates and lifts, / In all that humbles, sweetens, and consoles."

The Cathedral should be compared with Tennyson's *In Memoriam* and especially with Arnold's "Stanzas from the Grande Chartreuse" (1855), which deals with much the same problem of the quest for religious certitude by those later nineteenth-century thinkers

"Wandering between two worlds, one dead,
The other powerless to be born."

Compare also Longfellow's "The Golden Legend." For discussion see Bibliography under Shea, Strong, Quayle, and Bailey. The latter, p. 169, regards "The Cathedral" as "probably the most remarkable philosophic poem in American literature."

In form *The Cathedral* illustrates Lowell's mastery of "high seriousness" and "the grand style," although it contains bits of fun and some ornamentation as well as an occasional awkward line. The regularity and smoothness of the blank verse, in which Lowell wrote some twenty-five poems, is fairly typical in the limited variety of its cadences and pauses. Ferris Greenslet says in his chapter on "Lowell's Poetry" (*Lowell*, pp. 245–265) that "the quality of Lowell's poetic style at its very best is of a pithy and noble grandiloquence," and that this quality is especially represented in *The Cathedral*. The four other distinctive qualities Mr. Greenslet finds characteristic of Lowell's poetry are sincerity, a love of nature, a power of thought, and ideality.

Page 505. AGASSIZ

Lowell wrote this poem while in Rome. On the circumstances of composition see his letter to Norton, Feb. 26, 1874 (*Letters*, II, 115–116). Agassiz interested Lowell not only because of his rare personal winsomeness but because he was loyal both to science and to traditional religion. On the conflict between science and religion, see

B. J. Loewenberg's "The Controversy over Evolution in New England, 1859–1873," *New England Quarterly*, VIII, 232–257, and L. M. Shea's *Lowell's Religious Outlook*, pp. 100–113.

Note Lowell's attack (ll. 35 ff.) on the "public scandal, private fraud," associated with the Grant administration. On this subject consult V. L. Parrington's colorful analysis of "The Gilded Age," especially "The Great Barbecue," in *The Beginnings of Critical Realism in America*, pp. 7–47. Howells (*Literary Friends and Acquaintance*, p. 219) testifies that originally Lowell had a line in this poem indicating "too bitterly his disappointment with his country," which he "left out of the printed version, at the fervent entreaty of his friends." Lowell was attacked for what he did say in criticism of America and materialism, both here and in "An Ode for the Fourth of July, 1876." It was charged that residence in Europe had made him hostile to democracy, a charge which is amply refuted in his chief address to Englishmen ("Democracy," 1884); "never," says the historian J. F. Jameson, "did American democracy receive a better defense."

Compare his comment on Holmes, Emerson, and Hawthorne at the Saturday Club with his own earlier comments in *A Fable for Critics* and with Holmes's comments in the poem "At the Saturday Club."

Page 511. THREE MEMORIAL POEMS

These three poems appeared first in the *Atlantic Monthly* for June and August, 1875, and December, 1876. They were collected and published in book form in 1877 (really December, 1876) as *Three Memorial Poems*. Among contemporary reviews see those by W. D. Howells (*Atlantic Monthly*, March, 1877) and by J. V. Blake (*Radical Review*, May, 1877).

In the prefatory lines Lowell replied to those who attacked the second stanza of his poem on "Agassiz" (p. 505, above) as unpatriotic, showed his pride in his Puritan ancestry, and made clear his critical love of his country.

Page 512. ODE READ AT THE ONE HUNDREDTH ANNIVERSARY OF THE FIGHT AT CONCORD BRIDGE

For Lowell's explanation of the form of these poems see the portion of one of his letters to Thayer quoted in note on the "Commemoration Ode," above. It will be recalled that he said he wrote the poems primarily "for recitation," and that in this poem "harmony, without sacrifice of melody," was what he had "mainly in view." He used more three- and four-stress lines than in the other odes, and the last strophe is notable for the number of its anapestic substitutions. The first seven strophes embody Lowell's lyrical devotion to Freedom as evolved by our Puritan and Revolutionary ancestors, and they may well be read in the light of his lofty tribute to the Puritans and their heritage in his prose essay, "New England Two Centuries Ago" (*Works*, II, 1–76). Then Lowell turns to "graver thoughts"; he who had earlier exalted feeling at the expense of knowledge and traditional culture now hears the voice of Freedom saying (ll. 183–193) that she dwells only with Knowledge and "with men by culture trained and fortified," with men who obey divine law. (Cf. Freneau's "Rising Glory of America," Bryant's "The Antiquity of Freedom," and Whitman's "Over the Carnage.")

Page 515. UNDER THE OLD ELM

Lowell wrote J. B. Thayer, Jan. 14, 1877 (*Letters*, II, 188–189), "I think the 'Old Elm' the best of the three [Memorial Poems], mainly because it was composed after my college duties were over . . ." He said earlier, "I took advantage of the occasion [praising Washington] to hold out a hand of kindly reconciliation to Virginia. I could do it with the profounder feeling, that no family lost more than mine by the Civil War. Three nephews (the hope of our race) were killed in one or other of the Virginia battles, and three cousins on other of those bloody fields" (*Letters*, II, 141). On Lowell's political views of the difficult problems presented by the South after the war, see his essay on "Reconstruction" (1865), in his *Political Essays*. The war was to him a sacrament and a consecration; it abolished the sin of slavery and it proved that our people set the ideals of democratic nationality above material prosperity. In this essay, while he insisted on a peace which rested on a guarantee of the equal rights of black and white, he insisted that "our duty is not to punish but to repair. . . . Let us not harden our hearts against our white brethren, from whom interest and custom, those slyer knaves, whose fingers have felt about our own pockets, had stolen away their conscience and their sense of brotherhood." He opposed "any general confiscation of Rebel property" and "all irregular modes of levying contributions." He favored "conceding all that can be conceded without danger to the great principle [national unity] which has been at stake," and he was confident that the North and South would "live more harmoniously together in the future than in the past, now that the one rock of offence has been blasted out of the way."

The theme of the poem should be carefully compared and contrasted with that of the "Commemoration Ode" (p. 490, above). They have much in common, including their lofty dignity and their concern with communal thought and feeling and with civic responsibility. Yet the first, through its homage to Lincoln, exalts a disregard for traditionalism (strophe VI), while "Under the Old Elm," in viewing what Washington stood for through the memory of a century, exalts a respect for traditionalism and for organic continuity (strophes I and II) which were involved in the Federalistic spirit of which Washington was one of the chief spokesmen. Furthermore, while the

"Commemoration Ode" emphasizes the nation, "Under the Old Elm" emphasizes ultimately the influence of the self-controlled and self-poised individual (strophes II, IV, V). Lines 257–266, while applied to Washington, embody a noble expression of Lowell's mature ideal of "orbed" and "balanced" development of the individual "in perfect symmetry of self-control." Strophe VII celebrates Washington as the man who "shot union" through the chaotic colonies, and strophe VIII embodies Lowell's attempt at reconciliation as mentioned above. On the whole, the poem is certainly one of the most impressive of all our poems devoted to the tradition of political liberty and the good of all. On this important aspect of Lowell's significance, see the essay by Bliss Perry listed in the Bibliography.

Page 520. AN ODE FOR THE FOURTH OF JULY, 1876

Although this poem may not have an artistic finish equal to that of "Under the Old Elm," it probably represents the high-water mark of Lowell's mature thought in poetry.

Section I deals with the Revolution and the achievement of independence. Section II compares and contrasts the civilization in America which "the western traveller sees" with that of ancient Greece and Rome. Lowell says that in the West equality of manhood is "latent in the very sod" (l. 115), that no one can breath its air and not "grow humane." Incidentally, contrary to what some unsympathetic interpreters imagine, Lowell was fully conscious of the significance of the western frontier as the home of "distinctive Americanism" (see *Works*, VI, 203–205; V, 192; X, 22, 55, 93–94; *Letters*, I, 325; II, 169, 173, 248). Five years before F. J. Turner's epoch-making address on "The Significance of the Frontier in American History" (1893), Lowell in "The Independent in Politics" (1888) traced much of our distinctive equality, self-reliance, and optimism to the western frontier, although he did not ignore the manner in which these ideals were reinforced by European philosophies as well as the dangers involved in these ideals. In this "Ode" (ll. 149–150) he contrasts unfavorably our "inert prosperity, / This bovine comfort in the sense alone," with classical antiquity which "hid Beauty safe from Death in words or stone"; yet he believes that American potentialities are only partly developed, and that eventually America may concern itself with Beauty. Section III records Lowell's disillusionment with a democratic reliance on numbers rather than wisdom; evidence of "parasitic greed" had caused Lowell to lose his early faith in natural goodness, and to make him more realistic (see Nevins, *The Emergence of Modern America, 1865–1878*, Chap. VII). Section IV returns to a celebration of the Founders of the nation who directed their courses by "ancient wisdom channelled deep in law," who as Christian dualists "still believed in Heaven and Hell." The Puritans, as he had illustrated in "New England Two Centuries Ago," were not utopians but practical statesmen whose central ideal of civil liberty involved making men not masterless but self-mastered—"making man sole sponsor of himself." Eventually, strengthened by his studies in the classics, in the medieval Dante, and in Puritanism, Lowell came to believe that the state, the whole, can be no stronger than the sum of its parts, the individuals composing it, and this poem, the crown of his development, emphasizes the need of self-conquest guided by tradition.

Page 525. ENDYMION

First published in the *Atlantic Monthly* (Feb., 1888), and included in *Heartsease and Rue* (1888). In sending these verses to his publishers, Dec. 20, 1887, Lowell wrote: "I have at last managed to give what seems to me as much consecutiveness as they need to what have been a heap of fragments in my note-books for years. Longer revolution in my head might round it [the poem] better, but take it as a meteorolite, splintery still, but with some metallic iridescence here and there brought from some volcanic star. Let it come among poems of sentiment, and as the longest, first if possible." —Quoted by Scudder, *Biography*, II, 371–372.

The reader will recall that Endymion was a youthful shepherd of Mt. Latmus, in Caria, Asia Minor, who was beloved by the moon-goddess, Selene (Diana). Compare Lowell's treatment of the story with those of John Lyly and Keats. This "mystical comment" shows that Lowell's early mysticism (see *Letters*, I, 117, "One half of me is clear mystic and enthusiast . . ."), although reinforced by reason and traditionalism, vitalized his idealism to the last and gave his words a magic momentum suggesting more than they said. Just as in his first book he had viewed himself as the Red Cross Knight faring forth in the service of Una (his spirituelle bride Maria White) to succor the oppressed, so in his last great poem he pictures himself as Endymion worshipping his "heaven's queen" of beauty, truth, and freedom, a moon-goddess born of fancy who embraces him and departs, leaving him

"An inaccessible splendor to adore,
A faith, a hope of such transcendent worth
As bred ennobling discontent with earth."

Page 528. THE FUNCTION OF THE POET

It will be noticed that in this essay of 1855, as in his introduction to *The Biglow Papers*, Lowell tends to neglect the guidance of literary tradition and to argue that the immediate American scene alone is sufficient inspiration for a great literature.

Page 537. *From* THE LIFE AND LETTERS OF PERCIVAL

On Lowell's changing attitude toward the problem of whether American literature should deal with what is uniquely national or with what is universal, see B. T. Spencer, "A National Literature, 1837–1855," *American Literature*, VIII, 125–159 (May, 1936), and H. H. Clark, "Nationalism in American Literature," *University of Toronto Quarterly*, II, 492–519 (July, 1933). The view here expressed in connection with Percival had been adumbrated in Lowell's review of Longfellow's *Kavanagh* (which may have suggested his attitude); the review was entitled "Nationality in Literature" (*North American Review*, July, 1849).

On the subject of the criteria by which Lowell arrived at his opinion of romanticists as "a society of cripples," see H. H. Clark, "Lowell's Criticism of Romantic Literature," in Bibliography, above.

Page 540. *From* DANTE

This essay, entitled "The Shadow of Dante," appeared first in the *North American Review*, CXV, 139 ff. (July, 1872), and was reprinted in Lowell's *Among My Books*, Second Series, in 1876. Lowell also deals with Dante in *Appleton's New American Encyclopedia* (1870), and in the *Fifth Annual Report, Dante Society* (1886). Lowell and C. E. Norton (who translated Dante) were invited by Longfellow to constitute with him a Dante Club which met every Wednesday evening in the winter of 1865–1866 to discuss Longfellow's translation of Dante then in progress. Lowell's course in Dante at Harvard was his favorite, and his fresh, individual, and charming manner of interpreting this poet to his students has been vividly recorded by George E. Pond in an essay entitled "Lowell at Harvard," in *Liber Scriptorum* (New York, 1893), pp. 456 ff. While Bryant and Emerson brought the classicism of Homer and Plato, respectively, to bear on the American mind, Lowell and Longfellow were distinctive in preferring, and in introducing to the descendants of the Puritans, the Catholic medievalism of Dante. (For a brief discussion of attitudes toward Dante expressed by various Americans, see Emilio Goggio's "Dante Interests in Nineteenth Century America," *Philological Quarterly*, I, 192–201 [July, 1922]; see also T. W. Koch's extensive study, "Dante in America," in *Fifteenth Annual Report of the Dante Society* [Cambridge: 1896]. As early as 1854 in *Leaves from My Journal in Italy* (*Works*, I, 195), Lowell recognized the values of the dualism of Catholicism; see note on "The Cathedral," above.

LOWELL'S POETIC THEORY

Norman Foerster (*American Criticism*, pp. 146–147) summarizes Lowell's literary creed as follows:

"Literature is the ideal representation of human nature. Each literary work must have first of all a self-contained form, possessing such qualities as unity, design, proportion, clearness, power, economy, control, repose, sanity, impersonality. This form is organic; that is, the structure is determined from within by the 'soul' or animating conception, and the conception in turn is organic, proceeding from the writer's personal experience and cultural heritage. The faculty that images the whole and the necessary and harmonious relation of the parts is the plastic imagination. Form must be not only organic but ideal; that is, it must embody the real that resides in the actual. The faculty that images the ideal is the spiritual imagination. When the spiritual imagination acts in its ordinary capacity, representing the perdurable types of human nature, and in so doing achieves an elevated breadth, it may be termed the humanistic or ethical imagination. When it acts in its extraordinary capacity, revealing the life of the soul itself, and in so doing achieves height if need be at the expense of breadth, it is the ultimate spiritual imagination. Of this ultimate spiritual imagination, two kinds may be distinguished: an inferior kind that expresses momentary intuitions, and a superior kind that transforms the entire chaos of experience into a vision of the cosmos. In all its activities, the imagination must be guided by other human faculties, most of all by reason.

"Form determines quantitatively the beauty of a given work of art; spiritual imagination, guided by reason, determines it qualitatively. In the 'possible unity' of the greatest degree and the finest kind of beauty, we may conceive of the perfect work of art.

"The function of a work of art is to give delight. Of delight there are two general grades: first, the delight of recreation, when the more serious faculties are resting with a view to future working and the sportive faculties are free to confer charm upon leisure; and secondly, the joyful exercise of the higher faculties, or perhaps of all the faculties of mind and spirit working in harmony and so producing happiness rather than mere pleasure. For the fulfillment of both grades of delight, excellence of form is requisite; but the higher grade demands in addition moral or spiritual excellence—the contagion of a fine personality or the inspiration of an ideal vision of life."

To what extent did Lowell succeed in practicing his theories in his poetry?

OLIVER WENDELL HOLMES

CHRONOLOGY

1809 Born at Cambridge, Mass., August 29.
1824 Entered the orthodox stronghold, Phillips Academy, Andover, which only served to strengthen his already formed aversion to Calvinism.
1825 Entered Harvard.
1829 Graduated from Harvard, his revulsion against Calvinism strengthened by Unitarian influences there.
1830 Wrote verses for Harvard *Collegian* and Boston *Amateur*. Began and abandoned course of study for legal profession. Became well known through his popular "Old Ironsides."
1831–32 Articles by Holmes in the *New England Magazine* under title *The Autocrat of the Breakfast-Table* foreshadowed the articles twenty-five years later.
1833–35 Studied medicine in Paris, and traveled in France, Holland, Switzerland, Italy, England.
1836 Received M.D. from Harvard and began practice of medicine in Boston. Published *Poems* the humor of which did not help his medical reputation. Won Boylston prize for medical essay at Harvard.
1838–40 Professor of anatomy at Dartmouth.
1840 Married Amelia Lee Jackson.
1843 "The Contagiousness of Puerperal Fever," his best medical essay, and still recognized as important, aroused controversy in medical profession.
1847 Professor of Anatomy and Physiology at Harvard. 1847–1853, Dean of the Harvard Medical School.
1853 Delivered in Boston a Lowell Institute course of twelve lectures on *The English Poets of the Nineteenth Century.*
1857–58 *The Autocrat of the Breakfast-Table* appeared in the *Atlantic Monthly*. Published as book. 1858.
1860 *The Professor at the Breakfast-Table.*
1861 *Elsie Venner*, a novel.
1862 *Songs in Many Keys.*
1864 *Soundings from the Atlantic.*
1867 *The Guardian Angel*, a novel.
1872 *The Poet at the Breakfast-Table.*
1875 *Songs of Many Seasons.*
1879 *John Lothrop Motley: a Memoir.*
1880 *The Iron Gate and Other Poems.*
1882 Emeritus Professor.
1883 *Medical Essays. Pages from an Old Volume of Life.*
1885 *A Mortal Antipathy*, a novel. *Ralph Waldo Emerson* in the American Men of Letters Series.
1887 *Our Hundred Days in Europe. Before the Curfew and Other Poems.*
1891 *Over the Teacups.*
1894 Died in Boston on October 7.

BIBLIOGRAPHY

I. Bibliography

Ives, G. B. *A Bibliography of Oliver Wendell Holmes.* Boston: 1907. (Practically exhaustive. Pp. 243–286 contain a list of all biographies and criticism dealing with Holmes to 1907.)

II. Text

Works. Riverside Edition. Boston: 1891. 13 vols. (In 1892 the Memoirs, of Motley and Emerson were printed together, and the volume was added to the Riverside Edition as Vol. XI, the numbers of the three volumes of poems being changed to XII, XIII, and XIV.)

The Writings of Oliver Wendell Holmes. Standard Library Edition. Boston: 1892. 13 vols. (Printed from the plates of the Riverside Edition. The contents of the different volumes are the same, except that the poems occupy only two volumes, XII and XIII. Vol. XII contains the poems included in Vol. XI and the first 158 pages of XII of the Riverside Edition. After the publication of Morse's *Life and Letters*, those two volumes were added to the Standard Library Edition as Vols. XIV and XV.)

The Complete Poetical Works of Oliver Wendell Holmes, ed. by H. E. Scudder. Cambridge Edition. Boston: 1895. (The standard one-volume edition, with many useful head-notes and a chronological list of the poems, pp. 341–344.)

"Oration," in *The New England Society Orations.* New York: 1901. Vol. II, pp. 271–302. (This oration by Holmes in 1855 throws light on his political views, especially his view of the slaves as imperfectly human and in need of the compassionate protection of the whites, and his view of the greatness of the New England Federalistic tradition.)

"Four Letters Addressed to Coleman Sellers of Philadelphia," *Yale Review*, N.S. XIV, 410–413 (Jan., 1925).

"Hawthorne," *Atlantic Monthly*, XIV, 98–101 (July, 1864).

"Irving's Power of Idealization," *Critic*, III, 138–139 (March 31, 1883).

"Letter from Dr. Holmes [to Arthur Gilman], October 26, 1874," *Atlantic Monthly*, C, 715 (Nov., 1907).

"Light of Asia" [review of Sir Edwin Arnold's poem], *International Review*, pp. 345–372 (Oct., 1879).

"Old Books," [Buckingham's] *New England Magazine*, II, 46–49 (Jan., 1832).

"To John Pierpont, April 3, 1865" [a birthday poem], *Bookman*, XLIV, 626 (Feb., 1917)

"Tribute to Irving," *Massachusetts Historical Society Proceedings*, 1858–1860, pp. 418–422.

Esther B. Carpenter. *South County Studies.* Boston: 1924. ("With an introduction by Caroline Hagard, compiled largely from letters now first published by Oliver Wendell Holmes . . . There are twenty-six of these letters from Dr. Holmes, beginning in 1869 and ending in 1886.")

The Correspondence of John Lothrop Motley, ed. by G. W. Curtis. New York: 1889. 2 vols. (Contains many letters by Holmes.)

"Agassiz's Natural History" [review], *Atlantic Monthly*, I, 320–333 (Jan., 1858).

"Dr. Holmes at the Festival," *Quarterly Journal of the American Unitarian Association*, VI, 355–362 (July, 1859). ("A reply to the charges which various evangelical papers have brought against a recent article of his in the *Atlantic Monthly*, that it is *poisoning public opinion*.")

III. Biography and Criticism

Allen, G. W. *American Prosody.* New York: 1935, pp. 193–212. (Definitive scholarly survey of Holmes's use of meters and stanzas. Concludes that Holmes merely "used the old measures without contributing anything new to their handling except an urbane unself-consciousness and an epigrammatic polish" [p. 211].)

Bailey, E. J. *Religious Thought in the Greater American Poets.* Boston: 1922, pp. 137–157. (Holmes three religious tenets are: God is Love; worship is love of one's fellows; and the soul is immortal. Bailey slights science.)

Ball, James. *Dr. Oliver Wendell Holmes and His Works; Being a Brief Biographical and Critical Review.* London: 1878.

Ballantine, W. G. "Oliver Wendell Holmes as a Poet and as a Man," *North American Review*, CXC, 178–193 (August, 1909).

Brenner, Rica. *Twelve American Poets before 1900.* New York: 1933, pp. 169–198. (A good appreciative general essay, with some attention to his views of the relation between science and religion and to his technical skill as a poet.)

Brooks, Van Wyck. "Dr. Holmes: Forerunner of the Moderns," *Saturday Review of Literature*, XIV, 3–4, 13–15 (June 27, 1936). (A brief, spirited but undocumented essay emphasizing Holmes's revolt from Calvinism. Argues that in devoting *Elsie Venner* to the thesis that determinism, the absence of the individual's responsibility for wrongdoing, should inspire social sympathy, Holmes "played into the hands of Dr. Freud" and of "Dr. Marx.")

Brown, E. E. *Life of Oliver Wendell Holmes.* Boston: 1884. (Old-fashioned and discursive, but contains much evidence.)

"Centenary Study of Holmes," *Edinburgh Review*, CCXI, 414–434 (April, 1910).

Cheever, D. W. "Oliver Wendell Holmes the Anatomist," *Harvard Graduates' Magazine*, III, 154–159 (Dec., 1894).

Collins, John Churton. "The Poetry and Poets of America," in *Studies in Poetry and Criticism.* London: 1905.

Cooke, G. W. "Dr. Holmes at Fourscore," *New England Magazine*, N.S. I, 115–123 (Oct., 1889).

The Critic. Holmes Number, N.S. II (Aug. 30, 1884).

Crothers, S. M. *The Autocrat and His Fellow-Boarders.* Boston: 1909. (Previously published in the *Atlantic Monthly*, CIV, 237–244 [August, 1909].)

Curtis, G. W. *Literary and Social Essays.* New York: 1895, pp. 205–236. (A charmingly appreciative "discursive talk" on Holmes, stressing his grace and humor as a reaction from the Puritan temper of the New England of his ancestors. "No other author takes the reader into his personal confidence more closely than Holmes, and none reveals his personal temperament more clearly" [pp. 233–234]. Curtis pays tribute to Holmes's versatility and geniality, but neglects his philosophic thought and his scientific determinism.)

Eliot, C. W. "Oliver Wendell Holmes," *Harvard Graduates' Magazine*, XXXI, 457–465 (June, 1923). (The President of Harvard says this professor of anatomy was the most careful of men in preparation of his lectures, and very painstaking in experiments.)

Emerson, E. W. *The Early Years of the Saturday Club, 1855–1870.* Boston: 1918. (See index for numerous references to Holmes's part in this club.)

Fields, Annie. *Authors and Friends.* Boston: 1898, pp. 107–157. (A charming impressionistic essay, with many of Holmes's letters and *obiter dicta.* Emphasizes his conversational ability. Says he described Whitman as being "in an amorphous condition" [p. 133].)

Fuller, H. DeW. "Holmes," in *American Writers on American Literature*, ed. by John Macy. New York: 1931, pp. 153–163. (One of the best brief surveys, with about equal emphasis on his poetry, scientific thought, and his prose. Concludes that his interests in poetry and science "give a potency and range to his writings which . . . have never been surpassed in literature of so informal and so engaging a character" [p. 162], that "from the sum total of his writings emerges a great humanist—a man grounded in the culture of Western Europe" [p. 163] striving to reconcile a respect for tradition with a respect for free scientific inquiry as the basis of progress.)

Gavigan, W. V. "The Doctor Looks at Religion, Dr. Holmes and the Church," *Catholic World*, CXXXVII, 53–59 (April, 1933). (Describes Holmes's interest in the ceremony of the Catholic Church, and quotes his opinion that Catholicism is the most comforting religion, particularly to those who are dying. Cites *Elsie Venner* and *The Autocrat*.)

Gosse, Edmund. "An English View of the 'Autocrat,'" *Critic*, XXV, 382–383 (Dec. 1, 1894).

Grattan, C. H. "O. W. Holmes," *American Mercury*, IV, 37–41 (Jan., 1925). (Superficial and unsympathetic.)

Green, R. F. "Oliver Wendell Holmes: His Writings and Philosophy," *Proceedings of the Literary and Philosophical Society*, Liverpool, 1880–1881, XXXV, 215–247.

Hale, E. E. "Oliver Wendell Holmes," *The Critic*, XXV, 242–246 (Oct. 13, 1894).

—— "The Career of Oliver Wendell Holmes," *Review of Reviews*, XL, 84–86 (July, 1909).

Haweis, H. R. *American Humorists*. New York: 1882, pp. 37–66.

Hayakawa, Samuel I. *Oliver Wendell Holmes, Physician, Poet, and Essayist*. (A scholarly doctoral dissertation of 1934, available in manuscript at the Library of the University of Wisconsin. Chapter II [pp. 54–121] deals sympathetically with Holmes's view of "Science, Religion, and the Problem of Responsibility"; Chapter III [pp. 121–171] deals with his "Literary Theory." The work is elaborately documented, and it contains a full bibliography.)

Higginson, T. W. *Cheerful Yesterdays*. Boston: 1901. (See index.)

—— *Contemporaries*. Boston: 1899. (See index.)

—— *Old Cambridge*. New York: 1900, pp. 73–108.

Howe, M. A. DeW. *American Bookmen*. New York: 1902, pp. 265–286.

—— "Dr. Holmes, the Friend and Neighbor." *Yale Review*, N.S. VII, 562–578 (Apr., 1918).

—— "Holmes," in *Dictionary of American Biography*. New York: 1932. IX, 169–176. (The most up-to-date and authoritative brief life.)

Howells, W. D. "Oliver Wendell Holmes," in *Literary Friends and Acquaintance*. New York: 1900, pp. 146–177. (A realist and socialist gives random impressions of many sides of Holmes's personality. Genial and charming, but Holmes's limitations are recognized. Although kindly, he "liked his fences" and he "imagined no new rule of life, and no philosophy or theory of life.")

Hughes, J. L. "Oliver Wendell Holmes," *Canadian Magazine*, LX, 334–340 (Feb., 1923).

Jerrold, Walter. *Oliver Wendell Holmes*. London: 1893. (Chapters on the man, the poet [pp. 29–62], the novelist, the autocrat and teacher. Discursive, but cites considerable evidence. Claims [p. 43] that "even more than Walt Whitman is Holmes peculiarly national.")

Kennedy, W. S. *Oliver Wendell Holmes, Poet, Littérateur, Scientist*. Boston: 1883. (A fairly important early study.)

Knickerbocker, W. S. "His Own Boswell: a Note on the Poetry of Oliver Wendell Holmes," *Sewanee Review*, XLI, 454–466 (Oct.–Dec., 1933). (Brief but very stimulating. Finds Holmes distinctive in New England for being "so consistently personal" and for his adherence to "the world view of eighteenth-century British rationalists" or exponents of "cosmic benevolence." Touches on his literary and his political views.)

Kreymborg, Alfred. "Dr. Holmes and the New England Decline," in *Our Singing Strength*. New York: 1929, pp. 134–150. (Condescending. Practically ignores Holmes's philosophy, and views him merely as "a florist in verse" illustrating "the New England decline." "Holmes is now the least important poet of his group" [p. 135] because "he could react only to Pope and the rational grace of the French.")

Lang, Andrew. *Adventures among Books*. New York: 1905, pp. 81–96.

Lawton, W. C. *The New England Poets*. New York: 1898, pp. 232–254. (Discursive and superficial.)

Le Baron, G. "In the Autocrat's Library," *National Magazine*, V, 231–236 (Dec., 1896).

Linn, J. W. "Holmes as a Humorist," *University of Chicago Magazine*, II, 16–23 (Nov., 1909).

Lodge, H. C. *Certain Accepted Heroes and Other Essays*. New York: 1897, pp. 137–154. (Discursive and general, although appreciative.)

Lowell, J. R. "Elsie Venner" [review], in *The Round Table*. Boston: 1913, pp. 65–72. (Previously published in *Atlantic Monthly*, VII, 509–511 [Apr., 1861]. A glowing tribute to Lowell's old friend for his work in general, and a recognition that in this novel he "has struck a new vein of New-England romance," that the book is "full of wit and of sound thought.")

Ludlow, J. M. "Elsie Venner and Silas Marner," *Macmillan's Magazine*, IV, 305–309 (Aug., 1861).

Macy, John. "Holmes," in *The Spirit of American Literature*. New York: 1913, pp. 155–171. (Spirited appreciation. Holmes is America's "single great discursive essayist." "Only Hawthorne, of the New Englanders, equals him in unbroken perfection of style." Macy hardly touches the question of science *vs.* religion in Holmes.)

Matthews, Brander. "Holmes," in *Cambridge History of American Literature*, New York: 1918, II, 224–240. (One of the best general essays. Has high praise for his discursive essays, but thinks his serious poetry has formal polish at the expense of "depth of feeling and largeness of vision." In familiar verse he finds his blending of pathos and humor unsurpassed.)

May, Samuel. "Dr. Holmes with His Classmates," *Harvard Graduates' Magazine*, III, 159–162 (Dec., 1894).

Merrill, W. S. "The Centenary of the Autocrat," *Catholic World*, CXXXIV, 581–586 (Feb., 1932). (Sensible appreciation. Merrill regrets Holmes's lack of interest in Catholicism. See Gavigan.)

Meynell, Alice. *The Rhythm of Life and Other Essays*. London: 1905, pp. 60–67.

Mitford, Mary R. *Recollections of a Literary Life*. New York: 1852, pp. 399–410.

Morse, J. T. *Life and Letters of Oliver Wendell Holmes*. Boston: 1896. 2 vols. (Although uncritical, this is the fundamental source-book, with a great many of Holmes's letters. Reviewed by Jeannette Gilder in *The Critic*, XXVIII, 325–327, May 9, 1896.)

Onderdonk, J. L. *History of American Verse*. Chicago: 1901, pp. 268–279. (Superficial.)

Osler, Sir William. "Oliver Wendell Holmes," *Johns Hopkins Hospital Bulletin*, V, 85–88 (Oct., 1894). (A great scientist, in a public address, praises Holmes's contributions to science in "The Contagiousness of Puerperal Fever." Concludes that Holmes was "the most successful combination which the world has ever seen of the physician and the man of letters.")

Parrington, V. L. *The Romantic Revolution in America, 1800–1860*. New York: 1927, pp. 451–460. (To this economic determinist and humanitarian, Holmes is "only a minor figure in American literature" (p. 459); he was "an unsparing critic of romantic equalitarianism" and he extolled wealth as a means to leisure and cultivated living. Prejudiced as Parrington is, he is stimulating in analyzing Holmes's religious radicalism—his bitter science-bred attack on Calvinism and his extreme "harder-headed rationalism" [p. 454].)

Pritchard, J. P. "The Autocrat and Horace," *The Classical Weekly*, XXV, 217–223 (May 16, 1932). (An elaborately documented and valuable study, throwing much light not only on Holmes's knowledge of and kinship to Horace, but also on his literary theory in general.)

Roddis, L. H. "Medicine and the Muse, Oliver Wendell Holmes, M.D.," *Annals of Internal Medicine*, III, 717–723 (1930).

Savage, M. J. "The Religion of Holmes's Poems," *Arena*, XI, 41–54 (Dec., 1894). (Uncritical Unitarian praise of Holmes's religion as emphasizing a sense of human dignity which demanded a God better than man; an interest in life as developing; love for one's fellow men; and a belief in immortality. Fails to get at the scientific roots of his religion and his revolt from Calvinism, because Savage does not interpret the poems in the light of the prose.)

Selbie, R. H. "Holmes," *Manchester Quarterly*, XX, 232–258 (1901).

Slicer, T. R. "Oliver Wendell Holmes, the Friend of the World," in *From Poet to Premier, the Centennial Cycle, 1809–1909*. London: 1909, pp. 83–113.

Smalley, G. W. *Studies of Men*. New York: 1895, pp. 314–333.

Smith, J. E. Adams. *The Poet among the Hills; Oliver Wendell Holmes in Berkshire* . . . Pittsfield, Mass.: 1895.

Stearns, F. P. "Dr. Holmes," in *Cambridge Sketches*. Philadelphia: 1905, pp. 142–161.

Stedman, E. C. *Poets of America*. Boston: 1885, pp. 273–303. (A good essay, emphasizing Holmes's poems for occasions, and concluding that his prose is much more important and that his poetry owes much of its fame to his genial personality.)

Stephen, Leslie. *Studies of a Biographer*. London: 1907, II, 149–182. (This is one of the most penetrating essays on Holmes by one of the shrewdest of English philosophic critics.)

Stewart, George, Jr. *Evenings in the Library*. St. John, N. B.: 1878, pp. 52–73.

Strong, A. H. *American Poets and Their Theology*. Philadelphia: 1916, pp. 319–367. (Although didactic and written from the Calvinistic bias, this essay is relatively incisive in coming to grips with the basic elements of Holmes's religious view, which involved a faith in natural goodness and the notion that wrong-doers are not responsible for evil because it is a result of heredity and environment. Claims that Holmes confused hyper-Calvinism and Calvinism [pp. 340–341], and that he was a pioneer among writers of his group in bringing to Unitarian tenets the support of materialistic science.)

Ticknor, Caroline (ed.). *Dr. Holmes's Boston*. Boston: 1915.

Townsend, F. S. "The Religion of Oliver Wendell Holmes," *Methodist Review*, XCI, 605–611 (July, 1909).

Trowbridge, J. T. "Recollections of Oliver Wendell Holmes," *Atlantic Monthly*, XCI, 600–605 (May, 1903).

Turner, E. S. "The Autocrat's Theology; Unpublished Letters of Holmes," *Putnam's Magazine*, VI, 662–667 (Sept., 1909). (Shows Holmes's revulsion at the Congregational doctrine of predestination, defended by his correspondent, Rev. H. W. Parker, although Holmes himself accepted scientific determinism.)

Underwood, F. H. "Oliver Wendell Holmes," *Scribner's Monthly*, XVIII, 117–127 (May, 1879).

Viets, H. R. "Oliver Wendell Holmes, Physician," *American Scholar*, III, 5–11 (Winter, 1934).

Walsh, W. S. "Lowell and Holmes," in *Literary Life*. New York: 1882, II, 135–149. (The section on Holmes is based on David Macrae's description of Holmes as he delivered the inaugural lecture at the opening of the medical classes at Harvard.)

Wendell, Barrett. *A Literary History of America*. New York: 1911, pp. 407–425. (A penetrating analysis, centering on Holmes's attack on Calvinism, although Wendell neglects his scientific determinism. Concludes: "As in our final view of the New England Renaissance Ticknor seems its most eminent scholar, Longfellow its most typical poet, and Lowell its deepest humanist, so Holmes seems its one uncompromising rationalist" [p. 418].)

Werner, Dorothy L. *The Idea of Union in American Verse, 1776–1876*. Philadelphia: 1932. (A scholarly dissertation. See index for a large number of references to and discussions of Holmes's political poems. On his political views see also Parrington and Withington.)

Whittier, J. G. "Mirth and Medicine," in Whittier's *Works*, Standard Library Edition, VII, 374–382. (See also VI, 309–310, for a tribute on Holmes's seventy-fifth birthday. Whittier says Holmes "is Montaigne and Bacon under one hat." He praises "his genial nature, entire freedom from jealousy or envy, quick tenderness, large charity, hatred of sham, pretence, and unreality, and his reverent sense of the eternal and permanent.")

Winter, William. "Oliver Wendell Holmes," in *Old Friends*. New York: 1909, pp. 107–131. (Sentimental reminiscences.)

Winterich, J. T. "Romantic Stories of Books: Autocrat of the Breakfast-Table," *Publishers' Weekly*, CXIX, 317–321 (Jan. 17, 1931).

"Wit and Humor: Poems by Oliver Wendell Holmes" [review], *Quarterly Review*, CXXII, 232–235 (Jan., 1867).

Withington, Robert. "The Patriotism of the Autocrat," *Harvard Graduates' Magazine*, pp. 523–532 (June, 1928). (Holmes loved America, but he questioned democracy and preferred the tradition of the man of quality to that of the self-made man. He attacked vulgarity and humbug. He hoped for the Americanizing of religion, and he spoke out fearlessly for intellectual liberty.)

—— "A Note on the Autocrat, III and IV," *Modern Language Notes*, XLVI, 293 (May, 1931).

NOTES

GENERAL

Probably of all the major figures in American literature Holmes's fame has declined most in recent years. He is, however, important, first, because as a wit he represents a level of urbane and almost Augustan culture and social grace seldom if ever equalled in America; second, because of his grace and charm and depth of sentiment, of friendly recollection, of tender and humane emotion; and third, because he represents best, perhaps, the central nineteenth-century conflict between orthodox religion and science which had vast sociological results. It is seldom recognized by anthology readers unfamiliar with his complete works that his scientific determinism, his tendency to deny that the criminal is responsible for his acts, led to pity for the criminal. Holmes's advocacy that the criminal should not be punished but treated by psychiatrists as one morally sick renders him a pioneer in the succession of friends of the criminal which has culminated in Harry Elmer Barnes and Clarence Darrow today.

Page 543. OLD IRONSIDES

First printed in the Boston *Daily Advertiser* for Sept. 16, 1830, when Holmes was a law student at Harvard. The poem was reprinted throughout the nation, it prevented the destruction of the frigate *Constitution*, and first won Holmes fame. For details of composition see Morse's *Life*, I, 79–80.

THE BALLAD OF THE OYSTERMAN

This poem appeared in the *Amateur*, July 17, 1830, and is one of many ballads in which Holmes illustrates his distinctive ability to mingle sentiment and humor, the pathetic and the ridiculous. Compare in this respect Irving, to whom Holmes paid tribute.

Page 545. MY AUNT

This poem first appeared in the *New England Magazine*, Oct., 1831, and is one of the best illustrations of the ability mentioned above, applied to Holmes's immediate family. In his tendency to satirize, albeit in a kindly manner, eccentricities and departures from a norm of good sense, Holmes is akin to the classical and neo-classical writers whom he loved.

THE LAST LEAF

J. T. Morse (*Life*, I, 227) regards "The Last Leaf" as Holmes's best poem—better, even, than "The Chambered Nautilus." Governor Andrew told Holmes that Abraham Lincoln repeated the poem to him from memory as one of his favorites. Poe prized it highly. The poem illustrates Holmes's taste and tact and his subtle skill in exquisitely balancing drollery and sentiment. Notice his neo-classic tendency to satirize what is queer.

In commenting on the "somewhat singular measure" of the poem (see his note in Cambridge Edition, pp. 4–5) Holmes said that "so far as it was suggested by any previous poem, the echo must have come from Campbell's 'The Battle of the Baltic,' with its short terminal lines, such as the last of these two,

'By thy wild and stormy steep,
Elsinore.'

But I do not remember any poem in the same measure, except such as have been written since its publication." G. W. Allen (*American Prosody*, p. 209) concludes that the rhythm of this poem has "a lilt which is more musical than anything else Holmes ever wrote."

Page 546. POETRY: A METRICAL ESSAY

The note with which Holmes prefaced this poem, which is a sort of "progress of poesy," should be read with care. The development of Holmes's thought, embodying a nationalistic literary theory, may be outlined as follows:

Introduction: All men by nature are endowed by the poetic spirit, which works through associative recollection and which expresses itself through changing poetic forms.

Part I: Since all men share the poetic spirit, and its materials are remembered scenes, Holmes will enshrine in poetry his sweet recollections of his home and his local environment.

Part II: If the United States ever has another war, Holmes hopes it may inspire a national hymn comparable to the national hymns of France, Germany, and England. He refers proudly to his youthful heroic poem, "Old Ironsides."

Part III: Since war inspires the heroism which is the basis of *epic* poetry, let us celebrate those who nobly died in our war for independence in lays comparable to the *Iliad.*

Part IV: Since "man is still the same," *drama*, tracking "passions to their living source," offers a field for enduring art in America just as it did in Greece and Rome.

Part V: Poetry has its roots not "in verse alone" but in nature (even before science) and in language ("all nature links analogies" to the lexicon). Cf. Emerson's section on "Language" in *Nature;* Wordsworth's "Preface" of 1800 on language and nature. Rather than "Cowper's gloom or Chatterton's despair," Holmes advocates poetry of urbane and cheerful friendship. Although two of his friends (Charles Chauncey Emerson and Dr. James Jackson) have fallen prey to man's common mortality, he concludes that earth-inspired art is immortal, and outlasts the centuries and forgotten cities and graves.

Page 558. THE STATESMAN'S SECRET

Cf. Emerson's "Webster" (p. 191) and Whittier's "Ichabod" (p. 128). While the majestic Webster's idealism, Holmes says, is able to bring him "love unbought" and "a nation's homage nobler than its throne," he is in danger of yielding to the secret temptation to sacrifice his idealism (his abolitionism) for "a vulgar prize" (the presidency). Note the idealistic Holmes's view of practical politics: "party-fights are won by aiming low." During this period Holmes, like Emerson and Whittier, preferred to abandon the Union rather than abolition, although he later became an ardent unionist; see his "Union and Liberty" (p. 569) and note (p. 889). See also Holmes's more sympathetic poem, "The Birthday of Daniel Webster," written after Webster's death.

NON-RESISTANCE

Note that Holmes was not a pacifist. Cf. Lowell's "Commemoration Ode," ll. 131 ff.

Page 559.
AFTER A LECTURE ON WORDSWORTH

Holmes wrote this poem, and the one following on Shelley, to conclude lectures given at the Lowell Institute in Boston, in 1853, on English Poetry of the Nineteenth Century. These lectures have never been published, but they will be found reported in the Boston *Daily Evening Transcript,* March 23, 26, 30, April 2, 8, 9, 13, 16, 20, 23, 27, and May 2, 1853. Holmes especially praised the lyricism of Moore, Coleridge, Keats, and Shelley, although he is cautious in not subscribing to all of the philosophic and political ideas of the romanticists. Note that while elsewhere Holmes exalts literary traditionalism over nature as the poet's inspiration, in this poem he develops the theme that the Old World Wordsworth helps the New World to interpret and love the surpassing loveliness of its own natural scenery which shall eventually inspire a great poet as the crown of our national development.

Page 561. LATTER-DAY WARNINGS

In *The Autocrat of the Breakfast-Table,* in which this poem first appeared, it was preceded by the following paragraph: "I should have felt more nervous about the late comet, if I had thought the world was ripe. But it is very green yet, if I am not mistaken; and besides, there is a great deal of coal to use up, which I cannot bring myself to think was made for nothing. If certain things, which seem to me essential for a millennium, had come to pass, I should have been frightened; but they haven't" (*Writings,* I, 24). It should be noted that, although Holmes was exceedingly optimistic and even radical in his science-bred religious views (see *ibid.,* I, 113; IV, 255, for examples), he is realistic almost to the point of cynicism in his social views, as the present poem illustrates. Actually he knew that the selfishness and hypocrisy of mankind made any millennial views ridiculous. He sympathized with the oppressed philosophically, but in his actual social practice he was anything but an equalitarian. As his friend Howells said, "He liked his fences."

Page 562. THE CHAMBERED NAUTILUS

This poem first appeared in the *Atlantic Monthly,* Feb., 1858, in a section of *The Autocrat* introduced as follows: "Did I not say to you a little while ago that the universe swam in an ocean of similitudes and analogies? I will not quote Cowley, or Burns, or Wordsworth, just now, to show you what thoughts were suggested to them by the simplest natural objects, such as a flower or a leaf; but I will read you a few lines, if you do not object, suggested by looking at a section of one of those chambered shells to which is given the name of Pearly Nautilus . . . If you will look into Roget's Bridgewater Treatise, you will find a figure of one of these shells . . . of enlarging compartments successively dwelt in by the animal that inhabits the shell, which is built in a widening spiral. Can you find no lesson in this?" Holmes's idea of the "similitudes and analogies" between matter and mind suggests Emerson's similar theory developed in *Nature* (1836), that "Nature is the symbol of spirit," that "the laws of moral nature answer to those of matter as face to face in a glass," that the art of true poetry is to transmute spiritual ideas into images, to pierce abstract "rotten diction and fasten words again to visible things."

Emerson had also said that "all progress is an unfolding, like the vegetable bud," that man's growth may be likened to that of the shell-fish "which crawls out of its beautiful but stony case, because it no longer admits of its growth, and slowly forms itself a new house" (*Complete Works of Ralph Waldo Emerson*, Centenary ed., II, 124 and 330). Possibly this latter figure helped to suggest "The Chambered Nautilus" to Holmes. Cf. Emerson's "The Problem":

"how the fish outbuilt her shell,
Painting with morn each annual cell."

For Holmes has translated into poetry Emerson's idea of growth as a balanced, symmetrical expansion from a center. Although Holmes, whose intellectual roots were in the rational eighteenth century, may have been somewhat indifferent to some of the mysticism in Transcendentalism, it will be recalled that he wrote the biography of Emerson in the American Men of Letters series, that he confessed (*A Mortal Antipathy*, pp. 18–19) "thinking thoughts" and "using phrases . . . unconsciously borrowed" from Emerson, his "high-souled companion." Emerson's passage on the "shell-fish" was written at least seventeen years before "The Chambered Nautilus."

Holmes wrote to George Ticknor, "I should like to have you notice the rhythm of one poem . . . 'The Chambered Nautilus.' I am as willing to submit this to criticism as any I have written, in form as well as in substance, and I have not seen any English verse of just the same pattern" (Morse's *Life*, II, 278). G. W. Allen (*American Prosody*, pp. 207–209) says that "in none of his other poems do we find Holmes using such freely varied accents." He calls attention to the many reversed feet and interpolated spondees, as well as the pattern involving "the iambic pentameter, trimeter, and a final alexandrine, in the following scheme: $a_5a_3b_3bb_5c_3c_6$." Mr. Allen suggests that the combinations mentioned may possibly have been intended "to symbolize the crenulated and scalloped shell of the chambered nautilus." Holmes testified (*Life*, I, 226) that in writing the poem he experienced "the highest state of mental exaltation and the most crystalline clairvoyance, as it seemed to me, that had ever been granted to me—I mean that lucid vision of one's thought, and of all forms of expression which will be at once precise and musical, which is the poet's special gift, however large or small in amount of value."

THE LIVING TEMPLE

Note that following the Puritans' fear of the flesh, of the body, as the vessel of corruption, Holmes, taught by Darwinian evolution, glorifies the body in whose "wondrous frame" is the divine "Maker's glory seen." Although the decorous Holmes disliked Whitman, he shared the latter's general view of the divinity of the body. Whereas in the minds of traditional Christians, Holmes says, "'Nature' and 'Grace' have been contrasted with each other" as "two hostile Divinities in the Pantheon of post-classical polytheism," the "secret of the profound interest in 'Darwinianism'" is the fact that "it restores 'Nature' to its place as a true divine manifestation. It is that it removes the traditional curse from that helpless infant lying in its mother's arms. . . . If development upward is the general law of the race; if we have grown by natural evolution out of the cave-man, and even less human forms of life, we have everything to hope from the future. . . . We are entering on a new era, . . . the Revival of Humanity. . . . Sin, like disease, is a vital process. It is a function, and not an entity. It must be studied as a section of anthropology" (*Writings*, III, 304–306). On backgrounds see B. J. Loewenberg, "The Controversy over Evolution in New England," *New England Quarterly*, VIII, 232–257 (March, 1935). With Holmes's view of the body and of sin compare his friend Hawthorne's view in *The Marble Faun*, where he raises the question whether sin may be, like sorrow, "merely an element of human education, through which we struggle to a higher and purer state than we could otherwise have attained?" It should be noted, however, that Hawthorne has Kenyon answer, "I never did believe it." Compare and contrast Holmes's *Elsie Venner* and Hawthorne's *The Marble Faun* in their attitudes toward responsibility for sin and its results.

Page 563. THE DEACON'S MASTERPIECE

This poem, included in a section of *The Autocrat* in the *Atlantic Monthly*, Sept., 1858, is one of Holmes's many attacks, here in the form of a satirical allegory, on Calvinism. Perhaps his most extended and serious attack is his essay on Jonathan Edwards (*Writings*, VIII, 361–401), whose *The Freedom of the Will* (1754) was a masterpiece of logic. Holmes tries to show in this poem that a system based only on logic goes to pieces all at once. He wrote Mrs. Stowe, "I do not believe you or I can ever get the iron of Calvinism out of our souls." As in the case of Hawthorne, Calvinism seems to have dictated the *problems* with which Holmes was to deal—problems of the freedom of the will and the responsibility for sin. In discussing Edwards, whom he called "the salamander of divines," Holmes concluded, "We are all getting to be predestinarians as much as Edwards or Calvin was, only instead of universal corruption of nature derived from Adam, we recognize inherited congenital tendencies,—some good, some bad,—for which the subject of them is in no sense responsible" (*Writings*, VIII, 380). He wrote his greatest novel, *Elsie Venner*

(1861), in order "to test the doctrine of 'original sin' and human responsibility." He concluded that the heroine, poisoned by a rattlesnake before she was born, represented all those who receive "a moral poison from a remote ancestor" and that, since such sinners are not responsible, they are proper objects of pity. It should be noted that Holmes's attack on Calvinism is twofold. Although he scorns the "logical story" of Calvinism, he himself uses science as a means of establishing determinism; and he carries on the eighteenth-century a priori argument, based on humanitarianism, that since a human parent loves his child, God, being greater than we are, must love his children still more, and that therefore the Calvinists' God of wrath must be represented falsely. On one hand he appeals to logical science and to Darwinism; on the other he appeals to the testimony of parental love. He thus enlists both the head and the heart to combat Calvinism.

Page 566. THE TWO STREAMS

Just as "a pebble's edge" at their head-waters may cause two rivers to flow in different directions, so, as two men grow up and depart from "the heights of Will," a moment may determine divergencies which lead one to dark ways and the other to peace. One of Holmes's major interests as a prose writer was the undermining of Calvinistic predestination and the inculcation of the idea that man's will is limited and at the mercy of numerous external forces beyond his control. See note, below, on "Wind-Clouds and Star-Drifts."

Holmes discusses the charges that he borrowed the thought of the poem from Hopkins (*Writings*, VIII, 46), and concludes: "Captain, afterward Sir Francis Head, speaks of the showers parting on the Cordilleras, one portion going to the Atlantic, one to the Pacific. I found the image running loose in my mind, without a halter. It suggested itself as an illustration of the will, and I worked the poem out by the aid of Mitchell's School Atlas."

Page 567. HYMN OF TRUST

Holmes wrote Mrs. Stowe, "My creed . . . is to be found in the first two words of the Pater Noster . . . To me the Deity exists simply in human relations. He is a mere extension of what I know in humanity." See this long letter outlining his creed, quoted in Morse's *Life*, II, 245–254; see also *ibid.*, p. 147, and studies listed in Bibliography by Bailey, Hayakawa, Strong, and Townsend.

Page 568. A SUN-DAY HYMN

This optimistic Unitarian hymn is Holmes's finest utterance in this field, comparable to that of Addison in "The Spacious Firmament on High." Note his emphasis on God as love to be sought in truth—i.e., science. Whereas *Paradise Lost*, representing the Puritan tradition from which Holmes had revolted, regarded evil as existing "through God's high suffrance for the trial of man," to the Unitarian Holmes "all, save the clouds of sin, are thine!" See Morse's *Life*, I, ch. X, "The Doctor's Novels and Religious Teachings" (pp. 256–293).

BROTHER JONATHAN'S LAMENT FOR SISTER CAROLINE

On March 25, 1861, after Lincoln's inaugural address declaring the Union perpetual and to be maintained by force, and just before the South's attack on Fort Sumter, Holmes wrote this touching poem in which he views the secession of the South from the North as a temporary quarrel between sister and brother. Geography and kindred traditions make Union inevitable, he says, and he pleads that when Sister Caroline's "heart aches" she will be reunited with the brotherly North. Note that in December, however, of the same year, after Bull Run and the Trent Affair, Holmes wrote "Union and Liberty" (see note, below) urging the North to "Smite the bold traitors to freedom and law."

Page 569. PROLOGUE TO "SONGS IN MANY KEYS"

While Holmes thinks the War is most important, he hopes that these "idle leaves" produced in "forgetful ease" may in odd moments help to recall "the not unwelcome past." Note how many of Holmes poems are reminiscent.

UNION AND LIBERTY

Although Holmes was in philosophic and religious and scientific terms the spokesman of the liberal, the rational, the progressive, the humanitarian, and the partially monistic, in social, literary, and political terms he was relatively the spokesman of the traditional and the Federalistic. Abolition and kindred reform left him cold; see his defense of his view in a letter answering Lowell's impatience (Morse's *Life*, I, 298–301). He described himself as "an out-and-out republican in politics" (Morse, I, 298). "I go politically for equality,—I said,—and socially for *the* quality" (*The Professor at the Breakfast-Table*, p. 133). See "The Brahmin Caste," *Elsie Venner*, ch. I. Among Holmes's political poems are "A Ballad of the Boston Tea-Party"; "Lexington"; "Grandmother's Story of Bunker-Hill Battle"; "Old Ironsides"; "Daniel Webster"; "Brother Jonathan's Lament for Sister Caroline"; "Sherman's in Savannah"; "After the Fire"; "Welcome to the Nations"; "On the Death of President Garfield"; "Additional Verses to Hail Columbia." In the latter he develops the Federalistic view (cf. Lowell's essay "E Pluribus Unum") that

"Only Union's golden key
Guards the Ark of Liberty!"

These poems defending a coercive union as a safeguard of liberty should be read in the light of Holmes's impassioned address on "The Inevitable

Trial" (*Writings*, VIII, 78–120), on the Civil War and its issues, and in the light of his "Oration" before the New England Society in 1855. The latter is not included in his collected *Writings*, but is to be found in *The New England Society Orations* (New York, 1901), II, 271–302. See also in Bibliography, Robert Withington, "The Patriotism of the Autocrat," and Dorothy L. Werner, *The Idea of Union in American Verse (1776–1786)*.

TO MY READERS

Note that Holmes says, try as the poet will, his most "inward melodies" remain unknown and his "largest hope is unfulfilled." It will be seen in the prose representing his poetic theories (pp. 595 ff., above) that Holmes's rationalism did not prevent him from being highly mystical and subjective in his views of poetic creation.

Page 570. THE VOYAGE OF THE GOOD SHIP UNION

Compare Longfellow's "The Building of the Ship" and Lowell's "The Washers of the Shroud" (ll. 103 ff.).

Page 575. WIND-CLOUDS AND STAR-DRIFTS

Holmes's blank verse here is excellent and the poem approaches nearer than anything else he wrote to "the grand style." The poem was originally put into the mouth of the lonely Young Astronomer in *The Poet at the Breakfast-Table* (1872). The various sections of the poem are divided by extended and dramatically conceived theological discussions which serve as commentaries on the thought of the poem and which should be read by anyone who wishes to understand it in its full detail. In introducing the poem, Holmes (*Writings*, III, 141 ff.) deplores the fact that the pale student is "burning away, like his own midnight lamp, with only dead men's hands to hold, stretched out to him from the sepulchres of books, and dead men's souls imploring him from their tablets to warm them over again just for a little while in a human consciousness, when all this time [the Young Girl being present] there are soft, warm, living hands that would ask nothing better than to bring the blood back into those cold thin fingers, and gently caressing natures that would wind all their tendrils about the unawakened heart which knows so little of itself . . ." Holmes added that he did "not wish to be held responsible for some of his more daring thoughts . . ." Nevertheless, these thoughts square with those Holmes elsewhere expressed as his, and the poem may be taken as representing his revolt againt Calvinism, conceived as self-centered and obscurantist, in favor of a religion based on rationalistic science, progress, and a loving deity created in the image of humanitarian man. It is an attack on tradition, a defense of the view that because man's weakness is determined for the most part by forces beyond his control he is not entirely responsible for his shortcomings and so deserves not so much censure as pity. Section IX, on the "Rights" of man so created, should be compared with Holmes's essays on "Mechanism in Thought and Morals" and "Crime and Automatism" (*Writings*, VIII), where he develops the view expressed in *Elsie Venner* that "nine tenths of their [wrong-doers'] perversity comes from outside influences, drunken ancestors, abuse in childhood, bad company, from which you have been happily preserved, and for some of which you as a member of society, may be fractionally responsible" (*Writings*, V, 228). It is interesting to consider the extent to which Holmes's view that determinism ought to motivate pity for man in general and for wrong-doers in particular looks toward the view of modern social thinkers.

Page 586. EPILOGUE TO THE BREAKFAST-TABLE SERIES

In *The Autocrat of the Breakfast-Table*, which appeared in the opening numbers of the *Atlantic Monthly* (November, 1857, to October, 1858), and the sequels, *The Professor* (1859) and *The Poet* (1871), Holmes developed a semi-dramatic form with which he had experimented unsuccessfully more than a quarter of a century earlier in two papers in the *New England Magazine* for November, 1831, and February, 1832. Although the structure, involving one group of people slightly characterized and a slender narrative thread, resembles that of Goldsmith's *Citizen of the World* and Addison's *De Coverley Papers*, Holmes made the work highly original, skillfully maintaining the illusion of conversation, and vitalizing it with his own many-sided and sparkling personality in accordance with his sub-title, "Every Man His Own Boswell" (cf. "Epilogue," l. 26). In the poem, Holmes imagines that after a century he finds in an old bookstore his three books in the series, bound in one volume, and that he starts as he finds himself in the work. He indicates the basis of his writing in saying (ll. 57–64) that to him "the lowliest human heart" is a divine "altar" with all its passion, friendship, pity, love, and sorrow.

Page 587. PROGRAMME

This poem, written to introduce Holmes's mainly occasional *Songs of Many Seasons*, explains that most of the songs have been written for occasions by request of friends, and in spite of himself. He sums up his "varied strains" as treating "all the changes life can bring," from conviviality to "mourner's tears." He asks that we approach his poems "not to praise or blame" them but to share emotions common to "all our hearts."

FOR WHITTIER'S SEVENTIETH BIRTHDAY

ll. 21–28. Longfellow.

ll. 29–36. Emerson. Cf. "At the Saturday

Club" (ll. 13–160), on Emerson as "a winged Franklin." In Holmes's biography of Emerson he is cool toward Emerson's transcendentalism and as a rational scientist he emphasizes the Yankee common sense and practicality which Emerson shared with Franklin.

ll. 37–40. Lowell, creator of Hosea Biglow, who had just been appointed Minister to Spain, as Irving had been thirty-five years before.

ll. 40 ff. Whittier, George Herbert (1593–1633) was one of the most gentle and spiritual of the seventeenth-century lyricists.

Page 589. TWO SONNETS: HARVARD

As a scientific rationalist crusading against obscurantism, Holmes took particular pleasure in exalting the Harvard motto, "Veritas." See his letter to John O. Sargent (Feb. 19, 1878) accompanying these sonnets. Holmes there says in part (Morse's *Life*, I, 237): "The Harvard College of today wants no narrower, no more exclusive motto than Truth,—truth, which embraces all that is highest and purest in the precepts of all teachers, human or divine; all that is best in the creeds of all churches, whatever their name; but allows no lines of circumvallation to be drawn round its sacred citadel under the alleged authority of any record or of any organization.

"That is what I mean to express in these two squares of metrical lines wrought in the painful prolixity of the sonnet, a form of verse which suggests a slow minuet of rhythms stepping in measured cadences over a mosaic pavement of rhyme, and which not rarely combines a minimum of thought with a maximum of labor."

(This feeling may account for the fact that he wrote only three other sonnets—the sequence to Longfellow entitled "Our Dead Singer" (1882). All five sonnets adhere closely to the Italian form, which he handles with ease.)

Elsewhere (*Writings*, I, 111–113) Holmes reminds us of Shelley, the apostle of perfectibility. The Autocrat says that when enlightened philosophers remove the stone of "ancient error" or obscurantist traditionalism from human nature, which he likens to bleached grass, "then shall the nature which had lain blanched and broken rise in its full stature and native hues in the sunshine. Then shall God's minstrels build their nests in the hearts of a newborn humanity."

THE SILENT MELODY

A touching dramatic expression of the pathos of the poet who is unable to express his highest aim. See also "The Voiceless" (p. 565, above).

Page 590. THE IRON GATE

This poem was "read at the Breakfast given in honor of Dr. Holmes's Seventieth Birthday by the publishers of the *Atlantic Monthly*, Boston, December 3, 1879." It should be noted that, like Emerson, Holmes's life was crowned with a happy serenity and that he never gave way to the melancholy so characteristic of romanticists such as Shelley and Byron.

Page 591. AT THE SATURDAY CLUB

The Club came into existence late in the eighteen-fifties. It was without formal organization. Men such as Emerson, Longfellow, Lowell, Agassiz, Peirce, Hawthorne, Motley, Sumner, Whittier, and others dined together once a month at the Parker House. In this group of friends Holmes, the conversationalist and wit, coruscated most brilliantly. See Morse's *Life* (I, 243–244), and E. W. Emerson's *The Early Years of the Saturday Club, 1855–1870*.

Page 593. THE LYRE OF ANACREON

Written for the class reunion of 1885. Although Holmes wishes his poetry had caught "some fresher fancy's gleam," he rejoices that he has been able to celebrate the memories of his comrades in a spirit of love,—although Love is now figured not as a "sportive child" but "with spectacles and staff."

Page 595. HOLMES'S POETIC THEORY

Holmes's theories of prosody, growing out of his scientific interests, are embodied in his essay entitled "The Physiology of Versification" (*Writings*, VIII, 315–321). In this he connects the laws of versification with the respiration and the pulse. These, he says, are "the true timekeepers of the body," the normal person breathing at the rate of twenty times a minute. The octosyllabic measure is easiest to read, he says, because "it follows more exactly than any other measure the natural rhythm of expiration." On the same basis, Holmes thinks that the "heroic line" is less easy to read because usually not more than fourteen lines can be read in a minute. "If a breath is allowed to each line the respiration will be longer and slower than natural, and a sense of effort and fatigue will soon be the consequence." (See full discussion by G. W. Allen, *American Prosody*, pp. 193–211). Mr. Allen points out that Holmes's theory disregards the fact "that in enjambed octosyllabics, two, three, or several lines are read at one breath-sweep," and that in blank verse "the irregular variation of short and long breath-sweeps gives us the most pleasing effects."

As in the case of many other American poets, scholars have published little on Holmes's general literary theories. These are embodied partly in his poems—see, in this book, "Poetry: A Metrical Essay," "After a Lecture on Wordsworth," "After a Lecture on Shelley," "For the Meeting of the Burns Club," "The Voiceless," "Prologue to 'Songs in Many Keys,'" "To My Readers," "Bryant's Seventieth Birthday," "Epilogue to the Breakfast-Table Series," "Programme," "For

Whittier's Seventieth Birthday," "The Silent Melody," "At the Saturday Club," "The Lyre of Anacreon," "Invitâ Minervâ," and "To James Russell Lowell." Holmes's poetic theories as expressed in prose are briefly represented by the selections printed in this book, pp. 595–601.

In broad summary it may be said that his theories were somewhat as follows. Poetry is of mystical origin, the poet at best being but the mouthpiece of a beauty which is divine. There are two classes of poets, those inspired by genius and those inspired by talent. The former are the greater; their utterances transcend their will; they are true creators, channels for divine inspiration, whereas the others are either sensitive confessors or craftsmen. Like Irving, to whom Holmes paid high tribute, Holmes advocated combining sentiment and humor, each counteracting the extremes of the other. Although himself a scientist, Holmes insisted on the important distinction between scientific truth and the imaginative truth which is the realm of the poet; he attacked the "scientific" realism of which Zola and Flaubert were the heralds. (On backgrounds see Herbert Edwards's "Zola and the American Critics," *American Literature*, IV, 114–129, May, 1932.) Whereas quantitative and precise description was the object of scientific truth as the literary realists held, Holmes held that the true literary artist must take into account the human personality through which objective reality is refracted, that he must include such elements as illusion, emotion, imagination, and idealism. He characterized himself as "his own Boswell" and he reveled in reporting his own thoughts and emotions; but he insisted that the true poet must make an artesian attempt to bore through his subjectivity to the bed-rock of human nature which he has in common with the universality of men. As a scientist and a religious thinker, Holmes was radically hostile toward European traditionalism and radiantly optimistic about the possibilities of the New World and of Boston, "the Hub of the Universe." As a literary theorist, however, he held that "æsthetically speaking, America is after all a penal colony" (Morse's *Life*, II, 222), that our writers can profit not only by our "couple of centuries of half-starved civilization" but also by the rich literary tradition of Europe extending back to the ancients such as his favorite Horace, a tradition which he likened to "a still lakelet, a mountain tarn, fed by springs that never fail." Ultimately, then, although Holmes's literary theory is touched by some of the current romantic doctrines, it has an interesting kinship with that of such neoclassicists as Pope and the Augustans of whose urbanity and cheer Holmes is our most eminent spokesman. (See S. I. Hayakawa's *O. W. Holmes, Physician, Poet, Essayist*, 1934, a dissertation in manuscript available at the University of Wisconsin Library, ch. III, "Literary Theory," pp. 121–171; and J. P. Pritchard's "The Autocrat and Horace," *Classical Weekly*, XXV, 217–223, May 16, 1932.)

EMILY DICKINSON

CHRONOLOGY

It is not possible to put a record of Emily Dickinson's life into the chronological form used for other authors in this book. There are no dates to be entered for successive volumes of her work, as none were published while she was alive. There are few external events to be chronicled, since most of her life was spent apart from any glare of publicity.

1830 Born, December 10, in Amherst, Mass. Her father, Edward Dickinson, educated at Yale, a lawyer of some prominence, "a gentleman of the old school," was for nearly forty years treasurer of Amherst College. Emily's girlhood winsomely normal, with all the interests of other young people of similar standing, but with a penetrating keenness of mind and vigor of expression that enabled her humorously to puncture many of the little bubbles of social hypocrisy so dear to the traditionally minded. Among her more intimate friends of this period (and throughout life) was Helen Hunt Jackson, daughter of an Amherst professor, author of *Ramona*, etc.

1847 At Mount Holyoke Female Seminary, where she showed her independent spirit by rebelling against the observance of Christmas as a day of fasting. On her return home the next year she again took up work in Amherst Academy. The year before going to South Hadley she had begun the acquaintance with Susan Gilbert (later "Sister Sue") who was to become the most sympathetic and comprehending element in her life.

1854 Emily joined her father, then a member of Congress in Washington. She was socially popular, an excellent conversationalist, quick at repartee, and intelligently aware of the political scene of the day. There followed a visit to Philadelphia where she seems to have fallen in love with a young minister already married. Rather than bring unhappiness to another woman, she renounced this love. The extent to which this experience influenced the almost complete retirement of her later years can only be surmised.

1856 Emily's brother Austin and Susan Gilbert married and established their home adjoining the old Dickinson homestead. From this time on her chief outer interests seem to have centered in this new family, and to the wisely understanding "Sister Sue" went a constant flow of epigrammatic prose and poetic communication.

1862 Began her correspondence with Thomas Wentworth Higginson, sending him four poems, and asking his criticism and advice. He was at once greatly impressed by their unusual quality and in the ensuing correspondence gave the author suggestions for improving these and other poems sent later. It is significant that she never followed his views in regard to making her verse more nearly approach the traditional forms. Instead of doing that she usually sent some new verses. She knew what she wanted to write and fortunately was not amenable to his criticism. It is of record that she made two revisions at the suggestion of "Sister Sue," but otherwise she made little effort to change the original drafts. That she appreciated Higginson's advice, however, is shown by the fact that she referred to him as her "teacher."

1866 Her poem, "A narrow fellow in the grass," was printed in the *Springfield Republican*, February 14, under the title "The Snake." A copy had been given to the editor, Samuel Bowles, by "Sister Sue." A poem referred to as a "Valentine Extravaganza" seems to have been printed earlier in the same paper (February 26, 1852) from a copy that had been given to J. G. Holland. A third poem, under the title "Success," was published by Helen Hunt Jackson in *A Masque of Poets* (1878), one of the volumes of the "No Name Series." These three poems were, apparently, the only ones printed during the author's lifetime, and she never offered any for publication.

1870 T. W. Higginson visited Emily at Amherst, August 16.

1874 Her father died. Her mother became paralyzed the next year, dying in 1882. After the death of her father, Emily's retirement became almost complete.

1884 Breakdown in health.

1886 Died, May 15. She had requested that all her manuscripts and correspondence be destroyed, but upon examination of the mass of materials left, those responsible for carrying out her desires decided wisely that her own writings could not justifiably be lost. Her devoted sister Lavinia placed the poems in the hands of some friends, and the story of their posthumous publication appears below. A few more than nine hundred poems have so far been published, and Madame Bianchi may be expected to give the world still others from the material in her hands.

(The two books now available which are of supreme importance for the facts needed in understanding Emily Dickinson are those by her niece and literary executor, Martha Dickinson Bianchi. To these may be added a third, for intimate atmosphere, written by MacGregor Jenkins, who was a friend of the Dickinson family from childhood. See Bibliography below.)

BIBLIOGRAPHY

I. Bibliography

Hampson, A. L. (comp.) *Emily Dickinson: a Bibliography*. Northampton, Mass.: 1930. (According to the foreword, this does not claim to be exhaustive. It includes a list of studies about the poet, and names a few periodicals in which some of her poems were first printed.)

[Jones Library.] *Emily Dickinson: a Bibliography*. With a foreword by G. F. Whicher. Amherst, Mass.: 1930; second edition, 1931.

Starke, A. "Emily Dickinson as a Great Unknown," *American Book Collector*, V, 245–250 (Aug.–Sept., 1934).

II. Text

Poems. Three series. Boston: 1890, 1891, 1896. (The first collections of Emily Dickinson's poems. None were published during her lifetime. The poems were selected and arranged by "two of her friends," Mabel Loomis Todd and Thomas Wentworth Higginson, from manuscripts furnished by Emily's sister Lavinia. The first series has a brief but charmingly appreciative introduction by Mr. Higginson, the second has an introduction by Mrs. Todd. Higginson seems to have had little to do with the third series. The poems in each series were grouped under the headings: (1) Life, (2) Nature, (3) Love, and (4) Time and Eternity. A large number of the poems in these original collections were given titles "almost invariably supplied by the editors." Emily Dickinson, unlike most poets, made no effort to supply specific titles. The three volumes included about 450 poems.)

The Single Hound; Poems of a Lifetime, ed. with an introduction by Martha Dickinson Bianchi. Boston: 1914. (One hundred forty-seven additional poems selected from the almost daily "poetic flashes" by which Emily kept in touch with Sister Sue "a hedge away." The title is derived from the striking metaphor of the opening poem in which the Single Hound is identified with the soul's adventurous spirit.)

The Complete Poems of Emily Dickinson, ed. with introduction by M. D. Bianchi. Boston: 1924. (Reprints the poems in the above collections.)

Further Poems of Emily Dickinson, ed. with introduction by M. D. Bianchi and Alfred Leete Hampson. Boston: 1929. (Includes one hundred seventy-five poems not previously published.)

The Poems of Emily Dickinson, ed. with introduction by M. D. Bianchi and A. L. Hampson. Boston: 1930. (The indispensable Centenary Edition, published in connection with the widespread reputation attained by the poet's work at the time of the centenary celebration of her birth year. Includes all the poems published up to date of issue.)

Unpublished Poems of Emily Dickinson, ed. by M. D. Bianchi and A. L. Hampson. Boston: 1935. (A further gleaning of one hundred thirty-one poems from material not included in the Centenary Edition.)

Selected Poems of Emily Dickinson, ed. by Conrad Aiken. London: 1924. (An excellent selection from the earlier printed volumes, with a valuable introduction.)

"Unpublished Poems of Emily Dickinson," ed. by Margaret H. Barney and F. I. Carpenter, *New England Quarterly*, V, 217–220 (April, 1932). (Six poems which were among those sent to Thomas Wentworth Higginson for his criticism and comment between the years 1862 and 1875.)

Poems for Youth, ed. by Alfred Leete Hampson, with foreword by May Lamberton Becker and illustrations by George and Doris Hauman. Boston: 1934. (The first important selection made from Emily Dickinson's poems for a special group of readers.)

III. Biography and Criticism

Adams, Helen R. *The Prosody of Emily Dickinson*. (An unpublished doctoral dissertation of 1932 available at the Library of the University of Pennsylvania.)

Aiken, Conrad. "Emily Dickinson," *Bookman* (London) LXVII, 8–12 (Oct., 1924). Also in the *Dial*, LXXVI, 301–308 (April, 1924). See also his preface to her *Selected Poems* (1924). (This able modern poet and critic says, "Her poetry is perhaps the finest, by a woman, in the English language.")

Aldrich, T. B. "Un poète Manqué," in *Ponkapog Papers*, etc., Boston: 1907, pp. 83–86. (Regards her poems as distinguished for their "impossible rhyme, their involved significance, and their uninterrupted flute note of birds that have no continuous music." Suggests alterations in her work. This paper is an expansion of Aldrich's unsigned paper in the *Atlantic Monthly*, LXIX, 143–144 [Jan. 1892].)

Allen, G. W. *American Prosody*. New York: 1935, pp. 307–320. (A scholarly survey, concluding [p. 311], "aside from rimes, Emily Dickinson's versification is not a great deal more irregular than Emerson's. Her . . . originality lies more in the thought than in the metrical technique." See also Miles, Sherrer, Adams.)

Bianchi, Martha Dickinson. *Emily Dickinson Face to Face: Unpublished Letters, with Notes and Reminiscences*. Boston: 1932. (Written by the poet's niece, who inherited all the Dickinson manuscripts and memorabilia, this book is easily the most valuable one for a complete understanding of the background. An "intimately personal study," it illuminates the close relationship that existed between Emily and Susan Gilbert Dickinson, the "Sister Sue" of the letters. Pages 175–270 contain more than one hundred and fifty hitherto unpublished "Letters and Notes." A "Foreword" by A. L. Hampson [pp. ix–xx] furnishes a careful summary of the fluctuations of public interest in Emily Dickinson and her work.)

—— *The Life and Letters of Emily Dickinson.* Boston: 1924. (The authoritative formal biography, this book is of fundamental value in presenting all the more important basic facts necessary to an understanding of Emily Dickinson's life and poetry. Of particular value is the chapter entitled "Her Religion" [pp. 88–105].

Bloom, Margaret. "Emily Dickinson and Dr. Holland," *University of California Chronicle,* XXXV, 96–103 (Jan., 1933). (Since Emily was a close friend and admirer of Dr. Holland, author of novels which were best-sellers, Miss Bloom analyzes these novels as an index to his character and ideas. "For an all but disembodied spirit, isolated from human contacts, if that she were, Emily was for years in surprisingly close relation with the plain people of her time through their chosen apostle, Dr. Holland. It may be that she had her feet more firmly set in bourgeois soil than we have lately been led to believe." An interesting, well-presented paper, although the conclusion rests on inference rather than conclusive proof.)

Bradford, Gamaliel. "Emily Dickinson," in *Portraits of American Women.* Boston: 1919, pp. 229–257. (First appeared in *Atlantic Monthly,* CXXIV, 216–226 [August, 1919]. An impressionistic, somewhat rhapsodic study of her mind and character as seen in her writings. She is regarded as "puzzling, teasing, witching," and her "strange, chaotic verses" are "not so much verses as clots of fire, shreds of heaven, snatches of eternity." Of slight objective value to scholars.)

Brégy, Katherine. "Emily Dickinson: a New England Anchoress," *Catholic World,* CXX, 344–354 (Dec., 1924). (A brief but closely-reasoned and incisive study of her religious views, concluding that, as a mystic primarily concerned with the life of the spirit, "she was a seeker rather than a finder, a reacher out rather than a compasser of the Infinite" [p. 353]. Well documented. One of the most important studies of her religion.)

Brenner, Rica. *Twelve American Poets before 1900.* New York: 1933, pp. 267–295. (Mainly biographical, this is a sympathetic general essay, graceful and well-written.)

Brown, R. W. "A Sublimated Puritan," in *Lonely Americans.* New York: 1929, pp. 235–257. (Readable, sympathetic, impressionistic, with slight documentation, but with considerable insight into one aspect of Emily Dickinson's character. Thinks that her Puritan individualism made her rebellious, and her Puritan conscience compelled her to sublimate her desires—and so achieve greatness.)

Catel, Jean. "Sur Emily Dickinson, à propos de deux livres," *Revue Anglo-Américaine,* XIII, 140–144 (Dec., 1935). (An able discussion, by a distinguished French scholar, based on the biographies by Miss Pollitt and Mrs. Taggard.)

Chadwick, H. C. "Emily Dickinson: a Study," *Personalist,* X, 256–269 (Oct., 1929). (A charming summary of the more important known facts about the poet's life, without any fresh contribution.)

Comings, L. L. "Emily Dickinson," *Mount Holyoke Alumnæ Quarterly,* VIII, 133–139 (Oct., 1924).

Deutsch, Babette. "A Sojourn in Infinity," *Bookman,* LXIX, 303–306 (May, 1929). (An appreciative review of *Further Poems,* pointing out elements of greatness. "The present collection, while it does not diminish her stature by a cubit, can add nothing to it.")

Fletcher, J. G. "Woman and Poet," *Saturday Review of Literature,* I, 77–78 (Aug. 30, 1924).

Gorman, H. S. *The Procession of Masks.* Boston: 1923, pp. 43–54.

Hartley, M. *Adventures in the Arts.* New York: 1921, pp. 198–206.

Higginson, T. W. *Carlyle's Laugh and Other Surprises.* Boston: 1909, pp. 249–283. (Originally, "Emily Dickinson's Letters," *Atlantic Monthly,* LXVIII, 444–456 [Oct., 1891]. This record of her relation to the one man she called her "teacher" and who appreciated her insight and epigrammatic brilliance is of primary importance.)

Hillyer, R. "Emily Dickinson," *Freeman,* VI, 129–131 (Oct. 18, 1922).

Howells, W. D. "Poems of Emily Dickinson," *Harper's Magazine,* LXXXII, 318–321 (Jan., 1891). (Illustrates the fact that early critics did not neglect or disdain her poetry, which Howells thought "a distinctive addition to the literature of the world, and could not be left out of any record of it. This poetry is as characteristic of our life as our business enterprise, our political turmoil, our demagogism or our millionaires" [p. 318]. Suggests her affinity to Emerson.)

Jacoby, J. E. "L'esthétique de la sainteté: Emily Dickinson," in *Le mysticisme dans le pensée américain.* Paris: 1931, pp. 241–276. ("Elle est l'épousée, non pas du Christ, comme d'autres mystiques, mais de la Mort, de l'Eternité!")

Jenkins, MacGregor. *Emily Dickinson, Friend and Neighbor.* Boston: 1930. (Important first-hand testimony that, although she appeared to many to be a recluse, she was delightfully human and was regarded by her young neighbors as a "rare combination of the mystic and the playmate. . . . She never lost touch with the essentials of human life and experience" [p. 38]. She was "an enthralled observer.")

Keleher, Julia. "The Enigma of Emily Dickinson," *New Mexico Quarterly,* II, 326–332 (Nov., 1932). (Offers no convincing solution.)

Kreymborg, A. "A Tippler Leaning against the Sun," in *Our Singing Strength.* New York: 1929, pp. 193–205. (Although Kreymborg thinks her full of technical faults, "None the less, a careless critic cannot resist concluding: In a world so full of perfect poets, let us have at least one irresistibly imperfect" [p. 205]. An admirable, almost lyrical, impressionistic essay on her great gifts.)

Kurth, Paula. "Emily Dickinson in Her Letters," *Thought*, IV, 430–439 (Dec., 1929).

Lewisohn, Ludwig. *Expression in America*. New York: 1932, pp. 356–363. (Brief, but striking interpretation. "The wonder is not that she was a great poet amid the poverty and narrowness of her experience; the wonder is that there was born in that Amherst house so great a poet that she needed only that house and the seasons and a few books and one supreme and unfulfilled passion to make her one of the few great woman poets of all literature" [p. 362].)

Lowell, Amy. *Poetry and Poets*. Boston: 1930, pp. 88–108. (Says that her verse technique became "a great banner, the symbol of a militant revolt," to the *vers librists*. An important essay.)

Maynard, Theodore. "The Mystery of Emily Dickinson," *Catholic World*, CXXXIV, 70–81 (Oct., 1931).

McCarthy, William H. "We Temples Build," *Yale Review*, Spring, 1936.

McLean, S. R. "Emily Dickinson at Mount Holyoke," *New England Quarterly*, VII, 25–42 (March, 1934). (A scholarly article, casting some light on her early religious training and views.)

Miles, Susan. "The Irregularities of Emily Dickinson," *London Mercury*, XIII, 145–158 (Dec., 1925). (An ingenious essay, claiming that she was not naturally awkward nor a faulty rhymer, but that her irregularities were artistically adapted to express a world which lacked dovetailed regularity. Analyzes and classifies her approaches to rhymes, and tries to show a correlation between the idea of the verse and its approximation to rhyme. See also the study by Miss Sherrer.)

Moore, V. *Distinguished Women Writers*. New York: 1934, pp. 147–160.

Pohl, F. J. "The Emily Dickinson Controversy," *Sewanee Review*, XLI, 467–482 (Oct.–Dec., 1933). (Scholarly in method and interestingly written, but of decidedly questionable validity.)

Pollitt, Josephine. *Emily Dickinson: the Human Background of Her Poetry*. New York: 1930. (A fairly direct narrative which generally distinguishes between fact and fancy, except in its very tenuous theory of the identity of Emily's lover.)

Powell, Desmond. "Emily Dickinson," *Colorado College Publication*, General Series, No. 200 (May, 1934). (A vigorous, well-written and appreciative essay, concluding that she is more likely to endure for her love poems than for her philosophic ideas. Urges that the literary executives and relatives make it possible for readers to have a complete edition of her work.)

Sapir, Edward. "Emily Dickinson, a Primitive," *Poetry*, XXVI, 97–105 (May, 1925). (An impressionistic, sympathetic, sensitive review of *Complete Poems*. Thinks that she did not have a wide literary culture and that she was curiously blind to the materialism of her age. Thus isolated, she was a "primitive," and "we find the fruits of her healthy ignorances in a strange, unsought, and almost clairvoyant freshness.")

Sergeant, E. S. "An Early Imagist," *New Republic*, IV, 52–54 (Aug. 14, 1915).

Shackford, Martha H. "The Poetry of Emily Dickinson," *Atlantic Monthly*, CXI, 93–97 (Jan., 1913). (A gracious appreciation, buttressed by abundant illustrative quotations.)

Sherrer, Grace B. "A Study of Unusual Verb Constructions in the Poems of Emily Dickinson," *American Literature*, VII, 37–46 (March, 1935). (A scholarly article showing that her usage involving the omissions in the use of subjunctive and imperative moods is not as incorrect as generally supposed. "The subjunctive mood is the natural mode of expression to this writer, whose mind reacted subtly to the contradiction, uncertainty, and vagueness of the natural and spiritual worlds.")

Taggard, Genevieve. *The Life and Mind of Emily Dickinson*. New York: 1930. (The identification of the "lover" is necessarily inconclusive, and the style is somewhat novelistic. Provides a list of books about the poet, with annotations.)

Tate, Allan. "New England Culture and Emily Dickinson," *Symposium*, III, 206–226 (April, 1932). See also Tate's *Reactionary Essays on Poetry and Ideas*. New York: 1936, pp. 3–25. (Suggestive, rather high-handed assertions, without much proof. Tries to relate her to Hawthorne and James as in conflict with Nature [regarded as Death] by way of Puritan theology. Yet has minimized "supernatural proportions" of Puritanism, and "Mather would have burned her for a witch." See Brown.)

Taylor, W. F. *A History of American Letters*. New York: 1936, pp. 281–282. (Contains an extended bibliography, pp. 533–555.)

Todd, Mabel Loomis (ed.). *Letters of Emily Dickinson*. 2 vols. Boston: 1894. New and enlarged edition in 1 vol. New York: 1931. (The first important collection of biographical material.)

Trueblood, C. K. "Emily Dickinson," *Dial*, LXXX, 301–311 (April, 1926). (Although mainly undocumented, this brilliantly written critique is valuable in its peculiar subtlety and comprehensiveness. Emphasizes her "rare, subtle knowledge of the interiors of the spirit . . . Her retreat inward was to the bright observatories, and not the dark recesses of spirit." Her poetry has "the rarest of lyric asceticism.")

Untermeyer, L. "Colossal Substance," *Saturday Review of Literature*, March 16, 1929. See also his articles, "Emily Dickinson," *Saturday Review of Literature*, VI, 1169–1171 (July 5, 1930), and "Thoughts after a Centenary," *ibid.*, VII, 905–906 (June 20, 1931).

Van Doren, Carl. *American Literature: an Introduction.* Los Angeles: 1933, pp. 67–70. ("Her work approaches poetry's irreducible minimum, which is poetry's immortal part." Reprinted as "Epilogue" in the author's *Modern American Prose,* New York, 1934.)

Ward, A. C. "Emily Dickinson," in *American Literature, 1880–1930.* New York: 1932, pp. 43–52. (A stimulating critique, regarding her as "a major American poet—perhaps next to Whitman the greatest American poet of the last century . . . The inviolability of Selfhood was the substance and refrain of almost everything she wrote." Ward's notion, however, that "despair is at the bottom of her metaphysic" [p. 49] can hardly be accepted in the light of relevant studies by Bianchi [*Life and Letters*, pp. 88–105], Brégy, Brown, etc.)

Wells, Anna M. "Early Criticism of Emily Dickinson," *American Literature*, I, 243–259 (Nov., 1929). (A very valuable fully-documented assembly and interpretation of relevant evidence to 1915, with many incisive comments by the way. Shows that "until 1900, then, discussion of Emily Dickinson in the magazines was fairly plentiful. It was after the turn of the century that for fifteen years she became almost as obscure as she had been during her life." See also Miss Wells's discriminating review of books by Miss Pollitt, Mrs. Taggard, Jenkins, and Hampson in *American Literature*, II, 455–458, Jan., 1931.)

West, H. F. "Samuel F. Dickinson," *Dartmouth Alumni Magazine*, February, 1935. (Valuable for Emily Dickinson's ancestry and background.)

Whicher, G. F. "Emily Elizabeth Dickinson," in *Dictionary of American Biography*, V.

——"A Chronological Grouping of Some of Emily Dickinson's Poems," *Colophon*, Part XVI, (March, 1934).

—— "Emily Dickinson's Earliest Friend," *American Literature*, VI, 3–17 (March, 1934).

——"Poetry after the Civil War," in *American Writers on American Literature*, edited by John Macy. New York: 1931, pp. 374–388. (A brief but incisive analysis, in the light of the view that Whitman and Emily Dickinson "defined the poles of national feeling in their time." Emphasizes her devotion to nature and to introspection.)

Wood, Clement. "Emily Dickinson: the Shrinking Seer," in *Poets of America*. New York: 1925, pp. 82–96. (An ardent appreciation, profusely illustrated with quotations. Emphasizes her mysticism and concludes that "she wrote many more enduring poems than" Poe and Lanier, and that "she never sagged as low as each of them did.")

NOTES

Emily Dickinson's first book of *Poems* did not appear until 1890, and her *Complete Poems* were not collected until 1924. Such late publication, however, should not blind us to the fact that she *wrote* her poems at the time when Emerson, Whittier, Longfellow, and Holmes were doing their major work, and that her intellectual kinship is with them, as exponents of the older New England tradition, rather than with modern realists and pessimists and deterministic monists. It is true that the individuality of her poetic form and technique influenced modern poets. Even in this respect, however, Emerson was also a pioneer. And, like most New Englanders of the older school, Emily Dickinson was much more interested in *what* she had to say, in *ideas*, than she was in *how* she said it, in *form*. What were her ideas regarding man's relation to nature and the life of the senses? Man's relation to man as an individual and to mankind? To the world of divine spirit?

Let us summarize her reactions briefly, recalling the extent to which they are similar to Emerson's. First, although she rebelled, as Emerson did, against the theological dogmas of Puritanism, she was greatly indebted, as he was, to the general ethical fruits of Puritanism present in her environment—she inherited its moral earnestness, its dedication to the inward life of the spirit, its individualism and self-discipline. Second, like Emerson, she loved nature and its myriad beauties. Yet she recognized that these were fleeting, and that nature could be cruel; and she relied mainly as a dualist on the inward conviction that man is potentially a member of a permanent spiritual kingdom secure against change. Third, at a time when science and humanitarianism were exalted, Emily Dickinson subordinated both to mystical illumination and to individual responsibility: she supplemented rationalism with intuition and social sympathy with a belief that fundamentally man, endowed with free will, is the architect of his own fate. Fourth, although indifferent to mere outward time-serving conformity, she prized, like exponents of the classical and the Christian traditions, ethical guides such as the imitation of noble lives directed by the moral imagination. Fifth, Emily Dickinson followed Plato and Spenser and Emerson in transmuting physical love into divine love. Sixth, having sternly renounced a love which would have ruined the happiness of others, she became the psychological poet, of an interior life, recording, with whimsical feminine touches, her progress toward self-conquest. Her art became increasingly the psychological self-analysis of a singularly engaging spirit seeking mystical union with divine perfection. Seventh, like Emerson, she thought that beauty and truth and goodness are one, and that literary art ought to be not an end in itself but an organic by-product of spiritual striving; it should be direct, genuine, and simple, a truthful transcript of one's reaction to nature, to humanity, and to God.

Mr. F. O. Matthiessen has admirably summed up Emily Dickinson's dualism and centrality as it affects the quality of her poetry. He pays tribute to "her entire assurance that 'exhilaration is within,' that the outer world takes size, tone, and color from the inner, that the one season she really wants is 'midsummer in the mind.'

"Such balancing of light against dark, courage against despair, acceptance against longing, reveals again her understanding of Emerson's important affirmation that 'All things are double, one against another.' This constitutes the source of the dramatic urgency in her poems, since no drama can exist without this double grasp of good and evil; and Emily Dickinson's dramatic sense is preeminently the attribute that brings focus and significance to what would otherwise disperse into a confused series of tiny lyric ejaculations. . . .

"Her victory frequently lies in resignation or renunciation, in the perception of heroism in defeat; here it consists in quiet rejection of the world's values, in the discovery of its brutality. Such mastery of the world by rejection is a part of the New England strain: it is enacted by the most typical characters of Henry James as well as in the life of Jonathan Edwards. What gives Emily Dickinson's articulation of it peculiar vitality is her exact balance between abstraction and sensation. This delicate poise, as Allen Tate has remarked, constitutes the 'metaphysical' quality of her poetry. On the one hand, she does not lose herself wholly in a plunge into sensation as Whitman often did; on the other, she does not soar into the dry air of abstraction, as Emerson, despite his best intentions, was always too prone to do. As a result, the dramatic struggle of her spirit, though tightly centered in a narrow sphere, embraces a common human reality."—*Saturday Review of Literature*, XII, 12 (Jan. 18, 1936).

Poems on Nature

Page 603. THERE'S A CERTAIN SLANT OF LIGHT

Emily Dickinson is quite capable of describing external nature vividly and she mastered imagist etchings half a century before the Imagist movement (see Amy Lowell, Bibliography). It should be noted, however, as illustrated in this poem, that she is primarily concerned not with etching external nature but with the effect of certain natural phenomena on one's inward mood or consciousness: she is interested in the "internal difference" (l. 7). Note also her belief, held in common with Emerson and Coleridge, in the poem "To Hear an Oriole" (p. 604), that "The fashion of the ear/ Attireth that it hear," that ultimately the beauty of nature is "within" us.

I'LL TELL YOU HOW THE SUN ROSE

Note the characteristically feminine beauty of her description of the splendor of nature, vividly personified.

I LIKE TO SEE IT LAP THE MILES

Compare this sustained metaphor-poem of the train as a swift horse with modern poems by the professed Imagists such as Amy Lowell, Richard Aldington, Hilda Doolittle, J. G. Fletcher, Ezra Pound. (See Glenn Hughes, *Imagism and the Imagists*, Stanford, Calif.: 1931.) Note also the audacity and originality of her images, and her unique ability to suggest something "prodigious" in few words. Her combination of strictest economy and power of springing the imagination is almost unique in degree.

APPARENTLY WITH NO SURPRISE

While Emily Dickinson can view the realities of physical death whimsically, as in the reference to her "granite lip" in the next poem, she has less in common with the romantic notion of Wordsworth that "nature never did betray the heart that loved her" than with the view of the age of Darwin that nature is "red in tooth and claw." Here she confronts the fact that "an approving God," supposedly omnipotent and benevolent, permits nature (the frost) to play the part of an "assassin." Melville of course writes in a much more rebellious mood and in a different form, but he deals with the same theme in *Moby Dick* (1851).

Page 604. WHERE SHIPS OF PURPLE

Compare this colorful imagism in the interest of fantasy with similar poems by Sandburg.

Poems on Love

I GOT SO I COULD HEAR HIS NAME

Madame Bianchi (*Emily Dickinson Face to Face*, p. 51) writes: "The testimony of her closest contemporaries leaves no doubt that during her visit to Philadelphia, following her stay in Washington [in 1854], my aunt met the man who was henceforth to stand to her for the Power and the Glory, and with whom, in the phrase of the day, she 'fell in love.' These contemporaries were agreed that any further development of what was stated to be their mutual recognition of each other was impossible, owing to the fact that he was already married. According to them, the definite renunciation followed a brief interview in her father's house, and left a permanent effect upon my aunt's life and vision." This love, with its renunciation and sublimation, was the most crucial experience of her life, an experience which drove her to introspection and self-knowledge. In this poignant and lyrical poem in which the fused intensity of emotion and insight transcend the conventionalities of form she records the conquering of the agony of renunciation sufficiently to pray, even if somewhat blindly, in the hope that there is some Power that cares for and is superior to mankind.

HEART, WE WILL FORGET HIM

OF ALL THE SOULS

A WIFE AT DAYBREAK

The first poem is distinguished for its silvery melody. Note in these poems, which make a distinctive contribution to the great litany of love, the rise, in mystical vision of fulfillment, to a style of ecstatic elevation. (Cf. also "Title Divine," p. 605.) Eventually, through sublimation, physical love becomes transfigured in spiritual love—cf. Emerson's more impersonal and Platonic "Initial, Dæmonic, and Celestial Love," p. 215.

Poems on Inner Conflict and Self-Conquest

Page 605. AFTER GREAT PAIN

THEY SAY THAT "TIME ASSUAGES"

For a sensitive discussion of Emily Dickinson's "interiorization" in connection with her art, see Trueblood, Bibliography. Wrung out of a great central pain and renunciation of her womanhood, her poems such as these reveal singular power in recording psychological states. Although in her case these states seem to be perfectly normal and wholesome, her vogue among certain sorts of Freudian interpreters has no doubt been increased by the fact that, in a romantic age which has exhausted the exploitation of most aspects of strangeness and novelty in outward experience, Emily Dickinson's interiorization and her psychological adventurings represent a new sort of frontier. After Harte and Mark Twain exploited the West and Jack London Alaska, some readers imagine that Emily Dickinson's record of the inward life offers a new and strange hinterland for exploitation. Like the psychological and decorous Henry James, however, Emily Dickinson, inheritor of Puritanism, should not be confused with the decadent interiorists such as O'Neill or Joyce.

TO FIGHT ALOUD

TRIUMPH

GROWTH OF MAN

These poems record her attempt to "charge within" her bosom the "cavalry of woe" and her recognition that the highest kind of conquest is not physical but spiritual—self-conquest in the light of divine perfection. Although Emily Dickinson is not orthodox or narrowly sectarian, these ethical poems dealing with the conduct of human life show how deeply she is in accord with the central teaching of the Christian tradition, and they help to explain her relative indifference to the merely outward panaceas of contemporary humanitarians and reformers who sought utopia by re-making institutions. Like Emerson ("Self-Reliance") and Robinson ("The Man Against the Sky," p. 758), Emily Dickinson believed that man's growth "gravitates within" and is achieved not by outward means or social environment (cf. Lindsay) but by inward "solitary prowess" supported by patience and "distinct belief."

Page 606. WHAT SOFT, CHERUBIC CREATURES

Emily's anti-Victorian contempt for "soft, cherubic . . . gentlewomen" of "dimity convictions" who flee from the realistic aspects of "freckled human nature" tempts one to interpolate a word regarding her neglected social and political views. It was inevitable, in the light of her philosophy of centrality and self-conquest, that such matters should seem of remote importance to her. Yet her admiration for Dr. Holland and his bourgeois best-seller novels (see Bloom, in Bibliography) suggests that she was not so aloof from social interests and problems as often supposed. Her idolized lawyer-father was a strong Whig, and attended the Whig Convention in 1852 which sought, unsuccessfully, the nomination of Daniel Webster for the presidency. Mrs. Taggard (*Life and Mind of Emily Dickinson*, p. 192), says her father, the friend of the Unionist Webster, "distrusted the ideals of democracy, rabble movements and Jeffersonian individualism—his temperament could make a constitution, but never a revolution. Romantic politics and a sense of property are antithetical." Mrs. Taggard, however, thinks Emily "makes avowals on both sides." She liked "very well" (Bianchi, *Life and Letters*, p. 205) Theodore Parker, the Savonarola who lashed social and political corruption, although her father considered him "poison." Emily's closest friends, in addition to Dr. Holland, such as Col. Higginson and Samuel Bowles, Jr., fought, respectively, slavery and political corruption. Bowles edited the *Springfield Republican* of which Emily was a constant, enthusiastic reader; he attacked the corrupt James Fiske, Jr., and wrote the platform of a new reform movement based on lofty personal integrity (see G. S. Merriam, *Life and Times of Samuel Bowles*, 2 vols., New York: 1885). She disliked the "hateful, hard, successful face" as much as Hawthorne disliked Judge Pyncheon, exponent of smug and unscrupulous capitalism. In "Revolution Is the Pod" (*Poems*, 1930, p. 290) she compares revolution to a pod from which outworn systems fall in the wind. But she seems to imply that revolution is only a test of the genuine value of institutions in the face of an extreme inactivity as regards reform. Madame Bianchi concludes (*Life and Letters*, p. 81) that she had a grasp of European affairs and an interest in European statesmen that was unusual among the women of her day. On the whole, it is probable that a full investigation of her social and political views would show that they were in rather close accord with Emerson's, whom she resembles in so many other ways. It does not seem fair, then, to regard Emily Dickinson as a recluse who was completely blind to the secular struggles of her time, and its quest for social justice: an exponent of centrality, she was fundamentally conservative, but she was by no means uninterested in or unsympathetic toward attempts at reform. It is probable that if she had uttered her mind fully on this subject, her position would have been much like that of Lowell in "The Independent in Politics." It must not be forgotten that, as in the case of Emerson and Lowell, her centrality was tempered by her deep heritage of Christian charity. See, for example, her poem beginning, "If I can stop one heart from breaking."

READ, SWEET, HOW OTHERS STROVE

Like Emerson, Emily Dickinson managed to combine individualism with a profound respect for tradition—that is, for the inspiring record of the lives of others who had illustrated the ideal of self-conquest. Here she urges that one read how others "strove" and "renounced" until by so doing "we are stouter." It should be noted, however, that she pays allegiance not to mere antiquarianism or curiosity about the external idiosyncracies of past writers but to the classical-Christian doctrine of imaginative ethical imitation. (Cf. Plutarch's *Parallel Lives* and Thomas à Kempis's *Imitation of Christ*. See also Longfellow's "Psalm of Life," and consider Lowell's vast respect for culture and tradition.) There has been no exhaustive study of the extent to which Emily Dickinson followed her own advice about reading, although her letters contain numerous references to Plato, Dante, the Bible (especially the book of Revelation), the Brownings, George Eliot, Hawthorne, the Brontës, Sir Thomas Browne, Keats, De Quincey, Tennyson, Wordsworth, and Dickens (Bianchi, *Life and Letters*, pp. 80–81, 276, 294, 302, 318, 327, 240, 287, 311). "While Shakespeare remains," she said, "literature is firm" (*ibid.*, p. 294). She singled out Emerson's *Representative Men* to send Mrs. Higginson as "a little granite book you can lean upon." Emerson's volume of poems had been given her when she was nineteen, the year in which he collected and published in book form his "three challenges," "Nature," "The American Scholar," and "Divinity School Address." Emily's brother and sister eagerly read Emerson, and he stayed at their home when he lectured in Amherst. A girlhood friend, speaking of their common reading, says "Lowell was especially dear to us," and she recalls that Emily gave way to "a passionate fit of crying" brought on by a college tutor's statement that Lowell was inferior to Byron in style. According to Madame Bianchi (*Life and Letters*, p. 80), "She always read Frank Sanborn's letters in the columns of the *Springfield Republican* for their reflection of the art and literature of his period."

THE GLEAM OF AN HEROIC ACT

Cf. Emerson's poem "Heroism" (p. 199) and his great essay on this subject. It should be noted that Emily Dickinson looks upon the imagination not as a pander to Arcadian and aimless escape, as in the case of some of the romanticists, but rather as an inspiring means of envisaging an ethical heroism as the goal of all conduct. Her view of the imagination is essentially that of Milton, who said he aimed to realize in himself "a composition and pattern of the best and honorablest things" as these have been revealed by "the highest wisdom . . . in every age."

SUPERIORITY TO FATE

It should be noted that Emily Dickinson aligns herself with Emerson and Lowell, believers in man's free will and his power, through habitual self-discipline, of becoming the architect instead of the victim of outward circumstances, rather than with Holmes, who heralded the vogue of determinism in America.

ON THE BLEAKNESS OF MY LOT

'TIS LITTLE I COULD CARE

Instead of the chronic discontent and the yearning for the distant, the strange, and the indeterminate, so common among romanticists such as Shelley, one finds in Emily Dickinson's poetry serenity and an ability to find the miraculous in the near and the common. (Cf. Emerson and Whittier.) Far from voicing despair, as some deluded interpreters have imagined, she wrote characteristically, "I find ecstasy in living; the mere sense of living is joy enough" (Bianchi, *Life and Letters*, p. 275, in a letter of 1870 to Higginson). Of the first of these poems Ludwig Lewisohn wrote: "She can be of a compactness of expression and fullness of meaning not less than Goethean in Goethe's epigrammatic mood" (*Expression in America*, p. 359).

RENUNCIATION

Emily's renunciation of her already-married lover was the focal fact of most of her thinking, and it was based on a philosophy which emphasized what Emerson called the "Internal Check" which he traced to the classical Socrates, the Hindoos, and the mystical Quakers (Emerson's *Works*, IV, 140). The doctrine has been emphasized by many of the major American writers: see Bryant's *Prose Writings* (1884), I, p. 21; Whittier, *passim;* Longfellow's "The Golden Legend"; Lowell's "Ode to Happiness." Edgar Pelham (*Henry James*, 1927, p. 250) says rightly that the common denominator underlying most of James's novels is the "renunciation of something immensely valuable for the sake of something quite without price." In Robert Frost's "West-Running Brook" he says symbolically,

"It is this backward movement toward the source,
Against the stream, that most we see ourselves in,
The tribute of the current to the source."

(See G. R. Elliott's penetrating essay on Frost in *The Cycle of Modern Poetry*, Princeton, 1929, pp. 112–134.) Critics such as Paul Elmer More, Irving Babbitt, and Norman Foerster have based much of their work upon a philosophy which emphasizes this "Internal Check," or as Emily Dickinson says here, a liberal free-willed choosing of a "larger function," spiritual or at least distinctively human, as against a "smaller" function, temporal or animalistic.

Poems on Religion

Page 607. HE PREACHED UPON "BREADTH"

Although Emily Dickinson reacted against some of the outward rigor of her Puritan up-bringing, the Puritan sense of moral earnestness and self-discipline remained with her as much as it did in the case of Emerson. She represents, as Norman Foerster says (*Cambridge History of American Literature*, III, p. 32), the "last pale Indian-summer flower of Puritanism." With this poem expressing her impatience with the inside of the open mind in her day, compare Hawthorne's similar view in "The Celestial Railroad," in which he ridicules Unitarianism and the more expansive forms of Transcendentalism.

ARCTURUS

With this poem as an expression of the indifference of a mystic and a poet to science compare Whitman's "When I Heard the Learn'd Astronomer" (p. 695). Elsewhere Emily speaks of a color on solitary hills "that science cannot overtake,/ But human nature *feels*." Her view of science is also much like that of Whittier and Lowell—see pp. 807, 878. Note the characteristic ending of this poem, conveying whimsically her preference for the traditional, if poetic, view of Heaven.

AT LEAST TO PRAY IS LEFT

The second stanza of this poem especially illustrates Emily Dickinson's ability to soar like the intense mystical poets of the seventeenth century (cf. Herbert and Donne), although ll. 3–4 embody a degree of incertitude more distinctive of the nineteenth century. Yet in the poem "I Never Saw a Moor," on the same page, she says she is as "certain" of the existence of heaven "as if the chart were given."

I STEPPED FROM PLANK TO PLANK

For full discussion of her religious development, which fell somewhat short of absolute certitude, see the discriminating study by Miss Brégy listed in the Bibliography. The poem "Who Has Not Found" (p. 608), however, illustrates Emily Dickinson's view that one who fails in self-conquest here on earth will fail to reach the heaven above, as well as her emphasis upon love as that with which God furnishes her residence.

Page 608. THE SOUL'S SUPERIOR INSTANTS

I DID NOT REACH THEE

These terse and trenchant poems illustrate the fact that Emily Dickinson's faith rested securely not upon logic or history but upon mystical illumination of a high order. In relation to the first, compare the Puritan Cotton Mather's doctrine of the elect and his inward struggles to secure a visitation of spiritual insight. Note the ballad-like quality in the second poem, which sums up her dramatic Pilgrim's Progress. Madame Bianchi concludes, in her able chapter on Emily's religion (*Life and Letters*, pp. 95–96): "Brother Lawrence in the seventeenth century saying the smallest action for the love of God is all, and Emily saying 'The simplest solace with a loved aim has a heavenly quality,' are really more than paraphrase . . . She had the soul of a monk of the Middle Ages bound up in the flesh of Puritan descent, and, from Heaven knows where, all the fiery quality of imagination for which genius has been burned at the stake in one form or another since the beginning . . . She was not a pantheist, though she saw each tree and bush 'afire with God.'" Madame Bianchi goes on to testify that Emily was kindness incarnate toward all who knew her. "There must have been the most lofty, holy inspiration, indeed," she says, "to perfect such fragrant living . . . Awe summed up her attitude toward religion and love toward life."

THIS WORLD IS NOT CONCLUSION

Although Emily Dickinson's dualism, her faith in a permanent world of spiritual values transcending a fleeting world of sensuous phenomena, may not be as absolute as Catholic interpreters may wish, it would seem to be as clearly defined, at least, as that of Bryant (cf. "The Flood of Years"), of Whittier (cf. "Andrew Rykman's Prayer"), of Emerson (cf. "Threnody"), of Poe (cf. "Eureka"), and of most other nineteenth-century Americans.

POETIC THEORIES

Unlike most poets, Emily Dickinson left no extended discussion of her poetic theories, and her scattered remarks on the subject have never been assembled and interpreted. These theories can be sketched in their main outline, however, from her poems in this volume:

1. Poetry is a "corporeal illustration," a concrete bodying forth, of thought given by God, by "the Heavenly Grace." The poet transmutes the idea into an image ("Publication," p. 609, ll. 9–16). Cf. Emerson's theory of the fact and the symbol.

2. Poetry, in Emily Dickinson's case, is based on a rapture as of legacies "of *introspective* mines." Her deepest inspiration is within: she is the poet not of outward nature but of the inward life of the spirit ("To Tell the Beauty," p. 609).
3. Second only to the poet's inward psychological experience as an inspiration is literary *tradition*, or a knowledge of the psychological experience of others in the past. In the poem, "Unto My Books" (p. 609), note her delight in her books, her "kinsmen of the shelf" who are capable of transmuting a "wilderness without" to "bells within." Cf. her poem, "Read, Sweet, How Others Strove" (p. 606), for a corroborative view of the strengthening inspiration of traditionalism and of lofty examples of heroism in books. And see also her poem "There Is No Frigate Like a Book" (*Poems*, 1930, p. 46), the book being considered as the embodiment of "a human soul." Her favorite authors were Shakespeare, Sir Thomas Browne, the Brownings, the Brontës, and especially Emerson.
4. Like Emerson and Whittier, Emily Dickinson thought that the true poet "distills amazing sense/From ordinary meanings," and from the "familiar species." This "amazing sense" of spiritual realities is secure above the transience of the physical world: it is "exterior to Time" ("This Was a Poet," p. 608). Cf. Emerson (*Works*, I, 74), "The invariable mark of wisdom is to see the miraculous in the common."
5. Beauty, Truth, and Goodness are one. She concludes, discussing beauty and truth, that "the two are one" ("I Died for Beauty," p. 608). And she reckons "First Poets—then the Sun—then Summer—then the Heaven of God" (goodness), but concludes that the true poet can "comprehend the whole" ("I Reckon, When I Count at All"; also "Publication," p. 609). Like Emerson and Whittier, she is not an escapist or an exponent of art for art's sake: like them, she regards poetry as inspired by God and to be used as an avenue of approach to God, to the ultimate realities. Beauty is enough, but the highest beauty is the beauty of holiness, the by-product of life in harmony with divine law.

SIDNEY LANIER

CHRONOLOGY

1842 Born in Macon, Georgia, in home of a successful lawyer, February 3.

1857 After private tutoring, and having shown himself precocious in music, he entered sophomore class of Oglethorpe University, where his mind was opened to the value of modern science, and where he did much reading which included Jeremy Taylor, Keats, Carlyle, Tennyson.

1860 Graduated, and appointed a tutor.

1861–65 Member of Confederate Army. In prison for four months, where he translated poems from Heine and Herder.

1865–67 Returned home dangerously ill. Was in turn clerk in hotel, teacher, lawyer. Discouraged by conditions in South.

1867 Published *Tiger-Lilies*. Married Mary Day. Increased financial difficulties.

1868–72 Studied and practiced law in Macon. Opportunity to hear good orchestras and praise of his own music by German critics (1873) led him to decide to devote his life to music and poetry.

1873 Baltimore. Played in Peabody Orchestra.

1874 Anxious to write poems but handicapped by "dreadful struggle for bread."

1875 "Corn" and "The Symphony" published in *Lippincott's Magazine*.

1876 *Poems*.

1878 Composed "The Marshes of Glynn."

1879 Lecturer in English literature at Johns Hopkins University. Published *The Boy's Froissart*, first of a series of boys' books, written as "potboilers." Others were *The Boy's King Arthur* (1880), *The Boy's Mabinogion* (1881), and *The Boy's Percy* (1882).

1880 *The Science of English Verse*. Composed "Sunrise."

1881 Died of tuberculosis, September 7.

1883 *The English Novel and the Principle of Its Development*.

BIBLIOGRAPHY

I. Bibliography

The Cambridge History of American Literature. New York: 1918. II, 600–603.

Starke, A. H. *Sidney Lanier: A Biographical and Critical Study*. Chapel Hill, N. C.: 1933, pp. 455–473. (The most up-to-date bibliography. Includes books, uncollected poems and prose, uncollected poem outlines, unpublished letters, and much biographical and critical matter about Lanier. Individual poems are not included in this bibliography, but their dates and places of publication may be found in the text by means of the index.)

II. Text

Poems of Sidney Lanier. Edited by his wife, with a memorial by W. H. Ward. New York: 1884. (New editions 1891 and later. This is the authoritative text.)

Select Poems of Sidney Lanier, ed. with an introduction, notes, and bibliography by M. Callaway, Jr., New York: 1895.

Selections from Sidney Lanier, Prose and Verse, ed. with introduction and notes by H. W. Lanier. New York: 1916.

"A Commencement Address by Sidney Lanier," ed. by Jay B. Hubbell, *American Literature*, II, 385–404 (Jan., 1931). (Important "chiefly for Lanier's remarks on art and on Southern literature.")

Tiger-Lilies: a Novel. New York: 1867. (Very rare.)

Florida. Philadelphia: 1875.

Letters of Sidney Lanier: Selections from His Correspondence, 1866–1881. New York: 1899.

Music and Poetry. New York: 1898.

Retrospects and Prospects: Descriptive and Historical Essays. New York: 1899.

"Sidney Lanier and Paul Hamilton Hayne: Three Unpublished Letters," ed. by A. H. Starke, *American Literature*, I, 32–39 (March, 1929). (Letters from Lanier to Hayne, mainly on the latter's poems.)

The English Novel. New York: 1883; rev. ed., New York: 1897.

The Science of English Verse. New York: 1880.

Shakspere and His Forerunners, ed. by H. W. Lanier. New York: 1902. 2 vols.

Poem Outlines. New York: 1908.

III. Biography and Criticism

Allen, G. W. "Lanier," in *American Prosody*. New York: 1935, pp. 277–301. (Standard. Surveys *The Science of English Verse*, Lanier's use of meter, his phonetic reiterations, and his imagery. Concludes that he represents "an American culmination of melody in conventional meters," that "he is the best representative of his particular manner.")

Baskervill, W. M. *Southern Writers: Biographical and Critical Studies*. Nashville, Tenn.: 1897–1903. I, 137–298. (Readable general discussion. Divides Lanier's work into three periods. C. Furst [*Modern Language Notes*, XIV, 197–205, Nov., 1899] praises Baskervill's work but argues that chronology of Lanier's poems does not warrant the three-period classification.)

Bentzon, Th. [Mme Blanc.] "Un Musicien Poète. Sidney Lanier," *Choses et Gens d'Amé-*

rique. Paris: 1898, pp. 171–233. (Reprinted from *Revue de Deux Mondes*, CXLV, 307–341, Jan. 15, 1898. A discriminating and generous estimate of Lanier, introducing him to French readers, with some translations of his work.)

Bopes, C. F. "A Lost Occasional Poem by Sidney Lanier," *American Literature*, V, 269 (Nov., 1933).

Bourgeois, Yves R. "Sidney Lanier et Le Goffic," *Revue Anglo-Américaine*, VIII, 431–432 (Juin, 1931). (Discusses "The Revenge of Hamish.")

Boynton, P. H. *Literature and American Life.* Boston: 1936, pp. 577–585. (Emphasizes the difficulty with which Lanier overcame a tendency toward "saccharin amorosities." Concludes that "at his best he is not out of place in company with Bryant and Lowell and Morris and Arnold.")

Bradford, Gamaliel. "Sidney Lanier," in *American Portraits: 1875–1900.* Boston: 1922, pp. 59–83. (A readable and able analysis of Lanier as a man rather than as a poet. "Lanier lived in a spiritual whirlwind, until it snuffed him out.")

Brenner, Rica. *Twelve American Poets before 1900.* New York: 1933, pp. 296–320. (A graceful general essay, touching on most of Lanier's interests in a sympathetic manner.)

Cady, F. W. "Sidney Lanier," *South Atlantic Quarterly*, XIII, 156–173 (April, 1914). (A brief but discriminating critique based on the view that "immaturity is the key to any analysis of the work of Sidney Lanier.")

Clark, G. H. *Some Reminiscences and Early Letters of Sidney Lanier.* Macon, Ga.: 1907.

Fagin, N. B. "Sidney Lanier: Poet of the South," *Johns Hopkins Alumni Magazine*, XX, 232–241 (March, 1932).

Flournoy, M. H. *Essays: Historical and Critical.* Baltimore: 1928, pp. 89–96.

Foerster, Norman. "Lanier," in *Nature in American Literature.* New York: 1923, pp. 221–237. (A readable and detailed survey of Lanier's treatment of the scenery of the South and a judicial analysis of his philosophy as it relates to nature. Concludes that "nympholeptic longing" akin to that of "the unbridled romanticists, such as Rousseau and Shelley," "vitiates even his best work, such as the 'Hymns of the Marshes'" [p. 232].)

Furst, Clyde. "Concerning Sidney Lanier," *Modern Language Notes*, XIV, 197–205 (Nov., 1899). (A review of Lanier's *Music and Poetry* and discussion of Baskervill's "really splendid study." Argues, however, that the poems in their chronology do not support Baskervill's division of them into three periods. Reviews other treatments of Lanier.)

Garland, Hamlin. *Roadside Meetings.* New York: 1930, pp. 144–153. (A glowing tribute to Lanier as an inspiring and liberating spirit.)

Gilman, D. C. (ed.) *The Forty-Sixth Birthday of Sidney Lanier.* Baltimore: 1888. (Includes addresses, poems, and letters presented at the Johns Hopkins memorial meeting, Feb. 3, 1888.)

—— "Sidney Lanier: Reminiscences and Letters," *South Atlantic Quarterly*, IV, 115–122 (April, 1905). (Gilman was president of Johns Hopkins when Lanier lectured there.)

Gosse, Edmund. *Questions at Issue.* New York: 1893, pp. 78–81. (Brief critique. Claims that Lanier is "never simple, never easy.")

Graham, Philip. "Sidney Lanier's Thought in Relation to That of His Age," *University of Chicago Abstracts of Theses*, Humanistic Series, VI, 353–358 (1927–1928). (A summary of an elaborately-documented dissertation which surveys the development of Lanier's religious, economic, social, educational, and æsthetic theories, and shows their relation to those of his contemporaries. An important contribution, showing the range and vigor of Lanier's thought in its historical contexture. The evidence presented indicates that his romanticism was considerably balanced by conservative influences, notably his early Calvinistic training.)

—— "Lanier and Science," *American Literature*, IV, 288–292 (Nov., 1932). (Although he "refused to accept the doctrine of biological evolution," science strongly influenced his thought-patterns, his conceptions of art, his imagery, and his dislike for industrialism. He became "a poet voicing the pain incident to the conflict between the old and the new orders." Brief but valuable.)

—— "Lanier's Reading," *University of Texas Studies in English*, No. 11 (Sept. 1, 1931), pp. 63–89. (Despite an occasional slip, this survey, followed by a list of 419 titles, is an indispensable basis for any study of the development of Lanier's book-molded mind. Shows his special devotion, during different periods, to Carlyle, German romanticists, Keats and Poe, Shakespeare and the Bible, Anglo-Saxon writings, Chaucer, Malory and the romancers, Spencer and Huxley, and Tennyson, Browning, Swinburne and Whitman.)

Higginson, T. W. *Contemporaries.* Boston: 1899, pp. 85–101.

Huckel, Rev. Oliver. "The Genius of the Modern in Lanier," *Johns Hopkins Alumni Magazine*, XIV, 484–503 (June, 1926).

Kaufman, M. S. "Sidney Lanier, Poet Laureate of the South," *Methodist Review*, LXXXII, 94–107 (Fifth Series, XVI, Jan., 1900). (Emphasizes Lanier's character, "moral sanity," and the "pure, sweet, exhilarating atmosphere of his writings." Finds his optimism based on a faith in a firm order in the universe. Discusses his religious views, his exalted devotion to nature, and concludes that he is a "Christian pantheist." Not very scholarly.)

Kent, C. W. "A Study of Lanier's Poems," *Publications of the Modern Language Association*, VII,

33–63 (April, 1892). (Although the first part of this study [biography] has been superseded by Starke, and the second part [his reading] has been superseded by Graham, the third part, embodying a close analysis of Lanier's poems, is valuable. Sympathetic, well-documented, and thorough. See also G. W. Allen, above.)

King, F. A. "Sidney Lanier: Poet, Critic, and Musician," *Sewanee Review*, III, 216–230 (Feb., 1895).

Kuhl, E. P. "Sidney Lanier and Edward Spencer," *Studies in Philology*, XXVII, 462–476 (July, 1930). (A valuable article, printing for the first time Lanier's letter of April 1, 1875, describing the spiritual crisis after Howells's rejection of "Corn," a crisis which steeled his devotion to poetry. Admirable discussion of the whole situation. See Starke, below.)

Kreymborg, Alfred. *Our Singing Strength*. New York: 1929, pp. 161–171. (Thinks that Lanier built up his poetic theory before his poetic practice and that "he enslaved himself to form quite as restrictive as the conservative's abject prostration before classic conventions," that he needed "a little more of matter and less of manner." Finds him a studio poet, at once too technical and too didactic. The essay contains some fairly able æsthetic analyses of individual poems.)

Lorenz, Lincoln. *The Life of Sidney Lanier*. New York: 1935. (Lorenz says he was given access to "family records and permission to quote at discretion from unpublished letters," but he adds very little information to A. H. Starke's biography, which is much superior. Readable but sentimental. Sparsely documented.)

Macy, John. "Lanier," in *The Spirit of American Literature*. New York: 1913, pp. 309–323. ("Three volumes of unimpeachable poetry have been written in America: 'Leaves of Grass,' the thin volume of Poe, and the poetry of Sidney Lanier." Unlike Kreymborg, Macy claims "his theory followed his art." Brief and impressionistic. Concludes "he was unapproachably the best American poet of his generation.")

Malone, Kemp. "Sidney Lanier," *Johns Hopkins Alumni Magazine*, XXI, 244–249 (March, 1933). (Scholarly and stimulating.)

Miles, Dudley. "The New South: Lanier," *The Cambridge History of American Literature*. New York: 1918, Vol. II, 313–346. (A good comprehensive essay written with considerable critical detachment. Includes discussion of Lanier's prose works. Although Miles finds that "Lanier's thought is liable on analysis to be found commonplace and prosaic" [p. 343], he, unlike the Agrarians, praises him for his ability to combine a devotion to his Southern locality with a postwar "sympathy and comprehension in voicing the new idea of nationality" [p. 345].)

Mims, Edwin. *Sidney Lanier*. American Men of Letters Series. Boston: 1905. (Appreciative and graceful. Provides Southern background, and is an able and judicious interpretation, but does not attempt to appraise Lanier's standing among men of letters. Mims provides in the *Dictionary of American Biography* (X, 601–605) a most authoritative and up-to-date brief biography.)

Monroe, Harriet. "Rhythms of English Verse," in *Poets and Their Art*. New York: 1926, pp. 290–306. (Has little specifically on Lanier but concludes an interesting discussion agreeing with his view in *The Science of English Verse*. She says: "The analysis of poetic rhythm on the basis of musical notation seems so obvious as to make it incredible that Sidney Lanier should have been the first to apply it to English verse.")

More, P. E. "The Science of English Verse," in *Shelburne Essays*. First Series. New York: 1904, pp. 103–121. (A stimulating essay with occasional reference to Lanier. His "brilliant work is unexceptionable as a study of the *ideal* or *model* verse, but fails to consider the variance between the *ideal* and the *actual* rhythm." Says that a large part of T. W. Goodell's *Chapters on Greek Metric* deals with this very question, "and thus supplements Lanier's theory.")

Moses, M. J. *Literature of the South*. New York: 1910, pp. 358–383. (The best comprehensive work on the subject, useful in putting Lanier in his historical and geographical contexture.)

Northrup, M. H. "Sidney Lanier: Recollections and Letters," *Lippincott's Magazine*, LXXV, 302–315 (March, 1905).

Parks, E. W. "Introduction," in *Southern Poets*. New York: 1936, pp. xvii–cxlviii. (An up-to-date scholarly survey, very useful in relating Lanier to Southern backgrounds, political, economic, and religious, and to American poetic theory. Extensive annotated bibliography.)

Pattee, F. L. *A History of American Literature since 1870*. New York: 1915, pp. 274–288. (A readable and fairly judicious essay. "He is distinctively a transition figure." Originally "a disciple of Keats, a poet of merely sensuous beauty," Lanier was turned to a more elemental realism by his "close contact with life in its elemental conditions" in the Civil War. But "he was too excited, too impetuous, to finish anything. Poetry was a thing of rhapsodic outbursts, of tiptoe glimpses.")

Ransom, J. C. "Hearts and Heads," *American Review*, II, 554–571 (March, 1934). (A reply to Starke's "The Agrarians Deny a Leader" [see below] and a continuation of R. P. Warren's attack on Lanier. Attempts to show that, as Warren said, Lanier was completely unrealistic, sentimental, ineffectual, romantic, and inconsistent in his social ideas, and not, as Starke claimed, a "precursor" of Agrarianism. Writing with the militant Agrarian bias, Ransom condemns Lanier for what he regards as disloyalty to the South in his devotion, following the War, to the united nation. Fairly incisive, but harsh and partisan.)

Short, J. S. "Sidney Lanier at Johns Hopkins," *Johns Hopkins Alumni Magazine*, V, 7–24 (November, 1916).

"Sidney Lanier Commemoration," *Johns Hopkins Alumni Magazine*, XIV, 482–505 (June, 1926).

Snoddy, J. S. "Color and Motion in Lanier," *Poet-Lore*, XII, 558–570 (Oct.–Nov.–Dec., 1900). (An almost exhaustively-documented study of Lanier's words and phrases chosen to convey color and motion. Cf. Foerster, above. Shows how strikingly sensuous Lanier was.)

Snyder, H. N. *Modern Poets and Christian Teaching: Sidney Lanier*. New York: 1906. (The president of Oglethorpe College, which Lanier attended, emphasizes his Calvinistic training and conservative religious aspects.)

Starke, A. H. *Sidney Lanier: A Biographical and Critical Study*. Chapel Hill, N. C.: 1933. (This, the indispensable book for all Lanier students, assembles, in its 525 pages with over eight hundred notes, almost every scrap of information bearing on the poet's life and work. The book is impressive particularly in its objectivity, its mass of facts, precisely documented, although there is also considerable discriminating interpretation and criticism. Deals not only with Lanier's poetry, but with his social and economic views and with his many works of criticism and æsthetic theory. Reviewed by E. E. Leisy in *Southwest Review*, Winter, XVIII, 1–11 [1933], and by C. R. Anderson in *American Literature*, V, 275–279 [1933]. Starke, Mims, and Philip Graham have provided the key studies of Lanier.)

—— "The Agrarians Deny a Leader," *American Review*, II, 534–553 (March, 1934). (Attempts to show the range and modernness of Lanier's social views. See also Graham, above.)

—— "Lanier's Appreciation of Whitman," *American Scholar*, II, 398–408 (Oct., 1933). (Shows that along with Lanier's derogatory comments on Whitman there are other comments, hitherto unprinted, showing a sincere admiration for certain aspects of Whitman such as his democracy and nationalism. See the multitude of references to Whitman in Starke's long biography. See also Starke's "Sidney Lanier: Man of Science in the Field of Letters," *American Scholar*, II, 389–397 [Oct., 1933], and his "William Dean Howells and Sidney Lanier," *American Literature*, III, 79–82 [March, 1931]. Cf. E. P. Kuhl, above.)

Stedman, E. C. "The Late Sidney Lanier," in *Genius and Other Essays*. New York: 1911, pp. 250–253. Reprinted from *Critic*, I, 298 (Nov., 1881). (It is interesting to note that in Stedman's *Poets of America*, with extended essays on nine poets, Bayard Taylor is given an entire essay and Lanier is given less than three pages [449–451]. However, this may be explained by the fact that Stedman's book was in press when Lanier's collected *Poems* [1884] appeared.)

Stoddard, F. H. "The Ideal in Literature. A Review of 'The English Novel' by Sidney Lanier," *New Englander*, XLIII, 97–104 (Jan., 1884). (Praises Lanier's general spirit as a critic, but says "he fails in subtle differentiations" and that "he confuses the moral and the didactic" in condemning Fielding and Smollett.)

Strong, A. H. "Lanier," in *American Poets and Their Theology*. Philadelphia: 1916, pp. 371–418. (In view of the emphasis some interpreters have placed on Lanier's early Calvinism it is noteworthy that the militantly Calvinistic A. H. Strong concludes [pp. 399–400], "We find him in his later life skeptical with regard to churches and denominations and creeds, while yet he clung to his old beliefs with regard to sin and Christ and salvation. The external gave way to the internal. There was less and less of dependence upon self and upon human aid, but more and more dependence upon the infinite pity and love of God, as they are made known to us in Jesus Christ." Thinks "The Crystal," his "clearest confession of his faith in Christ," his "greatest poem." Although didactic and somewhat garrulous, this essay is useful in its assembly of evidence. Cf. Josiah Royce [*Spirit of Modern Philosophy*. Boston: 1892, pp. 442–446], who explained Lanier's teaching as denying the existence of evil. Also E. B. Pollard, "The Spiritual Message of Sidney Lanier," *Homiletic Review*, LXXIV, 91–95, August, 1917. See Voigt, below, and Snyder, above.)

Thorpe, H. C. "Sidney Lanier: A Poet for Musicians," *Musical Quarterly*, XI, 373–382 (July, 1925.) (His "musical instinct . . . caused him . . . to treat . . . language almost as tone, so that much of his poetry possesses a melodic fluency and color, which is only equalled by Poe." Thorpe illustrates this view by Lanier's [1] poems which have been set to music; [2] poems inspired by musical instruments, e.g., "The Symphony"; [3] poems about musicians; and [4] text for the Centennial Cantata. An interesting interpretation, by a specialist in music, of Lanier's poetry as it relates to music.)

Tolman, A. H. "Lanier's *Science of English Verse*," in *Gilman Memorial*. Baltimore: 1888, pp. 37–45. See also his discussion in *Views about Hamlet and Other Essays*. Boston: 1904, pp. 107–113. (Discriminating analysis by an able scholar.)

Turnbull, Frances. *The Catholic Man: A Study*. Boston: 1890. (A sentimental and romantic idealization of Lanier [as the character Paul] which helped to start the "Lanier legend." The Turnbulls were friends and benefactors of Lanier in Baltimore. Mrs. Turnbull was an art-patroness who had Annibale Gatti in 1893 paint "The Master Light of All Our Seeing," with Christ on the Mount shining on Lanier, an idea inspired by his poem "The Crystal.")

Voigt, G. P. "Lanier," in *The Religious and Ethical Element in the Major American Poets*. Bulletin of the Graduate School of the University of South Carolina, June 1, 1925, pp. 139–149. (A brief but generally judicious survey concluding that, although undenominational, Lanier accepted the general teachings of the Christian tradition as the basis of his work, and that this tradition conditioned his social criticism, his view of the moral value of music, his chivalry toward women, and his view of science. See Strong, above.)

Warren, R. P. "The Blind Poet: Sidney Lanier," *American Review*, II, 27–45 (November, 1933). (A somewhat violently partisan attempt to show Lanier's weaknesses in the light of "Agrarian" criteria. "Lanier failed [to see] that the nationalism mystically embodied in the 'Psalm of the West' was a nationalism of Trade." Warren claims that his "social program" is romantic nonsense: "This program is Love, and the instrument of its execution is music." "He was the final product of all that was dangerous in Romanticism." See Starke's reply, and see Graham, above, including his study of Lanier's reading in non-romantic fields. See also Strong and others who have emphasized the influence of Lanier's Calvinism.)

Weirick, Bruce. *From Whitman to Sandburg in American Poetry*. New York: 1924, pp. 73–83. (An appreciative discursive discussion, emphasizing Lanier's best work as "a lyric poet . . . in whom nature and religious elation mingle beautifully.")

Williams, S. T. "Lanier," in *American Writers on American Literature*, ed. by John Macy. New York: 1931, pp. 327–341. (A readable essay written with critical detachment. Emphasizes Lanier's "exaggerated moods" and feverish intensity as well as his "provinciality" and narrow didacticism illustrated in his treatment of novelists such as Fielding. Concludes that his *cor cordium* is found in a worship of nature which "is sometimes pagan.")

Wood, Clement. *Poets of America*. New York: 1925, pp. 68–81. (Discursive and appreciative. Concludes that Lanier was "of the clan of innovators. The irregular ode form had long been known in English poetry; but in his typical poems, he achieved a welding of musical form to the spoken word that was distinctly his own . . . The polyrhythmical chant and the shapely musical improvisation—these were America's first two contributions to the formal side of poetry" [p. 81].)

Woolf, W. P. "Sidney Lanier as Revealed in his Letters," *Sewanee Review*, VIII, 346–364 (July, 1900).

NOTES

GENERAL

Since Lanier was strongly conditioned by his Southern background, the student is urged to acquaint himself with the latest scholarly survey of that background, in terms political, social, and literary, in E. W. Parks's introduction to *Southern Poets* (1935) in American Writers Series.

One of the keys to Lanier's thought—his doctrine of etherealization—is found in *Retrospects and Prospects*, p. 6: "For as time flows on," he says, "man and nature steadily etherealize. As time flows on, the sense-kingdom continually decreases, and the soul-kingdom continually increases, *and this not by the destruction of sense's subjects, but by a system of promotions in which sensuous things constantly etherealizing, constantly acquire the dignity of spiritual things, and so diminish their own number and increase the other.*" According to R. P. Warren (see Bibliography), "This sentiment is a sort of text for Lanier's work, equally for his applause of science and his applause of small diversified farms, for 'The Psalm of the West,' and *The English Novel*, for 'The Marshes of Glynn' and his nationalism, for his admiration of Beethoven and his admiration of big business."

According to Stanley Williams (*American Writers on American Literature*, pp. 334–335): "Extraordinary technician, aspirer after beauty, he shrank, nevertheless, from dynamic, self-sufficient conceptions of art. Over his writings hovers the spirit of the first post-evolutionary religious ideas and also his prepossession for what he called 'the loveliness of morality.' To his wife he wrote: 'The beauty of holiness and the holiness of beauty mean one thing, burn as one fire, shine as one light.'

"Yet once safely within this paradise, Lanier gave himself freedom in feeling and expression. Here he could 'move with manly purity'; nay, he could let himself go in a thousand ardors over music, nature, love, human and divine. It is an interesting parodox, this wild fervor of Lanier within the confines of the respectable traditions of art. . . . For cut off by moral principles from half the themes which are the staples of modern poets, he yet sweeps us along on wings of fire, transfigures, exalts. This torrent of feeling in Lanier's poetry has been condemned; but it is, of course, a sincere expression of himself. He repeated the whirlwind of his life in the whirlwind of his poetry. This fault, if fault it really is, is again connected with his era. . . . He himself, then, knew his own weakness; his honest search for guidance is pitiful." For further backgrounds see, in addition to Parks's bibliography, the extensive and comprehensive bibliographies on all aspects of the age in A. C. Cole's, *The Irresistible Conflict, 1850–1865*, and Allan Nevins's *The Emergence of Modern America, 1865–1878*.

John Macy, representing the view of the æsthetic nationalists, concludes in his enthusiastic essay (*The Spirit of American Literature*) that Lanier "was unapproachably the best American poet of his generation," equalled only by Whitman and Poe.

Data regarding the composition of individual poems and the places of their first publication may be found in A. H. Starke's *Lanier* (1933).

Page 611. NIGHT AND DAY

The fact that Lanier was often inspired to write not by direct observation of nature but by books is illustrated in this early lyric in which the sunset is described figuratively as the Moor Othello, slaying the white Desdemona. Mr. Starke notes that he used the same figure in "The Dove" (1877), and that in *Tiger-Lilies*, his novel, he described moonlight on the mountains as Desdemona's "dainty white hand upon Othello's brow."

The sing-song pattern of this early poem suggests how much Lanier developed in his later poems in the direction of varied sound effects integrated with thought.

THE RAVEN DAYS

This, the most pessimistic of Lanier's poems, expresses the mood of desolation and despair which pervaded the South immediately following the Civil War. On backgrounds of the period as related to the poet, see Starke's *Lanier*, ch. VI, "Reconstruction." It should be remembered that there was difficulty not only in the South but in the nation at large. The Crédit Mobilier and Black Friday scandals, which may have colored Lanier's mood here, were to be followed by the Salary Grab, the panic of 1873, the Whiskey Ring, and the Boss Tweed régime in New York. Cf. also Lanier's "Spring and Tyranny," "Laughter in the Senate," "Nirvana," and "Barnacles." In general, however, Lanier had faith in progress and was optimistic about the future of the nation.

RESURRECTION

This poem first appeared in *The Round Table*, Oct. 24, 1868. It was revised for *Poems* (1884).

Lanier has a vision of the best men and empires of eighteen centuries past being resurrected in a regenerate state, a vision of the best of the past vitalizing the present. "Fain, fain am I, O Christ, to pass the grave."

Page 612. MAY THE MAIDEN

From the unfinished poem "The Jacquerie." This long poem, inspired by the chronicles of Froissart, was conceived while the poet was still in college. Planned at first as semi-operatic, it was to treat the relation of trade, which Lanier loathed, to the decline of chivalry and the growth of social unrest.

In sheer liquid beauty this lyric has hardly a peer in American literature. Note the superb vowel-harmony of the refrain of each stanza.

THAR'S MORE IN THE MAN THAN THAR IS IN THE LAND

Lanier was something of a pioneer in the matter of dialect poems and realism in the South, although the North had "The Biglow Papers" (1846–1867), and Lanier's own state had A. B. Longstreet's *Georgia Scenes* (1835) in prose. The present poem foreshadows "Corn," and it should be read in connection with his essay "The New South" in which, following the break-up of the plantation system caused by the War, he urged diversified farming on a small scale. On the disputed question of the relation of his program to that of the present "Agrarians" in the South, see the attack by the Agrarian, R. P. Warren ("The Blind Poet: Sidney Lanier," *American Review*, II, 27–45, Nov., 1933), a reply defending Lanier by A. H. Starke ("The Agrarians Deny a Leader," *American Review*, II, 534–53, March, 1934), and then a reply to Starke by J. C. Ransom (*American Review*, II, 554–71, March, 1934) defending Warren's attack on Lanier as completely unrealistic, romantic, sentimental, and inconsistent in his social ideas. It is clear of course that the poet was not always a practical economist and that he did not regard a love of his locality as inconsistent with a devotion to the welfare of a united nation.

It should be noted, however, that the poem symbolizes the masculine ethical view that it is not environment or external conditions but the individual's own exertion that results in success or failure. (Cf. the philosophy of Franklin's *Poor Richard's Almanac.*) Such a view may explain why Lanier had little sympathy with the schemes of social reformers who would regenerate men by changing merely outward factors.

Page 613. IN ABSENCE

Note that this expression of the lyrical ecstasy of love focuses on the (Platonic?) idea that "wife-love" and "God-love" are not opposed but rather supplement and reinforce each other.

THE SYMPHONY

A. H. Starke concludes (*Lanier*, p. 209) that this poem, "though certainly not the most effective nor the most beautiful of Lanier's poems, is, for the revelation it makes of his philosophy, without doubt the most significant." (See Mr. Starke's whole excellent discussion, pp. 201–211, to which I am indebted.) Briefly, Lanier attacks Trade for its inhumanities, voicing his protest successively through the violins (ll. 15 ff.), the flute (ll. 86 ff.), the clarionet (ll. 216 ff.), the horn (ll. 253 ff.), and the hautboy (ll. 325 ff.)—through his beloved music, which he defined as brotherly "love in search of a word." For the background of his growing conviction that "Our religions, our politics, our social life, our charities, our literature, nay, by Heavens! our music and our loves almost, are all meshed in unsubstantial concealments and filthy garnitures" by Trade, see his letter of April 17, 1872, to his friend Hayne (quoted by Starke, p. 201); his essay on "Paul H. Hayne's Poetry" (*Southern Magazine*, January, 1875); the *Tiger-Lilies* in which the villain Cranston is corrupted by Trade; his "Confederate Memorial Address" of April, 1870; and the following letter to Judge Logan E. Bleckley of Georgia, November 15, 1874: here Lanier explained his purpose to write "a long poem, founded on that strange uprising in the middle of the fourteenth century in France, called 'The Jacquerie.' It was the first time that the big hungers of *the People* appear in our modern civilization; and it is full of significance. The peasants learned from the merchant potentates of Flanders that a man who could not be a lord by birth, might be one by wealth; and so Trade arose, and overthrew Chivalry. Trade has now had possession of the civilized world for four hundred years: it controls all things, it interprets the Bible, it guides our national and almost all our individual life with its maxims; and its oppressions upon the moral existence of man have come to be ten thousand times more grievous than the worst tyrannies of the Feudal System ever were. Thus in the reversals of time, it is *now* the *gentleman* who must rise and overthrow Trade" (quoted by Mims, *Sidney Lanier*, p. 158).

On March 24, 1875, Lanier in Baltimore wrote his friend Gibson Peacock (quoted by Starke, p. 204), "Four days ago, a certain poem which I had vaguely ruminated for a week before took hold of me like a real James River ague, and I have been in a mortal shake with the same, day and night, ever since. I call it 'The Symphony': I personify each instrument in the orchestra, and make them discuss various deep social questions of the times, in the progress of the music. It is now nearly finished; and I shall be rejoiced thereat, for it verily racks all the bones of my spirit." Elsewhere he wrote, "It has so much of my heart in it that I feel a personal fate as inhering in it." The theme of the poem has been compared with that of *Unto This Last* by Ruskin, who combined a love of art and a hatred of trade. The much-quoted last line of the poem, summing up Lanier's philosophy, may have been suggested, as Starke says, by the definition of the French Romantic, Mme De Staël, with which Lanier was early familiar—"Music is love's only interpreter" (*Thorn-Fruit*, p. 13).

In its feeling for "the poor! the poor! the poor!" (l. 190) to be freed from the tentacles of industrialism by music as the symbol of love, does the poem essentially embody practical economic vision, class-hating humanitarianism, Christian charity, or a romantic and indeterminate sentimentality?

The very complex versification, its rich variety of cadences, its extensive use of feminine rhymes, and its contrasting tone-colors in rhymes (cf. horn passage, ll. 253 ff.), should be studied in the light of Lanier's own poetic theories illustrated in selections in this book, pp. 644–649, above. See the detailed analysis of the relation between Lanier's theory and practice in G. W. Allen, *American Prosody*, pp. 277–306, and H. C. Thorpe, "Lanier: A Poet for Musicians," *Musical Quarterly*, July, 1925.

Page 617. CORN

On circumstances of composition see Starke, *Lanier*, pp. 182 and 188–194. Lanier began this poem before "The Symphony." He sent "Corn" to Mr. M. M. Hurd (of Hurd and Houghton, who had published his *Tiger-Lilies*, and who owned the *Atlantic Monthly*) to be passed on to William Dean Howells, then editor of the *Atlantic*. Mr. Hurd sent Lanier Howells's letter of rejection in which Howells said that he "did not find it successful," that he thought readers would be mystified by the poem because he found no "connection between the apostrophe in the beginning and the bit of narrative at the close" and he felt that "neither was striking enough to stand alone" (see A. H. Starke, "William Dean Howells and Sidney Lanier," *American Literature*, III, 79–82, March, 1931). The letter stirred Lanier deeply, and he wrote Edward Spencer of its being the cause of a psychological conflict in "a high room, in Brooklyn, N. Y. . . . I led myself to an infinite height above myself, and meditated: and when evening came I found myself full of the ineffable contents of certainty and of perfect knowledge and of decision. I had become aware . . . that my business in life was to make poems . . . God must have his chorus." (This letter is printed and the situation is admirably discussed in E. P. Kuhl's "Sidney Lanier and Edward Spencer," *Studies in Philology*, XXVII, 462–476, July, 1930.)

Lines 1–51 show that the hitherto somewhat bookish poet is describing nature now with his eye on the object, although the details are harmonized and focused on a mood inspired by summer ripeness and drowsy bliss.

Lines 52–110, treating the corn as the type of "the poet soul-sublime," offer an interesting discussion of Lanier's view of the true poet's function. He "leads the vanward of his timid time." He teaches "selfless chivalry." He should be rooted in the concrete, the local and the particular, yet he should yield a harvest which is "universal" and in "select proportion." He should "marry new and old," earth and heaven, and reconcile "the dark and bright," helping the low and the high. Compare with his prose statements of the poet's function, pp. 644–649, above.

Lines 111–200, in harmony with "The Symphony" (see note above), embody an agrarian attack on the cotton-trade and get-rich-quick schemes which make men the prey of bankers. He tells a story of a poor farmer who became a victim of such schemes and had to run away to the West as a debtor. But he concludes that the misused land, like an old Lear, will yield to the Cordelia Spring and the South will be saved by corn.

In versification, G. W. Allen (*American Prosody*, p. 289) finds "Corn" represents the border-line between Lanier's "middle period" and his later, more varied prosodic manner. The poem is "composed mainly of pentameter lines, despite the fact that it has a large number of short lines which vary all the way from monometer to tetrameter."

Page 620. ACKNOWLEDGMENT

In an age of transition and indecision in religious belief, an age of conflict between head and heart, science and faith, Lanier is consoled in his vain attempt to reconcile sin and evil with God's benevolence by the peace he finds in his wife's love and her serene influence. Compare this poem with Matthew Arnold's "Dover Beach" (1867), which treats the same theme. These four sonnets, the third of which is one of the best Lanier ever wrote, continue the sonnets entitled "In Absence," written at the same time. Starke says that the improved quality of "Acknowledgment" is explained in part by Lanier's having profited by Bayard Taylor's criticism. Compare the chivalric attitude toward his wife with his attitude toward women in his commencement address of June 30, 1869, before the Furlow Masonic Female College of Americus, Georgia. (Lanier did not believe in women's voting.) It should be noted that he does not think that evil is dependent upon institutions.

Page 621. ROSE-MORALS

Compare Lanier's hope here expressed that his art may be a "virginal-prayerful art" with his poetic theory, p. 649, above.

PSALM OF THE WEST

This Centennial Ode was featured in bold type in *Lippincott's Magazine*, XVIII, 39–53 (July, 1876). After the sectionalism which culminated in civil strife, the Southern poet expresses his high faith in a united nation. The poem shows to what an extent Lanier, like Whitman, was a poet of democracy. In 1876, after reading *Leaves of Grass*, Lanier wrote Whitman (see Traubel, *With Walt Whitman in Camden*, 1906, opposite p. 208): "Although I entirely disagree with you in all points connected with artistic form, and in so much of the outcome of your doctrine as is involved in those poetic exposures of the person which your pages so unreservedly make, yet I feel sure that I understand you therein, and my dissent in these particulars becomes a very insignificant consideration in the presence of that unbounded delight which I take in the bigness and bravery of all your ways and thoughts. It is not known to me where I can find another modern song at once so large and so naïve: and the time needs to be told few things so much as the absolute personality of the person, the sufficiency of man's manhood *to* the man, which you have propounded in such large and beautiful rhythms." For full discussion see Starke, "Lanier's Appreciation of Whitman," *American Scholar*, Oct., 1933.

For backgrounds of the theme of "The Psalm of the West," see Dorothy L. Werner's *The Idea of Union in American Verse*, and see also the analysis of the poem in Starke's *Lanier*, pp. 248–252. The West is of course America, the Adam of lands, from whom was created the Eve of independent freedom whose centennial was then being celebrated. This noble national poem, an epitome of American history, has its key in the somewhat prettified figure (ll. 607–638) of the tournament between "Heart" (South) and "Head" (North) after which "Heart," overcome, says "*My love to my Beloved*" and they become "one flesh again!" (Jousts and tournaments were common forms of entertainment in the South both before and after the Civil War.) Although at times the imagination is strained and the imagery obscure, as Starke says, the poem is notable for the eight masculine and Miltonic sonnets (ll. 256–367) on Columbus in which Lanier did his best work in that form. Compare Lanier's dramatic-monologue treatment of Columbus in these sonnets with that of Freneau in "Pictures of Columbus" (pp. 10–22, above) and of Lowell in "Columbus" (pp. 440–444, above).

Planned as a symphony to create its own musical accompaniment, the poem "contains more metrical forms," according to G. W. Allen (*American Prosody*, p. 291), "than any other poem Lanier wrote. They are: (1) five-stress anapestic, with some short lines; (2) pentameter triplets; (3) four-plus-three measure; (4) pentameter in alternate rime; (5) four-plus-three; (6) pentameter triplets; (7) four-plus-two in alternate rime, six-line stanza; (8) alexandrines; (9) eight Italian sonnets; (10) headless octosyllabic couplets; (11) pentameter triplets; (12) octosyllabic couplets, some headless and some with an extra syllable; (13) pentameter triplets; (14) headless octosyllabic couplets; (15) four-plus-three quatrains; (16) headless octosyllabic couplets; (17) pentameter triplets; and (18) a four-stress stanza, riming *ababcc*. It is important to notice that this poem is iambic except for the beginning anapests, and that the different meters are not interwoven; *i.e.*, the poet passes directly from one measure to another, and irregularities within a particular meter are rare."

Page 631. EVENING SONG

This is one of Lanier's most beautiful lyrics. Lines 5–7, with their literary allusion, are reworked from his poem "Night."

THE STIRRUP-CUP

Although at times Lanier is sentimental, it should be noted that in his courageous facing of death one finds no self-pity.

A SONG OF ETERNITY IN TIME

Compare the Elizabethan Herrick's similar treatment of time and eternity. Note the intricate metrical pattern. Starke says this poem is revised from "Eternity in Time," published in 1870.

Page 632. SONG OF THE CHATTAHOOCHEE

This, the most widely popular of all Lanier's poems, is the simplest of his later attempts to produce music in words, although even here the meter has considerable variety. According to G. W. Allen's analysis (*American Prosody*, pp. 291–2). "The meter is mainly iambic, but most of the lines have one or two anapestic feet, sometimes the whole line being headless anapestic (cf. l. 5) . . . Each stanza begins and ends with the half-line repetend . . . These lines are always headless, as at the beginning of the poem . . . And they are always very closely parallel, both in thought and words. The cadences of the other lines of each stanza are subtly varied by skilful arrangement of the trisyllabic feet and initial truncation, the whole being worked out so that each stanza has a slightly different basic cadence from the other four."

Note that whereas Longfellow's "Excelsior" (1841) expresses the aspiring idealism of self-culture in "resisting all temptations" besetting the individual, the voice of duty calling him *upward*, the "Song of the Chattahoochee," in a more humanitarian period thirty-six years later, expresses devotion to community service. *Downward* [not upward] the "voices of Duty" call the river, to "be mixed with the main" and to turn the mills. Compare and contrast the ethical view embodied in these two poems, considering the advantages and disadvantages of each as a rule of conduct.

THE REVENGE OF HAMISH

Morgan Callaway (*Select Poems of Lanier*, p. 79) suggests as sources for this poem William Black's novel *Macleod of Dare* and Charles Mackay's *Maclaine's Child*. See Bourgeois in Bibliography, above. Note Lanier's hatred of injustice and abuse of power, and his deep pity for the mother whose child was killed. This swift, terse ballad, shorn of moralizing and embroidery, would seem to qualify Edmund Gosse's conventional charge that Lanier is "never simple, never easy." This charge is also refuted in "A Ballad of Trees and the Master." In "The Revenge of Hamish" Lanier uses the logaœdic dactylic meter.

Page 635. REMONSTRANCE

In this unusually denunciatory poem Lanier satirizes conventional theological opinions and creeds and their narrow bigotry and the resultant intolerance lurking in Church, Throne, and Hearth. Conventional Opinion, he says, killed Socrates and Christ, yet the latter still rules by "Love's authority." Lanier renounces Opinion for faith in "the love of love." Starke concludes (*Lanier*, pp. 418–419), "Through the entire body of Lanier's work we can trace this idea of the necessity to love, but the meaning of love has now become spiritualized and extended greatly. It is not earthly love, no longer even the love of Christ's commandment, nor Pauline charity. Nor is it, as Josiah Royce explained Lanier's teaching, love that denies the existence of evil. Rather is it love as the culmination of his theory of the etherealization constantly taking place in man, love as understanding tolerance, scientific truth, the solution of opposites, the one sure expression of the divine will, Christian love made into a philosophy and offered as a rational system for the solution of all problems that confront the individual and society. Indeed, Lanier has gone so far as to assert that of Christ's two commandments—to love the Lord with all our heart and to love our neighbor as ourself—the second is the essential one." Is Lanier, then, in the main a humanitarian believing that man's salvation is found in outward social service; or is he an exponent of centrality, believing that the roots of evil are within and that they are to be conquered by self-conquest; or does he unite a belief in centrality with a Christian belief in charity of heart as one of the traditional triune virtues?

Page 636. THE CRYSTAL

According to A. H. Strong (*American Poets and Their Theology*, pp. 407–8): "Lanier's greatest poem, to our mind, is 'The Crystal.' It is his greatest because it combines the most of critical judgment with the clearest confession of his faith in Christ." Shakespeare, Homer, Socrates, Buddha, Dante, Milton, Aeschylus, Lucretius, Marcus Aurelius, Thomas à Kempis, Epictetus, Behmen, Swedenborg, Langley [Langland], Caedmon, Emerson, Keats, Tennyson—all these "governor-spirits" have flaws. Only Christ is so flawless, so crystal-clear, that God's rays of truth and love can unhindered shine through him. On the other hand, Starke, (*Lanier*, p. 401) argues that in this poem "it is Jesus as the perfect man, the great exemplar of Christian teachings, not God nor of God save as all men may be of God, that Lanier apostrophizes. Lanier's theology was altogether too simple and reasonable to admit a trinity or a duality of divinity." Cf. also Lanier's view that "The Church is too hot . . ." p. 648, above.

Page 640. INDIVIDUALITY

In a letter to J. F. Kirk of June 15, 1880, accompanying this poem (quoted by Mims, pp. 316–317), Lanier explains his opposition to determinism and his view of man as distinct from nature: "I have been studying science, biology, chemistry, evolution, and all. It pieces on, perfectly, to those dreams which one has when one is a boy and wanders alone by a strong running river, on a day when the wind is high but the sky clear. These enormous modern generalizations fill me with such dreams again.

"But it is precisely at the beginning of that phenomenon which is the underlying subject of this poem, 'Individuality,' that the largest of such generalizations must begin, and the doctrine of evolution when pushed beyond this point appears to me, after the most careful examination of the evidence, to fail. It is pushed beyond this point in its current application to the genesis of species, and I think Mr. Huxley's last sweeping declaration is clearly parallel to that of an enthusiastic dissecter who, forgetting that his observations are upon dead bodies, should build a physiological conclusion upon purely anatomical facts.

"For whatever can be proved to have been evolved, evolution seems to me a noble and beautiful and true theory. But a careful search has not shown me a single instance in which such proof as would stand the first shot of a boy lawyer in a moot court, has been brought forward in support of an actual case of species differentiation.

"A cloud (see the poem) *may* be evolved; but not an artist; and I find, in looking over my poem, that it has made itself into a passionate reaffirmation of the artist's autonomy, threatened alike from the direction of the scientific fanatic and the pantheistic devotee."

For discussion see Graham, "Lanier and Science," *American Literature*, Nov., 1932.

Page 642. THE MARSHES OF GLYNN

"... Possibly the ever-charming 'Song of the Chattahoochee,' with its quiet simplicity and its feeling of river movement, is the most musical of his poems. In this sense, his work is not, on the whole, distinguished for its music, a good deal of it being harsh. Lanier's poems are musical, rather, because of the orchestral effect produced by such poems as 'The Marshes of Glynn' and 'Sunrise.' Most poets are melodic; a few, conspicuously Milton, with his 'organ quality,' are harmonic; Lanier is sometimes orchestral. In the Marsh Hymns we hear, not one melody artfully varied, but a bewildering succession of winding and darting melodies; we are aware of a full, rich, complex background of sound, of crescendo and decrescendo restlessly alternating, of a rapid tempo bespeaking eagerness and wonder, relieved perhaps too rarely by a brief tranquil interlude; and everywhere words are poured out lavishly like so many notes, not so much expressing a meaning as illustrating it."—Norman Foerster, *Nature in American Literature*, pp. 235–236.

Compare "The Marshes of Glynn" with Lanier's "Night and Day," twelve years earlier, as a measure of the growth of his prosodic art. "The Marshes of Glynn," says G. W. Allen (*American Prosody*, p. 292), "is anapestic, but the shifting of accents, initial truncation, and the frequent shifting of the number of syllables in the line from one to seventeen prevents the rhythm from becoming monotonous. All of these metrical devices are unmistakably intended primarily to produce the varying cadences of a musical composition. Few lines have precisely the same cadence, yet the meters ... give each verse a characteristic cadence, and the total effect is that of interlaced cadences." (Cf. ll. 4–6, 20, 71.)

Stanley Williams (*American Writers on American Literature*, p. 341) concludes that in such poems as this Lanier's "ecstasy before the splendor of Nature is sometimes pagan ... Here, perhaps, beneath all the wrappings of his broken life and confused writing, is the *cor cordium*."

Page 643. A BALLAD OF TREES AND THE MASTER

Mrs. Lanier has described the circumstances of the writing of this poem: "It was cold November weather. ... I was to go out for a little while to see a friend who was also ill. He urged me to go. As I went to change my house-dress for a warmer one, he began to write on a sheet of paper. I had been gone from the room perhaps fifteen or twenty minutes. When I came back he handed me the paper, saying, 'Take this to her and tell her that it is fresh from the mint.' It was 'The Ballad of Trees and the Master,' just as we have it without erasure or correction" (quoted by Starke, pp. 407–408).

Here, at last, literary allusiveness, affected involution, and luxuriance yield to perfect control and the swift, terse simplicity of perfect art.

In thought the poem is somewhat cryptic. Is it a poetical rendering of the story of Gethsemane? A tribute to Christ's courage? Or a celebration of the healing power of nature? Starke (p. 402) believes that Lanier regarded Christ not as divine but as a great ethical teacher, and that "the moral of the poem is not the meekness of Christ nor Lanier's tender love for Him: as in most of Lanier's poems, it is the healing effect of nature on the troubled spirit. The poem is a ballad of trees and the master, not of the master and trees, certainly not of the master alone. It is, therefore, not so much a Christian poem as a pagan one, a poem of kinship with nature, as one realizes even more when one reads it in connection with the pantheistic 'Sunrise' for which it was intended originally as an interlude."

Page 644 ff. LANIER'S POETIC THEORIES

It is odd that while some critics have attacked Lanier as an æsthete or technician thinking poetry "a mere matter of pleasing sounds," other critics, especially of the present, have attacked him as a didacticist, as unæsthetic in his insistence upon the beauty of holiness and the unity of beauty, truth, and goodness. These charges would appear to counteract each other, in part at least. He carried scientific investigation of artistic technique much farther even than the æsthetic Poe; yet, in his unreprinted essay entitled "Mazzini on Music" (*Independent*, June 27, 1878) he attacked the notion of art for art's sake, and elsewhere he said that "wherever there is a contest as between artistic and moral beauty, unless the moral side prevail, all is lost." (Quoted by Starke, p. 319.) In a letter of 1880 (p. 647, col. 1, ll. 40 ff., above) he insisted on "the sharpest distinction . . . between mere Technic and Inspiration." Indeed, his devotion to morality led him into serious pitfalls in *The English Novel* (1883) in denouncing novelists such as Richardson, Fielding, and Zola. What has been regarded as Lanier's moral didacticism has been interpreted as a disease bred by the florid chivalry of the sentimental South of his day. Although in practice Lanier is occasionally sentimental and few would defend his view of novelists such as Fielding, it should be carefully noted that his *theory* of the "beauty of holiness" and the unity of Beauty, Truth, and Goodness is essentially that of Emerson—a theory of honorable and ancient tradition which may be traced back through Milton and Spenser to its source in the classical Plato and Aristotle.

If Lanier's poetic theory approximates that of Poe in the many ways indicated above, is it superior or inferior in Lanier's greater interest in relating beauty to the conduct of life—to virtue? Compare and contrast their poetic practice. Of his own practice Lanier wrote: "I have frequently noticed in myself a tendency to a diffuse style; a disposition to push my metaphors too far, employing a multitude of words to heighten the patness of the image, and so making of it a *conceit* rather than a metaphor . . ." Did he transcend this tendency in "The Revenge of Hamish" and "A Ballad of Trees and the Master"?

l. 14. *one mighty impulse*, etc. On backgrounds of the doctrine of what Lanier regarded as the common basis of the arts see Graham, "Lanier and Science," *American Literature*, Nov., 1932. In *Music and Poetry*, a collection of essays, see also "From Bacon to Beethoven," pp. 1–24, and "Nature-Metaphors," pp. 95–114, and also the selection from p. 247 of *The Science of English Verse* reprinted on p. 645, above.

Page 645.

l. 13. *Time is the essential basis of rhythm.* Citing P. F. Baum's *Principles of English Versification* (Cambridge, 1923, pp. 56–65), Ada L. F. Snell's laboratory experiments, *Publications of Modern Language Association*, Sept., 1918, pp. 396–408, and her *Pause; a Study of Its Nature and Its Rhythmical Function in Verse* (Ann Arbor, 1918), G. W. Allen (*American Prosody*, p. 280) concludes that "laboratory experiments have shown that the actual time covered in the pronunciation of syllables in English verse varies so greatly that it is impossible either to write or read (naturally) a passage so that the series of sounds are even proportionately equal. Thus accent, instead of merely being convenient in marking sounds already rhythmical, is the *only* element in English verse which is sufficiently rhythmical for us to measure outside the laboratories of the physicist and the applied psychologist." (See also in *Music and Poetry* Lanier's essay on "The Physics of Music," pp. 47–67, and compare his emphasis on time at the expense of accent with Poe's similar theory in "The Rationale of Verse.") In subsequent discussion (*Science of English Verse*, pp. 74–94), while Lanier emphasizes temporal relation as "primary" rhythm, he lists four other elements of rhythm—accent, the phrase, the line, and the stanza. See also the discussion of this subject by P. E. More, A. H. Tolman, and Harriet Monroe in studies listed in Bibliography.

l. 51. See selections from Poe's *Eureka* in this book (pp. 271–275), and analysis of Poe's literary theory and practice as greatly indebted to Newtonian astronomy, in the Introduction to *Poe* (American Writers Series) by Miss Alterton and Hardin Craig.

Page 646.

ll. 33 ff. Note that Lanier, citing Herbert Spencer, explains "the awful struggle for existence" and evil as a necessary and essentially beneficent opposition in the world which results in "a beautiful and orderly principle of rhythm." Compare Whitman's Hegelian doctrine in "Chanting the Square Deific," p. 706, above.

l. 46. *genuine English utterances.* See Lanier's essay on "The Death of Byrhtnoth," and "Chaucer and Shakespeare," in *Music and Poetry*, pp. 136–196. With Jefferson and Longfellow, Lanier championed the view that "Our literature needs Anglo-Saxon iron; . . . we lack idiomatic bone and substance . . ."

Page 647.

Note, in the letter to his wife, Lanier's rapturous delight in music, in relation to which he thinks of poetry as "a mere tangent." (See Starke, *passim*, and H. C. Thorpe as noted in Bibliography.) In *Tiger-Lilies* Lanier has Felix Sterling sum up his philosophy when he says, "Music means harmony, harmony means love, and love means—God!" Cf. "The Symphony," especially the last line. Cf. Poe (p. 278, above), "It is in Music, perhaps, that the soul most nearly attains the great end for which, when inspired by the Poetic Sentiment, it struggles—the creation of supernal Beauty."

Page 648.

With Lanier's doctrine (in the letter to Bayard Taylor) that every poem must embody a central idea. artistically developed, with all details focused to give "unity of impression," compare Poe's theory of the short story and the poem (see his review of *Twice-Told Tales* and his review of Longfellow's *Ballads and Other Poems*, conveniently found in the Alterton-Craig *Poe*, pp. 343–364. See also "The Poetic Principle" in this book, pp. 275–286, above. It should be noted that in theory at least Lanier does not neglect matters of larger design and structure. Individual poems should be analyzed to ascertain to what extent he succeeded in practising his æsthetic theories.

WALT WHITMAN

CHRONOLOGY

1819 Born on a Long Island farm, May 31.
1823 Family moved to Brooklyn.
1832 Worked for printer of a local paper.
1836–39 Taught school on Long Island. Worked on newspapers part of time.
1841–48 Period of journalism and politics. His temperance tract, *Franklin Evans, or the Inebriate* (1841), a great success. Campaigned for Polk, 1844.
1848 Although never a fanatical abolitionist, he resigned editorship of the Democratic Brooklyn *Daily Eagle* when the proprietors criticized his anti-slavery articles. Trip to New Orleans; returned by way of Chicago.
1849–55 Worked with his father at carpentering. Did considerable reading, which included Homer, Epictetus, Scott. In 1849 he edited the Brooklyn *Freeman* (exponent of the Free-Soil Party) and during the next two years he wrote for periodicals.
1855 *Leaves of Grass* published, gaining for author an enthusiastic letter from Emerson. Working people indifferent to it. Second edition, 1856.
1855–61 Interested in poetry and politics. Made friends among all classes of people in New York. Edited Brooklyn *Daily Times*, 1857–1859.
1860 Enlarged third edition of *Leaves of Grass*. Other editions in 1867, 1871, and 1876.
1863–73 In Washington. During war gave time and strength to wounded in hospitals. Several government clerkships, one of which he lost when his superior discovered he was the author of the supposedly indecent *Leaves of Grass*. Period terminated by paralytic stroke which left him with broken health.
1865 *Drum-Taps*.
1871 *Democratic Vistas* (prose).
1874–84 Lived with George Whitman at Camden, N. J. 1884, bought small cottage.
1882 Final edition, *Leaves of Grass*. *Specimen Days*, prose.
1888 Another paralytic attack. *November Boughs* published.
1891 *Good-Bye, My Fancy*.
1892 Died at Camden on March 26.

BIBLIOGRAPHY

I. Bibliography

Allen, G. W. "Walt Whitman Bibliography, 1918–1934," *Bulletin of Bibliography Pamphlets*, No. 30. Boston: 1935. (Practically exhaustive for the dates indicated, this bibliography brings the lists in the *Cambridge History of American Literature* nearly up to date. Includes not only editions and reprints of Whitman, but also all studies about him.)

Holloway, Emory, and Saunders, Henry S. In the *Cambridge History of American Literature*, 1918, II, 551–581. (The most extensive basic bibliography, including poetry and prose published in periodicals.)

Shay, Frank. *The Bibliography of Walt Whitman*. New York: 1920. (Excellent up to its date. Does not include works about Whitman.)

Wells, Carolyn, and Goldsmith, A. F. *A Concise Bibliography of the Works of Walt Whitman*. Boston: 1922. (Includes fifty books about Whitman.)

II. Text

Leaves of Grass. Including "Sands at Seventy." 1st Annex, "Good-Bye My Fancy"; 2d Annex, "A Backward Glance O'er Travel'd Roads." Philadelphia: 1891–1892. (The last edition personally supervised by Whitman.)

The Complete Writings of Walt Whitman. Issued under the editorial supervision of his literary executors, Richard Maurice Bucke, Thomas B. Harned, and Horace L. Traubel. With additional bibliographical and critical material by Oscar Lovell Triggs. New York: 1902. 10 vols. (The standard edition of Whitman's writings: for items not included, see below.)

Leaves of Grass. Inclusive Edition, ed. by Emory Holloway. Garden City, N. Y.: 1925. (The indispensable edition.)

In Re Walt Whitman, ed. by his literary executors, Horace L. Traubel, Richard Maurice Bucke, and Thomas B. Harned. Philadelphia: 1893. (Includes three early reviews of *Leaves of Grass* written by Whitman himself and published anonymously.)

The Letters of Anne Gilchrist and Walt Whitman, ed. with an introduction by Thomas B. Harned. Garden City, N. Y.: 1918.

The Gathering of the Forces, ed. by Cleveland Rodgers and John Black. New York: 1920. 2 vols. (Editorials, essays, etc., written by Whitman as editor of the Brooklyn *Daily Eagle* in 1846 and 1847.)

The Uncollected Poetry and Prose of Walt Whitman, ed. with an introduction by Emory Holloway, Garden City, N. Y.: 1921. 2 vols. (Includes the early poems and stories and parts of Whitman's notebooks. The long biographical and critical introduction is finely documented and is indispensable for an understanding of the growth of Whitman's mind, although it is perhaps overenthusiastic in its judgment [p. lxxxiii] that *Leaves of Grass* is "the greatest single volume America has yet produced.")

The Half-Breed and Other Stories, ed. by Thomas Ollive Mabbott. New York: 1927.

Walt Whitman's Workshop, ed. with an introduction and notes by Clifton J. Furness. Cambridge, Mass.: 1928. (Includes "Notes for Lectures," "Anti-Slavery Notes," "The Eighteenth Presidency," and several introductions for *Leaves of Grass*—fresh materials which cast much new light on his political and literary theories. The detailed notes, pp. 185–265 are of great value.)

I Sit and Look Out, ed. by Emory Holloway and Vernolian Schwarz. New York: 1932. (Editorials, etc., from the Brooklyn *Daily Times*, 1857–1859.)

III. Biography and Criticism

Allen, G. W. *American Prosody*. New York: 1935, pp. 217–243. (A detailed and acute analysis, especially interesting in its demonstration of parallel structure and phonetic recurrence as the two main rhythmical principles of *Leaves of Grass*, principles derived mainly from the Bible. Refutes the conventional notion that in form Whitman was lawless. Of major importance.)

—— "Biblical Analogies for Walt Whitman's Prosody," *Revue Anglo-Américaine*, X, 490–507 (Aug., 1933). (Shows that, although Whitman has been commonly regarded as a pioneer in introducing a new form, he actually based his work on one of the oldest forms of expression. Scholarly.)

—— "Biblical Echoes in Whitman's Works," *American Literature*, VI, 302–315 (Nov., 1934). (Finds 160 allusions, most of which come from Genesis, Matthew, and Luke.)

Bailey, E. J. *Religious Thought in the Greater American Poets*. Boston: 1922, pp. 183–228. (A readable and generally sound essay. Emphasizes Whitman's lack of unity in his writings [p. 190], but finds in him considerable kinship with the Quakers [pp. 206–208]. Assembles evidence of Whitman's views on "God, Soul, Life, Death, and Immortality.")

Bailey, John. *Walt Whitman*. New York: 1926.

Barker, Portia. "Walt Whitman's Relations with Some New York Magazines," *American Literature*, VII, 274–301 (Nov., 1935). (A scholarly study throwing much light on the history of Whitman's reputation and showing that he exaggerated the hostility of the magazines toward him, although "only the *Saturday Press* and *The Critic* among New York magazines showed consistently a hearty, confident approval.")

—— "Walt Whitman and the *Atlantic Monthly*," *American Literature*, VI, 283–301. (An authoritative analysis, showing that the *Atlantic* veered "only slightly and very cautiously toward Whitman as the years passed.")

Barrus, Clara. *Whitman and Burroughs, Comrades*. Boston: 1931.

Bazalgette, Léon. *Walt Whitman; the Man and His Work*, tr. from the French by Ellen FitzGerald. New York: 1920.

Binns, H. B. *A Life of Walt Whitman*. New York: 1905.

Blodgett, Harold. *Walt Whitman in England*. Ithaca, N. Y.: 1934. (A comprehensive, scholarly book on the English attitude toward Whitman. Of great value.)

Boatright, Mody C. "Whitman and Hegel," *University of Texas Studies in English*, IX, 134–150 (July, 1929). (A scholarly study, showing parallelisms and suggesting that Whitman's idea of a cosmic consciousness unfolding through conflict toward divine ends may have come from Hegel.)

Brooks, Van Wyck. *America's Coming-of-Age*. New York: 1915, pp. 109–129. (A nationalist glorifies Whitman as "the precipitant of American character." Suggestive but of slight scholarly value.)

Bucke, R. M. *Walt Whitman*. Philadelphia: 1883. (Edited and partly written by Whitman.)

Burroughs, John. *Whitman: A Study*. Boston: 1896. (Reprinted as Vol. X of Burroughs's *Works*, Riverside Edition. Appreciative general interpretation of Whitman's ideas by a close friend whose information was based not only on writings but upon conversations. Yet he recognized serious shortcomings in *Leaves of Grass*—see pp. 149, 186, and 195 of the 1896 edition. Contains chapters on his ruling ideas and aims, his self-reliance, relation to art and literature, to life and morals, to culture, to his country and his times, to science and religion. For discussion of the extent of Whitman's own contributions to this book, see Furness, *Walt Whitman's Workshop*, pp. 214–220.)

Cairns, W. B. "Walt Whitman," *Yale Review*, N. S. VIII, 737–754 (July, 1919). (A discriminating discussion. Traces his egotism and democracy to transcendentalism, and finds his views of form and of sex the chief obstacles to his common acceptance.)

Campbell, Killis. "The Evolution of Whitman as Artist," *American Literature*, VI, 254–263 (Nov., 1934). (A scholarly analysis of Whitman's revisions in the various editions of *Leaves of Grass*. Concludes that these revisions show "a marked gain in taste," "a decided gain in picturesqueness and comeliness of phrase," and a "pronounced gain" in verse quality and cadence, except for the last decade of Whitman's life.)

—— "Miscellaneous Notes on Whitman," *University of Texas Studies in English*, XIV, 116–122 (July, 1934). (Bibliographical notes, literary echoes, coinages, textual errors in *Leaves of Grass*, use of the figure metanoia. Scholarly.)

Canby, H. S. *Classic Americans*. New York: 1931, pp. 308–351, (Although this essay somewhat disproportionately emphasizes Quakerism as an influence on Whitman, it is one of the best of the comprehensive critiques. Incisive and well-written.)

Carpenter, Edward. *Days with Walt Whitman, with Some Notes on His Life and Work.* London: 1906.

Carpenter, G. R. *Walt Whitman.* New York: 1909. (In English Men of Letters Series.)

Catel, Jean. *Rythme et langage dans l'édition des 'Leaves of Grass,' 1855.* Montpellier: 1930. (A scholarly thesis, approaching Whitman's poetry mainly as oratory.)

—— *Walt Whitman: la naissance du poète.* Paris: 1929. (An extensive book, subjecting Whitman to acute psychological analysis. "Nous avons montré que le sentiment du mal est enraciné au cœur même du poète des *Brins d'Herbe,* et que c'est probablement à ce sentiment que nous devons l'œuvre poétique de 1855" [p. 467].)

Cestre, Charles. "Walt Whitman, L'Inadapté—Le Mystique, Le Lyrique—Le Poète," *Revue Anglo-Américaine,* VII, 385–408, 481–504 (June and August, 1930); VIII, 19–41 (Oct., 1930). (Valuable.)

—— "Walt Whitman, Poet of Self," *University of California Chronicle,* XXV, 318–343 (July, 1923).

Clark, Grace D. "Walt Whitman in Germany," *Texas Review,* VI, 123–137 (Jan., 1921). (See also Anna Jacobson, "Walt Whitman in Germany since 1914," *Germanic Review,* I, 132–141 [April, 1926].)

Cooke, Alice L. "Whitman's Indebtedness to the Scientific Thought of His Day," *University of Texas Studies in English,* XIV, 89–115 (July, 1934). (A scholarly study of an important phase of Whitman's thought. Surveys his knowledge of science, his use of astronomy, geology, and other sciences, and his position as a mediator in the conflict between science and religion.)

—— "Whitman's Background in the Industrial Movements of His Time," *University of Texas Studies in English,* XV, 76–91 (July, 1935). (A well-documented study of "the evidence of Whitman's contact with trade-unionism and socialism." Although the influence is found to be indirect and by no means pronounced, this study shows that Whitman had more interest in social reform than is generally supposed.)

De Sélincourt, Basil. *Walt Whitman: a Critical Study.* London: 1914. (An extensive and acute analysis of Whitman's poetic form and style. Says Whitman "uses words and phrases more as if they were notes of music than any other writer . . . It was to him part of the virtue and necessity of life that its forms and processes were endlessly reduplicated; and poetry, which was delight in life, must somehow, he thought, mirror this elemental abundance" [p. 109].

Dowden, Edward. "The Poetry of Democracy: Walt Whitman," in *Studies in Literature, 1789–1877.* London: 1882. (First printed in the *Westminster Review,* July, 1871. Taine-like, Dowden considers Whitman's work as the inevitable expression of his democratic "surrounding society, the environment, the *milieu,* which has made such a phenomenon possible." In contrast to poetry which is the expression of an outworn aristocratic social order, Whitman's poetry is of great significance as a cross-section of the modern democratic age and environment. This stimulating essay may have aided Whitman in defining his own purpose. See Harold Blodgett, "Whitman and Dowden," *American Literature,* I, 171–182 [May, 1929].)

Erskine, John. "A Note on Whitman's Prosody," *Studies in Philology,* XX, 336–344 (July, 1923). (Thinks that Whitman's development of the rhythm of the phrase rather than of the line resulted from American habits in the reading of poetry. See also F. N. Scott, "A Note on Whitman's Prosody," *Journal of English and Germanic Philology,* VII, 134–153 [1908], and see especially G. W. Allen.)

Foerster, Norman. "Whitman," in *Nature in American Literature.* New York: 1923, pp. 176–220. (The authoritative treatment of the subject. Surveys the aspects of nature to which Whitman reacted, the senses he used most, his view of the naturalness of both individualism and humanitarianism. Compared with the dualistic Emerson, Whitman "leaves us at last with his gospel of individualism and his gospel of solidarity in violent conflict" [p. 218].)

—— "Whitman," in *American Criticism.* Boston: 1928, pp. 157–222. (An able attempt to present the logical articulation of Whitman's literary theories as grounded upon science and the democratic frontier spirit, and to appraise these theories. Concludes that, "He was a European romanticist modified by the American environment" [p. 216], and that Whitman's optimistic prophecy of the spirit which science and democracy would develop "has been falsified by the event"—by the rise of skepticism, cynicism, standardization, mechanistic determinism, and disillusionment revealed in current literature.)

Furness, C. J. "Walt Whitman's Politics," *American Mercury,* XVI, 459–466 (April, 1929). (Especially interesting in showing that Whitman studied Rousseau's *Contrat social* with care and sympathy.)

—— "Walt Whitman's Estimate of Shakespeare," *Harvard Studies and Notes in Philology and Literature,* XIV, 1–33 (1932). (A well-documented study, based in part on unpublished Whitmania, of his interest in and numerous and ambiguous judgments about Shakespeare. Finds Whitman "particularly indebted" to Shakespeare, but that because of his pose of complete independence he was "particularly concerned to conceal this indebtedness." Continues and supplements R. C. Harrison's able study of "Walt Whitman and Shakespeare," *Publications of the Modern Language Association,* XLIV, 1201–

1238 [Dec., 1929]. The first part of the late Mr. Harrison's paper, completed by Killis Campbell and R. A. Law, demonstrates Whitman's extensive knowledge of Shakespeare and his conception of Shakespeare as the soul of "feudal literature" as opposed to himself as the would-be soul of democratic literature. The second part of the paper presents a mass of parallel passages.)

Glicksberg, C. I. *Walt Whitman and the Civil War*. Philadelphia: 1933. (An important book, including much material from Whitman's manuscripts hitherto unpublished.)

Gohdes, C. L. F. "Whitman and Emerson," *Sewanee Review*, XXXVII, 79–93 (Jan., 1929). (See also J. B. Moore, "The Master of Whitman," *Studies in Philology*, XXIII, 77–89 [Jan., 1926]. Gohdes deals with the external and Moore with the internal evidence of Whitman's debt to Emerson. Ruth P. Pressley, in an unpublished dissertation, done at the University of Texas, on *Whitman's Debt to Emerson*, argues that the debt was greater than generally supposed.)

Gummere, F. B. "Whitman and Taine," in *Democracy and Poetry*. Boston: 1911, pp. 96–148. (A thoughtful essay by a distinguished authority on the nature of poetry. Emphasizes the paradox involved in Whitman's democratic celebration of the people *en masse* and his individualistic defiance, as a poet, of "convention, that is to say the active function of the community." "He cannot be the poet of democracy in its highest ideal who rejects the democratic idea of submission to the highest social order, to the spirit of the laws, to that imagined community" [p. 125]. "What Taine hated [individualism], Whitman loved . . . If Whitman, exponent of democratic art, thought that he could produce poetry as the expression of all the people, the *en masse*, voiced at will of the over-soul by his individual self, Taine, on the other hand, in an extreme democratic apotheosis of law, thought that he could explain poetry by convention, and could ground and found the everlasting science of it on the community" [pp. 131–132]. But actually Whitman, like Taine, does to a large extent regard poetry as determined by time and place, in America by frontier democracy and evolutionary science [see *Democratic Vistas*]; and furthermore, Gummere's view that Whitman was poetically lawless has been refuted by G. W. Allen—see above.)

Holloway, Emory. *Whitman: an Interpretation in Narrative*. New York: 1926.

—— "Whitman as Critic of America," *Studies in Philology*, XX, 345–369 (July, 1923). (Concludes that Whitman's optimistic faith and humanitarianism rendered his social criticism prophetic rather than realistically satirical. See also M. E. Curti, "Walt Whitman, Critic of America," *Sewanee Review*, XXXVI, 130–138 [April, 1928]. Curti argues that the growth of Whitman's mind from the "rampant national egotism of his youth" to the "mellow cosmopolitanism of the after the war period" is explained mostly by his disappointment at America's failure to fulfill his hopes and by his direct growing knowledge of people of other nations.)

Howard, Leon. "For a Critique of Whitman's Transcendentalism," *Modern Language Notes*, XLVII, 79–85 (Feb., 1932). (A suggestive study emphasizing the materialism present in Whitman's transcendentalism. See Gohdes and Moore on Whitman and Emerson.)

—— "Walt Whitman and the American Language," *American Speech*, V, 441–451 (Aug., 1930). (A scholarly study.)

Hungerford, Edward. "Walt Whitman and His Chart of Bumps," *American Literature*, II, 350–384 (Jan., 1931). (A scholarly exposition of Whitman's knowledge of phrenology, from which in part he seems to have derived his pervasive theories of "Amativeness" and "Adhesiveness." In the light of this source, Mr. Hungerford shows that it is unlikely that Whitman's love poems imply anything abnormal or degenerate.)

Jannaccone, P. *La Poesia di Walt Whitman e L'Evoluzionc delle Forme Ritmiche*. Torino, Italy: 1898.

Kennedy, W. S. *Reminiscences of Walt Whitman*. London: 1896. (Good on the last ten years of Whitman's life.)

Kreymborg, Alfred. "Whitman and the Democratic Cosmos," in *Our Singing Strength*. New York: 1929, pp. 206–230. (An impressionistic survey, jubilantly appreciative. In the same vein are John Macy, *The Spirit of American Literature* [New York: 1913], pp. 210–247, and Lewis Mumford, *The Golden Day* [New York: 1926], pp. 121–137. These nationalists glorify Whitman in large measure because he professed to express the distinctively American spirit rooted in science and democracy.)

Lowell, Amy. "Walt Whitman and the New Poetry," *Yale Review*, XVI, 502–519 (April, 1927). (The chief exponent of Imagism claims that her clan felt the influence of Whitman's independent spirit rather than his verse forms. See also P. M. Jones, "The Influence of Walt Whitman on the Origin of the 'Vers Libre,'" *Modern Language Review*, XI, 186–194 [April, 1916], and "Whitman in France," *ibid.*, X, 1–27 [Jan., 1915]. Also Catherine B. Ely, "Whitman and the Radicals as Poets of Democracy," *Open Court*, XXXVI, 594–601 [Oct., 1922], which contrasts Whitman and Pound, Sandburg, etc.)

More, P. E. "Walt Whitman," in *Shelburne Essays*, Fourth Series. Boston: 1906, 180–211. (A graceful and discriminating appraisal, finding the most constant and typical of Whitman's qualities in the sense he conveys of ceaseless indistinct motion. His devotion to the flux is related to his sensuous monism.)

Myers, H. A. "Whitman's Conception of the Spiritual Democracy, 1855–1856," *American Literature*, VI, 237–253 (Nov., 1934). (Argues that out of the American democracy of 1855, Whitman constructed an inner complement to the outer world, a spiritual democracy governed by two principles, one the unlimited individual, the other the equality of individuals. See Furness, Holloway, and also Cleveland Rodgers, "Walt Whitman the Poet of Democracy," *Mentor*, XI, 3–14 [Sept., 1923].)

Oppenheim, James. "Whitman," in *American Writers on America*, ed. by John Macy. New York: 1931, pp. 258–273. (A thoughtful judicial discussion. Finds that the excessive celebration of love "attains the dimension of a defect in Whitman. . . . There is too much sunshine, too much . . . boundless optimism . . . For Christ and Devil are the two poles in the human spirit, images of opposites. Goethe has not this one-sidedness, for verily there is the aspiring Faust and the destructive Mephisto. In this sense Whitman fails us, as he fails himself" [p. 269]. But see Miss Boatright's study of Hegel's influence and Whitman's "Chanting the Square Deific.")

Parrington, V. L. "The Afterglow of the Enlightenment—Walt Whitman," in *The Beginnings of Critical Realism in America*. New York: 1930, pp. 69–86. (A stimulating analysis of Whitman's political and social views in the light of formative factors—the Enlightenment, Jacksonianism, the humanitarian emotionalism of the fifties, Utopianism, monism, transcendentalism, the frontier, and evolutionary science. Recognizes that actually "today, with science become the drab and slut of war and industrialism, . . . Whitman's expansive hopes seem grotesque enough" [p. 85]. Nevertheless, even if his romantic hopes "have been belied by after events," Mr. Parrington held that Whitman was "a great figure, the greatest assuredly in our literature—yet perhaps only a great child . . . " [p. 86].)

Pattee, F. L. "Whitman," in *American Literature Since 1870*. New York: 1915, pp. 163–185. (An appreciative survey of Whitman's development by one of the most gifted of our nationalistic literary historians.)

Perry, Bliss. *Walt Whitman: His Life and Work*. Boston: 1906. (Revised, 1908. Judicious.)

Pound, Louise. "Walt Whitman and Italian Music," *American Mercury*, VI, 58–63 (Sept., 1925). See also her studies of "Walt Whitman and the French Language," *American Speech*, I, 421–430 (May, 1926); of "Walt Whitman's Neologisms," *American Mercury*, IV, 199–201 (Feb., 1925); and of "Walt Whitman and the Classics," *Southwest Review*, X, 75–83 (Jan., 1925). The latter, a vocabulary analysis, concludes that the classical loan element in his vocabulary is not so large or so striking as the Romance loan element. See also Leon Howard.)

Ross, E. C. "Whitman's Verse," *Modern Language Notes*, XLV, 363–364 (June, 1930). (Shows that Whitman considered the line as the unit: "A run-on line is rare in Whitman—so rare that it may be considered a 'slip.'")

Santayana, George. "The Poetry of Barbarism," in *Interpretations of Poetry and Religion*. New York: 1900, pp. 166–216. (A distinguished philosophic critic of conservative taste, Mr. Santayana finds that science, exalting change and promising progress, turns modern poets such as Whitman away from the past and "the sense of the moral identity of all ages," essential to enduring literature, and that Whitman's parade of "a mass of images without structure" has its analogy in the equalitarian "notion of an absolute democracy.")

Sherman, S. P. "Walt Whitman," in *Americans*. New York: 1922, pp. 153–185. (A readable undocumented essay which comes to grips with the central problem in Whitman's social thought—the problem of reconciling personal freedom with social authority. Mr. Sherman concluded that the problem was solved by Whitman's faith "that the American type of democratic government is the form best adapted to the production of the largest possible number of great and happy individuals." Finds in his poems "three great successive movements"—a pre-war "individualistic expansion"; "a movement of concentration corresponding to the period of the war"; and "a resumed movement of 'individualistic' expansion following the war, and spiritualized by it" [pp. 165–166].)

Speake, Marian R. *Contemporary American Criticism of Walt Whitman, 1855–92*. 1926. (An unpublished dissertation available at the Library of the University of Iowa.)

Stedman, E. C. "Walt Whitman," in *Poets of America*. Boston: 1885, pp. 349–395. (Stedman thinks that Whitman in his poems of sex violates the "law of reserve" [p. 369] which is instinctive in nature, that "Whittier, in this land, is a truer type of the people's poet" [p. 385]. But his praise of Whitman as a poet of America "gifted with language; feeling, imagination, and inspired by a determined purpose," did much in 1885 to break down prejudices against him.)

Stovall, Floyd. "Introduction" and "Bibliography," in *Walt Whitman*. New York: 1934, pp. xi–lxiii. (A well-documented and well-balanced study of the growth of Whitman's comprehensive religious, political, social, and literary theories in their genetic interrelations, and in the light of all up-to-date scholarship on the subject. The best essay of its length available. See also his "Main Drifts in Whitman's Poetry," *American Literature*, IV, 3–21 [March, 1932].)

Swinburne, A. C. "Under the Microscope," in *Complete Works*, ed. by Sir Edmund Gosse and T. J. Wise. London: 1926. 20 vols. XVI, 377–444. (Finds in Whitman "two distinct men of most inharmonious kinds; a poet and a formalist.")

Symonds, J. A. *Walt Whitman: a Study*. London: 1893. (Although old, this book offers a useful general introduction to the poet.)

Traubel, Horace. *With Walt Whitman in Camden*. New York: 1905–1912. 3 vols. (Includes Whitman's conversation in old age.)

Trowbridge, J. T. "Reminiscences of Walt Whitman," *Atlantic Monthly*, LXXXIX, 163–175 (Feb., 1902). (Throws light on Whitman's relations with Emerson.)

Ware, Lois. "Poetic Conventions in *Leaves of Grass*," *Studies in Philology*, XXVI, 47–57 (Jan., 1929). (A scholarly analysis, showing Whitman's careful use of alliteration, assonance, and parallelism. See Allen and Campbell.)

Wiley, Autrey Nell. "Reiterative Devices in *Leaves of Grass*," *American Literature*, I, 161–170 (May, 1929). ("Whitman's use of the reiterative devices shows a constant increase from 1855 to 1881. From a frequency of approximately twenty-two per cent in 1860, the use of the repetitive patterns increases to thirty-two per cent in 1867 and 1871 and thirty-eight per cent in 1881" [p. 170]. An important scholarly study, supporting the view of G. W. Allen and others that Whitman's verse is by no means lawless.)

NOTES

GENERAL

It is of the highest importance that, before attempting to judge Whitman as a whole, one should read his representative poems in chronological order and take into account not only his earlier radical work but also his later conservative work. For Whitman's mind developed or changed considerably. Professor Floyd Stovall, whose Introduction to *Whitman*, in the American Writers Series, is the best study yet made of the growth of Whitman's mind, has elsewhere summarized the main drifts in *Leaves of Grass* as follows: "(1) In politics, the drift from individualism to nationalism, with strong tendencies toward internationalism; (2) in general philosophy, the drift from love of freedom towards love of law; and (3) in religion, the drift from materialistic pantheism towards a highly spiritualized idealism. This direction of his development is also apparent in the changing themes that dominate his poetry from time to time. In the first period of the *Leaves* he was moved to poetic activity almost exclusively by his interest in life, especially life as sensation and spectacle. In the second period he was moved chiefly by the thought of death, and in the third period by the hope of immortality. The extent of his progress is clearly shown in his changing view of love as it is illustrated in the four key-poems of *Leaves of Grass*. Of these, the 'Song of Myself' celebrates man's self-love and arrogant pride in the possession of all life's material blessings, whereas the other three are concerned with unselfish love as manifested in some relation to death. 'Out of the Cradle Endlessly Rocking' describes how death by intensifying makes pure the love of man for woman; 'When Lilacs Last in the Dooryard Bloom'd' shows how death may exalt and consecrate the love of man for his fellowman; and 'Passage to India' reveals how in death the love of man for God is consummated and brought to fruition. These key-poems therefore mark the progress of a special personality, incorrectly supposed by Whitman to be typical, from youth to old age, and from love of self to love of God."—"Main Drifts in Whitman's Poetry," *American Literature*, March, 1932.

Stovall finds (*Whitman*, pp. xv, xvi) that Whitman drew much of his thought from liberal patterns of ideas developed by "the rationalism of the seventeenth century, by the intellectual and social enlightenment of the eighteenth, and by the empiricism of the nineteenth." Thus Whitman reflected "(1) the philosophy of progress, with its *a priori* method of reform and neglect of history; (2) faith in the innate goodness of man and the idealization of nature, illustrated in the revolutionary theories of Rousseau; (3) the idealism of German philosophy, particularly the Hegelian doctrine of a cosmic consciousness that unfolds through conflict and contradiction to divine ends; and (4) the scientific conception of nature as a reality independent of cosmic reason but determined by the processes of historical evolution. Much of the ambiguity of Whitman's writing is due to his uncritical acceptance of all these philosophies, which, though interrelated and developed one out of the other, are in many ways inconsistent."

Although Whitman has been claimed as the first of the modern realists, the herald of the "new poetry," it should be remembered that, unlike many of the modern materialists and determinists, he was essentially a mystic and that he represents mainly, according to V. L. Parrington, the afterglow of romanticism. "The millennial expectations that Whitman built upon science and democracy," concludes Norman Foerster (*American Criticism*, pp. 215–216), "we are now well aware, rested upon insecure foundations. But the weakness of his prophecy may be better accounted for otherwise. It is the result of his using, in the main unconsciously, the romantic tradition in which he must historically be placed. [For a suggestive development of many parallels between Rousseau and Whitman, see Bliss Perry's *Whitman*, pp. 277–280.] Gazing into the future, he saw there the romantic past from which he had averted his eyes. Notwithstanding his profession of modernity, his vision was in essentials that of the eighteenth and early nineteenth centuries, that of the naturistic stream of thought and feeling (with its modifying tributaries) running all the way from Shaftesbury to Emerson. He gives us the deism of Shaftesbury transcendentalized. The perfection of nature, the natural goodness of man, 'the great pride of man in himself' offset with an emotional humanitarianism—these are the materials of a structure only slightly colored with modernity. His politics, his ethics, his religion belong to the past, even that facile 'religiousness' which he hoped would suffuse and complete the work of science and democracy. Like Rousseau he cried 'Back to nature' and praised at once the ego and the average; and like him he spurned reason and exalted the emotions. Like Walter Scott he was fascinated with the beauty of the feudal order, which he hoped democracy might emulate while developing great personalities. Like Wordsworth he sought communion with his soul in the challenging presence of nature, and sang the glory of the humble and obscure in a language and rhythm intended to correspond with the tenor of their lives. Like Carlyle and Emerson in their most romantic years, he looked to Transcendental ideas for his conception of the soul and the universe. Like Emerson he extolled the virtue of self-reliance, authenticated not only by the romantic tradition but also by the example of the American frontier. In ideal Western personality he saw a kind of homespun equivalent of the old feudal splendor, and in his verse he sought to convey the energy, initiative, freedom, simplicity, and barbaric yawp of the pioneer. He was a European romanticist modified by the American environment. He was the last of the great romanticists and his death in 1892 symbolically coincided with the passing of the frontier."

According to Henry Seidel Canby, "On the intellectual side he was nearer to the Quakers than to the hearty vulgar. He was a half Quaker, with part of that half converted to Emersonism. Compare him to a man carrying a burning coal that he turns this way and that to see which wind will best fan it, and where is the tinder which it will ignite. Walt's personality was a glowing coal, and already in his youth his Quaker environment had taught him to look into his heart for the breath that came from God. His idea that the average man is an ideal temple of God because any excess above the average obscures the inner light, was Quaker also; and the assurance with which Walt Whitman, as a plain American, spoke to powers and principalities and, what was more courageous, to his conventional and orthodox fellow countrymen, was Quaker in its inspiration, if pagan in its audacity, and democratic in its nature. They will, said Charles Lamb of Quakers, endure no tyranny. And when the bright radiance of Emerson's moral idealism reached to Paumanok and seemed to answer his desire for a lofty spirituality common to all men, Whitman became the perfect channel through which a high potentiality of blended religious and physical emotions could be transformed into the concrete terms of an art. All of which means simply that the hearty pagan in Whitman first became Quaker, and then philosophical idealist and moralist, without losing its original apprehension of physical life. Keeping the enthusiasm of the religious emotions of the period of his youth, Whitman translated them into a religion for democracy that was pagan in its sensuousness, self-reliant in its spirituality, moral in its purpose, and above all idealistic, and this is the basis of his art. In no other country of the world could spiritual enthusiasm, a gusto for living, equalitarianism, a moral end, and absolute self-sufficiency in religious inspiration, have been so naturally and hence so successfully brought together and focused through one man's personality."—*Classic Americans*, pp. 312–313.

In reading *Leaves of Grass* one should constantly bear in mind Whitman's aim, which was, as he repeated many times, to record the emotions and thoughts of a representative personality against the contemporary American background of science and democracy. The "I" in "Song of Myself" and elsewhere is the communal and representative "I"—"what I assume you shall assume." Writing on Jan. 18, 1872, to Edward Dowden to "entirely accept" his article on *Leaves of Grass* (in the *Westminster Review*, July, 1871), Whitman concluded: "I would say that (as you of course see) the spine or verterber [sic] principle of my book is a model or ideal (for the service of the New World, & to be gradually absorbed in it) of a complete healthy, heroic, practical modern *Man*—emotional, moral, spiritual, patriotic—a grander better son, brother, husband, father, friend, citizen, than any yet—formed & shaped in consonance with modern science, with American Democracy, & with the requirements of current industrial & professional life—model of a Woman also, equally modern & heroic—a better daughter, wife, mother, citizen also, than any yet. I seek to typify a living Human Personality, immensely animal, with immense passions, immense amativeness, immense adhesiveness—in the woman immense maternity —& then, in both, immenser far a *moral conscience*. & in always realizing the direct & indirect control of the divine laws through all and over all forever."—Quoted by Bliss Perry, *Walt Whitman*, pp. 199–200.

Page 651. SONG OF MYSELF

Lest the crudities of this poem should discourage the reader from further study of Whitman, it should be pointed out that his later work shows much superiority both in artistry and soundness of thought. One should refrain from forming a judgment of Whitman as a whole until he has studied poems such as "When Lilacs Last in the Dooryard Bloom'd" and "Passage to India," and his prose such as "Democratic Vistas," in which he is sharply critical of the actual results of democracy. The "Song of Myself" illustrates Whitman's first philosophic period in its obsession with sensation and its glorification of freedom, self-love, arrogant pride, and equalitarianism.

Running through the poem are two major ideas. The first is Whitman's notion that he is "of every hue and caste . . ., of every rank and religion," a notion which he tries to illustrate by his endless catalogues and processions with which he identifies himself. This is the means by which he tries to give his poem universality—"What I assume you shall assume"; "In all people I see myself"; "All these I feel or am." The second idea involves his belief in the equality of all people, all things, and all experiences—"I am the poet of the Body and I am the poet of the Soul"; "I do not call one greater and one smaller." This equalitarianism, exalting the common and the sensual, rested upon quantitative and descriptive science. "I see," he says (l. 411) "that the elementary laws never apologize." And it rests on the pantheistic doctrine that things, men, and God are interfused and divinely one: "I hear and behold God in every object. . . . In the faces of men and women I see God, and in my own face in the glass" (ll. 1281–1285). It should be noted, however, that Whitman's interest in science was not inconsistent with his being a mystic (some interpreters have regarded the mystical experience recorded in section 5 of this poem as the key to his life) or with his refusing to believe in free will. "Hurrah for positive science! long live exact demonstration!" he says, yet "I but enter by them to an area of my dwelling" (ll. 485, 492). Stovall says of ll. 670–673: "Whitman accepted the theory of evolution, but he was inclined to the view that man is not limited in any way by his animal antecedents. His belief that environment is the chief factor in evolution connects him with Lamarck rather than with Darwin. It was on the strength of this belief that he expected a new race of people to develop in America."

In 1876, when Whitman stated reminiscently his purpose in *Leaves of Grass*, he emphasized saturating his ideas with "that vehemence of pride and audacity of freedom necessary to loosen the mind of still-to-be-form'd America from the accumulated folds, the superstitions, and all the long, tenacious and stifling anti-democratic authorities of the Asiatic and European past." To shock was thus part of his initial purpose.

Page 679. CROSSING BROOKLYN FERRY

"Living in Brooklyn or New York city from this time forward, my life, then, and still more the following years, was curiously identified with Fulton ferry, already becoming the greatest of its sort in the world for general importance, volume, variety, rapidity, and picturesqueness. Almost daily, later ('50 to '60), I cross'd on the boats, often up in the pilot-houses where I could get a full sweep, absorbing shows, accompaniments, surroundings. What oceanic currents, eddies, underneath—the great tides of humanity also, with ever-shifting movements! Indeed, I have always had a passion for ferries; to me they afford inimitable, streaming, never-failing, living poems. The river and bay scenery, all about New York island, any time of a fine day—the hurrying, splashing sea-tides—the changing panorama of steamers, all sizes, often a string of big ones outward bound to distant ports—the myriads of white-sail'd schooners, sloops, skiffs, and the marvellously beautiful yachts—the majestic Sound boats as they rounded the Battery and came along towards 5, afternoon, eastward bound—the prospect off towards Staten Island, or down the Narrows, or the other way up the Hudson—what refreshment of spirit such sights and experiences gave me years ago (and many a time since)! My old pilot friends, the Balsirs, Johnny Cole, Ira Smith, William White, and my young ferry friend, Tom Gere—how well I remember them all!"—Whitman, *Specimen Days.*

This poem embodies one of Whitman's most beautiful rhapsodies of the motley crowd and of his beloved Manhattan seen from the river. Note his characteristic identification with everyone and everything, an identification, he says, mystically, which transcends the limitations of time and place, and which includes (ll. 65–77) the common impulse to sin. G. W. Allen (*American Prosody*, p. 232) cites ll. 101–105 as an illustration of Whitman's "grammatical rhythm," or "the repetition of a certain sort of speech or grammatical construction"—cf. "Flow on," "flow with," "ebb with," "frolic on," "drench with," "cross from," "stand up."

Page 682. SONG OF THE OPEN ROAD

Although this poem is more artistic and better constructed than the "Song of Myself," it illustrates the same individualistic tendency of Whitman's earlier thought. While Emerson had held that "It is not more the office of man to receive all impressions, than it is to distinguish sharply between them" (*Journals*, III, 315), Whitman here teaches "the profound lesson of reception, nor preference nor denial" (l. 18), and he proclaims himself "loos'd of limits" (l. 53). Wisdom "is not susceptible of proof" (l. 79), being mystically instinctive. He discovers that "the secret of the making of the best persons, . . . is to grow in the open air and to eat and sleep with the earth" (ll. 71–72). It should be noted, however, that this equalitarian back-to-nature philosophy, defying all restraints, finds its sanction in Whitman's faith in progress, the celebration of which is the main theme of the poem. (For backgrounds see J. B. Bury, *The Idea of Progress* [1924], and Lois Whitney, *Primitivism and the Idea of Progress* [1934].) To Whitman life is simply "the procession of souls along the grand roads of the universe" (l. 182), souls to whom "adhesiveness" (l. 91) or benevolence is natural, souls who inevitably and without restriction "go toward the best" (l. 188). Yet, following Hegel, Whitman does not regard a faith in progress as precluding a "struggle" (l. 210). The poem contains many illustrations of the use of parallelism as a prosodic device.

Page 687. MIRACLES

This poem illustrates the manner in which Whitman's pantheism tended to make him see the miraculous in all the common things of nature. G. W. Allen (*American Prosody*, p. 226) has pointed out that structurally the poem consists of two "envelopes," a Biblical device involving parallelism in expressing similar ideas. Thus line 2, "As to me I know of nothing else but miracles," states a general idea, and lines 3–14 state parallel illustrations of the first idea, followed (ll. 15–16) by a reiteration of the initial idea (l. 2) as a conclusion. The last half of the poem follows the same plan. It should be noted that for the most part Whitman's poems are not lawless but follow an intricate law which is by no means novel, as many imagine, but which goes back at least as far as the ancient Hebrew scriptures.

ASSURANCES

As G. W. Allen has remarked, the structure of this poem constitutes a perfect "envelope." In its thought that Heavenly Death will compensate for all earth's horrors and mysteries the poem presages Whitman's later faith in immortality.

Page 688. OUT OF THE CRADLE ENDLESSLY ROCKING

Stovall writes: "The poem was based on an actual experience (see Holloway's *Whitman*, pp. 161–162); but 'leaping beyond' this experience, the poet discovers in it the means by which sexual love is spiritualized through death and transformed to the uses of poetical creation. The word *death*, the clue to this mystery, is uttered by the sea, symbol of the spiritual world. The bird is a symbol of the dæmon or genius of the poet" (*Whitman*, 1934, p. 407). In psychology the poem is related to the *Children of Adam* poems which embody Whitman's views of sex. G. W. Allen calls attention to the use of initial reiteration, one of the poet's characteristic devices, in the first three lines. The poem is usually regarded as one of Whitman's more artistic creations, while philosophically it shows him turning toward spiritual aspects of life. For further analysis of the poem see Louise Pound's "Note on Walt Whitman and Bird Poetry," *English Journal*, XIX, 31–36 (Jan., 1930).

Page 691. FACING WEST FROM CALIFORNIA'S SHORES

This is a sort of preview of "Passage to India" and its quest of internationalism.

FOR YOU O DEMOCRACY

Following Whitman's ardent espousal earlier of extreme individualism and states' rights, he here illustrates, on the eve of the Civil War, how he would "make the continent indissoluble" by "trilling these songs" of "the love of comrades." For Whitman's strong defence of an indissoluble Union as opposed to states' rights, see his *Gathering of the Forces* (ed. Rodgers and Black, I, 229–239). It is interesting to note that he seems to have found philosophic sanction of the Union in nature and science. "Contradictory as they are," the separate entity and the "imperial ensemble," both "are necessary," he said. "As the centripetal law were fatal alone, or the centrifugal law deadly and destructive alone, but together forming the law of eternal kosmical action, evolution, preservation, and life—so, by itself alone, the fullness of individuality, even the sanest, would surely destroy itself" (*Complete Prose Works*, 1914, p. 313).

RECORDERS AGES HENCE

This poem embodies Whitman's portrait of himself for posterity as "the tenderest lover." The licentious sexual love celebrated in his earlier poems becomes transmuted, during his hospital experiences as a nurse in the Civil War, to tender and unselfish compassion for the suffering. See Bibliography under Glicksberg.

I SAW IN LOUISIANA A LIVE-OAK GROWING

Note Whitman's growing recognition that, although trees (nature) may thrive in individual isolation, men cannot so thrive.

Page 692. I HEAR IT WAS CHARGED AGAINST ME

Replying to the charge that he "sought to destroy institutions," Whitman says he is "neither for nor against institutions" but for "the dear love of comrades." Like Lowell, Whitman eventually came to think that what counted was not institutions, although they were necessary safeguards, but great self-mastered individuals. Whitman is looking toward his later philosophy of Personalism embodied in *Democratic Vistas*.

I HEAR AMERICA SINGING

Note Whitman's delight in the rich variety of "strong melodious songs" by all sorts of American laborers.

GIVE ME THE SPLENDID SILENT SUN

This poem illustrates Whitman's inclusiveness in its sudden about-face in the middle—he loves not only nature but "faces and streets . . . incessant and endless." Cf. P. E. More's comments on Whitman's treatment of processions in relation to his pantheistic philosophy of the flux. G. W. Allen (*American Prosody*, p. 230), discussing

Whitman's use of initial repetition as an aspect of phonetic recurrences, praises his skill in interweaving his cadences in this poem. "The first cadence is distinguished by the reiteration of 'give me.' In the second strophe, the cadence is varied by brief repetitions; the second main cadence rings out clear and bold in the first four lines of section two and is achieved mainly by the reiteration of 'keep your . . .'; and then the poet quickly shifts to the first cadence for several lines, and plays variations throughout the remainder of the poem."

Page 693. PIONEERS! O PIONEERS!

Whitman returned from New Orleans by way of Chicago in 1848, and he went to Colorado in 1879. The frontier spirit, with its inculcation of equality, self-reliance, and optimism, powerfully reinforced his philosophy, which tended in the same direction. It should be noted especially that Whitman likes the frontiersmen's revolt from the European past (l. 17). As F. J. Turner, F. L. Paxson, Mrs. Lucy Hazard, and others have shown, the frontier accounts to a considerable extent for the development of qualities which are anti-European and distinctively and uniquely and democratically American. Emersonian transcendentalism, which brought Whitman "to a boil"—as he said—was itself strongly influenced by the frontier spirit, as E. L. Marchand has shown. For Whitman's references to the frontier environment, see also his poems "The Song of the Broad Axe," "Song of Occupations," "The Prairie Grass Dividing," "Thou Mother with Thy Equal Brood," and the section on "The Prairies" in *Specimen Days*. Whitman wrote concerning "Mississippi Valley Literature":

"Lying by one rainy day in Missouri to rest after quite a long exploration—first trying a big volume I found there of 'Milton, Young, Gray, Beattie and Collins,' but giving it up for a bad job—enjoying however for awhile, as often before, the reading of Walter Scott's poems, 'Lay of the Last Minstrel,' 'Marmion,' and so on—I stopp'd and laid down the book, and ponder'd the thought of a poetry that should in due time express and supply the teeming region I was in the midst of, and have briefly touch'd upon. One's mind needs but a moment's deliberation anywhere in the United States to see clearly enough that all the prevalent book and library poets, either as imported from Great Britain, or follow'd and *doppelgang'd* here, are foreign to our States, copiously as they are read by us all. But to fully understand not only how absolutely in opposition to our times and lands, and how little and cramp'd, and what anachronisms and absurdities many of their pages are, for American purposes, one must dwell or travel awhile in Missouri, Kansas and Colorado, and get rapport with their people and country.

"Will the day ever come—no matter how long deferr'd—when those models and lay-figures from the British islands—and even the precious traditions of the classics—will be reminiscences, studies only? The pure breath, primitiveness, boundless prodigality and amplitude, strange mixture of delicacy and power, of continence, of real and ideal, and of all original and first-class elements, of these prairies, the Rocky mountains, and of the Mississippi and Missouri rivers—will they ever appear in, and in some sort form a standard for our poetry and art? (I sometimes think that even the ambition of my friend Joaquin Miller to put them in, and illustrate them, places him ahead of the whole crowd.)" For full discussion of the actual literature of this section which so interested Whitman, see Dorothy A. Dondore, *The Prairie and the Making of Middle America* (Cedar Rapids, Iowa, 1926), and R. L. Rusk, *The Literature of the Middle Western Frontier* (2 vols., New York, 1925).

Page 695. WHEN I HEARD THE LEARN'D ASTRONOMER

Like Emerson, Whitman was considerably indebted to astronomy for reinforcing his religion with its faith in immutable laws, as opposed to the Puritans' faith in capricious and "illustrious providences." As a mystic rather than a rationalist, however, Whitman by no means thinks of science as telling the whole story. As in this poem, he prefers the "mystical" night to mere scientific "charts and diagrams" unvitalized by the religious imagination.

OUT OF THE ROLLING OCEAN THE CROWD

Holloway (*Uncollected Poetry and Prose*, I, lviii–lix) calls attention to the fact that Mrs. Ellen M. Calder, in an unpublished passage in a manuscript written for the *Atlantic Monthly* (June, 1907), claimed that this poem refers to Whitman's love for a married woman in Washington during the Civil War.

FROM PAUMANOK STARTING I FLY LIKE A BIRD

This poem embodies Whitman's literary aim inspired by the Civil War—his desire as a Unionist to "sing the idea of all," North, South, East, and West, of the "Western world one and inseparable," and then to sing "of each member of these States" individually. Whitman concluded "As I Sat by Blue Ontario's Shore" by saying, "As the wheel turns on its axle, so I find my chants turning finally on the war." For full discussion see Glicksberg.

Page 696. RISE O DAYS FROM YOUR FATHOMLESS DEEPS

This strong poem, showing that Whitman, no pacifist, was "fully satisfied" (l. 44) to see "warlike America rise" and Democracy "strike with vengeful stroke" (l. 33) to preserve a united nation, should be compared with Lowell's "The Washers of the Shroud." In general, however, Whitman was more of a pacifist than our other poets. For an interesting discussion, see Merle E.

Curti, "Poets of Peace and the Civil War," *World Unity*, X, 149–159 (June, 1932).

Page 697. COME UP FROM THE FIELDS FATHER

This dramatic story of a father and mother receiving news of the fatal wounding of their only son illustrates Whitman's deep compassion for the suffering the war involved, although he ardently demanded that it be carried on to keep the nation united.

Page 698. THE WOUND-DRESSER

This deeply-moving poem, realistic as it is, reveals a great-heartedness which no one, regardless of his artistic creed, can fail to venerate. Compare the spirit and the art of this poem with the "barbaric yawp" of "Song of Myself," and note how the experiences of the hospital wards during the war have deepened and mellowed Whitman's utterance and purged it of most of its former individualistic arrogance.

Page 699. OVER THE CARNAGE ROSE PROPHETIC A VOICE

With the key-thought of this poem ("affection shall solve the problems of freedom yet," rather than outward restraints) compare the climax of Emerson's essay on "Politics" (*Works*, III, 219) dealing with "the power of love" rather than "artificial restraints" as the basis of self-government.

TURN O LIBERTAD

This poem casts further light on Whitman's poetic aims in its demand that our singers turn from "the trailing glories of the past" (which he regards as "feudal") to "the future, greater than all the past." Cf. "Pioneers! O Pioneers!"

Page 700. YEARS OF THE MODERN

Whitman the nationalist here becomes interested in internationalism—"the solidarity of races" (l. 4). But the exponent of love hopes for this solidarity by means of having European aristocracies "broken" and kings "removed." Has his prophecy (reaffirmed in "Passage to India") that science, which has given us "the steamship, the electric telegraph," etc., will make all nations of "one heart" been progressively realized, or is it true that today divergent nationalisms are much less tolerant and more potentially perilous than in 1865? Whitman imagined that "free trade makes for solidarity" (Traubel, III, 366), and he testified, "every line I ever wrote . . . was animated by that feeling." Does Whitman's faith in science appear to minimize the fact that unless controlled by ethical ideals, science alone multiplies (a) individual and national aggressiveness in commerce and materialism, thus inviting conflicts, and science multiplies (b) man's ingenuity in manufacturing munitions to enforce clashing economic ambitions and so multiplies the power of the self-destruction of the race?

Page 701. WHEN LILACS LAST IN THE DOOR-YARD BLOOM'D

"Of all the days of the war," wrote Whitman in *Specimen Days*, "there are two especially I can never forget. Those were the day following the news, in New York and Brooklyn, of that first Bull Run defeat, and the day of Abraham Lincoln's death [April 15, 1865]. I was home in Brooklyn on both occasions. The day of the murder we heard the news very early in the morning. Mother prepared breakfast—and other meals afterward—as usual; but not a mouthful was eaten all day by either of us. We each drank half a cup of coffee; that was all. Little was said. We got every newspaper morning and evening, and the frequent extras of that period, and pass'd them silently to each other." (See also Whitman's "Death of Lincoln. Lecture deliver'd in New York, April 14, 1879 . . .") After the body of the martyred president had lain in state in Washington for six days, the funeral procession began, going through Philadelphia, New York, Chicago, and other cities to the burial place in Springfield, Illinois, where it arrived on May 4.

Stovall (*Whitman*, 1934, p. 410) writes: "As the representative of his nation, Whitman, in this poem, mourns the death of Lincoln, the ideal American. He uses three principal symbols: the star is Lincoln, the man (not the permanent spiritual self); the lilac is human love; the hermit thrush is the poet of the soul, and its song is the carol of death, the deliveress of the soul. As elsewhere in Whitman's poetry, the sea is the symbol of eternal life, the land of mortal life, and the shore of death that unites (and separates) the two, the 'dark mother' of the reborn soul. As in most elegies, the lament is for the death of the body, the consolation in the immortality of the soul. The lamentation includes the first twelve stanzas, the consolation the last three, beginning with stanza 14. Stanza 13 is transitional.

"One unusual and effective device in this elegy is the manner in which the reader is prepared for the consolation by the early introduction of the thrush and his persistent call, which, however, the poet cannot yet answer because he is held by the star and the lilac—by grief for his loved comrade and hero." As one of our greatest elegies the poem should be compared and contrasted with Milton's "Lycidas," Shelley's "Adonais," Tennyson's "In Memoriam," and Emerson's "Threnody."

Swinburne, in his earlier enthusiasm for Whitman, called this poem "the most sonorous nocturn ever chanted in the church of the world." And Bliss Perry (*Whitman*, p. 157) concluded that this poem "remains, with Lowell's 'Commemoration Ode,' as the finest imaginative product of the Civil War period. Never but once before, in 'Out of the Cradle Endlessly Rocking,' and never afterward, was Whitman capable of such sustained and deep-toned recitative, varied with lyric interludes of such pure beauty." G. W. Allen (*American Prosody*, 226–227) calls attention to the fact that in this poem "there is an extraordinarily effective use of the envelope, with the complete form in sections 8 (arranged *abcccccccd*), 11, and 12, and the incomplete form in sections 5 and 13 (introduction missing)"; he proceeds to give a detailed analysis of the poem as illustrative of the fact "that parallelism, or 'thought rhythm,' is the first rhythmical principle of *Leaves of Grass*."

Page 705. O CAPTAIN! MY CAPTAIN!

Although this poem on the death of Lincoln is probably the most widely popular of all Whitman's work, its rather conventional use of relatively regular meter and of rhymes and a refrain renders it by no means typical of the poems in *Leaves of Grass*. Whitman himself did not think highly of it, and he regretted that it distracted attention from the poems which he himself most prized.

Page 706. CHANTING THE SQUARE DEIFIC

The four aspects of Whitman's deity are: (1) Jehovah, or the relentless "mighty laws" of nature; (2) Christ-like "affection," the "Consolator"; (3) Satan, "plotting revolt" against any limitation of freedom; (4) Santa Spirita, or "the general soul" pervading all. It is possible that Whitman may have been led to include the third element (Satan, "comrade of criminals," the principle of ineradicable evil) by his study of Hegel, who merged good and evil and wrote of a cosmic consciousness unfolding through conflict to a divine end. (See M. C. Boatright, in Bibliography.) Whitman expresses a similar view of evil in "Song of Myself," "Crossing Brooklyn Ferry," "With Antecedents," "Song of the Universal," "Roaming in Thought," "This Compost," "Song of Prudence," and "By Blue Ontario's Shore." How does Whitman's view of the Santa Spirita immanent in all things relate to the Quaker's Inner Light to which he was devoted? (See H. S. Canby, in Bibliography.) With Emerson's view of poetic genius as an influx of the divine mind into the poet's mind, as "a larger imbibing of the common heart," compare Whitman's view (ll. 43–45) that this divinely-immanent "general soul" breathes "through these songs."

Page 707. ONE'S SELF I SING

If one is tempted at times to accuse Whitman of arrogant egotism, he should remember that generally his "I" is used in the communal and representative sense, as standing for "The Modern Man." Thus in "A Backward Glance" he explained the basis of *Leaves of Grass:* "This was a feeling or ambition to articulate and faithfully express in literary or poetic form, and uncompromisingly, my own physical, emotional, moral, intellectual, and æsthetic Personality, in the midst of, and tallying, the momentous spirit and facts of its immediate days, and of current America —and to exploit that Personality, identified with place and date, in a far more candid and comprehensive sense than any hitherto poem or book."

WHISPERS OF HEAVENLY DEATH

This poem, with its subdued beauty, represents many Whitman wrote on his intimations of immortality.

PROUD MUSIC OF THE STORM

Originally entitled "Proud Music of the Sea-Storm" in the *Atlantic Monthly* (February, 1869), this poem casts light on the development of Whitman's literary theory and, with other evidence of his considerable reading and knowledge of the arts, shows that he was by no means ignorant of world culture. In his slumber he dreams that the music of the storm is "blending with Nature's rhythmus all the tongues of nations" past and present, in Europe, Asia, and Africa, including not only their poetry but their dances, symphonies, and operas. (Cf. Louise Pound, "Whitman and Italian Music," *American Mercury*, Sept., 1925.) This dream of "man and art with Nature fused again" suggests "a new bard caroling in the West," the clew he had "sought so long." He would "take them all," these songs of all times and lands, and nourished by the art of man he would aim at "tallying life" in the real world and by this fusion arrive at "a new rhythmus." It should be noted that as Whitman grew older he became less contemptuous of Old World literature of the past: as a disciple of the evolutionists, he sees the present as "but a growth out of the past" ("Passage to India," l. 12), but according to the concept of progress the present must be better.

Page 710. PASSAGE TO INDIA

For a long quotation from Whitman's notebook containing the first prose sketch of this poem, see C. J. Furness, *Walt Whitman's Workshop* (pp. 200–201). Bliss Perry (*Whitman*, p. 195), quotes Whitman as saying of "Passage to India": "There's more of me, the essential, ultimate me, in that than in any of the poems . . . The burden of it is evolution—the one thing escaping the other—the unfolding of cosmic purposes."

Whitman was greatly impressed by the laying of the Atlantic Cable in 1866 and the opening in 1869 of the Suez Canal and the Union Pacific Railroad. He was confident that applied science, as illustrated in these exploits which facilitated communication, would effect "the marriage of continents" (l. 118) and cause all the peoples of the world to dwell together in brotherly unity. He saw the long history of the march of mankind from the ancient East to the West, from the times of "the mediæval navigators" down, as illustrating "God's purpose from the first." Now, the "rondure of the world at last accomplish'd," he thought that the "inscrutable purpose" of God was about to be accomplished here in America by the creation of a superior civilization based on the work of "captains and engineers" and "noble inventors" and "scientists," but crowned by the American poet who shall be "The true son of God . . . singing his songs." In this monistic utopia "Nature and Man shall be disjoin'd and diffused no more." This prophecy of the decline of nationalistic rivalries seems ironical in the light of the actual situation today, and Whitman does not seem to have foreseen other less humane results of science and industrialism, as already suggested above. From the beginning of section 7 on, Whitman treats the ancient search of explorers as a symbol of the search of the soul for God. Lines 175–193 have been called Miltonic because of their sublimity and majesty of utterance, although the indifference to sin and the general indeterminateness are hardly characteristic of the great Puritan. In commenting on Whitman's prophecy of "the true poet through whom is to be restored the divine trinity of God (the universal), Nature (the particular), and Man (the individual)," Stovall (*Whitman*, p. 411) concludes, "If Man here be understood as the community of human souls, Whitman's trinity becomes identical with Hegel's divine trinity of Father (Abstract Idea), Son (Nature), and Holy Ghost (the Church)." (See Boatright, in Bibliography.) It should be noted that in this poem, as representative of his third and last period, Whitman far transcends the materialism of his first period as represented by "Song of Myself." See his very long note on "Passage to India" in his "Preface, 1876" (Stovall, *Whitman*, pp. 337 ff.), where Whitman concludes that far more important than "the mightiest nationality" and "the best personalism" is "the only permanent and unitary meaning" of life, which he finds in the doctrine of immortality. "For, in my opinion," he says, "it is no less than this idea of immortality, above all other ideas, that is to enter into, and vivify, and give crowning religious stamp, to democracy in the New World." In *Democratic Vistas* (1871) our most ardent exponent of democracy found that "society, in these States, is canker'd, crude, superstitious, and rotten," and he concluded that "New World democracy . . . is, so far, an almost complete failure in its social aspects, and in really grand religious, moral, literary, and esthetic results" because "in any vigor, the element of the moral conscience, the most important, the verteber to State or man, seems to me either entirely lacking, or seriously enfeebled or outgrown." In this later period Whitman approached the criticism of American life illustrated so finely in Lowell's "An Ode for the Fourth of July, 1876." On Whitman as a critic of American life and politics see Bibliography under Holloway, Curti, Glicksberg, Furness, Myers, Sherman.

Page 715. THE BASE OF ALL METAPHYSICS

With the "base"—"the dear love of man for his comrade"—compare "I Hear It Was Charged against Me" (p. 692), and "Over the Carnage" (p. 699).

THOU MOTHER WITH THY EQUAL BROOD

This was first published as the title poem of the volume *As a Strong Bird on Pinions Free*, after Whitman read it by invitation at the commencement of Dartmouth College, June 26, 1872.

It has been said that for the most part Whitman represents not so much anything essentially new but rather "The Afterglow of the Enlightenment." And most of the ideas in this poem of eloquent ejaculated prophecy (ll. 76–77) may be found in the American representatives of the eighteenth-century Enlightenment, Thomas Paine (see Whitman's eulogistic Address in his memory in 1877 in *Specimen Days*), Philip Freneau, and Joel Barlow ("The Vision of Columbus," 1787). However, the doctrine of evolution has tended to give Whitman's faith in progress (of which this poem is a hymn) a deeper note. Although "the Past is also stored" in America, along with "priestly Asia" and "feudal Europe" (section 4), America represents the height of progress; and as a poet and prophet of her "endless Nationality," he would reject "the conceits of the poets of other lands" and ages and seek his poetic inspiration in the American frontier (section 2). He insists that without "moral wealth" our "proudest material civilization must remain in vain" (l. 87), and the "three peerless stars" guiding the republic are to him "Ensemble, Evolution, Freedom, / Set in the sky of Law." He foresees that the republic will be threatened with "moral consumption," but, in "Time's spirals rounding," he is confident as a believer in progress, that our "mystical Union" will enable us to "soar to the fulfillment of the future." Compare and contrast this poem with Lowell's "An Ode for the Fourth of July, 1876."

Page 718. THE MYSTIC TRUMPETER

This rhapsodic poem, first published in the *Kansas Magazine* (February, 1872), contributes to an understanding of Whitman's literary theories and aims. He imagines that the wind, as a trumpeter, conjures up the themes poets have dealt with hitherto: "the feudal world" and its glamorous pageantry (section 4); love (section 5); "war's alarums" (section 6); and dejection and the "humiliation of my race" (section 7). Then he commands the phantom trumpeter to sing to his soul "some vision of the future," of "a perfect world," a utopian vision of "Joy! joy! all over joy!"

In an article on "Whitman's 'The Mystic Trumpeter' as Autobiography" (*American Literature*, VII, 455–458, Jan., 1936), W. L. Werner analyzes the poem in detail, concluding, "The last five sections . . . seem to me to portray moods parallel to Whitman's own life: his early fondness for Scott's feudalism; his celebration of love in the early *Leaves;* the Civil War; his post-war despair at the evils of humanity; and his final optimism and ecstasy. Thus interpreted, the poem seems . . . a chronological summary of Whitman's poetic life."

Page 719. TO A LOCOMOTIVE IN WINTER

This poem illustrates Whitman's desire to devote poetry to the latest results of scientific invention and industrialism.

Page 720. SPIRIT THAT FORM'D THIS SCENE

This poem was not published until September 10, 1881, when it appeared in *The Critic*. It illustrates Whitman's pervading poetic theory that he could afford to be indifferent to artistic "rules precise and delicatesse," provided that his poems tallied with the "formless wild arrays" of the mountain peaks and gorges of nature. In *Specimen Days*, in a section entitled "An Egotistical 'Find,'" Whitman elaborated the idea of this poem with reference to his trip through the Colorado canyon country: "'I have found the law of my own poems,' was the unspoken but more-and-more decided feeling that came to me as I pass'd, hour after hour, amid all this grim yet joyous elemental abandon—this plenitude of material, entire absence of art, untrammel'd play of primitive Nature—the chasm, the gorge, the crystal mountain stream, repeated scores, hundreds of miles—the broad handling and absolute uncrampedness—the fantastic forms, bathed in transparent browns, faint reds and grays, towering sometimes a thousand, sometimes two or three thousand feet high—at their tops now and then huge masses pois'd, and mixing with the clouds, with only their outlines, hazed in misty lilac, visible."

ROAMING IN THOUGHT

In M. C. Boatright's study of "Whitman and Hegel" (see Bibliography), the following doctrines are found to be common to both: the universe is in a "fluid-like state"; the apparently chaotic flux has an order of its own, and change results from orderly development, the seeds of the future being contained in the past; contradictions of life can be reconciled by thinking of the universe as a vast organism exhibiting both unity and diversity; the universe is one, the material being in essence spiritual; good and evil are merged in each other; eternal struggle is necessary; whatever satisfies the soul is truth. Whitman and Hegel are unlike, however, in that Hegel arrived at his "conception of the universe by a process of logic," while Whitman reached his "by spiritual intuition, a sort of insight that is inherent in every individual."

Page 721. WHITMAN'S POETIC THEORY

For materials embodying the literary theory which guided Whitman's poetic practice, see the following, in addition to his "Preface to the 1855 Edition of *Leaves of Grass*" reprinted above: "Preface, 1876, *Leaves of Grass*"; "A Backward Glance o'er Travel'd Roads"; *Democratic Vistas;* prefaces to *As a Strong Bird on Pinions Free* (1872) and to *Two Rivulets* (1876); "Poetry in America Today" (1882); "Robert Burns as Poet and Person" (1886); "A Word about Tennyson" (1888); "American National Literature" (1891); "What Lurks behind Shakespeare's Historical Plays" (1888); poems such as "As I Sat Alone by Blue Ontario's Shore" (1856) and the following poems in this book (see also the notes on them), "For You O Democracy," "I Hear America Singing," "Pioneers! O Pioneers!" "Turn O Libertad," "Proud Music of the Storm," "Passage to India," "Thou Mother with Thy Equal Brood," "The Mystic Trumpeter," "Spirit That Form'd This Scene"; *The Gathering of the Forces*, II, 237–344, which reprints early book reviews, brief comments on such topics as "The Anti-Democratic Bearing of Scott's Novels," Milton, Carlyle, Coleridge, Keats and Longfellow, and his dramatic criticism; *Specimen Days* (1882); *Whitman's Workshop: a Collection of Unpublished Manuscripts*, edited by C. J. Furness (Cambridge: 1928), "Notes on Lecturing and Oratory" (pp. 33–38), "Notes for Lectures on Literature" (pp. 65–68), "Introductions intended for American Editions of *Leaves of Grass*" (pp. 115–137), and "Introduction to the London Edition of *Leaves of Grass*" (pp. 141–154). On Whitman's poetic theory in relation to his practice see the studies listed in the Bibliography under: Allen, Catel, De Sélincourt, Foerster, Erskine, Jannaccone, Ross, Stovall, Ware, Wiley.

Norman Foerster (*American Criticism*, p. 170) has summarized Whitman's literary creed as follows:

"There are many kinds of literature, because each age interprets life in its own special way; and each kind has its validity. Yet there is a best kind, not as yet realized. Broadly speaking, all the past kinds are expressions of feudalism and superstition. By virtue of the law of progress, the new age now dawning, the age of democracy and science, will be the best, and its literature will be the best. Therefore it is impossible to formulate the characteristics of the best literature on the basis of any literature already produced. Looking to the future rather than the past, the critic must be a revolutionary and a prophet. In formulating the new theory, such a critic will be guided by the characteristics of the age, as they are coming to clearness in America. These characteristics are, in the first place, Democracy, which is faith in the common man, belief in the greatness of spiritual individuality; and, in the second place, Science, which is faith in nature, belief in the glory of the physical. From these two is now being born a new religion, greater than either the Greek or the Hebrew. The function of the literature of the future will be to bring on the new age and eventually to give it full expression. And its law of expression must be natural—organic. The mode of expression suited to the régime of feudalism is becoming anachronistic, and we must now envisage a new mode suited to the régime of Democracy and Science."

To what extent did Whitman succeed in *practising* his poetic creed? Compare and contrast him with Whittier regarding the extent to which he has actually been accepted by the "powerful uneducated persons" whose spokesman Whitman professed to be?

VACHEL LINDSAY

CHRONOLOGY

1879 Born, Springfield, Illinois, November 10. Educated in the public schools. Before he was fourteen he had read Poe's "complete works, criticism and all, through and through."

1897–1900 Attended Hiram College, Ohio. Read standard authors, and experimented with drawing.

1900–03 Attended Art Institute of Chicago.

1904–05 At New York School of Art. Devoted himself to "drawing architecture, drawing sculpture, trying to draw the Venus of Milo, and imitating the Japanese Prints and Beardsley, and trying to draw like Blake and all such matters."

1905–09 Lectured to art classes of Y.M.C.A. (In Europe in 1906.)

1909–10 Lecturer for the Anti-Saloon League throughout central Illinois.

1912 Spent summer walking from Illinois to New Mexico, preaching "The Gospel of Beauty" and exchanging his poems, *Rhymes to Be Traded for Bread*, for food and shelter.

1913 Published his first book, *General Booth Enters into Heaven and Other Poems.*

1914 *Adventures While Preaching the Gospel of Beauty* (prose).

The Congo and Other Poems. Wins popularity, partly on account of his colorful and dramatic recital of his poems.

1915 *The Art of the Moving Picture* (prose).

1916 *A Handy Guide for Beggars* (prose).

1917 *The Chinese Nightingale and Other Poems.*

1920 *Daniel Jazz* (collection published in England).

The Golden Whales of California, and Other Rhymes in the American Language.

The Golden Book of Springfield. A prose picture of a Utopia to be shaped in the future by the influence of art and beauty.

1923 *Collected Poems.* (Revised edition, 1925.)

Going-to-the-Sun.

1923–24 Resident poet at Gulf Park College.

1925 Married Elizabeth Conner. Took up residence in Spokane, Washington.

1926 *Going-to-the-Stars,* including his poem on Andrew Jackson.

The Candle in the Cabin, made up mainly of somewhat saddened love poems.

1928 *Johnny Appleseed.*

1929 Returned to Springfield. *The Litany of Washington Street,* a collected series of political essays, punctuated by long quotations from Walt Whitman, with an essay on Whitman, "Statesman-Poet."

Rigamarole, Rigamarole.

Every Soul Is a Circus.

1931 December 5, suicide in the house in which he was born.

BIBLIOGRAPHY

I. Bibliography

No very extended formal bibliography of Vachel Lindsay is yet available. Much information may be found in E. L. Masters's *Vachel Lindsay,* A. E. Trombly's *Vachel Lindsay, Adventurer,* and other biographical and critical works entered below. See also Manly and Rickert's *Contemporary American Literature* (rev. by F. B. Millet. New York: 1929, pp. 221–223).

II. Text

Collected Poems. New York: 1923. Revised and illustrated ed., 1925. (Does not contain the poems in the following volumes of poetry: *Going-to-the-Sun* [1925]; *Going-to-the-Stars* [1926]; *The Candle in the Cabin* [1926]; *Johnny Appleseed and Other Poems* [1928]; *Every Soul Is a Circus* [1929].

The Art of the Moving Picture. New York: 1915. Revised Edition, 1922. (Prose.)

The Golden Book of Springfield. New York: 1920. (Prose.)

The Litany of Washington Street. New York: 1929. (Collected prose essays.)

Selected Poems. Edited by Hazelton Spencer. Modern Readers' Series. New York: 1931.

(For privately printed poems and pamphlets, see *Publishers' Weekly,* Sept. 29, 1923: and see biographical texts below.)

III. Biography and Criticism

Aiken, C. *Scepticisms.* New York: 1919, pp. 155–159. (A brief and unsympathetic essay, written on the assumption that Lindsay is a mere entertainer without ethical seriousness.)

Bartlett, A. H. "Voices from the Great Inland States: Illinois," *Poetry Review,* XV, 101–110 (March–April, 1924). (Deals with the work of Lindsay and of Carl Sandburg.)

Benjamin, P. L. "Vachel Lindsay—a Folk Poet," *Survey,* XLVI, 73–74 (Oct. 15, 1921).

Canby, H. S. "Vachel Lindsay," *Saturday Review of Literature,* VIII, 437 (Jan. 9, 1932).

Cooke, H. W. *Our Poets of Today.* New York: 1918.

Davies, C., and Lucas, L. "Two Aspects of Vachel Linday," *Poetry and the Play,* XI, 294–303 (Sept.–Nov., 1927).

Davison, E. "Nicholas Vachel Lindsay," in Squire, J. C., and others, *Contemporary American Authors.* New York: 1924, pp. 207–236. (A readable discursive critique, regarding Lindsay as "the most American of American poets." Likes his simplicity, garish color, healthy coarseness, and noise as opposed to his "shallow, artificial idealism.")

DeCasseres, B. "Five Portraits on Galvanized Iron," *American Mercury*, IX, 396–397 (Dec., 1926).

Drinkwater, John. "Two American Lives," *Quarterly Review* (London), CCLXVI, 122–135 (Jan., 1936). (Based on Harold Nicholson's *Dwight Morrow* and E. L. Masters's *Vachel Lindsay*.)

"An Evangelist in Rhyme," *Nation*, CXXXIII, 658 (Dec. 16, 1931).

Fiske, A. L. "Walking with Lindsay," *Commonweal*, XV, 409–411 (Feb. 10, 1932).

Frank, Glenn. "The Rodin of American Poetry," *The Century*, CII, 638–640 (August, 1921). (An appreciative discussion of "In Praise of Johnny Appleseed," with light on the development of the poem and a long quotation from the *London Spectator* regarding the poet.)

Graham, S. *Tramping with a Poet in the Rockies*. New York: 1922.

—— "Vachel Lindsay," *Spectator*, CXLVIII, 104 (Jan. 23, 1932).

Jones, L. *First Impressions*. New York: 1925, pp. 85–96.

—— "Vachel Lindsay: American Poet," *Christian Century*, XLVIII, 1619–1620 (Dec. 23, 1931).

Kreymborg, A. *Our Singing Strength*. New York: 1929, pp. 368–378. (A sympathetic survey of the main poems, with much good impressionistic criticism. Thinks that "most of the poems in the books of late years do not maintain the form of the earlier days" [p. 371] and that as a result of the War America "has outgrown and passed by its once darling Lindsay" [p. 378].)

Lindsay, V. *Adventures While Preaching the Gospel of Beauty*. New York: 1914.

—— "Adventures While Preaching Hieroglyphic Sermons," in *Collected Poems* (rev. ed., New York: 1925), pp. xvii–xlviii; and "Adventures While Singing These Songs," pp. 1–24.

—— *A Handy Guide for Beggars*. New York: 1916.

Lynd, R. *Books and Authors*. London: 1922, pp. 212–218.

Masters, E. L. *Vachel Lindsay: A Poet in America*. New York: 1935. (Although this book contains no bibliography and no precise documentation in footnotes, it is the best full-length study of Lindsay now available because it is based on personal intimacy and draws a mass of material from the poet's notebooks and letters and his wife's memories. Objectivity of interpretation is considerably marred, however, by Freudian and socialistic and sectional biases. Masters thinks Lindsay could have saved himself by finding an outlet in sex. He thinks the world owed him a living, and that men like Lindsay representing the agrarian West are "broken by Philistine persecution" of capitalism stemming from the East, "hunted down by the factory spirit which swelled the purses of slaughterhouse men, steel men, brokers and bankers, who made Chicago a soul possessed by torturing devils" [p. 271]. Masters glorifies Lindsay's Americanism, and concludes extravagantly that Lindsay's best poems "constitute the most considerable body of imaginative lyricism that any American has produced" [pp. 314–316].)

—— "Vachel Lindsay," *Bookman*, LXIV, 156–160 (Oct., 1926).

—— "The Tragedy of Vachel Lindsay," *American Mercury*, XXIX, 357–369 (July, 1933).

Maynard, T. "Vachel Lindsay: A Daniel in a Den of Buddhists," in *Our Best Poets*. New York: 1922, pp. 181–193. (Views Lindsay as a mystic. "With all his incidental weakness, Lindsay's intentions are essentially sound: his profundity is as surprising as his shallowness." Claims that "Harps in Heaven" is his most significant poem.)

Monroe, H. "Introduction," in *The Congo and Other Poems*. New York: 1914. (Gives a long quotation from Lindsay's letter which accompanied manuscripts when some of his poems were first published in *Poetry*—all about "the primitive singing of poetry." Miss Monroe praises Lindsay for re-establishing contact between the poet and the audience.)

—— *Poets and Their Art*. New York: 1932 (revised edition), pp. 21–28, 268–273. (An appreciative appraisal by the editor of *Poetry*. "From the first this poet has been led by . . . faith in beauty, in goodness, . . . in the splendor of common things and common experiences . . . Lindsay imparts a new flare of whimsical and colorful beauty to this American scene, and presents its extraordinary variety of emotion and mood.")

Munson, G. B. "Vachel Lindsay, Child-Errant," in *Destinations*. New York: 1928, pp. 67–74. (A sharply judicial critique from the conservative angle.)

O'Conor, N. J. "Vachel Lindsay: Poet-Prophet of the Middle West," *Landmark*, II, 805–808 (Dec., 1920).

Rittenhouse, J. B. "Vachel Lindsay," *South Atlantic Quarterly*, XXXII, 266–282 (July, 1933). (An important essay, based on first-hand material including many of Lindsay's letters to the author. Casts light on his relations with his mother and Harriet Monroe. Emphasizes his drawings and traces his political opinions to his father.)

Robinson, H. M. "The Ordeal of Vachel Lindsay," *Bookman*, LXXV, 6–9 (April, 1932).

Spencer, Hazelton. "Introduction," *Selected Poems of Vachel Lindsay*. New York: 1931, Modern Readers' Series. (An appreciative discussion, emphasizing Lindsay's distinctive lyric gifts in such poems as "The Chinese Nightingale." Incidentally, Lindsay's own recitals of about half the poems in this volume have been preserved on phonograph records now available at the Library of Columbia University.)

—— "The Life and Death of a Bard," *American Mercury*, XXV, 455–462 (April, 1932). (A brief appreciation and interpretation by a distinguished scholar, who concludes that as a bard rather than as a versifier "Lindsay clearly belongs with Emerson and Whitman" as at once the voice and the critic of our distinctively national democracy. Thinks he was "the greatest performer since Whitman," and the real "'driver' from first to last" in the New Poetry Movement. His prose shows that "the political idealism of his poetry was a conscious protest against political reality." Finds Lindsay's optimism and democracy essentially those of Emerson and Whitman.)

Trombly, A. E. *Vachel Lindsay, Adventurer*. Columbia, Mo.: 1929. (Ch. I, Biographical [with knowledge based on personal intimacy]; Ch. II, The Prose Books [originally published in *Southwest Review*, XIII, 459–468, Summer, 1928]; Ch. III, The Poems; Ch. IV, The Picture Books; Ch. V, Conclusion. Bibliography. A lucid, simple, sympathetic survey, with a good interpretation of the prose and poetry. Regards Lindsay as "the voice of the great masses of our people.")

Untermeyer, L. "Vachel Lindsay," *Saturday Review of Literature*, II, 236 (Oct. 25, 1925). (See also his discussion, *ibid.*, VIII, 368 [Dec. 12, 1931], in which he concludes that Lindsay's non-didactic lyrical poems are his greatest.)

Van Doren, C. "Salvation with Jazz: Vachel Lindsay," in *Many Minds*. New York: 1924, pp. 151–166. (A graceful essay. "All that was new in Mr. Lindsay's passion [for localistic nationalism] was its special object and method. He was the first to boost for beauty in the common American language" [p. 156]. "To the drive for a new localism there has succeeded a revolt from the village," and a general drift away from Lindsay's ideals toward satire and cynicism.)

Weirick, B. *From Whitman to Sandburg in American Poetry*. New York: 1924, pp. 204–210. (Brief but discriminating appreciation. "One poem like 'The Chinese Nightingale' will prove more effectual, one ventures, in the new warfare against the Philistines, than all his 'adventures,' rhymes to be sold for bread, and beating time to jazz and college yells.")

Wheeler, E. J. "An Illinois Art Revivalist," *Current Literature*, L, 320–323 (March, 1911).

Whipple, T. K. *Spokesmen*. New York: 1928, pp. 184–207. (A well-written and stimulating critique, developing the idea that Lindsay has two sides which he fails to integrate: he is "a faun trying to masquerade as a Sunday school superintendent . . . For him his poetry has had two functions: it has been either a refuge from actuality or a vehicle for edification. . . . The result, as usual, is instability, immaturity, and lack of integrity.")

"Why Vachel Lindsay Swears by the Log Cabin," *Literary Digest*, LXXXVIII, 50 (Feb. 20, 1926).

Wood, C. "Vachel Lindsay: Jazz and the Poet," in *Poets of America*. New York: 1925, pp. 229–245. ("Lindsay had from the start a burly, swaggering man-music, at times as softly sweet as bells heard over a hill, at times as enormous as the rumbling thunder deafening in the bell-tower." He has illustrated, however, "the gradual degradation of a great gift," partly as a result of the demands of his audiences. "They guffawed at the blare and the jitney comedy; and these are all he gives today, except for an occasional soapbox sermon" [p. 243]. A rather harsh critique, well illustrated, written from the artistic rather than from either the philosophical or social angle.)

NOTES

GENERAL

Although Lindsay has written several poems of considerable intrinsic value, he is probably most important as the spokesman of the tastes and ideas of the great mass of American people, especially in the Middle West in the nineteen-twenties, who gave him a far larger following than that of any other poet of the time. He is thus the representative voice of the agrarian, frontier, democratic, evangelical Middle West, and an inheritor of its humanitarian and utopian idealisms which stress the external and the social more than the inward and the individual. He is in line, essentially, with the liberal humanitarians such as Freneau, Barlow, Jefferson, of the early days, and with Walt Whitman. He opposed capitalism and urban industrialism, and he sought to recover in his crusade for "The New Localism" a fresh contact with the elemental springs of existence in small towns and the countryside; he sought a civilization of social justice which should eventually lead all men to express themselves in terms of beauty. In this way, the poet being rooted in his own soil and expressing the folkways of his group, we were supposed to secure a new poetry at once rich in variety and distinctively and uniquely American. It has been said by competent judges that, disregarding intrinsic values of art, Lindsay ranks with Emerson and Whitman in giving us a broad cross-section of the American mind of his period.

Lindsay was vastly more than a mere entertainer or an experimenter in sounds. But he did strive to restore to poetry its ancient birthright of being a chant or a song, and he followed Poe, Lanier, Swinburne, and Whitman (all of whom he greatly admired) in attention to rhythmical effects. Much as he liked the primitive and the barbaric, he was himself a carefully trained art-student and a painstakingly conscious craftsman in the musical technique and structure of verse.

"We will not accuse him of being a jazz poet," says T. K. Whipple (*Spokesmen*, pp. 202–203), "but merely insist that he used to be the master of a peculiarly spirited and infectious rhythm—and one, as he treated it, peculiarly American. At first one is tempted to say that this rhythm is not musical at all . . . that it is rhythm pure and simple, with no melody, no timbre. However, while it is true that the drums and taps are the most prominent instruments in Lindsay's orchestra, it is amazing, in the first place, what variety of effects he can get from them, from the shrill clash of the cymbals to the boom of the bass drum; and in the second place, if we listen attentively, we hear from time to time the sounds of flutes and violins. These are predominant throughout 'The Chinese Nightingale,' and are not absent from even so noisy a piece as 'The Santa Fé Trail.' . . .

"Indeed, one of Lindsay's chief merits is his use of variety in rhythm and tone-quality. He is a master both of gradual transition and of sharp contrast. His odes have lyric structure and arrangement; they are planned with definite effects and climaxes in mind. Furthermore, they have intellectual structure also. They are by no means mere riots of sound. See, for instance, how carefully 'The Congo' is made, with its three sections, each divided into two parts, with the refrain in each making the transition from the American negro to the African. And 'The Santa Fé Trail' evinces the same strong sense of form, the same ability to make the musical pattern and the intellectual plan define and enhance each other. No small part of the effectiveness of these pieces is derived from this classic quality, which may or may not have been suggested by the strophe, antistrophe, and epode of the Greek choric odes."

Page 733. A GOSPEL OF BEAUTY

Lindsay said that the three poems published under this title embody the "best brief expression of my gospel." This gospel involves a compound of agrarian democracy, evangelical religion, and æstheticism. Lindsay dislikes industrialism and "thundering commerce, fierce and bare" (l. 48). He honors the independent farmers who are lords of themselves and of their ancestral acres, which keep them in healthful contact with the primal and elemental springs of life. Unlike most of the other spokesmen of the New Poetry Movement, Lindsay is passionately devoted to Christianity as represented by the evangelical church and the Y.M.C.A. E. L. Masters (*Lindsay*, p. 298) observes rightly that he "never had the pantheism of Rousseau or Wordsworth," and he emphasizes Lindsay's deep debt to the teachings of the evangelist Alexander Campbell. Lindsay's lines 61–76, on the "Spirit-power" inspired by the "village church," should be read in connection with his prose work, *The Golden Book of Springfield* (1920), which presents a cathedral uniting all sects as the focal point in the utopian Springfield of 2018, a picture which illuminates the third poem in the present trilogy. In this prophesied utopia which "By faith shall rise redeemed" (l. 119), where Machinery and Trade are slaves and not rulers, "Music grows and Beauty is unchained" (l. 96), and "this beauty calls for valiant song" which shall make Springfield gleam as "The Artist's town of Bethlehem" (ll. 52, 84). This illustrates Lindsay's lifelong theme that beauty can be secured only as a by-product of a democratic, brotherly, humane civilization, that "Beauty is not directly pious, but does more civilizing in its proper hour than many sermons or laws." Just as Emerson said that beauty is the mark God sets upon individual virtue, so Lindsay saw beauty as the mark God sets upon civic virtue. The poem has a solemn beauty and sustained dignity in keeping with its subject and is unexcelled among Lindsay's social poems, which it is here included to represent.

Page 735. QUEEN MAB IN THE VILLAGE

This poem was included in Lindsay's pamphlet, *Rhymes To Be Traded for Bread* (1912). It represents a second group of his poems, those devoted to fairy-like "paths of wonder" (l. 56) and to lyricism for its own sweet beauty, without didactic intent. See also "The King of Yellow Butterflies" (p. 736) and "Aladdin and the Jinn" (p. 752), which also represent this group. Yet even this idyllic poem on Queen Mab, the fairy, suggests Lindsay's humanitarianism in his penitence for throwing "big rocks at pigeons" (l. 25) and picking "wailing daisies." Compare with Lowell's "Rhoecus" (p. 438), with Wordsworth's "She Was a Phantom of Delight," and with "Queen Mab" by his favorite Shelley. Lindsay cherished his dreams (p. 746, ll. 83–86), and he was a good deal of an escapist and romanticist in his indeterminate yearnings; see "Section V—Moon-Poems," *Collected Poems* (1923), pp. 229–249, and his Shelleyan volume *Going-to-the-Stars* (1926). Like Blake, whom he admired, Lindsay also wrote many songs of innocence and of childhood's fantasy.

Page 736. THE WEDDING OF THE ROSE AND THE LOTUS

Lindsay wrote, "The completion of the Panama Canal, the meeting of the waters of Asia and the West, and allied events, mean the making of new songs and arts the world over" (quoted, Masters, *Lindsay*, p. 222). With this Whitman-like utterance, compare Whitman's "Passage to India" (p. 710), prophesying a new benevolent internationalism as a result of the opening of the Suez Canal. Lindsay's beautiful symbolic poem, which sprang from the notation already cited, was illustrated by him in pamphlet form and distributed by Franklin K. Lane, Secretary of the Interior, to both houses of Congress on the first day of the Panama Exposition. Lindsay resented ("Foreword," *Collected Poems*, 1923, p. 17) the popular view that his poems were exclusively "a series of experiments in sound," and in repelling such a charge he cited this poem as an illustration of the fact that many of his poems used pictures,—hieroglyphs, as he called them—to symbolize ideas, in this case the union of the Occident and the Orient.

THE KING OF YELLOW BUTTERFLIES

See note on "Queen Mab in the Village," above.

GENERAL WILLIAM BOOTH ENTERS INTO HEAVEN

This poem, which first established Lindsay's national reputation, was written in 1912, following the death of the founder of the Salvation Army, and published in the magazine *Poetry*, January, 1913. "In my poem," wrote Lindsay, "I merely turned into rhyme as well as I could, word for word, General Booth's own account of his life, and the telegraph dispatches of his death after going blind. I set it to a tune that is not a tune, but a speech, a refrain used most frequently in the meetings of the Army on any public square to this day." It is odd that with his passionate desire to be the spokesman of unadulterated Americanism Lindsay should have established his reputation by a poem on an Englishman who founded an English institution, just as it is odd that he should have wandered homeless from coast to coast to teach each man he encountered the supreme duty of abiding at his own hearthstone. Lindsay's wanderings about New York at night had familiarized him with the colorful doings of the Salvation Army, with whose spiritual aims he was as an evangelist in profound sympathy. "Let us remember," says A. E. Trombly (*Lindsay*, 1929, p. 89), "that while the scene is so realistic as to have taken place in our city streets, it actually occurs in Heaven. The streets are those of Paradise; the actors are the poor mortals who, though rejected by humanity, are acceptable to Christ; and the passersby who stop to look on are God's saints. Literally, the poem is the apotheosis of the Salvation Army; symbolically, it is the apotheosis of all derelicts and the glorification of the most compelling aspect of Christianity, the humanity of Christ. The appeal to the imagination of Christendom through the Christian conception of Paradise, the verisimilitude of the scene, the humanity of Jesus, the fact that the poem voices the best of human aspirations and in a very human way, make for its profound spirituality." "The Congo" (1914), whose great success also depended on Lindsay's verve and high spirits and jazz rhythms, finds its climax in the third and last part which presents the Negro as shriven of his barbaric Voodoo superstitions and saved by Christianity. Compare also Lindsay's "I Heard Immanuel Singing," of which Masters (*Lindsay*, p. 216) says, "Lindsay never did anything more simply musical, more penetrated with that Bible feeling and imagery . . ." (On Lindsay's evangelical religion, see note on "A Gospel of Beauty," above.)

The success of the poem depended considerably on Lindsay's own public dramatic recital of it, in accordance with his view of the communal character of poetry, and his ability to arouse the enthusiasm and co-operation of large audiences. He has been likened to the wandering minstrels and bards of old in his interest in oral traditions and folk-art. Mr. Whipple (*Spokesmen*, p. 205) thinks that "his successes depend upon his sinking to a primitive or barbaric level—to the level of the negro, of the Salvation Army, of the child in 'Bryan, Bryan' and in 'John L. Sullivan,' of the mob in 'The Kallyope Yell,' and of the mythopœic savage in 'The Ghosts of the Buffaloes' and 'In Praise of Johnny Appleseed.'" He is the poet not of individual introspection like Emily Dickinson but of communal or group traditions of a broad character, and consequently his art and his rhythms are inspired by group-expressions—by his familiarity with hymn-singing, by vaudeville and screen actors keying their work to a large audience, and by western oratory designed to sway a crowd. Yet Lindsay's long training as a sophisticated art student entered unconsciously into these poems to enhance their colorful effectiveness in such lines (48–49) as

"The banjos rattled and the tambourines
Jing-jing-jingled in the hands of Queens."

Masters (*Lindsay*, p. 291), beginning with the strong first line of the poem, says: "The first foot is a molossus, that is, one of three long syllables. Syncopation is achieved by the use of pyrrhics, that is, feet composed of two short syllables. He interspersed trochees for swing and vigor, and anapests for running, romping, racing, banging drum effects, and for marching time. . . . Lindsay's genius dictated this fine onomatopœia. He did not by any rationale of verse say to himself that the drum speaks in the molossus, in spondees, and that people marching plant a foot down firmly and then lift the other one; nor that Salvationists hurrying to the corner go half leaping and bounding. He had in his mind the idea, the picture of the Salvation Army; his internal ear did the rest. It was a stroke of genius which no culture, no thinking, no discipline in verse, could ever have attained, or ever can attain. The very title of the poem is a miracle of inspiration."

Page 737. A NET TO SNARE THE MOONLIGHT

The agrarian Henry George was one of Lindsay's favorites, and he furnishes some of the texts in the poet's utopian *The Golden Book of Springfield*. (See Masters, *Lindsay*, pp. 266, 279.) This rather fairy-like little poem, compounded of dew and moonlight, suggests Lindsay's agrarian philosophy, his view that it is "our Father's mind" that "each poor man" should be given divinely-created "*land* to catch the rain." In general, of course, the spokesmen of the western frontier exalted not industrialism but agriculture. The notion that the farmer is close to God, because close to nature, goes back to eighteenth-century deism and the French physiocratic agrarians, who were among the teachers of the agrarian Jefferson, Lindsay's idol.

Page 738. ABRAHAM LINCOLN WALKS AT MIDNIGHT

Lindsay was born and died in a house owned by Lincoln's sister in Springfield, Illinois, within a stone's throw of the house in which Lincoln lived. In spite of Lindsay's own ardent Jeffersonianism he almost deified his fellow-townsman, the Republican Lincoln, as the voice of the democratic West, as a spokesman of the pioneer spirit. Just as the ghost of Hamlet's father betokened "something rotten in the state of Denmark," so Lindsay thinks that Lincoln's "mourning" ghost haunts Springfield on the eve of the World War because of "the sins of all the war-lords" and because

"Too many peasants fight, they know not why,
Too many homesteads in black terror weep."

This stately and dignified ballad, with its tragic beauty, Lindsay recited in an orotund and ominous tone with little variation; the poem represents his patriotic and war lyrics, and compares favorably with "Barbara Frietchie" and "Paul Revere's Ride." See also Lindsay's somewhat ludicrous poem on "The Statue of Old Andrew Jackson," who was another of his idols.

Lindsay's political and social philosophy, which has never been exhaustively studied, is expressed mainly in *Collected Poems* (pp. 71–105, 373–390), *The Golden Book of Springfield*, and especially in the prose *The Litany of Washington Street*. In the latter, as he says (p. 2), the "orations and litanies are held together by quotations from Whitman" and the book includes a reverent essay (pp. 54–64) on Whitman as "Statesman-Poet." In this exceedingly nationalistic and rather dramatically pictorial *Litany*, Lindsay says "I am a Jeffersonian," but he shows unexpected balance in presenting both Jefferson and Hamilton as extremists who are united and counterbalanced by Washington, constantly riding between them. "Always on Washington Street I see those three superb horsemen, Washington, Jefferson, and Hamilton, riding abreast. Washington in the middle on a much bigger, higher horse, never looking to the right or to the left . . . But if Jefferson must address Hamilton, he has to look around the General, and lean forward, which is difficult to do; or lag behind the General, which his pride will not permit. Thus I deride my favorite hero . . . Jefferson keeps near the southern curb, Hamilton near the northern curb; and I say that the three horses will move abreast till the day of doom, with the great plumed chief in the middle . . . Whoever rides after must ride behind the cavalcade of the General and his two aides, or else go afoot. . . . I say if he had the grand style, it was a good gift to the nation. . . . He still outbids Jefferson in the battle for the hearts of the people" (*Litany*, pp. 29–33). It should be noted, however, that Lindsay thought of Washington as molded by the American frontier: "George Washington, like all other United States citizens, was more influenced by red Indians than by anything brought over from Europe, be it a squire or a book." He was "a super-Indian chief in silk stockings" (*Litany*, p. 18). "For my part, I say that at the end of a thousand years, Jefferson's ideas will prevail, in the Washington cabinet meeting. But Hamiltonians are surely entitled to vote the other way" (*Litany*, p. 121). The poem, "The Virginians are Coming," originally planned as a summary for the *Litany* but published in *Every Soul Is a Circus*, shows his admiration for Robert E. Lee, and his longing for the breakdown of the modern economic system. Lindsay himself advocated pacifism, agrarianism, a redistribution of land, and other social reforms. "This My Song Is Made for Kerensky" regards the Russian Revolution as the dawn of a better order of government for and by the people. He explains "Why I Voted the Socialist Ticket" (*Poems*, p. 301), thinking that "our everlasting sinfulness" can be healed in "the polling places," which by God's providence will "make us sages with transfigured faces." Probably Lindsay's evangelicism leads him to place somewhat more emphasis than most socialists do on "everlasting sinfulness" and the divine will. But essentially he seems to represent a continuation of the tradition stretching from Jefferson and Paine and Freneau to modern radicals which seeks the cause and cure of evil in outward institutions rather than within the heart of the individual. That is why he can be so complacently the author of utopias.

THE SANTA-FÉ TRAIL

This characteristic but sometimes misunderstood poem embodies two different sides of Lindsay's work: his colorful and jazzy recording of the modernistic aspects of our American industrial civilization symbolized by the noisy procession of motor-cars; and his criticism of this soulless civilization devoid of beauty symbolized by the sweet song of the bird, the Rachel-Jane, telling of love and eternal youth. Although many readers hear only the noise in this poem, its main significance lies in the contrasting song of the bird.

Page 742. THE CHINESE NIGHTINGALE

Nearly everyone, including Lindsay, has agreed that this is by all odds his most coherently constructed and most hauntingly and delicately beautiful poem.

The poem illustrates how superbly Lindsay could transcend jazz and noise and crudity when he chose, as well as his characteristic ability to recognize the glory of romance and immutable beauty in the midst of the common-place and the squalid. As Mr. Bruce Weirick says (*From Whitman to Sandburg*, pp. 206–207), this "dream tale of a Chinese laundryman in San Francisco is more delicately tinged with the romance and oriental colorings of a musical comedy. It is sweet in spirit, elevated, and tender with a wistful love. It has the oriental background of Karma, of birth, death, rebirth, and death; but the red thread of love unites all the beads of these lovers' various half-remembered lives. The echo of these lives is the song of the Chinese nightingale, I take it, and it is that which gives the haunting melody,

> 'I remember, I remember
> That spring came on forever,
> That spring came on forever,'
> Said the Chinese nightingale.

Here we have the refrain still that was used so tellingly in 'The Congo' and 'General Booth,' but softened, and colored so as to unify and poetize the pictures that flow in kaleidoscopic change before us. And what magic pictures they are, that this mystical bird of the imagination nightly unrolls to the sight of this humble Chinese laundryman!" Compare the intermittent song of the nightingale with that of the Rachel-Jane in "The Santa-Fé Trail." Does Lindsay imply, as Whipple thinks (*Spokesmen*, p. 191), that "in all life only youth and love in springtime are memorable?" Note how much the tender beauty of the poem depends upon Lindsay's characteristic use of contrasts such as the lurid glimpse of the back-alleys of San Francisco and the exquisite dream of romance. Does the nightingale's song embody what is changeless as opposed to the changing aspects of actual surroundings? Compare Lindsay's use of the nightingale's song with the use which Whitman makes of the hermit thrush's song in "When Lilacs Last in the Dooryard Bloom'd" (p. 701).

Page 745. THE GHOST OF THE BUFFALOES

The "night before Christmas" sing-song and setting of this poem do not prevent it from serving as an impressive illustration of Lindsay's power in dealing with the primitive, colorful, vigorous, and romantic aspects of local traditions. Originally an exponent of poetry designed for what he called "The Higher Vaudeville," for choral chanting, Lindsay said that he was interested in securing "big contrasts" in his poems. Thus in "The Santa-Fé Trail" the song of the Rachel-Jane alternates with the blare of the noisy procession of motor-cars, and in "The Chinese Nightingale" the squalor of the back-alleys of San Francisco and the weary life of the laundryman are contrasted with the song of the nightingale. And in "The Ghost of the Buffaloes" the same sort of artistic purpose is served by the magical little flute-song of the wind in the chimney, conjuring him to dream (ll. 83–86), contrasting with the blood-curdling "a-la-la, a-la-la" of the Indians and the thunder of the buffaloes racing westward.

Page 746. IN PRAISE OF JOHNNY APPLESEED

Dr. Glenn Frank, writing in the same issue of the *Century* ("The Rodin of American Poetry," CII, 638–640, August, 1921) in which as editor he first published this poem by Lindsay, gives us an interesting side-light on the manner in which the poems were developed: "Mr. Lindsay, as he read the poem to audiences from week to week, found it growing and perfecting itself. The alteration of a line here, the revamping of a phrase there, the adding of a new stroke to the picture, were bringing out more effectively the overtones which are so much of the poem. We were frankly fascinated as we watched the poem grow from week to week, and delayed publication in order to catch the full benefit of the process." It appears, then, that Lindsay's poems were considerably molded by the successive and immediate reactions of audiences to whom the poems were orally presented: to him poetry was always communication, a sharing his thought with others, and he usually tested his attempts at communication empirically before publishing them. In this he resembled Mark Twain, who developed many of his stories in the same manner. Indeed, W. F. Taylor (*A History of American Letters*, New York, 1936, p. 398) says that "Lindsay is . . . a kind of folk poet, relating not to the philosophical school of American poets from Emerson through Moody, but to the back-country humorists and lecturers from Longstreet through Mark Twain and James Whitcomb Riley." (See Lindsay's "Three Poems about Mark Twain," *Collected Poems*, 1923, pp. 258–263.)

On the career of John Chapman, under the name of "Johnny Appleseed," see, besides the reference Lindsay gives (*Harper's Monthly Magazine*, November, 1871), Henry Chapin's book, *The Adventures of Johnny Appleseed* (New York, 1930), which contains an article by E. J. Lang entitled "Johnny Appleseed in Pittsburgh," also available in the *Western Pennsylvania Historical Magazine*, XIII, 256–260 (1930). Chapman (1775–1847), an eccentric, a sort of Roland of the Wild West, went forth before the host of pioneers, singing his songs of the Ancient of Days and planting his apple-orchards so that those who followed might enjoy the fruits of the earth. Lindsay, with his delight in folk-tales, takes "Johnny Appleseed" as a sort of symbol of the frontier spirit which vitalizes so much of his poetry and its religion of democracy. "Appleseed" is woven into the whole of *The Golden Book of Springfield*—see E. L. Masters's analysis (*Lindsay*, pp. 276–285). Masters throughout his book on Lindsay likens him to "Appleseed" and in commenting on this poem (p. 305), concludes, "All this allegory in which sowing of seed is the symbol of planting civilization refers to Lindsay himself. Johnny Appleseed is Lindsay. This poem lacks condensation, and because it is so excellent one wishes that somehow its wonderful material and imagery had been given the benefit of the file. With all its faults, however, it remains a remarkable poem, wholly original, and of really great import." The London *Spectator*, which printed the poem about the same time that it appeared in the *Century*, hailed Lindsay as a sort of modern Homer singing the great and strange revel of our race as it followed the setting sun to satisfy its hunger for land. The *Spectator* exulted in "this new welling up of the primitive" represented by Lindsay, and concluded that "technically and aesthetically his work is . . . full of the inaccuracy and vigor of mediaeval English or modern Russian woodcarvers."

Page 752. AN ARGUMENT

The two parts of this poem embody respectively two sides of Lindsay's own character—his robust, masculine delight in vigorous living illustrated by Henry Fifth, Hotspur, Macbeth, Falstaff, and Cæsar; and his evangelical and humanitarian utopianism. See note on "A Gospel of Beauty," and Masters's analysis (*Lindsay*, pp. 276–285) of the utopian *Golden Book of Springfield*. On the history of utopianism in America, see M. Kraus, "America and the Utopian Ideal in the 18th Century," *Mississippi Valley Historical Review*, XXII, 487–504 (March, 1936); Lewis Mumford, *The Story of Utopias* (1922); J. O. Hertzler, *The History of Utopian Thought* (1923). During Lindsay's youth a great many utopian books, especially novels, were published, the most notable being Edward Bellamy's *Looking Backward* (1888) and *Equality* (1897), and William Dean Howells's *A Traveler from Altruria* (1894); for full discussion see the interesting study by Allyn Forbes, "The Literary Quest for Utopia, 1880–1900," *Social Forces*, VI, 179–189 (1927).

THE UNPARDONABLE SIN

Lindsay illustrates here his ardent pacifism by a realistic detailing of the horrors of war and by indicating the irony of having opposing military powers "send forth rapine in the name of Christ."

Page 753. THE VOYAGE

This poem from *Every Soul Is a Circus* is taken to represent that volume and also *Going-to-the-Sun* (1923) and *Going-to-the-Stars* (1926). In the poems of these volumes, not included in *Collected Poems*, Masters (*Lindsay*, p. 313) says, "Lindsay achieved a purity of line and sound that is absent from his famous successes, those upon which his reputation first rested. A more refined taste will choose these rather than poems like 'The Congo,' and 'The Chinese Nightingale,' for the purpose of showing his genius in its finest manifestations. And one is almost led to believe that in those later books he was approaching the realization of an art which would have been the work of his genius purged at last of all dross, eccentricity and marring mannerisms." The poem embodies Lindsay's lyrical, fairy-like ideal of the poet—his desire to give a magical freshness to "The old sweet songs of Heaven/ And spring."

LINDSAY'S POETIC THEORIES

Lindsay's poetic theories await exhaustive analysis. They may be studied in *The Gospel of Beauty*, in the prefaces to his *Collected Poems* and to *Every Soul Is a Circus*, in his essays on "The Real American Language" (*American Mercury*, March, 1928) and on Whitman (in *The Litany of Washington Street*), and in *The Art of the Moving Picture*, with its section on hieroglyphics or symbols. These theories may also be studied in "The New Localism, an Illustrated Essay for the Village Statesman," published in 1912 in his *Vision, a Quarterly Journal of Æsthetic Appreciation of Life.* The main ideas in this essay, with its sub-title, "We Are Face to Face with Centralization," may be represented by the following quotations: "In brief, the New States' Rights is social, not political, an opportunity, not a legal system. It is based on a Renaissance of so many commission cities, dry villages, and school-centered country communities. This view of the state is the basis, not the consummation of the New Localism. . . . The devout dry town will establish the noble equivalent of the Oberammergau Passion Play, not necessarily a Bible drama, but a lofty and soul cleansing morality . . . Every little place will soon have its special calendar of outdoor festivals. The country High School, here and there, will produce not only its rhymer, but its poet, its orchestra of real composers, its own succession of sages, painters, Sibyls, its corn-field song, its festival insignia. . . . Not only will there be changes like these, but in all its passions and pursuits of the higher man, from novel writing to schools of philosophy, the best of our towns will bear the fruit called genius. . . . Many a stopping place will have its endowed ceramics and carvings, its special spice for the imagination, its peculiar proverb, its own type of men. . . . The New Localism will bring among its principal benefits what might be described as the Democratic Fine Arts, will bring an exquisite sensibility and powerful beauty making faculty among common men. . . . It [the Constitution of American art] will of course be unwritten. In many ways it will assume a parallel between itself and the political constitution. It will declare that bad taste is mob law, and good public taste is democracy. . . . Aesthetically speaking we are a mob on the prairie, and a despotism in cultured circles. The creative power represented by the Art Institute, Chicago, or the International Studio, or the Cathedral of St. John, Morningside Heights, or the Metropolitan Museum, fertilizing and helpful within a certain pale, but is European. The taste of the most radical, American-worshipping painters in New York is European. . . . Young Americans . . . should, if led by the spirit, wander over the whole nation in search of the secret of democratic beauty with their hearts at the same time overflowing with the righteousness of God. Then they should come back to their own hearth and neighborhood and gather a little circle of their own sort of workers about them and strive to make the neighborhood and home more beautiful and democratic and holy with their special art. . . . They should labor in their little circle expecting neither reward nor honors. . . . In their darkest hours they should be made strong by the vision of a completely beautiful neighborhood and the passion for a completely democratic art . . . *Religion, equality, and beauty!* By these America shall come into a glory that shall justify the yearnings of the sages for her perfection."

Lindsay's poetic creed may perhaps be roughly summarized as follows:

1. Beauty is the mark God sets upon *civic* virtue. "Ugliness is a kind of misgovernment." The beautiful and the good *of all* are the same thing, and the former is impossible without the latter. Hence the social welfare of the group must precede the creation of beautiful poems.
2. The poet must work from kin to kind, from the local and particular to the universal. "The things most worth while are one's own hearth and neighborhood. We should make our own home and neighborhood the most democratic, the most beautiful, and the holiest in the world" (*The Gospel of Beauty*, 1914). See also the foregoing quotation from "The New Localism."
3. The by-product of a happy community, poems involve communication, a sharing of their beauty with others, and hence should be capable of being effectively spoken or chanted by a group. Thus the manipulation of sound-effects and contrasts is important. Yet ultimately, "all poetry is first and last for the inner ear, and its final pleasures are for the soul, whispering in solitude . . . I petition that my verse be judged not as a series of experiments in sound, but for lifetime and even hereditary thoughts and memories of painting" ("Foreword," *Collected Poems*, 1923, pp. 7, 17).
4. As in moving pictures, other fine arts, such as painting, sculpture, architecture, and music, contribute to perfecting the perfect poem. (Cf. *The Art of the Moving Picture*. Lindsay's poems have been called a species of moving pictures. The subtitle of "The Chinese Nightingale" is "A Song in Chinese Tapestries.") The poet should be a close student of *all* the arts, and sensitive to their analogies and the possibilities of their cross-fertilization, Lessing's *Laokoön* notwithstanding.
5. "Poems written for pictures are to be judged by a Philosophy of Hieroglyphics," i.e., by the extent to which facts have been used as symbols of some broader human significance. The American poet should develop a system of "United States hieroglyphics" designed to focus attention on the fundamental symbols or patterns of ideas which represent life in America. The contemporary American scene is the best means by which a native poet may body forth the unseen. And since poetry is the flowering of a happy group-life or national life, our poetry ought to be distinctive of this group-life or distinctively American. As Taine (whom Lindsay studied) said, literature is determined by the poet's time, place, and race: it voices his unique nationality.

To what extent did Lindsay succeed in practicing these five ideals?

EDWIN ARLINGTON ROBINSON

CHRONOLOGY

1869 Born, Dec. 22, in village of Head Tide, Maine. Family moved soon to town of Gardiner to which the poet later referred as "Tilbury Town."

1891–93 At Harvard, until the death of his father obliged him to earn a living.

1896 *The Torrent and the Night Before,* his first collection of poems, privately printed.

1897 *The Children of the Night.* Includes some of the poems in the first volume, with many new ones. Robinson lived in New York and made his living in various ways, serving at one time as an inspector in the subway which was then being constructed.

1902 *Captain Craig.* (Revised edition, 1915.) President Theodore Roosevelt became interested in Robinson and gave him a clerkship in the New York Custom House, a position which he held from 1905 to 1910. After that he gave his entire time to poetry, living part of the time at the MacDowell Colony in New Hampshire, a colony of writers and artists.

1910 *The Town Down the River.*

1914 *Van Zorn.* A play.

1915 *The Porcupine.* A play.

1916 *The Man Against the Sky.*

1917 *Merlin.*

1920 *The Three Taverns. Lancelot.*

1921 *Avon's Harvest.*

1922 Awarded Pulitzer Prize, on the basis of his *Collected Poems* published the year before. New editions of the collected poems appeared in 1924, 1927, and 1929.

1923 *Roman Bartholow.*

1924 *The Man Who Died Twice.* (Awarded the Pulitzer Prize the following year.)

1925 *Dionysius in Doubt.*

1927 *Tristram.* (Awarded the Pulitzer Prize the following year.)

1928 *Sonnets, 1889–1927. Fortunatus.*

1929 *Cavender's House. Modred, a Fragment. The Prodigal Son.*

1930 *The Glory of the Nightingales.*

1931 *Matthias at the Door.*

1932 *Nicodemus.*

1933 *Talifer.*

1934 *Amaranth.*

1935 *King Jasper.* Died, April 6.

BIBLIOGRAPHY

I. Bibliography

Beebe, L. M., and Bulkley, R. J., Jr. *A Bibliography of the Writings of Edwin Arlington Robinson.* Cambridge, Mass.: 1931. (Contains a list of first editions and reprints, but no list of writings about Robinson.)

Edwin Arlington Robinson. A Collection of His Works from the Library of Bacon Callamore. Hartford: 1936. (A bibliography, with indication of where the poems first appeared. Includes valuable explanatory matter partly from the letters of Robinson to the collector.)

II. Text

Collected Poems by Edwin Arlington Robinson. New edition. New York: 1930.

Poems. Selected, with a preface, by Bliss Perry. New York: 1931.

The Glory of the Nightingales. New York: 1930.

Matthias at the Door. New York: 1931.

Nicodemus. New York: 1932.

Talifer. New York: 1933.

Amaranth. New York: 1934.

King Jasper. New York: 1935.

III. Biography and Criticism

App, A. J. "Edwin Arlington Robinson's Arthurian Poems," *Thought,* X, 468–479 (Dec., 1935).

Beebe, L. M. *Aspects of the Poetry of E. A. Robinson.* Cambridge, Mass.: 1928.

—— *Edwin Arlington Robinson and the Arthurian Legend.* Cambridge, Mass.: 1927.

Boynton, P. H. *Some Contemporary Americans.* Chicago: 1924, pp. 16–32. (A brief but judicious critique, emphasizing Robinson's timeless universality and essential serenity. "Mr. Robinson is never cynical toward the things that are more excellent.")

Brenner, R. *Ten Modern Poets.* New York: 1930, pp. 85–115. (Biographical.)

Brown, David. "Some Rejected Poems of Edwin Arlington Robinson," *American Literature,* VII, 395–414 (Jan., 1936). (A valuable scholarly article, casting considerable light upon his early literary aims.)

Cestre, C. "Amy Lowell, Robert Frost, and Edwin Arlington Robinson," *Johns Hopkins Alumni Magazine,* XIV, 363–388 (March, 1926).

—— *An Introduction to Edwin Arlington Robinson.* New York: 1930. (This is probably the best comprehensive book on the poet, by a distinguished French scholar and critic. The chapters are "A Modern Classic"; "Poetry of Emotion and Reflection"; "Treatment of Arthurian Legend"; "Interpretative and Dramatic Poetry"; "Humor"; and "Psychology." M. Cestre combines in an unusual degree both philosophical penetration and richness of æsthetic appreciation.)

—— "Avec Edwin Arlington Robinson dans L'Inferno de L'Art," *Revue Anglo-Américaine,* XII, 323–327 (April, 1935).

Conrad, L. H. "The Critic's Poet," *Landmark*, XV, 23–26 (Jan., 1933).

Cook, H. W. *Our Poets of Today*. New York: 1923, pp. 18–30.

Drinkwater, J. *The Muse in Council*. Boston: 1925, pp. 248–262. (This distinguished English critic and playwright concludes: "Mr. Robinson is in the true Greek tradition in this, that, whereas most of his fellow-countrymen who are poets see man beset by society, which is circumstance, he sees man beset by his own character." See also Drinkwater's essay on Robinson in the *Yale Review*, XI, 467–476 (April, 1922).

Evans, Nancy. "Edwin Arlington Robinson," *Bookman*, LXXV, 675–681 (Nov., 1932). (A valuable article based on a personal interview in which Robinson casts much light on his literary theories. He is also quoted as saying, "Mr. Morris was on the wrong track" in tracing the poet's transcendentalism to Josiah Royce.)

Fairclough, H. R. "The Classics and Our Twentieth Century Poets," *Stanford University Publications in Language and Literature*, II, 1–50 (1927). (In pp. 14–27 this eminent classical scholar discusses Robinson's traditional forms, his dramatic method, his aversion to sentimental love, his subordination of rhapsodies on nature to representative ethical aspects of mankind, and his aloofness and serenity which is characterized as Sophoclean. Mr. Fairclough concludes that Robinson was "deeply indebted to classical culture." A very important study.)

Farrar, J. (ed.) *The Literary Spotlight*. New York: 1924, pp. 116–124.

Flint, F. C. "Review of *Matthias at the Door*," *Symposium*, III, 237–248 (April, 1932).

Gorman, H. S. *The Procession of Masks*. Boston: 1923, pp. 15–39.

Hammond, J. "The Man Against the Sky—Edwin Arlington Robinson," *Personalist*, X, 178–184 (July, 1929).

Jones, L. *First Impressions*. New York: 1925, pp. 13–36.

Kilmer, J. *Literature in the Making*. New York: 1917, pp. 265–273.

Kreymborg, A. *Our Singing Strength*. New York: 1929, pp. 297–315. (Rather unsympathetic impressions of Robinson's poetry, book by book. Disparages his longer narrative poems. Emphasizes futility.)

Kunitz, S. J. (ed.) *Living Authors*. New York: 1932, pp. 344–346.

Ledoux, L. V. "Psychologist of New England," *Saturday Review of Literature*, XII, 3–4, 16, 18 (Oct. 19, 1935). (The poet's literary executor deals briefly with his relation to the "New England tradition of which he may have been the final flower.")

Lowell, A. "A Bird's-Eye View of E. A. Robinson," *Dial*, LXXII, 130–142 (Feb., 1922). (Robinson "straddles a period." He is a "dyed-in-the-wool New Englander . . . His insight into people is pure Yankee shrewdness . . . Two people and an atmosphere is Mr. Robinson's forte. Crowd his stage . . . and his edge becomes blunted." He falls short of Hardy in "poetry of soul . . . His vision is pointillistic." A sympathetic and discriminating discussion.)

—— *Tendencies in Modern American Poetry*. Boston: 1917, pp. 3–75. (A suggestive discussion in the light of imagistic criteria. On account of its date, the essay does not consider Robinson's important later work. Miss Lowell regarded Robinson as "the poet of the fleeting instant," praised his early work, but went far astray in condemning "Merlin" as "meandering" to a weak ending.)

Maynard, T. "Edwin Arlington Robinson: a Humorist Who Cannot Laugh," in *Our Best Poets*. New York: 1922, pp. 153–168. (A sympathetic and well-illustrated essay, dealing with Robinson's general attitude toward life. "Irony is the essence of his character." Concludes with the regret that he falls short of true greatness.)

Monroe, H. *Poets and Their Art*. New York: 1926, pp. 1–11. (A judicious brief essay. Finds "something akin" to Puritanism in Robinson. His main theme is the "heroic . . . struggle of highly strung sensitive souls to fulfill their manifest destiny." Pays special tribute to "The Master" and "The Man Who Died Twice.")

Morris, Lloyd. *The Poetry of Edwin Arlington Robinson*. New York: 1923. (Although this early book could not take into account Robinson's important later work, and although the book hardly runs to seventy pages, exclusive of bibliography, it is of special value in showing that Robinson was not a futilitarian but an idealist. Morris's theory that his view of life was strongly influenced by that of Josiah Royce at Harvard was refuted by Robinson himself—see Nancy Evans, above.)

Munson, G. B. *Destinations*. New York: 1928, pp. 57–66. (An unsympathetic judicial critique charging Robinson with negativity and finding his thought akin to that of Henry Adams. Munson thinks Robinson is over-rated.)

Pipkin, E. E. "The Arthur of Edwin Arlington Robinson," *English Journal*, XIX, 183–195 (March, 1930). (An excellent essay showing the ethical centrality of Robinson by means of cogent analyses of Arthur, Merlin, Guinevere, Tristram, etc. Emphasizes the profound humanity of the Arthurian characters, a humanity based on their being conceived dramatically in terms of their inner lives rather than in terms of mediaeval or romantic trappings.)

Redman, B. R. *Edwin Arlington Robinson*. New York: 1926.

Romig, Edna D. "Tilbury Town and Camelot," *University of Colorado Studies*, XIX, 303–326 (1932). (An elaborately documented but somewhat uncritical essay, attempting to prove that Robinson is a greater poet than Whitman, the

equal of Tennyson, and a "surer artist" than Wordsworth.)

Schonemann, F. "Der Lyriker der amerikanischen Skepsis," *Die Literatur*, XXXV, 446–448 (1933).

Squire, J. C. "Edwin Arlington Robinson," in *Contemporary American Authors*, edited by J. C. Squire. New York: 1928, pp. 121–148. (A well-balanced and well-written critique by an Englishman. After suggesting reasons why Robinson was almost unknown in England in 1928, Mr. Squire follows Mr. Drinkwater in emphasizing the classical and timeless aspect of the poet's reading of life. Concludes that he is "one of the best writers ever born in America," and "one of the most notable poets now enriching . . . English literature.")

St. Clair, G. "E. A. Robinson and Tilbury Town," *New Mexico Quarterly*, IV, 95–107 (May, 1934). (A clever and amusing essay dealing with the question of the realism of Robinson's portrayal of the people of New England, cast in the form of a dramatic monologue between Robinson, the Recording Spirit, and characters from Robinson's poems.)

Tate, Allan. "Again, O Ye Laurels," *New Republic*, LXXVI, 312–313 (Oct. 25, 1933). (Review of "Talifer," and general critique.)

Taylor, W. F. *A History of American Letters*. New York: 1936, pp. 339–347, with a very full bibliography, pp. 569–570. (An admirable, well-balanced and well-written interpretation and critique in brief space. Considers Robinson with Frost, Edith Wharton, and Willa Cather as representative of the "Central Currents in Poetry and Fiction" in the present century. Deals with his general position, his studies of character, his Arthurian romances, his psychological tales, and concludes that he is not a futilitarian but a spiritual explorer recognizing evil but seeing hope in the transcendental "Light.")

Theis, O. F. "Edwin Arlington Robinson," *Forum*, LI, 305–312 (Feb., 1914). (Stresses Robinson's detachment, originality, and psychological insight. Yet, "In the best sense of the word Robinson is an eclectic" [p. 311].)

Untermeyer, Louis. "Edwin Arlington Robinson," in *The New Era in American Poetry*. New York: 1919, pp. 111–135. (An impressionistic and discursive survey.)

Van Doren, M. *Edwin Arlington Robinson*. New York: 1927. (An able study, concluding that Robinson's fame as a major poet will ultimately rest not upon his short poems but upon his long narratives—a view of which Kreymborg disapproves.)

Weber, C. J. "The Cottage Lights of Wessex," *Colby Mercury*, VI, 64–67 (Feb., 1936). (Reminiscences of Robinson, and his relation to Thomas Hardy.)

Weirick, B. *From Whitman to Sandburg in American Poetry*. New York: 1924, pp. 184–192. (An unsympathetic discussion by a militant Westerner to whom Frost and Robinson represent "The Note of Futility." Robinson's is "a library culture. Much of his poetry is but the warmings over of English literature, . . . and is devoid of reference to the contemporary and the actual." He is distinguished for "a certain narrowness and stinginess," although he is a poet "of infinite polish.")

Whipple, T. K. *Spokesmen*. New York: 1928, pp. 45–69. (A discriminating but unsympathetic essay from a point of view mildly socialistic. Recognizes that although Robinson has been "strongly affected by the current pessimistic naturalism, . . . his philosophy . . . is a very much chastened and sobered transcendentalism." Admits that Robinson's comment on American life is "essentially the same as Emerson's—against conformity, uniformity, standardization, mechanization, . . . he opposes individualism, self-reliance, self-development." Yet Mr. Whipple thinks that "This repudiation of the world, this movement of desire away from reality, is . . . the central fact about Robinson.")

Wood, Clement. *Poets of America*. New York: 1925, pp. 119–41. (A discursive and dogmatic essay based on the conventional—and erroneous—view that Robinson has "a philosophy based upon a single postulate that man has failed, upon denial at core" [p. 140]. Emphasizes "the black despair of his heartsong." For contrary views see Drinkwater, Morris, Taylor, Whipple, Squire, and others above. Some of Mr. Wood's impressionistic criticism of individual poems is good.)

Zabel, M. D. "Edwin Arlington Robinson," *Commonweal*, XVII, 436–438 (Feb. 15, 1933). (Although Robinson may have written too much, "he chose the hard and solitary path of personal probity.")

NOTES

GENERAL

Robinson and Lindsay, representing roughly the general attitudes respectively of the East and the West, offer an interesting contrast. Robinson, heir of Puritanism and Transcendentalism, believes the cause and cure of evil is within the individual; Lindsay believes mainly that they are in society and social institutions. The first is essentially Federalistic, the second Jeffersonian and humanitarian. Hence Robinson deals mainly with ethical conflicts within the isolated individual; Lindsay deals mainly with groups or with propaganda for group reform—for prohibition, better parks, pacifism, socialism, etc. Robinson believes that only the few can save the many; Lindsay glorifies equalitarianism. Robinson devotes himself mainly to non-localized universal problems,

guided by tradition (cf. "The Man Against the Sky" and "Tristram"); Lindsay advocates and practices the "New Localism" and is in revolt against European traditionalism. Robinson uses older forms; Lindsay experiments with innovations in form. The first seeks a sophisticated ethical art for the contemplative few; the second seeks a broad oral art for the populace. Robinson, believing in progress only as regards individual self-conquest, tends to be somber; Lindsay, lyrically accepting the idea of rectilinear and continuous progress of the race, tends to be exuberant and optimistic. Robinson's art tends to achieve a fine integration, and a singular unity of thought, form, and mood; while Lindsay's art, excepting a few distinguished poems, tends to lack integration, finish, and harmony of atmosphere. With characteristic New England reserve, Robinson favors the relatively objective dramatic monologue; Lindsay, with Western outspokenness and directness, favors the more subjective lyric form. In broad terms, Robinson represents the individualism of the traditional East, and Lindsay represents the expansive and humanitarian West, with its anti-traditional frontier heritage of equality, optimism, and democracy. Together, they represent the two great traditions which run through American culture and which have been mutually useful in counteracting the tendency of each to approach an extreme.

"Robinson, as poet, deserves to be styled a modern classic, because he combines in harmonious union the old time qualities of intellectual acumen, broad humanity, universal appeal, decorum, sense of proportion and art of composition, with powers more recently developed as means of literary expression: imaginative coloring, sensuous richness, suggestive foreshortenings and word melody. A survey of his work yields the impression of wealth of vision and felicity of technique, together with a concern for what is most human in man: preference for the general, subordination of sensation to sensibility and of sensationalism to sense, propriety and reserve—all which remind us of ancient Greece and Rome, and of the Augustan age in France and in England. His occasional adaptations and variations of Greek themes fit so exactly with his own work that they seem to be a spontaneous retrospect of his thought towards the past. His most original creations, with all their keen analysis of the moods and idiosyncrasies of our time, bear the unmistakable stamp of the permanently human. . . . After all, Robinson harks back to Shakespeare, being keenly alive, like the poet of *The Tempest,* to the splendor of our higher nature, and sadly sensitive, like Prospero, to our inability to rise to the height of our aspirations."—Charles Cestre, *An Introduction to Edwin Arlington Robinson*, pp. 5–6, 55.

"His preoccupation is the spirit of man, not assailed and tortured by that movement of life which we call civilization, but seen, as it were, detached from this influence and laboring in all the ironies and aspirations of its own nature. Mr. Robinson is in the true Greek tradition in this, that, whereas most of his fellow-countrymen who are poets see man beset by society, which is circumstance, he sees mán beset by his own character, which is fate."—John Drinkwater, *The Muse in Council* (London, 1925), pp. 192–193.

Page 755. CREDO

In this magnificent early sonnet Robinson has given us the key to the philosophy which underlies most of his work: he recognizes *both* "the black and awful chaos of the night" (the blankly materialistic life of the senses) *and* "the coming glory of the Light" (our intuitions of a spiritual guidance transcending the life of the senses). Robinson, even more than Arnold, found himself between "two worlds," the world of science and the world of faith, and he is probably voicing his own view when he has Lancelot say,

"God, what a rain of ashes falls on him
Who sees the new and cannot leave the old!"

Touched by current pessimistic naturalism, a reader of Zola, Hardy, and their followers, he has devoted many poems to exploring dramatically the view of those who think life merely a "blind atomic pilgrimage" from nothing to nothing. On the other hand, as a native New Englander he had the blood of the Puritans and of the Transcendentalists in his veins. These two currents of thought, the naturalistic and the religious, run through most of Robinson's work. In the poem "The Children of the Night," he says "some are strong and some are weak," and that

"For those that never know the light,
The darkness is a sullen thing,"

that they alone "seem lost in Fortune's winnowing."

"It is the faith within the fear
That holds us to the life we curse."

In "L'Envoi" following the poems of *The Children of the Night* (*Collected Poems*, pp. 108–109), he records his consciousness of a "transcendent music," "a glad strain of some vast harmony"; he is confident that, "after time and place are overthrown, / God's touch will keep its one chord quivering." When Lancelot is defeated, he hears a Voice saying,

"Where the Light falls, death falls;
And in the darkness comes the Light. . . .
He rode on into the dark, under the stars.
And there were no more faces. There was nothing.
But always in the darkness he rode on,
Alone; and in the darkness came the Light."
(*Collected Poems*, p. 449).

See also the note below on "The Man Against the Sky," and Lloyd Morris's excellent chapter on

"Ideas" in *The Poetry of Edwin Arlington Robinson.* In line with Morris, T. K. Whipple (in *Spokesmen*, pp. 48–50), admitting that Robinson has been affected by pessimistic naturalism, sums up his thought as follows:

"... Does not—here is the very kernel of his thought—the fact that we do go on living prove that we do not accept naturalism as the complete truth? Something, somehow, has given us, in spite of the appearances, ground for faith and hope ... Perhaps our faith is illusory—as to that, Robinson cannot say; it suffices him that we all have it, that we have all caught glimpses of the Light, the Gleam, the Vision, the Word. ... His philosophy, in short, is a very much chastened and sobered transcendentalism. His inclination is to think that each of us has some sort of contact with the Infinite, which constitutes an inner illumination, an intuition of an absolute reality for which there is no explanation in the external, natural scheme of things. ... From this central tenet he develops the usual doctrines of transcendentalism: the need of self-reliance and self-development, of freedom and individualism. Since each has his own private revelation, the business of each is to make the most of it; and since all men share in the infinite mind, all men are important. The value of the individual is measured, if at all, only by his truth to himself."

CALVARY

This poem and many others suggest that while Robinson is hardly orthodox in his religious faith, he does have a deep respect for the general Christian tradition. If his early sonnet "For a Book by Thomas Hardy" (*Children of the Night*, p. 56), not included in his *Collected Poems*, indicates that the agnostic Hardy was an influence upon Robinson at one time, "A Christmas Sonnet" (p. 767) following Hardy's somewhat blasphemous poem on God's funeral, seems to suggest that he outgrew the influence of Hardy so far as his attitude toward Christianity is concerned. In "A Christmas Sonnet" he says "it will do no good" now to quibble "whether or not the cross was made of wood," for "something is here that was not here before." As we shall see, however, in the note to follow on "Tristram," Robinson was indebted not only to the Christian tradition, perhaps through transcendentalism, with its emphasis on body and spirit as well as intuitive faith, but also to the ancient classical tradition.

For comment on the three sonnets, "George Crabbe," "Zola," and "Oh for a Poet," see note below on Robinson's poetic theories.

Page 756. RICHARD CORY

This poem is presented as illustrative of many of Robinson's brief portraits which are characteristically dramatic. Note that he reveals to us only what life itself would reveal. We know Richard Cory only through his effect upon others.

Lloyd Morris (*Poetry of Robinson*, p. 69) observes that Robinson's doctrine of self-reliance and individualism derives from his belief that "each of us contains a spark of divinity, since we are all comprehended within the universal mind," and he concludes that "of all the characters he has created only those who have no light to follow—such characters as Tasker Norcross or Richard Cory or Briony—are really in his sense failures." It should be observed that although Robinson attacks democracy and sides with the Federalists (see "Demos and Dionysus, p. 767, and note, below), he almost invariably presents the rich man —Cory was "richer than a king"—in an unfavorable light. In "Cassandra" (*Collected Poems*, pp. 11–12) he says to materialistic America, "Your Dollar is your only Word." And he tells her that she disregards the guidance of the ages and tries to her peril to trample upon "the merciless old verities."

MINIVER CHEEVY

This poem is presented to illustrate the fact that, although capable of high seriousness, Robinson has a considerable vein of humor (see Cestre, *Robinson*, pp. 155–193), and also the fact that, while he may select mediæval themes for their universality, he regarded an attempt to escape to the Middle Ages from the commonplace present as ridiculous. Note the way in which the spondees concluding each verse enhance the ludicrous effect Robinson is trying to secure.

HOW ANNANDALE WENT OUT

Note Robinson's trenchant economy in this vivid little drama. A physician who also characterizes himself as liar and hypocrite, tells how he was called to attend his friend Annandale after some sort of accident which left him "a wreck, with hell between him and the end." It is implied that the physician, with "a slight kind of engine" (a hypodermic?), put Annandale out of his misery by killing him. Compare this realistic monologue with similar ones in Edgar Lee Masters's *Spoon River Anthology*, which appeared five years *after* this poem by Robinson. The rise of realism paralleled Robinson's development. The landmarks bearing on realistic literary theory are Howells's *Criticism and Fiction* (1891) and Hamlin Garland's *Crumbling Idols* (1894), although realism had been foreshadowed earlier. Stephen Crane's *Maggie, a Girl of the Streets* and *The Red Badge of Courage* appeared in 1892 and 1895 respectively, Frank Norris's *Octopus* in 1901, and Dreiser's *Sister Carrie* in 1900. For full discussion, with bibliographies, see Harry Hartwick, *The Foreground of American Fiction* (New York, 1934).

Page 757. FLAMMONDE

Note how effectively and artistically Robinson conveys the sense of the mystery of the identity, the past, and the "incommunicable ways" of this self-possessed and regal fifty-year-old "Prince of Castaways" who "borrowed graciously" for his living but helped the poor and the unfortunate.

Page 758. THE MAN AGAINST THE SKY

In this rich and majestic poem, whose theme is akin to that of Dante's *Paradiso*, and whose setting and atmosphere remind one of parts of Hardy's *Return of the Native*, Robinson has succeeded in blending the concrete image and the abstract idea in such a way as to give us a highly artistic presentation of the various paths of philosophic thought by which man may confront his universal destiny. The key to the structure of the poem is given in the flash-back, ll. 183–188. This representative man, "black-drawn against wild red," may, Robinson imagines, have taken one of five paths involving:

(1) "A vision answering a faith unshaken" (ll. 23–46), mystical and sublime.
(2) "An easy trust assumed of easy trials" (ll. 47–70), "seeing all things for the best."
(3) "A sick negation born of weak denials" (ll. 71–102), finding life "a sorry thing," a "lighted highway to the tomb."
(4) "A crazed abhorrence of an old condition" (ll. 103–136), of the fetters of one's past mistakes or misfortunes.
(5) "A blind attendance on a brief ambition" (ll. 137–178), which is fulfilled but which does not save one from destruction.

Each of us, Robinson says, must confront his destiny alone (l. 191), and he asks, if loss of faith in Heaven and Hell make life merely a "blind atomic pilgrimage" guided only by "crass chance," why we "care to stay alive" (l. 250). And he suggests that the fact that people do wish to continue living proves that they have faith in something transcending blank materialism. The poem is not a confession of nihilism, as casual readers sometimes imagine, but ultimately a positive affirmation of faith.

> "But this we know, if we know anything:
> That we may laugh and fight and sing
> And of our transience here make offering
> To an orient Word that will not be erased."

(See note on "Credo" above.) The life of the senses seems miserable and purposeless. But transcending the life of the senses each man has an intuition of a Light, or a Word, which bespeaks a spiritual guidance and heritage. When interviewed by Nancy Evans (see Bibliography), Robinson said, "If you want to find out about my 'Transcendentalism' [quotes were in his voice], read *The Man against the Sky* and *Matthias at the Door*—it's in those poems. It is impossible to believe that it is all for nothing—such waste would be inconceivable . . . The world is not a 'prison-house,' but a kind of spiritual kindergarten where bewildered infants are trying to spell God with the wrong blocks." (For a rich appreciation of the Dantesque beauty of "The Man Against the Sky," see Cestre, *Robinson*, pp. 60–66.)

Page 761. BEN JONSON ENTERTAINS A MAN FROM STRATFORD

In this dramatic monologue (cf. Browning's "My Last Duchess," etc.), Shakespeare's great rival and friend, classical Ben Jonson, talks discursively to an Alderman (l. 11) from Stratford who has known Shakespeare "from his origin" (l. 61) and whom Shakespeare has mentioned to Jonson as his friend and a man of "nimble element" above the "sad average" (ll. 17–25). Since Shakespeare is mentioned as "five and forty" (l. 129) and he was born in 1564, the time of the monologue must be 1609. Jonson and the Alderman are "buying beer" (l. 24)—and drinking it!—in a "grateful nook" (l. 306) in London. According to modern scholarly opinion, Shakespeare had just published his *Sonnets* (1609)—to which Robinson refers (l. 172) as the key to part of his autobiography—and he had written *Antony and Cleopatra* the year before, although it did not appear in print until the publication of the folio much later. In 1608, the year before, Shakespeare had left London and established himself at New Place, his comparatively rich home in his native Stratford. The prophecy of the coming of "a sunset spell / Thrown over him as over a glassed lake" (l. 327) was to be fulfilled in the relatively idyllic and serene plays, *Cymbeline*, acted in 1610, *The Winter's Tale*, acted in 1611, and *The Tempest*, acted in 1613. Each of these plays contains a sort of pastoral interlude glorifying the quiet of sylvan retirement as contrasted with the turmoil and corruption of cities and commerce with men; these interludes have been connected with Shakespeare's own retirement in the tiny town of Stratford after living in London. For a very readable but somewhat fictionized portrayal of Shakespeare's return to Stratford and its significance, see George Brandes's *William Shakespeare* (New York, 1920), pp. 670–690.

It should be noted that Jonson (and doubtless Robinson) is fascinated by the enigma of "this mad, careful, proud, indifferent Shakespeare" (l. 395), who has found life "hollow" (l. 261) and is convinced that "bugs and emperors / Go singularly back to the same dust" (ll. 298–304), and yet is "manor-bitten to the bone" (l. 115) and eager to amass "egregious shillings" to build the largest house in his home town. Robinson is of course chiefly interested here not in Shakespeare's plays but in the psychological problem presented by Shakespeare the man, whom we see vividly as seen by his contemporaries, in his habit as he lived.

It is also important to understand that the utterance regarding nihilism ("It's all Nothing," etc., l. 299) is dramatically attributed to Shakespeare, and that Robinson's own philosophy is quite different. See the note on "Credo," above. For an appreciation of the rich art of this poem, see Cestre, *Robinson*, pp. 131–134.

Page 766. THE MILL

Note Robinson's skill in approaching Robert Frost's way of dealing with Yankee character, his laconic under-statement, and use of setting. (Compare Frost's "The Death of the Hired Man.") How deftly and dramatically the details of this suicide are presented! Note also the beauty and economy of Robinson's descriptive touches—cf. "black water, . . . like starry velvet in the night . . ."

MR. FLOOD'S PARTY

Note the tender beauty of this portrait, blended of humor and pathos. The old derelict of Tilbury Town on his lonely way home tilts his jug once too often, sees two beings in himself, and presents one of the most engaging debates on record "with only two moons listening." The hilarity of the old man singing "For auld lang syne" until the "harmonious landscape rang" in the "silver loneliness of the night" contrasts pathetically with our knowledge that "there was not much that was ahead of him / And there was nothing in the town below" where friends had long since turned to strangers. This is one of the richest and most human of Robinson's many dramatic poems. Compare Robinson's attitude in this poem with Lindsay's attitude toward prohibition.

Page 767 A CHRISTMAS SONNET

See note on "Calvary," above.

DEMOS AND DIONYSUS

Because such long poems as this have not hitherto been available outside of Robinson's *Collected Poems*, many anthology-readers have erroneously imagined that he has had nothing to say about contemporary political and social tendencies in America. As a matter of fact, this poem and its companion, "Dionysus in Doubt" (*Collected Poems*, pp. 859–870), reveal Robinson as one of the most decisive and outspoken critics of the contemporary development of democratic standardization, regimentation, equalitarianism, materialism, and philistine indifference to individuality and beauty. With his roots deep in the soil of the Puritan elect and in Federalistic John Adams's New England, Robinson insists that

"the few shall save
The many, or the many are to fall."
("Demos," *Collected Poems*, pp. 471–472).

While Emerson as a political and social thinker wavered somewhat between quantity and quality, between "the greatest good of the greatest number" (*Works*, Centenary Edition, VII, p. 34) and a social ideal to be tested by its production of a few great self-reliant contributors to the spiritual heritage of the race, Robinson stands uncompromisingly for the latter ideal. He refracts his views dramatically through the mouth of the Olympian Dionysus, the god and giver of the grape and its wine. Dionysus calls democracy a "faith in something somewhere out of nothing" (l. 43), a "monster" full of "futilities and enormities" (ll. 86–88), an "octopus" distinguished for "essential devilishness" (ll. 98–100), a system which will render its dupes "a dislocated and unlovely mess / For undertakers" (ll. 290–291). In violence of expression on this subject, as well as in point of view, Robinson resembles Poe as a political and social thinker; see Ernest Marchand's "Poe as a Social Critic," *American Literature*, VI, 28–43. For, unlike John Adams, Robinson hates democracy not because it militates against the "good of all" as opposed to the good of one class, but because its philistine standardized equalitarianism is inimical to "romance and love and art" (l. 316), to the individual "self and soul" (l. 181). Robinson's indictment is thus distinctively that of a poet and a lover of æsthetic individuality. He foresees that feeling and fancy will be "whipped and rationed into reason" (ll. 187, 191–192), the individual "few that are peculiar" will "be ground to death" (ll. 196, 202), and love will "be subdued to studious procreation" (l. 164). The vision of the resultant "monotony and servitude" and "invertebrate futility" leaves him "sick at heart" (ll. 171–172, 177–178). Since Robinson believes that evil is of inward cause and cure, that man is not beset by society or institutions but by his own character, he has little of the humanitarian's zeal which is based on the possibility of legislating virtue by changing environment or institutions. Just as Emerson said the "masses are rude, lame, unmade, pernicious in their demands and influence," and that he wished only "to draw individuals out of them" (*Works*, VI, 249), so Robinson writes,

"Because one half of humankind
Lives here in hell, shall not the other half
Do any more than just for conscience' sake
Be miserable? Is this the way for us
To lead these creatures up to find the light,—
Or to be drawn down surely to the dark
Again?" (*Collected Poems*, pp. 126–127.)

Robinson of course regarded democracy as socialism in disguise and he identified it with the tyranny of the majority and with the totalitarian state. During the eleven years since Robinson wrote this critical poem, to what extent have his predictions come true, especially in Germany, Russia, and Italy? Compare and contrast Robinson and Lindsay in their views of democracy and socialism.

Page 772. TRISTRAM

For backgrounds see Maynadier, *The Arthur of the English Poets;* Dhaleine, *A Study of Tennyson's Idylls of the King;* and—in Bibliography—see studies of Robinson's treatment of the Arthurian legends by App, Beebe, Pipkin, Romig, and especially Cestre. Compare Robinson's treatment with that of Tennyson, Arnold, Swinburne, and Morris.

Nancy Evans (see Bibliography) quotes Robinson as saying: "I like to be familiar with my characters and their development before I start a poem. *Tristram* took two entire summers to write and I worked out its structure somewhat as a playwright would work out a play."

In Part I of *Tristram* the eighteen-year-old Isolt of Brittany is pictured watching the sea with her father, King Howel, and longing for the return of her lover, Tristram, who her father tells her has gone to attend the wedding of his uncle, old King Mark of Cornwall, and Isolt of Ireland.

In Part II Tristram is shown at night brooding by the Cornish Sea while he listens sullenly to the music celebrating the marriage of his uncle and Isolt, whom he himself has brought to this unholy marriage at the King's command. Tristram had not recognized the fact that he and Isolt loved each other in spite of the fact that he killed her kinsman Morhaus. King Mark sends in turn old Gouvernail, Tristram's mentor, and Queen Morgan, to request his nephew to return to the festival, but Tristram tells each to report that in celebrating the King's happiness he has made himself sick with wine. In reality he is heartsick and rebellious in his realization that he has forever separated himself from Isolt. The King is "vexed and vicious," and the section ends with an air of foreboding.

Part III, here reprinted, deals with the first of the two great love scenes between Tristram and Isolt of Ireland. The following extract from Professor Cestre's appreciative and penetrating *Introduction to Robinson* (pp. 98, 76, 102–105) may help the reader to envisage this part in relation to the whole poem, of which there are ten parts:

"The *Tristram*, which was published seven years after *Lancelot*, deserves for its stately structure, its dramatic force and its finish of expression, to be considered as the principal and commanding part of the trilogy on the Arthurian legend. . . .

[Unlike most of the others who have dealt with these legends], "he does not need to resort to spells of witches or fairies. His sole supernatural agencies are Time and Fate, that is, awful impersonations of the iron laws of change and of moral retribution. Under the sway of Time and Fate, his characters act according to the inner logic of men's moods, which change as men pass from youth to age, or as they shift from self-seeking to self-sacrifice, from weak indulgence to ideal aspiration, or the reverse. . . . He is the first poet, in the history of the English language, who has fully expressed the virtualities of the Arthurian legend in terms of symbolic beauty and human truth. . . .

"The composition is a model of the classic power of grasp and of rational ordering. The two great love scenes between Tristram and Isolt of Ireland—the supremely beautiful and tragic core of the poem—are incased in a prelude and a postlude, which bring in Isolt of Brittany, first as a girl, plaintively lamenting Tristram's departure, then as a wife, hearing of Tristram's death and plaintively mourning for his fate and hers. Thus framed in, the love drama takes place, at Tintagel, then at Joyous Gard, divided in the middle by Tristram's time of exile, during which he is induced by grief and pity to contract a marriage, which he will never consider as a binding union. The prelude makes us acquainted with the characters and their doings previous to the opening of the story; it serves as a preparation for the tragic events that are to follow, by creating an atmosphere of wistful expectation. The middle episode provides, as it were, a resting place, where we collect ourselves after the strain of the first act. In the postlude, we survey from a point of vantage the havoc worked by fate and death, and gradually come back to a state of comparative composure, where we give ourselves up to the spell of the becalmed melody and to the catharsis of pity and sorrow.

"The excellence of the poem lies chiefly in the picture of the uncontrollable, danger-fraught, fond passion which throws into each other's arms Tristram and Isolt, who cannot be united by the bonds of a lawful union. The poet's divining of the secrets of the heart, his lyrical genius and his power of dramatic emotion give him a high rank among the initiates of Apollo's mysteries. Concrete beauty—the setting of gorgeous nature, the entrancing loveliness of human faces, the winning spontaneity or awful stateliness of attitudes—accompanies the description of the feelings and makes it instant and real. The thrilling combination of sensuousness and spirituality appears in the very opening lines [ll. 40–47 of Part III], when Isolt, but dimly visible in the pale moonlight, slowly descends the grand staircase from the castle to meet Tristram. . . . The poet has associated love with death and fate, calling up the mighty antithesis which all great lyrists have sensed to be the most moving of dramatic themes."

ll. 292–295. *fate . . . Made hungry sport of these two.* One of the fascinating problems one confronts in studying Robinson is that of the precise quality of the fatalism which runs through so many of his poems and especially *Tristram.* "The very sharpest distinction must be drawn," according to Irving Babbitt (*Rousseau and Romanticism,* p. 190), "between the subrational fate of the emotional romanticist and the superrational fate of Greek tragedy. The fate of Æschylean tragedy, for instance, so far from undermining moral responsibility rather reinforces it. It is felt to be the revelation of a moral order of which man's experience at any particular moment is only an infinitesimal fragment. It does not seem, like the subrational fate of the emotional romanticist, the intrusion into the human realm of an alien power whether friendly or unfriendly." Is Robinson's "fate" like that of Hardy, which has been said to make human deeds seem only "throws of the dice in the blind night of chance," or is it more like that of Sophocles? (In Robinson's *Collected Poems* see his references to fate on pp. 381, 636, 648, 650, 652, 654, 662, 665, 666, 671, 674, 675, 676, 681, 682, 685, 686, 689.) The eminent classical scholar, H. R. Fairclough (see Bibliography), seems to have found Robinson at least as closely akin to Sophocles as to Hardy. His scholarly study in which he finds Robinson "deeply indebted to classical culture" is well worth reading.

ROBINSON'S POETIC THEORIES

Unlike most poets, Robinson left no extended prose statements regarding the aims or theories underlying his poetic practice. When I ventured to approach him directly regarding this matter, he wrote me (December 5th, 1934): "So far as I can make out, I haven't any literary theory or aim in literature except to do as well as I can what insists on being done. I have had to make this unsatisfactory sort of reply to many similar requests . . ." In his sonnet "Dear Friends" (*Collected Poems*, p. 83), he replied modestly to those who would reproach, counsel or pity him for what they regarded as "bubble-work," that his poems (games) such as they were might be "good glasses . . . to read the spirit through," and that "the shame I win for singing is all mine" while the gold he missed is theirs. Nevertheless, if Robinson seemed to obey the dictates of his individual genius and to be averse to being drawn into controversies regarding poetic theories, he has left many oblique expressions in his poems on authors which enable us to derive hints of his literary likes and dislikes and to envisage the general ideals he set for himself. In his sonnet "Oh for a poet" (p. 755, above), he revealed his distaste for "little sonnet-men" and for their mechanical "songs without souls, that flicker for a day." Here he yearned for a genuine poet to lighten the "dead gray" of "the barren age of ours" and to tell its meaning, giving America poetic fame "forevermore." As an apprentice Robinson shows himself as concerned especially with words and forms. In the sonnet beginning "The master and the slave" (*Collected Poems*, p. 95), he says that the poet must obey the demands of his form, must "understand the mission of his bondage," if he would command "the perfect word that is the poet's wand." "The sonnet is a crown, whereof the rhymes / Are for Thought's purest gold the jewel-stones."

In 1930, Robinson reviewed his early experiments in the eighteen-nineties in an article called "The First Seven Years" (*The Colophon*, Part IV). He characterizes himself in this formative period as "a certain juvenile and incorrigible fisher of words who thought nothing of fishing for two weeks to catch a stanza or even a line that he would not throw back into a squirming sea of language where there was every word but the one he wanted." Although he admitted being fascinated by "strange and iridescent and impossible words," what he chiefly sought, he says, was words which were "smooth and shining and subtle, and very much alive, and not too strange,"—words constituting a "new idiom." In this article, too, he testifies to being "violently excited over the structure and music of English blank verse" after having read widely in the English poets and having tried to render Cicero's first oration against Catiline into this form of which he was later to make such memorable use. He tells, also, of his experiments not only with sonnets and blank verse but with villanelles, ballades, and other forms. Indeed, it has been said that it is Robinson's "new idiom" in the old forms, his use of the rhythms of common speech within the conventional verse-pattern, which constitutes his chief distinction. Later, as reported by Nancy Evans (see Bibliography), Robinson said, "There is room for sufficient variation within the conventional forms of poetry. Poetry must be music, . . . not that it must jingle, but it *must be music*. Maybe it's possible to write free verse, but I've never read any. And it's not memorable. I cannot recall a single poem written in free verse, can you?" During this early period he seems for a time to have admired the decadent Verlaine (of whom he wrote a sonnet, *Collected Poems*, p. 96). When Verlaine and others such as Ibsen, Wagner, the Pre-Raphaelites, and the Parnassians were attacked by Max Nordau in his book *Degeneration* (1895), Robinson defended them obliquely by writing a "Poem for Max Nordau" (in Robinson's *The Torrent*, 1896, p. 33) embodying, with sardonic intent, all the things Nordau was known to dislike.

The "Ballade of Broken Flutes" (*Collected Poems*, pp. 77–78) seems to symbolize, in its "barren land" and the "ghostly band / Of skeletons in cold array," Robinson's view of the state of American literature in the eighteen-nineties. His are "The songs of one who strove to play / The broken flutes of Arcady," and he concludes wistfully that he has been obliged to abandon poetry "To fight where Mammon may decree." In "Rembrandt to Rembrandt" (*ibid.*, pp. 582–591), Robinson has the great artist talk to himself about the ostracism and the "bewildered and unhappy scorn" visited upon him because the philistine populace cannot appreciate the subtle play of "color and light" and the golden shadow of his later manner. And in this poem Robinson may be expressing, obliquely and dramatically, his own mood at America's indifference to him and to his lonely fidelity to his art. Nancy Evans quotes Robinson as saying to her, "Ideas are of course inseparable from the medium, but much memorable poetry is not important for what is said. . . . Somehow I feel that Whitman seems greater than he is. Anyway, I feel that whatever power he had was as a poet—not as a thinker."

What Robinson prized and sought most in poetry seems to have been fearless truth in treating high and universal themes. In "Zola" (p. 755, above) he says we have to conquer our "shamed indifference" before we can see in the "hideousness of Truth" the "divine heart of man," and he condemns the "squeamish and emasculate crusade / Against the grim dominion of his art." In an early sonnet "For a Book by Thomas Hardy" (*Children of the Night*, p. 56) Robinson seems sympathetic toward Hardy's "grand sad song" of "Life's wild infinity of mirth and woe." In his sonnet to "Thomas Hood" (*Collected Poems*, p. 91), Robinson speaks sympathetically of the "weird unrest" stirred by Hood's work as one who "cloaked his bitterness" at this "world of anguish and of sin" in "puns and pleasantries." Robinson's homage to "George Crabbe" (p. 755, above) is especially noteworthy, for he embodied "the sure strength that fearless truth endows," which "fashion cannot kill." The vigor of his "hard, human pulse" enables us to see the "emptiness" of many modern books which have been inspired by "the flicker, not the flame" of truth. Robinson's ultimate recognition that mere artistry will be inadequate unless it is organic with divine truth is expressed in "Octaves," stanza xix (*ibid.*, p. 106):

"Nor jewelled phrase nor mere mellifluous rhyme
Reverberates aright, or ever shall,
One cadence of that infinite plain-song
Which is itself all music. Stronger notes
Than any that have ever touched the world
Must ring to tell it—ring like hammer-blows,
Right-echoed of a chime primordial,
On anvils, in the gleaming of God's forge."

Such, then, were Robinson's main views of poetry and his aims in writing: in the eighteen-nineties America was in vital need of a genuine poet, but the indifference of philistines threatened to drive such a poet to serve Mammon; Robinson delighted at first in playing with words for their own beauty, but he came eventually to think that great poetry can derive only from fearless truth which vigorously confronts the grim facts of man's universal destiny.

To what extent did Robinson succeed in practicing his own theories?

GENERAL PRINCIPLES OF POETICS

Abercrombie, Lascelles. *The Theory of Poetry.* London: 1918.
—— *Principles of English Prosody.* London: 1923.
—— *The Idea of Great Poetry.* London: 1925.
—— *Poetry, Its Music and Meaning.* Oxford: 1932.
Alden, R. M. *An Introduction to Poetry.* New York: 1909. (Among the best of the books designed for beginners.)
Allen, G. W. *American Prosody.* New York: 1934. (Scholarly, comprehensive chapters on Freneau, Bryant, Poe, Emerson, Whittier, Longfellow, Holmes, Whitman, Lowell, Lanier, and Emily Dickinson. Indispensable for all students of American poetry. Contains an excellent introduction dealing with terms and principles, and bibliographies.)
Andersen, Johannes C. *The Laws of Verse.* Cambridge, England: 1928. (Stimulating.)
Andrews, C. E. *Writing and Reading of Verse.* New York: 1918. (Comprehensive and fresh.)
Atkins, J. W. H. *Literary Criticism in Antiquity.* Cambridge, England: 1934. 2 vols. (The best comprehensive survey of Greek and Roman theories; well-documented and well-balanced.)
Baldwin, Charles. *Ancient Rhetoric and Poetic.* New York: 1924.
—— *Mediæval Rhetoric and Poetic.* New York: 1928. (The two books by Baldwin are able, well-documented, and concise.)
Barfield, Owen. *Poetic Diction, A Study in Meaning.* London: 1928.
Baum, P. F. *The Principles of English Versification.* Cambridge, Mass.: 1922. (Authoritative.)
Bayfield, M. A. *The Measures of the Poets, a New System of English Prosody.* Cambridge, England: 1919. (An advanced work advocating prosodic reforms.)
Beeching, H. C. *Two Lectures Introductory to the Study of Poetry.* Cambridge, England: 1902.
Boas, George. *Philosophy and Poetry.* Norton, Mass.: 1932.
Bosanquet, Bernard. *A History of Æsthetic.* Second Edition, New York: 1917. (The standard history of European theory, with bibliography.)
Bremond, Henri. *Prayer and Poetry.* London: 1928. (A suggestive attempt to relate these.)
Bridges, Robert. *The Testament of Beauty.* Oxford: 1929.
Brown, S. J. *The Realm of Poetry; an Introduction.* London: 1921.
Buchanan, S. M. *Poetry and Mathematics.* New York: 1929.
Buck, P. M. *Literary Criticism.* New York: 1930. (Admirable discussions of poetic values, style, imagery, and genres. Bibliography.)
Butcher, S. H. *Aristotle's Theory of Poetry and Fine Art, with a Critical Text and Translation of the Poetics.* London: 1902. (Contains extensive scholarly comment on theses such as "imitation.")
Chapin, Elsa, and Thomas, R. *A New Approach to Poetry.* Chicago: 1929.
Clark, D. H. *Rhetoric and Poetic in the* [English] *Renaissance.* New York: 1922. (An able work.)
Coleridge, S. T. *Biographia Literaria,* ed. Shawcross. 2 vols. Oxford: 1907.
Cook, A. S. *The Art of Poetry.* Boston: 1892. (Contains the text and translation of the manuals on this subject by Horace, Vida, and Boileau.)
Cooper, Lane. *Aristotle on the Art of Poetry.* New York: 1913. ("An amplified version with supplementary illustrations for students of English.")
Courthope, W. J. *Life in Poetry: Law in Taste.* New York: 1901.
Cowl, R. *The Theory of Poetry in England.* London: 1914.
Croce, Benedetto. *Æsthetic as Science of Expression and General Linguistic.* Translated by D. Ainslee. London: 1922.
Crum, R. B. *Scientific Thought in Poetry.* New York: 1931. (A suggestive and scholarly work, with special attention to the poets' reaction to Newtonianism and Evolution. Bibliography.)
De Sélincourt, E. *The Study of Poetry.* English Assoc. Pamphlet, No. 40. Oxford: 1929.
—— "Rhyme in English Poetry," in *Essays and Studies by Members of the English Association,* Vol. VII, pp. 7–29. Oxford: 1921.
Dodds, Mrs. A. E. (Powell). *The Romantic Theory of Poetry.* London: 1926. (A useful survey from the standpoint of Crocean criteria.)
Eastman, Max. *The Enjoyment of Poetry and the Use of Criticism: Studies in the Relations of Criticism to Poetry in England.* New York: 1913. (Popular.)
Eliot, T. S. *The Use of Poetry.* Cambridge: 1933.
Erskine, John. *The Kinds of Poetry, and Other Essays.* New York: 1920.
Foerster, Norman. *American Criticism.* Boston: 1928. (Pages 241–257 provide an excellent outline of criteria for judicial criticism.)
Garrod, H. W. *Poetry and the Criticism of Life.* Cambridge, Mass.: 1931.
—— *The Profession of Poetry.* London: 1929.
Gayley, C. M., and Kurtz, B. P. *Methods and Materials of Literary Criticism: Lyric, Epic, and Allied Forms of Poetry.* Boston: 1920. (An in-

dispensable guide, with an elaborate bibliography.)
Gilbert, Katherine. *Studies in Recent Aesthetic.* Chapel Hill, N. C.: 1927.
Graves, Robert. *Poetic Unreason and Other Studies.* London: 1925.
Greene, W. C. *Plato's View of Poetry.* Cambridge, Mass.: 1918. Harvard Studies in Classical Philology, Vol. XXIX. (An authoritative scholarly study clearing up popular misunderstandings regarding Plato's view.)
Groom, Bernard. "Some Kinds of Poetic Diction," in *Essays and Studies by Members of the English Association,* Vol. XV, pp. 139–160. Oxford: 1922.
Hamer, Enid. *The Metres of English Prosody.* London: 1930. (An able analysis of principles and of the more important historical trends.)
Herford, C. H. *Is There a Poetic View of the World?* London: 1919.
Housman, A. E. *The Name and Nature of Poetry.* New York: 1933.
Hubbell, J. B., and Beaty, J. O. *An Introduction to Poetry.* Revised edition. New York: 1936. (Emphasizes meter and forms. Includes copious illustrations and bibliography, pp. 575–579.
Jacob, Cary F. *The Foundations and Nature of Verse.* New York: 1918. (A valuable scholarly study.)
Jennings, J. G. *An Essay on Metaphor in Poetry.* London: 1916.
Jesperson, Otto. "Notes on Metre," in *Linguistica, Select Papers.* London: 1933, pp. 249–274. (An authoritative essay by an outstanding philologist.)
Johnson, C. F. *Forms of English Poetry.* New York: 1904.
Kerr, W. P. *Form and Style in Poetry.* Edited by R. W. Chambers. London: 1928. (Important.)
Lanier, Sidney. *The Science of English Verse.* New York: 1880. (A suggestive attempt to show the identity of the laws of music and poetry.)
Lewis, B. R. *Creative Poetry, a Study of Its Organic Principle.* Stanford: 1931.
Liddell, M. H. *Brief Abstract of a New English Prosody, Based upon the Laws of English Rhythm.* Lafayette, Indiana: 1914. (A brief study endeavoring to show that wave-rhythms of thought underlie versification.)
Longinus. *On the Sublime.* Edited and translated by W. Rhys Roberts. London: 1899. (A great analysis of the "grand style" and of ways of approaching it. See T. R. Henn, *Longinus and English Criticism.* Cambridge, England: 1934.)
Lowes, J. L. *Convention and Revolt in Poetry.* Boston: 1919. (A learned and stimulating book, especially interesting in its discussion of free-verse and imagism.)
—— *The Road to Xanadu.* Boston: 1927. (An enormously scholarly study of "the ways of the imagination" in the creative processes of Coleridge who is considered as representative of the poet who draws upon his reading.)
MacDonald, Alexander. *The Primacy of Thought in Poetry.* London: 1928.
Masefield, John. *Poetry.* London: 1931.
Morris, A. R. *The Orchestration of the Metrical Line; an Analytical Story of Rhythmical Form.* Boston: 1925.
Murray, Gilbert. *The Classical Tradition in Poetry.* Cambridge: 1927. (Valuable.)
Murry, J. M. "The Nature of Poetry," in *Discoveries.* London: 1924.
Neilson, W. A. *Essentials of Poetry.* Boston: 1912.
Omond, T. S. *A Study of Metre.* London: 1920.
Perry, Bliss. *A Study of Poetry.* Boston: 1920. (Good introduction.)
Peterson, Houston. *The Melody of Chaos.* London: 1931.
Pound, Louise. *Poetic Origins and the Ballad.* New York: 1921.
Prescott, F. C. *The Poetic Mind.* New York: 1926. (A suggestive attempt to trace poetic inspiration to the subconscious.)
—— *Poetry and Myth.* New York: 1927.
Pyre, J. F. A. *A Short Introduction to English Versification.* New York: 1929. (The most authoritative and useful of the brief manuals.)
Quayle, Thomas. *Poetic Diction: a Study of the Eighteenth Century Verse.* London: 1924.
Raymond, G. L. *Poetry as a Representative Art.* New York: 1905.
Read, Herbert. *Form in Modern Poetry.* London: 1933.
—— *Phases of English Poetry.* New York: 1929.
Riding, L., and Graves, R. *A Survey of Modernist Poetry.* London: 1928. (A sympathetic and useful work.)
Roberts, Michael. *Critique of Poetry.* London: 1934.
Rylands, George. *Words and Poetry.* London: 1928.
Saintsbury, George. *History of English Prosody.* London: 1906–1910. 3 vols. (The standard treatment—in a delightful style.)
—— *Historical Manual of English Prosody.* London: 1914. (Valuable.)
Santayana, George. *Interpretations of Poetry and Religion.* New York: 1900. (Suggestive and valuable; see especially "The Elements of Poetry.")
Sikes, E. E. *The Greek View of Poetry.* London: 1931.
Smith, C. P. *Pattern and Variations in Poetry.* New York: 1932. (Not profoundly original, but interesting and stimulating.)
Smith, Egerton. *The Principles of English Metre.* London: 1923. (For the advanced student.)
Smithberger, Andrew, and McCole, Camille. *On Poetry.* New York: 1931. (An introductory book, with useful chapters on both versification and the theory of poetry, and with useful bibliographies.)
Snyder, E. D. *Hypnotic Poetry.* Philadelphia: 1930.
Sonnenshein, E. A. *What is Rhythm?* Oxford: 1925.

Sparrow, John. *Sense and Poetry.* New Haven: 1934. (On recent anti-traditional writers in England and America.)

Spindler, Robert. *Englische Metrik in ihren Grundzügen an Hand ausgewählter Textproben dargestellt.* München: 1927. (Valuable chapters on the major English poets.)

Stedman, E. C. *The Nature and Elements of Poetry.* Boston: 1892.

Stewart, G. R. *The Technique of English Verse.* New York: 1930. (A good study, interesting in its use of musical notation.)

Strunk, William. *English Metres.* Ithaca, N. Y.: 1935. (Ch. V, on "The Chief Metres of English Verse" in the light of their historical development, is especially important.)

Suares, André. *Musique et Poésie.* Paris: 1928.

Tillyard, E. M. W. *Poetry, Direct and Oblique.* London: 1934.

Tinker, Chauncey. *The Good Estate of Poetry.* Boston: 1929.

Verrier, Paul. *Essai sur les Principes de la Métrique Anglaise.* Paris: 1909. (Three large volumes of great scholarly value.)

Wells, H. W. *Poetic Imagery.* New York: 1924. (Although this refers especially to Elizabethan poetry and the "metaphysical conceit," the analysis of the metaphor is of great use to all students of poetry.)

Williams, Charles. *The English Poetic Mind.* London: 1932.

—— *Reason and Beauty in the Poetic Mind.* Oxford: 1933.

Williams, Ellis A. *An Anatomy of Poetry.* New York: n.d.

Wilson, Katherine M. *Sound and Meaning in English Poetry.* New York: 1930.

Wolfe, Humbert. *The Craft of Verse.* New York: 1928.

—— *Signpost to Poetry.* London: 1931.

—— *Romantic and Unromantic Poetry.* Bristol, England: 1933.

Wyld, H. C. *Studies in English Rhymes from Surrey to Pope.* London: 1923.

GENERAL INDEX

Authors' names and general headings are in black face type, titles are in italics, and first lines of poems are in roman type. Where a part or all of the first line of a poem is used as a title, the first line only is entered in italics as the title. Page numbers preceded by "*n*" refer to notes on selections.